Digital Information and Communication Technology and Its Applications

Hocine Cherifi Jasni Mohamad Zain
Eyas El-Qawasmeh (Eds.)

Digital Information and Communication Technology and Its Applications

International Conference, DICTAP 2011
Dijon, France, June 21-23, 2011
Proceedings, Part I

Springer

Volume Editors

Hocine Cherifi
LE2I, UMR, CNRS 5158, Faculté des Sciences Mirande
9, avenue Alain Savary, 21078 Dijon, France
E-mail: hocine.cherifi@u-bourgogne.fr

Jasni Mohamad Zain
Universiti Malaysia Pahang
Faculty of Computer Systems and Software Engineering
Lebuhraya Tun Razak, 26300 Gambang, Kuantan, Pahang, Malaysia
E-mail: jasni@ump.edu.my

Eyas El-Qawasmeh
King Saud University
Faculty of Computer and Information Science
Information Systems Department
Riyadh 11543, Saudi Arabia
E-mail: eyasa@usa.net

ISSN 1865-0929 e-ISSN 1865-0937
ISBN 978-3-642-21983-2 e-ISBN 978-3-642-21984-9
DOI 10.1007/978-3-642-21984-9
Springer Heidelberg Dordrecht London New York

Library of Congress Control Number: 2011930189

CR Subject Classification (1998): H, C.2, I.4, D.2

Typesetting: Camera-ready by author, data conversion by Scientific Publishing Services, Chennai, India

Printed on acid-free paper

Springer is part of Springer Science+Business Media (www.springer.com)

Preface

On behalf of the Program Committee, we welcome you to the proceedings of participate in the International Conference on Digital Information and Communication Technology and Its Applications (DICTAP 2011) held at the Université de Bourgogne.

The DICTAP 2011 conference explored new advances in digital information and data communications technologies. It brought together researchers from various areas of computer, information sciences, and data communications who address both theoretical and applied aspects of digital communications and wireless technology. We do hope that the discussions and exchange of ideas will contribute to the advancements in the technology in the near future.

The conference received 330 papers, out of which 130 were accepted, resulting in an acceptance rate of 39%. These accepted papers are authored by researchers from 34 countries covering many significant areas of digital information and data communications. Each paper was evaluated by a minimum of two reviewers.

We express our thanks to the Université de Bourgogne in Dijon, Springer, the authors and the organizers of the conference.

Proceedings Chairs DICTAP2011

General Chair

Hocine Cherifi	Université de Bourgogne, France

Program Chairs

Yoshiro Imai	Kagawa University, Japan
Renata Wachowiak-Smolikova	Nipissing University, Canada
Norozzila Sulaiman	University of Malaysia Pahang, Malaysia

Program Co-chairs

Noraziah Ahmad	University of Malaysia Pahang, Malaysia
Jan Platos	VSB-Technical University of Ostrava, Czech Republic
Eyas El-Qawasmeh	King Saud University, Saudi Arabia

Publicity Chairs

Ezendu Ariwa	London Metropolitan University, UK
Maytham Safar	Kuwait University, Kuwait
Zuqing Zhu	University of Science and Technology of China, China

Message from the Chairs

The International Conference on Digital Information and Communication Technology and Its Applications (DICTAP 2011)—co-sponsored by Springer—was organized and hosted by the Université de Bourgogne in Dijon, France, during June 21–23, 2011 in association with the Society of Digital Information and Wireless Communications. DICTAP 2011 was planned as a major event in the computer and information sciences and served as a forum for scientists and engineers to meet and present their latest research results, ideas, and papers in the diverse areas of data communications, networks, mobile communications, and information technology.

The conference included guest lectures and 128 research papers for presentation in the technical session. This meeting was a great opportunity to exchange knowledge and experience for all the participants who joined us from around the world to discuss new ideas in the areas of data communications and its applications. We are grateful to the Université de Bourgogne in Dijon for hosting this conference. We use this occasion to express our thanks to the Technical Committee and to all the external reviewers. We are grateful to Springer for co-sponsoring the event. Finally, we would like to thank all the participants and sponsors.

Hocine Cherifi
Yoshiro Imai
Renata Wachowiak-Smolikova
Norozzila Sulaiman

Table of Contents – Part I

Web Applications

Image Processing

Special Session (Visual Interfaces and User Experience (VIUE 2011))

Network Security

Ad Hoc Network

Cloud Computing

Data Compression

An Internet-Based Scientific Programming Environment

Michael Weeks

Georgia State University
Atlanta, Georgia, USA 30303
mweeks@ieee.org
http://carmaux.cs.gsu.edu

Abstract. A change currently unfolding is the move from desktop computing as we know it, where applications run on a person's computer, to network computing. The idea is to distribute an application across a network of computers, primarily the Internet. Whereas people in 2005 might have used Microsoft Word for their word-processing needs, people today might use Google Docs.

This paper details a project, started in 2007, to enable scientific programming through an environment based in an Internet browser. Scientific programming is an integral part of math, science and engineering.

This paper shows how the *Calq* system can be used for scientific programming, and evaluates how well it works. Testing revealed something unexpected. Google Chrome outperformed other browsers, taking only a fraction of the time to perform a complex task in *Calq*.

Keywords: Calq, Google Web Toolkit, web-based programming, scientific programming.

1 Introduction

How people think of a "computer" is undergoing a change as the line between the computer and the network blur, at least to the typical user. With Microsoft Word®, the computer user purchases the software and runs it on his/her computer. The document is tied to that computer since that is where it is stored. Google Docs® is a step forward since the document is stored remotely and accessed through the Internet, called by various names (such as cloud computing [1]). The user edits it from whatever computer is available, as long as it can run a web-browser. This is important as our definition of "computer" starts to blur with other computing devices (traditionally called embedded systems), such as cell-phones. For example, Apple's iPhone comes with a web-browser.

Programs like MATLAB® are heavily used in research [2], [3] and education [4]. A research project often involves a prototype in an initial stage, but the final product is not the prototyping code. Once the idea is well stated and tested, the researcher ports the code to other languages (like C or C++). Though

H. Cherifi, J.M. Zain, and E. El-Qawasmeh (Eds.): DICTAP 2011, Part I, CCIS 166, pp. 1–12, 2011.

those programming languages are less forgiving than the prototyping language, and may not have the same level of accompanying software, the final code will run much faster than the original prototype. Also, the compiled code might be included as firmware on an embedded system, possibly with a completely different processor than the original, prototyping computer. A common prototyping language is MATLAB, from the MathWorks, Inc.

Many researchers use it simply due to its flexibility and ease-of-use. MATLAB traces its development back to ideas in APL, including suppressing display, arrays, and recursively processing sub-expressions in parentheses [5]. There are other possibilities for scientific computation, such as the open source *Octave* software, and *SciLab*. Both of these provide a very similar environment to MATLAB, and both use almost the exact same syntax.

The article by Ronald Loui [6] argues that scripting languages (like MATLAB) make an ideal programming language for CS1 classes (the first programming language in a computer science curriculum). This point is debatable, but scripting languages undoubtedly have a place in education, alongside research.

This paper presents a shift from the local application to the web-browser application, for scientific prototyping and education. The project discussed here, called *Calq*, provides a web-based programming environment, using similar keywords and syntax as MATLAB. There is at least one other similar project [7], but unfortunately it does not appear to be functional. Another web-site (`http://artspb.com/matlab/`) has "IE MATLAB On Line," but it is not clear if it is a web-interface to MATLAB. *Calq* is a complete system, not just a front-end to another program.

The next section discusses the project design. To measure its effectiveness, two common signal processing programs are tested along with a computationally intensive program. Section 3 details the current implementation and experiment. Section 4 documents the results, and section 5 concludes this paper.

2 Project Design

An ideal scientific prototyping environment would be a simple, easily accessible programming interpreter. The user connects to the website [8], enters programming statements, and it returns the results via the browser. This is called *Calq*, short for *calculate* with the letter "q" to make it unique. The goal of this research project is to make a simple, flexible, scientific programming environment on-line, with open access. The intent is to supply a minimalist website, inspired by the Google search engine. It should be small, uncluttered, and with the input text box readily available. As an early prototyping and exploring environment, it should be lightweight enough to quickly respond, and compatible with MATLAB syntax so that working code can be copied and pasted from one environment into the other. *Calq* also works in portable devices like the iTouch.

Computing as a service is no new idea, but current research examines the role of the Internet in providing service oriented computing [9]. While this project is not service oriented computing in sense of business applications, it borrows the idea of using functions found on remote servers. It can give feedback that the user can quickly see (i.e., computation results, error messages as appropriate, graphs).

An end-user would not need to purchase, download nor install software. It could be used in classes, for small research projects, and for students to experiment with concepts and process data.

This project will provide much of the same usability found in programming environments like SciLab, Octave, and MATLAB. It will not be competition for these software products; for example, MATLAB software is well established and provides many narrow, technical extensions (functions) that the average user, and certainly the novice user, will not use. Examples include the aerospace toolbox, financial derivatives toolbox, and filter design toolbox. Note that the lack of a toolbox does not limit the determined user from developing his/her own supporting software.

2.1 Supported Programming Constructs

The programming language syntax for *Calq* is simple. This includes the `if...else` statement, and the `for` and `while` loops. Each block ends with an `end` statement. The *Calq* program recognizes these keywords, and carries out the operations that they denote. Future enhancements include a `switch...case` statement, and the `try...catch` statement.

The simple syntax works well since it limits the learning curve. Once the user has experimented with the assignment statements, variables, `if...else...end` statement, `for` and `while` loops, and the intuitive function calls, the user knows the vast majority of what he/she needs to know. The environment offers the flexibility of using variables without declaring them in advance, eliminating a source of frustration for novice programmers.

The main code will cover the basics: language (keyword) interpretation, numeric evaluation, and variable assignments. For example, the `disp` (display) function is built-in.

Functions come in two forms. Internal functions are provided for very common operations, and are part of the main *Calq* program (such as cos and sin). External functions are located on a server, and appear as stand-alone programs within a publicly-accessible directory. These functions may be altered (debugged) as needed, without affecting the main code, which should remain as "light-weight" as possible. External functions can be added at any time. They are executable (i.e., written in Java, C, C++, or a similar language), read data from standard-input and write to standard-output. As such, they can even be written in Perl or even a shell scripting language like Bash. They do not process *Calq* commands, but are specific extensions invoked by *Calq*. This project currently works with the external commands `load` (to get an example program stored on the server), `ls` (to list the remote files available to load), and `plot`.

2.2 Example Code

Use of an on-line scientific programming environment should be simple and powerful, such as the following commands.

```
t = 0:99;
x = cos(2*pi*5*t/100);
plot(x)
```

First, it creates variable t and stores all whole numbers between 0 and 99 in it. Then, it calculates the cosine of each element in that array multiplied by $2\pi 5/100$, storing the results in another array called x. Finally, it plots the results. (The results section refers to this program as "cosplot.")

3 Current Implementation

The first version was a CGI program, written in C++. Upon pressing the "evaluate" button on a webpage, the version 1 client sends the text-box containing code to the server, which responds with output in the form of a web-page. It does basic calculations, but it requires the server to do all of processing, which does not scale well. Also, if someone evaluates a program with an infinite loop, it occupies the server's resources.

A better approach is for the client to process the code, such as with a language like JavaScript. Google's Web Toolkit (GWT) solves this problem. GWT generates JavaScript from Java programs, and it is a safe environment. Even if the user has their computer process an infinite loop, he/she can simply close the browser to recover. A nice feature is the data permanence, where a variable defined once could be reused later that session. With the initial (stateless) approach, variables would have to be defined in the code every time the user pressed "evaluate". Current versions of *Calq* are written in Java and compiled to JavaScript with GWT. For information on how Google web toolkit was used to create this system, see [10].

A website has been created [8], shown in Figure 1. It evaluates real-valued expressions, and supports basic mathematic operations: addition, subtraction, multiplication, division, exponentiation, and precedence with parentheses. It also supports variable assignments, without declarations, and recognizes variables previously defined. *Calq* supports the following programming elements and commands.

– comments, for example:

```
% This program is an example
```

– calculations with +, -, /, *, and parentheses, for example:

```
(5-4)/(3*2) + 1
```

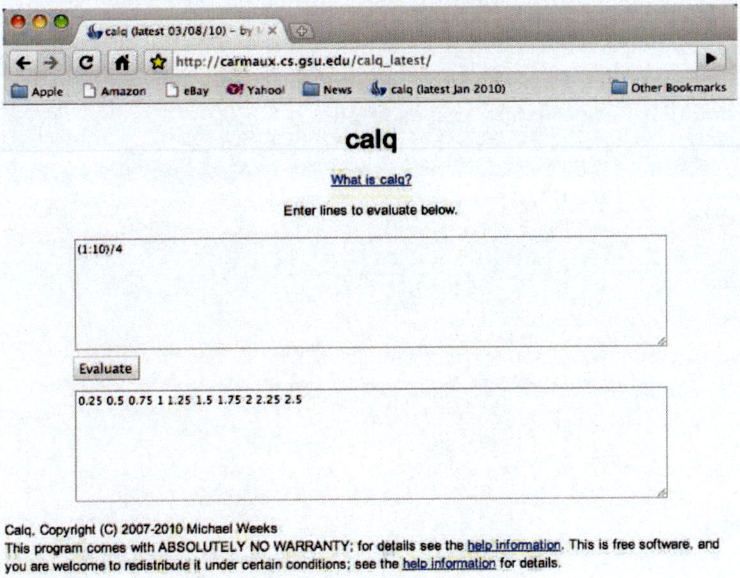

Fig. 1. The *Calq* web-page

- logic and comparison operations, like ==, >, <, >=, <=, !=, &&, ||, for example:

  ```
  [5, 1, 3] > [4, 6, 2]
  ```

  which returns values of 1.0, 0.0, 1.0, (that is, true, false, true).

- assignment, for example:

  ```
  x = 4
  ```

  creates a variable called "x" and stores the value 4.0 in it. There is no need to declare variables before usage. All variables are type double by default.

- arrays, such as the following.

  ```
  x = 4:10;
  y = x .* (1:length(x))
  ```

  In this example, `x` is assigned the array values 4, 5, 6, ... 10. The length of `x` is used to generate another array, from 1 to 7 in this case. These two arrays are multiplied point-by-point, and stored in a new variable called `y`.

  Note that as of this writing, ranges must use a default increment of one. To generate an array with, say, 0.25 increments, one can divide each value by the reciprocal. That is, `(1:10)/4` generates an array of 0.25, 0.5, 0.75, ... 2.5.

- display a message to the output (disp), for example:

```
disp('hello world')
```

- conditionals (if statements), for example:

```
if (x == 4)
    y = 1
else
    y = 2
end
```

Nested statements are supported, such as:

```
if (x == 4)
    if (y < 2)
        z = 1
    end
end
```

- loops (`while` and `for` statements), for example:

```
x = 1
while (x < 5)
    disp('hello')
    x = x + 1
end
```

Here is a similar example, using a `for` loop:

```
for x = 1:5
    disp('hello')
end
```

- math functions, including: `floor`, `ceil`, `round`, `fix`, `rand`, `abs`, `min`, `max`, `sqrt`, `exp`, `log`, `log2`, `log10`, `cos`, `sin`, `tan`, `acos`, `asin`, `atan`. These also work with arrays, as in the previous section's example.
- Fast Fourier Transform and its inverse, which includes support of imaginary numbers. For example, this code

```
x = 1:8;
X = fft(x);
xHat = ifft(X)
```

produces the following output, as expected.

```
        1            2            3            4
        5            6            7            8
```

3.1 Graphics Support

To support graphics, we need to draw images at run time. Figure 2 shows an example of this, a plot of a sinusoid. The numbers may look a little strange, because I defined them myself as bit-mapped images. Upon loading the web-page, the recipient's web-browser requests an image which is really a common gateway interface (CGI) program written in C. The program reads an array of floating-point numbers and returns an image, constructed based on the array.

The bit-map graphic example of Figure 2 demonstrates this idea of drawing images dynamically at run time. It proves that it can be done.

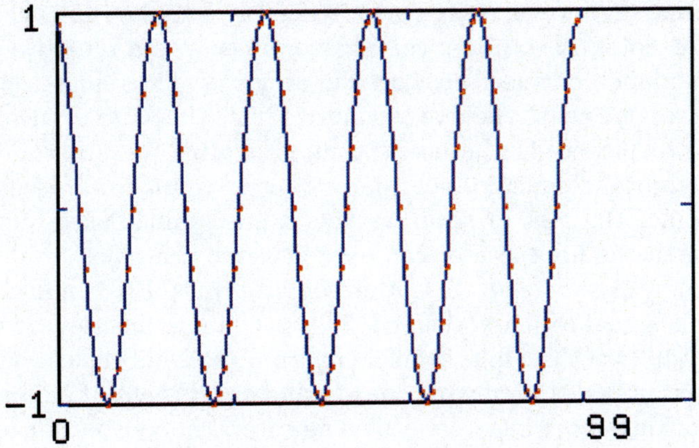

Fig. 2. Cosine plotted with *Calq*

3.2 Development Concerns

Making *Calq* as complete as, say MATLAB, is not realistic. For example, the MATLAB function `wavrecord` works with the local computer's sound card and microphone to record sound samples. There will be functions like this that cannot be implemented directly.

It is also not intended to be competition to MATLAB. If anything, it should complement MATLAB. Once the user becomes familiar with *Calq*'s capabilities, they are likely to desire something more powerful.

Latency and scalability also factor into the overall success of this project. The preliminary system uses a "watchdog timer," that decrements once per operation. When it expires, the system stops evaluating the user's commands. Some form of this timer may be desired in the final project, since it is entirely possible for the user to specify an infinite loop. It must be set with care, to respect the balance between functionality and quick response.

While one server providing the interface and external functions makes sense initially, demand will require more computing power once other people start using this system. Enabling this system on other servers may be enough to meet the demand, but this brings up issues with data and communications between servers. For example, if the system allows a user to store personal files on the *Calq* server (like *Google Docs* does), then it is a reasonable assumption that those files would be available through other *Calq* servers. Making this a distributed application can be done effectively with other technology like simple object access protocol (SOAP) [9].

3.3 Determining Success

Calq is tested with three different programs, running each multiple times on different computers. The first program, "cosplot," is given in an earlier section. The `plot` command, however, only partially factors into the run-time, due to the way it is implemented. The user's computer connects to a remote server, sends the data to plot, and continues on with the program. The remote server creates an image and responds with the image's name. Since this is an asynchronous call, the results are displayed on the user's computer after the program completes. Thus, only the initial connection and data transfer count towards the run-time. Additionally, since the plot program assigns a hash-value based on the current time as part of the name, the user can only plot one thing per "evaluate" cycle.

A second program, "wavelet," also represents a typical DSP application. It creates an example signal called `x`, defined to be a triangle function. It then makes an array called `db2` with the four coefficients from the Daubechies wavelet by the same name. Next, it finds the convolution of `x` and `db2`. Finally, it performs a down-sampling operation by copying every other value from the convolution result. While this is not efficient, it does show a simple approach. The program appears below.

```
tic

% Make an example signal (triangle)
x1 = (1:25)/25;
x2 = (51 - (26:50))/26;
x = [x1, x2];

% Compute wavelet coeffs
d0 = (1-sqrt(3))/(4*sqrt(2));
d1 = -(3-sqrt(3))/(4*sqrt(2));
d2 = (3+sqrt(3))/(4*sqrt(2));
d3 = -(1+sqrt(3))/(4*sqrt(2));
db2 = [d0, d1, d2, d3];

% Find convolution with our signal
h = conv(x, db2);

% downsample h to find the details
n=1;
for k=1:2:length(h)
```

```
        detail1(n) = h(k);
        n = n + 1;
    end

    toc
```

The first two examples verify that *Calq* works, and shows some difference in the run-times for different browsers. However, since the run-times are so small and subject to variations due to other causes, it would not be a good idea to draw conclusions based only on the differences between these times. To represent a more complex problem, the third program is the 5×5 square knight's tour. This classic search problem has a knight traverse a chessboard, visiting each square once and only once. The knight starts at row one, column one. This program demands more computational resources than the first two programs.

Though not shown in this paper due to length limitations, the "knight" program can be found by visiting the *Calq* website [8], typing `load('knight.m');` into the text-box, and pressing the "evaluate" button.

4 Results

The objective of the tests are to demonstrate this proof-of-concept across a wide variety of platforms. Tables 1, 2 and 3 show the results of running the example programs on different web-browsers. Each table corresponds to a different machine.

Initially, to measure the time, the procedure was to load the program, manually start a timer, click on the "evaluate" button, and stop the timer once the results are displayed. The problem with this method is that human reaction time could be blamed for any differences in run times. To fix this, *Calq* was expanded to recognize the keywords `tic`, `toc`, and `time`. The first two work together; `tic` records the current time internally, and `toc` shows the elapsed time since the (last) `tic` command. This does not indicate directly how much CPU time is spent interpreting the *Calq* program, though, and there does not appear to be a simple way to measure CPU time. The `time` command simply prints the current time, which is used to verify that `tic` and `toc` work correctly. That is, `time` is called at the start and end of the third program. This allows the timing results to be double-checked.

Loading the program means typing a `load` command (e.g., `load('cosplot');`, `load('wavelet');` or `load('knight.m');`) in the *Calq* window and clicking the "evaluate" button. Note that the system is case-sensitive, which causes some difficulty since the iPod Touch capitalizes the first letter typed into a text-box by default. The local computer contacts the remote server, gets the program, and overwrites the text area with it. Running the program means clicking the "evaluate" button again, after it is loaded.

Since the "knight" program does not interact with the remote server, run times reflect only how long it took the computer to run the program.

Table 1. Runtimes for different web-browsers in seconds, computer 1 (Intel Core 2 Duo 2.16 GHz, running Apple's Mac OS X 10.5.8)

Run	Chrome 5.0.307.11 beta	Firefox v3.6	Opera v10.10 Mac OS X	Safari v4.0.4 (5531.21.10)
cosplot 1	0.021	0.054	0.044	0.02
cosplot 2	0.004	0.053	0.046	0.018
cosplot 3	0.003	0.054	0.05	0.018
wavelet 1	0.048	0.67	0.813	0.162
wavelet 2	0.039	0.655	0.826	0.16
wavelet 3	0.038	0.675	0.78	0.16
knight 1	16	347	514	118
knight 2	16	352	503	101
knight 3	17	351	515	100

Table 2. Runtimes for different web-browsers in seconds, computer 2 (Intel Pentium 4 CPU 3.00 GHz, running Microsoft Windows XP)

Run	Chrome 4.1.249.1042 (42199)	Firefox v3.6.2	Opera v10.5.1 MS Windows	Safari v4.0.5 (531.22.7)	Windows Internet Explorer 8.0.6001.18702
cosplot 1	0.021	0.063	0.011	0.022	0.062
cosplot 2	0.005	0.059	0.009	0.022	0.078
cosplot 3	0.005	0.063	0.01	0.021	0.078
wavelet 1	0.068	0.795	0.101	0.14	1.141
wavelet 2	0.074	0.791	0.1	0.138	1.063
wavelet 3	0.071	0.852	0.099	0.138	1.078
knight 1	19	436	38	109	672
knight 2	18	434	38	105	865
knight 3	18	432	39	108	820

Table 3. Runtimes in seconds for computer 3 (iPod Touch, 2007 model, 8 GB, software version 3.1.3)

Run	Safari
cosplot 1	0.466
cosplot 2	0.467
cosplot 3	0.473
wavelet 1	2.91
wavelet 2	2.838
wavelet 3	2.867
knight 1	N/A

Running the "knight" program on Safari results in a slow script warning. Since the browser expects JavaScript programs to complete in a very short amount of time, it stops execution and allows the user to choose to continue or quit. On Safari, this warning pops up almost immediately, then every minute or so after this. The user must choose to continue the script, so human reaction time factors into the run-time. However, the default changes to "continue" allowing the user to simply press the return key.

Firefox has a similar warning for slow scripts. But the alert that it generates also allows the user the option to always allow slow scripts to continue. All run-times listed for Firefox are measured after changing this option, so user interaction is not a factor.

Windows Internet Explorer also generates a slow script warning, asking to stop the script, and defaults to "yes" every time. This warning appears about once a second, and it took an intolerable 1054 seconds to complete the knight's tour during the initial test. Much of this elapsed time is due to the response time for the user to click on "No." It is possible to turn this feature off by altering the registry for this browser, and the times in Table 2 reflects this.

Table 3 shows run-times for these programs on the iPod Touch. For the "knight" program, Safari gives the following error message almost immediately: "JavaScript Error ...JavaScript execution exceeded timeout." Therefore, this program does not run to completion on the iTouch.

5 Conclusion

As we see from Tables 1-3, the browser choice affects the run-time of the test programs. This is especially true for the third program, chosen due to its computationally intensive nature. For the first two programs, the run-times are too small (mostly less than one second) to draw conclusions about relative browser speeds. The iTouch took substantially longer to run the wavelet program (about three seconds), but this is to be expected given the disparity in processing power compared to the other machines tested. Surprisingly, Google's Chrome browser executes the third program the fastest, often by a factor of 10 or more. Opera also has a fast execution time on the Microsoft/PC platform, but performs slowly on the OS X/Macintosh. It will be interesting to see Opera's performance once it is available on the iTouch.

This paper provides an overview of the *Calq* project, and includes information about its current status. It demonstrates that the system can be used for some scientific applications.

Using the web-browser to launch applications is a new area of research. Along with applications like Google Docs, an interactive scientific programming environment should appeal to many people. This project provides a new tool for researchers and educators, allowing anyone with a web-browser to explore and experiment with a scientific programming environment. The immediate feedback aspect will appeal to many people. Free access means that disadvantaged people will be able to use it, too.

This application is no replacement for a mature, powerful language like MATLAB. But *Calq* could be used alongside it. It could also be used by people who do not have access to their normal computer, or who just want to try a quick experiment.

References

1. Lawton, G.: Moving the OS to the Web. IEEE Computer, 16–19 (March 2008)
2. Brannock, E., Weeks, M., Rehder, V.: Detecting Filopodia with Wavelets. In: International Symposium on Circuits and Systems, pp. 4046–4049. IEEE Press, Kos (2006)
3. Gamulkiewicz, B., Weeks, M.: Wavelet Based Speech Recognition. In: IEEE Midwest Symposium on Circuits and Systems, pp. 678–681. IEEE Press, Cairo (2003)
4. Beucher, O., Weeks, M.: Introduction to MATLAB & SIMULINK: A Project Approach, 3rd edn. Infinity Science Press, Hingham (2008)
5. Iverson, K.: APL Syntax and Semantics. In: Proceedings of the International Conference on APL, pp. 223–231. ACM, Washington, D.C (1983)
6. Loui, R.: In Praise of Scripting: Real Programming Pragmatism. IEEE Computer, 22–26 (July 2008)
7. Michel, S.: Matlib (on-line MATLAB interpreter), emiWorks Technical Computing, `http://www.semiworks.de/MatLib.aspx` (last accessed March 11, 2010)
8. Weeks, M.: The preliminary website for Calq, `http://carmaux.cs.gsu.edu/calq_latest`, hosted by Georgia State University
9. Papazoglou, M., Traverso, P., Dustdar, S., Leymann, F.: Service-Oriented Computing: State of the Art and Research Challenges. IEEE Computer, 38–45 (November 2007)
10. Weeks, M.: The Calq System for Signal Processing Applications. In: International Symposium on Communications and Information Technologies, pp. 121–126. Meiji University, Tokyo (2010)

Testing of Transmission Channels Quality for Different Types of Communication Technologies

Robert Bestak[1], Zuzana Vranova[2], and Vojtech Ondryhal[2]

[1] Czech Technical University in Prague, Technicka 2, 16627 Prague, Czech Republic
robert.bestak@fel.cvut.cz
[2] University of Defence, Kounicova 65, 66210 Brno, Czech Republic
{zuzana.vranova,vojtech.ondryhal}@unob.cz

Abstract. The current trend in communication development leads to the creation of a universal network suitable for transmission of all types of information. Terms such as the NGN or well-known VoIP start to be widely used. A key factor for assessing of the quality of offered services in the VoIP world represents the quality of transferred call. The assessment of the call quality for the above mentioned networks requires using new approaches. Nowadays, there are many standardized subjective and objective sophisticated methods of these speech quality evaluations. Based on the knowledge of these recommendations, we have developed testbed and procedures to verify and compare the signal quality when using TDM and VoIP technologies. The presented results are obtained from the measurement done in the network of the Armed Force Czech Republic.

Keywords: VoIP, signal voice quality, G.711.

1 Introduction

A new phenomenon so called the convergences of telephony and data networks in IP based principles leads to the creation of a universal network suitable for transmission of all types of information. Terms, such as the NGN (Next Generation Network), IPMC (IP Multimedia Communications) or well-known VoIP (Voice over Internet Protocol) start to be widely used. The ITU has defined the NGN in ITU-T Recommendation Y.2001 as a packet-based network able to provide telecommunication services and able to make use of multiple broadband, QoS (Quality of Service) enabled transport of technologies and in which service-related functions are independent of underlying transport-related technologies. It offers unrestricted access to users to different service providers. It supports generalized mobility which will allow consistent and ubiquitous provision of services to users. The NGN enables a wide number of multimedia services. The main services are VoIP, videoconferencing, instant messaging, email, and all other kinds of packet-switched communication services. The VoIP is a more specific term. It is a new modern sort of communication network which refers to transport of voice, video and data communication over IP network. Nowadays, the term VoIP, though, is really too limiting to describe the kinds of capabilities users seek in any sort of next-generation communications system. For that reason, a

H. Cherifi, J.M. Zain, and E. El-Qawasmeh (Eds.): DICTAP 2011, Part I, CCIS 166, pp. 13–23, 2011.

newer term called IPMC has been introduced to be more descriptive. A next generation system will provide much more than simple audio or video capabilities in a truly converged platform. Network development brings a number of user benefits, such as less expensive operator calls, mobility, multifunction terminals, user friendly interfaces and a wide number of multimedia services. A key criterion for assessment of the service quality remains the speech quality. Nowadays, there are many standardized subjective and objective sophisticated methods which are able to evaluate speech quality. Based on the knowledge of the above mentioned recommendations we have developed testbed and procedures in order to verify and compare the signal quality when using conventional TDM (Time Division Multiplex) and VoIP technologies. The presented outcomes are results obtained from the measurement done in the live network of the Armed Force Czech Republic (ACR).

Many works, such as [1], [2], or [3], address a problem related to subjective and objective methods of speech quality evaluation in VoIP and wireless networks. Some of papers only present theoretical works. Authors in [2] summarize methods of quality evaluation of voice transmission which is a basic parameter for development of VoIP devices, voice codecs, setting and operating of wired and mobile networks. Paper [3] focuses on objective methods of speech quality assessment by E-model. It presents the impact delay on R-factor when taking into account GSM codec RPE-LTP among others. Authors in [4] investigate effects of wireless-VoIP degradation on the performance of three state-of-the-art quality measurement algorithms: ITU-T PESQ, P.563 and E-model. Unlike the work of mentioned papers and unlike the commercially available communication simulators and analyzers, our selected procedures and testbed seem to be sufficient with respect to the obtained information for the initial evaluation of speech quality for our examined VoIP technologies.

The organization of this paper is as follows. In Section 2, we present VoIP technologies working in the real ACR communication network and CIS department VOIP testing and training base. Section 3 focuses on tests which are carried out in order to verify and compare the signal quality when using TDM and VoIP technologies. The measurements are done by using real communication technologies. In Section 4, we outline our conclusions.

2 VoIP Technologies in the ACR

As mention above, the world trend of modernization of communication infrastructure is characterized by convergence of phone and data networks of IP principles. Thus, implementation of VoIP technologies is a highly topical issue in the ACR. Two VoIP technologies operate in the ACR network, whereas one of them is represented by Cisco products and the other one by Alcatel-Lucent Omni-PCX Enterprise technology. Currently, it is necessary to solve not only problems with compatibility of these systems with regard to the net and users required services guarantee but also a number of questions related to reliability and security.

The CIS (Communication and Information Systems) department pays special attention to up-building of the high quality VoIP testing and training base.

2.1 Infrastructure of CIS Department VoIP Training Base

One the first system obtained to VoIP training base is Cisco CallManager Express. This product offers a complex solution of VoIP but has some restrictions. CallManager Express is a software running on Cisco router IOS (Internetwork Operating System) and can be managed only on Cisco devices on LAN (Local Area Network). Using of voice mail requires a special expensive Cisco router module. But CallManager Express offers modern telecommunications services, such as a phone book on Cisco IP phones via XML (eXtended Markup Language), DND (Do Not Disturb) feature or periodically push messages onto the screen of phones too. Typical connection scheme of training workplace equipped with CallManager Express is shown in Figure 1.

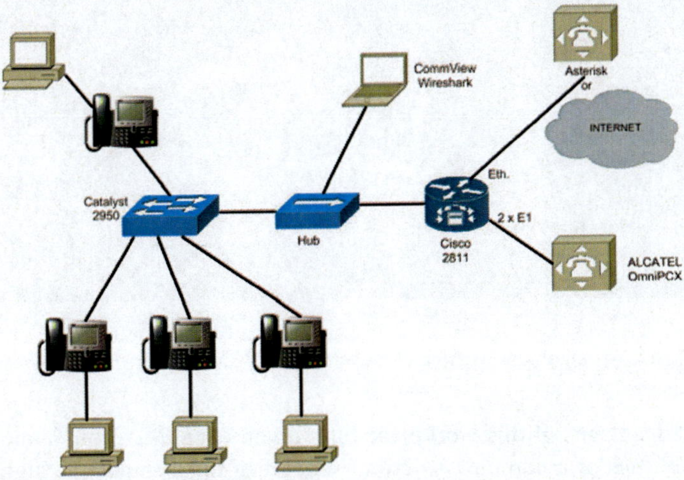

Fig. 1. Example of CallManager Express workplaces

The second workplace represents VoIP configuration of Alcatel-Lucent network devices. It consists of several Alcatel-Lucent devices. The key device is Alcatel-Lucent OmniPCX Enterprise communication server which provides multimedia call processing not only for Alcatel-Lucent, but also for TDM or IP phones and clients. The other devices are: L3 Ethernet switch Alcatel-Lucent OmniSwitch 6850 P24X, WLAN (wireless local area network) switch Alcatel-Lucent OmniAccess 4304, two Access points OAW-AP61, four WLAN phones Alcatel-Lucent 310/610 and TDM Alcatel-Lucent phones. The main part of the workplace is a common powerful PC running two key SW applications. For network management software Alcatel-Lucent OmniVista application is used and Alcatel-Lucent OmniTouch application is used as a server. The workplace is illustrated in Figure 2.

The Alcatel-Lucent OmniPCX Enterprise provides building blocks for any IP and/or legacy communications solution and open standard practices such as QSIG,

H.323, and SIP (Session Initiation Protocol). It offers broad scalability ranging from 10 to up 100 000 users and highly reliable solutions with an unmatched 99.999% uptime. The management of OmniPCX is transparent and easy with friendly GUI. One PC with running management software OmniVista can supervise the whole network with tens of communication servers.

Fig. 2. Arrangement of Alcatel-Lucent OmniPCX Enterprise workplace

The best advantages of this workplace built on an OmniPCX communication server are: possibilities of a complex solution, support of open standards, high reliability and security, mobility and the offer of advanced and additional services. The complexity of a communication server is supported by several building blocks. The main component is the Call Server which is the system control centre with only IP connectivity. One or more (possibly none) Media Gateways are necessary to support standard telephone equipment (such as wired digital or analogue sets, lines to the standard public or private telephone networks, DECT phone base stations). The scheme of communication server telephone system is shown in Figure 3.

There are no restrictions on using of terminals of only one manufacture (Alcatel-Lucent). Many standards and open standards such H.323 and SIP are supported. In addition, Alcatel-Lucent terminals offer some additional services. The high reliability is guaranteed by duplicating of call servers or by using passive servers in small branches. The duplicated server runs simultaneously with the main server. In the case of main server failure the duplicated one becomes a main server. In the case of loss of connection to main server, passive communication servers provide continuity of telephony services. It also controls interconnected terminals and can find out alternative connections through public network.

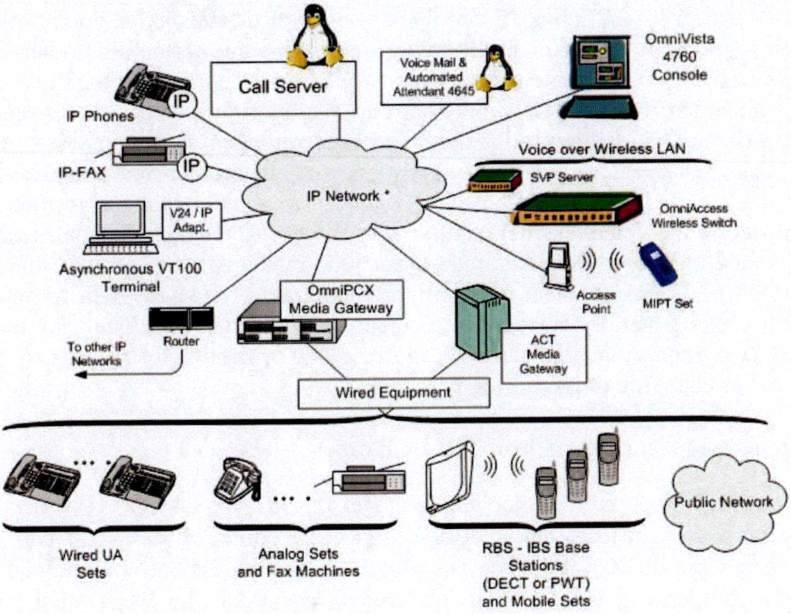

Fig. 3. Architecture of Alcatel-Lucent OmniPCX Enterprise telephone systems

The OmniPCX communication server supports several security elements. For example: the PCX accesses are protected by a strong limited live time password, accesses to PCX web applications are encrypted by using of the https (secured http) protocol, remote shell can be protected and encrypted by using of the SSH (secured shell) protocol, remote access to the PCX can be limited to the declared trusted hosts or further IP communications with IPTouch sets (Alcatel-Lucent phones) and the Media Gateways can be encrypted and authenticated, etc.

The WLAN switch Alcatel-Lucent OmniAccess 4304 can utilize the popular WiFi (Wireless Fidelity) technology and offers more mobility to its users. The WiFi mobile telephones Alcatel-Lucent 310/610 communicate with the call server through WLAN switch. Only „silly“ access points with integrated today common standards IEEE 802.11 a/b/g, can be connected to WLAN switch that controls the whole wireless network. This solution increases security because even if somebody obtains WiFi phones or access point, it doesn’t mean serious security risks. The WLAN switch provides many configuration tasks, such as VLAN configuration on access points or it especially provides roaming among the access points which increases the mobility of users a lot.

3 Measurement and Obtained Results

This part is devoted to measurement of the main telephone channel characteristics and parameters of both systems described in Section 2.

The measurement and comparison of the quality of established telephone connections are carried out for different alternates of systems and terminals. In accordance with relevant ITU-T recommendations series of tests are performed on TDM and IP channel created at first separately and after that in a hybrid network. Due to economic reasons we have had to develop testbed and procedures so as to get near to the required standard laboratory conditions. Frequency characteristics and delay are gradually verified. A different type of codecs is chosen as a parameter for verification of their impact on the voice channel quality. An echo of TDM voice channels and noise ratios are also measured. Separate measurement is made by using of the CommView software in the IP environment to determine the parameters MOS, R-factor, etc. The obtained results generally correspond to theoretical assumptions. Though, some deviations have been gradually clarified and resolved with either adjusting of testing equipment or changing of measuring procedures.

3.1 Frequency Characteristic of TDM Channel

Measurement is done at the telephone channel 0.3 kHz – 3.4 kHz. The measuring instruments are attached to the analogue connecting points on the TDM part of Alcatel-Lucent OmniPCX Enterprise. The aim of this measurement is a comparison of qualitative properties of TDM channels created separately by the system Alcatel-Lucent OmniPCX Enterprise with the characteristics of IP channel created on the same or other VoIP technology (see Figure 4).

By the dash-and-dot line, it is outlined the decrease of 3 dB compared with the average value of the level of the output signal which is marked with a dashed line. In the telephone channel bandwidth, 0.3 kHz – 3.4 kHz, the level of the measured signal is relatively stable. The results of measurement correspond to theoretical assumptions and show that the technology Alcatel-Lucent OmniPCX Enterprise fulfils the conditions of the standard in light of the provided width of transmitted zone.

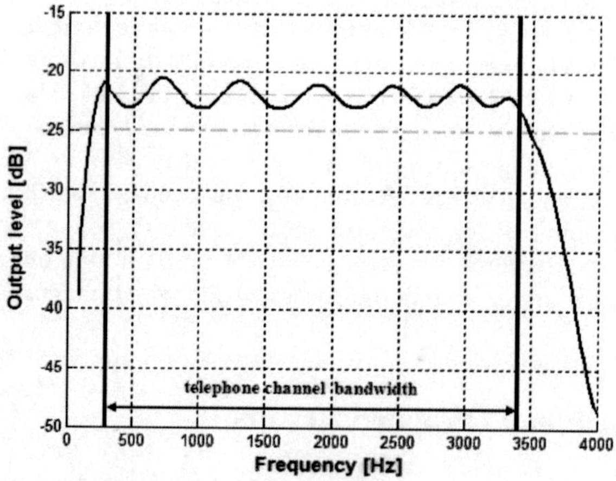

Fig. 4. Frequency characteristic of TDM channel

3.2 Frequency Characteristic of IP Channel

Alcatel-Lucent OmniPCX Enterprise IP Channel

The same type of measurement as in section 3.1 is done but the user interface of Alcatel-Lucent OmniPCX Enterprise is changed. Conversational channel is created between two Alcatel IP Touch telephones (see Figure 5).

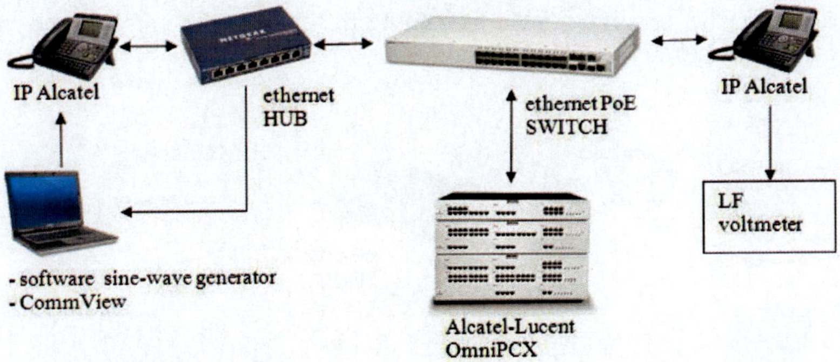

Fig. 5. Setting of devices when measuring frequency characteristic of IP channel (Alcatel-Lucent OmniPCX Enterprise)

The obtained results show that the technology Alcatel-Lucent OmniPCX Enterprise fulfills the conditions of the standard regarding the provided channel bandwidth in case of IP too (Figure 6).

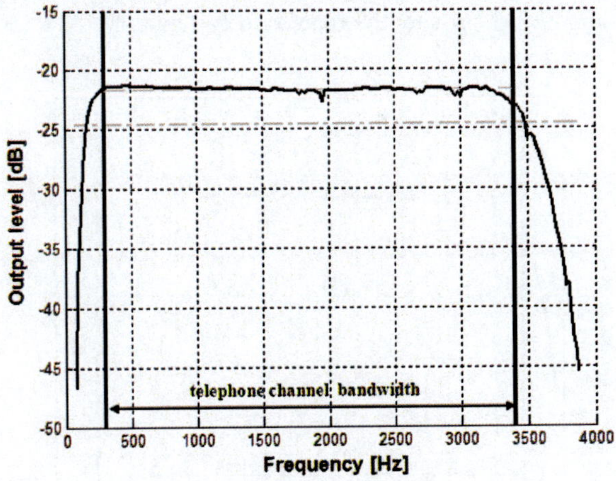

Fig. 6. Frequency characteristic of IP channel when using codec G.711 (Alcatel-Lucent OmniPCX Enterprise)

Linksys SPA-922 IP Channel with Codec G.711

Measurement is performed in the conversational channel populated by two phones Linksys SPA-922. The channel enables to link phones directly visavis with ordinary Ethernet cable without the use of call server. Thanks to this we gain almost ideal transmission environment without loss and delays.

As the generator sound card PC and the Program "The Generator" is used. The harmonious signal is used as the measuring signal which is steadily retuned in the required zone. The output of the sound card is connected through resistance divider and capacitor for the reasons of readjustment to the circuits of the telephone receiver. The connection setting is shown in Figure 7.

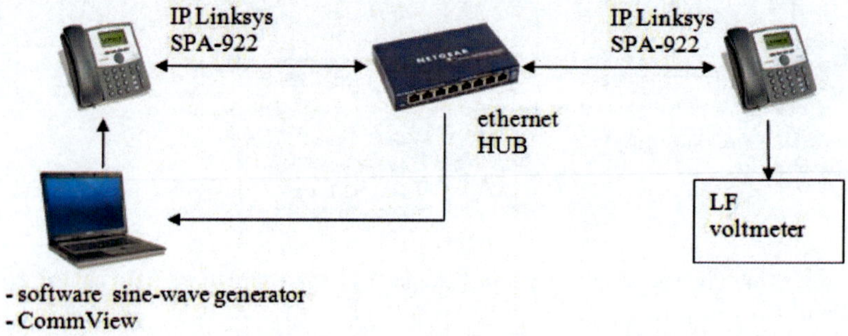

Fig. 7. Setting of devices when measuring frequency characteristic of IP channel (Linksys SPA-922)

Measurement is made for codec G.711 and obtained frequency characteristics are presented in Figure 8. As it can be observed, the telephones Linksys SPA-922 together with encoding G.711 provide the requested call quality.

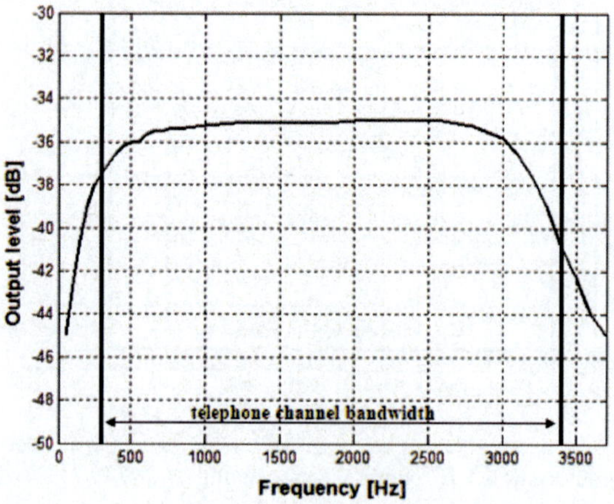

Fig. 8. Frequency characteristic of IP channel when using codec G.711 (Linksys SPA-922)

.Linksys SPA-922 IP Channel with Codecs G.729 and G.723.

Measurement is carried out under the same conditions as only for other types of codecs. Figure 9 illustrates that if the other types of codecs than G.711, in particular vocoders, are used, measurement by means of the first harmonic could be distorted. The same channel acts for the codecs G.723 and G.729 quite differently than in the previous scenario. The resulting curve is not a function of properties of the channel but it is strongly influenced by the operation of the used encoders.

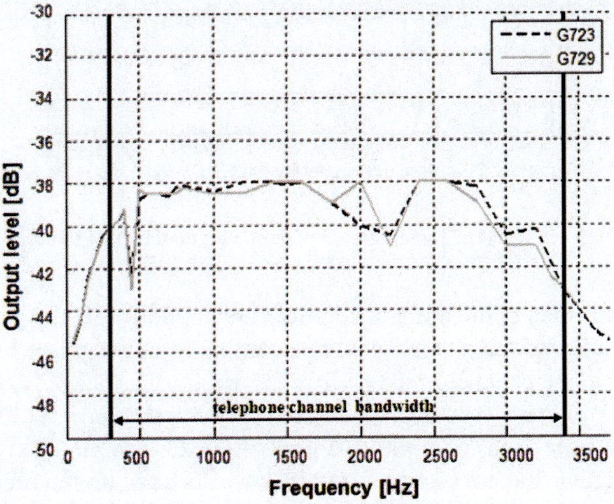

Fig. 9. Frequency characteristic of IP channel when using codecs G.729 and G.723

3.3 VoIP Technology Channel Delay Measurement

The setting of the workplace for the delay measurement is shown in Figure 10 and the results of measurement in Figures 11, 12.

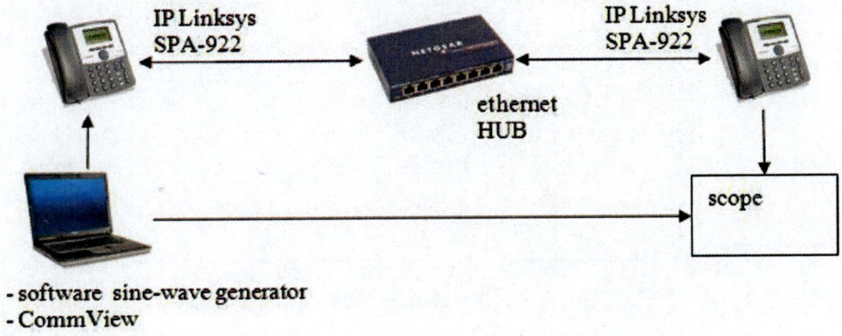

Fig. 10. Setting of devices when measuring the channel delay

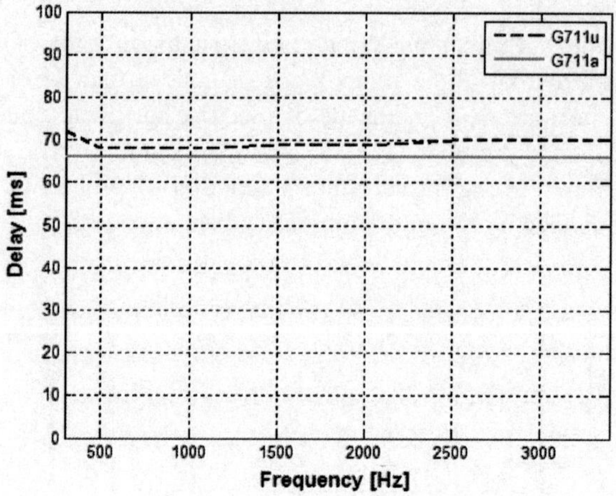

Fig. 11. Channel delay when using codec G.711

The obtained results confirm the theoretical assumptions that the packet delay and partly also the buffer of telephones would be concerned in the greatest extent with the resulting delays in the channel in the established workplace. The delay caused by A/D converter can be omitted. These conclusions apply for the codec G.711 (Figure 11). Additional delays are measured with the codecs G.723, and G.729 (Figure 12). The delay is in particular the consequence of the lower bandwidth required for the same length of packets, eventually of appropriate time demandingness of processing in the used equipment.

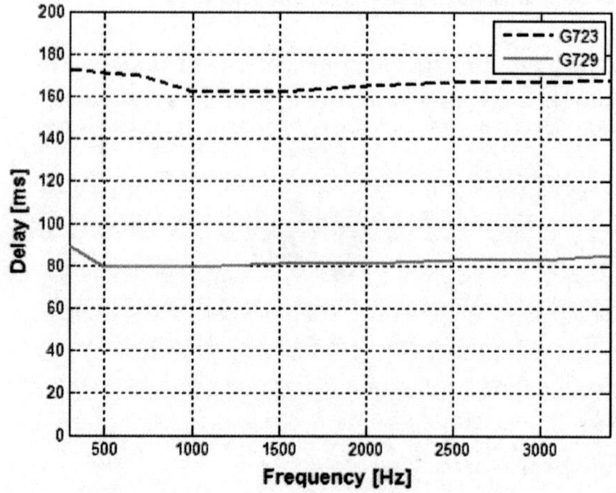

Fig. 12. Channel delay when using codecs G.723 and G.729

Notice that during the measurement of delays in the system Alcatel-Lucent OmniPCX Enterprise lower delay has been found for the codecs G.723 and G.729 (less than 31ms). During this measurement, another degree of framing is supposed. It was confirmed that the size of delay significantly depends not only on the type of codec, but also on the frame size. Furthermore, for the measurement of the delay for the systems Alcatel-Lucent OmniPCX Enterprise and Cisco connected in the network, the former system which includes codec G.729, brought into measurement significant delays. At the time, when used phones worked with the G.711 codec, the gateway driver had to convert the packets, thus, leading to the increase of delays up to 100ms, which may lead to degradation of quality of connection.

4 Conclusions

The paper analyses of the option of simple, fast and economically available verification of the quality of TDM and IP conversational channel for various VoIP technologies. By the process it went out of the knowledge of appropriate standards ITU-T series P defining the methods for subjective and objective assessment of transmission quality. The tests are carried out in the VOIP technologies set in the real communication network of the ACR.

Frequency characteristics of TDM and IP channels for different scenarios are evaluated. Furthermore, the parameter of delay, which may substantially affect the quality of transmitted voice in the VoIP network, is analyzed. Measurement is carried out for different types of codecs applicable to the tested network.

The obtained results have confirmed the theoretical assumptions. Furthermore, it is confirmed, how important the selection of network components is, in order to avoid the degradation of quality of voice communication because of inadequate increase of delay on the network. We also discovered deficiencies in certain internal system roles of the measured systems, which again led to the degradation of quality of transmitted voice, and will be addressed directly to the supplier of the technology.

Acknowledgment

This research work was supported by grant of Czech Ministry of Education, Youth and Sports No. MSM6840770014.

References

1. Falk, H.T., Ch, W.-Y.: Performance Study of Objective Speech Quality Measurement for Modern Wireless-VoIP Communications. EURASIP Journal on Audio, Speech, and Music Processing (2009)
2. Nemcik, M.: Evaluation of voice quality voice. Akusticke listy 2006/1, 7–13 (2006)
3. Pravda, I., Vodrazka, J.: Voice Quality Planning for NGN Including Mobile Networks. In: Twelve IFIP Personal Wireless Communications Conference, pp. 376–383. Springer, New York (2007)
4. Kuo, P.-J., Omae, K., Okajima, I., Umeda, N.: VoIP quality evaluation in Mobile wireless networks Advances in multimedia information processing. In: Third IEEE Pacific Rim Conference on Multimedia 2002. LNCS, vol. 2532, pp. 688–695. Springer, Heidelberg (2002)

Haptic Feedback for Passengers Using Public Transport

Ricky Jacob, Bashir Shalaik, Adam C. Winstanley, and Peter Mooney

Department of Computer Science, National University of Ireland,
Maynooth Co. Kildare, Ireland
{rjacob,bsalaik,adamw}@cs.nuim.ie

Abstract. People using public transport systems need two kinds of basic information - (1) when, where and which bus/train to board, and (2) when to exit the vehicle. In this paper we propose a system that helps the user know his/her stop is nearing. The main objective of our system is to overcome the 'neck down' approach of any visual interface which requires the user to look into the mobile screen for alerts. Haptic feedback is becoming a popular feedback mode for navigation and routing applications. Here we discuss the integration of haptics into public transport systems. Our system provides information about time and distance to the destination bus stop and uses haptic feedback in the form of the vibration alarm present in the phone to alert the user when the desired stop is being approached. The key outcome of this research is haptics being an effective alternative to provide feedback for public transport users.

Keywords: haptic, public transport, real-time data, gps.

1 Introduction

Haptic technology, or haptics, is a tactile feedback technology that takes advantage of our sense of touch by applying forces, vibrations, and/or motions to the user through a device. From computer games to virtual reality environments, haptics has been used for a long time [8]. One of the most popular uses is the Nintendo Wii controllers which give the user forced feedback while playing games. Some touch screen phones have integrated forced feedback to represent key clicks on screen using vibration alarm present on the phone. Research into the use of the sense of touch to transfer information has been going on for years. Van Erp, who has been working with haptics for over a decade, discusses the use of the tactile sense to supplement visual information in relation to navigating and orientating in a Virtual Environment [8]. Jacob et al [11] provided a summary of the different uses of haptics and how it is being integrated into GIS. Hoggan and Brewster [10] feel that with the integration of various sensors on a smartphone, it makes it an easier task to develop simple but effective communication techniques on a portable device. Heikkinen et al [9] states that our human "sense of touch is highly spatial and, by its nature, tactile sense depends on the physical contact to an object or its surroundings". With the emergence of smart phones that come enabled with various sensors like accelerometer, magnetometer, gyroscope, compass and GPS, it is possible to develop applications that provide navigation information in the form of haptic feedback [11] [13]. The "PocketNavigator"

H. Cherifi, J.M. Zain, and E. El-Qawasmeh (Eds.): DICTAP 2011, Part I, CCIS 166, pp. 24–32, 2011.

application which makes use of the GPS and compass helps the user navigate by providing different patterns of vibration feedback to represent various directions in motion. Jacob *et al* [12] describe a system which integrates OpenStreetMap data, Cloudmade Routing API [21], and pedestrian navigation and provides navigation cues using haptic feedback by making use of the vibration alarm in the phone. Pedestrian navigation using bearing-based haptic feedback is used to guide users in the general direction of their destination via vibrations [14]. The sense of touch is an integral part of our sensory system. Touch is also important in communicating as it can convey non-verbal information [9]. Haptic feedback as a means for providing navigation assistance to visually impaired have been an area of research over the past few years. Zelek augments the white cane and dog by developing this tactile glove which can be used to help a visually impaired user navigate [15].

The two kinds of information that people using public transport need are - (1) when, where and which bus/train to board, and (2) when to exit the vehicle to get off at the stop the user needs to go to. Dziekan and Kottenhoff [7] study the various benefits of dynamic real-time at-stop bus information system for passengers using public transport. The various benefits include - reduced wait time, increased ease-of use and a greater feeling of security, and higher customer satisfaction. The results of the study by Caufiled and O'Mahony demonstrate that passengers derive the greatest benefit from accessing transit stop information from real-time information displays [16]. The literature states that one of the main reasons individuals access real-time information is to remove the uncertainty when using public transit. Rehrl *et al* [17] discusses the need for personalized multimodal journey planners for the user who uses various modes of transport. Koskinen and Virtanen [18] discuss information needs from a point of view of the visually impaired in using public transport real time information in personal navigation systems. Three cases presented are: (1) using bus real time information to help the visually impaired to get in and leave a bus at the right stop, (2) boarding a train and (3) following a flight status. Bertolotto *et al* [4] describe a BusCatcher system. The main functionality provided include: display of maps, with overlaid route plotting, user and bus location, and display of bus timetables and arrival times. Turunen *et al* [20] present approaches for mobile public transport information services such as route guidance and push timetables using speech based feedback. Bantre *et al* [2] describes an application called "UbiBus" which is used to help blind or visually impaired people to take public transport. This system allows the user to request in advance the bus of his choice to stop, and to be alerted when the right bus has arrived. An RFID based ticketing system provides the user's destination and then text messages are sent by the system to guide the user in real time [1]. The Mobility-for-All project identifies the needs of users with cognitive disabilities who learn and use public transportation systems [5]. They present a socio-technical architecture that has three components: a) a personal travel assistant that uses real-time Global Positioning Systems data from the bus fleet to deliver just-in-time prompts; b) a mobile prompting client and a prompting script configuration tool for caregivers; and c) a monitoring system that collects real-time task status from the mobile client and alerts the support community of potential problems. There is mention about problems such as people falling asleep or buses not running on time are likely only to be seen in the world and not in the laboratory and thus not considered when designing a system for people to use[5]. While using public transport, the visually impaired or blind users found the most frustrating things to be 'poor clarity of stop announcements, exiting transit at wrong places, not finding a bus stop' among others [19]. Barbeau *et al* [3] describe a Travel Assistance Device (TAD) which aids transit riders with special needs in using public transportation. The three features of the TAD system are - a) The delivery of real-time auditory prompts to the transit rider via the cell phone informing them when they should request a stop, b) The delivery of an alert to the rider, caretaker and travel trainer when the rider deviates from the expected route and c) A webpage that allows travel trainers and caretakers to create new itineraries for transit riders, as well as monitor real-time rider location. Here the user uses a GPS enabled smartphone and uses a wireless headset connected via bluetooth which gives auditory feedback to the user when the destination bus stop is nearing. In our paper we describe a system similar to this [3] which can be used by any passenger using public transport. Instead of depending on visual or audio feedback which will require the user's attention, we intend to use haptic feedback in the form of vibration alarm with different patterns and frequencies to give different kinds of location based information to the user. With the vibration alarm being the main source of feedback in our system, it also takes into consideration of specific cases like "the passenger falling asleep on the bus" [5] and also users missing their stop due to inattentiveness or visual impairment[19].

2 Model Description

In this section we describe the user interaction model of our system. Figure 1 shows the flow of information across the four main parts of the system and is described here in detail. The user can download this application for free from our website. The user then runs the application and selects the destination bus stop just before boarding the bus. The user's current location and the selected destination bus stop are sent to the server using the HTTP protocol. The PHP script receiving this information stores the user's location along with the time stamp into the user's trip log table. The user's current location and the destination bus stop are used to compute the expected arrival time at the destination bus stop. Based on the user's current location, the next bus stop in the user's travel is also extracted from the database. These results are sent back from the server to the mobile device. Feedback to the user is provided using there different modes – Textual display, color coded buttons, and haptic feedback using vibration alarm. The textual display mode provides the user with three kinds of information – 1) Next bus stop in the trip, 2) Distance to the destination bus stop, 3) Expected arrival time at the destination bus stop. The color coded buttons are used to represent the user's location with respect to the final destination. Amber is used to inform the user that he has crossed the last stop before the destination stop where he needs to alight. The green color is used to inform the user that he is within 30 metres of the destination stop. This is also accompanied by the haptic feedback using high frequency vibration alert with a unique pattern, different from how it is when he receives a phone call/text message. Red color is used to represent any other location in the user's trip. The trip log table is used to map the user's location on a Bing map interface as shown in Figure 3. This web interface can be used (if he/she wishes to share) by the user's family and friends to view the live location of the user during the travel.

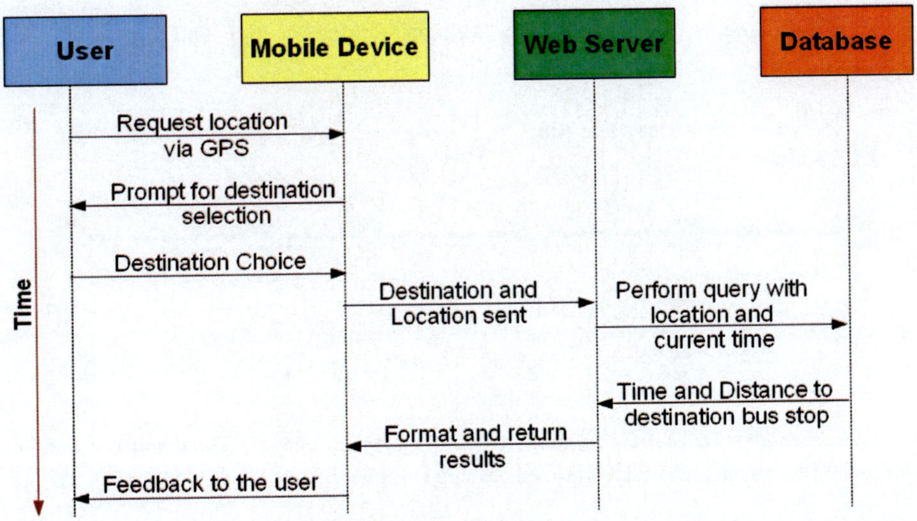

Fig. 1. User interaction model. It shows the flow of information across the four parts of the system as *Time* goes by.

The model of the route is stored in the MySQL database. Each route R is an ordered sequence of stops $\{d_s, d_0, ..., d_n, d_d\}$. The departure stop on a route is given by d_s and the terminus or destination stop is given by d_d. Each stop d_i has attribute information associated with it including: stop number, stop name, etc. Using the timetable information for a given journey R_i (say the 08:00 departure) along route R (for example 66 route) we store the timing for the bus to reach that stop. This can be stored as the number of minutes it will take the bus to reach an intermediate stop d_i after departing from d_s. This can also be stored as the actual time of day that a bus on journey R_i will reach a stop d_i along a given route R. This is illustrated in Figure 2. This model extends easily to incorporate other modes of public transportation including: long distance coach services, intercity trains, and trams.

A PHP script runs on the database webserver. Using the HTTP protocol the user's current location and their selected destination along route R is sent to the script. The user can select any choose any stop to begin their journey from d_s to d_n. This PHP script acts as a broken between the mobile device and the local spatial database which has store the bus route timetables. The current location (latitude, longitude) of the user at time t (given by u_t), on a given journey R_i along route R is stored in a separate table. The timestamp is also stored with this information. The same PHP script then computes and returns the following information back to the mobile device:

- The time in minutes, to the destination stops d_d from the current location of the bus on the route given by u_t
- The geographical distance, in kilometers, to the destination stop d_d from the current location of the bus on the route given by u_t
- The name, and stop number, of the next stop (between d_s and d_d)

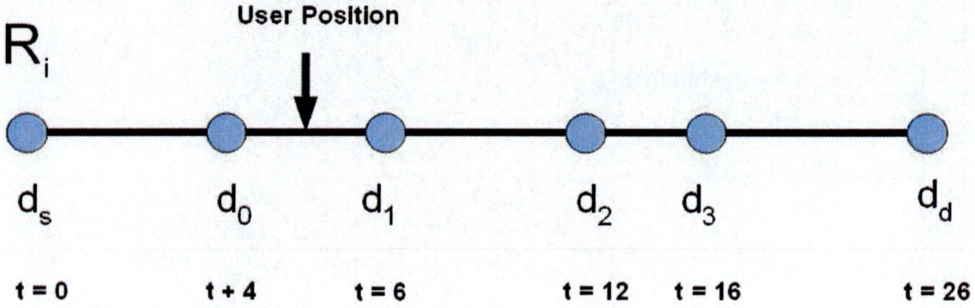

Fig. 2. An example of our route timetable model for a given journey R_i. The number of minutes required for the bus to reach each intermediate stop is shown *t*.

3 Implementation of the Model

Development was done in eclipse for Android using Java programming language. The Android Software Development Kit (SDK) supports the various sensors present in the phone. We tested this application by running it on the HTC Magic smart phone which runs on the Android Operating system. In order to test our concept we created a database in which we stored the time table of buses servicing stops from our University town (Maynooth) to Dublin. This is a popular route with tourists and visitors to our University. The timetable of the buses on the route was obtained from the DublinBus website [6]. MySQL database is used to store the bus time table data and also record the user's location with time stamp. A PHP script runs on the database webserver. Using the HTTP protocol the user location and the selected destination is sent to this script. This PHP script acts as the broker between the mobile devices our local spatial database which has the bus timings tables, the bus stop location table and a table to store the user position every time it is received with timestamps. The script computes and returns the following information back to the mobile device - 1) Time to the destination bus stop, 2) Distance to the destination bus stop, 3) Next bus stop in the route. These are computed based on the current location of the user when received by the script. The expected arrival time of the bus at the destination bus stop is computed and stored in a variable and sent to the mobile device initially when the journey begins. Thus it can be used as the alternative source for alerting the passenger if mobile connectivity is lost during the journey. A PHP script to display a map interface takes the value of the last known location of the user from the database and uses it to display user's current location. The interface also displays other relevant information like the expected time of arrival at destination, the distance to destination, and the next bus stop in the user's trip.

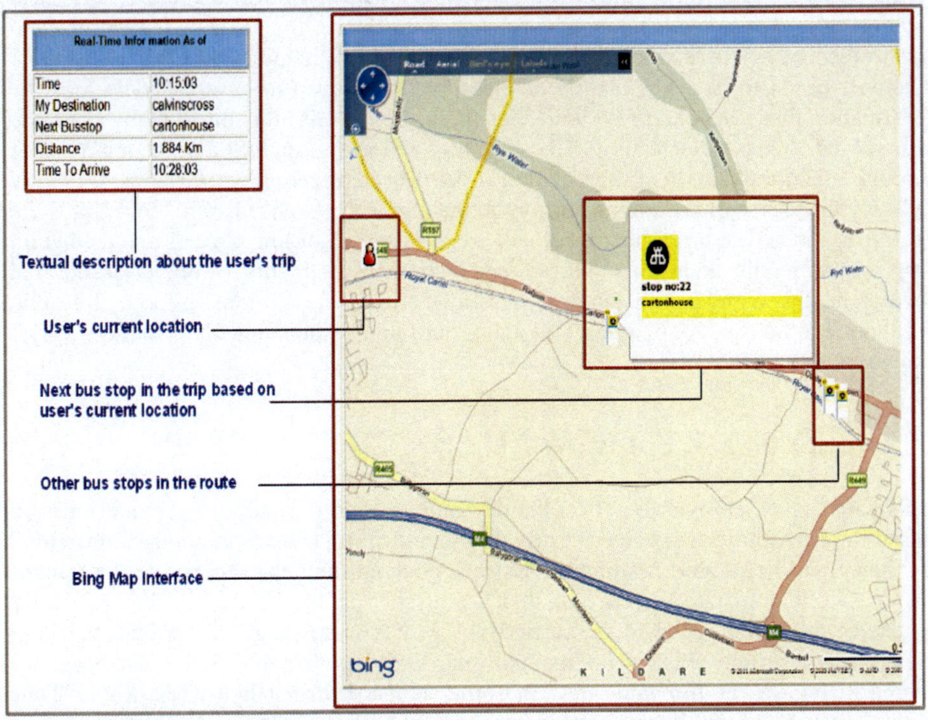

Fig. 3. The web interface displaying the user location and other relevant information

4 Key Findings with This Approach

To quantify motivation for this work we conducted a survey on public transport usage. We contacted 15 people for the survey and received 15 responses (mostly postgraduates and working personals). There are a number of important results from this survey, which was conducted online, which show that there is a need for an alert system similar to the one we have described in this paper. The majority (10 respondents) felt that the feedback from the in-bus display is useful. 11 of the 15 respondents had missed their stop while traveling by bus in the past. The most common reason for missing their stop was "since it was dark outside they hadn't noticed that their stop had arrived". The second most common reason was a result of passengers falling asleep on the bus where the response was "sleeping in the bus and thus not aware that their stop was approaching". The survey participants were asked what form of alert feedback they would most prefer. From the survey 'displaying user position on a map' and 'vibration alert to inform them of the bus stop' were the most selected options. The reasons for choosing the vibration alert feedback was given by 10 out of 15 who explained that they chose this since they don't need to devote all of their attention to the phone screen. The participants explained that since the phone is in their pockets/bag most of the time, the vibration alert would be a suitable form of feedback. Our system provides three kinds of feedback to the user with regard to arrival at destination stop. These feedback types are: textual feedback, the color coded buttons and haptic feedback. The textual and color coded feedback requires the user's attention. The user needs to have the screen of the application open to ensure he/she sees the information that has been provided. Thus the user will miss this information if he/she is involved in any other activity like listening to music, sending a text, or browsing through other applications in the phone. If the user is traveling with friends, it is very unlikely the user will have his attention on the phone [23]. Thus haptic feedback is the preferred mode for providing feedback to the user regarding arrival at destination stop. Haptic feedback ensures that the feedback is not distracting or embarrassing like a voice feedback and it also lets the user engage in other activities in the bus. Haptic feedback can be used by people of all age groups and by people with or without visual impairment.

5 Conclusion and Future Work

This paper gives an overview of a haptic-feedback based system to provide location based information for passengers using public transport. The vibration alarm provided by the system helps alert inattentive passengers about the bus as they near their destination. To demonstrate the success and use of such an application in the real-world extensive user trials need to be carried out with a wide range of participants from different age groups. Instead of manually storing the timetable into a database, we intend to import the timetable data in some standard format like KML/XML. Thus extending it to an alternate route in any region will be possible. With the positive feedback we received for the pedestrian navigation system using haptic feedback [11] [12], we feel that integration of haptic feedback with this location alert system will provide interesting research for future. In the future it is intended that our software will be developed to become a complete travel planner with route and location information based on haptic feedback. The continuous use of the vibrate function and the GPS with data transfer to the server can mean battery capacity may become an issue. Consequently, our software for this application must be developed with battery efficiency in mind. Over-usage of the vibrate function on the phone could drain the battery and this can cause distress and potential annoyance for the user [22].

Acknowledgments

Research in this paper is carried out as part of the Strategic Research Cluster grant (07/SRC/I1168) funded by Science Foundation Ireland under the National Development Plan. Dr. Peter Mooney is a research fellow at the Department of Computer Science and he is funded by the Irish Environmental Protection Agency STRIVE programme (grant 2008-FS-DM-14-S4). Bashir Shalaik is supported by a PhD studentship from the Libyan Ministry of Education. The authors gratefully acknowledge this support

References

1. Aguiar, A., Nunes, F., Silva, M., Elias, D.: Personal navigator for a public transport system using rfid ticketing. In: Motion 2009: Pervasive Technologies for Improved Mobility and Transportation (May 2009)
2. Bantre, M., Couderc, P., Pauty, J., Becus, M.: Ubibus: Ubiquitous computing to help blind people in public transport. In: Brewster, S., Dunlop, M.D. (eds.) Mobile HCI 2004. LNCS, vol. 3160, pp. 310–314. Springer, Heidelberg (2004)
3. Barbeau, S., Winters, P., Georggi, N., Labrador, M., Perez, R.: Travel assistance device: utilising global positioning system-enabled mobile phones to aid transit riders with special needs. Intelligent Transport Systems, IET 4(1), 12–23 (2010)
4. Bertolotto, M., O'Hare, M.P.G., Strahan, R., Brophy, A.N., Martin, A., McLoughlin, E.: Bus catcher: a context sensitive prototype system for public transportation users. In: Huang, B., Ling, T.W., Mohania, M.K., Ng, W.K., Wen, J.-R., Gupta, S.K. (eds.) WISE Workshops, pp. 64–72. IEEE Computer Society, Los Alamitos (2002)
5. Carmien, S., Dawe, M., Fischer, G., Gorman, A., Kintsch, A., Sullivan, J., James, F.: Socio-technical environments supporting people with cognitive disabilities using public transportation. ACM Transaction. Computer-Human Interactaction 12, 233–262 (2005)
6. Dublin Bus Website (2011), `http://www.dublinbus.ie/` (last accessed March 2011)
7. Dziekan, K., Kottenhoff, K.: Dynamic at-stop real-time information displays for public transport: effects on customers. Transportation Research Part A: Policy and Practice 41(6), 489–501 (2007)
8. Erp, J.B.F.V.: Tactile navigation display. In: Proceedings of the First International Workshop on Haptic Human-Computer Interaction, pp. 165–173. Springer, London (2001)
9. Heikkinen, J., Rantala, J., Olsson, T., Raisamo, R., Lylykangas, J., Raisamo, J., Surakka, J., Ahmaniemi, T.: Enhancing personal communication with spatial haptics: Two scenario based experiments on gestural interaction, Orlando, FL, USA, vol. 20, pp. 287–304 (October 2009)
10. Hoggan, E., Anwar, S., Brewster, S.: Mobile multi-actuator tactile displays. In: Oakley, I., Brewster, S. (eds.) HAID 2007. LNCS, vol. 4813, pp. 22–33. Springer, Heidelberg (2007)
11. Jacob, R., Mooney, P., Corcoran, P., Winstanley, A.C.: Hapticgis: Exploring the possibilities. In: ACMSIGSPATIAL Special 2, pp. 36–39 (November 2010)
12. Jacob, R., Mooney, P., Corcoran, P., Winstanley, A.C.: Integrating haptic feedback to pedestrian navigation applications. In: Proceedings of the GIS Research UK 19th Annual Conference, Portsmouth, England (April 2011)
13. Pielot, M., Poppinga, B., Boll, S.: Pocketnavigator: vibrotactile waypoint navigation for everyday mobile devices. In: Proceedings of the 12th International Conference on Human Computer Interaction with Mobile Devices and Services, ACM MobileHCI 2010, New York, NY, USA, pp. 423–426 (2010)
14. Robinson, S., Jones, M., Eslambolchilar, P., Smith, R.M, Lindborg, M.: "I did it my way": moving away from the tyranny of turn-by-turn pedestrian navigation. In: Proceedings of the 12th International Conference on Human Computer Interaction with Mobile Devices and Services, ACM MobileHCI 2010, New York, NY, USA, pp. 341–344 (2010)

15. Zelek, J.S.: Seeing by touch (haptics) for wayfinding. International Congress Series, 282:1108-1112, 2005. In: Vision 2005 - Proceedings of the International Congress held between 4 and 7, in London, UK (April 2005)
16. Caulfield, B., O'Mahony, M.: A stated preference analysis of real-time public transit stop information. Journal of Public Transportation 12(3), 1–20 (2009)
17. Rehrl, K., Bruntsch, S., Mentz, H.: Assisting Multimodal Travelers: Design and Prototypical Implementation of a Personal Travel Companion. IEEE Transactions on Intelligent Transportation Systems 12(3), 1–20 (2009)
18. Koskinen, S., Virtanen, A.: Public transport real time information in Personal navigation systems of a for special user groups. In: Proceedings of 11th World Congress on ITS (2004)
19. Marston, J.R., Golledge, R.G., Costanzo, C.M.: Investigating travel behavior of nondriving blind and vision impaired people: The role of public transit. The Professional Geographer 49(2), 235–245 (1997)
20. Turunen, M., Hurtig, T., Hakulinen, J., Virtanen, A., Koskinen, S.: Mobile Speech-based and Multimodal Public Transport Information Services. In: Proceedings of MobileHCI 2006 Workshop on Speech in Mobile and Pervasive Environments (2006)
21. Cloudmade API (2011), `http://developers.cloudmade.com/projects/show/web-maps-api` (last accessed March 2011)
22. Ravi, N., Scott, J., Han, L., Iftode, L.: Context-aware Battery Management for Mobile Phones. In: Sixth Annual IEEE International Conference on Pervasive Computing and Communications, pp. 224–233 (2008)
23. Moussaid, M., Perozo, N., Garnier, S., Helbing, D., Theraulaz, G.: The Walking Behaviour of Pedestrian Social Groups and Its Impact on Crowd Dynamics. PLoS ONE 5(4) (April 7, 2010)

Toward a Web Search Personalization Approach Based on Temporal Context

Djalila Boughareb and Nadir Farah

Computer science department
Annaba University, Algeria
{boughareb,farah}@labged.net

Abstract. In this paper, we describe the work done in the Web search personalization field. The proposed approach purpose is the understanding and identifying the user search needs using some information sources such as the search history and the search context focusing on temporal factor. These informations consist mainly of the day and the time of day. Considering such data, how can it improve the relevance of search results? That's what we focus on it in this work; The experimental results are promising and suggest that taking into account the day, the time of the query submission in addition to the pages recently been examined can be a viable context data for identifying the user search needs and furthermore enhancing the relevance of the search results.

Keywords: Personalized Web search, Web Usage Mining, temporal context and query expansion.

1 Introduction

The main feature of the World Wide Web is not that it allowed making available billions byte of information, but mostly that it has brought millions of users to make of the information search a daily task. In that task, the information retrieval tools are generally the only mediators between a search need and its partial or total satisfaction.

A wide variety of researches have improved the relevance of the results provided by the information retrieval tools. However, the explosion in the volume of the information available on the Web, which is measured at least 2.73 billion pages according to a recent statistics[1] made in December 2010; the low expression of the user query reflected in the fact that the users usually employ a few numbers of keywords to describe their needs average 2.9 words [7], for example, a user who's looking to purchase a *bigfoot 4x4* vehicle submits the query "*bigfoot*" to *AltaVista*[2] search engine will obtain among the ten most relevant documents, one document on football, five about animals, one about a production company and three about the chief of the *Miniconjou Lakota Sioux* and zero document about *4x4 vehicle*, but if we add the keyword "*vehicle*", all first documents returned by the search engine will be about vehicles, and will satisfy the user information needs; moreover, the reduced understanding of the user needs engender the low relevance of the retrieval results and its bad ranking.

---

[1] `http://www.worldwidewebsize.com/`

[2] `http://fr.altavista.com/`

H. Cherifi, J.M. Zain, and E. El-Qawasmeh (Eds.): DICTAP 2011, Part I, CCIS 166, pp. 33–44, 2011.

In order to overcome these problems, the information personalization has emerged as a promising field of research which can be defined as the application of data mining and machine learning techniques to build models of user behavior that can be applied to the task of predicting user needs and adapting future interactions with the ultimate goal of improved user satisfaction [1].

The purpose of this work is to develop a system prototype, which is able to both automatically identify the user information needs and retrieve relevant contents without requiring any action by the user. To do this, we have proposed: A user profiling approach to build user profiles or user models through some of information sources which can be extracted from the search history of the users using Web usage mining techniques. We have mainly taken into consideration temporal context in order to investigate the effectiveness of the time factor in understanding and identifying the search needs of the user, based on the heuristic that user browsing behavior changes according to the day and the time of query submission.

Indeed, we have observed that the browsing behavior changes according to the day and the time of day, *i.e.* the user browsing behavior during workdays are not the same as weekends for example. Driven by the browsing behaviors observation of 30 users during one month from January 01, 2010 to January 30, 2010, we have found that their search behavior varies according to the day and the hour, for example 12 surfers on average conducted research about sport field on Wednesday evening from 6pm and 13 on Thursday morning, nevertheless 14 surfers on average conducted research on their study domain on Monday afternoon between 2 pm and 7 pm. Generally, the searches have been focused on leisure websites on Saturday. Moreover, we developed a query expansion approach to resolve the short query problem based on the building models.

The remainder of this paper is organized as follows. Before describing the proposed approach in section 3, we present a state of the art in section 2. Section 4 presents the experiments and we discuss obtained results in section 5. Section 6 concludes the paper and outlines areas for future research.

2 State of the Art

In the large domain of the personalization, user modeling represents the main task. Indeed, a personalization system creates user profiles *a priori* and employs them to improve the quality of search responses [8], of provided web services [11, 14] or of web site design [2]. User modeling process can be divided into two main steps, data collection and profiles construction. Data collection consists of collecting relevant information about the users necessary to build user profiles; the information collected (age, gender, marital status, job...etc) may be:

-Explicitly inputted by the user via HTML forms and explicit feedback [14, 15] but due to the extra time and effort required from users this approach is not always fitting;

-Implicitly, in this case the user information's may be inferred from his/her browsing activity [4], from browsing history [19] and more recently from his/her search history [17], that contains information about the queries submitted by a particular user and the dates and times of those queries.

In order to improve the quality of data collected and thereafter the building models, some of researches combine explicit and implicit modeling approach, Quiroga and Mostafa [12] researches show that profiles built using the combination of explicit and implicit feedback improve the relevance of the results returned by their search systems, in fact they obtained 63% precision using explicit feedback alone, and 58% of precision using implicit feedback alone. Nevertheless, by the combination of the two approaches an approximately of 68% of precision was achieved. However, white [21] proves that there are no significant differences between profiles constructed using implicit and explicit feedback.

The profiles construction consist the second step of the user profiling process, it has as purpose to build the profiles from the collected data set based on machine learning algorithms like genetic algorithms [22], neural networks [10, 11], Bayesian networks [5] ... etc.

The employment of Web usage mining process (WUM) represents one of the main useful tools for user modeling in the field of Web search personalization, which has been used to analyze data collected about the search behavior of the users on the Web to extract useful knowledge. According to the final goal and the type of the application, researchers tempt to most exploit the search behavior such as a valuable source of knowledge.

Most existing web search personalization approaches are based mainly on search history and browsing history to build a user models or to expand the user queries. However, very little research effort has been focused on the temporal factor and its impact on the improvement of the web search results. In their work [9] Lingras and West proposed an adaptation of the K-means algorithm to develop interval clusters of web visitors using rough set theory. To identify the user behaviors, they were based on the number of web accesses, types of documents downloaded, and time of day (they divided the navigation time into two parts, day visit and night visit) but this presented a reduced accuracy of user's preferences over time.

Motivated by the idea that more accurate semantic similarity values between queries can be obtained by taking into account the timestamps in the log, Zhao et al. [23] proposed a time-dependent query similarity model by studying the temporal information associated with the query terms of the click-through data. The basic idea of this work is taking temporal information into consideration when modeling the query similarity for query expansion. They obtained more accurate results than the existing approaches which can be used for improving the personalized search experience.

3 Proposed Approach

The ideas presented in this paper are based on the observations cited above that the browsing behavior of the user changes according to the day and the hour. Indeed, it is obvious that the information needs of the user changes according to several factors known as the search context such as date, location, history of interaction and the current task. However, it may often maintain a pace well determined. For example, a majority of people visit the news each morning. In summary, the contribution of this work can be presented through the following points:

1. Exploiting temporal data (day and time of day) in addition to the pages recently been examined to identify the real search needs of the user motivated by the observed user browsing behavior and the following heuristics:

   - The user search behavior changes according to the day, i.e. during workdays the user browsing behavior is not the same as weekends for example surfers conducted research about leisure on Saturday;
   - The user search behavior changes according to the time of day and it may often maintain a well determined pace, for example a majority of people visit the news web sites each morning.
   - The information heavily searched in the last few instructions will probably be heavily searched again in the next few ones. Indeed, nearly 60% of users conducts more than one information retrieval search for the same information problem [20].

2. Exploiting temporal data (time spent in a web page) in addition to click through data to measure the relevance of web pages and to better rank the search results.

To do this, we have implemented a system prototype using a modular architecture. Each user access the search system home page is assigned a session ID, in which all the user navigation activities are recorded in a log file by the log-processing module. When the user submits an interrogation query to the system, the encoding module creates a vector of positive integers composed from the submitted query and information corresponding to the current research context (the day, the time of query submission and domain recently being examined). The created vector will be submitted to the class finder module. Based on the neural network models previously trained and embedded in a dynamically generated *Java* page the class finder module aims to catch the profile class of the current user. The results of this operation are supplied to the query expansion module for reformulating the original query based on the information included in the correspondent profile class. The research module's role is the execution of queries and results ranking based always on the information included in the profile class. In the following sections we describe in detail this approach, the experiments and the obtained results.

3.1 Building the User Profiles

A variety of artificial intelligence techniques have been used for user profiling, the most popular is Web Usage Mining which consists in applying data mining methods to access log files. These files which collect the information about the browsing history, including client IP address, query date/time, page requested, HTTP code, bytes served, user agent, and referrer, can be considered as the principal data sources in the WUM based personalization field.

To build the user profiles we have applied the mainly three steps in WUM process namely [3]: preprocessing, pattern discovery and pattern analysis to the access log files resulted from the Web server of the Computer Science department at *Annaba University* from January 01, 2009 to June 30, 2009, in the following sections we will focus on the first two steps.

3.1.1 Preprocessing

It involves two main steps are: first, the data cleaning which aims for filtering out irrelevant and noisy data from the log file, the removed data correspond to the records of graphics, videos and format information and the records with failed HTTP status codes;

Second, the data transformation which aims to transform the data set resulted from the previous step into an exploitable format for mining. In our case, after elimination the graphics and the multimedia file requests, the script requests and the crawler visits, we have reduced the number of requests from 26 084 to 17 040, i.e. 64% of the initial size and 10 323 user sessions of 30 minutes each one. We have been interested then in interrogation queries to retrieve keywords from the URL parameters (Fig. 1).

As the majority of users started their search queries from their own machines the problem of identifying users and sessions was not asked.

```
10.0.0.1 - - [16/Jan/2009:15:01:02 -0500] "GET /assignment-3.html HTTP/1.1" 200 8090
http://www.google.com/search?=course+of+data+mining&spell=1 Mozilla/4.0 (compatible; MSIE 6.0; NT 5.1;
SV1)"Windows
```

Fig. 1. An interrogation query resulting from the log file

3.1.2 Data Mining

In this stage, data mining techniques was applied to the data set resulted from the previous step. In order to build the user profiles we have brought the users who have conducted a search on a field *F*, in the Day *D* during the time interval *T* in the same profile class *C*, i.e., for this we have made a supervised learning based on artificial neural networks. Indeed, if we have proceeded to an unsupervised learning, we may be got a very disturbing number of classes, which do not allow us to achieve the desired goal of this approach, nor to test its effectiveness.

The edited network is an MLP (Multi Layer Perceptron) with a two hidden layers. The data encoding process was made as follows. An input vector $X\{[0,1]\}^p$with $p = 12$ is propagated from the input layer of four nodes to the output layer of eight nodes corresponding to the number of profile classes created, through two hidden layers (with 14, 12 nodes respectively). The input vector composed of four variables namely: the query, the day, the time of day and the domain recently being examined.

1. The query (q): we analyzed the submitted query based mainly on a keywords descriptor to find the domain targeted by the query; in our case we have created 4 vectors of terms for fields (computer science, sport, leisure and news). This analysis helps the system to estimate the domain targeted by the query. Other information can be useful to find the domain targeted by the query such as the type of the asked documents (e.g. if the user indicates that he is looking for pdf documents, this can promote computer science category. However, if the query contains the word video, it promotes the leisure category);
2. The day (d): The values that take the variable "day" correspond to the 7 days of the week.

3. The time of day (t): we divided the day into four browsing time: the morning (6:00 am to 11:59 am), the afternoon (noon to 3:59 pm), the evening (2:00 pm to 9:59 pm) and night (10:00 pm to 5:59 am).
4. The domain recently being examined (Rp): if that is the first user query this variable will take the same value of the variable query (q), otherwise the domain recently being examined will be determined by calculating similarity between the vector of the Web page and the 4 predefined descriptors of categories that contain the most common words in each domain, the vector page is obtained by *tf.idf* weighting scheme (the term frequency/inverse document frequency) described in the equation (1) [13].

$$\text{tf.idf} = \frac{\text{N}}{\text{T}} * \log\frac{\text{D}}{\text{DF}} \tag{1}$$

Where N is the number of times a word appears in a document, T is the total number of words in the same document, D is the total number of documents in a corpus and DF is the number of document in which a particular word is found.

3.2 User Profiles Representation

The created user profiles are represented through a weighted keyword vector, a set of queries and the examined search results; a page relevance measure has been employed to calculate the relevance of each page to her correspondent query.

Each profile class (pc_i) is described through an n-dimensional weighted keyword vector $V_i = \langle(k_1, w_1), (k_2, w_2), \dots \dots (k_n, w_3)\rangle$ and a set of queries, each query q_j is represented as an ordered vector of relevant pages to it. $q_j = \langle p_1, p_2, \dots . p_n\rangle$, where the relevance of a page $p_i$to the query q_j can be obtained based on the click-through data analysis by the following measure described in the equation (2). Grouping the results of the previous queries and assign them a weighing aims to enhance the relevance of the top first retrieved pages and better rank the system results. Indeed, information such as time spent on a page and the number of clicks inside, can help to determine the relevance of a page to a query and to all similar queries to it, this in order to better rank the returned results.

$$R(p_i, q_j) = \frac{T_v(p_i, q_j).\ NC}{\sum_{k=1}^{n} T_v(p_k, q_j)} \tag{2}$$

Here $T_v(p_i, q_j)$ measure the time that page p_i has been visited by the user who issued the query q_j, NC measure the number of clicks inside page p_i by the user who issued the query q_j and $\sum_{k=1}^{n} T_v(p_k, q_j)$ refers to the total number of times that all pages have been visited by the user who issued the query q_j.

3.3 Profiles Detection

This module tries to infer the current user profile by analyzing keywords describing his information needs and taking into account information corresponding to the current research context particularly the day, the time of query submission and information recently been examined to assign the current user to the appropriate profile class. To do this, the profiles detection module create a vector of positive integers composed from the submitted query and information corresponding to the current research context (the day, the query submission hour and domain recently being examined), the basic idea is that information heavily searched in the last few instructions will probably be heavily searched again in the next few ones. Indeed, in theme researches Spink et al. [18] show that nearly 60% of users had conducted more than one information retrieval search for the same information problem.

The created vector will be submitted to the neural network previously trained and embedded in a dynamically generated Java page in order to assign the current user to the appropriate profile class.

3.4 Query Reformulation

In order to reformulate the submitted query, the query reformulation module makes an expansion of that one with keywords resulting from similar queries to it to obtain a new query closer to the real need of the user and to bring back larger and better targeted results. The keywords used for expansion are derived from past queries which have a significant similarity with the current query, the basic hypothesis is that the top documents retrieved by a query are themselves the top documents retrieved by the past similar queries [20].

3.4.1 Query Similarity

Exploiting the past similar queries to extend the user query consists one of the most known methods in automatic query expansion field [6, 16]. We have based on this method to extend the user query. To do this, we have represented each query as a weighted keywords vector using *tf.idf* weighting scheme. We have employed the cosine similarity described in the equation (3) to measure the similarity $Sim(q_i, q_j)$ between queries. If a significant similarity between the submitted query and a past query is found, this one will be assigned to the query set Q_s, the purpose is to gather from the current profile class all queries whose exceed a given similarity threshold £ and employing them to extend the current submitted query.

$$Sim(q_i, q_j) = \frac{q_i \cdot q_j}{\|q_i\| \, \|q_j\|} \tag{3}$$

3.4.2 Query Expansion

As we have mentioned above, one of the most known problems in information retrieval is the low query expression reflected in the use of short queries. As a solution has been proposed to this problem, the query expansion which aims to support the user in his/her searches task through adding search keywords to a user query in order to disambiguate it and to increase the number of relevant documents retrieved. We have employed the first 10 keywords resulted from the most 5 similar queries to rewrite the original query q_0;

The weight of an added term P_t is obtained by averaging the weight of this term in Q_s queries where it appears.

$$P_t = \frac{\sum_i p_t}{k} \tag{4}$$

Where $\sum_i p_t$ is the sum of the weights of term t in k queries in Q_s where it appears k is the total number of queries containing the term t.

3.5 The Matching

In order to enhance the relevance of the top first retrieved pages and better rank results, we propose to include additional information like the page access frequency from previous queries results from similar queries. This can help to assign more accurate scores to the pages jugged relevance by the users having conducted a similar search queries. Based on the set of queries Q_s obtained in the previous step and contained all queries which have a significant similarity with the current one, we have defined a matching function described in the equation (5) as follow:

$$Match(q_i, p_j) = Sim(q_i, p_j) + nrank(p_j, Q_s) \tag{5}$$

$$nrank(p_j, Q_s) = \frac{\sum_k \sum_j R(p_j, q_k)}{\sum_i p_i \sum_q q_k} \tag{6}$$

Where $Sim(q_i, p_j)$ measure the cosine similarity between the page p_j vector and the query q_i vector, $nrank(p_j, Q_s)$ which is described in the equation (5) measures the average relevance of a page p_j in the query set Q_s based on the average time in which a page p_j has been accessed and the number of clicks inside compared with all others pages $(\sum_i p_i)$ resulted from all others similar queries $(\sum_q q_k)$. The $R(p_j, q_k)$ measure of the relevance of a page p_j to the query q_k have been defined above in the equation (2).

4 Experiments

We developed a Web-based Java prototype that provides an experimental validation of the neural network models. On the one hand, we mainly aimed to checking the ability of the produced models in catching the user profile according to: his/her query category, day, the query submission time and the domain recently being examined can be defined from pages recently visited, for this a vector of 4 values between] 0, 1] will be submitted to the neural network previously edited by *joone*[3] library, trained and embedded in a dynamically generated *Java* page.

The data set was divided into two separate sets including a training set and a test set. The training set consists of 745 vectors were used to build the user models while the test set which contains 250 vectors were used to evaluate the effectiveness of the user models. Results are presented in the following section.

[3] `http://sourceforge.net/projects/joone/`

The quality of an information search system may be measured by comparing the responses of the system with the ideal responses that the user expects to receive, based on two metrics commonly used in information retrieval are *recall* and *precision. Recall* measures the ability of a retrieval system to locate relevant documents in its index and *precision* measures its ability to not rank irrelevant documents.

In order to evaluate the user models and analyzing how the results quality can be influenced by the setting of the parameters involved in the user profiles. We have used a collection of 9 542 documents indexed by the *Lucene*[4] indexing API and we have been measuring the effectiveness of the implemented system in terms of *Top-n recall* and *Top-n precision* defined in the equations (7) and (8) respectively. For example, at n = 50, the top 50 search results are taken into consideration in measuring recall and precision. The obtained results are represented in the following section.

$$Top - n\ Recall = \frac{R_n}{M} \tag{7}$$

$$Top - n\ Precision = \frac{R_n}{N} \tag{8}$$

Where R_n represents the number of documents retrieved and relevant within n, M refers to the total number of relevant documents and N refer to the total number of documents retrieved.

5 Results and Discussion

Once the user models are generated, it is possible to carry out real tests as follows, we employed 15 users who build queries an average of 10 for each profile class. The experiments showed that over 80 submissions we obtain 6 errors of classification, i.e. 7,5%, we introduce the example of Profile class (pc_2) characterized by computer science students interested with leisure, (pc_7) characterized by users interested with leisure and (pc_8) characterized by users interested with music and videos, 1 vector from (pc_2) is classified in (pc_8) and 2 vectors are classified in (pc_7) that we don't consider this a classification error because profiles class can chair some characteristics and students browsing behavior will be similar than any other users browsing behavior over his scientific search.

Thereafter, in order to evaluate the expansion approach based on keywords involved from profile class caught, we tested the expansion of 54 queries and we obtain 48 good expansions, i.e. 88%. Taking the example of the query $q_0 = \langle programming, java \rangle$ submitted by a student who is recently examining a database course, in this period students in information and database system option were interested in a tutorial using Oracle framework. After reformulation step a new

[4] `http://lucene.apache.org/java/docs/index.html`

query $q' = \langle programming, java, Jbuilder, Oracle \rangle$ has been obtained. Another example the query $q_0 = \langle apple \rangle$after the expansion step, the system returns the query $q' = \langle apple, computer, Mac \rangle$ this because the recently examined pages were about computer science domain.

After analyzing user's judgments we observed that almost 76% of users were satisfied with the results provided by the system. The average Top-n recall and Top-n precision for 54 queries are represented in the following diagrams which show a comparison of the relevance of the Web Personalized Search System (*WePSSy*) results with *AltaVista, Excite* and *Google* search engine results.

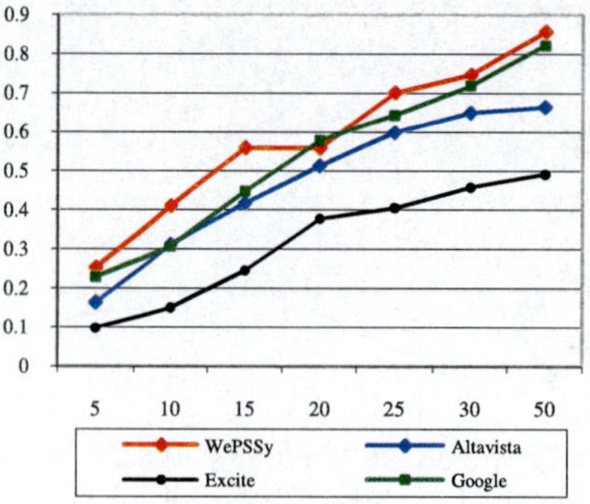

Fig. 2. Top-n recall (comparison of results obtained by the *WePSSy* system with *AltaVista, Excite* and *Google* search engine results)

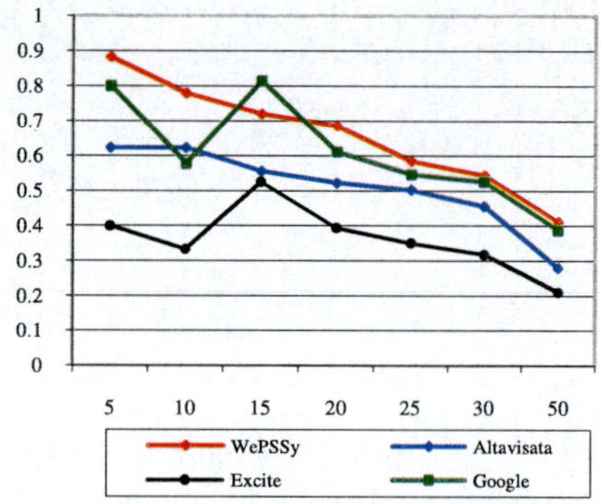

Fig. 3. Top-n precision (comparison of results obtained by the *WePSSy* system with *AltaVista, Excite* and *Google* search engine results)

6 Conclusion

In this paper, we have presented an information personalization approach for improving information retrieval effectiveness. Our study focused on temporal context information, mainly the day and time of day. We have attempted to investigate the impact of such data in the amelioration of the user models, the identification of the user needs and finally in the improvement of the relevance of search results. In fact, the built models prove its effectiveness and ability to assign the user to her/his profile class;

There are several issues for future work, for example, it would be interesting to support on an external semantic web resource (dictionary, thesaurus or ontology) for disambiguate query keywords and better identifying similar queries to the current one; also we attempt to enrich the data web house with other log files in order to test this approach in a wide area.

Moreover, we attempt to integrate this system as a mediator between surfers and search engines. To do this, surfers are called to submit their query to the system which detect their profile class and reformulate their queries before their submission to a search engine.

References

1. Anand, S.S., Mobasher, B.: Intelligent Techniques for Web Personalization. In: Carbonell, J.G., Siekmann, J. (eds.) ITWP 2003. LNCS (LNAI), vol. 3169, pp. 1–36. Springer, Heidelberg (2005)
2. Berendt, B., Hotho, A., Stumme, G.: Towards semantic web mining. In: Horrocks, I., Hendler, J. (eds.) ISWC 2002. LNCS, vol. 2342, pp. 264–278. Springer, Heidelberg (2002)
3. Cooley, R.: The Use of Web Structure and Content to Identify Subjectively Interesting Web Usage Patterns. ACM Transactions on Internet Technology (TOIT) 3, 102–104 (2003)
4. Fischer, G., Ye, Y.: Exploiting Context to make Delivered Information Relevant to Tasks and Users. In: 8th International Conference on User Modeling, Workshop on User Modeling for Context-Aware Applications, Sonthofen (2001)
5. Garcia, P., Amandi, A., Schiaffino, S., Campo, M.: Evaluating Bayesian Networks' Precision for Detecting Students' Learning Styles. Computers and Education 49, 794–808 (2007)
6. Glance, N.-S.: Community Search Assistant. In: Proceedings of the 6th International Conference on Intelligent User Interfaces, pp. 91–96. ACM Press, New York (2001)
7. Jansen, B., Spink, A., Wolfram, D., Saracevic, T.: From E-Sex to E-Commerce: Web Search Changes. IEEE Computer 35, 107–109 (2002)
8. Joachims, T.: Optimizing search engines using click through data. In: Proceedings of SIGKDD, pp. 133–142 (2002)
9. Lingras, P., West, C.: Interval set clustering of web users with rough k-means. Journal of Intelligent Information Systems 23, 5–16 (2004)
10. Mobasher, B., Dai, H., Luo, T., Nakagawa, M.: Improving the effectiveness of collaborative filtering on anonymous web usage data. In: Proceedings of the IJCAI 2001 Workshop on Intelligent Techniques for Web Personalization (ITWP 2001), Seattle, pp. 181–184 (2001)
11. Mobasher, B., Cooley, R., Srivastava, J.: Automatic personalization based on web usage mining. Communications of the ACM 43, 142–151 (2000)
12. Quiroga, L., Mostafa, J.: Empirical evaluation of explicit versus implicit acquisition of user profiles in information filtering systems. In: Proceedings of the 63rd Annual Meeting of the American Society for Information Science and Technology, Medford, vol. 37, pp. 4–13. Information Today, NJ (2000)
13. Salton, G., McGill, M.: Introduction to Modern Information Retrieval, New York (1983)
14. Shavlik, J., Eliassi-Rad, T.: Intelligent agents for web-based tasks: An advice taking approach. In: Working Notes of the AAAI/ICML 1998 Workshop on Learning for text categorization, Madison, pp. 63–70 (1998)
15. Shavlik, J., Calcari, S., Eliassi-Rad, T., Solock, J.: An instructable adaptive interface for discovering and monitoring information on the World Wide Web. In: Proceedings of the International Conference on Intelligent User Interfaces, California, pp. 157–160 (1999)
16. Smyth, B., Balfe, E., Freyne, J., Briggs, P., Coyle, M., Boydell, O.: Exploiting Query Repetition and Regularity in an Adaptive Community-Based Web Search Engine. Journal User Modeling and User-Adapted Interaction 14, 383–423 (2005)
17. Speretta, S., Gauch, S.: Personalizing search based user search histories. In: Proceedings of the 2005 IEEE/WIC/ACM International Conference on Web Intelligence, WI 2005, Washington, pp. 622–628 (2005)
18. Spink, A., Wilson, T., Ellis, D., Ford, N.: Modeling user's successive searches in digital environments, D-Lib Magazine (1998)

19. Trajkova, J., Gauch, S.: Improving Ontology-Based User Profiles. In: Proceedings of RIAO 2004, France, pp. 380–389 (2004)
20. Van-Rijsbergen, C.J.: Information Retrieval, 2nd edn. Butterworths, London (1979)
21. White, R.W., Jose, J.M., Ruthven, I.: Comparing explicit and implicit feedback techniques for web retrieval. In: Proceedings of the Tenth Text Retrieval Conference, Gaithersburg, pp. 534–538 (2001)
22. Yannibelli, V., Godoy, D., Amandi, A.: A Genetic Algorithm Approach to Recognize Students' Learning Styles. Interactive Learning Environments 14, 55–78 (2006)
23. Zhao, Q., Hoi, C.-H., Liu, T.-Y., Bhowmick, S., Lyu, M., Ma, W.-Y.: Time-Dependent Semantic Similarity Measure of Queries Using Historical Click-Through Data. In: Proceedings of 15th ACM International Conference on World Wide Web (WWW 2006). ACM Press, Edinburgh (2006)

On Flexible Web Services Composition Networks

Chantal Cherifi[1], Vincent Labatut[2], and Jean-François Santucci[1]

[1] University of Corsica, UMR CNRS, SPE Laboratory, Corte, France
[2] Galatasaray University, Computer Science Department, Istanbul, Turkey
chantalbonner@gmail.com

Abstract. The semantic Web service community develops efforts to bring semantics to Web service descriptions and allow automatic discovery and composition. However, there is no widespread adoption of such descriptions yet, because semantically defining Web services is highly complicated and costly. As a result, production Web services still rely on syntactic descriptions, key-word based discovery and predefined compositions. Hence, more advanced research on syntactic Web services is still ongoing. In this work we build syntactic composition Web services networks with three well known similarity metrics, namely Levenshtein, Jaro and Jaro-Winkler. We perform a comparative study on the metrics performance by studying the topological properties of networks built from a test collection of real-world descriptions. It appears Jaro-Winkler finds more appropriate similarities and can be used at higher thresholds. For lower thresholds, the Jaro metric would be preferable because it detect less irrelevant relationships.

Keywords: Web services, Web services Composition, Interaction Networks, Similarity Metrics, Flexible Matching.

1 Introduction

Web Services (WS) are autonomous software components that can be published, discovered and invoked for remote use. For this purpose, their characteristics must be made publicly available under the form of WS descriptions. Such a description file is comparable to an interface defined in the context of object-oriented programming. It lists the operations implemented by the WS. Currently, production WS use syntactic descriptions expressed with the WS description language (WSDL) [1], which is a W3C (World Wide Web Consortium) specification. Such descriptions basically contain the names of the operations and their parameters names and data types. Additionally, some lower level information regarding the network access to the WS is present. WS were initially designed to interact with each other, in order to provide a composition of WS able to offer higher level functionalities. Current production discovery mechanisms support only keyword-based search in WS registries and no form of inference or approximate match can be performed.

WS have rapidly emerged as important building blocks for business integration. With their explosive growth, the discovery and composition processes have become extremely important and challenging. Hence, advanced research comes from the semantic WS community, which develops a lot of efforts to bring semantics to WS

H. Cherifi, J.M. Zain, and E. El-Qawasmeh (Eds.): DICTAP 2011, Part I, CCIS 166, pp. 45–59, 2011.

descriptions and to automate discovery and composition. Languages exist, such as OWL-S [2], to provide semantic unambiguous and computer-interpretable descriptions of WS. They rely on ontologies to support users and software agents to discover, invoke and compose WS with certain properties. However, there is no widespread adoption of such descriptions yet, because their definition is highly complicated and costly, for two major reasons. First, although some tools have been proposed for the annotation process, human intervention is still necessary. Second, the use of ontologies raises the problem of ontology mapping which although widely researched, is still not fully solved. To cope with this state of facts, research has also been pursued, in parallel, on syntactic WS discovery and composition.

Works on syntactic discovery relies on comparing structured data such as parameters types and names, or analyzing unstructured textual comments. Hence, in [3], the authors provide a set of similarity assessment methods. WS Properties described in WSDL are divided into four categories: lexical, attribute, interface and QoS. *Lexical similarity* concerns textual properties such as the WS name or owner. *Attribute similarity* estimates the similarity of properties with more supporting domain knowledge, like for instance, the property indicating the type of media stream a broadcast WS provides. *Interface similarity* focuses on the WS operations input and output parameters, and evaluates the similarity of their names and data types. *Qos similarity* assesses the similarity of the WS quality performance. A more recent trend consists in taking advantage of the latent semantics. In this context, a method was proposed to retrieve relevant WS based on keyword-based syntactical analysis, with semantic concepts extracted from WSDL files [4]. In the first step, a set of WS is retrieved with a keyword search and a subset is isolated by analyzing the syntactical correlations between the query and the WS descriptions. The second step captures the semantic concepts hidden behind the words in a query and the advertisements in the WS, and compares them.

Works on syntactic composition encompasses a body of research, including the use of networks to represent compositions within a set of WS. In [5], the input and output parameters names are compared to build the network. To that end, the authors use a strict matching (exact similarity), an approximate matching (cosine similarity) and a semantic matching (WordNet similarity). The goal is to study how approximate and semantic matching impact the network small-world and scale-free properties. In this work, we propose to use three well-known approximate string similarity metrics, as alternatives to build syntactic WS composition networks. Similarities between WS are computed on the parameters names. Given a set of WS descriptions, we build several networks for each metrics by making their threshold varying. Each network contains all the interactions between the WS that have been computed on the basis of the parameters similarities retrieved by the approximate matching. For each network we compute a set of topological properties. We then analyze their evolution for each metric, in function of the threshold value. This study enables us to assess which metric and which threshold are the most suitable.

Our main contribution is to propose a flexible way to build WS composition networks based on approximate matching functions. This approach allows to link some semantically related WS that does not appear on WS composition networks based on strict equality of the parameters names. We provide a thorough study regarding the use of syntactic approximate similarity metrics on WS networks topology. The results of our experimentations allow determining the suitability of the metrics and the threshold range that maintains the false positive rate at an acceptable level.

In section 2, we give some basic concepts regarding WS definition, description and composition. Interaction networks are introduced in section 3 along with the similarity metrics. Section 4 is dedicated to the network properties. In section 5 we present and discuss our experimental results. Finally, in section 6 we highlight the conclusions and limitations of, and explain how our work it can be extended.

2 Web Services

In this section we give a formal definition of WS, explain how it can be described syntactically, and define WS composition.

A WS is a set of operations. An operation i represents a specific functionality, described independently from its implementation for interoperability purposes. It can be characterized by its input and output parameters, noted I_i and O_i, respectively. I_i corresponds to the information required to invoke operation i, whereas O_i is the information provided by this operation. At the WS level, the set of input and output parameters of a WS α are $I_\alpha = \bigcup I_i$ and $O_\alpha = \bigcup O_i$, respectively. Fig. 1 represents a WS labeled α with two operations numbered 1 and 2, and their sets of input and output parameters: $I_1 = \{a, b\}$, $O_1 = \{d\}$, $I_2 = \{c\}$, $O_2 = \{e, f\}$, $I_\alpha = \{a, b, c\}$, $O_\alpha = \{d, e, f\}$.

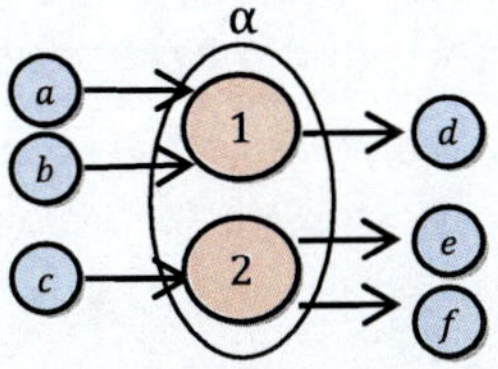

Fig. 1. Schematic representation of a WS α, with two operations 1 and 2 and six parameters a, b, c, d, e and f

WS are either syntactically or semantically described. In this work, we are only concerned by the syntactic description of WS, which relies on the WSDL language. A WS is described by defining messages and operations under the form of an XML document. A message encapsulates the data elements of an operation. Each message consists in a set of input or output parameters. Each parameter has a name and a data type. The type is generally defined using the XML schema definition language (XSD), which makes it independent from any implementation.

WS composition addresses the situation when a request cannot be satisfied by any available single atomic WS. In this case, it might be possible to fulfill the request by combining some of the available WS, resulting in a so-called *composite* WS. Given a request r with input parameters I_r, desired output parameters O_r and a set of available WS, one needs to find a WS α such that $I_r \supseteq I_{w\alpha}$ and $O_r \subseteq O_\alpha$. Finding a WS α that can fulfill r alone is referred to as WS discovery. When it is impossible for a single WS to fully satisfy r, one needs to compose several WS $\{\alpha, \beta, \dots, \eta\}$, so that for all

$\gamma \in \{\alpha, \beta, \ldots, \eta\}$, $I_\gamma$is required at a particular stage in the composition and $(O_\alpha \cup O_\beta \cup \ldots \cup O_\eta) \supseteq O_r$. This problem is referred to as WS composition. The composition thus produces a specification of how to link the available WS to realize the request.

3 Interaction Networks

An interaction network constitutes a convenient way to represent a set of interacting WS. It can be an object of study itself, and it can also be used to improve automated WS composition. In this section, we describe what these networks are and how they can be built.

Generally speaking, we define an interaction network as a directed graph whose nodes correspond to interacting objects and links indicate the possibility for the source nodes to act on the target nodes. In our specific case, a node represents a WS, and a link is created from a node α towards a node β if and only if for each input parameter in I_β, a similar output parameter exists in O_α. In other words, the link exists if and only if WS α can provide all the information requested to apply WS β. In Fig. 2, the left side represents a set of WS with their input and output parameters, whereas the right side corresponds to the associated interaction network. Considering WS α and WS β, all the inputs of β, $I_\beta = \{f\}$, are included in the outputs of α, $O_\alpha = \{d, e, f\}$, i.e. $I_\beta \subseteq O_\alpha$. Hence, α is able to provide all the information needed to interact with β. Consequently, a link exists between α and β in the interaction network. On the contrary, neither α nor β ($O_\alpha = \{d, e, f\}$, $O_\beta = \{g, h\}$), provide all the parameters required by γ ($I_\gamma = \{d, g\}$), which is why there is no link pointing towards γ in the interaction network.

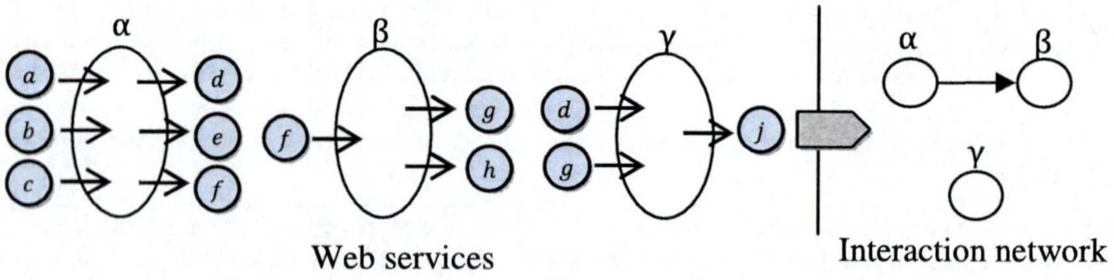

Fig. 2. Example of a WS interaction network

An interaction link between two WS therefore represents the possibility of composing them. Determining if two parameters are similar is a complex task which depends on how the notion of similarity is defined. This is implemented under the form of the matching function through the use of similarity metrics.

Parameters similarity is performed on parameter names. A matching function f takes two parameter names p_1 and p_2, and determines their level of similarity. We use an approximate matching in which two names are considered similar if the value of the similarity function is above some threshold. The key characteristic of the syntactic matching techniques is they interpret the input in function of its sole structure. Indeed, string-based terminological techniques consider a term as a sequence of character. These techniques are typically based on the following intuition: the more similar the strings, the more likely they convey the same information.

We selected three variants of the extensively used edit distance: Levenshtein, Jaro and Jaro-Winkler [6]. The edit distance is based on the number of insertions, deletions, and substitutions of characters required to transform one compared string into the other.

The Levenshtein metric is the basic edit distance function, which assigns a unit cost to all edit operations. For example, the number of operations to transform both strings *kitten* and *sitting* into one another is 3: 1) *k*itten (substitution of *k* with *s*) *s*itten; 2) sitt*e*n (substitution of *e* with *i*) sitt*i*n; 3) sittin (insertion of *g* at the end) sittin*g*.

The Jaro metric takes into account typical spelling deviations between strings. Consider two strings s_1 and s_2. A character a in s_1 is "in common" with s_2 if the same character a appears in about the place in s_2. In equation 1, m is the number of matching characters and t is the number of transpositions. A transposition is the operation needed to permute two matching characters if they are not farther than the distance expressed by equation 2.

$$d_j = \frac{1}{3}\left(\frac{m}{|s_1|} + \frac{m}{|s_2|} + \frac{m-t}{m}\right) \quad (1)$$

$$\left\lfloor \frac{\max\left(|s_1|, |s_2|\right)}{2} \right\rfloor - 1 \quad (2)$$

The Jaro-Winkler metric, equation 3, is an extension of the Jaro metric. It uses a prefix scale p which gives more favorable ratings to strings that match from the beginning for some prefix length l.

$$d_w = d_j + \left(lp\left(1 - d_j\right)\right) \quad (3)$$

The metrics score are normalized such that 0 equates to no similarity and 1 is an exact match.

4 Network Properties

The degree of a node is the number of links connected to this node. Considered at the level of the whole network, the degree is the basis of a number of measures. The minimum and maximum degrees are the smallest and largest degrees in the whole network, respectively. The average degree is the average of the degrees over all the nodes. The degree correlation reveals the way nodes are related to their neighbors according to their degree. It takes its value between -1 (perfectly disassortative) and $+1$ (perfectly assortative). In assortative networks, nodes tend to connect with nodes of similar degree. In disassortative networks, nodes with low degree are more likely connected with highly connected ones [7].

The density of a network is the ratio of the number of existing links to the number of possible links. It ranges from 0 (no link at all) to 1 (all possible links exist in the network, i.e. it is completely connected). Density describes the general level of connectedness in a network. A network is complete if all nodes are adjacent to each other. The more nodes are connected, the greater the density [8].

Shortest paths play an important role in the transport and communication within a network. Indeed, the geodesic provides an optimal path way for communication in a network. It is useful to represent all the shortest path lengths of a network as a matrix in which the entry is the length of the geodesic between two distinctive nodes. A measure of the typical separation between two nodes in the network is given by the average shortest path length, also known as average distance. It is defined as the average number of steps along the shortest paths for all possible pairs of nodes [7].

In many real-world networks it is found that if a node A is connected to a node B, and B is itself connected to another node C, then there is a high probability for A to be also connected to C. This property is called transitivity (or clustering) and is formally defined as the triangle density of the network. A triangle is a structure of three completely connected nodes. The transitivity is the ratio of existing to possible triangles in the considered network [9]. Its value ranges from 0 (the network does not contain any triangle) to 1 (each link in the network is a part of a triangle). The higher the transitivity is, the more probable it is to observe a link between two nodes possessing a common neighbor.

5 Experiments

In those experiments, our goal is twofold. First we want to compare different metrics in order to assess how the links creation is affected by the similarity between the parameters in our interaction network. We would like to identify the best metric in terms of suitability regarding the data features. Second we want to isolate a threshold range within which the matching results are meaningful. By tracking the evolution of the network links, we will be able to categorize the metrics and to determine an acceptable threshold value. We use the previously mentioned complex network properties to monitor this evolution. We start this section by describing our method. We then give the results and their interpretation for each of the topological property mentioned in section 4.

We analyzed the SAWSDL-TC1 collection of WS descriptions [10]. This test collection provides 894 semantic WS descriptions written in SAWSDL, and distributed over 7 thematic domains (education, medical care, food, travel, communication, economy and weapon). It originates in the OWLS-TC2.2 collection, which contains real-world WS descriptions retrieved from public IBM UDDI registries, and semi-automatically transformed from WSDL to OWL-S. This collection was subsequently re-sampled to increase its size, and converted to SAWSDL. We conducted experiments on the interaction networks extracted from SAWSDL-TC1 using the WS network extractor WS-NEXT [11]. For each metric, the networks are built by varying the threshold from 0 to 1 with a 0.01 step.

Fig. 3 shows the behavior of the average degree versus the threshold for each metric. First, we remark the behavior of the Jaro and the Jaro-Winkler curves are very similar. This is in accordance with the fact the Jaro-Winkler metric is a variation of the Jaro metric, as previously stated. Second, we observe the three curves have a sigmoid shape, i.e. they are divided in three areas: two plateaus separated by a slope. The first plateau corresponds to high average degrees and low threshold values. In this area the metrics find a lot of similarities, allowing many links to be drawn. Then, for small variations of the threshold, the average degree brutally decreases. The second plateau corresponds to average degrees comparable with values obtained for a threshold set at 1, and deserves a particular attention, because this threshold value causes links to appear only in case of exact match. We observe that each curve inflects at a different threshold value. The curves inflects at 0.4, 0.7 and 0.75 for Levenshtein, Jaro and Jaro-Winkler, respectively. Those differences are related to the number of similarities found by the metrics. With a threshold of 0.75, they retrieve 513, 1058 and 1737 similarities respectively.

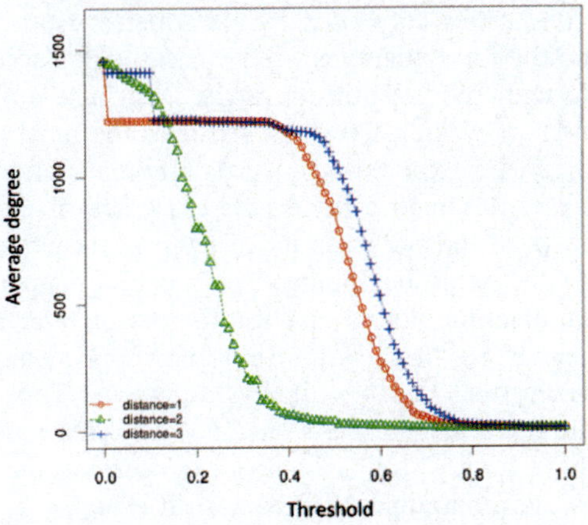

Fig. 3. Average degree in function of the metric threshold. Comparative curves of the Levenshtein (green triangles), Jaro (red circles) and Jaro-Winkler (blue crosses) metrics

To highlight the difference between the curves, we look at their meaningful part, ranging from the inflexion point to the threshold value of 1. We calculated the percentage of average degrees in addition to the average degree obtained with a threshold of 1 for different threshold values. The results are gathered in Table 1. For a threshold of 1, the average degree is 10 and the percentage reference is of course 0%. In the threshold area ranging from the inflexion point to 1, the average degree variation is always above 300%, which seems excessive. Nevertheless, this point needs to be confirmed. Let us assume that above 20% of the minimum average degree, results may be not acceptable (20% corresponding to an average degree of 12). From this postulate, the appropriate threshold is 0.7 for the Levenshtein metric, 0.88 for the Jaro metric. For the Jaro-Winkler metric, the percentage of 17.5 is reached at a threshold of 0.91, then it jumps to 25.4 at the threshold of 0.9. Therefore, we can assume that the threshold range that can be used is [0.7 ; 1] for Levenshtein, [0.88 ; 1] for Jaro and [0.91 ; 1] for Jaro-Winkler.

Table 1. Proportional variation in average degree between the networks obtained for some given thresholds and those resulting from the maximal threshold. For each metric, the smaller considered threshold corresponds to the inflexion point.

Threshold	0.4	0.5	0.6	0.7	0.75	0.8	0.9	1
Levenshtein	510	260	90	20	0	0	0	0
Jaro	-	-	-	370	130	60	10	0
Jaro-Winkler	-	-	-	-	350	140	50	0

To go deeper, one has to consider the qualitative aspects of the results. In other words, we would like to know if the additional links are appropriate i.e. if they correspond to parameters similarities having a semantic meaning. To that end, we analyzed the parameters similarities computed by each metric from the 20% threshold values and we estimated the false positives. As we can see in Table 2, the metrics can be ordered according to their score: Jaro returns the least false positives, Levenshtein stands between Jaro and Jaro-Winckler, which retrieves the most false positives. The score of Jaro-Winkler can be explained by analyzing the parameters names. This result is related to the fact this metric favors the existence of a common prefix between two strings. Indeed, in those data, a lot of parameters names belonging to the same domain start with the same beginning. The meaningful part of the parameter stands at the end. As an example, let us mention the two parameter names `Provide MedicalFlightInformation_DesiredDepartureAirport` and `Provide MedicalFlightInformation_DesiredDepartureDateTime`. Those parameters were considered as similar although the end parts have not the same meaning. We find that Levenshtein and Jaro have a very similar behavior concerning the false positives. Indeed, the first false positives that appear are names differing by a very short but very meaningful sequence of characters. As an example, consider: `ProvideMedicalTransportInformation_DesiredDepartureDateTime` and `ProvideNonMedicalTransportInformation_DesiredDepartureDateTime`. The string `Non` gives a completely different meaning to both parameters, which cannot be detected by the metrics.

Table 2. Parameters similarities from the 20% threshold values. 385 similarities are retrieved at the 1 threshold.

Metric	20% threshold value	Number of retrieved similarities	Number of false positives	Percentage of false positives
Levenshtein	0.70	626	127	20.3%
Jaro	0.88	495	53	10.7%
Jaro-Winkler	0.91	730	250	34.2%

To refine our conclusions on the best metric and the most appropriate threshold for each metric, we decided to identify the threshold values leading to false positives. With the Levenshtein, Jaro and Jaro-Winkler metric, we have no false positive at the thresholds of 0.96, 0.98, and 0.99, respectively. Compared to the 385 appropriate similarities retrieved with a threshold of 1, they find 4, 5 and 10 more appropriate similarities, respectively. In Table 3, we gathered the additional similarities retrieved by each metric. At the considered thresholds, it appears that Levenshtein finds some similarities that neither Jaro nor Jaro-Winkler find. Jaro-Winkler retrieves all the similarities found by Jaro and some additional ones. We also analyzed the average degree value at those thresholds. The network extracted with Levensthein does not present an average degree different from the one observed at a threshold of 1. Jaro and Jaro-Winkler networks show an average degree which is 0.52% above the one obtained for a threshold of 1. Hence, if the criterion is to retrieve 0% of false positives, Jaro-Winkler is the most suitable metric.

Table 3. Additional appropriate similarities for each metric at the threshold of 0% of false positives

Metric Threshold	Similarities
Levenshtein 0.96	GetPatientMedicalRecords_PatientHealthInsuranceNumber ~ SeePatientMedicalRecords_PatientHealthInsuranceNumber _GOVERNMENT-ORGANIZATION ~ _GOVERNMENTORGANIZATION _GOVERMENTORGANIZATION ~ _GOVERNMENTORGANIZATION _LINGUISTICEXPRESSION ~ _LINGUISTICEXPRESSION1
Jaro 0.98	_GOVERNMENT-ORGANIZATION ~ _GOVERNMENTORGANIZATION _LINGUISTICEXPRESSION ~_LINGUISTICEXPRESSION1 _GEOGRAPHICAL-REGION ~ _GEOGRAPHICAL-REGION1 _GEOGRAPHICAL-REGION ~ _GEOGRAPHICAL-REGION2 _GEOPOLITICAL-ENTITY ~ _GEOPOLITICAL-ENTITY1
Jaro-Winkler 0.99	_GOVERNMENT-ORGANIZATION ~ _GOVERNMENTORGANIZATION _GEOGRAPHICAL-REGION ~ _GEOGRAPHICAL-REGION1 _GEOGRAPHICAL-REGION ~ _GEOGRAPHICAL-REGION2 _GEOPOLITICAL-ENTITY ~ _GEOPOLITICAL-ENTITY1 _LINGUISTICEXPRESSION ~ _LINGUISTICEXPRESSION1 _SCIENCE-FICTION-NOVEL ~ _SCIENCEFICTIONNOVEL _GEOGRAPHICAL-REGION1 ~ _GEOGRAPHICAL-REGION2 _TIME-MEASURE ~ _TIMEMEASURE _LOCATION ~ _LOCATION1 _LOCATION ~ _LOCATION2

The variations observed for the density are very similar to those discussed for the average degree. At the threshold of 0, the density is rather high, with a value of 0.93. Nevertheless, we do not reach a complete network whose density is equal to 1. This is due to the interaction network definition, which implies that for a link to be drawn from a WS to another, all the required parameters must be provided. At the threshold of 1, the density drops to 0.006. At the inflexion points, the density for Levenshtein is 0.038, whereas it is 0.029 for both Jaro and Jaro-Winkler. The variations observed are of the same order of magnitude than those observed for the average degree. For the Levenshtein metric the variation is 533% while for both other metrics it reaches 383%. Considering a density value 20% above the density at the threshold of 1, which is 0.0072, this density is reached at the following thresholds: 0.72 for Levenshtein,

0.89 for Jaro and 0.93 for Jaro-Winkler. The corresponding percentages of false positives are 13.88%, 7.46% and 20.18%. Those values are comparable to the ones obtained for the average degree. Considering the thresholds at which no false positive is retrieved (0.96, 0.98 and 0.99), the corresponding densities are the same that the density at the threshold of 1 for the three metrics. The density is a property which is less sensible to small variations of the number of similarities than the average degree. Hence, it does not allow concluding which metric is the best at those thresholds.

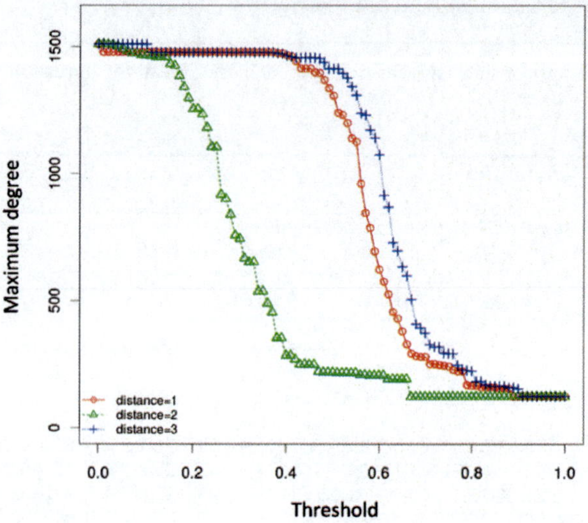

Fig. 4. Maximum degree in function of the metric threshold. Comparative curves of the Levenshtein (green triangles), Jaro (red circles) and Jaro-Winkler (blue crosses) metrics.

The maximum degree (cf. Fig. 4) globally follows the same trend than the average degree and the density. At the threshold of 0 and on the first plateau, the maximum degree is around 1510. At the threshold of 1, it falls to 123. Hence, the maximum degree is roughly multiplied by 10. At the inflexion points, the maximum degree is 285, 277 and 291 for Levenshtein, Jaro and Jaro-Winkler respectively. The variations are all of the same order of magnitude and smaller than the variations of the average degree and the density. For Levenshtein, Jaro and Jaro-Winkler the variations values are 131%, 125% and 137% respectively. Considering the maximum degree 20% above 123, which is 148, this value is approached within the threshold ranges [0.66,0.67], [0.88,0.89], [0.90,0.91] for Levenshtein, Jaro and Jaro-Winkler respectively. The corresponding maximum degrees are [193,123] for Levenshtein and [153,123] for both Jaro and Jaro-Winkler. The corresponding percentages of false positives are [28.43%, 26.56%], [10.7%, 7.46%] and [38.5%, 34.24%] . Results are very similar to those obtained for the average degree and the metrics can be ordered the same way. At the thresholds where no false positive is retrieved (0.96, 0.98 and 0.99), the maximum degree is not different from the value obtained with a threshold of 1. This is due to the fact few new similarities are introduced in this case. Hence, no conclusion can be given on which one of the three metric is the best.

As shown in Fig. 5, the curves of the minimum degree are also divided in three areas: one high plateau and one low plateau separated by a slope. A the threshold of 0, the minimum degree is 744. At the threshold of 1, the minimum degree is 0. This value corresponds to isolated nodes in the network. The inflexion points here appear latter: at 0.06 for Levenshtein and at 0.4 for both Jaro and Jaro-Winkler. The corresponding minimum degrees are 86 for Levenshtein and 37 for Jaro and Jaro-Winkler. The thresholds at which the minimum degree starts to be different from 0 are 0.18 for Levenshtein with a value of 3, 0.58 for Jaro with a value of 2, and 0.59 for Jaro-Winkler with a value of 1. The minimum degree is not very sensible to the variations of the number of similarities. Its value starts to increase at a threshold where an important number of false positive have been introduced.

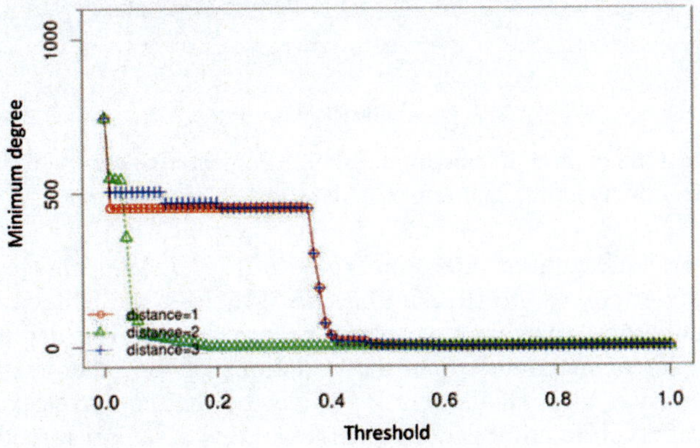

Fig. 5. Minimum degree in function of the metric threshold. Comparative curves of the Levenshtein (green triangles), Jaro (red circles) and Jaro-Winkler (blue crosses) metrics.

The transitivity curves (Fig. 6) globally show the same evolution than the ones of the average degree, the maximum degree and the density. The transitivity at the threshold of 0 almost reaches the value of 1. Indeed, the many links allow the existence of numerous triangles. At the threshold of 1, the value falls to 0.032. At the inflexion points, the transitivity values for Levenshtein, Jaro and Jaro-Winkler are 0.17, 0.14 and 0.16 respectively. In comparison with the transitivity at a threshold level of 1, the variations are 431%, 337%, 400%. They are rather high and of the same order than the ones observed for the average degree. Considering the transitivity value 20% above the one at a threshold of 1, which is 0.0384, this value is reached at the threshold of 0.74 for Levenshtein, 0.9 for Jaro and 0.96 for Jaro-Winkler. Those thresholds are very close to the one for which there is no false positive. The corresponding percentages of false positives are 12.54%, 6.76% and 7.26%. Hence, for those threshold values, we can rank Jaro and Jaro-Winkler at the same level, Levenshtein being the least performing. Considering the thresholds at which no false positive is retrieved, (0.96, 0.98 and 0.99), the corresponding transitivity are the same than the transitivity at 1. For this reason and by the same way than for the density and the maximum degree, no conclusion can be given on the metrics.

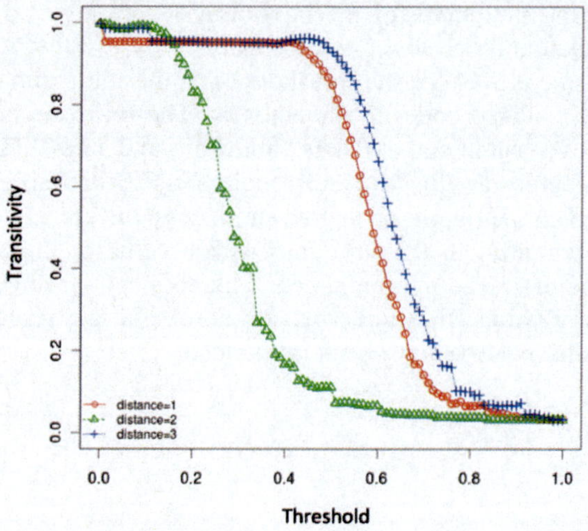

Fig. 6. Transitivity in function of the metric threshold. Comparative curves of the Levenshtein (green triangles), Jaro (red circles), and Jaro-Winkler (blue crosses) metrics.

The degree correlation curves are represented in Fig. 7. We can see that the Jaro and the Jaro-Winkler curves are still similar. Nevertheless, the behavior of the three curves is different from what we have observed previously. The degree correlation variations are of lesser magnitude than the variations of the other metrics. For low thresholds, curves start by a stable area in which the degree correlation value is 0. This indicates that no correlation pattern emerges in this area. For high thresholds the curves decrease until they reach a constant value (-0.246). This negative value reveals a slight disassortative degree correlation pattern. Between those two extremes, the curves exhibit a maximum value that can be related to the variations of the minimum degree and to the maximum degree. Starting from a threshold value of 1 the degree correlation remains constant until a threshold value of 0.83, 0.90 and 0.94 for Lenvenshtein, Jaro and Jaro-Winkler respectively.

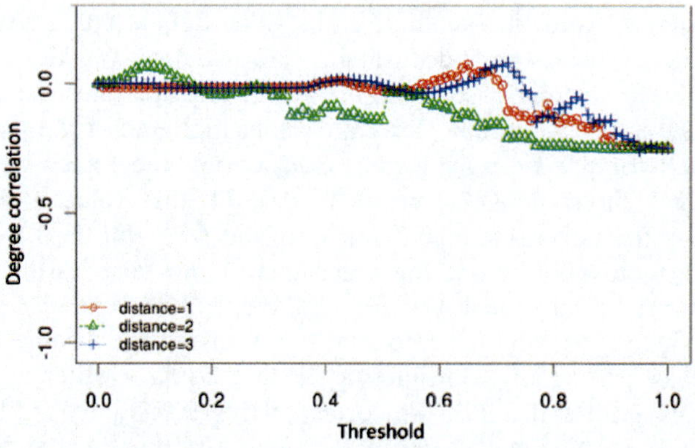

Fig. 7. Degree correlation in function of the metric threshold. Comparative curves of the Levenshtein (green triangles), Jaro (red circles) and Jaro-Winkler (blue crosses) metrics.

Fig. 8 shows the variation of the average distance according to the threshold. The three curves follow the same trends and Jaro and Jaro-Winkler are still closely similar. Nevertheless, the curves behavior is different from what we observed for the other properties. For the three metrics, we observe that the average distance globally increases with the threshold until it reaches a maximum value and then start to decrease. The maximum is reached at the thresholds of 0.5 for Levenshtein, 0.78 Jaro and 0.82 Jaro-Winkler. The corresponding average distance values are 3.30, 4.51 and 5.00 respectively. Globally the average distance increases with the threshold. For low threshold values the average distance is around 1 while for the threshold of 1, networks have an average distance of 2.18. Indeed, it makes sense to observe a greater average distance when the network contains less links. This means that almost all the nodes are neighbors of each other. This is in accordance with the results of the density which is not far from the value of 1 for small thresholds. We remark that the curves start to increase as soon as isolated nodes appear. Indeed, the average distance calculation is only performed on interconnected nodes. The thresholds associated to the maximal average distance correspond to the inflexion points in the maximum degree curves. The thresholds for which the average distance stays stable correspond to the thresholds in the maximum degree curves for which the final value of the maximum degree start to be reached. Hence from the observation of the average distance, we can refine the conclusions from the maximum degree curves by saying that the lower limit of acceptable thresholds is 0.75, 0.90 and 0.93 for Levenshtein, Jaro and Jaro-Winkler respectively.

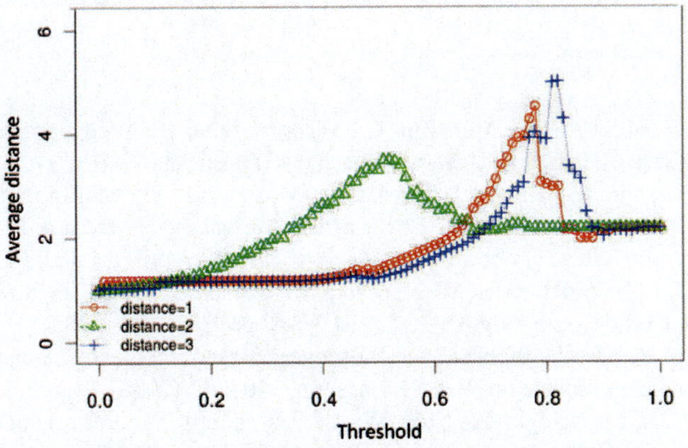

Fig. 8. Average distance in function of the metric threshold. Comparative curves of the Levenshtein (green triangles), Jaro (red circles) and Jaro-Winkler (blue crosses) metrics.

6 Conclusion

In this work, we studied different metrics used to build WS composition networks. To that end we observed the evolution of some complex network topological properties.

Our goal was to determine the most appropriate metric for such an application as well of the most appropriate threshold range to be associated to this metric. We used three well known metrics, namely Levenshtein, Jaro and Jaro-Winkler, especially designed to compute similarity relation between strings. The evolution of the networks from high to low thresholds reflects a growth of the interactions between WS, and hence, of potential compositions. New parameter similarities are revealed, and links are consequently added to the network, along with the threshold increase. If one is interested by a reasonable variation of the topological properties of the network as compared to a threshold value of 1, it seems that the Jaro metric is the most appropriate, as this metric introduces less false positives (inappropriate similarities) than the others. The threshold range that can be associated to each metric is globally [0.7,1], [0.89,1] and [0.91,1] for Levenshtein, Jaro and Jaro-Winkler, respectively. We also examined the behavior of the metrics when no false positive is introduced and new similarities are all semantically meaningful. In this case, Jaro-Winkler gives the best results. Naturally the threshold ranges are lower in this case, and the topological properties are very similar to the ones obtained with a threshold value of 1.

Globally, the use of the metrics to build composition networks is not very satisfying. As the threshold decreases, the false positive rate becomes very quickly prohibitive. This leads us to turn to an alternative approach. It consists in exploiting the latent semantics in parameters name. To extend our work, we plan map the names to ontological concepts with the use of some knowledge bases, such as WordNet [12] or DBPedia [13]. Hence, we could provide a large panel on the studied network properties according to the way similarities are computed to build the networks.

References

1. Christensen, E., Curbera, F., Meredith, G., Weerawarana, S.: Web Services Description Language (WSDL) 1.1, `http://www.w3.org/TR/wsdl`
2. Martin, D., Burstein, M., Hobbs, J., Lassila, O., McDermott, D., McIlraith, S., Narayanan, S., Paolucci, M., Parsia, B., Payne, T., Sirin, E., Srinivasan, N., Sycara, K.: OWL-S: Semantic Markup for Web Services, `http://www.w3.org/Submission/OWL-S/`
3. Wu, J., Wu, Z.: Similarity-based Web Service Matchmaking. In: IEEE International Conference on Semantic Computing, Orlando, FL, USA, pp. 287–294 (2005)
4. Ma, J., Zhang, Y., He, J.: Web Services Discovery Based on Latent Semantic Approach. In: International Conference on Web Services, pp. 740–747 (2008)
5. Kil, H., Oh, S.C., Elmacioglu, E., Nam, W., Lee, D.: Graph Theoretic Topological Analysis of Web Service Networks. World Wide Web 12(3), 321–343 (2009)
6. Cohen, W.W., Ravikumar, P., Fienberg, S.E.: A Comparison of String Distance Metrics for Name-Matching Tasks. In: International Workshop on Information Integration on the Web Acapulco, Mexico, pp. 73–78 (2003)
7. Boccaletti, S., Latora, V., Moreno, Y., Chavez, Y., Hwang, D.: Complex Networks: Structure and Dynamics. Physics Reports 424, 175–308 (2006)
8. Wasserman, S., Faust, K.: Social Network Analysis: Methods and Applications (1994)
9. Newman, M.-E.-J.: The Structure and Function of Complex Networks. SIAM Review 45 (2003)

10. SemWebCentral: SemWebCebtral.org, http://projects.semwebcentral.org/projects/sawsdl-tc/
11. Rivierre, Y., Cherifi, C., Santucci, J.F.: WS-NEXT: A Web Services Network Extractor Toolkit. In: International Conference on Information Technology, Jordan (2011)
12. Pease, A., Niles, I.: Linking Lexicons and Ontologies: Mapping WordNet to the Suggested Upper Merged Ontology. In: Proceedings of the IEEE International Conference on Information and Knowledge Engineering, pp. 412–416 (2003)
13. Universität Leipzig, Freie Universität Berlin, OpenLink: DBPedia.org website, http://wiki.dbpedia.org

Influence of Different Session Timeouts Thresholds on Results of Sequence Rule Analysis in Educational Data Mining

Michal Munk and Martin Drlik

Department of Informatics, Constantine the Philosopher University in Nitra, Tr. A. Hlinku 1,949 74 Nitra, Slovakia
{mmunk,mdrlik}@ukf.sk

Abstract. The purpose of using web usage mining methods in the area of learning management systems is to reveal the knowledge hidden in the log files of their web and database servers. By applying data mining methods to these data, interesting patterns concerning the users' behaviour can be identified. They help us to find the most effective structure of the e-learning courses, optimize the learning content, recommend the most suitable learning path based on student's behaviour, or provide more personalized environment. We prepare six datasets of different quality obtained from logs of the learning management system and pre-processed in different ways. We use three datasets with identified users' sessions based on 15, 30 and 60 minute session timeout threshold and three another datasets with the same thresholds including reconstructed paths among course activities. We try to assess the impact of different session timeout thresholds with or without paths completion on the quantity and quality of the sequence rule analysis that contribute to the representation of the learners' behavioural patterns in learning management system. The results show that the session timeout threshold has significant impact on quality and quantity of extracted sequence rules. On the contrary, it is shown that the completion of paths has neither significant impact on quantity nor quality of extracted rules.

Keywords: session timeout threshold, path completion, learning management system, sequence rules, web log mining.

1 Introduction

In educational contexts, web usage mining is a part of web data mining that can contribute to finding significant educational knowledge. We can describe it as extracting unknown actionable intelligence from interaction with the e-learning environment [1].

Web usage mining was used for personalizing e-learning, adapting educational hypermedia, discovering potential browsing problems, automatic recognition of learner groups in exploratory learning environments or predicting student performance [2]. Analyzing the unique types of data that come from educational systems can help us to find the most effective structure of the e-learning courses, optimize the learning content, recommend the most suitable learning path based on student's behaviour, or provide more personalized environment.

H. Cherifi, J.M. Zain, and E. El-Qawasmeh (Eds.): DICTAP 2011, Part I, CCIS 166, pp. 60–74, 2011.

But usually, the traditional e-learning platform does not directly support any of web usage mining methods. Therefore, it is often difficult for educators to obtain useful feedback on student's learning experiences or answer the questions how the learners proceed through the learning material and what they gain in knowledge from the online courses [3]. We note herein an effort of some authors to design tools that automate typical tasks performed in the pre-processing phase [4] or authors who prepare step-by-step tutorials [5, 6].

The data pre-processing itself represents often the most time consuming phase of the web page analysis [7]. We realized an experiment for purpose to find the an answer to question to what measure it is necessary to execute data pre-processing tasks for gaining valid data from the log files obtained from learning management systems. Specifically, we would like to assess the impact of session timeout threshold and path completion on the quantity and quality of extracted sequence rules that represent the learners' behavioural patterns in a learning management system [8].

We compare six datasets of different quality obtained from logs of the learning management system and pre-processed in different ways. We use three datasets with identified users' sessions based on 15, 30 and 60 minute session timeout threshold (STT) and three another datasets with the same thresholds including reconstructed paths among course activities.

The rest of the paper is structured subsequently. We summarize related work of other authors who deal with data pre-processing issues in connection with educational systems in the second chapter. Especially, we pay attention to authors who were concerned with the problem of finding the most suitable value of STT for session identification. Subsequently, we particularize research methodology and describe how we prepared log files in different manners in section 3. The section 4 gives the summary of experiment results in detail. Finally, we discuss obtained results and give indication of our future work in section 6.

2 Related Work

The aim of the pre-processing phase is to convert the raw data into a suitable input for the next stage mining algorithms [1]. Before applying data mining algorithm, a number of general data pre-processing tasks can be applied. We focus only on data cleaning, user identification, session identification and path completion in this paper.

Marquardt et al. [4] published a comprehensive paper about the application of web usage mining in the e-learning area with focus on the pre-processing phase. They did not deal with session timeout threshold in detail.

Romero et al. [5] paid more attention to data pre-processing issues in their survey. They summarized specific issues about web data mining in learning management systems and provided references about other relevant research papers. Moreover, Romero et al. dealt with some specific features of data pre-processing tasks in LMS Moodle in [5, 9], but they removed the problem of user identification and session identification from their discussion.

A user session that is closely associated with user identification is defined as a sequence of requests made by a single user over a certain navigation period and a user may have a single or multiple sessions during this time period. A session identification is a process of segmenting the log data of each user into individual access sessions [10]. Romero et al. argued that these tasks are solved by logging into and logging out from the system. We can agree with them in the case of user identification.

In the e-learning context, unlike other web based domains, user identification is a straightforward problem because the learners must login using their unique ID [1]. The excellent review of user identification was made in [3] and [11].

Assuming the user is identified, the next step is to perform session identification, by dividing the click stream of each user into sessions. We can find many approaches to session identification [12-16].

In order to determine when a session ends and the next one begins, the session timeout threshold (STT) is often used. A STT is a pre-defined period of inactivity that allows web applications to determine when a new session occurs. [17]. Each website is unique and should have its own STT value. The correct session timeout threshold is often discussed by several authors. They experimented with a variety of different timeouts to find an optimal value [18-23]. However, no generalized model was proposed to estimate the STT used to generate sessions [18]. Some authors noted that the number of identified sessions is directly dependent on time. Hence, it is important to select the correct space of time in order for the number of sessions to be estimated accurately [17].

In this paper, we used reactive time-oriented heuristic method to define the users' sessions. From our point of view sessions were identified as delimited series of clicks realized in the defined time period. We prepared three different files (A1, A2, A3) with a 15-minute STT (mentioned for example in [24]), 30-minute STT [11, 18, 25, 26] and 60-minute STT [27] to start a new session with regard to the setting used in learning management system.

The analysis of the path completion of user's activities is another problem. The reconstruction of activities is focused on retrograde completion of records on the path went through by the user by means of a back button, since the use of such button is not automatically recorded into log entries web-based educational system. Path completion consists of completing the log with inferred accesses. The site topology, represented by sitemap, is fundamental for this inference and significantly contributes to the quality of the resulting dataset, and thus to patterns precision and reliability [4].

The sitemap can be obtained using a crawler. We used Web Crawling application implemented in the used Data Miner for the needs of our analysis. Having ordered the records according to the IP address we searched for some linkages between the consecutive pages.

We found and analyzed several approaches mentioned in literature [11, 16]. Finally, we chose the same approach as in our previous paper [8]. A sequence for the selected IP address can look like this: A→B→C→D→X. In our example, based on the sitemap the algorithm can find out if there not exists the hyperlink from the page

D to our page X. Thus we assume that this page was accessed by the user by means of using a Back button from one of the previous pages.

Then, through a backward browsing we can find out, where of the previous pages exists a reference to page X. In our sample case, we can find out if there no exists a hyperlink to page X from page C, if C page is entered into the sequence, i.e. the sequence will look like this: A→B→C→D→C→X. Similarly, we shall find that there exists any hyperlink from page B to page X and can be added into the sequence, i.e. A→B→C→D→C→B→X.

Finally algorithm finds out that the page A contains hyperlink to page X and after the termination of the backward path analysis the sequence will look like this: A→B→C→D→C→B→A→X. Then it means, the user used Back button in order to transfer from page D to C, from C to B and from B to A [28]. After the application of this method we obtained the files (B1, B2, B3) with an identification of sessions based on user ID, IP address, different timeout thresholds and completing the paths [8].

3 Experiment Research Methodology

We aimed at specifying the inevitable steps that are required for gaining valid data from the log file of learning management system. Specially, we focused on the identification of sessions based on time of various length and reconstruction of student`s activities and influence of interaction of these two steps of data preparation on derived rules. We tried to assess the impact of this advanced techniques on the quantity and quality of the extracted rules. These rules contribute to the overall representation of the students' behaviour patterns. The experiment was realized in several steps.

1. Data acquisition – defining the observed variables into the log file from the point of view of obtaining the necessary data (user ID, IP address, date and time of access, URL address, activity, etc.).
2. Creation of data matrices – from the log file (information of accesses) and site-maps (information on the course contents).
3. Data preparation on various levels:

   3.1. with an identification of sessions based on 15-minute STT (File A1),
   3.2. with an identification of sessions based on 30-minute STT (File A2),
   3.3. with an identification of sessions based on 60-minute STT (File A3),
   3.4. with an identification of sessions based on 15-minute STT and completion of the paths (File B1),
   3.5. with an identification of sessions based on 30-minute STT and completion of the paths (File B2),
   3.6. with an identification of sessions based on 60-minute STT and completion of the paths (File B3).

4. Data analysis – searching for behaviour patterns of students in individual files. We used *STATISTICA Sequence, Association and Link Analysis* for sequence rules extraction. It is an implementation of algorithm using the powerful a-priori algorithm [29-32] together with a tree structured procedure that only requires one pass through data [33].
5. Understanding the output data – creation of data matrices from the outcomes of the analysis, defining assumptions.
6. Comparison of results of data analysis elaborated on various levels of data preparation from the point of view of quantity and quality of the found rules – patterns of behaviours of students upon browsing the course:
   6.1. comparison of the portion of the rules found in examined files,
   6.2. comparison of the portion of inexplicable rules in examined files,
   6.3. comparison of values of the degree of support and confidence of the found rules in examined files.

The contemporary learning management systems store information about their users not in server log file but mainly in relational database. We can find there high extensive log data of the students' activities. Learning management systems usually have built-in student monitoring features so they can record any student's activity [34].

The analyzed course consisted of 12 activities and 145 course pages. Students' records about their activities in individual course pages in learning management system were observed in the e-learning course in winter term 2010.

We used logs stored in relational database of LMS Moodle. LMS Moodle keeps detailed logs of all activities that students perform. It logs every click that students make for navigational [5]. We used records from mdl_log and mdl_log_display tables. These records contained the entities from the e-learning course with 180 participants. In this phase, log file was cleaned from irrelevant items. First of all, we removed entries of all users with the role other then student. After performing this task, 75 530 entries were accepted to be used in the next task.

These records were pre-processed in different manners. In each file, variable *Session* identifies individual course visit. The variable *Session* was based on variables *User ID*, *IP address* and timeout threshold with selected length (15, 30 and 60-minute STT) in the case of files X1, X2 and X3, where X = {A, B}. The paths were completed for each files BY separately, where Y = {1, 2, 3} based on the sitemap of the course.

Compared to the file X1 with the identification of sessions based on 15-minute STT (Table 1), the number of visits (costumer's sequences) decreased by approximately 7 % in case of the identification of sessions based on 30-minute STT (X2) and decreased by 12.5 % in case of the identification of sessions based on 60-minute STT (X3).

On the contrary, the number of frequented sequences increased by 14 % (A2) to 25 % (A3) and in the case of completing the paths increased by 12 % (B2) to 27 % (B3) in examined files.

Table 1. Number of accesses and sequences in particular files

File	Count of web accesses	Count of costumer's sequences	Count of frequented sequences	Average size of costumer's sequences
A1	70553	12992	71	5
A2	70553	12058	81	6
A3	70553	11378	89	6
B1	75372	12992	73	6
B2	75372	12058	82	6
B3	75439	11378	93	7

Having completed the paths (Table 1) the number of records increased by almost 7 % and the average length of visit/sequences increased from 5 to 6 (X2) and in the case of the identification of sessions based on 60-minute STT even to 7 (X3).

We articulated the following assumptions:

1. we expect that the identification of sessions based on shorter STT will have a significant impact on the quantity of extracted rules in terms of decreasing the portion of trivial and inexplicable rules,
2. we expect that the identification of sessions based on shorter STT will have a significant impact on the quality of extracted rules in the term of their basic measures of the quality,
3. we expect that the completion of paths will have a significant impact on the quantity of extracted rules in terms of increasing the portion of useful rules,
4. we expect that the completion of paths will have a significant impact on the quality of extracted rules in the term of their basic measures of the quality.

4 Results

4.1 Comparison of the Portion of the Found Rules in Examined Files

The analysis (Table 2) resulted in sequence rules, which we obtained from frequented sequences fulfilling their minimum support (in our case min s = 0.02). Frequented sequences were obtained from identified sequences, i.e. visits of individual students during one term.

There is a high coincidence between the results (Table 2) of sequence rule analysis in terms of the portion of the found rules in case of files with the identification of sessions based on 30-minute STT with and without the paths completion (A2, B2). The most rules were extracted from files with identification of sessions based on 60-minute STT; concretely 89 were extracted from the file A3, which represents over 88 % and 98 were extracted from the file B3, which represents over 97 % of the total number of found rules. Generally, more rules were found in the observed files with the completion of paths (BY).

Based on the results of Q test (Table 2), the zero hypothesis, which reasons that the incidence of rules does not depend on individual levels of data preparation for web log mining, is rejected at the 1 % significance level.

Table 2. Incidence of discovered sequence rules in particular files

Body	==>	Head	A1	A2	A3	B1	B2	B3	Type of rule
course view	==>	resource - final test requirements, course view	0	1	1	0	1	1	trivial
⋮	==>	⋮	⋮	⋮	⋮	⋮	⋮	⋮	⋮
course view	==>	view forum about ERD and relation schema	0	0	1	0	0	1	inexplicable
⋮	==>	⋮	⋮	⋮	⋮	⋮	⋮	⋮	⋮
course view	==>	view collaborative activities	1	1	1	1	1	1	useful
Count of derived sequence rules			63	78	89	68	81	98	
Percent of derived sequence rules (Percent 1's)			62.4	77.2	88.1	67.3	80.2	97.0	
Percent 0's			37.6	22.8	11.9	32.7	19.8	3.0	
Cochran Q test			Q = 93.84758, df = 5, p < 0.001						

The following graph (Fig. 1) visualizes the results of Cochran´s Q test.

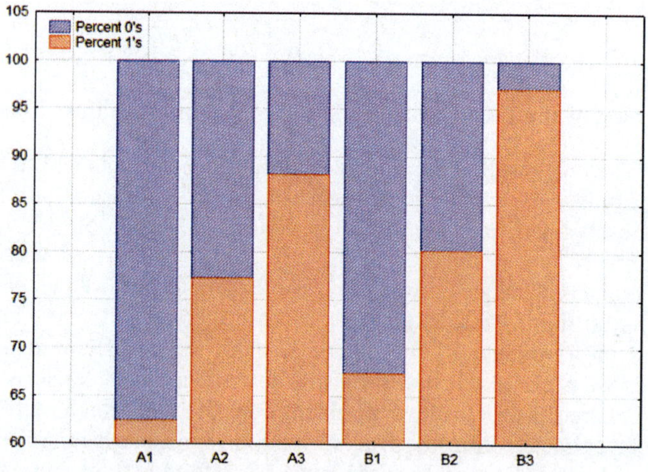

Fig. 1. Sequential/Stacked plot for derived rules in examined files

Kendall´s coefficient of concordance represents the degree of concordance in the number of the found rules among examined files. The value of coefficient (Table 3) is approximately 0.19 in both groups (AY, BY), while 1 means a perfect concordance and 0 represents discordance. Low values of coefficient confirm Q test results.

From the multiple comparisons (Tukey HSD test) was not identified homogenous group (Table 3) in term of the average incidence of the found rules. Statistically significant differences were proved on the level of significance 0.05 in the average incidence of found rules among all examined files (X1, X2, X3).

Table 3. Homogeneous groups for incidence of derived rules in examined files: (a) AY; (b) BY

File	Incidence	1	2	3	File	Incidence	1	2	3
A1	0.624	***			**B1**	0.673	***		
A2	0.772		***		**B2**	0.802		***	
A3	0.881			***	**B3**	0.970			***
Kendall Coefficient of Concordance			0.19459		**Kendall Coefficient of Concordance**			0.19773	

The value of STT has an important impact on the quantity of extracted rules (X1, X2, X3) in the process of session identification based on time.

If we have a look at the results in details (Table 4), we can see that in the files with the completion of the paths (BY) were found identical rules to the files without completion of the paths (AY), except one rule in case of files with 30-minute STT (X2) and three rules in case of the files with 60-minute STT (X3). The difference consisted only in 4 to 12 new rules, which were found in the files with the completion of the paths (BY). In case of the files with 15 and 30-minute STT (B1, B2) the portion of new files represented 5 % and 4 %. In case of the file with 60-minute STT (B3) almost 12 %, where also the statistically significant difference (Table 4c) in the number of found rules between A3 and B3 in favour of B3 was proved.

Table 4. Crosstabulations – AY x BY: (a) A1 x B1; (b) A2 x B2; (c) A3 x B3

(a)

A1\B1	0	1	Σ
0	33	5	38
	32.67 %	4.95%	37.62%
1	0	63	63
	0.00%	62.38%	62.38%
Σ	33	68	101
	32.67 %	67.33%	100%
McNemar (B/C)	$Chi^2 = 3.2$, df = 1, p = 0.0736		

Table 5. Crosstabulations - Incidence of rules x Types of rules: (a) A1; (b) A2; (c) A3

(a)

A1\Type	useful	trivial	inexp.
0	2	32	4
	9.52%	42.67%	80.00%
1	19	43	1
	90.48%	57.33%	20.00%
Σ	21	75	5
	100%	100%	100%
Pearson	$Chi^2 = 11.7$, df = 2, p = 0.0029		
Con. Coef. C	0.32226		
Cramér's V	0.34042		

(b)

A2\B2	0	1	Σ
0	19 18.81 %	4 3.96%	23 22.77%
1	1 0.99%	77 76.24%	78 77.23%
Σ	20 19.80 %	81 80.20%	101 100%
McNemar (B/C)	Chi^2 = 0.8, df = 1, p = 0.3711		

(b)

A2\Type	useful	trivial	inexp.
0	1 4.76%	19 25.33%	3 60.00%
1	20 95.24%	56 74.67%	2 40.00%
Σ	21 100%	75 100%	5 100%
Pearson	Chi^2 = 8.1, df = 2, p = 0.0175		
Con. Coef. C	0.27237		
Cramér's V	0.28308		

(c)

A3\B3	0	1	Σ
0	0 0.00%	12 11.88%	12 11.88%
1	3 2.97%	86 85.15%	89 88.12%
Σ	3 2.97%	98 97.03%	101 100%
McNemar (B/C)	Chi^2 = 4.3, df = 1, p = 0.0389		

(c)

A3\Type	useful	trivial	inexp.
0	0 0.00%	11 14.67%	1 20.00%
1	21 100.00%	64 85.33%	4 80.00%
Σ	21 100%	75 100%	5 100%
Pearson	Chi^2 = 3.7, df = 2, p = 0.1571		
Con. Coef. C	0.18804		
Cramér's V	0.19145		

The completion of the paths has an impact on the quantity of extracted rules only in case of files with the identification of sessions based on 60-minute timeout (A3 vs. B3). On the contrary, making provisions for the completion of paths in case of files with the identification of sessions based on shorter timeout has no significant impact on the quantity of extracted rules (X1, X2).

4.2 Comparison of the Portion of Inexplicable Rules in Examined Files

Now, we will look at the results of sequence analysis more closely, while taking into consideration the portion of each kind of the discovered rules. We require from association rules that they be not only clear but also useful. Association analysis produces the three common types of rules [35]:

- the useful (utilizable, beneficial),
- the trivial,
- the inexplicable.

In our case upon sequence rules we will differentiate same types of rules. The only requirement (validity assumption) of the use of chi-square test is high enough expected frequencies [36]. The condition is violated if the expected frequencies are lower than 5. The validity assumption of chi-square test in our tests is violated. This is the reason why we shall not prop ourselves only upon the results of Pearson chi-square test, but also upon the value of calculated contingency coefficient.

Contingency coefficients (Coef. C, Cramér's V) represent the degree of dependency between two nominal variables. The value of coefficient (Table 5a) is approximately 0.34. There is a medium dependency among the portion of the useful, trivial and inexplicable rules and their occurrence in the set of the discovered rules extracted from the data matrix A1, the contingency coefficient is statistically significant. The zero hypothesis (Table 5a) is rejected at the 1 % significance level, i.e. the portion of the useful, trivial and inexplicable rules depends on the identification of sessions based on 15-minute STT. In this file were found the least trivial and inexplicable rules, while 19 useful rules were extracted from the file (A1), which represents over 90 % of the total number of the found useful rules.

The value of coefficient (Table 5b) is approximately 0.28, while 1 means perfect relationship and 0 no relationship. There is a little dependency among the portion of the useful, trivial and inexplicable rules and their occurrence in the set of the discovered rules extracted from the data matrix File A2, the contingency coefficient is statistically significant. The zero hypothesis (Table 5b) is rejected at the 5 % significance level, i.e. the portion of the useful, trivial and inexplicable rules depends on the identification of sessions based on 30-minute timeout.

The coefficient value (Table 5c) is approximately 0.19, while 1 represents perfect dependency and 0 means independency. There is a little dependency among the portion of the useful, trivial and inexplicable rules and their occurrence in the set of the discovered rules extracted from the data matrix File A3, and the contingency coefficient is not statistically significant. In this file were found the most trivial and inexplicable rules, while portion of useful rules did not significantly increased.

Almost identical results were achieved for files with completion of the paths, too (Table 6). Similarly, the portion of useful, trivial and inexplicable rules is also approximately equal in case of files A1, B1 and files A2, B2. It corresponds with results from previous chapter (chapter 4.1), where were not proved significant differences in number of the discovered rules between files A1, B1 and files A2, B2. On the contrary, there was statistically significant difference (Table 4c) between A3 and B3 in favour of B3. If we have a look at the differences between A3 and B3 in dependency on types of rule (Table 5c, Table 6c), we observe increase in number of trivial and inexplicable rules in case B3, while the portion of useful rules is equal in both files.

The portion of trivial and inexplicable rules is dependent from the length of timeout by the identification of sessions based on time and independent from reconstruction of student`s activities in case of the identification of sessions based on 15-minute and 30-minute STT. Completion of paths has not impact on increasing portion of useful rules. On the contrary, impropriate chosen timeout may cause increasing of trivial and inexplicable rules.

Table 6. Crosstabulations - Incidence of rules x Types of rules: (a) B1; (b) B2; (c) B3. (U - useful, T – trivial, I – inexplicable rules. C - Contingency coefficient, V - Cramér's V.)

B1\ Type	**U**	**T**	**I**	**B2\ Type**	**U**	**T**	**I**	**B3\ Type**	**U**	**T**	**I**
0	2	27	4	**0**	2	15	3	**0**	0	3	0
	9.5%	36.0%	80.0%		9.5%	20.0%	60.0%		0.0%	4.0%	0.0%
1	19	48	1	**1**	19	60	2	**1**	21	72	5
	90.5%	64.0%	20.0%		90.5%	80.0%	40.0%		100.0%	96.0%	100.0%
Σ	21	75	5	Σ	21	75	5	Σ	21	75	5
	100%	100%	100%		100%	100%	100%		100%	100%	100%
Pear.	$Chi^2 = 10.6$, df = 2, p = 0.0050			**Pear.**	$Chi^2 = 6.5$, df = 2, p = 0.0390			**Pear.**	$Chi^2 = 1.1$, df = 2, p = 0.5851		
C	0.30798			**C**	0.24565			**C**	0.10247		
V	0.32372			**V**	0.25342			**V**	0.10302		

4.3 Comparison of the Values of Support and Confidence Rates of the Found Rules in Examined Files

Quality of sequence rules is assessed by means of two indicators [35]:

- support,
- confidence.

Results of the sequence rule analysis showed differences not only in the quantity of the found rules, but also in the quality. Kendall´s coefficient of concordance represents the degree of concordance in the support of the found rules among examined files. The value of coefficient (Table 7a) is approximately 0.89, while 1 means a perfect concordance and 0 represents discordancy.

From the multiple comparison (Tukey HSD test) five homogenous groups (Table 7a) consisting of examined files were identified in term of the average support of the found rules. The first homogenous group consists of files A1, B1, the third of files A2, B2 and the fifth of files A3, B3. Between these files is not statistically significant difference in support of discovered rules. On the contrary, statistically significant differences on the level of significance 0.05 in the average support of found rules were proved among files A1, A2, A3 and among files B1, B2, B3.

There were demonstrated differences in the quality in terms of confidence characteristics values of the discovered rules among individual files. The coefficient of concordance values (Table 7b) is almost 0.78, while 1 means a perfect concordance and 0 represents discordancy.

From the multiple comparison (Tukey HSD test) five homogenous groups (Table 7b) consisting of examined files were identified in term of the average confidence of the found rules. The first homogenous group consists of files A1, B1, the third of files A2, B2 and the fifth of files A3, B3. Between these files is not statistically significant difference in confidence of discovered rules. On the contrary, statistically significant differences on the level of significance 0.05 in the average confidence of found rules were proved among files A1, A2, A3 and among files B1, B2, B3.

Table 7. Homogeneous groups for (a) support of derived rules; (b) confidence of derived rules

(a)

File	Support	1	2	3	4	5
A1	4.330	****				
B1	4.625	****	****			
A2	4.806		****	****		
B2	5.104			****	****	
A3	5.231				****	****
B3	5.529					****
Kendall Coefficient of Concordance				0.88778		

(b)

File	Support	1	2	3	4	5
A1	26.702	****				
B1	27.474	****	****			
A2	27.762		****	****		
B2	28.468			****	****	
A3	28.833				****	****
B3	29.489					****
Kendall Coefficient of Concordance				0.78087		

Results (Table 7a, Table 7b) show that the largest degree of concordance in the support and confidence is among the rules found in the file without completing paths (AY) and in corresponding file with completion of the paths (BY). On the contrary, discordancy is among files with various timeout (X1, X2, X3) in both groups (AY, BY). Timeout by identification of sessions based on time has a substantial impact on the quality of extracted rules (X1, X2, X3). On the contrary, completion of the paths has not any significant impact on the quality of extracted rules (AY, BY).

5 Conclusions and Future Work

The first assumption concerning the identification of sessions based on time and its impact on quantity of extracted rules was fully proved. Specifically, it was proved that the length of STT has an important impact on the quantity of extracted rules. Statistically significant differences in the average incidence of found rules were proved among files A1, A2, A3 and among files B1, B2, B3. The portion of trivial and inexplicable rules is dependent from STT. Identification of sessions based on shorter STT has impact on decreasing portion of trivial and inexplicable rules.

The second assumption concerning the identification of sessions based on time and its impact on quality of extracted rules in term of their basic measures of quality was also fully proved. Similarly it was proved that shorter STT has a significant impact on the quality of extracted rules. Statistically significant differences in the average support and confidence of found rules were proved among files A1, A2, A3 and among files B1, B2, B3.

On the contrary, it was showed that the completion of paths has neither significant impact on quantity nor quality of extracted rules (AY, BY). Completion of paths has not impact on increasing portion of useful rules. The completion of the path has an impact on the quantity of extracted rules only in case of files with identification of sessions based on 60-minute STT (A3 vs. B3), while the portion of trivial and inexplicable rules was increasing. Completion of paths by the impropriate chosen STT may cause increasing of trivial and inexplicable rules. Results show that the largest degree of concordance in the support and confidence is among the rules found in the file without completion of the paths (AY) and in corresponding file with the completion of paths (BY). The third and fourth assumption were not proved.

From the previous follows, that the statement of several researchers about the number of identified sessions is dependent on time was proven. Experiment`s results showed that this dependency is not simple. The wrong STT choice could lead to the increasing of trivial and especially inexplicable rules.

Experiment has several weak places. At first, we have to notice that the experiment was realized based on data obtained from one e-learning course. Therefore, the obtained results could be misrepresented by course structure and used teaching methods. For generalization of the obtained findings, it would be needs to repeat the proposed experiment based on data obtained from several e-learning courses with various structures and/or various using of learning activities supporting course.

Our research indicates that it is possible to reduce the complexity of pre-processing phase in case of using web usage methods in educational context. We suppose that if the structure of e-learning course is relatively rigid and LMS provides sophisticated possibilities of navigation, the task of path completion can be removed from the pre-processing phase of web data mining because it has not significant impact on the quantity and quality of extracted knowledge. We would like to concentrate on further comprehensive work on generalization of presented methodology and increasing the data reliability used in experiment. We plan to repeat and improve proposed methodology to accumulate evidence in the future. Furthermore, we intend to investigate the ways of integration of path completion mechanism used in our experiment into the contemporary LMSs, or eventually in standardized web servers.

References

1. Ba-Omar, H., Petrounias, I., Anwar, F.: A Framework for Using Web Usage Mining to Personalise E-learning. In: Seventh IEEE International Conference on Advanced Learning Technologies, ICALT 2007, pp. 937–938 (2007)
2. Crespo Garcia, R.M., Kloos, C.D.: Web Usage Mining in a Blended Learning Context: A Case Study. In: Eighth IEEE International Conference on Advanced Learning Technologies, ICALT 2008, pp. 982–984 (2008)
3. Chitraa, V., Davamani, A.S.: A Survey on Preprocessing Methods for Web Usage Data. International Journal of Computer Science and Information Security 7 (2010)
4. Marquardt, C.G., Becker, K., Ruiz, D.D.: A Pre-processing Tool for Web Usage Mining in the Distance Education Domain. In: Proceedings of International Database Engineering and Applications Symposium, IDEAS 2004, pp. 78–87 (2004)
5. Romero, C., Ventura, S., Garcia, E.: Data Mining in Course Management Systems: Moodle Case Study and Tutorial. Comput. Educ. 51, 368–384 (2008)

6. Falakmasir, M.H., Habibi, J.: Using Educational Data Mining Methods to Study the Impact of Virtual Classroom in E-Learning. In: Baker, R.S.J.d., Merceron, A., Pavlik, P.I.J. (eds.) 3rd International Conference on Educational Data Mining, Pittsburgh, pp. 241–248 (2010)
7. Bing, L.: Web Data Mining. Exploring Hyperlinks, Contents and Usage Data. Springer, Heidelberg (2006)
8. Munk, M., Kapusta, J., Svec, P.: Data Pre-processing Evaluation for Web Log Mining: Reconstruction of Activities of a Web Visitor. Procedia Computer Science 1, 2273–2280 (2010)
9. Romero, C., Espejo, P.G., Zafra, A., Romero, J.R., Ventura, S.: Web Usage Mining for Predicting Final Marks of Students that Use Moodle Courses. Computer Applications in Engineering Education 26 (2010)
10. Raju, G.T., Satyanarayana, P.S.: Knowledge Discovery from Web Usage Data: a Complete Preprocessing Methodology. IJCSNS International Journal of Computer Science and Network Security 8 (2008)
11. Spiliopoulou, M., Mobasher, B., Berendt, B., Nakagawa, M.: A Framework for the Evaluation of Session Reconstruction Heuristics in Web-Usage Analysis. INFORMS J. on Computing 15, 171–190 (2003)
12. Bayir, M.A., Toroslu, I.H., Cosar, A.: A New Approach for Reactive Web Usage Data Processing. In: Proceedings of 22nd International Conference on Data Engineering Workshops, pp. 44–44 (2006)
13. Zhang, H., Liang, W.: An Intelligent Algorithm of Data Pre-processing in Web Usage Mining. In: Proceedings of the World Congress on Intelligent Control and Automation (WCICA), pp. 3119–3123 (2004)
14. Cooley, R., Mobasher, B., Srivastava, J.: Data Preparation for Mining World Wide Web Browsing Patterns. Knowledge and Information Systems 1, 5–32 (1999)
15. Yan, L., Boqin, F., Qinjiao, M.: Research on Path Completion Technique in Web Usage Mining. In: International Symposium on Computer Science and Computational Technology, ISCSCT 2008, vol. 1, pp. 554–559 (2008)
16. Yan, L., Boqin, F.: The Construction of Transactions for Web Usage Mining. In: International Conference on Computational Intelligence and Natural Computing, CINC 2009, vol. 1, pp. 121–124 (2009)
17. Huynh, T.: Empirically Driven Investigation of Dependability and Security Issues in Internet-Centric Systems. Department of Electrical and Computer Engineering. University of Alberta, Edmonton (2010)
18. Huynh, T., Miller, J.: Empirical Observations on the Session Timeout Threshold. Inf. Process. Manage. 45, 513–528 (2009)
19. Catledge, L.D., Pitkow, J.E.: Characterizing Browsing Strategies in the World-Wide Web. Comput. Netw. ISDN Syst. 27, 1065–1073 (1995)
20. Huntington, P., Nicholas, D., Jamali, H.R.: Website Usage Metrics: A Re-assessment of Session Data. Inf. Process. Manage. 44, 358–372 (2008)
21. Meiss, M., Duncan, J., Goncalves, B., Ramasco, J.J., Menczer, F.: What's in a Session: Tracking Individual Behavior on the Web. In: Proceedings of the 20th ACM Conference on Hypertext and Hypermedia. ACM, Torino (2009)
22. Huang, X., Peng, F., An, A., Schuurmans, D.: Dynamic Web Log Session Identification with Statistical Language Models. J. Am. Soc. Inf. Sci. Technol. 55, 1290–1303 (2004)
23. Goseva-Popstojanova, K., Mazimdar, S., Singh, A.D.: Empirical Study of Session-Based Workload and Reliability for Web Servers. In: Proceedings of the 15th International Symposium on Software Reliability Engineering. IEEE Computer Society, Los Alamitos (2004)

24. Tian, J., Rudraraju, S., Zhao, L.: Evaluating Web Software Reliability Based on Workload and Failure Data Extracted from Server Logs. IEEE Transactions on Software Engineering 30, 754–769 (2004)
25. Chen, Z., Fowler, R.H., Fu, A.W.-C.: Linear Time Algorithms for Finding Maximal Forward References. In: Proceedings of the International Conference on Information Technology: Computers and Communications. IEEE Computer Society, Los Alamitos (2003)
26. Borbinha, J., Baker, T., Mahoui, M., Jo Cunningham, S.: A comparative transaction log analysis of two computing collections. In: Borbinha, J.L., Baker, T. (eds.) ECDL 2000. LNCS, vol. 1923, pp. 418–423. Springer, Heidelberg (2000)
27. Kohavi, R., Mason, L., Parekh, R., Zheng, Z.: Lessons and Challenges from Mining Retail E-Commerce Data. Mach. Learn. 57, 83–113 (2004)
28. Munk, M., Kapusta, J., Švec, P., Turčáni, M.: Data Advance Preparation Factors Affecting Results of Sequence Rule Analysis in Web Log Mining. E+M Economics and Management 13, 143–160 (2010)
29. Agrawal, R., Imieliski, Swami, A.: Mining Association Rules Between Sets of Items in Large Databases. In: Proceedings of the 1993 ACM SIGMOD International Conference on Management of Data. ACM, Washington, D.C (1993)
30. Agrawal, R., Srikant, R.: Fast Algorithms for Mining Association Rules in Large Databases. In: Proceedings of the 20th International Conference on Very Large Data Bases. Morgan Kaufmann Publishers Inc., San Francisco (1994)
31. Han, J., Lakshmanan, L.V.S., Pei, J.: Scalable Frequent-pattern Mining Methods: an Overview. In: Tutorial notes of the Seventh ACM SIGKDD International Conference on Knowledge Discovery and Data Mining. ACM, San Francisco (2001)
32. Witten, I.H., Frank, E.: Data Mining: Practical Machine Learning Tools and Techniques. Morgan Kaufmann, New York (2000)
33. Electronic Statistics Textbook. StatSoft, Tulsa (2010)
34. Romero, C., Ventura, S.: Educational Data Mining: A Survey from 1995 to 2005. Expert Systems with Applications 33, 135–146 (2007)
35. Berry, M.J., Linoff, G.S.: Data Mining Techniques: For Marketing, Sales, and Customer Relationship Management. Wiley Publishing, Inc., Chichester (2004)
36. Hays, W.L.: Statistics. CBS College Publishing, New York (1988)

Analysis and Design of an Effective E-Accounting Information System (EEAIS)

Sarmad Mohammad

ITC- AOU - Kingdom of Bahrain
Tel.: (+973) 17407167; Mob.: (+973) 39409656
sarmad@aou.org.bh, sarmad1_jo@yahoo.com

Abstract. E-Accounting (Electronic Accounting) is a new information technology terminology based on the changing role of accountants, where advances in technology have relegated the mechanical aspects of accounting to computer networks. The new accountants are concerned about the implications of these numbers and their effects on the decision-making process.This research aims to perform the accounting functions as software intelligent agents [1] and integrating the accounting standards effectively as web application, so the main objective of this research paper is to provide an effective, consistent, customized and workable solution to companies that participate with the suggested OLAP accounting analysis and services. This paper will point out a guide line to analysis and design the suggested Effective Electronic-Accounting Information System (EEAIS) which provide a reliable, cost efficient and a very personal quick and accurate service to clients in secure environment with the highest level of professionalism, efficiency and technology.

Keywords: E-accounting, web application technology, OLAP.

1 Systematic Methodology

This research work developed a systematic methodology that uses Wetherbeis PIECES framework [2] (Performance, Information, Economics, Control, Efficiency and Security) to drive and support the analysis, which is a checklist for identifying problems with an existing information system. In support to the framework, advantages & disadvantages of e-Accounting compared to traditional accounting system summarized in *Table 1.*

The suggested system analysis methodology emphasizes to point out a guide lines (not framework) to build an effective E-Accounting system, Fig -1 illustrates EEAIS required characteristics of analysis guide lines, and the PIECES framework is implemented to measure the effectiveness of the system. The survey which includes [6] questions concerning PIECES framework (Performance, Information, Economics, Control, Efficiency, Security) about adoption of e-accounting in Bahrain have been conducted as a tool to measure the suggested system effectiveness. A Questionnaire has been conducted asking a group of 50 accountants about their opinion in order to indicate the factors that may affect the adoption of e-Accounting systems in organizations in Bahrain given in *Table 2*.

H. Cherifi, J.M. Zain, and E. El-Qawasmeh (Eds.): DICTAP 2011, Part I, CCIS 166, pp. 75–82, 2011.

2 Analysis of Required Online Characteristics of (EEAIS)

Main features of suggested e- accounting information system (EEAIS) are the following:

- Security and data protection are the methods and procedures used to authorize transactions, Safeguard and control assets [9].
- Comparability means that the system works smoothly with operations, personnel, and the organizational structure.
- Flexibility relates to the system's ability to accommodate changes in the organization.
- A cost/benefit relationship indicates that the cost of controls do not exceed their value to the organization compared to traditional accounting.

First step of EEAIS analysis is to fulfill required characteristics; some of these measures summarized in *Figure -1*, which should be implemented to ensure effective and efficient system.

3 Infrastructure Analysis

The EEAIS on line web site's infrastructure contains many specific components to be the index to the health of the infrastructure. A good starting point should include the operating system, server, network hardware, and application software. For each specific component, identify a set of detailed components [3] .For the operating system, this should include detailed components like CPU utilization, file systems, paging space, memory utilization, etc. These detailed components will become the focus of the monitors that will be used for ensure the availability of the infrastructure. *Figure -2* describes infrastructure components and flow diagram indicating operation steps. The application & business issues also will be included. Computerized accounting systems are organized by modules. These modules are separate but integrated units. A sales transaction entry will update two modules: Accounts Receivable/Sales and Inventory/Cost of Goods Sold. EEAIS is organized by function or task, usually have a choice of processing options on a "menu." will be discussed in design issue.

These issues are EEAIS characteristics (Security, Comparability, and Flexibility and Cost/Benefits relationship) used to clearly identify main features. Survey about adoption of e-accounting in Bahrain have been conducted to measure suggested system effectiveness and efficiency which includes important questions concerning PIECES, Performance, Information, Economics, Control, Efficiency, Security. A Questionnaire has been conducted asking a group of 50 accountants about their view regarding the adoption of e-Accounting systems in organizations in Bahrain given in *Table 2*. The infrastructure server, network hardware, and used tools (menu driven) that are the focus of the various system activities of e-accounting (application software) also included in the questionnaire to support analysis issue.

Table 1. E-Accounting compared to Traditional Accounting

E-Accounting	**Traditional Accounting**
1-Time & location flexibility 2-Cost-effective for clients. 3-Global with unlimited access to shared information 4-Self- paced	1 Time & location constraints 2- More expensive to deliver. 3-Local with limited accessed to shared information 4- Not Self-Paced, accountant –centered
5-Lack of Immediate feed-back in asynchronous e-accounting. 6-Non comfortable, anxiety, frustration and confusion to some clients. 7-Increased preparation time due to application software and Network requirement.	5-Motivating clients due to interaction & feedback with real accountant 6-Familiar to both individual & company due to cultivation of a social community. 7- Less preparation time needed.

Table 2. PIECES, Performance, Information, Economics, Control, Efficiency, Security. Questionnaire about adoption of e-accounting in Bahrain

	Questions	***YES***	***NO***	***Possibly/ Don't Know***
P	**Do you think that EEAIS implemented automated software intelligent agent standards will improve and maintain high performance accounting systems to ensure consistency, completeness and quality, reinforces and enhance services in your organization.**	68%	23%	9%
I	**Do you think that EEAIS will enable an excellent information communication between clients & your company?**	70%	20%	10%
E	**Do you think it is Cost-effective for clients to utilized on line EEAIS?**	48%	30%	22%
C	**Is EEAIS lack of accuracies, interaction and feed-back in online materials? Lack of client opportunity to ask accountant questions directly?**	57%	23%	20%
E	**Are there chances to improve the organization efficiency's in the absence of specific problems (Time, location constraints, slow response and eliminating paper works)?**	74%	16%	10%
S	**Is it more secure to adapt traditional accounting approach rather than e-accounting due to on line intruders?**	45%	34%	21%

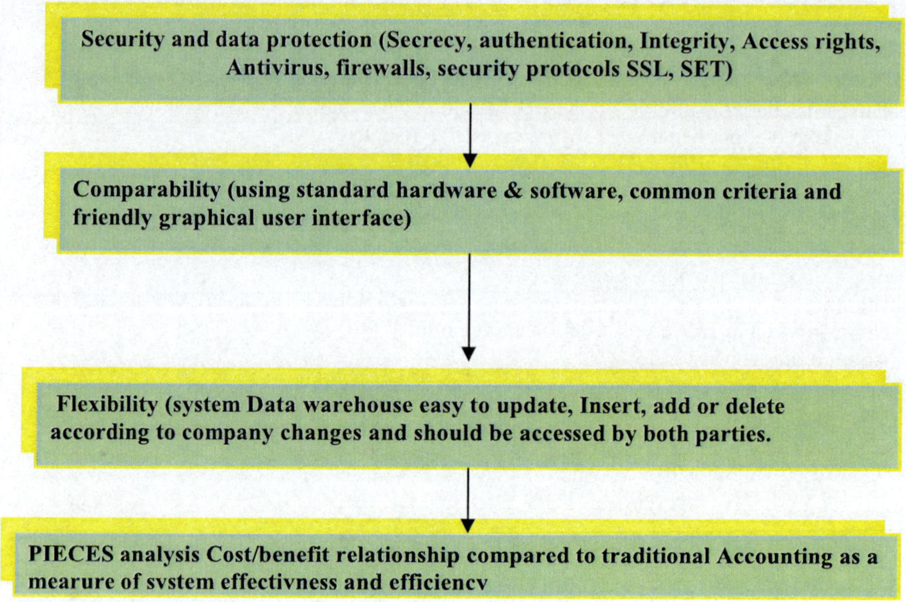

Fig. 1. Illustrates EEAIS required Analysis characteristics guide line

Figure-2 shows a briefing of the Infrastructure for suggested Efficient Electronic-Accounting Information System related to design issue, while *Figure-3* illustrates Design of OLAP Menu-Driven for EEAIS related to data warehouse as an application issue of E-accounting, the conclusions given in *Figure 4* which is the outcome of the survey (PIECES framework). There will be a future work will be conducted to design a conceptual frame work and to implement a benchmark work comparing suggested system with other related works to enhance EEAIS.

4 Application Issue

To understand how both computerized and manual accounting systems work [4], following includes important accounting services as OLAP workstation, of course theses services to be included in EEAIS:

- Tax and Business Advisory (Individual and Company)
- Payroll Services
- Invoice Solutions
- Business Start up Service
- Accounts Receivables Outsourcing
- Information Systems and Risk Management analysis.
- Financial Forecast and Projections analysis.
- Cash Flow and Budgeting Analysis
- Sales Tax Services
- Bookkeeping Service
- Financial Statements

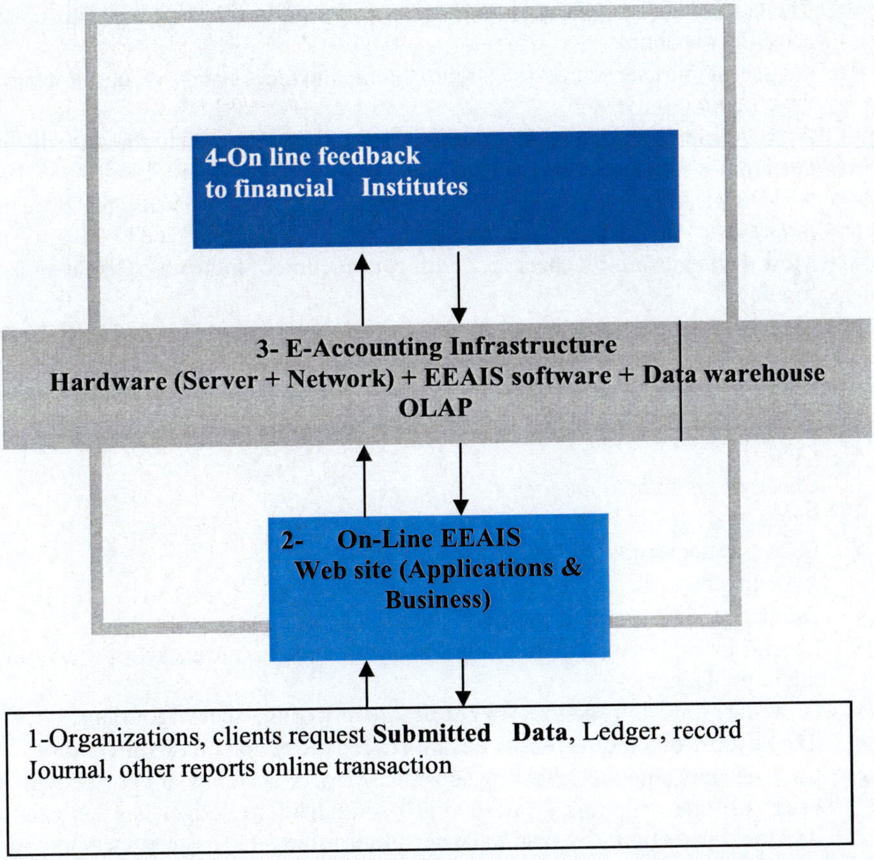

Fig . 2. Infrastructure of Efficient Electronic-Accounting Information System

5 Design Issues

The following will include suggested technical menu-driven software as intelligent Agents and data warehouse tools to be implemented in designed EEAIS.

- Design of the e-accounting system begins with the chart of accounts. The chart of accounts lists all accounts and their account number in the ledger.
- The designed software will account for all purchases of inventory, supplies, services, and other assets on account.
- Additional columns are provided in data base to enter other account descriptions and amounts.
- At month end, foot and cross foot the journal and post to the general ledger.
- At the end of the accounting period, where the total debits and credits of account balances in the general ledger should be equal.

- The control account balances are equal to the sum of the appropriate subsidiary ledger accounts.
- A general journal records sales returns and allowances and purchase returns in the company.
- A *credit memorandum* is the document issued by the seller for a credit to a customer's Accounts Receivable.
- A *debit memorandum* is the business document that states that the buyer no longer owes the seller for the amount of the returned purchases.
- Most payments are by check or credit card recorded in the cash disbursements journal.
- The cash disbursements journal have following columns in EEAIS 's data warehouse
- Check or credit card register
- Cash payments journal
- Date
- Check or credit card number
- Payee
- Cash amount (credit)
- Accounts payable (debit).
- Description and amount of other debits and credits.
- Special journals save much time in recording repetitive transactions and, posting to the ledger.
- However, some transactions do not fit into any of the special journals.
- The buyer debits the Accounts Payable to the seller and credits Inventory.
- Cash receipts amounts affecting subsidiary ledger accounts are posted daily to keep customer balances up to date [10]. A subsidiary ledger is often used to provide details on individual balances of customers (accounts receivable) and suppliers (accounts payable).

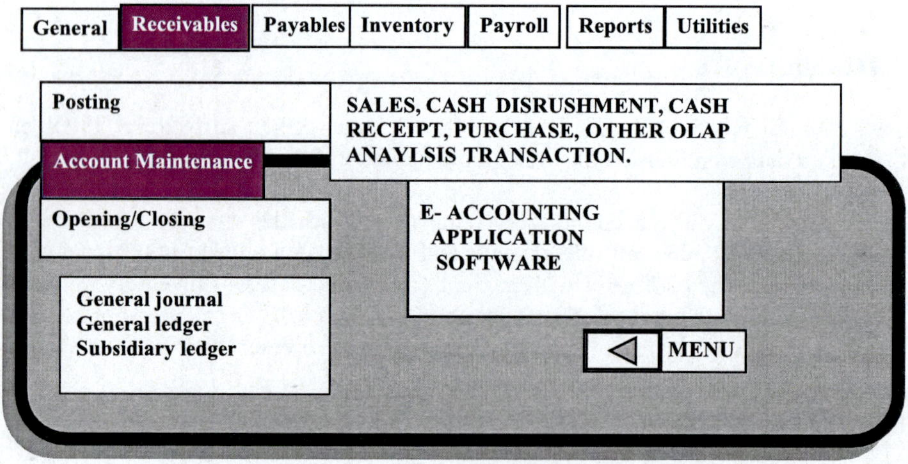

Fig. 3. Design of OLAP Menu-Driven for EEAIS related to data warehouse

6 Summary

This paper described a guide line to design and analysis an efficient, consistent, customized and workable solution to companies that participate with the suggested on line accounting services. The designed EEAIS provides a reliable, cost efficient and a very personal quick and accurate service to clients in secure environment. Questionnaire has been conducted to study and analysis an existing e-accounting systems requirements in order to find a priorities for improvement in suggested EEAIS.

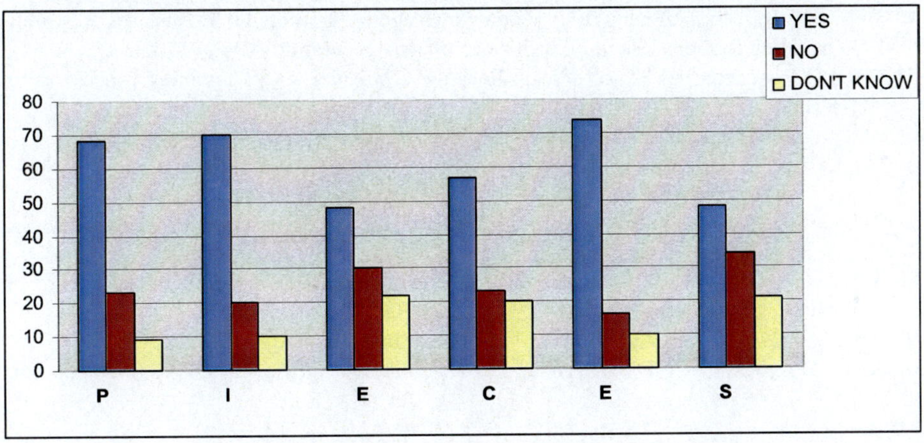

Fig. 4. PIECES Analysis outcomes

The outcomes of the PIECES survey shown in *Figure 4* indicate that more than 60% of accountants agree with the effectiveness of implementing EEAIS. The methodology is used for proactive planning which involves three steps: preplanning, analysis, and review process. *Figure -2* illustrates the infrastructure of EEAIS which is used to support the design associated with the methodology. The developed systematic methodology uses a series of issues to drive and support EEAIS design. These issues are used to clearly focus on the used tools of the system activities, so system perspective has a focus on hardware and software grouped by infrastructure, application, and business components. The support perspective is centered on design issue & suggested by menu driven given in *Figure-3* is based on Design of OLAP Menu-Driven for EEAIS related to data warehouse perspectives that incorporate tools. There will be a future work will be conducted to design and study a conceptual frame and to implement a benchmark work comparing suggested system with other related works to enhance EEAIS.

Acknowledgment

This Paper received a financial support towards the cost of its publication from the Deanship of Faculty of Information Technology at AOU, Kingdom of Bahrain.

References

1. Heflin, F., Subramanyam, K.R., Zhang, Y.: Regulation FD and the Financial Information Environment: Early Evidence. The Accounting Review (January 2003)
2. The PIECES Framework. A checklist for identifying problems with an existing information system, http://www.cs.toronto.edu/~sme/CSC340F/readings/PIECES.html
3. Tawfik, M.S.: Measuring the Digital Divide Using Digitations Index and Its Impacts in the Area of Electronic Accounting Systems. Electronic Account-ing Software and Research Site, http://mstawfik.tripod.com/
4. Gullkvist, B., Mika Ylinen, D.S.: Vaasa Polytechnic, Frontiers Of E-Business Research. E-Accounting Systems Use in Finnish Accounting Agencies (2005)
5. CSI LG E-Accounting Project stream-lines the acquisition and accounting process using web technologies and digital signature, http://www.csitech.com/news/070601.asp
6. Online Accounting Processing for Web Service E-Commerce Sites: An Empirical Study on Hi-Tech Firms, http://www.e-accounting.biz
7. Accounting Standards for Electronic Government Transactions and Web Services, http://www.eaccounting.cpa-asp.com
8. The Accounting Review, Electronic Data Interchange (EDI) to Improve the Efficiency of Accounting Transactions, pp. 703–729 (October 2002)
9. http://www.e-accounting.pl/ solution for e-accounting
10. Kieso, D.E., Kimmel, P.D., Weygandt, J.J.: E-accounting software pack-ages (Ph. D thesis)

DocFlow: A Document Workflow Management System for Small Office

Boonsit Yimwadsana, Chalalai Chaihirunkarn,
Apichaya Jaichoom, and Apichaya Thawornchak

Faculty of Information and Communication Technology,
Mahidol University 999 Phuttamonthon 4 Road, Salaya, Phuttamonthon
Nakhon Pathom 73170, Thailand
{itbyw,itcch}@mahidol.ac.th,
{picha_nat,apichayat}@hotmail.com

Abstract. Document management and workflow management systems have been widely used in large business enterprises to improve productivity. However, they still do not gain large acceptance in small and medium-sized businesses due to their cost and complexity. In addition, document management and workflow management concepts are often separated from each other. We combine the two concepts together and simplify the management of both document and workflow to fit small and medium business users. Our application, DocFlow, is designed with simplicity in mind while still maintaining necessary workflow and document management standard concepts including security. Approval mechanism is also considered. A group of actors can be assigned to a task, while only one of the team members is sufficient to make the group's decision. A case study of news publishing process is shown to demonstrate how DocFlow can be used to create a workflow that fits the news publishing process.

Keywords: Document Management, Workflow Management.

1 Introduction

Today's business organizations must employ rapid decision making process in order to cope with global competition. Rapid decision making process allows organizations to quickly drive the company forward according to the ever-changing business environment. Organizations must constantly reconsider and optimize the way they do business and bring in information systems to support business processes. Each organization usually makes strategic decisions by first defining each division's performance and result matrices, measure the matrices, analyze the matrices and finally intelligently report the matrices to the strategic teams consisting of the organization's leaders. Typically, each department or division can autonomously make a business decision that has to support the overall direction of the organization. It is also obvious that an organization must make a large number of small decisions to support a strategic decision. In another perspective, a decision makes by the board of executives will result in several small decisions made by various divisions of each organization.

In the case of small and medium size businesses (SMBs) including small branch offices, decisions and orders are usually confirmed by documents signed by heads at

H. Cherifi, J.M. Zain, and E. El-Qawasmeh (Eds.): DICTAP 2011, Part I, CCIS 166, pp. 83–92, 2011.

different levels. Thus, a large number of documents are generated until the completion of a process. A lot of times, documents must be reviewed by a few individuals before they can be approved and forwarded to the next task. This process can take a long time and involve many individuals. This can also create confusion in the area of document ownership and versions. Due to today business environment, an individual does not usually focus on one single task. A staff in an organization must be involved in different tasks and projects from within a single or several departments as a part of organizational integration effort. Hence, a document database must be created in order help individuals come back to review and approve documents later.

The document database is one of the earliest applications of information technology. Documents are transformed from paper form to electronic form. However, document management software or concept is one of the least deployed solutions in businesses. Proper file and folder management help company staffs organize documents so that they can work with and review documents in a repository efficiently to reduce operation costs and speed up market response [20]. When many staffs have to work together as a team or work with other staffs spanning different departments, a shared document repository is needed. Hence, a standard method for organizing documents must be defined. Different types of work environment have different standards. Common concepts of document and file storage management for efficient and effective information retrieval can be introduced. Various document management systems are proposed [1,3-5] and they have been widely accepted in various industries.

The World Wide Web is a document management platform that can be used to provide a common area for users to gain access and share documents. In particular hypertext helps alleviate various issues of document organization and information retrieval. Documents may no longer have to be stored as files in a file system without knowing their relationship. The success of hypertext can easily be seen from the success of the World Wide Web today. However, posting files online in the Internet or Intranet has a few obstacles. Not all staffs know how to put information or documents on websites, and they usually do not have access to the company's web server due to security reason. In addition, enforcing user access control and permission cannot be done easily. There are a number of websites that provide online services (cloud services) that allow members to post and share information on the websites such as Wikipedia [6] and Google Docs [7]. However, using these services lock users into the services of the websites. In order to start sharing documents and manage documents, one must register an account at a website providing the document management service, and place documents in the cloud. This usually violates typical business policy which requires that all documents must be kept private inside the company.

To accommodate a business policy on document privacy, documents must be kept inside the company. Shared file and folder repositories and document management systems should be deployed within a local area network to manage documents [19]. In addition, in a typical work environment, several people work with several version of documents that are revised by many people. This creates confusion on which version to use at the end. Several file and folder names can be created in order to reduce this confusion. However, this results in unnecessary files and folders which waste a lot of memory and creates confusion. In addition, sharing files and folders require careful monitoring of access control and file organization control at the server side which is not practical in an environment that has a large number of users.

Document management systems do not address how documents flow from an individual to another individual until the head department receives the final version of the document. The concept describing the flow of documents usually falls into the workflow management concept [14,17,18] which is tightly related to business process management. Defining workflows have become one of the most important tools used in business today. Various workflow information systems are proposed to make flow designation easier and more effective. Widely accepted workflow management systems are now developed and supported by companies offering solutions to enterprises such as IBM, SAP and Microsoft [9-11].

In short, document management system focuses on the management of electronic documents such as indexing and retrieving of documents [21]. Some of them may have version control and concurrency control built in. Workflow management system focuses on the transformation of business processes to workflow specification [17,18]. Monique [15] discussed the differences between document management software and workflow management software, and asserted that a business must clearly identify its requirements and choose which software to use.

In many small and medium businesses, document and workflow management systems are typically used separately. Workflow management systems are often used to define how divisions communicate systematically through task assignments and document flow assignments [18], while document management systems are used to manage document storages. When the two concepts are not combined, a staff must first search for documents from document management system, and put them into workflow management systems in order for the document to reach the decision makers.

Our work focuses on connecting document management system together with workflow management system in order to reduce the problem of document retrieval in workflow management system and workflow support in document management system. We propose a model of document workflow management system that combines document management system and workflow management system together. Currently, there are solutions that integrate document management software and workflow management software together such as [1,2] and ERP systems such as [11]. However, most solutions force users to switch to the solutions' document creation and management methods instead of allowing the users to use their favorite Word processing software such as Microsoft Word. In addition, the deployment of ERP systems require complex customized configurations to be perform in order to support the business environment [16].

2 DocFlow: A Document Workflow Management System

DocFlow is a document workflow management system that combines basic concept of document management system and workflow management system together to help small business manage business documents, tasks, and approval process. DocFlow system provides storage repository and document retrieval, versioning, security and workflow features which are explained as follows:

- Storage repository and Document Retrieval

  Documents are stored locally in file system normally supported by local filesystem in a server or Storage Area Network (SAN). When files are uploaded to the system, metadata of the documents, such as filenames, keywords, and dates, can be entered by the users and stored separately in DocFlow database. A major requirement is the support for various document formats. The storage repository will store documents in the original forms entered by the users. This is to provide support for different document formats that users would use. In Thailand, most organizations use Microsoft Office applications such as Microsoft Word, Microsoft Excel, Microsoft PowerPoint and Microsoft Visio to create documents. Other formats such as image- and vector-based documents (Adobe PDF, postscript, and JPEG), and archive-based documents such as (ZIP, GZIP, and RAR) documents are also supported. DocFlow refrains from enforcing another document processing format in order to integrate with other document processing software smoothly. The database is also designed to allow documents to be related to the workflow created by the workflow system to reduce the number of documents that have to be duplicated in different workflows.

- Versioning

Simple documents versioning are supported in order to keep the history of the documents. Users can retrieve previous versions of the documents and continue working from a selected milestone. Versioning helps users to create documents that are the same kind but use in different purpose or occasions. Users can define a set of documents under the same general target content and purpose type. Defining versions of documents are done by the users.

DocFlow supports group work function. If several individuals in a group edit the same documents at the same time and upload their own versions to the system, document inconsistency or conflict will occur. Thus, the system is designed with a simple document state management such that when an individual downloads documents from DocFlow, DocFlow will notify all members in the group responsible to process the documents that the documents are being edited by the individual. DocFlow does not allow other members of the group to upload new version of the locked documents until the individual unlock the documents by uploading new versions of the documents back to DocFlow. This is to prevent content conflicts since DocFlow does not have content merging capability found in specialized version control system software such as subversion [2]. During the time that the documents are locked, other group members can still download other versions of the documents except the ones that are locked. A newly uploaded document will be assigned a new version by default. It is the responsibility of the document uploader to specify in the version note that the new version of the document is an update from which version specifically.

- Security

All organizations must protect their documents in order to retain trade secrets and company internal information. Hence, access control and encryption are used. Access control information is kept in a separate table in the database based on standard access control policy [13] to implement authorization policy. A user can grant read-only, full access, or no access to another user or group based on his preference.

The integrity policy is implemented using Public Key Cryptography through the use of document data encryption and digital signing. For document encryption, we use symmetric key cryptography where the key are randomly and uniquely created for each document. To protect the symmetric key, public key cryptography is used. When a user uploads a document, each document is encrypted using a symmetric key (secret key). The symmetric key is encrypted using the document owner's public key, and stored in a key store database table along with other encrypted secret keys with document ID and user association. When the document owner gives permission to a user to access the file, the symmetric key is decrypted using the document owner's private key protected by a different password and stored either on the user's USB key drive or on the user's computer, and the symmetric key will be encrypted using the target user's public key and stored in the key store database table. The security mechanism is designed with the security encapsulation concept. The complexity of security message communications is hidden from the users as much as possible. The document encryption mechanism is shown in Figure 1.

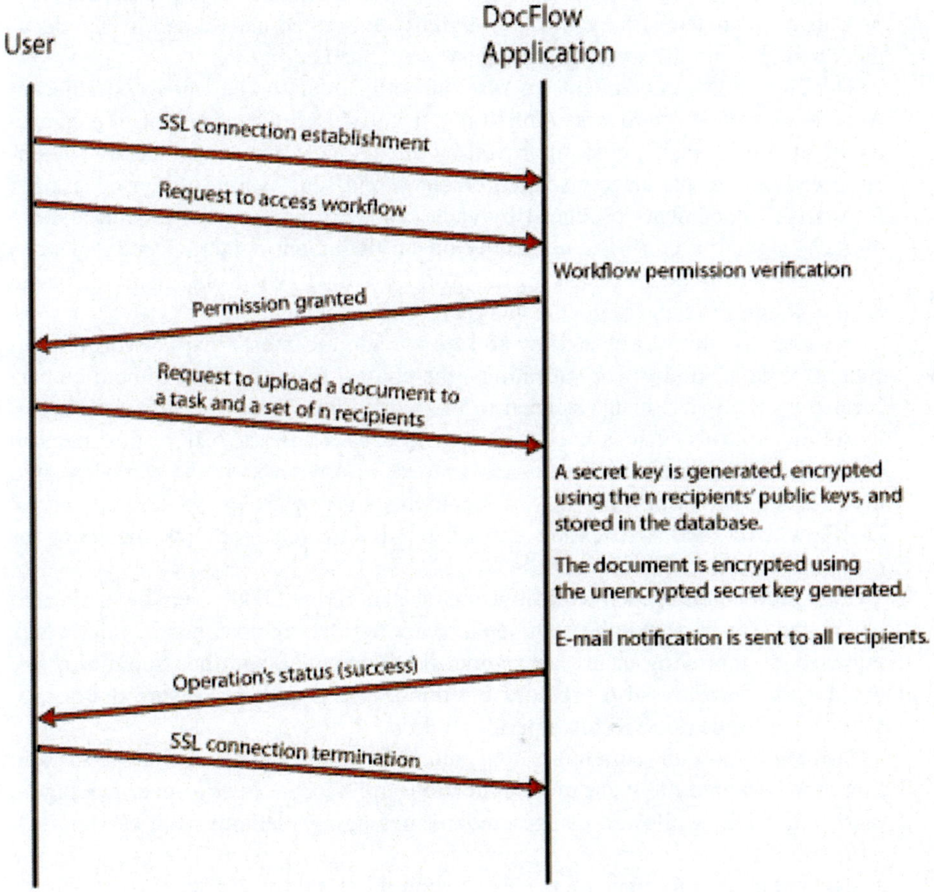

Fig. 1. Encryption mechanism of DocFlow

- Workflow

The workflow model of DocFlow system is based entirely on resource flow perspective [22]. A resource flow perspective defines workflow as a ternary relationship between tasks, actors and roles. A task is defined as a pair of document producing and consumption point. Each task involves the data that flow between a producer and a consumer. To simplify the workflow's tasks, each task can have only one actor or multiple actors. DocFlow provides user and group management service to help task and actors association. DocFlow focuses on the set of documents produced by an actor according to his/her roles associated with the task. A set of documents produced and confirmed by one of the task's actors determines the completion of a task. The path containing connected producer/consumer paths defines a workflow. In other words, a workflow defines a set of tasks. Each task has a start condition and an end condition describing the way the task takes action on prior tasks and the way the task activates the next task. A workflow has a start condition and an end condition as well. In our workflow concept, a document produced by an actor of each task is digitally encrypted and signed by the document owner using the security mechanism described earlier.

DocFlow allows documents to flow in both directions between two adjacent workflow's tasks. The reverse direction is usually used when the documents produced by a prior task are not approved by the actors in the current task. The unapproved documents are revised, commented and sent back to the prior task for rework. All documents produced by each task will have a new version and are digitally signed to confirm the identity of the document owner. Documents can only move on to the next task in the workflow only when one of the actors in each task approves all the documents received for the task.

In order to control a workflow and to provide the most flexible workflow to support various kinds of organizations, the control of a workflow should be performed by the individuals assigned to the workflow. DocFlow supports several workflow controls such as backward flow to send a specific task or document in backward direction of the flow, task skip to skip some tasks in the workflow, add new tasks to the workflow, and assignments of workflow and task members. DocFlow will send notification e-mails to all affected DocFlow members for every change related to the workflow.

It is important that each workflow and task should not take too many actions to be created. A task should be completed easily by placing documents into the task output box, approving or not approving the documents, and then submitting the documents. DocFlow also provides a reminder service to make sure that a specific task must be done within a period of time.

However, not all communication must flow through the workflow path. Sometimes behind the scene communications are needed. Peer-to-peer messaging communication is allowed using standard messaging methods such as DocFlow or traditional e-mail service. DocFlow allows users to send documents in the storage repository to other users easily without having to save them on the user's desktop first.

3 System Architecture and Implementation

DocFlow system is designed with three-tier architecture concept. It is implemented as a web-based system whose server-side consists of 4 major modules which are authentication, user and group management, document management and workflow management. The client-side module of the system is implemented using Adobe Flash and Adobe Flex technology while the server-side business process modules are implemented using PHP connecting to a MySQL database. Users use Web browser to access the system through https protocol. Adobe Flash and Flex technology allows simple and attractive interface. The client-side modules exchange messages with the server-side modules using web-services technology. Uploaded documents are stored in their original formats in a back-end SAN. The system architecture and details of each module are shown in Figure 2.

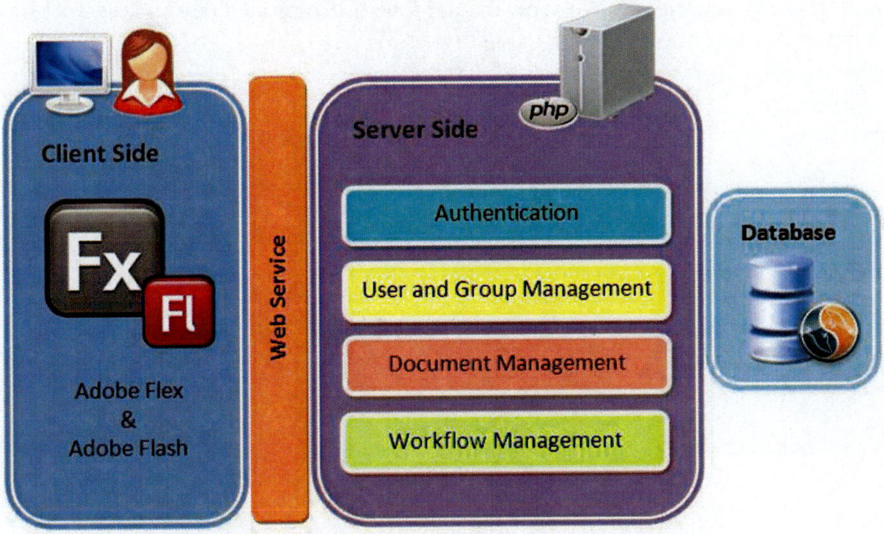

Fig. 2. DocFlow System Architecture

4 A Case of the Public Relation Division

Staffs in the public relation (PR) division at the Faculty of Information and Communication Technology, Mahidol University, Thailand, usually write news and events article to promote the faculty and the university. Normally there will be a few staffs who gather the content of the news and events in Thai language and pass it to a staff (news writer) who write each news. The news writer will forward the written news to another staff (English translator) who can translate the news from Thai to English. The news in both Thai and English will then be sent back to the news writer to make the final pass of the news before it is submitted to a group of faculty administrators (news Editor) who can approve the content of the news. The faculty administrator will then revise or comment on the news and events and send the revised document consisting of Thai and English versions back to the news writer who will make the final pass of the news.

Normally, the staffs communicate by e-mail and conversation. Since PR staffs have other responsibilities, often times the e-mails are not processed right away. There are a few times that one of the staffs forgets to take his/her responsible actions. Sometimes a staff completely forgets that there is a news article waiting for him/her to take action, and sometimes the staff forgets that he has already taken action. This delays the posting of the news update on the website and faculty newsletter.

Using DocFlow, assuming that the workflow for PR news posting is already established, the PR writer can post news article to the system and approve it so that the English translator can translate the news, view the news articles in progress in the workflow, and send news article back to the news writer to publish the news. There can be many English translators who can translate the news. However, only one English translator is sufficient to work on and approve the translated news. The workflow system for this set of tasks is depicted in Figure 3.

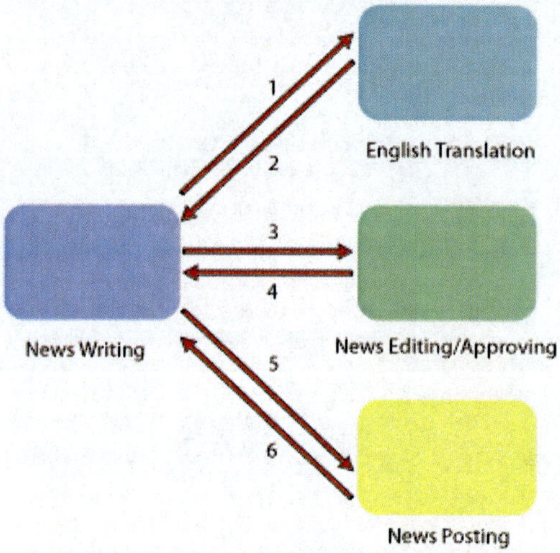

Fig. 3. News Publishing Workflow at the Faculty of ICT, Mahidol University consists of four actor groups categorized by roles. A task is defined by an arrow. DocFlow allows documents to flow from an actor to another actor. The state of the workflow system changes only when an actor approves the document. This change can be forward or backward depending on the actor's approval decision.

All PR staffs involving in news publishing can login securely through https connection and take responsible actions. Other faculty staffs who have access to DocFlow cannot open news article without permission from each document creator in the PR news publishing workflow. If one of the PR staffs forgets to complete a task within 2 business days, DocFlow will send a reminder via e-mail and system message to everyone in the workflow indicating a problem in the flow. In the aspect of document management system, if the news writer would like to look for news articles related to the faculty's soccer activities happening during December 2010, he/she can use document management service of DocFlow to search for the news articles which should also be displayed in different versions in the search results. Thus, DocFlow can help make task collaboration and document management simple, organized and effective.

5 Discussion and Future Works

DocFlow tries to be a simple workflow solution that can be used by anyone by retaining document formats. However, DocFlow does not integrate seamlessly into e-mail communication application such as Microsoft Outlook and Horde web-based e-mail service. This can increase the work that workers have to perform each day. Today, an organization uses many types of communication channels which can be categorized by medium and application types. The workflow and document management system should integrate common communication channels and formats together rather than create a new one. In addition, workflow should support team collaboration in such a way that task completion can be approved by a team consensus or decision maker.

Computer-supported task organization can significantly improve the performance of workers who collaborate. Confusion is reduced when workflows are clearly defined. Documents can be located quickly through document management system. Overall, each worker is presented with a clear workbook that share with other workers. The workbook has clear task assignments and progress level report. However, it is not possible to put all human tasks in a computerized workbook. Modelling human tasks sometimes cannot be documented and computerized. Computerized Workflow should be used largely to help making decisions, keeping milestones of tasks, and managing documents.

References

1. HP Automate Workflows, `http://h71028.www7.hp.com/enterprise/us/en/ipg/workflow-automation.html`
2. Xerox Document Management, `http://www.realbusiness.com/#/document-management/service-offerings-dm`
3. EMC Documentum, `http://www.emc.com/domains/documentum/index.htm`
4. Bonita Open Solution, `http://www.bonitasoft.com`
5. CuteFlow - Open Source document circulation and workflow system, `http://www.cuteflow.org`
6. Wikipedia, `http://www.wikipedia.org`
7. Google Docs, `http://docs.google.com`
8. Subversion, `http://subversion.tigris.org`
9. IBM Lotus Workflow, `http://www.ibm.com/software/lotus/products/workflow`

10. IBM Websphere MQ Workflow,
`http://www.ibm.com/software/integration/wmqwf`
11. SAP ERP Operations,
`http://www.sap.com/solutions/business-suite/erp/operations/index.epx`
12. Microsoft SharePoint, `http://sharepoint.microsoft.com`
13. Sandhu, R., Ferraiolo, D., Kuhn, R.: The NIST Model for Role Based Access Control: Towards a Unified Standard. In: Proceedings, 5th ACM Workshop on Role Based Access Control, Berlin, pp. 47–63 (2000)
14. van der Aalst, W., van Hee, K.: Workflow Management: Models, Methods, and Systems (Cooperative Information Systems). The MIT Press, Cambridge (2002)
15. Attinger, M.: Blurring the lines: Are document management software and automated workflow the same thing? Information Management Journal, 14–20 (1996)
16. Cardoso, J., Bostrom, R., Sheth, A.: Workflow Management Systems and ERP Systems: Differences, Commonalities, and Applications. Information Technology and Management 5, 319–338 (2004)
17. Basu, A., Kumar, A.: Research commentary: Workflow management issues in e-business. Information Systems Research 13(1), 1–14 (2002)
18. Stohr, E., Zhao, J.: Workflow Automation: Overview and Research Issues. Information Systems Frontiers 3(3), 281–296 (2001)
19. Harpaz, J.: Securing Document Management Systems: Call for Standards, Leadership. The CPA Journal 75(7), 11 (2005)
20. Neal, K.: Driving Better Business Performance with Document Management Processes. Information Management Journal 42(6), 48–49 (2008)
21. Paganelli, F., Pettenati, M.C., Giuli, D.: A Metadata-Based Approach for Unstructured Document Management in Organizations. Information Resources Management Journal 19(1), 1–22 (2006)
22. Wassink, I., Rauwerda, H., van der Vet, P., Breit, T., Nijholt, A.: E-BioFlow: Different Perspectives on Scientific Workflows, Bioinformatic Research and Development. Communications in Computer and Information Science 13(1), 243–257 (2008)

Computing Resources and Multimedia QoS Controls for Mobile Appliances

Ching-Ping Tsai[1,*], Hsu-Yung Kung[1], Mei-Hsien Lin[2], Wei-Kuang Lai[2], and Hsien-Chang Chen[1]

[1] Department of Management Information Systems, National PingTung University of Science and Technology, PingTung, Taiwan
{tcp,kung,m9456028}@mail.npust.edu.tw
[2] Department of Computer Science and Engineering, National Sun Yat-Sen University Kaohsiung, Taiwan
mslin@mail.npust.edu.tw, wklai@cse.nsysu.edu.tw

Abstract. The mobile network technology is rapid progress, but the computing resource has still been extremely limited. Therefore, the paper proposes the Computing Resource and Multimedia QoS Adaptation Control System for Mobile Appliances (CRMQ). It could control and adapt dynamically the resource usage ratio between the system processes and the application processes. To improve the battery life time of the mobile appliance, the proposed power adaptation control scheme is to dynamically adapt the power consumption of each medium stream based on its perception importance. The master stream (i.e., the audio stream) is allocated more electronic supply than the other streams (i.e., the background video). CRMQ system adapts the presentation quality of the multimedia service according to the available CPU, memory, and power resources. Simulation results reveal the performance efficiency of the CRMQ.

Keywords: Multimedia Streaming, Embedded Computing Resources, QoS Adaptation, Power Management.

1 Introduction

Mobile appliances that primarily process multimedia application is expected to become important platforms for pervasive computing. However, there are some problems, which include low bandwidth, available bandwidth varies quickly, and packet random loss, need to improve in the mobile network environment. The computing ability of the mobile appliance is limited, and the available bandwidth of mobile network is relatively unstable in usual [7]. Although mobile appliances have the mobility and convenience characteristic, the computing environment is characterized by unexpected variations of computing resources, such as network bandwidth, CPU ability, memory capacity, and battery life time. These mobile appliances should need to support multimedia quality of service (QoS) with limited computing resources [11]. The paper proposes Computing Resource and Multimedia QoS Adaptation Control system (CRMQ) for mobile appliances to achieve multimedia application services for mobile appliances based on the mobile network and the limited computational capacity status.

[*] Corresponding author.

H. Cherifi, J.M. Zain, and E. El-Qawasmeh (Eds.): DICTAP 2011, Part I, CCIS 166, pp. 93–105, 2011.

The rest of this paper is organized as follows. Section 2 introduces problem statement and preliminaries. Section 3 shows the system architecture of CRMQ. Section 4 presents the system implementation. Section 5 describes performance analysis. Conclusions are finally drawn in Section 6.

2 Problem Statement and Preliminaries

There exist many efficient bandwidth estimation schemes applicable in mobile network for multimedia streaming service [6], [8], [9]. Capone *et al.* referred to the packet-pair, TCP Vegas, and TCP Westwood, etc. and proposed TIBET (Time Intervals based Bandwidth Estimation Technique) [1], [12], [14] to estimate available bandwidth in mobile networks. The TIBET was time intervals based on bandwidth estimation technique. The average bandwidth (*Bw*) was used by equation (1), where n is the number of packets belonging to a connection, and L_i is the lengths of packets. The available bandwidth of mobile network varies greatly. In order to compute the available bandwidth flexibly and objectively, this paper integrates TIBET and MBTFRC [3] to obtain the available bandwidth of mobile network.

$$Bw_i = \frac{1}{T}\sum_{i=1}^{n} L_i = \frac{n\overline{L}}{T} = \frac{\overline{L}}{\frac{T}{n}} \tag{1}$$

Lin *et al.* proposed Measurement-Based TCP Friendly Rate Control (MBTFRC) protocol, which proposed a window-based EWMA (Exponentially Weighted Moving Average) filter with two weights, was used to achieve stability and fairness simultaneously [3].

The mobile appliances had limited computing, storage, and battery resources. Pasricha *et al.* proposed dynamic backlight adaptation for low-power handheld devices [2], [13]. Backlight power minimization can effectively extend battery life for mobile handheld devices [10]. Authors explored the use of a video compensation algorithm that induces power savings without noticeably affecting video quality. But before validate compensation algorithm, they selected 30 individuals to be a part of an extensive survey to subjectively access video quality when user viewed streaming video on a mobile appliance [15]. Showed the compensated stream and asked them to record their perceptions of differences in the video quality were to rule base. Besides, tuning the video luminosity and backlight levels could degrade the human perception of quality.

3 The System Architecture of CRMQ

The Computing Resource and Multimedia QoS Adaptation Control system (CRMQ) is for mobile appliances to achieve multimedia application services based on the mobile network and the limited computational capacity status [4], [5].

Fig. 1 depicts the CRMQ system architecture. The primary components of the Multimedia Server are Event Analyzer, Multimedia File Storage, and Stream Sender. Event Analyzer receives feedback information that includes multimedia requirement and the network status from the mobile client and delivers to response the media player size to the client site which computes consuming buffers. It sends the request to Multimedia File Storage and searching media files. Stream Sender sends media streams to Mobile Client from Multimedia-File Storage.

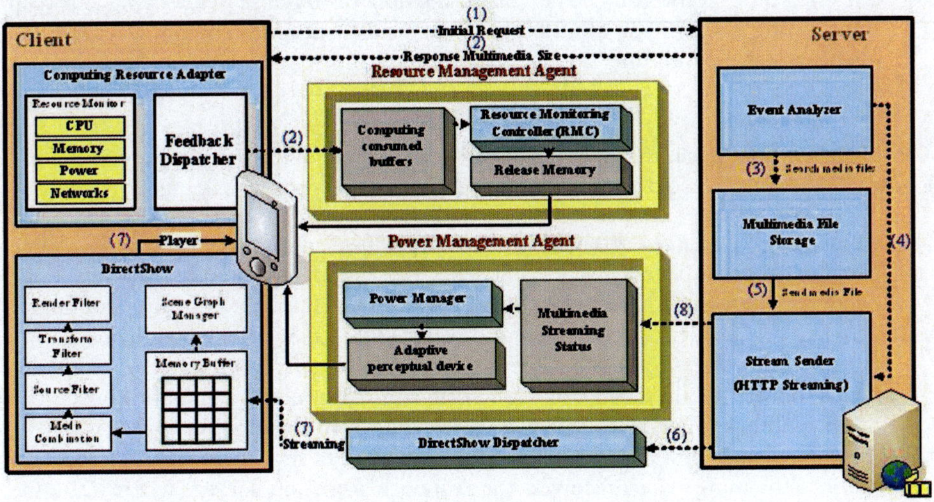

Fig. 1. The system architecture of CRMQ

The primary components of the Mobile Client are Computing Resources Adapter, Resource Management Agent, Power Management Agent, and DirectShow. The Computing Resources Adapter monitors the resource from the devices mainly, such as the CPU utilization, available memory, power status, and network status. The Feedback Dispatcher will send information to the multimedia server which is arguments of QoS decision. However, the Server will be response player size to the Resource Management Agent that computes consumed memory size mainly and monitors or controls the memory of the mobile devices which are called Resource Monitoring Controller(RMC), and trying to clear garbage memory when client requests media. The CRMQ system starts the Power Management Agent during the streaming is built and delivered by the Multimedia Server. It is according to the streaming status and the power information that adapts backlight brightness and volume level. The DirectShow Dispatcher finally receives the streaming and plays to the devices. The functions of system component are described as follows.

The Multimedia Server system is composed of three components, which are Event Analyzer, Multimedia File Storage, and Stream Sender.

(1) Event Analyzer: It received the connection and request/response messages from the mobile client. Based on the received messages, Event Analyzer notified the Multimedia File Storage to find the appropriate multimedia media file. According to the resource information of devices of the client and network status, Event Analyzer generated and sent corresponding events to the Stream Sender.

(2) Multimedia File Storage: It stored the multimedia files. Base on the request of mobile client, Multimedia File Storage retrieved the requested media segments and transferred the segments to the Stream Sender.
(3) Stream Sender: It adopted the standard HTTP agreement to establish a multimedia streaming connection. The main function of Stream Sender was to keep transmitting streams for the mobile client, and to provide streaming control. It also adapted the multimedia quality according to the QoS decision from the mobile client.

The Mobile Client system is composed of three components, which are Computing Resources Adapter, Resource Management Agent, and Power Management Agent.

(1) Computing Resources Adapter: It is the primary component of the Resource Monitor and the Feedback Dispatcher. The Resource Monitor analyzed the bandwidth information, memory load, and CPU utilization from the mobile appliance. If it needed to tune the multimedia QoS, QoS Decision transmitted the QoS decision message to the Feedback Dispatcher. It provided the current information of Mobile Client for the Server site and sent the computing resources of the mobile appliance to the Event Analyzer of Multimedia Server.
(2) Resource Management Agent: It will be computed to fix buffer sizes by equation (2) for streaming when received the response from the server, where D is the number of data packets. If the buffer size is not enough, it will be monitored the available memory and released surplus buffers.

$$\textit{Buffer Size} = \text{rate x 2 x } (D_{max} - D_{min}) \tag{2}$$

(3) Power Management Agent: It monitored the current power consumption information from the mobile appliance. To promote the mobile appliance power life time, the Power Manager adapted perceptual device power supportive level based on the scenario of playing stream.

The CRMQ system control procedures are described as follows.

Step(1):Mobile Client sends initial request to Multimedia Server and set up the connect session.
Step(2):Multimedia Server responses player size which requests media by the client. The Resource Management Agent will be computed buffer size and estimated the memory whether release it or not.
Step(3):Event Analyzer sends the media request to Multimedia File Storage and searches the media file.
Step(4):Event Analyzer sends the computing resource to the Stream Sender from the mobile devices.
Step(5):The media file sends to Stream Sender.
Step(6):Stream Sender is to estimate QoS of the media and to start transmission.
Step(7):DirectShow Render Filter renders stream is from the buffer and displays to client.
Step(8):According to media streaming status, power life time will be adapted perceptual device.

4 System Implementation

In this Section, we describe the design and implementation of main components of CRMQ system.

4.1 QoS Adaptive Decision Design

In order to implement the Multimedia QoS Decision, the CRMQ system collects the necessary information of mobile appliances which include available bandwidth, memory load, and CPU utilization. This paper adopts the TIBET and MBTFRC method to get the flexible and fairing available bandwidth. About the memory loading and CPU utilization, the CRMQ system uses some APIs from Microsoft Developer Network (MSDN) to compute the exact data. Multimedia QoS decision makes adaptive decision properly according to the mobile network bandwidth and the computing resources of the mobile appliance. Multimedia QoS is divided into multi-level. Fig. 2 depicts the Multimedia QoS Decision process. The operation procedure is as follows.

Step(1):Degrades the QoS: if media streaming is greater than available bandwidth, else going to step (2).
Step(2):Executes memory arrangement: if memory load is greater than 90%. Degrade the QoS: if the memory load is still higher, else going to step (3).
Step(3):Degrade the QoS: if CPU utilization is greater than 90%, else executing upgrade decision. Upgrade the QoS: if it passes the upgrade decision.

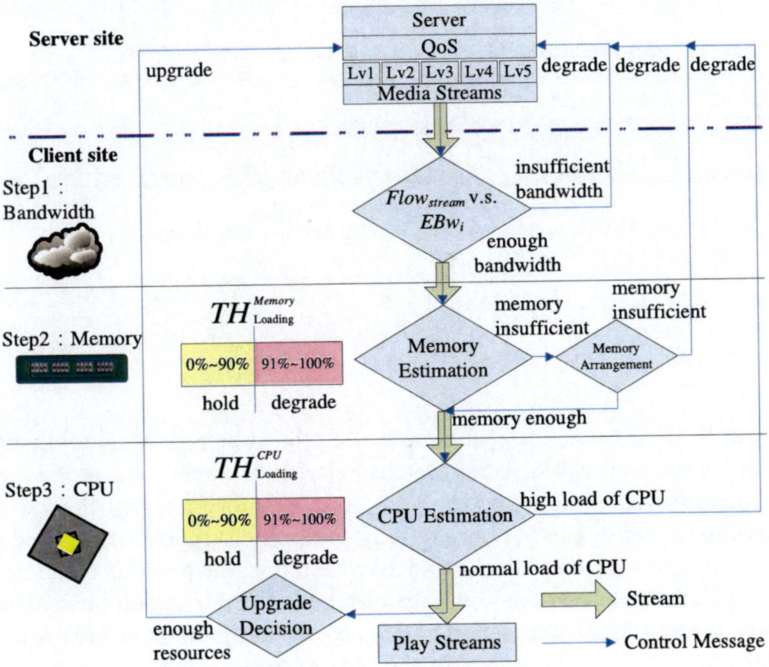

Fig. 2. Multimedia QoS decision procedures

4.2 Resource Management Control Scheme

Resource Monitoring Controller (RMC) monitors the available memory for the mobile devices in order to use more space. It could be satisfied requirements for memory in the high loading applications. The operation procedure algorithm is showed as follows.

```
MEMORYSTATUS memStat;
memset(&memStat, sizeof(MEMORYSTATUS), 0);
memStat.dwLength = sizeof(MEMORYSTATUS);
GlobalMemoryStatus(&memStat);

If ( memStat.dwMemoryLoad > $TH^{Mem}_{High}$ )
{
  If ((memStat.dwAvailPhys*100/memStat.dwTotalPhys)<$TH^{Mem}_{High}$ )
  {
   iFreeSize=64*1024*1024;
   char *pBuffer=new char[iFreeSize];
   int iStep=4*1024;
   for(int i=iStep-1 ; i<iFreeSize ; i+=iStep)
   {
    pBuffer[i]=0x0;
   }
   delete[]pBuffer;
  }
  else
  {
   HANDLE hProcessSnap;
   hProcessSnap=CreateToolhelp32Snapshot(TH32CS_SNAPPROCESS,0);
   PROCESSENTRY32 pe32;
   Pe32.dwSize = sizeof(PROCESSENTRY32);
   do{
      HANDLEhProcess=OpenProcess(PROCESS_SET_QUOTA,FALSE,
                      pe32.th32ProcessID);
      SetProcessWorkingSetSize(hProcess, -1, -1);
      CloseHandle(hProcess);
      } while(Process32Next(hProcessSnap, &pe32));
   CloseHandle( hProcessSnap );
  }
}
```

Owing to the RAM was different between the Object Storage Memory that saves a fixed virtual space and the Program Memory places the application programs in the WinCE devices mainly. However, the RMC was monitors usage at the system and user process on the Program Memory. It will release the surplus memory and recombine the decentralize memory block regularly. Therefore, the program could be used a large and continuous space. It provides the resource to devices when implement is the high load programs. Fig. 3 depicts the control flow design of Resource Monitoring Controller.

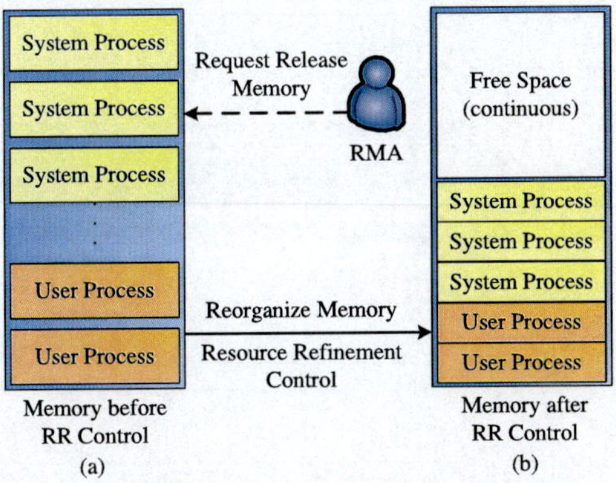

Fig. 3. Control flow of Resource Monitoring Controller

4.3 Power Management Control Scheme

According to the remaining battery life percentage, the perceptual device power supportive level can be adapted. Fig. 4 depicts the remaining battery life percentage threshold. The perceptual device includes backlight, audio, and network device.

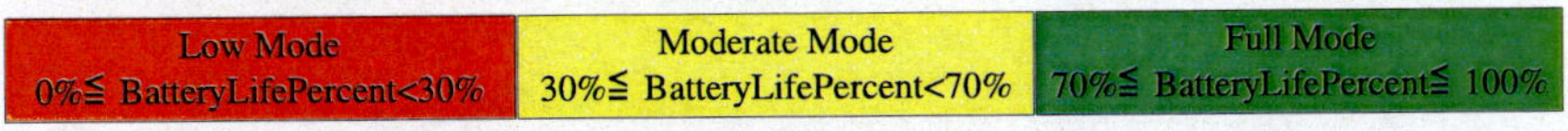

Fig. 4. The remaining battery life percentage threshold

Suppose the remaining battery life percentage is in the full mode. Fig. 5 depicts the adaptive perceptual device power supportive level. The horizontal axis is execution time. The order on Fig. 5 is divided into application start, buffering, streaming, and interval time. The vertical axis is device of power supportive and adaptive perceptual level. D0 is full on status. D1 is low on status. D2 is standby status. D3 is sleep status. D4 is off status. The perceptual device, which includes backlight, audio, and network, is adapted the different level based on the remaining battery life percentage mode. Figs. 5, 6, and 7 depict the perceptual device that is adapted level on the different mode.

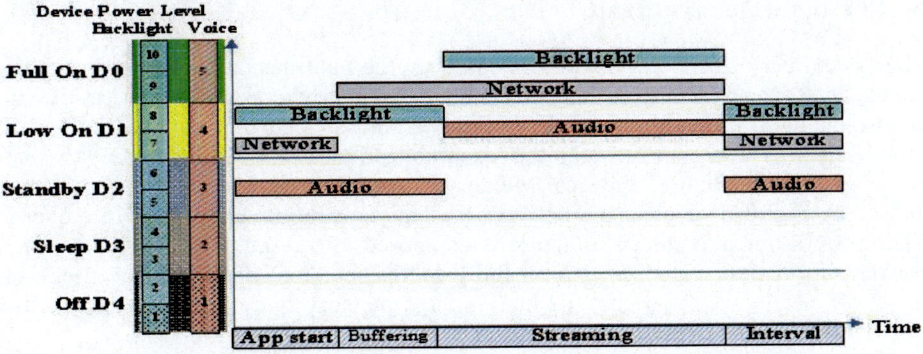

Fig. 5. Adaptive perceptual device power supporting level (full mode)

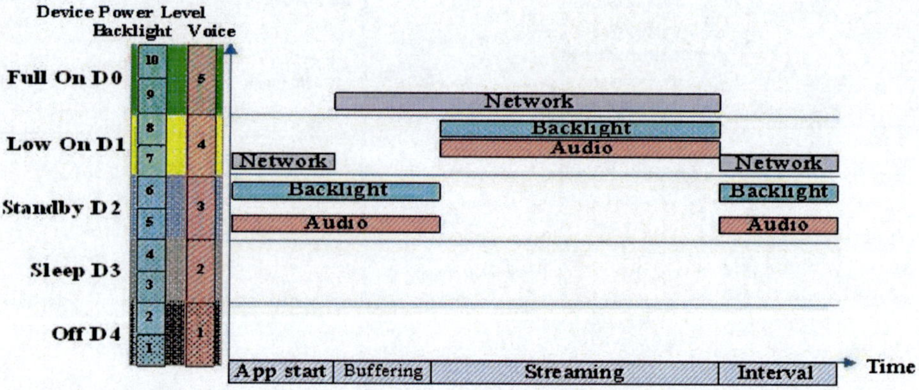

Fig. 6. Adaptive perceptual device power supporting level (moderate mode)

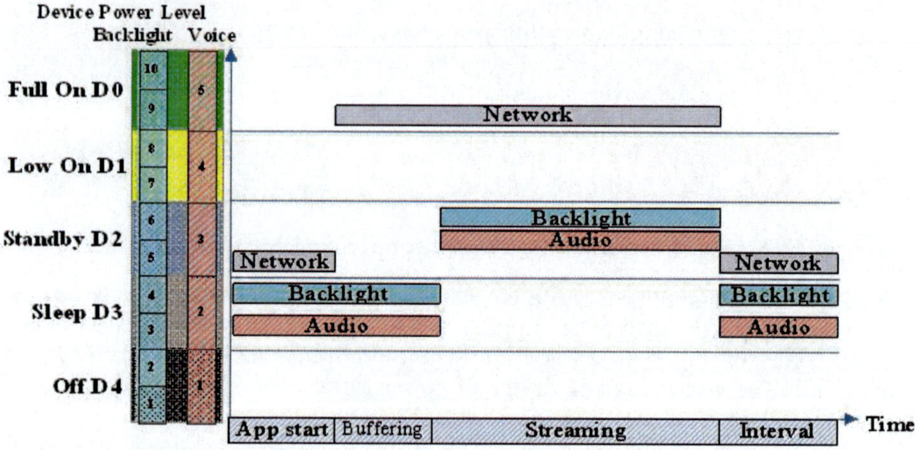

Fig. 7. Adaptive perceptual device power supporting level (low mode)

5 Performance Analysis

The system performance evaluation is based on the multimedia streaming of mobile client. The server will transmit the movie list to back the mobile client. The users can choose the interesting movie that they want. Fig. 8(a) depicts the resource monitor of mobile client. The users can watch the resource workload of the system currently that includes the utilization of Physical Memory, Storage Space, Virtual Address Space, and CPU. Fig. 8(b) depicts the network transmission information of mobile client. The network transmission information is composed of transmission information and packet information. Fig. 9(a) depicts the resource monitor controller. The user can break off or release the process to obtain a large memory space. Fig. 9(b) depicts the power management of the Power Monitor.

The practical implementation environment of CRMQ system includes a Dopod 900 with the Intel®PXA270 520 MHz CPU, the size of 49.73 MB RAM memory, and the

Windows Mobile 5.0 operating system to adopt as the mobile equipment. According to the scenario of appliance playing multimedia streaming of the mobile, the power management of mobile appliance can tune the backlight, audio, and network device power supportive level. Firstly, the system implements the experiment with the standby situation of the mobile appliance.

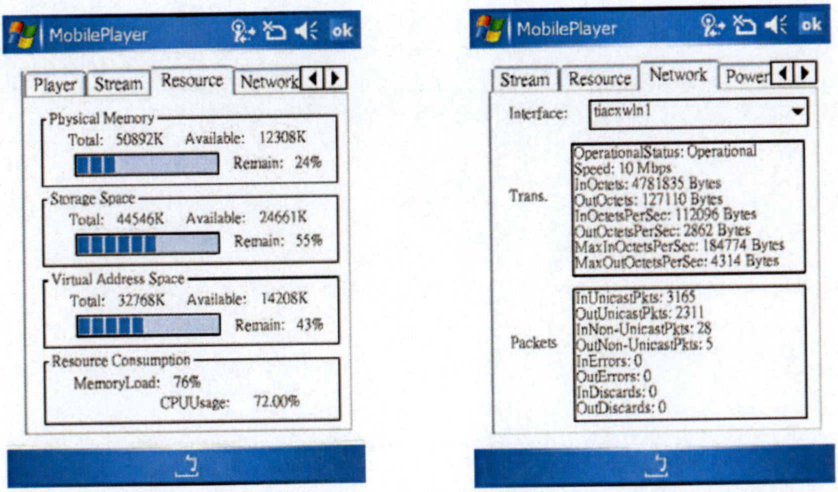

(a) (b)

Fig. 8. (a) The computing resource status information. (b) The network transmission information.

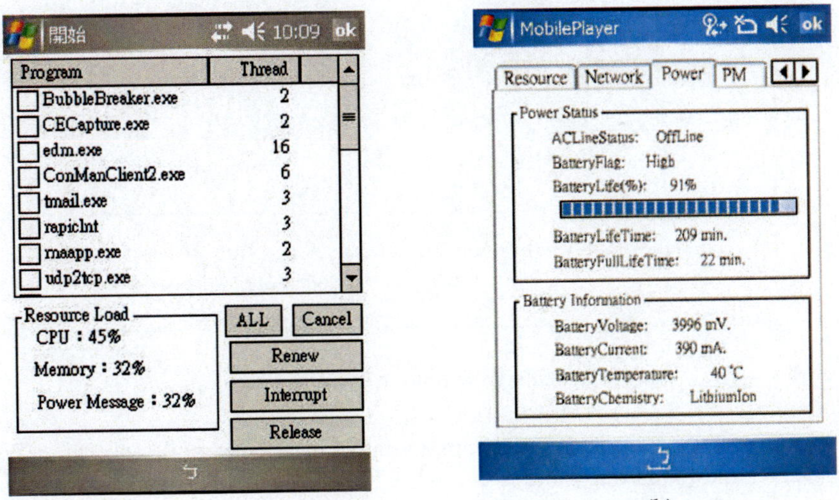

(a) (b)

Fig. 9. (a) UI of the resource monitor controller. (b) The power management of the Power Monitor.

Fig. 10 compares traditional mode and power management mode to explain the battery life percent variation. The battery consumption rate in power management mode decreases slowly than traditional mode. Therefore, the power management mode will has more battery life time. Fig. 11 compares traditional mode and power management mode to explain the battery life time variation. As shown in Fig. 11, the battery life time of power management mode is longer than the traditional mode.

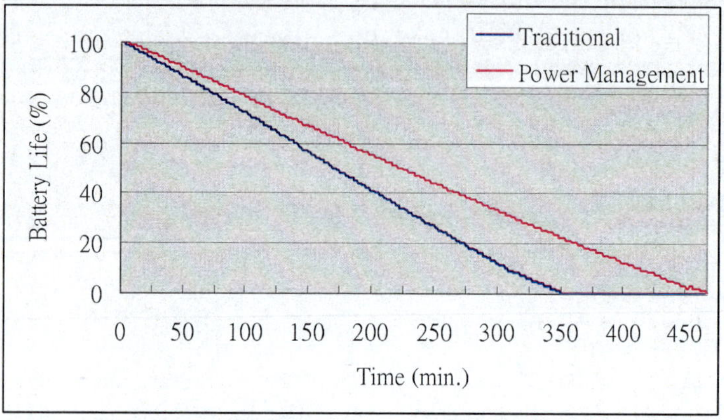

Fig. 10. Battery life percentage analysis (standby)

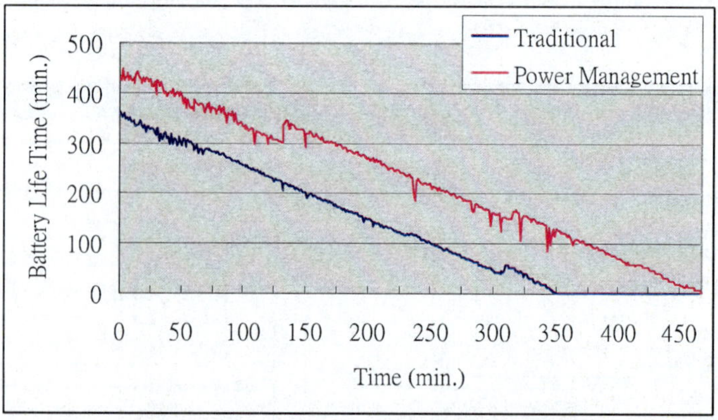

Fig. 11. Battery life time analysis (standby)

Fig. 12 depicts the variation of the computing resources of mobile appliance. With the elapse of time found that there is enough CPU utilization. The mobile client sent notify to server to adjust the QoS. The multimedia QoS was upgraded form level 2 QoS to level 4 QoS. On the other hand, choose the level 5 QoS at the beginning of playing streaming. Fig. 13 depicts the variation of the computing resources of mobile appliance. With the elapse of time, found the CPU utilization that was higher than

90%. The CRMQ system notify server to adjust the QoS as soon as possible. The multimedia QoS was degraded from level 5 QoS to level 4 QoS. When playing multimedia streaming with different mobile appliance platform and bandwidth, the multimedia QoS adaptive decision can adapt proper multimedia QoS according to the mobile computing environment.

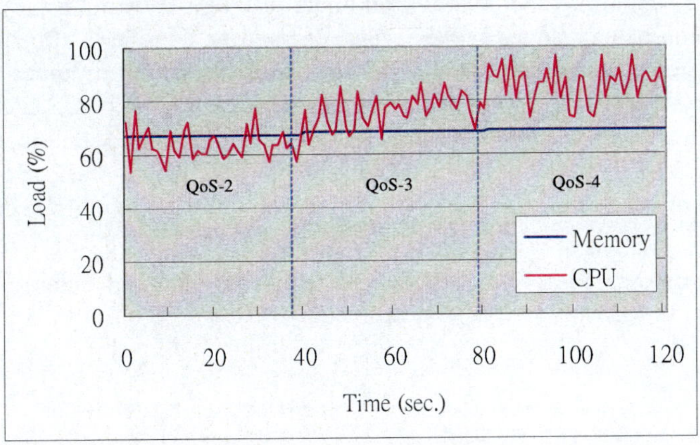

Fig. 12. The computing resources analysis of mobile appliance (upgrade QoS)

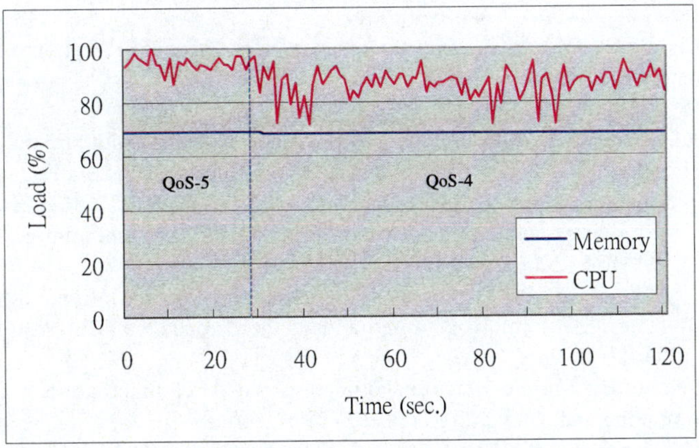

Fig. 13. The computing resources analysis of mobile appliance (degrade QoS)

6 Conclusions

The critical computing resource limitations of mobile appliances will be difficult to achieve the multimedia pervasive applications. To utilize the valuable computing resources of mobile appliances effectively, the paper proposes the Computing Resource and Multimedia QoS Adaptation Control system (CRMQ) for mobile appliances. The CRMQ system provides optimum multimedia QoS decision with mobile appliances based on the computing resources environment and network bandwidth. The resource management implement adapt and clean surplus memory that is not used or disperse to obtain a large memory size. The power management implements adapt device power supporting and quality level under different scenario of playing streaming. The whole battery power will be improved and be continued effectively. Using CRMQ system can promote perceptual quality and computing resources under playing streaming scenario with mobile appliances. Finally, the proposed CRMQ system is implemented and compared with the traditional WinCE-based multimedia application services. The results of performance reveal the feasibility and effectiveness of the CRMQ system which is capable of providing the smooth mobile multimedia services.

Acknowledgments. The research is supported by the National Science Council of Taiwan under the grant No. NSC 99-2220-E-020 -001.

References

1. Capone, A., Fratta, L., Martignon, F.: Bandwidth Estimation Schemes for TCP over Wireless Networks. IEEE Transactions on Mobile Computing 3(2), 129–143 (2004)
2. Henkel, J., Li, Y.: Avalanche: An Environment for Design Space Exploration and Optimization of Low-Power Embedded Systems. IEEE Transactions on Very Large Scale Integration (VLSI) Systems 10(4), 454–467 (2009)
3. Lin, Y., Cheng, S., Wang, W., Jin, Y.: Measurement-based TFRC: Improving TFRC in Heterogeneous Mobile Networks. IEEE Transactions on Wireless Communications 5(8), 1971–1975 (2006)
4. Muntean, G.M., Perry, P., Murphy, L.: A New Adaptive Multimedia Streaming System for All-IP Multi-service Networks. IEEE Transactions on Broadcasting 50(1), 1–10 (2004)
5. Yuan, W., Nahrstedt, K., Adve, S.V., Jones, D.L., Kravets, R.H.: GRACE-1: cross-layer adaptation for multimedia quality and battery energy. IEEE Transactions on Mobile Computing 5(7), 799–815 (2006)
6. Demircin, M.U., Beek, P.: Bandwidth Estimation and Robust Video Streaming Over 802.11E Wireless Lans. In: IEEE International Conference on Multimedia and Expo., pp. 1250–1253 (2008)
7. Kim, M., Nobe, B.: Mobile Network Estimation. In: ACM International Conference on Mobile Computing and Networking, pp. 298–309 (2007)
8. Layaida, O., Hagimont, D.: Adaptive Video Streaming for eMbedded Devices. IEEE Proceedings on Software Engineering 152(5), 238–244 (2008)
9. Lee, H.K., Hall, V., Yum, K.H., Kim, K.I., Kim, E.J.: Bandwidth Estimation in Wireless Lans for Multimedia Streaming Services. In: IEEE International Conference on Multimedia and Expo., pp. 1181–1184 (2009)
10. Lin, W.C., Chen, C.H.: An Energy-delay Efficient Power Management Scheme for eMbedded System in Multimedia Applications. In: IEEE Asia-Pacific Conference on Circuits and Systems, vol. 2, pp. 869–872 (2004)

11. Masugi, M., Takuma, T., Matsuda, M.: QoS Assessment of Video Streams over IP Networks based on Monitoring Transport and Application Layer Processes at User Clients. IEEE Proceedings on Communications 152(3), 335–341 (2005)
12. Parvez, N., Hossain, L.: Improving TCP Performance in Wired-wireless Networks by Using a Novel Adaptive Bandwidth Estimation Mechanism. In: IEEE Global Telecommunications Conference, vol. 5, pp. 2760–2764 (2009)
13. Pasricha, S., Luthra, M., Mohapatra, S., Dutt, N., Venkatasubramanian, N.: Dynamic Backlight Adaptation for Low-power Handheld Devices. IEEE Design & Test of Computers 21(5), 398–405 (2004)
14. Wong, C.F., Fung, W.L., Tang, C.F.J., Chan, S.-H.G.: TCP streaming for low-delay wireless video. In: International Conference on Quality of Service in Heterogeneous Wired/Wireless Networks, pp. 6–12 (2005)
15. Yang, G., Chen, L.J., Sun, T., Gerla, M., Sanadidi, M.Y.: Real-time Streaming over Wireless Links: A Comparative Study. In: IEEE Symposium on Computers and Communications, pp. 249–254 (2005)

Factors Influencing the EM Interaction between Mobile Phone Antennas and Human Head

Salah I. Al-Mously

Computer Engineering Department, College of Engineering,
Ishik University, Erbil, Iraq
salah.mously@ieee.org
http://www.salahalmously.info,
http://www.ishikuniversity.net

Abstract. This paper presents a procedure for the evaluation of the Electromagnetic (EM) interaction between the mobile phone antenna and human head, and investigates the factors may influence this interaction. These factors are considered for different mobile phone handset models operating in the GSM900, GSM1800/DCS, and UMTS/IMT-2000 bands, and next to head in *cheek* and *tilt* positions, in compliance with IEEE-standard 1528. Homogeneous and heterogeneous CAD-models were used to simulate the mobile phone user's head. A validation of our EM interaction computation using both Yee-FDTD and ADI-FDTD was achieved by comparison with previously published works.

Keywords: Dosimetry, FDTD, mobile phone antenna, MRI, phantom, specific anthropomorphic mannequin (SAM), specific absorption rate (SAR).

1 Introduction

Realistic usage of mobile phone handsets in different patterns imposes an EM wave interaction between the handset antenna and the human body (head and hand). This EM interaction due to the presence of the user's head close to the handheld set can be looked at from two different points of view;

Firstly, the mobile handset has an impact on the user, which is often understood as the exposure of the user to the EM field of the radiating device. The absorption of electromagnetic energy generated by mobile handset in the human tissue, SAR, has become a point of critical public discussion due to the possible health risks. SAR, therefore, becomes an important performance parameter for the marketing of cellular mobile phones and underlines the interest in optimizing the interaction between the handset and the user by both consumers and mobile phone manufacturers.

Secondly, and from a more technical point of view, the user has an impact on the mobile handset. The tissue of the user represents a large dielectric and lossy material distribution in the near field of a radiator. It is obvious, therefore, that all antenna parameters, such as impedance, radiation characteristic, radiation efficiency and total isotropic sensitivity (TIS), will be affected by the properties of the tissue. Moreover, the effect can differ with respect to the individual habits of the user in placing his hand around the mobile handset or attaching the handset to the head. Optimized user

H. Cherifi, J.M. Zain, and E. El-Qawasmeh (Eds.): DICTAP 2011, Part I, CCIS 166, pp. 106–120, 2011.

interaction, therefore, becomes a technical performance parameter of cellular mobile phones.

The EM interaction of the cellular handset and a human can be evaluated using either experimental measurements or numerical computations, e.g., FDTD method. Experimental measurements make use of the actual mobile phone, but with a simple homogeneous human head model having two or three tissues. Numerical computation makes use of an MRI-based heterogeneous anatomically correct human head model with more than thirty different tissues, but the handset is modeled as a simple box with an antenna. Numerical computation of the EM interaction can be enhanced by using semi- or complete-realistic handset models [1]-[3]. In this paper, a FDTD method is used to evaluate the EM interaction, where different human head models, i.e., homogeneous and heterogeneous, and different handset models, i.e., simple and semi-realistic, are used in computations [4]-[12].

2 Specific Absorption Rate (SAR)

It is generally accepted that SAR is the most appropriate metric for determining electromagnetic energy (EME) exposure in the very near field of a RF source [13]-[21]. SAR is expressed in watts per kilogram (W/kg) of biological tissue, and is generally quoted as a figure averaged over a volume corresponding to either 1 g or 10 g of body tissue. The SAR of a wireless product can be measured in two ways. It can be measured directly using body phantoms, robot arms, and associated test equipment (Fig. 1), or by mathematical modeling. The latter can be costly, and can take as long as several hours.

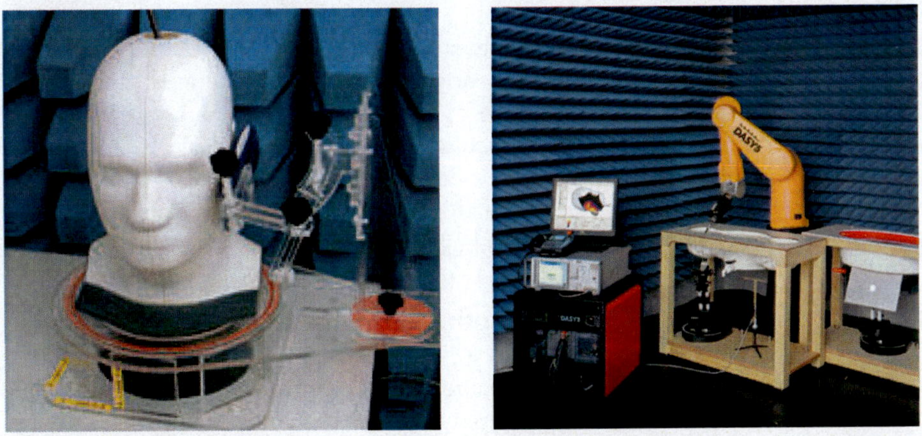

(a) (b)

Fig. 1. Different SAR measurement setups: (a) SAR measurement setup by IndexSAR company, http://www.indexsar.com, and (b) SAR measurement setup (DASY5) by SPEAG, http://www.speag.com

The concept of correlating the absorption mechanism of a biological tissue with the basic antenna parameters (e.g., input impedance, current, etc.) has been presented in many papers, Kuster [22], for example, described an approximation formula that provides a correlation of the peak SAR with the square of the incident magnetic field and consequently with the antenna current.

Using the FDTD method, the electric fields are calculated at the voxel edges, and consequently, the x, y and z-directed power components associated with a voxel are defined in different spatial locations. These components must be combined to calculate SAR in the voxel. There are three possible approaches to calculate the SAR: the 3-, 6-, and 12-field components approaches. The 12-field components approach is the most complicated but it is also the most accurate and the most appropriate from the mathematical point of view [23]. It correctly places all E-field components in the center of the voxel using linear interpolation. The power distribution is, therefore, now defined at the same location as the tissue mass. For these reasons, the 12-field components approach is preferred by IEEE-Std. 1529 [24].

The specific absorption rate is defined as:

$$SAR = \frac{\sigma_E}{2\rho}|\mathbf{E}|^2 = c\frac{dT}{dt} \qquad (1)$$

where c is the specific heat capacity, σ_E the electric conductivity, ρ the mass density of the tissue, **E** the induced electric field vector and dT/dt the temperature increase in the tissue.

Based on SCC-34, SC-2, WG-2 - Computational Dosimetry, IEEE-Std. 1529 [24], an algorithm has been implemented using a FDTD-based EM simulator, SEMCAD X [25], where for body tissues, the spatial-peak SAR should be evaluated in cubical volumes that contain a mass that is within 5% of the required mass. The cubical volume centered at each location should be expanded in all directions until the desired value for the mass is reached, with no surface boundaries of the averaging volume extending beyond the outermost surface of the considered region of the model. In addition, the cubical volume should not consist of more than 10% air. If these conditions are not met, then the center of the averaging volume is moved to the next location. Otherwise, the exact size of the final sampling cube is found using an inverse polynomial approximation algorithm, leading to very accurate results.

3 SAR Measurement and Computation Protocol

RF human exposure guidelines and evaluation methods differentiate between portable and mobile devices according to their proximity to exposed persons. Devices used in close proximity to the human body are evaluated against SAR limits. Devices used not close to the human body, can be evaluated with respect to Reference Levels or Maximum Permissible Exposure (MPE) limits for power density. When a product requires evaluation against SAR limits, the SAR evaluation must be performed using the guidelines and procedures prescribed by the applicable standard and regulation. While the requirements are similar from country to country, significant differences exist in the scope of the SAR regulations, the measurement standards and the approval requirements.

IEEE-Std. 1528 [13], EN 50360 [16] and EN 50361 [17], which replaced with the standard IEC 62209-1 [18], specify protocols and procedures for the measurement of the spatial-peak SAR induced inside a simplified model of the head of the users of mobile phone handsets. Both IEEE and IEC standards provide regulatory agencies with international consensus standards as a reference for accurate compliance testing.

The simplified physical model (phantom) of the human head specified in IEEE-Std. 1528 and IEC 62209-1 is the SAM. SAM has also been adopted by the European Committee for Electrotechnical Standardization (CENELEC) [16], the Association of Radio Industries and Businesses in Japan [19], and the Federal Communications Commission (FCC) in the USA [20]. SAM is based on the 90th percentile of a survey of American male military service personnel and represents a large male head, and was developed by the IEEE Standards Coordinating Committee 34, Subcommittee 2, Working Group 1 (SCC34/SC2/WG1) as a lossless plastic shell and an ear spacer. The SAM shell is filled with homogeneous fluid having the electrical properties of head tissue at the test frequency. The electrical properties of the fluid were based on calculations to give conservative spatial-peak SAR values averaged over 1 and 10 g for the test frequencies [26]. The electrical properties are defined in [13] and [27], with shell and ear spacer defined in [26]. The CAD files defining SAM show specific reference points and lines to be used to position mobile phones for the two compliance test positions specified in [13] and [26]. These are the *cheek*-position shown in Fig. 2(a) and the *tilt*-position shown in Fig. 2(b).

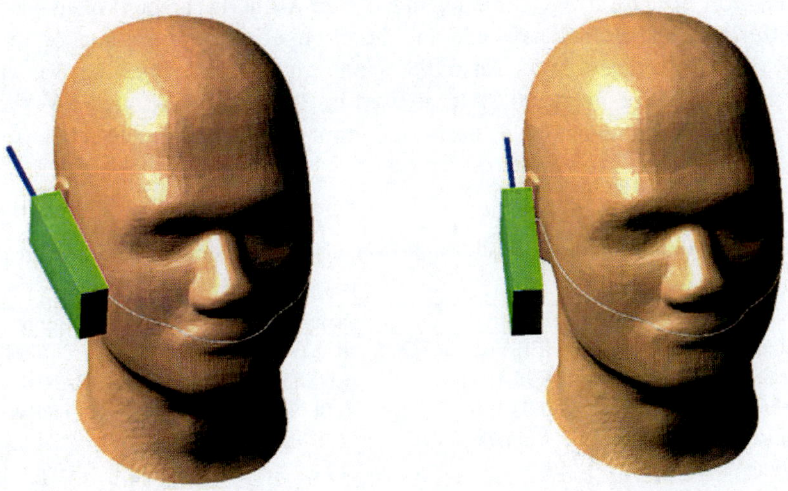

(a) (b)

Fig. 2. SAM next to the generic phone at: (a) *cheek*-position, and (b) *tilt*-position in compliance with IEEE-Std. 1528-2003 [13] and as in [26]

To ensure the protection of the public and workers from exposure to RF EM radiation, most countries have regulations which limit the exposure of persons to RF fields from RF transmitters operated in close proximity to the human body. Several organizations have set exposure limits for acceptable RF safety via SAR levels. The International Commission on Non-Ionizing Radiation Protection (ICNIRP) was launched as an independent commission in May 1992. This group publishes guidelines and recommendations related to human RF exposure [28].

4 SAR Exposure Limit

For the American National Standards Institute (ANSI), the RF safety sections now operate as part of the Institute of Electrical and Electronic Engineers (IEEE). IEEE wrote the most important publications for SAR test methods [13] and the standard safety levels [15].

The European standard EN 50360 specifies the SAR limits [16]. The limits are defined for exposure of the whole body, partial body (e.g., head and trunk), and hands, feet, wrists, and ankles. SAR limits are based on whole-body exposure levels of 0.08 W/kg. Limits are less stringent for exposure to hands, wrists, feet, and ankles. There are also considerable problems with the practicalities of measuring SAR in such body areas, because they are not normally modeled. In practice, measurements are made against a flat phantom, providing a conservative result.

Most SAR testing concerns exposure to the head. For Europe, the current limit is 2 W/kg for 10-g volume-averaged SAR. For the United States and a number of other countries, the limit is 1.6 W/kg for 1-g volume-averaged SAR. The lower U.S. limit is more stringent because it is volume-averaged over a smaller amount of tissue. Canada, South Korea and Bolivia have adopted the more-stringent U.S. limits of 1.6 W/kg for 1-g volume-averaged SAR. Australia, Japan and New Zealand have adopted 2 W/kg for 10-g volume-averaged SAR, as used in Europe [29]. Table 1 lists the SAR limits for the non-occupational users recommended in different countries and regions.

Table 1. SAR limits for non-occupational/unaware users in different countries and regions

	USA	**Europe**	**Australia**	**Japan**
Organization/Body	IEEE/ANSI/ FCC	ICNIRP	ASA	TTC/MPTC
Measurement method	C95.1	EN50360	ARPANSA	ARIB
Whole body averaged SAR	0.08 W/kg	0.08 W/kg	0.08 W/kg	0.04 W/kg
Spatial-peak SAR in head	1.6 W/kg	2 W/kg	2 W/kg	2 W/kg
Averaging mass	1 g	10 g	10 g	10 g
Spatial-peak SAR in limbs	4 W/kg	4 W/kg	4 W/kg	4 W/kg
Averaging mass	10 g	10 g	10 g	10 g
Averaging time	30 min	6 min	6 min	6 min

When comparing published results of the numerical dosimetric of SAR that is induced in head tissue due to the RF emission of mobile phone handsets, it is important to mention if the SAR values are based on averaging volumes that included or excluded the pinna. Inclusion versus exclusion of the pinna from the 1- and 10-g SAR averaging volumes is the most significant cause of discrepancies [26].

INCIRP Guidelines [28] apply the same spatial-peak SAR limits for the pinna and the head, whereas the draft IEEE-Std. C95.1b-2004, which were published later in 2005 [30], apply the spatial-peak SAR limits for the extremities to the pinnae (4 W/kg per 10-g mass rather than the 1.6 W/kg per 1g for the head). Some investigators [31], [32], treated the pinna in accordance with ICNIRP Guidelines, whereas others [33], [34], treated the pinna in accordance with the IEEE-Std. C95.1b-2004. For the heterogeneous head model with pressed air that was used in [4], [6], [9], [10] and [12], the pinna was treated in accordance with ICNIRP Guidelines.

5 Assessment Procedure of the EM Interaction

Assessment of the EM interaction of cellular handsets and a human has been investigated by many authors since the launch of second-generation systems in 1991. Different numerical methods, different human head models, different cellular handset models, different hand models, and different standard and non-standard usage patterns have been used in computations. Thus, varying results have been obtained. The causes of discrepancies in computations have been well investigated [26], [35]. Fig. 3 shows a block diagram of the proposed numerical computation procedure of both SAR induced in tissues and the antenna performance due to the EM interaction of realistic usage of a cellular handset using a FDTD method.

Assessment accuracy of the EM interaction depends on the following:

(a) *Mobile phone handset modeling.* This includes handset model (i.e., Dipole antenna, external antenna over a metal box, internal antenna integrated into a dielectric box, semi-realistic CAD model, and realistic *ProEngineer* CAD-based mode [3]), handset type (e.g., bar, clamshell, flip, swivel and slide), handset size, antenna type (e.g., whip, helix, PIF and MPA), and antenna position.
(b) *Human head modeling* (i.e., homogeneous phantoms including SAM, and heterogeneous MRI-based anatomically correct model). For the heterogeneous head model, the number of tissues, resolution, pinna thickness (pressed and non-pressed), and tissue parameters definition, all playing an important role in computing the EM interaction
(c) *Human hand modeling* (i.e., simple block, homogeneous CAD model, MRI-based model)
(d) *Positioning of handset, head and hand.* In the IEEE-Std. 1528-2003 [13], two handset positions with respect to head are adopted, *cheek* and *tilt*, but the hand position in not defined.
(e) *Electrical properties definition of the handset material and human tissues.*
(f) *Numerical method* (e.g., FDTD, FE, MoM, and hybrid methods). Applying the FDTD method, the grid-cell resolution and ABC should be specified in accordance with the available hardware for computation. Higher resolution and higher ABC needs a faster CPU and larger memory.

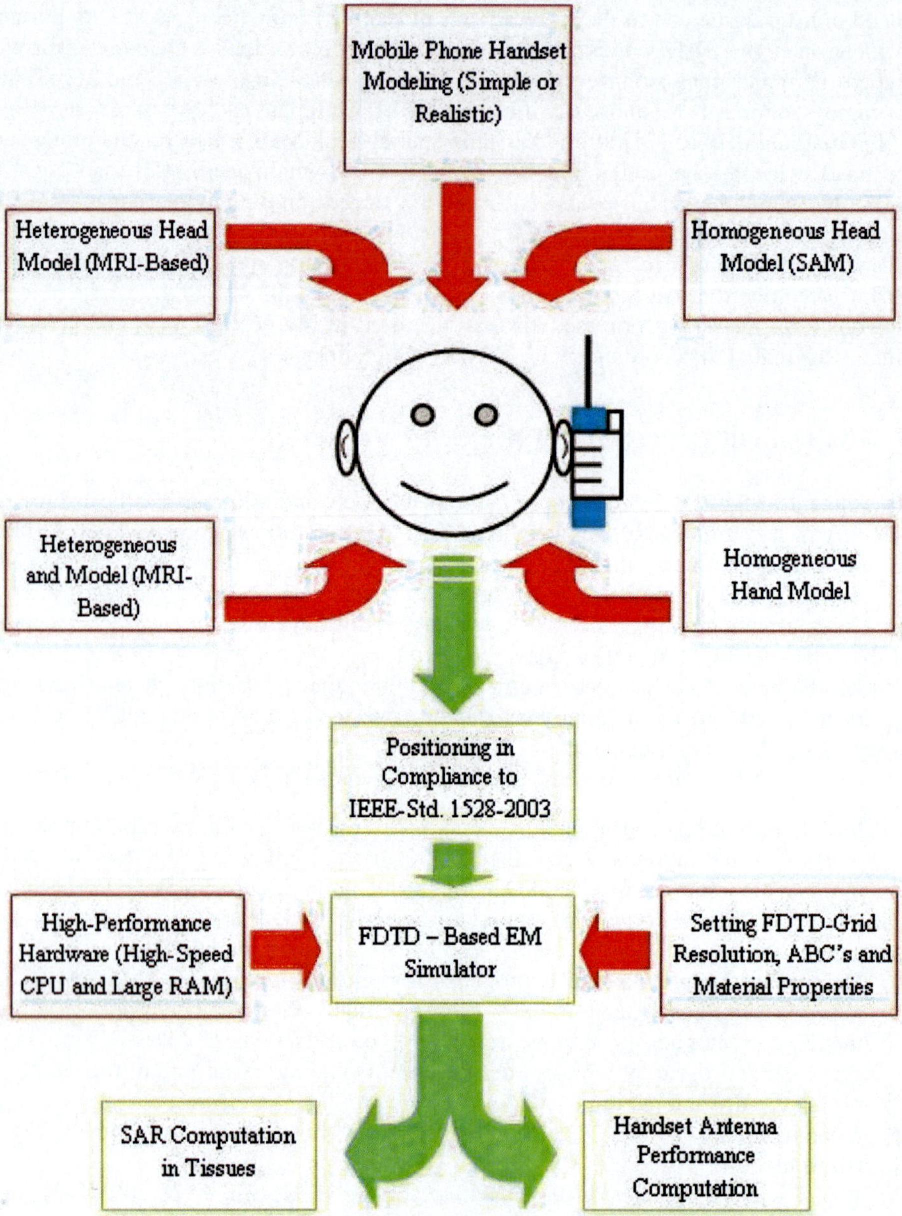

Fig. 3. A block diagram illustrating the numerical computation of the EM interaction of a cellular handset and human using FDTD method

6 Validation of the Numerical Dosimetric of SAR

Verification of our FDTD computation was performed by comparison with the numerical and practical dosimetric given in [26], where the spatial-peak SAR over 1g and 10g induced in SAM is computed due to the RF emission of a generic phone at 835 and 1900 MHz normalized to 1 W source power. Both Yee-FDTD and ADI-FDTD methods were applied for the numerical computation using SEMCAD X [25] and compared with the results presented in [26].

As described in [26], the generic mobile phone was formed by a monopole antenna and a chassis, with the excitation point at the base of the antenna. The antenna length was 71 mm for 835 MHz and 36 mm for 1900 MHz, and its square cross section had a 1-mm edge. The monopole was coated with 1 mm thick plastic having dielectric properties $\varepsilon_r = 2.5$ and $\sigma = 0.005$ S/m. The chassis comprised a PCB, having lateral dimensions of 40 × 100 mm and a thickness of 1 mm, symmetrically embedded in a solid plastic case with dielectric properties $\varepsilon_r = 4$ and $\sigma = 0.04$ S/m, lateral dimensions 42×102 mm, and thickness 21 mm. The antenna was mounted along the chassis centerline so as to avoid differences between right- and left-side head exposure. The antenna was a thick-wire model whose excitation was a 50-Ω sinusoidal voltage source at the gap between the antenna and PCB. Fig. 2 shows the generic phone in close proximity to a SAM phantom at *cheek* and *tilt*-position in compliance with IEEE-Std. 1528-2003 [13].

The simulation platform SEMCAD X incorporates automated heterogeneous grid generation, which automatically adapts the mesh to a specific setup. To align the simulated handset components to the FDTD grid accurately a minimum spatial resolution of $0.5 \times 0.5 \times 0.5$ mm^3 and a maximum spatial resolution of $3 \times 3 \times 3$ mm^3 in the *x*, *y*, and *z* directions was chosen for simulating the handset in hand close to head. A refining factor of 10 with a grading ratio of 1.2 was used for the solid regions during the simulations. The simulations assumed a steady state voltage at 835 and 1900 MHz, with a feed point of 50-Ω sinusoidal voltage source and a 1 mm physical gap between the antenna and the printed circuit board. The ABCs were set as a UPML-mode with 10 layers thickness, where the minimum level of absorption at the outer boundary was > 99.9% [25]. Table 2 explains the amount of the FDTD-grid cells needed to model the handset in close proximity to SAM at 835 and 1900 MHz, according to the setting parameters and values mentioned above.

Table 2. The generated FDTD-grid cell size of the generic phone in close proximity to SAM at *cheek* and *tilt* positions

Frequency	*Cheek*-position	*Tilt*-position
835 MHz	225 × 173 × 219 = 8.52458 Mcells	225 × 170 × 223 = 8.52975 Mcells
1900 MHz	191 × 139 × 186 = 4.93811 Mcells	191 × 136 × 186 = 4.83154 Mcells

The FDTD computation results, using both Yee-FDTD and ADI-FDTD methods, are shown in Table 3. The computed spatial-peak SAR over 1 and 10g was normalized to 1 W net input power as in [26], at both 835 and 1900 MHz, for comparison. The computation and measurement results in [26], shown in Table 3, were considered for sixteen participants where the mean and standard deviation of the SARs are presented.

The computation results of both methods, i.e., Yee-FDTD and ADI-FDTD methods, showed a good agreement with that computed in [26]. When using the ADI-FDTD method, an ADI time step factor of 10 was set during simulation. The minimum value of the time step factor was 1 and increasing this value made the simulation run faster. With a time step factor ≥12, the speed of simulation will be faster than Yee-FDTD method [25]. Two solver optimizations are used: firstly, optimization for speed, where the ADI factorizations of tridiogonal systems performed at each iteration and a huge memory were needed, and secondly, optimization for memory, where the ADI factorizations of tridiogonal systems performed at each iteration took a long run-time.

Table 3. Pooled SAR statistics that given in [26] and our computation, for the generic phone in close proximity to the SAM at *cheek* and *tilt*-position and normalized to 1 W input power

Frequency			835 MHz		1900 MHz	
Handset position			*Cheek*	*Tilt*	*Cheek*	*Tilt*
FDTD Computation in literature [26]	Spatial-peak SAR_{1g} (W/kg)	Mean	7.74	4.93	8.28	11.97
		Std. Dev.	0.40	0.64	1.58	3.10
		No.	16	16	16	15
	Spatial-peak SAR_{10g} (W/kg)	Mean	5.26	3.39	4.79	6.78
		Std. Dev.	0.27	0.26	0.73	1.37
		No.	16	16	16	15
Measurement in literature [26]	Spatial-peak SAR_{1g} (W/kg)		8.8	4.8	8.6	12.3
	Spatial-peak SAR_{10g} (W/kg)		6.1	3.2	5.3	6.9
Our FDTD Computation	Spatial-peak SAR_{1g} (W/kg)		7.5	4.813	8.1	12.28
	Spatial-peak SAR_{10g} (W/kg)		5.28	3.13	4.36	6.51
Our ADI-FDTD Computation	Spatial-peak SAR_{1g} (W/kg)		7.44	4.76	8.2	12.98
	Spatial-peak SAR_{10g} (W/kg)		5.26	3.09	4.46	6.72

The hardware used for simulation (Dell Desk-Top, M1600, 1.6 GHz Dual Core, 4 GB DDRAM) was incapable of achieving optimization for speed while processing the generated grid-cells ≥ **4**Mcells, and was also incapable of achieving optimization for memory while processing the generated grid-cells ≥ **10** Mcells. When using the Yee-FDTD method, however, the hardware could process up to 22 Mcells [6]. No hardware accelerator such as an Xware [25] was used in the simulations.

7 Factors Influencing the EM Wave Interaction between Mobile Phone Antenna and Human Head

The EM wave interaction between the mobile phone handset and human head has been reported in many papers. Studies concentrated firstly, on the effect of the human head on the handset antenna performance, including the feed-point impedance, gain, and efficiency [36]-[39], and secondly, on the impact of the antenna EM radiation on the user's head, caused by the absorbed power, and measured by predicting the induced specific absorption rate (SAR) in the head tissues [1]-[3], [40]-[55]. During realistic usage of cellular handsets, many factors may play an important role by increasing or decreasing the EM interaction between the handset antenna and the user's head. The factors influencing the interaction, include:

(a) **PCB and antenna positions** [7]; A hand-set model (generic mobile phone) formed by a monopole antenna and a PDB embedded in a chassis, with the excitation point at the base of the antenna, is simulated using FDTD-based EM-solver. Two cases were considered during the simulation; the first was varying the antenna+PCB position along the y-axis (chassis depth) with 9-steps, the second; was varying the antenna along the x-axis (chassis width) with 11-steps and keeping the PCB in the middle. The results showed that the optimum position for the antenna and PCB in hand-set close to head is the far right-corner for the right-hand users and the far left-corner for the left-hand users, where a minimum SAR in head is achieved.

(b) **Cellular handset shape** [4]; A novel cellular handset with a keypad over the screen and a bottom-mounted antenna has been proposed and numerically modeled, with the most handset components, using an FDTD-based EM solver. The proposed handset model is based on the commercially available model with a top-mounted external antenna. Both homogeneous and nonhomogeneous head phantoms have been used with a semirealistic hand design to simulate the handset in hand close to head. The simulation results showed a significant improvement in the antenna performance with the proposed handset model in hand close to head, as compared with the handset of top-mounted antenna. Also, using this proposed handset, a significant reduction in the induced SAR and power absorbed in head has been achieved.

(c) **Cellular handset position with respect to head** [8]; Both the computation accuracy and the cost were investigated in terms of the number of FDTD-grid cells due to the artifact rotation for a cellular handset close to the user's head. Two study cases were simulated to assess the EM coupling of a cellular handset and a

MRI-based human head model at 900 MHz; firstly, both handset and head CAD models are aligned to the FDTD-grid, secondly, handset close to a rotated head in compliance with IEEE-1528 standard. A FDTD-based platform, SEMCAD X, is used; where conventional and interactive gridder approaches are implemented to achieve the simulations. The results show that owing to the artifact rotation, the computation error may increase up to 30%, whereas, the required number of grid cells may increase up to 25%.

(d) **Human head of different originations** [11]; Four homogeneous head phantoms of different human origins, i.e., African female, European male, European old male, and Latin American male, with normal (non-pressed) ears are designed and used in simulations for evaluating the electromagnetic (EM) wave interaction between handset antennas and human head at 900 and 1800MHz with radiated power of 0.25 and 0.125 W, respectively. The difference in heads dimensions due to different origins shows different EM wave interaction. In general, the African female's head phantom showed a higher induced SAR at 900 MHz and a lower induced SAR at 1800 MHz, as compared with the other head phantoms. The African female's head phantom also showed more impact on both mobile phone models at 900 and 1800 MHz. This is due to the different pinna size and thickness that every adopted head phantom had, which made the distance between the antenna source and nearest head tissue of every head phantom was different accordingly

(e) **hand-hold position, Antenna type, and human head model type** [5], [6]; For a realistic usage pattern of mobile phone handset, i.e., *cheek* and *tilt*-positions, with an MRI-based human head model and semi-realistic mobile phone of different types, i.e., candy-bar and clamshell types with external and internal antenna, operating at GSM-900, GSM-1800, and UMTS frequencies, the following were observed; handhold position had a considerable impact on handset antenna matching, antenna radiation efficiency, and TIS. This impact, however, varied due to many factors, including antenna type/position, handset position in relation to head, and operating frequency, and can be summarized as follows.

1. The significant degradation in mobile phone antenna performance was noticed for the candy-bar with patch antenna. This is because the patch antenna is sandwiched between hand and head tissues during use, and the hand tissues acted as the antenna upper dielectric layers. This may shift the tuning frequency as well as decrease the radiation efficiency.
2. Owing to the hand-hold alteration in different positions, the internal antenna of candybar-type handsets exhibited more variation in total efficiency values than the external antenna. The maximum absolute difference (25%) was recorded at 900MHz for a candy-bar type handset with bottom patch antenna against HR-EFH at *tilt*-position.
3. Maximum TIS level was obtained for the candy-bar handheld against head at *cheek*-position operating at 1800 MHz, where a minimum total efficiency was recorded when simulating handsets with internal patch antenna.
4. There was more SAR variation in HR-EFH tissues owing to internal antenna exposure, as compared with external antenna exposure.

8 Conclusion

A procedure for evaluating the EM interaction between mobile phone antenna and human head using numerical techniques, e.g., FDTD, FE, MoM, has been presented in this paper. A validation of our EM interaction computation using both Yee-FDTD and ADI-FDTD was achieved by comparison with previously published papers. A review of the factors may affect on the EM interaction, e.g., antenna type, mobile handset type, antenna position, mobile handset position, etc., was demonstrated. It was shown that the mobile handset antenna specifications may affected dramatically due to the factors listed above, as well as, the amount of the SAR deposited in the human head may also changed dramatically due to the same factors.

Acknowledgment

The author would like to express his appreciation to Prof. Dr. **Cynthia Furse** at University of Utah, USA, for her technical advice and provision of important references. Special thanks are extended to reverent **Wayne Jennings** at Schmid & Partner Engineering AG (SPEAG), Zurich, Switzerland, for his kind assistance in providing the license for the SEMCAD platform and the numerical corrected model of a human head (HR-EFH). The author also grateful to Dr. **Theodoros Samaras** at the Radiocommunications Laboratory, Department of Physics, Aristotle University of Thessaloniki, Greece, to **Esra Neufeld** at the Foundation for Research on Information Technologies in Society (IT'IS), ETH Zurich, Switzerland, and to **Peter Futter** at SPEAG, Zurich, Switzerland, for their kind assistance and technical advices.

References

1. Chavannes, N., Tay, R., Nikoloski, N., Kuster, N.: Suitability of FDTD-based TCAD tools for RF design of mobile phones. IEEE Antennas & Propagation Magazine 45(6), 52–66 (2003)
2. Chavannes, N., Futter, P., Tay, R., Pokovic, K., Kuster, N.: Reliable prediction of mobile phone performance for different daily usage patterns using the FDTD method. In: Proceedings of the IEEE International Workshop on Antenna Technology (IWAT 2006), White Plains, NY, USA, pp. 345–348 (2006)
3. Futter, P., Chavannes, N., Tay, R., et al.: Reliable prediction of mobile phone performance for realistic in-use conditions using the FDTD method. IEEE Antennas and Propagation Magazine 50(1), 87–96 (2008)
4. Al-Mously, S.I., Abousetta, M.M.: A Novel Cellular Handset Design for an Enhanced Antenna Performance and a Reduced SAR in the Human Head. International Journal of Antennas and Propagation (IJAP) 2008 Article ID 642572, 10 pages (2008)
5. Al-Mously, S.I., Abousetta, M.M.: A Study of the Hand-Hold Impact on the EM Interaction of A Cellular Handset and A Human Head. International Journal of Electronics, Circuits, and Systems (IJECS) 2(2), 91–95 (2008)
6. Al-Mously, S.I., Abousetta, M.M.: Anticipated Impact of Hand-Hold Position on the Electromagnetic Interaction of Different Antenna Types/Positions and a Human in Cellular Communications. International Journal of Antennas and Propagation (IJAP) 2008, 22 pages (2008)

7. Al-Mously, S.I., Abousetta, M.M.: Study of Both Antenna and PCB Positions Effect on the Coupling Between the Cellular Hand-Set and Human Head at GSM-900 Standard. In: Proceeding of the International Workshop on Antenna Technology, iWAT 2008, Chiba, Japan, pp. 514–517 (2008)
8. Al-Mously, S.I., Abdalla, A.Z., Abousetta, Ibrahim, E.M.: Accuracy and Cost Computation of the EM Coupling of a Cellular Handset and a Human Due to Artifact Rotation. In: Proceeding of 16th Telecommunication Forum TELFOR 2008, Belgrade, Serbia, November 25-27, pp. 484–487 (2008)
9. Al-Mously, S.I., Abousetta, M.M.: User's Hand Effect on TIS of Different GSM900/1800 Mobile Phone Models Using FDTD Method. In: Proceeding of the International Conference on Computer, Electrical, and System Science, and Engineering (The World Academy of Science, Engineering and Technology, PWASET), Dubai, UAE, vol. 37, pp. 878–883 (2009)
10. Al-Mously, S.I., Abousetta, M.M.: Effect of the hand-hold position on the EM Interaction of clamshell-type handsets and a human. In: Proceeding of the Progress in Electromagnetics Research Symposium (PIERS), Moscow, Russia, August 18-21, pp. 1727–1731 (2009)
11. Al-Mously, S.I., Abousetta, M.M.: Impact of human head with different originations on the anticipated SAR in tissue. In: Proceeding of the Progress in Electromagnetics Research Symposium (PIERS), Moscow, Russia, August 18-21, pp. 1732–1736 (2009)
12. Al-Mously, S.I., Abousetta, M.M.: A definition of thermophysiological parameters of SAM materials for temperature rise calculation in the head of cellular handset user. In: Proceeding of the Progress in Electromagnetics Research Symposium (PIERS), Moscow, Russia, August 18-21, pp. 170–174 (2009)
13. IEEE Recommended Practice for Determining the Peak Spatial-Average Specific Absorption Rate (SAR) in the Human Head from Wireless Communications Devices: Measurement Techniques, IEEE Standard-1528 (2003)
14. Allen, S.G.: Radiofrequency field measurements and hazard assessment. Journal of Radiological Protection 11, 49–62 (1996)
15. Standard for Safety Levels with Respect to Human Exposure to Radiofrequency Electromagnetic Fields, 3 kHz to 300 GHz, IEEE Standards Coordinating Committee 28.4 (2006)
16. Product standard to demonstrate the compliance of mobile phones with the basic restrictions related to human exposure to electromagnetic fields (300 MHz–3GHz), European Committee for Electrical Standardization (CENELEC), EN 50360, Brussels (2001)
17. Basic Standard for the Measurement of Specific Absorption Rate Related to Exposure to Electromagnetic Fields from Mobile Phones (300 MHz–3GHz), European Committee for Electrical Standardization (CENELEC), EN-50361 (2001)
18. Human exposure to radio frequency fields from hand-held and body-mounted wireless communication devices - Human models, instrumentation, and procedures — Part 1: Procedure to determine the specific absorption rate (SAR) for hand-held devices used in close proximity to the ear (frequency range of 300 MHz to 3 GHz), IEC 62209-1 (2006)
19. Specific Absorption Rate (SAR) Estimation for Cellular Phone, Association of Radio Industries and businesses, ARIB STD-T56 (2002)
20. Evaluating Compliance with FCC Guidelines for Human Exposure to Radio Frequency Electromagnetic Field, Supplement C to OET Bulletin 65 (Edition 9701), Federal Communications Commission (FCC),Washington, DC, USA (1997)
21. ACA Radio communications (Electromagnetic Radiation - Human Exposure) Standard 2003, Schedules 1 and 2, Australian Communications Authority (2003)

22. Kuster, N., Balzano, Q.: Energy absorption mechanism by biological bodies in the near field of dipole antennas above 300 MHz. IEEE Transaction on Vehicular Technology 41(1), 17–23 (1992)
23. Caputa, K., Okoniewski, M., Stuchly, M.A.: An algorithm for computations of the power deposition in human tissue. IEEE Antennas and Propagation Magazine 41, 102–107 (1999)
24. Recommended Practice for Determining the Peak Spatial-Average Specific Absorption Rate (SAR) associated with the use of wireless handsets - computational techniques, IEEE-1529, draft standard
25. SEMCAD, Reference Manual for the SEMCAD Simulation Platform for Electromagnetic Compatibility, Antenna Design and Dosimetry, SPEAG-Schmid & Partner Engineering AG, `http://www.semcad.com/`
26. Beard, B.B., Kainz, W., Onishi, T., et al.: Comparisons of computed mobile phone induced SAR in the SAM phantom to that in anatomically correct models of the human head. IEEE Transaction on Electromagnetic Compatibility 48(2), 397–407 (2006)
27. Procedure to measure the Specific Absorption Rate (SAR) in the frequency range of 300MHz to 3 GHz - part 1: handheld mobile wireless communication devices, International Electrotechnical Commission, committee draft for vote, IEC 62209
28. ICNIRP, Guidelines for limiting exposure to time-varying electric, magnetic, and electromagnetic fields (up to 300 GHz), Health Phys., vol. 74(4), pp. 494–522 (1998)
29. Zombolas, C.: SAR Testing and Approval Requirements for Australia. In: Proceeding of the IEEE International Symposium on Electromagnetic Compatibility, vol. 1, pp. 273–278 (2003)
30. IEEE Standard for Safety Levels With Respect to Human Exposure to Radio Frequency Electromagnetic Fields, 3kHz to 300 GHz, Amendment2: Specific Absorption Rate (SAR) Limits for the Pinna, IEEE Standard C95.1b-2004 (2004)
31. Ghandi, O.P., Kang, G.: Inaccuracies of a plastic pinna SAM for SAR testing of cellular telephones against IEEE and ICNIRP safety guidelines. IEEE Transaction on Microwave Theory and Techniques 52(8) (2004)
32. Ghandi, O.P., Kang, G.: Some present problems and a proposed experimental phantom for SAR compliance testing of cellular telephones at 835 and 1900 MHz. Phys. Med. Biol. 47, 1501–1518 (2002)
33. Kuster, N., Christ, A., Chavannes, N., Nikoloski, N., Frolich, J.: Human head phantoms for compliance and communication performance testing of mobile telecommunication equipment at 900 MHz. In: Proceeding of the 2002 Interim Int. Symp. Antennas Propag., Yokosuka Research Park, Yokosuka, Japan (2002)
34. Christ, A., Chavannes, N., Nikoloski, N., Gerber, H., Pokovic, K., Kuster, N.: A numerical and experimental comparison of human head phantoms for compliance testing of mobile telephone equipment. Bioelectromagnetics 26, 125–137 (2005)
35. Beard, B.B., Kainz, W.: Review and standardization of cell phone exposure calculations using the SAM phantom and anatomically correct head models. BioMedical Engineering Online 3, 34 (2004), doi:10.1186/1475-925X-3-34
36. Kouveliotis, N.K., Panagiotou, S.C., Varlamos, P.K., Capsalis, C.N.: Theoretical approach of the interaction between a human head model and a mobile handset helical antenna using numerical methods. Progress In Electromagnetics Research, PIER 65, 309–327 (2006)
37. Sulonen, K., Vainikainen, P.: Performance of mobile phone antennas including effect of environment using two methods. IEEE Transaction on Instrumentation and Measurement 52(6), 1859–1864 (2003)
38. Krogerus, J., Icheln, C., Vainikainen, P.: Dependence of mean effective gain of mobile terminal antennas on side of head. In: Proceedings of the 35th European Microwave Conference, Paris, France, pp. 467–470 (2005)

39. Haider, H., Garn, H., Neubauer, G., Schmidt, G.: Investigation of mobile phone antennas with regard to power efficiency and radiation safety. In: Proceeding of the Workshop on Mobile Terminal and Human Body Interaction, Bergen, Norway (2000)
40. Toftgard, J., Hornsleth, S.N., Andersen, J.B.: Effects on portable antennas of the presence of a person. IEEE Transaction on Antennas and Propagation 41(6), 739–746 (1993)
41. Jensen, M.A., Rahmat-Samii, Y.: EM interaction of handset antennas and a human in personal communications. Proceeding of the IEEE 83(1), 7–17 (1995)
42. Graffin, J., Rots, N., Pedersen, G.F.: Radiations phantom for handheld phones. In: Proceedings of the IEEE Vehicular Technology Conference (VTC 2000), Boston, Mass, USA, vol. 2, pp. 853–860 (2000)
43. Kouveliotis, N.K., Panagiotou, S.C., Varlamos, P.K., Capsalis, C.N.: Theoretical approach of the interaction between a human head model and a mobile handset helical antenna using numerical methods. Progress in Electromagnetics Research, PIER 65, 309–327 (2006)
44. Khalatbari, S., Sardari, D., Mirzaee, A.A., Sadafi, H.A.: Calculating SAR in Two Models of the Human Head Exposed to Mobile Phones Radiations at 900 and 1800MHz. In: Proceedings of the Progress in Electromagnetics Research Symposium, Cambridge, USA, pp. 104–109 (2006)
45. Okoniewski, M., Stuchly, M.: A study of the handset antenna and human body interaction. IEEE Transaction on Microwave Theory and Techniques 44(10), 1855–1864 (1996)
46. Bernardi, P., Cavagnaro, M., Pisa, S.: Evaluation of the SAR distribution in the human head for cellular phones used in a partially closed environment. IEEE Transactions of Electromagnetic Compatibility 38(3), 357–366 (1996)
47. Lazzi, G., Pattnaik, S.S., Furse, C.M., Gandhi, O.P.: Comparison of FDTD computed and measured radiation patterns of commercial mobile telephones in presence of the human head. IEEE Transaction on Antennas and Propagation 46(6), 943–944 (1998)
48. Koulouridis, S., Nikita, K.S.: Study of the coupling between human head and cellular phone helical antennas. IEEE Transactions of Electromagnetic Compatibility 46(1), 62–70 (2004)
49. Wang, J., Fujiwara, O.: Comparison and evaluation of electromagnetic absorption characteristics in realistic human head models of adult and children for 900-MHz mobile telephones. IEEE Transactions on Microwave Theory and Techniques 51(3), 966–971 (2003)
50. Lazzi, G., Gandhi, O.P.: Realistically tilted and truncated anatomically based models of the human head for dosimetry of mobile telephones. IEEE Transactions of Electromagnetic Compatibility 39(1), 55–61 (1997)
51. Rowley, J.T., Waterhouse, R.B.: Performance of shorted microstrip patch antennas for mobile communications handsets at 1800 MHz. IEEE Transaction on Antennas and Propagation 47(5), 815–822 (1999)
52. Watanabe, S.-I., Taki, M., Nojima, T., Fujiwara, O.: Characteristics of the SAR distributions in a head exposed to electromagnetic field radiated by a hand-held portable radio. IEEE Transaction on Microwave Theory and Techniques 44(10), 1874–1883 (1996)
53. Bernardi, P., Cavagnaro, M., Pisa, S., Piuzzi, E.: Specific absorption rate and temperature increases in the head of a cellular-phone user. IEEE Transaction on Microwave Theory and Techniques 48(7), 1118–1126 (2000)
54. Lee, H., Choi, L.H., Pack, J.: Human head size and SAR characteristics for handset exposure. ETRI Journal 24, 176–179 (2002)
55. Francavilla, M., Schiavoni, A., Bertotto, P., Richiardi, G.: Effect of the hand on cellular phone radiation. IEE Proceeding of Microwaves, Antennas and Propagation 148, 247–253 (2001)

Measure a Subjective Video Quality Via a Neural Network

Hasnaa El Khattabi[1], Ahmed Tamtaoui[2], and Driss Aboutajdine[1]

[1] LRIT, Unité associée au CNRST, URAC 29, Faculté des Sciences,
Rabat, Morocco
[2] Institut National Des Postes et Télécommunications (INPT),
Rabat, Morocco
hasnaa.elkhattabi@yahoo.fr

Abstract. We present in this paper a new method to measure the quality of the video in order to change the judgment of the human eye by an objective measure. This latter predicts the mean opinion score (MOS) and the peak signal to noise ratio (PSNR) by providing eight parameters extracted from original and coded videos. These parameters that are used are: the average of DFT differences, the standard deviation of DFT differences, the average of DCT differences, the standard deviation of DCT differences, the variance of energy of color, the luminance Y, the chrominance U and the chrominance V. The results we obtained for the correlation show a percentage of 99.58% on training sets and 96.4% on the testing sets. These results compare very favorably with the results obtained with other methods [1].

Keywords: video, neural network MLP, subjective quality, objective quality, luminance, chrominance.

1 Introduction

Video Quality evaluation plays an important role in image and video processing. In order to change the human perception judgment by the machine evaluation, many researches were realized during the last two decades. Among the common methods we have, the mean squared error (MSE)[9], the peak signal to noise ratio (PSNR)[8, 14], the discrete cosine transform (DCT)[5, 6], and the decomposition in wavelets [13]. Another direction in this domain is based on the characteristics of the human vision system [2, 10, 11], like the contrast sensitivity function. One should note that in order to check the precision of these measures, these latter should be correlated with the results obtained using subjective quality evaluations, there exist two major methods concerning the subjective quality measure: double stimulus continuous quality scale (DSCQS) and single stimulus continuous quality evaluation (SSCQE) [3].

We present the video quality measure estimation via a neural network. This neural network predicts the observers mean opinion score (MOS) and the peak signal

H. Cherifi, J.M. Zain, and E. El-Qawasmeh (Eds.): DICTAP 2011, Part I, CCIS 166, pp. 121–130, 2011.

to noise ratio(PSNR) by providing eight parameters extracted from original and coded videos. The eight parameters are: the average of DFT differences, the standard deviation of DFT differences, the average of DCT differences, the standard deviation of DCT differences, the variance of energy of color, the luminance Y, the chrominance U and the chrominance V.

The network used is composed of an input layer with eight neurons corresponding to the extracted parameters, three intermediate layers (with 7, 5 and 3 neurons respectively) and an output layer with two neurons (PSNR, MOS). The function 'trainscg' (training scaled conjugate gradient) was used in the training stage. We have chosen DSCQ for the video subjective measure since the extraction of the parameters is performed on the two videos, original and coded.

In the second section we describe the subjective quality measure, in the third section we present the parameters of our work and the used neural network, and in the fourth section we give the results of our method and we end by a conclusion.

2 Subjective Quality Measurement

2.1 Presentation

There exist two major methods concerning the subjective quality measure: double stimulus continuous quality scale (DSCQS) and single stimulus continuous quality evaluation (SSCQE) [3].We have chosen DSCQS [3, 7] to measure the video subjective quality, since we deal with original and coded videos. We present to the observers the coded sequence A and the original B, without knowing which one is the reference video. For each sequence a quality score is then assigned, the processing continuation operates on the mean of differences of the two scores using a subjective evaluation scale (excellent, good, fair, poor, and bad) linked to a scale of values from 0 to 100 as shown in Figure 1.

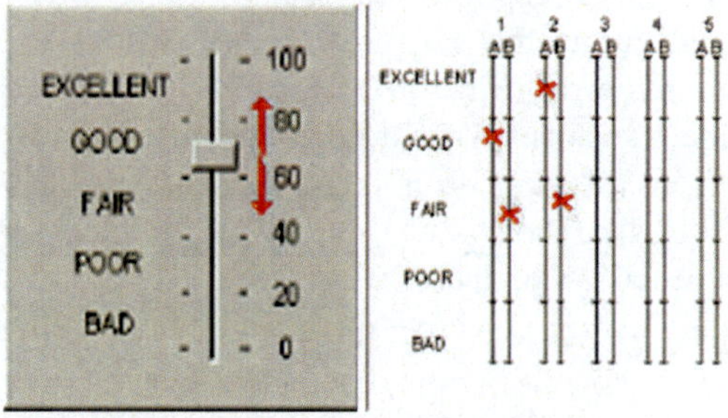

Fig. 1. Quality scale for DSCQS evaluation

2.2 Measurement

Examples of original sequences and their graduated shading versions that we used:

Akiyo original sequence,
Akiyo Coded / decoded with 24K bits/s,
Akiyo Coded / decoded with 64K bits/s,
Car phone original sequence,
Carphone Coded / decoded with 28K bits/s,
Carphone Coded / decoded with 64K bits/s,
Carphone Coded / decoded with 128K bits/s,

Fig. 2. Originals sequences

Each sequence lasts 3 seconds, and each test includes two presentations A and B, coming always from the same source clip, but one of them is coded while the other is the non coded reference video. The observers should note down the two sequences without being aware of the reference video. Its position varies according to a pseudo random sequence. The observers see each presentation twice (A, B, A, B), according to the trial format of table 1.

Table 1. The layout of DSCQS measure

Subject	Duration(seconds)
Presentation A	8-10
Break for notation	5
Presentation B	8-10
Break for notation	5
Presentation A(second time)	8-10
Break for notation	5
Presentation B(second time)	8-10
Break for notation	5

The number of observers was 13 persons. In order to let them have a valid opinion during the trials, we asked them to watch the original and graduated shading video clips. We did not take into consideration the results of this trial. On the quality scale of figure 1, the observers were writing their notes with a horizontal line to represent their opinion about the quality of a given presentation. The seized value represents the difference in absolute value between the presentations A and B.

3 Quality Evaluation

3.1 Parameters Extraction

The extraction of parameters is performed on blocks for which the size is 8*8 pixels, and the average is computed on each block. The eight features extracted from the input/output video sequence pairs are:

- Average of DFT difference (F1): This feature is computed as the average difference of the DFT coefficients between the original and coded image blocks.
- Standard deviation of DFT difference (F2): The standard deviation of the difference of the DFT coefficients between the original and encoded blocks is the second feature.
- Average of DCT difference (F3): This average is computed as the average difference of the DCT coefficients between the original and coded image blocks.
- Standard deviation of DCT difference (F4): The standard deviation of the difference of the DCT coefficients between the original and encoded blocks.
- The variance of energy of color (F5): The color difference, as measured by the energy in the difference between the original and coded blocks in the UVW color coordinate system. The UVW coordinates have good correlation with the subjective assessments [1]. The color difference is given by:

$$\Delta E = \sqrt{\Delta U^2 + \Delta V^2 + \Delta W^2} \tag{1}$$

- The luminance Y (F6): in the color space YUV, the luminance is given by the Y component. The difference of the luminance between the original and encoded blocks is used as a feature.
- The chrominance U (F7) and the chrominance V (F8): in the color space YUV, the chrominance U is given by the U component and the chrominance V is given by the V component. We compute the difference of the chrominance V between the original and encoded blocks and the same for the chrominance U.

The choice of parameters: the average of DFT differences, the standard deviation of DFT differences, the variance of energy of color, is based on the fact they concern the subjective quality [1] and the choice of the luminance Y, the chrominance U and V was made to get the information on the luminance and the color to predict the best possible subjective quality.

3.2 Multilayer Neural Networks

Presentation. Neural networks have the ability to learn complex data structures and approximate any continuous mapping. They have the advantage of working fast (after a training phase) even with large amounts of data. The results presented in this paper are based on multilayer network architecture, known as the multilayer perceptron (MLP). The MLP is a powerful tool that has been used extensively for classification, nonlinear regression, speech recognition, handwritten character recognition and many other applications. The elementary processing unit in a MLP is called a neuron or perceptron. It consists of a set of input synapses, through which the input signals are received, a summing unit and a nonlinear activation transfer function. Each neuron performs a nonlinear transformation of its input vector; the net input for unit j is given by:

$$net_j = \sum_i w_{ji} o_i + \theta_j \tag{2}$$

Where w_{ji} is the weight from unit i to unit j, o_i is the output of unit i, and θj is the bias for unit j.

MLP architecture consists of a layer of input units, followed by one or more layers of processing units, called hidden layers, and one output layer. Information propagates from the input to the output layer; the output signals represent the desired information. The input layer serves only as a relay of information and no information processing occurs at this layer. Before a network can operate to perform the desired task, it must be trained. The training process changes the training parameters of the network in such a way that the error between the network outputs and the target values (desired outputs) is minimized.

In this paper, we propose a method to predict the MOS of human observers using an MLP. Here the MLP is designed to predict the image fidelity using a set of key features extracted from the reference and coded video. The features are extracted from small blocks (say 8*8), and then they are fed as inputs to the network, which estimates the video quality of the corresponding block. The overall video quality is estimated by averaging the estimated quality measures of the individual blocks. Using features extracted from small regions has the advantage that the network becomes independent of video size. Eight features, extracted from the original and coded video, were used as inputs to the network.

Architecture. The multilayer perception (MLP) used here is composed of an input layer with eight neurons corresponding to the eight parameters (F1, F2, F3, F4, F5, F6, F7, F8), an output layer with two neurons presenting the subjective quality (MOS) and the objective quality, the peak signal to noise ratio (PSNR), and three intermediate hidden layers. The following figure presents this network:

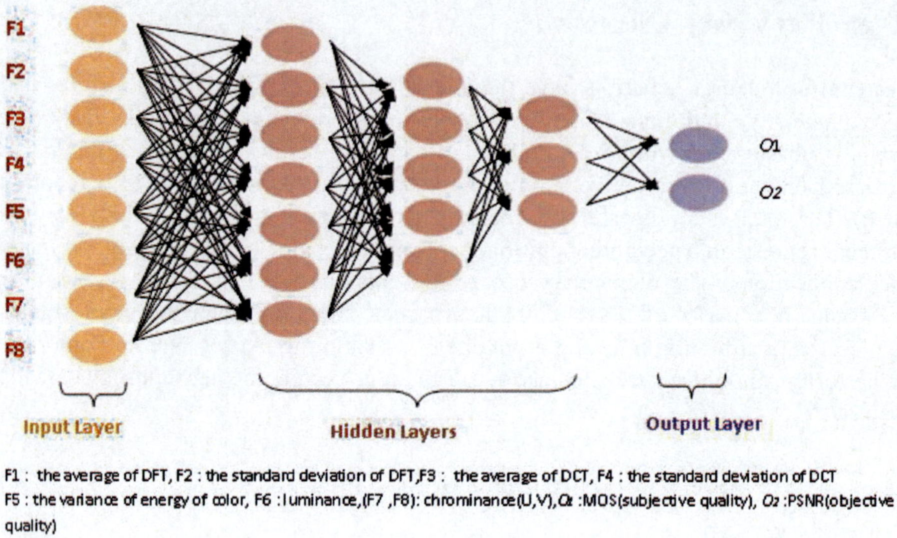

Fig. 3. MLP Network Architecture

Training. The training algorithm is the back propagation of the gradient with the use of the activation function sigmoid. This algorithm helps to update the weight values and biases that are randomly initialized to small values. The aim is to minimize the error criterion given by:

$$Er = 1/2\sum_{i=1}^{2} (t_i - O_i)^2 \tag{3}$$

Where i is the index of the output node, t_i is the desired output and O_i is the output computed by the network.

Network Training Algorithm

- The weights and the biases are initialized using small random values.
- The inputs and desired outputs are presented to the network.
- The actual outputs of the neural network are calculated by calculating the output of the nodes and going from the input to the output layer.
- The weights are adapted by backpropagating the error from the output to the input layer. That is,

$$w_{ji}(n+1) = w_{ji}(n) + \varepsilon\delta \tag{4}$$

Where the δ is the error propagated from node j, and ε is the learning rate. This process is done over all training patterns.

4 Experimental Results

The aim of this work is to estimate the video quality from the eight extracted using MLP network. We have used sequences coded in H.263 of type QCIF (quarter common intermediate format), whose size is 176*144 pixels*30 frames, and sequences CIF (common intermediate format) whose size is 352*288 pixels*30 frames. We end up with 11880 (22*18*30 blocks 8*8) values for each parameter per sequence QCIF and 47520 (44*36*30 blocks 8*8) values for each parameter per sequence CIF. The optimization of block quality is equivalent to the optimization of frame and sequence quality [1]. The experiment part is achieved in two steps: Training and testing.

In the MLP network training, five video sequences coded at different rates from four original video sequences (news, football, foreman and Stefan) were considered. The values of our parameters were normalized in order to reduce the computation complexity. This experiment was fully realized under Matlab (neural network toolbox).

The subjective quality of each of the coded sequences is assigned to the blocks of the same sequences. To make easier and accelerate the training, we used the function *trainscg* (training per scaled conjugate gradient). This algorithm is efficient for a large number of problems and it is much faster than other training algorithms. Furthermore its performances are not corrupted if the error is reduced, and does not require lot of memory to comply.

We use the neural network for an entirely different purpose. We want to apply it for the video quality prediction. Since no information on the network dimension is at our disposal, we will need to explore the set of all possibilities in order to refine our choice of the network configuration. This step will be achieved via a set of successive trials.

For the test, we used 13 coded video sequences at different rates from 6 original video sequences (News, Akiyo, Foreman, Carphone, Football and Stefan). We point out here that the test sequences were not used in the training. The performance of the network is given by the correlation coefficient [1], between the estimated output and the computed output of the sequence. This work is based on the following idea; In order to compute the subjective quality of the video, we need people to achieve it and of course it takes plenty of time. To avoid this hassle we thought of estimating this subjective measure via a convenient neurons network. This approach was recently used for video quality works [1, 12].

Several tests have been conducted to find the architecture of a neural network that would give us better results. And similarly several experiments have been tried to search the adequate number of parameters. The same criteria has been used for both parameters and architecture, which is based on the error between the estimated value and the calculated value at the network output in the training step. Since we used the supervised training, we do impose to the network an input and output. We obtained bad results when we worked with a minimum of parameters (five and four parameters), as well as more parameters (eleven parameters).

F. H. Lin and R. M. Mersereau [1] used the neurons network to compare their coder to the MPEG2 coder and estimated the MOS using as parameters: the average of DFT differences, the standard deviation of DFT differences, the mean absolute deviation of wepstrum differences, and the variance of UVW differences at the network entry. The results we obtained for the correlation show a percentage of 99.58% on training sets and 96.4% on the testing sets and the results obtained by F. H. Lin and R. M. Mersereau [1] for the correlation show a percentage of 97.77% on training sets and 95.04% on the testing sets. The results we obtained are much better than obtained by F. H. Lin and R. M. Mersereau [1].

Table 2. presents the computed, estimated (by the network) MOS and PSNR and their correlations. We can observe that our neural network is able to predict the measurements of MOS and PSNR, since the estimated values approach to the calculated values, and the values of correlations are satisfactory. We remark that the estimated values are not as exact as the ones that are computed, however they belong to the same quality intervals.

Table 2. Computed and estimated MOS and PSNR

Sequences	MOS computed	MOS estimated	PSNR computed	PSNR estimated	correlation
Akiyoqcif_64kbits/s	0.3509	0.2918	0.6462	0.5815	0.919
Carphoneqcif_128kbits/s	0.3790	0.2903	0.7859	0.7513	0.986
Footballcif_1.2Mbits/s	0.1257	0.1819	0.3525	0.5729	0.990
Foremanqcif_128kbits/s	0.3711	0.2909	0.8548	0.8055	0.998
Newscif_1.2Mbits/s	0.1194	0.1976	0.6153	0.5729	0.985
Stefancif_280kbits/s	0.3520	0.2786	0.2156	0.2329	0.970

5 Conclusion

The idea of this work is based on the fact that we try to substitute the human eye judgment by an objective method that makes easier the computation of the subjective quality, without the need of people presence. That saves us an awful lot of time, and avoid us the hassle of bringing over people. Sometimes we need to calculate the PSNR without the use of the original video, that's why we are adding in this work the PSNR estimation. We have tried to find a method that will allow us to compute the video subjective quality via a neural network by providing parameters (the average of DFT differences, the standard deviation of DFT differences, the average of DCT differences, the standard deviation of DCT differences, the variance of energy of color, the luminance Y, the chrominance U and the chrominance V) that are able to predict the video quality. The values of our parameters were normalized in order to reduce the computation complexity. This project was fully realized under Matlab (neural network toolbox). All our sequences are coded in the H.263 coder. It was very hard to get a network able to compute the quality of a given video. Regarding the testing, our network approaches the computed value. Several tests have been conducted to find the architecture of a neural network that would give us better results. And similarly several experiments have been tried to search the adequate number of parameters. The same criteria have been used for both parameters and architecture, which is based on the error between the estimated value and the calculated value at the network output in the training step. Since we used the supervised training, we do impose to the network an input and output. We obtained bad results when we worked with a minimum of parameters (five and four parameters), as well as several parameters (eleven parameters). We met some problems at the level of time, because the neural network takes a little more time at the level of the training step, and also at the level of database.

References

1. Lin, F.H., Mersereau, R.M.: Rate-quality tradeoff MPEG video encoder. Signal Processing : Image Communication 14, 297–300 (1999)
2. Wang, Z., Bovik, A.C.: Modern Image Quality Assessment. Morgan & Claypool Publishers, USA (2006)
3. Pinson, M., Wolf, S.: Comparing subjective video quality testing methodologies. In: SPIE Video Communications and Image Processing Conference, Lugano, Switzerland (July 2003)
4. Zurada, J.M.: Introduction to artificial neural system. PWS Publishiner Company (1992)
5. Malo, J., Pons, A.M., Artigas, J.M.: Subjective image fidelity metric based on bit allocation of the human visual system in the DCT domain. Image and Vision Computing 15, 535–548 (1997)
6. Watson, A.B., Hu, J., McGowan, J.F.: Digital video quality metric based on human vision. Journal of Electronic Imaging 10(I), 20–29 (2001)
7. Sun, H.M., Huang, Y.K.: Comparing Subjective Perceived Quality with Objective Video Quality by Content Characteristics and Bit Rates. In: International Conference on New Trends in Information and Service Science, niss, pp. 624–629 (2009)
8. Huynh-Thu, Q., Ghanbari, M.: Scope of validity of PSNR in image/video quality assessment. Electronics Letters 44(13), 800–801 (2008)
9. Wang, Z., Bovik, A.C.: Mean squared error: love it or leave it. IEEE Signal Process Mag. 26(1), 98–117 (2009)
10. Sheikh, H.R., Bovik, A.C., Veciana, G.d.: An Information Fidelity Criterion for Image Quality Assessment Using Natural Scene Statistics. IEEE Transactions on Image Processing 14(12), 2117–2128 (2005)

11. Juan, D., Yinglin, Y., Shengli, X.: A New Image Quality Assessment Based On HVS. Journal Of Electronics 22(3), 315–320 (2005)
12. Bouzerdoum, A., Havstad, A., Beghdadi, A.: Image quality assessment using a neural network approach. In: The Fourth IEEE International Symposium on Signal Processing and Information Technology, pp. 330–333 (2004)
13. Beghdadi, A., Pesquet-Popescu, B.: A new image distortion measure based on wavelet decomposition. In: Proc.Seventh Inter. Symp. Signal. Proces. Its Application, vol. 1, pp. 485–488 (2003)
14. Slanina, M., Ricny, V.: Estimating PSNR without reference for real H.264/AVC sequence intra frames. In: 18th International Conference on Radioelektronika, pp. 1–4 (2008)

Image Quality Assessment Based on Intrinsic Mode Function Coefficients Modeling

Abdelkaher Ait Abdelouahad[1], Mohammed El Hassouni[2], Hocine Cherifi[3], and Driss Aboutajdine[1]

[1] LRIT URAC- University of Mohammed V-Agdal-Morocco
a.abdelkher@gmail.com,
aboutaj@fsr.ac.ma
[2] DESTEC, FLSHR- University of Mohammed V-Agdal-Morocco
mohamed.elhassouni@gmail.com
[3] Le2i-UMR CNRS 5158 -University of Burgundy, Dijon-France
hocine.cherifi@u-bourgogne.fr

Abstract. Reduced reference image quality assessment (RRIQA) methods aim to assess the quality of a perceived image with only a reduced cue from its original version, called "reference image". The powerful advantage of RR methods is their "General-purpose". However, most introduced RR methods are built upon a non-adaptive transform models. This can limit the scope of RR methods to a small number of distortion types. In this work, we propose a bi-dimensional empirical mode decomposition-based RRIQA method. First, we decompose both, reference and distorted images, into Intrinsic Mode Functions (IMF), then we use the Generalized Gaussian Density (GGD) to model IMF coefficients. Finally, the distortion measure is computed from the "fitting errors", between the empirical and the theoretical IMF histograms, using the Kullback Leibler Divergence (KLD). In order to evaluate the performance of the proposed method, two approaches have been investigated : the logistic function-based regression and the well known Support vector machine-based classification. Experimental results show a high correlation between objective and subjective scores.

Keywords: RRIQA, IMF, GGD, KLD.

1 Introduction

Last years have witnessed a surge of interest to objective image quality measures, due to the enormous growth of digital image processing techniques: lossy compression, watermarking, quantization. These techniques generally transform the original image to an image of lower visual quality. To assess the performance of different techniques one has to measure the impact of the degradation induced by the processing in terms of perceived visual quality. To do so, subjective measures based essentially on human observer opinions have been introduced. These visual psychophysical judgments (detection, discrimination and preference) are made under controlled viewing conditions (fixed lighting, viewing distance, etc.), generate highly reliable and repeatable data, and are used to optimize the design of imaging processing techniques. The test plan for subjective video quality assessment is well guided by Video Quality Experts Group

H. Cherifi, J.M. Zain, and E. El-Qawasmeh (Eds.): DICTAP 2011, Part I, CCIS 166, pp. 131–145, 2011.

(VQEG) including the test procedure and subjective data analysis. A popular method for assessing image quality involves asking people to quantify their subjective impressions by selecting one of the five classes: Excellent, Good, Fair, Poor, Bad, from the quality scale (UIT-R [1]), then these opinions are converted into scores. Finally, the average of the scores is computed to get the Mean Opinion Score (MOS). Obviously, subjective tests are expensive and not applicable in tremendous number of situations. Objective measures aim to assess the visual quality of a perceived image automatically based on mathematics and computation methods are needed. Until now there is no one single image quality metric that can predict our subjective judgments of image quality because image quality judgments are influenced by a multitude of different types of visible signals, each weighted differently depending on the context under which a judgment is made. In other words a human observer can easily detect anomalies of a distorted image and judge its visual quality with no need to refer to the real scene, whereas a computer cannot. Research on objective visual quality can be classified in three folds depending on the information available. When the reference image is available the metrics belongs to the Full Reference (FR) methods. The simple and widely used Peak Signal -to -noise -Ratio (PSNR) and the Mean Structure Similarity Index (MSSIM) are both widely used FR metrics [2]. However, it is not always possible to get the reference images to assess image quality. When reference images are unavailable No Reference (NR) metrics are involved. No reference (NR) methods, which aim to quantify the quality of distorted image without any cue from its original version are generally conceived for specific distortion type and cannot be generalized for other distortions [3]. Reduced Reference (RR) is typically used when one can send side information with the processed image relating to the reference. Here, we focus on RR methods which provide a better trade-off between the quality rate accuracy and information required, as only small size of feature are extracted from the reference image. Recently, a number of authors have successfully introduced RR methods based on : image distortion modeling [4][5], human visual system (HVS) modeling [6][7], or finally natural image statistics modeling [8]. In [8], Z.wang et al introduced a RRIQA measure based on Steerable pyramids (a redundant transform of wavelets family). Although this method has known some success when tested on five types of distortion, it suffers from some weaknesses. First of all, steerable pyramids is a non-adaptive transform, and depends on a basis function. This later cannot fit all signals when this happens a wrong time-frequency representation of the signal is obtained. Consequently it is not sure that steerable pyramids will achieve the same success for other type of distortions. Furthermore, the wavelet transform provides a linear representation which cannot reflect the nonlinear masking phenomenon in human visual perception [9]. A novel decomposition method was introduced by Huang et al [10], named Empirical Mode decomposition (EMD). It aims to decompose non stationary and non linear signals to finite number of components : Intrinsic Mode Functions (IMF), and a residue. It was first used in signal analysis, then it attracted more researcher's attention. Few years later, Nunes et al [11] proposed an extension of this decomposition in the 2D case Bi-dimensional Empirical Mode Decomposition(BEMD). A number of authors have benefited from the BEMD in several image processing algorithms : image watermarking [12], texture image retrieval [13], and feature extraction [14]. In contrast to wavelet, EMD is nonlinear and adaptive method, it depends only on data since no basis function is needed. Motivated by the advantages of the BEMD, and to remedy the wavelet drawbacks discussed above, here we propose the use of BEMD as a representation domain. As distortions affects IMF coefficients and also their distribution. The investigation of IMF coefficients marginal distribution seems to be a reasonable choice. In the literature, most RR methods use a logistic function-based regression method to predict mean opinion scores from the values given by an objective measure. These scores are then compared in term of correlation with the existing subjective scores. The higher is the correlation, the more accurate is the objective measure. In addition to the objective measure introduced in this paper, an alternative approach to logistic function-based regression is investigated. It is an SVM-based classification, where the classification was conducted on each distortion set independently, according to the visual degradation level. The better is the classification accuracy the higher is the correlation of the objective measure with the HVS judgment. This paper is organized as follows. Section 2 presents the proposed IQA scheme. The BEMD and its algorithm are presented in Section 3. In Section 4, we describe the distortion measure. Section 5 explains how we conduct the experiments and presents some results of a comparison with existing methods. Finally, we give some concluding remarks.

2 IQA Proposed Scheme

In this paper, we propose a new IQA scheme based on the BEMD decomposition. This scheme provides a distance between a reference image and its distorted version as an output. This distance represents the error between both images and should have a good consistency with human judgment.

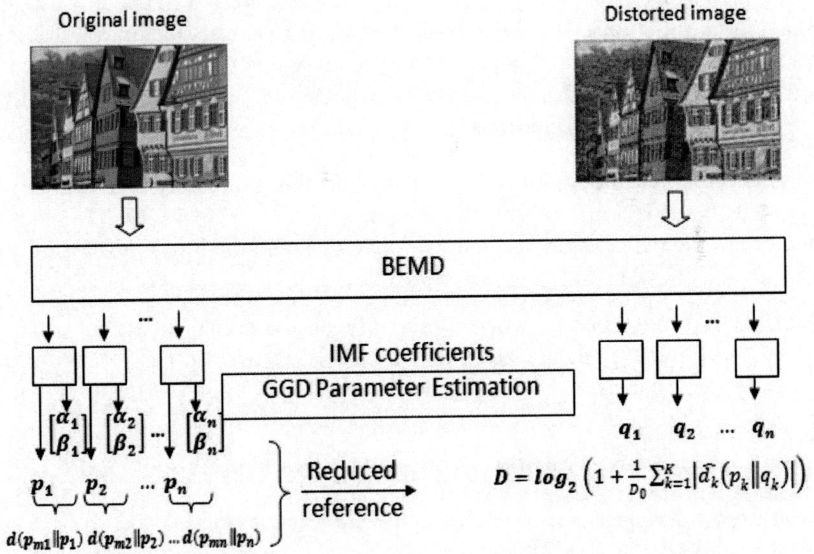

Fig. 1. The deployment scheme of the proposed RRIQA approach

The scheme consists in two stages as mentioned in **Fig.1**. First, a BEMD decomposition is employed to decompose the reference image at the sender side and the distorted image at the receiver side. Second, the features are extracted from the resulting IMFs based on modeling natural image statistics. The idea is that distortions make a degraded image appearing unnatural and affect image statistics. Measuring this unnaturalness can lead us to quantify the visual quality degradation. One way to do so is to consider the evolution of marginal distribution of IMF coefficients. This implies the availability of IMF coefficient histogram of the reference image at the receiver side. Using the histogram as a reduced reference raises the question of the amount of side information to be transmitted. If the bin size is coarse, we obtain a bad approximation accuracy but a small data rate while when the bin size is fine, we get a good accuracy but a heavier RR data rate. To avoid this problem it is more convenient to assume a theoretical distribution for the IMF marginal distribution and to estimate the parameters of the distribution. In this case the only side information to be transmitted consist of the estimated parameters and eventually an error between the the empirical distribution and the estimated one. The GGD model provides a good approximation of IMF coefficients histogram and this only with the use of two parameters (as explained in section 4). Moreover, we consider the fitting error between empirical and estimated IMF distribution. Finally, at the receiver side we use the extracted features to compute the global distance over all IMFs.

3 The Bi-dimensional Empirical Mode Decomposition

The Empirical Mode Decomposition (EMD) has been introduced [10] as a driven-data algorithm, since it is based purely on the properties observed in the data without predetermined basis functions. The main goal of EMD is to extract the oscillatory modes that represent the highest local frequency in a signal, while the remainders are considered as a residual. These modes are called Intrinsic Mode Functions (IMF). An IMF is a function that satisfies two conditions:

1- The function should be symmetric in time, and the number of extrema and zero crossings must be equal, or at most differ by one.
2- At any point, the mean value of the upper envelope, and the lower envelope must be zero.

The so called "sifting process" works iteratively on the signal to extract each IMF. Let $x(t)$ be the input signal, the algorithm of the EMD is summarized as follows : The sifting process consists in iterating from step 1 to 4 upon the detail signal $d(t)$

Empirical Mode Decomposition Algorithm

1. Identify all extrema of $x(t)$.
2. Interpolate between minima (resp. maxima), ending up with some envelope $e_{min}(t)$(resp. $e_{max}(t)$).
3. Compute the mean $m(t) = (e_{min}(t) + e_{max}(t))/2$.
4. Extract the detail $d(t) = x(t) - m(t)$.
5. Iterate on the residual $m(t)$.

until this later can be considered as zero mean. The resultant signal is designated as an IMF, then the residual will be considered as the input signal for the next IMF. The algorithm terminates when a stopping criterion or a desired number of IMFs is reached. After IMFs are extracted through the sifting process, the original signal $x(t)$ can be represented like this :

$$x(t) = \sum_{j=1}^{n} Imf_j(t) + m(t) \tag{1}$$

where Imf_j is the jth extracted IMF and n is the total number of IMFs.

In two dimensions (Bi-dimensional Empirical Mode Decomposition : BEMD), the algorithm remains the same as for a single dimension with a few changes : the curve fitting for extrema interpolation will be replaced with a surface fitting, this increases the computational complexity for identifying extrema and specially for extrema interpolation. Several two dimensions EMD versions have been developed [15][16], each of them uses its own interpolation method. Bhuiyan et al [17] proposed an interpolation based on statistical order filters. From a computational cost standpoint, this is a fast implementation, as only one iteration is required for each IMF. **Fig.2** illustrates an application of the BEMD on the "Buildings" image:

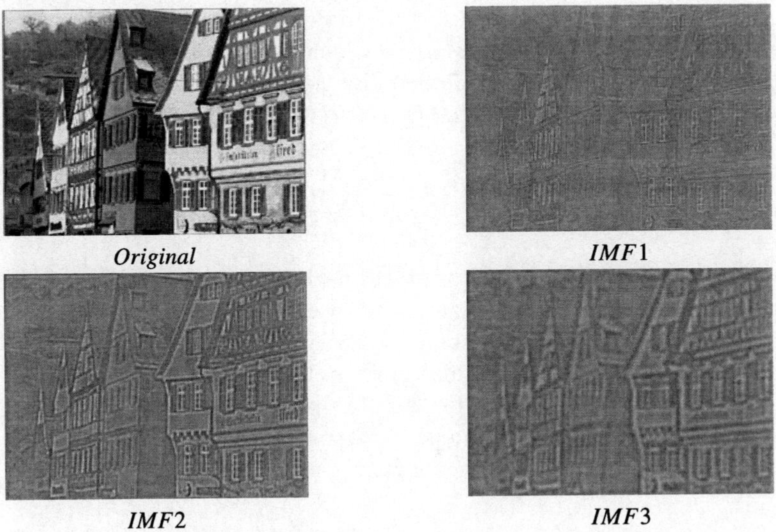

Fig. 2. The "Buildings" image decomposition using the BEMD

4 Distortion Measure

The resulting IMFs from an BEMD show the highest frequencies at each decomposition level, this frequencies decrease as the order of the IMF increases. For example, the first IMF contains a higher frequencies than the second one. Furthermore, in a particular

IMF the coefficients histogram exhibits a non Gaussian behavior, with a sharp peak at zero and heavier tails than the Gaussian distribution as can be seen in **Fig.3 (a)**. Such a distribution can be well fitted with a two parameters Generalized Gaussian Density (GGD) model given by:

$$p(x) = \frac{\beta}{2\alpha\Gamma(\frac{1}{\beta})} \exp(-(\frac{|x|}{\alpha})^{\beta}) \tag{2}$$

where $\Gamma(z) = \int_0^\infty e^{-t} t^{z-1} dt, z > 0$ represents the Gamma function, α is the scale parameter that describes the standard deviation of the density, and β is the shape parameter.

In the conception of an RR method, we should consider a transmission context, where an image in the sender side with a perfect quality have to be transmitted to a receiver side. The RR method consists in extracting relevant features from the reference image and use them as a reduced description. However, the selection of features is a critical step. On one hand, extracted features should be sensitive to a large type of distortions to guarantee the genericity, and also be sensitive to different distortion levels. On the other hand, extracted features should have a minimal size as possible. Here, we propose a marginal distribution-based RR method since the marginal distribution of IMF coefficients changes from a distortion type to another as illustrated in **Fig.3** (b), (c) and (d). Let us consider IMF_O as an IMF from the original image and IMF_D its corresponding from the distorted image. To quantify the quality degradation, we use the Kullback Leibler Divergence (KLD) which is recognized as a convenient way to compute divergence between two Probability Density Functions (PDFs). Assuming that $p(x)$ and $q(x)$ are the PDFs of IMF_O and IMF_D respectively, the KLD between them is defined as:

$$d(p\|q) = \int p(x) \log \frac{p(x)}{q(x)} dx \tag{3}$$

For this aim, the histograms of the original image must be available at the receiver side. Even if we can send the histogram to the receiver side it will increase the size of the feature significantly and causes some inconvenients. The GGD model provides an efficient way to get back coefficients histogram, so that only two parameters are needed to be transmitted to the receiver side. In the following, we note $p_m(x)$ the approximation of $p(x)$ using a 2- parameters GGD model. Furthermore, our feature will contains a third characteristic which is the prediction error defined as the KLD between $p(x)$ and $p_m(x)$:

$$d(p_m\|p) = \int p_m(x) \log \frac{p_m(x)}{p(x)} dx \tag{4}$$

In practice, this quantity can be computed as it follows:

$$d(p_m\|p) = \sum_{i=1}^{L} P_m(i) \log \frac{P_m(i)}{P(i)} dx \tag{5}$$

Where $P(i)$ and $P_m(i)$ are the normalized heights of the ith histogram bins, and L is the number of bins in the histograms. Unlike the sender side, at the receiver side we first

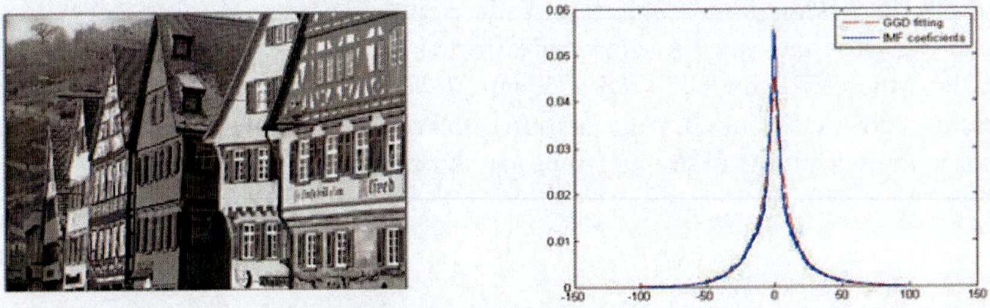

(*a*)

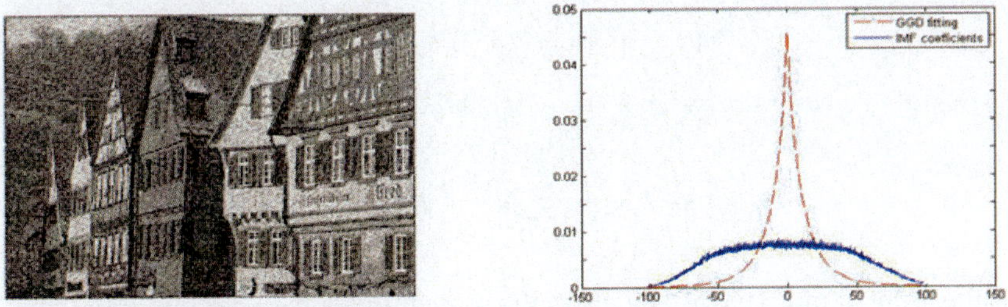

(*b*)

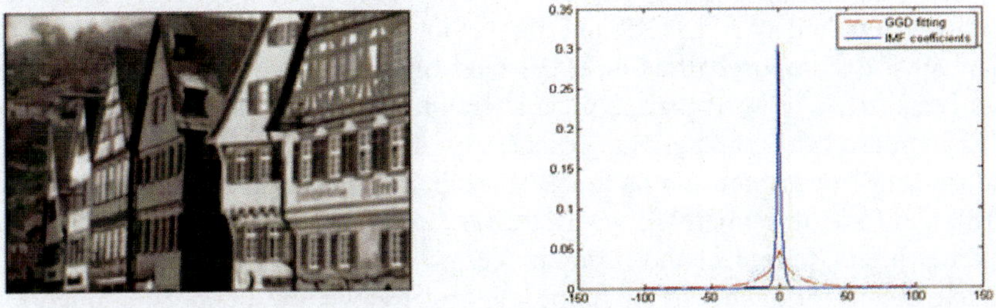

(*c*)

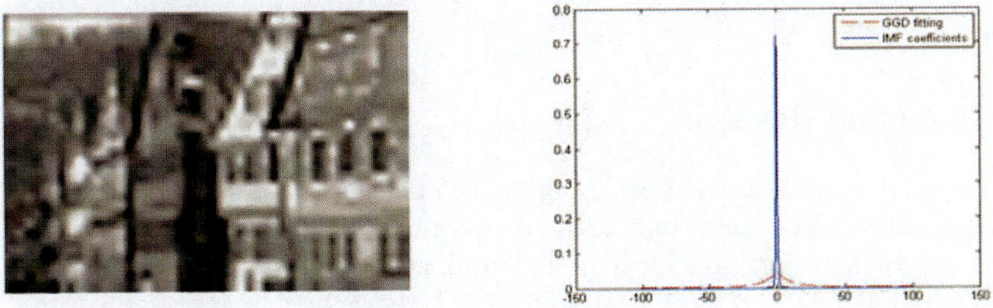

(*d*)

Fig. 3. Histograms of IMF coefficients under various distortion types. *(a)* original "Buildings" image, *(b)* white noise contaminated image, *(c)* blurred image, *(d)* transmission errors distorted image. *(Solid curves)* : histogram of IMF coefficients. *(Dashed curves)* : GGD model fitted to the histogram of IMF coefficients in the original image. The horizontal axis represents the IMF coefficients, while the vertical axis represents the frequency of these coefficients compute the KLD between $q(x)$ and $p_m(x)$ (equation (6)). We do not fit $q(x)$ with a GGD model cause we are not sure that the distorted image is still a natural one and consequently if the GGD model is still adequate. Indeed the distortion introduced by the processing can greatly modify the marginal distribution of the IMF coefficients. Therefore it is more accurate to use the empirical distribution of the processed image.

$$d(p_m\|q) = \int p_m(x)\log\frac{p_m(x)}{q(x)}dx \tag{6}$$

Then the KLD between $p(x)$ and $q(x)$ are estimated as:

$$\widehat{d}(p\|q) = d(p_m\|q) - d(p_m\|p) \tag{7}$$

Finally the overall distortion between an original and distorted image is as it follows:

$$D = \log_2(1 + \frac{1}{D_o}\sum_{k=1}^{K}|\widehat{d}^k(p^k\|q^k)|) \tag{8}$$

where K is the number of IMFs, p^k and q^k are the probability density functions of the kth IMF in the reference and distorted images, respectively. $\widehat{d^k}$ is the estimation of the KLD between p^k and q^k, and D_o is a constant used to control the scale of the distortion measure.

The proposed method is a real RR one thanks to the reduced number of features used : the image is decomposed into four IMFs and from each IMF we extract only three parameters $\{\alpha, \beta, d(p_m\|p)\}$ so that 12 parameters in the total. Increasing the number of IMF will increase the computational complexity of the algorithm and thus the size of the feature set. To estimate the parameters (α, β) we used the moment matching method [18], and for extracting IMFs we used a fast and adaptive BEMD [17] based on statistical order filters, to replace the sifting process which is time consuming.

To evaluate the performances of the proposed measure, we use the logistic function-based regression which takes the distances and provides the objective scores. Another alternative to the logistic function-based regression is proposed and it is based on SVM classifier. More details about the performance evaluation are given in the next section.

5 Experimental Results

Our experimental test was carried out using the LIVE database [19]. It is constructed from 29 high resolution images and contains seven sets of distorted and scored images, obtained by the use of five types of distortion at different levels. Set1 and 2 are JPEG2000 compressed images, set 3 and 4 are JPEG compressed images, set 5, 6 and 7 are respectively : Gaussian blur, white noise and transmission errors distorted images. The 29 reference images shown in **Fig.4** have very different textural characteristics, various percentages of homogeneous regions, edges and details.

To score the images one can use either the MOS or the Differential Mean Option Score (DMOS) which is the difference between "reference" and "processed" Mean Opinion Score. For LIVE database, the MOS of the reference images is equal to zero, and then the difference mean opinion score (DMOS) and the MOS are the same.

Fig. 4. The 29 reference images of the LIVE database

To illustrate the visual impact of the different distortions, **Fig.5** presents the reference image and the distorted images. In order to examine how well the proposed metric correlates with the human judgement, the given images have the same subjective visual quality according to the DMOS. As we can see, the distance between the distorted images and their reference image is of the same order of magnitude for all distortions.

In Fig.6, we show an application of the measure in equation (8) to five white noise contaminated images, as we can see the distance increases as the distortion level increases, this demonstrates a good consistency with human judgement.

The tests consist in choosing a reference image and one of its distorted versions. Both images are considered as entries of the scheme given in Fig.1. After feature extraction step in the BEMD domain a global distance is computed between the reference and distorted image as mentioned in equation (8). This distance represents an objective measure for image quality assessment. It produces a number and that number needs to be correlated with the subjective MOS. This can be done using two different protocols:

Logistic function based-regression. The subjective scores must be compared in term of correlation with the objective scores. These objective scores are computed from the values generated by the objective measure (the global distance in our case), using a nonlinear function according to the Video Quality Expert Group (VQEG) Phase I FR-TV [20]. Here, we use a four parameter logistic function given by :

$logistic(\gamma,D)=\frac{\gamma_1-\gamma_2}{1+e^{-(\frac{D-\gamma_3}{\gamma_4})}}+\gamma_2$, where $\gamma=(\gamma_1,\gamma_2,\gamma_3,\gamma_4)$. Then, $DMOS_p=logistic(\gamma,D)$

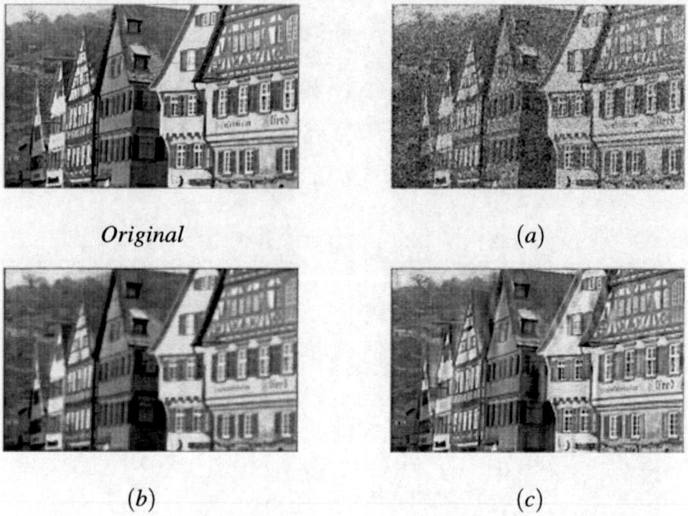

Fig. 5. An application of the proposed measure to different distorted images. ((a): white noise, D = 9.36, DMOS =56.68), ((b): Gaussian blur, D= 9.19, DMOS =56.17), ((c): Transmission errors, D= 8.07, DMOS =56.51).

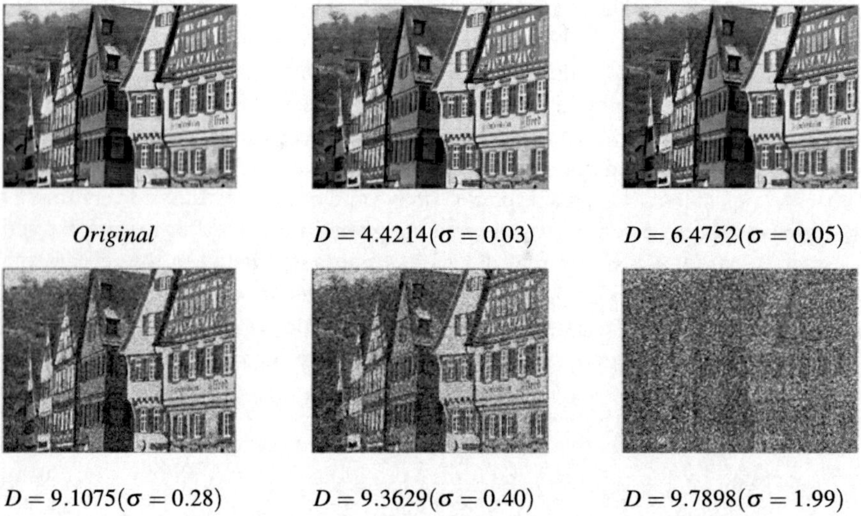

Fig. 6. An application of the proposed measure to different levels of Gaussian white noise contaminated images

Fig.7 shows the scatter plot of DMOS versus the model prediction for the JPEG2000, Transmission errors, White noise and Gaussian blurred distorted images. We can easily remark how well is the fitting specially for the Transmission errors and the white noise distortions.

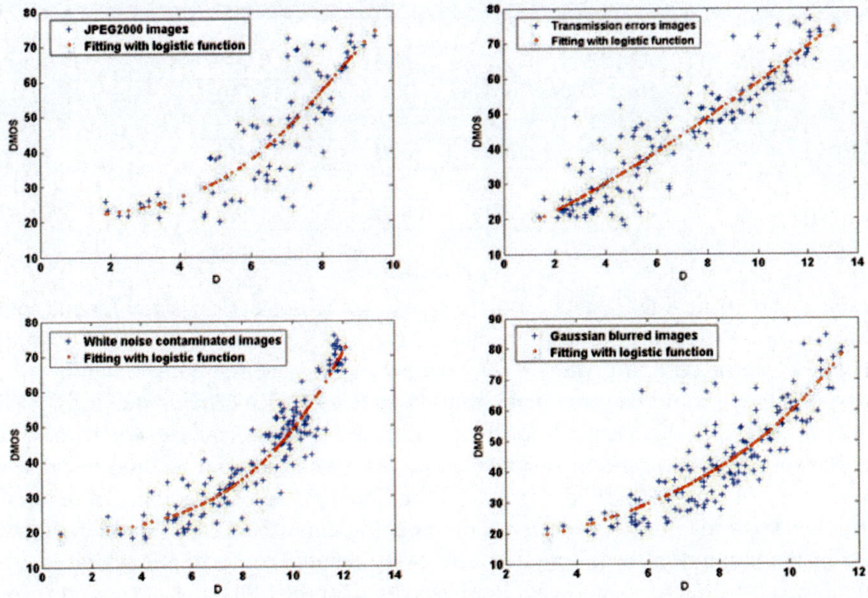

Fig. 7. Scatter plots of (DMOS) versus the model prediction for the JPEG2000, Transmission errors, White noise and Gaussian blurred distorted images

Once the nonlinear mapping is achieved, we obtain the predicted objective quality scores (DMOSp). To compare the subjective and objective quality scores, several metrics were introduced by the VQEG. In our study, we compute the correlation coefficient to evaluate the accuracy prediction and the Rank order coefficient to evaluate the monotonicity prediction. These metrics are defined as follows:

$$CC = \frac{\sum_{i=1}^{N}(DMOS(i) - \overline{DMOS})(DMOSp(i) - \overline{DMOSp})}{\sqrt{\sum_{i=1}^{N}(DMOS(i) - \overline{DMOS})^2}\sqrt{\sum_{i=1}^{N}(DMOSp(i) - \overline{DMOSp})^2}} \tag{9}$$

$$ROCC = 1 - \frac{6\sum_{i=1}^{N}(DMOS(i) - DMOSp(i))^2}{N(N^2 - 1)} \tag{10}$$

where the index i denotes the image sample and N denotes the number of samples.

Table 1. Performance evaluation for the quality measure using LIVE database

Dataset	Noise	Blur	Error
Correlation Coefficient (CC)			
BEMD	0.9332	0.8405	0.9176
Pyramids	0.8902	0.8874	0.9221
PSNR	0.9866	0.7742	0.8811
MSSIM	0.9706	0.9361	0.9439
Rank-Order Correlation Coefficient (ROCC)			
BEMD	0.9068	0.8349	0.9065
Pyramids	0.8699	0.9147	0.9210
PSNR	0.9855	0.7729	0.8785
MSSIM	0.9718	0.9421	0.9497

Table 1 shows the final results for three types : white noise, Gaussian blur and transmission errors. We report the results obtained for two RR metrics (BEMD, Pyramids) and two FR metrics (PSNR, MSSIM). As the FR metrics use more information we can expect than they should be more performing than RR metrics. This is true for MSSIM but not for the PSNR that perform poorly as compared to the RR metrics for all the types of degradation except for the noise perturbation. As we can see, our method ensures better prediction accuracy (higher correlation coefficients), better prediction monotonicity (higher Spearman rank-order correlation coefficients) than the steerable pyramids based method, and this for the white noise. Also comparing to PSNR which is a FR method, we can observe a significant improvements for the blur and transmission errors distortions.

We notice that we carried out other experiments for using the KLD between probability density functions (PDFs) by estimating the GGD parameters at the sender and the receiver side, but the results were not satisfying comparing to the proposed measure. This can be explained by the strength of the distortion that makes reference image lose its naturalness and then an estimation of the GGD parameters at the receiver side is not suitable. To go further, we thought to examine how an IMF behaves with a distortion type. For this aim, we conducted the same experiments as above but on each IMF separately. Table 2 shows the results.

As observed, the sensitivity of an IMF to the quality degradation changes depending on the distortion type and the order of the IMF. For instance, the performance decreases for the "Transmission errors" distortion as the order of the IMF increases. Also, some

Table 2. Performance evaluation using IMFs separately

	White Noise	Gaussian Blur	Transmission errors
IMF_1	CC = 0.91 ROCC = 0.90	CC = 0.74 ROCC = 0.75	CC = 0.87 ROCC = 0.87
IMF_2	CC = 0.75 ROCC = 0.73	CC = 0.82 ROCC = 0.81	CC = 0.86 ROCC = 0.85
IMF_3	CC = 0.85 ROCC = 0.87	CC = 0.77 ROCC = 0.73	CC = 0.75 ROCC = 0.75
IMF_4	CC = 0.86 ROCC = 0.89	CC = 0.41 ROCC = 0.66	CC = 0.75 ROCC = 0.74

IMFs are more sensitive for one set, while for the other sets it is not. A weighting factor according to the sensitivity of the IMF seems to be a good way to improve the accuracy of the proposed method. The weights are chosen in a way to give more importance for the IMFs which give better correlation values. To do so, the weights have been tuned experimentally, since no emerging combination can be applied in our case. Let us take the "Transmission errors" set for example, if w_1, w_2, w_3, w_4 are the weights for the $IMF_1, IMF_2, IMF_3, IMF_4$ respectively, then we should have $w_1 > w_2 > w_3 > w_4$. We change the value of $w_i, i = 1, ..., 4$ until reaching a better results. Some improvements have been obtained, but only for the Gaussian blur set as CC=0.88 and ROCC=0.87. This improvement around 5% is promising as the weighing procedure is very rough. One can expect further improvement by using a more refined combination of the IMF. Detailed experiments on the weighting factors remain for future work.

SVM-based classification. Traditionally, RRIQA methods use the logistic function-based regression to obtain objective scores. In this approach one extracts features from images and trains a learning algorithm to classify the images based on the feature extracted. The effectiveness of this approach is linked to the choice of discriminative features and the choice of the multiclass classification strategy [21]. M.saad et al [22] proposed a NRIQA which trained a statistical model using the SVM classifier, in the test step objective scores are obtained. Distorted images : we use three sets of distorted images. Set 1 :white noise, set 2 :Gaussian blur, set 3 : fast fading. Each set contains 145 images. The determination of the training and the testing sets has been realized thanks to the cross validation (leave one out). Let us consider a specific set (e.g white noise). Since the DMOS values are in the interval [0,100], this later was divided into five equal intervals]0,20],]20,40],]40,60],]60,80],]80,100] corresponding to the quality classes : Bad, Poor, Fair, Good Excellent, respectively. Thus the set of distorted images is divided into five subsets according to the DMOS associated to each image in the set. Then at each iteration we trained a multiclass SVM (five classes) using the leave one out cross validation. In other words each iteration involves using a single observation from the original sample as the validation data, and the remaining observations as the training data. This is repeated such that each observation in the sample is used once as the validation data.The Radial Basis Function RBF kernel was utilized and a feature selection step was carried out to select its parameters that give a better classification accuracy. The entries of the SVM are formed by the distances computed in equation (7). For the ith distorted image, $X_i = [d_1, d_2, d_3, d_4]$ represents the vector of features (only four IMFs are used). Table 3 shows the classification accuracy per set of distortion. In the worst case (Gaussian blur) only one out of ten images is misclassified.

Table 3. Classification accuracy for each distortion type set

Distortion type	Classification accuracy
White Noise	96.55%
Gaussian Blur	89.55%
Fast Fading	93.10%

In the case of logistic function-based regression, the top value of the correlation coefficient that we can obtain is equal to 1 as a full correlation between objective and subjective scores while for the classification case, the classification accuracy can be interpreted as the probability by which we are sure that the objective measure correlates well with the human judgment, thus a classification accuracy that equal to 100% is equivalent to a CC that equal to 1. This leads to a new alternative of the logistic function-based regression with no need to predicted DMOS. Thus, one can ask which one is more preferable? the logistic function-based regression or the SVM-based classification. From the first view, the SVM-based classification seems to be more powerful. Nevertheless this gain on performances is obtained at the price of an increasing complexity. On the one hand a complex training is required before one can use this strategy. On the other hand when this training step has been done the classification is straightforward.

6 Conclusion

A reduced reference method for image quality assessment is introduced, it's a new one since it is based on the BEMD, also the classification framework is proposed as an alternative of the logistic function-based regression. This later produces objective scores in order to verify the correlation with subjective scores, while the classification approach provides an accuracy rates which explain how the proposed measure is consistent with the human judgement. Promising results are given demonstrating the effectiveness of the method especially for the white noise distortion. As a future work, we expect to increase the sensitiveness of the proposed method to other types of degradations to the level obtained for the white noise contamination. We plan to use an alternative model for the marginal distribution of BEMD coefficients. The Gaussian Scale Mixture seems to be a convenient solution for this purpose. We also plan to extend this work to other types of distortion using a new image database.

References

1. UIT-R Recommendation BT. 500-10,Méthodologie d'évaluation subjective de la qualité des images de télévision. tech. rep., UIT, Geneva, Switzerland (2000)
2. Wang, Z., Bovik, A.C., Sheikh, H.R., Simoncelli, E.P.: Image quality assessment: From error visibility to structural similarity. IEEE Transactions on Image Processing 13(4), 1624–1639 (2004)
3. Wang, Z., Sheikh, H.R., Bovik, A.C.: No-reference perceptual quality assessment of JPEG compressed images. In: IEEE International Conference on Image Processing, pp. 477–480 (2002)
4. Gunawan, I.P., Ghanbari, M.: Reduced reference picture quality estimation by using local harmonic amplitude information. In: Proc. London Commun. Symp., pp. 137–140 (September 2003)
5. Kusuma, T.M., Zepernick, H.-J.: A reduced-reference perceptual quality metric for in-service image quality assessment. In: Proc. Joint 1st Workshop Mobile Future and Symp. Trends Commun., pp. 71–74 (October 2003)

6. Carnec, M., Le Callet, P., Barba, D.: An image quality assessment method based on perception of structural information. In: Proc. IEEE Int. Conf. Image Process., vol. 3, pp. 185–188 (September 2003)
7. Carnec, M., Le Callet, P., Barba, D.: Visual features for image quality assessment with reduced reference. In: Proc. IEEE Int. Conf. Image Process., vol. 1, pp. 421–424 (September 2005)
8. Wang, Z., Simoncelli, E.: Reduced-reference image quality assessment using a wavelet-domain natural image statistic model. In: Proc. of SPIE Human Vision and Electronic Imaging, pp. 149–159 (2005)
9. Foley, J.: Human luminence pattern mechanisms: Masking experiments require a new model. J. of Opt. Soc. of Amer. A 11(6), 1710–1719 (1994)
10. Huang, N.E., Shen, Z., Long, S.R., et al.: The empirical mode decomposition and the hilbert spectrum for non-linear and non-stationary time series analysis. Proc. Roy. Soc. Lond. A,. 454, 903–995 (1998)
11. Nunes, J., Bouaoune, Y., Delechelle, E., Niang, O., Bunel, P.: Image analysis by bidimensional empirical mode decomposition. Image and Vision Computing 21(12), 1019–1026 (2003)
12. Taghia, J., Doostari, M., Taghia, J.: An Image Watermarking Method Based on Bidimensional Empirical Mode Decomposition. In: Congress on Image and Signal Processing (CISP 2008), pp. 674–678 (2008)
13. Andaloussi, J., Lamard, M., Cazuguel, G., Tairi, H., Meknassi, M., Cochener, B., Roux, C.: Content based Medical Image Retrieval: use of Generalized Gaussian Density to model BEMD IMF. In: World Congress on Medical Physics and Biomedical Engineering, vol. 25(4), pp. 1249–1252 (2009)
14. Wan, J., Ren, L., Zhao, C.: Image Feature Extraction Based on the Two-Dimensional Empirical Mode Decomposition. In: Congress on Image and Signal Processing, CISP 2008, vol. 1, pp. 627–631 (2008)
15. Linderhed, A.: Variable sampling of the empirical mode decomposition of twodimensional signals. Int. J. Wavelets Multresolution Inform. Process. 3, 435–452 (2005)
16. Damerval, C., Meignen, S., Perrier, V.: A fast algorithm for bidimensional EMD. IEEE Sig. Process. Lett. 12, 701–704 (2005)
17. Bhuiyan, S., Adhami, R., Khan, J.: A novel approach of fast and adaptive bidimensional empirical mode decomposition. In: IEEE International Conference on Acoustics, Speech and Signal Processing, 2008 (ICASSP 2008), pp. 1313–1316 (2008)
18. Van de Wouwer, G., Scheunders, P., Van Dyck, D.: Statistical texture characterization from discrete wavelet representations. IEEE transactions on image processing 8(4), 592–598 (1999)
19. Sheikh, H., Wang, Z., Cormack, L., Bovik, A.: LIVE image quality assessment database. 2005-2010), `http://live.ece.utexas.edu/research/quality`
20. Rohaly, A., Libert, J., Corriveau, P., Webster, A., et al.: Final report from the video quality experts group on the validation of objective models of video quality assessment. ITU-T Standards Contribution COM, pp. 9–80
21. Demirkesen, C., Cherifi, H.: A comparison of multiclass SVM methods for real world natural scenes. In: Blanc-Talon, J., Bourennane, S., Philips, W., Popescu, D., Scheunders, P. (eds.) ACIVS 2008. LNCS, vol. 5259, pp. 752–763. Springer, Heidelberg (2008)
22. Saad, M., Bovik, A.C., Charrier, C.: A DCT statistics-based blind image quality index. IEEE Signal Processing Letters, 583–586 (2010)

Vascular Structures Registration in 2D MRA Images

Marwa Hermassi, Hejer Jelassi, and Kamel Hamrouni

BP 37, Le Belvédère 1002 Tunis, Tunisia
m.hermassi@gmail.com, kamel.hamrouni@enit.rnu.tn,
hejer_enit@yahoo.fr

Abstract. In this paper we present a registration method for cerebral vascular structures in the 2D MRA images. The method is based on bifurcation structures. The usual registration methods, based on point matching, largely depend on the branching angels of each bifurcation point. This may cause multiple feature correspondence due to similar branching angels. Hence, bifurcation structures offer better registration. Each bifurcation structure is composed of a master bifurcation point and its three connected neighbors. The characteristic vector of each bifurcation structure consists of the normalized branching angle and length, and it is invariant against translation, rotation, scaling, and even modest distortion. The validation of the registration accuracy is particularly important. Virtual and physical images may provide the gold standard for validation. Also, image databases may in the future provide a source for the objective comparison of different vascular registration methods.

Keywords: Bifurcation structures, feature extraction, image registration, vascular structures.

1 Introduction

Image registration is the process of establishing pixel-to-pixel correspondence between two images of the same scene. It's quite difficult to have an overview on the registration methods due to the important number of publications concerning this subject such as [1] and [2]. Some authors presented excellent overview of medical images registration methods [3], [4] and [5]. Image registration is based on four elements: features, similarity criterion, transformation and optimization method. Many registration approaches are described in the literature. Geometric approaches or feature-feature registration methods, volumetric approaches also known as image-image approaches and finally mixed methods. The first methods consist on automatically or manually extracting features from image. Features can be significant regions, lines or points. They should be distinct, spread all over the image and efficiently detectable in both images. They are expected to be stable in time to stay at fixed positions during the whole experiment [2]. The second approaches optimize a similarity measure that directly compares voxel intensities between two images. These registration methods are favored for registering tissue images [6]. The mixed methods are combinations between the two methods cited before. [7] Developed an approach based on block matching using volumetric features combined to a geometric algorithm, the Iterative

H. Cherifi, J.M. Zain, and E. El-Qawasmeh (Eds.): DICTAP 2011, Part I, CCIS 166, pp. 146–160, 2011.

Closest Point algorithm (ICP). The ICP algorithm uses the distance between surfaces and lines in images. Distance is a geometric similarity criterion, the same as the Hausdorff distance or the distance maps such as used in [8] and [9]. The Euclidian distance is used to match points features,. Volumetric criterion are based on points intensity such as the Lowest Square (LS) criterion used in monomodal registration, correlation coefficient, correlation factor, Woods criterion [10] and the Mutual Information [11]. Transformation can be linear such as affine, rigid and projective transformations. It can be non linear such as functions base, Radial Basis Functions (RBF) and the Free Form Deformations (FFD). The last step in the registration process is the optimization of the similarity criterion. It consists on maximizing or minimizing the criterion. We can cite the Weighed Least Square [12], the one-plus-one revolutionary optimizer developed by Styner and al. [13] and used by Chillet and al. in [8]. An overview of the optimization methods is presented on [14]. The structure of the cerebral vascular network, shown in figure 1, presents anatomical invariants which motivates for using robust features such as bifurcation points as they are a stable indicator for blood flow.

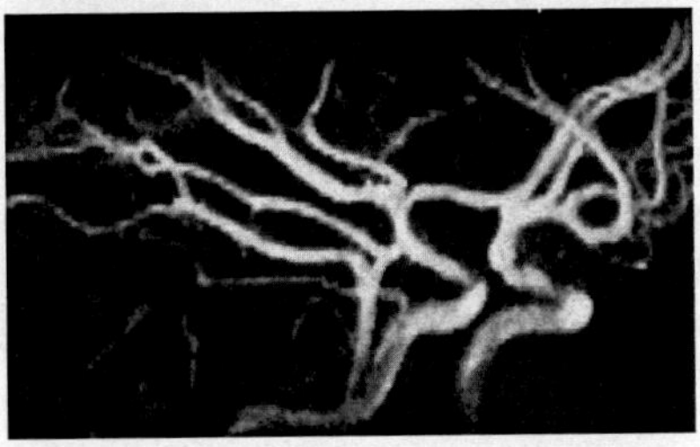

Fig. 1. Vascular cerebral vessels

Points matching techniques are based on corresponding points on both images. These approaches are composed of two steps: feature matching and transformation estimation. The matching process establishes the correspondence between two features groups. Once the matched pairs are efficient, transformation parameters can be identified easily and precisely. The branching angles of each bifurcation point are used to produce a probability for every pair of points. As these angles have a coarse precision which leads to similar bifurcation points, the matching won't be unique and reliable to guide registration. In this view Chen et al. [15] proposed a new structural characteristic for the feature-based retinal images registration.

The proposed method consists on a structure matching technique. The bifurcation structure is composed of a master bifurcation point and its three connected neighbors. The characteristic vector of each bifurcation structure is composed the normalized branching angles and lengths. The idea is to set a transformation obtained from the feature matching process and to perform registration then. If doesn't work, another solution has to be tested to minimize the error. We propose to use this technique to vascular structures in 2D Magnetic Resonance angiographic images.

2 Pretreatment Steps

2.1 Segmentation

For the segmentation of the vascular network, we use its connectivity characteristic. [16] proposes a technique based on the mathematical morphology which provides a robust transformation, the morphological construction. It requires two images: a

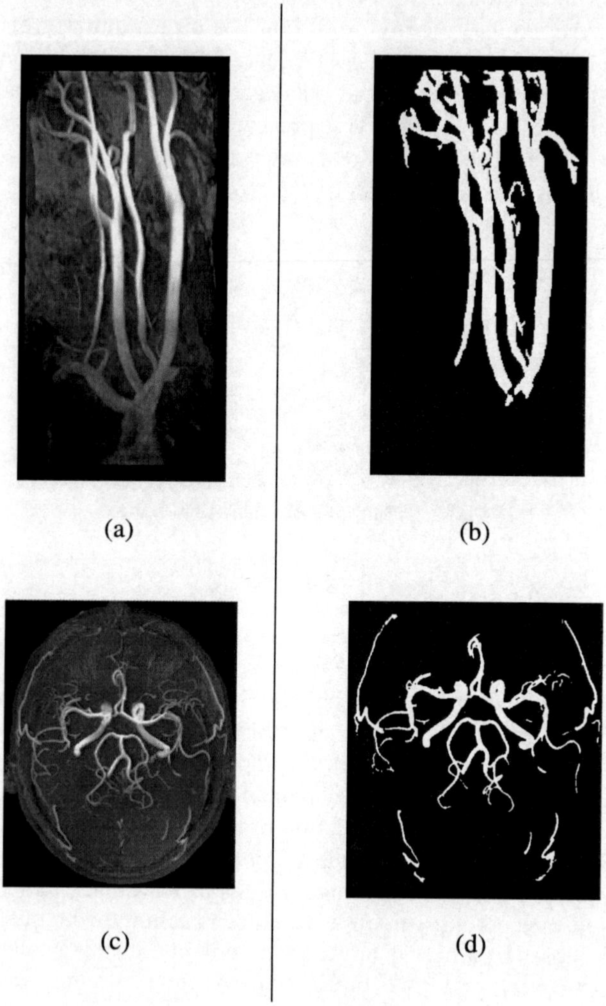

Fig. 2. Segmentation result. (a) and (c) Original image. (b) and (d)Segmented image.

mask image and a marker image and operates by iterating until idem potency a geodesic dilatation of the marker image with respect to the mask image. Applying a morphological algorithm, named "Toggle mapping", on the original image followed by a transformation "top hat" which extract clear details of the image provides the mask image. The size of the structuring element is chosen in a way to improve first the vascular vessels borders in the original image, and then to extract all the details which belong to the vascular network. These extracted details may contain other parasite or pathological objects which are not connected to the vascular network. To eliminate these objects, we apply the suppremum opening with linear and oriented structuring elements. The resulting image will be considered as the marker image. The morphological construction is finally applied with the obtained mask and marker images. The result of image segmentation is shown on figure 2.

2.2 Skeletonization

Skeletonization consists on reducing a form in a set of lines. The interest is that it provides a simplified version of the object while keeping the same homotopy and isolates the related elements. Many skeletonization approaches exist such as topological thinning, distance maps extraction, analytical calculation and the burning front simulation. An overview of the skeletonization methods is presented in [17]. In this work, we opt for a topological thinning skeletonization. It consists on eroding little by little the objects' border until the image is centered and thin. Let X be an object of the image and B the structuring element. The skeleton is obtained by removing from X the result of erosion of X by B.

$$XoB^i = X \setminus ((((X \ominus B^1) \ominus B^2) \ominus B^3) \ominus B^4) . \tag{1}$$

The B^i are obtained following a Π/4 rotation of the structuring element. They are four in number shown in figure 3. Figure 4 shows different iterations of skeletonization of a segmented image.

Fig. 3. Different structured elements, following a Π/4 rotation

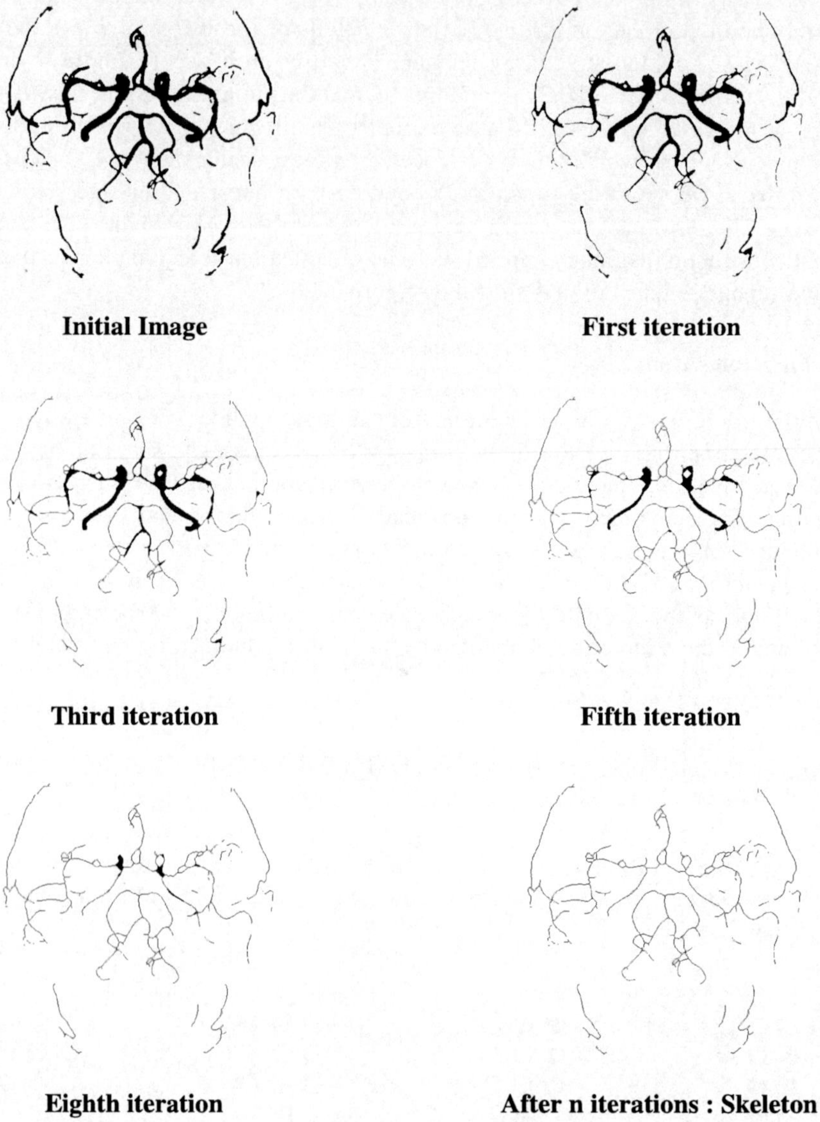

Fig. 4. Resulting skeleton after applying an iterative topological thinning on the segmented image

3 Bifurcation Structures Extraction

It is natural to explore and establishes a vascularization relation between two angiographic images because the vascular vessels are robust and stable geometric transformations and intensity change. In this work we use the bifurcation structure, shown on figure 5, for the angiographic images registration.

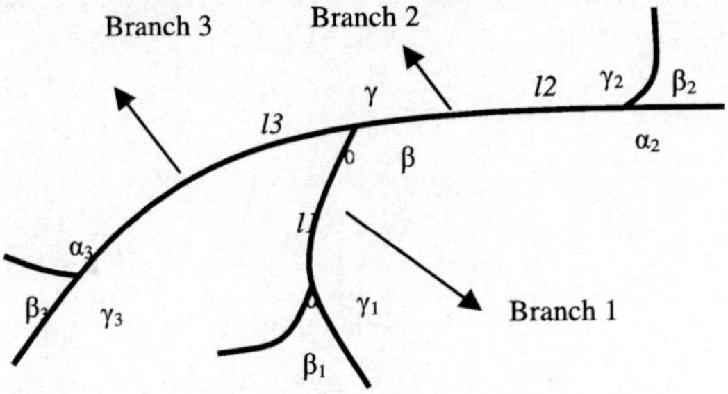

Fig. 5. The bifurcation structure is composed of a master bifurcation point and its three connected neighbors

The structure is composed of a master bifurcation point and its three connected neighbors. The master point has three branches with lengths numbered 1, 2, 3 and angles numbered α, β, and γ, where each branch is connected to a bifurcation point. The characteristic vector of each bifurcation structure is:

$$\tilde{x} = [l_1, \alpha, \alpha_1, \beta_1, \gamma_1, l_2, \beta, \alpha_2, \beta_2, \gamma_2, l_3, \alpha_3, \beta_3, \gamma_3] \quad . \tag{2}$$

Where l_i and α_i are respectively the length and the angle normalized with:

$$\begin{cases} l_i = length \quad of \quad the \quad branch \quad i \Big/ (\sum_{i=1}^{3} lengthes \quad i) \\ \alpha_i = angle \quad of \quad the \quad branch \quad i \quad in \quad degrees/360° \end{cases} \quad . \tag{3}$$

In the angiographic images, bifurcations points are obvious visual characteristics and can be recognized by their T shape with three branches around. Let P be a point of the image. In a 3x3 window, P has 8 neighbors Vi (i∈{1..8}) which take 1 or 0 as value. Pix is the number of pixel corresponding to 1 in the neighborhood of P is:

$$Pix(P) = \sum_{i=1}^{8} Vi \quad . \tag{4}$$

Finally, the bifurcation points of the image are defined by:

$$Pts\_bifurcation=\{\text{the points } P_{(i,j)} \text{ as } Pix(P_{(i,j)})\geq 3;(i,j)\in(m,n) \text{ where } m \text{ and } n \text{ are the dimensions of the image}\}\ . \quad (5)$$

To calculate the branching angles, we consider a circle of radius R and centered in P [18]. This circle intercepts the three branches in three points (I1, I2, I3) with coordinates respectively (x_1, y_1), (x_2, y_2) and (x_3, y_3). The angle of each branch relative to the horizontal is given by:

$$\theta_i = arctg(\frac{y_i - y_0}{x_i - x_0}) \quad . \quad (6)$$

Where θ_i is the angle of the ith branch relative to the horizontal and (x_0, y_0) are the coordinates of the point P. The angel vector of the bifurcation point is written:

$$Angle\_Vector=\left[\alpha=\theta_2-\theta_1 \quad \beta=\theta_3-\theta_2 \quad \gamma=\theta_1-\theta_3\right] \quad . \quad (7)$$

Where θ_1, θ_2 et θ_3 correspond to the angles of each branch of the bifurcation point relative to the horizontal. After the localization of the bifurcation points, we start the tracking of the bifurcation structure. The aim is the extraction of the characteristic vector. Let P be the master bifurcation point, P_1, P_2 and P_3 three bifurcation points, neighbors of P. To establish if there is a connection between P and its three neighbors we explore its neighborhood. We proceed like presented in algorithm 1 and shown in figure 6.

Algorithm 1. Search of the connected neighbors

V ← P

Repeat

In a 3x3 window of V search for Vi = 1
If true then is Vi a bifurcation point
Until Vi corresponds to a bifurcation point.

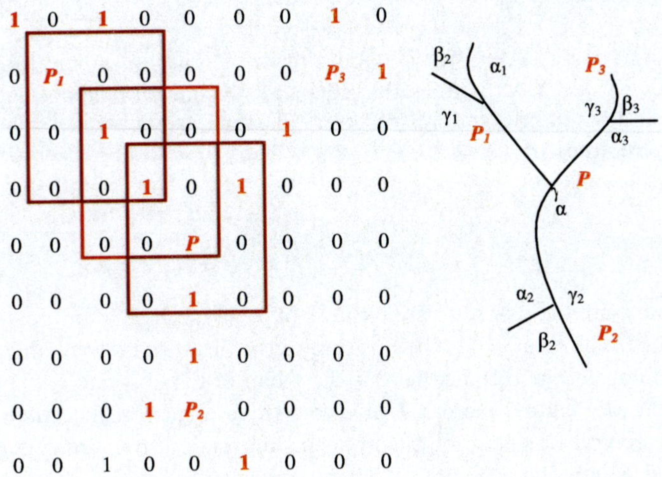

(a) (b)

Fig. 6. Feature vector extraction. (a) Example of search in the neighborhood of the master bifurcation point. (b) Master bifurcation point, its neighbors ad its angles and their corresponding angles.

Each point of the structure is defined by its coordinates. So, let (x_0, y_0), (x_1, y_1), (x_2, y_2) et (x_3, y_3) be the coordinates respectively of P, P_1, P_2 et P_3. We have:

$$\begin{cases} l_1 = d(P,P_1) = \sqrt{(x_1 - x_0)^2 + (y_1 - y_0)^2} \\ l_2 = d(P,P_2) = \sqrt{(x_2 - x_0)^2 + (y_2 - y_0)^2} \\ l_3 = d(P,P_3) = \sqrt{(x_3 - x_0)^2 + (y_3 - y_0)^2} \end{cases} . \tag{8}$$

$$\begin{cases} \alpha = \theta_2 - \theta_1 = arctg(\frac{x_2 - x_0}{y_2 - y_0}) - arctg(\frac{x_1 - x_0}{y_1 - y_0}) \\ \beta = \theta_3 - \theta_2 = arctg(\frac{x_3 - x_0}{y_3 - y_0}) - arctg(\frac{x_2 - x_0}{y_2 - y_0}) \\ \gamma = \theta_1 \_ \theta_3 = arctg(\frac{x_1 - x_0}{y_1 - y_0}) - arctg(\frac{x_3 - x_0}{y_3 - y_0}) \end{cases} . \tag{9}$$

Where l_1, l_2 et l_3 are respectively the branches' lengths that connect P to P_1, P_2 and P_3. θ_1, θ_2 and θ_3 are the angles of the branches relative to the horizontal and α, β and γ are the angles between the branches. Angles and distances have to be normalized according to (3).

4 Feature Matching

The matching process seeks for a good similarity criterion among all the pairs of structures. Let X and Y be the features groups of two images containing respectively a number M_1 and M_2 of bifurcation structures. The similarity measure $s_{i,j}$ on each pair of bifurcation structures is:

$$s_{i,j} = d(x_i, y_j) \quad . \tag{10}$$

Where x_i and y_j are the characteristic vectors of the ith and the jth bifurcation structures in both images. The term d(.) is the measure of the distance between the characteristic vectors. The considered distance here is the mean of the absolute value of the difference between the feature vectors. Unlike the three angles of the unique bifurcation point, the characteristic vector of the proposed bifurcation structure contains classified elements, the length and the angle. This structure facilitates the matching process by reducing the multiple correspondences' occurrence as shown on figure 7.

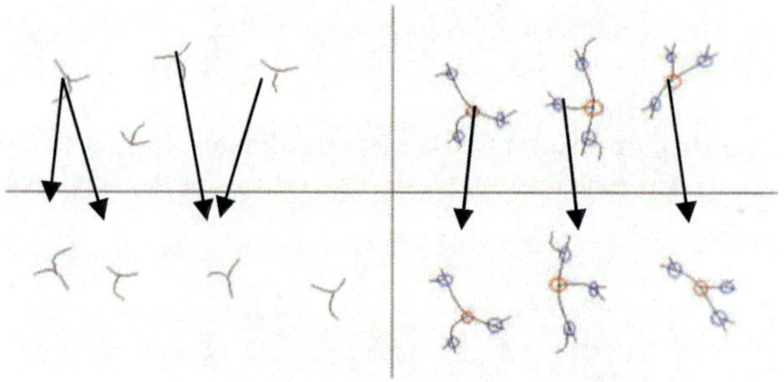

Fig. 7. Matching process. (a) The bifurcation points matching may induce errors due to multiple correspondences. (b) Bifurcation structures matching.

5 Registration: Transformation Model and Optimization

Registration is the application of a geometric transformation based on the bifurcation structures on the image to register. We used the linear, affine and projective transformations. We observed that in some cases, the linear transformation provides a better result than the affine transformation but we note that in the general case, the affine transformation is robust enough to provide a good result, in particular when the image go through distortions. Indeed, this transformation is sufficient to match two images of the same scene taken from the same angle of view but with different positions. The affine transformation has generally four parameters, t_x, t_y, θ and s which transform a point with coordinates (x_1, y_1) into a point with coordinates (x_2, y_2) as follow:

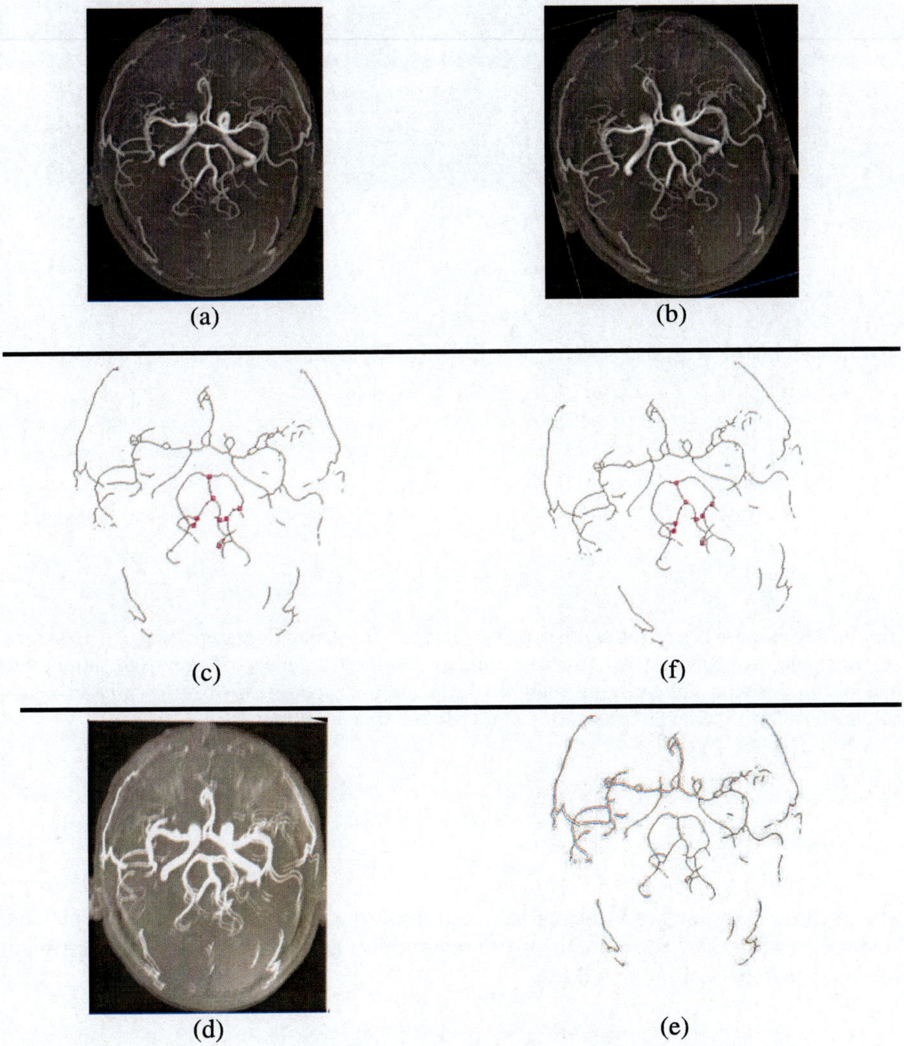

Fig. 8. Registration result. (a) An angiographic image. (b) A second angiographic image with a 15° rotation compared to the first one. (c)The mosaic angiographic image. (d) Vascular network and matched bifurcation structures of (a). (e) Vascular network and matched bifurcation structures of (b). (f) Mosaic image of the vascular network.

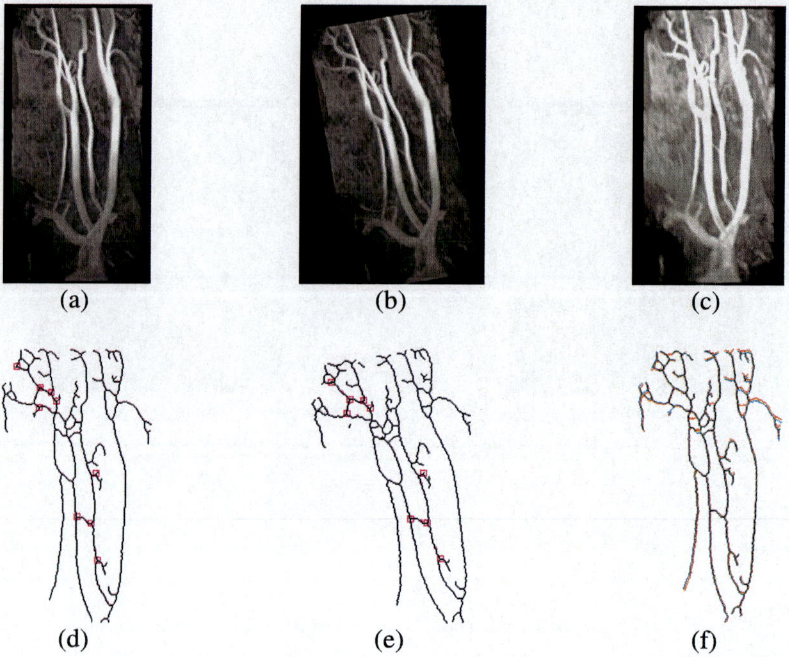

Fig. 9. Registration result for another pair of images. (a) An angiographic image. (b) A second angiographic image with a 15° rotation compared to the first one. (c)The mosaic angiographic image. (d) Vascular network and matched bifurcation structures of (a). (e) Vascular network and matched bifurcation structures of (b). (f) Mosaic image of the vascular network.

$$\begin{pmatrix} x_2 \\ y_2 \end{pmatrix} = \begin{pmatrix} t_x \\ t_y \end{pmatrix} + s \cdot \begin{pmatrix} \cos\theta & -\sin\theta \\ \sin\theta & \cos\theta \end{pmatrix} \cdot \begin{pmatrix} x_1 \\ y_1 \end{pmatrix} \quad . \tag{11}$$

The purpose is to apply an optimal affine transformation which parameters realize the best registration. The refinement of the registration and the transformation estimation can be simultaneously reached by:

$$e_{(pq,mn)} = d(M(x_p, y_q), M(x_m, y_n)) \quad . \tag{12}$$

Here $M(x_p, y_q)$ and $M(x_m, y_n)$ are respectively the parameters of the estimated transformation from pairs (x_p, y_q) and (x_m, y_n). d(.) is the difference. Of course, successful candidates for the estimation are those with good similarity s. We retain finally the pairs of structures that generate transformation models verifying a minimum error e. e is the mean of the squared difference between models.

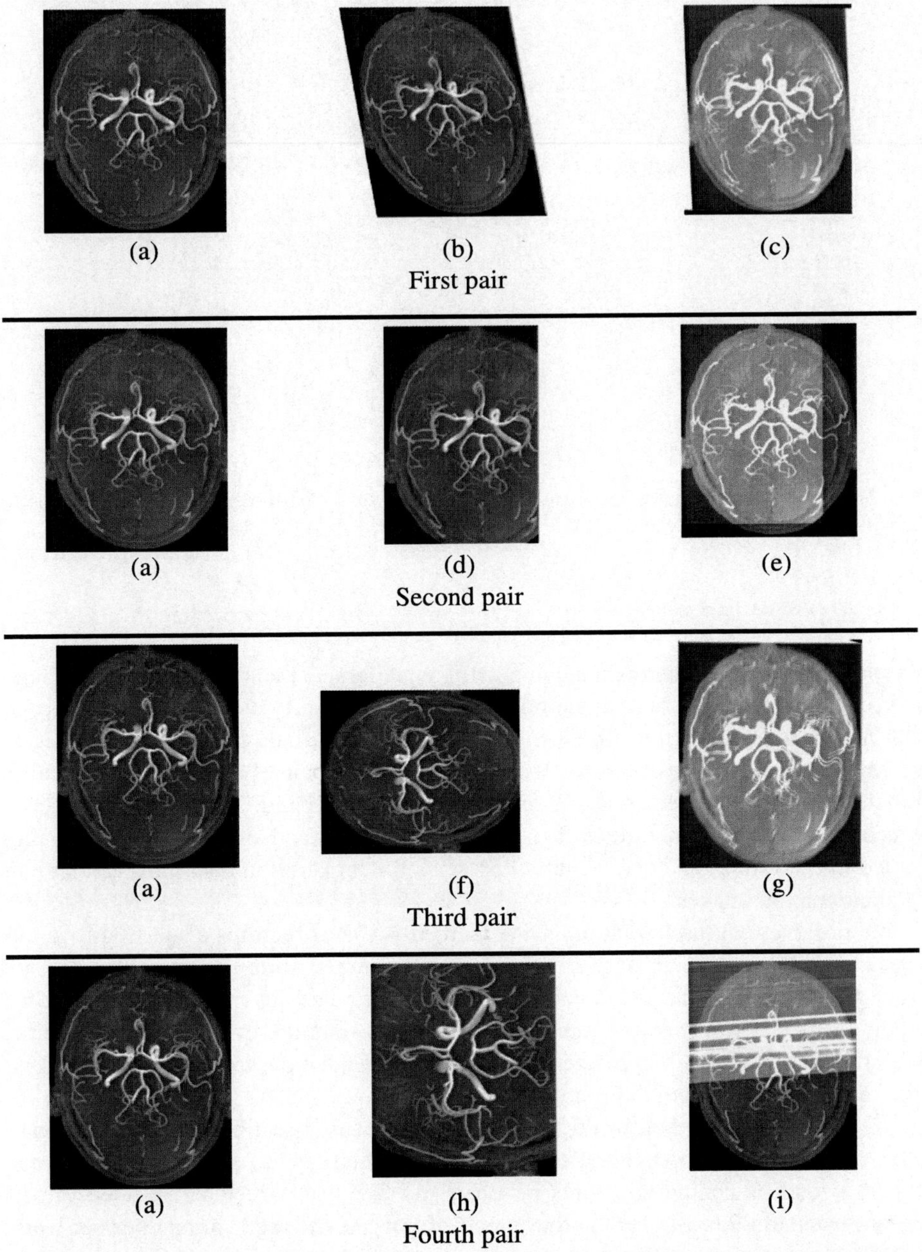

Fig. 10. Registration result on few different pairs of images. (a) Angiographic image. (b) Angiographic image after a 10° declination. (c) Registration result of the first pairs. (d) ARM image after sectioning. (e)Registration result for the second pair. (f) ARM image after 90° rotation. (g) Registration result for the third pair. (h) Angiographic image after 0,8 resizing, sectioning and 90° rotation. (i) Registration result of the fourth pair.

(a) (b) (c)

Fig. 11. Registration improvement result. (a) Reference image. (b)Image to register (c) Mosaic image.

6 Experimental Results

We proceed to the structures matching using equations (1) and (10) to find the initial correspondence. The structures initially matched are used to estimate the transformation model and refines the correspondence. Figures 8(a) and 8(b) shows two angiographic images. 8(b) has been rotated by 15°. For this pair of images, 19 bifurcation structures has been detected and give 17 good matched pairs. The four best matched structures are shown in figures 8(d) and 8(e). The aligned mosaic images are presented in figure 8(c) and 8(f). Figure 9 presents the registration result for another pair of angiographic images.

We observe that the limitation of the method is that it requires a successful vascular segmentation. Indeed, poor segmentation can infer various artifacts that are not related to the image and thus distort the registration. The advantage of the proposed method is that it works even if the image undergoes rotation, translation and resizing. We applied this method on images which undergoes rotation, translation or re-sizing. The results are illustrated in Figure 10.

We find that the method works for images with leans, a sectioning and a rotation of 90 °. For these pairs of images, the bifurcation structures are always 19 in number, with 17 good branching structures matched and finally 4 structures selected to perform the registration. But for the fourth pair of images, the registration does not work. For this pair, we detect 19 and 15 bifurcation structures that yield to 11 matched pairs and finally 4 candidate structures for the registration. We tried to improve the registration by acting on the number of structures to match and by changing the type of transformation. We obtain 2 pairs of candidate structures for the registration of which the result is shown in Figure 11.

7 Conclusion

This paper presents a registration method on the vascular structures in 2D angiographic images. This method involves the extraction of a bifurcation structure consisting of master bifurcation point and its three connected neighbors. Its feature vector is composed of the branches' lengths and branching angles of the bifurcation structure. It is invariant to rotation, translation, scaling and slight distortions. This method is effective when the vascular tree is detected on MRA image.

References

1. Brown, L.G.: A survey of image registration techniques. ACM: Computer surveys, tome 24(4), 325–376 (1992)
2. Zitova, B., Flusser, J.: Image registration methods: a survey. Image and Vision Computing 21(11), 977–1000 (2003)
3. Antoine, M.J.B., Viergever, M.A.: A Survey of Medical Image Registration. Medical Image analysis 2(1), 1–36 (1997)
4. Barillot, C.: Fusion de Données et Imagerie 3D en Médecine, Clearance report, Université de Rennes 1 (September 1999)
5. Hill, D., Batchelor, P., Holden, M., Hawkes, D.: Medical Image Registration. Phys. Med. Biol. 46 (2001)
6. Passat, N.: Contribution à la segmentation des réseaux vasculaires cérébraux obtenus en IRM. Intégration de connaissance anatomique pour le guidage d'outils de morphologie mathématique, Thesis report (September 28, 2005)
7. Ourselin, S.: Recalage d'images médicales par appariement de régions: Application à la création d'atlas histologique 3D. Thesis report, Université Nice-Sophia Antipolis (January 2002)
8. Chillet, D., Jomier, J., Cool, D., Aylward, S.R.: Vascular atlas formation using a vessel-to-image affine registration method. In: Ellis, R.E., Peters, T.M. (eds.) MICCAI 2003. LNCS, vol. 2878, pp. 335–342. Springer, Heidelberg (2003)
9. Cool, D., Chillet, D., Kim, J., Guyon, J.-P., Foskey, M., Aylward, S.R.: Tissue-based affine registration of brain images to form a vascular density atlas. In: Ellis, R.E., Peters, T.M. (eds.) MICCAI 2003. LNCS, vol. 2879, pp. 9–15. Springer, Heidelberg (2003)
10. Roche, A.: Recalage d'images médicales par inférence statistique. Sciences thesis, Université de Nice Sophia-Antipolis (February 2001)
11. Bondiau, P.Y.: Mise en œuvre et évaluation d'outils de fusion d'image en radiothérapie. Sciences thesis, Université de Nice-Sophia Antipolis (November 2004)
12. Commowick, O.: Création et utilisation d'atlas anatomiques numériques pour la radiothérapie. Sciences' Thesis, Université Nice–Sophia Antipolis (February 2007)
13. Styner, M., Gerig, G.: Evaluation of 2D/3D bias correction with 1+1ES optimization. Technical Report, BIWI-TR-179, Image science Lab, ETH Zürich (October 1997)
14. Zhang, Z.: Parameter Estimation Techniques: A Tutorial with Application to Conic Fitting. International Journal of Image and Vision Computing 15(1), 59–76 (1997)

15. Chen, L., Zhang, X.L.: Feature-Based Retinal Image Registration Using Bifurcation Structures (February 2009)
16. Attali, D.: Squelettes et graphes de Voronoï 2D et 3D. Doctoral thesis, Université Joseph Fourier - Grenoble I (October 1995)
17. Jlassi, H., Hamrouni, K.: Detection of blood vessels in retinal images. International Journal of Image and Graphics 10(1), 57–72 (2010)
18. Jlassi, H., Hamrouni, K.: Caractérisation de la rétine en vue de l'élaboration d'une méthode biométrique d'identification de personnes. In: SETIT (March 2005)

Design and Implementation of Lifting Based Integer Wavelet Transform for Image Compression Applications

Morteza Gholipour

Islamic Azad University, Behshahr Branch, Behshahr, Iran
gholipour@iaubs.ac.ir

Abstract. In this paper we present an FPGA implementation of 5/3 Discrete Wavelet Transform (DWT), which is used in image compression. The 5/3 lifting-based wavelet transform is modeled and simulated using MATLAB. DSP implementation methodologies are used to optimize the required hardware. The signal flow graph and dependence graph are derived and optimized to implement the hardware description of the circuit in Verilog. The circuit code then has been synthesized and realized using Field Programmable Gate Array (FPGA) of FLEX10KE family. Post-synthesis simulations confirm the circuit operation and efficiency.

Keywords: DWT, Lifting Scheme Wavelet, DSP, Image compression, FPGA implementation.

1 Introduction

The Discrete Wavelet Transform (DWT) followed by coding techniques would be very efficient for image compression. The DWT has been successfully used in other signal processing applications such as speech recognition, pattern recognition, computer graphics, blood-pressure, ECG analyses, statistics and physics [1]-[5]. The MPEG-4 and JEPG 2000 use the DWT for image compression [6], because of its advantages over conventional transforms, such as the Fourier transform. The DWT has the two properties of no blocking effect and perfect reconstruction of the analysis and the synthesis wavelets. Wavelet transforms are closely related to tree-structured digital filter banks. Therefore the DWT has the property of multiresolution analysis (MRA) in which there is adjustable locality in both the space (time) and frequency domains [7]. In multiresolution signal analysis, a signal decomposes into its components in different frequency bands.

The very good decorrelation properties of DWT along with its attractive features in image coding, have conducted to significant interest in efficient algorithms for its hardware implementation. Various VLSI architectures of the DWT have presented in the literature [8]-[16]. The conventional convolution based DWT requires massive computations and consumes much area and power, which could be overcome by using the lifting based scheme for the DWT introduced by Sweldens [17], [18]. The Lifting-based wavelet, which is also called as the second generation wavelet, is based entirely on the spatial method. Lifting scheme has several advantages, including "in-place"

H. Cherifi, J.M. Zain, and E. El-Qawasmeh (Eds.): DICTAP 2011, Part I, CCIS 166, pp. 161–172, 2011.

computation of the wavelet coefficients, integer-to-integer wavelet transform (IWT) [19], symmetric forward and inverse transform, etc.

In this paper we have implemented 5/3 lifting based integer wavelet transform which is used in image compression. We have used the DSP algorithms and signal flow graph (SFG) methodology to improve the performance and efficiency of our design. The remaining of the paper is organized as follows. In Section 2, we will briefly describe the DWT, the lifting scheme and the 5/3 wavelet transform. High level modeling, hardware implementation and simulation results are presented in Section 3. Finally, a summary and conclusion will be given in Section 4.

2 Discrete Wavelet Transform

DWT, which provides a time-frequency domain representation for the analysis of signals, can be implemented using filter banks. Another framework for efficient computation of the DWT is called *lifting scheme* (LS). These approaches are briefly described in the following subsections.

2.1 Filter Banks Method

Filters are one of the most widely used signal processing functions. The basic block in a wavelet transform is a filter bank, shown in Fig. 1, which consists of two filters. The forward transform uses analysis filters $\tilde{h}$ (low-pass) and $\tilde{g}$ (high pass) followed by downsampling. A discrete signal S is fed to these filters. The output of the filters is downsampled by two which results in high pass and low pass signals, denoted by d (detail) and a (approximation), respectively. These signals have half as much samples as the input signal S. The inverse transform, on the other hand, first upsamples the *HP* and *LP* signals and then uses two synthesis filters h (low-pass) and g (high-pass) and then the results are added together. In a perfect reconstruction filter bank the resulting signal is equal to original signal.

The DWT performs multiresolution signal analysis, in which the decomposition and reconstruction processes can be done in more than one level as shown in Fig. 2. The samples generated by the high pass filters are completely decomposed, while the other samples generated by the low pass filters are applied to the next-level for further decomposition.

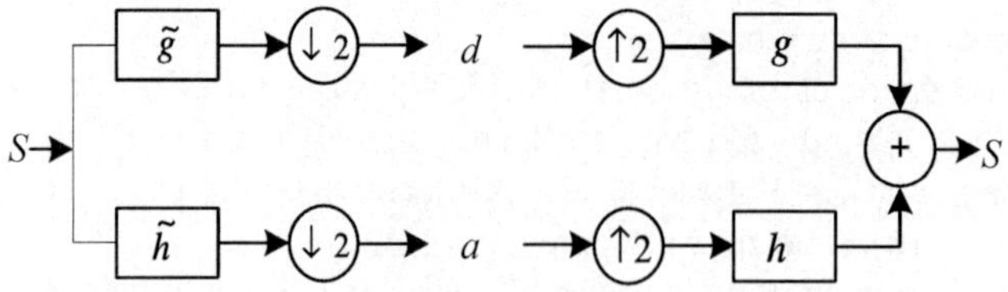

Fig. 1. Filter bank structure of discrete wavelet transform

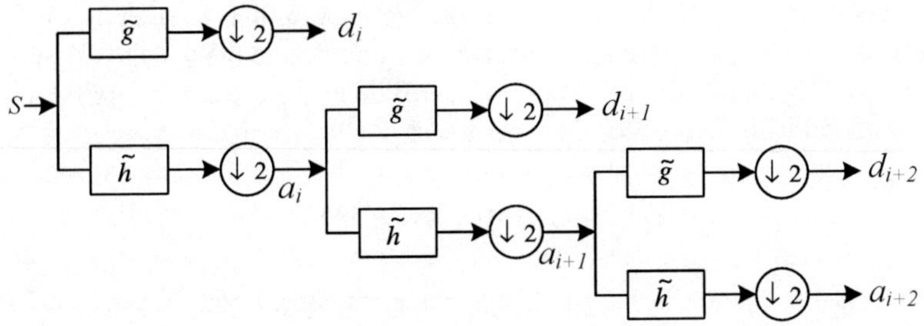

Fig. 2. Two level decomposition of DWT

2.2 Lifting Scheme Wavelet Transform

The Lifting Scheme (LS) is a method to improve some specific properties of a given wavelet transform. The lifting scheme, which is called second generation of wavelets, was first introduced by Sweldens [17]. The lifting scheme entirely relies on the spatial domain and compared to the filter bank structure has great advantages of better computational efficiency in terms of lower number required multiplications and additions. This results in lower area, power consumption and design complexity when implemented as VLSI architectures. The lifting scheme can be easily implemented by hardware due to its significantly reduced computations. Lifting has other advantages, such as "in-place" computation of the DWT, integer-to-integer wavelet transforms (which are useful for lossless coding), etc.

In the lifting-based DWT scheme, the high-pass and low-pass filters are broken up into a sequence of upper and lower triangular matrices [18]. The LS is consists of three steps, namely, Split (also called Lazy Wavelet Transform), Predict, and Update. These three steps are depicted in Fig. 3(a). The first step splits the input signal x into even and odd samples,

$$x_e = x(2n) \tag{1}$$

$$x_o = x(2n+1)$$

In the predict step, the even samples $x(2n)$ is used to predict the odd samples $x(2n+1)$ using a prediction function P. The difference between the predicted and original values will produce high-frequency information, which replaces the odd samples:

$$y(2n+1) = x_o(2n+1) - P(x_e) \tag{2}$$

This is the detail coefficients g_{j+1}. The even samples can represent a coarser version of the input sequence at half the resolution. But, to ensure that the average of the signal is preserved, the detail coefficients are used to update the evens. This is done in update step which generates approximation coefficients f_{j+1}. In this stage the even samples are updated using the following equation:

$$y(2n) = x_e + U(y(2n+1)) \tag{3}$$

in which U is the update function. The inverse transform could easily be found, exchanging the sign of the predict step and the update step and apply all operations in reversed order as shown in Fig. 3 (b).

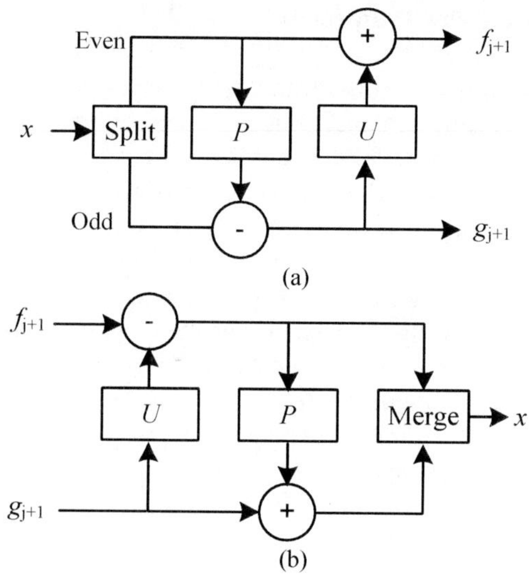

Fig. 3. The lifting scheme, (a) forward transform, (b) inverse transform

The LS transform can be done in more than one level. The f_{j+1} becomes the input for the next recursive stage for the transform as shown in Fig. 4. The number of data elements processed by the wavelet transform must be a power of two. If there are 2^n data elements, the first step of the forward transform will produce 2^{n-1} approximation and 2^{n-1} detail coefficients. As we can see in both predict and update steps, every time we add or subtract something to one stream. All the samples in the stream are replaced by new samples and at any time we need only the current streams to update sample values. It is the other property of lifting in which the whole transform can be done in-place, without the need for temporary memory. This in-place property reduces the amount of memory required to implement the transform.

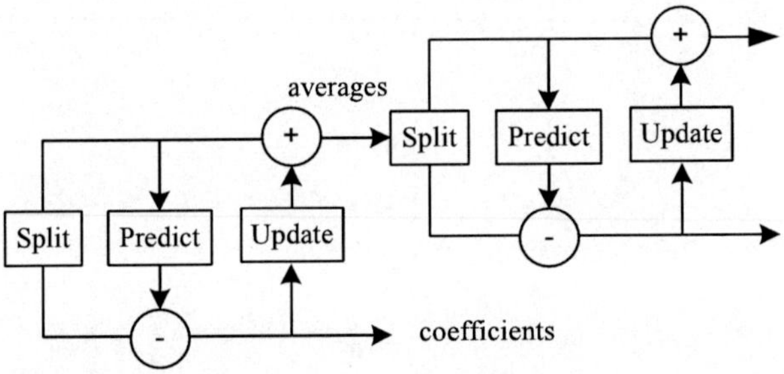

Fig. 4. The two stages in the lifting scheme wavelet

2.3 The 5/3 Lifting Based Wavelet Transform

The 5/3 wavelet which is used in the JPEG 2000 lossless compression, which is also known as CDF (2,2) is a member of the family of the Cohen-Daubechies-Feauveau biorthogonal wavelets. It is called 5/3 wavelet because of the filter length of 5 and 3 for the low and high pass filters, respectively. The CDF wavelets are expressed as CDF$(n,\tilde{n})$ [20], in which the dual numbers of $(n,\tilde{n})$ indicates the vanishing factor of n in both predict and update steps. The decomposition wavelet filters of CDF(2,2) are expressed as follows

$$\tilde{g}_{(2,2)} : \frac{\sqrt{2}}{4}.(1,-2,1) \tag{4}$$

$$\tilde{h}_{(2,2)} : \frac{\sqrt{2}}{8}.(-1,2,6,2,-1) \tag{5}$$

The wavelet and scaling function graphs of CDF(2,2), shown in Fig. 5, can be obtained by convolving the impulse δ with high pass and low pass filters, respectively. The CDF biorthogonal wavelets have three key benefits: 1) they have finite support. This preserves the locality of image features, 2) the scaling function $\varphi(x)$ is always symmetric, and the wavelet function $\psi(x)$ is always symmetric or antisymmetric, which is important for image processing operations, 3) the coefficients of the wavelet filters are of the form $z/2^n$ with z integer and n a natural numbers. This means that all divisions can be implemented using binary shifts. The lifting equivalent steps of CDF(2,2), which its functional diagram is shown in Fig. 6, can be expressed as follows:

$$\text{Split step:} \quad s_i \leftarrow x_{2i}, \quad d_i \leftarrow x_{2i+1} \tag{6}$$

$$\text{Predict step:} \quad d_i \leftarrow d_i - \tfrac{1}{2}(s_i + s_{i+1}) \tag{7}$$

$$\text{Update step:} \quad s_i \leftarrow s_i + \tfrac{1}{4}(d_{i-1} + d_i) \tag{8}$$

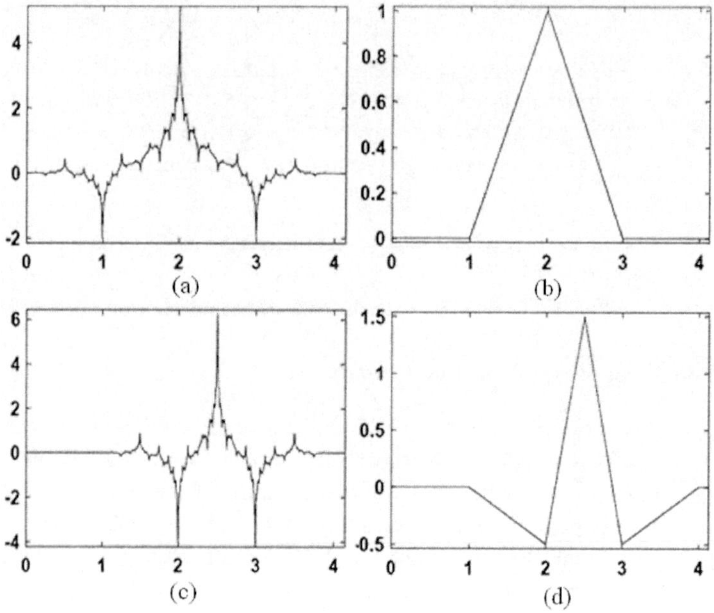

Fig. 5. The graphs for wavelet and scaling functions of CDF(2,2), (a) decomposition scaling function φ, (b) reconstruction scaling function φ, (c) decomposition wavelet function ψ, (d) reconstruction wavelet function ψ

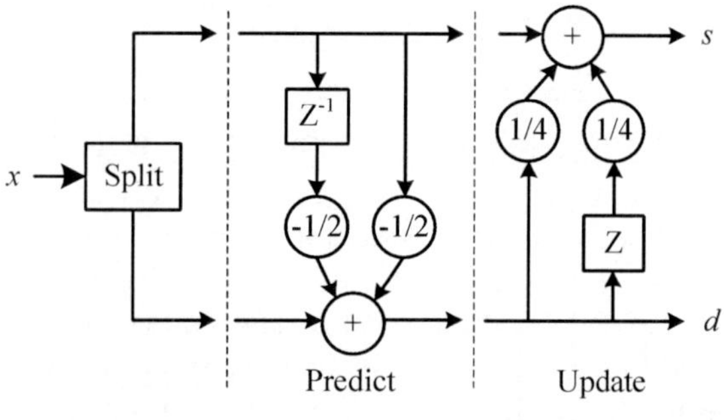

Fig. 6. The lifting scheme for CDF (2,2)

2.4 Image Compression

Wavelet transform can be utilized in a wide range of applications, including signal processing, speech compression and recognition, denoising, biometrics and others. One of the important applications is in JPEG 2000 still image compression. The JPEG 2000 standard introduces advances in image compression technology in which the image coding system is optimized for efficiency, scalability and interoperability in different multimedia environments.

The JPEG 2000 compression block diagram is shown in Fig. 7 [21]. At the encoder, the source image is first decomposed into rectangular tile-components (Fig. 8). A wavelet discrete transform is applied on each tile into different resolution levels, which results in a coefficient for any pixel of the image without any compression yet. These coefficients can then be compressed more easily because the information is statistically concentrated in just a few coefficients. In DWT, higher amplitudes represent the most prominent information of the signal, while the less prominent information appears in very low amplitudes. Eliminating these low amplitudes results in a good data compression, and hence the DWT enables high compression rates while retains with good quality of image. The coefficients are then quantized and the quantized values are entropy encoded and/or run length encoded into an output bit stream compressed image.

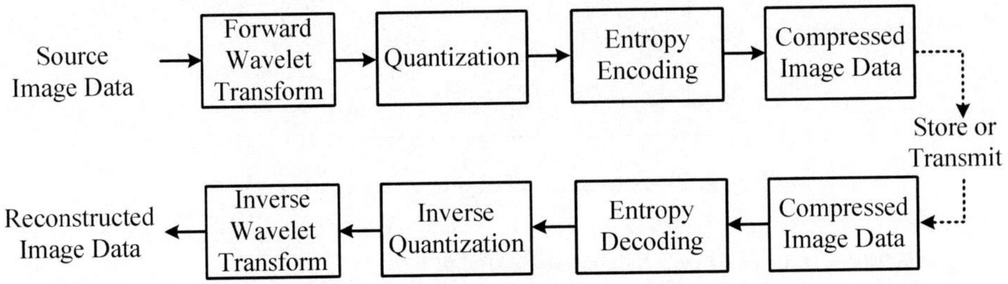

Fig. 7. Block diagram of the JPEG 2000 compression, (a) encoder side, (b) decoder side

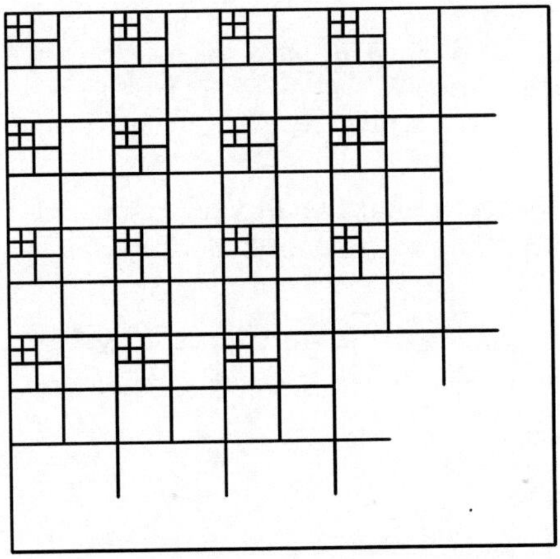

Fig. 8. Image tiling and Discrete Wavelet Transform of each tile

3 Implementation of 5/3 Wavelet Transform

In this section we present detail description of the design flow used to implement the hardware of 32-bit integer-to-integer lifting 5/3 wavelet transform, which is shown in Fig. 9. A 32-bit input signal *sig* is fed to the circuit and it calculates the output low and high frequency coefficients, denoted by *approximation* and *detail*, respectively. The *clk* signal is the input clock pulse and each *eon* period indicates one output data. Note that the output will be ready after some delay which is required for circuit operation. The design flow starts from behavioral description of 5/3 wavelet transform in MATLAB's Simulink [22] and its verification. After DSP optimization of the model it will be ready for hardware design and implementation.

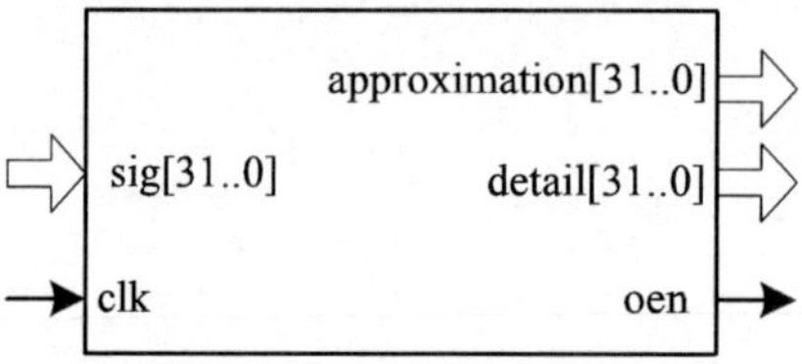

Fig. 9. Block diagram of implemented hardware

3.1 Behavioral Model of 5/3 Wavelet Transform

As the first step, the 5/3 wavelet transform is modeled and simulated using Simulink, with the model shown in Fig. 10. A test data sequence of values (6, 5, 1, 9, 5, 11, 4, 3, 5, 0, 6, 4, 9, 6, 5, 7) is then applied to this model and simulation outputs, which are shown in Fig. 11, are compared to the values calculated by MATLAB's internal functions as

```
x=[6 5 1 9 5 11 4 3 5 0 6 4 9 6 5 7];
lsInt = liftwave('cdf2.2','int2int');
[cAint,cDint] = lwt(x,lsInt)
```

Comparison results verify correct functionality of this model. Fig. 12 shows an example of the data flow in 5/3 lifting wavelet for 8 clock cycles.

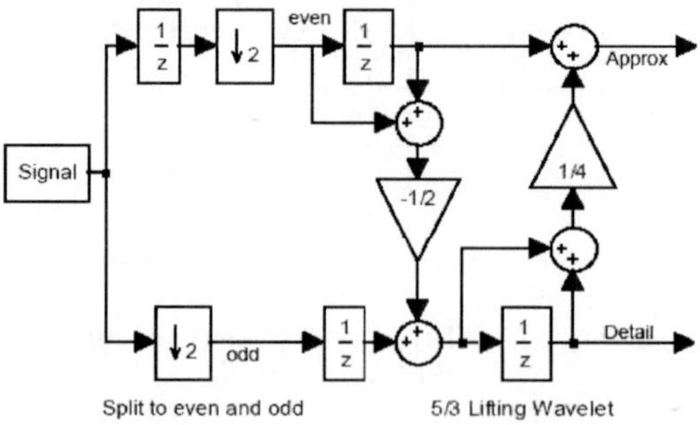

Fig. 10. Simulink model for 5/3 wavelet transform

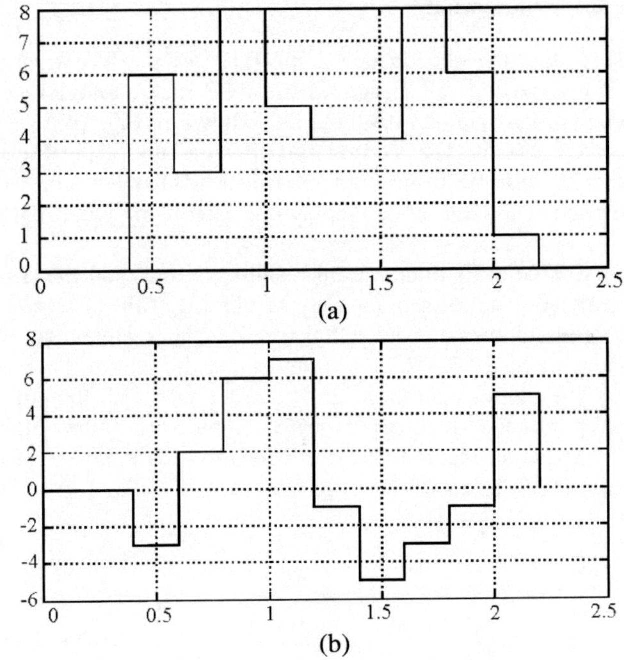

Fig. 11. Simulation output of 5/3 wavelet transform model using Simulink, (a) Approximation coefficients (b) Detail coefficients

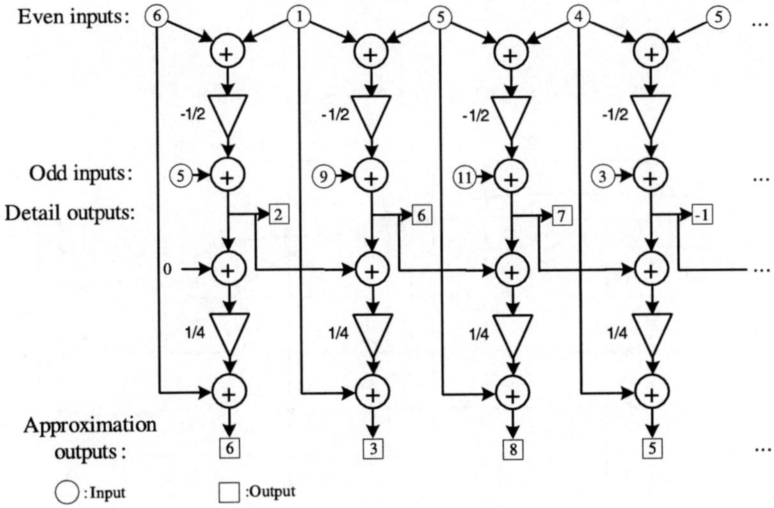

Fig. 12. An example of 5/3 lifting wavelet calculation

3.2 Hardware Implementation

At the next design step, the dependence graph (DG) of the 5/3 structure is derived using the SFG shown in Fig. 13, based on the DSP methodologies. Then we have used difference equations obtained from the DG, shown in Fig. 14, to write the Verilog description of the circuit. The Verilog code is simulated using Modelsim and its results are compared with the results obtained by MATLAB to confirm the correct operation of the code. The HDL code then synthesized using Quartus-II and realized with FPGA.

Post-synthesis simulation is done on the resulting circuit and the results are compared with the associated output generated by MATLAB. Table 1 shows the summary report of the implementation on FLEX10KE FPGA. Our implementation uses 323 of 1728 logic elements of EPF10K30ETC144 device, while requires no memory blocks. In order to verify the circuit operation in all the design steps, the simulations were done on various input data and the results were compared with the outputs calculated by MATLAB. A sample simulation waveform for input data pattern of (6, 5, 1, 9, 5, 11, 4, 3, 5, 0, 6, 4, 9, 6, 5, 7) is shown in Fig. 15.

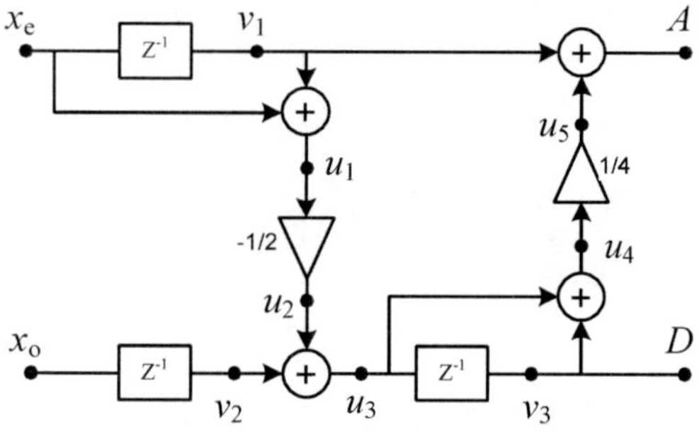

$$N_1 = \{x_e, x_o, v_1, v_2, v_3\}$$

$$N_2 = \{u_1, v_1, v_2, v_3\}$$

$$N_3 = \{u_2, v_1, v_2, v_3\}$$

$$N_4 = \{u_3, v_1, v_3\}$$

$$N_5 = \{u_4, v_1\}$$

$$N_6 = \{u_5, v_1\}$$

$$N_7 = \{A, D\}$$

Fig. 13. SFG of the 5/3 wavelet transform

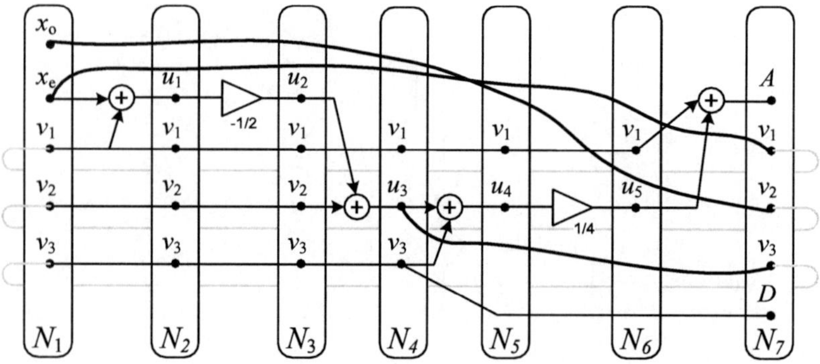

Fig. 14. Dependence graph of the 5/3 wavelet transform

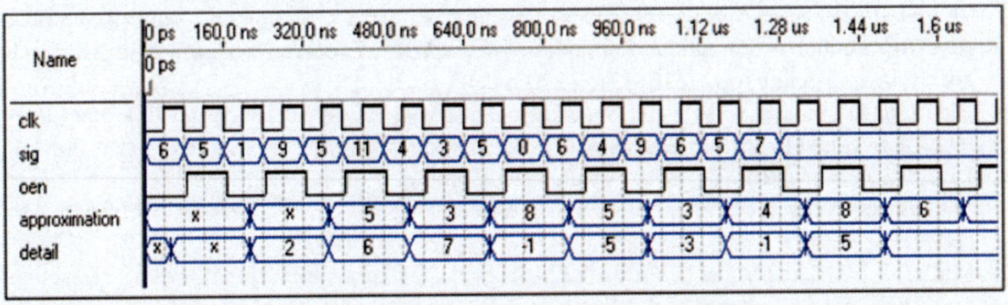

Fig. 15. A sample simulation waveform

Table 1. Synthesis report

Family	FLEX10KE
Total logic elements	323 / 1,728 (19 %)
Total pins	98 / 102 (96 %)
Total memory bits	0 / 24,576 (0 %)
Device	EPF10K30ETC144-1X

4 Summary and Conclusions

In this paper we implemented 5/3 lifting based wavelet transform which is used in image compression. We described the lifting based wavelet transform, and designed an integer-to-integer 5/3 lifting wavelet. The design is modeled and simulated using MATLAB's Simulink. This model is used to derive signal flow graph (SFG) and dependence graph (DG) of the design, using DSP optimization methodologies. The hardware description of this wavelet transform module is written in Verilog code using the obtained DG, and is simulated using Modelsim. Simulations were done to confirm correct operation of each design step. The code has been synthesized and realized successfully and implemented on the FPGA device of FLEX10KE. Post-synthesis simulations using Modelsim verifies the circuit operation.

References

1. Quellec, G., Lamard, M., Cazuguel, G., Cochener, B., Roux, C.: Adaptive Nonseparable Wavelet Transform via Lifting and its Application to Content-Based Image Retrieval. IEEE Transactions on Image Processing 19(1), 25–35 (2010)
2. Yang, G., Guo, S.: A New Wavelet Lifting Scheme for Image Compression Applications. In: Zheng, N., Jiang, X., Lan, X. (eds.) IWICPAS 2006. LNCS, vol. 4153, pp. 465–474. Springer, Heidelberg (2006)
3. Sheng, M., Chuanyi, J.: Modeling Heterogeneous Network Traffic in Wavelet Domain. IEEE/ACM Transactions on Networking 9(5), 634–649 (2001)

4. Zhang, D.: Wavelet Approach for ECG Baseline Wander Correction and Noise Reduction. In: 27th Annual International Conference of the IEEE-EMBS, Engineering in Medicine and Biology Society, pp. 1212–1215 (2005)
5. Bahoura, M., Rouat, J.: Wavelet Speech Enhancement Based on the Teager Energy Operator. IEEE Signal Processing Letters 8(1), 10–12 (2001)
6. Park, T., Kim, J., Rho, J.: Low-Power, Low-Complexity Bit-Serial VLSI Architecture for 1D Discrete Wavelet Transform. Circuits, Systems, and Signal Processing 26(5), 619–634 (2007)
7. Mallat, S.: A Theory for Multiresolution Signal Decomposition: the Wavelet representation. IEEE Trans. Pattern Anal. Mach. Intell. 11, 674–693 (1989)
8. Knowles, G.: VLSI Architectures for the Discrete Wavelet Transform. Electronics Letters 26(15), 1184–1185 (1990)
9. Lewis, A.S., Knowles, G.: VLSI Architecture for 2-D Daubechies Wavelet Transform Without Multipliers. Electronics Letter 27(2), 171–173 (1991)
10. Parhi, K.K., Nishitani, T.: VLSI Architectures for Discrete Wavelete Transforms. IEEE Trans. on VLSI Systems 1(2), 191–202 (1993)
11. Martina, M., Masera, G., Piccinini, G., Zamboni, M.: A VLSI Architecture for IWT (Integer Wavelet Transform). In: Proc. 43rd IEEE Midwest Symp. on Circuits and Systems, Lansing MI, pp. 1174–1177 (2000)
12. Das, A., Hazra, A., Banerjee, S.: An Efficient Architecture for 3-D Discrete Wavelet Transform. IEEE Trans. on Circuits and Systems for Video Tech. 20(2) (2010)
13. Tan, K.C.B., Arslan, T.: Shift-Accumulator ALU Centric JPEG2000 5/3 Lifting Based Discrete Wavelet Transform Architecture. In: Proceedings of the 2003 International Symposium on Circuits and Systems (ISCAS 2003), vol. 5, pp. V161–V164 (2003)
14. Dillen, G., Georis, B., Legat, J., Canteanu, O.: Combined Line-Based Architecture for the 5-3 and 9-7 Wavelet Transform in JPEG2000. IEEE Transactions on Circuits and Systems for Video Technology 13(9), 944–950 (2003)
15. Vishwanath, M., Owens, R.M., Irwin, M.J.: VLSI Architectures for the Discrete Wavelet Transform. IEEE Trans. on Circuits and Systems II: Analog and Digital Signal Processing 42(5) (1995)
16. Chen, P.-Y.: VLSI Implementation for One-Dimensional Multilevel Lifting-Based Wavelet Transform. IEEE Transactions on Computers 53(4), 386–398 (2004)
17. Sweldens, W.: The Lifting Scheme: A New Philosophy in Biorthogonal Wavelet Constructions. In: Proc. SPIE, vol. 2569, pp. 68–79 (1995)
18. Daubechies, I., Sweldens, W.: Factoring Wavelet Transforms into Lifting Steps. J. Fourier Anal. Appl. 4(3), 247–269 (1998)
19. Calderbank, A.R., Daubechies, I., Sweldens, W., Yeo, B.L.: Wavelet Transform that Map Integers to Integers. ACHA 5(3), 332–369 (1998)
20. Cohen, A., Daubechies, I., Feauveau, J.: Bi-orthogonal Bases of Compactly Supported Wavelets. Comm. Pure Appl. Math. 45(5), 485–560 (1992)
21. Skodras, A., Christopoulos, C., Ebrahimi, T.: The JPEG 2000 Still Image Compression Standard. IEEE Signal Processing Magazine, 36–58 (2001)
22. MATLAB ® Help, The MathWorks, Inc.

Detection of Defects in Weld Radiographic Images by Using Chan-Vese Model and Level Set Formulation

Yamina Boutiche

Centre de Recherche Scientifique et Technique en Soudage et Contrôle CSC
Route de Dely Brahim BP. 64 Cheraga,
Algiers, Algeria
Boutiche_y@yahoo.fr

Abstract. In this paper, we propose a model for active contours to detect boundaries' objects in given image. The curve evolution is based on Chan-Vese model implemented via variational level set formulation. The particularity of this model is the capacity to detect boundaries' objects without need to use gradient of the image, this propriety gives its several advantages: it allows to detect both contours with or without gradient, it has ability to detect automatically interior contours, and it is robust in the presence of noise. For increasing the performance of model, we introduce the level sets function to describe the active contour, the more important advantage to use level set is the ability to change topology. Experiments on synthetic and real (weld radiographic) images show both efficiency and accuracy of implemented model.

Keywords: Image segmentation, Curve evolution, Chan-Vese model, EDPs, Level set.

1 Introduction

This paper is concerned with image segmentation, which plays a very important role in many applications. It consists of creating a partition of the image u_0 into subsets R_i called *regions*. Where, no region is empty, the intersection between two regions is empty, and the union of all regions cover the whole image. A region is a set of connected pixels having common properties that distinguish them from the pixels of neighboring regions. Those ones are separated by contours. However, we distinguish, in literature, two ways of segmenting images, the first one is called *based–region segmentation*, and second is named *based-contour segmentation*.

Nowadays, and given the importance of segmentation, multiple studies and a wide range of applications and mathematical approaches are developed to reach good quality of segmentation. The techniques based on variational formulations and called *deformable models* are used to detect objects in a given image u_0 using theories of curves evolution [1]. The basic idea is: from an initial curve C which is given; to deform the curve till surrounded the objects' boundaries, under some constraints from the image. There are two different approaches within variational segmentation:

H. Cherifi, J.M. Zain, and E. El-Qawasmeh (Eds.): DICTAP 2011, Part I, CCIS 166, pp. 173–183, 2011.

edge-based models such as the active contours "snakes" [2], and *region-based methods* such as Chan-Vese model [3].

Almost all edge-based models mentioned above use the gradient of the image u_0 to locate the objects' edges. Therefore, to stop the evolving curve an edge-function is used, which is strictly positive inside homogeneous regions and near zero on the edges, it is formulated as follow:

$$g(|\nabla u_0|) = \frac{1}{1+|\nabla(G_\sigma * u_0)|^2} \quad . \tag{1}$$

The operator gradient is well adapted to a certain class of problems, but can be put in failure in the presence of strong noise and can become completely ineffective when boundaries' objects are very weak. On the contrary, the approaches biased region avoid the derivatives of the image intensity. Thus, it is more robust to the noises, it detects objects whose boundaries cannot be defied or are badly defined through the gradient, and it automatically detects interior contours [4][5].

In problems of curve evolution, including snakes, the level set method of Osher and Sethian [6][7] has been used extensively because it allows for automatic topology changes, cusps, and corners. Moreover, the computations are made on a fixed rectangular grid. Using this approach, geometric active contour models, using a stopping edge-function, have been proposed in [8][9][10], and [11].

Region-based segmentation models are often inspired by the classical work of Mumford -Shah [12] where it is argued that segmentation functional should contain a data term, regularization on the model, and regularization on the partitioning. Based on the Mumford -Shah functional, Chan and Vese proposed a new model for active contours to detect objects boundary. The total energy to minimize is described, essentially, by the averages intensities inside and outside the curve [3].

The paper is structured as follows: the next section is devoted to the detailed review of the adopted model (Chan-Vese). In the third section, we formulate the chan-vese model via the level sets function, and the associated Euler-Lagrange equation. In section 4, we present the numerical discretization and algorithm implemented. In section 5, we discuss a various numerical results on synthetic and real weld radiographic images. We conclude this article with a brief conclusion in section 6.

2 Chan-Vese Formulation

The more popular and older region-based segmentation is the Mumford-Shah model in 1989 [12]. Much works have been inspired from this model, for example the model, called "*Without edges*", which was proposed by Chan and Vese in 2001 [3], on what we focus in this paper. The main idea of *without edges model* is to consider the information inside regions, not only at their boundaries. Let us present this model: let u_0 be the original image, c the evolving curve, and c_{in} , c_{out} two unknown constants. Chan and Vese propose the following minimization problem:

$$F_{in}(c) + F_{out}(c) = \int_{inside(c)} |u_0(x,y) - c_{in}|^2 dx\, dy + \int_{outside(c)} |u_0(x,y) - c_{out}|^2 dx\, dy \ . \quad (2)$$

where the constants c_{in}, c_{out} depending on c, they are defined as the averages of u_0 inside and outside c, respectively.

We look for minimizing (2), if we note c_0 the minimum of (2); it is obvious that $c_0$is the boundary of the object, because the fitting term given by (2) is superior or equal zero, always. So its minimum is when $F_{in}(c) \approx 0$ and $F_{out}(c) \approx 0$:

$inf\{F_{in} + F_{out}\} \approx 0 \approx F_{in}(c_0) + F_{out}(c_0)$. so $F_{in}(c_0) \approx 0 \Rightarrow u_0(x,y) \approx c_{in}$
$F_{out}(c_0) \approx 0 \Rightarrow u_0(x,y) \approx c_{out}$. Where inf is an abbreviation for infimum

As formulations show, we obtain a minimum of (2) when we have homogeneity inside and outside a curve, in this case wet have $c = c_0$,it is the boundary of object (See fig. 1).

Chan and Vese had added some regularizing terms, like the length of curve c, and the area of the region inside c. Therefore, the functional become:

$$F(c_{in}, c_{out}, c) = \mu . Length(c) + v . Area(inside(c)) + \lambda_1 \int_{inside(c)} |u_0(x,y) - c_{in}|^2 dx\, dy$$
$$+ \lambda_2 \int_{outside(c)} |u_0(x,y) - c_{out}|^2 dxdy \ . \quad (3)$$

where $\mu, v \geq 0, \lambda_1, \lambda_2 > 0$ are constant parameters, we note that in almost all practical experiences cases, we set $v = 0, \lambda_1 = \lambda_2 = 1$.

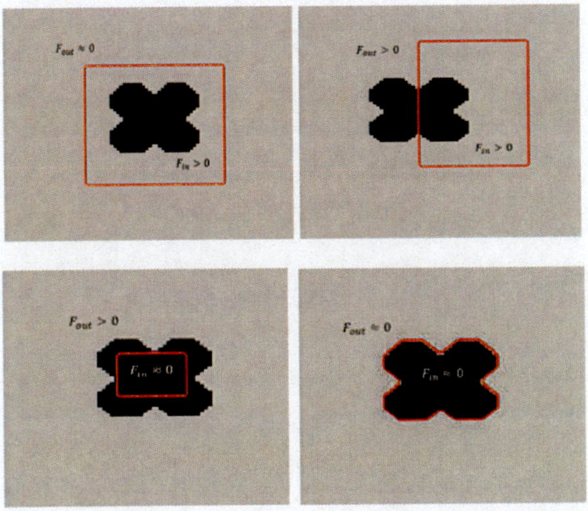

Fig. 1. All possible cases in the curve position, and corresponding values of the $F_{in}(c)$ and $F_{out}(c)$

3 Level Set Formulation of the Chain-Vese Model

The level set method evolves a contour (in two dimensions) or a surface (in three dimensions) implicitly by manipulating a higher dimensional function, called level set $\Phi(X,t)$. The evolving contour or surface can be extracted from the zero level set $C(X,t) = \{\Phi(X,t) = 0\}$. The advantages of using this method is the possibility to manage automatically the topology changes of curve in evolution, however, the curve C can be divided into two or three curves, inversely, several curves may merge and become a single curve (Osher,2003). By convention we have:

$$\begin{cases} c = \partial w = \{(x,y) \in \Omega : \emptyset(x,y) = 0\}, \\ inside(c) = w = \{(x,y) \in \Omega : \emptyset(x,y) > 0\}, \\ outside(c) = \Omega \backslash \overline{w} = \{(x,y) \in \Omega : \emptyset(x,y) < 0\}. \end{cases}$$

where $w \subset \Omega$ is open, and $c = \partial w$. Fig. 2 illustrates the above description of level set function.

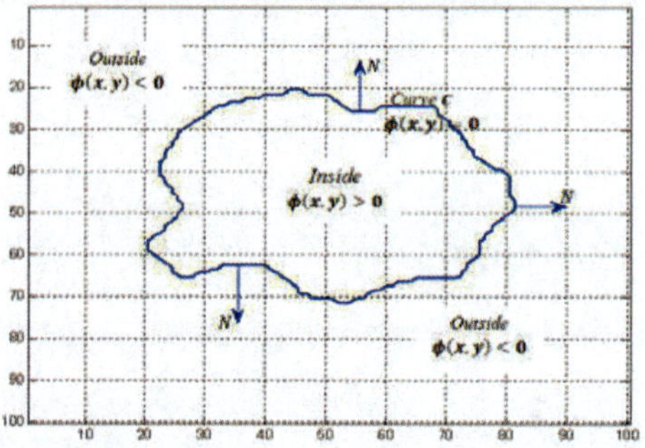

Fig. 2. Level sets function, curve $c = \{(x,y) : \phi(x,y) = 0\}$

Now we focus on presenting Chan-Vese model via level set function. To express the inside and outside concept, we call Heaviside function H defined as follow:

$$H(z) = \begin{cases} 1, & if\ z \geq 0 \\ 0, & if\ z < 0 \end{cases}, \quad \delta_0(z) = \frac{d}{dz} H(z), \quad Z \in \mathbb{R} \tag{4}$$

Using level set $\phi(x,y)$ to describe curve $c(x,y)$ and Heaviside function, the formulation (3) can be written as:

$$F(c_{in}, c_{out}, \phi) = \mu . \int_\Omega \delta(\phi(x,y)) |\nabla\phi(x,y)| dxdy$$
$$+ v \int_\Omega H(\phi(x,y))\, dxdy + \lambda_1 \int_\Omega |u_0(x,y) - c_{in}|^2 H(\phi(x,y)) dx\, dy$$
$$+ \lambda_2 \int_\Omega |u_0(x,y) - c_{out}|^2 \left(1 - H(\phi(x,y))\right) dx\, dy . \tag{5}$$

Where the first integral express the length curve, that is penalized by μ. The second one presents the area inside the curve, which is penalized by v.

Using level set $\phi(x,y)$ the constants c_{in} and c_{out} can be expressed easily:

$$c_{in} = average(u_0) \quad on\ \phi \geq 0 \\ = \frac{\int_\Omega u_0(x,y)H(\phi(x,y))dxdy}{\int_\Omega H(\phi(x,y))dxdy}. \tag{6}$$

$$c_{out} = average(u_0) \quad on\ \phi < 0 \\ = \frac{\int_\Omega u_0(x,y)\left(1-H(\phi(x,y))\right)dxdy}{\int_\Omega \left(1-H(\phi(x,y))\right)dxdy}. \tag{7}$$

If we use the Heaviside function as it has already defined (equation 4), the functional will be no differentiable because H is not differentiable. To overcome this problem, we consider slightly regularized version of H. There are several manners to express this regularization; the one used in [3] is given by:

$$H_\varepsilon(z) = \frac{1}{2}\left(1 + \frac{2}{\pi}\arctan\left(\frac{z}{\varepsilon}\right)\right) \qquad \delta_\varepsilon(z) = \frac{1}{\pi}\cdot\frac{\varepsilon}{\varepsilon^2+z^2}. \tag{9}$$

where ε is a given constant and $z \in \mathbb{R}$.

This formulation is used because it is different of zero everywhere as their graphs show on fig. 3. However, the algorithm tendencies to compute a global minimize, and the Euler-Lagrange equation (10) acts on all level curves, this that allows, in practice, obtaining a global minimizer (object's boundaries) independently of the initial curve position. More detail, comparisons with another formulation of H, and influence of ε value may be find in [3].

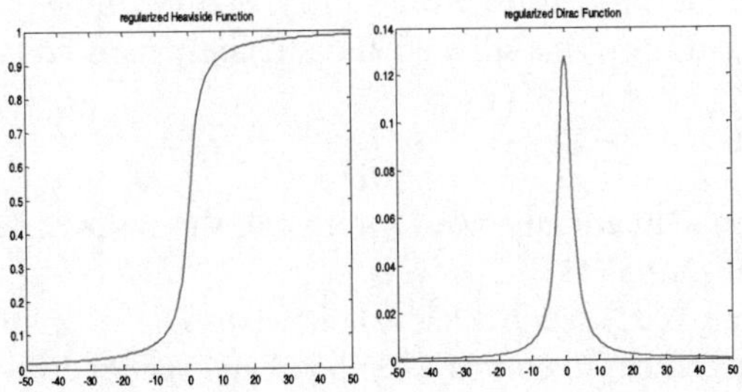

Fig. 3. The Heaviside and Dirac function for $\varepsilon = 2.5$

To minimize the formulation (5) we need their associated Euler-Lagrange equation, this one is given in [3] as follow:

$$\frac{\partial \phi}{\partial t} = \delta_\varepsilon(\phi)\left[\mu \operatorname{div}\left(\frac{\nabla\phi}{|\nabla\phi|}\right) - v - \lambda_1(u_0 - c_{in})^2 + \lambda_2(u_0 - c_{out})^2\right] = 0\,. \tag{10}$$

with $\phi(0, x, y) = \phi_0(x, y)$ is the initial level set function which is given.

4 Implementation

In this section we present the algorithm of the Chan-Vese model formulated via level set method implemented during this work.

4.1 Initialization of Level Sets

Traditionally, the level set function is initialized to a signed distance function to its interface. In almost works this one is a circle or a rectangle. This function is used widely thanks to its propriety $|\nabla\phi| = 1$ which simplifies calculations [13]. In traditional level set, re-initialize ϕ is used as a numerical remedy for maintaining stable curve evolution [8], [9], [11]. Re-initialize ϕ consists to solve the following re-initialization equation [13]:

$$\frac{\partial \phi}{\partial t} = sign(\phi_0)(1 - |\nabla\phi|)\,. \tag{11}$$

Much works, in literature, have been devoted to the re-initialization problem [14], [15]. Unfortunately, in some cases, for example ϕ_0 is not smooth or it is much steeper on one side of the interface than other, the resulting zero level of function ϕ can be moved incorrectly [16]. In addition, and from the practical viewpoints, the re-initialization process is complicated, expensive, and has side effects [15]. For this, there are some recent works avoiding the re-initialization such as the model proposed in [17].

More recently, the level set function is initialized to a binary function, which is more efficient and easier to construct practically, and the initial contour can take any shape. Further, the cost for re-initialization is efficiently reduced [18].

4.2 Descretization

To solve the problem numerically, we have to call the finite differences, often, used for numerical discretization [13].

To implement the proposed model, we have used the simple finite difference schema (forward difference) to compute temporal and spatial derivatives, so we have:

- Temporal discretization:
- $\frac{\partial \phi}{\partial t} = \frac{\phi_{i,j}^{n+1} - \phi_{i,j}^{n}}{\Delta t}$

- Spatial discretization

$$\nabla^x \phi_{i,j} = \frac{\phi_{i+1,j} - \phi_{i,j}}{\Delta x}$$

$$\nabla^y \phi_{i,j} = \frac{\phi_{i,j+1} - \phi_{i,j}}{\Delta y}$$

4.3 Algorithm

We summarize the main procedures, of the algorithm as follow:

Input: Image u_0, Initial curve position IP, parameters $\lambda_1,\ \lambda_2,\ \mu,\ v,\ \Delta t,\ \varepsilon$ Number of iterations N.
Output: Segmentation Result
Initialize Φ_0 to binary function
For all N *Iterations* do
Calculate c_{in} and c_{out} using equations (6,7)
Calculate Curvature Terms K;
Update Level Set Function
$$\Phi_{ij}^{n+1} = \Phi_{ij}^{n} + \Delta t.\delta(\phi_{i,j}).\left[\mu.K_{i,j} - v - \lambda_1(u_0(i,j) - c_{in})^2 + \lambda_2(u_0(i,j) - c_{out})^2\right]$$
Keep ϕ a binary function:
$\phi = 1\ if\ \phi > 0, otherwise, \phi = -1.$
End

5 Experimental Results

First of all, we note that our algorithm is implemented via Matlab 7.0 on 3.06-GHz and 1Go RAM, intel Pentium IV.

Now, let us present some of our experimental outcomes of the proposed model. The numerical implementation is based on the algorithm for curve evolution via level-sets. Also, as we have already explained, the model utilizes the image statistical information (average intensities inside and outside) to stop the curve evolution on the objects' boundaries, for this it is less sensitive to noise and it has better performance for images with weak edges. Furthermore, the *C-V* model implemented via level set can well segment all objects in a given image. In addition, the model can extract well the exterior and the interior boundaries. Another important advantage of the model is its less sensitive to the initial contour position, so this one can be anywhere on the image domain. For all the following results we have setting $\Delta t = 0.1$, $\varepsilon = 2.5$, and $\lambda_1 = \lambda_2 = 1$.

The result of segmentation on Fig.4 summarizes much of those advantages. From the initial contour, which is on the background of the image, the model detects all the boundaries' objects; even those are inside the objects (interior boundaries) as: door, windows, and the write on the house's roof...so on. Finally, we Note that we have the same outcome for any initial contour position.

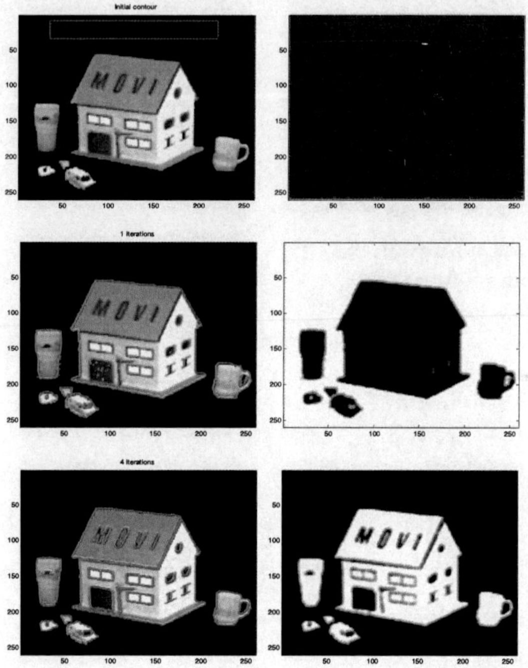

Fig. 4. Detection of different objects from a noisy image independently of curve initial position, with extraction of the interior boundaries. We set $\mu = 0.1; \quad v = 30. \ CPU\ time = 14.98s$.

Now, we want to show the model ability to detect weak boundaries. So we choose a synthetic image which contains four objects with different intensities as follow: Fig. 5 (b): 180, 100, 50, background =200; Fig. 5 (c): 120, 100, 50, background =200. As segmentation results show (Fig. 5) : the model failed to extract boundaries' object which have strong homogeneous intensity (Fig. 5(b)), but when the intensity is slightly different Chan-Vese model can detect this boundaries (Fig.5(c)). Note also, *C-V* model can extract objects' boundaries but it cannot give the corresponding intensity for each region: all objects on the image result are characterized by the same intensity (c_{in}) even though they have different intensities in the original image (Fig.5(d)) and (Fig.5(e)).

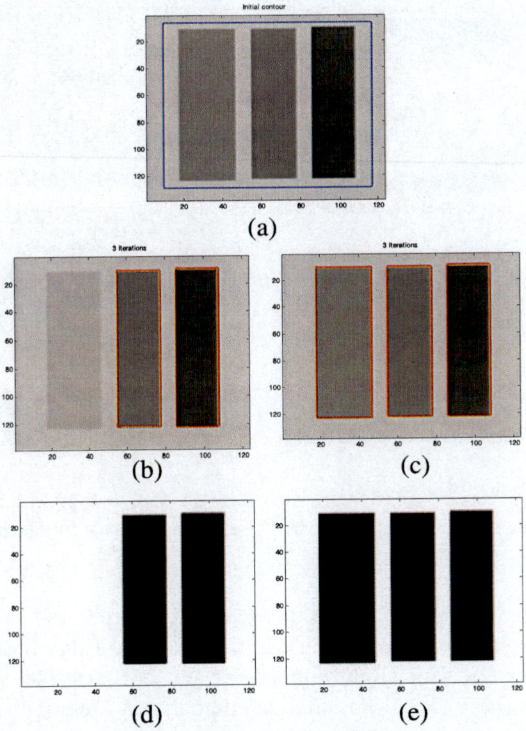

Fig. 5. Results for segmenting multi-objects with three different intensities (a) Initial contour. Column (b) result segmentation for 180, 100, 50, background =200. Column (c) result segmentation for 120, 100, 50, background =200. For both experiences we set $\mu = 0.1;\ \ v = 20.\ CPU\ time = 38.5s.$

Our target focuses on the radiographic image segmentation, applied to the detection of defects that could happen during the welding operation; it's about automatic control operation named *Non Destructive Testing* (*NDT*). The results obtained have been represented in the following figures:

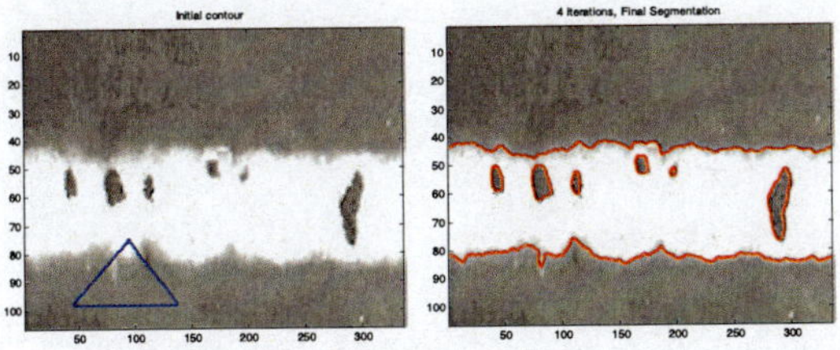

Fig.6. Detection of all defects in weld defects radiographic image $\mu = 0.2;\ v = 20,$ $CPU\ time = 14.6s$

Another example of radiographic image on which we have added a Gaussian noise ($\sigma^2 = 0.005$), and without any preprocessing of the noise image (filtering). The model can detect boundaries of defects very well, even though the image is nosy.

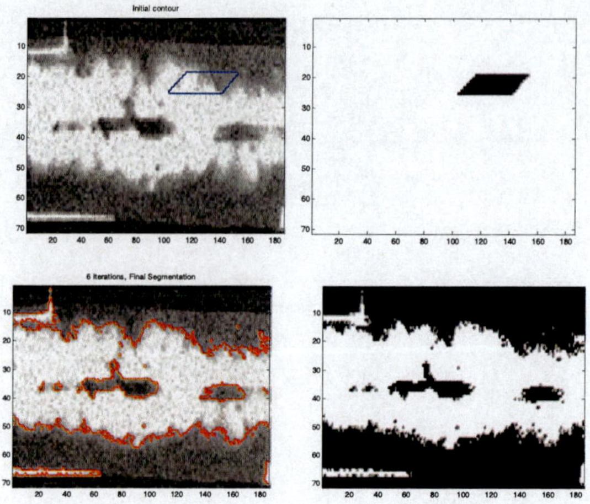

Fig. 6. Detection of defects in noisy radiographic image first column the initial and final contours, second one, the corresponding of the initial and final binary function. $\mu = 0.5;\ v = 20$, $CPU\ time = 13.6s$.

An example of radiographic image that we cannot segmented by Edge-based model because of their very weak boundaries; in this case the Edge-based function (equation 1) is never ever equal or slight equal zero and curve doesn't stop evolution till vanishes. As results show, the *C-V* model can detect very weak boundaries.

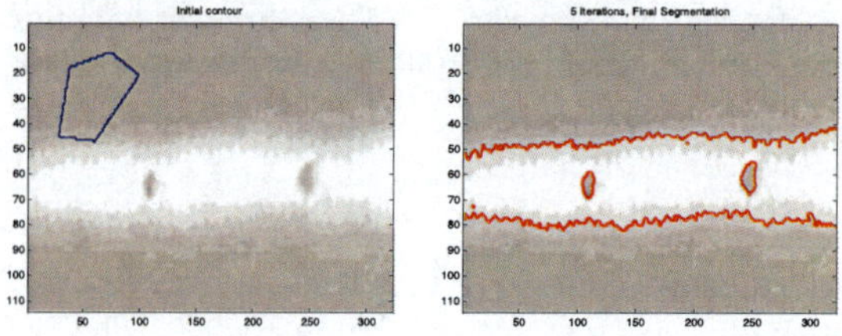

Fig. 7. Segmentation of radiographic image with very weak boundaries. $\mu = 0.1;\ v = 20$. $CPU\ time = 38.5s$.

Note that the proposed algorithm has less computational complexity and it converge in few iterations, by consequent, CPU time is reduced.

6 Conclusion

The algorithm was proposed to detect contours in given images which have gradient edges, weak edges or without edges. By using statistical image information, evolve contour stops in the objects boundaries. From this, The *C-V* model benefits a several advantages including robustness even with noisy data, and automatic detection of interior contours. Also, the initial contour can be anywhere in the image domain.

Before closing this paper, it is important to remember that *Chan-Vese* model separates two regions, so we have as a result the background presented with constant intensity (c_{out}) and all objects presented with (c_{in}). To extract objects with their corresponding intensities; we have to use multiphase or multi-region model. That is our aim for future work.

References

1. Dacorogna, B.: Introduction to the Calculus of Variations. Imperial College Press, London (2004) ISBN: 1-86094-499-X
2. Kass, M., Witkin, A., Terzopoulos, D.: Snakes: Active Contour Models, Internat. J. Comput. Vision 1, 321–331 (1988)
3. Chan, T., Vese, L.: An Active Contour Model without Edges. IEEE Trans. Image Processing 10(2), 266–277 (2001)
4. Zhi-lin, F., Yin, J.-w., Gang, C., Jin-xiang, D.: Jacquard image segmentation using Mumford-Shah model. Journal of Zhejiang University SCIENCE, 109–116 (2006)
5. Herbulot, A.: Mesures statistiques non-paramétriques pour la segmentation d'images et de vidéos et minimisation par contours actifs. Thèse de doctorat, Université de Nice - Sophia Antipolis (2007)
6. Osher, S., Sethin, J.A.: Fronts Propagating with Curvature-dependent Speed: Algorithms based on Hamilton–Jacobi formulation. J. Comput. Phys. 79, 12–49 (1988)
7. Osher, S., Paragios, N.: Geometric Level Set Methods in Imaging, Vision and Graphics, pp. 207–226. Springer, Heidelberg (2003)
8. Caselles, V., Catté, F., Coll, T., Dibos, F.: A Geometric Model for Active Contours in image processing. Numer. Math. 66, 1–31 (1993)
9. Malladi, R., Sethian, J.A., Vemuri, B.C.: A Topology Independent Shape Modeling Scheme. In: Proc. SPIE Conf. on Geometric Methods in Computer Vision II, San Diego, pp. 246–258 (1993)
10. Malladi, R., Sethian, J.A., Vemuri, B.C.: Evolutionary fronts for topology- independent shape modeling and recovery. In: Eklundh, J.-O. (ed.) ECCV 1994. LNCS, vol. 800, pp. 3–13. Springer, Heidelberg (1994)
11. Malladi, R., Sethian, J.A., Vemuri, B.C.: Shape Modeling with Front Propagation: A Level Set Approach. IEEE Trans. Pattern Anal. Mach. Intell. 17, 158–175 (1995)
12. Mumford, D., Shah, J.: Optimal approximations by piecewise smooth functions and associated variational problems. Commun. Pure Appl. Math. 42(4) (1989)
13. Osher, S., Fedkiw, R.P.: Level Set Methods and Dynamic Implicit Surfaces. Springer, Heidelberg (2003)
14. Peng, D., Merriman, B., Osher, S., Zhao, H., Kang, M.: A PDE-based Fast Local Level Set Method. J. omp. Phys. 155, 410–438 (1999)
15. Sussman, M., Fatemi, E.: An Efficient, Interface-preserving Level Set Redistancing algorithm and its Application to Interfacial Incompressible Fluid Flow. SIAM J. Sci. Comp. 20, 1165–1191 (1999)
16. Han, X., Xu, C., Prince, J.: A Topology Preserving Level Set Method For Geometric deformable models. IEEE Trans. Patt. Anal. Intell. 25, 755–768 (2003)
17. Li, C., Xu, C., Gui, C., Fox, M.D.: Level Set without Re-initialisation: A New Variational Formulation. In: IEEE Computer Society Conference on Computer Vision and Pattern Recognition (2005)
18. Zhang, K., Zhang, L., Song, H., Zhou, W.: Active Contours with Selective Local or Global Segmentation: A New Formulation and Level Set Method. Elsevier Journal, Image and Vision Computing, 668–676 (2010)

Adaptive and Statistical Polygonal Curve for Multiple Weld Defects Detection in Radiographic Images

Aicha Baya Goumeidane[1], Mohammed Khamadja[2], and Nafaa Nacereddine[1]

[1] Centre de recherche Scientifique et Technique en Soudage et Controle, (CSC), Cheraga Alger, Algeria
ab_goumeidane@yahoo.fr, nafaa.nacereddine@enp.edu.dz

[2] SP_Lab, Electronic Dept., Mentouri University, Ain El Bey Road, 25000 Constantine, Algeria
m_khamadja@yahoo.fr

Abstract. With the advances in computer science and artificial intelligence techniques, the opportunity to develop computer aided technique for radiographic inspection in Non Destructive Testing arose. This paper presents an adaptive probabilistic region-based deformable model using an explicit representation that aims to extract automatically defects from a radiographic film. To deal with the height computation cost of such model, an adaptive polygonal representation is used and the search space for the greedy-based model evolution is reduced. Furthermore, we adapt this explicit model to handle topological changes in presence of multiple defects.

Keywords: Radiographic inspection, explicit deformable model, adaptive contour representation, Maximum likelihood criterion, Multiple contours.

1 Introduction

Radiography is one of the old and still effective NDT tools. X-rays penetrate welded target and produce a shadow picture of the internal structure of the target [1]. Automatic detection of weld defect is thus a difficult task because of the poor image quality of industrial radiographic images, the bad contrast, the noise and the low defects dimensions. Moreover, the perfect knowledge of defects shapes and their locations is critical for the appreciation of the welding quality. For that purpose, image segmentation is applied. It allows the initial separation of regions of interest which are subsequently classified. Among the boundary extraction based segmentation techniques, active contour or snakes are recognized to be one of the efficient tools for 2D/3D image segmentation [2]. Broadly speaking a snake is a curve which evolves to match the contour of an object in the image. The bulk of the existing works in segmentation using active contours can be categorized into two basic approaches: edge-based approaches, and region-based ones. The edge-based approaches are called so because the information used to

H. Cherifi, J.M. Zain, and E. El-Qawasmeh (Eds.): DICTAP 2011, Part I, CCIS 166, pp. 184–198, 2011.

drawn the curves to the edges is strictly along the boundary. Hence, a strong edge must be detected in order to drive the snake. This obviously causes poor performance of the snake in weak gradient fields. That is, these approaches fail in the presence of noise. Several improvements have been proposed to overcome these limitations but still they fail in numerous cases [3][4][5][6][7][8][9] [10][11]. With the region- based ones [12] [13][14][15][16][17][18][19] [20], the inner and the outer region defined by the snake are considered and, thus, they are well-adapted to situations for which it is difficult to extract boundaries from the target. We can note that such methods are computationally intensive since the computations are made over a region [18][19].

This paper deals with the detection of multiple weld defects in radiographic films, and presents a new region based snake which exploits a statistical formulation where a maximum likelihood greedy evolution strategy and an adaptive snake nodes representation are used. In Section 2 we detail the mathematical formulation of the snake which is the basis of our work. Section 3 is devoted to the development of the proposed progression stategy of our snake to increase the progression speed. In section 4 we show how we adapt the model to the topology in presence of multiple defects. Results are shows in Section 5. We draw the main conclusions in section 6.

2 The Statistical Snake

2.1 Statistical Image Model

Let $C = \{c_0, c_1, ..., c_{N-1}\}$ be the boundary of a connected image region R_1 of the plane and R_2 the points that do not belong to R_1. if x_i is the gray-level value observed at the ith pixel, $\mathbf{X} = \{x_i\}$ the pixel grey levels, p_x the grey level density, and $\phi_x = \{\phi_1, \phi_2\}$ the density parameters (i.e., $p(x_i) = p(x_i|\phi_1)$ for $i \in R_1$ and$p(x_i) = p(x_i|\phi_2)$ for $i \in R_2$). The simplest possible region based model is characterized by the following hypothesis: conditional independence (given the region contour, all the pixels are independent); and region homogeneity, i.e., all the pixels in the inner (outer) region have identical distributions characterized by the same ϕ_x. Thus the likelihood function can be written as done in [13] [14]

$$p(\mathbf{X}|C, \phi_x) = \prod_{i \in R_1} p(x_i|\phi_1) \prod_{i \in R_2} p(x_i|\phi_2) \tag{1}$$

2.2 Evolution Criterion

The purpose being the estimation of the contour C of the region R_1 with K snake nodes, then this can be done by exploiting the presented image model by using the MAP estimation since:

$$p(C|\mathbf{X}) = p(C)p(\mathbf{X}|C) \tag{2}$$

and then

$$\hat{C}_{MAP} = \arg\max_C p(C)p(\mathbf{X}|C) \tag{3}$$

Since we assume there is no shape prior and no constraints are applied to the model, then $p(C)$ can be considered as uniform constant and then removed from the estimation. Moreover Model image parameters must be added in the estimation, then:

$$\hat{C}_{MAP} = \arg\max_{C} p(\mathbf{X}|C) = \arg\max_{C} p(\mathbf{X}|C, \phi_x) = \hat{C}_{ML} \quad (4)$$

Hence the MAP estimation is reduced to ML (Maximum likelihood) one. Estimating C implies also the estimation of the parameter model ϕ_x. Under the maximum likelihood criterion, the best estimates of ϕ_x and C denoted by $\hat{\phi_x}$ and $\hat{C}$ are given by:

$$(\hat{C}, \hat{\phi_x})_{ML} = \arg\max_{C,\phi_x} \log p(\mathbf{X}|C, \phi_x) \quad (5)$$

The log function is included d as it allows some formal simplification without affecting the location of the maximum. Since solving (5) simultaneously with respect to C and ϕ_x would be computationally very difficult, then an iterative scheme is used to solve the equation:

$$\hat{C}^{t+1} = \arg\max_{C} \log p(\mathbf{X}|C, \hat{\phi_x}^t) \quad (6)$$

$$\hat{\phi_x}^{t+1} = \arg\max_{\phi_x} \log p(\mathbf{X}|\hat{C}^{t+1}, \phi_x) \quad (7)$$

Where $\hat{C}^t$ and $\hat{\phi_x}^t$ are the ML estimates of C and ϕ_x respectively at the iteration t.

2.3 Greedy Evolution

The implementation of the snake evolution (according to(6)) uses the greedy strategy, which evolves the curve parameters in an iterative manner by local neighborhood search around snake points to select new ones which maximize $\log p(\mathbf{X}|C, \hat{\phi_x}^t)$. The used neighborhood is the set of the eight nearest pixels.

3 Speeding the Evolution

The region-based snakes are known for their high computational cost. To reduce this cost we have associated two strategies:

3.1 Neighborhood Reducing and Normal Evolution

In [20], authors choose to change the search strategy of the pixels being candidates to maximize $\log p(\mathbf{X}|C, \hat{\phi_x}^t)$. For each snake node, instead of searching the new position of this node among the 8-neighborhood positions, the space search is reduced from 1 to 1/4 by limiting the search to the two pixels laying in normal directions of snake curve at this node. This has speeded up four times the snake progression. In this work we decide to increase the search deep to reach the four pixels laying in the normal direction as shown in Fig.1.

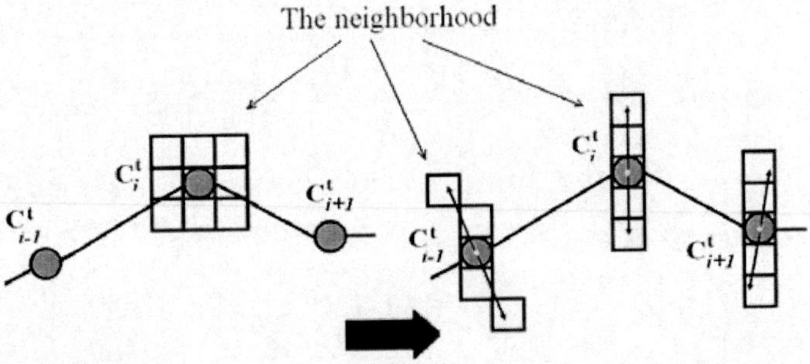

Fig. 1. The new neighborhood: from the eight nearest pixels to the four nearest pixels in the normal directions

3.2 Polygonal Representation and Adaptive Segments Length

An obvious reason for choosing the polygonal representation is for the simplicity of its implementation. Another advantage of this description is when a node is moved; the deformation of the shape is local. Moreover, it could describe smooth shapes when a large number of nodes are used. However increase the nodes number will decrease the computation speed. To improve progression velocity, nodes number increases gradually along the snake evolution iterations through an insertion/deletion procedure. Indeed, initialization is done with few points and when the evolution stops, points are added between the existing points to launch the evolution, whereas other points are removed.

Deletion and Insertion Processes. The progression of the snake will be achieved through cycles, where the number of the snake points grow with a insertion/deletion procedure. In the cycle 0, the initialization of the contour begin with few points. Thus, solving (6) is done quickly and permits to have an approximating segmentation of the object as this first contour converges. In the next cycle, points are added between initial nodes and a mean length $MeanS$ of obtained segments is computed. As the curve progresses towards its next final step, the maximum length allowed will be related to $MeanS$ so that if two successive points c_i and c_{i+1} move away more than this length, a new point is inserted and then the segment $[c_i \; c_{i+1}]$ is divided. On the other hand, if the distance of two consecutive points is less than a defined threshold (TH)these two points are merged into one point placed in the middle of the segment $[c_i \; c_{i+1}]$. Moreover, to prevent undesired behavior of the contour, like self intersections of adjacent segments, every three consecutive points c_{i-1}, c_i, c_{i+1} are checked, and if the nodes c_{i-1} and c_{i+1} are closer than $MeanS/2$, c_i is removed (the two segments are merged) as illustrated in Fig.2. This can be assimilated to a regularization process to maintain curve continuity and prevent overshooting. When convergence is achieved again (the progression stops) new points are added and a new$MeanS$ is computed. A new cycle can begin. The process is repeated until no progression is noted after a new cycle is begun or no more points could be added. This is achieved when the distance between every two consecutive points is less then the threshold TH. Here, the end of the final cycle is reached.

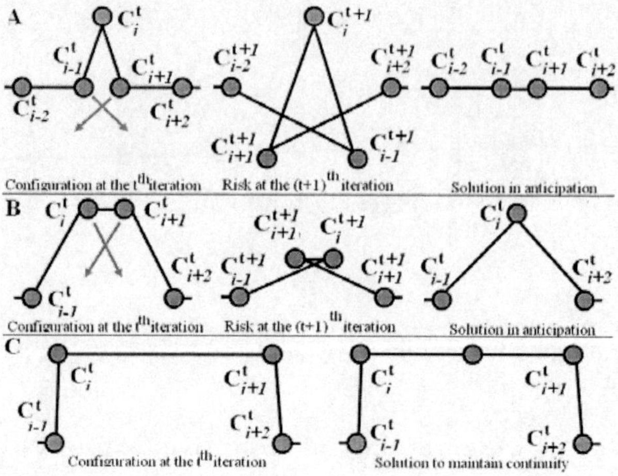

Fig. 2. Regularization procedure: A and B Avoiding overshooting by merging segments or nodes, C Maintaining the continuity by adding nodes if necessary

3.3 Algorithms

Since the kernel of the method is the Maximum Likelihood (ML) estimation of the snake nodes by optimizing the search strategy (reducing the neighborhood), we begin by presenting the algorithm related to the ML criterion, we have named **AlgotithmML**. Next to this algorithm we present the algorithm of the regularization we have just named **Regularization**. These two algorithms will be used by the algorithm which describes the evolution of the snake over a cycle. We have called this algorithm **AlgorithmCycle**. The overall method algorithm named **OverallAlgo** is given after the three quoted algorithms. For all these algorithms $MeanS$ and TH are the mean segment length and the threshold shown in the section 3.2 α is a constant related to the continuity maintenance of the snake model. ε is the convergence threshold.

Algorithm 1. AlgorithmML

input : M nodes $C = [c_0, c_1, \ldots, c_{M-1}]$,
output: C^{ML}, ML
Begin;
Step 0 : Estimate $\phi_x(\phi_1, \phi_2)$inside and outside C;
Step 1 : Update the polygon according to:
$c_j^{ML} = \arg \max_{n_j \in N(c_j)} \log p(\mathbf{X}|[c_1, c_2, \ldots, n_j, \ldots, c_M], \phi_x)$ $N(c_j)$ is the set of the four nearest pixels laying in the normal direction of c_j. This will be repeated for all the polygon points;
Step 2 :Estimate ϕ_x^{ML} for C^{ML} and ML as: $ML = \log p(\mathbf{X}|C^{ML}, \phi_x^{ML})$;
End

Algorithm 2. Regularization

input : M nodes $C = [c_0, c_1, \ldots, c_{M-1}]$, $MeanS$, TH, α
output: C^{Reg}
Begin;
Step 0: Compute the M segments length: $S\_lenght(i)$;
Step 1: **for** *all i (i=1,...,M)* **do**
    if $S\_length(i) < TH$ **then**
        Remove c_i and c_{i+1} and replace them by a new one in the middle of $[c_i c_{i+1}]$
    end
    if $S\_length(i) > \alpha * MeanS$ **then**
        insert a node in the middle of $[c_i c_{i+1}]$
    end
end
Step 2 :**for** *all triplet* (c_{i-1}, c_i, c_{i+1}) **do**
    if c_{i-1} *and* c_{i+1} *are closer than* $MeanS/2$ **then**
        Remove c_i
    end
end
End

Algorithm 3. AlgorithmCycle

input : Initial nodes $C^0_{cy} = [c^0_{cy-1}, c^0_{cy-2}, \ldots, c^0_{cy-N-1}]$, $MeanS$, TH, α,ε
output: The estimates $\hat{C}_{cy}$, $\hat{L}_{cy}$ of the current cycle
Begin
Step 0: Set $t = 0$ (iteration counter) and $C^t_{cy} = C^0_{cy}$
    Compute $MeanS$ of the N initial segments
Step 1: Estimate $\phi^t_{x_{cy}}(\phi_1, \phi_2)$ inside and outside C^t_{cy}
    $L1 = \log p(\mathbf{X}|C^t_{cy}, \phi^t_{x_{cy}})$
    Perform **AlgorithmML**(C^t_{cy})
Step 2 : Recover ML and C^{ML}
    $L2 = ML, C^{t+1}_{cy} = C^{ML}$
    Perform **Regularization**(C^{t+1}_{cy}, $MeanS$, TH, α)
if $|L1 - L2| > \varepsilon$ **then**
    $C^t_{cy} = C^{Reg}$
    go to **step 1**
    else
    $\hat{L}_{cy} = L2$
    go to end
end
End

Algorithm 4. OverallAlgo

input : Initial nodes C^0, $MeanS$, TH, α, ε
output: Final contour $\hat{C}$

Begin
Step 0 :Compute $MeanS$ of the all segments of C^0
Step 1 :Perform **AlgorithmCycle**(C^0, ε, TH, α, $MeanS$)
Step 2 : Recover $\hat{L_{cy}}$ and the snake nodes $\hat{C_{cy}}$
Step 3 :Insert new nodes to launch the evolution
if *no node can be inserted* **then**
  $\hat{C} = \hat{C_{cy}}$
  Go to **End**
end

Step 4 :Creation of C^{New} because of the step 3
Step 5 :Perform **AlgorithmML**(C^{New})
Recover ML, Recover C^{ML}
if $\hat{L}_{cy} - ML < \varepsilon$ **then**
  $\hat{C} = \hat{C_{cy}}$
  go to **End**
end

Step 6 :$C^0 = C^{ML}$
Go to step 1
End

4 Adapting the Topology

The presented adaptive snake model can be used to represent the contour of a single defect. However, if there is more than one defect in the image, the snake model can be modified so that it handles the topological changes and determines the corresponding contour of each defect. We will describe here the determination of critical points where the snake is split for multiple defect representation. The validation of each contour will be verified so that invalid contour will be removed.

4.1 The Model Behavior in the Presence of Multiple Defects

In presence of multiple defects, the model curve will try to surround all these defects. From this will result one or more self intersections of the curve, depending of the number of the defects and their positions with respect to the initial contour. The critical points where the curve is split, are the self intersection points. The apparition of self intersection implies the creation of loops which are considered as valid if they are not empty. It is known that an explicit snake is represented by a chain of ordered points . Then, if self intersections occur, their points are inserted in the snake nodes chain first and then, are stored in a vector named Vip in the order they appear by running through the nodes chain. Obviously each intersection point will appear twice in this new chain. For convenience, we define a loop as a points chain which starts and finishes with the same intersection point without encountering another intersection point. After a loop is detected, isolated and its validity is checked, then, the corresponding intersection point is removed from Vip and thus can be considered as an ordinary point in the remaining curve. This will permit to detect loops born from two or more self intersections.

This can be explained from an example: Let $C_n = \{c_1, c_2, ..., c_n\}$, with n=12, be the nodes chain of the curve shown in the Fig. 3, with c_1 as the first node (in grey in the figure). These nodes are taken in the clock-wise order in the figure. This curve, which represents our snake model, has undergone two self intersections, represented by the points we named c_{int1} and c_{int2}, when it tries to surround the two shapes. These two points are inserted in the chain nodes representing the model to form the new model points as following: $C_n^{new} = \{c_1^{new}, c_2^{new}, ..., c_n^{new}\}$, with n=16 and $c_4^{new} = c_{int1}$, $c_6^{new} = c_{int2}$, $c_{13}^{new} = c_{int2}$, $c^{new}c_{14} = c_{int1}$. After this modification, the vector Vip is formed by: Vip=[c_{int1} c_{int2} c_{int2} c_{int1}]=[c_4^{new} c_6^{new} c_{13}^{new} c_{14}^{new}].

Thus, by running through the snake nodes chain in the clock-wise sense, we will encounter $Vip(1)$ then $Vip(2)$ and so on...By applying the loop definition we have given, and just by examining Vip the loops can be detected. Hence, the first detected loop is the one consisting of the nodes between $Vip(2)$ and $Vip(3)$

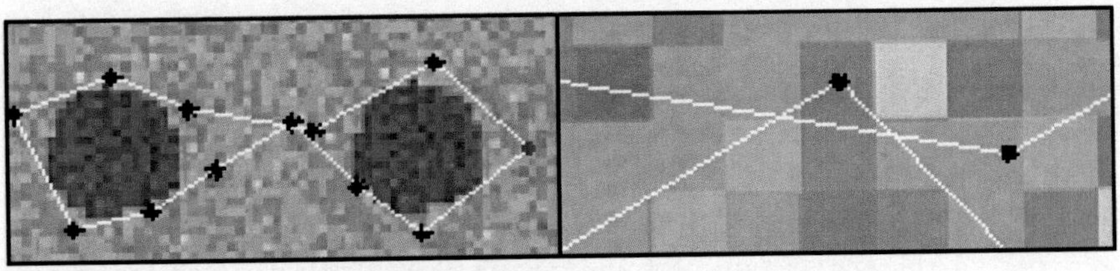

Fig. 3. At left self intersection of the polygonal curve, at right Zoomed self intersections

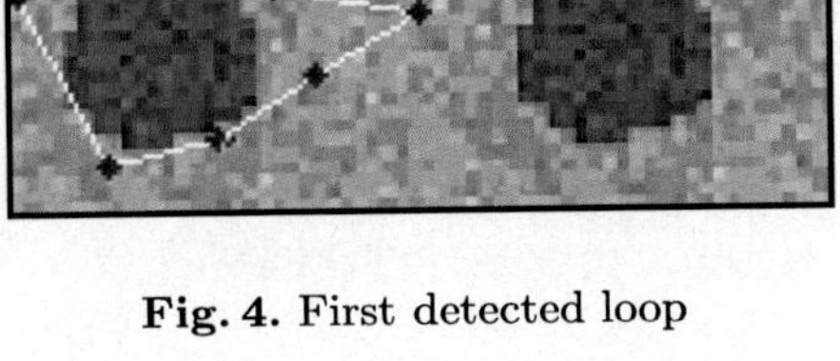

Fig. 4. First detected loop

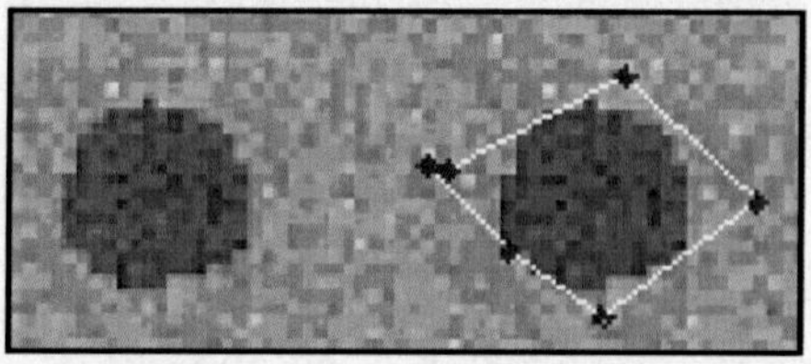

Fig. 5. Second detected loop

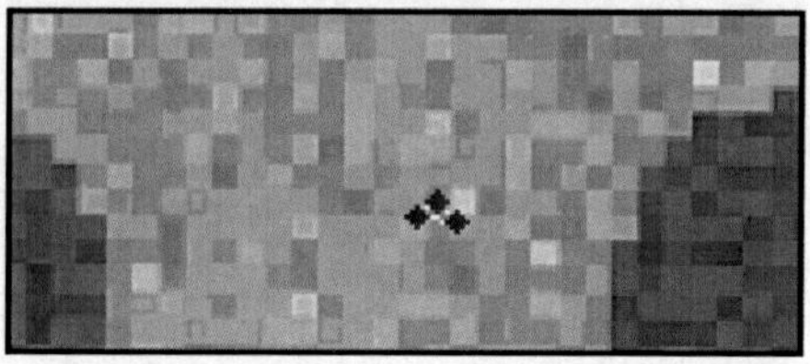

Fig. 6. Third detected loop, it is empty and then it is an invalid one

ie. $\{c_6^{new}, c_7^{new}, ..., c_{12}^{new}\}$, ($c_6^{new}$ being equal to c_{13}^{new}). This first loop, shown on the Fig. 4, is separated from the initial curve, its validity is checked (not empty) and c_6^{new}, c_{13}^{new} are deleted from Vip and then considered as ordinary nodes in the remaining curve. Now, Vip equals $[c_4^{new} \quad c_{14}^{new}]$. Therefore, the next loop to be detected is made up of the nodes that are between c_4^{new} and c_{14}^{new}. It should be noted that we have to choose the loop which do not contain previous detected loops nodes (except self-intersection's points). In this case the new loop consists of the node's sequence $\{c_{14}^{new}, c_{15}^{new}, c_{16}^{new}, c_1^{new}, ..., c_3^{new}\}$ (c_4^{new} being equal to c_{14}^{new}). This loop, which is also separated from the remaining snake curve, is illustrated in the Fig 5. Once Vip is empty, we check the remaining nodes in the remaining snake curve. These nodes constitute also a loop as shown in Fig. 6.

To check the validity of a loop, we had just to see the characteristics of the outer region of the snake model at the first self intersections, like for example the mean or(and) the variance. If the inside region of the current loop have similar characteristics of the outside region of the overall polygonal curve at the first intersection (same characteristics of the background) then this loop is not valid,and, it will be rejected. On the other hand, a loop which holds few pixels (a valid loop must contain a minimum number of pixels we have named $MinSize$) is also rejected because there are no weld defects that have such little sizes.

The new obtained curves (detected valid loops) will be treated as independent ones, i.e. the algorithms quoted before are applied separately on each detected loop. Indeed, their progressions depend only on the object they contain.

5 Results

The snake we proposed, is tested first on a synthetic image consisting of one complex object (Fig.8). This image is corrupted with a Gaussian distributed noise . The image pixels grey levels are then modeled with a Gaussian distribution with mean and variance μ and σ^2 respectively. The estimates of ϕ_x with i=1, 2 are the mean and the variance of pixels grey levels inside and outside the polygon representing the snake. The Gaussian noise parameters of this image are $\{\mu_1, \sigma_1\} = \{70, 20\}$ for the object and $\{\mu_2, \sigma_2\} = \{140, 15\}$ for the background.

First, we begin by showing the model behavior without regularization. Fig.7 gives an example of the effect of the absence of reularization procedures. Indeed, the creation of undesirable loops is then inescapable.

We show after the behavior of the association of the algorithms **AlgorithmML**, **AlgorithmCycle**, **Regularization** and **Algorithm** with $\alpha = 1.5$, $TH = 1$, $\varepsilon = 10^{-4}$ on this image (Fig.8). The model can track concavities and although the noisy considered image, the object contour is correctly estimated.

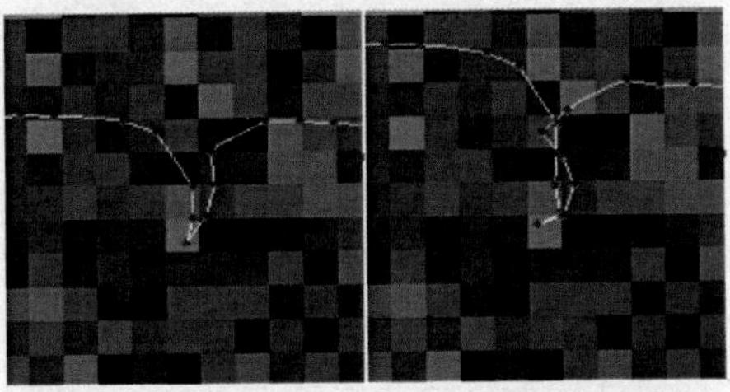

Fig. 7. Undesirable loops creation without regularization

Furthermore, the model is tested on weld defect radiographic images containing one defect as shown in Fig.9. Because the industrial or medical radiographic images, follow, in general, Gaussian distribution and that is due mainly to the differential absorption principle which governs the formation process of such images. The initial contours are sets of eight points describing circles crossing the defect in each image, the final ones match perfectly the defects boundaries.

After having tested the behavior of the model in presence of one defect, we show in the next two figures its capacity of handling topological changes in presence of multiple defect in the image (Fig.10, Fig.11), where the minimal size of a defect is chosen to be equal to three pixels ($MinSize = 3$). The snake surrounds the defects, splits and fits successfully their contours.

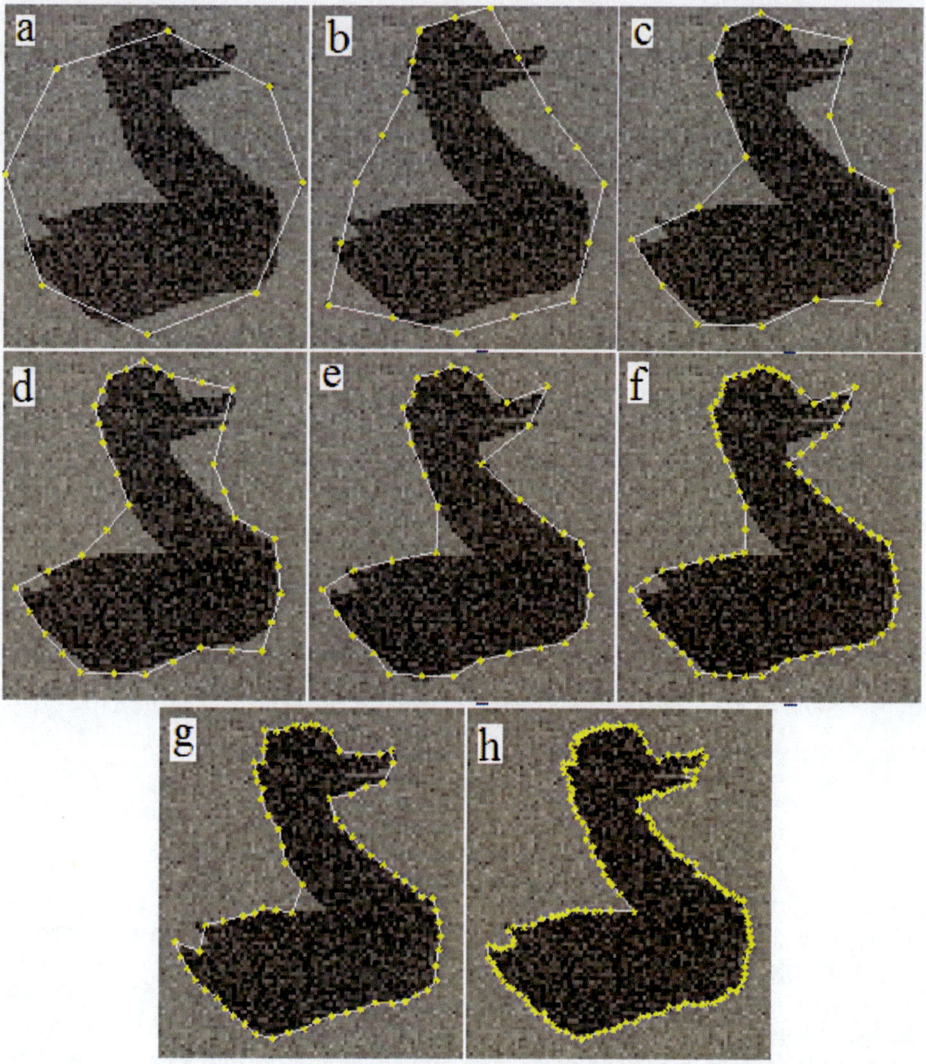

Fig. 8. Adaptive snake progression in case of synthetic images, a) initialization: start of the first cycle, b) first division to launch the evolution and the start of the second cycle , c) iteration before the second division d) second division e) iteration before the third division f) third division g) iteration before the last iteration, h) final rsult

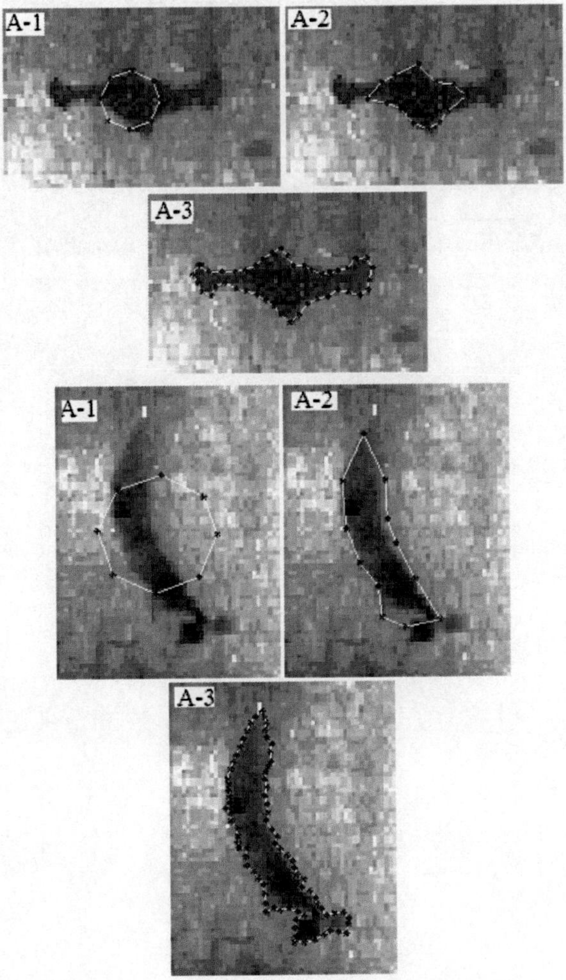

Fig. 9. Adaptive snake progression in case of radiographic images: A1 initial contours, A2 intermediate contours, A3 final contours

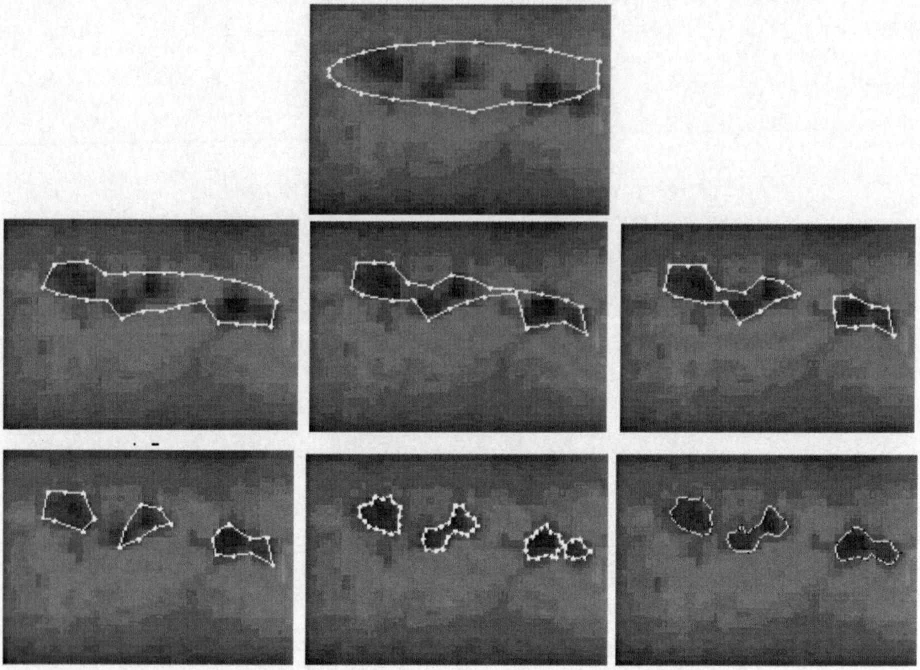

Fig. 10. Adaptive snake progression in presence of multiple defects

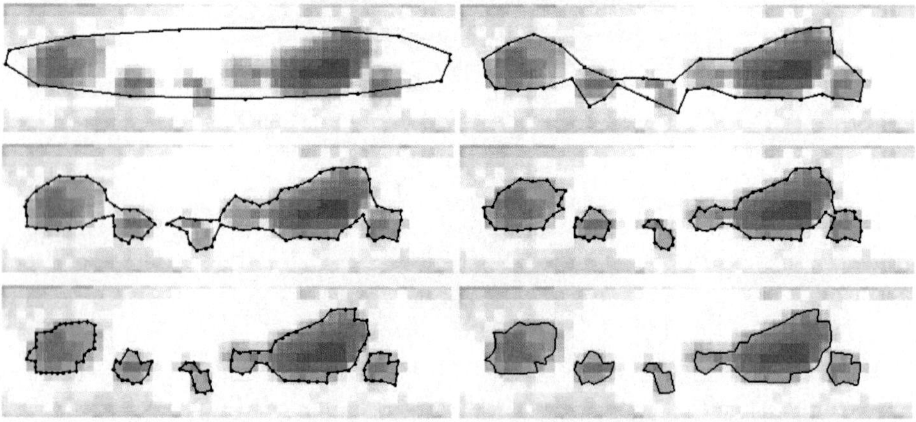

Fig. 11. Adaptive snake progression in presence of multiple defects

6 Conclusion

We have described a new approach of boundary extraction of weld defects in radiographic images. This approach is based on statistical formulation of contour estimation improved with a combination of additional strategies to speed up the progression and increase in an adaptive way the model nodes number. Moreover the proposed snake model can split successfully in presence of multiple contours and handle the topological changes. Experiments, on synthetic and radiographic images, show the ability of the proposed technique to give quickly a good estimation of the contours by fitting almost boundaries.

References

1. Halmshaw, R.: The Grid: Introduction to the Non-Destructive Testing in Welded Joints. Woodhead Publishing, Cambridge (1996)
2. Kass, M., Witkin, A., Terzopoulos, D.: Snakes: Active Contour Models. International Journal of Computer Vision, 321–331 (1988)
3. Xu, C., Prince, J.: Snakes, Shapes, and gradient vector flow. IEEE Transactions on Images Processing 7(3), 359–369 (1998)
4. Jacob, M., Blu, T., Unser, M.: Efficient energies and algorithms for parametric snakes. IEEE Trans. on Image Proc. 13(9), 1231–1244 (2004)
5. Tauber, C., Batatia, H., Morin, G., Ayache, A.: Robust b-spline snakes for ultrasound image segmentation. IEEE Computers in Cardiology 31, 25–28 (2004)
6. Zimmer, C., Olivo-Marin, J.C.: Coupled parametric active contours. IEEE Trans. Pattern Anal. Mach. Intell. 27(11), 1838–1842 (2005)
7. Srikrishnan, V., Chaudhuri, S., Roy, S.D., Sevcovic, D.: On Stabilisation of Parametric Active Contours. In: CVPR 2007, pp. 1–6 (2007)
8. Li, B., Acton, S.T.: Active Contour External Force Using Vector Field Convolution for Image Segmentation. IEEE Trans. on Image Processing 16(8), 2096–2106 (2007)
9. Li, B., Acton, S.T.: Automatic Active Model Initialization via Poisson Inverse Gradient. IEEE Trans. on Image Processing 17(8), 1406–1420 (2008)
10. Collewet, C.: Polar snakes: A fast and robust parametric active contour model. In: IEEE Int. Conf. on Image Processing, pp. 3013–3016 (2009)
11. Wang, Y., Liu, L., Zhang, H., Cao, Z., Lu, S.: Image Segmentation Using Active Contours With Normally Biased GVF External Force. IEEE signal Processing 17(10), 875–878 (2010)
12. Ronfard, R.: Region based strategies for active contour models. IJCV 13(2), 229–251 (1994)
13. Dias, J.M.B.: Adaptive bayesian contour estimation: A vector space representation approach. In: Hancock, E.R., Pelillo, M. (eds.) EMMCVPR 1999. LNCS, vol. 1654, pp. 157–173. Springer, Heidelberg (1999)
14. Jardim, S.M.G.V.B., Figuerido, M.A.T.: Segmentation of Fetal Ultrasound Images. Ultrasound in Med. & Biol. 31(2), 243–250 (2005)
15. Ivins, J., Porrill, J.: Active region models for segmenting medical images. In: Proceedings of the IEEE Internation Conference on Image Processing (1994)
16. Abd-Almageed, W., Smith, C.E.: Mixture models for dynamic statistical pressure snakes. In: IEEE International Conference on Pattern Recognition (2002)

17. Abd-Almageed, W., Ramadan, S., Smith, C.E.: Kernel Snakes: Non-parametric Active Contour Models. In: IEEE International Conference on Systems, Man and Cybernetics (2003)
18. Goumeidane, A.B., Khamadja, M., Naceredine, N.: Bayesian Pressure Snake for Weld Defect Detection. In: Blanc-Talon, J., Philips, W., Popescu, D., Scheunders, P. (eds.) ACIVS 2009. LNCS, vol. 5807, pp. 309–319. Springer, Heidelberg (2009)
19. Chesnaud, C., Réfrégier, P., Boulet, V.: Statistical Region Snake-Based Segmentation Adapted to Different Physical Noise Models. IEEE Transaction on PAMI 21(11), 1145–1157 (1999)
20. Nacereddine, N., Hammami, L., Ziou, D., Goumeidane, A.B.: Region-based active contour with adaptive B-spline. Application in radiographic weld inspection. Image Processing & Communications 15(1), 35–45 (2010)

A Method for Plant Classification Based on Artificial Immune System and Wavelet Transform

Esma Bendiab and Mohamed Kheirreddine Kholladi

MISC Laboratory, Department of Computer Science,
Mentouti University of Constantine, 25017, Algeria
Bendiab_e@yahoo.fr, Kholladi@yahoo.com

Abstract. Leaves recognition plays an important role in plant classification. Its key issue lies in whether selected features are stable and have good ability to discriminate different kinds of leaves. In this paper, we propose a novel method of plant classification from leaf image set based on artificial immune system (AIS) and wavelet transforms. AISs are a type of intelligent algorithm; they emulate the human defense mechanism and they use its principles, to give them the power to be applied as a classifier. In addition, the wavelet transform offers fascinating features for texture classification. Experimental results show that using artificial immune system and wavelet transform to recognize leaf plant image is possible, and the accuracy of recognition is encouraging.

Keywords: Artificial Immune System (AIS), Dendritic Cell Algorithm (DCA), Digital wavelet transform, leaves classification.

1 Introduction

Artificial immune systems (AIS) are relatively new class of meta-heuristics that mimics aspects of the human immune system to solve computational problems [1-4]. They are massively distributed and parallel, highly adaptive and reactive and evolutionary where learning is native. AIS can be defined [5] as the composition of intelligent methodologies, inspired by the natural immune system for the resolution of real world problems.

Growing interests are surrounding those systems due to the fact that natural mechanisms such as: recognition, identification, and intruders' elimination, which allow the human body to reach its immunity. AISs suggest new ideas for computational problems. Artificial immune systems consist of some typical intelligent computational algorithms [1,2] termed immune network theory, clone selection , negative selection and recently the danger theory[3] .

Though, AISs has successful applications which are quoted in literature [1-3]; the self non self paradigm, which performs discriminatory process by tolerating self entities and reacting to foreign ones, was much criticized for many reasons, which will be described in section 2. Therefore, a controversial alternative way to this paradigm was proposed: the danger theory [4].

The danger theory offers new perspectives and ideas to AISs [4,6]. It stipulates that the immune system react to danger and not to foreign entities. In this context, it is a

H. Cherifi, J.M. Zain, and E. El-Qawasmeh (Eds.): DICTAP 2011, Part I, CCIS 166, pp. 199–208, 2011.

matter of distinguishing non self but harmless from self but harmful invaders, termed: antigen. If the labels self and non self were to be replaced by interesting and non interesting data, a distinction would prove beneficial. In this case, the AIS is being applied as a classifier [6].

Besides, plant recognition is an important and challenging task [7-10] due to the lack of proper models or representation schemes. Compared with other methods, such as cell and molecule biology methods, classification based on leaf image is the first choice for plant classification. Sampling leaves and photogening them are low-cost and convenient. Moreover, leaves can be very easily found and collected everywhere. By computing some efficient features of leaves and using a suitable pattern classifier, it is possible to recognize different plants successfully.

Many works have been focused on leaf feature extraction for recognition of plant. We can especially mention [7-10]. In [7], authors proposed a classification method of plant classification based on wavelet transforms and support vector machines. The approach is not the first in this way, as authors in [8] have earlier used the support vector machines as an approach of plants recognition but using the colour and the texture features space. In [9], a method of recognizing leaf images based on shape features using and comparing three classifiers approaches was introduced. In [10], the author proposes a method of plants classification based on leaves recognition. Two methods called the gray-level co-occurrence matrix and principal component analysis algorithms have been applied to extract the leaves texture features.

This paper proposes a new approach for classifying plant leaves. The classification resorts to the Dendritic cell algorithm from danger theory and uses the wavelet transform as space features. The Wavelet Transform [11] provides a powerful tool to capture localised features and gives developments for more flexible and useful representations. Also, it presents constant analysis of a given signal by projection onto a set of basic functions that are scaled by means of frequency variation. Each wavelet is a shifted scaled version of an original or mother wavelet. These families are usually orthogonal to one another, important since this yields computational efficiency and ease of numerical implementation [7].

The rest of the paper is organized as follows. Section 2 contains relevant background information and motivation regarding the danger theory. Section 3 describes the Dendritic Cell Algorithm. In section 4, we define the wavelet transform. This is followed by Sections 5, presenting a description of the approach. This is followed by experimentations in section 6. The paper ends with a conclusion and future works.

2 The Danger Theory

The main goal of the immune system is to protect our bodies from invading entities, called: antigens, which cause damage and diseases.

At the outset, the traditional immune theory considers that the protection was done by distinguishing self and non self inside the body and by eliminating the non self. Incompetent to explain certain phenomena, the discriminating paradigm in the immune system presents many gaps, such [3]:

- There is no immune reaction to foreign bacteria in the guts or to the food which we eat although both of them are foreign entities.
- The system does not govern to body changes, even self changes as well.
- On the other hand, there are certain auto immune processes which are useful like some diseases and certain types of tumours that are fought by the immune system (both attacks against self) and successful transplants.

So, a new field in AIS emerges, baptized the danger theory, which offers an alternative to self non self discrimination approach. The danger theory stipulates that the immune response is done by reaction to a danger not to a foreign entity. In the sense, that the immune system is activated upon the receipt of molecular signals, which indicate damage or stress to the body, rather than pattern matching in the self non self paradigm. Furthermore, the immune response is done in reaction to signals during the intrusion and not by the intrusion itself.

These signals can be mainly of two nature [3,4]: safe and danger signal. The first indicates that the data to be processed, which represent antigen in the nature, were collected under normal circumstances; while the second signifies potentially anomalous data. The danger theory can be apprehended by: the Dendritic Cells Algorithm (DCA), which will be presented in the following section.

3 The Dendritic Cell Algorithm

The Dendritic Cell Algorithm (DCA) is a bio-inspired algorithm. It was introduced by Greensmith and al [6,12] and has demonstrated potential as a classifier for static machine learning data [12,13], as a simple port scan detector under both off-line conditions and in real time experiments [13-17]. The DCA accomplished the task of classification per correlation, fusion of data and filtering [16].

Initial implementations of the DCA have provided promising classification accuracy results on a number of benchmark datasets. However, the basic DCA uses several stochastic variables which make its systematic analysis and functionality understanding very difficult. In order to overcome those problems, a DCA improvement was proposed [17]: the dDCA (deterministic DCA). In the this paper, we focus on the new version. Its Pseudo code can be found in [17].

The dDCA is based population algorithm in which each agent of the system is represented by a virtual cell, which carries out the signal processing and antigen sampling components. Its inputs take two forms, antigens and signals. The first, are elements which act as a description of items within the problem domain. These elements will later be classified. While the second ones are a set dedicated to monitor some informative data features. Signals can be on two kinds: 'safe' and 'danger' signal. At each iteration *t*, the dDCA inputs consist of the values of the safe signal *St*, the danger signal *Dt* and antigens *At*. The dDCA proceeds on three steps as follows:

1. Initialization

The DC population and algorithm parameters are initialized and initial data are collected.

2. Signal Processing and Update phase

All antigens are presented to the DC population so that each DC agent samples only one antigen and proceeds to signal processing. At each step, each single cell i calculates two separate cumulative sums, called $CSMi$ and Ki, and it places them in its own storage data structure. The values CSM and K can be given by Eq.(1) and (2) respectively :

$$CSM = St + Dt \tag{1}$$

$$K = Dt - 2St \tag{2}$$

This process is repeated until all presented antigens have been assigned to the population. At each iteration, incoming antigens undergo the same process. All DCs will process the signals and update their values $CSMi$ and Ki. If the antigens number is greater than the DC number only a fraction of the DCs will sample additional antigens.

The DCi updates and cumulates the values $CSMi$ and Ki until a migration threshold Mi is reached. Once the $CSMi$ is greater than the migration threshold Mi, the cell presents its temporary output Ki as an output entity $Kout$. For all antigens sampled by DCi during its lifetime, they are labeled as normal if Kout < 0 and anomalous if Kout > 0.

After recording results, the values of $CSMi$ and Ki are reset to zero. All sampled antigens are also cleared. DCi then continues to sample signals and collect antigens as it did before until stopping criterion is met.

3. Aggregation phase

At the end, at the aggregation step, the nature of the response is determined by measuring the number of cells that are fully mature. In the original DCA, antigens analysis and data context evaluation are done by calculating the mature context antigen value (MCAV) average. A representation of completely mature cells can be done. An abnormal MCAV is closer to the value 1. This value of the $MCAV$ is then thresholded to achieve the final binary classification of normal or anomalous. The $K\alpha$ metric, an alternative metric to the $MCAV$, was proposed with the dDCA in [21]. The $K\alpha$ uses the average of all output values $Kout$ as the metric for each antigen type, instead of thresholding them to zero into binary tags.

4 The Wavelet Transform

Over the last decades, the wavelet transform has emerged as a powerful tool for the analysis and decomposition of signals and images at multi-resolutions. It is used for noise reduction, feature extraction or signal compression. The wavelet transform proceeds by decomposing a given signal into its scale and space components. Information can be obtained about both the amplitude of any periodic signal as well as when/where it occurred in time/space. Wavelet analysis thus localizes both in time/space and frequency [11].

The wavelet transform can be defined as the decomposition of a signal g (t) using a series of elemental functions called: wavelets and scaling factors.

$$g[t] = \sum_{m \in z} \sum_{n \in z} \langle x, \Psi_{m,n} \rangle . \Psi_{m,n}[t] \quad (3)$$

In wavelet decomposition, the image is split into an approximation and details images. The approximation is then split itself into a second level of approximation and detail. The image is usually segmented into a so-called approximation image and into so-called detail images. The transformed coefficients in approximation and detail sub-images are the essential features, which are as useful for image classification. A tree wavelet package transform can be constructed [11]. Where *S* denotes the signal, *D* denotes the detail and *A* the approximation, as shown in Fig.1.

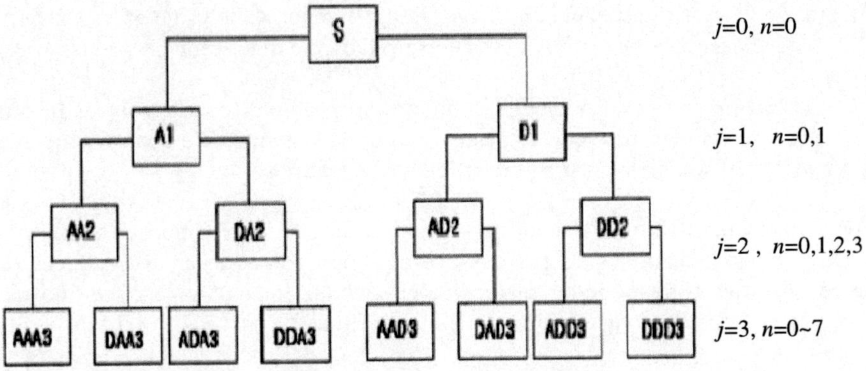

Fig. 1. The tree-structured wavelets transform

For a discrete signal, the decomposition coefficients of wavelet packets can be computed iteratively by Eq. (4):

$$x_{2n,j+1}^{k} = \sum_{l} h_{l-2k}\, x_{n,j}^{l} \quad ; \quad x_{2n+1,j+1}^{k} = \sum_{l} g_{l-2k}\, x_{n,j}^{l} \quad (4)$$

Where: $x_{n,j} = \{x_{n,j}^{k}\}$ is the decomposition coefficient sequence of the nth node at level j of the wavelet packet tree.

5 A Method of Leaf Classification

An approach based on artificial immune system ought to describe two aspects:

1. The projection and models advocating of immune elements in the real world problem.

2. The use of the appropriate immune algorithm or approach to solve the problem.

These two aspects are presented in following sections.

5.1 Immune Representation Using the dDCA

For sake of clarity, before describing the immune representation, we must depict the feature space. In this paper, we consider the decomposition using the wavelet package transform in order to get the average energy [11]. This is as follows:

The texture images are decomposed using the wavelet package transform. Then, the average energy of approximation and detail sub-image of two level decomposed images are calculated as features using the formulas given in (5) as follows:

$$E = \frac{1}{N \times N} \sum_{i=1}^{N} \sum_{j=1}^{N} |f(x, y)| \tag{5}$$

Where: N denotes the size of sub-image, $f(x, y)$ denotes the value of an image pixel.

Now, we describe the different elements used by the dDCA for image classification:

- **Antigens:** In AIS, antigens symbolize the problem to be resolved. In our approach, antigens are leaves images set to be classified. We consider the average energy of wavelet transform coefficients as features.

For texture classification, the unknown texture image is decomposed using wavelet package transform and a similar set of average energy features are extracted and compared with the corresponding feature values which are assumed to be known in a priori using a distance vector formula, given in Eq.6:

$$D(j) = \sum_{i=1}^{N} abs\,[f_i(x) - f_j(j)] \tag{6}$$

Where; $f_i\ (x)$ represents the features of unknown texture, while $f_i(j)$ represents the features of known j^{th} texture.

So:

- **Signals:** Signals input correspond to information set about a considered class. In this context, we suggest that:

  1. Danger signal: denote the distance between an unknown leaf texture features and known j texture features.

  2. Safe signal: denote the distance between an unknown leaf texture features and known j' texture features.

The two signals can be given by D_{danger} and D_{safe} as described in Eq. 7 and 8 at the manner of Eq. (6)

$$\text{Danger signal} = D_{danger} = \sum_{i=1}^{N} abs\,[f_i\,(x) - f_j\,(j)] \tag{7}$$

$$\text{Safe signal} = D_{safe} = \sum_{i=1}^{N} abs\,[f_i\,(x) - f_j\,(j')] \tag{8}$$

5.2 Outline of the Proposed Approach

In this section, we describe the proposed approach in the context of leaves image classification. The approach operates as follows:

Initialisation

At first, the system is initialized by setting various parameters, such: Antigens collection and signals input construction. At the same time of collecting leaves image, signals are constructed progressively.

The known leaves images, selected from labelled set, are decomposed using the wavelet package transform. Then, the average energy of approximation and detail sub-image of two level decomposed images are calculated as features using the formulas given Eq. (5).

Each leaf image (antigen), collected from the leaves image collection, is decomposed using wavelet package transform and a similar set of average energy features are extracted, (two labelled images selected randomly) and compared with the corresponding feature values which are assumed to be known in a priori using a distance vector formula, given in Eq. 6, in order to construct danger D_{danger} and the safe D_{safe} signals as in Eq. 7 and 8. Both streams are presented to the dDCA.

Signal Processing and Update Phase

Data Update: we collect leaves image and we choose randomly two images from labelled images set. Then, we assess the danger D_{danger} and the safe D_{safe} signals, as given in Eq.7 and 8. Both streams are presented to the dDCA. (This process is repeated until the number of images present at each time *i*, is assigned to all the DC population).

Cells Cycle: The DC population is presented by a matrix, in which rows correspond to cells. Each row-cell *i* has a maturation mark *CSMi* and a temporary output *Ki*.

For each cell *i*, a maturation mark *CSMi* is evaluated and a cumulatively output signal *Ki* is calculated as follows:

$$CSMi = D_{danger}\, t + D_{safe}\, t \qquad \text{and} \qquad Ki = D_{danger}\, t - 2\, D_{safe}\, t$$

When data are present, cells cycle is continually repeated. Until the maturation mark becomes greater than a migration threshold *Mi* (*CSMi* > *Mi*). Then, the cell prints a context: *Kout*, it is removed from the sampling population and its contents are reset after being logged for the aggregation stage. Finally, the cell is returned to the sampling population.

This process is repeated (cells cycling and data update) until a stopping criteria is met. In our case, until the iteration number is met.

Aggregation Phase

At the end, at the aggregation phase, we analyse data and we evaluate their contexts. In this work, we consider only the *MCAV* metric (the Mature Context Antigen Value), as it generates a more intuitive output score. We calculate the mean mature context value (MCAV: The total fraction of mature DCs presenting said leaf image is divided by the total amount of times by which the leaf image was presented. So, semi mature context indicates that collected leaf is part of the considered class. While, mature context signifies that the collected leaf image is part of another class.

More precisely, the MCAV can be evaluated as follows: for all leaves images in the total list, leaf type count is incremented. If leaf image context equals one, the leaf type mature count is incremented. Then, for all leaves types, the MCAV of leaf type is equal to mature count / leaf count.

6 Results and Discussion

In our approach, the classifier needs more information about classes in order to give a signification indication about the image context. For this, we have used a set of leaves images. The samples typically include different green plants, with simple backgrounds, which imply different colour and texture leaves, with varying lighting conditions. Thus, in order to form signals inputs. The collection is presented during the run time with the image to be classified.

During the experiment, we select 10 kinds of plants with 100 leaf images for each plant. Leaves images database is a set of web collection, some samples are shown in Fig.2. The size of the plant leaf images is 240*240. The following experiments are designed for testing the accuracy and efficiency of the proposed method. The experiments are programmed using Matlab 9.

Algorithm parameters are important part in the classification accuracy. Hence, we have considered 100 cells agent in the DC population and 100 iterations as stopping criteria which coincides to the leaves images number. The maturation mark is evaluated by *CSMi*. For an unknown texture of a leaf image, if $CSMi=D_{danger}+D_{safe} =D_{danger}$. the unknown texture have a high chance to be classified in the jth texture, if the distance $D\ (j)$ is minimum among all textures.

As far as, if $CSMi=D_{danger}+D_{safe} =D_{safe}$ the unknown texture have a high chance to be classified in the $j'^{\ th}$ texture, if the distance $D\ (j')$ is the minimum.

To achieve a single step classification, a migration threshold *Mi* is introduced that can take care of data in overlapping the different leaves texture. The migration threshold *Mi* is fixed to one of the input signals. In the sense that if *CSMi* tends towards one of the two signals, this is implies that one of the two signals tends to zero. So, we can conclude that the pixel have more chance to belong to one of the signals approaching zero.

Fig. 2. Samples of images used in tests

In order to evaluate the pixel membership to a class, we assess the metric *MCAV*. Each leaf image is given a *MCAV* coefficient value which can be compared with a threshold. In our case, the threshold is fixed at 0,90. Once a threshold is applied, it is then possible to classify the leaf. Therefore, the relevant rates of true and false positives can be shown.

We can conclude from the results that the system gave encouraging results for both classes vegetal and soil inputs. The use of the wavelet transform to evaluate texture features enhance the performance of our system and gave recognition accuracy of 85% .

7 Conclusion and Future Work

In this paper, we have proposed a classification approach for plant leaf recognition based on the danger theory from artificial immune systems. The leaf plant features are extracted and processed by wavelet transforms to form the input of the dDCA.

We have presented our preliminary results obtained in this way. The experimental results indicate that our algorithm is workable with a recognition rate greater than 85% on 10 kinds of plant leaf images. However, we recognize that the proposed method should be compared with other approach in order to evaluate its quality.

To improve it, we will further investigate the potential influence of other parameters and we will use alternative information signals for measuring the correlation and representations space. Also, we will consider the leaves shapes beside leaves textures.

References

1. De Castro, L., Timmis, J. (eds.): Artificial Immune Systems: A New Computational Approach. Springer, London (2002)
2. Hart, E., Timmis, J.I.: Application Areas of AIS: The Past, The Present and The Future. In: Jacob, C., Pilat, M.L., Bentley, P.J., Timmis, J.I. (eds.) ICARIS 2005. LNCS, vol. 3627, pp. 483–497. Springer, Heidelberg (2005)
3. Aickelin, U., Bentley, P.J., Cayzer, S., Kim, J., McLeod, J.: Danger theory: The link between AIS and IDS? In: Timmis, J., Bentley, P.J., Hart, E. (eds.) ICARIS 2003. LNCS, vol. 2787, pp. 147–155. Springer, Heidelberg (2003)
4. Aickelin, U., Cayzer, S.: The danger theory and its application to artificial immune systems. In: The 1th International Conference on Artificial Immune Systems (ICARIS 2002), Canterbury, UK, pp. 141–148 (2002)
5. Dasgupta, D.: Artificial Immune Systems and their applications. Springer, Heidelberg (1999)
6. Greensmith, J.: The Dendritic Cell Algorithm. University of Nottingham (2007)
7. Liu, J., Zhang, S., Deng, S.: A Method of Plant Classification Based on Wavelet Transforms and Support Vector Machines. In: Huang, D.-S., Jo, K.-H., Lee, H.-H., Kang, H.-J., Bevilacqua, V. (eds.) ICIC 2009. LNCS, vol. 5754, pp. 253–260. Springer, Heidelberg (2009)
8. Man, Q.-K., Zheng, C.-H., Wang, X.-F., Lin, F.-Y.: Recognition of Plant Leaves Using Support Vector Machine. In: Huang, D.-S., et al. (eds.) ICIC 2008. CCIS, vol. 15, pp. 192–199. Springer, Heidelberg (2008)
9. Singh, K., Gupta, I., Gupta, S.: SVM-BDT PNN and Fourier Moment Technique for Classification of Leaf Shape. International Journal of Signal Processing, Image Processing and Pattern Recognition 3(4) (December 2010)
10. Ehsanirad, A.: Plant Classification Based on Leaf Recognition. International Journal of Computer Science and Information Security 8(4) (July 2010)
11. Zhang, Y., He, X.-J., Huang, J.-H.H.D.S., Zhang, X.-P., Huang, G.-B.: Texture Feature-Based Image Classification Using Wavelet Package Transform. In: Huang, D.-S., Zhang, X.-P., Huang, G.-B. (eds.) ICIC 2005. LNCS, vol. 3644, pp. 165–173. Springer, Heidelberg (2005)
12. Greensmith, J., Aickelin, U., Cayzer, S.: Introducing Dendritic Cells as a Novel Immune-Inspired Algorithm for Anomaly Detection. In: Jacob, C., Pilat, M.L., Bentley, P.J., Timmis, J.I. (eds.) ICARIS 2005. LNCS, vol. 3627, pp. 153–167. Springer, Heidelberg (2005)
13. Oates, R., Greensmith, J., Aickelin, U., Garibaldi, J., Kendall, G.: The Application of a Dendritic Cell Algorithm to a Robotic Classifier. In: The 6th International Conference on Artificial Immune (ICARIS 2006), pp. 204–215 (2007)
14. Greensmith, J., Twycross, J., Aickelin, U.: Dendritic Cells for Anomaly Detection. In: IEEE World Congress on Computational Intelligence, Vancouver, Canada, pp. 664–671 (2006b)
15. Greensmith, J., Twycross, J., Aickelin, U.: Dendritic cells for anomaly detection. In: IEEE Congress on Evolutionary Computation (2006)
16. Greensmith, J., Aickelin, U., Tedesco, G.: Information Fusion for Anomaly Detection with the Dendritic Cell Algorithm. Journal Information Fusion 11(1) (January 2010)
17. Greensmith, J., Aickelin, U.: The deterministic dendritic cell algorithm. In: Bentley, P.J., Lee, D., Jung, S. (eds.) ICARIS 2008. LNCS, vol. 5132, pp. 291–302. Springer, Heidelberg (2008)

Adaptive Local Contrast Enhancement Combined with 2D Discrete Wavelet Transform for Mammographic Mass Detection and Classification

Daniela Giordano, Isaak Kavasidis, and Concetto Spampinato

Department of Electrical, Electronics and Informatics Engineering
University of Catania, Viale A. Doria, 6, 95125 Catania, Italy
{dgiordan,ikavasidis,cspampin}@dieei.unict.it

Abstract. This paper presents an automated knowledge-based vision system for mass detection and classification in X-Ray mammograms. The system developed herein is based on several processing steps, which aim first at identifying the various regions of the mammogram such as breast, markers, artifacts and background area and then to analyze the identified areas by applying a contrast improvement method for highlighting the pixels of the candidate masses. The detection of such candidate masses is then done by applying locally a 2D Haar Wavelet transform, whereas the mass classification (in benign and malignant ones) is performed by means of a support vector machine whose features are the spatial moments extracted from the identified masses. The system was tested on the public database MIAS achieving very promising results in terms both of accuracy and of sensitivity.

Keywords: Biomedical Image Processing, X-Ray, Local Image Enhancement, Support Vector Machines.

1 Introduction

Breast cancer is one of the main causes of cancer deaths in women. The survival chances are increased by early diagnosis and proper treatment. One of the most characteristic early signs of breast cancer is the presence of masses. Mammography is currently the most sensitive and effective method for detecting breast cancer, reducing mortality rates by up to 25%. The detection and classification of masses is a difficult task for radiologists because of the subtle differences between local dense parenchymal and masses. Moreover, in the classification of breast masses, two types of errors may occur: 1) the *False Negative* that is the most serious error and occurs when a malignant lesion is estimated as a benign one and 2) the *False Positive* that occurs when a benign mass is classified as malignant. This type of error, even though it has no direct physical consequences, should be avoided since it may cause negative psychological effects to the patient. To aid radiologists in the task of detecting subtle abnormalities

H. Cherifi, J.M. Zain, and E. El-Qawasmeh (Eds.): DICTAP 2011, Part I, CCIS 166, pp. 209–218, 2011.

in a mammogram, researchers have developed different image processing and image analysis techniques. In fact, a large number of *CAD (Computer Aided Diagnosis)* systems have been developed for the detection of masses in digitized mammograms, aiming to overcome such errors and to make the analysis fully automatic. There is an extensive literature (one of the most recent is proposed by Sampat *el al.* in [11]) on the development and evaluation of CAD systems in mammography, especially related to microcalcifications detection, which is a difficult task because a) masses are often ill-defined and poor in contrast, b) the lack of adipose tissue in young subjects [1], and c) normal breast tissue, such as blood vessels, often appear as a set of linear structures.

Many of the existing approaches use clustering techniques to segment the mammogram and are able to identify effectively masses but suffer from inherent drawbacks: they do not use spatial information about the masses and they exploit a-priori knowledge about the image under examination [6] and [10]. Differently, there exist approaches based on edge detection techniques that identify masses in a mammogram [12], [14], [15] whose problem is that they are not always capable to identify accurately the contour of the masses.

None of the existing methods can achieve perfect performance, i.e., there are either false positive or false negative errors, so there's still room for improvement in breast mass detection. In particular, as stated in [7], the performance of all the existing algorithms, in terms of accuracy and sensitivity, is influenced by the masses' shape, size and tissue type and models that combine knowledge on the nature of mass (e.g. gray-level values, textures and contour information) with a detection procedure that extracts features from the examined image, such as breast tissue, should be investigated in order to achieve better performance. With this aim in this paper we propose a detection system that first highlights the pixels highly correlated with candidate masses by a specific contrast stretching function that takes into account the image's features. The candidate mass detection is then performed by applying locally 2D discrete wavelets on the enhanced image, differently from existing wavelet-based methods [4], [9] and [17] that detect mass by considering the image as a whole (i.e. applying the wavelet globally). The screening of the detected candidate masses is performed by using a-priori information on masses. The final masses classification (in benign or malignant) is achieved by applying a Support Vector Machine (SVM) that uses mass shape descriptors as features.

This paper is organized as follows: in the next section an overview of the breast mass is presented. Section 3 shows the overall architecture of the proposed algorithm, whereas Section 4 describes the experimental results. Finally, Section 5 points out the concluding remarks.

2 Breast Malignant Mass

Breast lesions can be divided in two main categories: *microcalcifications* (group of small white calcium spots) and *masses* (a circumscribed object brighter than its surrounding tissue). In this paper we deal with mass analysis, which is a difficult problem because masses have varying sizes, shape and density. Moreover, they exhibit poor image contrast and are highly connected to the surrounding parenchymal tissue density. Masses are defined as space-occupying lesions that are characterized by their shapes and margin properties and have a typical size ranging from 4 to 50 mm. Their shape, size and margins help the radiologist to assess the likelihood of cancer. The evolution of a mass during one year is quite important to understand its nature, in fact no changes might mean a benign condition, thus avoiding unnecessary biopsies. According to morphological parameters, such as shape and type of tissue, a rough classification can be made, in fact, the morphology of a lesion is strongly connected to the degree of malignancy. For example, masses with a very bright core in the X-Rays are considered the most typical manifestation of malignant lesions. For this reason, the main aim of this work is to automatically analyze the mammograms, to detect masses and then to classify them as *benign* or *malignant*.

3 The Proposed System

The proposed CAD , which aims at increasing the accuracy in the early detection and diagnosis of breast cancers, consists of three main modules:

- A pre-processing module that aims at eliminating both eventual noise introduced during the digitization and other uninteresting objects;
- A mass detection module that relies on a contrast stretching method that highlights all the pixels that likely belong to masses with respect to the ones belonging to the other tissues and on a wavelet-based method that extracts the candidate masses taking as input the output image of the contrast stretching part. The selection of the masses (among the set of candidates) to be passed to the the classification module is performed by exploiting a-priori information on masses.
- A mass classification module that works on the detected masses with the end of distinguishing the malignant masses from the benign ones.

Pre-processing is one of the most critical steps since the accuracy of the overall system strongly depends on it. In fact, the noise affecting the mammograms makes their interpretation very difficult, hence a preprocessing phase is necessary to improve their quality and to enable a more reliable features extraction phase. Initially, to reduce undesired noise and artifacts introduced during the digitization process, a median filter to the whole image is applied. For extracting only the breast and reducing the removing the background (e.g. labels, date, etc.), the adaptive thresholding, proposed in [3] and [2], based on local enhancement by means of Difference of Gaussians (DoG) filter, is used.

The first step for detecting masses is to highlights all those pixels that are highly correlated with the masses. In detail, we apply to the output image of the

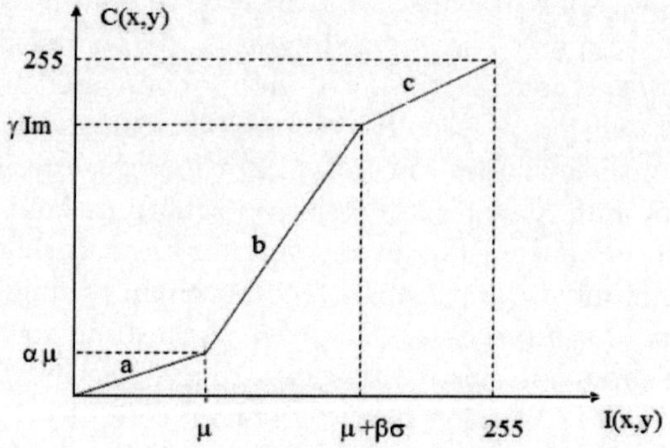

Fig. 1. Contrast Stretching Function

pre-processing level, $I(x, y)$, a *pixel based transformation* (see fig. 1) according to the formula (1), where the cut-off parameters are extracted directly by the image features, obtaining the output image $C(x, y)$.

$$C(x,y) = \begin{cases} I(x,y) \cdot a & \text{if } 0 < I(x,y) < x_1 \\ y_1 + (I(x,y) - x_1) \cdot b & \text{if } x_1 < I(x,y) < x_2 \\ y_2 + (I(x,y) - x_2) \cdot c & \text{if } x_1 < I(x,y) < 255 \end{cases} \tag{1}$$

where (x_1, y_1) and (x_2, y_2) (cut-off parameters) are set to $x_1 = \mu$ and $y_1 = \alpha \cdot \mu$, $x_2 = \mu + \beta \cdot \sigma$ and $y_2 = \gamma \cdot I_M$; with μ, σ and I_M that represent, respectively, the mean, the standard deviation and the maximum, of the image gray levels. The parameters a, b, c are strongly connected and computed according to the following equations:

$$a = \frac{\alpha \cdot \beta}{\mu} \; b = \frac{\gamma I_M - \alpha\mu}{(\mu+\beta\alpha)-\mu} \; c = \frac{255-\gamma I_M}{255-(\mu+\beta\alpha)} \tag{2}$$

with $0 < \alpha < 1$, $\beta > 0$ and $\gamma > 0$ to be set experimentally. Fig. 2-b shows the output image when $\alpha = 0.6$, $\beta = 1.5$ and $\gamma = 1$. These values have been identified by running a genetic algorithm on the image training set (described in the result section). We used the following parameters for our genetic algorithm: binary mutation (with probability 0.05), two-point crossover (with probability 0.65) and normalized geometric selection (with probability 0.08). These values are intrinsically related to images, with trimodal histogram, as the one shown in fig. 2-a. In fig. 2-b, it is possible to notice that those areas with a higher probability of being masses are highlighted in the output image.

To extract the candidate masses a 2D Wavelet Transform is then applied to the image $C(x, y)$. Although there exist many types of mother wavelets, in this work we have used the Haar wavelet function due to its qualities of computational performance, poor energy compaction for images and precision in image reconstruction [8]. Our approach follows a multi-level wavelet transformation of

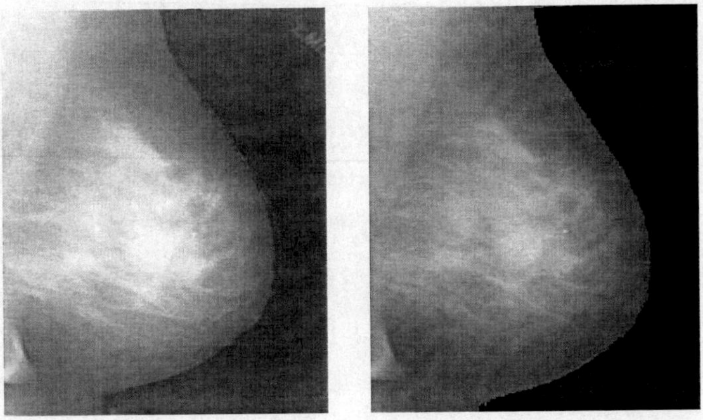

(a) (b)

Fig. 2. a) Example Image $I(x, y)$, b) Output Image $C(x, y)$ with $\alpha = 0.6$, $\beta = 1.5$ and $\gamma = 1$

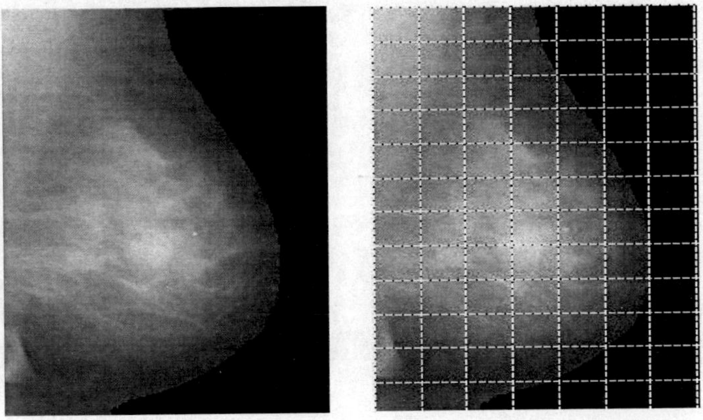

(a) (b)

Fig. 3. a) Enhanced Image $C(x, y)$ and b) Image with NxN masks

the image, applied to a certain number of masks (square size NxN) over the image, instead of applying it to the entire image (see fig. 3); this eliminates the high value of the coefficients due to the intensity variance of the breast border with respect to background.

Fig. 4 shows some components of the nine images obtained during the wavelet transformation phase.

After wavelet coefficients estimation, we segment these coefficients by using a region-based segmentation approach and then we reconstruct the above three levels, achieving the images shown in fig. 5. As it is possible to notice, the mass is well-defined in each of the three considered levels.

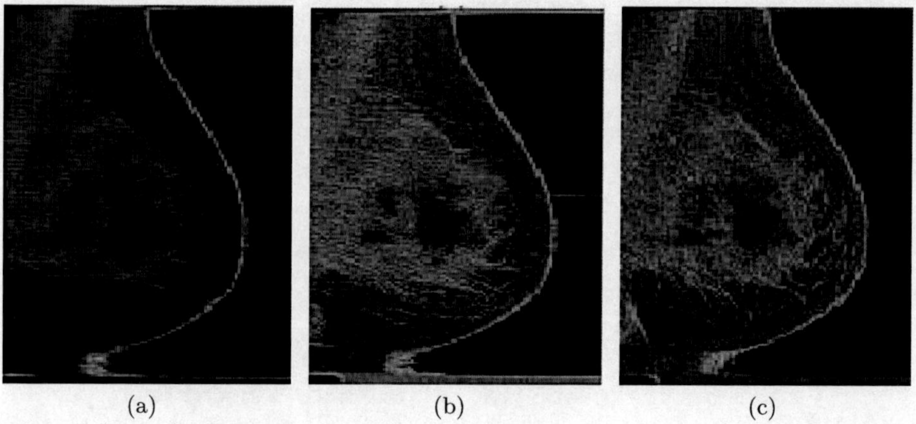

Fig. 4. Examples of Wavelet components: (a) 2nd level - horizontal; (b) 3rd level - horizontal; (c) 3rd level - vertical

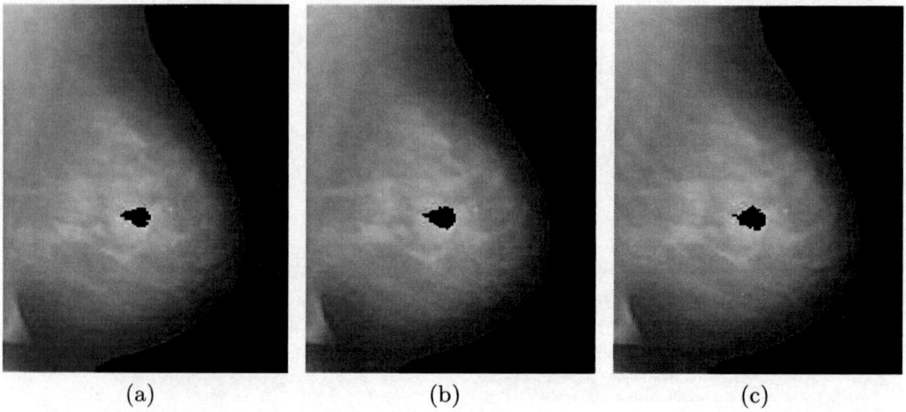

Fig. 5. Wavelet reconstructions after components segmentation of the first three levels: (a) 1st level reconstruction; (b) 2nd level reconstruction; (c) 3rd level reconstruction

The last part of the processing system aims at discriminating, from the set of identified candidate masses, the masses from vessels, granular tissues that have comparable sizes with the target objects. The lesions we are interested in have oval shape with linear dimensions in the range $[4 - 50]$ mm. Hence, in order to remove the very small or very large objects and to reconstruct the target objects, erosion and closing operators (with a kernel 3x3) have been applied. Afterwards, the shape of the identified masses are improved by applying a *region growing* algorithm. The extracted masses are further classified in benign or malignant by using a Support Vector Machine, with radial basis function [5] as kernel, that works on the spatial moments of such masses. The considered spatial moments, used as discriminant features, are: 1) *Area*, 2) *Perimeter*, 3) *Compactness* and 4) *Elongation*. Indeed area and perimeter provide us information about the object dimensions, whereas from compactness and elongation we derive information about how the lesions look like. In fig.6 an example of how the proposed system works is shown.

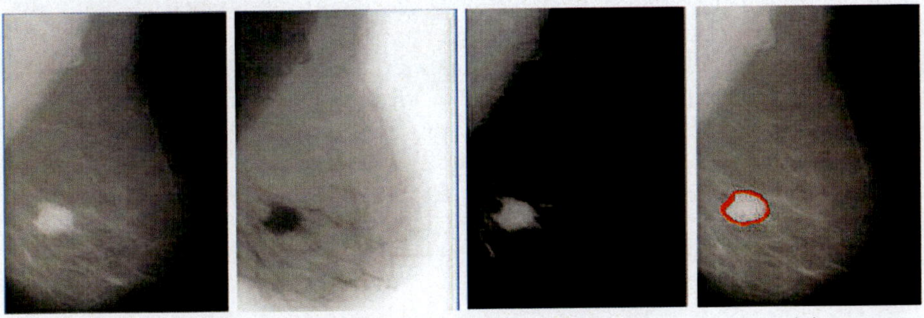

(a) (b) (c) (d)

Fig. 6. a) Original Image, b) Negative, c) Image obtained after the contrast stretching algorithm and d) malignant mass classification

3.1 Experimental Results

The data set for the performance evaluation consisted of 668 mammograms extracted from the Image Analysis Society database (MIAS) [13]. We divided the entire dataset into two sets: the learning set (386 images) and the test set (the remaining 282 images). The 282 test images contained in total 321 masses and the mass detection algorithm identified 292 masses, whose 288 were true positives whereas 4 were false positives. The 288 true positives (192 benign masses and 96 malignant masses) were used for testing the classification stage. In detail, the evaluation of the performance of the mass classification was done by using 1) the **sensitivity (SENS)**, 2) the **specificity (SPEC)** and 3) the **accuracy (ACC)** that integrates both the above ratios and are defined as follows:

$$Accuracy = 100 \cdot \frac{TP + TN}{TP + TN + FP + FN} \tag{3}$$

$$Sensitivity = 100 \cdot \frac{TP}{TP + FN} \tag{4}$$

$$Specificity = 100 \cdot \frac{TN}{TN + FP} \tag{5}$$

Where TP and TN are, respectively, the true positives and the true negatives, whereas FP and FN are, respectively, the false positives and the false negatives. The achieved performance over the test sets is reported in Table 1.

Table 1. The achieved Performance

	TP	FP	TN	FN	Sens	Spec	Acc
Mass Classification	86	12	181	9	90.5%	93.7%	92.7%

The achieved performance, in terms of sensitivity, are surely better than other approaches that use similar methods based on morphological shape analysis and global wavelet transform, such as the ones proposed in [16], [9], where both sensitivity and specificity are less than 90% for mass classification, whereas our approach reaches an average performance of about 92%. The sensitivity ratio of the classification part shows that the system is quite effective in distinguishing benign to malignant masses as shown in fig. 7. Moreover, the obtained results are comparable with the most effective CADs [11] that achieve averagely an accuracy of about 94% and are based on semi-automated approaches.

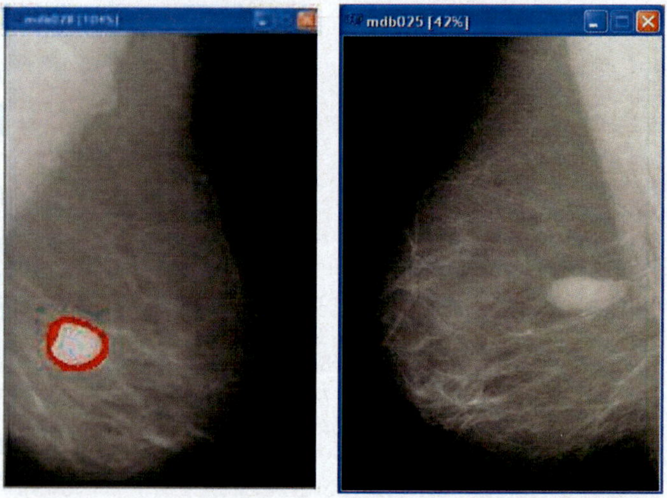

(a) (b)

Fig. 7. a) Malignant mass detected by the proposed system and b) Benign Mass not detected

4 Conclusions and Future Work

This paper has proposed a system for mass detection and classification, capable of distinguishing malignant masses from normal areas and from benign masses. The obtained results are quite promising taking into account that the system is almost fully automatic. Indeed, most of the thresholds or parameters used are strongly connected to the image features and are not set manually. Moreover, our system outperforms the existing CAD systems for mammography because of the reliable enhancement system integrated with the local 2D wavelet transform, although mass shape, mass size and breast tissue influence should be investigated. Therefore, further work will focus on expanding the system by combining existing effective algorithms (the Laplacian, the Iris filter, the pattern matching) in order to make the system more robust especially for improving the sensitivity.

References

1. Egan, R.: Breast Imaging: Diagnosis and Morphology of Breast Diseases. Saunders Co Ltd. (1988)
2. Giordano, D., Spampinato, C., Scarciofalo, G., Leonardi, R.: EMROI extraction and classification by adaptive thresholding and DoG filtering for automated skeletal bone age analysis. In: Proc. of the 29th EMBC Conference, pp. 6551–6556 (2007)
3. Giordano, D., Spampinato, C., Scarciofalo, G., Leonardi, R.: An automatic system for skeletal bone age measurement by robust processing of carpal and epiphysial/metaphysial bones. IEEE Transactions on Instrumentation and Measurement 59(10), 2539–2553 (2010)
4. Hadhou, M., Amin, M., Dabbour, W.: Detection of breast cancer tumor algorithm using mathematical morphology and wavelet analysis. In: Proc. of GVIP 2005, pp. 208–213 (2005)
5. Kecman, V.: Learning and Soft Computing, Support Vector Machines, Neural Networks and Fuzzy Logic Models. MIT Press, Cambridge (2001)
6. Kom, G., Tiedeu, A., Kom, M.: Automated detection of masses in mammograms by local adaptive thresholding. Comput. Biol. Med. 37, 37–48 (2007)
7. Oliver, A., Freixenet, J., Marti, J., Perez, E., Pont, J., Denton, E.R., Zwiggelaar, R.: A review of automatic mass detection and segmentation in mammographic images. Med. Image Anal. 14, 87–110 (2010)
8. Raviraj, P., Sanavullah, M.: The modified 2D Haar wavelet transformation in image compression. Middle-East Journ. of Scient. Research 2 (2007)
9. Rejani, Y.I.A., Selvi, S.T.: Early detection of breast cancer using SVM classifier technique. CoRR, abs/0912.2314 (2009)
10. Rojas Dominguez, A., Nandi, A.K.: Detection of masses in mammograms via statistically based enhancement, multilevel-thresholding segmentation, and region selection. Comput. Med. Imaging Graph 32, 304–315 (2008)
11. Sampat, M., Markey, M., Bovik, A.: Computer-aided detection and diagnosys in mammography. In: Handbook of Image and Video Processing, 2nd edn., pp. 1195–1217 (2005)
12. Shi, J., Sahiner, B., Chan, H.P., Ge, J., Hadjiiski, L., Helvie, M.A., Nees, A., Wu, Y.T., Wei, J., Zhou, C., Zhang, Y., Cui, J.: Characterization of mammographic masses based on level set segmentation with new image features and patient information. Med. Phys. 35, 280–290 (2008)
13. Suckling, J., Parker, D., Dance, S., Astely, I., Hutt, I., Boggis, C.: The mammographic images analysis society digital mammogram database. Exerpta Medical International Congress Series, pp. 375–378 (1994)

14. Suliga, M., Deklerck, R., Nyssen, E.: Markov random field-based clustering applied to the segmentation of masses in digital mammograms. Comput. Med. Imaging Graph 32, 502–512 (2008)
15. Timp, S., Karssemeijer, N.: A new 2D segmentation method based on dynamic programming applied to computer aided detection in mammography. Med. Phys. 31, 958–971 (2004)
16. Wei, J., Sahiner, B., Hadjiiski, L.M., Chan, H.P., Petrick, N., Helvie, M.A., Roubidoux, M.A., Ge, J., Zhou, C.: Computer-aided detection of breast masses on full field digital mammograms. Med. Phys. 32, 2827–2838 (2005)
17. Zhang, L., Sankar, R., Qian, W.: Advances in micro-calcification clusters detection in mammography. Comput. Biol. Med. 32, 515–528 (2002)

Texture Image Retrieval Using Local Binary Edge Patterns

Abdelhamid Abdesselam

Department of Computer Science,
College of Science,
Sultan Qaboos University, Oman
ahamid@squ.edu.om

Abstract. Texture is a fundamental property of surfaces, and as so, it plays an important role in the human visual system for analysis and recognition of images. A large number of techniques for retrieving and classifying image textures have been proposed during the last few decades. This paper describes a new texture retrieval method that uses the spatial distribution of edge points as the main discriminating feature. The proposed method consists of three main steps: First, the edge points in the image are identified; then the local distribution of the edge points is described using an LBP-like coding. The output of this step is a 2D array of LBP-like codes, called LBEP image. The final step consists of calculating two histograms from the resulting LBEP image. These histograms constitute the feature vectors that characterize the texture. The results of the experiments that have been conducted show that the proposed method significantly improves the traditional edge histogram method and outperforms several other state-of-the art methods in terms of retrieval accuracy.

Keywords: Texture-based Image Retrieval, Edge detection, Local Binary Edge Patterns.

1 Introduction

Image texture has been proven to be a powerful feature for retrieval and classification of images. In fact, an important number of real world objects have distinctive textures. These objects range from natural scenes such as clouds, water, and trees, to man-made objects such as bricks, fabrics, and buildings.

During the last three decades, a large number of approaches have been devised for describing, classifying and retrieving texture images. Some of the proposed approaches work in the image space itself. Under this category, we find those methods using edge density, edge histograms, or co-occurrence matrices [1-4, 20-22]. Most of the recent approaches extract texture features from transformed image space. The most common transforms are Fourier [5-7, 18], wavelet [8-12, 23-27] and Gabor transforms [13-16]. This paper describes a new technique that makes use of the local distribution of the edge points to characterize the texture of an image. The description is represented by a 2-D array of LBP-like codes called LBEP image from which two histograms are derived to constitute the feature vectors of the texture.

H. Cherifi, J.M. Zain, and E. El-Qawasmeh (Eds.): DICTAP 2011, Part I, CCIS 166, pp. 219–230, 2011.

2 Brief Review of Related Works

This study considers some of the state-of-the art texture analysis methods recently described in literature. This includes methods working in a transformed space (such as wavelet, Gabor or Fourier spaces) and some methods working in the image space itself, such as edge histogram- and Local Binary Pattern-based methods. All these techniques have been reported to produce very good results.

2.1 Methods Working in Pixel Space

Edge information is considered as one of the most fundamental texture primitives [29]. This information is used in different forms to describe texture images. Edge histogram (also known as gradient vector) is among the most popular of these forms. A gradient operator (such as Sobel operator) is applied to the image to obtain gradient magnitude and gradient direction images. From these two images a histogram of gradient directions is constructed. It records the gradient magnitude of the image edges at various directions [12].

LBP-based approach was first introduced by Ojala et al.in 1996 [20]. It uses an operator called Local Binary Pattern (LBP in short), characterized by its simplicity, accuracy and invariance to monotonic changes in gray scale caused by illumination variations. Several extensions of the original LBP-based texture analysis method were proposed since then, such as a rotation and scaling invariant method [21], and a multi-resolution method [22]. In its original form, LBP operator assigns to each image pixel the decimal value of a binary string that describes the local pattern around the pixel. Figure.1 illustrates how LBP code is calculated.

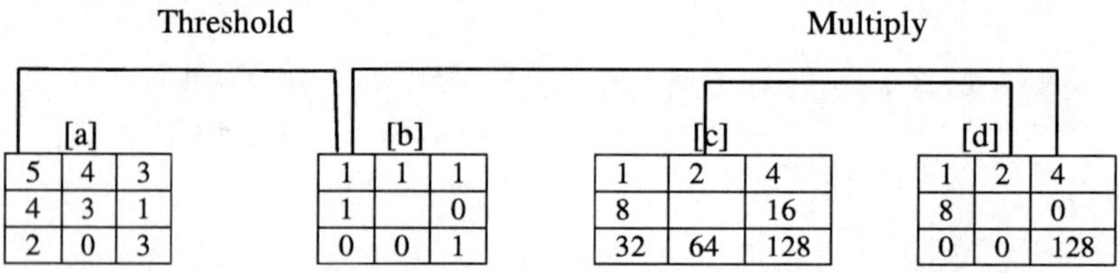

[a] A sample neighbourhood [b] Resulting bit-string [c] LBP mask [d]=[b]x[c];
LBP=1+2+4+8+128=143

Fig. 1. LBP Calculation

2.2 Methods Working in Transformed Space

In late 80's physiological studies on the visual cortex suggested that visual systems of primates use multi-scale analysis, Beck et al [17]. Gabor transform was among the first techniques to adopt this approach, mainly because of its similarity with the response found in visual cells of primates. The main problem with Gabor-based approaches is their slowness [15]. Wavelet-based approaches became a good alternative since they produce good results in a much faster time. Various variants of wavelet decompositions were proposed. The pyramidal wavelet decomposition was the most in use until recently, when complex wavelets transform (CWT) [23-24] and more specifically the Dual Tree Complex Wavelet Transform (DT-CWT) [25-27] were introduced and reported to produce better results for texture characterization. The newly proposed methods are characterized by their shift invariance property and they have a better directional selectivity (12 directions for DT-CWT, 6 for most Gabor wavelets and CWT, while there are only 3 for traditional real wavelet transforms). In most cases, texture is characterized by the energy, and or the standard deviation of the different sub-bands resulting from the wavelet decomposition. More recently a new Fourier-based multi-resolution approach was proposed [18]; it produces a significant improvement over traditional Fourier-based techniques. In this method, the frequency domain is segmented into rings and wedges and their energies, at different resolutions, are calculated. The feature vector consists of energies of all the rings and wedges produced by the multi-resolution decomposition.

3 Proposed Method

The proposed method characterizes a texture by the local distribution of its edge pixels. This method differs from other edge-based techniques by the way edginess is described: it uses LBP-like binary coding. This choice is made because of the simplicity and efficiency of this coding. It also differs from LBP-based techniques by the nature of the information that is coded. LBP-based techniques encode all differences in intensity around the central pixel. In the proposed approach, only significant changes (potential edges) are coded. This is in accordance with two facts known about the Human Visual System (HVS): It can only detect significant changes in intensity, and edges are important clues to HVS, when performing texture analysis [30].

3.1 Feature Extraction Process

The following diagram shows the main steps involved in the feature extraction process of the proposed approach:

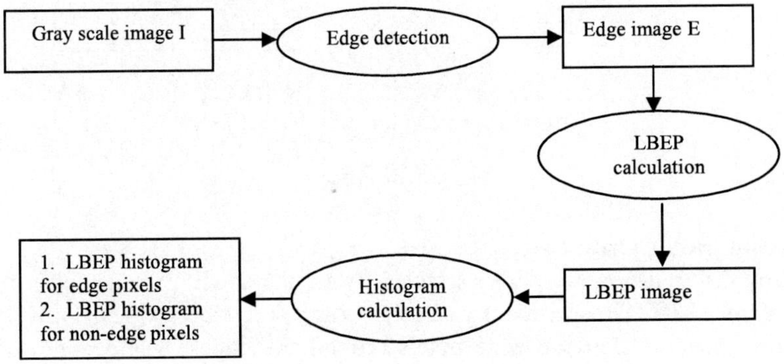

Fig. 2. Feature extraction process

3.1.1 Edge Detection

Three well known edge detection techniques Sobel, Canny and Laplacian of Gaussian (LoG) were tested. Edge detection using Sobel operator is the fastest among the three techniques but is also the most sensitive to noise, which leads to a much deteriorated accuracy for the retrieval process. Canny algorithm produces a better characterization of the edges but is relatively slow which affects sensibly the speed of the overall retrieval process. LoG is chosen as it produces a good trade-off between execution time and retrieval accuracy.

3.1.2 Local Binary Edge Pattern Calculation

The local distribution of edge points is represented by the LBEP image that results from correlating the binary edge image E and a predefined LBEP mask M. Formula (1) shows how LBEP image is calculated.

$$LBEP(i,j) = \sum_{s=0}^{K-1} \sum_{t=0}^{K-1} E\left(i - \tfrac{K}{2} + s, j - \tfrac{K}{2} + t\right).M(s,t) \quad (1)$$

Where *M* is a mask of size *K* x *K*

This operation applies an LBP-like coding to E. Various LBEP masks have been tested: an 8-neighbour mask, a 12-neighbour mask and a 24-neighbour mask. The use of 24-neighbour mask slows down sensibly the retrieval process (mainly at the level of histogram calculation) without significant improvement in the accuracy. Further investigation showed that 12-neighbour mask leads to better retrieval results. Figure.3 shows the 8- and 12-neighbourhood masks that have been considered.

1	2	4
128		8
64	32	16

a)- 8-neighbour mask M
0<=E(i,j)<=255

		1		
	128	256	2	
64	2048		512	4
	32	1024	8	
		16		

b)- 12-neighbour mask M.
0<=E(i,j)<=4095

Fig. 3. LBEP masks

3.1.3 Histogram Calculation

Two normalized histograms are extracted from the LBEP image. The first one considers only LBEP image pixels related to edges (i.e. where E(i,j)=1). It describes the locale distribution of the edge pixels around the edges. The second histogram considers only the LBEP image pixels related to non-edge pixels (i.e. where E(i,j)=0).

It describes the local distribution of edge pixels around non-edge pixels. This separation between edge and non-edge pixels leads to a better characterization of the texture. It distinguishes between textures having similar overall LBEP histogram but distributed differently among edge and non-edge pixels. Resulting histograms constitute the feature vectors that describe the texture.

3.2 Similarity Measurement

Given two texture images I and J, each represented by two normalized k-dimensional feature vectors f^{x}_{1} and f^{x}_{2}.; where x=I or J. The dissimilarity between I and J is defined by formula (2):

$$D(I,J)=(d1+d2)/2; \quad (2)$$

Where

$$d1 = \sum_{l=1}^{l=k} \left| f_1^i(l) - f_1^j(l) \right|$$

$$d2 = \sum_{l=1}^{l=k} \left| f_2^i(l) - f_2^j(l) \right|$$

4 Experimentation

4.1 Test Dataset

The dataset used in the experiments is made of 76 gray scale images selected from the Brodatz album downloaded in 2009 from:

[http://www.ux.uis.no/~tranden/brodatz.html].

Images that have uniform textures (i.e. similar texture over the whole image) were selected. All the images are of size 640 x 640 pixels. Each image is partitioned into 25 non-overlapping sub-images of size 128 x 128, from which 4 sub-images were chosen to constitute the image database (i.e. database= 304 images) and one sub-image to be used as a query image (i.e. 76 query images).

4.2 Hardware and Software Environment

We have conducted all the experiments on an Intel Core 2 (2GHz) Laptop with 2 GB RAM. The software environment consists of MS Windows 7 professional and Matlab7.

4.3 Performance Evaluation

To evaluate the performance of the proposed approach, we have adopted the well-known efficacy formula (3) introduced by Kankahalli et al. [19]

$$Efficacy = \eta_T = \begin{cases} n/N & if \quad N \leq T \\ n/T & if \quad N > T \end{cases} \tag{3}$$

Where

n is the number of relevant images retrieved by the CBIR system, N is the total number of relevant images that are stored in the database, and T is the number of images displayed on the screen as a response to the query.

In the experimentation that has been conducted N=4, and T=10 which means Efficacy=n/4;

Several state-of-the-art retrieval techniques were included in the investigation. Three multi-resolution techniques : Dual-Tree Complex Wavelet Transform using means and standard deviations of the sub-bands similar to the one described in [26], traditional Gabor Filters technique using means and standard deviations of the different sub-bands as described in [16], and a 3-level multi-resolution Fourier described in [18]. Two single-resolutions techniques were also included; they are LBP-based technique proposed by [20], and the classical edge histogram technique as described in [28].

5 Results and Discussion

Table.1 summarizes the results of the experiment and Figure.4 shows a sample of results produced by the 6 methods included in the experiment.

Table 1. Comparing performance of the proposed method (LBEP) and some other state-of-the-art techniques

MRFFT= Multi-resolution Fourier-based technique
DT-CWT(μ, σ)= Dual-Tree Complex Wavelet approach using 4 scales and 6 orientations.
Gabor(μ, σ): Gabor technique using 3 scales and 6 orientations.
LBP= LBP-based technique
LBEP= Proposed technique
Edge Histogram technique

Technique	Efficacy (n_{10}) %
LBP	98
LBEP (Proposed method)	98
MRFFT	97
Gabor(μ, σ)	96
DT-CWT(μ, σ)	96
Edge Histogram	73

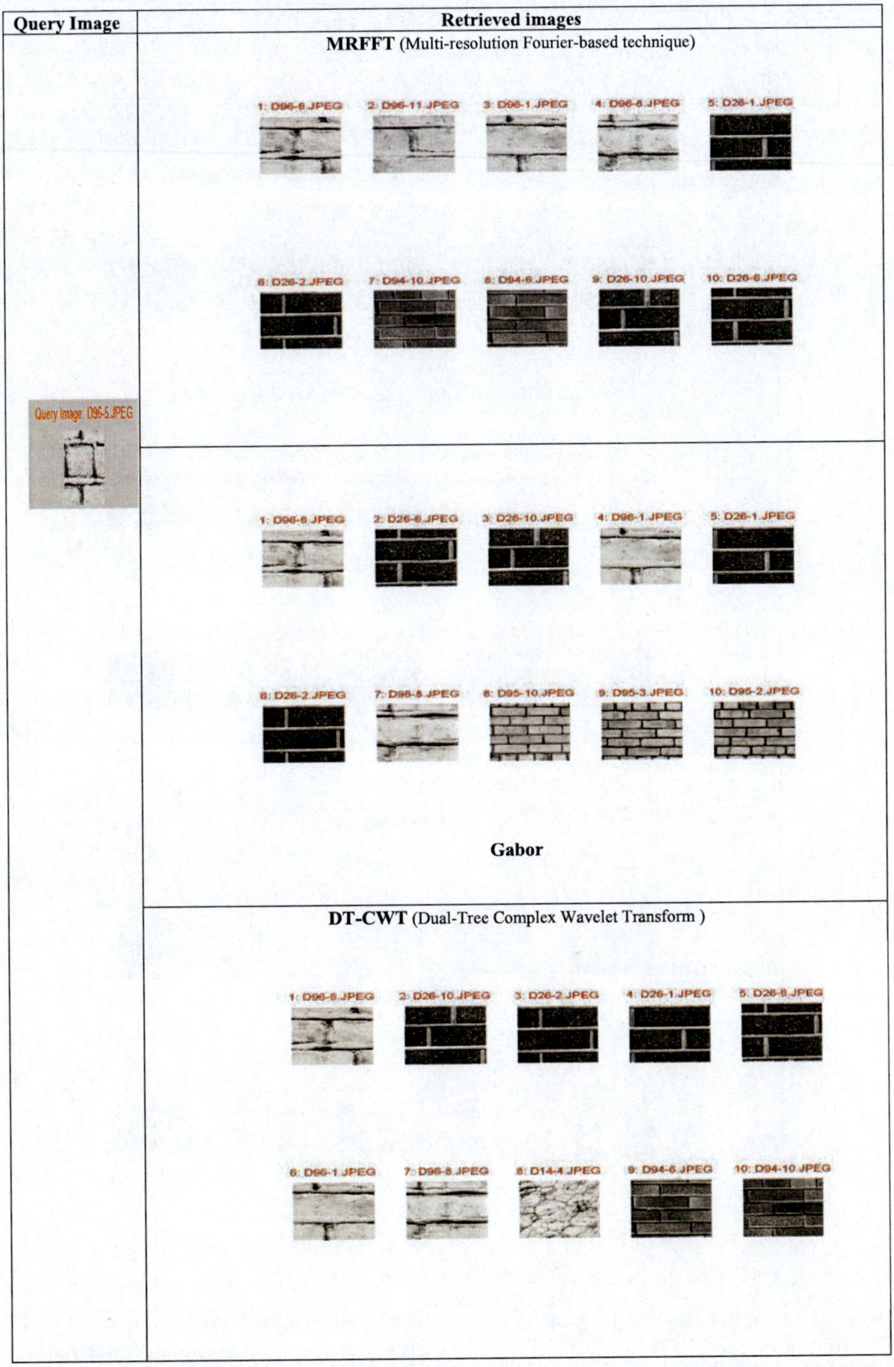

Fig. 4. Retrieval results for the proposed method(LBEP) and 5 other techniques included in the study. Retrieved images are sorted by decreasing value of similarity score from left to right and top to bottom.

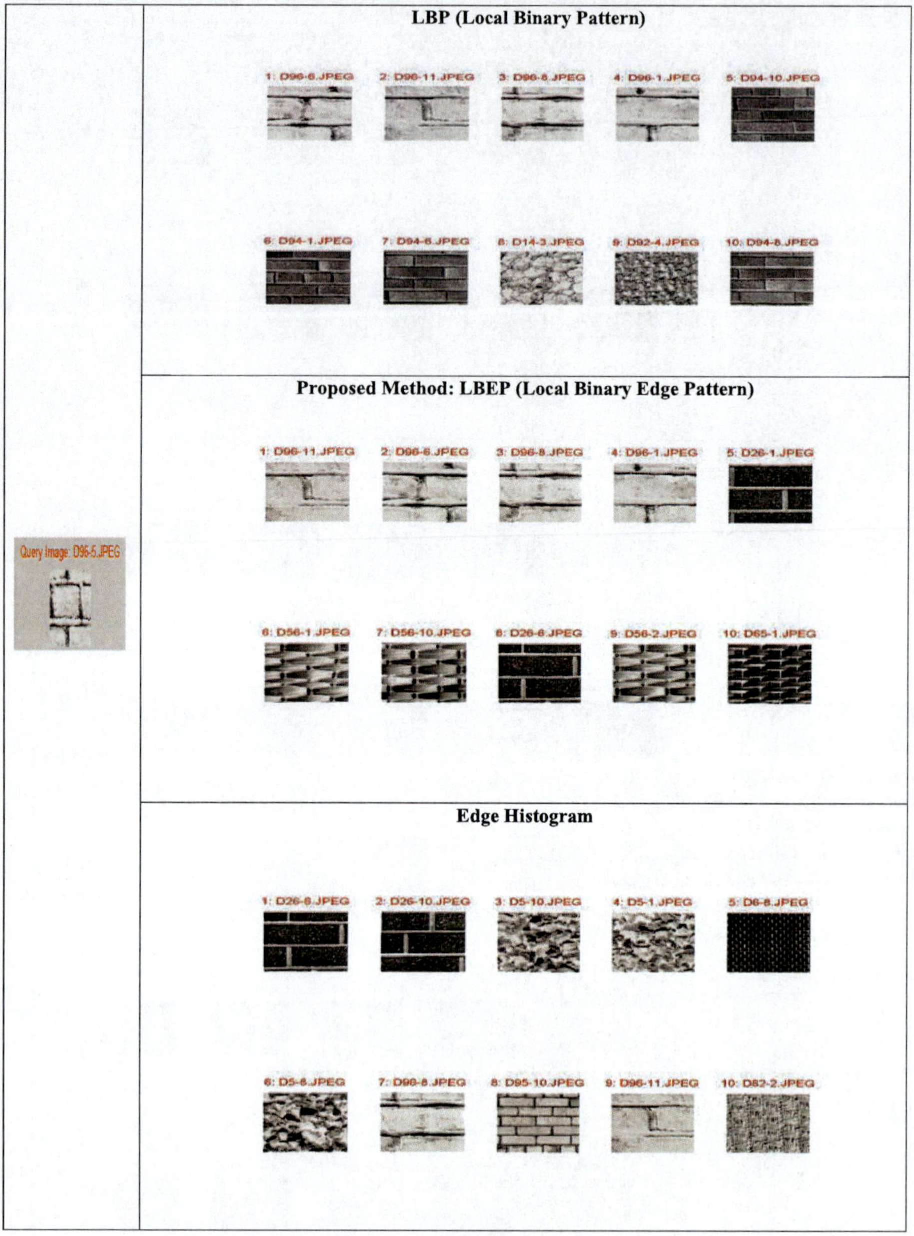

Fig. 4. (*continued*)

Two main conclusions can be made from the results shown in Table.1:

First, although, edge Histogram and LBEP techniques are based on edge information, the accuracy of LBEP is far better than the one obtained by Edge Histogram technique (98% against 73%). This shows the importance of the local distribution of edges and the effectiveness of the LBP coding in capturing this information.

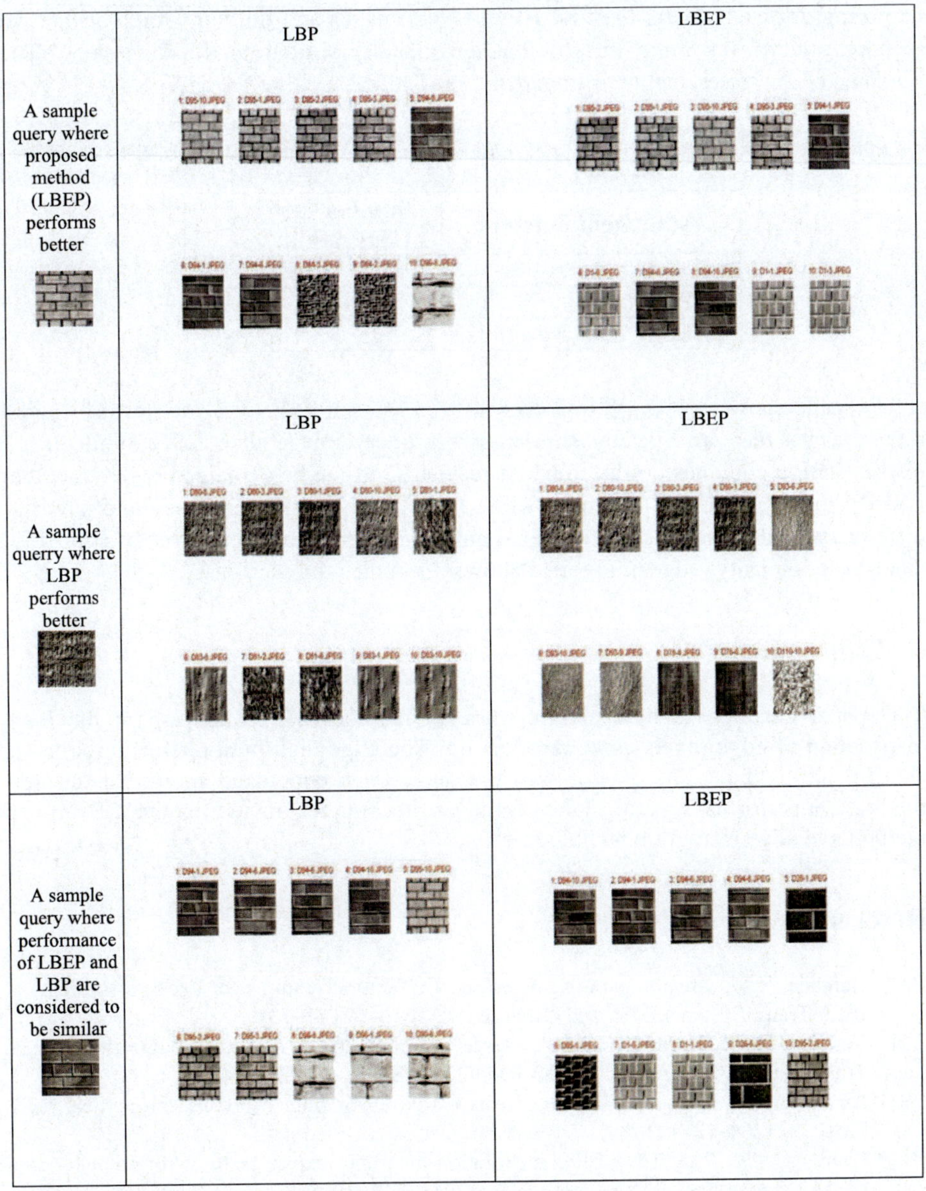

Fig. 5. Sample results of the experiment conducted to compare visually outputs of the two methods LBP and LBEP

Secondly, with 98% accuracy, LBP and LBEP have the best performance among the 6 techniques included in the comparison.

In order to better estimate the difference in performance between LBP and LBEP techniques, we decided to adopt a more qualitative approach that consists of exploring, for each query, the first 10 retrieved images and find out which of the two techniques retrieves more images that are visually similar to the query one. The outcome of this assessment is summarized on Table.2.

Table 2. Comparing visual similarity of retrieved images for both LBP and LBEP techniques

Assessment outcome	Number of queries	%
LBEP is better	38	50.00%
LBP is better	13	17.11%
LBEP & LBP are similar	25	32.89%

The table shows that in 38 queries (out of a total of 76), LBEP retrieval included more images that are visually similar to the query image than LBP. While in 13 queries LBP techniques produced better results. This can be explained by the fact that LBEP similarity is based on edges while LBP retrieval is based on simple intensity differences and as mentioned earlier, human being is more sensitive to significant changes in intensity (edges). Figure.5 shows 3 samples for each case.

6 Conclusion

This paper describes a new texture retrieval method that makes use of the local distribution of edge pixels as texture feature. The edge distribution is captured using an LBP-like coding. The experiments that have been conducted show that the new method outperforms several state of the art techniques including the LBP-based method and edge histogram technique.

References

[1] Haralick, R.M., Shanmugam, K., Dinstein, J.: Textural features for image classification. IEEE Trans. Systems, Man and Cybernetics 3, 610–621 (1973)
[2] Conners, R.W., Harlow, C.A.: A theoretical comparison of texture algorithms. IEEE Trans. Pattern Analysis and Machine Intelligence 2, 204–222 (1980)
[3] Amadasun, M., King, R.: Textural features corresponding to textural properties. IEEE SMC 19, 1264–1274 (1989)
[4] Fountain, S.R., Tan, T.N.: Efficient rotation invariant texture features for content-based image retrieval. Pattern Recognition 31, 1725–1732 (1998)
[5] Tsai, D.-M., Tseng, C.-F.: Surface roughness classification for castings. Pattern Recognition 32, 389–405 (1999)
[6] Weszka, C.R., Dyer, A., Rosenfeld: A comparative study of texture measures for terrain classification. IEEE Trans. System, Man and Cybernetics 6, 269–285 (1976)
[7] Gibson, D., Gaydecki, P.A.: Definition and application of a Fourier domain texture measure: Application to histological image segmentation. Comp. Biol. 25, 551–557 (1995)

[8] Smith, J.R., Transform, S.-F.: features for texture classification and discrimination in large image databases. In: International Conference on Image Processing, vol. 3, pp. 407–411 (1994)
[9] Kokare, M., Biswas, P.K., Chatterji, B.N.: Texture image retrieval using rotated wavelet filters. Pattern Recognition Letters 28, 1240–1249 (2007)
[10] Huang, P.W., Dai, S.K.: Image retrieval by texture similarity. Pattern Recognition 36, 665–679 (2003)
[11] Huang, P.W., Dai, S.K.: Design of a two-stage content-based image retrieval system using texture similarity. Information Processing and Management 40, 81–96 (2004)
[12] Huang, P.W., Dai, S.K., Lin, P.L.: Texture image retrieval and image segmentation using composite sub-band gradient vectors. J. Vis. Communication and Image Representation 17, 947–957 (2006)
[13] Daugman, J.G., Kammen, D.M.: Image statistics gases and visual neural primitives. In: IEEE ICNN, vol. 4, pp. 163–175 (1987)
[14] Jain, A.K., Farrokhnia, F.: Unsupervised texture segmentation using Gabor filters. Pattern Recognition 24, 1167–1186 (1991)
[15] Bianconi, F., Fernandez, A.: Evaluation of the effects of Gabor filter parameters on texture classification. Pattern Recognition 40, 3325–3335 (2007)
[16] Zhang, D., Wong, A., Indrawan, M., Lu, G.: Content-based image retrieval using Gabor texture features. In: Pacific-Rim Conference on Multimedia, Sydney, Australia, pp. 392–395 (2000)
[17] Beck, J., Sutter, A., Ivry, R.: Spatial frequency channels and perceptual grouping in texture segregation. Computer Vision Graphics and Image Processing 37, 299–325 (1987)
[18] Abdesselam, A.: A multi-resolution texture image retrieval using Fourier transform. The Journal of Engineering Research 7, 48–58 (2010)
[19] Kankahalli, M., Mehtre, B.M., Wu, J.K.: Cluster-based color matching for image retrieval. Pattern Recognition 29, 701–708 (1996)
[20] Ojala, T., Pietikäinen, M., Harwood, D.: A Comparative study of texture measures with classification based on feature distributions. Pattern Recognition 29, 51–59 (1996)
[21] Ojala, T., Pietikäinen, M., Mäenpää, T.: Gray scale and rotation invariant texture classification with local binary patterns. In: Vernon, D. (ed.) ECCV 2000. LNCS, vol. 1842, pp. 404–420. Springer, Heidelberg (2000)
[22] Ojala, T., Pietikaeinen, M., Maeenpaea, T.: Multiresolution gray-scale and rotation invariant texture classification with local binary patterns. IEEE Transactions On Pattern Analysis and Machine Intelligence 24, 971–987 (2002)
[23] Kokare, M., Biswas, P.K., Chatterji, B.N.: Texture image retrieval using new rotated complex wavelet filters. IEEE Trans. On Systems, Man, and Cybernetics, B. 35, 1168–1178 (2005)
[24] Kokare, M., Biswas, P.K., Chatterji, B.N.: Rotation-invariant texture image retrieval using rotated complex wavelet filters. IEEE Trans. On Systems, Man, and Cybernetics B. 36, 1273–1282 (2006)
[25] Selesnick, I.W.: The design of approximate Hilbert transform pairs of wavelet bases. IEEE Trans. Signal Processing 50, 1144–1152 (2002)
[26] Celik, T., Tjahjadi, T.: Multiscale texture classification using dual-tree complex wavelet transform. Pattern Recognition Letters 30, 331–339 (2009)
[27] Vo, A., Oraintara, S.: A study of relative phase in complex wavelet domain: property, statistics and applications in texture image retrieval and segmentation. In: Signal Processing Image Communication (2009)

[28] Haralick, R.M., Shapiro, L.G.: Computer and robot vision, vol. 1. Addison-Wesley, Reading (1992)
[29] Varna, M., Garg, R.: Locally invariant fractal features for statistical texture classification. In: 11th International Conference on Computer Vision, Rio de Janeiro, Brazil, vol. 2 (1987)
[30] Deshmukh, N.K., Kurhe, A.B., Satonkar, S.S.: Edge detection technique for topographic image of an urban / peri-urban environment using smoothing functions and morphological filter. International Journal of Computer Science and Information Technologies 2, 691–693 (2011)

Detection of Active Regions in Solar Images Using Visual Attention

Flavio Cannavo[1], Concetto Spampinato[2], Daniela Giordano[2], Fatima Rubio da Costa[3], and Silvia Nunnari[2]

[1] Istituto Nazionale di Geofisica e Vulcanologia, Sezione di Catania, Piazza Roma, 2, 95122 Catania, Italy
flavio.cannavo@ct.ingv.it

[2] Department of Electrical, Electronics and Informatics Engineering University of Catania, Viale A. Doria, 6, 95125 Catania, Italy
{dgiordan,cspampin,snunnari}@dieei.unict.it

[3] Max Planck Institute for Solar System Research Max-Planck-Str. 2, 37191 Katlenburg-Lindau, Germany
rubio@mps.mpg.de

Abstract. This paper deals with the problem of processing solar images using a visual saliency based approach. The system consists of two main parts: 1) a pre-processing part carried out by using an enhancement method that aims at highlighting the Sun in solar images and 2) a visual saliency based approach that detects active regions (events of interest) on the pre-processed images. Experimental results show that the proposed approach exhibits a precision index of about of 70% and thus it is, to some extent, suitable to allow detection of active regions, without human assistance, mainly in massive processing of solar images. However, the recall performance points out that at the current stage of development the method has room for improvements in detecting some active areas, as shown the F-score index that at presently is about 60%.

1 Introduction

The Sun is a fascinating object, and, although it is a rather ordinary star, it is the most studied and the closest star to the earth. Sun's observations allow the discovery of a variety of physical phenomena that keep surprising solar physicists. Over the last couple of decades, solar physicists have increased our knowledge of both the solar interior and the solar atmosphere. Nowadays, we realize that solar phenomena are on the one hand very exciting, but on the other also much more complex than we could imagine. Indeed, intrinsically three dimensional, time dependent and usually non-linear phenomena on all wavelengths and time scales, accessible to present day instruments, can be observable. This poses enormous challenges for both observation and theory, requiring the use of innovative techniques and methods. Moreover, knowledge about the Sun can be also used to understand better the physics of other stars. Indeed, the Sun provides a unique laboratory for understanding fundamental physical processes

H. Cherifi, J.M. Zain, and E. El-Qawasmeh (Eds.): DICTAP 2011, Part I, CCIS 166, pp. 231–241, 2011.

such as magnetic field generation and evolution, particle acceleration, magnetic instabilities, reconnection, plasma heating, plasma waves, magnetic turbulence and so on. We can, therefore, regard the Sun as the Rosetta stone of astro-plasma physics.

The state-of-art in solar exploration, e.g. [2] and [10], indicates that such phenomena may be studied directly from solar images at different wavelengths, taken from telescopes and satellites. Despite several decades of research in solar physics, the general problem of recognizing complex patterns (due to the Sun's activities) with arbitrary orientations, locations, and scales remains unsolved. Currently, these solar images are manually analyzed by solar physicists to find interesting events. This procedure, of course, is very tedious, since it requires a lot of time and human concentration and it is also error prone. This problem becomes increasingly evident with the growing number of massive archives of solar images produced by the instrumentation located at the ground-based observatories or aboard of satellites. Therefore, there is the necessity to develop automatic image processing methods to convert this bulk of data in accessible information for the solar physicists [14]. So far, very few approaches have been developed for automatic solar image processing. For instance, Qu *et al.* in [9] use image processing techniques for automatic solar flare tracking, whereas McAteer *et al.* in [8] propose a region-growing method combined with boundary-extraction to detect interesting regions of magnetic significance on the solar disc. The main problem of these approaches is that they use a-priori knowledge (e.g. the size, the orientation, etc..) of the events to be detected, thus making their application to different images almost useless. In order to accommodate the need of automatic solar images analysis and to overcome the above limit, in this paper we propose an approach based on the integration between standard image processing techniques and visual saliency analysis for the automatic detection of remarkable events in Sun activity. The paper is organized as follows: in Section 2 we report a summary of Sun activities with particular emphasis on the phenomena of interest. Section 3 describes briefly the visual saliency algorithm. Section 4 describes the proposed system pointing out the integration between the visual saliency algorithm and image processing techniques. In Section 5, the implemented software tool is described. Finally, the experimental results and the concluding remarks are given, respectively, in Section 6 and in Section 7.

2 Solar Activity

The solar activity is the process by which we understand the behavior of the Sun in its atmosphere. The behavior of the Sun and its pattern purely depend upon the surface magnetism of the Sun. The solar atmosphere is deemed to be part of the Sun layers above the visible surface, the photosphere. The photosphere is the outer visible layer of the Sun and it is only about 500 km thick. A number of features can be observed in the photosphere [1], i.e.:

- **Sunspots** are dark regions due to the presence of intense magnetic fields and consist of two parts: the umbra, which is the dark core of the spot, and the penumbra ("almost shadow"), which surrounds it.
- **Granules** are the common background of the solar images and have an average size of about 1000 km and a lifetime approximately of 5 minutes.
- **Solar faculae** are bright areas located near Sunspots or in Polar Regions. They have sizes of 0.25 arcsec and life duration between 5 minutes and 5 days.

  The chromosphere is the narrow layer (about 2500 km) of the solar atmosphere just above the photosphere. In the chromosphere the main observable features are:

  - **Plages** (Fig. 1): are bright patches around Sunspots.
  - **Filaments** (Fig. 1): dense material, cooler than the surrounding seen in $H\alpha$[1] as dark and thread-like features.
  - **Prominences** (Fig. 1): are physically the same phenomenon than filaments, but are seen projecting out above the limb.

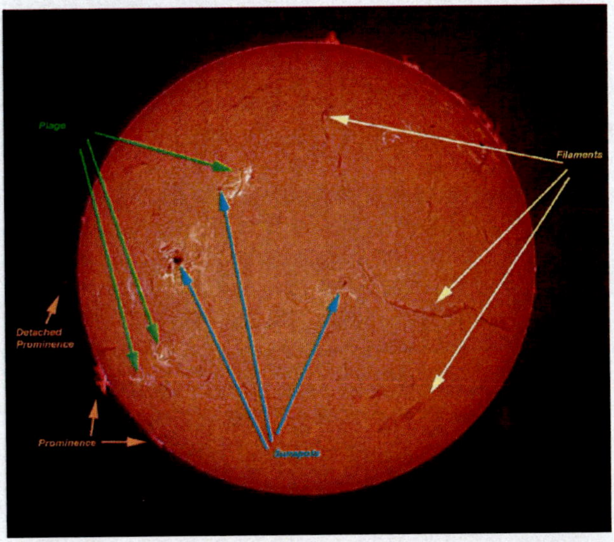

Fig. 1. Sun features

The corona is the outermost layer of the solar atmosphere, which extends out various solar radius, becoming the solar wind. In the visible band it is six orders of magnitude fainter than the photosphere. There are two types of coronal structures: those with open magnetic field lines and those with closed magnetic field lines: 1) **Open-field regions**, known as coronal holes,

[1] H-alpha ($H\alpha$) is a red visible spectral line created by hydrogen.

essentially exist at the solar poles and are the source of the fast solar wind (about 800 km/s), which essentially moves plasma from the corona out into interplanetary space, appear darker in ExtremeUltraViolet and X-ray bands and 2)**Closed magnetic field lines** commonly form active regions, which are the source of most of the explosive phenomena associated with the Sun.

Other features seen in the solar atmosphere are solar flares and coronal mass ejections which are due to sudden increase in the solar luminosity due to unstable release of energy. In this paper we propose a visual saliency-based approach to detect all the Sun features here described from full-disk Sun images.

3 The Saliency-Based Visual Algorithm

The saliency-based algorithm used in this paper follows a bottom-up philosophy according to the biological model proposed by Itti and Koch in [6] and it is based on two elements: 1) a saliency map that provides a biologically plausible model of visual attention based on color and orientations features and aims at detecting the areas of potential interest and 2) a mechanism for blocking or for routing the information flow toward fixed positions. More in detail, the control of visual attention is managed by using features maps, which are further integrated into a saliency map that codifies how much an event is salient with respect to the neighboring zones. Afterwards, a "winner take all" mechanism selects the region with the greatest saliency in the saliency map, in order of decreasing saliency. An overview of the used approach is shown in Fig. 2. The input image is firstly decomposed into a set of Gaussian pyramids and then low-level vision features (colors, orientation and brightness) are extracted for each Gaussian level. The low level features are combined in topographic maps (features maps) providing information about colors, intensity and objects orientation. Each feature map is computed by linear "center-surround" operations (according to the model shown in Fig. 2) that reproduce the human receptive field and are implemented as differences between fine and coarse levels of the Gaussian pyramids. The features maps are then combined into conspicuity maps. Afterwards, these conspicuity maps compete for the saliency, i.e. all these maps are integrated, in a purely bottom-up manner, into a *saliency map*, which topographically codifies the most interesting zones. The maximum of this saliency map defines the most salient image location, to which the focus of attention should be directed. Finally, each maximum is iteratively inhibited in order to allow the model to direct the attention toward the next maximum.

Visual saliency has been used in many research areas: biometrics [3], [11] , video surveillance [12], medical image processing/retrieval [7] but never applied to solar physics. In this paper we have used the Matlab Saliency Toolbox freely downloadable from at the link: *http://www.saliencytoolbox.net*. The code was originally developed as part of Dirk B. Walther's PhD thesis [13] in the Koch Lab at the California Institute of Technology.

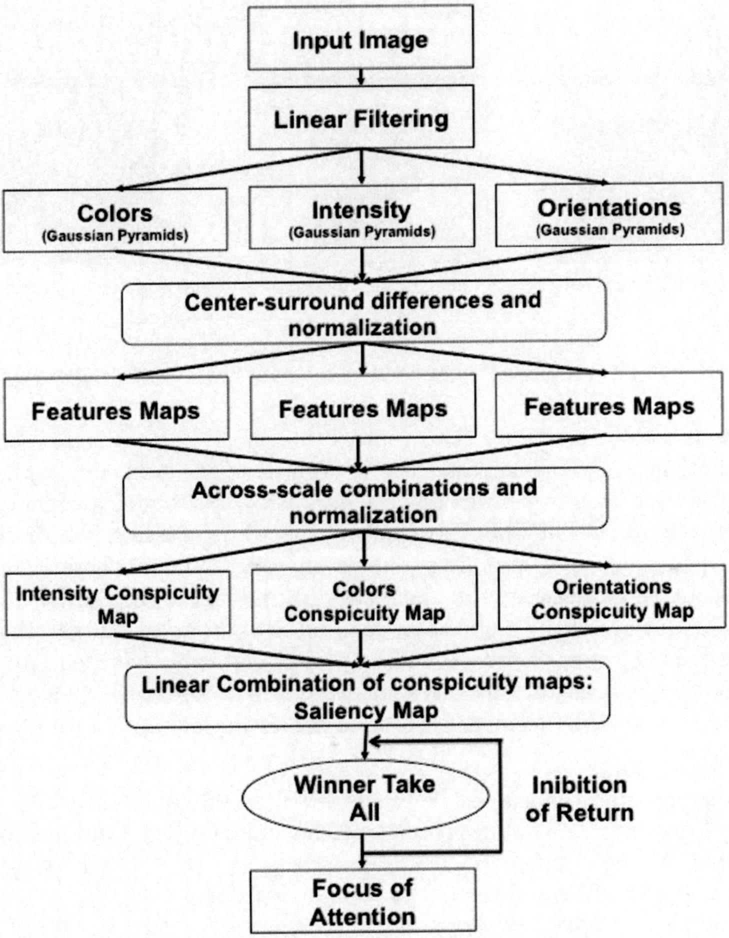

Fig. 2. Architecture of visual saliency algorithm

4 The Proposed System

The proposed system detects events in solar images by performing two steps: 1) image pre-processing to detect the Sun area and 2) event detection carried out by visual saliency on the image obtained at the previous step. The image pre-processing step is necessary since the visual saliency approach fails in detecting the events of interest if applied directly to the original image, as shown in Fig. 3.

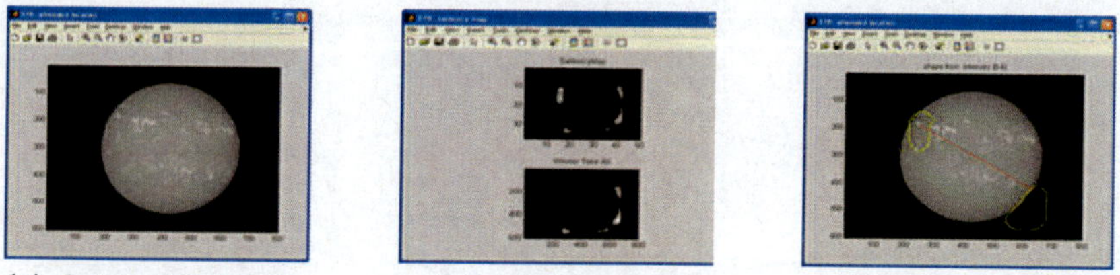

(a) Original Solar Images (b) Saliency Map (c) Two detected events

Fig. 3. The visual saliency algorithm fails if applied to the original images

As it is possible to notice, the event at the most bottom-right part of the image is not an event of interest since it is outside the Sun area while we are interested in detecting events inside the Sun-disk. This is a clear example when the visual saliency is not able to detect events by processing the original Sun images and this problem is mainly due to the edge effects: there is, indeed, a strong discontinuity, between the black background where the Sun disk is placed and the solar surface of the globe itself, leading to an orientation map that affects the whole saliency map in visual saliency model above described. In order to allow saliency analysis to find the solar events of interest we process the raw solar images by an enhancement technique consisting of the following steps:

- **Sun detection**:
  - Thresholding the gray-scale image with the 90th-percentile.
  - Calculating the center of mass of the main object found through the thresholding.
  - Finding the Sun radius by the Hough transform.
- **Background suppression**:
  - Setting the background level at the mean value grey level calculated in the Sun border for minimizing the contrast.
- **Image intensity values adjustment**:
  - Mapping the intensity values of the original image to new ones so as that 1% of data is saturated at low and high intensities of the original image. This increases the contrast of the final image.

An example of events detection is shown in Fig. 4: 1) the original solar image (Fig. 4-a) is thresholded with the 90th-percentile (Fig. 4-b), then the border of the

Sun is extracted (Fig. 4-c) by using the Canny filter. Afterwards the background is removed and the grey levels are adjusted, as above described, obtaining the final image (Fig. 4-d) to be passed to the visual saliency algorithm in order to detect the events of interest (Fig. 4-e).

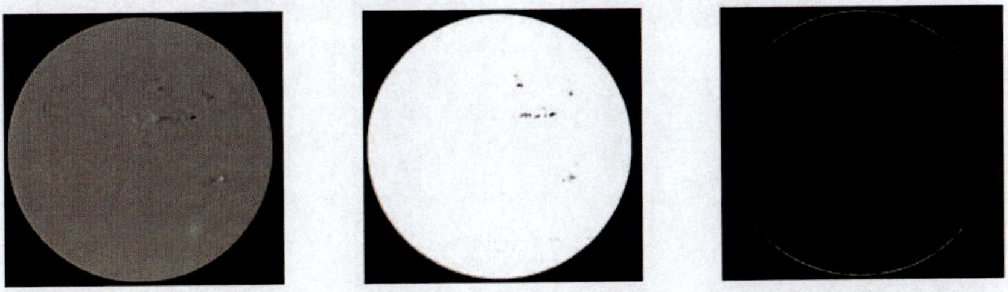

(a) Original Solar Images (b) Thresholded Image (c) Edge Detection

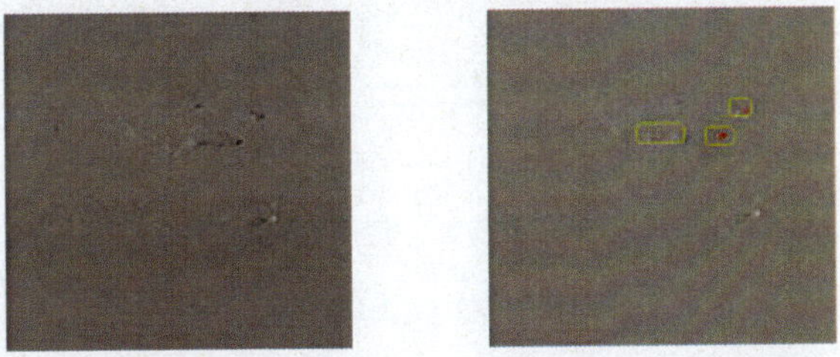

(d) Background Removal (e) The detected events

Fig. 4. Output of each step of the proposed algorithm

5 DARS: The Developed Toolbox

Based on the method described in the previous section we have implemented a software tool, referred here as DARS (Detector of Active Regions in Sun Images) which automatically performs pre-processing steps focused on enhancing the original image and then applies the saliency analysis. The DARS software has been developed in Matlab and its GUI is shown in Fig. 5:

As it is possible to notice, DARS is provided with the following functions:

- handling an image (load into memory, write to files, reset);
- performing manual (i.e. user driven) image enhancement (by applying spatial and morphological filters) to make the original image more suitable for analysis;
- performing automatic enhancement of the original image (see the Auto button) according to the algorithms described below;
- running the Saliency Toolbox to perform Saliency Analysis

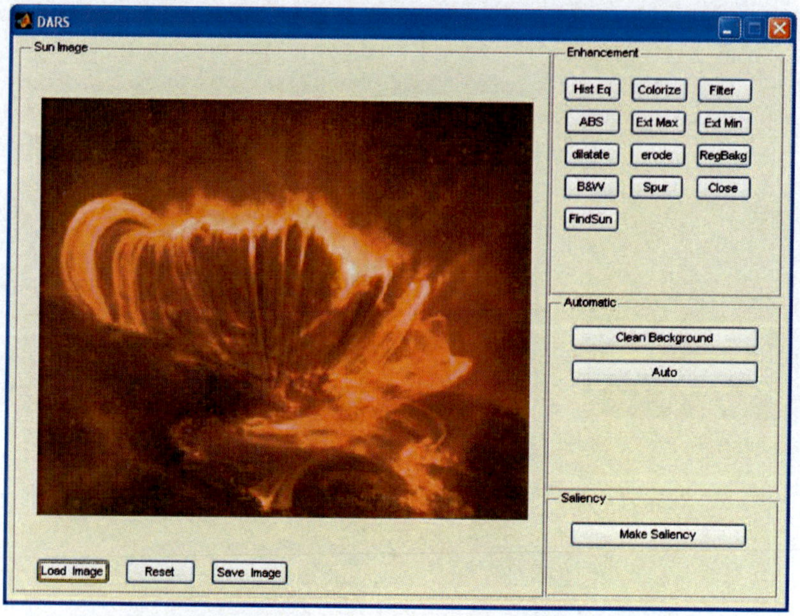

Fig. 5. The DARS GUI with an example of solar flare image

The set of image enhancement processing function includes:

- *HistEqu* this function performs image equalization;
- *Colorize* allows to obtain a color image from a grey-scale one;
- *Filter* performs different kind of image filtering;
- *Abs* performs the following mathematical operation: 2*abs(I)-mean(I). This helps to point out in evidence the extreme values of the image;
- *ExtMax* computes extended maxima over the input images;
- *ExtMin* computes extended minima over the input image;
- *Dilate* applies the basic morphological operation of dilate;
- *RegBack* suppresses the background;
- *B&W* thresholds the image;
- *Spur* removes spur pixels;

The tool is freely downloadable at the weblink *www.i3s-lab.ing.unict.it/dars.html.*

6 Experimental Results

To validate the proposed approach, we considered a set 270 of solar images provided by the MDI Data Services & Information (*http://soi.stanford.edu/data/*). In particular, for the following analysis we considered the images of magnetograms and of $H\alpha$ solar images, which are usually less affected by instrumentation noise. The data set was preliminary divided into two sets here referred to as the Calibration set and the Test set. The Calibration set, consisting of 30 images, was taken into account in order to calibrate the software tool for the subsequent test phase. The calibration phase had two main goals:

1. determine the most appropriate sequence of pre-processing steps (e.g. Subtract background image, equalize etc.)
2. determine the most appropriate set of parameters required by the Saliency algorithm, namely the lowest and highest surround level, the smallest and largest c-s (center-surround) delta and the saliency map level [6].

While goal 1 was pursued on a heuristically basis, to reach goal 2 a genetic optimization approach [5] has been considered. The adopted scheme is the following: images in the calibration set were submitted to a human expert who was required to identify the location of significant events. Subsequently the automatic pre-processing of images in the calibration set was performed. The resulting images were then processed by the saliency algorithm in an optimization framework whose purpose was to determine the optimal parameters of the saliency algorithm, i.e. the ones that maximize the number of events correctly detected. The set of parameters obtained for the images of the calibrations are shown in Table 1:

Table 1. Values of the saliency analysis parameters obtained by using genetic algorithms

Parameter	Value
Lowest surround level	3
Highest surround level	5
Smallest c-s delta	3
Largest c-s delta	4
Saliency map level	5

In order to assess the performance of the proposed tool in detecting active areas in solar images, we have adopted a well-known approach in binary classification, i.e. measures of the quality of classification are built from a confusion matrix, which records correctly and incorrectly detected examples for each class. In detail, outcomes are labeled either as positive (p) or negative (n) class. If the outcome from a prediction is p and the actual value is also p, then it is called a true positive (TP); however if the actual value is n then it is said to be a false positive (FP). Conversely, a true negative has occurred when both the prediction outcome and the actual value are n, and false negative is when the prediction outcome is n while the actual value is p. It is easy to understand that in our case the number of TN counts is zero, since it doesn't make sense to detect not active areas. Bearing in mind this peculiarity the following set of performance indices, referred to as Precision, Recall and F-score can be defined, according with expressions (1), (2) and (3):

$$Precision = 100 \cdot \frac{TP}{TP + FP} \quad (1)$$

$$Recall = 100 \cdot \frac{TP}{TP + FN} \quad (2)$$

$$F - score = \frac{2 \cdot Precision \cdot Recall}{Precision + Recall} \quad (3)$$

All the performance may vary from 0 to 100, respectively, in the worst and in the best case. From expressions (1) and (2) it is evident that while the precision is affected by TP and FP, the recall is affected by TP and FN. Furthermore the F-score takes into account both the precision and the recall indices giving a measure of the test's accuracy. Application of these performance indices in the proposed application gives the values reported in Table 2.

Table 2. Achieved Performance

True Observed (TO)	Precision	Recall	F-score
900	70.5% ± 4.5%	56.9% ± 2.8%	61.8% ± 1.3%

It is to be stressed here that these values were obtained assuming that close independent active regions may be regarded as a unique active region. This aspect thus refers with the maximum spatial resolution of the visual tool. As a general comment we can say that about 70% of Precision represents a quite satisfactory rate of event correctly detected for massive image processing. Since recall is lower than precision it is obvious that the proposed tool has a rate of FN higher than FP, i.e. DARS has some difficulties in recognizing some kind of active areas. This is reflected in an F-score of about 60%. On the other hand there is a variety of different phenomena occurring in Sun surface, as pointed out in Section 2, thus it is quite difficult to calibrate the image processing tool to detect all these kind of events.

7 Concluding Remarks

In this paper we have proposed a system for supporting solar physicians in the massive analysis of solar images based on the Itti and Koch model for visual attention. The precision of the proposed method was about 70%, whereas the recall was lower, thus highlighting some difficulties in recognizing some active areas. Future developments will regard the investigation of the influence of the events' nature (size and shape) on the system's performance. Such analysis may provide us advises to modify automatically the method, according to the peculiarities of different events, in order to achieve better performance. Moreover, image pre-processing techniques, such as the one proposed in [4] will be also integrated to remove more effectively the background and to handle noise due to instrumentation.

References

1. Rubio da Costa, F.: Chromospheric Flares: Study of the Flare Energy Release and Transport. PhD thesis, University of Catania, Catania, Italy (2010)
2. Durak, N., Nasraoui, O.: Feature exploration for mining coronal loops from solar images. In: Proceedings of the 20th IEEE International Conference on Tools with Artificial Intelligence, Washington, DC, USA, vol. 1, pp. 547–550 (2008)
3. Faro, A., Giordano, D., Spampinato, C.: An automated tool for face recognition using visual attention and active shape models analysis, vol. 1, pp. 4848–4852 (2006)
4. Giordano, D., Leonardi, R., Maiorana, F., Scarciofalo, G., Spampinato, C.: Epiphysis and metaphysis extraction and classification by adaptive thresholding and DoG filtering for automated skeletal bone age analysis. In: Conf. Proc. IEEE Eng. Med. Biol. Soc., pp. 6552–6557 (2007)
5. Goldberg, D.E.: Genetic Algorithms in Search, Optimization and Machine Learning, 1st edn. Addison-Wesley Longman Publishing Co., Inc., Boston (1989)
6. Itti, L., Koch, C., Niebur, E.: A model of saliency-based visual attention for rapid scene analysis. IEEE Transactions on Pattern Analysis and Machine Intelligence 20(11), 1254–1259 (1998)
7. Liu, W., Tong, Q.Y.: Medical image retrieval using salient point detector, vol. 6, pp. 6352–6355 (2005)
8. McAteer, R., Gallagher, P., Ireland, J., Young, C.: Automated boundary-extraction and region-growing techniques applied to solar magnetograms. Solar Physics 228, 55–66 (2005)
9. Qu, M., Shih, F.Y., Jing, J., Wang, H.: Solar flare tracking using image processing techniques. In: ICME, pp. 347–350 (2004)
10. Rust, D.M.: Solar flares: An overview. Advances in Space Research 12(2-3), 289–301 (1992)
11. Spampinato, C.: Visual attention for behavioral biometric systems. In: Wang, L., Geng, X. (eds.) Behavioral Biometrics for Human Identification: Intelligent Applications, ch. 14, pp. 290–316. IGI Global (2010)
12. Tong, Y., Konik, H., Cheikh, F.A., Guraya, F.F.E., Tremeau, A.: Multi-feature based visual saliency detection in surveillance video, vol. 7744, p. 774404. SPIE, CA (2010)
13. Walter, D.: Interactions of Visual Attention and Object Recognition: Computational Modeling, Algorithms, and Psychophysics. PhD thesis. California Institute of Technology,Pasadena, California (2006)
14. Zharkova, V., Ipson, S., Benkhalil, A., Zharkov, S.: Feature recognition in solar images. Artif. Intell. Rev. 23, 209–266 (2005)

A Comparison between Different Fingerprint Matching Techniques

Saeed Mehmandoust[1] and Asadollah Shahbahrami[2]

[1] Department of Information Technology
University of Guilan, Rasht, Iran
saeedmehmandoust@gmail.com
[2] Department of Computer Engineering
University of Guilan, Rasht, Iran
shahbahrami@guilan.ac.ir

Abstract. Authentication is a necessary part in many information technology applications such as e-commerce, e-banking, and access control. Design of an efficient authentication system which covers vulnerabilities of ordinary systems such as password-based, token-based, and biometric-based is so important.Fingerprint is one of the best modalities for online authentication due to its suitability and performance. Different techniques for fingerprint matching have been proposed. The techniques are classified into three main categories, correlation based, minutia based, and non-minutia based. In this paper we try to evaluate thesetechniquesin terms of performance. The shape context algorithm has better accuracy, while it has lower performance than the other algorithms.

Keywords: Fingerprint Matching, Shape Context, Gabor Filter, Phase Only Correlation.

1 Introduction

Modern information technology society needs user authentication as an important part in many areas. These areas of application are access control to important places, vehicles, smart homes, e-health, e-payment, and e-banking [1],[2],[3].

These applications exchange personal, financial or health data which needs to remain private. Authentication is the process of positively verifying the identity of a user in a computer system to allow access to resources of the system [4]. An authentication process is comprised of two main stages, enrollment and verification. During enrollment some personal secret data is shared with the authentication system. These secret data will be checked to be correctly entered to the system through verification phase. There are three different kinds of authentication systems. In the first kind, a user is authenticated by a shared secret password. Applications of such a method can be varied to control access to information systems, e-mail,and ATMs. Many studies have shown the vulnerabilities of such system [5],[6],[7].

One problem with password-based systems is that memorizing long strong passwords is difficult for human users and on the other hand short memorable ones are

H. Cherifi, J.M. Zain, and E. El-Qawasmeh (Eds.): DICTAP 2011, Part I, CCIS 166, pp. 242–253, 2011.

often can be guessed or attacked by dictionary attacks. The second kind of authentication system is done when a user presents something called token, in her possession to the authentication system. The token is a secure electronic device that participates in authentication process Tokens can be for example, smart cards, USB-tokens, OTPs, and any other similar device probably with processing and memory resources [8].

Tokens also suffer from some kinds of vulnerabilities when used solely as they can be easily stolen or lost. Token security is seriously depends on its tamper-resistant hardware and software. The third method of authentication is the process of recognizing and verifying users via unique personal features known as biometrics. Biometric refers to automatic recognition of an individual based on her behavioral and/or physiological characteristic [1].These features can be fingerprint, iris, and hand scans, etc. Biometrics strictly connect a user with her features and cannot be stolen or forget. Biometric systems have also some security issues. Biometric feature set called biometric templates, potentially can be revealed to unauthorized persons.

Biometrics are less easily lent or stolen than tokens and passwords. Biometric features are always associated with users and there is no need for them to do any but to present the biometric factor. Hence the use of biometric for authentication is easier for users. In addition biometrics is a solution for situations that traditional systems are not able to solve, like non-repudiation. Results in[4] show that a stable biometric template should not be deployed in single factor mode as it can be stolen or copied during a long period.

It has been investigated in [4] that fingerprint has a nice balance between its features among all other modalities of biometrics. Fingerprint authentication is a convenient biometric authentication for users. Fingerprints are proved to be very distinctive and permanent although they temporarily have slight changes due to skin conditions. It has developed many live-scanners which can easily capture proper fingerprint images.

A fingerprint matching algorithm compares two given fingerprints, generally called enrolled and input fingerprint and returns a similarity score. The result can be presented as a binary decision showing matched or unmatched. Matching fingerprint images is a very difficult problem, mainly due to the large variability in different impressions of the same finger called intra-class variation. The main factors responsible for intra-class variations are displacement, rotation, partial overlap, non-linear distortion, pressure and skin conditions, noise, and feature extraction errors [9],[10].

On the other hand, images from different fingers may sometimes appear quite similar due to small inter-class variations. Although the probability that a large number of minutiae from impressions of two different fingers will match is extremely small fingerprint matchers aim to find the best alignment. They often tend to declare that a pair of the minutiae is matched even when they are not perfectly coincident.

A large number of automatic fingerprint matching algorithms have been proposed in the literature. We need on-line fingerprint recognition systems, to be deployed in commercial applications. There is still a need to continually develop more robust systems capable of properly processing and comparing poor quality fingerprint images; this is particularly important when dealing with large scale applications or when small area and relatively inexpensive low quality sensors are employed. Approaches to fingerprint matching can be coarsely classified into three families [10].

Correlation-based matching which two fingerprint images are superimposed and the correlation between the corresponding pixels is computed for different alignments. Minutiae-based matching which is the most popular and widely used technique, being the basis of the fingerprint comparison made by fingerprint examiners. Minutiae are extracted from the two fingerprints and stored as sets of points in the two dimensional plane. Minutiae-based matching essentially consists of finding the alignment between the template and the input minutiae feature sets that result in the maximum number of minutiae pairings. The third technique is non-minutiae feature-based matching minutiae extraction is difficult in extremely low-quality fingerprint images. While some other features of the fingerprint ridge pattern like local orientation and frequency, ridge shape, texture information may be extracted more reliably than minutiae, their distinctiveness as well as persistence is generally lower. The approaches belonging to this family compare fingerprints in terms of features extracted from the ridge pattern. Few matching algorithms operate directly on gray scale fingerprint images. Most of them require that an intermediate fingerprint representation be derived through a feature extraction stage.

In this paper, we try compare different fingerprint matching algorithms. For this purpose we first introduce each technique. Then each of matching algorithmis implemented on a PC platform using MATLB software. Then we discuss the performance of each technique.

The rest of paper is organized as follows. In section 2 we look at the different matching techniques in detail. Section 3 discusses implementation results of the fingerprint matching algorithms. In section 4 we provide some conclusions.

2 Fingerprint Matching Algorithms

2.1 Three Categories of Matching Algorithms

A fingerprint matching algorithm compares the input and enrolled fingerprint patterns and it calculates a matching score. There are three main categories for fingerprint matching algorithms. The first category is correlation-based algorithms which correlation between the input and enrolled images is computed for different alignments. Second kind of algorithm is minutiae-based ones. Minutia-based matching is the most widely used algorithm in fingerprint matching as minutia extraction can be done with high consistency. Fingerprint minutia which can be ridge ending or bifurcation, as shown in Fig.1 are extracted from the two fingerprints images and stored as sets of points in the two dimensional coordination.

Minutiae-based matching essentially consists of finding the alignment between the template and the input minutiae feature sets that result in the maximum number of minutiae pairings. The last matching category is non-minutiae matching which extract other features of the fingerprint ridge pattern. The advantage of this kind of algorithms is that such non-minutia features can be extracted more reliably in low quality images [7]. A minutia matching is the most well-known and widely used algorithm for fingerprint matching, thanks to its strict analogy with the way forensic experts compare fingerprints and its acceptance as a proof of identity in the courts of law in almost all countries around the world [17].

Let P and Q be the representation of the template and input fingerprint, respectively. Unlike in correlation-based techniques, where the fingerprint representation coincides with the fingerprint image, here the representation is a variable length feature vector whose elements are the fingerprint minutiae. Each minutia in the form of ridge ending or ridge bifurcation may be described by a number of attributes, including its location in the fingerprint image and orientation. Most common minutiae matching algorithms consider each minutia as a triplet $m = (x, y, \theta)$ that indicates theminutia location coordinates and the minutia angle θ.

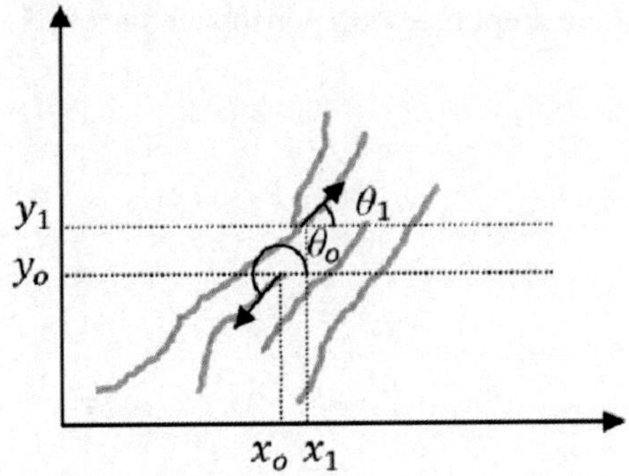

Fig. 1. Minutia representation

2.2 Correlation Based Techniques

Having the template and the input fingerprint images, a measure of their diversity is the sum of squared differences between the intensities of the corresponding pixels. $SSD(P, Q) = |P - Q|^2$. The diversity between the two images is minimized when the cross-correlation between P and Q is maximized. So cross correlation a measure of the image similarity. Due to the displacement and rotation of the two impressions of a same fingerprint, their similarity cannot be simply computed by superimposing P and Q and calculating the cross correlation. Direct cross correlating usually leads to unacceptable results due to image brightness, contrast, vary significantly across different impressions. In addition a direct cross correlating is computationally very expensive. As to the computational complexity of the correlation technique, some approaches have been proposed in the literature to achieve efficient implementations. Phase-Only-correlation (POC) function has been proposed for fingerprint matching algorithm. The POC technique has been applied for biometric matching applications [17]. POC algorithm is considered to have high robustness against fingerprint image degradation. In this paper we choose POC algorithm as an index for the correlation based fingerprint matching techniques.

Consider two $N_1 \times N_2$images,$p(n_1, n_2)$and $q(n_1, n_2)$, where we assume that the index ranges are $n_1 = -M_1 \dots M_1(M_1 > 0)$ and $n_2 = -M_2 \dots M_2(M_2 > 0)$. $P(k_1, k_2)$and$Q(k_1, k_2)$ denote the 2D DFTs of the two images. $P(k_1, k_2)$and$Q(k_1, k_2)$ are given similarly by

$$P(k_1,k_2) = \sum_{n_1,n_2} p(n_1,n_2) W_{N_1}^{k_1 n_1} W_{N_2}^{k_2 n_2}$$
$$= A_P(k_1,k_2) e^{j\theta_P(k_1,k_2)} \quad (1)$$

$$Q(k_1,k_2) = \sum_{n_1,n_2} q(n_1,n_2) W_{N_1}^{k_1 n_1} W_{N_2}^{k_2 n_2}$$
$$= A_Q(k_1,k_2) e^{jQ(k_1,k_2)} \quad (2)$$

where $k_1 = -M_1 \ldots M_1$, $k_2 = -M_2 \ldots M_2$, $W_{N_1} = e^{-j\frac{2\pi}{N_1}}$ and $W_{N_2} = e^{-j\frac{2\pi}{N_2}}$. $A_P(k_1,k_2)$and$A_Q(k_1,k_2)$ are amplitude components and $e^{j\theta_P(k_1,k_2)}$ and $e^{j\theta_Q(k_1,k_2)}$are phase components .

The cross-phase spectrum $\widehat{R_{FG}}(k_1,k_2)$is defined as

$$\widehat{R_{PQ}}(k_1,k_2) = \frac{P(k_1,k_2)\overline{Q(k_1,k_2)}}{|P(k_1,k_2)\overline{Q(k_1,k_2)}|}$$
$$= e^{j\theta(k_1,k_2)} \quad (3)$$

The POC function $\widehat{r_{pq}}(n_2,n_2)$ is the 2d inverse DFT of $\widehat{R_{PQ}}(k_1,k_2)$ and is given by

$$\widehat{r_{pq}}(n_2,n_2) = \frac{1}{N_1 N_2} \sum_{k_1,k_2} \widehat{R_{PQ}}(k_1,k_2) W_{N_1}^{-k_1 n_1} W_{N_2}^{-k_2 n_2} \quad (4)$$

When $p(n_1,n_2) = q(n_1,n_2)$ which means that we have two identical images, the POC function will be given by $\widehat{r_{pp}}(n_1,n_2)$ has the value 1 if $n_1 = n_2 = 0$ and otherwise equals to 0. The most important property of POC function compared to the ordinary correlation is the accuracy in image matching. When two images are similar, their POC function has a sharp peak. When two images are not similar, the peak drops significantly. The height of the POC function can be used as a good similarity measure for fingerprint matching. Other important properties of the POC function used for fingerprint matching is that it is not influenced by image shift and brightness change, and it is highly robust against noise. However the POC function is sensitive to the image rotation, and hence we need to normalize the rotation angle between the registered fingerprint $p(n_1,n_2)$ and the input fingerprint $q(n_1,n_2)$ in order to perform the high-accuracy fingerprint matching [15].

2.3 Minutia Based Techniques

In minutiae based matching, minutiae are first extracted from the fingerprint images and stored as sets of points on a two-dimensional plane. Matching essentially consists of finding the alignment between the template and the input minutiae sets that result in the maximum number of pairings.

$$\begin{pmatrix} \Delta x \\ \Delta y \\ \Delta\theta \end{pmatrix} = \begin{pmatrix} p_x^{ref} \\ p_y^{ref} \\ p_\theta^{ref} \end{pmatrix} - \begin{pmatrix} q_x^{ref} \\ q_y^{ref} \\ q_\theta^{ref} \end{pmatrix} \quad (5)$$

The alignment set $R_{\Delta x,\Delta y,\Delta\theta} = \{(r_x^1, r_y^1, r_\theta^1) \dots (r_x^n, r_x^n, r_x^n)\}$is calculated using (6). The alignment process is calculated according to all possible combinations transformation parameters.

$$R_{\Delta x,\Delta y,\Delta\theta} = \begin{pmatrix} r_x^i \\ r_y^i \\ r_\theta^i \end{pmatrix} = \begin{pmatrix} cos\Delta\theta & -sin\Delta\theta & 0 \\ sin\Delta\theta & cos\Delta\theta & 0 \\ 0 & 0 & 1 \end{pmatrix} \begin{pmatrix} q_{x-}^{ref} q_x^{ref} \\ q_{y-}^{ref} q_y^{ref} \\ q_\theta^i \end{pmatrix} + \begin{pmatrix} q_x^{ref} \\ q_y^{ref} \\ 0 \end{pmatrix} + \begin{pmatrix} \Delta x \\ \Delta y \\ \Delta\theta \end{pmatrix}$$

$$= \begin{pmatrix} cos\Delta\theta & -sin\Delta\theta & 0 \\ sin\Delta\theta & cos\Delta\theta & 0 \\ 0 & 0 & 1 \end{pmatrix} \begin{pmatrix} q_{x-}^{ref} q_x^{ref} \\ q_{y-}^{ref} q_y^{ref} \\ q_\theta^i \end{pmatrix} + \begin{pmatrix} p_x^{ref} \\ p_y^{ref} \\ \Delta\theta \end{pmatrix} \quad (6)$$

The overall matching is segmented into 3 units, Pre-process, Transformation and Comparison. Pre-processing selects reference points form P and Q and calculates transformation parameters. Transformation unit transforms input minutia Q *to* $R_{\Delta x,\Delta y,\Delta\theta}$. Comparison unit computes the matching score S. If this score is higher than a predefined matching score threshold the matching process is halted and the score is sent to output.

The process of finding an optimal alignment between the template and the input minutiae sets can be modeled as point pattern matching. Recently, the shape context, a robust descriptor for point pattern matching was proposed in the literature. Shape context, is applied in fingerprint matching by enhancing with minutiae type and angle details. A modified matching cost between shape contexts, by including the application specific contextual information, improves the accuracy of matching when compared with the original minutia techniques. To reduce computation for practical use, a simple pre-processing step termed elliptical region filtering is applied in removing spurious minutiae prior to matching.

The approach has been enhanced in [16]. It applied in matching a pair of fingerprints whose minutiae are modeled as point patterns. To provide the necessary background for our explanation, we briefly summarize below how the shape context is constructed for the set of filtered minutiae of a fingerprint. They will be used in matching the minutiae of the fingerprint.

Basically, there are four major steps in the shape context based fingerprint matching. First constructing shape context which means for everyminutiap_i, a coarse histogram $h_i$of the relative coordinates of the remaining $n-1$ minutiae is computed.

$$h_i(k) = \#\{q \neq p_i : (q - p_i) \in bin(k)\} \quad (7)$$

To measure the cost of matching two minutias, one on each of the fingerprints, the following equation based on (8) static is used:

$$C_{ij} \equiv C(p_i, q_j) = \frac{1}{2}\sum_{k-1}^{K} \frac{[h_i(k)-h_j(k)]^2}{h_i(k)+h_j(k)} \quad (8)$$

The set of all costs $C_{ij}$for all pairs of minutiae p_i on the first and $q_i$on the second fingerprint are similarly computed. The second step is to minimize matching cost. Given all costs C_{ij}in the current iteration, this step attempts to minimize the total matching cost using the equation below.

$$H(\pi) = \sum_i C(p_i, q_{\pi(i)}) \tag{9}$$

Here, π is a permutation enforcing a one-to-one correspondence between minutiae on the two fingerprints.The third step is warping by Thin Plate Spline (TPS) transformation. Given the set of minutiae correspondences, this step tries to estimate a modeling transformation T: $R^2 \rightarrow R^2$ using TPS to warp one onto the other. The objective is to minimize bending energy of the TPS interpolation by$f(x,y)$as:

$$I_f = \iint_{R^2} \left(\frac{\partial^2 f}{\partial x^2}\right) + 2\left(\frac{\partial^2 f}{\partial x \partial y}\right) + \left(\frac{\partial^2 f}{\partial y^2}\right) dx\, dy \tag{10}$$

This and the previous two steps are repeated for several iterations before the final distance that measures the dissimilarity of the pair of fingerprints is computed. Finally we calculate final distance$D$ by:

$$D = D_{sc} + \alpha D_{ac} + \beta D_{be} \tag{11}$$

Where D_{sc} is the shape context cost that is calculated after iterations, D_{ac} is an appearance cost, and D_{be} is the bending energy. Both α and β are constants determined by experiments [16].

2.4 Non-minutia Matching

Three main reasons induce designers of fingerprint recognition techniques to search for additional fingerprint distinguishing features, beyond minutiae. Additional features may be used in conjunction with minutiae to increase system accuracy and robustness. It is worth noting that several non-minutiae feature based techniques use minutiae for pre-alignment or to define anchor points. Reliably extracting minutiae from extremely poor quality fingerprints is difficult. Although minutiae may carry most of the fingerprint discriminatory information, they do not always constitute the best tradeoff between accuracy and robustness for the poor quality fingerprints [17].

Non-minutiae-based methods may perform better than minutiae-based methods when the area of fingerprint sensor is small. In fingerprints with small area, only 4–5 minutiae may exist and in that case minutiae-based algorithm do not behave satisfactorily. Global and local texture information sources are important alternatives to minutiae, and texture-based fingerprint matching is an active area of research. Image texture is defined by spatial repetition of basic elements, and is characterized by properties such as scale, orientation, frequency, symmetry, isotropy, and so on.

Local texture analysis has proved to be more effective than global feature analysis. We know that most of the local texture information is contained in the orientation and frequency images. Several methods have been proposed where a similarity score is derived from the correlation between the aligned orientation images of the two fingerprints. The alignment can be based on the orientation image alone or delegated to a further minutiae matching stage.

The most popular technique to match fingerprints based on texture information is the FingerCode [17]. The fingerprint area of interest is tessellated with respect to the core point. A feature vector is composed of an ordered enumeration of the features extracted from the local information contained in each sector specified by the tessellation. Thus the feature elements capture the local texture information and the ordered enumeration of the tessellation captures the global relationship among the local contributions. The local texture information in each sector is decomposed into separate channels by using a Gabor filter-bank. In fact, the Gabor filter-bank is a well-known technique for capturing useful texture information in specific band-pass channels as well as decomposing this information into bi-orthogonal components in terms of spatial frequencies.

Therefore, each fingerprint is represented by a fixed-size feature vector, called the FingerCode. The element of the vector denotes the energy revealed by the filter j in cell i, and is computed as the average absolute deviation(AAD) from the mean of the responses of the filter j over all the pixels of the cell i. Matching two fingerprints is then translated into matching their respective Fingercodes, which is simply performed by computing the Euclidean distance between two Fingercodes. Fig. 2 shows the diagram of fingercode matching system.

In [17] they obtained good results by tessellating the area of interest into 80 cells, and by using a bank of eight Gabor filters. Therefore, each fingerprint is represented by a 80 ×8 = 640 fixed-size feature vector, called the Fingercode. The elementV_{ij}denotes theenergy revealed by the filter j in cell i, and is computed as the average absolute deviation from the mean of the responses of the filter j over all the pixels of the cell i. Here$i$ = 1…80 is the cell index and j = 1…8 is the filter index.

$$V_{ij} = \frac{1}{n_i}\left(\sum_{C_i} |g(x, y: \theta_j, 0.1) - \bar{g_\iota}\right) \qquad (12)$$

Where$C_i$is the ith cell of the tessellation, $n_i$is the number of pixels in C_i, the Gabor filter expression$g(\ )$ is defined by Equation (12) and $\bar{g_\iota}$is the mean value of g over the cell C_i. Matching two fingerprints is then translated into matching their respective Fingercodes, which is simply performed by computing the Euclidean distance between two Fingercodes. The even symmetric two-dimensional Gabor filter has the following form:

$$g(x, y: \theta, f) = exp\left\{-\frac{1}{2}\left[\frac{x_\theta^2}{\sigma_x^2} + \frac{y_\theta^2}{\sigma_y^2}\right]\right\}.\cos\,(2\pi f . x_\theta) \qquad (13)$$

The orientation of the filter is θ, and $[x_\theta, y_\theta]$is the coordinates of [x, y] after a clockwise rotation of the Cartesian axes by an angle of (90°– θ). One critical point in Fingercode approach is the alignment of the grid defining the tessellation with respect to the core point. When the core point cannot be reliably detected, or it isclose to the border of the fingerprint area, the FingerCode of the input fingerprint may be incompleteor incompatible with respect to the template[17].

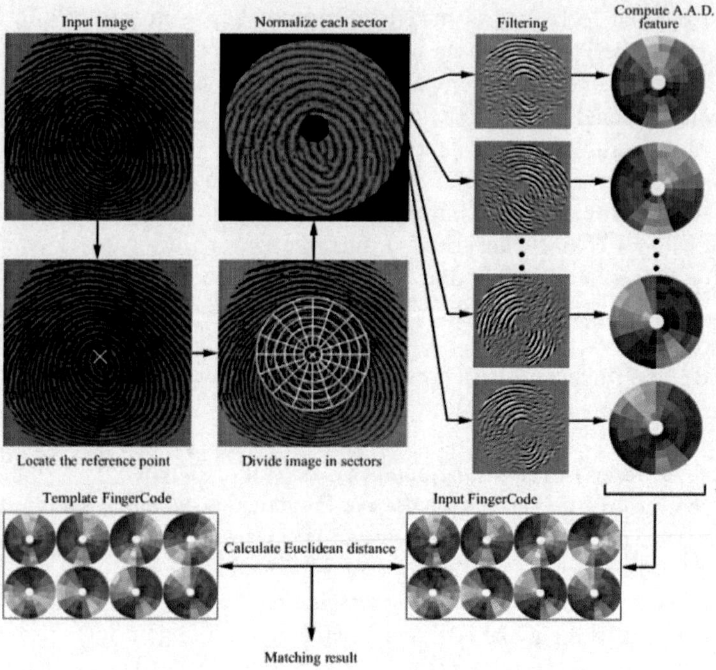

Fig. 2. Diagram of finger code matching algorithm [17]

3 Implementation Results

Using FVC2002 databases, two sets of experiments areconducted to evaluate discriminating ability of each algorithm POC, Shape context and Fingercode algorithm. The other important parameter we want to measure for each algorithm is speed of matching. The platform we used had a 2.4 GHz Core 2 Duo CPU with 4 Giga bytes of RAM. Obviously the result of comparisons will be in terms of this hardware circumstance and cannot be compared directly to other platforms. So the goal of the comparison is to show the situation of speed and accuracy parameters with respect to each other in each algorithm.

3.1 Accuracy Analysis

The similarity degrees of all matched minutiae and unmatchedminutiae are computed. If the similarity degree betweena pair of minutiae is higher than or equal to a threshold,they are inferred as a pair of matched minutiae; otherwise,they are inferred as a pair of unmatched minutiae. When thesimilarity degree between a pair of unmatched minutiae ishigher than or equal to a threshold and inferred as a pair ofmatched minutiae, an error called false match occurs. Whenthe similarity degree between a pair of matched minutiae islower than a threshold and inferred as a pair of unmatchedminutiae, an error called false non-match occurs. The ratio offalse matches to all unmatched minutiae is called false matchrate (FMR), and the ratio of false non-matches to all matched minutiae is called false non-match rate (FNMR). By changing the threshold, we obtain a receiver operating characteristic (ROC) curve with false match rate as*x*-axis and false non-match rate as *y*-axis. The accuracy of each algorithm in terms of False Match Rate (FMR), False Non-match Rate (FNMR), and Equal Error rate (EER) are evaluated. The EER denotes the error rate at the threshold *t* for which both FMR and FNMR are identical. The EER is an important indicator, a finger print system is rarely used at the operating point corresponding to EER, and often another threshold is set corresponding to a pre-specified value of FMR. The accuracy requirements of a biometric verification system are very much application dependent. For example, in forensic applications such as criminal identification, it is the false-non-match rate that is of more concern than the false match rate: that is, we do not want to miss identifying a criminal even at the risk of manually examining a large number of potential false matches identified by the system. At the other extreme, a very low false match rate maybe the most important factor in a highly secure access control application, where the primary objective is to not let in any impostors. Zero FNMR is defined as the lowest FMR at which no false non-matches occur and Zero FMR is defined as the lowest FNMR at which no false matches occur[13].

Fig. 3 shows the ROC curve and EER for the POC algorithm. As it is showed by arrow the EER value is 2.1%. Fig. 4 shows the ROC curve and EER for the shape context algorithm. The EER point is showed by arrow in 1%. Fig. 3 shows the ROC curve and EER for the Fingercode algorithm. We obtained the EER value of 1.1% for Fingercode algorithm. These results are shown in Table 1.

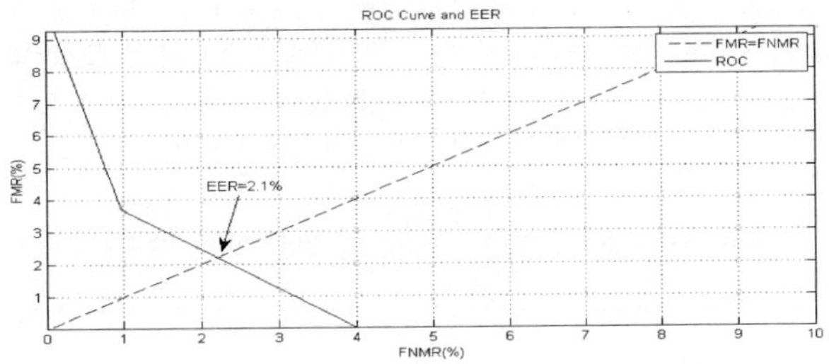

Fig. 3. ROC Curve and EER for POC Algorithm

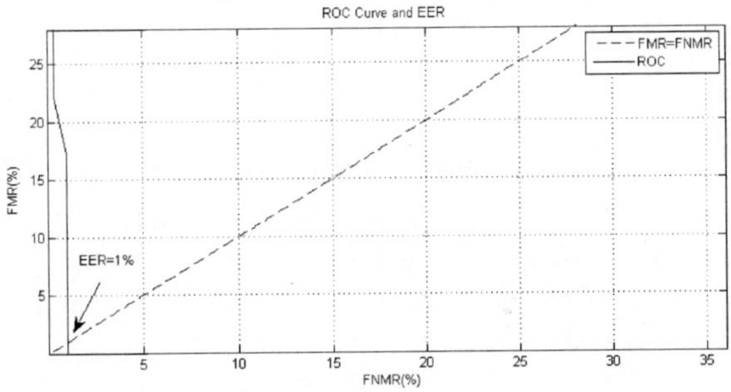

Fig. 4. ROC Curve and EER for Shape Context Algorithm

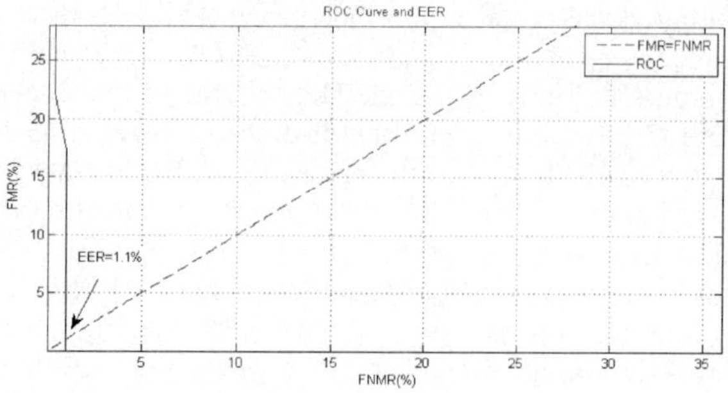

Fig. 5. ROC Curve and EER for Fingercode Algorithm

Table 1. Accuracy Analysis for Fingercode Algorithm

Accuracy Analysis of Each Algorithm	EER(%)
POC	2.1
Shape Context	1
Fingercode	1.1

3.2 Speed Evaluation

Even though CPU time cannot be considered as an accurate estimate of computational load, it could provide an idea on how efficient fingerprint matching algorithm is in comparison with the other two algorithms. Table 2 shows the CPU time result as a metric for speed measurement of each fingerprint algorithm.

Table 2. Speed Analysis for Fingercode Algorithm

Speed Analysis of Each Algorithm	CPU-Time(s)
POC	1.078
Shape Context	2.56
Fingercode	1.9

4 Conclusions

In this paper three main classes of fingerprint matching algorithms have been studied. Each algorithm was implemented in MATLAB programming tool and some evaluations in term of accuracy and performance have been performed.The POC algorithm has better results in terms of performance of matching but it has lower accuracy than other algorithms. The shape context has better accuracy but it has lower performance than the others. Fingercode approach has balanced results in terms of speed and accuracy.

References

1. Ogorman, L.: Comparing Passwords, Tokens, and Biometrics for User Authentication. Proceeding of IEEE 91(12), 2021–2040 (2003)
2. Pan, S.B., Moon, D., Kim, K., Chung, Y.: A Fingerprint Matching Hardware for Smart Cards. IEICE Electronics Express 5(4), 136–144 (2008)
3. Bistarelli, S., Santini, F., Vacceralli, A.: An Asymmetric Fingerprint Matching Algorithm for Java Card. In: Proceeding of 5thInternational Conference on Audio- and Video-Based Biometric Person Authentication, pp. 279–288 (2005)
4. Fons, M., Fons, F., Canto, E., Lopez, M.: Hardware-Software Co-design of a Fingerprint Matcher on Card. In: Proceeding of IEEE International Conference on Electro/Information Technology, pp. 113–118 (2006)
5. Jain, A.K., Ross, A., Prabhakar, S.: An Introduction to Biometric Recognition. IEEE Transactions on Circuits and Systems for Video Technology 14(1), 4–20 (2004)
6. Han, S., Skinner, G., Potdar, V., Chang, E.: A Framework of Authentication and Authorization for E-health Services. In: Proceeding of 3rd ACM Workshop on Secure Web Services, pp. 105–106 (2006)
7. Ribalda, R., Glez, G., Castro, A., Garrido, J.: A Mobile Biometric System-on-Token System for Signing Digital Transactions. IEEE Security and Privacy 8(2), 1–19 (2010)
8. Maltoni, D., Maio, D., Jain, A.K., Prabhakar: Handbook of Fingerprint Recognition. Springer Professional Computing. Springer, Heidelberg (2009)
9. Chen, T., Yau, W., Jiang, X.: Token-Based Fingerprint Authentication. Recent Patents on Computer Science, pp. 50–58. Bentham Science Publishers Ltd (2009)
10. Moon, D., Gil, Y., Ahn, D., Pan, S., Chung, Y., Park, C.: Fingerprint-Based Authentication for USB Token Systems. In: Chae, K.-J., Yung, M. (eds.) WISA 2003. LNCS, vol. 2908, pp. 355–364. Springer, Heidelberg (2004)
11. Grother, P., Salamon, W., Watson, C., Indovina, M., Flanagan, P.: MINEX II: Performance of Fingerprint Match-on-Card Algorithms. NIST Interagency Report 7477 (2007)
12. Fons, M., Fons, F., Canto, E., Lopez, M.: Design of a Hardware Accelerator for Fingerprint Alignment. In: Proceeding of IEEE International Conference on Field Programmable Logic and Applications, pp. 485–488 (2007)
13. Maltoni, D., Maio, D., Jain, A.K., Prabhakar, S.: Habdbook of Fingerprint Recognition, 2nd edn. Spriner Professional Computing (2009)
14. Kwan, P.W.H., Gao, J., Guo, Y.: Fingerprint Matching Using Enhanced Shape Context. In: Proceeding of 21st IVCNZ Conference on Image and Vision Computing, pp. 115–120 (2006)
15. Ito, K., Nakajima, H., Kobayashi, K., Aoki, T., Higuchi, T.: A Fingerprint Matching Algorithm Using Phase-only correlation. IEICE Transaction on Fundamentals 87(3) (2004)
16. Blongie, S., Malik, J., Puzicha, J.: Shape Matching and Object Recognition Using Shape Context. IEEE Transaction on PAMI 24, 509–522 (2002)
17. Jain, A.K., Prabhakar, S., Hong, L., Pankanti, S.: Filterbank-based fingerprint matching. IEEE Transaction on Image Processing 9, 846–859 (2000)

Classification of Multispectral Images Using an Artificial Ant-Based Algorithm

Radja Khedam and Aichouche Belhadj-Aissa

Image Processing and Radiation Laboratory, Faculty of Electronic and Computer Science,
University of Science and Technology Houari Boumediene (USTHB),
BP. 32, El Alia, Bab Ezzouar, 16111, Algiers, Algeria
rkhedam@usthb.dz, rkhedam@yahoo.com

Abstract. When dealing with unsupervised satellite images classification task, an algorithm such as K-means or ISODATA is chosen to take a data set and find a pre-specified number of statistical clusters in a multispectral space. These standard methods are limited because they require *a priori* knowledge of a probable number of classes. Furthermore, they also use random principles which are often locally optimal. Several approaches can be used to overcome these problems. In this paper, we are interested in approach inspired by the clustering of corpses and larval observed in real ant colonies. Based on previous works in this research field, we propose an ant-based multispectral image classifier. The main advantage of this approach is that it does not require any information on the input data, such as the number of classes, or an initial partition. Experimental results show the accuracy of obtained maps and so, the efficiency of developed algorithm.

Keywords: Remote sensing, image, classification, unsupervised, ant colony.

1 Introduction

Research in social insect behavior has provided computer scientists with powerful methods for designing distributed control and optimization algorithms. These techniques are being applied successfully to a variety of scientific and engineering problems. In addition to achieving good performance on a wide spectrum of "static" problems, such techniques tend to exhibit a high degree of flexibility and robustness in a "dynamic" environment. In this paper our study concerns models based on insects self-organization among which we focus on Brood sorting model in ant colonies.

In ant colonies the workers form piles of corpses to clean up their nests. This aggregation of corpses is due to the attraction between the dead items. Small clusters of items grow by attracting workers to deposit more items; this positive feedback leads to the formation of larger and larger clusters. Worker ants gather larvae according to their size, all larvae of the same size tend to be clustered together. An item is dropped by the ant if it is surrounded by items which are similar to the item it is carrying; an object is picked up by the ant when it perceives items in the neighborhood which are dissimilar from the item to be picked up.

H. Cherifi, J.M. Zain, and E. El-Qawasmeh (Eds.): DICTAP 2011, Part I, CCIS 166, pp. 254–266, 2011.

Deneubourg *et al.* [3] have proposed a model of this phenomenon. In short, each data (or object) to cluster is described by n real values. Initially the objects are scattered randomly on a discrete 2D grid which can be considered as a toroidal square matrix to allow the ants to travel from one end to another easily. The size of the grid is dependent on the number of objects to be clustered. Objects can be piled up on the same cell, constituting heaps. A heap thereby represents a class. The distance between two objects can be calculated by the Euclidean distance between two points in R^n. The centroid of a class is determined by the center of its points. An *a prior* fixed number of ants move onto the grid and can perform different actions. Each ant moves at each iteration, and can possibly drop or pick up an object according to its state. All of these actions are executed according to predefined probabilities and to the thresholds for deciding when to merge heaps and remove items from a heap.

In this paper we shall describe the adaptation of the above ant-based algorithm to classify automatically a remotely sensed data. The most important modifications are linked to the nature of satellite data and to the definition of thematic classes.

The remainder of the paper is organised as follows. Section 2 briefly introduces the problem domain of remotely sensed data classification, and Section 3 reviews previous work on ant-based clustering. Section 4 presents the basic ant-based algorithm as reported in the literature, and in Section 5 we describe the principles of the proposed ant-based classifier applied to real satellite data. The employed simulated and real test data sets, results and evaluation measures are presented and discussed in Section 6. Finally Section 7 provides our conclusion.

2 Classification of Multispectral Satellite Data

Given the current available techniques, remote sensing is recognized as a timely and cost-effective tool for earth observation and land monitoring. It constitutes the most feasible approach to both land surface change detection, and land-cover information required for the management of natural resources. The extraction of land-cover information is usually achieved through supervised or unsupervised classification methods.

Supervised classification requires prior knowledge of the ground cover in the study site. The process of gaining this prior knowledge is known as ground-truthing. With supervised classification algorithms such as Maximum Likelihood or minimum of distance, the researcher locates areas on the unmodified image for which he knows the type of land cover, defines a polygon around the known area, and assigns that land cover class to the pixels within the polygon. This process known as training step is continued until a statistically significant number of pixels exist for each class in the classification scheme. Then, the multispectral data from the pixels in the sample polygons are used to train a classification algorithm. Once trained, the algorithm can then be applied to the entire image and a final classified image is obtained.

In unsupervised classification, an algorithm such as K-means or Isodata, is chosen that will take a remotely sensed data set and find a pre-specified number of statistical clusters in multispectral space. Although these clusters are not always equivalent to actual classes of land cover, this method can be used without having prior knowledge of the ground cover in the study site.

The standard approaches of K-means and Isodata are limited because they generally require the a priori knowledge of a probable number of classes. Furthermore, they also use random principles which are often locally optimal. Among the approaches that can be used to outperform those standard methods, Monmarché [14] reported the following methods: Bayesian classification with AutoClass, genetic-based approaches and ant-based approaches. In addition, we can suggest approaches based on swarm intelligence [1] and cellular automata [4], [9].

In this work, we present and largely discuss an unsupervised classification approach inspired by the clustering of corpses and larval sorting activities observed in real ant colonies. This approach was already proposed with preliminary results in [7], [8]. Before giving details about our approach, it seems interesting to survey ant-based clustering in the literature.

3 Previous Works on Ant-Based Data Clustering

Data clustering is one of those problems in which real ants can suggest very interesting heuristics for computer scientists. The idea of an ant-based algorithm is specifically derived from research into the Pheidole pallidula [3], Lasius niger and Messor sancta [2] species of ant. These species sort larvae and/or corpses to form clusters. The phenomenon that is observed in these experiments is the aggregation of dead bodies by workers. If dead bodies, or more precisely items belonging to dead bodies, are randomly distributed in space at the beginning of the experiment, the workers will form clusters within a few hours.

An early study in using the metaphor of biological ant colonies related to automated clustering problems is due to Deneubourg *et al.* [3]. They used a population of randomly moving artificial ants to simulate the experimental results seen with real ants clustering their corpses. Two algorithms were proposed as models for the observed experimental behaviour, of chief importance, the item pickup and drop probability mechanism. From this study the model which, least accurately modelled the real ants was the most applicable to automated clustering problems in computer science. Lumer and Faieta [12] extended the model of Deneubourg *et al.,* modifying the algorithm to include the ability to sort multiple types, in order to make it suitable for exploratory data analysis. The proposed Lumer and Feita ant model has subsequently been used for data-mining [13], graph-partitioning [10] and text-mining [5]. However, the obtained number of clusters is often too high and convergence is slow. Therefore, a number of modifications were proposed [6] [17], among which Monmarché *et al.* [15] have suggested applying the algorithm twice. The first time, the capacity of all ants is 1, which results in a high number of tight clusters. Subsequently the algorithm is repeated with the clusters of the first pass as atomic objects and ants with an infinite capacity. After each pass K-means clustering is applied for handling small classification errors. Monmarché's ant-based approach called "AntClass" gives good clustering results [7], [8].

In the context of global image classification under the classical Markov Random Field (MRF) assumption, Ouadfel and Batouche [17] showed that ant colony system produces equivalent or better results than other stochastic optimization methods like simulated annealing and genetic algorithm. On the other hand Le Héragarat-Mascle et al. [11] proposed an ant colony optimization for image regularization based on a non-stationary Markov modelling and they applied this approach on a simulated image and on actual remote sensing images of Spot 5 satellite. The common point of these two works is that the ant-based strategy is used as an optimization method which needs necessary an initial configuration to be regularized under the markovian hypothesis.

In the next section, we present the general outline of the basic ant-algorithm as reported in the literature [14], [15], [16].

4 Principles of the Basic Clustering Ant-Based Algorithm

The basic ant-based clustering algorithm is presented as follows [14], [15]:

- Randomly place the ants on the board.
- Randomly place objects on the board at most one per cell.
- Repeat:
- For each ant do:
    - Move the ant
    - If the ant does not carry any object then if there is an object in the eight neighboring cells of the ant, the ant possibly picks up the object;
    - Else the ant possibly drops a carried object, by looking at the eight neighboring cells around it.
- Until stopping criteria is met.

Initially the ants are scattered randomly on the 2D board. The ant moves on the board and possibly picks an object or drops an object. The movement of the ant is not completely random. Initially the ant picks a direction randomly then the ant continues in the same direction with a probability, otherwise it generates a new random direction. On reaching the new location on the board the ant may possibly pick up an object or drop an object, if it is carrying one. The heuristics and the exact mechanism for picking up or dropping an object are explained below. The stopping criterion for the ants, here, is the upper limit on the number of times through the repeat loop. The ants cluster the objects to form heaps. A heap is defined as a collection of two or more objects. A heap is spatially located in a single cell.

4.1 Heuristic Rules of Ants

The following parameters are defined for a heap and are used to construct heuristics for the classifier ant-based algorithm [16].

Let consider a heap $T = \{o_1, o_2, \ldots, o_{nT}\}$ with n_T objects o_i $(i = 1, \ldots, n_T)$. Five statistical parameters are computed as follows:

- Maximum distance between two objects in a heap *T:*

$$d^*(T) = \max_{(i,j)\in\{1,..,n_T\}^2}\{d(o_i, o_j)\}. \tag{1}$$

Where $d(o_i, o_j)$ is the Euclidean distance between the two objects o_i, and o_j.

- Mean distance between two objects o_i, and o_j of a heap *T:*

$$\bar{d}(T) = \frac{2}{n_T(n_T-1)}\sum_{(i,j)\in\{1,..,n_T\}^2} d(o_i, o_j). \tag{2}$$

-Mass center of all the objects in a heap *T:*

$$O_{center}(T) = \frac{1}{n_T}\sum_{i\in\{1,..,n_T\}}\{o_i\}. \tag{3}$$

- Maximum distance between all the objects in a heap *T* and its mass center:

$$d^*_{O_{center}}(T) = \max_{i\in\{1,..,n_T\}}\{d(o_i, O_{center}(T))\}. \tag{4}$$

- Mean distance between the objects of *T* and its mass center:

$$\bar{d}_{O_{center}}(T) = \frac{1}{n_T}\sum_{i\in\{1,..,n_T\}} d(o_i, O_{center}(T)). \tag{5}$$

Most dissimilar object in the heap T is the object which is the farthest from the center of this heap.

4.2 Ants Mechanism of Picking Up and Dropping Objects

In this section, we recall the most important mechanisms used by ants to pick up and drop objects in a heap. These mechanisms are presented in details in [16].

Picking up objects

If an ant does not carry any object, the probability $\mathrm{P_p(T)}$ of picking up an object in the heap T depends on the following cases:

1. If the heap T contains only one object ($n_T = 1$), then it is systematically picked up and so $P_p(T) = 1$.
2. If the heap T contains two objects ($n_T = 2$), then $P_p(T)$ depends both on $\bar{d}_{O_{center}}(T)$ and $\bar{d}(T)$, and it equals to $\min\{(\bar{d}_{O_{center}}(T)/\bar{d}(T)),\ 1\}$.
3. If the heap T contains more than two objects ($n_T > 2$), the probability $P_p(T) \approx 1$ only when $\bar{d}_{O_{center}}(T) \ll d^*_{O_{center}}(T)$.

Dropping objects

If an ant carries an object o_i, the probability $P_d(o_i, T)$ of dropping the object o_i in the heap T depends on the following cases:

1. The object o_i is dropped on a neighbouring empty cell and $P_d(o_i, T) = 1$.
2. The object o_i is dropped on a neighbouring single object ó if the two objects o_i and ó are close enough to each other according to a dissimilarity threshold expressed as a percentage of the maximum dissimilarity in the database.
3. The object o_i is dropped on a neighbouring heap T if o_i is close enough to $O_{center}(T)$, on again, according to another dissimilarity threshold.

Some parameters are added in the algorithm in order to accelerate the convergence of the classification process. Also, they allow achieving more homogeneous heaps with few misclassifications. These parameters are simple heuristics and are defined as follows [16]:

a) An ant will be able to pick up an object of a heap T only if the dissimilarity of this object with $O_{center}(T)$ is higher than a fixed threshold T_{remove}.

b) An ant will be able to drop an object on a heap T only if this object is sufficiently similar to $O_{center}(T)$ compared to a fixed threshold T_{create}.

In the next section, we describe our unsupervised multispectral image classification method that discovers automatically the classes without additional information, such as an initial partitioning of the data or the initial number of clusters.

5 Principles of Ant-Based Image Classifier

The ant-based classifier presented in this study follows the general outlines of the principles mentioned above. Recall that our method is not an improvement over existing ones, because the existing ant-based approaches were developed and applied to classify a mono dimensional numerical data randomly distributed on a square grid. In the field of satellite multispectral image classification, these approaches have not been yet applied. They could be adapted to the nature of remotely sensed data: the pixels to classify are multidimensional (a number of spectral channels) and not randomly positioned in the image. The pixels are virtually picked by the ants; they could not change their location. The main introduced modifications are as follows:

1. A multispectral image is assimilated to a 2D grid.
2. The grid size is defined as the multispectral image dimension.
3. To simulate the toroidal shape of the grid we connect virtually the boarders of the multispectral image. When an ant reaches one end of the grid, it disappears and reappears on the side opposite of the grid.
4. Pixels to classify are not randomly scatter on the grid. Each specified pixel is positioned on one cell of the grid.
5. The mechanisms for picking up and dropping pixels are not physical but virtual. In image classification, spatial location of pixels must be respected.
6. The movement of ants on the grid is stochastic. It has a probability of 0.6 to continue straightly and a probability of 0.4 to change a direction. In this case, an ant has a chance on two to turn of 45 degrees on the right or left.
7. The distance between two pixels X and Y on the cluster (heap) is computed using a multispectral radiometric distance given by:

$$d = \sqrt{\sum_{i=1}^{Nb} (x_i - y_i)^2} \tag{6}$$

Where x_i and y_i are respectively the radiometric values of pixel X and pixel Y in the ith spectral band. *Nb* is number of considered spectral bands.

The algorithm is run until convergence criterion is met. This criterion is obtained when all pixels are tested (ants assigned one label for each pixel). T_{create} and T_{remove} are user specified thresholds according to the nature of data.

As mentioned on the most papers related on this stochastic ant-based algorithm, the created initial partition is compound of too many homogenous classes and with some free pixels left alone on the board, because the algorithm is stopped before convergence which would be too long to obtain. We therefore propose to add to this algorithm (step 1) a more deterministic and convergent component through a deterministic ant-based algorithm (step 2) whose characteristics are:

1. Only one ant is considered.
2. Ant has a deterministic direction and an internal memory to go directly to free pixels.
3. The capacity of the ant is infinite, it becomes able to handle heap of objects.

At the end of this second algorithm which operates on two steps, alls pixels are assigned and the real number of classes is very well approximated.

6 Experimental Results and Discussion

The presented ant-based classifier has been tested first on simulated data and then on real remotely sensed data.

6.1 Application on Simulation Data

Fig. 1 shows a 256 x 256 8-bit gray scale image created to specifically validate our algorithm. It is a multi-band image which synthesized a multispectral image with three spectral channels (Fig. a.1, Fig. b.1 and Fig. c.1) and five different thematic classes: water (W), dense vegetation (DV), bare soil (BS), urban area (UA), and less dense vegetation (LDV). RGB composition of this image is given on Fig. 2.

During simulation, we have tried to respect the real spectral signature of each class. We have used ENVI's Z profiles to interactively plot the spectrum (all bands) for some samples from each thematic class (Fig. 3).

Fig. a.1. Band 1

Fig. b.1. Band 2

Fig. c.1. Band 3

Fig. 1. Simulated multiband image

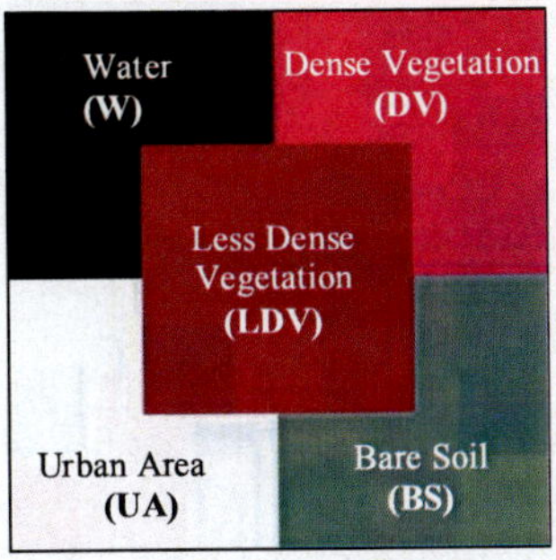

Fig. 2. RGB composition of the three simulated bands

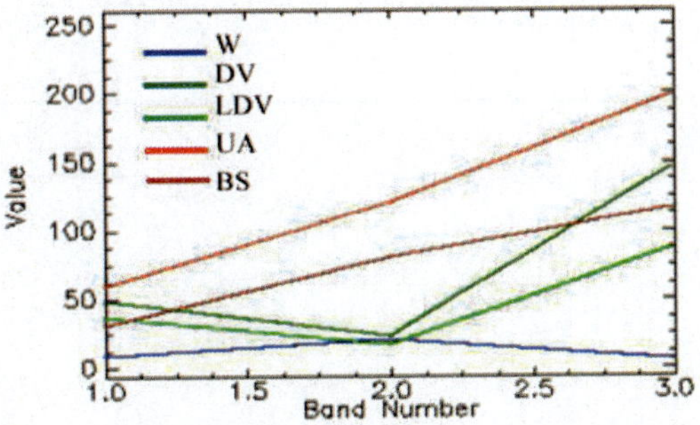

Fig. 3. Spectral signatures of the five classes

Results of step 1 with 100 ants and 250 ants are given respectively on Fig. 4 and Fig. 5. Results of step 1 followed by step 2 with 100 ants and 250 ants are given respectively by Fig. 6 and Fig. 7. However, Fig. 8 shows the final result obtained with 250 ants at the convergence. Also, graphs of Fig. 9 give the influence of the ants number on the discovered classes number and the free pixels number. For all these results T_{create} and T_{remove} are taken respectively equal to 0.011 and 0.090.

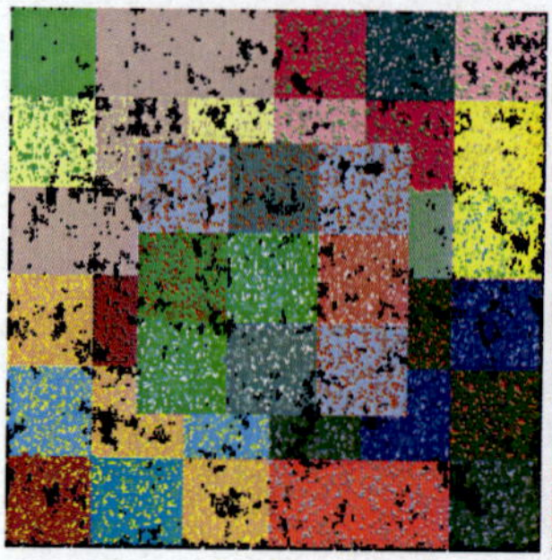

Fig. 4. Result with 100 ants Step 1

Fig. 5. Result with 250 ants Step 1

Fig. 6. Result with 100 ants Step 1 + Step 2

Fig. 7. Result with 250 ants (Step 1 + Step 2)

Fig. 8. Result with 250 ants (Step 1 + Step 2) (convergence)

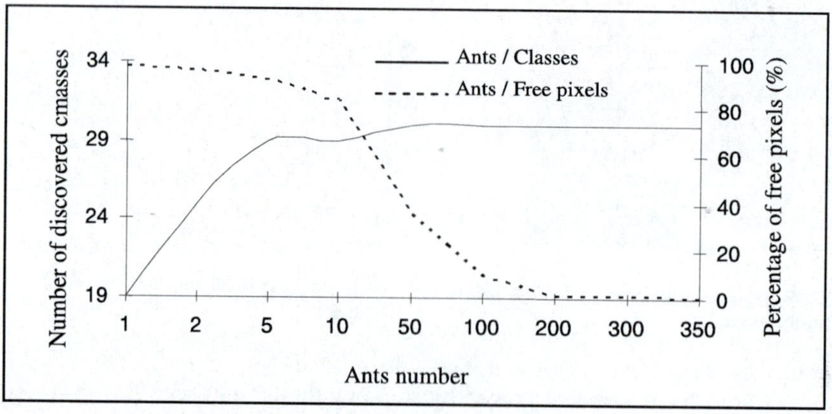

Fig. 9. Influence of ants number on discovered classes number and free pixels number

From the above results (Fig. 9), it appears that an ant is able to detect 19 sub classes in the 05 main classes of the simulated image, but it can visit only 2% of image pixels and leaves, therefore, 98% free pixels. With 100 ants, the number of classes increased to 30 and the number of pixels free fall to 9% (Fig. 4). With 250 ants all pixels are visited (0% free pixels), but the number of classes remains constant (Fig. 5). This is explained by the fact that firstly, an ant does not look a pixel already tagged by the previous ant, and secondly, the decentralization mode function of the algorithm causes that each ant has a vision of its local environment, and does not continue the work of another ant. Thus, we introduced the deterministic algorithm (step 2) to classify the free pixels not yet tested (Fig. 6 and Fig. 7) and then merge the similar classes (Fig. 8).

Finally, the adapted ant-based approach has a good performance for classification of numerical multidimensional data but it is necessary to choose the appropriate values of the ant-colony's parameters.

6.2 Application on Satellite Multispectral Data

The used real satellite data consists of a multispectral image acquired on 3rd June, 2001 by ETM+ sensor of LandSat-7 satellite. This multi-band image of six spectral channels (respectively centered around red, green, blue, and infra red frequencies) and with a spatial resolution of 30 m (size of a pixel is 30 x 30 m^2), covers a north-eastern part of Algiers (Algeria). Fig.10 shows the RGB composition of the study area. We can see the international airport of Algiers, the USTHB University and two main zones: an urban zone (three main urban cities: Bab Ezzouar, Dar El Beida and El Hamiz) located at the north of the airport, and an agricultural zone with bare soils located at the south of the airport.

Consideration of this real data has required other values of T_{create} and T_{remove} parameters. They have been chosen empirically equal to 0.008 and 0.96 respectively. Since the number of pixels to classify is the same as for the simulated image (256x256), then the number of 250 ants was maintained. Intermediate results are given on Fig. 11 and Fig. 12. The final result is presented on Fig. 13. Furthermore, in Fig. 14, we give a different result for other values of T_{create} and T_{remove} (0.016 and 0.56).

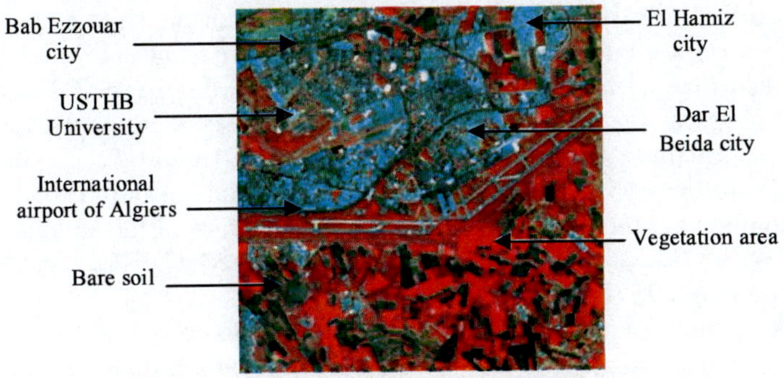

Fig. 10. RGB composition of real satellite image

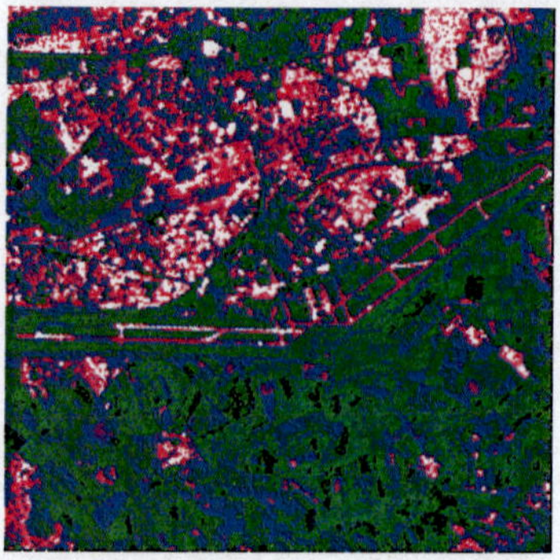

Fig. 11. Result with 250 ants (0.8% of free pixels)

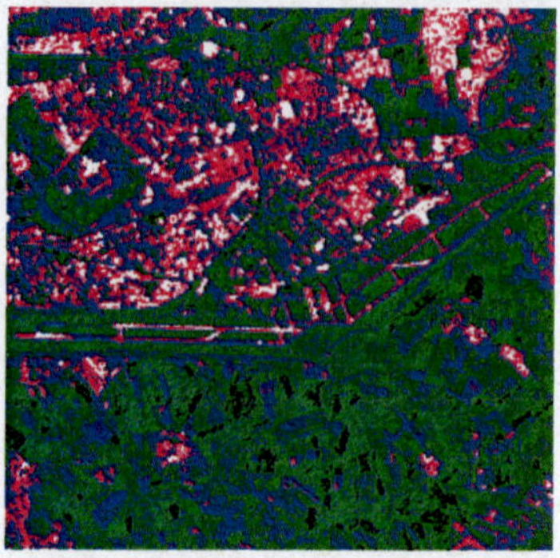

Fig. 12. Classification of free pixels

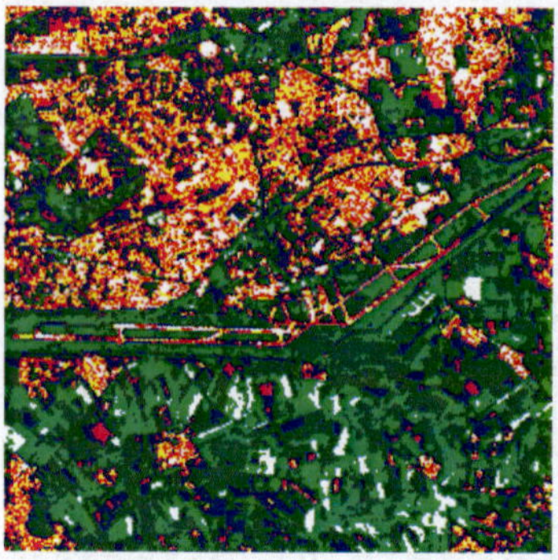

Fig 13. Final result *(T_{create} = 0.008 and T_{remove} = 0.96)*

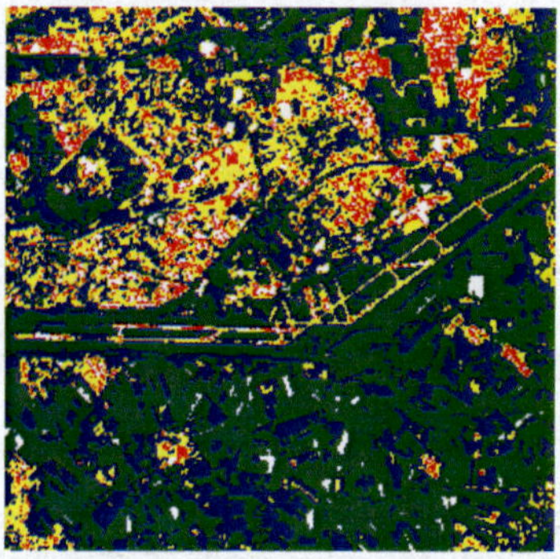

Fig. 14. Final result *(T_{create} = 0.016 and T_{remove} = 0.56)*

With 250 ants, most of the pixels are classified into one of the 123 discovered classes (Fig. 11). Most of the 0.8% free pixels located on the right edge and bottom edge of the image are labeled in the second step (Fig. 12) during which the similar classes are also merged to obtain a final partition of well separated 07 classes (Fig. 13). However, as we see in Fig. 13, the classification result is highly dependent on T_{create} and T_{remove} values. Indeed, with T_{create} equal to 0016 and T_{remove} equal to 0.56, the obtained result has 05 classes, where the vegetation class (on the south part of the airport) is dominant, which does not match the ground truth of the study area. But we are much closer to that reality, with the 07 classes obtained when T_{create} equal to 0.008 and T_{remove} equal to 0.96 (Fig. 14).

The spectral analysis of the obtained classes allows us to specify the thematic nature of each of these classes as follows: dense urban, medium dense urban, less dense urban, bare soil, covered soil, dense vegetation, and less dense vegetation.

7 Conclusion and Outlook

We have presented in this paper an ant-based algorithm for unsupervised classification of remotely sensed data. This algorithm is inspired by the observation of some real ant colony behaviour exploiting the self-organization paradigm. Like all ant-based clustering algorithms, no initial partitioning of the data is needed, nor should the number of clusters be known in advance. In addition, as it has been clearly shown in this study, these algorithms have the capacity to work with any kind of data that can be described in term of similarity/dissimilarity function, and they impose no assumption on the distribution model of the data or on the shape of the clusters they work with. However, the ants are clearly sensitive to the threshold for deciding when to merge heaps (T_{create}) and remove items (T_{remove}) from a heap, especially when dealing with a real data.

Further work should focus on:

1. Setting the different parameters automatically.
2. Testing other similarity functions such as Hamming distance or Minkowski distance in order to reduce the initial number of classes.
3. Considering other sources of inspiration from real ant's behaviour, for example, ants can communicate between them and can exchange objects. Ant pheromones can be also introduced to reduce the free pixels.

References

1. Bonabeau, E., Dorigo, M., Theraulaz, G.: Swarm Intelligence: From Natural to Artificial Systems. Oxford University Press, New York (1999)
2. Chretien, L.: Organisation Spatiale du Materiel Provenant de lexcavation du nid chez Messor Barbarus et des Cadavres douvrieres chez Lasius niger (Hymenopterae: Formicidae). PhD thesis, Universite Libre de Bruxelles (1996)
3. Deneubourg, J.L., Goss, S., Francs, N., Sendova-Franks, A., Detrain, C., Chretien, L.: The dynamics of collective sorting: Robot-Like Ant and Ant-Like Robot. In: Meyer, J.A., Wilson, S.W. (eds.) Proceedings First Conference on Simulation of adaptive Behavior: from animals to animates, pp. 356–365. MIT Press, Cambridge (1991)
4. Gutowitz, H.: Cellular Automata: Theory and Experiment. MIT Press, Bradford Books (1991)
5. Handl, J., Meyer, B.: Improved Ant-Based Clustering and Sorting. In: Guervós, J.J.M., Adamidis, P.A., Beyer, H.-G., Fernández-Villacañas, J.-L., Schwefel, H.-P. (eds.) PPSN 2002. LNCS, vol. 2439, pp. 913–923. Springer, Heidelberg (2002)
6. Kanade, P.M., Hall, L.O.: Fuzzy ants as a clustering concept. In: 22nd International Conference of the North American Fuzzy Information Processing Society, NAFIPS, pp. 227–232 (2003)
7. Khedam, R., Outemzabet, N., Tazaoui, Y., Belhadj-Aissa, A.: Unsupervised multispectral classification images using artificial ants. In: IEEE International Conference on Information & Communication Technologies: from Theory to Applications (ICTTA 2006), Damas, Syrie (2006)

8. Khedam, R., Belhadj-Aissa, A.: Clustering of remotely sensed data using an artificial Ant-based approach. In: The 2nd International Conference on Metaheuristics and Nature Inspired Computing, META 2008, Hammamet, Tunisie (2008)
9. Khedam, R., Belhadj-Aissa, A.: Cellular Automata for unsupervised remotely sensed data classification. In: International Conference on Metaheuristics and Nature Inspired Computing, Djerba Island, Tunisia (2010)
10. Kuntz, P., Snyers, D.: Emergent colonization and graph partitioning. In: Proceedings of the Third International Conference on Simulation of Adaptive Behaviour: From Animals to Animats, vol. 3, pp. 494–500. MIT Press, Cambridge (1994)
11. Le Hégarat-Mascle, S., Kallel1, A., Descombes, X.: Ant colony optimization for image regularization based on a non-stationary Markov modeling. IEEE Transactions on Image Processing (submitted on April 20, 2005)
12. Lumer, E., Faieta, B.: Diversity and Adaptation in Populations of Clustering Ants. In: Proceedings Third International Conference on Simulation of Adaptive Behavior: from animals to animates, vol. 3, pp. 499–508. MIT Press, Cambridge (1994)
13. Lumer, E., Faieta, B.: Exploratory database analysis via self-organization (1995) (unpublished manuscript)
14. Monmarché, N.: On data clustering with artificial ants. In: Freitas, A. (ed.) AAAI 1999 & GECCO-99 Workshop on Data Mining with Evolutionary Algorithms, Research Directions, Orlando, Florida, pp. 23–26 (1999)
15. Monmarché, N., Slimane, M., Venturini, G.: AntClass: discovery of clusters in numeric data by an hybridization of an ant colony with the K-means algorithm. Technical Report 213, Laboratoire d'Informatique de l'Université de Tours, E3i Tours, p. 21 (1999)
16. Monmarché, N.: Algorithmes de fourmis artificielles: applications à la classification et à l'optimisation. Thèse de Doctorat de l'université de Tours. Discipline: Informatique. Université François Rabelais, Tours, France, p. 231 (1999)
17. Ouadfel, S., Batouche, M.: MRF-based image segmentation using Ant Colony System. Electronic Letters on Computer Vision and Image Analysis, 12–24 (2003)
18. Schockaert, S., De Cock, M., Cornelis, C., Kerre, C.E.: Efficient clustering with fuzzy ants. In: Proceedings Trim Size: 9in x 6in FuzzyAnts, p. 6 (2004)

PSO-Based Multiple People Tracking

Chen Ching-Han and Yan Miao-Chun

Department of CSIE, National Central University
320 Taoyuan, Taiwan
{pierre,miaochun}@csie.ncu.edu.tw

Abstract. In tracking applications, the task is a dynamic optimization problem which may be influenced by the object state and the time. In this paper, we present a robust human tracking by the particle swarm optimization (PSO) algorithm as a search strategy. We separate our system into two parts: human detection and human tracking. For human detection, considering the active camera, we do temporal differencing to detect the regions of interest. For human tracking, avoid losing tracking from unobvious movement of moving people, we implement the PSO algorithm. The particles fly around the search region to get an optimal match of the target. The appearance of the targets is modeled by feature vector and histogram. Experiments show the effectiveness of the proposed method.

Keywords: Object Tracking; Motion Detection; PSO; Optimization.

1 Introduction

Recently, visual tracking has been a popular application in computer vision, for example, public area surveillance, home care, and robot vision, etc. The abilities to track and recognize moving objects are important. First, we must get the moving region called region of interest (ROI) from the image sequences. There are many methods to do this, such as temporal differencing, background subtraction, and change detection. The background subtract method is to build background model, subtract with incoming images, and then get the foreground objects. Shao-Yi et al.[1] build the background model, subtract with incoming image and then get the foreground objects. Saeed et al.[2] do temporal differencing to obtain the contours of the moving people. In robot vision, considering the active camera and the background changes all the time, we implement our method with temporal differencing.

Many methods has been proposed for tracking, for instance, Hayashi et.al [3] use the mean shift algorithm which modeled by color feature and iterated to track the target until convergence. [4, 5] build the models like postures of human, then according to the models to decide which is the best match to targets. The most popular approaches are Kalman filter [6], condensation algorithm [7], and particle filter [8]. But the method for multiple objects tracking by particle filter tends to fail when two or more players come close to each other or overlap. The reason is that the filters' particles tend to move to regions of high posterior probability.

H. Cherifi, J.M. Zain, and E. El-Qawasmeh (Eds.): DICTAP 2011, Part I, CCIS 166, pp. 267–276, 2011.

Then we propose the optimization algorithm for object tracking called particle swarm optimization (PSO) algorithm. PSO is a new population based on stochastic optimization technique, has received more and more attentions because of its considerable success in solving non-linear, multimodal optimization problems. [9-11] implement a multiple head tracking searched by PSO. They use a head template as a target model and count the hair and skin color pixels inside the search window and find the best match representing the human face. Xiaoqin et.al[12] propose a sequential PSO by incorporating the temporal continuity information into the traditional PSO algorithm. And the parameters in PSO are changed adaptively according to the fitness values of particles and the predicted motion of the tracked object. But the method is only for single person tracking.

In addition, temporal differencing is a simple method to detect motion region, but the disadvantage is that if the motion is unobvious, it would get a fragment of the object. This will cause us to track failed. So, we incorporate PSO into our tracking.

The paper is organized as follows. Section 2 introduces human detection. In Section 3, a brief PSO algorithm and the proposed PSO-based tracking algorithm are presented. Section 4 shows the experiments. Section 5 is the conclusion.

2 Human Detection and Labeling

In this section, we present the method how to detect motion, segment and label each region by 8-connected components. Each moving person has its own label.

2.1 Motion Detection

Due to the background may change when robot or camera move, we do temporal differencing to detect motion.

A threshold function is used to determine change. If f(t) is the intensity of frame at time t, then the difference between f(t) and f(t-1) can be presented as

$$\Delta D = |\ ft(x, y) - ft - 1(x, y)| \tag{1}$$

A motion image M(t) can be extracted by a threshold as

$$M(t) = \begin{cases} 1, & \text{if } \Delta D > threshold \\ 0, & \text{if } \Delta D < threshlod \end{cases} \tag{2}$$

If the difference is large than the threshold, it is marked as an active pixel.

The morphological binary operations in image processing, dilation and erosion, are used. Dilation is used to join the broken segments. Erosion is used to remove the noise such as the pixels caused by light changed or fluttering leaves. Dilation and erosion operations are expressed as (3) and (4), respectively.

Let A and B are two sets of 2-D space. $\hat{B}$ means the reflection of set B.

Dilation:

$$A \oplus B = \{z \mid (\hat{B})_z \cap A \neq \phi\} \tag{3}$$

Erosion:

$$A\Theta B=\left\{z \mid (\hat{B})_z \subseteq A\right\} \tag{4}$$

Then we separate our image into equal-size blocks, and count the active pixels in each block. If the sum of the active pixels is greater than the threshold (a percentage of block size*block size), the block is marked as an active block which means it is a part of the moving person. Then connect the blocks to form an integrated human by 8-connected components. Fig. shows the result.

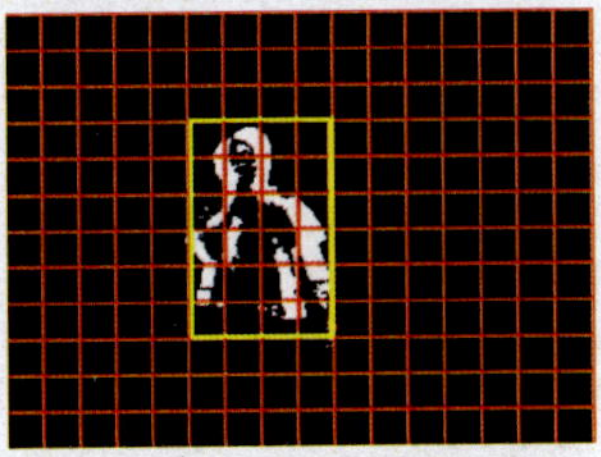

Fig. 1. The blocks marked as active ones

Remark 1. In the printed volumes, illustrations are generally black and white (halftones), and only in exceptional cases, and if the author is prepared to cover the extra costs involved, are colored pictures accepted. Colored pictures are welcome in the electronic version free of charge. If you send colored figures that are to be printed in black and white, please make sure that they really are legible in black and white. Some colors show up very poorly when printed in black and white.

2.2 Region Labeling

Because we assume to track multiple people, the motion detection may bring many regions. We must label each active block so as to do individual PSO tracking. The method we utilize is 8-connected components. From Fig.2, each region has its own label indicating an individual.

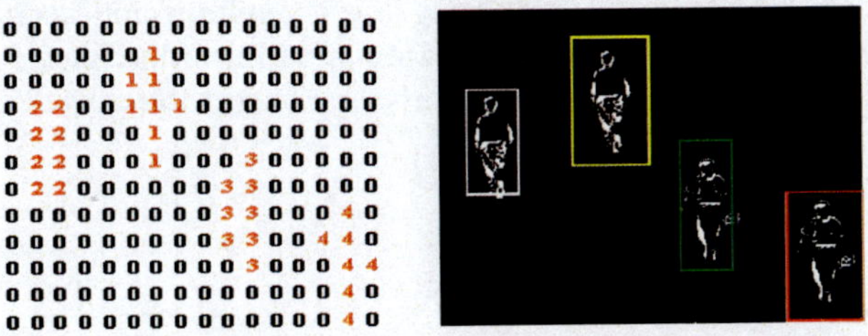

(a) (b)

Fig. 2. Region labeling. (a) the blocks marked as different labels; (b) segmenting result of individuals.

2.3 PSO-Based Tracking

The PSO algorithm is first developed by Kennedy and Eberhart in 1995. The algorithm is inspired by the social behavior of bird flocking. In PSO, each solution is a bird of the flock and is referred to as a particle. At each iteration, the birds tried to reach the destination and influenced by the social behavior. It has been applied successfully to a wide variety of search and optimization problems. Also, a swarm of n individuals communicate either directly or indirectly with one another search directions.

3 PSO-Based Tracking

The PSO algorithm is first developed by Kennedy and Eberhart in 1995. The algorithm is inspired by the social behavior of bird flocking. In PSO, each solution is a bird of the flock and is referred to as a particle. At each iteration, the birds tried to reach the destination and influenced by the social behavior. It has been applied successfully to a wide variety of search and optimization problems. Also, a swarm of n individuals communicate either directly or indirectly with one another search directions.

3.1 PSO Algorithm

The process is initialized with a group of particles (solutions),[x1,x2,…,xn] . (N is the number of particles.) Each particle has corresponding fitness value evaluated by the object function. At each iteration, the *i*th particle moves according to the adaptable velocity which is of the previous best state found by that particle (for individual best), and of the best state found so far among the neighborhood particles (for global best).

The velocity and position of the particle at each iteration is updated based on the following equations:

$$v(t) = v(t-1) + \varphi 1\big(P(t) - x(t-1)\big) + \varphi 2(Pg(t) - x(t-1)) \tag{5}$$

$$X(t) = X(t-1) + V(t) \tag{6}$$

where $\boldsymbol{\varphi}1$, $\boldsymbol{\varphi}2$ are learning rates governing the cognition and social components. They are positive random numbers drawn from a uniform distribution. And to allow particles to oscillate within bounds, the parameter Vmax is introduced:

$$Vi = \begin{cases} Vmax, \mathit{if}\ Vi > Vmax \\ -Vmax, \mathit{else\ if}\ Vi < -Vmax \end{cases} \tag{7}$$

3.2 Target Model

The process is initialized with a group of particles (solutions),[x1,x2,…,xn] . (N is the number of particles.) Each particle has corresponding fitness value evaluated by the object function. At each iteration, the *i*th particle moves according to the adaptable.

Our algorithm localized the people found in each frame using a rectangle. The motion is characterized by the particle x_i=(x, y, weight, height, H, $\bar{f}$) where (x, y) denotes the position of 2-D translation of the image, (weight, height) is the weight and height of the object search window, H is the histogram and $\bar{f}$ is the feature vector of the object search window. In the following, we introduce the appearance model.

The appearance of the target is modeled as color feature vector(proposed by Mohan S *et.al* [13]) and gray-level histogram. The color space is the normalized color coordinates (NCC). Because the R and G values are sensitive to the illumination, we transform the RGB color space to the NCC. Here are the transform formulas:

$$r = \frac{R}{R+G+B} \tag{8}$$

$$g = \frac{G}{R+G+B} \tag{9}$$

Then the feature represented for color information is the mean value μ, of the 1-D histogram (normalized by the total pixels in the search window). The feature vector for the characterizing of the image is:

$$\bar{f} = (\mu R, \mu G) \tag{10}$$

Which

$$\mu R = \frac{\sum_{i=1}^{n} Ri}{n} \tag{11}$$

$$\mu G = \frac{\sum_{i=1}^{n} Gi}{n} \tag{12}$$

The distance measurement is the

$$D(m,t) = |\bar{f}m - \bar{f}t| = \sum_{R,G} |\mu m - \mu t| \tag{13}$$

where D(m, t) is the Mahattan distance between the search window(target found representing by f) and the model(representing by m).

Also, the histogram which is segmented to 256 bins records the luminance of the search window. Then the intersection between the search window histogram and the target model can be calculated. The histogram intersection is defined as follows:

$$HI(m,t) = \frac{\sum_{j=1}^{n} \min(H(m,j), H(t,j))}{\sum_{j=1}^{n} H(t,j)} \tag{14}$$

The fitness value of *i*th particle is calculated by

$$F_i = \rho 1 * D(m,t) + \rho 2 * HI(m,t) \tag{15}$$

where ρ1 and ρ2 are the weights of the two criteria, that is the fitness value is a weighted combination.

Because similar colors in RGB color space may have different illumination in gray level, we combine the two properties to make decisions.

3.3 PSO Target Tracking

Here is the proposed PSO algorithm for multiple peoples tracking. Initially, when the first and two frames come, we do temporal differencing and region labeling to decide how many individual people in the frame, and then build new models for them indicating the targets we want to track. Then as new frame comes, we calculate how many people are in the frame. If the total of found people (represented by F) is greater than the total of the models (represented by M), we build a new model. If F<M, we find out that existing objects occluded or disappear. This situation we discuss in the next section. And if the F=M, we represent PSO tracking to find out where the position of each person exactly. Each person has its own PSO optimizer. In PSO tracking, the particles are initialized around the previous center position of the tracking model as a search space. Each particle represents a search window including the feature vector and the histogram and then finds the best match with the tracking model. This means the position of the model at present. The position of each model is updated every frame and motion vector is recorded as a basis of the trajectory. We utilize the PSO to estimate the position at present.

The flowchart of the PSO tracking process is showed in Fig. 3.

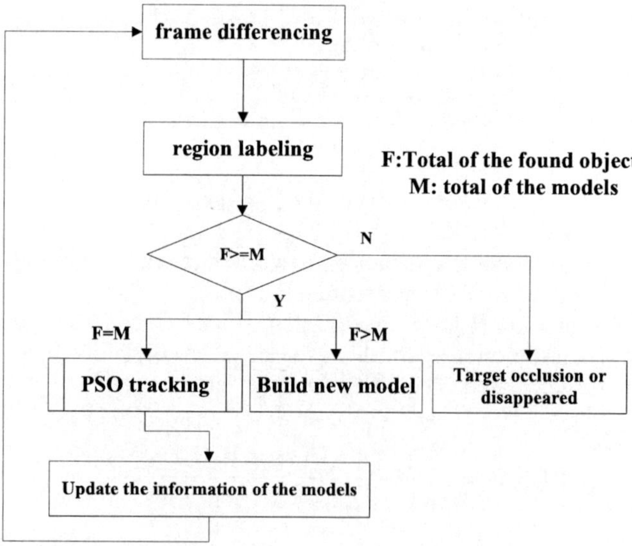

Fig. 3. PSO-based multiple persons tracking algorithm

If the total of the targets found is less than the total of the models, we assume there is something occluded or disappeared. In this situation, we match the target list we found in this frame with the model list, determine which model is unseen. And if the position of the model in previous frame plus the motion vector recorded before is out of the boundaries, we assume the model has exited the frame, or the model is occluded. Then how to decide the occlusive model in this frame? We use motion vector information to estimate the position of this model in this frame. The short segmentation of the trajectory is considered as linear. Section 4 will show the experiment result.

4 Experimental Results

The proposed algorithm is simulated by Borland C++ on Window XP with Pentium 4 CPU and 1G memory. The image size (resolution) of each frame is 320*240 (width*height) and the block size is 20*20 which is the most suitable size.

The block size has a great effect on the result. If the block size is set too small, then we will get many fragments. If the block size is set too large and the people walk too close, it will judge this as a target. The factor will influence our result and may cause tracking to fail. Fig. 4(a) is the original image demonstrating two walking people. From Fig. 4(b), we can see that a redundant segmentation came into being. Then Fig. 4(d) resulted only one segmentation.

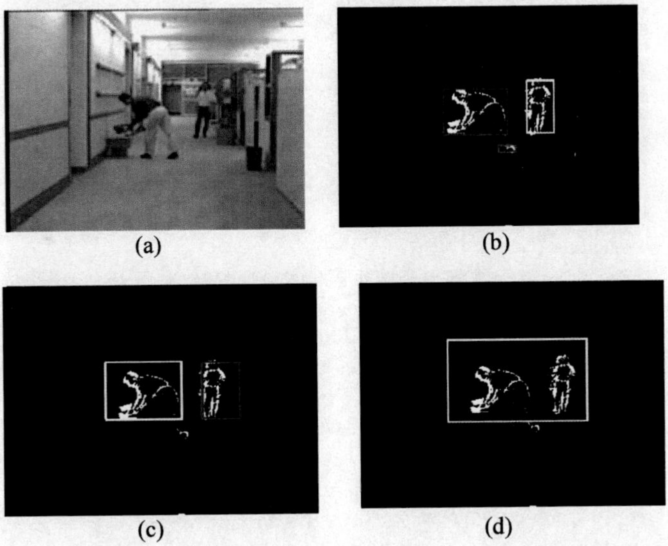

Fig. 4. Experiment with two walking people. (a) The original image of two people; (b) lock size=10 and 3 segmentations; (c) block size=20 and 2 segmentations; (d) 4 block size=30 and 1 segmentation.

The followings are the result of multiple people tracking by the proposed PSO based tracking. Fig. 5 shows the two people tracking. They are localized by two different color rectangles to show their position (the order of the pictures is from left to right, top to down). And Fig. 6 shows the three people tracking without occlusion. From theses snapshots, we can see that our algorithm works on multiple people tracking.

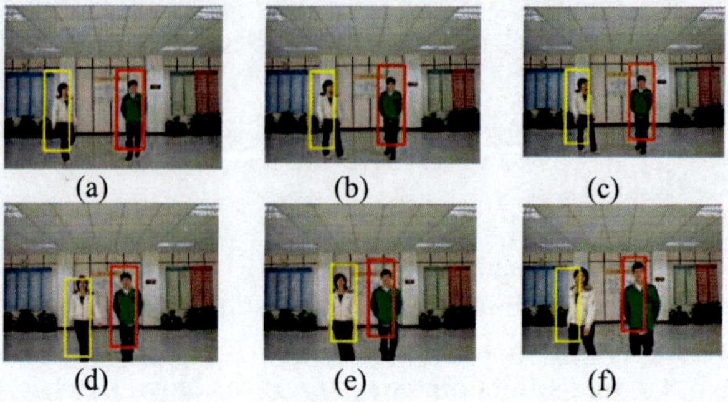

Fig. 5. Two peoples tracking

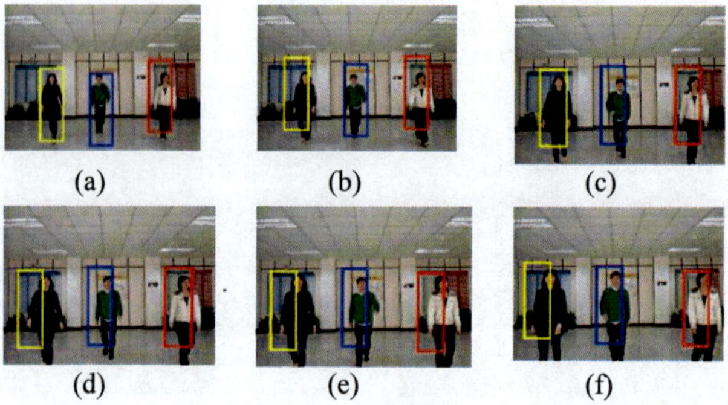

Fig. 6. Three peoples tracking

The next experiment is the occlusion handled. The estimated positions of the occlusive people are localized by the model position recorded plus the motion vector. We use a two-person walking video Fig. 7(a) is the original image samples extracted from a two-people moving video. They passed by, and Fig. 8 is the tracking result.

Fig. 7. Original images extracted from video

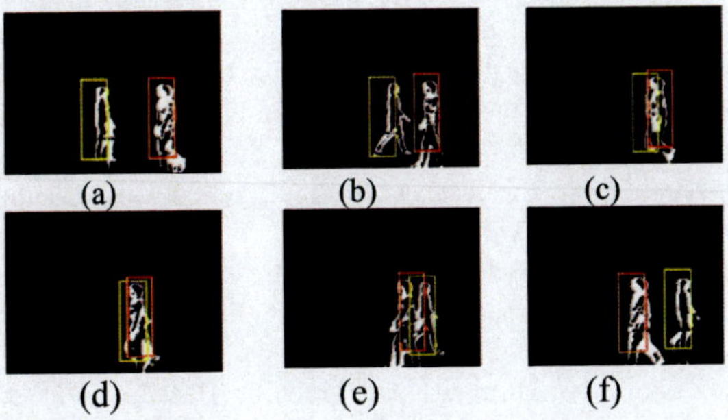

Fig. 8. Tracking result under occlusion

5 Conclusion

A PSO-based multiple persons tracking algorithm is proposed. This algorithm is developed on the application frameworks about the video surveillance and robot vision. The background may change when the robot moves, so we do temporal differencing to detect motion. But a problem is that if the motion is unobvious, we may fail to track. Tracking is a dynamic problem. In order to come up with that, we use PSO tracking as a search strategy to do optimization. The particles present the position, width and height of the search window, and the fitness values are calculate. The fitness function is a combined equation of the distance of the color feature vector and the value of the histogram intersection. When occluded, we add the motion vector plus the previous position of the model. The experiments above show our algorithm works and estimate the position exactly.

References

1. Shao-Yi, C., Shyh-Yih, M., Liang-Gee, C.: Efficient moving object segmentation algorithm using background registration technique. IEEE Transactions on Circuits and Systems for Video Technology 12(7), 577–586 (2002)
2. Ghidary, S.S., Toshi Takamori, Y.N., Hattori, M.: Human Detection and Localization at Indoor Environment by Home Robot. In: IEEE International Conference on Systems, Man, and Cybernetics, vol. 2, pp. 1360–1365 (2000)
3. Hayashi, Y., Fujiyoshi, H.: Mean-Shift-Based Color Tracking in Illuminance Change. In: Visser, U., Ribeiro, F., Ohashi, T., Dellaert, F. (eds.) RoboCup 2007: Robot Soccer World Cup XI. LNCS (LNAI), vol. 5001, pp. 302–311. Springer, Heidelberg (2008)
4. Karaulova, I., Hall, P., Marshall, A.: A hierarchical model of dynamics for tracking people with a single video camera. In: Proc. of British Machine Vision Conference, pp. 262–352 (2000)
5. von Brecht, J.H., Chan, T.F.: Occlusion Tracking Using Logic Models. In: Proceedings of the Ninth IASTED International Conference Signal And Image Processing (2007)
6. Erik Cuevas, D.Z., Rojas, R.: Kalman filter for vision tracking. Measurement, August 1-18 (2005)

7. Hu, M., Tan, T.: Tracking People through Occlusions. In: ICPR 2004, vol. 2, pp. 724–727 (2004)
8. Liu, Y.W.W.Z.J., Liu, X.T.P.: A novel particle filter based people tracking method through occlusion. In: Proceedings of the 11th Joint Conference on Information Sciences, p. 7 (2008)
9. Sulistijono, I.A., Kubota, N.: Particle swarm intelligence robot vision for multiple human tracking of a partner robot. In: Annual Conference on SICE 2007, pp. 604–609 (2007)
10. Sulistijono, I.A., Kubota, N.: Evolutionary Robot Vision and Particle Swarm Intelligence Robot Vision for Multiple Human Tracking of A Partner Robot. In: CEC 2007, 1535 - 1541(2007)
11. Sulistijono, I.A., Kubota, N.: Human Head Tracking Based on Particle Swarm Optimization and genetic algorithm. Journal of Advanced Computational Intelligence and Intelligent Informatics 11(6), 681–687 (2007)
12. Zhang, X., Steve Maybank, W.H., Li, X., Zhu, M., Zhang, X., Hu, W., Maybank, S., Li, X., Zhu, M.: Sequential particle swarm optimization for visual tracking. In: IEEE Int. Conf. on CVPR, pp. 1–8 (2008)
13. KanKanhalh, M.S., Jian Kang Wu, B.M.M.: Cluster-Based Color Matching for Image Retrieval. Pattern Recognition 29, 701–708 (1995)

A Neuro-fuzzy Approach of Bubble Recognition in Cardiac Video Processing

Ismail Burak Parlak[1,2,*], Salih Murat Egi[1,5], Ahmet Ademoglu[2], Costantino Balestra[3,5], Peter Germonpre[4,5], Alessandro Marroni[5], and Salih Aydin[6]

[1] Galatasaray University, Department of Computer Engineering, Ciragan Cad. No:36 34357 Ortakoy, Istanbul, Turkey
[2] Bogazici University, Institute of Biomedical Engineering, Kandilli Campus 34684 Cengelkoy, Istanbul, Turkey
[3] Environmental&Occupational Physiology Lab. Haute Ecole Paul Henri Spaak, Brussels, Belgium
[4] Centre for Hyperbaric Oxygen Therapy, Military Hospital,B-1120 Brussels, Belgium
[5] Divers Alert Network (DAN) Europe Research Committee B-1600 Brussels, Belgium
[6] Istanbul University, Department of Undersea Medicine, Istanbul, Turkey
bparlak@gsu.edu.tr

Abstract. 2D echocardiography which is the golden standard in clinics becomes the new trend of analysis in diving via its high advantages in portability for diagnosis. By the way, the major weakness of this system is non-integrated analysis platform for bubble recognition. In this study, we developed a full automatic method to recognize bubbles in videos. Gabor Wavelet based neural networks are commonly used in face recognition and biometrics. We adopted a similar approach to overcome recognition problem by training our system through real bubble morphologies. Our method does not require a segmentation step which is almost crucial in several studies. Our correct detection rate varies between 82.7-94.3%. After the detection, we classified our findings on ventricles and atria using fuzzy k-means algorithm. Bubbles are clustered in three different subjects with 84.3-93.7% accuracy rates. We suggest that this routine would be useful in longitudinal analysis and subjects with congenital risk factors.

Keywords: Decompression Sickness, Echocardiography, Neural Networks, Gabor Wavelet, Fuzzy K-Means Clustering.

1 Introduction

In professional and recreational diving, several medical and computational studies are developed to prevent unwanted effects of decompression sickness. Diving

* This research is supported by Galatasaray University, Funds of Academic Research and Divers Alert Network (DAN) Europe.

H. Cherifi, J.M. Zain, and E. El-Qawasmeh (Eds.): DICTAP 2011, Part I, CCIS 166, pp. 277–286, 2011.

tables, timing algorithms were the initial attempts in this area. Even if related procedures decrease the physiological risks and diving pitfalls, a total system to resolve relevant medical problems has not yet developed. Most of the decompression illnesses (DCI) and side effects are classified as unexplained cases though all precautions were taken into account. For this purpose, researchers focus on a brand new subject; the models and effects of micro emboli. Balestra et al. [1] showed that the prevention of DCI and strokes are related to bubble physiology and morphology. By the way, studies between inter subjects and even same subjects considered in different dives could cause big variations in post decompression bubble formations [2].

During last decade, bubble patterns were analyzed in the form of sound waves and recognition procedures were built up using Doppler ultrasound in different studies [3,4]. This practical and generally handheld modality is always preferred for post decompression surveys. However these records are limited to venous examinations and all existent bubbles in circulation would not be observed. The noise interference and the lack of any information related to emboli morphology are other restrictions.

2D Echocardiography which is available in portable forms serves as a better modality in cardiologic diagnosis. Clinicians who visualize bubbles in cardiac chambers count them manually within recorded frames. This human eye based recognition would cause big variations between trained and untrained observers [5]. Recent studies tried to resolve this problem by an automatization in fixed region of interests (ROI) placed onto Left Atrium (LA) or pulmonary artery [6,7]. Moreover, variation in terms of pixel intensity and chamber opacification were analyzed by Norton et al. to detect congenital shunts and bubbles [8]. It is obvious that an objective recognition in echocardiography is always a difficult task due to image quality. Image assessment and visual interpretation are correlated with probe and patient stabilization. The experience of clinicians, acquisition setup and device specifications would also limit or enhance both manual and computational recognition. Furthermore, inherent speckle noise and temporal loss of view in apical four chambers are major problems for computerized analysis.

In general, bubble detection would be considered in two different ways. Firstly, bubbles would be detected in a human based optimal ROI (for example LA, pulmonary artery, aorta) which is specifically known in heart. Secondly, bubbles would be detected in whole cardiac chambers and they might be classified according to spatial constraints. Even the first approach has been studied through different methods. The second problem has not yet been considered. Moreover, these two approaches would be identified as forward and inverse problems. In this paper, we aimed to resolve cardiac microemboli through secondary approach. Artificial Neural Networks (ANN) proved their capabilities of intelligent object recognition in several domains. Even single adaptation of ANN would vary in noisy environments; a good training phase and network architecture provide results in acceptable range. Gabor wavelet is a method to detect, filter or, reconstruct spatio-temporal variant object forms. It would be integrated with ANN in face recognition and biometrics [9,10,11] and preferred as an imitator of human wise recognition. We followed same reasoning in video based detection. Bubbles were spatially mapped via their centroids in whole heart. Therefore, spatially distributed bubbles might be treated as a regular data set and would be clustered onto different segments. For this purpose, detected bubbles might be clustered using fuzzy k-means algorithm into two major segments; ventricles and atria. It is known that bubbles in atrium and especially in left atria are the principle factor of those different illnesses in diving.

Post decompression records in echocardiography are considered to detect micro bubbles and to survey unexplained decompression sickness which is commonly examined by standardized methods such as dive computers and tables. Moreover, classified bubbles over atria would be a potential risk for probable unexplained DCI, hypoxemia. Even if there are some limitation factors to lead accurate detection rates such image quality, Transthoracic Echocardiography (TTE) and acquisition protocol, we propose that our findings would offer a better interpretation of existent bubbles to comprehend how morphology alter during circulation and blood turbulence.

In our study, we detect microemboli in whole heart without preprocessing or cardiac segmentation. We hypothesize that full automatic recognition and spatial classification should be taken into account for long term studies in diving and congenital risky groups. We conclude that atrial bubble distribution and its temporal decay would be a useful tool in long term analysis.

2 Methods

We performed this analysis on three male professional divers. Each subject provided written informed consent before participating to join the study. Recording and archiving are performed using Transthoracic Echocardiography (3-8 Mhz, MicroMaxx, SonoSite Inc, WA) as imaging modality. For each subject, three different records lasting approximately three seconds are archived with high resolution avi format. Videos are recorded with 25 frames per second (fps) and 640x480 pixels as resolution size. Therefore, for each patient 4000-4500 frames are examined. All records are evaluatued double blinded by two trained clinicians on bubble detection.

In this study Gabor kernel which is generalized by Daugman [12] is utilized to perform the Gabor Wavelet transformation. Gabor Transform is preferred in human wise recognition systems. Thus, we followed a similar reasoning for the bubbles in cardiology which are mainly detected depending on clinician visual perception.

$$\Psi_i(\vec{x}) = \frac{\left\|\vec{k_i}\right\|^2}{\sigma^2} e^{-\frac{\left\|\vec{k_i}\right\|^2 \left\|\vec{x}\right\|^2}{2\sigma^2}} [e^{i\vec{k_i}\vec{x}} - e^{-\frac{\sigma^2}{2}}] \tag{1}$$

Here each Ψ surface is identified with $\overrightarrow{k_i}$ vector. $\overrightarrow{k_i}$ vector is engendered through Gauss function with standard deviation σ. The central frequency of ith is defines as;

$$\overrightarrow{k_i} = \begin{pmatrix} k_{ix} \\ k_{iy} \end{pmatrix} = \begin{pmatrix} k_v \cos(\theta_\mu) \\ k_v \sin(\theta_\mu) \end{pmatrix} \tag{2}$$

where;

$$k_v = 2^{\frac{2-v}{2}} \tag{3}$$

$$\theta_\mu = \mu \frac{\pi}{8} \tag{4}$$

The v and μ s express five spatial frequency and eight orientations, respectively. These structure is represented in Fig. 2.

Our hierarchy in ANN is constructed as feed forward neural network which has three main layers. While hidden layer has 100 neurons, output layer has one output neuron. The initial weight vectors are defined using *Nguyen Widrow* method. Hyperbolic tangent function is utilized as transfer function during learning phase. This function is defined as it follows;

$$\tanh(x) = \frac{e^{2x} - 1}{e^{2x} + 1} \tag{5}$$

Our network layer is trained with candidate bubbles whose contrast, shape and resolution are similar to considered records. 250 different candidate bubble examples are manually segmented from different videos apart from TTE records in this paper. Some examples from these bubbles are represented in Fig. 1.

All TTE frames within this study which may contain microemboli are firstly convolved with Gabor kernel function. Secondly, convolved patterns are transferred to ANN. Output layer expressed probable bubbles onto the result frame and gave their corresponding centroids.

Fuzzy K-Means Clustering Algorithm is found as a suitable data classification routine in several domains. Detected bubbles would be considered as spatial points in heart which is briefly composed by four cardiac chambers. Even the initial means would affect the final results in noisy data sets. We hypothesize that there will be two clusters in our image and their spatial locations do not change drastically if any perturbation from patient or probe side does not occur.

We initialize our method by setting two the initial guesses of cluster centroids. As we separate ventricles and atrium, we place two points on upper and lower parts. Our frame is formed by 640x480 pixels. Therefore, the cluster centre of ventricles and atrium is set to 80x240 and 480x240 respectively. As this method iterates, in the next steps we repeat to assign each point in our data set according to its closest mean. The degree of membership is performed through Euclidean distance. Therefore, all points will be assigned to two groups; ventricles and atrium.

We can summarize our Fuzzy K-Means method as it follows;

```
Set initial means: mean_ventricle mean_atrium
While(there is no change in means)
   m=1 to maximum point number
   n=1 to 2
   Calculate degree of membership:U(m,n) of point x_m in Cluster_n
   For each cluster (1_to_2)
     Evaluate the fuzzy means with respect to new assigned points
   End_For
End_While
```

3 Results

In all subjects who were staying in post decompression interval, we found microemboli in four cardiac chambers. These detected bubbles in all frames were gathered into one spatial data set for each subject. Data sets were interpreted via fuzzy k-means method in order to cluster them within the heart. Detection and classification results are given in Table 1 and 2.

In our initial phase of detection, we had the assumption of variant bubble morphologies for ANN training phase in Fig. 1. As it might be observed in Fig. 3, detected nine bubbles are located in different cardiac chambers. Their shapes and surfaces are not same but resemble to our assumption.

Even if all nine bubbles in Fig. 3 would be treated as true positives, manual double blind detection results revealed that bubbles # 5, 8 and 9 are false positives. We observe that our approach would recognize probable bubble spots through our training phase but it may not identify nor distinguish if a detected spot is a real bubble or not. In this case of Fig. 3 it might be remarked that false positives are located on endocardial boundary and valves. These structures are generally continuously visualized without fragmentation. However patient and/or probe movements may introduce convexities and discontinuities onto these tissues which will be detected as bubbles.

We performed a comparison between double blind manual detection and ANN based detection in Table 1. Our bubble detection rates are between 82.7-94.3% (mean 89.63%). We observe that bubbles are mostly located in right side which is a physiological effect. Bubbles in circulation would be filtered in lungs. Therefore fewer bubbles are detected in left atria and ventricle.

In the initiation phase of fuzzy k-means method we set our spatial cluster means on upper and lower parts of image frame whose resolution is 640x480 pixels. These upper and lower parts correspond to ventricles and atrium by hypothesis as the initial guess. When the spatial points were evaluated the centroids moved iteratively. We reached the final locations of spatial distributions in 4-5 iterations . Two clusters are visualized in Fig. 4.

In order to evaluate the correctness of detection and the accuracy of bubble distribution, all records were analyzed double blinded. The green ellipse zones illustrate major false positive regions; endocardial boundary, valves and speckle shadows. In Table 1, we note that detection rates may differ due to visual speculation of human bubble detection in boundary zones, artifacts or within suboptimal frames. As it is shown in Table 2, the spatial classification into two clusters with fuzzy k-means were achieved for both detection approaches; manual and ANN based in order to compare how classification might be affected by computerized detection. In Table 2 we note that our classification rates are between 84.3-93.7% (mean 90.48%). We should note that classification rates through manual detection were 82.18-88.65% (mean 84.73%).

Fig. 1. Bubble examples for ANN training phase(right side),Binarized forms of bubble examples (left side)

Table 1. Evaluation of detection results

	Detected Bubbles			Detection Rate of ANN(%)	
	ANN	Clinician1	Clinician2	Through Clinician1	Through Clinician2
Subject #1	475	405	428	82.71	89.01
Subject #2	1396	1302	1287	92.78	91.53
Subject #3	864	818	800	94.37	92

Table 2. Evaluation of classification results

	Ventricular		Atrial	
	Bubbles	Clustering Rate(%)	Bubbles	Clustering Rate(%)
Subject #1	288	87.65	187	89.23
Subject #2	915	84.32	481	91.85
Subject #3	587	92.19	277	93.76

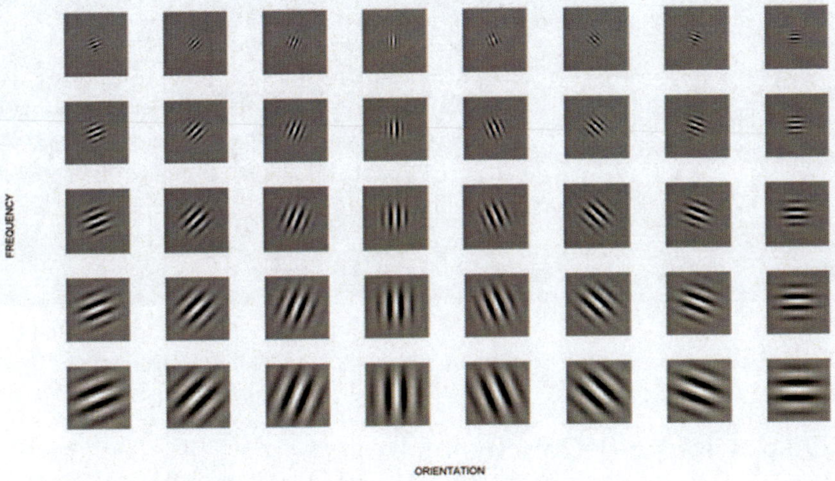

Fig. 2. Gabor wavelet for bubble detection

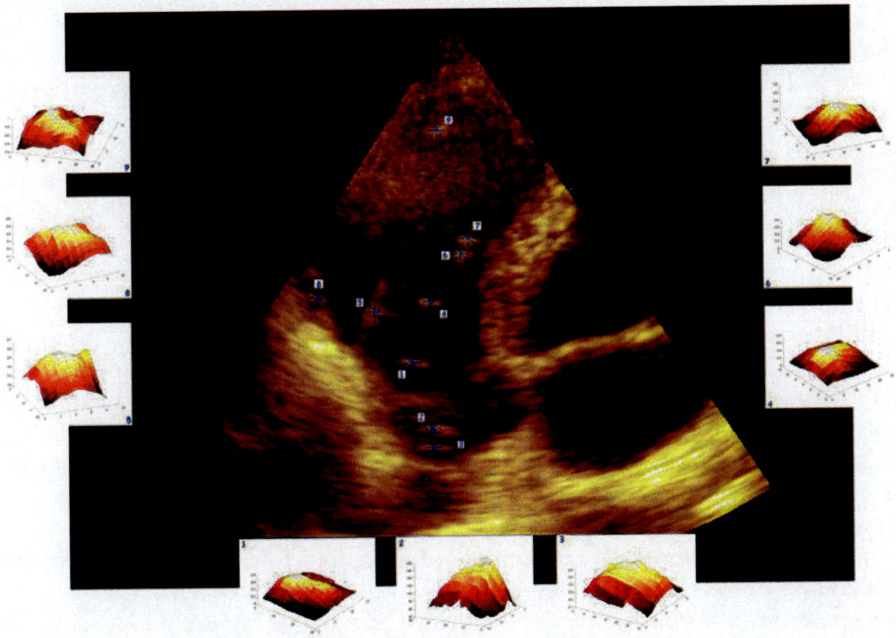

Fig. 3. Detection results and Bubble Surfaces

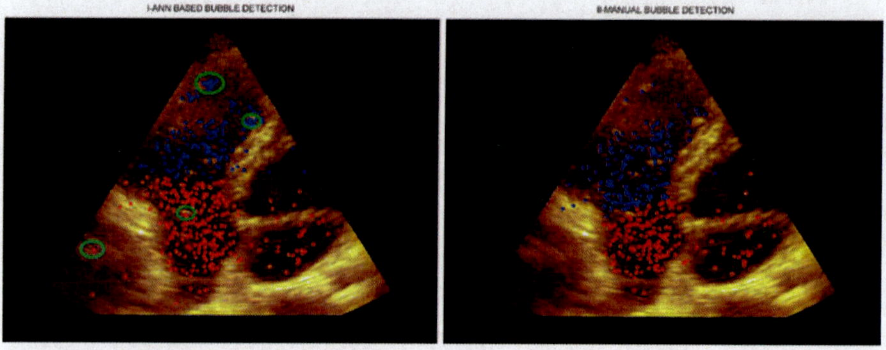

Fig. 4. Classification results on both ANN and Manual Detection

4 Discussion and Conclusion

Post decompression period after diving consist the most risky interval for probable incidence of decompression sicknesses and other related diseases due to the formations of free nitrogen bubbles in circulation. Microemboli which are the main cause of these diseases were not well studied due to imaging and computational restrictions.

Nowadays, mathematical models and computational methods developed by different research groups propose a standardization in medical surveys of decompression based evaluations. Actual observations in venous gas emboli would reveal the effects of decompression stress. Nevertheless, the principal causes under bubble formations and their incorporations into circulation paths are not discovered. Newer theories which maintain the principles built on Doppler studies, M-Mode Echocardiograhy and Imaging propose further observations based on the relationship between arterial endothelial tissues and bubble formations. On the other hand, there is still the lack and fundamental need of quantitative analysis on bubbles in a computational manner.

For this purposes, we proposed a full automatic procedure to resolve two main problems in bubble studies. Firstly we detected synchronously microemboli in whole heart by mapping them spatially through their centroids. Secondly, we resolved the bubble distribution problem within ventricles and atria. It is clear that our method would offer a better perspective for both recreational and professional dives as an inverse approach. On the other hand, we note that both detection and clustering methods might suffer from blurry records. Even if apical view of TTE offered the advantage of complete four chambers' view, we were limited to see some chambers with a partial aspect due to patient or probe movement during recording phase. Therefore, image quality and clinician experience are crucial for good performance in automatic analysis. Moreover, resolution, contrast, bubble brightness, fps rates are major factors in ANN training phase. These factors would affect detection rates. When resolution size, whole frame contrast differ it is obvious that bubble shape and morphologies would be altered. It is also remarkable to note that bubble shapes are commonly modeled as ellipsoids but in different acquisitions where inherent noise or resolutions are main limitations, they would be modeled as lozenges or star shapes as well.

Fuzzy k-means clustering which is a preferred classification method in statistics and optimization offered accurate rates as it is shown in Table 2. Although mitral valves and endocardial boundary introduced noise and false positive bubbles, two segments are well segmented for both manual and automatic detection as it is shown in Fig. 4 and Table 2. The major speculation zone in Fig. 4 is valve located region. Their openings and closings introduce a difficult task of classification for automatic decision making. We remark that suboptimal frames due to patient movement and shadowing artifacts related to probe acquisition would lead accurate clustering. It is also evident that false positives onto lower boundaries push the fuzzy central mean of atrium towards lower parts.

In this study, ANN training is performed by candidate bubbles with different morphologies in Fig. 1. In the prospective analysis, we would train our network hierarchy through non candidate bubbles to improve accuracy rates of detection. As it might be observed in Fig. 3 false positive bubbles intervene within green marked regions. These regions consist of endocardial boundary, valves and blurry spots towards the outside extremities. We conclude that these non bubble structures which lower our accuracy in detection and classification might be eliminated with this secondary training phase.

References

1. Balestra, C., Germonpre, P., Marroni, A., Cronje, F.J.: PFO & the diver. Best Publishing Company, Flagstaff (2007)
2. Blatteau, J.E., Souraud, J.B., Gempp, E., Boussuges, A.: Gas nuclei, their origin, and their role in bubble formation. Aviat Space Environ. Med. 77, 1068–1076 (2006)
3. Tufan, K., Ademoglu, A., Kurtaran, E., Yildiz, G., Aydin, S., Egi, S.M.: Automatic detection of bubbles in the subclavian vein using doppler ultrasound signals. Aviat Space Environ. Med. 77, 957–962 (2006)
4. Nakamura, H., Inoue, Y., Kudo, T., Kurihara, N., Sugano, N., Iwai, T.: Detection of venous emboli using doppler ultrasound. European Journal of Vascular & Endovascular Surgery 35, 96–101 (2008)
5. Eftedal, O., Brubakk, A.O.: Agreement between trained and untrained observers in grading intravascular bubble signals in ultrasonic images. Undersea Hyperb. Med. 24, 293–299 (1997)
6. Eftedal, O., Brubakk, A.O.: Detecting intravascular gas bubbles in ultrasonic images. Med. Biol. Eng. Comput. 31, 627–633 (1993)
7. Eftedal, O., Mohammadi, R., Rouhani, M., Torp, H., Brubakk, A.O.: Computer real time detection of intravascular bubbles. In: Proceedings of the 20th Annual Meeting of EUBS, Istanbul, pp. 490–494 (1994)
8. Norton, M.S., Sims, A.J., Morris, D., Zaglavara, T., Kenny, M.A., Murray, A.: Quantification of echo contrast passage across a patent foramen ovale. In: Computers in Cardiology, pp. 89–92. IEEE Press, Cleveland (1998)

9. Shen, L., Bai, L.: A review on gabor wavelets for face recognition. Pattern Anal. Applic. 9, 273–292 (2006)
10. Hjelmas, E.: Face detection a survey. Comput. Vis Image Underst. 83, 236–274 (2001)
11. Tian, Y.L., Kanade, T., Cohn, J.F.: Evaluation of gabor wavelet based facial action unit recognition in image sequences of increasing complexity. In: Fifth IEEE International Conference on Automatic Face and Gesture Recognition, Washington, pp. 229–234 (2002)
12. Daugman, J.G.: Complete discrete 2D gabor transforms by neural networks for image analysis and compression. IEEE Trans. Acoustics Speech Signal Process 36, 1169–1179 (1988)

Three–Dimensional Segmentation of Ventricular Heart Chambers from Multi–Slice Computerized Tomography: An Hybrid Approach

Antonio Bravo[1], Miguel Vera[2], Mireille Garreau[3,4], and Rubén Medina[5]

[1] Grupo de Bioingeniería, Universidad Nacional Experimental del Táchira, Decanato de Investigación, San Cristóbal 5001, Venezuela
abravo@unet.edu.ve
[2] Laboratorio de Física, Departamento de Ciencias, Universidad de Los Andes–Táchira, San Cristóbal 5001, Venezuela
[3] INSERM, U 642, Rennes, F-35000 France
[4] Laboratoire Traitement du Signal et de l'Image, Université de Rennes 1, Rennes 35042, France
[5] Grupo de Ingeniería Biomédica, Universidad de Los Andes, Facultad de Ingeniería, Mérida 5101, Venezuela

Abstract. This research is focused on segmentation of the heart ventricles from volumes of Multi Slice Computerized Tomography (MSCT) image sequences. The segmentation is performed in three–dimensional (3–D) space aiming at recovering the topological features of cavities. The enhancement scheme based on mathematical morphology operators and the hybrid–linkage region growing technique are integrated into the segmentation approach. Several clinical MSCT four dimensional (3–D + t) volumes of the human heart are used to test the proposed segmentation approach. For validating the results, a comparison between the shapes obtained using the segmentation method and the ground truth shapes manually traced by a cardiologist is performed. Results obtained on 3–D real data show the capabilities of the approach for extracting the ventricular cavities with the necessary segmentation accuracy.

Keywords: Segmentation, mathematical morphology, region growing, multi slice computerized tomography, cardiac images, heart ventricles.

1 Introduction

The segmentation problem could be interpreted as a clustering problem and stated as follows: given a set of data points, the objective is to classify them into groups such that the association degree between two points is maximal if they belong to the same group. This association procedure detects the similarities between points in order to define the structures or objects in the data.

In this paper, the segmentation is applied in order to extract the anatomical structures shape such as left and right ventricles in Multi Slice Computerized Tomography (MSCT) images of the human heart.

H. Cherifi, J.M. Zain, and E. El-Qawasmeh (Eds.): DICTAP 2011, Part I, CCIS 166, pp. 287–301, 2011.

MSCT is a non–invasive imaging modality that provides the necessary space and time resolution for representing 4–D (volume + time) cardiac images. Images studies in cardiology are used to obtain both qualitative and quantitative information of the heart and vessels morphology and function. Assessment of cardiovascular function is important since Cardio–Vascular Disease (CVD) is considered the most important cause of mortality. Approximately 17 million people die each year, representing one third of the deaths in the world [1]. Most of 32 million strokes and heart attacks occurring every year are caused by one or more cardiovascular risk factors such as hypertension, diabetes, smoking, high levels of lipids in the blood or physical inactivity. About 85% of overall mortality of middle- and low-income countries is due to CVD and it is estimated that CVD will be the leading cause of death in developed countries [2].

Several studies in cardiac segmentation, especially focused on segmenting the cardiac cavities have been reported. Among them are:

- A hybrid model for left ventricle (LV) detection in computed tomography (CT) images has been proposed by Chen *et al.* [3]. The model couples a segmenter, based on prior Gibbs models and deformable models with a marching cubes procedure. A external force based on a scalar gradient was considered to achieve convergence. Eight CT studies were used to test the approach. Results obtained on real 3–D data reveals the good behavior of the method.
- Fleureau *et al.* [4,5], proposed a new technique for general purpose, semi-interactive and multi-object segmentation in N-dimensional images, applied to the extraction of cardiac structures in MSCT imaging. The proposed approach makes use of a multi-agent scheme combined with a supervised classification methodology allowing the introduction of a priori information and presenting fast computing times. The multi-agent system is organized around a communicating agent which manages a population of situated agents (associated to the objects of interest) which segment the image through cooperative and competitive interactions. The proposed technique has been tested on several patient data sets, providing first results to extract cardiac structures such as left ventricle, left atrium, right ventricle and right atrium.
- Sermesant [6] presented a 3–D model of the heart ventricles that couples electrical and biomechanical functions. Three data types are used to construct the model: the myocardial geometry obtained from a canine heart, the orientation of muscular fibers, and parameters of electrophysiological activity extracted from the FitzHugh–Nagumo equations. The model allows the ventricular dynamics simulation considering the electromechanical function of the heart. This model is also used for segmentation of image sequences followed by the extraction of cardiac function indexes. The accuracy of clinical indexes obtained is comparable with results reported in the literature.
- LV endocardial and epicardial walls are automatically delineated using an approach based on morphological operators and the gradient vector flow snake algorithm [7]. The Canny operator is applied to images morphologically filtered in order to obtain an edge map useful to initialize the snake. This initial border is optimized to define the endocardial contour. Then,

the endocardial border is used as initialization for obtaining the epicardial contour. The correlation coefficient calculated by comparing manual and automatic contours estimated from magnetic resonance imaging (MRI) was 0.96 for the endocardium and 0.90 for the epicardium.
- A method for segmenting the LV from MRI was developed by Lynch *et al.* [8]. This method incorporates prior knowledge about LV motion to guide a parametric model of the cavity. The model deformation was initially controlled by a level–set formulation. The state of the model attained by the level–set evolution was refined using the expectation maximization algorithm. The objective was to fit the model to MRI data. The correlation coefficient obtained by a linear regression analysis of results obtained using six databases with respect to manual segmentation was 0.76.
- Van Assen *et al.* [9] developed a semi–automatic segmentation method based on a 3–D active shape model. The method has the advantage of being imaging modality independent. The LV shape was obtained for the whole cardiac cycle in 3–D MRI and CT sequences. A point–to–point distance was one of the metrics used to evaluate the performance of this method. The average value of the distances obtained for the CT sequences was 1.85 mm.
- A model–based framework for detection of heart structures has been reported by Ecabert *et al.* [10]. The heart is represented as a triangulated mesh model including RV, LV, atria, myocardium, and great vessels. The heart model is located near the target heart using the 3–D generalized Hough transform. Finally, in order to detect the cardiac anatomy parametric and deformable adaptations are applied to the model. These adaptations do not allow removal or insertion of triangles to the model. The deformation is attained by triangle correspondence. The mean point–to–surface error reported when applying the model–based method to 28 CT volumes was 0.82 ± 1.00 mm.
- Recently, the whole heart is segmented using an automatic approach based on image registration techniques reported by Zhuang *et al.* [11]. The approach considers the locally affine registration method to detect the initial shapes of the atria, ventricles and great vessels. The adaptative control point status free–form deformations scheme is then used in order to refine the initial segmentation. The method has been applied to 37 MRI heart volumes. The rms surface–to–surface error is lower than 4.5 mm. The volume overlap error is also used to establish the degree of overlap between two volumes. The overlap error obtained ($mean \pm standard\ \ deviation$) was 0.73 ± 0.07.

The objective of this research is developing an automatic human heart ventricles segmentation method based on unsupervised clustering. This is an extended version of the clustering based approach for automatic image segmentation presented in [12]. In the proposed extension, the smoothing and morphological filters are applied in 3–D space as well as the similarity function and the region growing technique. In this extension, the extraction of the right ventricle (RV) is also considered. The performance of the proposed method is quantified by estimating the difference between the cavities shapes obtained by our approach with respect to shapes manually traced by a cardiologist. The segmentation error is quantified by using a set of metrics that has been proposed and used in the literature [13].

2 Method

An overview of the proposed method is shown on pipeline in Figure 1: first, a preprocessing stage is used to exclude information associated with cardiac structures such as the left atrium and the aortic and pulmonary vessels. Moreover, in the first stage, the seed points located inside the target region are estimated. Next, the smoothing and morphological filters are used to improve the ventricles information in the 3–D volumes. Finally, a confidence connected region growing algorithm is used for classifying the LV, RV and background regions. This algorithm is an hybrid–linkage region growing algorithm that uses a feature vector including the gray–level intensity of each voxel and the simple statistics as mean and standard deviation calculated in a neighborhood around the current voxel.

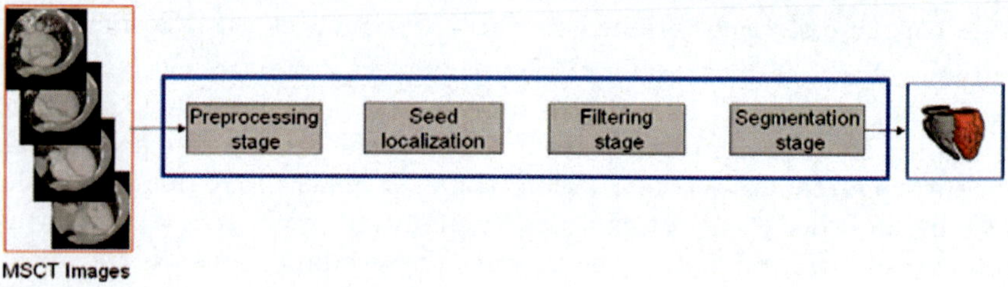

Fig. 1. Pipeline for cardiac cavities segmentation

2.1 Data Source

Two human MSCT databases are used. The acquisition process is performed using the helical computed tomography General Electric medical system, Light Speed^{64}. The acquisition has been triggered by the R wave of the electrocardiography signal. The dataset contains 20 volumes to describe the heart anatomical information for a cardiac cycle. The resolution of each volume is $(512 \times 512 \times 325)$ voxels. The spacing between pixels in each slice is 0.488281 mm and the slice thickness is 0.625 mm. The image volume is quantized with 12 bits per voxel.

2.2 Preprocessing Stage

The MSCT databases of the heart are cut at the level of the aortic valve to exclude certain anatomical structures. This process is performed according to following procedure:

1. The junction of the mitral and aortic valves is detected by a cardiologist. This point is denoted by V_{MA}. Similarly, the point that defines the apex is also located (point denoted by V_{APEX}).

2. The detected points at the valve and apex are joined starting from the V_{APEX} point and ending at point V_{MA} using a straight line. This line constitutes the anatomical heart axis. The direction of the vector with components (V_{APEX},V_{MA}) defines the direction of the heart axis.
3. A plane located at the junction of the mitral and aortic valves (V_{MA}) is constructed. The direction of the anatomical heart axis is used as the normal to the plane (see Figure 2).

Fig. 2. An heart volume with a cutting plane

4. A linear classifier is designed to divide each MSCT volume into two half–volumes $\mathcal{V}_1$ (voxels to exclude) and $\mathcal{V}_2$ (voxels to analyze). This linear classifier separates the volume considering a hyperplane decision surface according to discriminant function in (1). In this case, the normal vector orientation to the hyperplane in three–dimensional space corresponds to the anatomical heart axis direction established in the previous step.

$$g(\mathbf{v}) = \mathbf{w}^t \cdot \mathbf{v} + \omega_0 \ , \tag{1}$$

where $\mathbf{v}$ is the voxel to analyze, $\mathbf{w}$ is the normal to the hyper–plane and ω_0 is the bias [14].
5. For each voxel $\mathbf{v}$ in a MSCT volume, the classifier implements the following decision rule: Decide that the voxel $\mathbf{v} \in \mathcal{V}_1$ if $g(\mathbf{v}) \geq 0$ or $\mathbf{v} \in \mathcal{V}_2$ if $g(\mathbf{v}) < 0$.

This stage is also used for establishing the seed points required in the clustering algorithm. The midpoint (V_M) of the line described by V_{MA} and V_{APEX} points is computed. The seed point for the left ventricle is located at this midpoint. Figure 3 shows the axial, coronal and sagittal views of the MSCT volume after applying the pre–processing procedure described previously.

2.3 Volume Enhancement

The information inside the ventricular cardiac cavities is enhanced using the Gaussian and averaging filters. A discrete Gaussian distribution could be expressed as a density mask according to (2).

$$G(i,j,k) = \frac{1}{\left(\sqrt{2\pi}\right)^3 \sigma_i \sigma_j \sigma_k} \exp - \left(\frac{i^2}{2\sigma_i^2} + \frac{j^2}{2\sigma_j^2} + \frac{k^2}{2\sigma_k^2} \right), \ \ 0 \leq i,j,k \leq n \ , \tag{2}$$

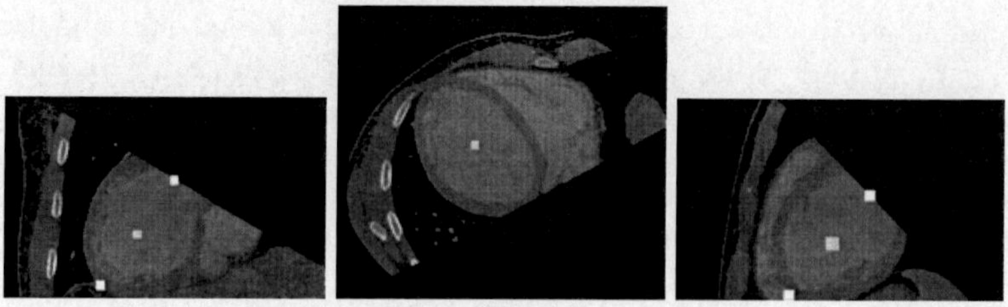

(a) (b) (c)

Fig. 3. The points V_{MA} and V_{APEX} are indicated by the white squares. The seed point is indicated by a gray square. (a) Coronal view. (b) Axial view. (c) Sagittal view.

where n denotes the mask size and σ_i, σ_j and σ_k are the standard deviation applied at each dimension. The processed image ($\mathbf{I}_{\text{Gauss}}$) is a blurred version of the input image.

An average filter is also applied to the input volumes. According to this filter, if a voxel value is greater than the average of its neighbors (the $m^3 - 1$ closest voxels in a neighborhood of size $(m \times m \times m)$ plus a certain threshold ε, then the voxel value in the output image is set to the average value, otherwise the output voxel is set equal to the voxel in the input image. The output volume ($\mathbf{I}_\text{P}$) is a smoothed version of the input volume $\mathbf{I}_\text{O}$. The threshold value ε is set to the standard deviation of the input volume (σ_O).

The gray scale morphological operators are used for implementing the filter aimed at enhancing the edges of the cardiac cavities. The proposed filter is based on the top–hat transform. This transform is a composite operation defined by the set difference between the image processed by a closing operator and the original image [15]. The closing ($\bullet$) operator is also a composite operation that combines the basic operations of erosion ($\ominus$) and dilation ($\oplus$). The top–hat transform is expressed according to (3).

$$\mathbf{I} \bullet \mathbf{B} - \mathbf{I} = (\mathbf{I} \oplus \mathbf{B}) \ominus \mathbf{B} - \mathbf{I} \ , \tag{3}$$

where $\mathbf{B}$ is a set of additional points known as structuring element. The structuring element used corresponds to an ellipsoid whose dimensions vary depending on the operator. The major axis of the structuring element is in correspondence with Z-axis and the minor axes are in correspondence with the axes X- and Y- of the databases

A modification of the basic top–hat transform definition is introduced. The Gaussian smoothed image is used to calculate the morphological closing. Finally, the top–hat transform is calculated using (4), the result is a volume with enhanced contours.

$$\mathbf{I}_{\text{BTH}} = (\mathbf{I}_{\text{Gauss}} \oplus \mathbf{B}) \ominus \mathbf{B} - \mathbf{I}_{\text{Gauss}} \ . \tag{4}$$

Figure 4 shows the results obtained after applying to the original images (Figure 3) the Gaussian, the average and the top–hat filters. The first row shows

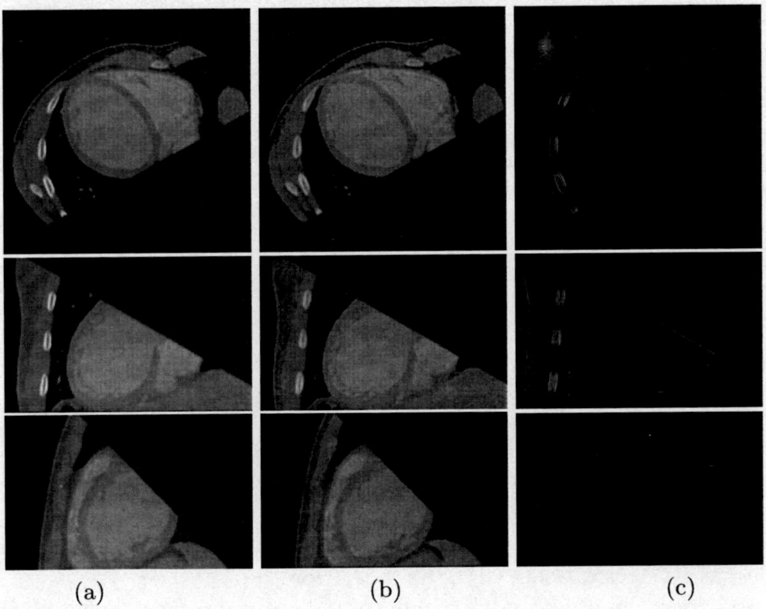

Fig. 4. Enhancement stage. (a) Gaussian smoothed image. (b) Averaging smoothed image. (c) The top–hat image.

the enhancement images for the axial view, while second and third rows show the images in the coronal and sagittal views, respectively.

The final step in the enhancement stage consists in calculating the difference between the intensity values of the top–hat image and the average image. This difference is quantified using a similarity criterion [16]. For each voxel $v\ _{\mathbf{I_{BTH}}}(i,j,k) \in \mathbf{I}_{\mathrm{BTH}}$ and $v\ _{\mathbf{I_P}}(i,j,k) \in \mathbf{I}_{\mathrm{P}}$ the feature vectors are constructed according to (5).

$$\begin{array}{lcl} \mathbf{pv}_{\mathbf{I_{BTH}}} & = & [i_1, i_2, i_3] \\ \mathbf{pv}_{\mathbf{I_P}} & = & [a,\ b,\ c\ ] \end{array}, \tag{5}$$

where i_1, i_2, i_3, a, b, c are obtained according to (6). In Figure 5.a, i_1 represents the gray level information of the voxel at position (i, j, k) (current voxel), i_2 and i_3 represent the gray level values for the voxels $(i, j+1, k)$ and $(i, j, k+1)$, respectively. i_1, i_2, i_3 are defined in the top–hat 3–D image. Figure 5.b shows the voxels in the average 3–D image where the intensities a, b, c are defined.

$$\begin{array}{ll} i_1 = v\ _{\mathbf{I_{BTH}}}(i,j,k), & a = v\ _{\mathbf{I_P}}(i,j,k) \\ i_2 = v\ _{\mathbf{I_{BTH}}}(i,j+1,k), & b = v\ _{\mathbf{I_P}}(i,j+1,k) \\ i_3 = v\ _{\mathbf{I_{BTH}}}(i,j,k+1), & c = v\ _{\mathbf{I_P}}(i,j,k+1) \end{array}. \tag{6}$$

The differences between $\mathbf{I}_{\mathrm{BTH}}$ and $\mathbf{I}_{\mathrm{P}}$ obtained using similarity criterion are stored into a 3–D volume ($\mathbf{I}_{\mathrm{S}}$). Each voxel of the similarity volume is determined according to equation (7).

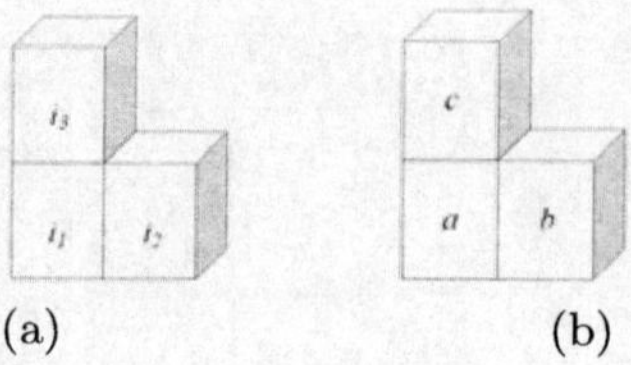

Fig. 5. Similarity features vectors components. a) Voxels in $\mathbf{I_{BTH}}$. b) Voxels in $\mathbf{I_P}$.

$$v_{\mathbf{I_S}}(i,j,k) = \sum_{r=1}^{6} d_r \ , \tag{7}$$

where $d_1 = (i_1 - i_2)^2$, $d_2 = (i_1 - i_3)^2$, $d_3 = (i_1 - b)^2$, $d_4 = (i_1 - c)^2$, $d_5 = (i_2 - a)^2$ and $d_6 = (i_3 - a)^2$.

Finally, a data density function $\mathbf{I_D}$ [17] is obtained by convolving $\mathbf{I_S}$ with a unimodal density mask (2). The density function establishes the degree of dispersion in $\mathbf{I_S}$. The process described previously, is applied to all volumes of the human MSCT database.

Figure 6 shows the image enhanced obtained after applying the similarity criteria. In this image the information associated to the boundaries of the LV and RV are enhanced with respect to other anatomical structures that are present in the MSCT volume. The results of the enhancement stage are shown (Figure 6) in the axial, coronal and sagittal views.

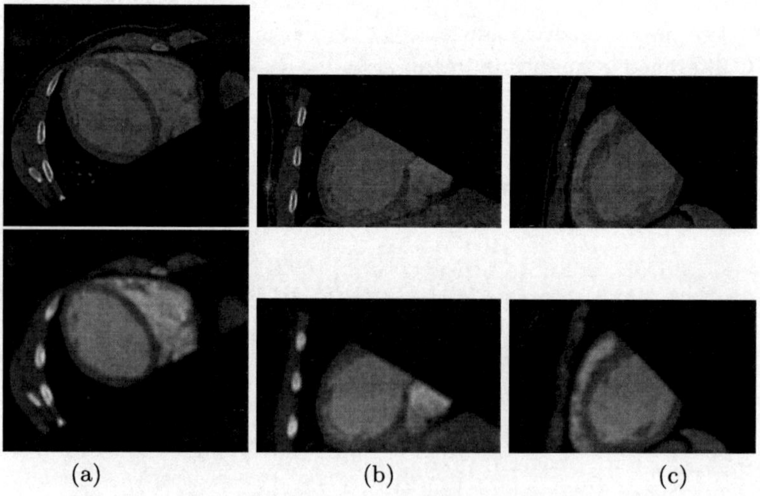

Fig. 6. Final enhancement process, top row shows the original image, bottom row shows the enhanced image. (a) Axial view.(b) Coronal view. (c) Sagittal view.

2.4 Hough Transform Right Ventricle Seed Localization

In this work, the Generalized Hough Transform (GHT) is applied to obtain the RV border in one MSCT slice. From the RV contour, the seed point required to initialize the clustering algorithm is computed as the centroid of this contour. The RV contour detection and seed localization are performed on the slice on which the LV seed was placed (according to procedure described in section 2.2)

The GHT proposed by Ballard [18] has been used to detect objects, with specific shapes, from images. The proposed algorithm consists of two stages: 1) training and 2) detection. During the training stage, the objective is to describe a pattern of the shape to detect. The second stage is implemented to detect a similar shape in an image not used during the training step. A detailed description of the training and detection stages for ventricle segmentation using GHT was presented in [12]. Figure 7 shows the results of the RV contour detection in the MSCT slice.

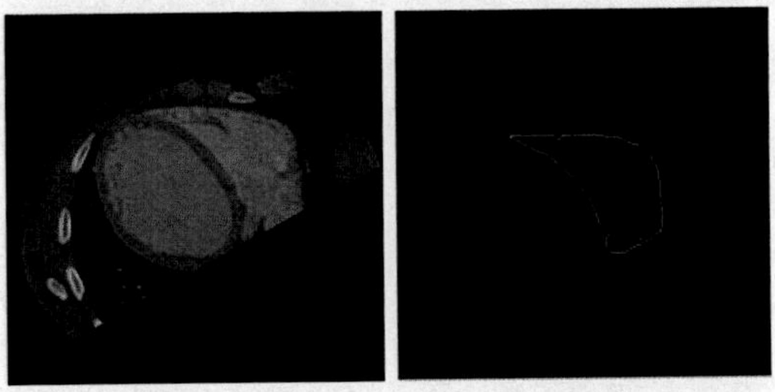

(a) (b)

Fig. 7. Seed localization process. (a) Original image. (b) Detected RV contour.

2.5 Segmentation Process

The proposed segmentation approach is a region–based method that uses the hybrid–linkage region growing algorithm in order to group voxels into 3–D regions. The commonly used region growing scheme in 2–D is a simple graphical seed–fill algorithm called pixel aggregation [19], which starts with a seed pixel and grows a region by appending connected neighboring pixels that reaches a certain homogeneity criterion. The 3–D hybrid–linkage technique starts also with a seed that lies inside the region of interest and spreads to the p–connected voxels that have similar properties. This region growing techniques, also known as confidence connected region growing, assign a property vector to each voxel where the property vector depends on the $(l \times l \times l)$ neighborhood of the voxel.

The algorithmic form of the hybrid–linkage clustering technique is as follows:

1. The seed voxel (v_s) defined in the section 2.2 is taken as the first to analyze.
2. A initial region is established as a neighborhood of voxels around the seed.
3. The mean ($\bar{v}_s$) and standard deviation (σ_s) calculated in the initial region are used to define a range of permissible intensities given by $[\bar{v}_s - \tau\sigma_s, \bar{v}_s + \tau\sigma_s]$, where the scalar τ allows to scale the range.

4. All voxels in the neighborhood are checked for inclusion in the region. In this sense, each voxel is analyzed in order to determine if its gray level value satisfies the condition for inclusion in current region. If the intensity value is in the range of permissible intensities the voxel is added to the region and it is labeled as a foreground voxel. If the gray level value of the voxel is outside the permitted range, it is rejected and marked as a background voxel.
5. Once all voxels in the neighborhood have been checked, the algorithm goes back to Step 4 to analyze the $(l \times l \times l)$ new neighborhood of the next voxel in the image volume.
6. Steps 4–5 are executed until region growing stops.
7. The algorithm stops when no more voxels can be added to the foreground region.

Multiprogramming based on threads is considered in the hybrid–linkage region growing algorithm in order to segment the two ventricles. A first thread segments the LV and the second thread segments the RV. These processes start at same time (running on a single processor) considering the time division multiplexing ability (switching between threads) associated with threads–based multiprogramming. This implementation allows to speed up the segmentation process.

The region–based method output is a binary 3–D image where each foreground voxel is labeled to one and the background voxels are labeled to zero. Figure 8 shows the results obtained after applying the proposed segmentation approach, in order to illustrate, the left ventricle is drawn in red while the right ventricle in green. The bi–dimensional images shown in the Figure 8 represent the results obtained by applying the segmentation method to the 3–D enhanced image (axial, coronal and sagittal planes) shown in the second row of Figure 6. These results show that a portion of the right atrium is also segmented. To avoid this problem, the hyperplane used to exclude anatomical structures (see section 2.2) must be replaced by a hypersurface that considers the shape of the wall and valves located between the atria and ventricles chambers.

The cardiac structures extracted from real three–dimensional MSCT data are visualized with Marching Cubes. Marching cubes has long been employed as a standard indirect volume rendering approach to extract iso–surfaces from 3–D volumetric data [20,21,22]. The binary volumes obtained after the segmentation

(a) (b) (c)

Fig. 8. Results of segmentation process. (a) Axial view.(b) Coronal view. (c) Sagittal view.

process (section 2.5), represent the left and right cardiac ventricles. The reconstruction of these cardiac structures is performed using the Visualization Toolkit (VTK) [23].

2.6 Validation

The proposed method is validated by calculating the difference between the obtained ventricular shapes with respect to the ground truth shapes, estimated by an expert. The methodology proposed by Suzuki *et al.* [13] is used to evaluate the performance of the segmentation method. Suzuki's quantitative evaluation methodology is based on calculating two metrics that represent the contour error (E_C) and the area error (E_A). Suzuki formulation is performed in 2–D space, the contour and area errors expressions can be seen in [13, p. 335]. The 3–D expressions of the Susuki metrics are shown by the equations (8) and (9).

$$E_C = \frac{\sum_{x,y,z \in R_E} [a_P(x,y,z) \oplus a_D(x,y,z)]}{\sum_{x,y,z \in R_E} a_D(x,y,z)} , \tag{8}$$

$$E_A = \frac{|\sum_{x,y,z \in R_E} a_D(x,y,z) - \sum_{x,y,z \in R_E} a_P(x,y,z)|}{\sum_{x,y,z \in R_E} a_D(x,y,z)} , \tag{9}$$

where:

$$a_D(x,y,z) = \begin{cases} 1, & (x,y,z) \in R_D \\ 0, & \text{otherwise} \end{cases} , \quad a_P(x,y,z) = \begin{cases} 1, & (x,y,z) \in R_P \\ 0, & \text{otherwise} \end{cases} , \tag{10}$$

where R_E is the 3–D region corresponding to the image support, R_D is the region enclosed by the surface traced by the specialist, R_P is the region enclosed by the surface obtained by the proposed approach, and $\oplus$ is the exclusive OR operator.

The Dice coefficient (Eqs. 11) [24] is also used in the validation. This coefficient is maximum when a perfect overlap is reached and minimum when two volumes do not overlap at all. The maximum value is one and the minimum is zero.

$$Dice\ Coefficient = \frac{2\,|R_D \bigcap R_P|}{|R_D| + |R_P|} \tag{11}$$

3 Results

A region–based segmentation method has been applied to MSCT medical data acquired on a GE Lightspeed tomograph with 64 detectors. The objective was to extract the left and right ventricles of the heart from the whole database. The proposed method is implemented using a multi–platform object–oriented methodology along with C++ multiprogramming and using dynamic memory handling. Standard libraries such as the Visualization Toolkit (VTK) are used.

In this section, the qualitative and quantitative results that show the accuracy behavior of the algorithm are provided. These results are obtained by applying

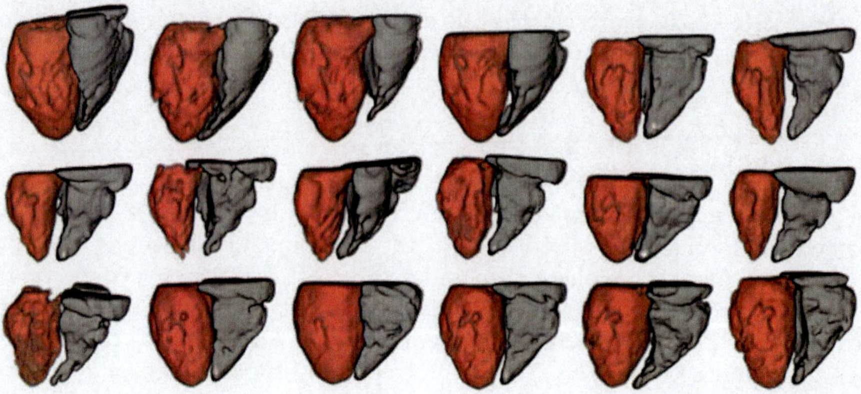

Fig. 9. Iso–surfaces of the cardiac structures between 10% and 90% of the cardiac cycle. First database

our approach to two MSCT cardiac sequences. Qualitative results are shown in Figure 9 and Figure 10 in which the LV is shown in red and the RV is shown in gray. These figures show the internal walls of the LV and the RV reconstructed using the iso–surface rendering technique based on marching cubes.

Quantitative results are provided by quantifying the difference between the estimated ventricles shapes with respect to the ground truth shapes, estimated by an expert. The ground truth shapes are obtained using a manual tracing process. An expert trace the left and right ventricles contours in the axial image plane of the MSCT volume. From this information the LV and RV ground truth shapes are modeled. These ground truth shapes and the shapes computed by the proposed hybrid segmentation method are used to calculate the Susuki metrics (see section 2.6). For left ventricle, the average area error obtained (*mean* ± *standard deviation*) with respect to cardiologist was 0.72% ± 0.66%. The maximum average area error was 2.45% and the minimum was 0.01%. These errors have been calculated considering 2 MSCT sequences (a total of 40 volumes). The area errors obtained for LV are smaller to values reported in [12].

Comparison between the segmented RV and the surface inferred by cardiologist showed that the minimum area errors of 3.89%. The maximum area error for the right ventricle was 14.76%. The mean and standard deviation for the area error was 9.71% ± 6.43%. In table 1, the mean, the maximum (max), the minimum (min) and the standard deviation (std) for contour error calculated according to Eqs. (8) are shown.

Dice coefficient is also calculated using equation (11) for both 4–D segmented database. In this case, the overlap volume error was 0.91 ± 0.03, with maximum value of 0.94 and minimum value of 0.84. The average of the Dice coefficient is close to value reported for left ventricle in [11], (0.92 ± 0.02), while the dice coefficient estimated for the right ventricle is 0.87 ± 0.04 which is greater than the value reported in [11].

The proposed hybrid approach takes 3 min to extract the cavities per MSCT volume. The computational cost to segment the entire sequence is 1 hour. The test involved 85,196,800 voxels (6500 MSCT slices). The machine used for the experimental setup was based on a Core 2 Duo 2GHz processor with 2Gb RAM.

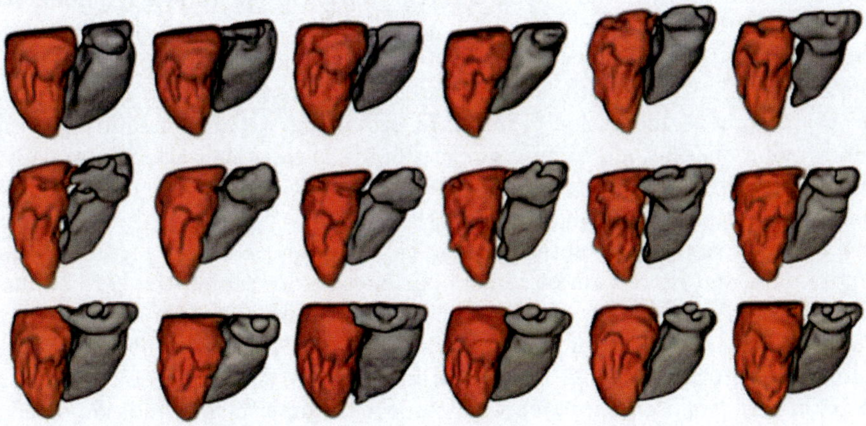

Fig. 10. Iso–surfaces of the cardiac structures between 10% and 90% of the cardiac cycle. Second database.

Table 1. Contour errors obtained for the MSCT processed volumes

	E_C [%]	
	Left Ventricle	**Right Ventricle**
min	11.15	14.21
mean	11.94	15.93
max	12.25	17.04
std	0.27	1.51

4 Conclusions

A methodology of image enhancement combined with a confidence connected region growing technique and multi-threaded dynamical programming have been introduced in order to develop a usefull hybrid approach to segment the left and right ventricles from cardiac MSCT imaging. The approach is performed in 3–D to take into account space topological features of the left and right ventricle while improving the computation time.

The input MSCT images are initially preprocessed as described in Section 2.2 in order to exclude certain anatomical structures as left and right atria. The 3–D volumes obtained after preprocessing are enhanced using morphological filters. The unsupervised clustering scheme used allows to analyze 3–D regions in order to detect the voxels that fulfil with the grouping condition. This condition is constructed by taking into account a permissible range of intensities useful for discriminating the differents anatomical structures contained in the MSCT images. Finally, a binary 3–D volume is obtained where the voxels labeled as one represent the cardiac cavities. This information is visualized using an iso–surface rendering technique. The validation was performed based on the methodologies proposed in [13] and [24]. The validation stage shows that errors are small.

The segmentation method does not require any prior knowledge about the heart chambers anatomy and provides an accurate surface detection for the LV cavity. A limitation of the approach in the RV segmentation process including the seed selection procedure is that it detects a portion of the right atrium. However as our segmentation results are promising we are currently working for improving the method aiming at performing the segmentation from MSCT images taking into account the shape of the wall and valves located between the atria and the ventricles.

As a further research, a more complete validation is necessary, including tests on more data and extraction of clinical parameters describing the cardiac function. This validation stage could also include a comparison of estimated parameters, such as the volume and the ejection fraction with respect to results obtained using other imaging modalities including MRI or ultrasound. A comparison of the proposed approach with respect to different methods reported in the literature is also proposed.

Acknowledgment

The authors would like to thank the Investigation Dean's Office of Universidad Nacional Experimental del Táchira, Venezuela, CDCHT from Universidad de Los Andes, Venezuela and ECOS NORD–FONACIT grant PI–20100000299 for their support to this research. Authors would also like to thank H. Le Breton and D. Boulmier from the Centre Cardio Pneumologique in Rennes, France for providing the human MSCT databases.

References

1. WHO: Integrated management of cardiovascular risk. The World Health Report 2002 Geneva, World Health Organization (2002)
2. WHO: Reducing risk and promoting healthy life. The World Health Report 2002 Geneva, World Health Organization (2002)
3. Chen, T., Metaxas, D., Axel, L.: 3D cardiac anatomy reconstruction using high resolution CT data. In: Barillot, C., Haynor, D.R., Hellier, P. (eds.) MICCAI 2004. LNCS, vol. 3216, pp. 411–418. Springer, Heidelberg (2004)
4. Fleureau, J., Garreau, M., Hernández, A., Simon, A., Boulmier, D.: Multi-object and N-D segmentation of cardiac MSCT data using SVM classifiers and a connectivity algorithm. Computers in Cardiology, 817–820 (2006)
5. Fleureau, J., Garreau, M., Boulmier, D., Hernández, A.: 3D multi-object segmentation of cardiac MSCT imaging by using a multi-agent approach. In: 29th Conf. IEEE Eng. Med. Biol. Soc., pp. 6003–6600 (2007)

6. Sermesant, M., Delingette, H., Ayache, N.: An electromechanical model of the heart for image analysis and simulation. IEEE Trans. Med. Imag. 25(5), 612–625 (2006)
7. El Berbari, R., Bloch, I., Redheuil, A., Angelini, E., Mousseaux, E., Frouin, F., Herment, A.: An automated myocardial segmentation in cardiac MRI. In: 29th Conf. IEEE Eng. Med. Biol. Soc., pp. 4508–4511 (2007)
8. Lynch, M., Ghita, O., Whelan, P.: Segmentation of the left ventricle of the heart in 3-D+t MRI data using an optimized nonrigid temporal model. IEEE Trans. Med. Imag. 27(2), 195–203 (2008)
9. Assen, H.V., Danilouchkine, M., Dirksen, M., Reiber, J., Lelieveldt, B.: A 3D active shape model driven by fuzzy inference: Application to cardiac CT and MR. IEEE Trans. Inform. Technol. Biomed. 12(5), 595–605 (2008)
10. Ecabert, O., Peters, J., Schramm, H., Lorenz, C., Von Berg, J., Walker, M., Vembar, M., Olszewski, M., Subramanyan, K., Lavi, G., Weese, J.: Automatic model-based segmentation of the heart in CT images. IEEE Trans. Med. Imaging 27(9), 1189–1201 (2008)
11. Zhuang, X., Rhode, K.S., Razavi, R., Hawkes, D.J., Ourselin, S.: A registration–based propagation framework for automatic whole heart segmentation of cardiac MRI. IEEE Trans. Med. Imag. 29(9), 1612–1625 (2010)
12. Bravo, A., Clemente, J., Vera, M., Avila, J., Medina, R.: A hybrid boundary-region left ventricle segmentation in computed tomography. In: International Conference on Computer Vision Theory and Applications, Angers, France, pp. 107–114 (2010)
13. Suzuki, K., Horiba, I., Sugie, N., Nanki, M.: Extraction of left ventricular contours from left ventriculograms by means of a neural edge detector. IEEE Trans. Med. Imag. 23(3), 330–339 (2004)
14. Duda, R., Hart, P., Stork, D.: Pattern classification. Wiley, New York (2000)
15. Serra, J.: Image analysis and mathematical morphology. A Press, London (1982)
16. Haralick, R.A., Shapiro, L.: Computer and robot vision, vol. I. Addison–Wesley, USA (1992)
17. Pauwels, E., Frederix, G.: Finding salient regions in images: Non-parametric clustering for images segmentation and grouping. Computer Vision and Image Understanding 75(1,2), 73–85 (1999); Special Issue
18. Ballard, D.: Generalizing the hough transform to detect arbitrary shapes. Pattern Recog. 13(2), 111–122 (1981)
19. Gonzalez, R., Woods, R.: Digital image processing. Prentice Hall, USA (2002)
20. Salomon, D.: Computer graphics and geometric modeling. Springer, USA (1999)
21. Livnat, Y., Parker, S., Johnson, C.: Fast isosurface extraction methods for large image data sets. In: Bankman, I.N. (ed.) Handbook of Medical Imaging: Processing and Analysis, pp. 731–774. Academic Press, San Diego (2000)
22. Lorensen, W., Cline, H.: Marching cubes: A high resolution 3D surface construction algorithm. Comput. Graph. 21(4), 163–169 (1987)
23. Schroeder, W., Martin, K., Lorensen, B.: The visualization toolkit, an object-oriented approach to 3D graphics. Prentice Hall, New York (2001)
24. Dice, L.: Measures of the amount of ecologic association between species. Ecology 26(3), 297–302 (1945)

Fingerprint Matching Using an Onion Layer Algorithm of Computational Geometry Based on Level 3 Features

Samaneh Mazaheri[2], Bahram Sadeghi Bigham[2], and Rohollah Moosavi Tayebi[1]

[1] Islamic Azad University, Shahr-e-Qods Branch,Tehran, Iran
Moosavi_tayebi@shahryariau.ac.ir
[2] Institute for Advanced Studies in Basic Science (IASBS)
Department of Computer Science & IT, RoboCG Lab, Zanjan, Iran
{S.mazaheri,b_sadeghi_b}@iasbs.ac.ir

Abstract. Fingerprint matching algorithm is a key issue of the fingerprint recognition, and there already exist many fingerprint matching algorithms. In this paper, we present a new approach to fingerprint matching using an onion layer algorithm of computational geometry. This matching approach utilizes Level 3 features in conjunction with Level 2 features for matching. In order to extract valid minutiae and valid pores, we apply some image processing steps on input fingerprint, at first. Using an Onion layer algorithm, we construct nested convex polygons of minutiae, and then based on polygons property, we perform matching of fingerprints; we use the most interior polygon in order to calculate the rigid transformations parameters and perform level 2 matching, then we apply level 3 matching. Experimental results on FVC2006 show the performance of the proposed algorithm.

Keywords: Image Processing, Fingerprint matching, Fingerprint recognition, Onion layer algorithm, Computational Geometry, Nested Convex Polygons.

1 Introduction

Fingerprint recognition is a widely popular but a complex pattern recognition Problem. It is difficult to design accurate algorithms capable of extracting salient features and matching them in a robust way. There are two main applications involving fingerprints: fingerprint verification and fingerprint identification. While the goal of fingerprint verification is to verify the identity of a person, the goal of fingerprint identification is to establish the identity of a person. Specifically, fingerprint identification involves matching a query fingerprint against a fingerprint database to establish the identity for an individual. To reduce search time and computational complexity, fingerprint classification is usually employed to reduce the search space by splitting the database into smaller parts (fingerprint classes) [1]. There is a popular misconception that automatic fingerprint recognition is a fully solved problem since it was one of the first applications of machine pattern recognition. On the contrary, fingerprint recognition is still a challenging and important pattern recognition problem. The real challenge is matching fingerprints affected by:

H. Cherifi, J.M. Zain, and E. El-Qawasmeh (Eds.): DICTAP 2011, Part I, CCIS 166, pp. 302–314, 2011.

- High displacement or rotation which results in smaller overlap between template and query fingerprints (this case can be treated as similar to matching partial fingerprints),
- Non-linear distortion caused by the finger plasticity,
- Different pressure and skin condition and
- Feature extraction errors which may result in spurious or missing features.

The approaches to fingerprint matching can be coarsely classified into three classes: Correlation-based matching, Minutiae-based matching and Ridge-feature-based matching. In correlation-based matching, two fingerprint images are superimposed and the correlation between corresponding pixels is computed for different alignments. During minutiae-based matching, the set of minutiae are extracted from the two fingerprints and stored as a sets of points in the two dimensional plane. Ridge-feature-based matching is based on such feature as orientation map, ridge lines and ridge geometry.

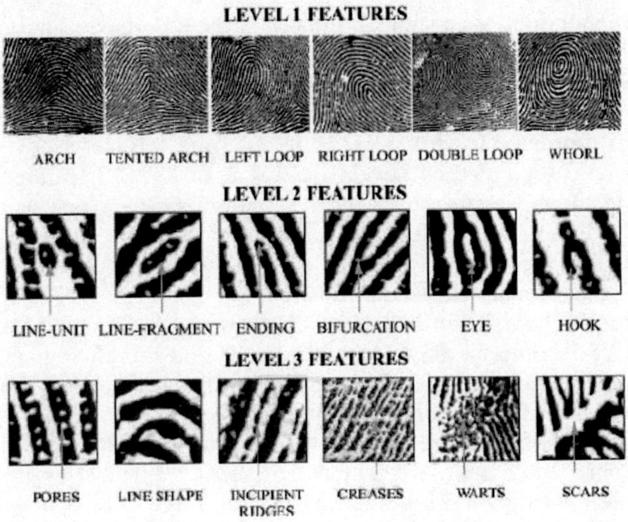

Fig. 1. Fingerprint features at Level 1, Level 2 and Level 3 [2, 3]

The information contained in a fingerprint can be categorized into three different levels, namely, Level 1 (pattern), Level 2 (minutiae points), and Level 3 (pores and ridge contours).

The vast majority of contemporary automated fingerprint authentication systems (AFAS[1]) are minutiae (Level 2 features) based [4]. Minutiae-based systems generally rely on finding correspondences[2] between the minutiae points present in "query" and "reference" fingerprint images. These systems normally perform well with high-quality fingerprint images and a sufficient fingerprint surface area. These conditions, however, may not always be attainable.

---

[1] Automated Fingerprint Authentication Systems.

[2] A minutiae in the "query" fingerprint and a minutiae in the "reference" fingerprint are said to be corresponding if they represent the identical minutiae scanned from the same finger.

In many cases, only a small portion of the "query" fingerprint can be compared with the "reference" fingerprints as a result, the number of minutiae correspondences might significantly decrease and the matching algorithm would not be able to make a decision with high certainly. This effect is even more marked on intrinsically poor quality fingerprints, where only a subset of the minutiae can be extracted and used with sufficient reliability. Although minutiae may carry most of the fingerprint's discriminatory information, they do not always constitute the best trade-off between accuracy and robustness. This has led the designers of fingerprint recognition techniques to search for other fingerprint distinguishing features, beyond minutiae which may be used in conjunction with minutiae (and not as an alternative) to increase the system accuracy and robustness. It is a known fact that the presence of level 3 features in fingerprints provides minutiae detail for matching and the potential for increased accuracy.

Ray et al. [5] have presented a means of modeling and extracting pores (which are considered as highly distinctive Level 3 features) from 500 ppi fingerprint images. This study showed that while not every fingerprint image obtained with a 500 ppi scanner has evident pores, a substantial number of them do have. Thus, it is a natural step to try to extract Level 3 information, and use them in conjunction with minutiae to achieve robust matching decisions. In addition, the fine details of level 3 features could potentially be exploited in circumstances that require high-confidence matches.

The types of information that can be collected from a fingerprint's friction ridge impression can be categorized as Level 1, Level 2, or Level 3 features as shown in Figure 1. At the global level, the fingerprint pattern exhibits one or more regions where the ridge lines assume distinctive shapes characterized by high curvature, frequent termination, etc.

These regions are broadly classified into arch, loop, and whorl. The arch, loop, and whorl can further be classified into various subcategories, by noticing Delta and core. Features of Level 1 comprise these global patterns and morphological information. They alone do not contain sufficient information to uniquely identify fingerprints but are used for broad classification of fingerprints.

Level 2 features or minutiae refer to the various ways that the ridges can be discontinuous. These are essentially Galton characteristics, namely ridge endings and ridge bifurcations. A ridge ending is defined as the ridge point where a ridge ends abruptly. A bifurcation is defined as the ridge point where a ridge bifurcates into two ridges.

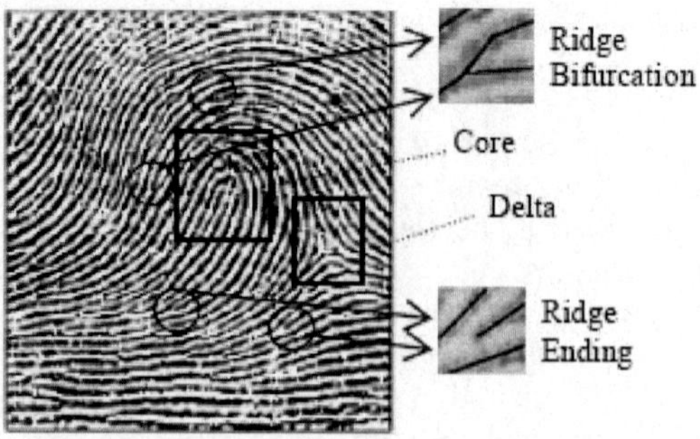

Fig. 2. Singular Points (Core & Delta) and Minutiae (ridge ending & ridge bifurcation)

Minutiae are the most prominent features, generally stable and robust to fingerprint impression conditions. Statistical analysis has shown that Level 2 features have sufficient discriminating power to establish the individuality of fingerprints [6]. Level 3 features are the extremely fine intra ridge details present in fingerprints [7]. These are essentially the sweat pores and ridge contours. Pores are the openings of the sweat glands and they are distributed along the ridges.

Studies [8] have shown that density of pores on a ridge varies from 23 to 45 pores per inch and 20 to 40 pores should be sufficient to determine the identity of an individual. A pore can be either open or closed, based on its perspiration activity. A closed pore is entirely enclosed by a ridge, while an open pore intersects with the valley lying between two ridges as shown in Figure 3.

The pore information (position, number and shape) are considered to be permanent, immutable and highly distinctive but very few automatic matching techniques use pores since their reliable extraction requires high resolution and good quality fingerprint images. Ridge contours contain valuable Level 3 information including ridge width and edge shape. Various shapes on the friction ridge edges can be classified into eight categories, namely, straight, convex, peak, table, pocket, concave, angle, and others as shown in Figure 4. The shapes and relative position of ridge edges are considered as permanent and unique.

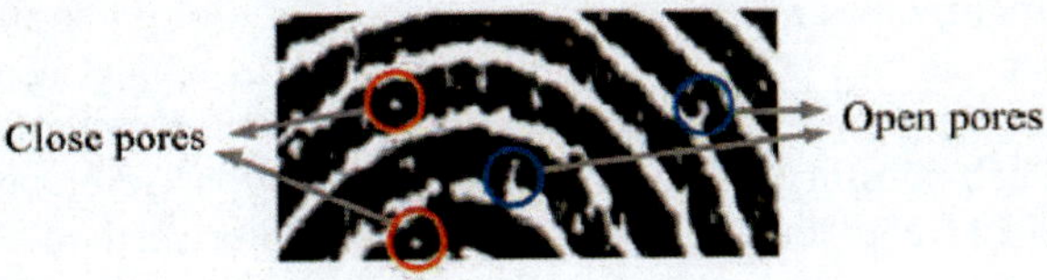

Fig. 3. Open and closed pores [9]

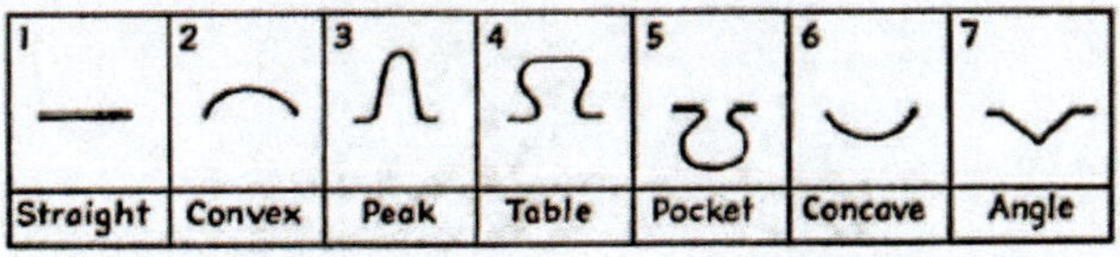

Fig. 4. Characteristics of ridge contours and edges [8]

On the perpetual quest for perfection, a number of techniques devised for reducing FAR[3] and FRR[4] were developed; computational geometry being one of such techniques [10]. Matching is usually based on lower-level features determined by singularities in the finger ridge pattern known as minutiae. Given the minutiae representation of fingerprints, fingerprint matching can simply be seen as a point matching problem. As mentioned before, two kinds of minutiae are adopted in matching: ridge ending and ridge bifurcation. For each minutia usually extract three features: type, the coordinates and the orientation.

---

[3] False Acceptance Rate.

[4] False Rejection Rate.

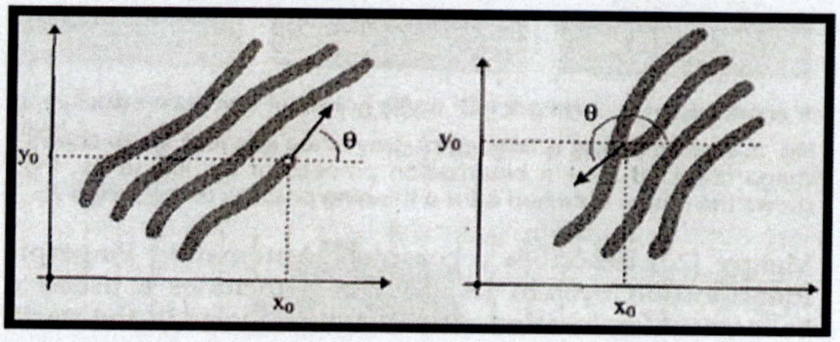

Fig. 5. Two types of minutiae, ridge ending and ridge bifurcation with their orientations

Where θ is the orientation and (x_0, y_0) is the coordinate of minutiae. M. Poulos et al. develop an approach that constructs nested polygons based on pixels brightness; this method needs some image processing techniques [11].

Another geometric topologic structure, *Nested Convex* Polygons (NCP) [12, 13], used in [14], Khazaee and others establish a matching using minutiae. This approach was invariant from translation and rotation. They also had a local matching with using of the most interior polygon (Reference Polygon) and then apply global matching. They use reference polygon that is unique for every fingerprint; this uniqueness helps to reject non matching fingerprints with minimum process and time. We use in our approach, this point of view and continue this idea to use it for pores and ridges in level 3 features. In this paper, we proposed a new fingerprint matching method that utilizes Level 3 features (pores and ridge contour) in conjunction with Level 2 features (minutiae) for matchingusing of the most interior polygon (reference polygon) and apply matching in 2 levels. Three main steps of our proposed method are:

1) Minutiae extraction and matching in level 2
2) Pores extraction and matching in level 3
3) Fingerprint recognition

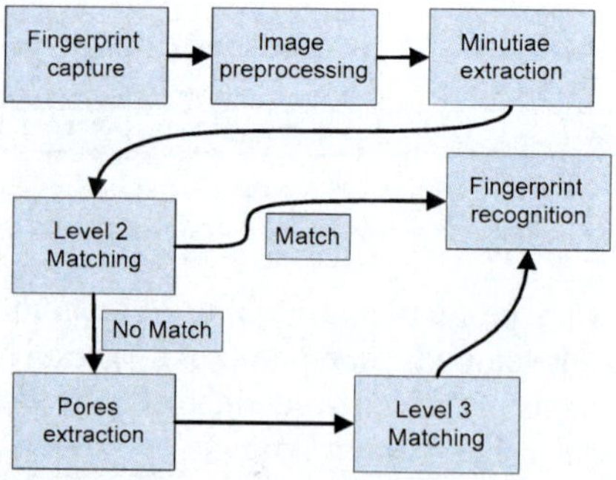

Fig. 6. The proposed fingerprint recognition system

In Section 2, we introduce nested convex polygons [13]. In section 3, we describe matching approach. Then, in section 4, show how we can construct a NCP with minutiae and pores. A new approach for fingerprint matching using NCP is described in section 5. Experimental results on FVC2006 are presented in Section 6. The paper is concluded in Section 7.

2 Nested Convex Polygons

Let $S=\{x_1,x_2,...,x_n\}$ denote n points in two dimensional spaces. We use Quick Hall algorithm iteratively to construct nested polygons [13].

Algorithm1: *Construct Nested Convex Polygons (CNCP)*
Input: $S=\{x_1,x_2,...,x_n\}$, $K=\{\}$, $depth=0$
Output: *Nested Convex polygons with their depth*

```
While (N (S )>0){
    K ={};
    K ={quickhall (S );
    S =S −K ;
    StorePolygon Properties (K ,depth );
   depth++;
}//end of while
```

Where $N(S)$ is the number of minutia in S, $quickhall()$ method find the convex layer of given point set and *Store Polygon Propertise* is a method that stores the reference polygon properties and its depth finally.

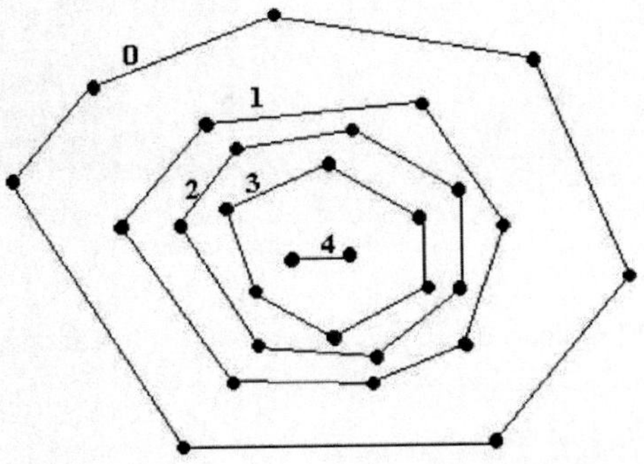

Fig. 7. Nested polygons constructed from point set

3 Fingerprint Matching

The purpose of fingerprint matching is to determine whether two fingerprints are from the same finger or not. In order to this, the input fingerprint needs to align with the template fingerprint represented by its minutiae pattern [15]. The following rigid transformation can be performed:

$$F_{s,\Delta\theta,\Delta x,\Delta y}\begin{pmatrix} x_{temp} \\ y_{temp} \end{pmatrix} = s\begin{pmatrix} \cos\Delta\theta & -\sin\Delta\theta \\ \sin\Delta\theta & \cos\Delta\theta \end{pmatrix}\begin{pmatrix} x_{input} \\ y_{input} \end{pmatrix} + \begin{pmatrix} \Delta x \\ \Delta y \end{pmatrix}$$

Where $(s,\Delta\theta,\Delta x,\Delta y)$ represent a set of rigid transformation parameters: (scale, rotation, translation). In our research, we assume that the scaling factor between input and template image is identical since both images are captured with the same device.

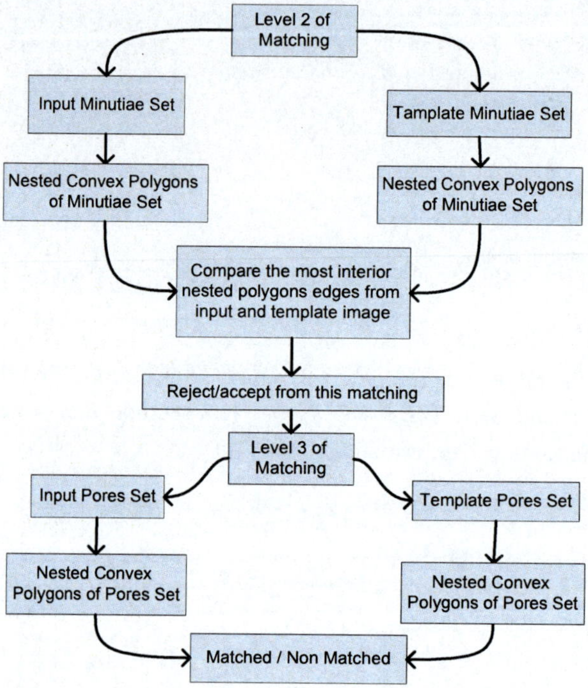

Fig. 8. Flow chart of generic fingerprint identification system

4 Constructed Nested Polygons

Let $Q=((x_1^Q,y_1^Q,\theta_1^Q,t_1^Q)...(x_n^Q,y_n^Q,\theta_n^Q,t_n^Q))$ denote the set of n minutiae in the input image ((x, y): location of minutiae, ?: orientation field of minutiae, t: minutiae type, end or bifurcation);

And $P=((x_1^P,y_1^P,\theta_1^P,t_1^P)...(x_n^P,y_n^P,\theta_n^P,t_n^P))$ denote the set of m minutiae in template image [14].

Table 1. Data structure used for comparing fingerprint images in level 2.Y: Dependent on fingerprint transformation, N: independent of it

Feature	**Fields**			
Minutiae Point	X : (Y)	Y: (Y)	θ : (Y)	Type: (N)
Polygon Edges	Length: (N)	θ_1 : (N)	θ_2 : (N)	Type1: (N) / Type2: (N)

Table 2. Data structure used for comparing fingerprint images in level 3.Y: Dependent on fingerprint transformation, N: independent of it

Feature	**Fields**			
Pore Point	X : (Y)	Y: (Y)	θ : (Y)	Type: (N)
Polygon Edges	Length: (N)	θ_1 : (N)	θ_2 : (N)	Type1: (N) / Type2: (N)

Table1 shows features that we use in level 2 matching and table2 shows the features we use in level 3 matching. In the table1, Length is the length of edge; $?_1$ is the angel between the edge and the orientation field at the first minutiae point; $Type_1$ denote minutiae type of the first minutiae [10].

Using onion layer algorithm we construct nested polygons; for every fingerprint we store edge properties that mentioned in table1 of the reference polygon, plus its depth, and Minutiae points features that mentioned in first row of table1 in database as template (fingerprint Registration). Also, we construct nested polygons for pores

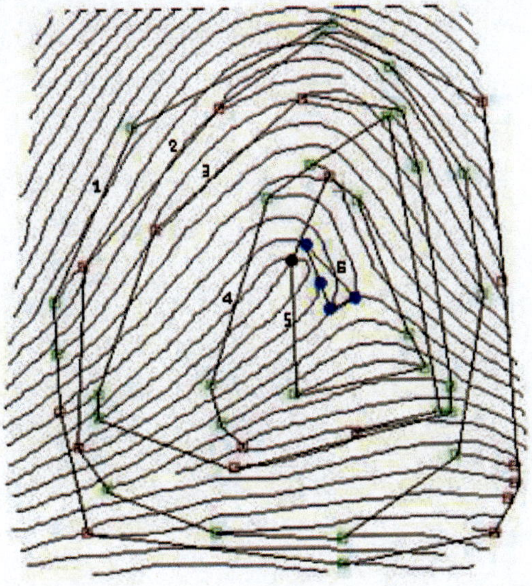

Fig. 9. Fingerprint with minutiae and its nested polygons

and for every fingerprint store edge properties that mentioned in table2 of the reference polygon, plus its depth, and pore points features that mentioned in first row of table2 in database as template (fingerprint Registration).

At the Figure 9 the polygon at depth 6 is the reference polygon that used for level 2 matching in order to calculate rigid transformation parameters; these parameters apply to the whole remain minutiae of input fingerprint in order to align with template fingerprint, then level 3 matching is employed, and if the score of matching is higher than predefined threshold, two fingerprints are identical, otherwise they are from different fingers.

5 Fingerprint Registration and Matching Based on NCP

The purpose of fingerprint matching is to determine whether two fingerprints are from the same finger or not. At this step input fingerprint image goes through preprocessing, NCPs construction and determining its class like registration step. Afterward depend on Identification (1?n matching) or verification (1?1 matching) we perform matching. In verification mode we do not have to determine the class of fingerprint; retrieve fingerprint from database template and perform matching. But the purpose of identification is to identify unknown person, so in this mode, the class of input fingerprint is detect and matching of unknown fingerprint with templates at that class continue until happen a matching or rejection at the end. We divided registration in two steps: firstly, in preprocessing step, some image processing techniques that customize for fingerprint, like segmentation, normalization, Gabor filter and etc apply on fingerprint input image [16]. Next, Binarization and thinning are employed and valid minutiae are extracted from thin image.

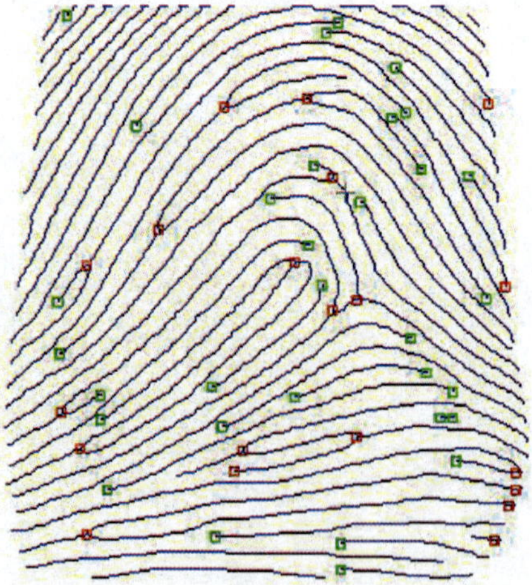

Fig. 10. Final results of pre-processing steps

Secondly, we apply onion layer algorithm and construct NCPs. We store invariant feature (table1) for reference polygon plus its depth and variant features for other polygons in the database as a template. We also do the same procedure for pores and apply onion layer algorithm and construct NCPs for them too and store invariant feature (table2) for reference polygon plus its depth and variant features for other polygons in the database as a template. Following steps elaborate our algorithm in identification mode.

Some abbreviations that we use in algorithm:

- **RP**: Reference Polygon
- **RT**: Reference Triangle
- **P_i**: RP of input fingerprint image
- **P_t**: RP of template fingerprint image
- **β_i**: angle between two adjacent edges of RP in RT of input fingerprint image
- **β_t**: angle between two adjacent edges of RP in RT of template fingerprint image
- Other abbreviations are interpreted base on table1 and table2.

Algorithm 2 [14]:

1. Compare input and template RP depth:

$$D = \left| Dept(P_i) - Dept(P_t) \right| \tag{1}$$

2. If $D \geq 2$, then two fingerprints are not from same finger, so matching reject at this step.

3. Otherwise select one of the P_i edges (E_i) and find corresponding edge in P_t; two edges are corresponding (equal) if satisfy four following conditions:

$$Len(E_i) - Len(E_t) \prec T_1 \tag{2}$$

$$Type_1(E_i) = Type_1(E_t) \tag{3}$$

$$Type_2(E_i) = Type_2(E_t) \tag{4}$$

$$\theta_{i1} - \theta_{t1} \prec T_2 \text{ And } \theta_{i2} - \theta_{t2} \prec T_2 \tag{5}$$

Where, T_1 and T_2 are respectively thresholds of length of edges, and minutia angle and orientation of edge, respectively.

4. Repeat step 3, until find two adjacent edges in P_i that have two adjacent edges corresponding in P_t. If such couple adjacent edges don't exist in two RPs, matching reject at this step.

5. Using of such couple adjacent edges, a triangle constructed as Reference Triangle (RT). One more step needed to ensure that two triangles are exactly corresponded, that's satisfied with following condition:

$$|\beta_i - \beta_t| \prec T_3 \tag{6}$$

Where, T_3 is threshold of angle between two adjacent edges in two RT.

6. using of RT, calculate the rigid transformation parameters $(\Delta\theta, \Delta x, \Delta y)$.

7. Achieve the number of corresponding minutiae pairs. Given an alignment $(\Delta\theta, \Delta x, \Delta y)$, minutiae of input fingerprint are mapped into template fingerprint. Judging they are matched or not according to equations (7);

$$m = \{yes, if \sqrt{(x_i - x_{temp})^2 + (y_i - y_{temp})^2} \le r_0 \ and \ Type_i = Type_t \ and \ |\theta_i - \theta_t| \prec \theta_0 \quad no, otherwise \tag{7}$$

Where, r_0 and $?_0$ are thresholds of distance and orientation respectively.

8. Similarity calculates according to equation (8);

$$p = \frac{2n}{m+q} \times 100 \tag{8}$$

Where, m and q are the number of minutiae in two fingerprints and n is the number of matched minutiae. If p be greater than predefined value, so two fingerprint are the same, otherwise go back to step 3. This iteration continues until either no candidate at step 4 exists, or accepts at step 9.

6 Experimental Results

We perform experiments using the fingerprint database of FVC 2006 to evaluate the correctness of algorithm in this paper and show the results of experiments. The experiment uses DB1_a in database FVC 2006 [17]. Each database contained 800

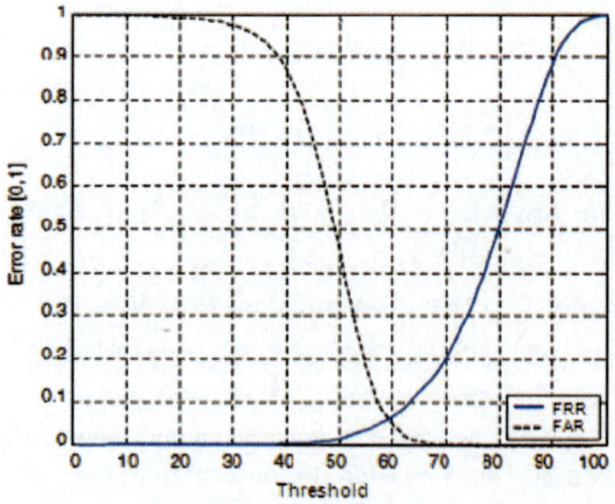

Fig. 11. EER-curve on DB1_a, FVC2006 obtained

fingerprints from 100 different fingers and in each database dry, wet, scratched, distorted and markedly rotated fingerprints were also adequately represented. We compare our results with *Cspn* algorithm in FVC 2006 in terms of FRR and FAR; this comparison shows the accuracy of new algorithm.

The best value for threshold is cross point of two curves. Our algorithm has less error than Cspn at this point.

7 Conclusion

In this paper, we have developed a new approach to fingerprint matching using an onion layer algorithm of computational geometry. This matching approach utilizes Level 3 features (pores and ridge contour) in conjunction with Level 2 features (minutiae) for matching. Using an Onion layer algorithm, we construct nested convex polygons of minutiae, and then based on polygons property, we perform matching of fingerprints; we use the most interior polygon in order to calculate the rigid transformations parameters and perform level 2 matching, then we apply level 3 matching. The theory analysis of computational complexity shows that the NCP approach for fingerprint matching is more efficient than the standard minutiae based matching algorithms. Three main steps of our proposed method for fingerprint matching are: Minutiae extraction and perform matching in level 2, Pores extraction and perform matching in level 3 and then fingerprint recognition. The most important characteristics of the proposed algorithm are: fast identification, very fast in rejection, more accurate than classic minutiae matching. Another advantage of proposed algorithm is that none of image processing techniques are require for matching.

Our future objective is considering new computational geometry structure for matching and classification in order to more resistant against noise and poor quality fingerprints.

References

1. Bebis, G., Deaconu, T., Georgiopoulos, M.: Fingerprint Identification Using Delaunay Triangulation. In: IEEE International Conference on Information Intelligence and Systems (1999)
2. The Thin Blue Line (2006), `http://www.policensw.com/info/fingerprints/finger06.html`
3. van de Nieuwendijk, H.: Fingerprints (2006), `http://www.xs4all.nl/~dacty/minu.htm`
4. Maio, D., Maltoni, D., Cappelli, R., Wayman, J.L., Jain, A.K.: FVC 2000: Fingerprint Verification Competition. IEEE Transactions on Pattern Analysis and Machine Intelligence 24(3), 402–412 (2002)
5. Ray, M., Meenen, P., Adhami, R.: A novel approach to fingerprint pore extraction. In: Southeastern Symposium on System Theory, pp. 282–286 (2005)
6. Pankanti, S., Prabhakar, S., Jain, A.K.: On the Individuality of Fingerprints. IEEE Trans. Pattern Anal. Mach. Intell 24(8), 1010–1025 (2002)
7. CDEFFS: The ANSI/NIST Committee to Define an Extended Fingerprint Feature Set (2006), `http://fingerprint.nist.gov/standard/cdeffs/index.html`

8. Ashbaugh, D.R.: Quantitative-Quantitative Friction Ridge Analysis: An Introduction to Basic and Advanced Ridgeology. CRC Press, Boca Raton (1999)
9. Jain, A.K., Chen, Y., Demirkus, M.: Pores and Ridges: High-Resolution Fingerprint Matching Using Level 3 Features. PAMI 29(1), 15–27 (2007)
10. Wang, C., Gavrilova, L.: Delaunay Triangulation Algorithm for Fingerprint Matching. In: The 3rd IEEE International Symposium of Voronoi Diagrams in Science and Engineering (2006)
11. Poulos, M., Magkos, E., Chrissikopoulos, V., Alexandris, N.: Secure Fingerprint Verification Based on Image Processing Segmentation Using Computational Geometry Algorithms. In: Proceedings of the IASTED International Conference on Signal Processing, Pattern Recognition, and Apllications, Rhodes Island, Greece, June 30-July 2. ACTA Press (2003)
12. Rourke, J.O.: Computational Geometry. Cambridge University Press, Cambridge (1995)
13. Sack, J.-R., Urrutia, J.: Handbook of Computational Geometry. Elsevier, Amsterdam (2000)
14. Khazaei, H., Mohades, A.: Fingerprint Matching and Classification using an Onion Layer algorithm of Computational Geometry. International Journal of Mathematics and Computers in Simulation 1(1) (2007)
15. Jiang, X.D., Yau, W.Y.: Fingerprint minutiae matching based on the local and Global Structures. In: Proceedings of the 15th International Conference on Pattern Recognition (2000)
16. Maltoni, D., Maio, D., Jain, A.K., Prabhakar, S.: Handbook of Fingerprint Recognition. Springer, Heidelberg (2003)
17. `http://bias.csr.unibo.it/fvc2006/`

Multiple Collaborative Cameras for Multi-Target Tracking Using Color-Based Particle Filter and Contour Information

Victoria Rudakova, Sajib Kumar Saha, and Faouzi Alaya Cheikh

Gjøvik University College, Norway
rozzmarine@gmail.com, to_sajib_cse@yahoo.com, faouzi.cheikh@hig.no

Abstract. Multi-target tracking is a active research field nowadays due to its wide practical applicability in video processing. While talking about Multi-target tracking, 'multi-target occlusion' is a common problem that needs to be addressed. Lots of work has been done using multiple cameras for handling 'multi-target occlusion'; however most of them require camera calibration parameters that make them impractical for outdoor video surveillance applications. The main focus of this paper is to reduce the dependency on camera calibration for multiple camera collaboration. In this perspective Gale-Shapley algorithm (GSA) has been used for finding stable matching between two or more camera views, while more robustness on tracking of objects has been ensured by combining multiple cues such object's boundary information of the object with color histogram. Efficient tracking of object ensures proficient reckoning of target depicting parameter (i.e. apparent color, height and width information of the object) as a consequence better camera collaboration. The simulation results prove the validity of our approach.

Keywords: surveillance; multiple camera tracking; multi-people tracking; particle filtering.

1 Introduction

Object tracking has received tremendous attention in the video processing community due to its numerous potential applications in video surveillance, human activity analysis, traffic monitoring, etc. Recently the focus of the community is on multi-target tracking (MTT) that requires determining the number as well as the dynamics of targets. However, due to several factors, reliable target tracking still remains a challenging domain of research. The underlying difficulties behind multi-target tracking are founded mostly upon the apparent similarity of targets and multi-target occlusion. MTT for targets whose appearance is distinctive is comparatively easier since it can be solved reasonably well by using multiple independent single-target trackers. However, MTT for targets whose appearance is similar such as pedestrians in crowded scenes is a much more difficult task. In addition with this MTT must deal with multi-target occlusion, namely, the tracker must separate the targets and assign them correct labels. Computational complexity also plays an important role, as in most applications

H. Cherifi, J.M. Zain, and E. El-Qawasmeh (Eds.): DICTAP 2011, Part I, CCIS 166, pp. 315–326, 2011.

the tracking should be real time. All these issues make target tracking or multi-object tracking a challenging task even today.

The contribution of that paper (based on the thesis work [33]) is to use color and size information of the object for multi camera collaboration in order to reduce the dependency on camera calibration.

2 Previous Works

Most of the early works for MTT were based on monocular video [1]. A widely accepted approach that addresses many problems of MTT is based on a joint state-space representation that infers the joint data association [2, 3]. A binary variable has been used by MacCormick and Blake [4] to identify foreground objects and then a probabilistic exclusion principle has been used to penalize the hypothesis where two objects occlude. In [5], the likelihood is calculated by enumerating all possible association hypotheses. Zhao and Nevatia [6, 7] used a different 3D shape model and joint likelihood for multiple human segmentation and tracking. Tao et al. [8] proposed a sampling-based multiple-target tracking method using background subtraction. Khan et al. in [9] proposed a Markov chain Monte Carlo (MCMC)-based particle filter which uses a Markov random field to model motion interaction. Smith et al. presented a different MCMC-based particle filter to estimate the multi-object configuration [10]. McKenna et al. [11] presented a color-based system for tracking groups of people. Adaptive color models are used to provide qualitative estimates of depth ordering during occlusion. Although the above solutions, which are based on a centralized process, can handle the problem of multi-target occlusion in principle, they impose a hign computational cost due to the complexity introduced by the high dimensionality of the joint-state representation which grows exponentially in terms of the number of objects tracked.

Several researchers proposed decentralized solutions for multi-target tracking. In [12] the multi-object occlusion problem has been solved by using multiple cameras where the cameras are separated widely in order to obtain visual information from wide viewing angles and offer a possible 3D solution. The system needs to pass the subjects identities across cameras when the identities are lost in a certain view by matching subjects across camera views. Therefore, the system needs to match subjects in consecutive frames of a single camera and also match subjects across cameras in order to maintain subject identities in as many cameras as possible. Although this cross view correspondence is related to wide baseline stereo matching, traditional correlation based methods fail due to the large difference in viewpoint [13].

Yu and Wu [14] and Wu et al. [15] used multiple collaborative trackers for MTT modeled by a Markov random network. This approach demonstrates the efficiency of the decentralized method. The decentralized approach was carried further by Qu et al. [16] who proposed an interactively distributed multi-object tracking framework using a magnetic-inertia potential model.

However, using multiple cameras raises many additional challenges. The most critical difficulties presented by multi-camera tracking are to establish a consistent label correspondence of the same target among the different views and to integrate the information from different camera views for tracking that is robust to significant and persistent occlusion.

Many existing approaches address the label correspondence problem by using different techniques such as feature matching [17, 18], camera calibration and/or 3D environment model [18, 19], and motion-trajectory alignment [20]. A kalman filter based approach has been proposed in [13] for tracking multiple object in indoor environment. Here in addition to apparent color, apparent height, landmark modality, homography and epipolar geometry has been used for multi-camera cooperation. Qu et al. in [1] presented a distributed Bayesian framework for multiple-target tracking using multiple collaborative cameras. The distributed Bayesian framework avoids the computational complexity inherent in centralized methods that rely on joint-state representation and joint data association. Epipolar geometry has been used for multi-camera collaboration. However, dependency on epipolar geometry makes that approach impractical, since the angle of view with respect to each camera has to be known very accurately, which is challenging for outdoor video surveillance due to environmental maladies.

3 Proposed Framework

3.1 Bayesian Sequential Estimation

The Bayesian sequential estimation helps to estimate a posterior distribution noted as $p(x_{0:t}|z_{1:t})$ or its marginal $p(x_t|z_{1:t})$, where $x_{0:t}$ includes a set of all states up to time t and $z_{1:t}$ - set of all the observations up to time t accordingly. The evolution of the state sequences $\{x_t, t \in N\}$ of a target is given by equation 1; and the observation model is given by equation 2:

$$x_t = f_t(x_{t-1}, v_{t-1}) \tag{1}$$

$$z_t = h_t(x_t, u_t) \tag{2}$$

Where f_t: $\mathbb{R}^{n_x} \times \mathbb{R}^{n_v} \rightarrow \mathbb{R}^{n_x}$ and h_t: $\mathbb{R}^{n_x} \times \mathbb{R}^{n_u} \rightarrow \mathbb{R}^{n_z}$ can be both linear and non-linear, and v_t and u_t are sequences of i.d.d. process noise and measurement noise respectively; at the same time n_v and n_u are their dimensions.

In Bayesian context, the tracking problem can be considered as recursive calculation of some belief degree in the state x_t at time step t, given the data observation $z_{1:t}$. That is, we need to construct a probability density function $p(x_t|z_{1:t})$. It is assumed that initial state of the system (also called prior) is given.

$$p(x_0|z_0) = p(x_0) \tag{3}$$

Then, the posterior distribution $p(x_t|z_{1:t})$ can be calculated by the following two steps given in equations (4) and (5).

Prediction:

$$p(x_t|z_{1:t-1}) = \int p(x_t|x_{t-1})p(x_{t-1}|z_{1:t-1})\, dx_{t-1} \tag{4}$$

Update:

$$p(x_t|z_{1:t}) = \frac{p(z_t|x_t)p(x_t|z_{1:t-1})}{p(z_t|z_{1:t-1})} = \frac{p(z_t|x_t)p(x_t|z_{1:t-1})}{\int p(z_t|x_t)p(x_t|z_{1:t-1})\, dx_{t-1}} \tag{5}$$

In equation (5) the denominator is normalization constant and it depends on the likelihood function $p(z_t|x_t)$ - as described by equation (2). But presented recursive propagation is just a conceptual solution and can't be applied in practice.

However Monte-carlo simulation [26] with sequential importance sampling (SIS) technique, allows us to approximate equations 4 and 5 in the discreet form:

Prediction:

$$p(x_t|z_{0:t-1}) \approx \sum_{n=1}^{N_s} p(x_t|x_{t-1}^{(n)})\omega_{t-1}^{(n)} \tag{6}$$

Update:

$$p(x_t|z_{0:t}) \approx \sum_{n=1}^{N_s} \omega_t^{(n)}\, \delta(x_t - x_{t-1}) \tag{7}$$

Where $\omega_t^{(n)} \infty \frac{p(z_t|x_t^{(n)})p(x_t^{(n)}|x_{t-1}^{(n)})}{q(x_t^{(n)}|x_{t-1}^{(n)}, z_{0:t})}\omega_{t-1}^{(n)}$ as well as $\sum_{n=1}^{N_s} \omega_t^{(n)} = 1$

Nonetheless in order to avoid degeneracy (one of the common problems with SIS) re-sampling of the particles need to be done. Therefore, the main idea is to update the particles whose contribution to the approximation to $p(x_t|z_{1:t})$ is almost zero and pay attention to the more promising particles. It generates a new set $\{\tilde{x}_t^{(n)}, N_s^{-1}\}_{n=1}^{N_s}$ by re-sampling with replacement N_s times from an approximate discreet representation of $p(x_t|z_{0:t})$, so that $Pr(\tilde{x}_t^{(n)} = x_t^{(m)}) = \omega_t^{(m)}$ and weights must be reset to $\omega_t^{(n)} = \frac{1}{N_s}$ (we denote it N_s^{-1}).

For this paper we have used the re-sampling scheme proposed in [27].

State estimate:

The mean state ('mean' particle, 'mean'shape or weighted sum of particles) has been used.

$$\varepsilon[X_t] = \sum_{n=1}^{N_s} \omega_t^{(n)} x_t^{(n)} \tag{8}$$

3.2 Modeling of Densities

3.2.1 Target Representation

Since ellipse can provide more precise shape information than a bounding box [28], simple 5D parametric ellipse has been used in order to decrease computational costs, and at the same time, it is sufficient to represent the tracking results (see figure 1). Therefore, one state x_t^i is defined by $x_t^i = (cx_t^i, cy_t^i, a_t^i, b_t^i, \rho_t^i)$, where i is target index, t - current time, (cx, cy) - coordinates of the center of ellipse, (a, b) major and minor axis, and ρ - orientation angle.

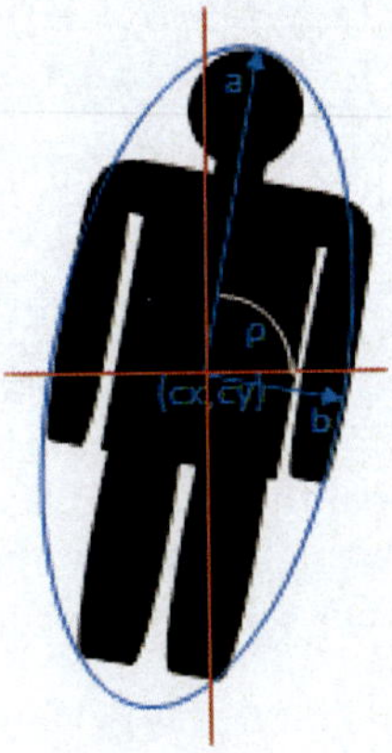

Fig. 1. Ellipse representation for describing a human body

3.2.2 Local Observation Model

As a local likelihood $p\left(z_t^i \middle| x_t^{i,(n)}\right)$, single cue - color histogram like [29] has been used. Color models are obtained in the Hue-Saturation-Value (HSV) color space in order to decouple chromatic information from shading effects. As for the bin numbers, N; we have used $N_h = N_s = 8$ and $N_v = 4$.

3.3.3 State Dynamics Model

Lucas-Kanade (LK) optical flow algorithm [30] has been used for motion estimation.

3.3.4 Interaction Model

When targets start to interact with each other (i.e., occlusion), we cannot rely on the motion based proposal anymore, hence magnetic-repulsion inertia re-weighting scheme [29] stand on random based proposal has been used instead of the re-weighting scheme proposed in [31]; since [29] gives better results than [31] in our experiment.

3.3 Improved Contour Detection for Moving Object

One important consideration for state dynamics model is how to include prediction of ellipse parameters a, b and ρ. Until now it was possible to predict only the center coordinates (cx, cy) of the ellipse based on the LK optical flow [30] calculation. At the same time parameters a, b and ρ propagate according to random-based prediction which is not very effective sometimes since it can lead to over-expanding or over-squeezing of the ellipse bounds. Hence to overcome this problem objects' contour information has been considered for calculating a, b and ρ.

Detecting the contour information consists of three phases like in [32]; in the first phase gradient information has been extracted since it is much less affected by the quantization noise and abrupt change of illumination. Sobel operators has been used instead of Roberts operators or Prewitt operators, as they are generally less computation expensive and more suitable for hardware realizations [32].

$$f_E(x,y,t) = |f(x,y,t) * H_X| + |f(x,y,t) * H_Y| \quad (9)$$

$$\text{Where } H_X = \frac{1}{4}\begin{bmatrix} -1 & 0 & 1 \\ -2 & 0 & 2 \\ -1 & 0 & 1 \end{bmatrix} \text{ and } H_Y = \frac{1}{4}\begin{bmatrix} -1 & -2 & -1 \\ 0 & 0 & 0 \\ 1 & 2 & 1 \end{bmatrix}$$

Where, $f(x, y, t)$ denotes a pixel of a gray-scale image, $f_E(x, y, t)$ denotes the gradient of the pixel, H_X and H_Y denote the horizontal and the vertical transform matrix, respectively.

In the second phase three frame differencing scheme [32] has been used instead of commonly used two frame differencing method for better detection of moving objects contour. The operation is detailed in the following equation

$$D(x,y,\Delta t) = |f_E(x,y,t) - f_E(x,y,t-1)| \cdot |f_E(x,y,t) - f_E(x,y,t+1)| \quad (10)$$

The background contour in an image resulted from such a gradient-based three-frame differencing can be largely eliminated, whereas the contours of moving objects can be remarkably enhanced.

In the third phase a step of eight-connectivity testing is appended with three-frame differencing for the sake of noise reduction.

Once the contours of moving objects have been detected using the above mentioned procedure, then (cx,cy) detected by particle filter has been used to calculate a', b', ρ'. The calculation of a' is quiet simple, in fact it is the distance of a point $(x_{a'}, y_{a'})$, that is the farthest form (cx,cy) within a certain perimeter defined by $(cx, cy, a, b+\frac{b}{3}, \rho \pm 5^o)$. Then $\rho' = \tan^{-1}(\frac{y_{a'} - cy}{x_{a'} - cx})$ can be calculated. Now b' is the distance of farthest point $(x_{b'}, y_{b'})$, which makes $90^o \pm 5^o$ angle with respect to line joining (cx,cy) and $(x_{a'}, y_{a'})$.

Now the ellipse that tracks the object(s) has been defined by the parameters $(cx, cy, a_{new}, b_{new}, \rho_{new})$ where $a_{new} = 0.4 * a + 0.6 * a'$, $b_{new} = 0.4 * b + 0.6 * b'$ and $\rho_{new} = 0.4 * \rho + 0.6 * \rho'$

If for any reason (shadow, occlusion etc; Fig. 7), the calculated a' becomes unreliable (i.e. $a' < \frac{a}{3}$ or $a' > 2 * a$) then while calculating a_{new}, the weighting factors (0.5, 0.5) may be used instead of (0.4, 0.6); and the last used (from known previous frame) value of a' will be used (if the value of a' is taken from a frame which is not more than 5 frames before from the current frame). Otherwise the factor becomes (1, 0). Same is true for b', ρ'.

3.4 Multi-camera Data Fusion

In order to correctly associate corresponding targets (assign the same identity of objects irrespective of camera views) Gale-Shapley algorithm (GSA) [24] has been used, that uses color, height and width information of the detected object in 2 camera views. Each time a new object appears in the camera view(s) its normalized color histogram (normalized by apparent height and width; we will refer it to as initialized histogram) has been stored in the camera view(s), at the same time the corresponding labeling of objects with respect to one reference camera has been done by using GSA that uses the histogram distance between objects of two different camera views to generate the preference lists for objects. For system using more than 2 cameras that labeling should be done for all the cameras with respect to one reference camera. Once labeling has been done each camera can work independently and track individually. Once an occlusion occurs in the reference camera then the histogram distance of objects has been calculated by considering the normalized color histogram of objects (of that frame) with respect to its initialized histogram on that camera view; and then occluded object has been identified by comparing the histogram distances of objects that are in interaction. Once an (or more) occlusion has been detected then the idea becomes is to figure out which camera can be suggested for that object, for that perspective the reference camera will look for that object in the camera to its right. If that object is also occluded there then the reference camera will look for that object in the camera on its left to it to check whether that object is occluded on that camera view or no and so on.

4 Experimental Result

4.1 Experimental Setup

Two USB Logitec web cameras have been used. All the video sequences with people were recorded from these cameras. For the initialization of the targets the code implemented in [31] has been used.

Several experimental camera set-ups were tested, where people number, their activities (hand-shaking, walking and occluding each other) and also illumination (daylight, artificial room light) varied. Original videos were recorded with the frame size of 640×480. For our tests it was decided to decrease the frame size to 320×240 to lower computational costs needed for processing one frame. For all the sequences, we use 50 particles for each target.

4.2 Experimental Analysis

For tracking of individual object the model proposed here that combines border information of the object with particle filter information gives better result than using only particle filter information (see figure 2, 3; in figure 2 the tracker wraps considerable amount of background data). Even though the processing introduced here takes some extra time (17 ms per frame for the configuration similar as [32]) it is negligible compared to the time taken by particle filter additionally it does not depend on the number of objects present in the sequence; it ensures better tracking and overall good performance of the proposed framework.

The proposed methodology ensures quality tracking and gives constant labeling of objects irrespective of camera views. For all the tested video sequences (15 video sequences $\times$ 2 camera views (with overlapping field of view)) the tracking and labeling of objects were appropriate, unless the objects were too away from (more than 8 meters) the camera.

Fig. 2. Tracking of objects using partilcle filter only

Fig. 3. Tracking of objects using partilcle filter augmented with edge information of the object

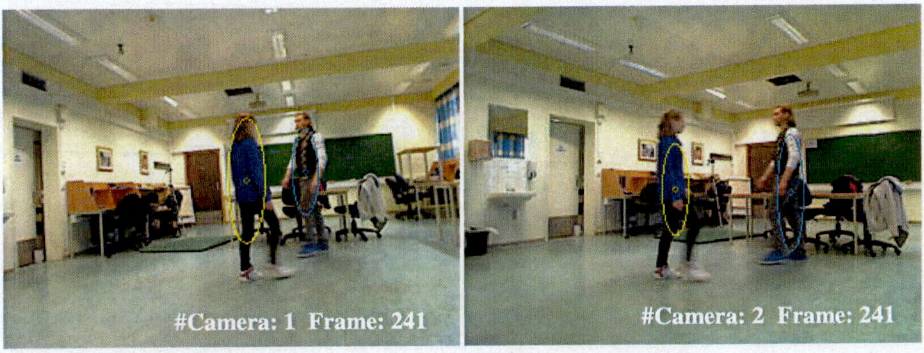

Fig. 4. Video sequences obtained from two camera views and tracking of objects (where the color of ellipses ensures that the objects are labeled correctly irrespective of camera views)

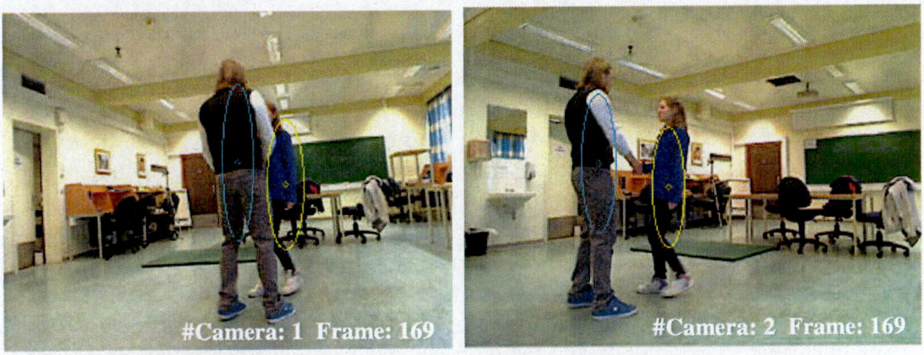

Fig. 5. Video sequences obtained from two camera views and tracking of objects

Fig. 6. Video sequences where the yellow tracker loses its target

Fig. 7. Video sequence where detected border of the objects is not sufficient

5 Conclusion and Discussion

Provided that epipolar geometry is not a sufficient solution for multi-camera data fusion, an innovative methodology for multi-camera data fusion has been proposed based on Gale-Shapley Algorithm. The idea of the proposed methodology here is not to check the correctness of coordinates of tracked objects in the image coordinate system (like most of the systems do), but to maintain correct identities of targets among the different camera views (see figure 4, 5). While maintaining same identity of object(s) across camera views or identifying occluded object based on normalized color histogram it's very important that the tracked ellipse should cover the object sufficiently and should contain as less as possible data from background, which has been ensured here by combining information with particle filter. As a consequence the proposed methodology ensures quality tracking and accurate labeling of objects across camera views.

It has been observed that when the object becomes too away from the camera (more than 8 meters) then the tracker loses its track (see figure 6). Even though HSV color space has been used to ignore the lightness effect of object with respect to the camera distance, it does not give so robust result in reality. Hence some more advanced color space can be used.

While detecting the ellipse based on border information of the object, still we are using the centroid information of the ellipse detected by particle filter. Hence geometric formula can be used for more robust detection of centroid(s)

One major short-coming of the proposed approach (like any other color based detection) is that for objects of apparent similarity (objects wearing similar cloths and having same height and width) the system may not work properly.

References

1. Qu, W., Schonfeld, D., Mohamed, M.: Distributed Bayesian multiple-target tracking in crowded environments using multiple collaborative cameras. EURASIP Journal on Applied Signal Processing (1), 21–21 (2007)
2. Bar-Shalom, Y., Jammer, A.G.: Tracking and Data Association. Academic Press, San Diego (1998)

3. Hue, C., Cadre, J.-P.L., P´erez, P.: Sequential Monte Carlo methods for multiple target tracking and data fusion. IEEE Transactions on Signal Processing 50(2), 309–325 (2002)
4. MacCormick, J., Blake, A.: A probabilistic exclusion principle for tracking multiple objects. International Journal of Computer Vision 39(1), 57–71 (2000)
5. Gordon, N.: A hybrid bootstrap filter for target tracking in clutter. IEEE Transactions on Aerospace and Electronic Systems 33(1), 353–358 (1997)
6. Zhao, T., Nevatia, R.: Tracking multiple humans in crowded environment. In: Proceedings of the IEEE Computer Society Conference on Computer Vision and Pattern Recognition (CVPR 2004), Washington, DC, USA, vol. 2, pp. 406–413 (June-July 2004)
7. Zhao, T., Nevatia, R.: Tracking multiple humans in complex situations. IEEE Transactions on Pattern Analysis and Machine Intelligence 26(9), 1208–1221 (2004)
8. Tao, H., Sawhney, H., Kumar, R.: A sampling algorithm for detection and tracking multiple objects. In: Proceedings of IEEE International Conference on Computer Vision (ICCV 1999) Workshop on Vision Algorithm, Corfu, Greece (September 1999)
9. Khan, Z., Balch, T., Dellaert, F.: An MCMC-Based Particle Filter for Tracking Multiple Interacting Targets. In: Pajdla, T., Matas, J(G.) (eds.) ECCV 2004. LNCS, vol. 3024, pp. 279–290. Springer, Heidelberg (2004)
10. Smith, K., Gatica-Perez, D., Odobez, J.-M.: Using particles to track varying numbers of interacting people. In: Proceedings of the IEEE Computer Society Conference on Computer Vision and Pattern Recognition (CVPR 2005), San Diego, Calif, USA, vol. 1, pp. 962–969 (June 2005)
11. McKenna, S.J., Jabri, S., Duric, Z., Rosenfeld, A., Wechsler, H.: Tracking groups of people. Computer Vision and Image Understanding 80(1), 42–56 (2000)
12. Lee, L., Romano, R., Stein, G.: Monitoring activities from multiple video streams: Establishing a common coordinate frame. IEEE Transactions on Pattern Analysis and Machine Intelligence, 758–767 (2000); Special Issue on Video Surveillance and Monitoring
13. Chang, T.-h., Gong, S.: Tracking Multiple People with a Multi-Camera System. In: IEEE Workshop on Multi-Object Tracking (2001)
14. Yu, T., Wu, Y.: Collaborative tracking of multiple targets. In: Proceedings of the IEEE Computer Society Conference on Computer Vision and Pattern Recognition (CVPR 2004), Washington, DC, USA, vol. 1, pp. 834–841 (June-July 2004)
15. Wu, Y., Hua, G., Yu, T.: Tracking articulated body by dynamic Markov network. In: Proceedings of 9th IEEE International Conference on Computer Vision (ICCV 2003), Nice, France, vol. 2, pp. 1094–1101 (October 2003)
16. Qu, W., Schonfeld, D., Mohamed, M.: Real-time interactively distributed multi-object tracking using a magnetic-inertia potential model. In: Proceedings of 10th IEEE International Conference on Computer Vision (ICCV 2005), Beijing, China, vol. 1, pp. 535–540 (October 2005)
17. Cai, Q., Aggarwal, J.K.: Tracking human motion in structured environments using a distributed-camera system. IEEE Transactions on Pattern Analysis and Machine Intelligence 21(11), 1241–1247 (1999)
18. Kelly, P.H., Katkere, A., Kuramura, D.Y., Moezzi, S., Chatterjee, S., Jain, R.: An architecture for multiple perspective interactive video. In: Proceedings of 3rd ACM International Conference on Multimedia (ACM Multimedia 1995), San Francisco, Calif, USA, pp. 201–212 (November 1995)
19. Black, J., Ellis, T.: Multiple camera image tracking. In: Proceedings of 2nd IEEE International Workshop on Performance Evaluation of Tracking and Surveillance (PETS 2001), Kauai,Hawaii, USA (December 2001)

20. Lee, L., Romano, R., Stein, G.: Monitoring activities from multiple video streams: establishing a common coordinate frame. IEEE Transactions on Pattern Analysis and Machine Intelligence 22(8), 758–767 (2000)
21. Hue, C., Le Cadre, J.-P., Pérez, P.: Sequential monte carlo methods for multiple target tracking and data fusion. IEEE Transactions on Signal Processing 50(2), 309–325 (2002)
22. Pérez, P., Hue, C., Vermaak, J., Gangnet, M.: Color-based probabilistic tracking. In: Heyden, A., Sparr, G., Nielsen, M., Johansen, P. (eds.) ECCV 2002. LNCS, vol. 2350, pp. 661–675. Springer, Heidelberg (2002)
23. Gale, D., Shapley, L.S.: College admissions and the stability of marriage. American Mathematical Monthly 69, 9–14 (1962)
24. http://en.wikipedia.org/wiki/Stable_marriage_problem
25. Guraya, F.F.E., Bayle, P.-Y., Cheikh, F.A.: People tracking via a modified CAMSHIFT algorithm (2009)
26. Maskell, S., Gordon, N.: A tutorial on particle Filters for on-line nonlinear/non-Gaussian Bayesian tracking. IEEE Transactions on Signal Processing 50, 174–188 (2001)
27. Kitagawa, G.: Monte Carlo: Filter and smoother for non-Gaussian nonlinear state space models. Journal of Computational and Graphical Statistics 5(1), 1–25 (1996)
28. Chen, T., Lin, Y.-C., Fang, W.-H.: A Video-Based Human Fall Detection System For Smart Homes. YieJournal of the Chinese Institute of Engineers 33(5), 681–690 (2010)
29. Nummiaro, K., Koller-Meier, E., Gool, L.V., Gaal, L.V.: Object tracking with an adaptive color-based particle Filter (2002), http://www.koller-meier.ch/esther/dagm2002.pdf
30. Bouguet, J. Y.: Pyramidal implementation of the Lucas Kanade feature tracker: Description of the algorithm. Intel Corporation Microprocessor Research Labs (2002), http://robots.stanford.edu/cs223b04/algo_tracking.pdf
31. Blake, A., Isard, M.: The Condensation algorithm - conditional density propagation and applications to visual tracking. In: Advances in Neural Information Processing Systems (NIPS 1996), December 2-5, pp. 36–41. The MIT Press, Denver (1996)
32. Zhao, S., Zhao, J., Wang, Y., Fu, X.: Moving object detecting using gradient information, three-frame-differencing and connectivity testing. In: Sattar, A., Kang, B.-h. (eds.) AI 2006. LNCS (LNAI), vol. 4304, pp. 510–518. Springer, Heidelberg (2006)
33. Rudakova, V.: Probabilistic framework for multi-target tracking using multi-camera: applied to fall detection. Master thesis, Gjøvik University College (2010)

Automatic Adaptive Facial Feature Extraction Using CDF Analysis

Sushil Kumar Paul[1], Saida Bouakaz[2], and Mohammad Shorif Uddin[3]

[1] LIRIS Lab, SAARA Research Team, University Claude Bernard Lyon1, France
paulksushil@yahoo.com
[2] LIRIS Lab, SAARA Research Team, University Claude Bernard Lyon1, France
saida.bouakaz@liris.cnrs.fr
[3] Department of Computer Science and Engineering, Jahangirnagar University, Savar, Dhaka, Bangladesh
shorifuddin@gmail.com

Abstract. This paper proposes a novel adaptive algorithm to extract facial feature points automatically such as eyes corners, nostrils, nose tip, and mouth corners in frontal view faces, which is based on histogram representing CDF approach. At first, the method adopts the Viola-Jones face detector to detect the location of face and the four relevant regions such as right eye, left eye, nose, and mouth areas are cropped in a face image. Then the histogram of each cropped relevant region is computed and its CDF value is employed by varying different threshold values to create a new filtering image in an adaptive way. The connected component of interested area for each relevant filtering image is indicated our respective feature region. A simple linear search and a contour algorithm are applied to extract our desired corner points automatically. The method was tested on a large BioID face database and the experimental results have achieved average success rates of 95.56%.

Keywords: Connected component, corner point detection, face recognition, histogram representing cumulative distribution function (CDF), linear search.

1 Introduction

Face analysis such as facial features extraction and face recognition is one of the most flourishing areas in computer vision like identification, authentication, security, surveillance system, human-computer interaction, psychology and so on [1]. Facial features extraction is the initial stage for face recognition in the field of vision technology. The most significant feature points are eyes corners, nostrils, nose tip, and mouth corners. These are the key components for face recognition [2], [3]. Eyes are the most crucial facial feature for face analysis because of its inter-ocular distance, which is constant among people and unaffected by moustache or beard [3]. Eyes and mouth also convey facial expressions. Another valuable face feature points are nostrils because nose tip is the symmetry point of both right and left side face regions and nose indicates the head pose and it is not impacted by facial expressions [4]. Therefore, face recognition is distinctly influenced by these feature points.

H. Cherifi, J.M. Zain, and E. El-Qawasmeh (Eds.): DICTAP 2011, Part I, CCIS 166, pp. 327–338, 2011.

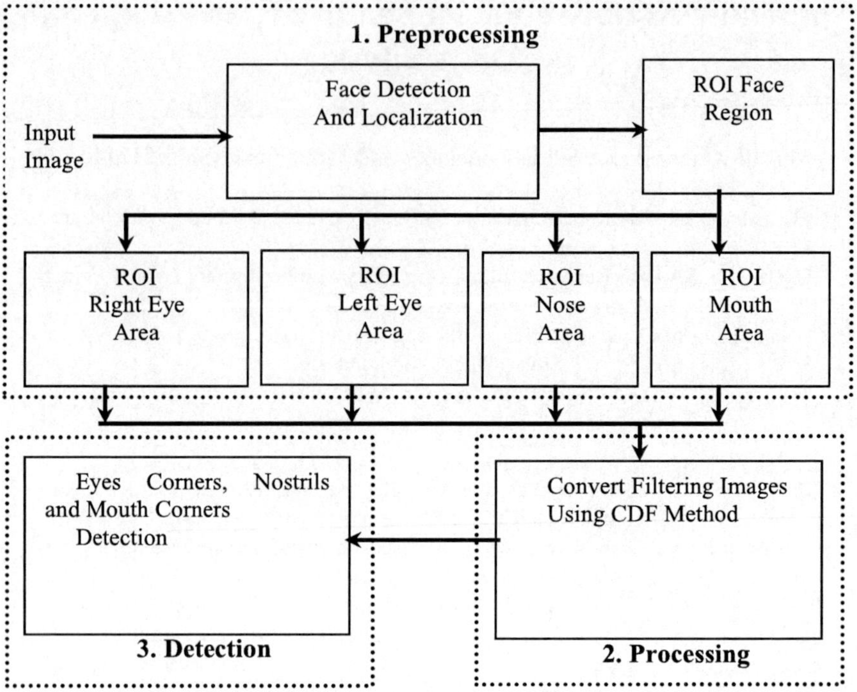

Fig. 1. Block diagram of proposed feature extraction algorithm

Currently, Active Shape Model (ASM) and Active Appearance Model (AAM) are extensively used for face alignment and tracking [5]. Facial feature extraction methods could be divided in two categories: texture-based and shape-based methods. Texture-based methods take local texture e.g. pixel values around a given specific feature point instead of concerning all facial feature points as a shape (shape-based methods). Some texture-based facial feature extraction algorithms are: hierarchical 2-level wavelet networks for facial feature localization [6], facial point detection using log Gabor wavelet networks by employing geometry cross-ratios relationships[7], neural-network-based eye-feature detector by locating micro-features instead of entire eyes[8]. Some shape-based facial feature extraction algorithms including AAM, based on face detectors are: view-based active wavelet network [9], view-based direct appearance models [10]. The combination of texture- and shape-based algorithms are: elastic bunch graph matching [11], AdaBoost with Shape Constrains [12], 3D Shape Constraint using Probabilistic-like Output [13]. Wiskott et al. [11] represented faces by a rectangular graph which is based on Gabor wavelet transform and each node labelled with a set of complex Gabor wavelet coefficients. Cristinacce and Cootes [12] used the Haar features based AdaBoost classifier combined with the statistical shape model. In both ASM and AAM, a model is built for predefined points by using the test images and then an iterative scheme is applied to this model in detecting feature points. Most of the above mentioned algorithms are not entirely reliable due to variation in pose, illumination, facial expression, and lighting condition and high computational complexity. So, it is indispensable to develop robust, automatic, and accurate facial feature point localization algorithms, which are capable in coping different imaging conditions.

In this paper, we propose a robust adaptive algorithm based on histogram representing cumulative distribution function (CDF) scheme that extracts the facial feature points in a fast as well as accurate way under varying illuminations, expressions and lighting conditions. Figure 1 shows the block diagram of our proposed algorithm that includes preprocessing, main processing and detection blocks. The preprocessing block detects the face and crops the face, right eye, left eye, nose, and mouth areas. The processing block is responsible for four ROIs such as right eye, left eye, nose, and mouth areas and then converts into binary images. The detection block detects the corner points of four ROIs. The remainder of the paper is organized as follows. Section 2 describes the region of interest (ROI) detection. In section 3, we present the mathematical description of CDF method, which form the basis for our approach, and then we explain the facial feature point detection with the algorithmic details. Section 4 shows the experimental results of our facial feature extraction system. Finally we conclude the paper along with highlighting future work directions in section 5.

2 Region of Interest Detection

A rectangular portion of an image to perform some other operation and also to reduce the computational cost for further processing is known as region of interest (ROI). By applying the Viola-Jones face detector algorithm, the detected face region is cropped first then we divide the face area vertically into upper, middle and lower parts [14].

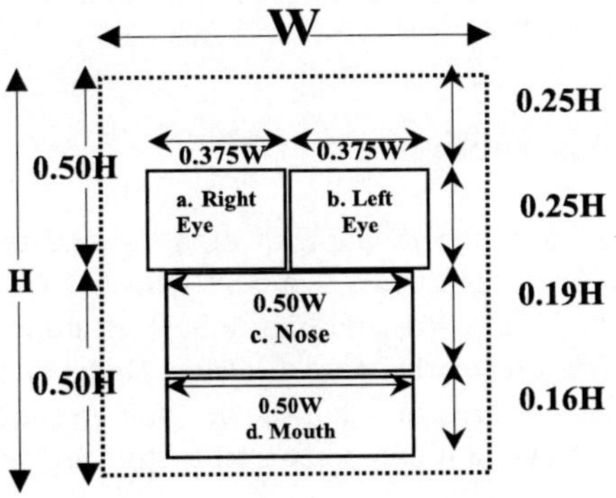

Fig. 2. Location and size of four ROIs of face image such as (a.) Right Eye (Size:0.375W×0.25H, (b.) Left Eye (Size:0.375W×0.25H,(c.) Nose (Size: 0.50W×0.19H), and (d.) Mouth (Size: 0.50W×0.16H) where, W=Image Width and H=Image Height.

From the human frontal face structure concept, eyes, nose, and mouth areas are situated in upper, middle, and lower portions of the face image, respectively. Again, the upper portion is partitioned horizontally into left and right segments for isolating right and left eyes, respectively.

Finally, the smallest ROI regions are segmented for right and left eyes, nose, and mouth in order to increase the detection rate. Figure 1, Figure 2, and Figure 3(d) are shown the block diagram of our proposed algorithm, location and size of four ROIs and cropped images, respectively.

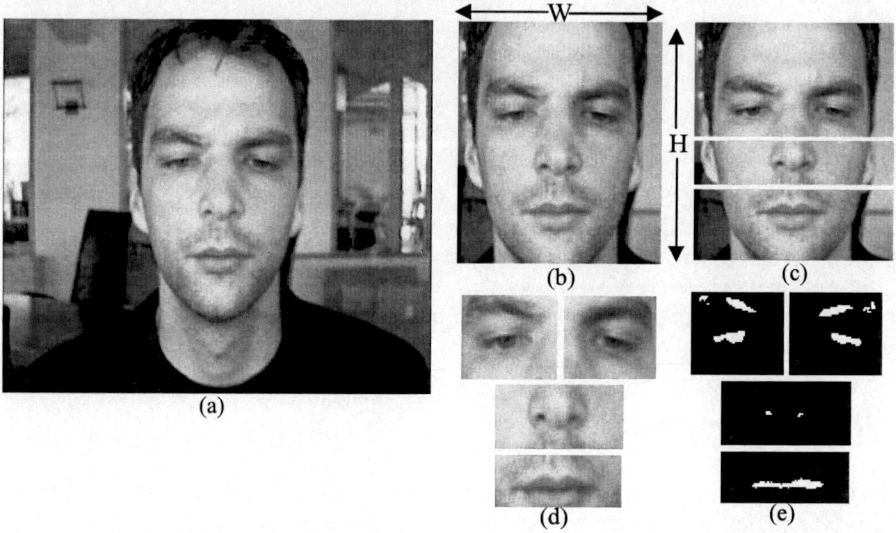

Fig. 3. Procedure of our proposed algorithm: (a) Input image, (b) Detected and cropped the face, (c) Face is divided into three vertical parts, which are indicated eyes, nose and mouth areas, (d) Four ROIs show the exact right and left eyes, nose and mouth regions, (e) Applying CDF method, all of the four ROIs are converted into new filtering images.

3 Facial Features Extraction

Our proposed method exhibits the location of eight crucial feature points including four corner points for right and left eyes, two points for nostrils and two corner points for mouth as shown in the Figure 3(d) and Figure 3(e). Feature points are extracted by an adaptive approach. To create the new filtering (binary) images, the following mathematical concepts are applied on each of the four original cropped (ROIs) gray scale images such as right eye, left eye, nose and mouth regions (see Figure 3(d) and Figure 3(e))[16],[17].

$$P_{I(x,y)}(v) = P(I(x,y)=v) = \frac{n_v}{N} \qquad \text{where, } 0 \le v \le 255 \tag{1}$$

$$CDF_{I(x,y)}(v) = \sum_{i=0}^{V} P_{I(x,y)}(i) \tag{2}$$

$$I_{FI}(x,y) = \begin{cases} 255 & \text{when} \quad CDF(I(x,y)) \le Th \\ 0 & \text{otherwise} \end{cases} \tag{3}$$

Where, I(x,y) is denoted by each of the four original cropped gray scale images, $P_{I(x,y)}(v)$ is the histogram representing probability of an occurrence of a pixel of gray level v, n_v is the number of pixels and N(width×height) is the total number of pixels, and $CDF_{I(x,y)}(v)$ is the histogram representing cumulative distribution function(CDF) up to the gray level v for an image I(x,y)[16],[17], where $0 \leq v \leq 255$. The CDF (v) is measured by summing up the all histogram values from gray level 0 to v. The new filtering image, $I_{FI}(x,y)$ is achieved when CDF value is not exceeded the threshold value Th and the $I_{FI}(x, y)$ image only contains the white pixels of our specific desired connected component area. Figure 3(e) is shown the respective white pixel's connected component of all filtering images for right eye, left eye, nose, and mouth region. Two different groups of threshold values are used for our evaluation purpose. One for eyes and mouth regions ($0.01 \leq Th \leq 0.10$) and other for nose region ($0.001 \leq Th \leq 0.010$) because nostrils contain minimum numbers of low intensity pixels of original image compare to eyes and mouth region (see Figure 4) [4].

3.1 Eye and Mouth Corner Points Detection

A simple linear search concept is applied on right eye, left eye, and mouth filtering images to detect the first white pixel locations as the candidate points: (1) starting from bottom-left position for right corner points and (2) starting from bottom-right position for left corner points to search upward direction. The located first white pixel's positions are the candidate corner points.

3.2 Nostrils and Nose Tip Detection

A contour algorithm, using connected component, is applied on nose filtering image to select the last (right nostril) and the previous last (left nostril) contours from bottom to upward direction. Then the last and the previous last contour's element locations are sorted as an ascending order according to horizontal direction(x-value). The locations of the last element (right nostril point) of the last contour and the first element (left nostril point) of the previous the last contour are the candidate nostrils. Nose tip is computed as the mid point between nostrils because the nose tip conveys the highest gray scale value so that nose filtering image shows insufficient information about it(see the middle filtering image of Figure 3(e))[6], [18].

All of the detected eight corner points are indicated as 'black plus symbols', and only calculated nose tip is indicated as 'black solid circle' as shown in Figure 5.

3.3 Proposed Algorithm

The proposed algorithm is organized by three sections, which are included "preprocessing", "processing", and "detection" sections (see Figure 1). The preprocessing section detects the face and its location and then crops the face, right and left eyes, nose, and mouth regions in an image. We assume that as a frontal face image, the eyes, nose, and mouth are located in upper half, middle and lower parts, respectively, in an image (see Figure 2 and Figure 3). In the processing section, the cropped images i.e. four ROIs such as right eye, left eye, nose, and mouth are converted into filtering images by applying CDF method (using equations (1),(2), & (3)) [16],[17]. Applying simple linear search and contour concepts on these filtering images, the detection section finds out the all facial feature points such as right and left eye corners, nostrils, and mouth corners. The step by step procedures of our proposed algorithm are described as follows.

Preprocessing Section

1. Input: $I_{whole\text{-}face\text{-}window}(x,y)$ =Frontal face gray scale image having head and shoulder (whole face window)(see Figure 3(a)).
2. Detect and localize the face by applying the OpenCV face detection algorithm [19].
3. Detect the regions of interest (ROI) for face, right and left eyes, nose, and mouth by applying the OpenCV ROI library functions [19] and then we build the following new images.

   (a) $I_{face}(x,y)$ =New image having only face area and its size is W×H(see Figure 2 and Figure 3(b)) Where, W=image width, H=image height.

   (b) $I_{eye\text{-}right}(x,y)$ =New image having only right eye area and its size is 0.375W×0.25H(see Figure 2 and Figure 3(d)).

   (c) $I_{eye\text{-}left}(x,y)$ =New image having only left eye area and its size is 0.375W×0.25H(see Figure 2 and Figure 3(d)).

   (d) $I_{nose}(x,y)$ =New image having only nose area and its size is 0.50W×0.19H(see Figure 2 and Figure 3(d)).

   (e) $I_{mouth}(x,y)$ =New image having only mouth area and its size is 0.50W×0.16H(see Figure 2 and Figure 3(d)).

Processing Section

4. Apply CDF method(using equations (1),(2), & (3)) [16],[17] on the above four ROIs such as $I_{eye\text{-}right}(x,y)$, $I_{eye\text{-}left}(x,y)$, $I_{nose}(x,y)$, and $I_{mouth}(x,y)$ images(see Figure 3(d)) and convert it into new filtering(binary) images such as $I_{FI\_eye\text{-}right}(x,y)$, $I_{FI\_eye\text{-}left}(x,y)$, $I_{FI\_nose}(x,y)$, and $I_{FI\_mouth}(x,y)$ for different threshold values(see Figure 3(e)).

Detection Section

5. (a) A simple linear search concept is applied on filtering images such as $I_{FI\_eye\text{-}right}(x,y)$, $I_{FI\_eye\text{-}left}(x,y)$, and $I_{FI\_mouth}(x,y)$ for eyes and mouth corner points, then find out the first white pixel location as bottom-up approach. To locate for all corner points :(1) starting searches from bottom-left position for right corner points and (2) starting searches from bottom-right position for left corner points.

   (b) Apply the OpenCV contour library function on filtering image, $I_{FI\_nose}(x,y)$ for nostrils; then consider the locations of the last(right nostril point) and the first (left nostril point) elements for the last and the previous last contours as a bottom-up approach where, the contour's element locations are sorted horizontally (x-direction) as an ascending order[19].

(c) Calculate a mid point between nostrils for nose tip.

6. At last, the detected points are transferred to the $I_{face}(x,y)$ image (see Figure 3(b) and Figure 5).

4 Experimental Results

4.1 Face Database

The work described in this paper is used head-shoulder BioID face database [15].The dataset with the frontal view of a face of one out of 23 different test persons consists of 1521 gray level images having properties of different illumination, face area, complex background with a resolution of 384×286 pixel. During evaluation, some images are omitted due to :(1) detecting false region (not face) by Viola-Jones face detector [14] and (2) person with large size eye glasses and highly dense moustache or beard as a complex background property of an image.

4.2 Results

The proposed algorithm was primarily developed and tested on Code::Blocks the open source, cross-platform combine with c++ language, and GNU GCC compiler. Some OpenCV library functions were used for face detection and localization, cropping and also connected component (contour algorithm) purpose [19]. During evaluation, two different groups of threshold values were used for our CDF analysis (using equations (1), (2), & (3)) [16], [17]. One is $0.01 \leq Th \leq 0.10$ for locating eyes and mouth corner points and other is $0.001 \leq Th \leq 0.010$ for locating nostrils. Figure 4 shows the detection rate of eight corner points by using different threshold values. Figure 4(a) shows single nostril, both nostrils and overall detection rate for nostrils and Figure 4(b) shows single corner, both corners and overall detection rate for right eye, left eye, and mouth corner points. The combination of single corner and both corners detection rate is considered as the overall detection rate. Threshold values

Table 1. Table of feature points detection rate

Features	Detection Rate (%) for both Points/ Corners	Detection Rate (%) for single Point/ Corner	Overall Detection Rate (%)	Threshold Value for CDF
Right Eye	84.82	13.10	97.92	0.070
Left Eye	80.46	17.56	98.02	0.060
Nostrils	75.00	10.42	89.58	0.004
Mouth	86.71	10.02	96.73	0.060
Average	81.75	13.82	95.56	-

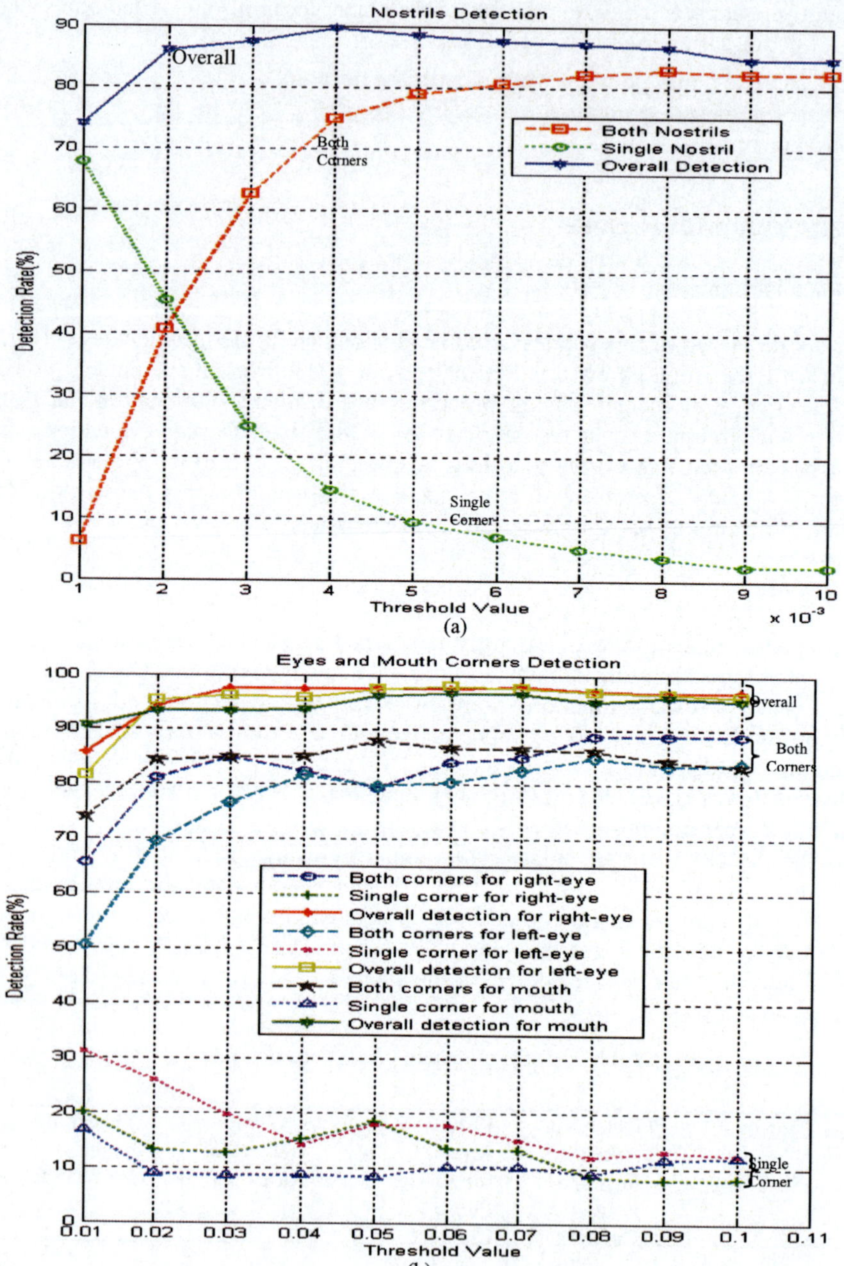

(b)

Fig. 4. Detection Rate using different threshold values of CDF method on BioID face database: (a) Nostrils Detection Curves (Single, Both, Overall), (b) Eyes and Mouth Corners Detection Curves (Single, Both, Overall)

Table 2. Comparisons with 2-level GWN [6] and GFBBC [2]

Algorithms	Average Detection rate (%)
2-level GWN	92.87
GFBBC	93.00
Ours	95.56

0.070, 0.060, 0.004, and 0.060 produce the detection rates 97.92%, 98.02%, 89.58%, and 96.73% for right-eye corners, left-eye corners, nostrils, and mouth corners, respectively. Table 1 indicates the results of our facial feature extraction algorithm, where the overall average detection rate is 95.56%. We compared our algorithm with R.S. Feris, et al. [6] and D. Vukadinovic, M. Pantic [2]. The comparison results are shown in table 2. Some of the detection results are shown in the Figure 5.

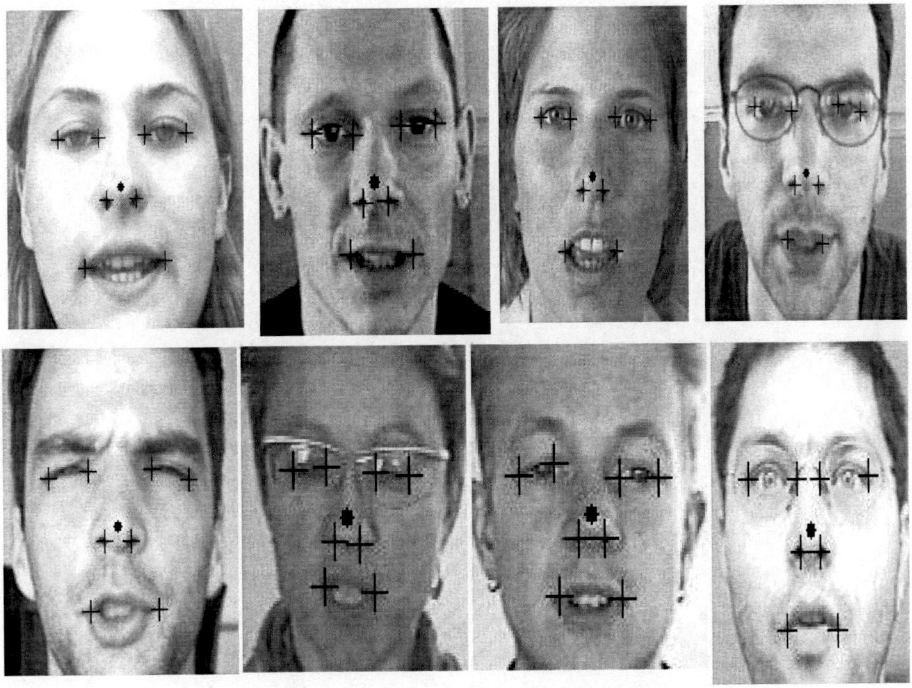

Fig. 5. Result of detected feature points:(a) Some true detection, (b) Some single nostril detection and (c) Some false detection

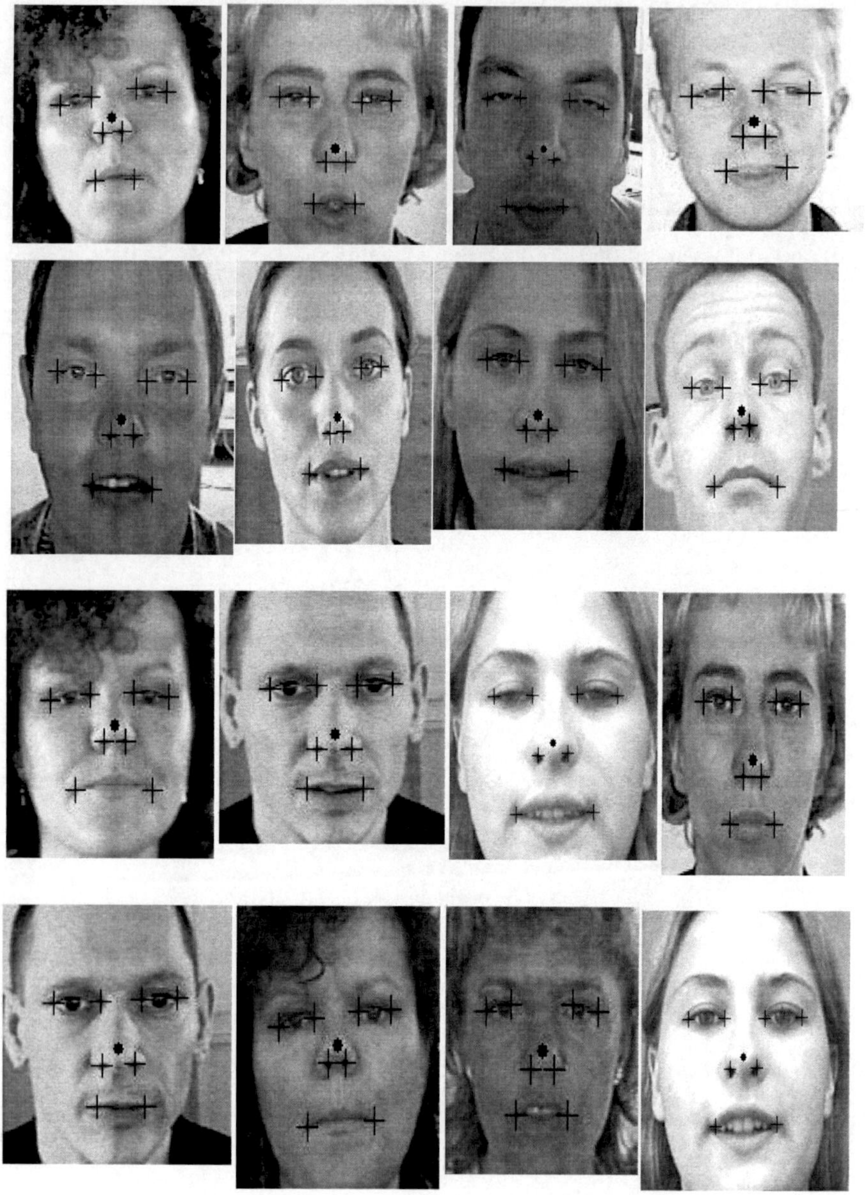

(a)

Fig. 5. (*Continued*)

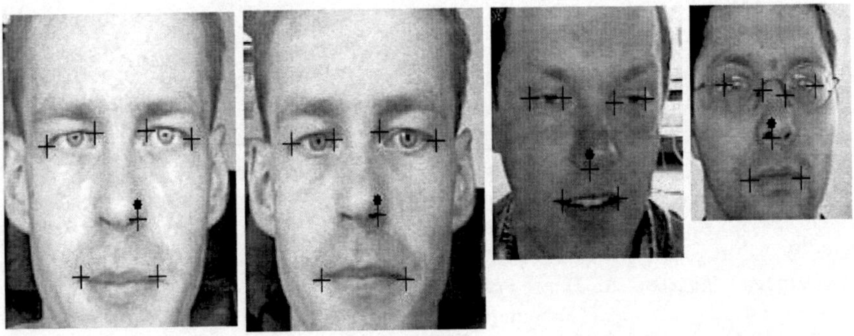

(b)

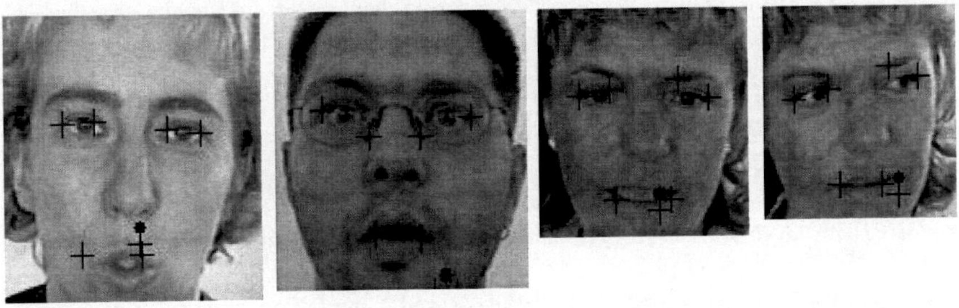

(c)

Fig. 5. *(Continued)*

5 Conclusion and Future Work

In this paper, we have shown how salient facial features are extracted based on histogram representing CDF method in an adaptive manner combined with face detector, simple linear search, and also connected component concepts i.e. contour algorithm in various expression and illumination conditions in an image. Image segments are converted into filtering images with the help of CDF approach by varying different threshold values instead of applying morphological operations. Our algorithm was assessed on free accessible BioID gray scale frontal face database. The experimental results confirmed the higher detection rate as compare to other well known facial feature extraction algorithms.

Future work will concentrate to improve the detection rate of both corner points instead of single corner point, to find the other prominent facial features such as eyebrows corners, eyeballs, upper and lower lips of mouth and face recognition, as well.

Acknowledgment

This research has been supported by the EU Erasmus Mundus Project-eLINK (east-west Link for Innovation, Networking and Knowledge exchange) under External Cooperation Window-Asia Regional Call (EM ECW-ref. 149674-EM-1-2008-1-UK-ERAMUNDUS).

References

1. Zhao, W., Chellappa, R., Phillips, P.J., Rosenfeld, A.: Face Recognition: A Literature Survey. ACM Computing Surveys 35(4) (December 2003)
2. Vukadinovic, D., Pantic, M.: Fully Automatic Facial Feature Point Detection Using Gabor Feature Based Boosted Classifiers. In: IEEE International Conference on Systems, Man and Cybernetics Waikoloa, Hawaii, October 10-12 (2005)
3. http://eprints.um.edu.my/877/1/GS10-4.pdf
4. Chew, W.J., Seng, K.P., Ang, L.-M.: Nose Tip Detection on a Three-Dimensional Face Range Image Invariant to Head Pose. In: Proceedings of The International Multi Conference of Engineers and Computer Scientists, Hong Kong, March 18-20, vol. I (2009)
5. Matthews, I., Baker, S.: Active Appearance Models Revisited. Int'l Journal Computer Vision 60(2), 135–164 (2004)
6. Feris, R.S., et al.: Hierarchical Wavelet Networks for Facial Feature Localization. In: Proc. IEEE Int'l Conf. Face and Gesture Recognition, pp. 118–123 (2002)
7. Holden, E., Owens, R.: Automatic Facial Point Detection. In: Proc. The 5th Asian Conf. on Computer Vision, Melbourne, Australia, January 23-25 (2002)
8. Reinders, M.J.T., et al.: Locating Facial Features in Image Sequences using Neural Networks. In: Proc. IEEE Int'l Conf. Face and Gesture Recognition, pp. 230–235 (1996)
9. Hu, C., et al.: Real-time view-based face alignment using active wavelet networks. In: Proc. IEEE Int'l Workshop Analysis and Modeling of Faces and Gestures, pp. 215–221 (2003)
10. Yan, S., et al.: Face Alignment using View-Based Direct Appearance Models. Int'l J. Imaging Systems and Technology 13(1), 106–112 (2003)
11. Wiskott, L., et al.: Face Recognition by Elastic Bunch Graph. Matching. IEEE Trans. Pattern Analysis and Machine Intelligence 19(7), 775–779 (1979)
12. Cristinacce, D., Cootes, T.: Facial Feature Detection Using AdaBoost with Shape Constrains. In: British Machine Vision Conference (2003)
13. Chen, L., et al.: 3D Shape Constraint for Facial Feature Localization using Probabilistic-like Output. In: Proc. IEEE Int'l Workshop Analysis and Modeling of Faces and Gestures, pp. 302–307 (2004)
14. Viola, P., Jones, M.J.: Robust Real-time Object Detection. International Journal of Computer Vision 57(2), 137–154 (2004)
15. BioID Face Database, http://www.bioid.com/downloads/facedb/index.php
16. Kim, J.-Y., Kim, L.-S., Hwang, S.-H.: An Advanced Contrast Enhancement Using Partially Overlapped Sub-Block Histogram. IEEE Transactions On Circuits And Systems For Video Technology 11(4) (2001)
17. Asadifard, M., Shanbezadeh, J.: Automatic Adaptive Center of Pupil Detection Using Face Detection and CDF Analysis. In: Proceedings of The International Multi Conference of Engineers and Computer Scientists, Hong Kong, March 17-19, pp. 130–133 (2010)
18. Jahanbin, S., et al.: Automated Facial Feature Detection from Portrait and Range Images. In: IEEE Southwest Symposium on Image Analysis and Interpretation, March 24-26 (2008)
19. http://sourceforge.net/projects/opencvlibrary/files/opencv-win/2.0/OpenCV-2.0.0a-win32.exe/download

Digital Characters Machine

Jaume Duran Castells and Sergi Villagrasa Falip

Universitat de Barcelona, Pg. de la Vall D'Hebron, 171,
08035, Barcelona, Spain
jaumeduran@ub.edu
La Salle - Universitat Ramon Llull, Quatre Camins, 2,
08022, Barcelona, Spain
sergiv@salle.url.edu

Abstract. In this paper, we will focus on the study of digital characters and existing technologies of creation. The type of character is increasing and in the future, they may assume many main roles. Digital characters must overcome issues, as Uncanny Valley to ensure the viewer does not reject them because of their low credibility. This statement makes us challenge the need to work with metrics to measure the degree of plausibility of a character.

Keywords: Visualization, Characters, Digital Cinema, Uncanny Valley.

1 Introduction

The film industry has been the driving force that has guided the biggest advances in the field of Computer Graphics (CG). Now we have faster computers to make possible what was impossible earlier due to computational cost of calculation. This increment of performance is followed by an increase in detail and more simulation to achieve perfection in the digital synthesis. But, at some moment, the increase of the computer's performance needs to converge with the ability to create a perfect and completely believable CG character.

To be able to see these vicissitudes in a film, several things are important: a minimal level of computer's performance from 1 Teraflops, real shaders and a perfect simulation of the nature and behavior of light. With all of this, we can create an avatar, but this will still from the emotional response of a human to establish a familiarity relation. The empathy of the spectator to the avatar has to be perfect so as not to provoke rejection (Uncanny Valley, Mori, 1970) [1].

For this research, we investigated the film and technological evolution to conclude that when we will be able to recreate virtual humans without being recognizable, avatars of the actors are made with ones and zeros.

2 CG Characters

We use the term "Flop" (transactions per second capable of making a processor) to measure computing power.

H. Cherifi, J.M. Zain, and E. El-Qawasmeh (Eds.): DICTAP 2011, Part I, CCIS 166, pp. 339–344, 2011.

Another important factor is: the correlation between the number of transistors with a processor and their computational power. In this sense, Moore's Law [2] can indicate a vision of the future growth of computing power. Moore's Law as applied to computing states that approximately every 18 months, the number of transistors doubles that can include an integrated circuit. It should be noted that the power increase is not only based on the number of transistors. A machine with an Exaflop is near the capacity of processing "raw" estimate of the human brain.

To create *The Last Starfighter* (Nick Castle, 1984) a Cray supercomputer called X-MP was used, with a cost of $15 million at that time (1984-1985). Only Phong Shading and not Textures were used to generate the render.

Using a modern computer, we tried to emulate the production costs of *Starfighter*: with a 3 Ghz Quad Pentium Extreme and a polygonal model of the Gunstar ship, the render with a resolution of 2K takes less than a second to generate one image. Thus, we could generate the entire film in one day.

With the same assumption, and following Moore's law, we could conclude that the power of a Cray supercomputer of today is the same as a regular PC in the next 25 years. In fact, according to that law, the ability to implement transistors doubles every 6 months. Progress is not linear but exponential. We can suppose therefore, that in few years we will have the power of supercomputers inside common PCs, and with them, we may generate real characters in a short time [3, 4, 5].

In fact, this technology already exists: the LightStage, a mechanism to capture CG realistic 3D models of any person has already been implemented in some films, for example, from *Spider-Man 2* (Sam Raimi, 2004) or *Spider-Man 3* (Sam Raimi, 2007) to *Avatar* (James Cameron, 2010).

3 The Voight-Kampff Machine

The Voight-Kampff is used primarily by Blade Runners (*Blade Runner*, Ridley Scott, 1982) to determine if a suspect is truly human by measuring the degree of his empathic response through carefully worded questions and statements (Fig. 1).

The future is just a round the corner and the phenomenon of virtual actors will become a reality very soon, but some problems are already known. There is a need for good communication between the creator of these virtual actors and the production team, operation rights, and marketing of these films, where these “actors” are integrated.

This trend leads to the possibility that often the quality level required by the producer does not conform to the budget agreed with the company. To address this situation, we propose a scoring system that measures how far the virtual actor is to the Uncanny Valley and how close to the human is it. For instance, a scale from 0 to 10, where 0 to 5 falls into de Uncanny Valley means that the films have a poor level of virtual characters and may affect the audience and critics, and of course, the box office profits. Or the virtual actors may score 10, which it means that the virtual actors are perfect and indistinguishable from a real human (Fig. 2).

Our Voight-Kampff, as a clear reference to the Blade Runner machine, could do this measurement but only from the Valley area forward. We will not have to score the empathy. We will measure human likeness to obtain a score that tell us instantly if the virtual actor falls into the Uncanny Valley or what degree of likeness it can have with the audience.

This measure would be based in two levels: Scoring, the visual aspect, and is the realism of the skin, eyes, hair, and so on; and the animation itself, the subtle movement of the eyes, a bulge of the face skin, the breathing, the natural movement of the body, and so on. We would score of all aspects separately, but with an averaged final value.

Fig. 1. The Voight-Kampff (*Blade Runner*, Ridley Scott, 1982)

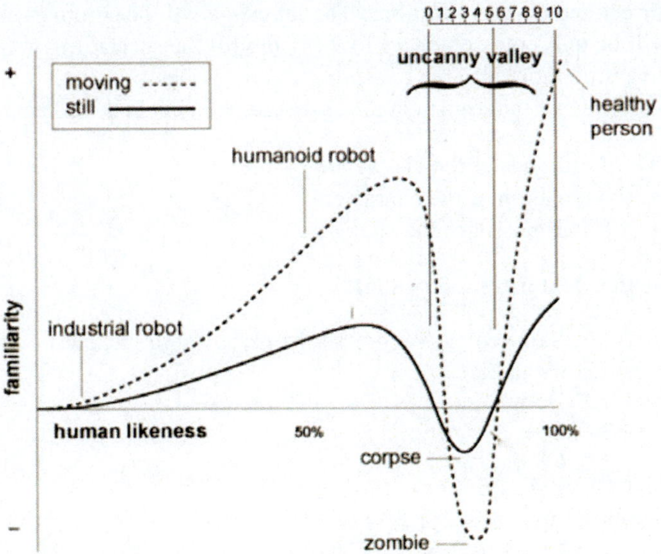

Fig. 2. Uncanny Valley with the scoring method

To make the metric proposed we know others types of measurements used in psychology and neuropsychology for the assessment of user emotions that may be useful in our research.

For instance, it is very difficult to define the meaning of emotion, but there is a consensus that emotions can differ and can be measured [6]. One of the most important studies and replicated in numerous researches to ensure its validity within diverse cultural frameworks is the IAPS (International Affective Picture System [7]). In this system, the emotions are grouped into three variables: "Valence" or level of happiness; "Activation" or level of excitement (also called Arousal); and "Dominance" or level of control sensation. To measure these three levels, the system uses the SAM (Self-Assessment Manikin [8]), a pictorial scale where the user scores between a maximum (9) and a minimum (1) value, the feeling that an image, video, sound, music, is good or not. Nowadays, in communication and multimedia frameworks, we find researches, which are using this measurement system, with most of them, focused on evaluating both the user's behavior in front of some information, such as the usability or accessibility of the interfaces [9, 10].

In other study, we try other questions referring to the visual animation aspects.

4 A Method for a Digital Character Machine

The method that we're working is based on several questions about a few issues like aesthetics and animation of the character.

Each issue split apart in more branches and more detailed questions.

All of these issues will be a weighted and will result in a clear final number that tell us how close are the character of uncanny valley, or if the character are into de uncanny valley or even if the character overpass the uncanny valley.

Working for the machine, each concept will be detailed with a simple question test with several direct and simple questions. The language will be common language and the answers will be only four sentences for easy job for the spectator.

Deep inside a little more into the questions and the issues.

First, we want to score the realism of the character. We split in three items for do this:

- Aesthetics of the character.
- Animation of the character.
- Environment of the character.

1. Aesthetics (texturing and model):

    1.1. Skin (color, brightness, wrinkles, fat tissue, etc.).
    1.2. Head hair.
    1.3. Body hair.
    1.4. Eyes.
    1.5. Cloth.

2. Animation:

    2.1. Facial.
        2.1.1. Muscles behind the skin.

2.1.2. Muscles around the eyes (orbicularis oculi).
2.1.3. Muscles around the mouth (orbicularis oris).
2.1.4. Expression of the eyes.
2.2. Chest.
2.3. Head.
2.4. Arms.
2.5. Legs.
2.6. Walking.
2.7. Running.
2.8. Standing.

3. Environment:

3.1. Lighting over the character.
3.2. HRDI.

The questions linked to each issue must be direct and easy.

· Instance I.

Look the character "x" in this video. Look his face and the expression of the eyes. Is credible his expression? Do you believe that is realistic?

With this question we score from one to four the degree of realism of the character. This score will weighted with other questions of the section of animation and the face. Scoring the eyes has more weight that scoring the mouth for instance because in the face, framed on the eyes, is the major focus for the spectator and the base of a credible character.

· Instance II.

Scoring the aesthetics, the model of the character.

Look the character "x". Pay attention of his skin. The brightness, is the skin too dry? Look the wrinkles, creases and the hair… How good is the skin of this character?

Answers:

A. Very artificial. No detail.
B. Good skin look but no detail like wrinkles.
C. Good skin. Normal.
D. Great skin. High detail.

And so on progressively for all groups and subgroups that we want to score.

When we have all the scoring for the entire question, we weight each question depending of its importance for realism of the character. This final number tells us how close or how good is the character overall.

5 Conclusions

We are in working progress making all the questions for the test and the weighting for each issue.

When we have this questions and the scoring, making a test for any film with a CG character we can detect how good is a CG character and how close is the character of uncanny valley and may provoque de rejection of the spectator.

Also we can detect if one character is real person or CG making more complex and key questions.

We conclude that our approach is just the first step towards building a complete machine for scoring the human likeness and advertising to fall in Uncanny Valley and the value of level of perfection of the virtual actor.

In *Blade Runner*, the Voight-Kampff machine measures bodily functions, such as respiration, "blush response", heart rate, and eye movement, in response to emotionally provocative questions. In our machine, maybe some functions could be measured, such as eye movement and respiration, for detecting a virtual actor.

In future work, we plant to implement the machine (the test) that measures human likeness and will finally pass the test to the audience. As said Holden (Morgan Paull) to Leon (Brion James) in the film, "It's a test, designed to provoke an emotional response… Shall we continue?".

References

1. Mori, M.: Bukimi no Tani. In: Macdorman, K.F., Minato, T. (eds.) The Uncanny Valley, vol. 7 (4), Energy, USA (2005)
2. Moore, G.E.: Cramming More Components on To Integrated Circuits, vol. 38(8). Electronics, USA (1965)
3. Duran, J.: Guía para ver y analizar Toy Story (1995) John Lasseter. Nau llibres - Octaedro, Valencia - Barcelona (2008)
4. Villagrasa, S., Duran, J.: La credibilidad de las imágenes generadas por ordenador en la comunicación mediada. In: II Congreso Internacional de la Asociación Española de Investigación de la Comunicación, Malaga, Spain, February 3-5 (2010)
5. Villagrasa, S., Duran, J., Fonseca, D.: The Motion Capture and its Contribution in the Facial Animation. In: V International Conference on Social and Organizational Informatics and Cybernetics, Orlando, Florida, USA, July 10-13 (2009)
6. Boehner, K., Depaula, R., Dourish, P., Sengers, P.: How emotion is made and measured. International Journal Human Computer Studies 65(4), 275–291 (2007)
7. Lang, P.J., Bradley, M.M., Cuthbert, B.N.: International affective picture system: affective ratings of pictures and instruction manual. University of Florida, NIME. University of Florida, Gainesville, USA (2005)
8. Bradley, M.M.: Measuring emotion: the self-assessment manikin and the semantic differential. Journal of Behavior Therapy and Experimental Psychiatry, 46–59 (1994)
9. Fonseca, D., et al.: An image-centred search and indexation system based in user's data and perceived emotion. In: ACM MM 2008, International Workshop on HCC, Vancouver, Canada, pp. 27–34 (2008)
10. Fonseca, D., et al.: User's experience in the visualization of architectural images in different environments. In: IV International Multiconference on Society, Cybernetics and Informatics, Orlando, Florida, USA, vol. 2, pp. 18–22 (2010)

CREA: Defining Future Multiplatform Interaction on TV Shows through a User Experience Study

Marc Pifarré, Eva Villegas, and David Fonseca

GTM-Grup de Recerca en Tecnologies Mèdia LA SALLE - UNIVERSITAT RAMON LLULL, Barcelona, Spain
{mpifarre,evillegas,fonsi}@salle.url.edu

Abstract. Television programs use to involve a passive role by the viewer. The aim of the project described in this article is about changing the roll of the viewer to become a participant. To achieve this goal it is necessary to define a type of application that does not yet exist. The way to get information on how to create a positive user experience of an interactive television game show concept has been to involve users on the product concept definition phase.Applying user experience exploration techniques centered on users needs and desires the main factors that would affect the user in case of developing this concept have been obtained. Using a qualitative strategic design method is possible to achieve well-defined and subtle information regarding the motivations and desirable game mechanics for the future users.

Keywords: User experience, Usability, User Involvement, Psychology, Co-Reflection, Television.

1 Introduction

Television Game Shows are one of the more traditional genres of audiovisual entertainment. The classical questions and answers contest still working today, and still motivating the viewers, either from a television studio or from a couch in their house.

CREA project proposes what should be the next evolutionary step for television game shows. There have been attempts to induce the interaction of the viewers from home using through mobile phone computer, but the response from users has not been sufficiently representative as to change the concept of program. The key to define this change lies not only in the improvement of new technologies but in the motivation of users to use them. The focus of this project focuses on how to motivate users to participate in televised contests by using new technologies. Starting from this premise a study focused on user's needs and desires has been conducted to define a concept of interaction in televised game shows that really encourages the viewer to become involved.

The CREA project was aimed at defining requirements regarding a non existing product. The hiring company asked the Userlab team for a study about how an interactive quiz television show should be. The goal was de definition of a game in

H. Cherifi, J.M. Zain, and E. El-Qawasmeh (Eds.): DICTAP 2011, Part I, CCIS 166, pp. 345–354, 2011.

which the user would participate remotely through several multimedia devices, a hybrid between conventional television quiz show and a quiz videogame.

To define a compelling game play mechanics and a user's motivating interaction, a qualitative baseline study was conducted to gather the factors that would lead users to a satisfactory experience.

1.1 Methodological Design

The challenge on this study was mainly methodological. Due to the lack of a prototype on which apply the tests was difficult to design a test taken into account most of existing usability techniques. The context of the study was well defined then was not appropriate to apply techniques only based on ethnographic or participant observation, as it was necessary to generate information from a non-natural scenario.

The final methodological design consists in combining various qualitative techniques of user experience and creates an "ad hoc" technique in order to cover the needs raised on this project.

In order to define the premises to be implemented on the first prototype the qualitative study was divided in two parts:

- Exploration: The exploration phase aims to define the strengths and weaknesses about the current interaction on media platforms regarding quiz games.
- Immersion: The immersion phase is designed to extract a concept definition about a multi-platform interaction game during TV game show broadcasting.

To meet the objectives of both parts of the study specific methods of exploration and definition of user experience were applied to each phase.

1.2 Sample

The sample of users for the first phase of the project was divided in two profiles:

- Expert users: an expert user is someone familiar with participating in televised game shows.
- Medium users: is the kind of user that has not a clear willingness to participate fiscally in a televised game show.

Both user profiles made the same test separately. The number of users was 11 on the expert users group and 10 on the medium users group.

2 Exploration Phase

To carry out this phase of the test technique, it has been applied focus BLA:

Bipolar Laddering (BLA) method is defined as a psychological exploration technique, which points out the key factors of the user experience with a concrete product or service. This system allows knowing which concrete characteristics of the product cause users' frustration, confidence or gratitude (between many others). BLA method works on positive and negative poles to define the strengths and weaknesses of the product. Once the element is obtained the laddering technique is going to be applied to define the user experience relevant details. The object of a laddering interview is to uncover how product attributes, usage consequences, and personal values are linked in a person's mind. The characteristics obtained through laddering application will define what specific factors make consider an element as strength or as a weakness. Once the element is been defined, the interviewer ask to the user for a solution of the problem in the case of negative elements or an improvement in the case of positive elements.

2.1 BLA Performing

BLA performing consists in three steps:

1. Elicitation of the elements: The test starts from a blank template for the positive elements (strengths) and another exactly the same for the negative elements (weaknesses). The interviewer will ask the users to mention what aspects of the product they like best or help them in their goals or usual tasks. The elements mentioned need to be summarized in one word or short sentence.
2. Marking of elements: Once the list of positive and negative elements is done, the interviewer will ask the user to score each one from 1 (lowest possible level of satisfaction) to 10 (maximum level of satisfaction).
3. Elements definition: Once the elements have been assessed, the qualitative phase starts. The interviewer reads out the elements of both lists to the user and apply the laddering interviewing technique asking for a justification of each one of the elements (Why is it a positive element? Why this mark?). The answer must be a specific explanation of the concrete characteristics that make the mentioned element a strength or weakness of the product.

Before starting the focus BLA group session participants spend 40 minutes playing quiz games using the following platforms:

1. Fixed console (Wii, PS3): The game used was *Buzz.*
2. Nintendo DS: The game used was *Who wants to be a millionaire?*
3. Mobile Phone: The game used was *Trivial Pursuit.*
4. Web game of an existing TV Show: The game used was *Bocamoll*, a quiz television program from TV· channel, that had a website game on line.

2.2 Results of Exploration Phase

The type of data obtained in the exploratory phase were used to identify the strengths and weaknesses of current devices, this technique was used to identify wants and needs to be meaningful for future applications.

The following will show some of the results achieved by applying the method focus BLA (Bipolar laddering) to illustrate the information obtained in this phase of the project.

In the elicitation phase of expert user group the following table of results was obtained.

Table 1. Table of negative elements of *Bocamoll* web game, expert group

Negative elements	*User 1*	*User 2*	*User 3*	*User 4*	*User 5*	*User 6*	*User 7*	*User 8*	*User 9*	*User 10*	*User 11*	*Mention*	*Average*
Sometimes the correct answer is not accepted.	1	1	1	1	3	1	1	1	1	0	0	100%	1,00
Inadequate response time.	2	1	4	2	3	1	2	2	1	5	3	100%	2,36
If you don't know an answer, is not allowed to skip.	0	3	0	0	2	0	1	4	1	1	0	100%	1,09
It don't give the correct answer.	2	2	3	2	2	2	2	0	2	4	3	100%	2,18
Some questions are repeated.	2	2	3	4	3	4	1	3	3	1	1	100%	2,45

The table of negatives elements shows the results obtained with focus BLA technique. The 5 elements have a mention of 100% which means that are relevant issues to all of the users. The lowest ranked element was NE1: *Sometimes doesn't accept the correct answer.* Since each element has a subjective justification we can see the reasons for the low valuation of the users.

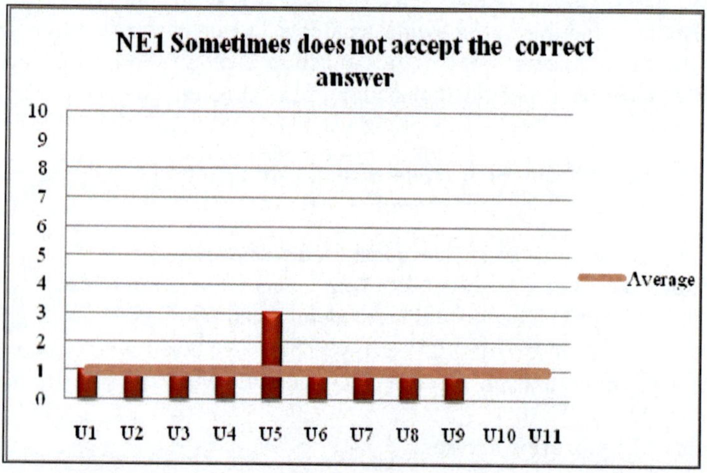

Fig. 1. Scores of negative element 1 (NE1), expert group

Each of the elements obtained in the table has a subjective justification of the problem and offers a solution generated by the consensus of the group. In case there is no consensus, the proposed solutions are registered separately regarding the percentage of users agree to each solution.

Table 2. Table of negative elements of mobile phone game, expert group

Negative elements	*User 1*	*User 2*	*User 3*	*User 4*	*User 5*	*User 6*	*User 7*	*User 8*	*User 9*	*User 10*	*User 11*	*Mention*	*Average*
Screen size	4	4	2	1	6	1	3	-	3	-	2	81,82%	2,89
Difficulty using keyboard	-	-	-	1	-	1	-	5	0	4	5	54,55%	2,67
Interaction with other players	5	3	-	-	3	3	3	4	-	4	3	72,73%	3,50

In case one of the users do not identify the element defined by the group as a problem (or strong point in case of positive elements) will not score such element as it is not relevant enough for him/her.

During the exploration phase were obtained two tables of results, positive and negative elements, for each of the devices tested.

This information allows having a clear idea of the main strengths and weaknesses of each type of game interaction regarding the device. That helps to define a starting point to carry out the new prototype design.

3 Immersion Phase

Once defined the main factors that affect the user in major gaming platforms is intended to obtain information about the motivations and game mechanics that should be included in a television contest (quiz) in which the user can remotely participate during the program broadcast.

The immersion phase is designed to extract a definition about desirable's multi-platform interaction during the TV show broadcasting. To achieve this goal an exploration technique based on visual elements has been applied.

The visual elements, with which users are asked to work, are a series of cards that represent different types of interaction elements that help users to define their ideal interaction and game mechanics.

There are four types of cards:

1. Interaction Scenarios: Scenarios are reproduced in which the user can interact remotely, as a living room, bedroom, and sitting on a train or an airport.
2. Devices: Cards that reproduce devices interfaces to real size. The devices are: mobile phone, computer screen, television screen and iPhone.
3. Interface elements: Interface elements will be divided into minimum units and provided with the same size as the devices, so users can repeat the same item with different devices.
4. Blank Cards: All cards/scenarios described above will be mirrored in blank to the same size to allow the user create new items in any category.

Fig. 2. Example of visual element cards

When users receive the artwork start working by groups of 3 or 4 people and defined as they would like to interact with a game of this type. The premise given is the following "*Imagine that while the quiz contest Bocamoll is on air you have the chance of play from your mobile, your laptop or your TV like a videogame. Tell us how you like running a contest of this kind using the material you have*".

From this premise users combine the visual elements and proposed the ideal game mechanics. To filter surface information a detailed explanation of each step was requested of each proposal, thus eliminating much of the information that can be unreflective by the user.

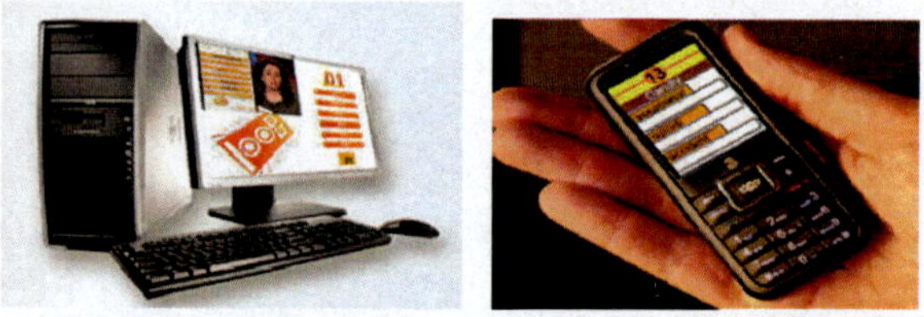

Fig. 3. Example of visual elements cards put it in a device interface

Each of these images is composed of several visual elements; users organize those elements to configure a desirable interface depending on the device they use.

Depending on the type of device the interface elements change significantly. For instance on case of mobile phone users opt to remove the television broadcasting due the small interface space they had. This premise was obtained when users realized that due to the large amount of space occupied by the emission interface could not read or interact comfortably with the interactive elements on screen.

3.1 Results of Immersion Phase

Immersion phase helped to identify key problems for each device tested.

Mobile Phone

Interface

The principal condition while designing an interface for game shows for mobile phones is the limited screen size. If the options for interaction and information are not easily identifiable, the application tends to cause rejection.

This factor has been mentioned for both profiles of user's during the exploration phase and has been manifested through the design proposals at the immersion phase.

Interaction Suitable

Prioritize the interactive part. To solve the problem of screen size, it was reached at a consensus solution: you must prioritize the interactive part of the competition in the mobile phone interface. Users do not wish to appear on the mobile interface the TV broadcast. The only reason is the lack of interface area, because when they raised the possibility of interaction with more spacious interfaces (e.g. computer) always have preferred to see both the television broadcast and interactive options simultaneously.

What if the user does not have a television in front? The response from users has been to resolve this situation including optional audio during interaction with the game. In this way the user could play the game using the speech program. Although users were not there to explain, you should consider the inclusion of visual reinforcement of interface for tests that may be confused just listening to them.

Computer

Interface

The computer is certainly the device that gives users more interaction options. The interface desired by the computer includes the interactive part and the television broadcast at the same time.

The distribution of the screen should be stable and consistent, so that one side always appears the interactive part and on the other side the game show broadcasting.

Interaction Suitable

The problems of interaction that appear on other platforms virtually disappear with the computer. There are two elements that cause this to happen: mouse and keyboard. Both are tools that give the resources to successfully interact with any type of test included in the game show.

Touch PDA or Smart Phone

Interface

The screen size of PDAs, iPhone, Nintendo DS and similar devices is much greater than that of conventional phones. This factor significantly affects the display of the interface and allows that it may be more complex. Users, in cases of interaction with a TV game show, have included items that did not want the mobile phone interface such as punctuation, which would be fixed in a corner or rankings data.

Interaction Suitable

Tactile interaction is the most important distinguishing feature of this type of device. This factor determines the approach of interaction that was defined for mobile phones, since in any case be raised by the use of buttons in response. Tactile devices in the selection of an item screen (how to choose the correct answer) may be pressing on the screen. This advantage presents a comparative offense for users who would play through a buttons mobile phone.

Television

Although the TV does not have a high level of interaction, it has an interface very generous in space, and in this case it can represent both the interactive information (time, position, rank, etc.) and the game show emission.

Interface
Television is the device more intuitive for users because the default is to associate a broadcast TV quiz to it.

In this case the distribution of the interface follows the same model has been proposed with the computer, half the screen to broadcast the program and the other half by the game interaction.

Interaction Suitable
Unlike the computer case, the interaction allowed through the television device is very limited due to the only tool users have is the remote control.

Users are more inclined to navigate with arrows than with numbers, since they considered as more intuitive. Users consider that navigation with numbers was a complicated interaction.

4 Multiplayer Competition

One of the most interesting results obtained in this project is the multiplayer concept applied to this game context.

Users have clearly defined elements of motivation inspired by on line games design, especially when they talked about rankings or game rooms.

Some users have mentioned the *Liga Marca* or Facebook's *Farmville* to define a desirable interaction with a TV quiz game. The factor of competitiveness and social interaction offered a clear motivation for the users.

Users have defined two types of virtual multiplayer spaces in which competing both online users and physical users located on the TV set.

Generic Rooms
The generic rooms would allow a game in large group as large cities or neighborhoods, in this kind of virtual room user's town compete as a team.

User should be able to identify himself individually within the group where he is participating, is important the user to know the number of total participants inside the group and what position does he respect the other players.

It has also appeared to be an interesting factor to meet the users personally. For example, within the group *Barcelona (Sants area)* would not be surprising that there are two or more acquaintances. This is a motivating factor for the user, but the applications should leave always the option to participate anonymously.

The generic room is a motivator for two primary reasons:

1. The sense of community motivates users by default. Taking part for your city, your neighborhood and competing against other cities or groups arouses user's motivation.
2. The user has the feeling that is possible to win if there are a reasonable number of competitors. Though the user can have references to inter-group (groups against groups) and intra-group (individual regarding the rest of the group) is very important and advisable to give the user the reference of his global position (all the players respect him) because is a desired reference point and a major motivation.

Configurable Rooms
Another type of virtual play rooms very attractive for users is the configurable rooms. In this case the user would play against a selection of users picked by him. Thus there could be games between members of a family, or friends (playing against each other), or members of the same company playing against others (e.g. finance department against marketing department) at any case the players would be always known by the user.

Within this category has also emerged the option of "challenge" in this case the game would be a "one on one" between players, challenging other users to see who gets better marks.

Options as rankings and rooms do not have to be mutually exclusive; the user should be able to play for his department and also for his city or neighborhood at the same time.

5 Other Motivations

The following points summarize the main motivation issues in case they were able to interact synchronously with the kind of television quiz show defined in this project.

1. The Application Should Be Free

Users have shown a systematic refusal to pay per game or per time. They would accept a fee to download a software but do not accept the idea of paying for fraction of time or game.

2. The television show format must be designed taking in account the user's remote interaction.

It has been noticed the need for an integrated design of the contest, which affects the television program design itself. It is important that the questions presented and the structure of the program is designed to interact using different types of interface and devices.

3. This type of application must be developed on existing device.

Users do not want a new device to play the contest. The implementation, whatever it is, must be using a device already used by the user.

4. It should have prizes

It is important for users to win a prize. Both users' profiles have stated that the possibility of winning a gift would be a great motivation. Was also noted the importance for the user if he/her hear about an acquaintance has won a prize.

6 Conclusions

The following points summarize the main issues to take in account in case an application as the described on this project were able to be developed.

1. The sync interaction with the show broadcasting is clearly motivating

The fact of interacting with a program being broadcast at real time (not necessarily live) is a great motivation element for the users; in fact this is a basic condition, since most of the users would not participate in case the game was not synchronized by the TV show.

2. A quick interaction is needed
Users do not want to write. This is a premise of interaction that has been almost unanimously, the final application should be quick and easy, if the user has to write, it their motivation drop down. This principle also applicable for a computer interaction, this is a factor to be considered while designing the final application.

3. Don't dismiss the voice as interaction model.
Although now it is technically difficult, the voice interaction style seems a good solution for this type of application. The answer by voice would avoid many problems such as writing, overloading the interface errors or pressing a button. On the other hand, although users had the option of voice response, also would like to have the option of interact digitally, since it is not always convenient to have to speak loudly to play the game.

4. The time scores
One of the principles that have been established for this type of game is that the response time has to score, e.g. the score obtained for both the correct answer as to respond quickly. This score shared between accuracy and time has to be applied in order to avoid the user frustration in short term, removing him right away or giving the impression that it is not possible to win.

5. Multiplayer Competition
The factor of competitiveness and social interaction offered a clear motivation for the users. Users have clearly defined elements of motivation inspired by on line social games design. This can be the success key in this kind of game.

References

1. Gauntlett, D.: Creative Explorations: New Approaches to Identities and Audiences. Routledge, New York (2007)
2. Sanders, E.: Information, Inspiration and Co-creation. In: Proceeding of the 6th International Conference of the European Academy of Design. University of the Arts, Bremen (2005)
3. Neimeyer, R.A.: Features, Foundations and Future Directions. In: Neimeyer, R.A., Mahoney, M.J. (eds.) Constructivism in Psychotherapy. American Association, Washington (1995)
4. Jensen, B. G.: The Role of the Artifact in Participatory Design Research. In: Design Communication. 3rd Nordcode Seminar&Workshop, Lyngby-Denmark (2004)
5. Pifarré, M.: Bipolar Laddering (BLA): a Participatory Subjective Exploration Method on User Experience. In: Dux 2007: Conference on Designing for User Experience, Chicago-USA (November 2007)
6. Södergard, C.: Mobile Television-technology and User Experiences, VTT Information technology (2003)
7. Tomico, O., Pifarré, M., Lloveras, J.: Analyzing the Role of Constructivist Psychology Methods into User Subjective Experience Gathering Techniques for Product Design. In: ICED 2007: International Conference on Engineering Design, Paris-France (August 2007)

Visual Interfaces and User Experience: Augmented Reality for Architectural Education: One Study Case and Work in Progress

Ernest Redondo[1], Isidro Navarro[1], Albert Sánchez[2], and David Fonseca[3]

[1] Departamento de Expresión Gráfica Arquitectónica I, Universidad Politécnica de Cataluña, Barcelona Tech. Escuela Técnica Superior de Arquitectura de Barcelona, ETSAB, Avda Diagonal 649, 2, 08028, Barcelona, Spain
ernesto.redondo@upc.edu, isidro.navarro@upc.edu
[2] Departamento de Expresión Gráfica Arquitectónica II, Universidad Politécnica de Cataluña, Escuela Politécnica Superior de Edificación de Barcelona, EPSEB, C/. Gregorio Marañón, 44-50, 3. 08028, Barcelona, Spain
asri@telefonica.net
[3] GTAM, Grup de Recerca en Tecnologies Mèdia, Enginyeria La Salle, Universitat Ramon Llull, C/ Quatre Camins 2, 08022, Barcelona, Spain
fonsi@salle.url.edu

Abstract. In this paper we present the first conclusions of an educational research project which seeks to evaluate, throughout the academic training period, and by the use of Augmented Reality (AR) technology, the graphic and spatial capabilities of undergraduate and master's degree in architecture, construction, urbanism and design students. The project consists of twelve case studies to be carried out in several university centers. Currently, after the first case study has been finalised, it has been demonstrated that by combining the use of an attractive technology, to create dynamic photomontage for visual evaluation of virtual models in a real environment, and by the user-machine interaction that involves AR, students feel more motivated and the development and evolution of their graphic competences and space skills increased in shorter learning periods, improving their academic performance. For this experiment we have used mobile phones, laptops, as well as low cost AR applications.

Keywords: Augmented reality, Educational research, Architectural graphic representation.

1 Introduction

The objective of this special session is to share research or development works focused on evaluating and improving both the visual interface of an application and the user interaction experience. Particularly, the aim of this educational research is to evaluate the use of AR when teaching architecture, urbanism, construction and design at either undergraduate or masters level. It also focuses on the development of students'

H. Cherifi, J.M. Zain, and E. El-Qawasmeh (Eds.): DICTAP 2011, Part I, CCIS 166, pp. 355–367, 2011.

graphical and spatial skills, and the improvement of their academic performance via the use of mobile phones, laptops, as well as low cost AR applications.

In our case – based in the field of teaching research in the aforementioned areas, which are usually grouped in university centers and in architecture representation and visual communication departments, where equivalent studies hardly exist - the main contribution to scientific knowledge, is the carrying out of different case studies in which satisfaction, usability of AR technology, and improvement of students academic performance is being evaluated. This research goes on to demonstrate that by using NPR (Non Photorealistic Render) 3D modeling and low cost AR applications on portable devices, in indoors and outdoors environments, students acquire a high level of graphic training in a very short period of time, allowing them to create virtual and interactive photomontages, very useful for the evaluation of the visual impact of their projects without wasting extra time learning to use complex computer applications. They can instantly check their first sketches in a real site – known as photomontage 3D in real time - retaking the tradition of the architectural photomontage, whose usefulness has been proved in the professional and academic environment as a way to evaluate future projects.

We assume that students, digital natives, are common users of ICT, feel attracted to them, they can quickly learn how to use them in an intuitive way, and improve their use in a self-taught way. But most of the times they are not adequately trained about it. We try to exploit their attraction in order to study how these technologies and its implementation, with the use of new teaching methodologies, have an impact on their three-dimensional visualisation and free manipulation of architecture forms. At the same time, we want to find out if this issue can help to improve their performance in spatial comprehension processes and their graphical representation skills, from as early as the start of their academic years. The way we use the AR technology by means of user-machine interaction, enhances spatial coordination and encourages observation and manipulation of virtual objects. It´s easy to use and needs only of very basic virtual modelling training in order to be visualised, encouraging the student to develop the ability of reading and represent geometric shapes on the computer, which could be useful for future professionals. Avoids, therefore, complex systems and keeps in touch with the creative process.

To reach this goal it is necessary to advance in architecture understanding and in specific educational methods; which is why this study is carried out in different universities, on individuals with different academic skill levels and subjects, involving new teaching strategies, methodologies, materials and didactic tools designed within the TIC scope. They all are being properly validated and tested, both for the academic performance improvement achieved, and for the satisfaction or usability of the applications and computing devices that have been used.

In this sense, and as a teaching research project which involved large groups of students in regular courses, the solution adopted was to study how AR is integrated in different subjects, depending on its specific contents. We use laptops or school netbooks, and with them 3D models have been generated and visualized on site, always using educational software like Gimp, SketchUP, Autocad, 3Ds Max, and exporting them using plug-in or AR free applications, such as Build-Ar or Mr Planet, Ar-media Inglobe Technologies or Junaio in order to be viewed through a web camera connected to a computer, or using 3G standard mobile devices Android or iOs based.

2 Background and Current State of the Problem

2.1 Background

The background of this research should be found in first place in the work of the authors whose main purpose is the graphical academic training of future architects, as well as the development of new strategies that enhance academic performance. In particular, we have now shown [1] that freehand drawing, realised in digital boards, tablets, or Ipads, is more than an acceptable substitute for traditional drawing, and its utilisation, combined with TIC, improves the student graphical instruction and their academic performance.

We have also published studies of academic urban retrieval, including AR Technology, [2],[3] in low cost mobile devices, as well as works about teaching improvement using digital image [4]. Similar studies to ours, related to spatial abilities development for engineering students that use AR, have also been recently published[5]. These studies focus in the editing of educational content to incorporate AR markers and, somehow, ensure and confirm the initial hypothesis of this research.

Secondly, it is worth to state briefly the concept of the architectural photomontage as a graphical register, the main idea of our proposal. It's based on merging photographic picture, which represents a real environment, and a virtual model, and matching both vanishing points [6]. Projects adjustments related to their location and scale, the design of furniture elements and indoor and outdoor spaces, as well as technical documentation queries on real site, are competences and skills that future architects, town planners or designers, have to acquire during their academic training.

For all of the above, new tools like AR, which allow in site design adjustments during the model creation process, are needed. In this sense, digital image has hardly overcome intentionality, perspective fitting problems, and tonal adjustments of traditional architectural photomontage, which has a long tradition from the beginning of the XX century. There are many examples like the Mies studies of 1921 for the skyscraper Friedrichstrasse of Berlín [7], or the studies of El Lissizitky, in 1925 for the building Der Wolkënbugel [8], who superimposed his drawings over images using conventional graphics techniques. Later on, utopian proposals and the new technological advances, attached to the pop aesthetic of the 60's in Europe and Japan led iconic images of these photo montages in which the colour brought expressiveness. Special mention needs to be made in this respect of the works of the Team X collectives [9], Archigram[10] or Superstudio[11]. Recently, the new proposals of digital photo montages, break with the traditional perspective rules, for, in pseudo realistic collages, transmit more the poetic idea of their projects rather than their own future concretion. Contemporary references are the works from J.Nouvel[12] S.Hall[13], MVRDV Herzon & de Meuron[14] etc.

As we have already mentioned, despite the use of recent digital representation techniques, these proposals, add nothing. They do not provide interactive and real time checking strategies, and do not take advantage of new interconnection and information sharing possibilities between users and participants on the project.

2.2 Current State of the Augmented Reality Technology

The technology that helps to overcome all these limitations and which we are going to evaluate and incorporate to the teaching system is AR. Their creators [15] define AR as a virtual reality variation, where the user can see the real world with virtual objects, mixed or superimposed. In contrast to virtual reality, AR does not replace the real environment, instead it uses the real environment as a background to be registered. The final result is a dynamic image of a 3D virtual model superimposed on a real time video of the environment. This scene is shown to the user on a computer screen or other devices, as projectors, or digital board, using special glasses or in a 3g cell phone. This sensitive experience is essential for this technology rising. The main problem in architecture is to resolve the integration between virtual objects and real images. Any overlap must be accurate and at the right scale in order for those models to match its hypothetic situation and size in the real scene.

This technology, which has been recently commercialized, covers different areas. If we focus on our specific fields of study, we would highlight the book edition applications, where trackers are added to show additional information. The best example of this is Magicbook[16]. In the field of education specific applications for maths and geometry have been studied [17][18]. In architecture the use of AR is anecdotic; the precedents in this field are the indoor studies [19] [20]. In Tinmith project, outdoors works have been also done. Other semi-immersive proposals which incorporate AR over screens in the study of urban projects are projects as Arthur[21], the Luminous Table[22] or the Sketchand+Benchworks[23], where different data entry devices are combined in a virtual theatre. More recently,[24][25] different tests on building renovation have been realized. Within urban planning, we should mention [26] and in the infrastructure of the construction enginery [27]. In architecture teaching the following stand out [28][29][30][31], devoted to objects design and to other more general teaching applications. There are some baseline surveys about the utility of these technologies on professional architecture companies [32] which had shown a big interest for it.

In our opinion, the quantum leap and dissemination of this technology is due to its accessibility from mobile phones thanks to the libraries ARToolkitPlus [33]. Mobile Ar software applications appear continuously, we should mention MARA from Nokia or Layar, the first application of generalist use available both for Iphone users as for Android Os based phones. In 2010, Junaio appears, the first markerless open-use application. It works with multimedia content (videos, renders, 3d models) and registration is based on real environment images recognition, instead of markers. Moreover, low cost AR plug-in for programmes as GoogleSketchUp are generalising the use of this technology, but mostly indoors.

2.3 The Problem to Solve

The challenge we have to face year after year, is the incorporation, within the educational training process, of digital technologies. We are convinced students feel strongly attracted to them and teachers do not always know how they should be introduced. From the educational centers, however, there is a constant reminder that we should keep traditional strategies perhaps for fear of distorting the contents of the fields due to the complexity that some traditional computer applications have. This approach focuses on drawings production or final presentation, instead of promoting the generation of ideas or increase spatial and graphical skills. Given how students feel towards these new type of technologies and the intuitive use of AR and NPR, we should study how it affects on the performance of future professionals, giving priority to the contents and to the architectural concepts, instead of focusing on learning the various computer' tools. Therefore it has been decided that it would be useful to create a multidisciplinary team of investigators with knowledge in all the different areas implied. Together with that team, we are designing new teaching strategies where tools and materials are being developed in the ICT and AR environment. Furthermore, we have already done several feasibility trials through the *Laboratorio de Modelado Virtual de la Ciudad, LMVC* from CPSV, *Centro de Política de Suelo y Valoración* of the Barcelona Tech. University, which demonstrate that low cost equipment and free applications are useful to carry out planned research.

Fig. 1. AR application sample used for the study and the virtual reconstruction of architectural heritage in the roman city of Gerunda, Girona, Spain, carried out by the authors in the LMVC

3 General Methodology: Case Study

3.1 Methodology

The general methodology used is that of a study of case, which is often used in educational evaluations. For this research, the case will consist of postgraduate and master degree students groups. A new educational proposal will be tested, looking at both quantitative and qualitative reviews. Augmented reality will be incorporated to their learning training as a technology for visualization and understanding of the architectural forms, as well as a graphical synthesis tool to show how different theoretical concepts are developed. We separate methodology into two different stages.

3.1.1 Qualitative Investigation

Within every study of case a few *Contents* will be established. These will be structured in accordance with a General Learning Program and will depend on the specific subject content, in every school period. The hierarchy of knowledge to be acquired, before and after every course, should be clear and close to Bloom's taxonomy [34]. It is a matter of relying on a structure that allows teachers to evaluate skills improvement on every level. This objective of every course relies on the fact that students are more or less familiar with the new technologies. – it aims to prove that when teachers use TIC tools, students pay more attention, academic performance increases, and they show more interest in carrying out the exercises proposed. In addition, we want to prove that once they use AR to visualize their proposals, performance and graphical skills increase even more. Students often do not show interest and are not motivated when they use traditional methodologies.

Materials and didactic contents. For the development of every course it is necessary to create some didactic contents adapted to the subject and to the specificity of the proposed tests. We´ll will work in coordination with the individuals responsible for the subject who will be in charge of the virtual construction exercises. In many cases it will be necessary to carry out a brief training or make some specific user manuals for 3dsoftware or 3D modelling.

Equipments. Because of the importance of computer technology in this study we will describe the equipment used. In short, the basic equipment was made up of portable computers and even netbooks Toshiba NB200 owned by students themselves. These were provided with a second simple webcam, Logitech model C200. This allowed to see indoor RA models RA using 20x20 cm. Markers. The virtual models were generated by Google SketchUp (each student had a free license for this programme) and were then exported to AR using the free plug-in Ar-media Inglobetechnologies's whose duration of 30 seconds allows for basic adjustments. Alternatively, the teacher exports an AR model using the professional application ArExporter 2.0, so that students can see it for an unlimited time using the free viewer ArPlayer 2.0, once received by wifi or USB pen drive. In advanced courses, we work with the students' own portable computers and educational licenses for different computer applications, GoogleSketcupPro, AutoCAD, 3DStudio max, Revit, Rhyno, Photoshop. We use plugins and viewers from AR-Media in its educational version, or even Build-Ar and MrPlanet, other free AR's applications that allow the use of two or more markers simultaneously. This is useful for wide range viewing, because at least one marker must be recognized and visible. For such viewings, students use a webcam Hercules Dualpix of 1 Mb viewing the models up to 12 meters of distance with 50x50cm trackers, and always avoiding direct lighting. Model size could reach 16 Mb. To work outdoors, with long distances, a webcam of high range, 5 Mp, Logitech C910 has been used making possible to view models of 25 Mb up to 25 meters away on 50x50 cm. Markers. We have successfully tested the 3D models visualization using the application *Junaio* using mobile phones. In this case it is still necessary to reduce models to 2000 polygons and apply low-resolution textures.

3.1.2 Quantitative Research

It refers to the part of the work dedicated to the compilation of information. We have considered: *Participants.* There will be selected an experimental students group and a control one if feasible. They will follow an ordinary course. The group size will vary but it will have a minimum of 15 students to make sure there is a significant population sample. For this reason it may be necessary to repeat the experiment. *Measurement and evaluation of academic performance.* As we described we'll try to work with two groups of students, once finished every process the teachers from both groups will evaluate the results together. *Students satisfaction surveys.* Using a specific questionnaire every student is asked about his performance assessment, about the amount of hours he or she has dedicated to the RA daily, and to consider if the educational resources have been appropriate to the complexity of the exercise. We use SEEQ based questionnaires as an instrument of evaluation and auto evaluation by students (Students ' Evaluation of Educational Quality [35]. In a similar way *Applications usability and used hardware will be evaluated.* We take user concepts parameterization [36] from ISO norm 9241-11 using a specific survey form, that will depend on the resources and computer technology used in every course.

4 Case Study

4.1 Master Course: New Computer Technologies for Spatial Analysis and Their Application to Urban Design Processes in the Master and Graphic Expression in Architecture and Urban Projection: University of Guadalajara, Mexico

4.1.1 Main Purpose and Objectives of the Course

To try to solve the aforementioned deficiencies and to increase master's students skills, all of which are native users of digital technology, most by force of events, and expert users of both computer and traditional graphical techniques, including collage, we propose an academic experiment that tries to increase their competences in computer graphics generation in a new area, the AR, which allows to study, on site, virtual models, and their application on urban projects design. For this purpose, we present a case study of implementation of these new teaching methodologies targeted to Master of Graphic Expression Processes of CUAAD-UDG students. It has been developed in outdoor environments, still an unreported option because most of AR software is designed for indoor environments use. The greatest challenge was how to overcome the difficulties in carrying out these experiments with students that were not aware of these technologies, and that have a multidisciplinary profile. The activity was focused on architects, graphic and industrial designers, who have to work together, a practice unusual in its center. Therefore, teamwork has been a considerable effort of the course. The results of these experiments are perfectly described into the theme of this special session on Visual Interfaces and User Experiences, since the main objective of this experiment is to improve perceptual and expressive abilities, as well as professional performance of our students, in a short time. By using visual interfaces such as AR, students have achieved remarkable results. It should be noted in this case the merge of previous experience and the students' desire to learn anything new.

4.1.2 Methodological Proposal for Educational Innovation in the Master Course

Taking into account the background described, we wanted to go one step further raising a dynamic and real time 3d photomontage updated version. We use for it standard devices like portable computer and free or low cost software. A perfectly available option if AR's applications are optical-registration based. Our contribution is the transfer of these AR technologies to education processes, specifically to an Urban design master course. Students have different profiles and they are supposed to work in multidisciplinary groups. Instead of fixed images and traditional photomontages, generation, we work on 3D and interactive photomontages registered on a real environment. Our aim is to demonstrate the usefulness and advantages of this technology for education, where flexibility and responsiveness allows addressing diverse problems. In this way we can work on 3d simple models from an urban scale to an object design for furniture, positioning and scaling them adequately.

4.1.3 Study of Case, Educational Materials and Valuation

In our work, the case focuses on groups of students of the Master on Processes and Graphical Expression in Architecture and Urban Projection; a multidisciplinary group of 24 licentiates in architecture, urbanism, graphical and industrial design who we have experimented with. The agenda was a combination of lectures and laboratory indoor and outdoor practices. More specifically in the Cultural University Center of the University of Guadalajara, Mexico, which is under construction. A previous urban model was proposed, and students were required to come up with diverse contributions on facades and also propose urban furniture around public central square. As we have described basic AR software was used. 4 theoretical classes of one hour and a half were given, and we spent 15 hours of practices in the classroom, distributed in four sessions. In one of the meetings there was a guided tour of the place, after that, the urban modelling began and some facades from the city were added to this basic model. Working areas were defined for each group and they all developed an urban setting project. It included the design of the attached real facades, urban furniture and the corporate identity. The designed objects were viewed by AR in the exterior and in the foyer of the CUUAD for a first evaluation. After that we worked in the area of the project to test models and for scale, vanishing points, and perspective adjustment. The visualization was carried out by means of personal computers and webcams, using 30x30cm trackers, which were initially designed for indoor viewing. We achieved consistent visualizations up to 12mts of distance. Exceptionally in this case to obtain video images, the process was recorded with a video camera Sony Handicam CCD-TRV-138 using a graphics card Dazzle Hollywood DV connected to a laptop (Fig. 2).

Fig. 2. Newspaper stand project visualization using AR technology at the Center Telmex. Guadalajara, Jalisco, Mexico

4.1.4 Evaluation of the Study

The course evaluation was based both on attendance to the course (it was over 95%) and the final delivery note. We have carried out one more objective evaluation based on a questionnaire, it had questions relative to the degree of satisfaction, usefulness and global valuation of the system. In addition, we asked about how this methodology helped the students to improve their competitions and skills on graphical computer science, beyond current knowledge. Anonymous surveys were distributed to all students and they were required to rate questions from 1 to 5. Students percentage of participation was 67 %. All questions got a score of 5 in 94% of the answers. In this context the experimental group has overcome fully the result of the control group, pupils from previous year course. They worked in the same urban project but did not add the AR technology to it. So their final participation did not exceed 45 %.

4.1.5 Particular Conclusions, Discussion and Future Work

As preliminary conclusions of our work, considering the acquired experience, we must highlight the following: In this Study of case, it has been demonstrated that the use of mobile devices like laptop equipped with webcams and combined with low cost applications of augmented reality, are an acceptable substitute of the traditional photomontage technologies. It allows dynamic viewing of the students' virtual models sited on their future emplacement, even in outdoor environments. With these results in mind, these strategies allow academic and professional performance improvement; shortening urban projects development time, and promote their creativity whether they are architects, town planners, designers, etc.

5 Work in Progress

In parallel, we are conducting two case studies to evaluate academic performance. The first is a supervised activity aimed at the implementation of new digital technologies in building construction and maintenance processes, within the course of Graphic Expression III at the School of Engineering Building in Barcelona. The purpose and objectives are the implementation of AR technology in the teaching of engineering and building areas. This item could offer potential advantages in all stages of the construction processes, from conceptual design, to the management and maintenance of the building systems throughout its life. It seems useful in staking tasks, or control facilities too. In the field of interpretation and communication, where this technology would facilitate the interpretation of drawings, technical documentation and other specifications. These systems can generate a real image superimposed on a specific stage of the construction process and by joining a database, can show different levels of information based on each user's queries. This, in turn, is heterogeneous, and with different needs and requirements. In the present case, interior spaces of existing buildings, the following could be considered for example: the need to know about the building loads of an area, its thermal behavior, or the location of certain facilities. All of them possible virtual models that overlap to real space, and should contribute to a better understanding of the building, and to a greater efficiency in construction processes, rehabilitation or building maintenance. Arises, therefore, the desirability of using a variety of tools related to AR technology, during a supervised activity, where the student will be able to transmit to other participants a more constructive and technical knowledge on the building where he/she works. Somehow, they must, "complete" constructive information on their surrounding space. The goal is twofold: first, to evaluate the possibility of using this technology in indoor environments, tied to construction and maintenance processes, so that the user acquire more technical knowledge of their environment, and secondly, with the application of these emerging techniques, we will try to develop new alternative teaching methods to the traditional ones, that would return in greater efficiency and academic performance. Teaching experience so far unreported. (Fig. 3).

Fig. 3. Sample images illustrating the models generated by teachers for project and case study evaluation

The second case we are developing is in the subject of Representation Systems II in the third-year Architecture degree. Polytechnic School of Architecture La Salle Tarragona, Universitat Ramon Llull, the purpose of which is the application of advanced 3D rendering systems for volumetric description of architecture students' projects. This is intended as a tool in the decisions of the architectural design process. The application of augmented reality technology in the design process must allow a better perception of volumetric integration that will facilitate the understanding of the architectural proposal. Like the case of the University of Guadalajara, we present a teaching application of augmented reality techniques. On this case, the students are in an intermediate stage of their university studies and their habits in projects definition are just beginning. The working hypothesis is to see how much AR techniques can help the student in the initial process of projects elaboration. These space-control skills may be important in the formal decisions and to implement their proposals. The definition of contents is appropriate to an educational activity for a project course. This will aim to provide a better understanding of these new techniques. Cases will also be tested in different size scales.

6 General Conclusions and Discussion

Regarding the project in its educational aspect, we have shown that using ICT, pupils with very little prior training specific to AR but motivated by these technologies, using a comprehensive educational strategy which combines the visualization and modeling 3D, incorporating agile digital graphics tools with a high level of usability, substantial improvements in academic performance and spatial awareness capabilities area obtained in a short time with a high degree of acceptance by them. We tested these strategies in a case study, supplemented with two different educational groups, and in the first one we've got a very remarkable improvement in performance. As we understand, in education, the most important are the concepts to study and to represent in each case, so that the rendering technology helps, enhances and facilitates the idea discussion and allows a rapid assessment and review of projects. We don´t try to generate realistic images or final nice presentations, but working models, prototypes faster and easier to manipulate. In the immediate future we´ll repeat the experiments on larger group samples of participants, preparing more control groups at different levels of future architects, planners and building engineers, in order to obtain more reliable data and to obtain global conclusions.

From the point of view of the applicability of these strategies, the preliminary conclusion is that they require large trackers to be valid for distances of less than 25 meters and in optimal lighting conditions, serving to work outdoors in optimum environmental conditions. Also, if the virtual model must be viewed at a distance, it requires reorientation to be projected onto a tilted tracker, eg 45 degrees that is more easily recognizable. Instead we have had no problems with file sizes, with Ar-media, models can run more than 5 MB. Another drawback in this case, is that open space registration requires a simple topographic base. In all these cases access to the virtual model is carried out from the personal computer that runs a file compiled on the display. However, we have proven that if you have good coverage Wiimax or a modem it is possible to download the file using a Dropbox application. This option is applicable in indoor wireless coverage. Slowness and network capacity can be a problem if it has to transmit a large file.

If the model registration is carried out at shorter distances, about 12 feet or even less, small tracker, wireless and basic equipment is the best option, because lighting conditions are under control and models are displayed stably. The drawback in these cases is the displacements of the webcam, which implies that when the tracker is out of sight of the camera's field of view, the model disappears. In this case the solution is the use of multimarker AR applications where the virtual model is repeated properly shifted depending on the distance and markers position, models have to be simpler, and in this case viewer freedom of movement is a bit restricted. The last option and probably the most suitable for the vision of virtual buildings and objects at distances beyond 25 meters is tested with makerless applications like "Junaio" where the model registration is based on the recognition of a previous image of the place. The problem here is the same in terms of telephone coverage and availability of 3G handsets, as well as low resolution and detail of the virtual models currently limited to 2000 polygons, the use of texture sizes equivalent to 512x5123 pixels, and having to predefine the images that act as markers preferably taken with the phone itself. For future work in this technical aspect we are evaluating the possibility of viewing the models with AR Vuzix glasses or similar, connected to a laptop or mobile phone, which would solve the problem of light contrast of LED and LCD backlit screens in outdoor environments, used in the first configuration. However, this immersive system is still too expensive.

References

1. Redondo, E., Santana, G.: Metodologías docentes basadas en interfases táctiles para la docencia del dibujo y los proyectos arquitectónicos. Revista Arquitecturasrevista (6), 90–105 (2010)

2. Redondo, E.: Intervenciones virtuales en un entorno urbano. La recuperación de la trama viaria del barrio judío de Girona. ACE: Architecture, City and Environment 12, 77–97 (2010)
3. Redondo, E.: Un caso de estudio de investigación aplicada. La recuperación de la trama viaria del Barrio Judío de Girona mediante realidad aumentada. Revista EGA de los Departamentos de Expresión Gráfica de España. núm 16 (2010)
4. Fonseca, D., Fernández, J.A., Garcia, O.: Comportamiento Plausible de agente virtuales: Inclusión de parámetros de usabilidad emocional a partir de imágenes fotográficas. In: Callaos, N., Baralt, J., Orlando (eds.) International Institute of Informatics and Systemics. Memorias CISCI 2007, vol. 1, pp. 142–152 (2007)
5. Saorín, Gutierrez, M., Martín Dorta, N.Y., Contero, M.: Design and Validation of an Augmented Book for Spatial Abilities Development in Engineering Students. Computer & Graphics 34(1), 7–91 (2009)
6. Moliner, X.: El fotomuntatge arquietctònic. El cas de Mies van der Rohe. Tesis doctoral, Universidad de Girona. España (2010)
7. Mies van der Rohe, L.: `http://www.miessociety.org/legacy/projects/friedrichstrasse-office-building/`
8. Lissitzky-Kuppers, Sophie El Lissitzky, life, letters, texts. Thames and Hudson, 414 p. (1980)
9. Team X, `http://www.team10online.org/`
10. Archigram Archival Project, `http://archigram.westminster.ac.uk/project.ph`
11. Dempsey, A.: Estilos, escuelas y movimientos. Superstudio. Ed. Blume, Barcelona. 304 pp (2002)
12. Jean Nouvel 1994-2002, El Croquis, nº 112/113, Madrid, 347 pp (2002)
13. Steven Hall, architect. 2004-2008, El Croquis, n. º141, Madrid. 249 pp (2008)
14. MVRDV 1997-2002, Stacking and layering, El Croquis, nº 111, Madrid 275 pp (2002)
15. Azuma, R., Baillot, Y., Behringer, R., Feiner, S., Julier, S., MacIntyre, B.: Recent Advances in Augmented Reality. IEEE Computer Graphics and Applications 21(6), 34–47 (2001)
16. Billinghurst, M., Kato, H., Poupyrev, I.: The MagicBook (2001)
17. Kaufmann, H.: Construct3D: An Augmented Reality Application for Matthematics and Geometry Education. In: Proceeding of ACM Multimedia Conference 2002, pp. 656–657 (2002)
18. Juan, M., Beatrice, F., Cano, J.: An Augmented Reality System for Learning the Interior of the Human Body. In: The 8th IEEE International Conference on Advanced Learning Technologies (ICALT 2008), Santander, Spain, pp. 186–188 (2008)
19. Mlkawi, A.Y., Srinivasan, R.: Building Performance Visualization Using Augmented Reality. In: En: International Conference on Computer Graphics and Vision (14º), Bory CZ Rep. Proceedings of the Fourteenth International Conference on Computer Graphics and Vision,Bory CZ, pp. 122–127 (2004)
20. Piekarsky, W.Y., Thomas, B.: Tinmith-Metro: New Outdoor Techniques for Creating CityModels with an Augmented Reality Wearable Computer. In: 5th International Symposium on Wearable Computers, Zurich, CH, pp. 31–38 (2001)
21. Broll, J., Lindt, J., Ohlenburg, M., Wittkämper, C., Yuan, T., Novotny, C., Mottram.: ARTHUR: A Collaborative Augmented Environment for Architectural Design and UrbanPlanning. In: Proceedings of Seventh International Conference on Humans and Computers (7^a), Taiwan, New Jersy, pp. 102–109 (2004)

22. Ben-Joseph, H., Ishii, J., Underkoffler, B.: URBAN Simulation and the Luminous Planning Table: Bridging the Gap between the Digital and the Tangible por. Journal of Planning and Education Research (21), 196–203 (2001)
23. Seichter, H.Y., Schnabel, M.A.: Digital and Tangible Sensation: An Augmented Reality Urban Design Studio. In: Proceedings of the 10th International Conference on Computer Aided Architectural Design Research in Asia (10^a), Delhi, India, vol. 2, pp. 193–202 (2005)
24. Sánchez, J., Borro, D.: Automatic Augmented Video Creation for Markerless Environments. In: Proceedings of the 2nd International Conference on Computer Vision Theory and Application (VISAPP 2007), Barcelona, Spain, pp. 519–522 (2007)
25. Tonn, C., Petzold, F., Bimber, O., Grundhö, F.A., Donath, D.: Spatial Augmented Reality for Architecture Desiging and Planning with and within Existing Buildings. International Journal of Architectural Computing 6(1), 41–58 (2008)
26. Kato, H., Tachibana, K., Tanabe, M., Nakajima, T., Fukuda, Y.: A City-Planning system based on Augmented Reality with a Tangible Interface. In: Proceedings of the Second IEEE and ACM International Symposium on Mixed and Augmented Reality (ISMAR 2003), Tokio, Japan, pp. 340–341 (2003)
27. Schall, G., Mendez, E., Kruijff, E.: Handheld Augmented Reality for underground infrastructure visualization. Pers. Ubiquit Comput. (13), 281–192 (2009)
28. Salles, J.M., Capó, J., Carreras, J., Galli, R., Gamito, M.: A4D: Augmented Reality 4D System for Architecture and Building Construction. In: CONVR 2003, Zurich, Switzerlan, September 24, pp. 71–76. Virginia Tech (2003)
29. Liarokapis, F., Petridis, P., Lister, P.F., White, M.: Multimedia Augmented Reality Interface for E-Learning (MARIE). World Transactions on Engineering and Technology Education, UICEE 1(2), 173–176 (2002)
30. Haller, M., Holm, R., Volkert, J., Wagner, R.A.: VR based safety training in a petroleum refinery. In: The 20th Annual Conf. of the European Association of CG, Eurographics, Milano, Italy (1999)
31. Ruiz, A., Urdiales, C., Fernandez Ruiz, J., Sandoval, F.: Ideación Arquitectónica Asistida Mediante Realidad Aumentada, Innovación en Telecomunicaciones V-1 - V-8 (2004)
32. Xiangyu, W., Ning, G.U., Marchant, L.: An empirical study on designers' perception of augmented reality within an architectural firm. ITcom 13, 536–552 (2008)
33. Wagner, D.: Handheld Augmented Reality. Thesis Doctoral. Graz University of Technology, Graz, Austria (2007)

Communications in Computer and Information Science: Using Marker Augmented Reality Technology for Spatial Space Understanding in Computer Graphics

Malinka Ivanova[1] and Georgi Ivanov[2]

[1] Technical University of Sofia, College of Energetics and Electronics, Blvd. Kl. Ohridski 8, Sofia 1000, Bulgaria
m_ivanova@tu-sofia.bg
[2] University of Edinburgh, School of Informatics, Appleton Tower, Crichton Street, Edinburgh, EH8 9LE, UK
G.Ivanov@sms.ed.ac.uk

Abstract. In this paper the experience gained at using low-cost interactive marker augmented reality (AR) technology during course Computer graphics is presented. The preliminary exploration of AR technology adoption for learning enhancing and understanding of spatial spaces is done and several benefits are identified and analyzed via a model. Software and tools for AR learning objects development are explored and one solution is chosen from the point of view students to be involved not only in an interactive learning process, but also to be part of an authoring process. A model of usage of a virtual learning environment with access to AR learning objects is created to support students' participation during the course. The students' opinion is gathered and the results describe AR as promising and effective technology that allows spatial spaces to be examined in detail and that supports creative thinking and development of more realistic 3D scenes.

Keywords: augmented reality, computer graphics, spatial understanding, AR authoring tools, interactive learning environment.

1 Introduction

Applied computer graphics is a unique part of a computer science education in that it bridges among mathematics, physics phenomenon, art, and engineering techniques.

Computer graphics course examines the technical aspects of picture generation from geometrical models taking into consideration time, memory and quality aspects of the algorithms that are used. Laboratory practices are planned for applying the theoretical knowledge and receiving new skills working with the software package 3DSMax converting them into realistic spatial solutions. Realization of realistic three dimensional scenes or object models requires precise modeling, arranging of objects, choosing of color patterns, lights, effects and cameras. This is possible not only at utilization of theoretical knowledge about construction of 3D space, but also after

H. Cherifi, J.M. Zain, and E. El-Qawasmeh (Eds.): DICTAP 2011, Part I, CCIS 166, pp. 368–379, 2011.

detailed examination, visual mapping and understanding of the real spatial approaches. Gardner describes the spatial abilities as an important component of human intelligence where a mental model of the spatial world is forming [1]. A survey with a first year mechanical engineering students about their spatial abilities is done by Nagy-Kondor and the results point that many students have a problem when they have to imagine a spatial figure, to reconstruct and represent of the projection [2]. The 3D presentation of Augmented Reality (AR) technology can be used to provide novel learning opportunities for spatial understanding. According to Horizon report [3] simple AR will be adopted for two to three years giving the opportunity for gaining rich learning experience.

Augmented Reality is described commonly as combined computer-generated virtual objects/ environments with real objects/environments, often to enhance or annotate what can be discerned by the human user [4]. Virtual 2D or 3D computer graphics objects are augmented with real world creating the sensation that virtual objects are presented in the real world. The virtual objects display information that the students cannot directly detect with their own senses. Marker and markerless AR applications are experimented for educational purposes. More simple and low-cost solution is marker pattern creation with combination of web camera usage and computer. AR authoring software tools need for creating 3D objects, marker patterns and tags, for objects rendering and positioning in 3D space. AR effect can be created without using markers, it is the so called markerless AR that uses special equipment for placing virtual elements in a digital world. Markerless AR has not yet advanced to the point where it's possible to provide a simple way for the public to use the technology.

Two AR techniques: the magic mirror and the magic lens are known to extend the real environments. The magic mirror technique requires a computer/television monitor behind the area that is being captured by an AR video camera. The magic lens technique is a different approach utilizing a standard computer monitor or as complex as a Head-Mounted Display (HMD) allowing an image of the real world to be seen with added AR elements [5].

In this paper AR applications utilized in several learning scenarios from chemistry, biology, astronomy, automotive engineering are explored to identify the benefits of AR technology for a learning process and also the possibilities for integration of AR learning objects in a learning environment to be seen. Exploration and summarization of approaches for marker AR learning objects development is done and a solution of an authoring tool is chosen. In a case study two different learning scenarios have been carefully designed based on human-computer interaction principles so that meaningful virtual information is presented in an interactive and engaging way. The advantages of marker AR technology for enhancement of an individual's learning experience and better understanding of spatial spaces are discussed after taking the students' comments.

2 State-of-the-Art of Learning Scenarios with AR Technology

The literature overview shows that AR provides exciting tools for students to learn and explore new things in more interesting ways in different science subject domains.

There are many studies conducted to prove that AR implemented in classroom help to improve the learning process and a few of them are examined below.

AR in chemistry education is investigated in [6] exploring how students interact and learn with AR and physical models of amino acids. Several of students like AR technology, because the models are portable and easy to make, allowing them to observe the structures in more details and also to receive a bigger image. Other students feel uncomfortable using the AR markers; they prefer to interact with ball-and-stick physical models in order to get a feeling of physical contact. The research provides guidelines concerning designing the AR environment for classroom settings.

In the biology area, a learning system on interior human body is produced to present the human organs in details when students need such knowledge [7]. The analysis point that there is no significant differences using both visualization systems (Head-Mounted Display and a typical monitor) and students consider these systems as a useful and enjoyable tool for learning of the interior of the human body.

In astronomy, the AR technology is applied as a method for better students' understanding of sun-earth system concepts of rotation/revolution, solstice/equinox, and seasonal variation of light and temperature [8]. The authors report that the usage of visual and sensory information creates a powerful learning experience for the students, improving significantly their understanding and reducing misunderstandings. The analysis implies that learning complex spatial phenomena is closely linked to the way students control the time and way they are able to manipulate virtual 3D objects.

An AR system for automotive engineering education is developed to support teaching/learning of the disassemble/assemble procedure of automatic transmission of a vehicle. The system consists of vehicle transmission, set of tools and mechanical facilities, two video cameras, computer with developed software, HMD glasses, two LCD screens and software that provides instructions on assembling and disassembling processes of real vehicle transmission. Overlaying of 3D instructions on the technological workspace can be used as an interactive educational step-by-step guide. The authors conclude that this AR system makes educational process more interesting and intuitive, the learning process is easier and financially more effective [9].

Development of AR books contributes to enhancing the learning process too, allowing the final user to experience a variety of sensory stimuli while enjoying and interacting with the content [10]. In a preliminary evaluation with five adults the author founds the AR book's features impact learning in several ways: enhance its value as an educational material, easier understanding of the visualized text, audio-visual content is more attractive than standard text books.

AR books technology is currently suitable to implement in storytelling, giving possibilities for visualization of 3D animation virtual model appearing on the current pages using the AR display and interacting with pop-up avatar characters from any perspective view [11].

Several advantages to integrate AR technology in education are identified during the examination of AR implementation in educational practices. Utilizing AR for learning stimulates creative thinking among students, enhances their comprehension in concrete subject domain and increase the understanding of spatial spaces. In several unattractive science subjects AR technology can stand as a motivation tool for conduction of students their own explorations and as a supportive tool of theory learning in an interesting and enjoyable way. AR proposes a safe environment for students to practice skills and conduct experiments.

The key benefits of AR technology are summarized in [12] : excels at conveying spatial and temporal concepts; multiple objects can be placed in relative context to one another or relative to objects in the real world; maximizes impact, creates contextual awareness, enhances engagement, and facilitates interaction; heightens understanding with kinesthetic learners; provides a high degree of engaging, self-paced interaction, and maintains interest; improves communication, learning retention, and interaction with others; includes both professionally built content and an AR content building tool suite.

Several AR system affordances are described in [13] in context of environmental design education: rapid and accurate object identification, invisible feature identification and exploration; the layering of multiple information sources; readily apparent object relationships; and easy manipulation of perspectives.

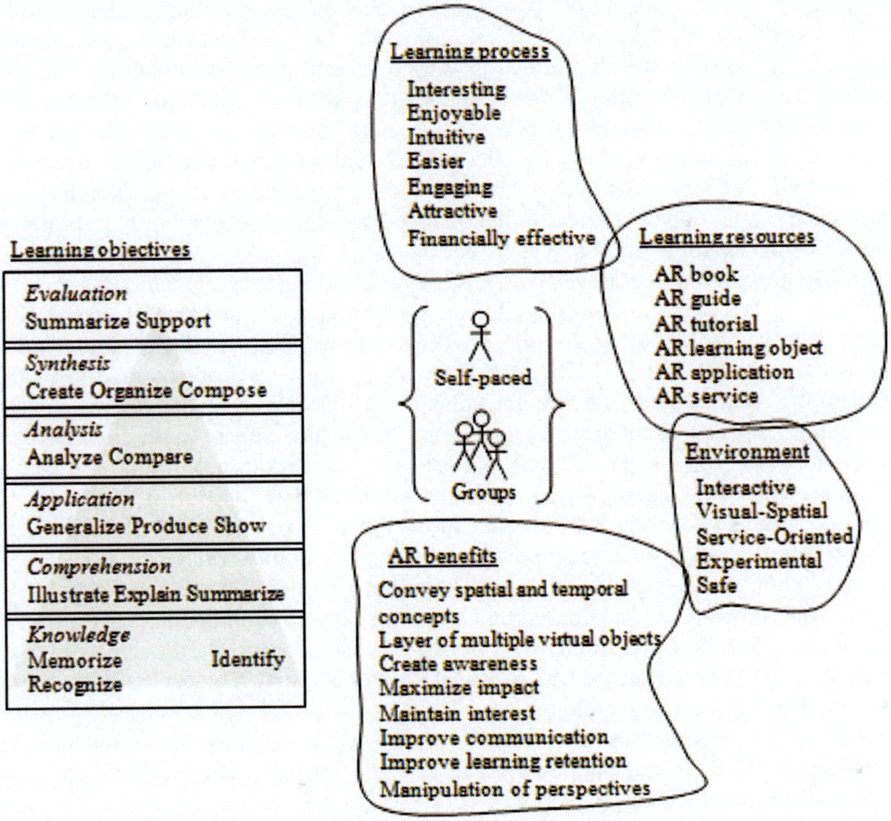

Fig. 1. Benefits of AR technology for learning

A generalized model about the benefits of AR technology for learning is summarized via Figure 1. A student (alone or in a group) can be involved in a learning process according to preliminary defined learning objectives (Bloom taxonomy is used here) utilizing environment with learning resources/services (including marker AR learning objects (LO)) and achieving knowledge/skills taking advantages of AR technology.

2 Software and Tools

Exploration of AR software features is done with aim an appropriate tool for automated authoring of marker AR LO to be chosen. The information is gathered from web sites and scientific papers with studies and practices and it is summarized in Table 1.

ARToolKit (http://www.hitl.washington.edu/artoolkit/) is a C and C++ language software library for building AR applications. ARToolKit is originally developed by Dr. Hirokazu Kato, and its ongoing development is being supported by the Human Interface Technology Laboratory (HIT) at the University of Washington, HIT Lab NZ at the University of Canterbury, New Zealand, and ARToolworks, Inc, Seattle. Among of its features are the following: single camera position/orientation tracking, tracking code that uses simple black squares, the ability to use any square marker patterns, easy camera calibration code, fast enough for real time AR applications. A development environment such as Microsoft Visual Studio 6 and Microsoft Visual Studio .NET 2003 or other free available needs for toolkit building. Currently it is maintained as an open source project hosted on SourceForge with commercial licenses available from ARToolWorks.

ARTag (http://www.artag.net/) is a C++ and C# library which started as an extension to ARToolkit. Currently it comes bundled with an OpenGL-based SDK which makes it a standalone solution. ARTag is developed by Mark Fiala when he was working at the National Research Council of Canada's Institute of Information Technology. This library is freely unavailable after December 2010 due to licensing restrictions. ARTag recognizes special black-and-white square markers, finds the pose, and then sets the model view matrix. ARTag markers allow the software to calculate where to insert virtual elements so that they appear properly in the augmented image. Among ARTag advantages (in comparison with ARToolkit) are increased computing processing power, uses more complex image processing and digital symbol processing to achieve a higher reliability and immunity to lighting.
Support for camera capture is based on OpenCV's CvCam library for USB2 cameras, IEEE-1394 cameras from Point Grey research are also supported. 3D objects in WRL (VRML), OBJ (Wavefront, Maya), ASE (3D-Studio export) files can be loaded from disk and displayed as augmentations.

Studierstube (http://studierstube.icg.tu-graz.ac.at/) is a software framework for development (C/C++ language coding) of AR and virtual reality applications. This framework is invented to develop the worldwide first collaborative AR application. Later the focus changed to support mobile AR applications development. Studierstube is a product of Graz University of Technology. Studierstube for PC is freely available for download under GPL, while Studierstube ES for mobile phones is available commercially. It builds on the scene graph library Coin3D and features the device management framework OpenTracker. Additionally, ADAPTIVE Communication

Environment (to extend Studierstube's network communication abilities), Coin3D-2, and TinyXML library can be utilized.

Goblin XNA (http://graphics.cs.columbia.edu/projects/goblin/index.htm) is a platform for research on 3D user interfaces, including mobile AR and virtual reality, with an emphasis on games. It is developed from Colombia University and it is written in C# and based on the Microsoft XNA platform. The platform currently supports 6DOF (six degree of freedom) position and orientation tracking using marker based camera tracking through ARTag with OpenCV or DirectShow, and InterSense hybrid trackers. Physics is supported through BulletX and Newton Game Dynamics. Networking is supported through Lidgren library.

osgART (http://www.artoolworks.com/community/osgart/) is a new software development toolkit (C++ library) developed by the HITLab NZ and distributed by ARToolworks, Inc., which simplifies the development of AR or mixed reality applications by combining the well-known ARToolKit tracking library with OpenSceneGraph. The library offers 3 main functionalities: high level integration of video input, spatial registration, and photometric registration. With osgART, users gain the benefit of all the features of OpenSceneGraph (high quality renderer, multiple file type loaders, community nodekits like osgAL, etc.). The user can develop and prototype interactive applications that can use tangible interaction (in C++, Python, Lua, Ruby, etc.).

ARMedia Plugin for Autodesk 3DMax (http://www.inglobetechnologies.com/en/new_products/arplugin_max/info.php) allows experimentation with the AR technology inside 3D modeling software, visualizing 3D products directly in the real physical space which surrounds them, also models can be visualized out of the digital workspace directly on users' desktop or in any physical location, by connecting a simple webcam and by printing a suitable code. By means of the ARmedia Exporter users can create and publish AR files autonomously. Files created by the Exporter can be visualized on any computer with the freely available ARmedia Player, without the need of having Autodesk 3dsMax and the Plugin installed.

ATOMIC (http://www.sologicolibre.org/projects/atomic/en/index.php) is a project to create a new authoring tool suitable for children. Initially developed to create AR applications and mind maps. ATOMIC Authoring Tool is FLOSS software developed under the GPL license. ATOMIC is a cross-platform software, developed for non-programmers, for creation of small and simple AR applications.

DART (http://www.cc.gatech.edu/dart/aboutdart.htm) is designed to support rapid prototyping of AR experiences, to overlay graphics and audio on a user's view of the world. DART is built as a collection of extensions to the Macromedia Director multimedia-programming environment. The DART system consists of: (1) A Director Xtra to communicate with cameras, the marker tracker, hardware trackers and sensors, and distributed memory. (2) A collection of director behavior palettes that contains drag and drop behaviors for controlling the functionality of the AR application, from low-level device control to high level actors and actions.

AMIRE is a project about the efficient creation and modification of augmented reality (AR) and mixed reality (MR) applications. AMIRE provides the tools for authoring AR/MR applications based on a library of components.

Table 1. Features of AR software and tools

Product	Type	Features	Prerequisite (for Windows OS)	License
ARToolKit	Library	single camera position, tracking code that uses simple black squares, use of any square marker patterns, easy camera calibration code, fast for real time AR apps	- Microsoft Visual Studio 6 and Microsoft Visual Studio .NET 2003 - DSVideoLib - GLUT SDK - DirectX runtime	-GNU GPL/ARTool Kit -Commercial -Dual license
ARTag	Library	increased computing processing power, more complex image processing, a higher reliability and immunity to lighting	-Ogre3D Software Development Kit -OpenCV \STLport -P5 Glove Software development kit	License restrictions
Studierstube	Framework for development	- AR applications – collaborative, mobile	-VisualStudio 2005 -External components	- PC - GPL - mobile phones - commercially
Goblin XNA	Library	3D scene manipulation and rendering, 6DOF position and orientation tracking, networking, creation of classical 2D interaction components	-Microsoft Visual Studio 2008 -XNA Game Studio -Newton Game Dynamics SDK 1.53 -ALVAR or Artag	BSD License
osgART	Library	support of multiple video inputs, integration of high level video object, video shader concept, generic marker concept, API in C++ ,Python, Lua, Ruby, C# and Java	- Visual Studio .NET 2003 - OpenSceneGraph - ARToolKit.	osgART Standard Edition - GNU GPL license
ARMedia	Plugin for 3DSMax	stand alone, web, mobile apps, tracking techniques, marker library and generator, exporter, lighting debug mode, antialiasing, support animations, scene configuration	-ARMedia Player -3DSMax software - Apple QuickTime	Trial, PLE, Commercial
ATOMIC	Authoring Tool	choice of pattern and object, run and execute wrl files	-JAVA RT	GPL license
DART	A collection of extensions to the Macromedia Director	coordinate 3D objects, video, sound, and tracking information, communicate with cameras, the marker tracker, hardware trackers and sensors, and distributed memory	-Macromedia Director 8.5 or newer -Direct X 9.0b Runtime -Shockwave Player	Trial, Commercial

Examination of products' features, prerequisites for Windows OS and license from one hand and the context of usage from other hand lead to decision making about utilization of the appropriate tool for AR LO development. Experimentation with ARMedia Plugin for Autodesk 3DMax is chosen because of several reasons: (1) Autodesk 3DMax environment is well-known by authors and it is studied by students during the course Computer graphics. In this case the students can play a role not only of content consumers, but also can be involved in authoring and learning process, working on their projects (including AR technology). (2) ARMedia Plugin is easy and fast for installation and configuration by educators and students. (3) AR LO can be visualized on any computer with the freely available ARmedia Player, without the need of having Autodesk 3DSMax and the Plugin installed (if they are consumers).

3 Case Study – Marker AR in Computer Graphics

AR is a promising technology in educational sector, but it is important to ascertain whether it can support learning in Computer graphics subject in an effective way. The following hypothesis in this study is suggested: marker AR can be effectively combined with traditional learning methods to help students understand complex concepts and analyze spatial spaces during practical laboratories where they create 3D models and scenes. Two interactive scenarios are designed and demonstrated to Computer graphics course. The first scenario is called "Project-based learning" and it represents a gallery of 3D models and scenes to introduce students to possible problems in their project working. The second one is called "Learning by AR representation" and the tutorial is designed consisting of several marker AR learning objects about vector and raster hardware input, output and interactive computer graphics devices. The participants are students in the second year of their bachelor degree from Computer Science and Electronics specialty. They are divided administratively in three groups of 20 students. Qualitative responses are collected from the students based on the "thinking aloud" technique [14] and the method of "informal interview" [15].

The project based learning (PBL) is an important factor for generic (problem solving, communication, creative thinking, decision making, management) and specific technical skills acquired by students studying Computer graphics course [16]. It enables them to understand in details given topics reconstructing complex models and scenes from the real world (interior, exterior) or creating new imaginary solutions (e.g. cosmic scene). The PBL model proposed in [17] is applied and includes the following steps: (1) Introducing students to the state of the art problems and showing the huge potential of working topics; (2) Identification of challenging problems and solving the problems by students; (3) Setting up the driving questions what has to be accomplished and what content has to be studied; (4) Introducing students to the environment for problem solving (including collecting and managing its main components when students organize their PLEs) with 3 main components: digital resources (marker AR gallery, tutorials, best practices, papers), web-based applications/tools and free hosted services; (5) The process of the actual investigation is performed: how the tasks can be completed that require higher-level and critical thinking skills, such as analysis, synthesis and evaluation of information; (6) Guidance is provided when students need it (through student-educator interactions, peer counselling, guiding, project templates, etc.); (7) Assessment of the students' knowledge and competences as a result of the project work.

AR gallery is developed to support the first step of PBL model when students have to choose a topic for implementation. AR gallery consists of free available 2D pictures of models and scenes, created with 3DSMax software and also the previews works of alumni. The students from past years in this first step were involved in 3D realistic modeling via these 2D pictures, talking about shapes, space, perspectives, light and rendering effects, color patterns, materials and maps. This year, the AR gallery is presented to students giving them access to marker AR learning objects and possibility to interact with 3D models/scenes as long as they wish to understand the physical phenomena, art techniques or engineering methods (Figure 2). This allowed the exploration of the potential benefits of AR technologies for learning in Computer graphics course. AR gallery could be viewed locally or over the Internet, using only low-cost system of webcam and computer.

One part of students prefers to work on their projects in self-paced mode and others are grouped in two or three. Self-paced learning is chosen by individuals who wish independently to direct the processes of doing and learning and they feel bored and frustrated when they have to work in a group. Group-based learning is characterized with agreement among students about the pieces that can be created, with good communication, ideas transferring and decision making. It removes the barriers of individual thinking and understanding and offers students with multiple arguments which encourage thinking in different aspects and learning from each other. It also forces and motivates weaker students to improve their work/learning and to join the collaborative union that eventually helps them to feel stronger in a given topic.

Fig. 2. Learning objects from marker AR gallery

In the second scenario the main strategy is based on learning by AR representation. According to the curriculum of the Computer graphics course, one topic is devoted to the understanding of input, output, interactive raster and vector devices. To present a more engaging way of learning, 3D representations of the hardware is combined with human-computer interaction techniques. Students are able to examine the 3D information about raster and vector concepts and their realizations in a given hardware solution. The aim of these marker AR learning objects (organized in a tutorial) is to combine traditional methods (i.e. textbook reading with 2D pictures) with interactive AR technologies to understand how such computer graphics hardware devices look like in reality from different perspectives. The 3D representations are available for students and they are able to perform basic interactions on them such as rotations, translations and scaling operations (Figure 3). Several 3D models in this tutorial are created by students and educators, others are found through Google search as free available models.

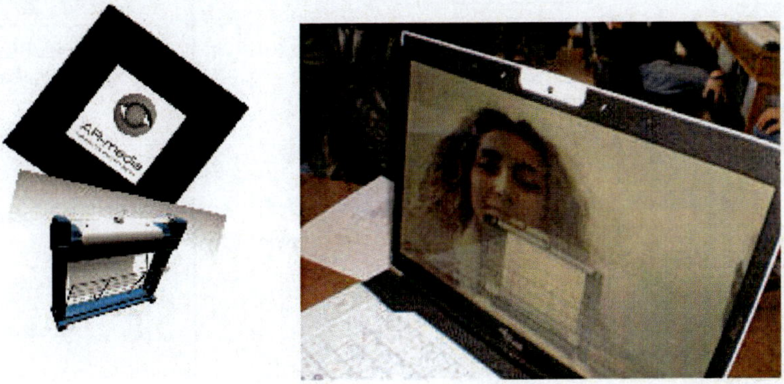

Fig. 3. Marker AR Tutorial

The AR patterns are presented to the students in the lecture time and they have a possibility to interact with AR models during laboratory practices and at home in informal way in time they wish.

The free hosted learning management system Edu20 is utilized for students' facilitation of learning scenarios, access to AR content/patterns and social interactions. A model of a virtual learning environment (VLE) is created to support the effective students' participation during the course (Figure 4), actively using AR technology.

The students' opinion after experimentation about effectiveness of marker AR technology for learning in the designed learning scenarios is gathered. The students are asked to comment on the effectiveness of AR learning objects in their preparation for project working and studying of topic about computer graphics hardware devices. Also, they are asked to share their opinion about the potential of AR technology usage as an additional tool for learning the Computer graphics course. As far as the students' feedback is concerned, all of them agreed the presented technology is very promising and should be applied in the classroom in the future. Most of them are impressed with the ease of use, the flexibility and the capabilities of the learning interface. They commented that the marker AR LO can enhance interaction and engagement with the subject matter. The spatial spaces can be examined in details that support creation of more realistic 3D models and scenes. Several students pointed out that the use of AR technology is an impressive method for easier learning, memorizing and understanding the theories and concepts in Computer graphics. Among the advantages of AR technology students include the possibility to observe supplementary digital information, to see the model details and the opportunity to manipulate intuitively the virtual information, repeating LO as many times as they need. However, almost all students make benevolent comments about the fact that only a few scenarios with several LO are implemented. Several of them express their enthusiasm and ideas to prepare models and scenes that could be utilized as parts of AR gallery and AR tutorial.

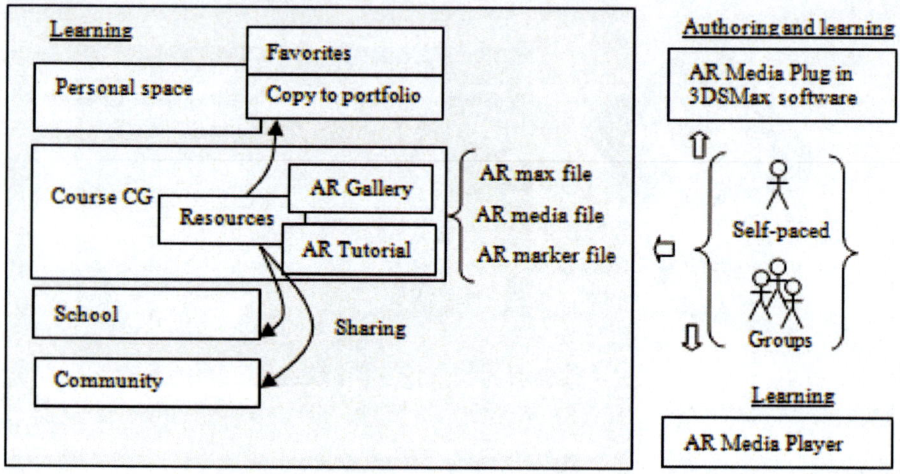

Fig. 4. A model of VLE with AR technology

4 Conclusion

In this paper, a low-cost interactive environment including AR technology for learning improving and spatial spaces understanding is presented. The innovation of the solution is that it can propose students high interactive human-computer interface for models manipulation and thus observing the details in 3D space. The software for AR content development is explored with aim an authoring tool to be chosen. The effect of the made choice is increased of the fact that students are involved not only in interaction with AR learning objects, but also in an authoring process of 3D learning objects. The results of the case study show the positive opinion of students about the future usage of marker AR technology in the course Computer graphics. They are impressed by the possibility of multi-modal visualization, practical exploration of the theory, and an attractive and enjoyable way for learning. The AR technology can be applied in self-paced learning, where individual learners are able to manage their directions of exploration as well as in group-based learning where communication, ideas sharing and interaction among participants are among the main methods for learning.

References

1. Gardner, H.: Frames of mind: the theory of multiple intelligences. Basic Books, New York (1983)
2. Nagy-Kondor, R.: Spatial ability of engineering students. Annales Mathematicae et Informaticae 34, 113–122 (2007), http://www.kurims.kyoto-u.ac.jp/EMIS/journals/AMI/2007/ami2007-nagy.pdf
3. Johnson, L., Levine, A., Smith, R., Stone, S.: The 2010 Horizon Report. The New Media Consortium, Austin (2010)
4. Augmented reality – Wikipedia, http://en.wikipedia.org/wiki/Augmented_reality
5. Augmented reality: A practical guide (2008), http://media.pragprog.com/titles/cfar/intro.pdf
6. Chen, Y.: A study of comparing the use of augmented reality and physical models in chemistry education. In: Proceedings of the ACM International Conference on Virtual Reality Continuum and its Application, Hong Kong, China, June 14-June 17, pp. 369–372 (2006)
7. Juan, C., Beatrice, F., Cano, J.: An Augmented Reality System for Learning the Interior of the Human Body. In: Eighth IEEE International Conference on Advanced Learning Technologies, ICALT 2008, Santander, Cantabri, pp. 186–188 (2008)
8. Shelton, B., Hedley, N.: Using Augmented Reality for Teaching Earth-Sun Relationships to Undergraduate Geography Students. In: First IEEE International Augmented Reality Toolkit Workshop, Darmstadt, Germany (2002)
9. Farkhatdinov, I., Ryu, J.: Development of Educational System for Automotive Engineering based on Augmented Reality. In: Proceedings of the ICEE and ICEER 2009 International Conference on Engineering Education and Research, Korea (2009), http://robot.kut.ac.kr/papers/DeveEduVirtual.pdf
10. Dias, A.: Technology enhanced learning and augmented reality: An application on mulltimedia interactive books. International Business & Economics Review 1(1) (2009)
11. Billinghurst, M., Kato, H., Poupyrev, I.: The MagicBook-Moving Seamlessly between Reality and Virtuality. IEEE Computer Graphics and Applications 21(3), 6–8 (2001)
12. Jochim, S.: Augmented Reality in Modern Education (2010), http://augmentedrealitydevelopmentlab.com/wp-content/uploads/2010/08/ARDLArticle8.5-11Small.pdf
13. Blalock, J., Carringer, J.: Augmented Reality Applications for Environmental Designers. In: Pearson, E., Bohman, P. (eds.) Proceedings of World Conference on Educational Multimedia, Hypermedia and Telecommunications, pp. 2757–2762. AACE, Chesapeake (2006)
14. Dix, J., Finlay, J., Abowd, D., Beale, R.: Human-Computer Interaction, 3rd edn. Prentice Hall Europe, Pearson (2004)
15. Valenzuela, D., Shrivastava, P.: Interview as a Method for Qualitative Research. Presentation, http://www.public.asu.edu/~kroel/www500/Interview%20Fri.pdf
16. Thomas, W.: A Review of Research on Project Based Learning (March 2000), http://www.bobpearlman.org/BestPractices/PBL_Research.pdf
17. Shtereva, K., Ivanova, M., Raykov, P.: Project Based Learning in Microelectronics: Utilizing ICAPP. Interactive Computer Aided Learning Conference, Villach, Austria, September 23-25 (2009)

User Interface Plasticity for Groupware

Sonia Mendoza[1], Dominique Decouchant[2,3], Gabriela Sánchez[1], José Rodríguez[1], and Alfredo Piero Mateos Papis[2]

[1] Departamento de Computación, CINVESTAV-IPN, D.F., Mexico
smendoza@cs.cinvestav.mx,
gsanchez@computacion.cs.cinvestav.mx
rodriguez@cs.cinvestav.mx,
[2] Depto. de Tecnologías de la Información, UAM-Cuajimalpa, D.F., Mexico
decouchant@correo.cua.uam.mx
amateos@correo.cua.uam.mx
[3] C.N.R.S. - Laboratoire LIG de Grenoble, France

Abstract. Plastic user interfaces are intentionally developed to automatically adapt themselves to changes in the user's working context. Although some Web single-user interactive systems already integrate some plastic capabilities, this research topic remains quasi-unexplored in the domain of Computer Supported Cooperative Work. This paper is centered on prototyping a plastic collaborative whiteboard, which adapts itself: 1) to the *platform*, as being able to be launched from heterogeneous computer devices and 2) to each *collaborator*, when he is detected working from several devices. In this last case, if the collaborator agrees, the whiteboard can split its user interface among his devices in order to facilitate user-system interaction without affecting the other collaborators present in the working session. The distributed interface components work as if they were co-located within a unique device. At any time, the whiteboard maintains group awareness among the involved collaborators.

Keywords: plastic user interfaces, context of use, multi-computer and multi-user collaborative environments, group awareness.

1 Introduction

The increasing proliferation of heterogeneous computers and the unstoppable progress of communication networks allow to conceive the user [2] as a nomadic entity that evolves within a multi-computer and multi-user environment where he employs several devices and systems to collaborate with other users anytime anywhere. However, an interactive system cannot display the same user interface on small, medium and big screens of such a multi-computer environment.

The automatic transposition of an interactive system from a PC to a smartphone results non-feasible, due to their so different displaying, processing, storage and communication capabilities. The most obvious solution to cope with this problem focus on reducing the size of user interface components in order to display them in a unique view [5]. However, this primitive solution affects usability because manipulating these components might be difficult for the user.

H. Cherifi, J.M. Zain, and E. El-Qawasmeh (Eds.): DICTAP 2011, Part I, CCIS 166, pp. 380–394, 2011.

User interface plasticity [4] allows interactive systems to manage variations based on: 1) the *user* (e.g., detecting when he is interacting with the system from several devices), 2) the *environment* (e.g., hiding personal information when a unauthorized person is approaching to the screen), and 3) the hardware and software *platforms* (e.g., screen size and operating system capabilities), while preserving a set of quality criteria (e.g., usability and continuity).

In the domain of single-user interactive systems, user interface plasticity has been mainly studied through the development of prototypes and the definition of some concepts and models. However, this topic remains quasi-unexplored in the domain of groupware systems, despite the imminent need to provide the user interface of these systems with adaptability to contextual changes, e.g., components should be shown (hidden) in order to supply (to filter reduntant) group awareness information during distributed (face-to-face) interactions.

In this paper, we apply some adaptability principles to the development of a plastic collaborative whiteboard that is able: 1) to remodel its user interface in order to be launched from heterogeneous devices, and 2) to redistribute a user's interface (without disrupting the other collaborators of the working session) when detecting he is working from different devices. We specially select the collaborative whiteboard application because its functional core is relatively simple, whereas its user interface allows us to focus on our main goal: to study how plasticity principles can be successfully applied to adapt the collaborators' interface and whether they are relevant in the field of the groupware systems.

After providing a background of the plasticity problem for single-user systems (Section 2), we present an analysis of the adaptability properties of the most relevant plastic interactive systems (Section 3). Afterwards, we apply and adapt some adaptability principles to design and implement the proposed plastic collaborative whiteboard (Section 4). Then, we describe some achieved results that allow us to show how our application facilitates both user-system and user-user interactions due to its plastic capacities (Section 5). Finally, some important extensions concludes our proposal (Section 6).

2 Background: Plasticity for Single-User Systems

Plasticity [4] is defined as the capability of interactive systems to adapt themselves to changes produced in their context of use, while preserving a set of predefined quality properties, e.g., usability. The *context of use* [2] involves three elements: 1) the *user* denotes the human being who is using the interactive system; 2) the *platform* refers to the available hardware and software of the user's computers; and 3) the *environment* concerns the physical and social conditions where interaction takes place. Plasticity is achieved from two approaches [4]:

a) *Redistribution* reorganizes the user interface (UI) on different platforms. Four types are identified: 1) from a *centralized organization to another one*, whose goal is to preserve the centralization state of the UI, e.g., migration from a PC to a PDA; 2) from a *centralized one to a distributed one*, which distributes the UI among several platforms; 3) from *a distributed one to a centralized one*, whose effect is to concentrate the UI into one platform; and 4) from a *distributed organization to another one*, which modifies the distribution state of the UI.

b) *Remodeling* reconfigures the UI by inserting, suppressing, and substituting all or some UI components. Transformations apply to different abstraction levels: 1) *intra-modal*, when the source components are retargeted within the same modality, e.g., from graphical interaction to graphical one; 2) *inter-modal*, when the source components are retargeted into a different modality, e.g., from graphical interaction to hapic one; and 3) *multi-modal*, when remodeling uses a combination of intra- and inter-modal transformations.

Both plasticity approaches consider some factors that have a direct influence when adapting the user interface of single-user interactive systems [4]:

a) The *adaptation granularity* denotes the UI unit that can be remodeled and redistributed. Four adaptation grains are identified: 1) *pixel* shares out any UI component among multiple displays; 2) *interactor* represents the UI smallest unit supporting a task, e.g., a "save" button; 3) *workspace* refers to a space supporting the execution of a set of logically related tasks, e.g., a printing window; and 4) *total* affects the whole UI by modifications.

b) The *user interface deployment* concerns the installation of the UI in the host platform following: 1) *static deployment*, which means that UI adaptation is performed when the system is launched and from then no more modifications are carried out; or 2) *dynamic deployment*, which means that remodeling and redistribution are performed on the fly.

c) The *meta-user interface* (meta-UI) consists of a set of functions that evaluate and control the state of a plastic system. Three types of meta-IUs are identified: 1) *meta-UI without negotiation*, which makes observable the adaptation process without allowing the user to participate; 2) *meta-UI with negotiation*, which is required when the system cannot decide between different adaptation forms, or when the user wants to control the process outcome; and 3) *plastic meta-UI*, which instantiates the adequate meta-UI when the system is launched.

3 Related Work

On the basis of the previously introduced factors, we analyze the most important plastic interactive systems. The majority of them are single-user systems, although others only provide a basic support for cooperative work. Few systems automatically remodel and redistribute their user interface, while others invite the user to participate to the adaptation process.

The Sedan-BouillonWeb site [1] promotes the tourist sites of Sedan and Bouillon cities. It allows the user to control the redistribution of the site main page between two devices. The heating control system [4] allows the user to administrate the temperature of his house rooms from different hardware and software platforms. Unlike these single-user interactive systems, Roomware [9] supports working groups, whose members are co-located in a physical room; this system aims to add computing capabilities to real objects (e.g., walls and tables) in order to explore new interaction forms. The ConnecTables system [11] facilitates transitions from individual work to cooperative one, allowing the users to couple two personal tablets to dynamically create a shared workspace.

The first plastic capability, the *context of use*, refers to the user interface adaptation to the *user*, the *platform* and the *environment*. The Sedan-Bouillon Web site adapts to: 1) the *user* as it identifies him when he is working from different devices; and 2) the *platform* as it can be accessed from PC and PDA. The heating control system adapts to the software/hardware *platforms* because it can be launched as Web and stand-alone applications, and it allows to consult the room temperature from heterogeneous devices. Likewise, Roomware is able to run on three special devices: 1) DynaWall, a large wall touch-sensitive device; 2) InteracTable, a touch-sensitive plasma display into a tabletop; and 3) CommChair, which combines an armchairs with a pen-based computer. A variation of *platform* adaptation is implemented by ConnecTable*s* that allows to physically/logically couple two tablets to create a shared space.

There are four types of UI *redistribution* that result from the 2-permutation with repetition allowed on a set of two possible transition states: *centralization* and *distribution*. The Sedan-Bouillon Web site supports all types of redistribution, e.g., full replication or partial distribution of the workspaces between different devices. Roomware supports transitions: 1) *centralized-distributed*, when sharing out the UI among the three smartboards of DynaWall; 2) *distributed-centralized*, when reconcentrating the UI in an InteracTable or CommChair; and 3) *centralized-centralized*, when migrating the UI from an InteracTable to a CommChair and vice-versa. ConnecTables only supports UI transitions from a *distributed organization* to a *centralized one* and vice-versa, when two tablets are respectively coupled and decoupled. Finally, the heating control only proposes a *centralized organization* of their UI.

Remodeling consists in reconfiguring the UI components at the *intra-*, *inter-* or *multi-modal* abstraction levels. All the analyzed systems are *intra-modal* as their source components are retargeted within the same graphical modality.

The *adaptation granularity* defines the deep grain (i.e., *pixel*, *interactor*, *workspace*, *total*) in which the UI can be transformed. The heating control system remodels its UI at the *total* and *interactor* grains; the first grain means that the PC and PDA user interfaces are graphical, whereas those of the mobile phone and watch are textual; the second grain means that the PC user interface is displayed on one view, whereas that of the PDA is structured into three views (one per room) through which the user navigates using tabs. The Sedan-Bouillon Web site remodels its UI at the *workspace* grain as the presentation (size, position and alignment) of the Web main page title, content and navigation bar is modified when this page is loaded from a PDA. Roomware uses the *pixel* grain when the UI is distributed on the three smartboards of DynaWall. Finally, ConnecTables also redistributes its UI at the *pixel* grain, allowing the user to drag-and-drop an image from one tablet to another when they are in coupled mode.

The *user interface deployment* can be *static* or *dynamic*. The Sedan-Bouillon Web site provides on the fly redistribution of its workspaces. Likewise, ConnecTables dynamically creates a shared workspace (or personal ones) when two users couple (or decouple) their tablets. The heating control and Roomware only provide *static deployment*.

The Sedan-Bouillon Web site is the unique system that provides a *meta-user interface with negotiation*, because the user cooperates with the system for the redistribution of the UI workspaces (e.g., Web page title and navigation bar).

Currently, the adaptability of groupware applications is being analyzed as a side issue of the development of augmented reality techniques, which mainly rely on redistribution. The studied systems do not consider neither the *user* and *environment* elements of the context of use, nor most of the factors that affect the user interface. Thus, we explore whether a plastic groupware application can be developed from the plasticity principles defined for single-user systems.

4 Development of a Plastic Collaborative Whiteboard

Applying the plasticity approaches and factors of single-user interactive systems (cf. Section 2), we developed a plastic collaborative whiteboard. This application is able to remodels and redistributes its user interface in response to changes occurred in the *platform* and *user* elements of the context of use. Firstly, we describe a MVC-based design of this groupware application. Afterwards, we focus on implementation issues related with the display space management of handheld devices. Finally, we present some results by means of a scenario that highlights the benefits to provide groupware applications with plastic capabilities.

4.1 MVC Architecture-Based Design

The design of the plastic collaborative whiteboard is based on the architectural style Model-View-Controller (MVC) [7]. We prefer it to other styles (e.g., PAC* [8]) as, from our point of view, the MVC principles (several views for a model) match better with the plasticity principles (several user interfaces for an application). Thus, MVC simplifies the application structural representation before and after applying any plastic adaptation. MVC also facilitates software reutilization by modeling the application as independent interrelated components.

The basic MVC architecture consists of a *model*, which represents the application data; a *controller*, which interprets user input; and a *view*, which handles output. Like many MVC variants, our plastic collaborative whiteboard implements view-controller pairs as combined components. As shown in Fig. 1, the MVC tree contains the root node, R, and three child nodes, H1, H2 and H3. At runtime, the R node view-controller is in charge of: 1) creating an application instance, 2) coordinating its children, and 3) communicating with other distributed application instances. The R node model stores information about these tasks (e.g., remote instance identifier or active children). The R node children are:

The *H1 node* authenticates the collaborator. Its view-controller receives the collaborator identification (e.g., a name/password pair or a real-time photo of his face) from a specific window. Then, the H1 view-controller calls the corresponding model functions to validate the collaborator identity. Finally, the H1 view-controller notifies its father of the validation result.

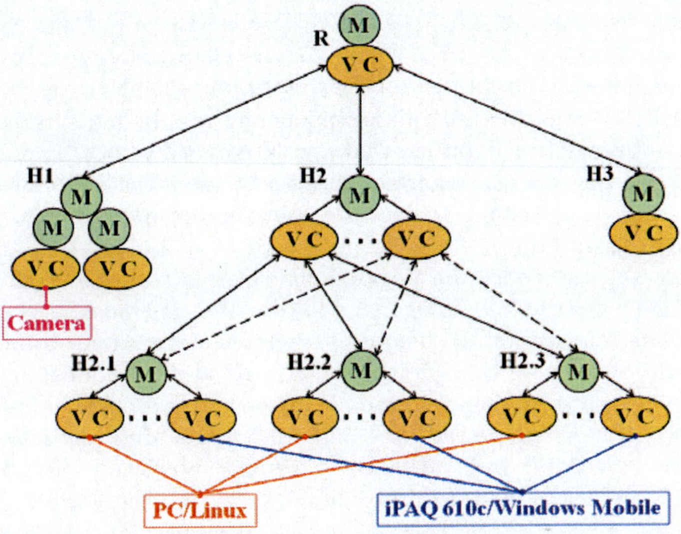

Fig. 1. MVC-Based Architecture of the Plastic Collaborative Whiteboard

The *H2 node* administrates the collaborative whiteboard. Its view-controller receives the collaborator's input (e.g., clicks on the drawing area), whereas its model maintains a log of each collaborator's actions (e.g., created figures/texts and their dimensions, coordinates, and used paintbrushes and colors). The H2 node contains three children nodes:

1) The *H2.1 node* manages the toolbar, which is composed of several figures, paintbrushes, and colors. The H2.1 view-controller calls the corresponding model functions in order to highlight the current tools (e.g., figure and color) chosen by the local collaborator.

2) The *H2.2 node* administrates the drawing area. Its view-controller calls the corresponding H2.2 model functions that calculate the 2D dimensions and coordinates of each figure and text displayed on the screen. The H2.2 view-controller communicate with its remote pairs in order to provide and obtain the productions accomplished by respectively the local collaborator and the remote ones. The H2.2 model saves each figure and text properties (e.g., type, outline, color, size, position and creator).

3) The *H2.3 node* manages the group awareness bar. Its view-controller manages the collaborators' status (e.g., present/absent) in the working session and coordinates with its remote pairs to organize each collaborator's name, photo and status in order of arrival. The H2.3 model stores relevant information about collaborators (e.g., identifier and incoming/leaving time).

The *H3 node* manages the *redistribution meta-user interface with negotiation* (cf. Section 2). Its view-controller is activated if the collaborator: 1) logs on to the plastic collaborative whiteboard from another device or 2) explicitly requests the meta-user interface. The H3 model stores the redistribution configuration of the user interface components selected by the local collaborator.

As we saw in Section 2, the *adaptation granularity* of an application determines how deep its user interface is going to be metamorphosed. In the case of our plastic collaborative whiteboard, the adaptation granularity is the *workspace* because: 1) it is a suitable unit when remodeling and redistributing the application user interface to computers that own a reduced screen; and 2) from the user's point of view, the user interface is easier to use if the metamorphosis concerns a set of logically connected tasks rather than some unrelated interactors or the whole user interface.

Regarding the H3 node, the plastic collaborative whiteboard supports the *user interface redistribution* categorized as *distributed organization to another distributed one* (cf. Section 2). The user interface state moves from: 1) a *fully replicated state*, where all the workspaces (H1, H2 and H3 nodes) appear in the multiple devices used by the same user to log on to the working session, toward 2) a *distributed state*, where the H2.1 and H2.3 nodes are hosted by one of the user's devices, according to his decision. This user interface redistribution aims to facilitate user-system and user-user interactions (see Section 5).

The *context of use* (cf. Section 2) for the plastic collaborative whiteboard includes the *user* and *platform* elements, as it can adapt itself: 1) to the platform characteristics at starting time, and 2) to the collaborator identity when he is detected working from two computer devices. In the first case, the plastic collaborative whiteboard performs *inter-modal remodeling* (cf. Section 2) of the H1 node because, in computers equipped with a camera and the OpenCV (Open Source Computer Vision) library, the identification data only consists of the collaborator's picture that is automatically taken by OpenCV and processed by a face recognition system [6], which is in charge of identifying him. Otherwise, the identification data only refers to the collaborator name and password. In the second case, when the collaborator is working from two computer devices, the plastic collaborative whiteboard performs *intra-modal remodeling* because it remains providing a graphical interaction support.

Remodeling and redistribution of the H2.1 and H2.3 nodes are performed on the fly, while the collaborative whiteboard is running. Thus, the *user interface deployment* is fully *dynamic*. As we discuss in the next section, the visible area (corresponding to the physic display of handheld devices) managed by the H2.2 node needs to be remodeled too.

4.2 JSE and JME-Based Implementation

Because application portability [3] is an important property of plastic interactive systems, we select the Java SE and Java ME to implement the proposed collaborative whiteboard on the following heterogeneous platforms: 1) PCs/Linux, 2) a SMARTBoard/MacOS, 3) a PDA HP iPAQ 6945/Windows Mobile 5.0, and 4) a smartphone HP iPAQ 610c/Windows Mobile 6.0. Most developers usually design and implement interactive systems only for PC. However, when the interaction device capabilities (e.g., screen size) are reduced, the management of some computer resources (e.g., display space) becomes especially difficult in the case of groupware applications. Moreover, if collaborators are immersed in a multi-device environment, the implementation of user interfaces becomes more difficult because the user's cognitive load should not be increased. Otherwise, the application usability might be put in jeopardy

In order to satisfy this requirement, we implemented three prototypes of the collaborative whiteboard for large and medium screens (e.g., SMARTBoard and PC) and five prototypes for small screens (e.g., handheld), from which some were discarded. Thus, we conducted a basic usability study of these prototypes using questionnaires proposed to 25 master/PhD students of our institution during two working sessions (the former lasted 30 minutes, whereas the latter took 50 minutes). We observed that, in the case of large and medium screens, the interviewees preferred the Microsoft Paint-like prototype because most of them already knew Microsoft Paint, so they are more acquainted with it.

Selecting a prototype for small screens depends not only on the organization and appearance of the user interface components but also on their functionality to accomplish the planned tasks. Four of the five prototypes propose a user interface including more than one window, whereas the one of the fifth prototype are made of one unique window. On this respect, we observed that most of the interviewees preferred this last one for two reasons: 1) they do not have to navigate through several windows; and 2) the number of pen clicks required to perform the planned tasks remains reduced.

Because the plastic collaborative whiteboard implementation for big/medium screens is relatively easy, in the next section we describe the specific implementation for both smartphone iPAQ 610c and PDA iPAQ 6945, as the functions developed for these devices can be applied to any kind of handheld.

User Interface Workspaces

The smartphone display surface, manipulable for programmers, is 240 width $\times$ 269 height px^2. If the OS menu bar located at the bottom is suppressed, the display surface height increases to 360 px, but the area occupied by this menu bar is not manipulable (see Fig. 2a). On the other hand, the PDA display surface is 240 width $\times$ 188 height px^2. Unlike the smartphone, the PDA area used by this OS menu bar can be configured. By removing this menu bar, the display surface height rises to 214 px (see Fig. 2b). The upper part of this area is tactile, whereas the complement bottom one is writable but not readable. Thus, the tactile area increases to 240×195 px^2.

Fig. 2 also shows the position of each workspace within the display surface of the handheld devices. In both of them, the *group awareness bar* is shown in an horizontal way at the bottom of the display surface. Particularly, in the PDA, this workspace occupies an area of 240×19 px^2 in order to take advantage of the whole non-tactile area, as it does not need data input from the collaborator (see Fig. 2a). In the smartphone, this workspace is reduced to 240×10 px^2 in order to maximize the drawing area, while supporting homogeneous vertical scrolling jumps (see Fig. 2b). The *group awareness bar* is always accessible to the collaborator in order to provide him with updated presence information.

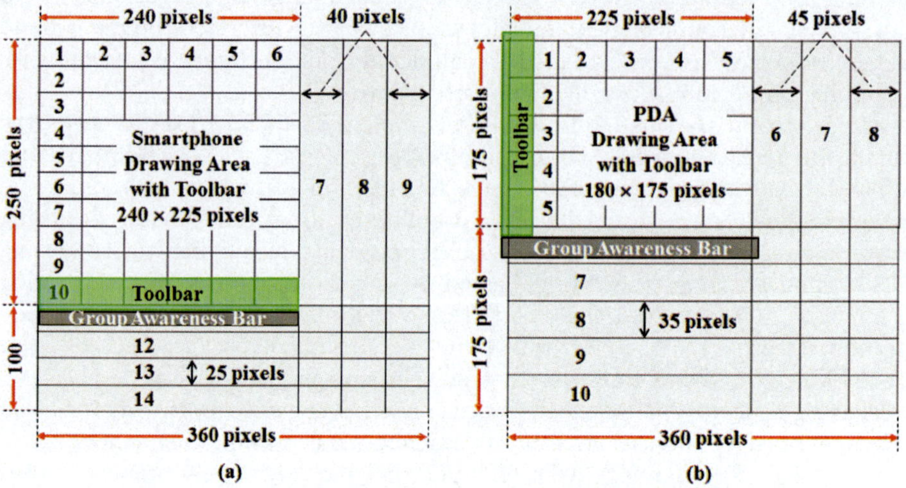

Fig. 2. Drawing Area Division for the HP iPAQ 610c and 6945

In the smartphone, the *toolbar* is placed on top of the group awareness bar in order to reserve enough space to create a quasi-squared rectangular drawing area, similar to the drawing area provided on computers with big or medium screen. Thus, this workspace occupies an area of 240 width $\times$ 34 height px^2 and is composed of two rows of interactors, e.g., figures, colors and paintbrushes (see Fig. 2a). In the PDA, the *toolbar* is vertically placed on the left side of the display surface in order to define once more a quasi-squared drawing area. Thus, this workspace uses an area of 34 width $\times$ 195 height px^2 and contains two columns of interactors (see Fig. 2b). Anyway, the *toolbar* can be temporarily hidden by the user in order to make the visible drawing area larger.

Scrolling the Shared Drawing Area

The *drawing area* of the plastic collaborative whiteboard comprises the surface unused by the previous workspaces, i.e., 240$\times$225 px^2 for the smartphone and 206$\times$195 px^2 for the PDA. However, the *drawing area* can be increased when needed in order to have the same size regardless of the heterogeneity of the host devices, e.g., PC, PDA and smartphone. Thus, when the whiteboard application runs on handheld devices, the *drawing area* can be bigger than the display surface requiring vertical and horizontal scrollbars to navigate across it. Local scrolling does not affect remote collaborators.

As JME does not provide any primitives to implement scrolling, we implement four invisible scrollbars, one for each side of the display surface: 1) two horizontal bars for up-down scrolling and 2) two vertical bars for left-right scrolling. To handle them, a suitable manipulation technique involves sliding the pen on the corresponding scrollbar towards the desired direction. The drag and drop manipulation technique for traditional scrollbars is quite appropriate for mouse computers, but when applying to pen computers, some users dislike the feeling of scratching the display surface with the pen tip [10].

Scrollbar implementation firstly entails verifying whether handheld devices are able to acquire the coordinates when sliding the pen on the display surface. The PDA does not support it, so scrolling only works when the pen taps on the area managed by each scrollbar. This limitation implies constraints for the design of the *drawing area*, which has to be reduced in order to implement such scrollbars. When the *toolbar* is hidden in the PDA (see Fig. 2b), the *drawing area* width is reduced from 240 to 225 px, so that the left and right vertical scrollbars respectively measure 8 and 7 px width, which is sufficient enough to select and activate these scrollbars, while maximizing the *drawing area* and supporting homogeneous scrolling hops. When the *toolbar* is shown in the PDA (see Fig. 2b), the *drawing area* width is reduced from 206 to 180 px in order to reserve 13 px width for each scrollbar (the right one and left one). In the same way, the *drawing area* height is reduced to 175 px in order to reserve 10 px height for each scrollbar (the top one and the bottom one).

As previously mentioned, the smartphone owns the capability to read coordinates, so there is no need to reduce the *drawing area*. When the *toolbar* is shown (see Fig. 2a), the *drawing area* (240×225 px^2) is divided into 6 columns of 40 px each and 9 rows of 25 px each. Otherwise, the *drawing area* (240×250 px^2) is increased by 1 row and the *group awareness bar* remodels itself by increasing its height from 10 to 19 px (like that of the PDA). On the other hand, when the *toolbar* is shown in the PDA (see Fig. 2b), the *drawing area* (180×175 px^2) is divided into 4 columns of 45 px each and 5 rows of 35 px each. Otherwise, the *drawing area* (225×175 px^2) is increased by 1 column.

The dimensions of the whole *drawing area* have been fixed to 360 width × 350 height px^2. Thus, the display surface of both smartphone and PDA has to be considered as a window the user moves within the *drawing area*. To implement this window, the smartphone *drawing area* gains 3 columns and 4 rows (see gray area in Fig. 2a), whereas the PDA *drawing area* is increased by 3 columns and 5 rows (see gray area in Fig. 2b). For instance, if the *toolbar* is shown in the smartphone, the user has to slide the pen five times on the horizontal scrollbar located at the bottom of the *drawing area*, in order to see the content of the non-visible rows (the one hidden by the *toolbar* plus the four augmented ones). Each time the user slides the pen, the resulting vertical hop measures 25 px. However, when the *toolbar* is hidden, the user has to slide just two times (50 px per hop) as multiples of 25 px are used to make scrolling easy for him.

The following algorithm generalizes horizontal scrolling on the *drawing area* using vertical scrollbars located at the left and the right of display surface. The input parameters of this algorithm are: 1) the coordinate x of the point $p(x, y)$ generated by the user when sliding the pen on such scrollbars; 2) the width of the mobile device screen (variable x'); 3) the presence or absence of workspaces (e.g., *toolbar* and *group awareness bar*) placed all along the display surface height (variable *isThere_VerWS*); 4) the width of such workspaces (variable *verWS_Width*); 5) the placement of such workspaces, i.e., the value "1" indicates that they are located at the left side of the display surface and "0" indicates that they are placed at the right side (variable *is_verWS_AtLeft*); 6) the width of the vertical scrollbars respectively located at the left (variable *leftSB_Width*) and the right (variable *rightSB_Width*) of the display surface; 7) the maximal number of hops allowed to cover the whole *drawing area* in an horizontal way (variable *maxHorHop*); and 8) the number of rectangles hidden by such vertical workspaces (variable *hiddenRect*). The number of horizontal hops (*horHop*) to visualize a specific part of the *drawing area* serves as input and output parameter.

```
Input: x, x', isThere_VerWS, verWS_Width, is_verWS_AtLeft,
leftSB_Width, rightSB_Width, horHop, maxHorHop, hiddenRect
Output: horHop
1:  if isThere_VerWS then //there are workspaces
       if is_verWS_AtLeft then //workspaces are at left side
          if verWS_Width < x and horHop > 0 and
             x < (verWS_Width + leftSB_Width) then
5:           horHop ← horHop - 1 //sliding on left scrollbar
          else
             if x < x' and (x' - rightSB_Width) < x and
                horHop < (maxHorHop + hiddenRect) then
                horHop ← horHop + 1 //sliding on right scrollbar
10:    else //workspaces are at right side
          if x > (x' - (verWS_Width + rightSB_Width)) and
             x < (x' - verWS_Width) and
             horHop < (maxHorHop + hiddenRect) then
             horHop ← horHop + 1 //sliding on right scrollbar
15:       else
             if x > 0 and x < leftSB_Width and horHop > 0 then
                horHop ← horHop - 1 //sliding on left scrollbar
    else //there are no workspaces
       if x < 0 and x < leftSB_Width and horHop > 0 then
20:       horHop ← horHop - 1 //sliding on left scrollbar
       else
          if x < x' and (x' - rightSB_Width) < x and
             horHop < maxHorHop then
             horHop ← horHop + 1 //sliding on right scrollbar
25: return horHop
```

From the line 1 to 17, the algorithm horizontally scrolls the *drawing area*, while verifying whether a vertical workspace is located at the left (see line 2) or at the right (see line 10) of the display surface. If a workspace is shown, the algorithm considers its width and verifies whether the coordinate x produced when tapping the pen on the display surface corresponds to the area reserved to the left vertical scrollbar (see lines 5 and 17) or the right vertical one (see lines 9 and 14). If any workspace does not exist or it is hidden, the algorithm carries out the same verifications, but the calculus of the horizontal hops (variable *horHop*) needed to visualize the left part (see line 20) or the right part (see line 24) of the *drawing area* are obviously different. When scrolling to the left, the variable *horHop* has to be bigger than 0. This restriction indicates that the user already moves to the right of the *drawing area* at least once. When scrolling to the right, the variable *horHop* has to be smaller than a maximal value, which varies depending on whether a vertical workspace is present.

We do not present the vertical scrolling algorithm as it is very similar to the horizontal scrolling one.

5 Use Scenario of the Plastic Collaborative Whiteboard

To illustrate the plastic capabilities of the collaborative whiteboard, let us consider the following scenario: *Kim* logs on to the application from a camera-equipped PC/Linux connected to the wired network. The whiteboard first took a picture of *Kim*'s face [6] to authenticate her and so authorizes her to initiate a collaborative working session. Then, the whiteboard displays its user interface in a unique view, which contains three workspaces: 1) a toolbar, 2) a drawing area, and 3) a group awareness bar. She recovers a document draft jointly initialized with her colleagues during a past session. The group awareness bar indicates that *Kim* is the only collaborator present in the current session.

Few minutes later *Jane*, who is traveling by bus, uses her PDA/Linux to log on to the application, which authenticates her by means of her name and password. After welcoming *Jane*, the whiteboard also shows its user interface in a unique view containing the three workspaces. By means of them, *Jane* can perceive *Kim*'s presence and her document draft proposals. In a simultaneous way, *Kim*'s group awareness bar displays *Jane*'s photo, name and status.

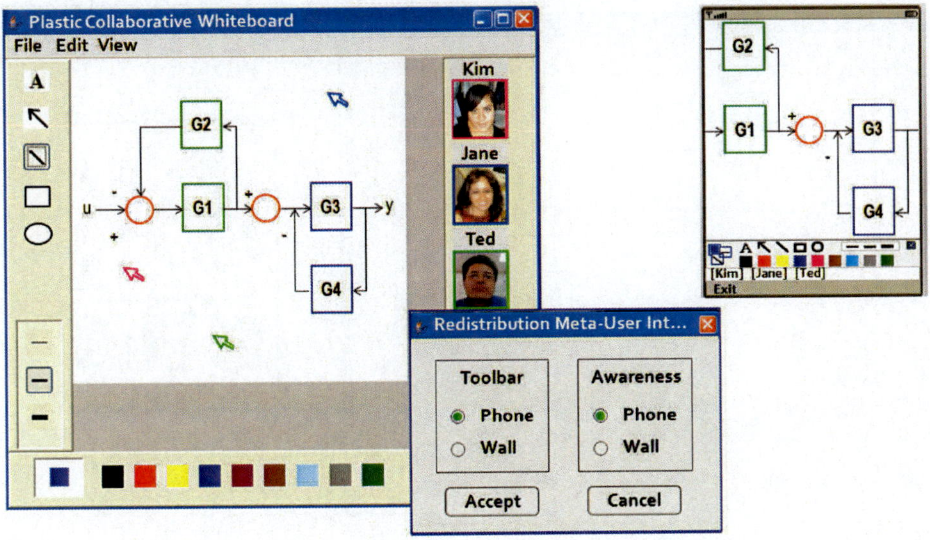

Fig. 3. The Plastic Whiteboard Running on Ted's Devices

As *Jane* is using her PDA, the group awareness bar is placed at the bottom of the view, where each present collaborator's name is shown in order of arrival. The toolbar, situated above the group awareness bar, shows the tools (e.g., figure, paintbrush and color) selected by *Jane* just before logging out of the last session. At this point, the working session between *Kim* and *Jane* is established. Thus, when one of them draws on the drawing area, the other can observe the effects of her actions in a quasi-synchronous way.

Some time later, *Ted* logs on to the application firstly from his wall-sized computer/MacOS and then from his smartphone/Windows Mobile. The whiteboard instance running on the computer authenticates him via the face recognition system, whereas the whiteboard instance running on the smartphone identifies him via his name and password. *Kim*'s and *Jane*'s group awareness bar shows that *Ted* just logged on to the session and, in a symmetrical way, he perceives *Kim*'s and *Jane*'s presence (see Fig. 3). Then, *Ted* starts working with the same context (e.g., selections and tools) of the last session he left.

At the moment the application detects him interacting with two devices, it displays a redistribution meta-user interface (meta-UI) on the wall-sized computer in order to invite him to participate in the plastic adaptation of his interaction interface (see Fig. 3). From this meta-UI, *Ted* selects the smartphone to host the group awareness bar and the toolbar, but also he decides to maintain the toolbar on the wall-sized computer. As a result of this adaptation, the smartphone hosts the group awareness bar and the toolbar, whereas the wall-sized computer maintains the toolbar and the drawing area (see Fig. 4). Thus, the toolbar is displayed on both devices that allow him: 1) to produce in a more efficient way or 2) to invite a colleague to take part of the document production.

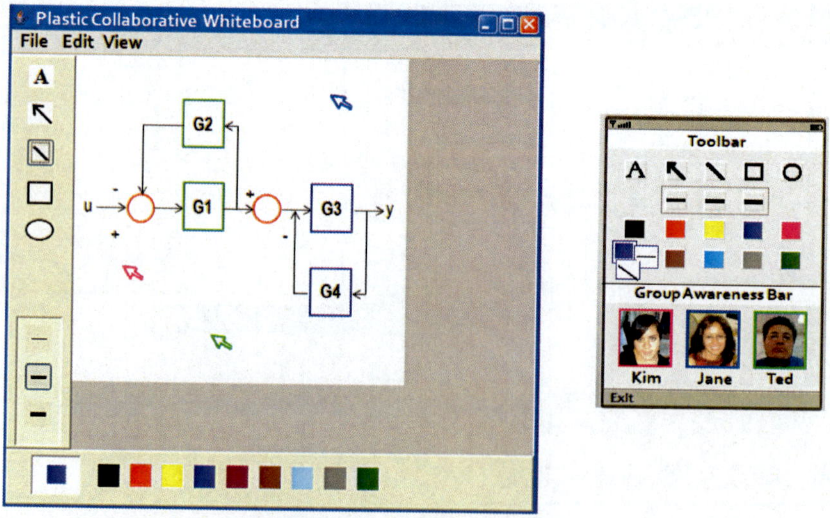

Fig. 4. The Plastic Collaborative Whiteboard After UI Redistribution

Because the smartphone does not display the drawing area, the toolbar size has been increased allowing to offer more tools, whereas the group awareness bar can now show each collaborator's name and photo (see Fig. 4).

Putting the toolbar on a wall-sized computer introduces several problems. For instance, in our scenario, *Ted* might not be able to reach the toolbar at the top of the wall-sized computer. By means of the multi-computer approach [10], he can use: 1) his smartphone, like a palette of oil-painting, to select a paintbrush type, a color or a figure and 2) his wall-sized computer, like a canvas board, to draw. Like a traditional oil painter, *Ted* can tap on a color icon with his pen to change the pen color. This multi-computer approach also allows *Ted* to work with *Kim* and *Jane* in a remote way. Moreover, a *Ted*'s colleague might meet him in his office to participate in the session. In this case, both of them have a smartphone, but they physically share the wall-sized computer to produce.

6 Conclusion and Future Work

The unavoidable heterogeneity of emergent hardware and software platforms has forced the software developers to adapt their applications (e.g., browsers and games) to a subset of these platforms in order to increase their availability and usage. On the other hand, our way of working is evolving due to important advances in communication and information technologies. Until now, the user work was mainly centralized on one single computing device (e.g., a PC). More and more people are using a set of computers in a dynamic way, e.g., one may use two or more laptops, whereas others may use a wall-sized computer as well as PDAs. Thus, designing and developing applications and suitable supports for multi-computer and multi-user environments become a unavoidable task.

User interface plasticity provides a means to structure the plastic adaptation process of such applications. This research topic is being studied in the domain of single-user systems, where several concepts, prototypes and reference models [2] have been proposed. However, in the domain of groupware applications, the adaptability of end-user applications starts being studied as a side issue of the design and implementation of augmented reality techniques. Thus, these research works only focus on the platform, leaving aside the users and the environment.

Some of the factors influencing the user interface of single-user interactive systems (e.g., *state recovery* and *adaptation granularities*, *user interface deployment*, and *technological spaces*) can also be applied to groupware applications in order to provide them with the plasticity property. However, others factors (e.g., *context of use* and *redistribution meta-user interface*) need to be adapted to the particular requirements of groupware applications. Particularly, the re-definition of the *context of use* needs to consider: 1) a group of collaborators instead of a user only; and 2) their spacial interaction form (remote vs. face to face) in order to consequently adapt the user interface, e.g., suppression of the group awareness bar when some collaborators are co-located. On the other hand, the *redistribution meta-user interface* with plasticity seems to be suited to groupware applications, because it has also to be adapted to the collaborative working context; for example, let us suppose a group of co-located collaborators, everybody owning a PDA and having access to a common wall-sized computer; in order to avoid conflicts among collaborators, the meta-user interface should not show the drawing area as a redistributable workspace, but it should provide some consensus policies for other workspaces, e.g., the toolbar, when being candidates for redistribution.

This study opens the research field of plastic user interfaces for collaborative environments. From the results of this research effort, we can imagine the possibility to define plastic generic concepts and mechanisms that can be adapted to different kinds of groupware applications.

References

1. Balme, L., Demeure, A., Calvary, G., Coutaz, J.: Sedan-Bouillon: A Plastic Web Site, In: INTERACT 2005 Workshop on Plastic Services for Mobile Devices, pp. 1-3, Rome (2005)
2. Calvary, G., Coutaz, J., Thevenin, D., Limbourg, Q., Souchon, N., Bouillon, L., Florins, M., Vanderdonckt, J.: Plasticity of User Interfaces: A Revised Reference Framework. In: 1st International Workshop on Task Models and Diagrams for User Interface Design, pp. 127–134. INFOREC Publishing House, Bucharest (2002)
3. Coulouris, G.F., Dollimore, J., Kindberg, T.: Distributed systems: concepts and design, 4th edn. Addison-Wesley, Reading (2005)
4. Coutaz, J., Calvary, G.: HCI and Software Engineering: Designing for User Interface Plasticity. In: The Human-Computer Interaction Handbook: Fundamentals, Evolving Technologies, and Emerging Applications - Human Factors and Ergonomics Series, pp. 1107–1118. CRC Press, New York (2008)
5. Crease, M.: A Toolkit of Resource-Sensitive, Multimodal Widgets, PhD Thesis, Department of Computer Science, University of Glasgow (2001)
6. García, K., Mendoza, S., Olague, G., Decouchant, D., Rodríguez, J.: Shared Resource Availability within Ubiquitous Collaboration Environments. In: Briggs, R.O., Antunes, P., de Vreede, G.-J., Read, A.S. (eds.) CRIWG 2008. LNCS, vol. 5411, pp. 25–40. Springer, Heidelberg (2008)
7. Giesecke, S.: Taxonomy of architectural style usage. In: 2006 Conference on Pattern Languages of Programs, pp. 1–10. ACM Press, Portland (2006)
8. Kammer, P.J., Taylor, R.N.: An architectural style for supporting work practice: coping with the complex structure of coordination relationships. In: 2005 International Symposium on Collaborative Technologies and Systems, pp. 218–227. IEEE Computer Society, St Louis (2005)
9. Prante, T., Streitz, N.A., Tandler, P.: Roomware: Computers Disappear and Interaction Evolves. IEEE Computer 37(12), 47–54 (2004)
10. Rekimoto, J.: A Multiple Device Approach for Supporting Whiteboard-Based Interactions. In: 1998 Conference on Human Factors in Computing Systems, pp. 344–351. ACM Press, Los Angeles (1998)
11. Tandler, P., Prante, T., Müller, C., Streitz, N., Steinmetz, R.: Connectables: Dynamic Coupling of Displays for the Flexible Creation of Shared Workspaces. In: 14th Annual ACM Symposium on User Interface Software and Technology, pp. 11–20. ACM Press, Orlando (2001)

Mobile Phones in a Retirement Home: Strategic Tools for Mediated Communication

Mireia Fernández-Ardèvol

Research Program "Mobile Communication, Economy and Society"
IN3 – Open University of Catalonia
c/ Roc Boronat, 117, 7th floor. E-08018 Barcelona (Catalonia, Spain)
mfernandezar@uoc.edu

Abstract. By means of a case study we explore how the residents of a retirement home use mobile telephony. This is part of wider research on mobile communication among the elderly population in the metropolitan area of Barcelona (Catalonia, Spain). A qualitative approach, based on semi-structured interviews, allows the exploration of social perceptions, representations and use of the technology to better understand the processes in operation here. We analyze the position that mobile telephony occupies in the personal system of communication channels (PSCC) and we observe that the mobile phone has become a central channel and a strategic tool for seniors who have moved from their private household to a retirement home, while intensity of telephony use is kept low. Taking into account the available evidence on mobile appropriation in the golden age, the first results of the case study are presented and discussed here.

Keywords: Mobile telephony, Retirement home, Elderly population, Barcelona (Catalonia, Spain), Personal System of Communication Channels.

1 Introduction

Ever since the first stages of the popularization of mobile telephony, the relationship between age and different patterns of adoption and use has been discussed (for instance [1] or [2]). At present, the likelihood of being a mobile user is always below the average among the senior population, but high compared to other information and communication technologies (see [3] for a discussion on the European Union). For instance, in Catalonia three out of four persons between 65 and 74 years old are mobile users, a figure clearly below the population average of 93% (population from 16 to 74 years old) [4]. Nevertheless, this difference is decreasing and a general trend can be identified "toward the general diffusion of mobile communication within the whole population, with age continuing to specify the type of use rather than the use itself" [5, p. 41].

A complete analysis of use and appropriation of mobile communication must take into account the senior population, the least studied cohort in this field and the most important age group in demographic terms in Europe [6]. The effective age at which

H. Cherifi, J.M. Zain, and E. El-Qawasmeh (Eds.): DICTAP 2011, Part I, CCIS 166, pp. 395–406, 2011.

mobile communication has been incorporated is a key point. Thus, it is of great interest to study the current situation and the future evolution of adoption and use in the golden age. Future studies, as well, should take into account the evolution of mobile use as those that began to use mobile phones during their youth get older. At present, however, we are focused on individuals who have been introduced to mobile communication late in their lives (at the age of 50 or at the age of 85, for instance).

Personal communication is affected by age, and so are the information and communication technologies (ICT) mediating these communications [7]. Aging is related to socio-cultural aspects; thus personal values and interests change over one's lifetime. Moreover, aging shapes physical characteristics as well: from cognition or reading capacity, to more basic abilities, like handling small featured devices. Indeed, "in a very literal sense, older adults may perceive technology differently than younger adults do" [8]. The effective use of mobile devices is not only related to technical issues but also to communicative habits, which among the elderly are mainly centered on the maintenance of family relationships [9, 10, 11].

The aim of this paper is to contribute with empirical evidence to better understand the processes in operation for the acceptance, or rejection, of mobile telephony among the senior population. For doing so, we developed a qualitative empirical research project in the metropolitan area of Barcelona (Catalonia, Spain). In this paper our interest is focused on individuals living in a retirement home, as the particularities of their housing might condition the kind of communication media individuals can access. The preliminary results of the case study are presented and discussed in this paper following a description of the analytical framework of the research. Lastly, conclusions are presented.

2 Analytical Framework

Available evidence points to the fact that elderly persons are less inclined to use mobile communication; however, they are "catching up to the levels of mainstream innovation, but largely lag behind in the use of new services integrated into the technology" [12, p.191]. Recent statistics on the use of mobile phones and the use of advanced mobile services confirm this trend in Europe [13]. Regarding paths of use, older people would most likely use mobile phones only in emergencies, unexpected or micro-coordination situations [10, 11, 14, 15] in which they consider that it is the most efficient tool to communicate with.

The pressure to have a phone often comes from their social interactions [16]. "Initial use is characterized by caution" [9, p.14]; however, once the elderly person becomes accustomed to it, the device is gradually incorporated in all activities of everyday life. It seems that the members of the elderly person's personal network are usually the proactive part of this specific mediated communication [15, 16]. This is true at least in the first stages of adoption, while some differences in the pattern of use have been described for different countries. For instance, in northern Italy [17] or in England [10], reported uses by the elderly are more basic than in Finland [9]. In any case, the main service is voice calls, with very little acceptance of SMS [1, 2, 16, 18].

It seems clear that, from the elderly perspective, use depends on personal willingness as well as on the expectations that others place on them to use mobile features. Nevertheless, reluctance could turn into acceptance if the service meets the needs of the person [16]. In addition, the device must demonstrate an acceptable level of usability, compared to other means of communication that would satisfy similar communicative necessities of the individual.

Moreover, the use of mobile phones must be understood in terms of the personal system of communication channels (PSCC) of each individual. We define this as the set of communications channels that are used on a regular basis: fixed phone, mobile phone, Internet, face-to-face communication and even letters or telegrams. Each person would identify a different set of channels in their everyday life activity. The set of channels might be framed by individual attitudes and aptitudes, as well as by personal interests and socially imposed interests or pressures (see [3]).

Accessibility and availability of communication tools become critical aspects, as it is use, but not ownership, which is the key element that defines PSCC. To this effect, we would like to explore whether the mobile phone is a peripheral tool or a central tool for users living in a retirement home; as the trend detected in our previous work, based both on empirical research [19] and on the analysis of available secondary data [3], indicates that mobile telephony does not appear to be a central means of communication in the PSCC of the elderly.

3 Empirical Approach: Methodology and Case Study

The qualitative fieldwork of this case study is based on semi-structured interviews conducted in a retirement home located in the metropolitan area of Barcelona (Catalonia, Spain). Our focus is centered on mobile users living in the dwelling. Semi-structured interviews constitute an effective method to capture the links among different aspects of social practices and representations. To triangulate information, fieldwork includes direct observation of the handset; thus, whenever possible and pertinent, a picture of the interviewee's phone is taken and the interviewer observes, as well, how the individual handles the device. Additional interviews were held with non-mobile users living in the retirement home, the social worker and other professionals at the center to get a better picture of the available telephone services.

This case study belongs to wider ongoing research in which sampled individuals are selected following four axes. The first one is age, with two broad cohorts: younger seniors (60-74 years old) and older seniors (75+ years old); gender; housing (own home or retirement home) and educational level (up to secondary level, and secondary level or higher). Therefore, in this paper we are presenting the first results from a specific subset of the sample.

Statistics indicate that non-users still constitute a significant group among seniors (see above). This is the reason why we include non-mobile users in our studies, as their subjective experience will bring relevant information to better understand their relationship –acceptation or rejection– with mobile telephony.

3.1 The Retirement Home Under Study

The studied retirement home is a relatively new dwelling, opened in 2005. It is a combined care facility designed for seniors with different degrees of dependency. Some of the residents receive public funding to be able to afford monthly fees, as this is a private center linked to the public system through the city council and the government of Catalonia. With a total of 117 residential places distributed both in individual and double rooms, one of the floors is devoted to less dependent residents, which constitute our collective of interest. They are mostly autonomous persons who need some personal support, with some individuals needing a higher degree of personal support due to physical disabilities.

In the dwelling, fixed telephony can be both a collective and a private tool. There is a public phone box in the building that only operates with coins (credit cards and prepaid cards are not accepted); while the phone in the reception area can be used by residents at a symbolic price of 1 Euro per call, regardless of the destination and duration. Local calls to fixed phones are markedly cheaper while this could be a price close to the average peak-hour price when the destination is a mobile phone. Those who want to use the in-room landline must bring their own fixed handset and pay, as well, 1 symbolic Euro per call. On the other hand, there is never any charge for incoming calls. Incoming calls are announced over the public address system for those who don't have an in-room fixed phone. Calls can be answered on any of the community phones located on each floor of the retirement home.

Regarding other means of communication, neither computers nor Internet connections are available for residents. Indeed, individuals we talked to had never used the Internet before moving to the dwelling. In addition, TV sets are available in common areas while private televisions and radios are allowed in rooms –in double rooms two TV sets can be installed. Few residents have pay-television channels in their respective rooms, a service not available in common areas.

The media repertoire is completed with mobile telephony, which always is a personal and private device.

3.2 Studied Individuals

There were 12 mobile owners in our collective of interest. Among them, 10 agreed to participate in the research and were recorded during the interview. In addition, we interviewed two other individuals who had an in-room landline but did not have a mobile phone. Interviews took place in December 2010 and January 2011. Table 1 gathers selected characteristics of the interviewed mobile owners.

With a clear majority of older seniors (7), there are more women than men (8 vs. 2) as must be expected in these age cohorts. Except for one person, all individuals have primary studies or lower; a reflection of the low access to education of the generation that was born around the Spanish Civil War. Regarding communication technologies, there is an owner that does not use the mobile phone who, at the same time, is the only person in the sample with an in-room fixed phone. Finally, there are no Internet users in the sample, while all of the interviewees used to have a landline at home.

Table 1. Selected characteristics of mobile owners in the case study (10 individuals)

	N		N
Gender			
Female	8	**Communication technologies**	
Male	2	Mobile owner	10
Age group		Mobile user	9
60-74 (younger seniors)	3	In-room fixed phone	1
75 + (older seniors)	7	Used to have a landline at home	10
Level of studies		Internet users	0
Primary or lower	9		
Secondary or higher	1		
	10		

While the general degree of dependence is low, it is worth noting that three persons suffer from mobility impairment, with one woman unable to walk due to a degenerative disease. Moreover, up to five individuals showed slightly impaired cognition.

4 Initial Results

In general, we can observe that the mobile phone is the main phone for the 9 effective users. It constitutes a key tool for mediated communication with the closest personal network, while face-to-face meetings are usually important and frequent. In addition, the residents can use other resources in the dwelling both on a regular basis or occasionally.

For instance, two persons mention that in case they don't answer the mobile, their relatives will call them on the fixed dwelling phone. On the other hand, two other individuals regularly combine the use of the collective fixed phone and their personal mobile. In this sense, a woman (age 73) explains that she has a very short list of contacts in her phonebook. This is the selected set of numbers she talks to with her mobile. For all other numbers, she uses the phone box in the home. For more expensive calls, to relatives living in the south of Spain, she takes advantage of her daughter's flat landline rate. On the other hand, another woman (age 86) sometimes calls her children with her mobile; they do not pick up on purpose and call her back on the dwelling fixed line. Strategies of cost minimization are in operation here as, maybe, these women show a higher use of telephony than other elderly residents.

We already mentioned that one owner does not use the mobile phone. A woman (age 96) keeps the handset always turned off in the closet. She rejects this kind of telephony and prefers using her in-room landline, as it is easier to handle calls. Indeed, she only needs to dial the reception number and they put her through to the requested number. To justify her election, she points to usability problems (she mentions visual problems); but she also indicates she wants to pay for her phone calls (mobile communication costs are assumed by her son). The mobile handset is a novelty for her and she refers to it as an object belonging to her son, the person who brought it about three months before our interview.

Indeed, interviewed users consider the mobile phone a really useful tool and declare that they would get a new one in case their handset was broken. In some cases the phone means connection to them (man 82, woman 75 years old) while in others it means company (woman 82) as the person feels she is not alone. However, they describe moderate and low intensity of use of the device. In the next paragraphs we discuss a selected set of relevant characteristics regarding the way the mobile phone is perceived and used by the 9 individuals in the case study that have effectively incorporated the mobile phone in their everyday life.

4.1 How Fixed Is the Mobile Phone?

Some individuals use the mobile as if, in some respects, it were a landline. They tend to leave the handset in their room (5 out of 9 individuals do) and bring it with them on selected occasions. The handset can even be kept in the room always plugged in (2 individuals describe this). These users agree on, explicitly or tacitly, certain specific times in which they will be in their room to answer incoming calls. The negotiation process can include, as well, an explicit request from relatives to always be reachable by mobile phone. In this sense, those who always bring the handset with them usually explain that they follow the advice of close relatives who would become worried if they did not answer a call. Security and safety reasons [5], here, are not explained in first person terms (such as "just in case I have an emergency and need help") but in terms of what third persons, their beloved, would think if they were not reachable. This might be related to the low level of ability they show with the handset (as discussed in sections 4.4. and 4.5).

Two persons, a man (age 82) and a woman (age 86) do not consider it necessary to bring the handset with them when they leave the home because their respective children accompany them. On the contrary, a woman who usually leaves the phone plugged in (age 75) always brings her cell phone with her when leaving the retirement home, as she needs it to coordinate and/or micro-coordinate (Ling, 2004) once she arrives at her destination.

In fact, the mobile phone is often perceived as a substitute for the former home landline. The most significant example corresponds to a woman (age 87) who was given a mobile phone when she first entered a nursing home, before moving to her current dwelling. Her grandson took care of keeping the same fixed number she previously had so that she could still be in touch with her whole network. Another example is that of a woman (age 75) who explains that she used to have the mobile handset just for emergencies and barely used it, while at present; all her mediated communications are held through the mobile. These behaviors are in keeping with the general agreement that an in-room landline is not needed when you have a mobile phone.

4.2 The Phone Is Made to Work

The mobile phone is always kept on. This can be due to the fact that the majority of the interviewees do not know how to switch the handset off, or how to set it to silent. Therefore, it would seem that they do not have a strategy regarding this point.

However, a man (age 72) summarizes the way most users perceive the mobile handset by telling us that "the phone is made to work",[1] so there is no need to switch it off or to silence it.

When directly asked if they turn off the phone or set it to silent in specific situations they tend to answer that there is no danger of an interruption as they don't have too many incoming calls, or, alternatively, because all the members of their network know which is the proper time during the day to call them. If an incoming call could create an uncomfortable situation, such as during a doctor visit, they just switch the phone off. In this sense, nobody reports being reprimanded for this behavior. A woman (age 64) mentions that she personally never sets the phone to silent –she prioritizes her relatives being able to reach her– however, when she is with her son he can set it to silent in places like cinemas.

Lastly, the phone can stay turned off for long periods of time due to a mistake or if it falls and breaks into pieces. Users need help to fix the device and they turn to both dwelling staff or to their relatives.

4.3 Voice: The Main Service

Voice calls constitutes the only service used by studied individuals. Other embedded services, in general, are not used or even known about. For instance, few individuals were able to identify incoming SMS on their handset, while none of them are able to read them. Some individuals do not recognize the icon on the screen, or refer to text messages with incorrect words or expressions. Only one woman (age 75) had ever tried to send an SMS: a couple of weeks before our conversation she was encouraged and assisted by one of the workers at the home, who helped her to send it. But she never got an answer as the friend she wrote to did not even know how to read text messages.

Incoming calls are almost always answered, as long as the user hears the mobile. Three individuals, however, describe their selective practices. First, a woman (age 87) only answers calls that correspond to names in her phonebook while any other number will be ignored. Indeed, she mentioned that "[in the mobile] there are no numbers [just names]"[2]. Following the same logic, a second woman (age 86) only picks up calls with a specific ringtone. She explains that the rest of incoming calls are *wrong calls* so there is no need to answer them. In both cases, users are only able to communicate by mobile phone with those contacts that another person had put in the phonebook for them. Finally, a man (age 82) affirms that he never answers a call if he does not recognize the number. This can refer to phone numbers or to contact names displayed on the screen of the handset.

4.4 Usability

Some individuals complained about not being more proficient with the handset, while others just tell us that they only use what they are interested in. This is the case of a man (age 72) who tells us that he wants the mobile "just for speaking and

[1] Original in Spanish: "el teléfono es para que vaya", author translation.
[2] Original in Catalan: "[al mòbil] no hi números [només noms]", author translation.

listening … I don't want to do anymore with it"[3]. He even compares mobile phones with computers, by stating that they are more difficult for seniors.

Physical impairments are mentioned as restrictions to use, as expressed by a woman (age 87) who needs light and brightness to manipulate her black handset. In addition, cognitive abilities can limit mobile use, as well, among the majority of the individuals we surveyed. In this sense, individuals' descriptions clearly show that it can be difficult to remember a set of instructions to access specific embedded functions of the handset. In this regard, two women (ages 76 and 87) mentioned they had instructions written down to look at in case they forget specific routines. One of them had already learned some processes and no longer needs to refer to her notes. However, both women appreciate having the instructions written down, just in case.

Some individuals are able to explain the kind of mistakes they make while others are not clear about what it is going on with the handset. It seems, in this sense, that clamshells are easier to use than older handset models, as there is no need to lock or unlock the keypad; while those designed for elderly people can be more user-friendly. There is only one user with a handset specially designed for seniors and who reported some difficulties handling the device due to reduced mobility problems (see Appendix for selected pictures of the devices).

However, despite the difficulties we describe regarding use of the handset, when questioned about it, users evaluate the mobile phone as an easy-to-use device. This might be because of the general perception that this technology is currently considered to be a basic one, or it may also be because they use the phone regularly and, therefore, it has become incorporated in their everyday life.

4.5 Assisted Users

Individuals in this case study can be described as assisted mobile users. Based on [3], we can state that assisted users show at least two of these characteristics: (1) Very basic features: they only identify the green button (to answer calls) and the red button (to hang up) on the handset. (2) Limited number of calls: they dial numbers directly, as their phonebook is empty or they are not able to use it. Alternatively, they are only able to call those numbers that somebody else has put in the handset phonebook for them. (3) Only voice: SMS or any other service beyond voice communication is not used or even understood. (4) Non-portable mobile: they leave the handset permanently in a fixed place, and on some occasions it may be permanently plugged in. (5) Always on: they do not know how to turn the phone off or how to set it to silent. (6) Missed calls: they are not able to indentify missed calls. (7) They never manipulate the handset, disassembling or assembling it to fix it (for instance, when it falls). Or, (8) in prepaid plans, they need help to increase available airtime.

In consequence, assisted users generally need the help of another person to use the mobile phone. What we have observed is that a relative, or a caregiver, takes care of the configuration of the device, while the user may tend to upset the configuration unintentionally. Thus, users do with the mobile phone what they have been told to do

[3] Original in Spanish: "Sólo para hablar y escuchar… ya no quiero hacer nada más con él", author translation.

-or what they can remember to do; while they show no autonomy because they do not feel they can control the device. Therefore, they don't explore the handset, usually to avoid causing damage.

5 Conclusions

Mobile users in the retirement home appreciate the device, which constitutes the main channel for mediated communication with their closest network. In some cases it even constitutes the only telephone they use, while in others they combine it with different available fixed phones. Thus, we observe a high degree of acceptance of the technology among mobile owners, despite the substantial usability problems they report.

Access to communication media changes when a person moves from a private household to a retirement home –as do many other aspects of everyday life. Therefore, the personal system of communication channels is redefined. In this sense, for mobile users the handset increases its centrality because a landline, which is a very important tool in private households among Catalan seniors, is not available as it was previously.

Like all information and communication technologies, network effects are in operation here with regard to the popularization of given services. Thus, aside from personal abilities to perform tasks with the mobile phone, the abilities of those individuals that constitute the personal network of the seniors become transcendent. In this sense, it is impossible to get used to text messaging if there is nobody to share them with.

On the other hand, expectations that relatives place on each individual also shape effective use. As these seniors do not explore the capabilities of the handset, they only do what they are told to do. Thus, we observe how one's closest relatives are highly involved in the maintenance of the mobile phone, as they are with other aspects of the elderly person's life. Therefore, it is possible to state that, within this studied sample, the closest individuals in the personal support network seems to play a key role regarding, first of all, the effective adoption of mobile telephony and, secondly, the kind of use of this specific phone and the rest of the phones in the dwelling.

Usability problems among the interviewed individuals are mainly related to diminished physical and cognitive capacities. This shapes the ability, or inability, to perform specific tasks with the handset and, therefore, the evaluation of the user experience. In the evaluation process, which can be more or less explicit, individuals might be considering the communication repertoire available in the retirement home and the specific characteristics and usability of available devices. In this context, fixed phones show lower levels of usability compared with mobile phones. This is why mobile telephony is beginning to be accepted among those seniors who were at one time reluctant to adopt it.

Summing up, while studied seniors follow common trends already described for elderly persons in general, it is clear that housing characteristics shape the way mobile telephony is accepted and used in everyday life. Therefore, the study of a retirement home constitutes relevant research as it allows the identification of relevant particularities of the appropriation process of mobile telephony among specific groups of senior citizens.

Acknowledgments. The author would like to acknowledge all the interviewed individuals. Main informants and facilitators for this case study were Fuensanta Fernández, Ana Moreno and Susanna Seguer. Lidia Arroyo provided useful comments. The usual disclaimer applies.

References

1. Ling, R.: Adolescent girls and young adult men: two sub-cultures of the mobile telephone. Revista de Estudios de Juventud 52, 33–46 (2002)
2. Ling, R.: The Mobile Connection: the Cell Phone's Impact on Society. Morgan Kaufmann, San Francisco (2004)
3. Fernández-Ardèvol, M.: Interactions with and through mobile phones: what about the elderly population? In: ECREA Conference 2010, Hamburg, October 12-15 (2010)
4. FOBSIC: Enquesta sobre l'equipament i l'ús de les Tecnologies de la Informació i la Comunicació (TIC) a les llars de Catalunya (2010). Volum II. Usos individuals. Fundació Observatori per a la Societat de la Informació de Catalunya, FOBSIC (2010), http://www.fobsic.net/opencms/export/sites/fobsic_site/ca/Documentos/TIC_Llars/TIC_Llars_2010/TIC_Llars_2010_Volum2_usos.pdf (last accessed January 2011)
5. Castells, M., Fernández-Ardèvol, M., Qiu, J.L., Sey, A.: Mobile Communication and Society: A Global Perspective. MIT Press, Cambridge (2006)
6. Giannakouris, K.: Ageing characterises the demographic perspectives of the European societies. Eurostat Statistics in Focus, 72/2008 (2008), http://epp.eurostat.ec.europa.eu/cache/ITY_OFFPUB/KS-SF-08-072/EN/KS-SF-08-072-EN.PDF (last accessed, September 2010)
7. Charness, N., Parks, D.C., Sabel, B.A. (eds.): Communication, technology and aging: opportunities and challenges for the future. Springer Publishing Company, New York (2001)
8. Charness, N., Boot, W.R.: Aging and information technology use: potential and barriers. Current Directions in Psychological Science 18(5), 253–258 (2009)
9. Oskman, V.: Young People and Seniors in Finnish 'Mobile Information Society'. Journal of Interactive Media in Education 02, 1–21 (2006)
10. Kurniawan, S.: Older people and mobile phones: A multi-method investigation. International Journal of Human-Computer Studies 66, 889–901 (2008)
11. Kurniawan, S., Mahmud, M., Nugroho, Y.: A Study of the Use of Mobile Phones by Older Persons. In: CHI 2006, Montréal, Quebec, Canada, April 22-26 (2006)
12. Karnowski, V., von Pape, T., Wirth, W.: After the digital divide? An appropriation-perspective on the generational mobile phone divide. In: Hartmann, M., Rössler, P., Höflich, J. (eds.) After the Mobile Phone? Social Changes and the Development of Mobile Communication, Berlin, pp. 185–202 (2008)
13. Eurostat: Statistics on the Use of Mobile Phohe [isoc_cias_mph], Special module 2008: Individuals - Use of advanced services, last updated 09-08-2010 (2010), http://appsso.eurostat.ec.europa.eu/nui/show.do?dataset=isoc_cias_mph&lang=en (last accessed August 2010)

14. Hashizume, A., Kurosu, M., Kaneko, T.: The Choice of Communication Media and the Use of Mobile Phone among Senior Users and Young Users. In: Lee, S., Choo, H., Ha, S., Shin, I.C. (eds.) APCHI 2008. LNCS, vol. 5068, pp. 427–436. Springer, Heidelberg (2008)
15. Mohd, N., Hazrina, H., Nazean, J.: The Use of Mobile Phones by Elderly: A Study in Malaysia Perspectives. Journal of Social Sciences 4(2), 123–127 (2008)
16. Ling, R.: Should We be Concerned that the Elderly don't Text? The Information Society 24, 334–341 (2008)
17. Conci, M., Pianesi, F., Zancanaro, M.: Useful, Social and Enjoyable: Mobile Phone Adoption by Older People. In: Gross, T., Gulliksen, J., Kotzé, P., Oestreicher, L., Palanque, P., Prates, R.O., Winckler, M. (eds.) INTERACT 2009. LNCS, vol. 5726, pp. 63–76. Springer, Heidelberg (2009)
18. Lenhart, A.: Cell phones and American adults. They make just as many calls, but text less often than teens. Full Report. Pew Internet & American Life Project (September 2010), http://www.pewinternet.org/~/media//Files/Reports/2010/PIP_Adults_Cellphones_Report_2010.pdf
19. Fernández-Ardèvol, M.: Mobile Telephony among the Elders: first results of a qualitative approach. In: Kommers, P., Isaías, P. (eds.) Proceedings of the IADIS International Conference e-Society 2011 (2011)

Appendix: Selected Mobile Phones in the Retirement Home

1) Classical handsets

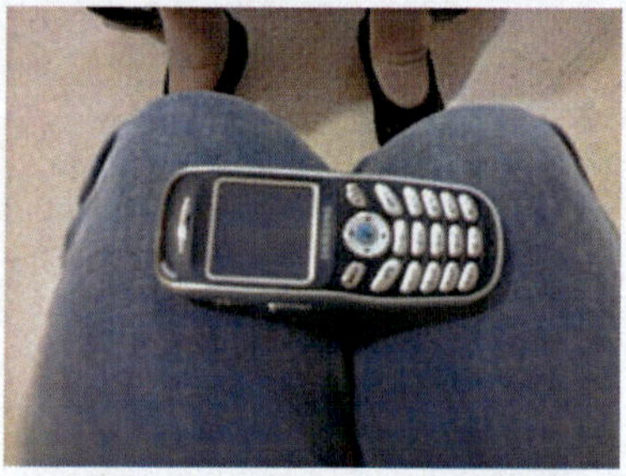

2) Clamshell handsets

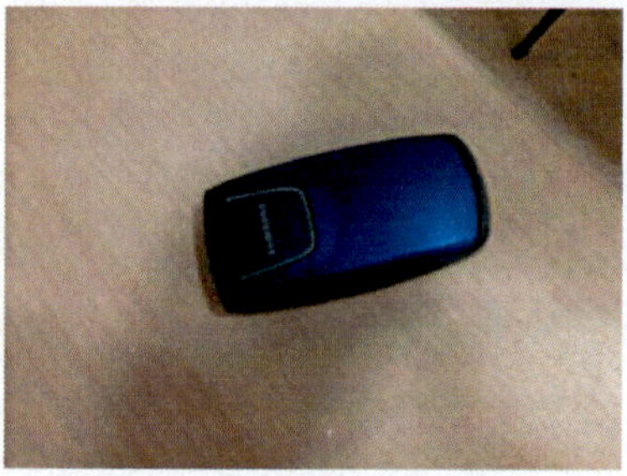

3) Handset designed for elders

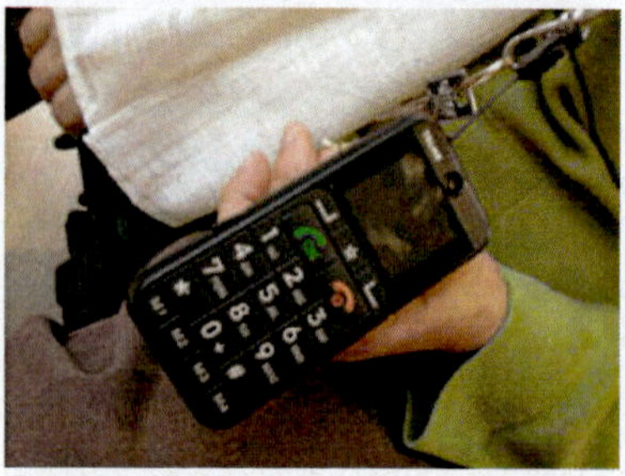

Source: fieldwork.

Mobile Visualization of Architectural Projects: Quality and Emotional Evaluation Based on User Experience

David Fonseca[1], Ernest Redondo[2], Isidro Navarro[2],
Marc Pifarré[1], and Eva Villegas[1]

[1] GTAM – Grup de Recerca en Tecnologies Mèdia, Enginyeria La Salle,
Universitat Ramon Llull. C/ Quatre Camins 2. 08022. Barcelona, Spain
{fonsi,mpifarre,evillegas}@salle.url.edu
[2] Departamento de Expresión Gráfica Arquitectónica I,
Universidad Politécnica de Cataluña. Barcelona Tech. Escuela Técnica
Superior de Arquitectura de Barcelona, ETSAB,
Avda Diagonal 649, 2. 08028. Barcelona, Spain
{ernesto.redondo,isidro.navarro}@upc.edu

Abstract. The visualization of architectural design has always been associated with physical models, exhibition panels and displays on computer screens, usually in a large format. However, technological developments in the past decades have produced new devices such as handheld PCs, pocket PCs, and Smartphones that have increasingly larger screens and more sophisticated technical characteristics. The emergence of these devices has made both the non expert and advanced user a consumer of such devices. This evolution has created a new workflow that enables on-site management and decision making through the viewing of information on those devices. In this paper, we will study the basic features of the architectural image to provide a better user experience for browsing these types of images on mobile devices' limited and heterogeneous screen sizes by comparing the results with traditional and immersive environments.

Keywords: Visualization, Small Screen Devices, Quality and Emotional Evaluations, Image Transcoding and adaptation, User Experience.

1 Introduction

Mobile phones are now a part of many aspects of everyday life. Modern Smartphones can not only make calls, but also play music, take and store photographs, browse the Internet and send email [1]. The research community is exploring the different possibilities these devices offer users, ranging from optimizing the presentation of information and creating an augmented reality, to studies more focused on user interaction. Undoubtedly, one of the most researched themes on the use of these new technologies is information visualization (IV). IV is a well-established discipline that proposes graphical approaches to help users better understand and make sense of large volumes of information [2]. The small screens of handheld devices provide a clear imperative to designing visual information carefully and presenting it in the

H. Cherifi, J.M. Zain, and E. El-Qawasmeh (Eds.): DICTAP 2011, Part I, CCIS 166, pp. 407–416, 2011.

most effective way. Limited screen size makes it difficult to display large information spaces (e.g., maps, photographs, web pages, etc. [3]).

Among the various lines of research associated with mobile communication technology, the spotlight falls on web contents and geographical information retrieval frameworks in an attempt to resolve, searches and access information. Screen resolution, the resolution and size of the image and the type of connection or transfer rates of map locations or routes have been widely studied, where quick and constant updates are vital. In those environments, the simplification of information is very important. In the case of photographic images and architectural frameworks, this simplification is more difficult to achieve without sacrificing important information. Therefore, it is essential to employ efficient visualization mechanisms that guarantee straightforward and understandable access to relevant information. Meanwhile, the major limitation from a user's viewpoint is moving away from data volume (or time-to-wait) to screen size because of the brisk development of hardware technologies that improve the connections [4].

In this paper, we propose a novel point of view in the research on image visualization, which is specifically focused on architectural images. The main contribution of our work is the evaluation of user experience when viewing images in three different environments: computer screen, HMD (Head Mounted Display) and mobile phone; and to define the best range of compression and color model of the image to generate an optimal visual experience. To carry out our work, and based on the methodology and results of previous phases [5], we focus on the evaluation of the perceived quality and the relationship between the color model and level of compression and their influence on the user's emotional framework. This approach is intended to complement traditional studies where user perception and the characteristics of the human visual system have received little attention [6].

2 Related Work

2.1 Traditional vs. Mobile Visualization

Compared to other screens, mobile devices have many restrictions to consider when developing visualization applications [7]:

- Displays are very limited due to smaller size, lower resolution, fewer colors, and other factors.
- The width/height aspect ratio differs greatly from the usual 4:3.
- Onboard hardware, including the CPU, memory, buses, and graphic hardware is much less powerful.
- Connectivity is slower, affecting interactivity when a significant quantity of data is stored on remote databases.

Without a doubt, the most important initial restriction is the limited display area, which impacts on the effort required by users in their interaction with software on handheld devices and can reduce their ability to complete search-type tasks [8]. Also, users of Smartphones often incur further costs both in monetary terms and response time as wireless data transfer rates are generally slower than those available on networked desktop computers. Response times to data requests are longer and unproductive user 'wait time' increases. It is assumed that the optimization of the size and image resolution will help improve visualization in such devices and create a more efficient transfer of information and, therefore, an improvement in data connection.

2.2 Browsing Images

Several techniques had been proposed to display large chunks of information intended for web page display on mobile devices [3], which are usually unsuitable for displaying images and maps. The most common technique is to provide users with panning and zooming capabilities that allow them to select the portion of space to view. With these techniques the sizes and resolutions of the images remain the same, but, as previously noted, the transmission or display speeds can be reduced. The image adaptation problem has also been studied by researchers for some time [4]. Most of them identify three areas of client variation: network, hardware, and software, and their corresponding image distillation functions: file size reduction, color reduction, and format conversion [9].

Browsing large photos, drawings, or diagrams, is more problematic on mobile devices. To reduce the number of scroll and zoom operations required for browsing, researchers are adapting text visualization techniques such as RSVP (rapid serial visual presentation) to enable users to view information through selected portions of a picture [4]. For example, some studies propose an RSVP browser for photographs that use an image-processing algorithm to identify possible points of interest, such as people's faces. User evaluation results indicate that the browser works well with group photos but is less effective with generic images such as those taken from the news. From an architectural perspective, the new portable devices are gaining acceptance as useful tools at a construction site [10]. Software applications previously confined to desktop computers are now available on the construction site and the data is accessible through a wireless Internet connection [11].

2.3 New Framework for Adaptative Delivery

Client device capability, network bandwidth, and user preferences are becoming increasingly diverse and heterogeneous. To create the best value among all system variables (user, interface and message), various proposals have recently been generated all focused on the generation of information transcoding [12, 13]. In short, these systems proposed a framework for determining when and how to transcode images in an HTTP proxy server while focusing their research on saving response time by JPEG/GIF compression, or color-to-grayscale conversion. Many media processing technologies can be used to improve the user's experience within a heterogeneous network environment [13]. These technologies can be grouped into five categories: information abstraction, modality transformation, data transcoding, data prioritization, and purpose classification.

In the research for this paper, we focused on studying data transcoding technology (the process of converting the data format according to client device capability), and in particular the evaluation of user behaviour during the visualization of images that undergo a change in color system, compression format, or both operations. Based on the results of this experiment and compared with those from other environments analyzed (computer screen, projector screen, HMD), it was concluded that the first experimental approach to the architectural image features should be based on the visual environment to improve the communication for a particular user. To analyze our research proposal, two working hypotheses will be enunciated and expanded:

- H1: Images with less detail and a better differentiation between figure and ground (usually infographic images) are more amenable to high compression without loss of quality awareness.
- H2: Architectural images in black and white do not convey the entire message (they lose information about materials and lighting), and their quality and emotional affect is reduced on smaller screens (on a mobile screen) compared to larger ones (computer and HMD) because of the very difficult to see detailed information.

3 Methodology and Procedure

We have employed two models of images in the test design: the first is a representative selection from the IAPS system [14], tested in several previous studies (for example [15, 16, 17]), which were used as control images and placed at the beginning (7 images) and at the end (7 images) of the test. The second group of images related to the architectural project have been split into the following diverse sub-groups: infographic images generated by computer (18 images), explanatory photographic images of a concrete project (Bridge AZUD, Ebro River in Zaragoza, Spain, Isidro Navarro, 2008, 19 images), composition panels (used in the course "Informatics Tools, Level 2.," Architectural Degree, La Salle, Ramon Llull University, 7 images), and HDR photographic images (6 images). Our two models combine original images of the IAPS system (color images with a resolution of 1024x768) and architectural color images (with resolutions between 800x600 and 4900x3500). There are also images that have been modified in terms of color (converted to black and white), and level of compression (JPG changes into JPG2000 with compression rates of between 80% and 95%).

We used JPEG 2000 (an international standard ISO-15444 developed in open source code) because of its most obvious benefit [18]: its increased compression capability which is especially useful in high resolution images [19, 20]. Another interesting aspect of the JPG2000 format is the ROI (region-of-interest) coding scheme and spatial/SNR scalability that provide a useful functionality of progressive encoding and display for fast database access as well as for delivering various resolutions to terminals with different capabilities in terms of display and bandwidth [4]. Regarding the type of images, the test method involved the following steps:

- If the test is performed using a PowerPoint® presentation, the test facilitator explains the basic objective, and collects general information about the test environment (local time, date, place, and information about the screen). In other cases, the on-line system implemented in previous phases is responsible for capturing some of the information about the display and user data [21]. For mobile environment, we have chosen a PPT visualization because of the preliminary test that showed low usability of our web system [21] on small screens (we need a lot of "panning actions").
- The facilitator (or web system) displays the two previous images to test the evaluation methodology. Without providing a definite time limit, the facilitator explains the manner in which the user must evaluate the images.
- Finally, the user evaluates the images on three levels (valence, arousal, and quality perceived) using the SAM test (Fig.1 original model paper or Fig 2. on-line version). Once the user completes the evaluation, the system automatically jumps to the subsequent image. If the user is unable to complete the evaluation, the concepts are left unmarked within the system.

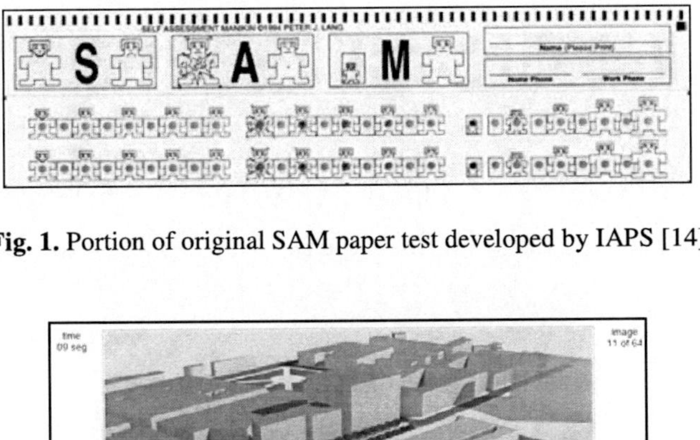

Fig. 1. Portion of original SAM paper test developed by IAPS [14]

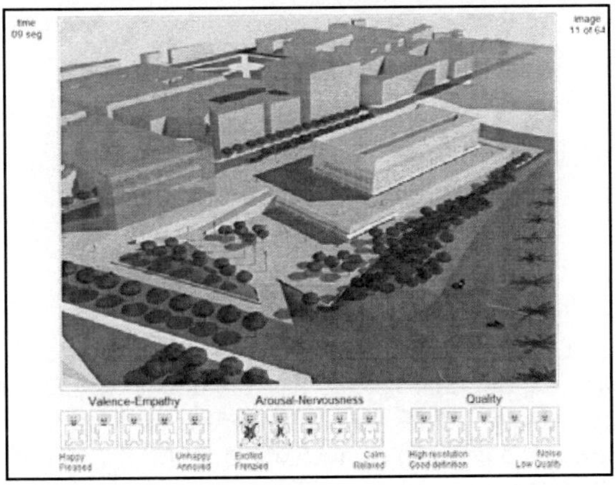

Fig. 2. On-line SAM test developed in previous phases [5]

The test was conducted with three different screens:

- **Generic computer screen**: 17" diagonal distance with a resolution of 1280x1024 and 0,4–0,5m between user and the screen. A sampled of 34 users was involved in the evaluation: 12 women (Average Age (Av): 27,7; Standard Deviation (SD): 7,2) and 22 men (Av: 28,86; SD: 7,01).
- **Head Mounted Display** (5DT HMD 800-40): 0,49" equivalent to 44" at 2m visualization (real visualization distance: 0,03–0,04m), resolution of 800x600 per display. We tested 14 users: 6 women (Av: 25,83; SD: 6,36) and 8 men (Av: 27,25; SD: 6,45).
- **Smartphone** (Nokia n97 mini): 3.2", resolution of 640x360 and 0,3–0,4m of distance visualization. We tested 20 users: 10 women (Av: 28,7; SD: 4,74) and 10 men (Av: 26,5; SD: 6,47).

4 Methodology and Procedure

The first analysis we performed was to compare the overall quality perceived by users in the evaluation of architectural images in the three environments tested:

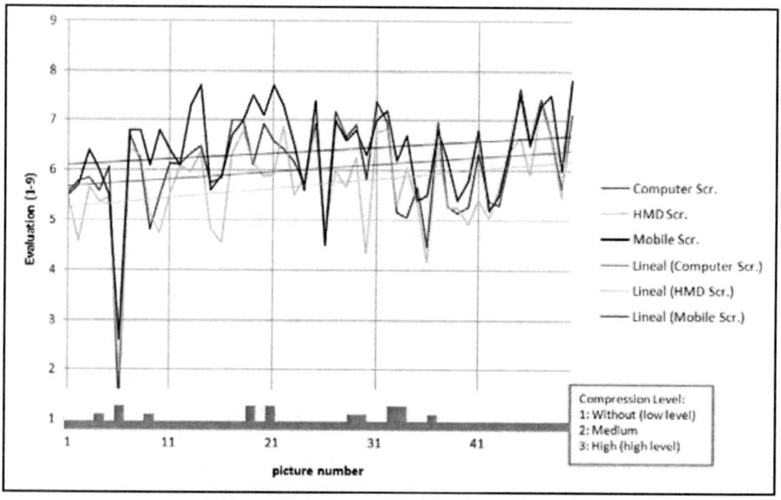

Fig. 3. Overall quality evaluation

It became clear that the best quality assessment was yielded by viewing on a mobile screen (even though this screen has the lower resolution). Including the control images, the average is 6,27 (SD:1,87) for viewing on a mobile screen, 5,71 (SD: 1,85) for viewing on a computer screen and 5,54 (SD: 1,63) for the use of HMD. It is emphasized that the only image with a significantly lower resolution value (picture n° 6, 200x142), was the worst rated (Av: 2,6; SD :1,6), about 40% lower than in high compression cases (8 pictures with 95% compression rate: 4,7; SD :2,09). Based on these initial results and the statement of Hypothesis 1, it should now be checked if the infographic images can support a high level of compression without lowering its assessment by users:

Table 1. Infographic image. Average of image quality based on the device screen.

Img.Nº	Resolution	Color /Compr.	Mobile	Computer	HMD
8	4000x2600	Original	5,50	5,56	5,42
	800x520	80%	6,10	4,81	5,13
10	2400x1700	Original	6,40	5,84	5,67
	800x567	90%	6,00	5,59	5,38
	200x142	95%	2,60	1,34	1,96
21	800x600	Original	7,70	6,48	6,38
	800x600	B&w	6,80	5,48	4,75
18	1800x1200	Original	6,40	6,14	5,54
	1800x1200	B&w	5,60	5,74	4,83
25	3200x1800	Original	7,00	6,99	6,79
	3200x1800	B&w	5,90	5,85	4,54

To check the relevance of the differences we have realized a statically analysis comparing the variances and the averages with an ANOVA study. There is a statistically significant difference with a significance level above 90% ($\alpha = 0.1$), between mobile device and HMD screen, so the mobile screen quality is significantly higher ($P(t) = 0.061$). Also, there is a statistically significant difference with a significance level above 80% between mobile device and standard computer screen (17"-19"), so the mobile screen quality is significantly higher ($P(t) = 0.177$). With these results we would be able to affirm that to match the perceived quality of these environments:

- We conclude that in the case of infographic images, a high compression (between 80 and 90%) can be easily supported without significantly lowering its assessment in respect of the original, especially on a mobile screen: Original Av: 6,6; SD: 1,85; compressed images 80–90% Av: 6,05; SD: 2,11. In the other environments studied, when the original is compressed between 80 and 90% there is a perceived reduction in quality of between 10 and 15%, allowing us to conclude that this is within a tolerable and recommended range.
- In HMD device we need to increase the image resolution or decrease the compression performed.
- In mobile screen visualization, we can further increase the degree of image compression because of the limited size and resolution of the device.
- In both cases, the ranges of variation of infographic images (compression or modification of the resolution) can be about 20% over the original.

In line with previous phases of our investigation [5], in the case of conversion to black and white a sharp reduction is seen, regardless of the resolution and level of compression of the infographic image: about 13% on mobile and computer screen, and 25% on HMD. This information tells us that the use of black and white in architectural framework is not valid.

We then investigated whether the previous statement can be extended to photographic images, thereby corroborating hypothesis 2:

Table 2. Photographic image. Average of image quality based on the device screen

Img.Nº	Resolution	Color / Compr.	Mobile	Computer	HMD
34	2000x1220	Original	7,00	7,18	6,00
	2000x1220	80%	6,80	6,97	6,50
	2000x1220	90%	7,70	6,59	5,92
	2000x1220	95%	7,50	6,12	6,17
	2000x1220	b/n	5,40	5,67	5,33
	2000x1220	B&w --- 80%	6,30	5,84	4,33
	2000x1220	B&w --- 90%	6,20	5,18	5,29
35	2000x1333	Original	6,60	6,66	5,67
	2000x1333	B&w	6,50	6,16	5,50
32	2000x1333	Original	7,40	6,94	6,79
	2000x1333	80%	6,80	6,91	6,25
	2000x1333	95%	6,7	5,05	6,04
52	2816x1880	Original	7,50	7,64	6,67
	2816x1880	B&w	6,50	6,56	5,92
	2816x1880	HDR	7,30	7,43	7,29
55	2816x1880	Original	7,50	6,69	6,67
	2816x1880	B&w	6,00	5,63	5,46
	2816x1880	HDR	7,80	7,12	7,75

Again, we can see how the visualization on small screens, in comparison with the other environments tested, allows for higher compression levels without greatly affecting the perceived quality. In the case of color images, these support the compression regardless of the viewing environment, but not with the black–and-white images, which even without compression are perceived to be of lower quality than color.

The values in the table below show the degree of significance obtained from the implementation of the "Student t test" for samples with unequal variances. Those values below the limit set to $\alpha = 0.2$ (acceptable value for a sample of only 20 users), meant that there was a statistical difference in the values obtained and therefore should be considered as a remarkable difference between environments:

Table 3. Significance level of differences observed in photographic images by device

	Quality		Valence		Arousal	
	CS. vs. Mobile	HMD. Vs. Mobile	CS. vs. Mobile	HMD. Vs. Mobile	CS. vs. Mobile	HMD. Vs. Mobile
Color without compression	0.344	0.103	0,00001	0,0002	0.047	0,0004
Color with 80% comp.	0.070	0.091	0.054	0.023	0.208	0.141
Color with 95% comp.	0.043	0.028	0.015	0.024	0.198	0.008
Grey Scale without compression	0.481	0.256	0.081	0.455	0.347	0.206
Grey Scale with compression (80-90-95%)	0.134	0.102	0.007	0.195	0.301	0.100

In conclusion, both working hypotheses have been proven, which means that the display of images on small format screens generate greater empathy from the user (to be linked to the perceived quality of emotion [21]), including for images with high compression or that are in black-and-white, which are the least suited for use in architectural environments.

References

1. Sousa, R., Nisi, V., Oakley, I.: Glaze: A visualization framework for mobile devices. In: Gross, T., Gulliksen, J., Kotzé, P., Oestreicher, L., Palanque, P., Prates, R.O., Winckler, M. (eds.) INTERACT 2009. LNCS, vol. 5726, pp. 870–873. Springer, Heidelberg (2009)
2. Carmo, M.B., Afonso, A.P., Matos, P.P.: Visualization of geographic query results for small screen devices. In: Proceedings of the 4th ACM Workshop on Geographical Information Retrieval (GIR 2007), pp. 63–64. ACM, New York (2007)
3. Burigat, S., Chittaro, L., Gabrielli, S.: Visualizing locations of off-screen objects on mobile devices: A Comparative Evaluation of Three Approaches. In: Proceedings of the 8th Conference on Human-Computer Interaction with Mobile Devices and Services (MobileHCI 2006), pp. 239–246. ACM, New York (2006)
4. Chen, L., Xie, S., Fan, X., Ma, W.Y., Zhang, H.J., Zhou, H.Q.: A visual attention model for adapting images on small devices. J. Multimed Syst. 9(4), 353–364 (2003)
5. Fonseca, D., Garcia, O., Duran, J., Pifarre, M., Villegas, E.: An image-centred "search and indexation system" based in user's data and perceived emotion. In: Proceeding of the 3rd ACM International Workshop on Human-Centered Computing, pp. 27–34. ACM, New York (2008)
6. Fan, X., Xie, X., Ma, W., Zhang, H.Z.: visual attention based image browsing on mobile devices. In: Proceedings of the 2003 International Conference on Multimedia and Expo (ICME), pp. 53–56. IEEE Computer Society, Los Alamitos (2003)
7. Chittaro, L.: Visualizing information on mobile devices. J. Computer 39(3), 40–45 (2006)
8. Jones, S., Jones, M., Deo, S.: Using keyphrases as search result surrogates on small screen devices. J. Personal and Ubiquitous Computing 8(1), 55–68 (2004)
9. Smith, J.R., Mohan, R., Li, C.S.: Content-based transcoding of images in the internet. In: Proceedings of 5th Int. Conf. on Image Processing (ICIP 1998), pp. 7–11 (1998)
10. Saidi, K., Hass, C., Balli, N.: The value of handheld computers in construction. In: Proceedings of the 19th International Symposium on Automation and Robotics in Construction, Washington (2002)
11. Lipman, R.: Mobile 3D visualization for steel structures. J. Automation in Construction 13, 119–125 (2004)
12. Han, R., Bhagwat, P., LaMIare, R., Mummert, T., Perret, V., Rubas, J.: Dynamic Adaptation in an image transcoding proxy for mobile web browsing. J. IEEE Pers. Commun. 5(6), 8–17 (1998)
13. Ma, W., Bedner, I., Chang, G., Kuchinsky, A., Zhang, H.: Framework for adaptive content delivery in heterogeneous network environments. In: Proceedings of SPIE (Multimedia Comput Network) The Smithsoniana/NASA Astrophysics Data System, pp. 86–100 (2000)
14. Lang, P., Bradley, M., Cuthbert, B.: International affective picture system (IAPS): Technical manual and affective ratings. Technical Report, Gainesville, USA (1997)
15. Houtveen, J., Rietveld, S., Schoutrop, M., Spiering, M., Brosschot, J.: A repressive coping style and affective, facial and physiological responses to looking at emotional pictures. J. of Psychophysiology 42, 265–277 (2001)

16. Aguilar, F., Verdejo, A., Peralta, M., Sánchez, M., Pérez, M.: Expirience of emotions in substance abusers exposed to images containing neutral, positive, and negative affective stimuli. J. Drug and Alcohol Dependece 78, 159–167 (2005)
17. Verschuere, B., Crombez, G., Koster, E.: Cross cultural validation of the IAPS. Technical report, Ghent University, Belgium (2007)
18. Bernier, R.: An introduction to JPEG 2000. J. Library Hi Tech News 23(7), 26–27 (2006)
19. Hughitt, V., Ireland, J., Mueller, D., Simitoglu, G., Garcia Ortiz, J., Schmidt, L., Wamsler, B., Beck, J., Alexandarian, A., Fleck, B.: Helioviewer.org: Browsing very large image archives online using JPEG2000. In: American Geophysical Union, Fall Meeting, Smithsonian/NASA Astrophysics Data (2009)
20. Rosenbaum, R., Schumann, H.: JPEG2000-based image communication for modern browsing techniques. In: Proceedings of the SPIE (Image and Video Communications and Processing) International Society for Optical Engineering, pp. 1019–1030 (2005)
21. Fonseca, D., Garcia, O., Navarro, I., Duran, J., Villegas, E., Pifarre, M.: Iconographic web image classification based on open source technology. In: IIIS Proceedings of the 13th World Multi-Conference on Systemics, Cybernetics and Informatics (WMSCI 2009), Orlando, vol. 3, pp. 184–189 (2009)

Semi-Automatic Hand/Finger Tracker Initialization for Gesture-Based Human Computer Interaction

Daniel Popa, Vasile Gui, and Marius Otesteanu

"Politehnica" University of Timisoara, Faculty of Electronics and Telecommunications,
Bd. V. Parvan nr. 2, 300223 Timisoara, Romania
{gheorghe.popa,vasile.gui,marius.otesteanu}@etc.upt.ro

Abstract. Many solutions are available in the literature for tracking body elements for gesture-based human-computer interfaces, but most of them leave open the problem of tracker initialization or use manual initialization. Solutions for automatic initialization are also available, especially for 3D environments. In this paper we propose a semi-automatic method for initialization of a hand/finger tracker in monocular vision systems. The constraints imposed for the semi-automatic initialization allow a more reliable identification of the target than in the case of fully automatic initialization and can also be used to secure the access to a gesture-based interface. The proposed method combines foreground/background segmentation with color, shape, position and time constraints to ensure a user friendly and safe tracker initialization. The method is not computationally intensive and can be used to initialize virtually any hand/finger tracker.

Keywords: tracker initialization, hand/finger tracking, HCI, gesture-based interfaces, semi-supervised tracking.

1 Introduction

The development of the computers during the last decades conducted to their expansion in almost all areas of modern life. As a consequence, the necessity for more natural interfaces between the human users and the computers emerged. Traditional input devices like mouses, keyboards, touchpads or touchscreens do not provide natural interfaces.

Recently more and more research in the field of Human Computer Interaction (HCI) focuses on developing gesture-based interfaces. A very popular approach for gesture-based HCI relies on devices that visually track the movements of the user [1]. Gestures are expressive body movements containing spatial and temporal variation [2] and the computer must use intelligent algorithms in order to be able to recognize the meaning of a specific gesture.

Since gesture-based interfaces require some intelligence in the perception of the user's actions, they are categorized as intelligent HCIs [3].
A considerable amount of work in gesture recognition has been conducted in the field of computer vision and [3], [4] and [5] contain good surveys on this subject.

H. Cherifi, J.M. Zain, and E. El-Qawasmeh (Eds.): DICTAP 2011, Part I, CCIS 166, pp. 417–430, 2011.

A vision based gesture recognition system is usually composed of three main components [6]: image preprocessing, tracking, and gesture recognition. Image preprocessing is a preliminary step in which the frames are prepared for analysis through various procedures which reveal and express in a simplified form important data (features) necessary to locate the target (hand, finger, face). The tracking part is responsible for tracking the target from frame to frame based on the data obtained from the image preprocessing step. Finally, the gesture recognition part is responsible for deciding whether the user is performing a meaningful gesture.

An important aspect concerning the practical applicability of vision-based gesture recognition systems and of the video trackers, in general, is the initialization of the tracker. The initialization of the tracker is the process in which the tracker identifies for the first time the object to be tracked. The initialization can be implemented in various ways, depending on the nature of the target and the tracking principle. Considering the degree of involvement of a human operator, the tracker initialization can be classified as manual or automatic.

In the case of manual initialization, a human supervisor needs to indicate the target object to the tracker (e.g. indicate using a pointing device). This type of initialization may be suitable in order to prove the functional principle of a tracker or gesture recognition system [7], [8], [9] but is generally not adequate for practical applications like gesture-based interfaces.

The automatic initialization does not require any intervention from a human supervisor. In this case the system must be able to automatically identify the target and focus on it [10], [11], [12].

This paper presents a semi-automatic method to initialize a finger tracker used in a single camera, vision-based gesture recognition system. The semi-automatic character of the initialization comes from the fact that the tracker initializes automatically, only when the target hand/finger appears in a specific area of the image.

In many applications a completely automatic initialization of the tracker is preferable to a semi-automatic one. However, automatic initialization requires more flexibility in hand detection, leaving more room for unintended gesture detection. Since in the proposed approach initialization occurs only in the specified area, the probability of unintended tracker initialization (i.e. the tracker should not be initialized when a user hand moves around the interest area if the user did not confirmed his intention to access the interface) is reduced. Also the constraints imposed for a semi-automatic initialization allow a more reliable identification of the target, which makes it an attractive option not only for the particular case of dynamic gesture-based interfaces but also for the more general category of the semi-supervised trackers. Semi-supervised trackers learn the target model in the first frame, then, during the tracking process perform no updates (or perform insignificant updates), therefore it is important to have a reliable model of the target from the initialization phase.

In the next section an overview of other tracker initialization solutions is provided. The third section contains the description of the proposed algorithm. The experimental results and the conclusions are presented in sections 4 and 5.

2 Related Work

Although many solutions have been proposed in the literature for gesture recognition and tracking body elements (e.g. face, hand, fingers), most of them leave open the initialization problem or use manual initialization [8], [9], [13], focusing on the tracking problem.

3D vision systems can provide a good framework for the automatic initialization of the tracker, based on the additional information provided by a stereo camera system [11].

In systems based on monocular vision it is very difficult to recognize the target in various (often ambiguous) poses and therefore a fully automatic initialization is hard to implement in this case. Many authors use color information to initialize trackers. In [14] face tracker initialization relies on the color probability density. In [15] colored and textured rectangular patches are used for automatic initialization of a human body tracker. Color is also the most widely used feature for hand/finger detection. A popular approach is to use skin color based detection as skin hue has relatively low variation between people. A review of skin chromaticity models can be found in [16]. The main advantage of the hue is its invariance to illumination changes. Nevertheless, the hue is unreliable at low illumination levels, for objects which are achromatic or have low saturations and for bright or excessively illuminated objects (nearly white objects). Under certain assumptions, color and motion cues can be used to perform automatic initialization of hand trackers [17], [18].

Shape information has also widely been used to detect hands. Edge detectors can be used to obtain shape information of the hand/fingers, but many edges may also result from background objects and from hand texture. Edges, color information and decision trees are used in [19] for detecting hands and fingers.

Background subtraction is a fast and powerful technique used in video segmentation [20]-[23]. Although background subtraction can provide useful information for hand/finger tracking and tracker initialization, it is not really effective when used alone. In [24] background subtraction is combined with morphological operations for hand detection. Background subtraction combined with color and/or shape information has also a great potential for automatic hand/finger tracker initialization [24].

3 Proposed Method

The proposed method was developed for the initialization of a finger (index) tracker used in dynamic gesture recognition. The method can be used to initialize a hand or finger tracker in a monocular vision environment. The tracker can only be initialized by the presence of the hand, in a specific position and in a specific area of the image. To guide the user on the required hand pose and location, while waiting for the initialization of the tracker, a hand contour is displayed on a monitor, over the image captured by the camera used by the HCI as shown in fig. 1.

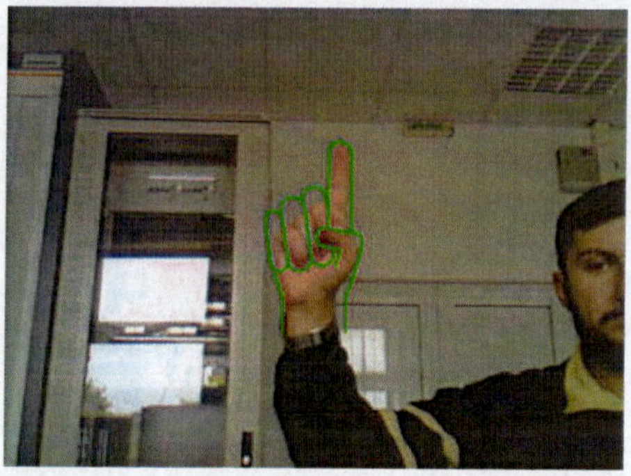

Fig. 1. Screen capture from the CONFIRM state

3.1 Conditions for Hand/Finger Detection

The tracker for which the proposed method was developed is part of a dynamic gesture recognition system. Therefore tracking should only start when a user wants to use the gesture based interface. When the tracker's target is a hand or a finger, an object in a frame must fulfill simultaneously the following criteria in order to trigger the initialization of the tracker:

- foreground object
- color (skin)
- shape/pose
- location within the image

First of all, the target object (i.e. hand/finger) must be a foreground object. In fact, this is a general condition that can be applied for trackers of any type, as normally the target of a tracker is a foreground object.

Another characteristic of the target is the uniform color (skin color).

The first two criteria significantly reduce the data for processing, but a third criterion of shape/pose is required in order to distinguish a hand/finger from other skin colored foreground objects. Also the constraints on shape/pose together with those on location within the image help in avoiding false triggering of the tracker initialization. The hand may have various appearances in a monocular vision frame. Accidental triggering of the tracker initialization must be avoided, because the user must consciously start using the gesture based interface.

3.2 The Hand Detection Algorithm

A preliminary processing of the video stream for the detection of the hand/finger is background subtraction. Background subtraction is an important step towards hand segmentation, resulting in considerable reduction of the processing data. For applications where the assumption that the only foreground object in the scene is the hand to track, this step can directly locate the position of the hand. Such an assumption is generally not acceptable for practical situations and therefore additional steps are required to distinguish the hand/finger to track from the other foreground objects.

The next step of processing implements the color criterion which is applied to the foreground objects detected in the previous step. HSV color space is useful for indentifying the skin colored objects. Skin appears to have the same hue for all humans (except for albinos) [14]. Different races' skins differ only in color saturation (i.e. dark-skinned people have greater saturation, while light-skinned people have lower saturation). Considering this property, a simple threshold based skin detector can be implemented in order to discriminate between skin and non-skin foreground objects. Two auxiliary binary images are generated using thresholds in the 3 dimensions of the HSV color space:

- an image of valid skin color pixels – in which the pixel positions for which all the skin color criteria are fulfilled are set to white and the remaining pixels are set to black and
- an image of pixels which cannot be directly classified as skin or non-skin – in which the pixel positions for which the hue is not reliable are set to white and the remaining pixels are set to black.

A confidence interval in the H domain is defined so that it covers the hue range for normal human skin color. Thresholds are also required in the S and V domains in order to identify the pixels for which the hue is not reliable:

- pixels with too low saturation,
- pixels with too low brightness (value),
- pixels with too high brightness.

In the saturation domain a single threshold is required in order to identify the pixels with a too low saturation. A minimal and a maximal threshold are imposed in the value (brightness) domain.

Pixels with a reliable hue, within the skin confidence interval, are considered skin colored pixels and marked correspondingly in the image of valid skin pixels. Pixels which do not fit the limitations in the saturation and value domains do not present a reliable hue. These pixels cannot be directly classified as skin or non-skin colored, based on their hue and therefore they are marked in a separate auxiliary image. A decision whether these pixels are to be considered skin or not is made latter, based on the shape and location constraints.

The shape/pose and location criteria are implemented together using a hand shaped binary mask. This mask is used together with the auxiliary binary images obtained after the previous step for detection of the hand presence. Thresholds are applied on the percentages of pixel matches in order to decide whether a hand is detected or not. First, the region of interest of the image of valid hue skin colored pixels is compared with the hand shaped mask. Both images are binary, and a pixelwise comparison is made in order to determine the percentage of matching pixels. The percentage of matching pixels in the two images is compared with a threshold to decide whether further investigation of non-reliable hue pixels is necessary. If the percentage of matching pixels is below this threshold, no reliable decision can be made on the hand presence, and in this case the hand is considered not detected. If the percentage is above this threshold, the second auxiliary image is taken into account. If any non-reliable hue pixels were marked in the second auxiliary image, they will be used to increase the matching percentage. White pixels from the second auxiliary image, which correspond to positions within the hand mask, are classified as skin colored and those which correspond to positions outside the mask are classified as non-skin colored. The matching percentage is recalculated and compared with a new threshold (higher than the one used at the previous step). The hand is considered detected only if the percentage is above this threshold. The values of the thresholds were determined experimentally, in order to allow a comfortable initialization, while avoiding false hand detection.

3.3 Tracker Initialization

The hand detection procedure described above is the basic part of the proposed tracker initialization method. In order to avoid false triggering, the tracker is not initialized after the first detection of the hand. A state machine controls the tracker initialization and the basic tracking functions. Three states are defined:

- SEARCH,
- CONFIRM and
- FOUND.

Fig. 2 presents the three states and the possible transitions between them. Fig. 3 presents the outline of the tracker initialization process. The first two processing steps – background subtraction and color space analysis – are applied to all frames regardless of the current state. Then the processing is state dependent and different tasks are performed in each state.

The system starts in the SEARCH state. In this state, at each frame, hand detection is attempted. When the hand is successfully detected, the system advances to the next state: CONFIRM. The purpose of the CONFIRM state is to ensure that the user wants to communicate through the gesture-based interface (i.e. to avoid accidental triggering of the tracking). The CONFIRM state is maintained for a minimum time interval, Tmin. There is also an upper limitation, Tmax, of the time spent in the CONFIRM state, in order to allow the system to return to the search state if the initial detection of the target is not confirmed. The user is aware that he must keep the hand in the required position for a short time interval (Tmin) in order to trigger the tracker, and therefore we found reasonable to impose a value of Tmax of approximately 2×Tmin.

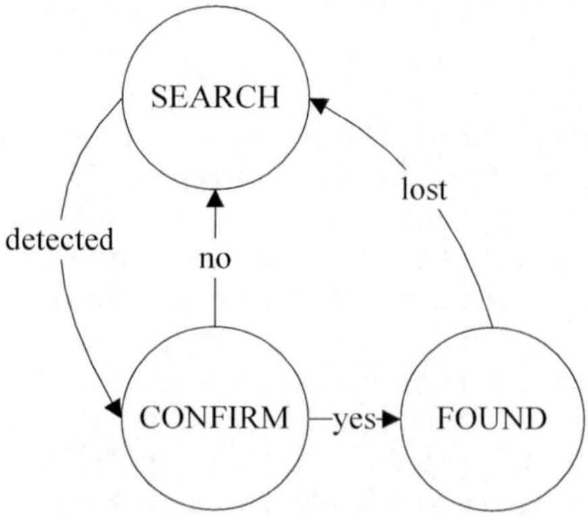

Fig. 2. State machine diagram

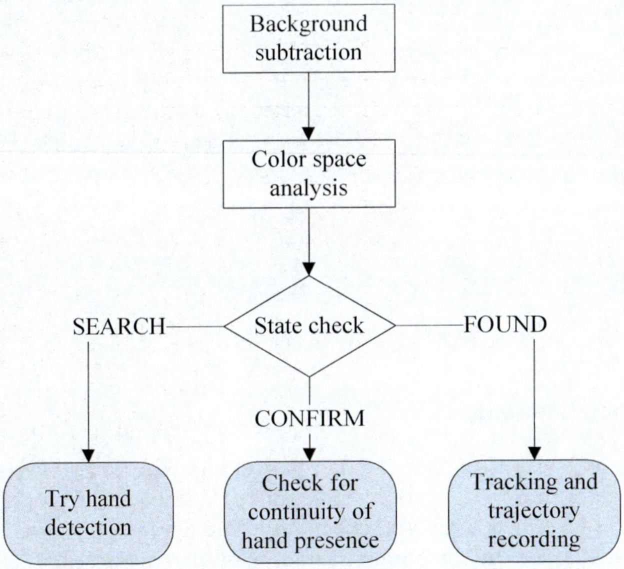

Fig. 3. Flowchart of frame processing for hand detection

While the system is in the CONFIRM state, the user should maintain the hand in the required position. In this state, for each frame, a decision about the hand presence is made. Two counters are updated every frame and help deciding when to leave the CONFIRM state:

- a time/frame counter – counts the time (or the number of frames) elapsed since the beginning of the current CONFIRM state – and
- a hand detection success counter – a measure of hand detection rate.

The hand detection counter starts at 1 and is incremented with every frame in which the hand is detected. For every frame in which the hand is not detected the counter is decremented, but the decrement operation is limited to 0 (i.e. no decrementing takes place when the counter value is 0).

While the time counter is between Tmin and Tmax, the system may try to advance to the third state. At any moment within this time interval, if the hand detection success counter exceeds a specific threshold (approximately 70% of the number of frames processed during Tmin), the tracker is initialized at the current location of the hand and the system advances to the 3-rd state, FOUND. If the hand detection success counter does not reach the required threshold before Tmax elapses, the tracker is not initialized and the system returns to the SEARCH state.

The FOUND state corresponds to the basic tracking operations, which are not the object of this paper. The system remains in this state as long as the target is not declared lost by the tracking algorithm. The target is assumed lost only if it is not detected for a relatively long interval of time. When the target is considered lost, the system returns to the SEARCH state and the initialization procedure restarts.

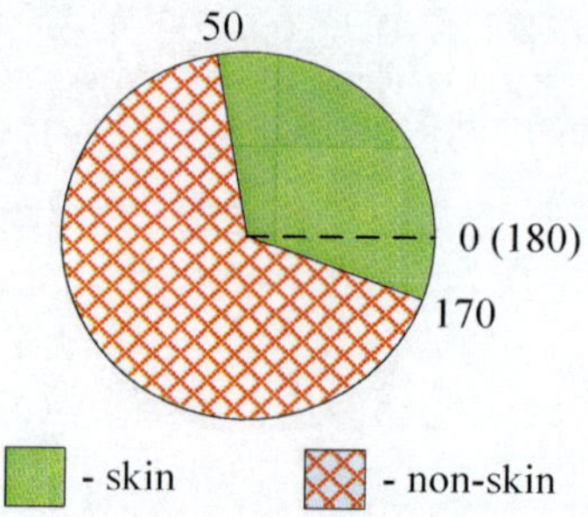

Fig. 4. Circular representation of the 8-bit hue

3.4 Implementation Details

The proposed method was implemented as part of a dynamic hand gesture recognition system. The algorithm was used for the initialization of a CamShift based hand tracker [7] and of a finger tracker, respectively. The application was developed using Microsoft Visual C++. In the implementation of the application, OpenCV library functions were used for various tasks like video capture (from camera or from previously recorded *.avi files), background subtraction, color space conversions, pixelwise operations etc. The video sequences were acquired using a common webcam at 640×480 resolution and approximately 15 fps.

The background subtraction was implemented using the codebook based method available in OpenCV.

The thresholds in the HSV color space used to identify the reliable hue skin pixels and the non-reliable hue pixels were set based on experiments. OpenCV uses 8 bits to represent each of the H, S and V components of a pixel. S and V cover each the full range available on 8 bits, [0 – 255]. H (hue) which is defined as an angle should range from 0 to 360. In order to fit the 8 bit representation, in OpenCV, all hue values are divided by 2 and therefore the range is reduced to [0 – 180], as shown in fig. 4.

Reliable hue pixels have saturation above 30, and value between 40 and 245. We determined empirically, by calculating hue histograms for manually selected skin colored areas that the appropriate range for hue was [170 – 180] and [0 – 50]. It can be noticed in fig. 4 that the two intervals are actually contiguous due to the circular definition of the hue (180 and 0 represent the same color).

During the SEARCH and CONFIRM states a hand contour is displayed on a monitor to guide the user on the required hand pose and location as shown in fig. 1. A rectangular binary mask is applied at the location of the displayed hand contour to verify the shape/pose and location criteria. The two binary images obtained after the color space processing in the area of the rectangular hand mask, corresponding to the image in fig. 1, are presented in fig. 5.

A global threshold of 60% is used for matching pixels in the rectangular region, where the hand mask is applied. Some areas within the hand mask are considered critical and therefore, tighter matching thresholds, of 70 - 85%, are applied separately to each of these areas. Fig. 6 presents the matching result image (white pixels indicate a match) and the 5 critical rectangular areas where the tighter thresholds are applied.

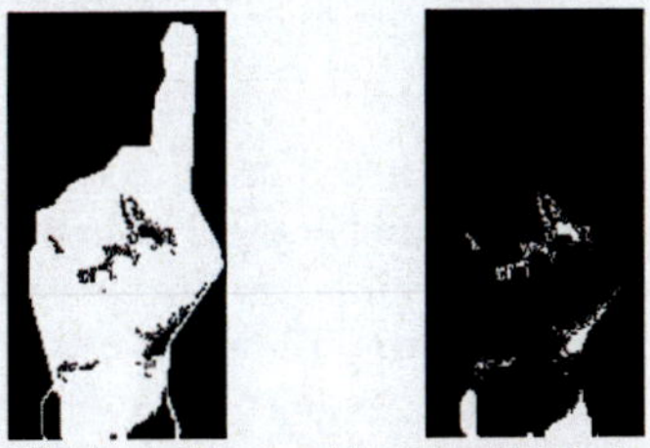

a) valid hue skin b) non-reliable hue

Fig. 5. Binary images after color space analysis in the hand mask region

White pixels indicate matching and black pixels indicate non-matching. In the example in fig. 6 regions 1 and 4 have 100% matched pixels, regions 3 and 5 have 99% and region 2 has 93%.The tightest thresholds, of 85% are used for regions 1, 4, 3 and 5, while for region 2 a 70% threshold is used.

Region 1 should virtually contain 100% non-skin pixels, while region 4 should contain 100% skin pixels, regardless of the proportionality between hand/finger dimensions.

Regions 3 and 5 should contain non-skin pixels and they are treated together by applying an overall matching percentage threshold of 85%. The two regions are treated together to allow a more comfortable initialization procedure. Sometimes, one of them may have a lower matching percentage while the other virtually has 100% matching. Such an imbalance between the two regions may appear due to hand tilt and/or left/right position shift.

In region 2, a 70% threshold is applied. This region should contain skin pixels. The low threshold used for this region is due to the fact that the matching percentage in this region is heavily influenced by two factors:

- the thickness of the index finger (the matching percentage lowers for users with thin fingers) and
- the possible tilt or position shift of the index finger with respect to the ideal position indicated by the guiding hand contour.

The global threshold is more relaxed, because, while the hand mask is unique, different users have different hand/finger dimensions proportionalities.

In our experiments the time limits used for the CONFIRM state were Tmin = 1s (15 frames) and Tmax = 2s (30 frames).

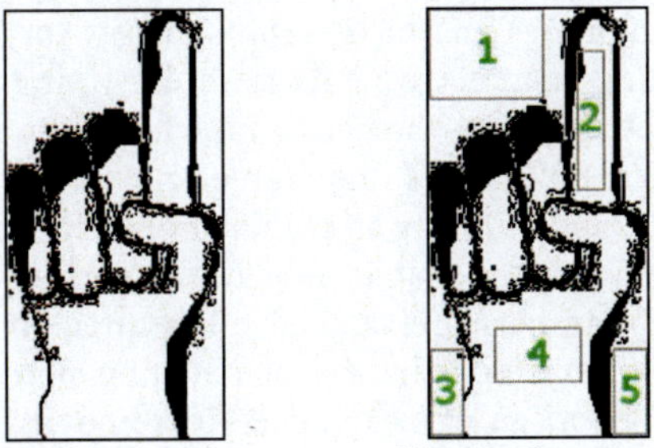

a) matching result b) critical areas

Fig. 6. Matching pixels in the rectangular hand mask region

4 Experiments and Results

The proposed tracker initialization method was tested with different backgrounds, both with daylight and artificial lighting. A number of 25 tests were performed by 3 users.

The histograms of the global matching percentages for 6 tracker initializations (1 with daylight and 1 with artificial lighting for each of the 3 users) are presented in fig. 7. In each case the frames taken into account begin with the frame in which the hand is detected for the first time and end with the frame in which the tracker is initialized.

It can be observed that in a single case – artificial light 2 – percentages below 60% are obtained. The 6 matching percentages below the 60% threshold correspond to frames in which the user's hand was not aligned correctly with the guiding hand-shaped contour. It can also be observed that in the other 5 cases all the matching percentages are higher than 65%.

In 5 of the cases presented in fig. 7 the CONFIRM state ends after the minimum time interval, while for the other case – artificial light 2 – 2 additional frames are necessary before advancing to the FOUND state and initializing the tracker.

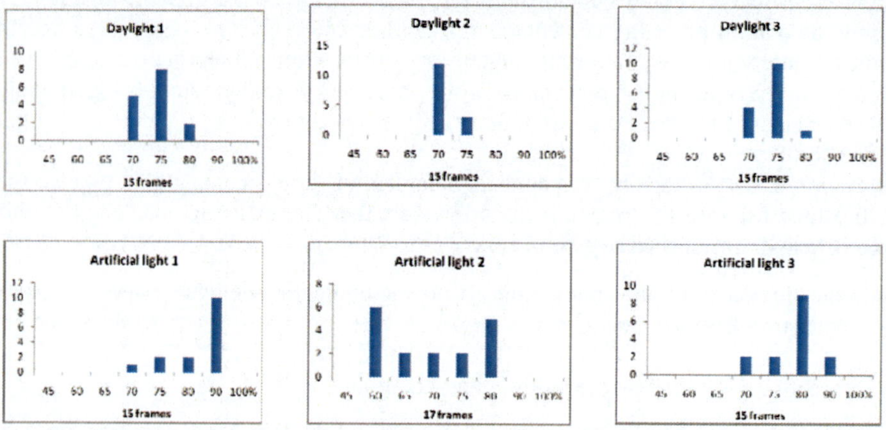

Fig. 7. Histograms of global matching percentages in the rectangular hand mask region

Tracker initialization experiments were analyzed for the 25 cases (15 with daylight and 10 with artificial lighting) and table 1 summarizes the results obtained from the point of view of matching percentages and thresholds fitting.

Considering each of the five threshold based detection criteria, detection was successful in more than 87% of all the frames processed in the CONFIRM state. Actually a success rate below 90% was obtained only for the region 2 criterion. The hand is considered detected in a frame only if all the five criteria are met, and this happened for 78% of the frames analyzed. The last three columns of the table present the minimum, the maximum and the mean matching percentages corresponding to each of the 5 criteria. The mean was calculated by removing 3% of the worse and 3% of the best matching percentages. Low matching percentages correspond to frames in

Table 1. Summary of the initialization results

	Criteria passed [%]	Min %	Max %	Mean %
Global	92	48	82	73
Region 1	96	76	100	97
Region 2	87	0	100	88
Region 4	91	39	100	94
Regions 3,5	95	80	99	96
All	78			

which the user's hand did not fit correctly the indicated shape. The results obtained indicate that the chosen combination of criteria allows the system to correctly identify the frames in which the user's hand is present at the required location.

The histogram of the number of frames spent by the system in the CONFIRM state is presented in fig. 8. In 19 of the 25 tests the tracker initialization occurred after the minimum time interval (15 frames – 1s at 15 fps)

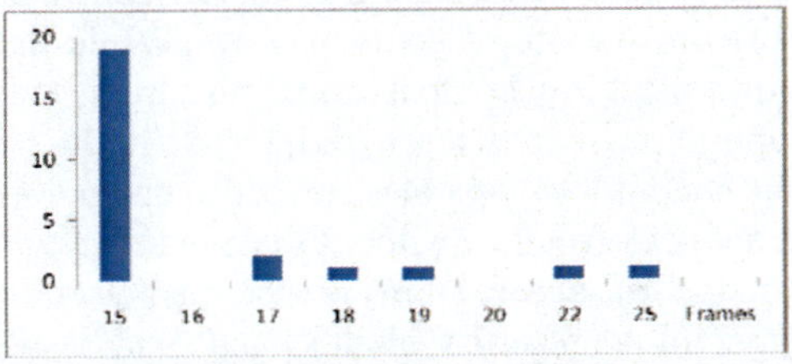

Fig. 8. Histogram of the number of frames in the CONFIRM state for the 25 experiments

Only in 2 cases, in which the user moved the hand slightly around the guiding contour in order to test the limits of the detection capacity, more than 20 frames were necessary to accomplish the requirements for tracker initialization. The measured time intervals considered in fig. 8 do not take into account the time necessary to the user to fit the hand correctly to the guiding shape. The average time needed to fit the hand to the guiding shape was below 3 s. This illustrates that the proposed method allows the user to easily initialize the tracker.

Additionally, the system was tested for resistance to false triggering. For this purpose three types of tests were performed:

- random movements of the hand were performed around the initialization area,
- human subjects moving around the initialization area and
- global lighting change (most part of the image appeared as foreground).

In the first case, when random hand movements were performed in the initialization area, the system advanced occasionally from the SEARCH to the CONFIRM state, but no false initialization occurred, as the conditions imposed in the CONFIRM state to allow the tracker initialization were not met.

For the second test scenario, when human subjects moved around the initialization area, no false hand detection occurred and the system remained in the SEARCH state.

The resistance to false initialization due to global lighting changes was tested using 5 different backgrounds both for increasing and decreasing lighting. During the tests performed no false hand detection occurred and the system remained in the SEARCH state. When skin-like background was used, it was observed that, due to the lighting change, some areas of the background appeared as foreground and therefore 2 criteria (foreground object and color) were met for these areas, but during the tests performed no such area happened to take the shape of the hand required for the initialization. The probability for such an area to take the required hand shape and size, at the required location in the image in order to trigger a false tracker initialization is extremely low. Therefore we can consider that lighting changes in the scene are unlikely to cause false initializations, regardless of the background used.

The tests for resistance to false triggering combined with the results of the 25 tests for tracker initialization indicate the reliability of the proposed method.

5 Conclusions

The proposed method proved to be reliable for hand/finger tracker initialization. The method is easy to use from the user's point of view. While the multiple conditions imposed for initialization need low computational resources, they are able to provide a quick initialization and to prevent false triggering. The multi-cue approach allow the proposed initialization method to operate correctly under very different lighting conditions, with different backgrounds, without the need to readjust the settings of the thresholds. The advantage of a safe start is obtained at the price of a reduced flexibility regarding the initial position of the hand, and restrictions regarding the hand color uniformity (i.e. the user may not wear gloves, have extremely dirty hands etc.).

The four detection criteria together with the time constraints imposed provide a user friendly initialization procedure. The time interval when the user must keep the hand in a given pose at a specific location is short enough in order not to be considered a drawback and it is long enough to significantly reduce the chances of false triggering.

The proposed method can be used with a large variety of hand/finger trackers, as it only identifies the time when the object to be tracked is present at the specified location so that the tracker can start and no restrictions are imposed on the tracking algorithm.

Acknowledgement

The research reported in this paper was developed in the framework of a grant funded by the Romanian Research Council (CNCSIS) with the title "Statistic and semantic modeling in image sequences analysis", ID 931, contr. 651/19.01.2009.

References

1. Gavrila, D.M.: The visual analysis of human movement: a survey. Computer Vision and Image Understanding 73(1), 82–98 (1999)
2. Wang, T.S., Shum, H.Y., Xu, Y.Q., Zheng, N.N.: Unsupervised Analysis of Human Gestures. In: IEEE Pacific Rim Conference on Multimedia, pp. 174–181 (2001)
3. Karray, F., Alemzadeh, M., Saleh, J.A., Arab, M.N.: Human-Computer Interaction: Overview on State of the Art. International Journal on Smart Sensing and Intelligent Systems 1(1), 137–159 (2008)
4. Wu, Y., Huang, T.: Vision-Based Gesture Recognition: A Review. In: Proceedings of the International Gesture Recognition Workshop, pp. 103–115 (1999)
5. Pavlovic, V.I., Sharma, R., Huang, T.S.: Visual Interpretation of Hand Gestures for Human-Computer Interaction: A Review. IEEE Transactions on Pattern Analysis and Machine Intelligence 19(7), 677–695 (1997)
6. Moeslund, T., Nrgaard, L.: A Brief Overview of Hand Gestures used in Wearable Human Computer Interfaces. Technical Report CVMT 03-02, Computer Vision and Media Technology Laboratory, Aalborg University, DK (2003)
7. Popa, D., Simion, G., Gui, V., Otesteanu, M.: Real time trajectory based hand gesture recognition. WSEAS Transactions on Information Science and Applications 5(4), 532–546 (2008)
8. Sidenbladh, H., Black, M.J., Fleet, D.J.: Stochastic tracking of 3D human figures using 2D image motion. In: Vernon, D. (ed.) ECCV 2000. LNCS, vol. 1843, pp. 702–718. Springer, Heidelberg (2000)
9. Dargazany, A., Solimani, A.: Kernel-Based Hand Tracking. Australian Journal of Basic and Applied Sciences 3(4), 4017–4025 (2009)
10. Shell, H.S.M., Arora, V., Dutta, A., Behera, L.: Face feature tracking with automatic initialization and failure recovery. In: IEEE Conference on Cybernetics and Intelligent Systems (CIS), pp. 96–101 (2010)
11. Schmidt, J., Castrillon, M.: Automatic Initialization for Body Tracking - Using Appearance to Learn a Model for Tracking Human Upper Body Motions. In: 3rd International Conference on Computer Vision Theory and Applications (VISAPP), pp. 535–542 (2008)
12. Xu, J., Wu, Y., Katsaggelos, A.: Part-based initialization for hand tracking. In: 17th IEEE International Conference on Image Processing (ICIP), pp. 3257–3260 (2010)
13. Coogan, T., Awad, G.M., Han, J., Sutherland, A.: Real time hand gesture recognition including hand segmentation and tracking. In: Bebis, G., Boyle, R., Parvin, B., Koracin, D., Remagnino, P., Nefian, A., Meenakshisundaram, G., Pascucci, V., Zara, J., Molineros, J., Theisel, H., Malzbender, T. (eds.) ISVC 2006. LNCS, vol. 4291, pp. 495–504. Springer, Heidelberg (2006)
14. Bradski, G. R.: Computer vision face tracking as a component of a perceptual user interface. Intel Technology Journal Q2 (1998), `http://developer.intel.com/technology/itj/archive/1998.htm`
15. Ramanan, D., Forsyth, D.A.: Finding and tracking people from the bottom up. In: IEEE Computer Society Conference on Computer Vision and Pattern Recognition (CVPR 2003), vol. 2, pp. 467–474 (2003)
16. Terrillon, J., Shirazi, M., Fukamachi, H., Akamtsu, S.: Comparative performance of different skin chrominance models and chrominance spaces for the automatic detection of human faces in color images. In: Proceedings of the International Conference on Automatic Face and Gesture Recognition (FG), pp. 54–61 (2000)

17. Barhate, K.A., Patwardhan, K.S., Roy, S.D., Chaudhuri, S., Chaudhury, S.: Robust shape based two hand tracker. In: Proc. IEEE International Conference on Image Processing (ICIP 2004), pp. 1017–1020 (2004)
18. Yuan, Q., Sclaroff, S., Athitsos, V.: Automatic 2D Hand Tracking in Video Sequences. In: Seventh IEEE Workshops on Application of Computer Vision WACV/MOTIONS 2005, vol. 1, pp. 250–256 (2005)
19. Caglar, M.B., Lobo, N.: Open hand detection in a cluttered single image using finger primitives. In: Proceedings of the IEEE Computer Society Conference on Computer Vision and Pattern Recognition, New York, pp. 148–153 (2006)
20. Stauffer, C., Eric, W., Grimson, L.: Adaptive background mixture models for real-time tracking. In: Proc. IEEE Computer Vision and Pattern Recognition (CVPR), pp. 2246–2252 (1999)
21. Elgamal, A., Duraiswami, R., Harwood, D., Davis, L.S.: Background and foreground modeling using nonparametric kernel density estimation for visual surveillance. Proceedings of the IEEE 90(7), 1151–1162 (2002)
22. Ianăşi, C.N., Gui, V., Toma, C.I., Pescaru, D.: A fast algorithm for background tracking in video surveillance using nonparametric kernel density estimation. In: Facta Universitatis, Niš, Serbia and Montenegro, Series Electronics and Energetics, vol. 18(1), pp. 127–144 (2005)
23. Stolkin, R., Florescu, I., Kamberov, G.: An adaptive background model for CAMSHIFT tracking with a moving camera. In: Proc. 6th International Conference on Advances in Pattern Recognition, pp. 261–265. World Scientific Publishing, Calcutta (2007)
24. Salleh, N.S.M., Jais, J., Mazalan, L., Ismail, R., Yussof, S., Ahmad, A., Anuar, A., Mohamad, D.: Sign Language to Voice Recognition: Hand Detection Techniques for Vision-Based Approach. In: Current Developments in Technology-Assisted Education, FORMATEX, Spain, pp. 967–972 (2006)

Security Evaluation for Graphical Password

Arash Habibi Lashkari[1], Azizah Abdul Manaf[1], Maslin Masrom[2], and Salwani Mohd Daud[1]

[1] Advanced Informatics School, Universiti Technologi Malaysia (UTM), Kuala Lumpur, Malaysia
[2] Razak School of Engineering and Advanced Technology, Universiti Technologi Malaysia (UTM), Kuala Lumpur, Malaysia
a_habibi_l@hotmail.com, azizah07@ic.utm.my, maslin@ic.utm.my, salwani@ic.utm.my

Abstract. Nowadays, user authentication is one of the important topics in information security. Text-based strong password schemes could provide with certain degree of security. However, the fact that strong passwords being difficult to memorize often leads their owners to write them down on papers or even save them in a computer file. Graphical Password or Graphical user authentication (GUA) has been proposed as a possible alternative solution to text-based authentication, motivated particularly by the fact that humans can remember images better than text. All of Graphical Password algorithms have two different aspects which are usability and security. This paper focuses on security aspects of algorithms that most of researchers work on this part and try to define security features and attributes. Unfortunately, till now there isn't a complete evaluation criterion for graphical password security. At first, this paper tries to study on most of GUA algorithm. Then, collects the major security attributes in GUA and proposed an evaluation criterion.

Keywords: Pure Recall-Based GUA, Cued Recall-Based GUA, Recognition Based GUA, Graphical Password, Security, Attack Patterns, Brute force, Dictionary attack, Guessing Attack, Spyware, Shoulder surfing, Social engineering Attack, Password Entropy, Password Space.

1 Introduction

The term "Picture Superiority Effect" coined by researchers to describe Graphical-Based Passwords (GBP) reflects the effect of GBP's as a solution to conventional password techniques. Furthermore, such a term underscores the impact of GBP's in that the "effect" is on account of the fact that graphics and texts are easier to commit to memory than conventional password techniques.

Initially, the concept of Graphical User Authentication (GUA) (Graphical Password or Graphical Image Authentication (GIA)) described by Blonder [6], one image would appear on the screen whereupon the user would click on a few chosen regions of the image. If the user clicked in the correct regions then the user would be authenticated. Memorability of passwords and the efficiency of input images are two major key human factors. Memorability has two perspectives:

H. Cherifi, J.M. Zain, and E. El-Qawasmeh (Eds.): DICTAP 2011, Part I, CCIS 166, pp. 431–444, 2011.

- The process of selecting and the encoding of the password by the user.
- Defining the task that user has to undertake to retrieve the password.

The graphical user authentication (GUA) system requires a user to select a memorable image. Such a selection of memorable images would depend on the nature of the image itself and the specific sequence of click locations. Images with meaningful content will support the user's memorability.

2 Graphical Authentications Methods

Most of articles from 1995 till 2010 describe that Graphical Authentication Techniques are categorised into three groups:

2.1 Pure Recall Based Techniques

Users reproduce their passwords, without having the chance to use the reminder marks of system. Although easy and convenient, it appears that users do not quite remember their passwords. Table 1 shows some of the algorithms which were created based on this technique.

Table 1. Pure Recall Based Techniques Ordered by Date

Algorithm	Proposed Date	Created By
Draw a Secret (DAS)	1999	Jermyn Ian et al.
Passdoodle	1999	Christopher Varenhorst
Grid Selection	2004	Juaie Thorpe, P.C. Van Oorschot
Syukri	2005	Syukri, et al.
Qualitative DAS (QDAS)	2007	Di Lin, et al.

2.2 Cued Recall Based Techniques

Here, the system provides a framework of reminders, hints and gestures for the users to reproduce their passwords or make a reproduction that would be much more accurate. Table 2 lists some of the algorithms which were created based on this technique.

Table 2. Cued Recall Based Techniques Ordered by Date

Algorithm	Proposed Date	Created By
Blonder	1996	Greg E. Blonder
Passlogix v-Go	2002	Passlogic Inc. Co.
VisKey SFR	2003	SFR Company
PassPoint	2005	Susan Wiedenbeck, et al.
Pass-Go	2006	-
Passmap	2006	Roman V. Vamponski
Background DAS (BDAS)	2007	Paul Duaphi

2.3 Recognition Based Techniques

Here, users select pictures, icons or symbols from a bank of images. During the authentication process, the users have to recognise their registration choice from a grid of image. Research has shown that "90% of users can remember their password after one or two months" [15]. Table 3 shows some of the algorithms which were created based on this technique.

Table 3. Recognition Based Techniques Ordered by Date

Algorithm	Proposed Date	Created By
Passface	2000	Sacha Brostoff , M. Angela Sasse
Déjà vu	2000	Rachna Dhamija, drian Perrig
Triangle	2002	Leonardo Sobrado , J-Canille Birget
Movable Frame	2002	Leonardo Sobrado , J-Canille Birget
Picture Password	2003	Wayne Jansen, et al.
WIW	2003	Shushuang Man, et al.
Story	2004	Darren Davies, et al.

In the following section the GUA's algorithms will review and study.

3 Pure Recall Based Techniques

Passdoodle

Passdoodle is a graphical user authentication (GUA) algorithm made up of handwritten designs or text, drawn with a stylus onto a touch sensitive screen. It has been confirmed that doodles are more difficult to crack as there is a theoretically larger number of possible doodle passwords than text passwords [3]. Fig. 1 shows a sample of the Passdoodle algorithm.

Draw a Secret (DAS)

This method consisted of an interface that had a rectangular grid of size G * G, which allowed the user to draw a simple picture on a 2D grid as in Fig. 2. Each cell in this grid is earmarked by discrete rectangular coordinates (x,y). As clearly evidenced in the Fig. 2, the coordinate sequence made by the drawing is:

(2,2), (3,2), (3,3), (2,3), (2,2), (2,1)

The stroke should be a sequence of cells which does not contain a pen up event. Hence the password is defined as some strokes, separated by the pen up event. At the time of authentication, the user needs to re-draw the picture by creating the stroke in exactly the same order as in the registration phase. If the drawing hits the exact grids and in the same order, the user is authenticated [7].

Grid Selection

In 2004, a research was conducted on the complexity of the DAS technique based on password length and stroke count by Thorpe and Orschot. Their study showed that the item which has the greatest effect on the DAS password space is the number of strokes. This means that for a fixed password length, if a few strokes are selected then the password space will significantly decrease. To enhance security, Thorpe and Orschot created a "Grid Selection" technique. As shown in Fig. 3, the selection grid has a large rectangular region to zoom in on, from the grid which the user selects their key for their password. This definitely increases the DAS password space [10].

Qualitative DAS (QDAS)

The QDAS method was created in 2007 as a boost to the DAS method, by encoding each stroke. The raw encoding consists of its starting cell and the order of qualitative direction change in the stroke vis-a-vie the grid. A directional change is when the pen passes over a cell boundary in a direction in variance to the direction of the pass in the previous cell boundary. Research has shown that the image which has a hot spot is pivotal as a background image [5]. Fig. 4 shows a sample of QDAS password.

Syukri

In 2005 Syukri et al. proposed a system where authentication is kicked in when the users draw their signatures utilising the mouse. The sample of Syukri can be seen in Fig. 5 [1]. This technique has a two step process, registration and verification. During the registration stage, the user will be required to draw his signature with the mouse, whereupon the system will extract the signature area and either enlarge or scale-down the signatures, rotating the same if necessary (Alternatively known as normalising). The information will later be stored in the database. The verification stage initially receives the user input, where upon the normalisation takes place, and then extracts the parameters of the signature. By using a dynamic updateable database and the geometric average means, verification will be performed [1].

Fig. 1. An Example of a Passdoodle

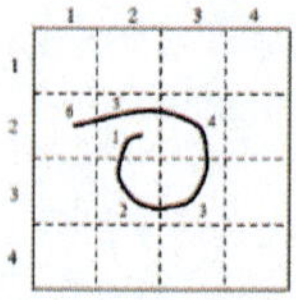

Fig. 2. Draw a Secret (DAS)

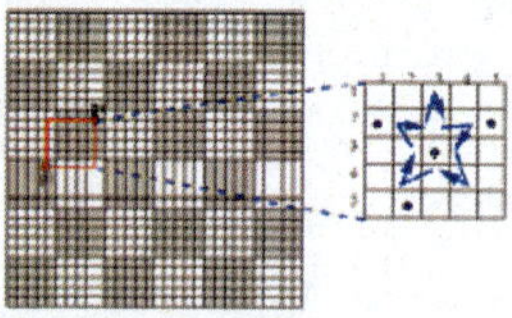

Fig. 3. A Sample of Grid Selection

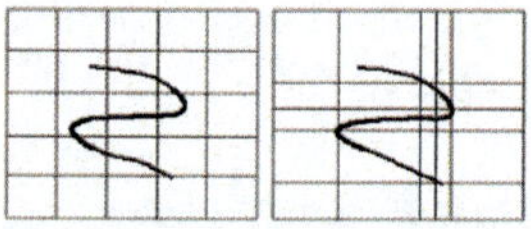

Fig. 4. A Sample of Qualitative DAS

4 Cued Recall-Based Techniques

Blonder

Greg E. Blonder, in 1966 created a method wherein a pre-determined image is presented to the user on a visual display so that the user should be able point to one or more predetermined positions on the image (tap regions) in a predetermined order as a way of pointing out his or her authorisation to access the resource. Blonder maintained that the method was secure according to the millions of different regions [18]. Fig. 6 shows a sample of the Blonder password.

Fig. 5. A Sample of Syukri

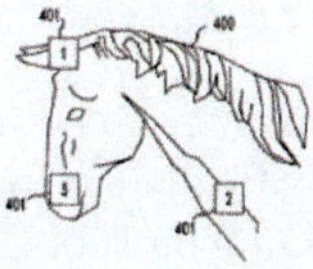

Fig. 6. A Sample of Blonder

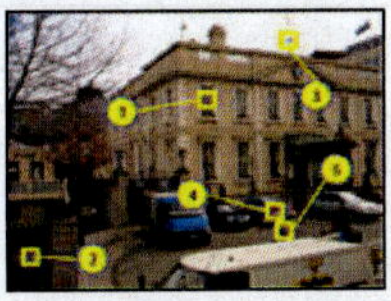

Fig. 7. A Sample of Passpoint

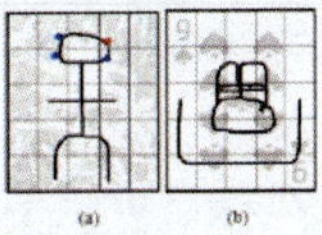

Fig. 8. A Sample of BDAS

PassPoint

In 2005, the PassPoint was created in order to cover the image limitations of the Blonder Algorithm. The picture could be any natural picture or painting but at the same time had to be rich enough in order for it to have many possible click points. On the other hand the existence of the image has no role other than helping the user to remember the click point. This algorithm has another flexibility which makes it possible for there to be no need for artificial pictures which have pre selected regions to be clicked like the Blonder algorithm. During the registration phase the user chooses several points on the picture in a certain sequence. To log in, the user only needs to click close to the chosen click points, and inside some adjustable tolerable distance, say within 0.25 cm from the actual click point [17]. Fig. 7 shows a sample of the PassPoint password.

Background DAS (BDAS)

Created in 2007, this method added a background image to the original DAS, such that both the background image and the drawing grid is the key to cued recall. The user begins by trying to have a secret in mind which is made up of three points from different categories. Firstly the user starts to draw using the point from a background image. Then the next point of user is that the user's choice of the secret is affected by various characteristics of the image. The last alternative for the user is a mix of the two previous methods [11]. Fig. 8 shows a sample of BDAS algorithm.

PASSMAP

Analysis on passwords has shown that a good password is hard to commit to memory besides this a password which is easy to remember is too short and simple to be secured. A survey in human memory has confirmed that a landmark on a well-known journey is fairly easy. For example, Fig. 9 shows a sample of a PassMap password for a passenger who wants to take a trip to Europe. Referring to the Figure below, it will be easy to memorise the trip in a map [14].

Passlogix v-Go

Passlogix Inc. is a commercial security company located in New York City USA. Their scheme, Passlogix v-Go, utilises a technique known as "Repeating a sequence of actions" meaning creating a password in a chronological sequence. Users select their background images based on the environment, for example in the kitchen, bathroom, bedroom or others (See Fig. 10). User can click on a series of items in the image as password. For example in the kitchen environment a user can: prepare a meal by selecting a fast food from the refrigerator and put on the hot plate, select some vegetables and wash them, then put them on the launch desk [10].

VisKey SFR

VisKey is a one of the recall based authentication schemes commercialised by SFR Company in Germany which was created specifically for mobile devices such as PDAs. To form a password, all users need to do is to tap their spots in sequence (Fig. 11) [10].

Pass-Go

In 2006, this scheme being created as an improvement of the DAS algorithm, keeping the advantages of the DAS whilst adding some extra security features. Pass-Go is a grid-based scheme which requires a user to select intersections, instead of cells, thus the new system refers to a matrix of intersections, rather than cells as in DAS (Fig. 12) [8].

Fig. 9. A Sample of PASSMAP

Fig. 10. A Sample of Passlogix v.Go

Fig. 11. A Sample of VisKey SFR

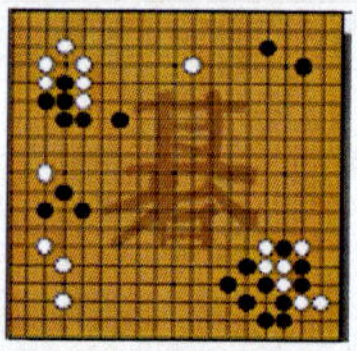

Fig. 12. A Sample of Pass-Go

5 Recognition-Based Techniques

Passface

In 2000, this method was developed by the idea to choose a face of humans as a password. Firstly, a trial session starts with the user in order to have an adventure for the real login process. During the registration phase the user chooses whether their image password should be a male or female picture, then chooses four faces from decoy images as the future password (Fig. 13). According to research [2], this is one of the algorithms which cover most of the usability features like ease of use, and straightforward creation and recognition.

Déjà vu

This algorithm created in 2000, starts by allowing users to select a specific number of pictures from a large image portfolio. The pictures are created by random art which is one of hash visualisation algorithms. One initial seed is given for starters and then one random mathematical formula is generated defining the color value for each pixel in the image. The output will be one random abstract image. The benefit of this method is that as the image depends completely on its initial seed, so there is no need for saving the picture pixel by pixel and only the seeds need to be stored in the trust server. During authentication phase, the user should pass through a challenging set where his portfolio mixes with some decoy images; the user will be authenticated if he is able to identify his password among the entire portfolio as illustrated in Fig. 14 [12].

Fig. 13. A Sample of Passface

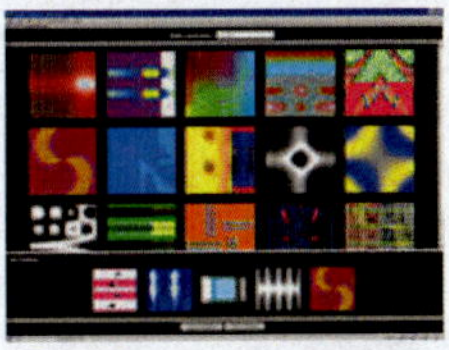

Fig. 14. A Sample of Déjà vu

Fig. 15. A Sample of Triangle

Fig. 16. A Sample of Moveable Frame

Triangle

A group in 2002 proposed the triangle algorithm based on several schemes to resist the Shoulder surfing attack. The first scheme named, triangle as shown in Fig. 15, randomly places a set of N objects (a few hundred or a few thousand) on the screen. Additionally, there is a subset of K pass objects previously chosen and memorised by the user. The system will select the placement of N objects randomly in the log-in phase [9].

Movable Frame

The moveable frame algorithm proposed in 2002 had a similar idea to that of triangle method. However in its case the user had to select three objects from K objects in the login phase. As it is shown in Fig. 16, only 3 pass objects are displayed at any given time and only one of them is placed in a movable frame. The user must move the frame until the three objects line up one after the other. These operations minimise the random movements involved in finding the password [9].

Picture Password

This algorithm was designed especially for handheld devices like Personal Digital Assistant (PDA) in 2003. According to Fig. 17, during enrollment, the user selecting a theme identifying the thumbnail photos to be applied and then registers a sequence of thumbnail images that are used as a future password. If the device is powered on, then the user must input the true sequence of images but after successful log-in the user can change the password [4].

Story

The Story Algorithm that was proposed in 2004, categorised the available pictures into nine categories namely animals, cars, women, foods, children, men, objects, natures and sports (Fig. 18). This algorithm was proposed by Carnegie Mellon University to be used for different purposes. In this method the user selects the password from the mixed pictures in the nine categories in order to make a story [8].

Where Is Waldo (WIW)

In order to offer resistance against shoulder surfing, in 2003 another algorithm that uses a unique code for each picture was proposed. The user selects some picture as a password. This picture must be found in the log-in phase before the user can type the related unique code in a text box. The argument is that it is very hard to dismantle this kind of password even if the whole authentication process is recorded on video as there is no mouse click to give away the pass-object information. The log-in screen of this graphical password algorithm is shown in Fig. 19 [16].

Fig. 17. A Sample of Picture Password

Fig. 18. A Sample of Story Algorithm

Fig. 19. A Sample of WIW Algorithm

6 Evaluations

Regarding to our survey on most of the researches from 1996 till 2010, there are many reports on security evaluation of GUA algorithm in different aspects. Some of the researchers focus on attacks and evaluate finding the related attacks to GUA algorithm. Some other researchers focus on password spaces and try to define some formula for calculating the number of possible passwords in each algorithm. But regarding to these researches till now, there isn't a complete evaluation framework or criteria that cover all aspects of security for GUA algorithm [8]. In this section we will define the evaluation framework and try to evaluate all algorithms based on this evaluation. Fig. 20 shows the 3 attributes of security in GUA algorithm that we named Magic Triangle.

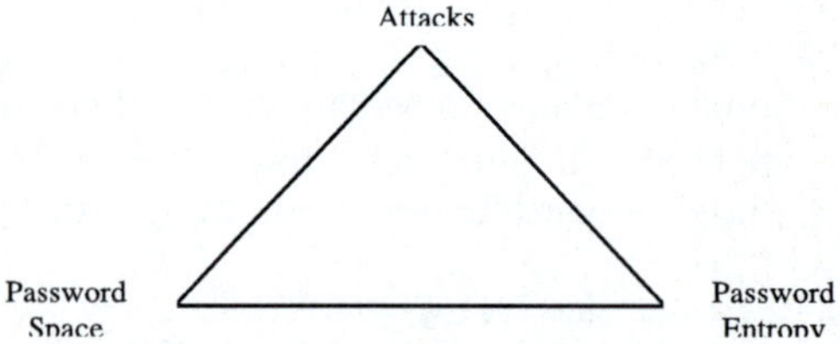

Fig. 20. Magic triangle for GUA security evaluation

6.1 Attacks

Very little research has been done to study the difficulty of attacking graphical passwords. Because graphical passwords are not widely used in practice, there is no report on real cases of attacking graphical passwords [19]. Here we define the GUA possible attacks based on International Attacks Patterns standard (CAPEC 2010) and briefly exam these attacks for breaking graphical passwords. Then make a comparison among section five perused algorithms based on GUA attacks.

Brute Force Attack

This is an attack which tries every possible combination of password status in order to break the password. It is more difficult for this attack to be successful in graphical passwords than textual passwords because the attack programs must create all mouse motions to imitate the user password, especially for recall based graphical passwords. The main item which helps in the resistance to brute force attacks is having a large password space. Some graphical password techniques have proved to have a larger password space in comparison with textual passwords [8].

Dictionary Attack

This is an attack in which the attacker starts by using the words in the dictionary to test whether the user choose them as a password or not. The brute force technique is used to implement the attack. This sort of attack is more successful in the textual password. Although the dictionary attack is proved to be in some of the recall base graphical algorithm [12] [17], an automated dictionary attack will be much more complex than a text based dictionary attack [8].

Spyware Attack

This is a special kind of attack where tools are initially installed on a user's computer and then start to record any sensitive data. The movement of the mouse or any key being pressed will be recorded by this sort of malware. All the data that has been recorded without notifying the user is then reported back out of the computer. Except for a few instances, using only key logging or key listening spyware cannot be used to break graphical passwords as it is not proved whether the movement of the mouse spyware can be an effective tool for breaking graphical passwords. Even if the mouse tracking is saved, it is not sufficient for breaking and finding the graphical password. Some other information such as window position and size, as well as timing information are needed to complete this kind of attack [8].

Shoulder Surfing Attack

It is obvious from the name of this attack, that sometimes it is possible for an attacker to find out a person's password by looking over the person's shoulder. Usually this kind of attack can be seen in a crowded place where most people are not concerned about someone standing behind them when they are entering a pin code. The more modern method of this attack can be seen when there is a camera in the ceiling or wall near the ATM machine, which records the pin numbers of users. So it is really recommend that users try to shield keypad to protect their pin number from attackers [8].

Social Engineering Attack (Description Attack)

This is an attack in which an attacker, through interaction with one of the employees about the organization, manages to impersonate an authorised employee. This may lead the 'impersonator' to gain an identity which is the first step of his hacking process. Sometimes the attacker cannot gather enough information about the organisation or a valid user. In such a situation the attacker will most likely try to contact another employee. The cycle is repeated until the attacker manages to get an authorized identity of one of the personnel.

Guessing Attack

Through Guessing Attack a lot of users try to choose their password based on their personal information like the name of their pets, passport number, family name and so forth, the attacker attempts to guess the password by trying these possible passwords [14].

In the following section we put together the comparison table for these attacks based on the surveys. Some parts of the table are filled in based on the previous survey and papers [6] [11], even as much as we try to complete them, the parts that are still not filled will be considered as future work [8].

Compare GUA Algorithms Based on Attacks

Table 4, 5 and 6 shows a comparative on three categories of GUA algorithms based on common attacks which gathered with previous survey that in these tables "Y" means resistance to attack, "N" means non-resistance to attack, and "-" means there isn't research focus on this part till now [18] [19] [14].

Table 4. The Attack Resistance in Pure Recall-Based Techniques

Algorithms	Attacks					
	Brute Force	Dictionary	Spyware	Shoulder Surfing	Social Engineering	Guessing
DAS	N	Y	N	Y	N	Y
Passdoodle	-	-	-	Y	-	-
Grid Selection	-	-	-	Y	-	-
Syukri	N	Y	N	Y	N	Y
QDAS	-	-	-	Y	-	-

Table 5. The Attack Resistance in Cued Recall-Based Techniques

Algorithms	Attacks					
	Brute Force	Dictionary	Spyware	Shoulder Surfing	Social Engineering	Guessing
Blonder	Y	N	N	Y	N	Y
Passlogix	Y	-	-	Y	-	Y
PassPoint	Y	N	N	Y	N	Y
BDAS	-	-	-	Y	-	-
PASSMAP	N	-	-	Y	-	Y
VisKey SFR	Y	N	N	Y	N	-
Pass-Go	Y	-	-	-	N	Y

Table 6. The Attacks Resistance in Recognition-Based Techniques

Algorithms	Attacks					
	Brute Force	Dictionary	Spyware	Shoulder Surfing	Social Engineering	Guessing
PassFace	N	N	Y	N	N	N
Déjà vu	N	Y	Y	N	Y	N
Triangle	N	Y	-	Y	Y	N
Movable Frame	N	N	Y	Y	-	-
Picture Password	N	-	N	N	-	-
Story	N	-	-	N	-	N
WIW	-	-	-	N	-	-
GUABRR	-	-	Y	Y	Y	Y

The Table 4 and 5 shows that, quit a vast survey needs to find out the vulnerabilities of each graphical password algorithm to five common attacks, which recommends to be done in future. All cued based algorithms are vulnerable to brute force attack, but at the same time pure based algorithm are resistant to this attack. Most pure recall based algorithms are vulnerable to dictionary and spyware attack. Most of algorithms in both categories are resistant to shoulder surfing attack.

According to table 6, in Triangle, Movable frame and GUABRR omitting mouse clicks make the algorithm resistance on shoulder surfing attack but unfortunately there is not much research on Spyware and Guessing attacks.

6.2 Password Space

Users can pick any element for their password in GUA; the raw size of password space is an upper bound on the information content of the distribution that users choose in practice. It is not possible to define a formula for password space but for all algorithms it is possible to calculate the password space or the number of passwords that can be generated by the algorithm [8] [19]. Now, this section will define and calculate the password space for previous algorithms then make a comparative analysis.

In the text-based passwords a password space is:

Space= M^N

Where N is the length of the password, and M is the number of characters excluding "space" [19]. For example, in textual passwords with length of 6 characters that can select the capital and small characters, the password space will be:

Space = 52^6

In the GUA, for the Passface algorithm with N rounds and M pictures in each round, the password space will be [8] [19]:

Space = M^N

In the Blonder algorithm and Passlogix with N number of pixels on the image and M number of locations to be clicked, the password space will be [19]:

Space = N^M

Table 7 shows the comparison between previous algorithms and the newly proposed algorithm based on password space [8] [19].

Table 7. Comparative Table Based on "Graphical Space"

Algorithm	Formula
Textual (with 6 characters length include capital and small alphabets)	52 ^ 6
Textual (6 characters: capital and small alphabets and numbers)	62 ^ 6
Image selection similar to Passface (4 runs, 9 pictures)	9 ^ 4
Click based algorithm similar to Passpoint (4 loci and assuming 30 salient points)	30 ^ 4

6.3 Password Entropy

Password entropy is usually used to measure the security of a generated password, which conceptually means how hard to blindly guess out the password. For simplicity, assume all passwords are evenly distributed, the password entropy of a graphic password can then be calculated as follows [20] [21].

$$\text{Entropy} = N \log_2 (|L||O||C|)$$

In other words, Graphical password entropy tries to measure the probability that the attacker obtains the correct password based on random guessing [20].

In the above formula, N is the length or number of runs, L is locus alphabet as the set of all loci, O is an object alphabet and C is color of the alphabet [8]. For example in a point click GUA algorithm that runs for four rounds and has 30 salient points with 4 objects and 4 colors then:

$$\text{Entropy} = 4 * \text{Log2}\ (30*4*4) = 35.6$$

In an image selection algorithm with 5 runs and in each run selects 1 from 9 images then:

$$\text{Entropy} = 5 * \text{Log2}\ (9) = 15.8$$

Now, table 8 shows the comparison between previous algorithms and the new proposed algorithm [20] [21].

Table 8. Comparative Table Based on "Password Entropy"

Algorithm	Formula	Entropy (bits)
Textual (with 6 characters length include capital and small alphabets)	$6 * \text{Log}_2 (52)$	34.32
Textual (with 6 characters length include capital and small alphabets and numbers)	6 * Log2 (62)	35.70
Image selection similar to Passface (4 runs, 9 pictures)	4 * Log2 (9)	12.74
Click based algorithm similar to Passpoint (4 loci and assuming 30 salient points)	4 * Log2 (30)	19.69

7 Conclusion

User authentication is the most critical element in the field of Information Security. Most of the research results from 1996 to 2010 show that people are able to recognize and remember combinations of geometrical shapes, patterns, textures and colors better than meaningless alphanumeric characters, making the graphical user authentication to be greatly desired as a possible alternative to textual passwords. At first, this paper study on three categories of GUA algorithms namely Pure-Recall, Cued-Recall and Recognition based. As there isn't a complete security evaluation framework for GUA algorithms, in the next step, this paper has proposed a new GUA security evaluation framework namely magic triangle evaluation. In the last part, the paper tries to define the proposed evaluation attributes and evaluate the GUA algorithms based on evaluation for making the comparison table. Finally, regarding to the comparison table and result of evaluation, paper tries to discuss about analysis and evaluation.

References

[1] Eljetlawi, A.M.: Study And Develop A New Graphical Password System, University Technology Malaysia, Master Dissertation (2008)

[2] Eljetlawi, A.M., Ithnin, N.: Graphical Password: Comprehensive Study Of The Usability Features of The Recognition Base Graphical Password Methods. In: Third International Conference on Convergence and Hybrid Information Technology. IEEE, Los Alamitos (2008)

[3] Varenhorst, C.: Passdoodles: A Lightweight Authentication Method.Massachusetts Institute of Technology, Research Science Institute (2004)
[4] Darren, D., Fabian, M., Michael, K.: On User Choice In Graphical Password Schemes. In: Proceedings of the 20th Annual Computer Security Applications Conference. IEEE, Canada (2004)
[5] Lin, D., Dunphy, P., Olivier, P., Yan, J.: Graphical Passwords And Qualitative Spatial Relations. In: Proceedings of the 3rd Symposium on Usable Privacy and Security. ACM, Pennsylvania (2007)
[6] Blonder, G.E.: Graphical Password, U.S. Patent No. 5559961 (1996)
[7] Ian, J., Mayer, A., Monrose, F., Reiter, M.K., Rubin, A.D.: The Design and Analysis of Graphical Passwords. In: Proceedings of The Eighth USENIX Security Symposium, pp. 1–14. USENIX Association (1999)
[8] Lashkari, A.H., Towhidi, F.: Graphical User Authentication (GUA). Lambert Academic Publishing, Germany (2010) ISBN: 978-3-8433-8072-0
[9] Sobrado, L., Birget, J.-C.: Graphical Passwords. The Rutgers Scholar, an Electronic Bulletin for Undergraduate Research 4 (2002)
[10] Hafiz, M.D., Abdullah, A.H., Ithnin, N., Mammi, H.K.: Towards Identifying Usability And Security Features of Graphical Password in Knowledge Based Authentication Technique. IEEE, Los Alamitos (2008)
[11] Dunphy, P., Yan, J.: Do Background Images Improve "Draw A Secret" Graphical Passwords? In: Proceedings of the 14th ACM Conference On Computer And Communications Security, Alexandria, Virginia, USA (2007)
[12] Dhamija, R., Perrig, A.: 'Déja vu: A User Study. Using Images For Authentication. In: The Proceeding of the 9th USENIX Security Symposium (2000)
[13] Dhamija, R.: Hash Visualisation In User Authentication. In: Proceedings of CHI 2000. ACM The Hague (2000)
[14] Yampolskiy, R.V.: User Authentication Via Behavior Based Passwords. IEEE Explore (2007)
[15] Komanduri, S., Hutchings, D.R.: Order and Entropy in Picture Passwords. In: Proceedings of Graphics Interface, Canadian Information Processing Society, Ontario, Canada (2008)
[16] Man, S., Hong, D., Matthews, M.: A Shoulder-Surfing Resistant Graphical Password Scheme – Wiw. In: Proceedings of International Conference On Security And Management, Las Vegas, NV (2003)
[17] Wiedenbeck, S., Watersa, J., Birgetb, J.-C., Brodskiyc, A., Memon, N.: Design And Longitudinal Evaluation of A Graphical Password System, pp. 102–127. Academic Press, Inc., London (2005a)
[18] Wiedenbeck, S., Birget, J.-C., Brodskiy, A.: Authentication Using Graphical Passwords: Effects of Tolerance And Image Choice. In: Symposium On Usable Privacy and Security (SOUPS), Pittsburgh, PA, USA (2005b)
[19] Suo, X., Zhu, Y., Scott, G., Owen: Graphical Passwords: A Survey. In: Proceedings of the 21st Annual Computer Security Applications. IEEE, Los Alamitos (2005)
[20] Li, Z., Sun, Q., Lian, Y., Giust, D.D.: An Association-Based Graphical Password Design Resistant To Shoulder-Surfing Attack, University of Cagliari, Italy. IEEE, Los Alamitos (2005)
[21] Qibin Sun, Z.L., Jiang, X., Kot, A.: An Interactive and Secure User Authentication Scheme For Mobile Devices. In: Supported By The A-Star Serc Mobile Media TSRP Grant No 062 130 0056. IEEE, Los Alamitos (2008)

A Wide Survey on Botnet

Arash Habibi Lashkari[1], Seyedeh Ghazal Ghalebandi[2], and Mohammad Reza Moradhaseli[3]

[1] Advanced Informatics School, Universiti Technologi Malaysia (UTM), Kuala Lumpur, Malaysia
a_habibi_l@hotmail.com
[2] Computer Science and Information Technology Department, University of Malaya (UM), Kuala Lumpur, Malaysia
gazelle.ghalebandi.it@gmail.com
[3] Center of technology and innovation (R&D), UCTI, Kuala Lumpur, Malaysia
m.moradhaseli@gmail.com

Abstract. Botnets are security threat now days, since they tend to perform serious internet attacks in vast area through the compromised group of infected machines. The presence of command and control mechanism in botnet structure makes them stronger than traditional attacks. Over course of the time botnet developer have switched to more advanced mechanism to evade each of which new detection methods and countermeasures. As our knowledge , existing survey on botnets area have just focused on determining different attributes of botnet behavior, hence this paper attempts to introduce botnet with a famous bot sample for defined behavior that provides obvious view on botnets and its feature. This paper is based on our two previous accepted papers of botnets on IEEE conferences namely ICCSIT 2011 and ICNCS 2010.

Keywords: Botnet, p2p Botnet, IRC botnet, HTTP botnet, Command and Control Models (C&C).

1 Introduction

Highest rising usage of the Internet-based communication which is contains thousands of connected networks have shifted security practitioner ' focus on to protect whatever are passed through these connections to evade malicious behavior of cyber criminal. But over the time the developers improve their protection or detection methods, attackers create new way of evasion.

Botnets are emerging threat with thousand of infected computers. According to recent report [25], the extents of the botnets' damage are becoming more critical day by day. Botnets has made an effort to control zombies remotely and instruct them by commands from Botmaster. The way Botmaster conduct bots relay on architecture of botnet command and control mechanism such as IRC, HTTP, DNS, or P2P-based [24]. At this point, we turn our attention to presenting our study to grasp botnets. According the recent papers, in [5] intuition behind this paper is to propose key metrics on botnet structure but while the sample of bots are not covered there. Also in

H. Cherifi, J.M. Zain, and E. El-Qawasmeh (Eds.): DICTAP 2011, Part I, CCIS 166, pp. 445–454, 2011.

[24] it has been focusing on characteristics of botnet without pointing at performance of key metrics on botnet structure. Thereby this complementary paper makes effort to cover the gaps in which it could somehow manifest their underlying techniques of botnets structure. By doing so, the researchers can improve their detection or prevention methods to deal with growing number of botnets.

For the sake of discussion, but without loss of generality, we define botnet as follow:

Botnet is a group of compromised computers. Botmasters are responsible to send and receive command and control to bot clients. Bots are not more than a software program which can create botnets by downloading that software or by clicking on infected email [1]. A vulnerable computer can be a member of centralized control model which is able to communicate with others infected computer. A Botmaster devotes a server to work as a command center (figure 1) [2].

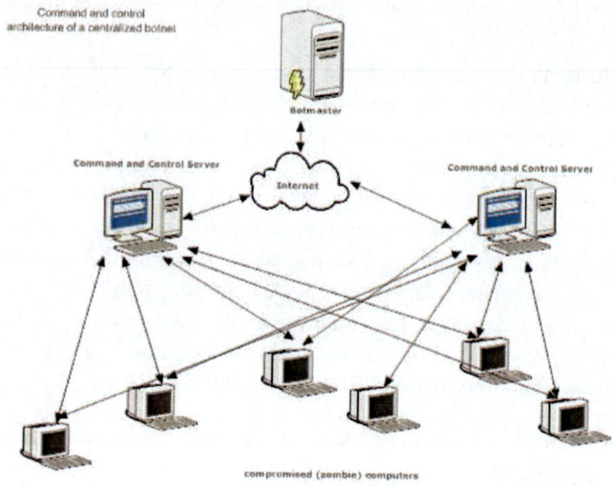

Fig. 1. Communication of botnet components

2 Botnet Protocols

There are different classification to address properties of botnets such as command and control mechanism, protocol, infection method, type of attack and etc. first of all this paper attempts to map which protocol are used and reveal the existing bots based on each protocol.

2.1 IRC

Internet Relay Chat (IRC) was just a channel which capable users to talk together real-time. After a while malicious behaviors exploits vulnerabilities of these channels and applied it for nefarious purpose [17]. Agobot is one of the earlier kind of

IRC-based botnets which is found end of 2002, this bot include major component such as command and control mechanism, capable of launching DoS attacks, defense mechanism like patching vulnerability and traffic sniffing and gather sensitive information [8]. They exploit Local Authority Subsystem Service vulnerability of windows operating system. In contrast with worms, bots like Agobots will continue victimize others so that PC's owner unaware about what is going on in their PC [26].

2.2 P2P

P2P botnet's concept represents a distributed malicious software networks. This new botnet technology which making them more resilient to previous protocols such as IRC or HTTP due to increase survivability as well as to covert identities of operators. In contrast of IRC, estimating P2P botnet's size is difficult [27].

2.2.1 Parasite

Parasite is one type of P2P botnets. Its structure exploits P2P network and its members are limited to vulnerable hosts exist inside P2P network. Hence all bots exits in the network can find the other bots due to P2P protocol. It is convenient and simple to create P2P botnets through this way because all bots are chosen from existing network. In this type of P2P botnet, bot peers and normal peers are mixed together therefore in order to collect more information in such network, legitimate nodes can be chosen as sensor to help in monitoring issue [4]. In 2008, Srizbi bot become well-known as a world's worst spamming botnet. Srizbi can run inside the kernel on infected host quite stealthy within a network driver which uses TCP/IP parameter. It is used rootkit techniques to hide its file so that can bypass firewalls. It can be identified through TCP fingerprinting of operating system on infected host [31].

2.2.2 Leeching

Leeching is the other class of p2p botnet upon a p2p network and it exploits protocols of that network within C&C structure which vulnerable hosts are chosen through the internet so that they will participate in and become the member of existing network. Leeching type is looks like parasite but differs in bootstrap point, it means parasite does not have a bootstrap steps but leeching has. After a peer is compromised it has some files, so this file is used to make sure commands from Botmaster is forwarded in proper peer.[5]. According to [4] the earlier version of storm bot belongs to leeching class of P2P botnets. Strom bot propagates by using email which includes text so that attempts to trick victim into opening the attachments or clicking the link inside the body of email content. The attachments could be a copy of storm binary. The goal is to copy storm binary to victim's machine. To evade detection, exploit code would be changed periodically. After the victim installed the code that machine is being infected [33].

2.2.3 Bot-Only

Other type of p2p botnet is called bot-only which totally differs from 2 others because it has own network. Also it uses bootstrap mechanism, and Botmasters in this type of botnet are flexible even to construct new C&C protocol [5]. Nugache can be put to this class of P2P botnet, after the peer list is created, since the encryption P2P channel must be set up between client and servant, Nugache peers will join to network through exchanging the RSA key. After these steps an internal protocol is used to determine listening port number and peer's list IP address, as well as to identify peer as a client or servant. Moreover it will check binaries may need to update. Bootstrap controls peer list [34].

2.3 HTTP

Bobax is known as HTTP-based bot so that it tends to create spam. A template and a list of email addresses are required to send its email. It uses Dynamic DNS provider, and also plaintext HTTP which is used to communicate with HTTP-based C&C server [10].

3 Command and Control Models (C&C)

The command and control mechanism used to instruct botnets. They direct botnets to operate some tasks such as deny service, spamming, try to find new system to order more bots and etc [8].

3.1 Centralized C&C Model

There are two types of botnet centralized C&C server. they are called pull style and push style where commands are download (pull) by bots or sent to bots (push). Each centralized C&C is set up by Botmaster. Typically it depends on the way a Botmaster instructs bots; in push style the Botmaster has direct control on botnet, so that any infected host is connected to the C&C server , then they should be wait the command. In pull style the Botmaster does not have direct control on botnet, hence in order to receive commands, the bots interact the C&C server periodically [9]. Over the years empirical research indicates centralized C&C servers can be easily detect. As such Interruption of command and control is led to a useless botnet. Figure 2 shows centralized command and communication mechanism.

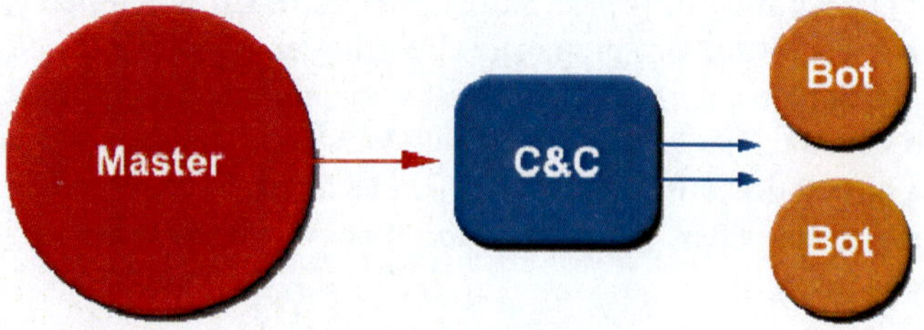

Fig. 2. Centralized C&C mechanism

SDBot is an IRC-based botnet which uses centralized command and control mechanism. First it starts by establishing a connection to server through command like NICK and USER, PING and PONG, JOIN and so on. Next step is to expect other commands such as PRIVMSG, NOTICE, and TOPIC IRC message [8].

3.2 P2P-Based C&C Model

In P2P botnets C&C server is concealed, then detection is become harder. After a peer enters to the network and contract to the other peers, finally it can become a member of that network. Hence frequently updates its database through interacting with others peers. By now this peer can play role as command and controller. Therefore commands are being sent via this peer to the remaining peers [7].

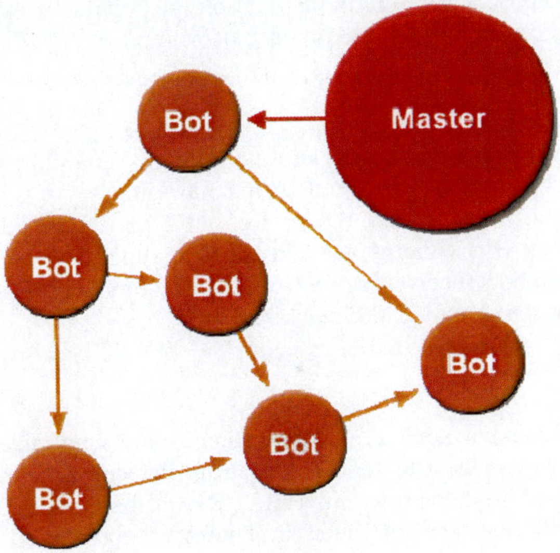

Fig. 3. P2P-based C&C mechanism

Storm botnet employ P2P network structure as his C&C infrastructure to disseminate commands to the peers. They tend to participate in illicit behavior such as email spam, phishing attacks, instant messaging o attacks, etc. Botmaster partitions botnet and assigns a unique encryption keys to each partition so that employ each partition individually in order to illicit activity. Since a storm binary is installed on a victim's machine, a 128-bit ID is generated so that a peer-list file is created which includes ID where is the 128-bit node ID, IP address, UDP PORT in hexadecimal format. New infected node joins botnet and the peer-list file is used to join and finding available updates of nodes [22].

3.3 Unstructured C&C Model

Unstructured C&C model is known as a random. In this model there is no active connection between victim and bot. likewise, bot does not have any information about any more than one other bot. command sender or Botmaster encrypts command messages and randomly scans the internet and deliver it to another bot when it is being detected. Finding single bot, it would not be lead to detection full botnet. Advantages include difficult to being detected or taken down. And disadvantages include latency and scalability [29].

4 Botnet Behaviors

We make effort to grasp botnet behavior by review several related paper. Through accomplishing our survey, it makes us clear that botnets tend to perform common serious attacks such as distributed denial service attack, spamming, sniffing, etc, in large scales based on their nature which recruit vulnerable systems to accomplish their nefarious purpose. Therefore in this section the behaviors and characteristics are mentioned including one bot sample for each of which.

4.1 DDOS Attack

BlackEnergy is a HTTP-based botnet and the primarily goal directs to DDoS attacks. Messages interact with these bots and their controlling servers include information about bot's ID and unique build ID for the bot binary. Build ID is used to keep tracking of updates. BlackEnergy uses base64 encoding of commands to covert the attacker [13]. Once bots receive from a Botmaster a command which indicated DDoS attack, all of them start to attack defined target [14].

4.2 Spam

Mybot is one of the bots that uses IRC protocol and centralized structure for its connection. This bot is used to send spam. From detection prospective, researchers have found bots will send spam within same URLs if they belong to the same botnet. This result supports that fact bot clients in a same group (botnet) involve with same instruction from bot master [3].

4.3 Phishing

Since botnets enable attackers to control a large number of compromised computers, they are being considered as a threat to internet systems. Hence they tend to use bots to attack against other systems such as identity theft [16]. Phishing is known for its online financial fraud through stealing personal identity. Coreflood is a bot which is responsible for phishing. This bot takes order from command and control remotely so that it makes it capable to keep track of HTTP traffics [15].

4.4 Steal Sensitive Data

Attackers conduct bots in compromised machines to retrieve sensitive data from infected host. There are several bots which evolve with steal information such as Agobot and SDBot. Besides the spying, these bots send out ideal commands to run different program and function in order to achieve their goals. Spybot is a popular bot which uses different functions to gain information from infected hosts such as listing RSA password and so on [17].

5 Infection Mechanisms

Infected mechanism refers the way bots use to find new host. Earlier infection mechanisms include horizontal scans and vertical scans, where horizontal is applied on single port within a defined address range, and vertical is applied on single IP address within a defined range of port number [8]. The recently methods are appeared to improve traditional techniques such as socially engineered malware links attached or embedded in email or remotely exploiting vulnerabilities on a host machine. Bots participate in malicious behavior automatically over internet. In contrast with earlier variations, presence of Botmaster makes them more sophisticated thereby bots can be controlled [30].

5.1 Web Download

Web download command has 2 parameters; URL and file path so that first one is used for download data and the other one is used for store those data. Through these commands, IP addresses of target are obtained [18]. Commands and updates are frequently accessed within query web servers via infected hosts [20].

5.2 Mail Attachments

Mail-attachment is a file sent along with an e-mail message. Unexpected e-mail with the fake attachment can be considered suspicious, if the sender is not known. Clickbot is a HTTP-based bot spreads through email message. They direct attacker by open or download those attachments which may contain advertisements. Clickbots are instructed from Botmaster. They tend to achieve IP and they have ability to disguise IP address of PC which they attempts to exploit that its vulnerability, hence it is difficult to detect Clickbot to finding them at web server logs [11] [12].

5.3 Automatically Scan, Exploit and Compromise

Recruiting new host is a most important part of botnet creation mission in order to spread widely. It can be ascertained by vulnerability scanning. To accomplish this goal, large number of infected hosts should attempt to identify exploitable vulnerabilities in the other new hosts. For example FTP services suffer a buffer overflow exploit. Hence large range of IP addresses are being searched for this vulnerability. Therefore founded IP addresses are considered in a distinct log file. After all several log files are compiled together in order to exploitation of vulnerabilities [19].

6 Taxonomy

By investigation about botnets and their structure and also their malicious behavior, it is required to classify threats in more aspects which are related to possible defenses.

The goal is to identify most effective approach to treat botnets and classifying key properties of botnets types. In this part we present to review important attributes of botnets [6]. The performance measurements of botnets can be considered by determination of three dimensions as below:

6.1 Efficiency

Communication efficiency of each botnet can be used as a major factor to evaluate a botnet [6]. It means how fast a command is delivered from a Botmaster to a botnet. Since in p2p botnets where there is no plot among command sender and receiver, so efficiency is considered as a measure for determine distance between peers. It determines the reliability of delivered command in such botnet whether or not the command is successfully received [5].

6.2 Effectiveness

Effectiveness is used to determine the extent of damaged which is caused by a particular botnet directly. On the hand the size of botnets represents effectiveness of botnets [5] [6].

6.3 Available Bandwidth

If normal usage of bandwidth is subtracted from maximum network bandwidth, the result will be the available bandwidth [5].

6.4 Robustness

Robustness of network is expressed by the measure such as distributed degree and clustering [5].if there are two pairs of nodes so that they have a shared node in their pairs, local transitivity will measures the chance of that unshared nodes in each pairs will be able to have connection together. Hence robustness of network is applying this fact to measure redundancy [6].

7 Conclusion

Since botnets start to appear as the forthcoming danger to internet, this paper focused on botnet characteristics to grasp more detailed behavior on their mechanism which could be well preparation for future study as well as thwarting botnet communication. It has been summarized most major characteristics of botnet including botnet protocols, and moreover the command and control structures are described, also botnet behavior covered to address serious attacks took our attention to study. The infection mechanism section includes completing point of view through considering architecture of existing botnet attacking method. The last part of this paper, Taxonomy, tends to meet different aspect of botnets characteristics. We provided name of bots which well-known for their related task as a member of botnets on each section to shed light on in the context of botnet structure.

References

1. Brodsky, A., Brodsky, D.: A Distributed Content Independent Method for Spam Detection, University of Winnipeg, Winnipeg, MB, Canada, R3B 2E9, Microsoft Corporation, Redmond, WA, USA (2007)
2. Cole, A., Mellor, M., Noyes, D.: Botnets: The Rise of the Machines (2006)
3. Botnets: The New Threat Landscape, Cisco Systems solutions (2007)
4. Shirley, B., Mano, C.D.: Sub-Botnet Coordination Using Tokens in a Switched Network. Department of Computer Science Utah State University, Logan, Utah (2008)
5. Davis, C.R., Fernandez, J.M., Neville, S., McHugh, J.: Sybil attacks as a mitigation strategy against the Storm botnet, École Polytechnique de Montréal, University of Victoria, Dalhousie University (2008)
6. Li, C., Jiang, W., Zou, X.: Botnet: Survey and Case Study, National Computer network Emergency Response technical, Research Center of Computer Network and Information Security Technology Harbin Institute of Technology, China (2010)
7. Dagon, D., Gu, G., Lee, C.P., Lee, W.: A Taxonomy of Botnet Structures. Georgia Institute of Technology, USA (2008)
8. Dittrich, D., Dietrich, S.: Discovery techniques for P2P botnets, Applied Physics Laboratory University of Washington (2008)
9. Dittrich, D., Dietrich, S.: P2P as botnet command and control: a deeper insight. Applied Physics Laboratory University of Washington, Computer Science Department Stevens Institute of Technology (2008)
10. Stinson, E., Mitchell, J.C.: Characterizing Bots' Remote Control Behavior, Department of Computer Science. Stanford University, Stanford (2008)
11. Cooke, E., Jahanian, F., McPherson, D.: The Zombie Roundup: Understanding, Detecting, and Disrupting Botnets. Electrical Engineering and Computer Science Department University of Michigan (2005)
12. Naseem, F., Shafqat, M., Sabir, U., Shahzad, A.: A Survey of Botnet Technology and Detection, Department of Computer Engineering University of Engineering and Technology, Taxila, Pakistan 47040. International Journal of Video & Image Processing and Network Security IJVIPNS-IJENS 10(01) (2010)
13. Gu, G., Zhang, J., Lee, W.: BotSniffer: Detecting Botnet Command and Control Channels in Network Traffic, School of Computer Science, College of Computing Georgia Institute of Technology Atlanta, GA (2008)
14. Milletary, J.: Technical Trends in Phishing Attacks, US-CERT (2005)
15. Nazario, J.: BlackEnergy DDoS Bot Analysis, Arbor Networks (October 2007)
16. McLaughlin, L.: Bot Software Spreads, Causes New Worries. IEEE Distributed Systems Online 1541-4922 © (2004)
17. Daswani, N., Stoppelman, M.: the Google Click Quality and Security Teams, The Anatomy of Clickbot.A, Google, Inc. (2007)
18. Provos, N., Holz, T.: Virtual honeypot: tracking botnet (2007)
19. Ianelli, N., Hackworth, A.: Botnets as a Vehicle for Online Crime, CERT/Coordination Center (2005)
20. Yegneswaran, P.B.V.: An Inside Look at Botnets, Computer Sciences Department University of Wisconsin, Madison (2007)
21. Royal, P.: On the Kraken and Bobax Botnets, DAMBALLA (April 9, 2008)
22. Wang, P., Aslam, B., Zou, C.C.: Peer-to-Peer Botnets: The Next Generation of Botnet Attacks. School of Electrical Engineering and Computer Science. University of Central Florida, Orlando (2010)

23. Wang, P., Wu, L., Aslam, B., Zou, C.C.: A Systematic Study on Peer-to-Peer Botnets. School of Electrical Engineering & Computer Science University of Central Florida Orlando, Florida 32816, USA (2009)
24. Mitchell, S.P., Linden, J.: Click Fraud: what is it and how do we make it go away, Thinkpartnership (2006)
25. Mori, T., Esquivel, H., Akella, A., Shimoda, A., Goto, S.: Understanding Large-Scale Spamming Botnets From Internet Edge Sites, NTT Laboratories 3-9-11 Midoricho Musashino Tokyo, Japan 180-8585, UW – Madison 1210 W. Dayton St. Madison, WI 53706-1685, Waseda University 3-4-1 Ohkubo, Shinjuku Tokyo, Japan (2010)
26. Holz, T., Steiner, M., Dahl, F., Biersack, E., Freiling, F.: Measurements and Mitigation of Peer-to-Peer-based Botnets: A Case Study on StormWorm, University of Mannheim, Institut Eur´ecom, Sophia Antipolis (2008)
27. Holz, T.: Spying with bots, Laboratory for Dependable Distributed Systems at RWTH Aachen University (2005)
28. Lu, W., Tavallaee, M., Ghorbani, A.A.: Automatic Discovery of Botnet Communities on Large-Scale Communication Networks, University of New Brunswick, Fredericton, NB E3B 5A3, Canada (2009)
29. Zhu, Z., Lu, G., Chen, Y., Fu, Z.J., Roberts, P., Han, K.: Botnet Research Survey, Northwestern Univ., Evanston, IL (2008)
30. Zhu, Z., Lu, G., Fu, Z.J., Roberts, P., Han, K., Chen, Y.: Botnet Research Survey, Northwestern University, Tsinghua University (2008)
31. Li, Z., Hu, J., Hu, Z., Wang, B., Tang, L., Yi, X.: Measuring the botnet using the second character of bots, School of computer science and technology, Huazhong University of Science and Technology, Wuhan, China (2010)

Alternative DNA Security Using BioJava

Mircea-Florin Vaida[1], Radu Terec[1], and Lenuta Alboaie[2]

[1] Technical University of Cluj-Napoca, Faculty of Electronics, Telecommunications and Information Technology, Departament of Communications, 26 – 28 Gh. Baritiu, 400027, Cluj-Napoca, Romania, Phone: (+40) 264 401810
Mircea.Vaida@com.utcluj.ro, RaduTerec@gmail.com
[2] Alexandru Ioan Cuza University of Iasi, Romania, Faculty of Computer Science, Berthelot, 16, Iasi, Romania
adria@infoiasi.ro

Abstract. This paper presents alternative security methods based on DNA. From the alternative security methods available, a DNA algorithm was implemented using symmetric coding in BioJava and MatLab. As results, a comparison has been made between the performances of different standard symmetrical algorithms using dedicated applications. In addition to this, we also present an asymmetric key generation and DNA security algorithm. The asymmetric key generation algorithm starts from a password phrase. The asymmetric DNA algorithm proposes a mechanism which makes use of more encryption technologies. Therefore, it is more reliable and more powerful than the OTP DNA symmetric algorithm.

Keywords: DNA security, BioJava, asymmetric cryptography.

1 Introduction

With the growth of the information technology (IT) power, and with the emergence of new technologies, the number of threats a user is supposed to deal with grew exponentially. For this reason, the security of a system is essential nowadays. It doesn't matter if we talk about bank accounts, social security numbers or a simple telephone call. It is important that the information is known only by the intended persons, usually the sender and the receiver.

In the domain of security, to ensure the confidentiality property two main approaches can be used: that of symmetrical and asymmetrical cryptographic algorithms. Cryptography consists in processing plain information [1], [2], applying a cipher and producing encoded output, meaningless to a third-party who does not know the key. Symmetrical algorithms use the same key to encrypt and decrypt the data, while asymmetric algorithms use a public key to encrypt the data and a private key to decrypt it. By keeping the private key safe, you can assure that the data

H. Cherifi, J.M. Zain, and E. El-Qawasmeh (Eds.): DICTAP 2011, Part I, CCIS 166, pp. 455–469, 2011.

remains safe. The disadvantage of asymmetric algorithms is that they are computationally intensive. Therefore, in security a combination of asymmetric and symmetric algorithms is used.

In the future it is most likely that the computer architecture and power will evolve. Such systems might drastically reduce the time needed to compute a cryptographic key. As a result, security systems need to find new techniques to transmit the data securely without relying on the existing pure mathematical methods.

We therefore use alternative security concepts [9]. The major algorithms which are accepted as alternative security are the elliptic, vocal, quantum and DNA encryption algorithms. Elliptic algorithms are used for portable devices which have a limited processing power, use a simple algebra and relatively small ciphers.

The quantum cryptography is not a quantum encryption algorithm but rather a method of creating and distributing private keys. It is based on the fact that photons send towards a receiver changing irreversibly their state if they are intercepted. Quantum cryptography was developed starting with the 70s in Universities from Geneva, Baltimore and Los Alamos.

In [18] two protocols are described, BB84 and BB92, that, instead of using general encryption and decryption techniques, verify if the key was intercepted. This is possible because once a photon is duplicated, the others are immediately noticed. However, these techniques are still vulnerable to the Man-in-the-Middle and DoS attack.

DNA Cryptography is a new field based on the researches in DNA computation [4] and new technologies like: PCR (Polymerase Chain Reaction), Microarray, etc. DNA computing has a high level computational ability and is capable of storing huge amounts of data. A gram of DNA contains 10^{21} DNA bases, equivalent to 10^8 terabytes of data. In DNA cryptography we use existing biological information from DNA public databases to encode the plaintext [7], [12].

The cryptographic process can make use of different methods. In [9] the *one-time pads* (OTP) algorithms are described, which is one of the most efficient security algorithms, while in [15] a method based on the DNA splicing technique is detailed. In the case of the *one-time pad* algorithms, the plaintext is combined with a secret random key or *pad* which is used only once. The pad is combined with the plaintext using a typical modular addition, or an XOR operation, or another technique. In the case of [15] the start codes and the pattern codes specify the position of the introns, so they are no longer easy to find. However, to transmit the spliced key, they make use of public-key secured channel.

Additionally, we will describe an algorithm which makes use of asymmetric cryptographic principles. The main idea is to avoid the usage of both purely mathematical symmetric and asymmetric algorithms and to use an advanced asymmetric algorithm based on DNA. The speed of the algorithm should be quite high because we make use of the powerful parallel computing possibilities of the DNA. Also, the original asymmetric keys are generated starting from a user password to avoid their storage.

This paper is structured in 5 sections. In section 2 we present some general aspects about the genetic code. In section 3 we show 2 algorithms for the symmetric DNA implementation, a MatLab implementation and one realized in BioJava. We will also expose the limitation imposed by these platforms. In section 4 we describe an advanced asymmetric DNA encryption algorithm. We will conclude this paper in section 5 where a comparison between the obtained results is made and the conclusions and possible continuations of our work are presented.

2 General Aspects about Genetic Code

There are 4 nitrogenous bases used in making a strand of DNA. These are adenine (A), thymine (T), cytosine (C) and guanine (G). These 4 bases (A, T, C and G) are used in a similar way to the letters of an alphabet. The sequence of these DNA bases will code specific genetic information [7].

In our previous work we used a one-time pad, symmetric key cryptosystem [19]. In the OTP algorithm, each key is used just once, hence the name of OTP. The encryption process uses a large non-repeating set of truly random key letters. Each pad is used exactly once, for exactly one message. The sender encrypts the message and then destroys the used pad. As it is a symmetric key cryptosystem, the receiver has an identical pad and uses it for decryption. The receiver destroys the corresponding pad after decrypting the message. New message means new key letters. A cipher text message is equally likely to correspond to any possible plaintext message. Cryptosystems which use a secret random OTP are known to be perfectly secure.

By using DNA with common symmetric key cryptography, we can use the inherent massively-parallel computing properties and storage capacity of DNA, in order to perform the encryption and decryption using OTP keys. The resulting encryption algorithm which uses DNA medium is much more complex than the one used by conventional encryption methods.

To implement and exemplify the OTP algorithm, we downloaded a chromosome from the open source NCBI GenBank. As stated, in this algorithm the chromosomes are used as cryptographic keys. They have a small dimension and a huge storage capability. There is a whole set of chromosomes, from different organisms which can be used to create a unique set of cryptographic keys. In order to splice the genome, we must know the order in which the bases are placed in the DNA string.

The chosen chromosome was "*Homo sapiens FOSMID clone ABC24-1954N7 from chromosome 1*". It's length is high enough for our purposes (37983 bases).

GenBank offers different formats in which the chromosomal sequences can be downloaded:

- GenBank,
- GenBank Full,
- FASTA,
- ASN.1.

We chose the FASTA format because it's easier to handle and manipulate. To manipulate the chromosomal sequences we used BioJava API methods, a framework for processing DNA sequences. Another API which can be used for managing DNA sequences is offered by MatLab. Using this API, a dedicated application has been implemented [10].

In MatLab, the plaintext message was first transformed in a bit array. An encryption unit was transformed into an 8 bit length ASCII code. After that, using functions from the Bioinformatics Toolbox, each message was transformed from binary to DNA alphabet. Each character was converted to a 4-letter DNA sequence and then searched in the chromosomal sequence used as OTP, [19].

Next, we will present an alternative implementation which makes use of the BioJava API.

The core of BioJava is actually a symbolic alphabet API, [20]. Here, sequences are represented as a list of references to singleton symbol objects that are derived from an alphabet. The symbol list is stored as often as possible. The list is compressed and uses up to four symbols per byte.

Besides the fundamental symbols of the alphabet (A, C, G and T as mentioned earlier), the BioJava alphabets also contain extra symbol objects which represent all possible combinations of the four fundamental symbols. The structure of the BioJava architecture together with its most important APIs is presented below:

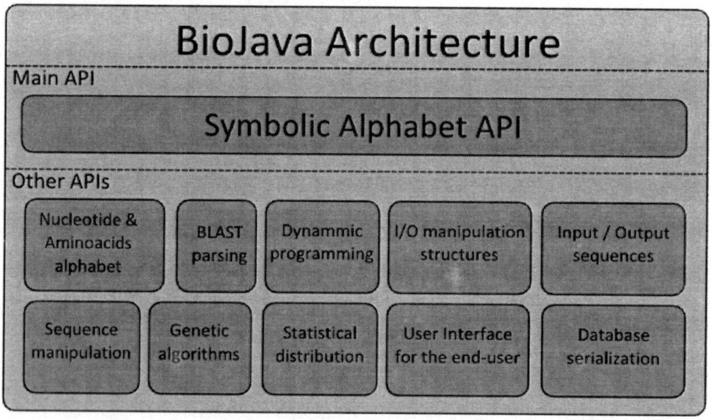

Fig. 1. The BioJava Architecture

By using the symbol approach, we can create higher order alphabets and symbols. This is achieved by multiplying existing alphabets. In this way, a codon can be treated as nothing more than just a higher level alphabet, which is very convenient in our case. With this alphabet, one can create views over sequences without modifying the underlying sequence.

In BioJava a typical program starts by using the sequence input/output API and the sequence/feature object model. These mechanisms allow the sequences to be loaded from a various number of file formats, among which is FASTA, the one we used. The obtained results can be once more saved or converted into a different format.

3 DNA Cryptography Implementations

In this chapter we will start by presenting the initial Java implementation of the symmetric OTP encryption algorithm, [19]. We will then continue by describing the corresponding BioJava implementation and some drawbacks of this symmetric algorithm.

3.1 Java Implementation

Due to the restrictions that limit the use of JCE, the symmetric cryptographic algorithm was developed using OpenJDK, which is based on the JDK 6.0 version of the Java platform and does not enforce certificate verification. This algorithm involves three steps: key generation, encryption and decryption.

In this algorithm, the length of the key must be exactly the same as the length of the plaintext. In this case, the plaintext is the secret message, translated according to the following substitution alphabet: 00 – A, 01 – C, 10 – G and 11 – T. Therefore, the length of the key is three times the length of the secret message. So, when trying to send very long messages, the length of the key would be huge. For this reason, the message is broken into fixed-size blocks of data. The cipher encrypts or decrypts one block at a time, using a key that has the same length as the block.

The implementation of block ciphers raises an interesting problem: the message we wish to encrypt will not always be a multiple of the block size. To compensate for the last incomplete block, padding is needed. However, this DNA Cipher will not use a standard padding scheme but a shorter version (a fraction) of the original key. The only mode of operation implemented by the DNA Symmetric Cipher is ECB (Electronic Code Book). ECB mode has the disadvantage that the same plaintext will always encrypt to the same ciphertext, when using the same key.

As we mentioned, the DNA Cipher applies a double encryption in order to secure the message we want to keep secret. The first encryption step uses a substitution cipher.

For applying the substitution cipher a HashMap object was used. HashMap is a java.util class that implements the Map interface. These objects associate a value to a specified unique key in the map. Each character of the secret message is represented by a combination of 3 DNA bases.

The result after applying the substitution cipher is a string containing characters from the DNA alphabet (A, C, G and T). This will further be transformed into a byte array, together with the key. The exclusive or operation (XOR) is then applied to the key and the message in order to produce the encrypted message.

When decrypting an encrypted message, it is essential to have the key and the substitution alphabet. While the substitution alphabet is known, being public, the key is kept secret and is given only to the addressee. Any malicious third party won't be able to decrypt the message without the original key.

For the decryption, the received message is XOR-ed with the secret key which results in a DNA-based text. This text is then broken into groups of three characters and with the help of the reverse map each such group will be replaced with the corresponding letter. The reverse map is the inverse of the one used for translating the original message into a DNA message. This way the receiver is able to read the original secret message.

A powerful implementation should consider medical analysis of a patient. In [8] an improved DNA algorithm is proposed.

3.2 BioJava Implementation

In this approach, we use more steps to obtain the DNA code starting from the plaintext. For each character from the message we wish to encode, we first apply the *get_bytes()* method which returns an 8bit ASCII string of the character we wish to encode. Further, we apply the *get_DNA_code()* method which converts the obtained 8 bit string, corresponding to an ASCII character, into DNA alphabet. The function returns a string which contains the DNA-encoded message.

The *get_DNA_code()* method is the main method for converting the plaintext to DNA encoded text. For each 2 bits from the initial 8 bit sequence, corresponding to an ASCII character, a specific DNA character is assigned: 00 – A, 01 – C, 10 – G and 11 – T. Based on this process we obtain a raw DNA message.

Table 1. DNA encryption test sequence

```
Plaintext message: „test"
ASCII message: 116 101 115 116
Raw DNA message: „TCACGCCCTATCTCA"
```

The coded characters are searched in the chromosome chosen as session key at the beginning of the communication. The raw DNA message is split into groups of 4 bases. When such a group is found in the chromosome, its base index is stored in a vector. The search is made between the first characters of the chromosome up to the 37983th. At each new iteration, a 4 base segment is compared with the corresponding 4 base segment from the raw DNA message. So, each character from the original string will have an index vector associated, where the chromosome locations of that character are found.

The *get_index()* method effectuates the parsing – the comparison of the chromosomal sequences and creates for each character an index vector. To parse the sequences in the FASTA format specific BioJava API methods were used.

BioJava offers us the possibility of reading the FASTA sequences by using a FASTA stream which is obtained with the help of the SeqIOTools class. We can pass through each of the sequences by using a *SequenceIterator* object. These sequences are then loaded into an *Sequence* list of objects, from where they can be accessed using the *SequneceAt()* mrthod.

In the last phase of the encryption, for each character of the message, a random index from the vector index is chosen. We use the *get_random()* method for this purpose. In this way, even if we would use the same key to encrypt a message, we would obtain a different result because of the random indexes.

Since the algorithm is a symmetric one, for the decryption we use the same key as for encryption. Each index received from the encoded message is actually pointing to a 4 base sequence, which is the equivalent of an ASCII character.

So, the *decode()* method realizes following operations: It will first extract the DNA 4 base sequences from the received indexes. Then, it will convert the obtained raw DNA message into the equivalent ASCII-coded message. From the ASCII coded message we finally obtain the original plaintext. And with this, the decryption step is completed.

The main vulnerability of this algorithm is that, if the attacker intercepts the message, he can decode the message himself if he knows the coding chromosomal sequence used as session key.

4 BioJava Asymmetric Algorithm Description

In this chapter we will present in detail an advanced method of obtaining DNA-encoded messages. It relies on the use of an asymmetric algorithm and on key generation starting from a user password.

We will also present a pseudo-code description of the algorithm.

4.1 Asymmetric Key Generation

Our first concern when it comes to asymmetric key algorithms was to develop a way in which the user was no longer supposed to deal with key management authorities or with the safe storage of keys. The reason behind this decision is fairly simple: both methods can be attacked. Fake authorities can pretend to be real key-management authorities and intruders may breach the key storage security. By intruders we mean both persons who have access to the computer and hackers, which illegally accessed the computer.

To address this problem, we designed an asymmetric key generation algorithm starting from a password. The method has some similarities with the RFC2898 symmetric key derivation algorithm [21]. The key derivation algorithm is based on a combination of hashes and the RSA algorithm. Below we present the basic steps of this algorithm:

- **Step 1:** First, the password string is converted to a byte array, hashed using SHA256 and then transformed to BigInteger number. This number is transformed in an odd number, *tmp*, which is further used to apply the RSA algorithm for key generation.
- **Step 2:** Starting from *tmp* we search for 2 random pseudo-prime number p and q. The relation between *tmp, p* and q is simple: $p < tmp < q$. To spare the computational power of the device, we do not compute traditionally if p and q are prime but make primality tests.
- A primality test determines the probability according to which a number is prime. The sequence of the primality test is the following: First, trial

divisions are carried out using prime numbers below 2000. If any of the primes divides this BigInteger, then it is not prime. Second, we perform base 2 strong pseudo-prime test. If this BigInteger is a base 2 strong pseudo-prime, we proceed on to the next step. Last, we perform the strong Lucas pseudo-prime test. If everything goes well, it returns true and we declare the number as being pseudo-prime.

• **Step 3:** Next, we determine Euler totient: *phi* = (p - 1) * (q - 1) ; and *n* = p*q;

• **Step 4:** Next, we determine the public exponent, *e*. The condition imposed to *e* is to be coprime with *phi.*

• **Step 5:** Next, we compute the private exponential, *d* and the CRT (Chinese Reminder Theorem) factors: *dp*, *dq* and *qInv*.

• **Step 6:** Finally, all computed values are written to a suitable structure, waiting further processing.

• The public key is released as the public exponent, *e* together with *n*.

• The private key is released as the private exponent, *d* together with *n* and the CRT factors.

The scheme of this algorithm is presented below:

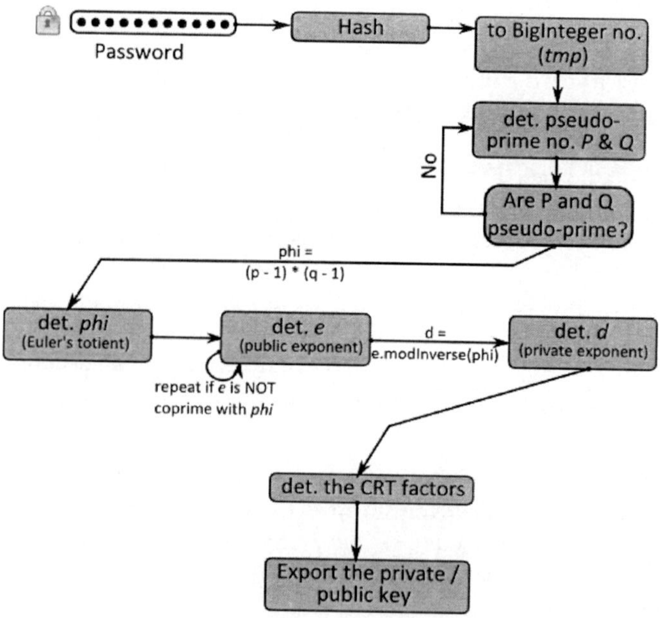

Fig. 2. Asymmetric RSA compatible key generation

In comparison with the RFC2898 implementation, here we no longer use several iterations to derive the key. This process has been shown to be time consuming and provide only little extra security. We therefore considered it safe to disregard it.

The strength of the key-generator algorithm is given by the large pseudo-prime numbers it is using and of course, by the asymmetric algorithm. By using primality tests one can determine with a precision of 97 – 99% that a number is prime. But most importantly, the primality tests save time. So, the average computation time, including appropriate key export, for the whole algorithm is 143 ms. After the generation process was completed, the public or private key can be retrieved using the static *ToXmlString* method.

Next, we will illustrate the algorithm through a short example. Suppose the user password is “DNACryptography”. Starting from this password, we compute its hash with SHA256. The result is shown below. This hashed password is converted into the BigInteger number *tmp*. Starting from it, and according to the algorithm described above, we generate the public exponent *e* and the private exponent *d*.

Table 2. Asymmetric DNA encryption test sequence

```
user password: "DNACryptography"
hashed password: "ed38f5aa72c3843883c26c701dfce03e0d5d6a8d"
tmp = 845979413928639845587469165925716582498797231629929694
      46756202517881375676359726620829895211 2229
e = 1063
d = 622097271837183006931454033440940850476686457179854307 8
    2067931848646161930033787072523479660987299191525204542
    4327429202622472207387685378317736890998257538720690765
    466158123868118572427782935
```

We conducted several tests and the generated keys match the PKCS #5 specifications. Objects could be instantiated with the generated keys and used with the normal system-build RSA algorithm.

4.2 Asymmetric DNA Algorithm

The asymmetric DNA algorithm proposes a mechanism which makes use of three encryption technologies. In short, at the program initialization, both the initiator and its partner generate a pair of asymmetric keys. Further, the initiator and its partner negotiate which symmetric algorithms to use, its specifications and of course, the codon sequence where the indexes of the DNA bases will be looked up. After this initial negotiation is completed, the communication continues with normal message transfer. The normal message transfer supposes that the data is symmetrically encoded, and that the key with which the data was encoded is asymmetrically encoded and attached to the data. This approach was first presented in [17].

Next, we will describe the algorithm in more detail and also provide a pseudo-code description for a better understanding.

Step 1: At the startup of the program, the user is asked to provide a password phrase. The password phrase can be as long or as complicated as the user sees fit. The password phrase will be further hashed with SHA256.

Step 2: According to the algorithm described in section 4.1, the public and private asymmetric keys will be generated. Since the pseudo-prime numbers p and q are randomly chosen, even if the user provides the same password for more sessions, the asymmetric keys will be different.

Step 3: The initiator selects which symmetric algorithms will be used in the case of normal message transfer. He can choose between 3DES, AES and IDEA. Further, he selects the time after which the symmetric keys will be renewed and the symmetric key length. Next, he will choose the codon sequence where the indexes will be searched. For all this options appropriate visual selection tools are provided.

Step 4: The negotiation phase begins. The initiator sends to its partner its public key. The partner responds by encrypting his own public key with the initiators public key. After the initiator receives the partner's public key, he will encrypt with it the chosen parameters. Upon receiving the parameters of the algorithms, the partner may accept or propose his own parameters. In case the initiators parameters are rejected, the parties will chose the parameters which provide the maximum available security.

Step 5: The negotiation phase is completed with the sending of a test message which is encrypted like any regular message would be encrypted. If the test message is not received correctly by any of the two parties or if the message transfer takes too much time, the negotiation phase is restarted. In this way, we protect the messages from tampering and interception.

Step 6: The transmission of a normal message. In this case, the actual data will be symmetrically encoded, according to the specifications negotiated before. The symmetric key is randomly generated at a time interval t. The symmetric key is encrypted with the partner's public key and then attached to the message. So, the message consists in the data, encrypted with a symmetric key and the symmetric key itself, encrypted with the partner's public key. We chose to adopt this mechanism because symmetric algorithms are faster than asymmetric ones. Still, in this scenario, the strength of the algorithm is equivalent to a fully asymmetric one because the symmetric key is encrypted asymmetrically. The procedure is illustrated below:

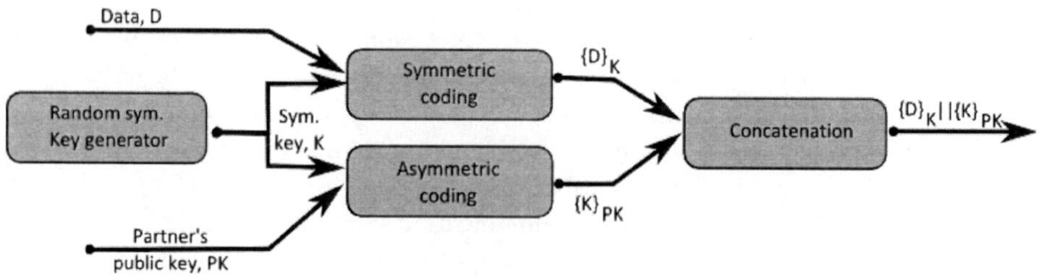

Fig. 3. Encryption scheme

Next, the obtained key will be converted into a byte array. The obtained array will be converted to a raw DNA message, by using a substitution alphabet. Finally, the raw DNA message is converted to a string of indexes and then transmitted.

The decryption process is fairly similar. The user converts the index array back to raw DNA array and extracts the ASCII data. From this data he will decipher the symmetric key used for that encryption, by using its private key. Finally the user will obtain the data by using the retrieved symmetric key. At the end of the communication, all negotiated data is disregarded (symmetric keys used, the asymmetric key pair and the codon sequence used).

5 Conclusions and Compared Results

In this chapter we will present the results we obtained for the symmetric algorithm implementation along with the conclusions of our present work.

Our first goal was to compare the time required to complete the encryption/decryption process. We compared the execution time of the DNA Symmetric Cipher with the time required by other classical encryption algorithms. We chose a random text of 360 characters, in string format which was applied to all tests.

The testing sequence is:

Table 3. Testing sequence

```
k39pc3xygfv(!x|jl+qo|9~7k9why(ktr6pkiaw|gwnn&aw+be|r|*4u+rz$
wm)(v_e&$dz|hc7^+p6%54vp*g*)kzlx!%4n4bvb#%vex~7c^qe_d745h40i
$_2j*6t0h$8o!c~9x4^2srn81x*wn9&k%*oo_co(*~!bfur7tl4udm!m4t+a
|tb%zho6xmv$6k+#1$&axghrh*_3_zz@0!05u*|an$)5)k+8qf0fozxxw)_u
pryjj7_|+nd_&x+_jeflua^^peb_+%@03+36w)$~j715*r)x(*bumozo#s^j
u)6jji@xa3y35^$+#mbyizt*mdst&h|hbf6o*)r2qrwm10ur+mbezz(1p7$f
```

To be able to compute the time required for encryption and decryption, we used the public static *nanoTime*() method from the *System* class which gives the current time in nanoseconds. We called this method twice: once before instantiating the Cipher object, and one after the encryption. By subtracting the obtained time intervals, we determine the execution time.

It is important to understand that the execution time varies depending on the used OS, the memory load and on the execution thread management. We therefore measured the execution time on 3 different machines:

- **System 1:** Intel Core 2 Duo 2140, 1.6 GHz, 1 Gb RAM, Vista OS
- **System 2:** Intel Core 2 Duo T6500, 2.1 GHz, 4 Gb RAM, Windows 7 OS
- **System 3:** Intel Dual Core T4300, 2.1 GHz, 3 Gb RAM, Ubuntu 10.04 OS

Next, we present the execution time which was obtained for various symmetric algorithms in the case of the first, second and the third system, for different cases:

Table 4. Results obtained for System 1

Analysis results for Vista OS							
DES	Encryption	50	26	1.03	0.81	0.84	0.84
	Decryption	1.63	0.35	0.33	0.32	0.34	0.36
AES	Encryption	80	26	0.92	0.95	0.88	0.54
	Decryption	27	2.09	0.30	22.26	0	0.14
Blowfish	Encryption	65	10.91	25	24	0.15	1.45
	Decryption	3	1.87	1.72	29	1.09	1
3DES	Encryption	82	24	2.41	25	2.12	1.42
	Decryption	1.56	1.42	26	1.23	1.41	0.66
BIO sym. algorithm	Encryption	4091	4871	4875	4969	4880	4932
	Decryption	6.29	4.19	4.19	4.19	4.19	4.19

Table 5. Results obtained for System 2

Analysis results for Windows 7							
DES	Encryption	34	1.43	1.09	1.2	1.73	1.19
	Decryption	0.75	0.37	0.44	0.42	0.38	0.37
AES	Encryption	28	1.3	1.16	0.07	1.77	0.82
	Decryption	0.12	0.14	2.09	0.9	2.09	0.16
Blowfish	Encryption	22	28.4	6.2	4	1.6	2.83
	Decryption	2.24	2.21	1.8	1.8	1.8	1.71
3DES	Encryption	41	6.59	2.78	2.62	2.69	2.12
	Decryption	1.12	1.78	1.24	1.74	1.48	1
BIO sym. algorithm	Encryption	3970	3884	3887	3901	3900	3910
	Decryption	4.19	4.19	4.19	2.09	4.19	2.09

Table 6. Results obtained for System 3

Analysis results for Ubuntu 10.04							
DES	Encryption	12.64	0.9	0.61	0.59	0.61	0.56
	Decryption	1.24	0.45	0.44	0.45	0.43	0.41
AES	Encryption	0.66	0.6	0.63	0.63	0.62	0.63
	Decryption	0.66	0.71	0.64	0.64	0.19	0.19
Blowfish	Encryption	37.07	32	19	13	15	14
	Decryption	0.81	0.77	0.81	0.58	0.74	0.59
3DES	Encryption	14	11	17.7	10.21	10.11	13
	Decryption	0.77	0.79	0.78	0.6	0.6	0.6
BIO sym. algorithm	Encryption	1896	1848	1857	1846	1850	1850
	Decryption	2.62	13.1	1.83	1.31	1.57	2.62

Below, we will illustrate the maximum, mean, olimpic (by eliminating the absolute minimum and maximum values) and minimum encryption and decryption time for the Symmetric Bio Algorithm.

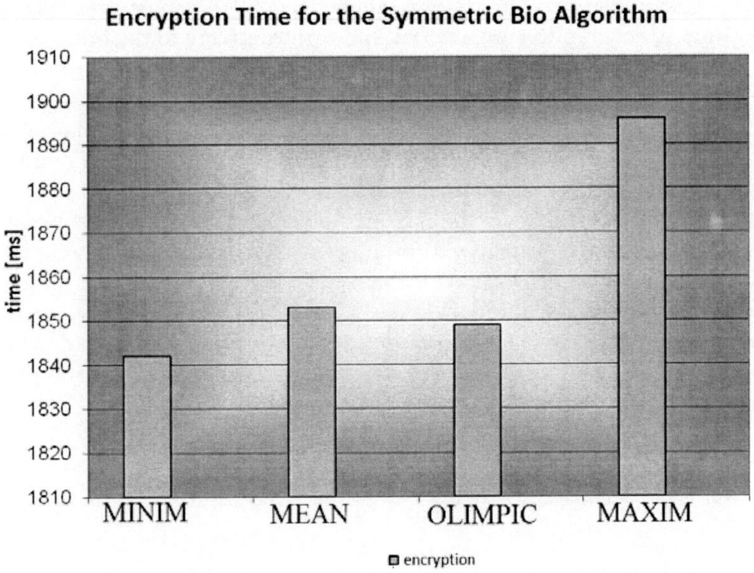

Fig. 4. Encryption time for the Symmetric Bio Algorithm

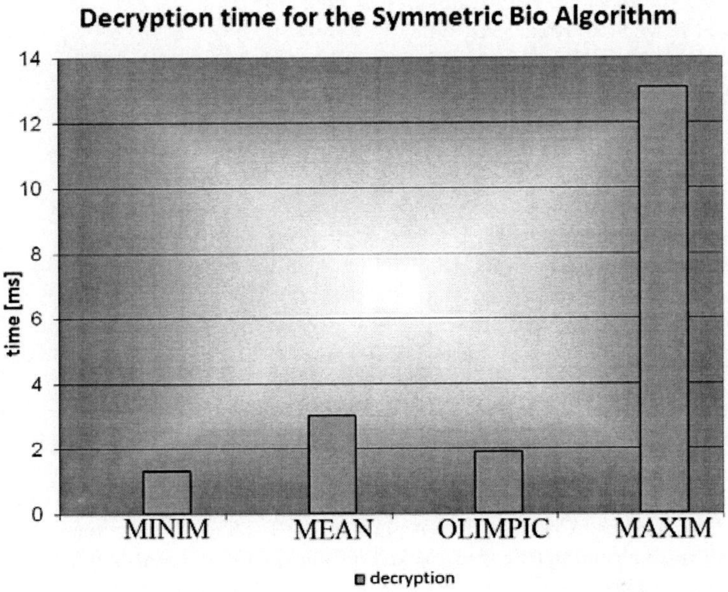

Fig. 5. Decryption time for the Symmetric Bio Algorithm

First of all, we can notice that the systems 1 and 2 (with Windows OS) have larger time variations for the encryption and decryption processes. The third system, based on the Linux platform, offers a better stability, since the variation of the execution time is smaller.

As seen from the figures and tables above, the DNA Cipher requires a longer execution time for encryption and decryption, comparatively to the other ciphers. We would expect these results because of the type conversions which are needed in the case of the symmetric Bio algorithm. All classical encryption algorithms process array of bytes while the DNA Cipher is about strings. The additional conversions from string to array of bytes and back make this cipher to require more time for encryption and decryption then other classic algorithms.

However, this inconvenience should be solved with the implementation of full DNA algorithms and the usage of Bio-processors, which would make use of the parallel processing power of DNA algorithms.

In this paper we proposed an asymmetric DNA mechanism that is more reliable and more powerful than the OTP DNA symmetric algorithm. As future developments, we would like to make some test for the asymmetric DNA algorithm and increase its execution time.

Acknowledgments. This work was supported by CNCSIS–UEFISCSU, project number PNII – IDEI 1083/2007-2010.

References

1. Hook, D.: Beginning Cryptography with Java. Wrox Press (2005)
2. Kahn, D.: The codebrakers. McMillan, New York (1967)
3. Schena, M.: Microarray analysis. Wiley-Liss (July 2003)
4. Adleman, L.M.: Molecular computation of solution to combinatorial problems. Science 266, 1021–1024 (1994)
5. Schneier, B.: Applied cryptography: protocols, algorithms, and source code in C. John Wiley & Sons Inc., Chichester (1996)
6. Java Cryptography Architecture. Sun Microsystems (2011), `http://java.sun.com/j2se/1.4.2/docs/guide/security/CryptoSpec.html`
7. Genetics Home Reference. U.S. National Library of Medicine (2011), `http://ghr.nlm.nih.gov/handbook/basics/dna`
8. Hodorogea, T., Vaida, M.F.: Blood Analysis as Biometric Selection of Public Keys. In: 7 th International Carpathian Control Conference ICCC 2006, Ostrava – Beskydy, Czech Republic, May 29-31, pp. 675–678 (2006)
9. Gehani, A., LaBean, T., Reif, J.: DNA-Based Cryptography. DIMACS Series in Discrete Mathematics and Theoretical Computer Science (LNCS), vol. 54. Springer, Heidelberg (2004)
10. Tornea, O., Borda, M., Hodorogea, T., Vaida, M.-F.: Encryption System with Indexing DNA Chromosomes Cryptographic Algorithm. In: IASTED International Conference on Biomedical Engineering (BioMed 2010), Innsbruck, Austria, paper 680-099, February 15-18, pp. 12–15 (2010)

11. Wilson, R. K.: The sequence of Homo sapiens FOSMID clone ABC14-50190700J6, submitted to (2009), http://www.ncbi.nlm.nih.gov
12. DNA Alphabet. VSNS BioComputing Division (2011), http://www.techfak.uni-bielefeld.de/bcd/Curric/PrwAli/node7.html#SECTION00071000000000000000
13. Wagner, Neal R.: The Laws of Cryptography with Java Code. [PDF] (2003)
14. Schneier, B.: Description of a New Variable-Length Key, 64-Bit Block Cipher (Blowfish). In: Anderson, R. (ed.) FSE 1993. LNCS, vol. 809, Springer, Heidelberg (1994)
15. Amin, S.T., Saeb, M., El-Gindi, S.: A DNA-based Implementation of YAEA Encryption Algorithm. In: IASTED International Conference on Computational Intelligence, San Francisco, pp. 120–125 (2006)
16. BioJava (2011), http://java.sun.com/developer/technicalArticles/javaopensource/biojava/
17. Nobelis, N., Boudaoud, K., Riveill, M.: Une architecture pour le transfert électronique sécurisé de document, PhD Thesis, Equipe Rainbow, Laboratories I3S – CNRS, Sophia-Antipolis, France (2008)
18. Techateerawat, P.: A Review on Quantum Cryptography Technology. International Transaction Journal of Engineering, Management & Applied Sciences & Technologies 1, 35–41 (2010)
19. Vaida, M.-F., Terec, R., Tornea, O., Ligia, C., Vanea, A.: DNA Alternative Security, Advances in Intelligent Systems and Technologies. In: Proceedings ECIT 2010 – 6th European Conference on Intelligent Systems and Technologies, Iasi, Romania, October 07-09, pp. 1–4 (2010)
20. Holland, R.C.G., Down, T., Pocock, M., Prlić, A., Huen, D., James, K., Foisy, S., Dräger, A., Yates, A., Heuer, M., Schreiber, M.J.: BioJava: an Open-Source Framework for Bioinformatics. Bioinformatics (2008)
21. RSA Security Inc. Public-Key Cryptography Standards (PKCS) PKCS #5 v2.0: Password-Based Cryptography Standard (2000)

An Intelligent System for Decision Making in Firewall Forensics

Hassina Bensefia[1] and Nacira Ghoualmi[2]

[1] Department of Computer Science, Bordj Bou Arreridj University, 34000 Bordj Bou Arreridj, Algeria
[2] Department of Computer Science, Badji Mokhtar University of Annaba, 23000 Annaba, Algeria
{Bensefia_hassina,Ghoualmi}@yahoo.fr

Abstract. The firewall log files trace all incoming and outgoing events in a network. Their content can include details about network penetration attempts and attacks. For this reason firewall forensics becomes a principal branch in computer forensics field. It uses the firewall log files content as a source of evidence and leads an investigation to identify and solve computer attacks. The investigation in firewall forensics is a too delicate procedure. It consists of analyzing and interpreting the relevant information contained in firewall log files to confirm or refute the attacks occurrence. But log files content is mysterious and difficult to decode. Its analysis and interpretation require a qualified expertise. This paper presents an intelligent system that automates the firewall forensics process and helps in managing, analyzing and interpreting the firewall log files content. This system will assist the security administrator to make suitable decisions and judgments during the investigation step.

Keywords: Firewall Forensics, Computer Forensics, Investigation, Evidence, Log files, Firewall, Multi-agent.

1 Introduction

The computer crime is a serious and spiny problem. Several organizations lost their productivity and reputation because of various direct and indirect attacks without any legal recourse. As a reaction to computer crime, forensic science was introduced in the computer security field in the aim to establish a judicial system able to discover computer crimes and prosecute its perpetrators. Then computer forensics emerges as a new discipline enabling the collection of information from computer systems and networks to apply investigation methods in order to determine the information which proves the occurrence of any computer crime. This information is considered as an evident proof and will be submitted to the court of law [4]. Log files which are an important source of audit in a computer system trace all the events occurring during its activity. Log files content can include details about any exceptional, suspected or unwanted event [3]. Then the log files generated by the network components like servers, routers and firewalls are sources of evidence for computer forensics [5]. As the firewall is the single input and output for a network, it represents the ideal location

H. Cherifi, J.M. Zain, and E. El-Qawasmeh (Eds.): DICTAP 2011, Part I, CCIS 166, pp. 470–484, 2011.

for recording all the events occurring in a network. Regarding this important role and position, firewall forensics imposes itself as a branch in computer forensics field. The investigation in firewall forensics is based on the inspection and revision of firewall log files content which constitutes a vital source of evidence. But log files content is huge and has ASCII (American Standard Code for Information Interchange) format. It is mysterious to read and difficult to manage. Its interpretation requires knowledge related to the log file format itself and qualified skills in information, network administration, protocols, vulnerabilities, attacks and hacking techniques [3]. The security administrator who is responsible for the security of the network is implied in the firewall forensics process. Face to any network attack, he must do investigation to solve the attack and make his own decision and judgment about the attack. But he always finds difficulties to manage and analyze the huge firewall log files content which is a tedious task. Then our contribution consists of designing and developing an intelligent system in order to help the security administrator to exploit, manage and analyze the firewall log files content. This system will conduct automatically the firewall forensics process and assist the security administrator in interpreting firewall log files content. Then the security administrator will be able to make the best decisions and judgments about attacks during the investigation step which is a delicate procedure in the firewall forensics process. The rest of the paper is organized as follows. Section 2 defines the computer forensics concept and the importance of the log files in computer forensics. Section 3 introduces the firewall forensics. Section 4 develops the methodology that we adopted to design our proposed system. Section 5 describes our system and its components. Section 6 gives a preview on our system implementation and its execution results. Section 7 summarizes our conclusion and perspectives.

2 Computer Forensics

Computer forensics is an emergent science in computer security field [1]. It applies law to illegitimate use of computer systems in the aim to solve the computer crime and make it admissible in a tribunal [3]. The process of computer forensics consists first of collecting data from computer systems and network components. Then it employs an investigation to retrace malicious events and identify attacks. The finality is to discover the identity of the attacker and obtain accusatory judicial evidence [3]. The evidence is the set of data which can trace systems and networks activities and confirm or refute any attack occurrence [1]. The evidence depends on attack type and may exist in three main locations: the victim system, the attacker system or in the network components which are situated between the victim system and the attacker system.

The investigation is an important step in computer forensics. It is a procedure that allows solving any attack after it has occurred [2]. It analyzes the collected information to verify if an attack has occurred. The investigation can determine the time of intrusion, the attack nature, the attack author and the traces that he left behind him, the penetrated systems, the methods used to accomplish the attack and the routing borrowed by the attacker [1]. The objective of the investigation is providing the sufficient judicial evidence to prosecute the attack author.

Computer Logging is a functionality that records the events happening in a host during the execution of an application or a network service such as a mail server, a web server or a Domain Name Server (DNS). The recording takes the form of a file with an ASCII (American Standard Code for Information and Interchange) structure which is called log file [7]. Each entry in the log file is a line which represents a request received by the host, the host response and the request processing time. So the log file reports all the activities and events related to the user and system behavior. It can include traces of any suspected activity. The relevant information in log files content has major interest during the resolution of an attack [4]. Therefore log files are an important source of evidence for computer forensics [3] [12] [13]. At the occurrence of any attack, the information contained in log files must be carefully verified during the investigation step in order to obtain accusatory evidence.

3 Firewall Forensics

The firewall is a vital element for the security of a private network [7] [8]. It implements an access control policy for the traffic exchanged between the private network and internet in the aim to allow or deny its transit. The Firewall is the single input and output of a network. So it represents the ideal location for recording the network activities. The firewall log files report all the network incoming and outgoing activities. They can give details about the TCP/IP traffic passing cross the firewall and the malicious activities happening in the network. Then the relevant information contained in firewall log files is an indispensable source of evidence for the investigation and a tool to discover computer crimes. As a consequence firewall forensics was introduced in computer forensics as new axis [5]. We define firewall forensics as the collection and analysis of firewall log files content in the objective of identifying penetration attempts and determine attacks targeting a network protected by a firewall [7].

Fig. 1 shows an extract of the log file content of Microsoft proxy server which is an application gateway firewall. We give significance of the first input of this log file which is:

16/01/02, 10:50:39, 193.194.77.227, 193.194.77.228, TCP, 1363, 113, SYN, 0, 193.194.77.228, -,-

- 16/01/02: is the reception date of the TCP/IP packet.
- 10:50:39: is the reception time of the TCP/IP packet.
- 193.194.77.227: is the source IP address. It is the IP address of the system that sends the TCP/IP packet.
- 193.194.77.228: is the destination IP address. It is the IP address of the system which will receive the TCP/IP packet.
- TCP: is the protocol used to transmit the TCP/IP packet.
- 1363: is the source port number. It indicates the ongoing application on the system which has sent the packet.
- 113: is the destination port. It indicates the application in execution on the system which will receive the packet.
- SYN: is the value of the TCP flag which indicates the establishment of connection.

- 0: this field indicates the result of the proxy filtering rule. If it is 0, it indicates that the TCP/IP packet is rejected. If it is 1, the TCP/IP packet is accepted.
- 193.194.77.228: is the IP address of the gateway receiving the TCP/IP packet.
- -: is an empty field.

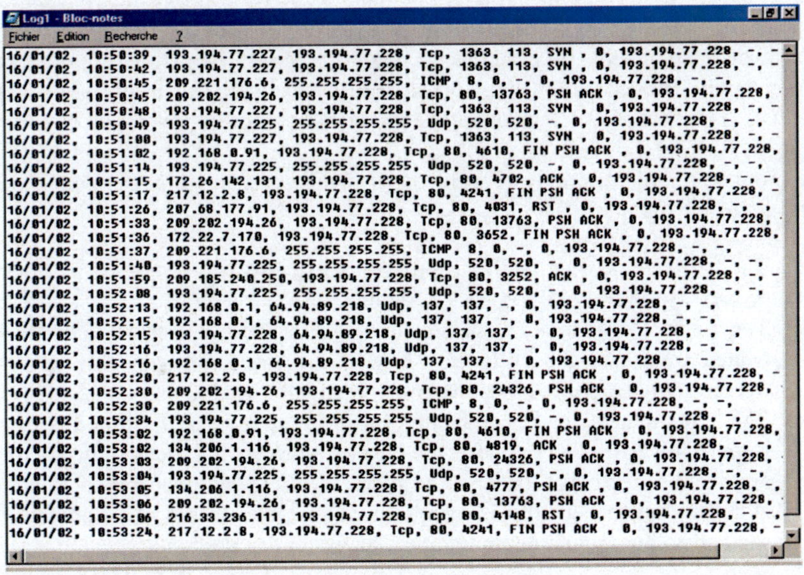
Log1 - Bloc-notes
Fichier Edition Recherche ?

```
16/01/02, 10:50:39, 193.194.77.227, 193.194.77.228, Tcp, 1363, 113, SYN , 0, 193.194.77.228, -, -
16/01/02, 10:50:42, 193.194.77.227, 193.194.77.228, Tcp, 1363, 113, SYN , 0, 193.194.77.228, -, -
16/01/02, 10:50:45, 209.221.176.6, 255.255.255.255, ICMP, 8, 0, -, 0, 193.194.77.228, -, -,
16/01/02, 10:50:45, 209.202.194.26, 193.194.77.228, Tcp, 80, 13763, PSH ACK , 0, 193.194.77.228,
16/01/02, 10:50:48, 193.194.77.227, 193.194.77.228, Tcp, 1363, 113, SYN , 0, 193.194.77.228, -, -
16/01/02, 10:50:49, 193.194.77.225, 255.255.255.255, Udp, 520, 520, -, 0, 193.194.77.228, -, -,
16/01/02, 10:51:00, 193.194.77.227, 193.194.77.228, Tcp, 1363, 113, SYN , 0, 193.194.77.228, -, -
16/01/02, 10:51:02, 192.168.0.91, 193.194.77.228, Tcp, 80, 4610, FIN PSH ACK , 0, 193.194.77.228,
16/01/02, 10:51:14, 193.194.77.225, 255.255.255.255, Udp, 520, 520, -, 0, 193.194.77.228, -, -,
16/01/02, 10:51:15, 172.26.142.131, 193.194.77.228, Tcp, 80, 4702, ACK , 0, 193.194.77.228, -, -,
16/01/02, 10:51:17, 217.12.2.8, 193.194.77.228, Tcp, 80, 4241, FIN PSH ACK , 0, 193.194.77.228, -
16/01/02, 10:51:26, 207.68.177.91, 193.194.77.228, Tcp, 80, 4031, RST , 0, 193.194.77.228, -, -,
16/01/02, 10:51:33, 209.202.194.26, 193.194.77.228, Tcp, 80, 13763, PSH ACK , 0, 193.194.77.228,
16/01/02, 10:51:36, 172.22.7.170, 193.194.77.228, Tcp, 80, 3652, FIN PSH ACK , 0, 193.194.77.228,
16/01/02, 10:51:37, 209.221.176.6, 255.255.255.255, ICMP, 8, 0, -, 0, 193.194.77.228, -, -,
16/01/02, 10:51:40, 193.194.77.225, 255.255.255.255, Udp, 520, 520, -, 0, 193.194.77.228, -, -,
16/01/02, 10:51:59, 209.185.240.250, 193.194.77.228, Tcp, 80, 3252, ACK , 0, 193.194.77.228, -, -
16/01/02, 10:52:08, 193.194.77.225, 255.255.255.255, Udp, 520, 520, -, 0, 193.194.77.228, -, -,
16/01/02, 10:52:13, 192.168.0.1, 64.94.89.218, Udp, 137, 137, -, 0, 193.194.77.228, -, -,
16/01/02, 10:52:15, 192.168.0.1, 64.94.89.218, Udp, 137, 137, -, 0, 193.194.77.228, -, -,
16/01/02, 10:52:15, 193.194.77.228, 64.94.89.218, Udp, 137, 137, -, 0, 193.194.77.228, -, -,
16/01/02, 10:52:16, 193.194.77.228, 64.94.89.218, Udp, 137, 137, -, 0, 193.194.77.228, -, -,
16/01/02, 10:52:16, 192.168.0.1, 64.94.89.218, Udp, 137, 137, -, 0, 193.194.77.228, -, -,
16/01/02, 10:52:20, 217.12.2.8, 193.194.77.228, Tcp, 80, 4241, FIN PSH ACK , 0, 193.194.77.228, -
16/01/02, 10:52:30, 209.202.194.26, 193.194.77.228, Tcp, 80, 24326, PSH ACK , 0, 193.194.77.228,
16/01/02, 10:52:30, 209.221.176.6, 255.255.255.255, ICMP, 8, 0, -, 0, 193.194.77.228, -, -,
16/01/02, 10:52:34, 193.194.77.225, 255.255.255.255, Udp, 520, 520, -, 0, 193.194.77.228, -, -,
16/01/02, 10:53:02, 192.168.0.91, 193.194.77.228, Tcp, 80, 4610, FIN PSH ACK , 0, 193.194.77.228,
16/01/02, 10:53:02, 134.206.1.116, 193.194.77.228, Tcp, 80, 4819, ACK , 0, 193.194.77.228, -, -,
16/01/02, 10:53:03, 209.202.194.26, 193.194.77.228, Tcp, 80, 24326, PSH ACK , 0, 193.194.77.228,
16/01/02, 10:53:04, 193.194.77.225, 255.255.255.255, Udp, 520, 520, -, 0, 193.194.77.228, -, -,
16/01/02, 10:53:05, 134.206.1.116, 193.194.77.228, Tcp, 80, 4777, PSH ACK , 0, 193.194.77.228, -,
16/01/02, 10:53:06, 209.202.194.26, 193.194.77.228, Tcp, 80, 13763, PSH ACK , 0, 193.194.77.228,
16/01/02, 10:53:06, 216.33.236.111, 193.194.77.228, Tcp, 80, 4148, RST , 0, 193.194.77.228, -, -,
16/01/02, 10:53:24, 217.12.2.8, 193.194.77.228, Tcp, 80, 4241, FIN PSH ACK , 0, 193.194.77.228, -
```

Fig. 1. Extract of Microsoft proxy server 2.0 log file

4 Methodology

To achieve our objective and build an intelligent system that helps the security administrator in the firewall forensics process, we divide the global process of firewall forensics into four main enchained steps which are partially parallel:

1. Collection: this step allows the collection of only the relevant information contained in firewall log files.
2. Inspection: it analyzes the collected information to check whether suspected events exist or not.
3. Investigation: it determines the significance of any suspected event in order to confirm if the event is malicious or normal behavior.
4. Notification: if the event is malicious, this step will generate a detailed report about the investigation result which will be transmitted to the security administrator.

There is no standard format for firewall log files. Each firewall generates log files in a proprietor format. So the collection step requires expertise to understand the firewall log files format. The inspection step also requires expertise to discover suspected events in firewall log files content. To determine the significance and the goal of a suspected event, the investigation step needs a qualified knowledge. A multi-agent system will be the most suitable approach to build our system [10] [11]. We employ cognitive agents. Our motivation is justified by the diversity of expertise required in the three main phases of the firewall forensics process (collection, inspection and investigation). The agents can collaborate in order to contribute to the forensics process which represents a complex problem beyond their individual capacities and knowledge. This collaboration is expressed by exchange of information between the agents. A partial parallelism is needed also between the phases of this complex process.

We propose a multi-agent system for the firewall forensics process which consists of three cognitive agents:

1. The collector agent is dedicated for the collection step. Its collects and processes the firewall log files content.
2. The inspector agent is dedicated for the inspection step. It identifies suspected events in the collected firewall log files content. This agent must transmit any suspected event to the investigator agent.
3. The investigator agent is dedicated for both the investigation and notification steps. This agent has to check the suspected event and determine its significance and objective in order to confirm or refute the occurrence of attack. If attack is confirmed, the investigator agent generates a detailed report and sends it to the security administrator as a security alert.

5 Architecture of the Proposed System

Fig. 2 illustrates the global architecture of our proposed system. Considering a private network connected to internet which is protected by a firewall. The firewall logging functionality is activated to generate daily log files in a specific format which is proprietor to the deployed firewall. Our proposed system proceeds by the rotation of the ongoing log file at regular time intervals which results of an instantaneous copy of the ongoing log file. The collector agent reads the instantaneous log file copy. It takes into account only the packets that have been accepted by the firewall. Then it extracts the important fields of every accepted activity and saves them in a data base called activity base. The inspector agent inspects the activity base to identify suspected events and send them to the investigator agent. This latter determines the signification and the objective of the suspected activity. If the suspected activity is confirmed as a malicious activity, the investigator develops a detailed report about this activity and sends it to the security administrator. All the reports generated by the investigator are saved in a data base called archives base. Our system includes two interfaces. The user interface allows the interaction between the security administrator and the system. The expert interface allows experts to update the agents knowledge.

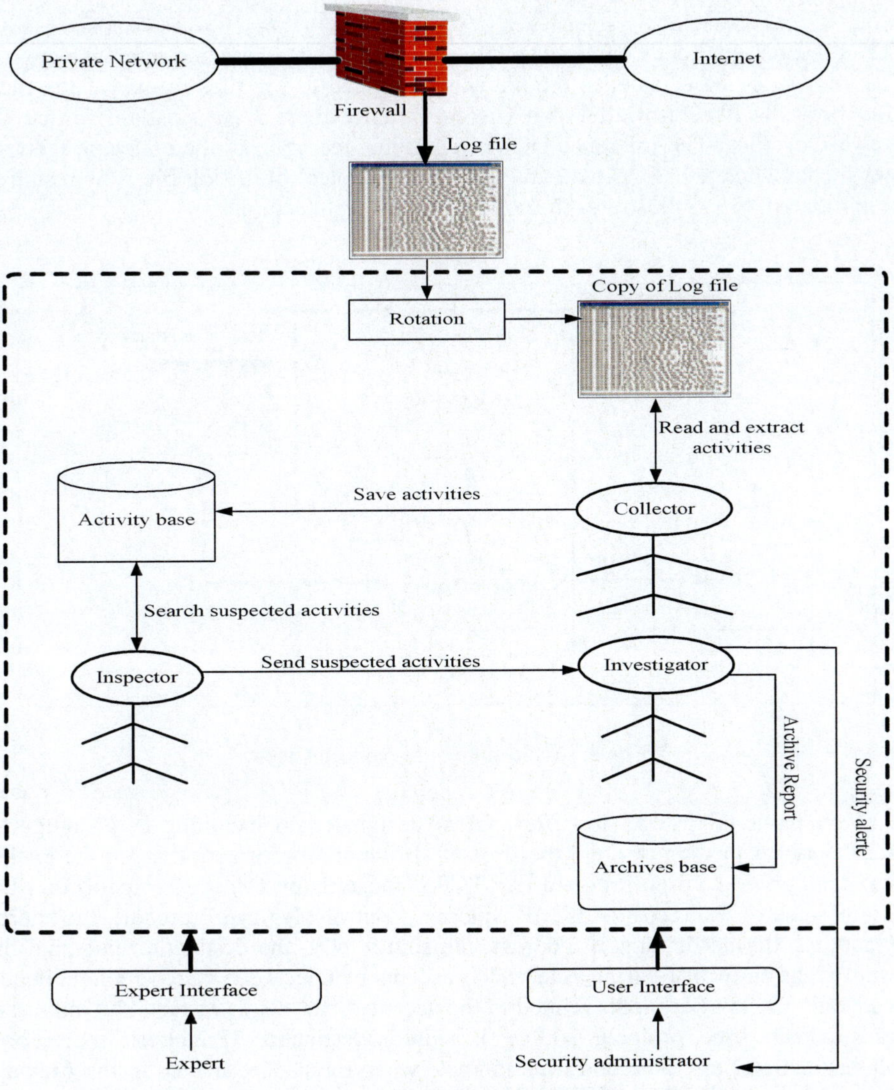

Fig. 2. Architecture of the proposed system

As follows, we will give a detailed description of our system components and show the agents reasoning and communication.

5.1 Collector Agent

The collector agent is a cognitive agent having knowledge base and inference engine. The knowledge base includes the knowledge related to log files format of the most used firewalls like Firewall-1 and Cisco Pix since there is no standard format for firewall log files. The inference engine represents the brain of the collector agent. It uses the knowledge base to read and process the content of the log file copy resulting from rotation. Fig. 3 illustrates the collector agent architecture.

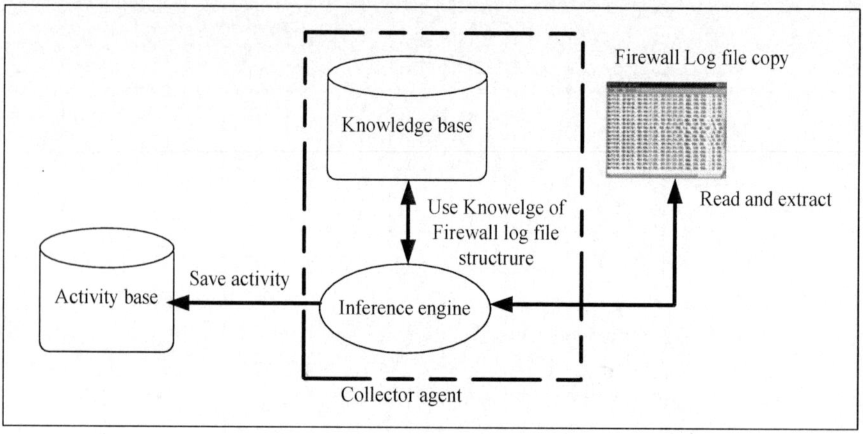

Fig. 3. Architecture of the collector agent

Every input in firewall log file content designates an incoming or an outgoing TCP/IP packet passing through the firewall. It includes information about the packet like: date, time, the used protocol like TCP (Transmission Control Protocol) or UDP (User Datagram Protocol) or ICMP (Internet Control Message Protocol), the source IP address, the destination IP address, the source port, the destination port and the result of the firewall filtering rule which accepts or rejects the packet. The collector treats only the log file inputs related to the accepted packets. It extracts the important fields as date, time, protocol, source IP address, destination IP address, source port and destination port. Date and time indicate when the packet arrived to the firewall. Protocol, source IP address, destination IP address, source port and destination port are the essential elements in a communication. The firewall inspects TCP/IP packets according to these elements. So the interpretation of any log file input depends on the significance of the essential elements of communication which means the purpose achieved by the communication. We consider the extracted essential communication elements as a record that we call activity. So the collector saves this record in the activity base.

The reasoning of the collector agent follows these steps:

1. Take a copy of the firewall log file.
2. Read the input of the firewall log file copy.
3. If the packet is rejected by the firewall, go to step 2.
4. If the packet is accepted by the firewall, extract the essential elements of communication according to the log file format of the deployed firewall.
5. Save the extracted elements (activity) in the activity base.
6. If it is the end of log file copy go to step 1 else go to step 2.

5.2 Activity Base

We propose this data base to facilitate the inspection of the firewall log file content which is a difficult operation on the log file copy. Fig. 4 illustrates the activity base structure. Each record in this data base summarizes a TCP/IP packet accepted by the firewall. It includes the essential elements of communication which form an activity. Every record in the activity base is composed of the following fields: activity number, activity nature and the communication elements which are: date, time, protocol, source IP address, destination IP address, source port and destination port. The Activity number is an integer that acts as the identifier of the activity. It will be incremented at every activity insertion in the activity base. The activity nature field will contain the character string "NOR" if the activity is normal. Else if the activity is suspected and may be malicious, the activity nature field will contain the string "MAL". This field must be filled up by the inspector agent after inspecting the activity.

Activity number	Activity nature	Date	Time	IP source	IP destination	Protocol	Source port	Destination port

Fig. 4. Activity base structure

5.3 Inspector Agent

It is a cognitive agent that integrates knowledge base and inference engine. The Knowledge base includes the knowledge about all the threats that can involve one or more than one element of the five essential communication elements: source IP address, destination IP address, source port, destination port and protocol. The inspector uses this knowledge to inspect firewall log files content. To create the inspector knowledge base, we use a concise document which is written by Robert Graham titled Firewall Forensics (What am I seeing?) [6]. This document gives the significance of the port numbers, IP addresses and ICMP messages that can be often observed by firewall users in firewall log files content. Then the inspector knowledge base contains what we call the predefined suspected activities related to one or more than one of the five essential communication elements. The inference engine is the brain of the inspector agent. As shown in Fig. 5, it exploits the predefined suspected activities to inspect the activity base records. When an activity is inspected as a suspected activity, it will be automatically sent to the investigator agent. The reasoning of the inspector agent respects the following steps:

1. Access to the activity base record in a sequential order.
2. Compare the fields of the activity base record to the predefined suspected activities fields.
3. If the activity is normal, the inspector will mark the field activity nature with "NOR".
4. If the activity is suspected, the inspector will mark the field activity nature with "MAL" and will send the suspected record to the investigator agent.
5. Go to step 1.

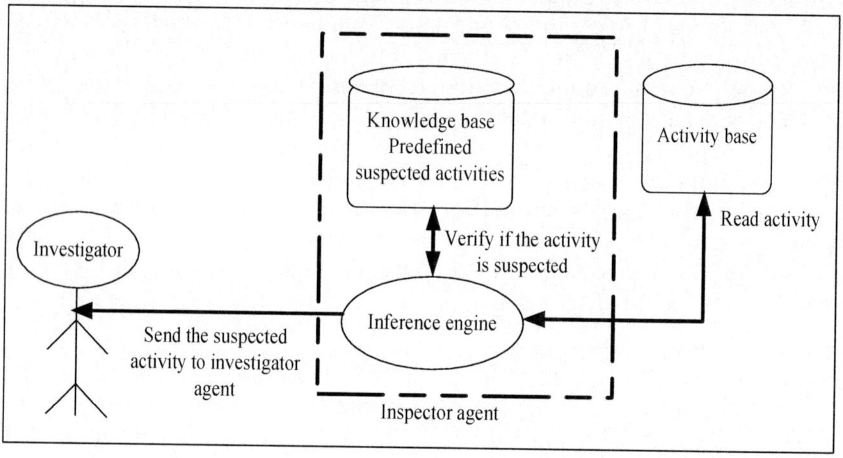

Fig. 5. Architecture of the inspector agent

5.4 Investigator Agent

It is a cognitive agent which is endowed with knowledge base and inference engine. The Knowledge base contains the knowledge related to the interpretation of the firewall log files content. For conceiving this knowledge base, we exploit the document written by Robert Graham entitled FAQ: Firewall Forensics (What am I seeing?) which explains the significance of some port numbers and IP addresses [6]. The investigator knowledge base includes 112 production rules. We give examples of some rules:

- Rule 1: IF {Protocol= TCP and Destination port=0} THEN {Attempt to identify the operating system}.
- Rule 2: IF {Protocol= UDP and Destination port=0} THEN {Attempt to identify the operating system}.

- Rule 3: IF {Protocol=UDP and Source port=68 and Destination address=255.255.255.255 and destination port=67} THEN {Response of a DHCP server to the request of a DHCP client}.
- Rule 4: IF {Protocol= TCP and Destination port=7} THEN {Connection to the TCPMUX service of an IRIX machine}.

Fig. 6 describes the investigator agent architecture. Being the brain of the investigator agent, the inference engine exploits the knowledge base to interpret any suspected activity transmitted by the inspector agent. If the suspected activity is a malicious action, the inference engine will generate a report including details about this malicious activity and sends it as a security alert to the security administrator. This report will be stored in a data base called archives base. This is the reasoning followed by the investigator agent:

1. Receive the suspected activity transmitted by the inspector agent.
2. Search the applied rules in the knowledge base.
3. Execute the selected rules to obtain the interpretation of the suspected activity.
4. If the interpretation indicates a malicious activity then generate a report including the malicious activity and its interpretation.
5. If the interpretation indicates a normal activity, then send a message to the inspector agent to mark the activity as normal "NOR" in the activity base and go to step 1.
6. Send the generated report as a security alert to the security administrator and save a copy of this alert in the archives base. Go to step 1.

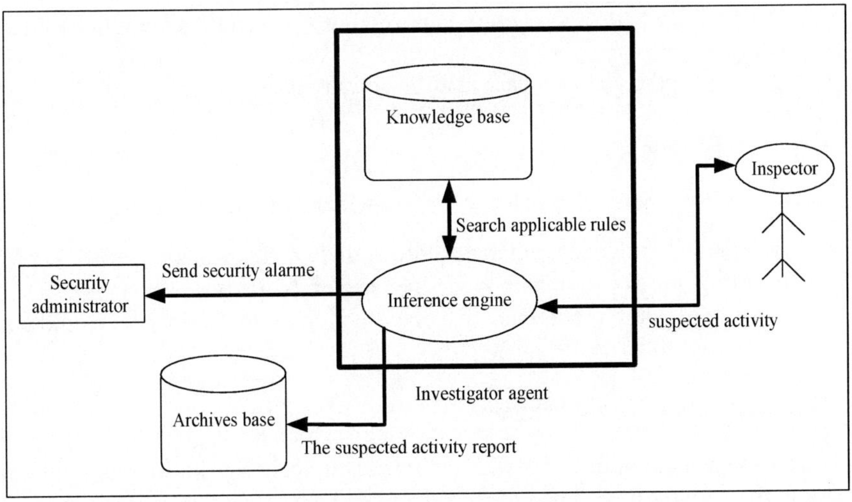

Fig. 6. Architecture of the investigator agent

5.5 Archives Base

Fig. 7 gives a preview of the archives base. This data base gathers all the reports generated by the investigator agent during a year. The structure that we propose for the archives base consists of three linked tables. The first table indexes the month in the year. The second table indexes the day in the month. The third table contains the reports generated which are indexed by day. We have adopted this structure to help the security administrator to interrogate the archives base in a late time.

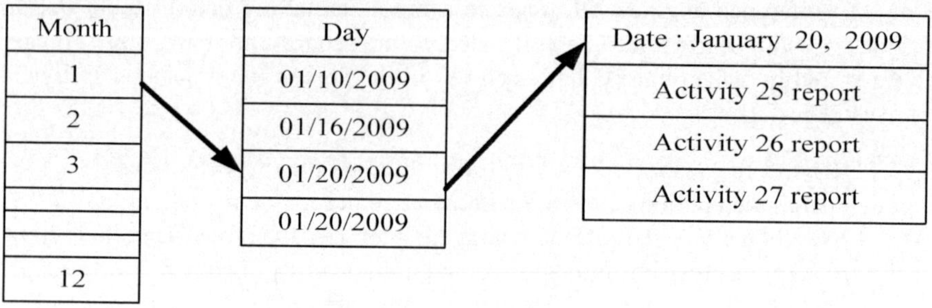

Fig. 7. Archives base structure

5.6 User Interface

The user interface will be used by the security administrator to interact with the system when he conducts an investigation or faces attacks. This interface allows him to:

- Determine whether an activity is normal or suspected and obtain its interpretation.
- Interrogate the archives base and the activity base

5.7 Expert Interface

This interface allows experts to manage the knowledge of the agents like:

- Introducing knowledge related to firewalls log file formats.
- Inserting new rules in the knowledge base of the investigator agent.
- Introducing new predefined suspected activities in the inspector knowledge base.

5.8 Communication between Agents

The collector agent communicates with the inspector agent by sharing the information existing in the activity base. Then we use the blackboard model as a mean of communication between the collector agent and the inspector agent. When the collector puts down an activity, the inspector inspects it by determining if it is a suspected activity or not. The inspector agent and the investigator agent do not share a common information zone. So we employ the actor model in order to allow communication between them. The two agents will communicate by sending messages. Fig. 8 and Fig. 9 show the models adopted respectively for the communication between the collector agent and the inspector agent and the communication between the inspector agent and the investigator agent.

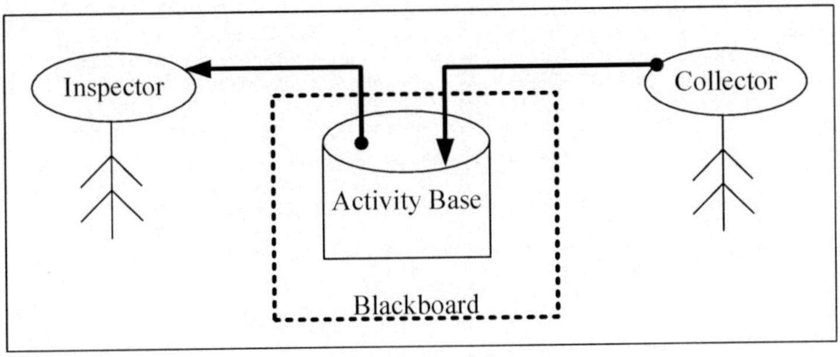

Fig. 8. Communication between the collector agent and the inspector agent

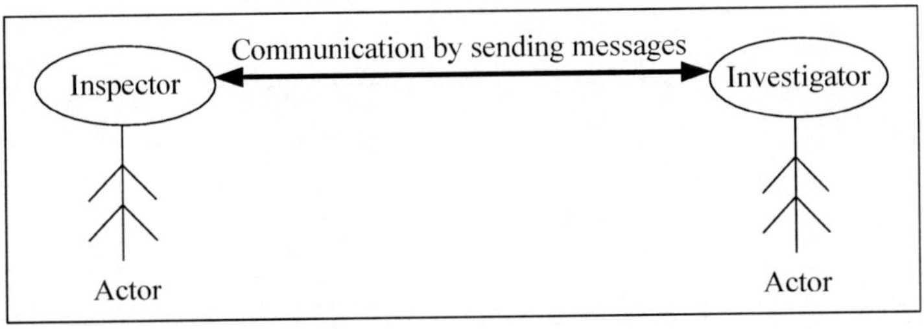

Fig. 9. Communication between the inspector agent and the investigator agent

6 Implementation of the Proposed System and Results

We have implemented the proposed system with Java language because it offers many advantages like the object oriented programming, multitasking application and multiplatform portability. To show the ability of our implemented system in inspecting and investigating firewall log files, we give some execution results through this short extract of Microsoft proxy server 2.0 log file which is described in Fig.10.

The collector agent reads the log file inputs. It extracts only the important fields related to the packets which have been accepted by the firewall and stores them as records in the activity base. The inspector agent inspects the activity base records. If the record presents a normal activity, it fixes its activity nature field with "NOR". If the record is suspected as malicious activity, the inspector agent sets its activity nature field as "MAL" and sends this record to the investigator agent. Fig. 11 gives a snapshot of the activity base content.

```
04/11/08, 03:36:52, 136.199.55.156, 193.194.77.225, ICMP, 8, 0, -, 0, 193.194.77.228, -, -,
04/11/08, 03:36:55, 136.199.55.156, 193.194.77.225, Udp, 520, 520, -, 0, 193.194.77.228, -, -,
04/11/08, 03:36:58, 204.29.239.23, 193.194.77.222, Tcp, 1240, 53, -, 1, 193.194.77.228, -, -,
04/11/08, 03:37:08, 193.194.77.222, 204.29.239.23, Tcp, 53, 1240, -, 1, 193.194.77.228, -, -,
04/11/08, 03:37:10, 130.79.68.209, 193.194.77.227, Tcp, 3125, 23, -, 0, 193.194.77.228, -, -,
04/11/08, 03:37:14, 216.33.236.111, 193.194.77.226, Tcp, 1896, 1, -, 0, 193.194.77.228, -, -,
04/11/08, 03:37:23, 193.194.23.121, 193.194.77.229, Udp, 1132, 22, -, 1, 193.194.77.228, -, -,
04/11/08, 03:37:30, 134.206.1.116, 193.194.77.228, ICMP, 8, 0, -, 0, 193.194.77.228, -, -,
04/11/08, 03:37:43, 134.206.1.116, 193.194.77.228, ICMP, 8, 0, -, 0, 193.194.77.228, -, -,
04/11/08, 03:37:56, 134.206.1.116, 193.194.77.228, ICMP, 8, 0, -, 0, 193.194.77.228, -, -,
04/11/08, 03:38:01, 0.0.0.0, 255.255.255.255, Udp, 67, 68, -, 1, 193.194.77.228, -, -,
04/11/08, 03:38:08, 193.194.77.220, 255.255.255.255, Udp, 68, 67, -, 1, 193.194.77.228, -, -,
04/11/08, 03:38:10, 193.194.78.35, 193.194.77.224, Udp, 1234, 0, -, 1, 193.194.77.228, -, -,
04/11/08, 03:38:15, 193.194.75.190, 193.194.77.225, Tcp, 1526, 11, -, 1, 193.194.77.228, -, -,
04/11/08, 03:38:18, 193.194.75.190, 194.193.77.225, Tcp, 1752, 98, -, 1, 193.194.77.228, -, -,
04/11/08, 03:39:23, 193.194.77.225, 255.255.255.255, Udp, 138, 138, -, 0, 193.194.77.228, -, -,
04/11/08, 03:39:37, 193.194.78.35, 193.194.77.228, Tcp, 1768, 80, SYN, 0, 193.194.77.228, -, -,
04/11/08, 03:39:53, 193.194.68.20, 193.194.77.226, Tcp, 143, 143, -, 0, 193.194.77.228, -, -,
04/11/08, 03:39:53, 193.194.68.20, 193.194.77.226, Tcp, 110, 110, -, 0, 193.194.77.228, -, -,
04/11/08, 03:39:53, 193.194.68.20, 193.194.77.226, Tcp, 25, 25, -, 1, 193.194.77.228, -, -,
04/11/08, 03:39:58, 80.89.196.27, 255.255.255.255, Tcp, 4998, 80, SYN, 0, 193.194.77.228, -, -,
04/11/08, 03:40:11, 193.194.242.145, 193.194.77.230, Tcp, 3240, 1243, -, 1, 193.194.77.228, -, -,
04/11/08, 03:40:33, 64.94.89.218, 193.194.77.228, ICMP, 8, 0, -, 0, 193.194.77.228, -, -,
04/11/08, 03:40:46, 169.254.1.22, 193.194.77.222, Udp, 161, 161, -, 1, 193.194.77.228, -, -,
04/11/08, 03:41:10, 193.194.77.225, 255.255.255.255, Udp, 520, 520, -, 0, 193.194.77.228, -, -,
```

Fig. 10. A short extract of Microsoft Proxy Server 2.0 log file

Activity number	Activity nature	Date	Time	IP Source	IP Destination	Protocol	Source Port	Destination Port
01	NOR	04/11/08	03:36:58	204.29.239.23	193.194.77.222	Tcp	1240	53
02	NOR	04/11/08	03:37:08	193.194.77.222	204.29.239.23	Tcp	53	1240
03	MAL	04/11/08	03:37:23	193.194.23.121	193.194.77.229	Udp	1132	22
04	MAL	04/11/08	03:38:01	0.0.0.0	255.255.255.255	Udp	67	68
05	NOR	04/11/08	03:38:08	193.194.77.220	255.255.255.255	Udp	68	67
06	MAL	04/11/08	03:38:10	193.194.78.35	193.194.77.224	Udp	1240	0
07	MAL	04/11/08	03:38:15	193.194.75.190	193.194.77.225	Tcp	1526	11
08	MAL	04/11/08	03:38:18	193.194.75.190	194.193.77.225	Tcp	1752	98
09	MAL	04/11/08	03:39:53	193.194.68.20	193.194.77.226	Tcp	25	25
10	MAL	04/11/08	03:40:11	193.194.242.145	193.194.77.230	Tcp	3240	1243
11	MAL	04/11/08	03:40:46	169.254.1.22	193.194.77.222	Udp	161	161

Fig. 11. The activity base records

Table 1. Investigator reasoning results

Activity number	Investigator reasoning results
03	Request for remote access and control of the system.
04	Request sent by a DHCP client to a DHCP server.
06	Attempt to identify the operating system.
07	Request to list the active processes on a Unix machine.
08	Connection to linuxconf of a Linux machine.
09	Attempt to scan the SMTP service by Sscan.
10	Remote access to the Trojan horse Sub-7.
11	The IP source address is tampered.

The investigator agent uses its rule base to undertake reasoning about the malicious records. It gives an interpretation of each record in the aim to confirm or refute the inspector decision. Table 1 displays the results of the investigator reasoning which demonstrates that all the records are malicious activities except activity number 04 which is a normal activity.

In general the IP source address 0.0.0.0 is a tampered address but according to the investigator reasoning, when this address is used with IP destination address 255.255.255.255 and Udp protocol and respectively the source and destination ports 67 and 68, it indicates a request sent by a DHCP client to a DHCP server. When a DHCP client starts, it has no IP address. It uses 0.0.0.0 as source IP address to send a request to the network on the port 68. Then the activity number 04 is not malicious. It is a normal activity. The investigator agent sends a message to the inspector agent to mark the activity number 04 as normal "NOR" in the activity base.

7 Conclusion and Perspectives

Our proposed system represents an intelligent tool having the following strong points:

- Managing and exploiting the voluminous and mysterious firewall log files content.
- Identifying suspected activities in the mass of information contained in firewall log files.
- Interpreting and notifying any confirmed malicious activity.
- Summarizing all the TCP/IP packets passing through the firewall in the activity base. This data base can help the security administrator to study the network activity and make statistics about the nature of traffic passing through the firewall.
- Archiving reports about all malicious activities in the archives base. This data base is well structured and it can be easily interrogated in an offline mode by the security administrator.

Our proposed system can accomplish the firewall forensics process automatically. It helps the security administrator to take the best decisions to achieve an investigation thanks to the expertise instituted in the agents. As perspective, we envisage extending the knowledge of the agents and exploit the archives base to study the behavior of attackers and create their profiles.

References

1. Bensefia, H.: Fichiers Logs: Preuves Judiciaires et Composant Vital pour Forensics. Review of Scientific and Technical Information (RIST) 15(01-02), 77–94 (2005)
2. Carrier, B., Spafford, E.H.: Getting physical with the digital investigation process. International Journal of digital evidence 2(2) (2003)
3. Yasinsac, A., Manzano, Y.: Policies to Enhance Computer and Network Forensics. In: Workshop on Information Assurance and Security, United States Military Academy, West Point, pp. 289-295 (2001)

4. Sommer, P.: Digital Footprints: Assessing Computer Evidence, Criminal Law Review, Special Edition, pp. 61-78 (1998)
5. Casey, E.: Digital Evidence and Computer Crime: Forensic Science, Computers, and the Internet. Book review. Academic Press, San Diego (2000)
6. FAQ: Firewall Forensics (What am I seeing ?), http://www.capnet.state.tx.us/firewall-seen.html (last visit October 2010)
7. Bensefia, H.: La conception d'une base de connaissances pour l'investigation dans Firewall Forensics. Master thesis. Centre of Research in Technical and Scientific Information, Algeria (2002)
8. Lodin, W., Schuba, L.: Firewalls fend off invasions from the net. IEEE spectrum 35(2) (1998)
9. Chown, T., Read, J., DeRoure, D.: The Use of Firewalls in an Academic Environment. JTAP-631, Department of Electronics and Computer Science. University of Southampton (2000)
10. Ferber, J.: Introduction aux systèmes multiagents. Inter Editions (2005)
11. Boissier, O., Guessoum, Z.: Systèmes Multi-agents Défis Scientifiques et Nouveaux usages. Hermès (2004)
12. Murray, C.P.: Network Forensics. University of Minnesota, Morris (2000)
13. Sommer, P.: Downloads, Logs and Captures: Evidence from cyberspace. Computer Journal of Financial Crime, 138-152 (1997)

Static Parsing Steganography

Hikmat Farhat[1], Khalil Challita[1], and Joseph Zalaket[2]

[1] Computer Science Department
Notre Dame University, Lebanon
{kchallita,hfarhat}@ndu.edu.lb
[2] Computer Science Department
Holy Spirit University of Kaslik , Lebanon
josephzalaket@usek.edu.lb

Abstract. In this paper we propose a method for hiding a secret message in a digital image that is based on parsing the cover image instead of changing its structure. Our algorithm uses a divide-and-conquer strategy and works in $\Theta(n \log n)$ time. Its core idea is based on the problem of finding the longest common substring of two strings. The key advantage of our method is that the cover image is not modified, which makes it very difficult for any steganalysis technique based on image analysis to detect and extract the message from the image.

Keywords: Steganography, steganalysis, cover media, stego-media, stego-key, image parsing.

1 Introduction

Steganography is the art of exchanging secret information between two parties. Usually it requires that the very existence of the message is unknown. Steganography embeds the secret message in a harmless looking cover, such as a digital image file [6,7]. In addition, the embedded message can be encrypted to hide the content of the message in case of exposure. The need for steganography is obvious but what is less obvious is the need for more research in the field. Simple techniques are easily detectable and there is a whole of field of defeating steganogrphic techniques called steganalysis [8]. As it is always the case, advances in steganography are usually countered by advances in steganalysis which makes it a constantly evolving field.

Since most steganographic system use digital images as cover, the whole field has borrowed methods and ideas from the closely related fields of watermarking and fingerprinting which also manipulate digital audio and video, for the purpose of copyright. Even though, in principle, many aspect of images can be manipulated, in reality most stego systems aim for the preservation of the visual integrity of the image. Early stego systems goals was to make changes not detectable by the human eye [15]. This feature is not enough because statistical method can detect the changes in the image even if it is not visible. Image compression also plays a role in steganography because it was found that on many occasions the result depend on the compression scheme used.

H. Cherifi, J.M. Zain, and E. El-Qawasmeh (Eds.): DICTAP 2011, Part I, CCIS 166, pp. 485–492, 2011.

Most existing methods have limitations concerning the message size, the security of the system against attackers and efficiency. In this paper we present a new method for steganography called Static Parsing Steganography (SPS). The word *static* refers to the fact that the structure of the cover media remains intact. SPS generates a separate file to be sent to the receiver who will be able to retrieve the secret message from the cover media. Our algorithm uses the longest common substring (LCS) algorithm as a subroutine to find *all* the bits of the secret message within the cover image. It is worth noting that SPS makes use of a divide-and-conquer strategy to hide the secret message, and runs in $\Theta(n\, logn)$ time. As we shall see, its main advantage is the reduced size of the output file, compared to other more straightforward methods.

This paper is divided as follows. In Section 2 we briefly talk about steganography and steganalysis. In Section 3 we describe current steganographic techniques in digital images. The Static Parsing Steganography (SPS) method is discussed in Section 4. Finally, and before concluding, we show some experimental results in Section 5.

2 Steganography and Steganalysis

A steganographic system is a mechanism that embeds a secret message m in a cover object c using a secret shared k. The result is a stego object s which carries the message m. Formally we defined the stegosystem as a pair of mappings (F, G) with F serves as the embedding function and G as the extraction function.

$$s = F(c, m, k)$$
$$m = G(s, k)$$

If M is the set of all possible messages then the embedding capacity of the stegosystem is $\log_2 M$ bits. The embedding efficiency is defined as

$$e = \frac{\log_2 M}{d(c, s)}$$

The set of all cover objects C is sampled using a probability distribution $P(c)$ with $c \in C$, giving the probability of selecting a cover object c. If the key and message are selected randomly then the Kullback-Leibler distance

$$KL(P|Q) = \sum_{c \in C} P(c) \log \frac{P(c)}{Q(c)}$$

gives a measure of the security of the stegosystem. The three quantifiers defined above: capacity, efficiency and security are the most important requirements that must be satisfied for any steganographic system. In reality, determining the best embedding function from a cover distribution is an NP-hard problem[1]. In addition, combining cryptography and steganography adds another layer of security [12]. Before embedding a secret message using steganography, the message is first encrypted. The receiver then should have both the stego-key in order to retrieve the encrypted information and the cryptographic key in order to decrypt it.

Steganalysis is the art of detecting messages hidden by stegosystems [9]. There are different types of attacks against such systems [3,14]. In one such attack, the *Known cover attack*, the original cover object and the stego-object are available for analysis. The idea in this attack is to compare the original media with the stego-media and note the differences. These differences may lead to the emergence of patterns that would constitute a signature of a known steganographic technique. A different approach to steganalysis is to model images using a feature vector as in blind steganalysis and capture the relationship between the change in the feature vector to the change rate using regression [13]. Yet another approach is based on the Maximum Likelihood principle [11] The concept of steganographic security, in the statistical sense, has been formalized by Cachin[1] by using an information-theoretic model for steganography. In this model the action of detecting hidden messages is equivalent to the task of hypothesis testing. In a perfectly secure stegosystem the eavesdropper has no information at all about the presence of a hidden message.

3 Steganographic Techniques in Digital Images

It would be helpful to review the encoding scheme of some image formats. The GIF format is a simple encoding of the RGB colors for each pixel using an 8-bit value. The color is not specified directly, rather the index into a 256 element array is selected. After the encoding the whole image is compressed using LZW lossless technique. In the JPEG format, first each color is converted from RGB format to YC_BC_R where the luma (Y) component representing the brightness of the pixel is treated differently than the chroma components (C_BC_R) which represent color difference. The difference of treatment is due to the fact that the human eye discerns changes in the brightness much more than color changes. Doing such a conversion allows greater compression without a significant effect on perceptual image quality. One can achieve higher compression rate this way because the brightness information, which is more important to the eventual perceptual quality of the image, is confined to a single channel. Once this is done for each component the discrete cosine transform (DCT)is computed to transform 8x8 pixel blocks of the image into DCT coefficients. The coefficients are computed as

$$F(u,v) = \sum_{x=0}^{7}\sum_{y=0}^{7} G(x,y) \cos\frac{(2x+1)\pi u}{16} \cos\frac{(2x+1)\pi v}{16} \qquad (1)$$

After the DCT is completed the coefficients $F(u,v)$ are quantized using elements from a table.

Many different steganographic methods have been proposed during the last few years. Most of them can be seen as substitution systems (which are based on the Least Significant Bit (LSB) encoding technique). Such methods try to substitute redundant parts of a signal with a secret message. Their main disadvantage is the relative weakness against cover modifications. Other more robust techniques fall within the *transform domain* where secret information is embedded in the transform space of the signal such as the frequency domain. We next describe some of these methods.

The most popular method for steganography is the Least Significant Bit (LSB) encoding [3]. Using any digital image, LSB replaces the least significant bits of each byte by the hidden message bits. Depending on the image format the resulting changes made by the least-significant bits are visually detectable or not [12]. For example, the GIF format is susceptible to visual attacks while JPEG being in the frequency domain as shown in equation (1) is less prone to such attacks.

The first publicly available stegnographic system was JSteg [16]. Its algorithm replaces the least-significant bit of the DCT coefficients with the message data. Because JSteg does not require a key, an attacker knowing the existence of the message will be able to recover it. Due to its simplicity LSB embedding of JSteg is the most common method implemented today. However, many steganalysis techniques have been developed to counter JSteg [20]. One can show that there is JPEG steganogrphic limit with respect to the current steganalysis methods[4,18,17].

Other stegosystems include the Transform domain method [19,10] which works in similar way as watermarking uses by using a large area of the cover image to hide messages which makes these method robust against attacks. The main disadvantage of such methods, however, is that one cannot send large messages because there is a trade-off between the size of the message and robustness against attack. What concerns us most in this paper is the fact that almost all steganographic methods applied on digital images change the structure and statistics of the images in when a hidden message is embedded in them.

4 Static Parsing Steganography

In this paper we propose a new secret key steganographic method that does not modify the structure of the image. The Static Parsing Steganography (SPS) algorithm takes as input a cover image and a secret message, and after some computations outputs a binary file. The output file is then sent to the receiver who simply has to reverse the encoding process in order to retrieve the hidden message. The main idea of SPS is based on a divide-and-conquer strategy to encode the secret message based on the cover image.

4.1 Description of the Algorithm

SPS consists of 2 main steps.

1. A cover image (that both the sender and receiver share), and the secret message to be sent are converted into bits. Let us denote the output files by Image1 and Secret1, respectively.

2. In this step, we encode the secret message Secret1 based on Image1. The idea is based on the problem of finding the longest common substring of two strings using a generalized suffix tree, which can be done in linear time [5]. The algorithm uses a divide-and-conquer strategy and works as follows. It starts with the whole bits of Secret1 and tries to find a match of all the bits of Secret1 in Image1. If this is the case, it stores the indexes of the start and end bits of Secret1 that occur within Image1 in an output file Output1. If not, the algorithm recursively tries to find a match of the first and second halves of Secret1 in Image1. It keeps repeating the process until all the bits of Secret1 have been matched with some bits of Image1.

We next give a pseudo-code on how the algorithm works.

Denote by LCS(S1, S2) the algorithm that finds the longest common subsequence of S1 that appears in S2, and returns true if the whole of S1 occurs in S2. We allow this modification of the algorithm (i.e. LCS) in order to simplify the implementation of SPS we next describe.

```
SPS(secretMessage, coverImage);
  if LCS(secretMessage, coverImage) is true,
       then store the positions of the indexes of the start
            and end bits of Secret that occur within Image
            the output file Output,
       else SPS(LeftPart-secretMessage, coverImage),
            SPS(RightPart-secretMessage, coverImage),
 return Output,
```

Example 1. Assume that the cover image is 100010101111 and that the secret message is 1010. Then the output file would be 58, since 1010 occurs in 100010101111 starting from index 5 (assuming that the first index is numbered 1).

Example 2. Assume that the cover image is Image = 110101001011000 and that the secret message is Secret = 11111010. This encoding requires 4 recursive calls of SPS. Indeed, the first call returns false since Secret does not appear in Image. After the first recursive call, we evaluate SPS(1111,110101001011000) and SPS(1010,110101001011000). The former requires 2 additional recursive calls: SPS(11,110101001011000), and the latter none, since 1010 appears in Image from index 4 to 7. The call SPS(11,110101001011000) returns 12.
So the output file contains 121247.

4.2 Time Complexity

The running time of SPS can be determined by the recurrence relation $T(n) = 2T(n/2) + O(n)$.

This is because the recursive call divides the problem into 2 equal subproblems, and the local work which is determined by LCS requires $O(n)$ time.

The solution of this recurrence is $\Theta(n\, logn)$ [2].

5 Implementation and Results

We implemented SPS on a Mac Pro with Quad-Core 2.8 GHz and 4 GB of Ram. We selected 8 different sizes of text messages (ranging from 1 KB to 500 KB) to test SPS. Concerning the cover images used, two image formats were selected: JPEG and BMP.

In the below table, we give some results of using SPS without the Longest Common Substring problem. Instead, we encode the secret message one byte at a time.

Message size (KB)	Output file (KB)
10	31
100	143
200	228
500	715
1000	1125

Fig. 1. Encoding 1 byte at a time

As we can see from Figure 1, the size of the output file is linear with respect to the size of the cover image because we are processing the hidden message one byte at a time.

By combining LCS to SPS, the size of the output file can be reduced approximately by a factor of 20.

We applied this method to 24-bit JPEG, and BMP images.

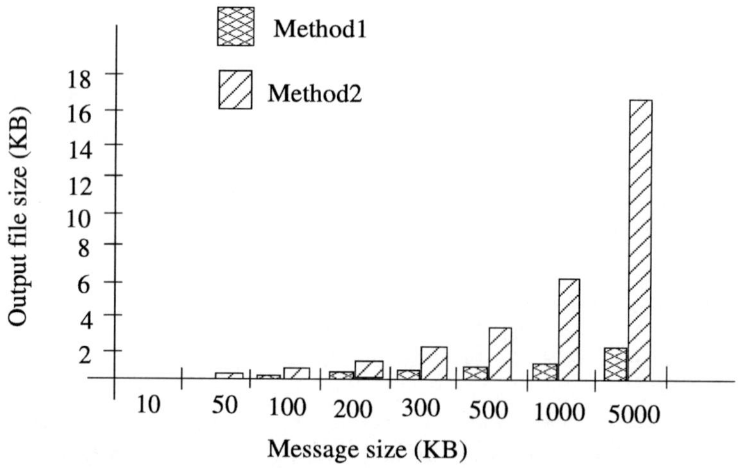

Fig. 2. Comparison between both encoding methods.

We show in Figure 2 the different sizes of the output files that result after applying both methods on a 256x256 JPEG image.

In Figure 2, Method2 refers to the process of encoding 1 byte at a time, and Method1 refers to our newly designed and implemented method. Obviously, Method1 is much more efficient than Method2, and produces an output file much smaller than the one produced by Method2.

It is clear that Method1 results in the generation of an output file that is much more larger than the one generated by Method2 (i.e. the one that uses LCS as a subroutine). On the other hand, it is easy to check that (in practice) Method1 runs in linear time since we compare 1 byte of the secret message to the bytes of the cover image, if we assume that the latter is big enough compared to the secret message to be sent.

6 Conclusion

We presented in this paper a new steganographic technique that allows us to hide a secret message without modifying the cover object. Indeed, Static Parsing Steganography searches for the locations sequences of bits of the secret message that appear in the cover image and saves their locations in an outpt file. The latter is then sent to the receiver who is assumed to share the cover image with the sender. Static Parsing Steganography uses the longest common substring (LCS) problem to find the largest occurrence of bits of the secret message within the cover image. Furthermore, SPS makes use of a divide-and-conquer strategy to hide the secret message. We also showed in this paper that the running time of SPS is $\Theta(n\, logn)$. The main advantage of SPS is the reduced size of the output file, compared for example with the version of SPS that does not use LCS as a subroutine, but instead encodes one byte of the secret message at a time.

References

1. Cachin, C.: An information-theoretic model for steganography. In: Aucsmith, D. (ed.) IH 1998. LNCS, vol. 1525, pp. 306–318. Springer, Heidelberg (1998)
2. Cormen, Leiserson, Rivest, Stein.: Introduction to algorithms, 2nd edn. The MIT press, Cambridge (2001)
3. Dunbar, B.: A detailed look at steganographic techniques and their use in an open-systems environment. Sans InfoSec Reading Room (2002)
4. Fridrich, J., Pevný, T., Kodovský, J.: Statistically undetectable jpeg steganography: dead ends challenges, and opportunities. In: Proceedings of the 9th Workshop on Multimedia & Security, pp. 3–14. ACM, New York (2007)
5. Gusfield, D.: Algorithms on strings, trees, and sequences. Cambridge university press, Cambridge (1997)
6. Huaiqing, W., Wang, S.: Cyber warfare: Steganography vs. steganalysis. Communications of the ACM 47(10), 76–82 (2004)
7. Fridrich, M.G.J.: Practical steganalysis of digital images - state of the art. Security and Watermarking of Multimedia Contents IV 4675, 1–13 (2002)

8. Johnson, N., Jajodia, S.: Steganalysis of images created using current steganography software. In: Workshop on Information Hiding (1998)
9. Johnson, N., Jajodia, S.: Steganalysis: The investigation of hidden information. In: Proc. of the 1998 IEEE Information Technology Conference (1998)
10. Katzenbeisser, Petitcolas: Information hiding: Techniques for steganography and watermarking. Artech House, Boston (2000)
11. Ker, A.D.: A fusion of maximum likelihood and structural steganalysis. In: Furon, T., Cayre, F., Doërr, G., Bas, P. (eds.) IH 2007. LNCS, vol. 4567, pp. 204–219. Springer, Heidelberg (2008)
12. Krenn, R.: Steganography and steganalysis. Whitepaper (2004)
13. Lee, K., Westfeld, A., Lee, S.: Generalised category attack—improving histogram-based attack on JPEG LSB embedding. In: Furon, T., Cayre, F., Doërr, G., Bas, P. (eds.) IH 2007. LNCS, vol. 4567, pp. 378–391. Springer, Heidelberg (2008)
14. Lin, E.T., Delp, E.J.: A review of data hiding in digital images. In: Proceedings of the Image Processing, Image Quality, Image Capture Systems Conference (1999)
15. Shirali-Shahreza, M., Shirali-Shahreza, S.: Collage steganography. In: Proceedings of the 5th IEEE/ACIS International Conference on Computer and Information Science (ICIS 2006), Honolulu, HI, USA, pp. 316–321 (July 2006)
16. Upham, D.: Steganographic algorithm JSteg, `http://zooid.org/paul/crypto/jsteg`
17. Westfeld, A., Pfitzmann, A.: Attacks on steganographic systems. In: Pfitzmann, A. (ed.) IH 1999. LNCS, vol. 1768, pp. 61–76. Springer, Heidelberg (2000)
18. Yu, X., Wang, Y., Tan, T.: On estimation of secret message length in jsteg-like steganography. In: Proceedings of the Pattern Recognition, 17th International Conference on (ICPR 2004), pp. 673–676. IEEE Computer Society, Los Alamitos (2000)
19. Zahedi Kermani, M.J.Z.: A robust steganography algorithm based on texture similarity using gabor filter. In: IEEE 5th International Symposium on Signal Processing and Information Technology (2005)
20. Zhang, T., Ping, X.: A fast and effective steganalytic technique against jsteg-like algorithms. In: SAC 2003, pp. 307–311. ACM, New York (2003)

Dealing with Stateful Firewall Checking

Nihel Ben Youssef and Adel Bouhoula

Higher School of Communication of Tunis(Sup'Com)
University of Carthage, Tunisia
{nihel.benyoussef,adel.bouhoula}@supcom.rnu.tn

Abstract. A drawback of stateless firewalls is that they have no memory of previous packets which makes them vulnerable to specific attacks . A stateful firewall is connection-aware, offering finer-grained control of network traffic. Unfortunately, configuring stateful firewalls is highly error prone. That is due to the potentially large number of entangled filtering rules, besides the difficulty for the administrator to apprehend the stateful filtering notions. In this paper, we propose the first formal and automatic method to check whether a stateful firewall reacts correctly according to a security policy given in an high level declarative language. When errors are detected, some feedback is returned to the user in order to correct the firewall configuration. We show that our method is both correct and complete. Finally, it has been implemented in a prototype of verifier based on a satisfiability solver modulo theories (SMT). The results obtained are very promising..

1 Introduction

Firewalls are among the most commonly used mechanisms for improving the security of enterprise networks. A network firewall resides on a network node (host or Router). Its role is to inspect all the forwarding traffic. Based on its configuration, the firewall makes a decision regarding what action (accept or deny) to perform on a given packet. The firewall configuration is composed by a set of ordered rules. Each rule consists on conditions and an action. A firewall is stateless if the rule's conditions are based on header information in a packet such as source address, destination address, protocol, source port and destination port. In such case, the firewall treats each packet in isolation. A firewall is stateful if it decides the fate of a packet not only by examining its header information but also the packets that the firewall has accepted previously. The stateful packet inspection is deployed by modern firewall products, such as Cisco PIX Firewalls [14], CheckPoint FireWall-1 [12] and Netfilter/IPTables [9]. Its main advantage is to avoid security holes that could result from stateless filtering and specially caused by spoofing attacks. The following example illustrates threats generated by stateless Netfilter/IPTables rules:

```
r1. iptables -A forward -s 192.168.0.0/16 -d 10.1.1.1 -p tcp - -dport 80 -A accept
r2. iptables -A forward -s 10.1.1.1 -d 192.168.0.0/16 -p tcp - -sport 80 -A accept
```

The rules above allow the access of machines in the private network *192.168.2.0/24* to the web server *10.1.1.1*.

H. Cherifi, J.M. Zain, and E. El-Qawasmeh (Eds.): DICTAP 2011, Part I, CCIS 166, pp. 493–507, 2011.

As shown in figure 1, a hacker can spoof the web server address and forge malicious packets, intended to sensitive private machines, and having as source port *80*. The firewall will accept it by applying the second filtering rule. To patch up such vulnerability, the stateful version of our example consists on allowing only the legal web traffic initiated from the private network. The firewall keeps track of the state of the web connection traveling across it. Only packets matching a known connection state will be allowed; others will be rejected. Stateful packet inspection is presented in details in section 2.

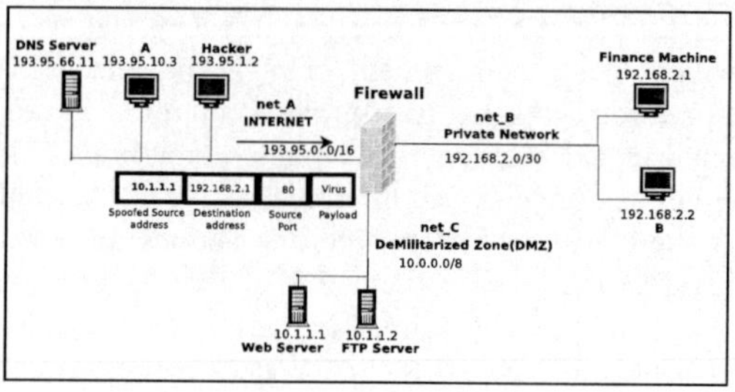

Fig. 1. A stateless Firewall Vulnerability

Although a variety of stateful firewall products have been available and deployed on the Internet for some time , most firewalls are plagued with policy errors. A finding confirmed by the study undertaken by Wool[17]. We can distinguish mainly two reasons: First, the difficulty for an administrator to familiarize with the stateful filtering notions and second, the existence of configuration constraints. The main constraint is that the filtering rules of a firewall configuration FC file are treated in the order in which they are read in the configuration file, in a *switch-case* fashion.

For instance, if two filtering rules associate different actions to the same flow type, then only rule with the lower order is really applied. This is in contrast with the security policy SP, which is a set of rules considered without order. In this case, the action taken, for the flow under consideration, can be the one of the non executed rule. For example, let insert the following rule at the top of the previous configuration:

```
r1. iptables -A forward -s 192.168.2.0/24 -d 10.0.0.0/8 -A deny
r2. iptables -A forward -s 192.168.0.0/16 -d 10.1.1.1 -p tcp - -dport 80 -A accept
r3. iptables -A forward -s 10.1.1.1 -d 192.168.0.0/16 -p tcp - -sport 80 -A accept
```

The first rule is configured to deny all the outbound traffic coming from the sub-network 192.168.2.0/24 to the demilitarized zone. Hence, if Finance machine attempts to reach the web server, it will be blocked by applying the first matching rule r_1 and this is in contrast with the security policy we aim to establish. As stated by Chapman [20], safely configuring firewall rules has never been an easy task. Since, firewall configurations are low-level files, subject to special configuration constraints in order to ensure an efficient real time processing by specific devices. Whereas, the security policy SP , used to express global security requirements, is generally specified in high-level declarative language easy to understand. Hence, this make verifying the conformance of a firewall configuration F C to a security policy SP a daunting task. Particularly, when it is to analyze the impact of the inter-actions of a large number of rules on the behavior of a firewall.

Benefiting from the well-established rule based model of stateless firewalls, the research results for such firewalls have been numerous. Several methods have been proposed [16,4,1,2,25,22] for the detection of inter-rule conflicts in FC. These work are limited to the problem conflict avoidance, and do not consider the more general problem of verifying whether a stateless firewall reacts correctly with respect to a given SP. Solutions are studied in [8,18,24,15] for the analysis of stateless firewalls' behavior. These methods require some final user interactions by sending queries through a verification tool. Such manual solutions can be tedious when checking discrepancies with respect to complicated security requirements. In [6],[13] and [11] the authors address the problem of automatic verification by providing automatic translation tool of the security requirements (SP), specified in a high level language, into a set of ordered stateless filtering rules (i.e. a FC). Therefore, these methods can handle the whole problem of conformance of FC to SP, but the validity of the compilation itself has not been proved. In particular, the FC rules obtained may be in conflict. In other part, some researches, such as [5] and [10], have proposed to present a model for stateful filtering engines. But the question: *how to check whether stateful firewalls are correctly configured with respect to a given security policy* remains unanswered. Although, the study conducted in [3] proposes a black-box test of configured stateful firewalls, only the analyze of the FTP protocol's sessions is elaborated and the output is limited to the generation of counter-examples. That should give idea about the firewall's behavior. But, no information are given about the rule(s) causing the discovered discrepancies.

In this paper, we propose an automatic and generic method for checking whether a stateful firewall is well configured with respect to a security policy, given in an expressive enough declarative language. Furthermore, the proposed method ensures conflicts avoidance within the SP that we aim to establish and returns key elements for the correction of a flawed FC. Our method has been implemented as a prototype which can be used either in order to validate an existing stateful FC ($\mathbf{S}\_FC$) with respect to a given

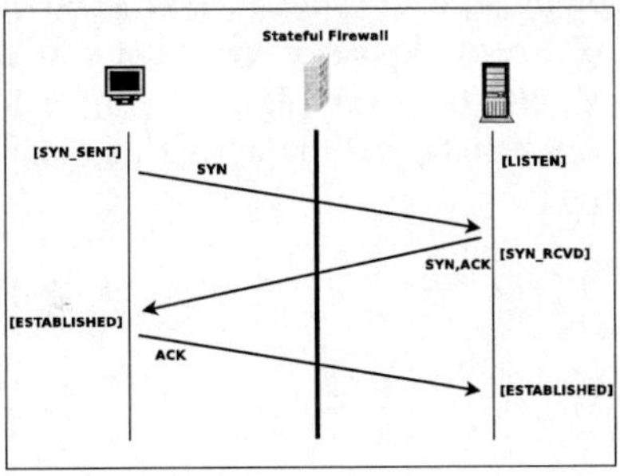

Fig. 2. Tracking the TCP Protocol

SP or downstream of a compiler of SP. It can also be used in order to assist the updates of FC, since some conflicts may be created by the addition or deletion of filtering rules.

The remainder of this paper is organized as follows. In Section 2, we introduce the stateful Packet Inspection. Section 3 settles the definition of the problems addressed in the paper, in particular the properties of soundness and completeness of a **S**_FC with respect to a SP. In Section 4, we present an inference system introducing the proposed method and prove its correctness and completeness. Finally, in Section 5, we show some experiments on a case study.

2 Stateful Packet Inspection

Connection-tracking is the basis of stateful firewalls. It refers to the ability to maintain state information about a connection as an entry in a state table. Every entry holds a laundry list of information that uniquely identifies the communication session it represents. Such information might include source and destination IP address information, flags, sequence and acknowledgment numbers, and more. Entries are inserted in and removed from the state table according to the packets the firewall is examining. In this case, connection related fields like connection states ('new','established','related') are checked. These states vary greatly depending on application/protocol used.

2.1 TCP Protocol

Web application (HTTP), for instance, uses TCP as a transport layer. TCP is a connection-oriented protocol. the state of its communication sessions can be solidly defined. TCP tracks the state of its connections with flags. Figure 2 illustrates the TCP three-way handshake connection establishment. The connection stage LISTEN is occurred when a host is waiting for a request to start a connection. A host is in the stage SYN-SENT when it has sent out a SYN packet and is waiting for the proper SYN-ACK reply. SYN-RCVD is the stage when a host has received a SYN packet and is replying with its SYN-ACK reply. Finally, ESTABLISHED is the state a connection is in after its necessary ACK packet has been received.The initiating host goes into this state after receiving a SYN-ACK, as the responding host does after receiving the lone ACK.

Various firewall products handle the tracking of state in many different ways. Netfilter/Iptables is a among popular firewall products. When a connection is begun using a tracked protocol, Netfilter/IPTables adds a state table entry for the connection in question.

For example, let we deal with the example given in section 1. The security policy states that the private network has the right to access the web server. The Stateful Iptables rules should be as follows:

```
r1. iptables -A forward -s 192.168.0.0/16 -d 10.1.1.1 -p tcp - -dport 80 -m state
--state NEW,ESTABLISHED -A accept
r2. iptables -A forward -s 10.1.1.1 -d 192.168.0.0/16 -p tcp - -sport 80 -m state
--state ESTABLISHED -A accept
```

Once a syn packet that initiates a TCP connection is sent from the pivate network and accepted by the first rule above that allows a NEW connection, the following connection table entry is created:

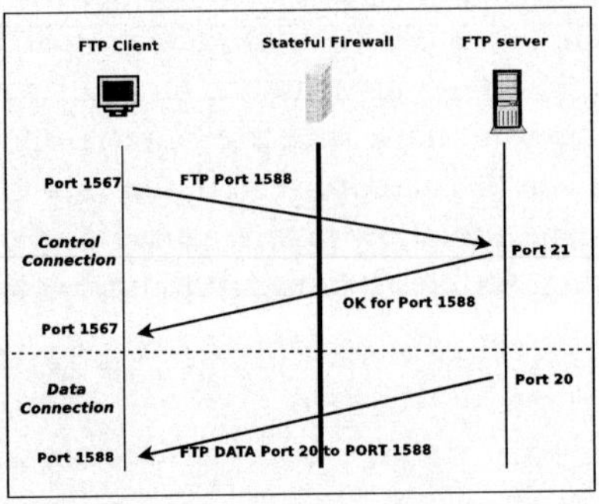

Fig. 3. Tracking the FTP Protocol

```
tcp 6 50 SYN_SENT src=192.168.2.1 dst=10.1.1.1 sport=1506 dport=22 [UNREPLIED]
src=10.1.1.1 dst=192.168.2.1 sport=80 dport=1506 use=1
```

When a syn-ack packet arrives, the firewall accepts it by applying the second rule and the entry in the connection tracking table is modified as follows:

```
tcp 6 65 SYN_RCVD src=192.168.2.1 dst=10.1.1.1 sport=1506 dport=22 src=10.1.1.1
dst=192.168.2.1 sport=80 dport=1506 use=1
```

One can see that the TCP connection state changes to SYN-RCVD, while the tracked connection-state changes from NEW to ESTABLISHED. We note that the tracked connection states (NEW, ESTABLISHED, etc.) are different from the TCP connection establishment states (SYN-SENT, SYN-RCVD, etc.). Finally, when the last part of the three-way TCP connection establishment handshake, an ack packet arrives from the client, the first rule accepts it as ESTABLISHED state. The connection-tracking entry becomes:

```
tcp 6 41 ESTABLISHED src=192.168.2.1 dst=10.1.1.1 sport=1506 dport=22 [ASSURED]
src=10.1.1.1 dst=192.168.2.1 sport=80 dport=1506 use=1
```

The TCP state of the connection is altered to ESTABLISHED and the connection-tracking state of the connection is modified to ASSURED.
For a stateful firewall to be able to truly facilitate all types of TCP connections, it must have some knowledge of the application protocols being run, especially those that behave in nonstandard ways. File Transfer Protocol (FTP) [23] is an application protocol that is used to transfer files between two hosts by using TCP protocol. However, standard FTP uses an atypical communication exchange when initializing its data channel. The states of the two individual TCP connections that make up an FTP session can be tracked in the normal fashion. However, the state of the FTP connection obeys different rules.

When a client wants to connect to a remote FTP server, the client sends a request to connect to the server on the well-known port 21. This first step is called the control connection. After that, the client sends to the server a PORT command to specify the port number that he will use for the data connection. After this PORT command is received, the server uses its well-known port 20 to connect back to this new port. This connection is called the data connection. This process is illustrated in figure 3. We should note that multimedia protocols, such as H.323, Real Time Streaming Protocol (RTSP), work similarly to FTP through a stateful firewall with more connections and complexity. Specific filtering rules have to be created to inspect the control connection and its *related* traffic. This can be accomplished in the case of FTP by adding the state option RELATED. For instance, to allow private network in figure 1 to access the FTP server *10.1.1.2*, the following Netfilter/Iptables rules are necessary:

```
r1. iptables -A forward -s 192.168.0.0/16 -d 10.1.1.2 -p tcp - -dport 21 -m state
--state NEW,ESTABLISHED,RELATED -A accept
r2. iptables -A forward -s 10.1.1.2 -d 192.168.0.0/16 -p tcp - -sport 21 -m state
--state ESTABLISHED,RELATED -A accept
```

2.2 UDP Protocol

Unlike TCP, UDP (User Datagram Protocol) is a connectionless transport protocol. a stateful firewall must track a UDP connection in a pseudo-stateful manner, keeping track of items specific to its connection only. Because UDP has no sequence numbers or flags, the only items on which we can base a sessions state are the IP addressing and port numbers used by the source and destination hosts.
DNS(Domain Name System) is a system used to translate domain names meaningful to humans into the numerical identifiers associated with networking equipment for the purpose of locating and addressing these devices worldwide. DNS primarily uses User Datagram Protocol (UDP) on port number 53 to serve requests. For instance, to allow private network in figure 1 to access the DNS server *193.95.66.11*, the following Netfilter/Iptables rules are necessary:

```
r1. iptables -A forward -s 192.168.0.0/16 -d 193.95.66.11 -p udp - -dport 53 -m state
--state NEW,ESTABLISHED -A accept
r2. iptables -A forward -s 193.95.66.11 -d 192.168.0.0/16 -p udp - -sport 53 -m state
--state ESTABLISHED -A accept
```

2.3 ICMP Protocol

ICMP(Internet Control Message Protocol), like UDP, really is not a stateful protocol. However, like UDP, it also has attributes that allow its connections to be pseudo-statefully tracked. ICMP is often used in a request/reply-type usage.The most popular example of an application that uses this request/reply form is ping (Packet Internet Groper Protocol) [19]. It sends echo requests and receives echo reply messages which might be an easy-track way. ICMP is also used to return error messages when a host or protocol can not do so on its own, in what can be described as a response message. ICMP response-type messages are precipitated by requests by other protocols (TCP, UDP). For example, if during a UDP communication session a host can no longer keep up with the speed at which it is receiving packets, UDP offers no method of letting the other party know to slow down transmission. However, the receiving host can send an ICMP source quench message to let the sending host know to slow down transmission of packets. However, if the firewall blocks this message because it is not part of the normal UDP session, the host that is sending packets too quickly does not know that an issue has come up, and it continues to send at the same speed, resulting in lost packets at the receiving host. Stateful firewalls must consider such *related* traffic when deciding what traffic should be returned to protected hosts. For the above example in section 2.2 , the following Netfilter/Iptables rule should be inserted:

```
r3. iptables -A forward -s 193.95.66.11 -d 192.168.2.0/24 -p icmp -m state
--state RELATED -A accept
```

3 Formal Properties

The main goal of this work consists in checking whether a stateful firewall is well configured. As stated previously, stateful rules should be themselves conform to the application'behavior and should be configured correctly by respecting the order constraint in filtering rules. In other terms, we propose a formal method to verify that the stateful firewall configuration **S_**FC is sound and complete with respect to a given SP. In this section, we define formally these notions.

We consider a finite *domain* $\mathcal{P}$ containing all the headers of packets possibly incoming to or outgoing from a network.

A *stateful firewall configuration* (**S_**FC) is a finite sequence of *filtering rules* of the form **S_**$FC = (r_i \Rightarrow A_i)_{0 \leq i < n}$. Each precondition r_i of a rule defines a filter for packets of $\mathcal{P}$. Each r_i is made of the following main fields: the source, the destination, the protocol, the port and the state. The source and destination fields correspond to one or more machines identified by an IPv4 address and a mask coded both on 4 bytes. The protocol is either `TCP`, `UDP` or `ICMP`. The port field is a number coded on 2 bytes and the state field is either `NEW`, `ESTABLISHED` or `RELATED` for the case of Netfilter/Iptables. These values vary with the vendors definitions of stateful filtering/stateful inspection. Until the next section, we just consider a function dom mapping each r_i into the subset of $\mathcal{P}$ of filtered packets. Each right member A_i of a rule of **S_**FC is an *action* defining the behaviour of the firewall on filtered packets: $A_i \in \{accept, deny\}$. This model describes a generic form of **S_**FCwhich are used by most firewall products such as CISCO, *Access Control List*, stateless `IPTABLES`, `IPCHAINS` and *Check Point Firewall...*

A *security policy* (SP) is a set SP of formula defining whether packets are accepted or denied.

In Section 4, we only consider the definition domain of SP, partitioned into $dom(SP) = \bigcup_{A \in \{accept, deny\}} SP_A$.

SP is called *consistent* if $SP_{accept} \cap SP_{deny} = \emptyset$.

A **S_**FC is *sound* with respect to a SP if the action undertaken by the firewall for each forwarding packet, (i.e. the action of the first filtering rule matching the packet) is the same as the one defined by the SP.

Definition 1 (soundness). **S_**FC *is sound with respect to* SP *iff for all* $p \in \mathcal{P}$, *if there exists a rule* $r_i \Rightarrow A_i$ *in* **S_**FC *such that* $p \in dom(r_i)$ *and for all* $j < i$, $p \notin dom(r_j)$ *then* $p \in SP_{A_i}$.

$$\text{recurcall}\ \frac{((r \Rightarrow A), \mathbf{S}\_FC), D}{\mathbf{S}\_FC, D \cup dom(r)} \quad \text{if } dom(r) \setminus D \subseteq SP_A$$

$$\text{success}\ \frac{\emptyset, D}{\text{success}} \quad \text{if } D \supseteq dom(SP)$$

$$\text{failure}\ \frac{\mathbf{S}\_FC, D}{\text{fail}(fst(\mathbf{S}\_FC), D)} \quad \text{if no other rule applies}$$

Fig. 4. Inference System

A $\mathbf{S}\_FC$ is *complete* with respect to a SP if the action defined by the SP for each packet p is really undertaken by the firewall.

Definition 2 (completeness). $\mathbf{S}\_FC$ *is complete with respect to* SP *iff for all* $p \in \mathcal{P}$ *and* $A \in \{accept, deny\}$*, if* $p \in SP_A$ *then there exists a rule* $r_i \Rightarrow A$ *in* $\mathbf{S}\_FC$ *such that* $p \in dom(r_i) \setminus \bigcup_{j<i} dom(r_j)$.

4 Proposed Method

We propose in this section necessary and sufficient conditions for the simultaneous verification of the properties of soundness and completeness of a $\mathbf{S}\_FC$ with respect to a SP. The conditions are presented in an inference system shown in Figure 4. The rules of the system in Figure 4 apply to couples $(\mathbf{S}\_FC, D)$ whose first component $\mathbf{S}\_FC$ is a sequence of filtering rules and whose second component D is a subset of $\mathcal{P}$. This latter subset represents the accumulation of the sets of packets filtered by the rules of $\mathbf{S}\_FC$ processed so far.

We write $C \vdash_{SP} C'$ is C' is obtained from C by application of one of the inference rules of Figure 4 (note that C' may be a couple as above or one of success or fail) and we denote by $\vdash^*_{SP}$ the reflexive and transitive closure of $\vdash_{SP}$.

The main inference rule is recurcall . It deals with the first filtering rule $r \Rightarrow A$ of the $\mathbf{S}_FC$given in the couple. The condition for the application of recurcall is that the set of packets $dom(r)$ filtered by this rule and not handled by the previous rules (i.e. not in D) would follow the same action A as defined by the the security policy.

Hence, successful repeated applications of recurcall ensures the soundness of the $\mathbf{S}_FC$with respect to the SP.

The success rule is applied under two conditions. First, recurcall must have been used successfully until all filtering rules have been processed (in this case the first component $\mathbf{S}\_FC$ of the couple is empty). Second, the global domain of the security policy must be included in D. This latter condition ensures that all the packets treated by the security policy are also handled by the firewall configuration (completeness of $\mathbf{S}\_FC$).

There are two cases for the application of failure. In the first case, failure is applied to a couple $(\mathbf{S}\_FC, D)$ where $\mathbf{S}\_FC$ is not empty. It means that recurcall has failed on this couple and hence that the $\mathbf{S}_FC$is not sound with respect to the SP. In this case, failure returns the first filtering rule of $\mathbf{S\_}FC$ as a example of rule which is not correct, in order to provide help to the user in order to correct the $\mathbf{S\_}FC$. In the second case, failure is applied to $(\emptyset, D)$. It means that success has failed on this couple and that the $\mathbf{S_}FC$is not complete with respect to the SP. In this case, D is returned and can be used in order to identify packets handled by the SP and not by the $\mathbf{S\_}FC$.

Let us now prove that the inference system of Figure 4 is correct and complete. From now on, we assume given a $\mathbf{S\_}FC = r_0 \Rightarrow A_0, \ldots, r_{n-1} \Rightarrow A_{n-1}$ with $n > 0$.

In the correctness theorem below, we assume that SP is consistent. In our previous work [21], we present a method for checking this property.

Theorem 1 (correctness). *Assume that the security policy SP is consistent. If $(\mathbf{S\_}FC, \emptyset) \vdash^*_{SP}$ success then the firewall configuration $\mathbf{S\_}FC$ is sound and complete with respect to SP.*

Proof. $If(\mathbf{S\_}FC, \emptyset) \vdash^*_{SP}$ success then we have $(\mathbf{S\_}FC, \emptyset) \vdash_{SP} (\mathbf{S\_}FC_1, D_1) \vdash_{SP} \ldots \vdash_{SP} (\mathbf{S\_}FC_n, D_n) \vdash_{SP}$ success, where $\mathbf{S\_}FC_n = \emptyset$, all the steps but the last one are recurcall and $dom(SP) \subseteq D_n$. We can easily show by induction on i that for all $1 \leq i \leq n$, $D_i = \bigcup_{j<i} dom(r_j)$. Let $D_0 = \emptyset$.

Assume that there exists $p \in \mathcal{P}$ and $r_i \Rightarrow A_i$ in $\mathbf{S\_}FC$ $(i < n)$ such that $p \in dom(r_i) \setminus \bigcup_{j<i} dom(r_j)$.

It follows that $p \in dom(r_i) \setminus D_i$, and, by the condition of recurcall that $p \in SP_{A_i}$. Hence $\mathbf{S\_}FC$ is sound with respect to SP. g condition is true:$\forall r_i \Rightarrow A'$, $dom(r_i) - \cup_{j<i} dom(r_j) \subseteq SP_{A'}$.

Let $A \in \{accept, deny\}$ and $p \in SP_A$. By the condition of the inference rule success, $p \in D_n = \bigcup_{j<i} dom(r_j)$. Let i be the smallest integer k such that $p \in dom(r_k)$. It means that $p \in dom(r_i) \setminus \bigcup_{j<i} dom(r_j)$. As above, it follows that $p \in SP_{A_i}$, and hence that $A_i = A$, by the hypothesis that SP is consistent. Therefore, $\mathbf{S\_}FC$ is complete with respect to SP.

Theorem 2 (completeness). *If the firewall configuration $\mathbf{S\_}FC$ is sound and complete with respect to the security policy SP then $(\mathbf{S\_}FC, \emptyset) \vdash^*_{SP}$ success.*

Proof. Assume that $\mathbf{S\_}FC$ it is sound and complete with respect to SP. The soundness implies that for all $i < n$ and all packet $p \in dom(r_i) \setminus \bigcup_{j<i} dom(r_j)$, $p \in SP_{A_i}$.

It follows that $(\mathbf{S\_}FC, \emptyset) \vdash_{SP} (\mathbf{S\_}FC_1, D_1) \vdash_{SP} \ldots \vdash_{SP} (\mathbf{S\_}FC_n, D_n)$ with $D_i = \bigcup_{j<i} dom(r_j)$ for all $i \leq n$ and $\mathbf{S\_}FC_n = \emptyset$, by application of the inference recurcall. Moreover, the completeness of $\mathbf{S\_}FC$ implies that every $p \in dom(SP)$ also belongs to D_n. Hence $(\mathbf{S\_}FC_n, D_n) \vdash_{SP}$ success, and altogether $(\mathbf{S\_}FC, \emptyset) \vdash^*_{SP}$ success.

Theorem 3 (soundness of failure). *If $(\mathbf{S\_}FC, \emptyset) \vdash^*_{SP}$ fail then the firewall configuration $\mathbf{S\_}FC$ is not sound or not complete with respect to the security policy SP.*

Proof. Either we can apply iteratively the recurcall rule starting with $(\mathbf{S\_}FC, \emptyset)$, until we obtain $(\emptyset, \bigcup_{j<n} dom(r_j))$, or one application of the recurcall rule fails. In the latter case, there exists $i < n$ such that $dom(r_i) \setminus \bigcup_{j<i} dom(r_j) \not\subseteq SP_{A_i}$. Therefore, there exists $p \in \mathcal{P}$ such that $p \in dom(r_i) \setminus \bigcup_{j<i} dom(r_j)$ and $p \notin SP_{A_i}$. It follows that $\mathbf{S\_}FC$ is not sound with respect to the security policy SP.

If $(\mathbf{S\_}FC, \emptyset) \vdash^*_{SP} (\emptyset, \bigcup_{j<n} dom(r_j))$ using recurcall but the application of the success rule to the last couple fails, then there exists $A \in \{accept, deny\}$ and $p \in SP_A$ such that $p \notin \bigcup_{j<n} dom(r_j)$. It follows that $\mathbf{S\_}FC$ is not complete with respect to the security policy SP.

Since the application of the inferences to $(SP, \emptyset)$ always terminates, and the outcome can only be success or fail, it follows immediately from the Theorem 1 that if the firewall configuration $\mathbf{S\_}FC$ is not sound or not complete with respect to the security policy SP, then $(\mathbf{S\_}FC, \emptyset) \vdash^*_{SP}$ fail (completeness of failure).

To summarize the above results, we have the following sufficient and necessary conditions for

Soundness: $\forall i < n, dom(r_i) \setminus \bigcup_{j<i} dom(r_j) \subseteq SP_{A_i}$,

Completeness: soundness and $dom(SP) \subseteq \bigcup_{i<n} dom(r_i)$.

Table 1. Stateful Firewall Configuration to be Verified

	src_adr	*dst_adr*	*src_port*	*dst_port*	*protocol*	*state*	*action*
r_1	193.95.66.11	192.168.2.0/30	53	*	udp	Established	accept
r_2	10.1.1.1	192.168.2.2	80	*	tcp	New	accept
r_3	192.168.2.0/31	193.95.66.11	*	53	udp	New, Established	accept
r_4	10.1.1.1	192.168.2.2	80	*	tcp	Established	accept
r_5	193.95.0.0/16	10.1.1.2	*	21	tcp	New, Established, Related	accept
r_6	192.168.2.2	10.1.1.1	*	80	tcp	New, Established	accept
r_7	192.168.2.0/30	10.0.0.0/8	*	*	*	*	deny
r_8	10.1.1.2	193.95.0.0/16	21	*	tcp	Established, Related	accept

5 Automatic Verification Tool

In this section, we present the automation of the verification of soundness and completeness of a $\mathbf{S\_}FC$ with respect to a SP. For this purpose, we have used Yices [7], as a recent SMT(Satisfiability modulo theories) solver which permits to implement the inputs and to solve the satisfiability of formulas, corresponding to the conditions in section 4, in theories such as arrays, scalar types, lamda expressions and more. The first input of our verification tool is a set of stateful firewall rules. Each rule is defined by a priority order and made of the following main fields: the source, the destination, the protocol, the state and the port. In order to illustrate the verification procedure proposed, we have chosen to apply our method to a case study of a corporate network shown in Figure 1. The network is divided into three zones delineated by branches of a firewall whose initial configuration $\mathbf{S\_}FC$ corresponds to the rules in Table 1.

The **Security Policy SP** that should be respected contains the following directives.

sp_1 : `net_B` has not the right to access to `net_C`, except the machine `B` that has only the right to access to the `WEB server`.
sp_2 : `net_B` has the right to access to the `DNS server`.
sp_3 : `net_A`, except the machine `A`, has the right to access to the `FTP server`.

```
root@nihel:/home/nihel/Desktop/yices-1.0.21/bin# ./yices -e soundness.ys

 loading security policy....
 loading firewall rules....
sat
(= ips1 10)
(= ips2 1)
(= ips3 1)
(= ipd1 192)
(= protocol tcp)
(= state new)
(= ips4 1)
(= ipd2 168)
(= ipd3 2)
(= ipd4 2)
(= sport 80)
(= dport 193)
(= (sp 11) false)
(= (sp 12) true)
(= (sp' 11) false)
(= (sp' 12) false)
(= (sp 21) false)
(= (sp 22) false)
(= (sp 23) false)
(= (sp' 21) false)
(= (sp 31) false)
(= (sp 32) false)
(= (sp' 31) false)
(= (sp' 32) false)
(= (r 1) false)
(= (r 2) true)
(= (r 3) false)
```

Fig. 5. Soundness verification

Bellow, we note that sp_{ij} and sp'_{ij} respectively the conditions and the exceptions of the policy directive sp_i. In our case, a **stateful** firewall configuration should consider that, for instance,

$\mathbf{sp_{11}}$: **The traffic from** `net_B` **to** `net_C` **is denied.**
$\mathbf{sp_{12}}$: **The** `WEB server` **should not initiate the connection with** `net_B`.
$\mathbf{sp'_{11}}$: **The machine** `B` **has the right to initiate the connection to the** `WEB server`.
$\mathbf{sp'_{12}}$: **The** `WEB server` **has the right to accept the connection initiated by the machine** `B`.

Our goal is to verify that the configuration $\mathbf{S}\_FC$ of Table 1 is conform to the security policy SP by checking the soundness and the completeness properties.

5.1 Soundness Verification

We proceed to the verification of the firewall configuration soundness. The satisfiability result obtained is displayed in Figure 5.

The outcome shows that the firewall configuration $\mathbf{S}\_FC$ is not sound with respect to the security policy SP, i.e. that there exists some packets that will undergo an action different of that imposed by the security policy. It indicates also that r_2 is the first rule that causes this discrepancy precisely with the directive sp_{12}. Indeed, the model returned corresponds to a packet accepted by the firewall through the rule r_2 while it should be refused according to the first directive of the security policy. As stated in section 1, such packet should be denied to avoid spoofing attacks: An external machine can spoof the ip address 10.1.1.1 and send a malicious packet to the machine 192.168.2.2, the firewall will accept it through r_2. However, this is prohibited by our security policy and our tool mentions it.

This conflict can be resolved by altering the action of the rule r_2.

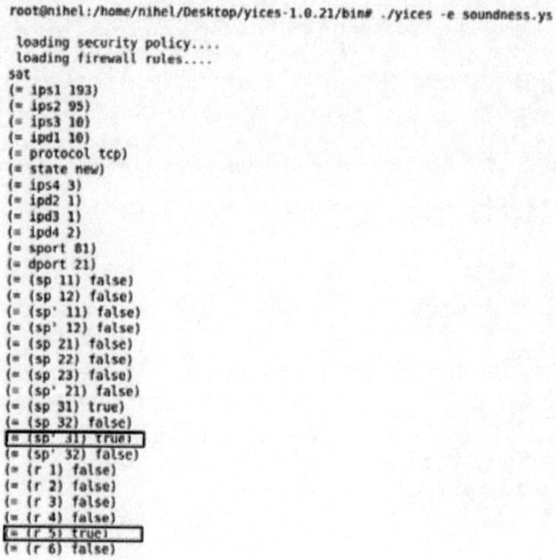

```
root@nihel:/home/nihel/Desktop/yices-1.0.21/bin# ./yices -e soundness.ys

 loading security policy....
 loading firewall rules....
sat
(= ips1 193)
(= ips2 95)
(= ips3 10)
(= ipd1 10)
(= protocol tcp)
(= state new)
(= ips4 3)
(= ipd2 1)
(= ipd3 1)
(= ipd4 2)
(= sport 81)
(= dport 21)
(= (sp 11) false)
(= (sp 12) false)
(= (sp' 11) false)
(= (sp' 12) false)
(= (sp 21) false)
(= (sp 22) false)
(= (sp 23) false)
(= (sp' 21) false)
(= (sp 31) true)
(= (sp 32) false)
(= (sp' 31) true)
(= (sp' 32) false)
(= (r 1) false)
(= (r 2) false)
(= (r 3) false)
(= (r 4) false)
(= (r 5) true)
(= (r 6) false)
```

Fig. 6. Second Soundness Check

Table 2. A sound Stateful Firewall Configuration

	src_adr	*dst_adr*	*src_port*	*dst_port*	*protocol*	*state*	*action*
r_1	193.95.66.11	192.168.2.0/30	53	*	udp	Established	accept
r_2	10.1.1.1	192.168.2.2	80	*	tcp	New	deny
r_3	192.168.2.0/31	193.95.66.11	*	53	udp	New, Established	accept
r_4	10.1.1.1	192.168.2.2	80	*	tcp	Established	accept
r_5	193.95.10.3	10.1.1.2	*	21	tcp	New	deny
r_6	193.95.0.0/16	10.1.1.2	*	21	tcp	New, Established, Related	accept
r_7	192.168.2.2	10.1.1.1	*	80	tcp	New, Established	accept
r_8	192.168.2.0/30	10.0.0.0/8	*	*	*	*	deny
r_9	10.1.1.2	193.95.0.0/16	21	*	tcp	Established, Related	accept

Once correcting **S**_FC the soundness check algorithm detects an ultimate flawed rule which is r_5. Figure 6 indicates that r_5 is in conflict with the exception of the security directive sp_3. Indeed, according to sp'_{31}, the machine A (193.95.10.3) has not the right to access to the FTP server (10.1.1.2). However, the effective part of r_5, which is the real set of packets considered by this rule, is accepting this traffic. This conflict can be resolved by adding a rule immediately preceding the rule r_5, which allows to implement correctly the third directive exception indicated by the given model. Table 2 presents the entire modification resulted from our soundness firewall checking.

5.2 Completeness Verification

After the soundness property has been established, we conduct the verification of the completeness of the stateful firewall configuration. We obtained the satisfiability result displayed in Figure 7.

According to this outcome, the configuration **S**_FC is not complete with respect to the security policy SP: some packets handled by the security policy are not treated by

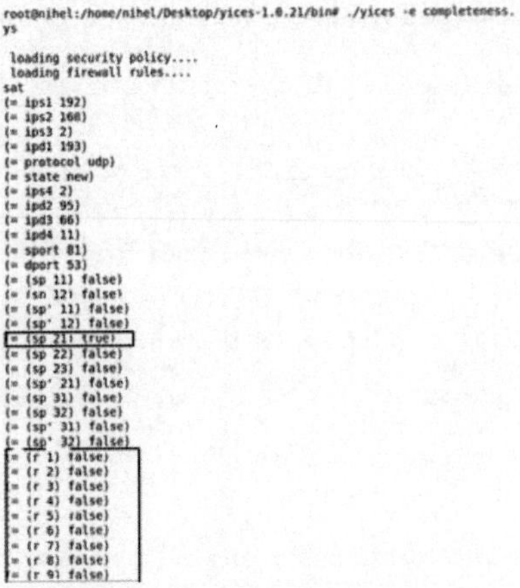

Fig. 7. Completeness verification

the filtering rules. Essentially, the model given in Figure 7 shows that at least one packet considered by the security directive sp_2 is not treated by the firewall configuration. Indeed, the rule r_3 addresses only a subnetwork of `net_B`. The packet corresponding to the model returned belongs to another part of `net_B`, which is untreated. One possible solution would be to change the mask used in the destination address of the rule r_3 to consider all the second directive domain. Once correcting $\mathbf{S}\_FC$, we conduct again the completeness check algorithm. As shown in Figure 8, the security directive sp_2 is not yet completely considered by the firewall configuration. Indeed, the outcome shows that the *related* icmp packets corresponding to the UDP traffic between `net_A` and the `DNS server` is omitted in $\mathbf{S}\_FC$. Our solution is to add the missing rule at the end of the firewall configuration. The sound and complete firewall configuration we obtained is presented in Table 3.

Fig. 8. Second Completeness verification

Table 3. A sound and Complete Stateful Firewall Configuration

	src_adr	*dst_adr*	*src_port*	*dst_port*	*protocol*	*state*	*action*
r_1	193.95.66.11	192.168.2.0/30	53	*	udp	Established	accept
r_2	10.1.1.1	192.168.2.2	80	*	tcp	New	deny
r_3	192.168.2.0/30	193.95.66.11	*	53	udp	New, Established	accept
r_4	10.1.1.1	192.168.2.2	80	*	tcp	Established	accept
r_5	193.95.10.3	10.1.1.2	*	21	tcp	New	deny
r_6	193.95.0.0/16	10.1.1.2	*	21	tcp	New, Established, Related	accept
r_7	192.168.2.2	10.1.1.1	*	80	tcp	New, Established	accept
r_8	192.168.2.0/30	10.0.0.0/8	*	*	*	*	deny
r_9	10.1.1.2	193.95.0.0/16	21	*	tcp	Established, Related	accept
r_{10}	193.95.66.11	192.168.2.0/30	*	*	icmp	related	accept

We note that YICES validates the three properties after the modifications taken in Sections 5.1 and 5.2 by displaying in each case an unsatisfiability result.

6 Conclusion

In this paper, we propose a first formal method for certifying automatically that a stateful firewall configuration is sound and complete with respect to a given security policy. Otherwise, the method provides key information helping users to correct configuration errors. Our formal method is both sound and complete and offers full-coverage of all possible IP packets used in production environments. Finally, our method has been implemented based on a satisfiability solver modulo theories. The experimental results obtained show the efficiency of our approach. As further work, we are currently working on an extension of our new technique to provide automatic resolution of firewall misconfigurations.

References

1. Abbes, T., Bouhoula, A., Rusinowitch, M.: Inference system for detecting firewall filtering rules anomalies. In: Proc. of the 23rd Annual ACM Symp. on Applied Computing (2008)
2. Al-Shaer, E., Hamed, H.: Discovery of policy anomalies in distributed firewalls. IEEE Infocomm (2004)
3. Brucker, A., Wolff, B.: Test-sequence generation with hol-testGen with an application to firewall testing. In: Gurevich, Y., Meyer, B. (eds.) TAP 2007. LNCS, vol. 4454, pp. 149–168. Springer, Heidelberg (2007)
4. Benelbahri, M., Bouhoula, A.: Tuple based approach for anomalies detection within firewall filtering rules. In: 12th IEEE Symp. on Computers and Communications (2007)
5. Gouda, M., Liu, A.X.: A Model of Stateful Firewalls and its Properties. In: Proc. of International Conference on Dependable Systems and Networks, DSN 2005 (2005)
6. Cupens, F., Cuppens-Boulahia, N., Sans, T., Miege, A.: A formal approach to specify and deploy a network security policy. In: Second Workshop on Formal Aspects in Security and Trust, pp. 203–218 (2004)
7. Dutertre, B., Moura, L.: The yices smt solver (2006), `http://yices.csl.sri.com/tool-paper.pdf`

8. Eronen, P., Zitting, J.: An expert system for analyzing firewall rules. In: Proc. of 6th Nordic Workshop on Secure IT Systems (2001)
9. Netfilter/IPTables (2005), `http://www.netfilter.org/`
10. Buttyan, L., Pek, G., Thong, T.: Consistency verification of stateful firewalls is not harder than the stateless case. Proc. of Infocommunications Journal LXIV (2009)
11. Hamdi, H., Mosbah, M., Bouhoula, A.: A domain specific language for securing distributed systems. In: Second Int. Conf. on Systems and Networks Communications (2007)
12. CheckPoint FireWall-1 (March 25, 2005), `http://www.checkpoint.com/`
13. Bartal, Y., Mayer, A.J., Nissim, K., Wool, A.: Firmato: A novel firewall management toolkit. In: IEEE Symposium on Security and Privacy (1999)
14. Cisco PIX Firewalls (March 25, 2005), `http://www.cisco.com/`
15. Lui, A.X., Gouda, M., Ma, H., Ngu, A.: Firewall queries. In: Proc. of the 8th Int. Conf. on Principles of Distributed Systems, pp. 197–212 (2004)
16. Pornavalai, C., Chomsiri, T.: Firewall policy analyzing by relational algebra. In: The 2004 Int. Technical Conf. on Circuits/Systems, Computers and Communications (2004)
17. Wool, A.: A quantitative study of firewall configuration errors. IEEE Computer 37(6) (2004)
18. Mayer, A., Wool, A., Ziskind, E.: Fang: A firewall analysis engine. In: Proc. of the 2000 IEEE Symp. on Security and Privacy, pp. 14–17 (2000)
19. Postel, J.: Internet control message protocol. RFC 792 (1981)
20. Chapman, D.B.: Network (in) security hrough IP packet filtering. In: Proceedings of the Third Usenix Unix Security Symposium, pp. 63–76 (1992)
21. Ben Youssef, N., Bouhoula, A.: Automatic Conformance Verification of Distributed Firewalls to Security Requirements. In: In Proc. of the IEEE Conference on Privacy, Security, Risk and Trust, PASSAT (2010)
22. Alfaro, J.G., Bouhalia-cuppens, N., Cuppens, F.: Complete analysis of configuration rules to guarantee reliable network security policies. In: IEEE Symposium on Security and Privacy (May 2006)
23. Postel, J., Reynolds, J.: File transfer protocol. RFC 959 (1985)
24. Liu, A.X., Gouda, M.: Firewall Policy Queries. Proceeding of IEEE Transactions on Parallel and Distributed Systems (2009)
25. Yuan, L., Chen, H., Mai, J., Chuah, C.-N., Su, Z., Mohapatra, P.: Fireman: a toolkit for firewall modeling and analysis. In: IEEE Symposium on Security and Privacy (May 2006)

A Novel Proof of Work Model Based on Pattern Matching to Prevent DoS Attack

Ali Ordi[1], Hamid Mousavi[2], Bharanidharan Shanmugam[1], Mohammad Reza Abbasy[1], and Mohammad Reza Najaf Torkaman[1]

[1] Universiti Teknologi Malaysia, Advance Informatics School (AIS), KL, Malaysia
oali2@live.utm.my, bharani@ic.utm.my,
{ramohammad2,rntmohammad2}@live.utm.my
[2] Multimedia University, Faculty of Engineering (FOE), Cyberjaya, Malaysia
Sepentamino@hotmail.com

Abstract. One of the most common types of denial of service attack on 802.11 based networks is resource depletion at AP side. APs meet such a problem through receiving flood probe or authentication requests which are forwarded by attackers whose aim are to make AP unavailable to legitimate users. The other most common type of DoS attack takes advantage of unprotected management frame. Malicious user sends deauthentication or disassociation frame permanently to disrupt the network. However 802.11w has introduced a new solution to protect management frames using WPA and WPA2, they are unprotected where WEP is used. This paper focuses on these two common attacks and proposes a solution based on letter envelop protocol and proof-of-work protocol which forces the users to solve a puzzle before completing the association process with AP. The proposed scheme is also resistant against spoofed puzzle solutions attack.

Keywords: Network, Wireless, Client Puzzle, Letter Envelop, Denial of Service attack, Connection request flooding attack, Spoofed disconnect attack.

1 Introduction

Wireless networks are finding a special position in the digital world. Despite growing the popularity of IEEE 802.11 based network, they are vulnerable to many attacks [1]. Several security methods and standards like WPA2, EAP, 802.11i, and 802.11w have been ratified to fix some of these vulnerabilities. However many serious attacks still threaten this type of networks [2] like Denial of service or DoS attack that targets the availability of the network services.

There are two modes in which wireless networks operate: ad-hock mode and infrastructure mode [3]. This paper focuses on infrastructure mode in which a non-AP station (STA) tries to connect to an access point (AP) to exchange data with network. STAs must authenticate themselves to AP before exchanging data. Despite the benefits of authentication process and also association process, there are several signs that they are prone to become an avenue for denying service [4]. In other words, an attacker can forward flood authentication or association request frames using spoofed MAC address to exhaust the AP's resources [5].

H. Cherifi, J.M. Zain, and E. El-Qawasmeh (Eds.): DICTAP 2011, Part I, CCIS 166, pp. 508–520, 2011.

There are two most common types of DoS attack on wireless network in infrastructure mode: connection request flooding that leads to resources depletion attack and deauthentication and disassociation attack [6].

In the first scenario, attacker sends flood connection request frames whether probe, authentication or association request towards AP. Authentication process has been designed as a stateful process. So AP has to allocate an amount of its memory to each request to store STA information. As a result, if AP receives a large number of request frames over a relatively short time, it will encounter a serious problem: memory exhaustion [7].

The next scenario, i.e. Deauthentication and disassociation attack or spoofed disconnect attack, takes advantage of a flaw in IEEE standard 802.11 where management frames are left unprotected [8]. IEEE standard 802.11w employs message integrity code (MIC) to protect management frames. MIC uses shared secret key which is derived by EAPOL 4-way handshake process. This means standard 802.11w can be used where WPA or WPA2 is used as security protocol [9]. Hence, attacker can send spoofed deauthentication or disassociation frames to disrupt the network connections where WEP or other security protocol is used. As a result, legitimate STA will have to pass authentication and association processes after each attack, if he or she wants to keep its connection. Frequently forwarding deauthentication or disassociation management frames by attacker, makes AP unavailable to legitimate users.

Since APs are not able to distinguish between the legitimate management frame and spoofed management frame, finding an efficient and effective anti-DoS scheme is very difficult [10]. Several security methods and even standards are being used to prevent DoS attacks. However they are not able to eliminate the threat of this type of attack on wireless network completely. Even some of them add extra overhead on AP's resources that raises the probability of running resources depletion attack [6].

This paper proposes a new solution to protect 802.11 based networks against two types of DoS attack, which are the connection request flooding attack and spoofed disconnect attack. To do so, the proposed scheme takes advantage of client puzzle and letter envelop protocols.

This paper is organized as the following: The next section will explain the details of the connection request flooding attack as well as spoofed disconnect attack on 802.11 based networks in infrastructure mode. Section 3will deal with client puzzle protocol. In Section 4, the details of proposed solution will be discussed. The analysis of the security of this approach based on probability theory and client puzzle protocol's general properties will be provided before the conclusion.

2 DoS Attack on Wireless Network

Fayssal and Uk Kim [11] have classified wireless network attacks in six categories: Identity spoofing, Eavesdropping, Vulnerability, Denial of Service (DoS), Replay, and Rogue Access Point attacks.

Dos Attacks as one of the most common attacks against 802.11 based networks employ useless traffic such as beacon, probe request, association, authentication, ARP, and data flood. This cumulative traffic degrades the performance of the wireless network and even hinders normal user to access network resources.

There are several types of DoS attack including:

1. Authentication frame attack whose aim to de-authenticate current connectivity from AP
2. AP association and authentication buffer overflow or connection request flooding attack
3. Physical layer attack
4. Disassociation and deauthentication attack or spoofed disconnect attack
5. Network setting attack

This paper focuses on two of these attacks: connection request flooding attack and abusing disassociation and deauthentication management frame which called Farewell attack [12] or spoofed disconnect attack.

2.1 Spoofed Disconnect Attack

IEEE 802.11i states that the relationship between STA and AP places in one of the four following states:

1. Initial start state, unauthenticated, unassociated
2. Authenticated and not associated
3. Authenticated and associated
4. Authenticated, associated and 802.1x authenticated

As shown in Fig.1, after identifying the certain AP and completing the mutual authentication process using exchanging several authentication messages, both AP and STA move to state 2; authenticated and not associated state. In this stage STA sends association request to AP. As soon as receiving the AP's association response frame, both AP

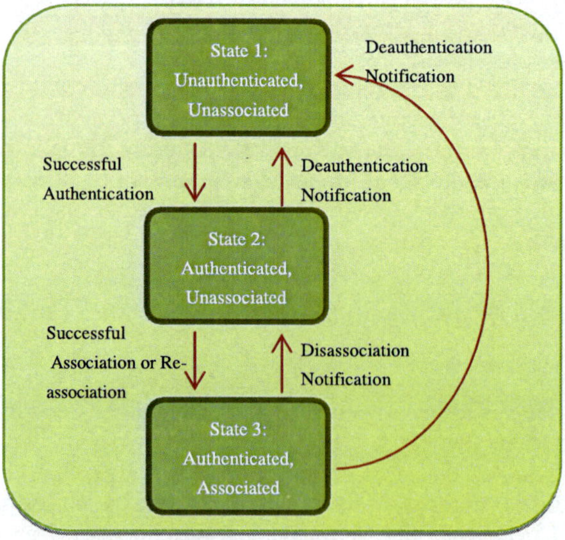

Fig. 1. Relationship between state variables and services

and STA come to state 3. If they are in an open-system authentication network, they will be able to exchange data in state 3. Otherwise, if shared-key authentication is used, AP and STA will complete 802.1x authentication process and migrate to state 4.

According to IEEE standard 802.11,if a disassociation frame is received, both associated peers will move from state 3 or 4 back to state 2.Similarly, a deauthentication frame forces both AP and STA to transit to state 1 no matter whether they were in state 2, 3 or 4. Since standard 802.11 has left these management frames unprotected, they have become a valuable target for DoS attacks. Even though, IEEE standard 802.11w solves this problem by protecting management frames, 802.11wtakes advantage of WPA and WPA2 security protocol. in other words, the wireless networks that use other security protocol such as WEP are still prone to spoofed disconnect attack. Technically, 802.11w has been disabled in capable APs by default and needs to be enabled manually. Therefore, in such circumstances malicious users simply launch spoofed disconnect attack using broadcasting spoofed deauthentication and disassociation frames.[13]

2.2 Connection Request Flooding Attack

As mention in previous sub section, IEEE standard 802.11i defines four different states that AP and STA place in one of them respectively. To move to each state, AP and STA need to exchange several messages. They pursue the following procedure.

Initially STA sends probe request frame to find an AP and AP replies by probe response frame including some necessary information to establish connection. To jump to state 2, STA forwards authentication request message and receives AP's reply through authentication response frame. Finally, association request and response messagesare exchanged to bring AP and STA to state 3.As shown in figure 2, Beacon frames which periodically are broadcasted by AP, paly an alternative role for probe process: probe request and response messages.

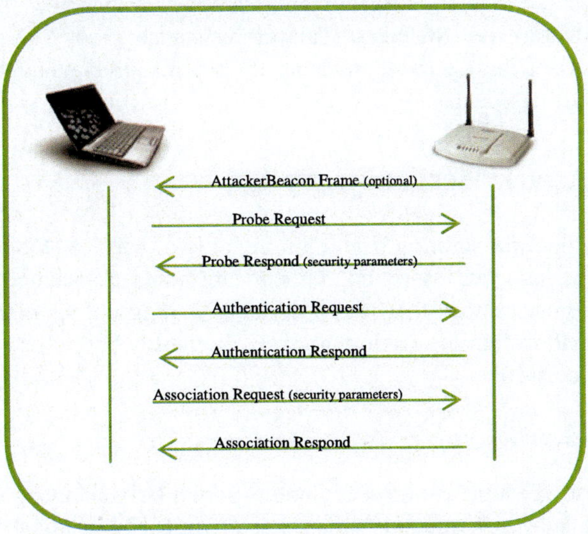

Fig. 2. 802.11 (Open System) authentication and Association procedure

During the above procedure, AP has to store some STA information in each state which is used for moving to superior states. Being stateful, authentication and association procedure is susceptible to exhaust the memory resources. Attacker simply sends out flood requests towards AP. As a result, these flooding requests exhaust AP's finite storage resources and leave AP in an overload status. Consequently, AP would not be able to serve legitimate users. This type of attack can be run based on each of the three types of requests: probe request, authentication request, and association request. [13] Like spoofed disconnect attack, Attackers exploit spoofed MAC addresses to launch such an attack.

3 Client-Puzzle Based Anti-DoS Attack Scheme

Initially the client puzzle scheme has been introduced by Dwork and Naor[14] to combat junk mail. Later, Jules and Brainard [15] took advantage of cryptographic client puzzle scheme to defend against resource depletion attack in servers. They followed the aim of balancing resource (CPU and Memory) consumption between both sides of a communication. In their method, client which is intended to connect to a server has to spend some time in order to solve a puzzle which has been established by server. Hence attacker will not able to flood request messages before solving their respective puzzles in a relatively short time.

To prevent connection request flooding attack that leads to resource depletion attack on wireless network, several schemes have been proposed based on client puzzle protocol[16] [17] [18]. As APs involve serious computational and storage resources limitation compared to server, these practices may bring up other resources depletion for wireless network like computational resources depletion or even memory exhaustion.

In [19], authors discuss the specifications of a good cryptographic puzzle scheme included of: Puzzle fairness, Computation guarantee, Efficiency, Adjustability of difficulty, Correlation-free, Stateless, Tamper-resistance, and Non-parallelizability while [17] categorizes these puzzles in terms of CPU resource-exhausting and memory resource-exhausting puzzles.

4 Anti-DoS Attack Mechanism Design

As mentioned earlier, our solution is going to repel two types of DoS attack; resource depletion which is launched by probe, authentication and association flood requests and spoofed disconnect attack that is run through sending out spoofed deauthentication and disassociation frames. To do that, we will employ both client puzzle and letter-envelop protocols[20].

4.1 Puzzle Construction

As it turns out, to prevent resource depletion, particularly memory exhausting, the proposed scheme consumes memory as little as possible. To establish the puzzle, AP initially generates two random numbers, N_i and K. The length of N_i, L, can be changed from zero to sixty three bits to adjust the puzzle difficulty. AP considers K as a 32-bit number. To create the pattern, AP calculates six values between zero and 127 using N_i. Then AP needs to consider a 128-bit number and marks its six bit positions which are computed in previous stage. If LSB (N_i) =0 then the value of each position will be opposite of the value of its peer. Otherwise they peer to peer will have the same value. AP after creating the pattern establishes hash function h_0 using N_i, AP's MAC address, L, and H_K as parameters. Whenever AP receives a probe request frame, it will send a probe response frame back containing h_0, L, and H_K. STA extracts these values and finds N_i by brute force method. Then STA generate a 32-bit random number, R, and calculates H_R=hash (R). Then STA creates the pattern using N_i and applies it over H_R. STA sends an authentication request frame containing H_R, and h_0. Finally AP verifies the pattern to decide whether accept or deny the request.

The following procedure describes the proposed solution step by step. Table 1 summarizes the notations that are used in this procedure.

Table 1. Proposed Scheme Notation

Notation	Description
K	32-bit random number generated by AP
N_i	The puzzle answer
L	The length of N_i
X	The numerical value of 7 first bit of N_i
Y	The numerical value of 7 second bit of N_i
Z	LSB(N_i)
hash	A cryptography hash function - MD5
MAC_x	MAC Address of station x
R	32-bit random number generated by STA
$\neq$	Not equal
V(x)	The value of the xth bit

1. Generate 32-bit random number K and calculate H_K = hash (K)[1]
2. Generate L-bit random number N_i ($0 \leq L \leq 63$)
3. Calculate the following equation:

   $$h_0 = hash\ (N_i \| H_K \| L \| MAC_{AP})$$
4. Extract 7 first and second bits of N_i and calculate the corresponding numerical values, x and y.($0 \leq x \leq 127$, $0 \leq y \leq 127$)
5. Calculate $x' = 2 \times x$ and $y' = 2 \times y$ and subtract from 127if needed ($x' < 128$, $y' < 128$)

[1] This process is performed only once when AP comes up.

6. Calculate $x'' = 2 \times x'$ and $y'' = 2 \times y'$ and subtract from 127 if needed $(x'' < 128, y'' < 128)$
7. Consider z =LSB(N_i)
8. Create a pattern based on z, x, x', x'', y, y', y''

   If z=0 then V(x) ≠V(y), V(x') ≠V (y'), V (x'') ≠V(y'')

   If z=1thenV(x)=V(y), V(x')=V (y'), V (x'')=V(y'')

   For example if x=**24** and y=**65** then

   i. $x' = 2 \times x = 2 \times 24 = \mathbf{48}$and $y' = 2 \times y = 2 \times 65 = 130 > 128 \Rightarrow y' = 130 - 127 = \mathbf{3}$
   ii. $x'' = 2 \times x' = 2 \times 48 = \mathbf{96}$and $y'' = 2 \times y' = 3 \times 2 = \mathbf{6}$
   iii. If z=1 then the values of these 6 positions must be as following:
      1. Value of 65th bit = Value of 24th bit
         a. E.g. if V(24)= 0 then V(65) must be zero.
      2. Value of 3rd bit = Value of 48th bit
      3. Value of 96th= Value of 6th bit
   iv. If z=0 then the values of these 6 positions must be as following:
      1. Value of 65th bit≠Value of 24th bit
         a. E.g. if V(24)= 0 then V(65) must be 1.
      2. Value of 3rdbit≠Value of 48th bit
      3. Value of 6th ≠ Value of 96th bit
9. In probe respond frame, add h_0, H_K, L

When a STA applies for communication through probe request, AP forwards puzzle's information including h_0, H_K, and L by probe response frame.

To complete the communication procedures, STA pursues the following steps:

10. Extract H_K, h_0, L
11. Make up the following equation and find N_i by using of brute force method:

    h_0 = hash (N_i || H_K || L || MAC_{AP})
12. Generate 32-bit random number R and calculate H_R= hash(R)
13. Extract 7 first and second bits of N_i and calculate the corresponding numerical value (x, y)
14. Calculate $x' = 2 \times x$ and $y' = 2 \times y$ and subtract from 127 if needed (x'<128, y'<128)
15. Calculate $x'' = 2 \times x'$ and$y'' = 2 \times y'$ and subtract from 127 if needed (x"<128, y"<128)
16. Consider z =LSB (N_i)

17. If z=0 then the value bits of positions y, y', y" of H_R should be change to the ***opposed*** value of bits of positions x, x', x" respectively.
18. If z=1 then the value bits of positions y, y', y" of H_R should be change to the ***same*** value of bits of positions x, x', x" respectively.
19. Send h_0 and changed H_R to AP through authentication request frame
20. Store R and H_K

Generally, APs expect to meet authentication requests frames including puzzle solution after expiring certain time, t_{exp}, based on difficulty which is determined by L. Otherwise AP discard the received authentication request frames. When AP receives an authentication request frame, after t_{exp}, do the following steps to verify the solution:

21. Check the h_0 to verify the validity of puzzle
22. Look up the received H_R within associated H_R list to prevent flood repetitious puzzle (also to prevent reply attack). If AP finds the received H_R in associated H_R list, the frame is discarded.
23. Compare H_R to pattern which has been formed in stage 8

As we utilize MD5 as hash algorithm, number 127 is used in stages 5, 6, 14, and 15 because the output of this type of hash function is 128 bits (in stage 12),and so a vailable positions are between 0 and 127.

When stage 23 is passed, based on the handshaking procedure, AP forwards authentication respond frame and allocates a certain size of memory for STA's information along with H_R.

AP can adjust the puzzle difficulty by means of L when it senses the attack. A variable, δ, help AP to sense the attack. Δ shows the number of services which AP can serve based on available resources. When a probe request is received, δ is decreased. Even though, Ni changes periodically based on predefined time, the following rules are applied by AP:

- If δ has not been changed during N_i life time, old N_i would be valid for next cycle.
- If δ is less than 25% of available resources, then N_i immediately will be replaced with a new and stronger one (L would be larger).

However, at any time when AP realizes that attack has been eliminated, it would back to its normal activities. In other word, it decreases the difficulty of N_i, i.e. L, even down to zero.

4.2 Anti-spoofed Disconnect Attack Mechanism

Disassociation and deauthentication frames body include a field that called reason code that shows why these frames have been issued.

Table 2. Reason codes

Reason Code	Description
2	Previous authentication no longer valid
3	Deauthenticated because sending STA is leaving (or has left) IBSS or ESS
4	Disassociated due to inactivity
5	Disassociated because AP is unable to handle all currently associated STAs
6	Class 2 frame received from non-authenticated STA
7	Class 3 frame received from non-associated STA
8	Disassociated because sending STA is leaving (or has left) BSS
9	STA requesting (re)association is not authenticated with responding STA

As listed in Table 2[21], deauthentication or disassociation frame is issued in following three scenarios[2]:

1. When the STA goes offline; reason code 3 or 8.
2. When the AP goes offline; reason code 3.
3. When AP terminates some current associated STAs because it cannot serve all STAs; reason code 5.

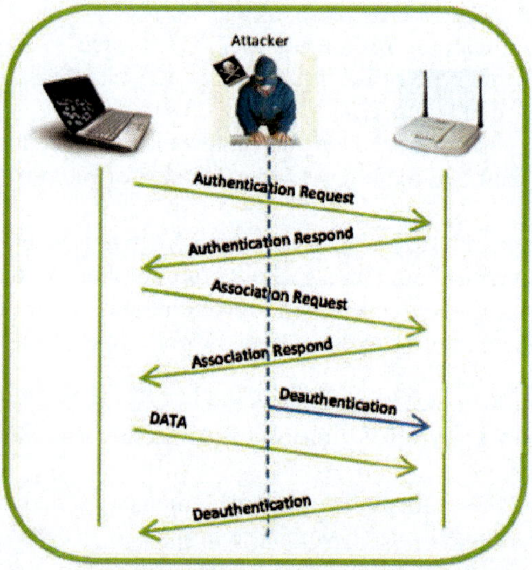

Fig. 3. Deauthentication attack

In each aforementioned scenario, when a STA or AP receives a deauthentication or disassociation frame in our proposed scheme, before terminating the connection, they do the following stage:

[2] If STA has not been passed the state 2 or 3 infigure 1, the frame would be discarded; reason code = 2,6,7,9.

1. *Scenario 1*
   a. STA sends R through the deauthentication or disassociation frame to AP.
   b. AP calculates H'_R=hash(R) and compares to stored H_R.
   c. If $H'_R \approx H_R$, AP terminates the communication, otherwise AP discards the frame.

2. *Scenario 2*
   a. AP broadcast K through deauthentication frame to all STAs.
   b. STAs calculate H'_K=hash (K) and compare to stored H_K.
   c. If H'_K=H_K, STAs terminate the communication, otherwise they discard these frame.

Since Scenario 3 occurs rarely [22], STAs ignore disassociation frames for this case in our scheme.

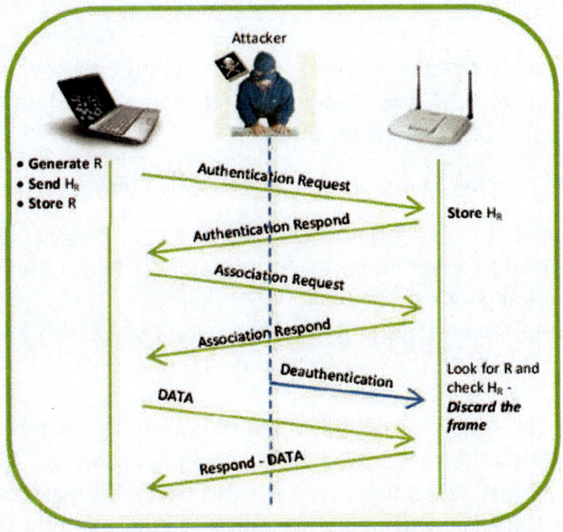

Fig. 4. Anti- Farewell attack mechanism

5 Security Analysis

The main purpose of this paper is to put an attacker in troubles when he or she wants to forward too many authentication requests towards AP. To do so, the following general conditions [23] should be satisfied:

Computation guarantee and Adjustability of difficulty: We assume that hash functions resist against pre-image solution, so the attacker has to only solve the puzzle through brute force approach. Hence, he or she needs enough time to find the correct solution. In other words, the attacker has to look for the solution in a range of 2^L possible answers. Even though this range may be reduced to $2^{L/2}$ possible answers [24], he or she still has to spend enough time to find the puzzle's solution. Moreover, AP can simply increase L, the difficulty of the puzzle, when it senses the attack or decrease L when the attack subsides.

Correlation free and Tamper-resistance: An attacker cannot learn Ni by examining the other STA's answers, because in our scheme each STA should implement the pattern over its own H_R that is normally unique.

Efficiency: This scheme resists against the puzzle verification attack where an attacker forwards too many authentication requests with fake solution. That means the puzzle verification is done just by looking for correct pattern in a received H_R, a significantly low computational process.

Puzzle fairness: When AP receives an authentication request containing puzzle solution during the lifetime of t_{exp}, the frame is discarded. As a result, the attacker has to wait until the t_{exp} is expired. So he or she will have much limited time to attack with certain N_i.

Stateless: AP normally allocates a fixed- memory to store the puzzle information: h_0 and corresponding pattern. Hence, since the puzzle acts as stateless function, AP never meets memory exhausting in a short time.

In addition to these general conditions, our scheme also meets two more conditions:

1. AP generates Ni after predefined time iff δ has been changed. Consequently AP preserves its resources for more cycles unlike [17] which producing Ni periodically even without any request.
2. We use MD5 as the hash algorithm whose output of 128-bit. Undoubtedly, using SHA1 or other algorithms needs to modify stages 4, 5, 6, 13, 14, and 15

If an attacker wants to reach correct pattern without solving the puzzle, he or she will have to try 128×128×2 different cases. If the attacker can launch 1500 spoofed frame per second [25], at least 21 seconds is needed to check all these cases. Considering this time and δ, the attacker will be forced to find N_i through brute force if he or she wants to run efficient attack.

Furthermore, when AP receives a probe request, it does not store any information related to STA. So the increasing the requests cannot exhaust the AP's resources. Moreover, the memory allocated to h_0 and corresponding pattern is cleared after changing the N_i, meaning that the algorithm uses a fixed-size memory to handle the puzzle.

Additionally, AP in stage 22 of the proposed algorithm, checks the received H_R with existing associated H_Rs. AP will discard frame If H_R exits. As a result, this stage guarantees our scheme as an anti-replay attack mechanism.

6 Conclusion

This paper offered an anti-DoS attack solution based on the proof-of-work protocol and one way hard function. The proposed scheme protects 802.11 based networks against both resource depletion attacks which are launched through flood probe, authentication, and association requests as well as spoofed disconnect attack. This solution also protects the 802.11 based networks against forged solution of the client puzzle which may bypass the client puzzle protocol. Furthermore, it decreases the verification process significantly. The future study can focus on finding a smarter mechanism to realize DoS attack to adjust parameter L.

References

[1] Nasreldin, M., Aslan, H., El-Hennawy, M., El-Hennawy, A.: WiMax Security. In: 22nd International Conference on Advanced Information Networking and Applications - Workshops (Aina Workshops 2008), pp. 1335–1340 (2008)

[2] Yu, P.H., Pooch, U.W.: A Secure Dynamic Cryptographic And Encryption Protocol For Wireless Networks. In: EUROCON 2009, pp. 1860–1865. IEEE, St.-Petersburg (2009)

[3] Gast, M.: 802.11® Wireless Networks The Definitive Guide. O'Reilly, Sebastopol (2005)

[4] Bellardo, J., Savage, S.: 802.11 Denial-of-Service Attacks:Real Vulnerabilities and Practical Solutions. In: SSYM 2003 Proceedings of the 12th conference on USENIX Security Symposium, Washington, D.C., USA, vol. 12 (2003)

[5] He, C., Mitchell, J.C.: Security analysis and improvements for IEEE802.11i. In: Proceedings of the 12th Annual Network and Distributed System Security Symposium (NDSS 2005), pp. 90–110 (2005)

[6] Liu, C.-H., Huang, Y.-Z.: The analysis for DoS and DDoS attacks of WLAN. In: Second International Conference on MultiMedia and Information Technology, pp. 108–111 (2010)

[7] Bicakci, K., Tavli, B.: Denial-of-Service attacks and countermeasures in IEEE 802.11 wireless networks. Computer Standards & Interfaces 31(5), 931–941 (2009)

[8] Ding, P., Holliday, J., Celik, A.: Improving The Security of Wireless LANs By Managing 802.1x Disassociation. In: First IEEE Consumer Communications and Networking Conference,CCNC 2004, pp. 53–58 (2004)

[9] IEEE Std 802.11w^{TM} (September 30, 2009)

[10] Zhang, Y., Sampalli, S.: Client-based Intrusion Prevention System for 802.11 Wireless LANs. In: IEEE 6th Intemational Conference on Wireless and Mobile Computing. Networking and Communications, Niagara Falls, Ontario, pp. 100–107 (2010)

[11] Fayssal, S., Kim, N.U.: Performance Analysis Toolset for Wireless Intrusion Detection Systems. In: IEEE 2010 International Conference on High Performance Computing and Simulation (HPCS), Caen, France, pp. 484–490 (2010)

[12] Nguyen, T.D., Nguyen, D.H.M., Tran, B.N., Vu, H., Mittal, N.: A lightweight solution for defending against deauthentication/disassociation attacks on 802.11 networks, pp. 1–6. IEEE, Los Alamitos (2008)

[13] Dong, Q., Gao, L., Li, X.: A New Client-Puzzle Based DoS-Resistant Scheme of IEEE 802.11i Wireless Authentication Protocol. In: 3rd International Conference on Biomedical Engineering and Informatics (BMEI 2010), pp. 2712–2716 (2010)

[14] Dwork, C., Naor, M.: Pricing via Processing or Combatting Junk Mail, pp. 139–147. Springer, Heidelberg (1992)

[15] Jules, A., Brainard, J.: A Cryptographic Countermeasure against Connection Depletion Attacks, pp. 151–165. IEEE Computer Society, Los Alamitos (1999)

[16] Shi, T.-j., Ma, J.-f.: Design and analysis of a wireless authentication protocol against DoS attacks based on Hash function. Aerospace Electronics Information Engineering and Control 28(1), 122–126 (2006)

[17] Dong, Q., Gao, L., Li, X.: A New Client-Puzzle Based DoS-Resistant Scheme of IEEE 802.11i Wireless Authentication Protocol. In: 3rd International Conference on Biomedical Engineering and Informatics (BMEI 2010), pp. 2712–2716 (2010)

[18] Laishun, Z., Minglei, Z., Yuanbo, G.: A Client Puzzle Based Defense Mechanism to Resist DoS Attacks in WLAN. In: 2010 International Forum on Information Technology and Applications, pp. 424–427. IEEE Computer Society, Los Alamitos (2010)

[19] Abliz, M., Znati, T.: A Guided Tour Puzzle for Denial of Service Prevention. In: 2009 Annual Computer Security Applications Conference, pp. 279–288 (2009)

[20] Nguyen, T.N., Tran, B.N., Nguyen, D.H.M.: A Lightweight Solution For Wireless Lan: Letter-Envelop Protocol. IEEE, Los Alamitos (2008)

[21] IEEE Std 802.11™ (June 12, 2007)

[22] Nguyen, T.D., Nguyen, D.H.M., Tran, B.N., Vu, H., Mittal, N.: A lightweight solution for defending against deauthentication/disassociation attacks on 802.11 networks, pp. 1–6. IEEE, Los Alamitos (2008)

[23] Abliz, T.Z.M.: A Guided Tour Puzzle for Denial of Service Prevention. In: 2009 Annual Computer Security Applications Conference, pp. 279–288 (2009)

[24] Patarin, J., Montreuil, A.: Benes and Butterfly Schemes Revisited. In: Won, D.H., Kim, S. (eds.) ICISC 2005. LNCS, vol. 3935, pp. 92–116. Springer, Heidelberg (2006)

[25] Feng, W.-C., Kaiser, E., Feng, W.-C., Luu, A.: The Design and Implementation of Network Puzzles. In: Proceedings of IEEE 24th Annual Joint Conference of the IEEE Computer and Communications Societies, INFOCOM 2005, Miami, Florida, USA, pp. 2372–2382 (2005)

[26] Nasreldin, M., Aslan, H., El-Hennawy, M., El-Hennawy, A.: WiMax Security. In: 22nd International Conference on Advanced Information Networking and Applications - Workshops (Aina Workshops 2008), pp. 1335–1340 (2008)

[27] Dwork, C., Naor, M.: Pricing via Processing or Combatting Junk Mail, pp. 139–147. Springer, Heidelberg (1992)

A New Approach of the Cryptographic Attacks

Otilia Cangea and Gabriela Moise

Petroleum-Gas University of Ploiesti, Romania
Romania, 100680 Ploiesti, 39 Bucuresti Blvd.
ocangea@upg-ploiesti.ro,
gmoise@upg-ploiesti.ro

Abstract. In this paper, there is presented the taxonomy of possible attacks on ciphers in the cryptographic systems. The main attack techniques are linear, differential and algebraic cryptanalysis, each of them having particular features regarding the design of algorithms techniques. The cryptographic algorithms have to be designed to resist different kinds of attacks, so the mathematical functions of the encryption algorithms have to satisfy the cryptographic properties defined by Shannon. The paper proposes a new approach on the cryptographic attacks using an error regulation-based cryptanalysis.

Keywords: cryptographic attacks, intermediate key, error regulation-based cryptanalysis, fuzzy controller.

1 Introduction

The cryptographic attacks are techniques used to decipher a ciphertext without knowing the cryptographic keys. There are several types of attacks, according to the cryptographic techniques that are used.

The cryptographic systems are built on Shannon's principle regarding the confusion and diffusion principles [1]. The confusion refers to a complex relationship between the plaintext and the ciphertext, therefore a cryptanalyst cannot use this relation in order to uncover the cryptographic key. The diffusion principle means that every bit of the plaintext and every bit of the cryptographic key affects a lot of bits of the ciphertext.

In 1883, Kerckhoff formulated the principle that a cryptosystem should be secure even if everything about the system, except the key, is public knowledge [2]. The principle is known as Kerckhoffs' law, which was revised later by Shannon as follows: "the enemy knows the system being used" and known as Shannon's maxima [1].

The schema of a cryptosystem is presented in Fig. 1.

There are two main types of cryptosystems: symmetric-key cryptosystems and asymmetric-key cryptosystems. In a symmetric-key cryptosystem, the encryption key and the decryption key are the same or can be derived one from the other. In an asymmetric-key cryptosystem, there is no relationship between the encryption and the

H. Cherifi, J.M. Zain, and E. El-Qawasmeh (Eds.): DICTAP 2011, Part I, CCIS 166, pp. 521–534, 2011.

decryption keys. Depending on the mode of codification, either a whole block of the message coded using the same key or bit by bit using different keys, the ciphers can be divided into block ciphers or stream ciphers.

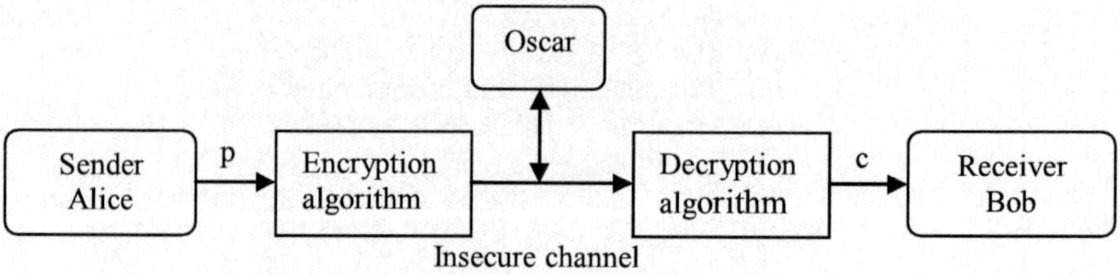

Fig. 1. Schema of a cryptosystem

In the schema above, the attacker, namely Oscar, intercepts the ciphertext (*c*) and tries to recover the decryption key or the plaintext (*p*). Oscar can only read the message or he can change it and transmit to Bob a decayed ciphertext.

In this paper, there are presented various types of cryptographic attacks and it is proposed a new approach using an *error regulation-based cryptanalysis*.

The paper is organized as follows:

- the taxonomy of cryptographic attacks, emphasizing the mostly used techniques, namely linear, differential, and algebraic cryptanalysis;
- the proposal of a new model of cryptographic attack, i.e. error regulation-based cryptanalysis. The innovation consists in implementing the cryptographic attacks technique using the intermediate keys, on the basis of a feedback-type controller that performs the regulation of the cryptographic key;
- experimental results obtained using the proposed attack technique;
- conclusions that underline the most important contributions of the paper.

2 Taxonomy of the Cryptographic Attacks

There are various cryptographic attacks. The sure attack is the brute force attack that consists in trying all the possible keys. This is not feasible while the lengths of the keys are bigger (nowadays the keys have at least 1024 bits) and the complexity of the algorithms causes a longer response time.

In order to define the taxonomy of the cryptographic attacks, one has to consider the information known by the cryptanalyst [3] and, within the taxonomies generated by these criteria, the cryptographic algorithms. The cryptanalyst known information refers to sets of plaintexts or ciphertexts and he has to uncover the cryptographic key. In the case of asymmetric cryptosystem, the cryptanalyst may possess the encryption key and has to find the decryption key.

The taxonomy of the cryptanalysis is presented in Fig. 2.

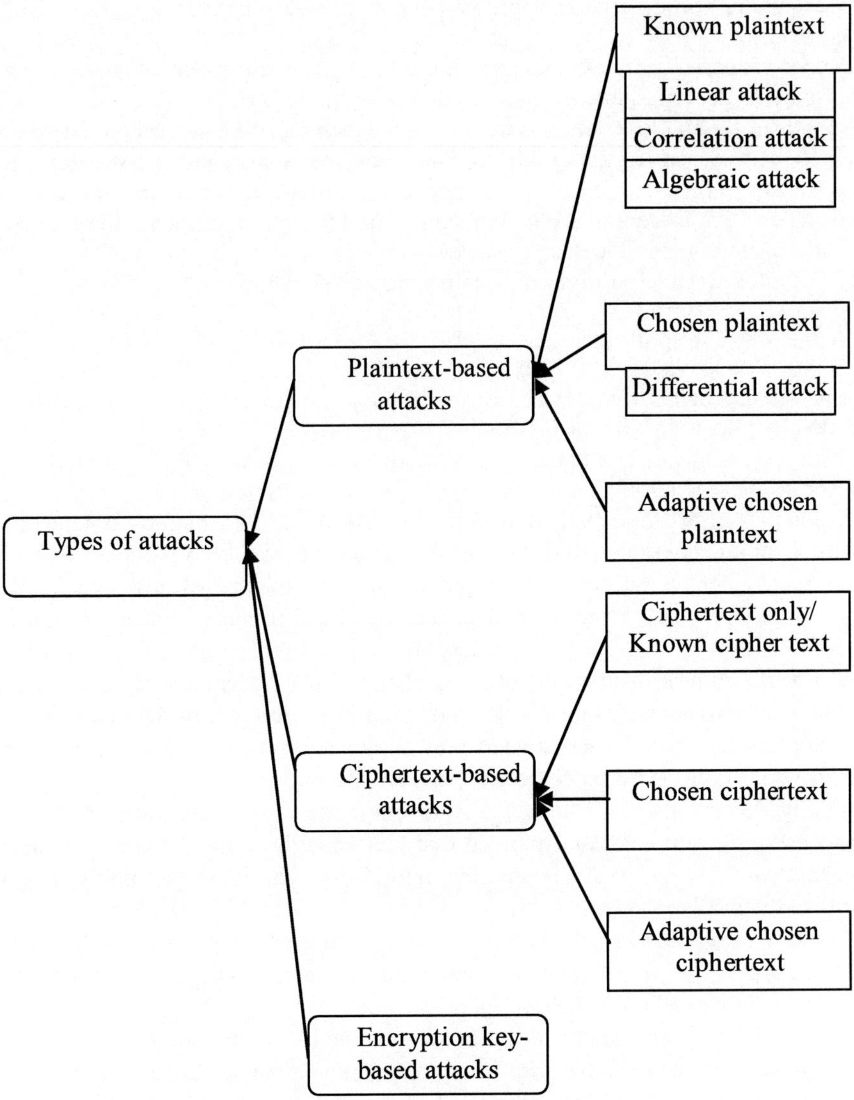

Fig. 2. Taxonomy of the cryptanalysis

In a known-plaintext attack, one (Oscar, in Fig. 1, for example) possesses a set of pairs of plaintexts and corresponding ciphertexts obtained with a certain key.

In a chosen-plaintext attack, one is able to prior choose a set of plaintexts, to encrypt them and to analyze the results.

Adaptive-chosen plaintext attack is based on the fact that one is able to choose in an adaptive (interactive) way a set of plaintexts and to obtain the corresponding ciphertext using a fixed key. In an adaptive chosen plaintext, a cryptanalyst adapts the attack based on prior results.

In a ciphertext-only attack, one possesses a set of ciphertexts (encoded with the same key).

Chosen-ciphertext attack enables the cryptanalyst to prior choose a set of ciphertexts, to decrypt them and to analyze the results.

Adaptive-chosen ciphertext allows the choice of a set of ciphertexts in an adaptive (interactive) way and obtaining the corresponding plaintexts (with a fixed key). In an adaptive chosen plaintext, a cryptanalyst adapts the attack based on prior results.

Encryption key-based attack is defined by the fact that one knows the encryption key and tries to uncover the decryption key.

The cryptographic algorithms use mainly statistical methods.

2.1 Linear Cryptanalysis

Matsui and Yamagishi first devised linear cryptanalysis in an attack on FEAL. It was extended by Matsui [4] to attack DES.

Linear cryptanalysis is a known plaintext attack which uses a linear approximation to describe the behavior of the block cipher. Given sufficient pairs of plaintext and corresponding ciphertext, bits of information about the key can be obtained, and increased amounts of data will usually give a higher probability of success.

There have been a variety of enhancements and improvements to the basic attack. Langford and Hellman [5] introduced an attack called differential-linear cryptanalysis that combines elements of differential cryptanalysis with those of linear cryptanalysis. Also, Kaliski and Robshaw [6] showed that a linear cryptanalytic attack using multiple approximations might allow a reduction in the amount of data required for a successful attack. Other issues, such as protecting ciphers against linear cryptanalysis, have also been considered by Nyberg [7] and Knudsen [8].

Initially, Matsui used 2^{47} known plaintext-ciphertext pairs and later, in 1994, he refined the algorithm and demonstrated that it is enough to use 2^{43} known plaintext-ciphertext pairs [4]. He implemented the algorithm in the C programming language and broke the DES cipher.

The number of necessary known plaintexts and the time depend on the number of rounds of the DES cipher. The results obtained by Matsui, using a PA-RISC/66MHz HP9750 computer and published in [9], are:

"8-round DES is breakable with 2^{21} known-plaintexts in 40 seconds;

12-round DES is breakable with 2^{33} known-plaintexts in 50 hours;

16-round DES is breakable with 2^{47} known-plaintexts faster than an exhaustive search for 56 key bits."

The main idea of the linear cryptanalysis is to approximate the non-linear block using the following expression:

$$\left(\underset{i\in\{1,\ldots,64\}}{\oplus} P(i)\right) \oplus \left(\underset{j\in\{1,\ldots,64\}}{\oplus} C(j)\right) = \underset{k\in\{1,\ldots,56\}}{\oplus} K(k)\,. \tag{1}$$

where:

P, C, K represent 64-bits plaintext, 64-bits ciphertext, 56-bits key respectively, and i, j, k indicate fixed bit locations.

The equation holds with a probability p for randomly plaintext and its corresponding ciphertext. The probability $p \neq 1/2$ and the bias (magnitude) $|p - 1/2|$ state the effectiveness of linear approximation. The algorithms used to determine one bit and multiple bits of information about the key are based on a maximum likelihood method.

Matsui found the following linear approximation to break the DES cipher. For example, in order to break a 16-round DES using 2^{47} known plaintext pairs, it is enough to solve the following equation:

$$\begin{aligned} &P_H(7)\oplus P_H(18)\oplus P_H(24)\oplus P_L(12)\oplus P_L(16)\oplus C_H(15)\oplus C_L(7)\oplus C_L(18)\oplus C_L(24)\oplus \\ &C_L(29)\oplus F_{16}(C_L,K_{16})[15]=K_1(19)\oplus K_1(23)\oplus K_3(22)\oplus K_4(44)\oplus K_7(22)\oplus K_8(44) \\ &\oplus K_9(22)\oplus K_{11}(22)\oplus K_{12}(44)\oplus K_{13}(22)\oplus K_{15}(22) \end{aligned} \quad (2)$$

where:

P_H represents the left 32 bits of P

P_L represents the right 32 bits of P

C_H represents the left 32 bits of C

C_L represents the right 32 bits of C

K_i represents the intermediate key in the i-th round

F_i represents the function used in the i-th round

$A[i]$ means the bit from the i-th position of the vector A

$A[i_1,i_2,\ldots,i_k]=A[i_1]\oplus[i_2]\ldots\oplus A[i_k]$

2.2 Differential Cryptanalysis

Differential cryptanalysis is a chosen plaintext attack that means the attacker selects inputs and examines the outputs trying to find the key. The method was developed by Biham and Shamir and presented in [10]. The differential cryptanalysis is based on the following observation: the attacker knows that for a particular ΔP ($\Delta P = P_i \oplus P_j$ is called input difference), a particular value ΔC ($\Delta C = C_i \oplus C_j$ is called output difference) occurs with a high probability. The pair (C_i, C_j) represents the corresponding ciphertexts of the plaintexts pair (P_i, P_j). The pair $(\Delta P, \Delta C)$ is called differential characteristic.

Each S-box has associated a difference distribution table [11], in which each row corresponds to a given input difference and each column corresponds to a given output difference. The entries of the table represent the number of occurrences of the output difference value (ΔC) corresponding to the given input difference (ΔP).

The input of any S-box has 6 bits and the output has 4 bits, so observing the differential behavior of any S-box, there are 64^2 possible inputs pairs (X_1, X_2).

If $S(X_1) = Y_1$, $S(X_2) = Y_2$ and $\Delta X = X_1 \oplus X_2$, then $\Delta Y = Y_1 \oplus Y_2$.

Y_1, Y_2 and ΔY can have 16 possible values. The distribution on the differential output ΔY can be calculated by counting the occurrence of each value ΔY, when (X_1, X_2) varies on each 64^2 value.

The difference distribution table of S_1 is presented in Table 1.

Table 1. The difference distribution table of S1

Input x'	Output y'															
	0	1	2	3	4	5	6	7	8	9	A	B	C	D	E	F
00	64	0	0	0	0	0	0	0	0	0	0	0	0	0	0	0
01	0	0	0	6	0	2	4	4	0	10	12	4	10	6	2	4
02	0	0	0	8	0	4	4	4	0	6	8	6	12	6	4	2
03	14	4	2	2	10	6	4	2	6	4	4	0	2	2	2	0
...	...	...	...	...	...	...	...	...	...	...	...	...	...	...	...	...
3E	4	8	2	2	2	4	4	14	4	2	0	2	0	8	4	4
3F	4	4	4	2	4	0	2	4	4	2	4	8	8	6	2	2

The differential distribution is highly non-uniform; for example, for $\Delta X = 02$, $\Delta Y = 0,1,2,4,8$ with the probability 0 and $\Delta Y = 3, A$ with the probability $\frac{8}{64}$.

So, it can be derived Table 2 for $\Delta X = 02$.

Table 2. ΔY occurrences for $\Delta X = 02$

ΔY	0	1	2	3	4	5	6	7	8	9	A	B	C	D	E	F
Occurs	0	0	0	8	0	4	4	4	0	6	8	6	12	6	4	2

$02 \rightarrow F$ has 2 occurrences; calculating, it can be observed that the input pairs can be:

$$\begin{matrix} X_1 = 1 = 000001 \\ X_2 = 3 = 000011 \end{matrix} \quad \text{or} \quad \begin{matrix} X_2 = 1 = 000001 \\ X_1 = 3 = 000011 \end{matrix} \tag{3}$$

and

$$S_1(1) \oplus S_1(3) = S_1(3) \oplus S_1(1) = 15 \tag{4}$$

In order to determine the key, let us consider two inputs to S_1, 0 and 2, $0 \oplus 2 = 2$ and the output difference as F, according to the schema presented in Fig.3.

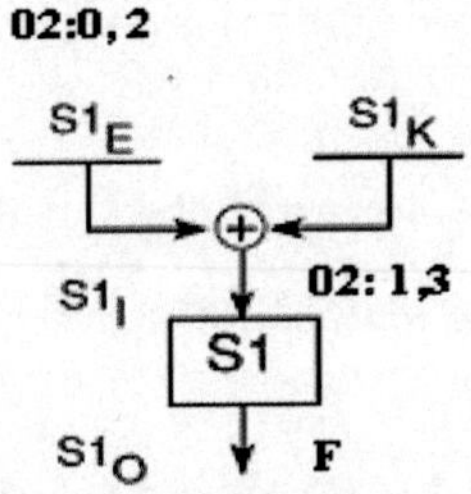

Fig. 3. Key determining schema for a differential cryptanalysis

The corresponding relations are:

$$\begin{array}{ll} 1 \oplus 0 = 1 & 1 \oplus 2 = 3 \\ 3 \oplus 0 = 3 & 3 \oplus 2 = 1 \end{array} \tag{5}$$

and the possible keys are $\{1, 3\}$.

Considering more input and output differences, one can obtain more sets of possible keys. Intersecting these sets, it can be obtained the key used to the 1st round of the DES algorithm.

2.3 Algebraic Cryptanalysis

The algebraic attack is faster than the attacks presented above for some ciphers. This attack was presented by Courtois and Meier in 2003 for the stream cipher [12]. The algebraic cryptanalysis is a method used against both types of ciphers, i.e. stream cipher and block cipher, with a particular success on the stream cipher (special for LFSR-based keystream generator). The main idea of the algebraic attacks consists in finding a system of equations which expresses the dependence outputs (O)-inputs (I) and in solving of this system. A solution of the system gives the secret key.

The possible classes of equations relevant for the algebraic cryptanalysis are:

"• Class 1. Low-degree multivariate I/O relations;

• Class 2. I/O equations with a small number monomials (can be of high or low degree);

• Class 3. Equations of very low degree (between 1 and 2), low non-linearity and extreme sparsity that one can obtain by adding additional variables" [13].

An example of a system of nonlinear equations between the initial state of the LFSR, $k\ (l\ bits)$ and the output of keystream bit is:

$$\begin{aligned} f(k) &= z^0 \\ f(L(k)) &= z^1 \\ f(L(k)) &= z^2 \end{aligned} \tag{6}$$

where L is a linear update function and z^t represents the output of the keystream bit. Techniques to solve the system use the Linearization algorithms (XL, XSL) or Gröbner bases.

The algebraic attack is a new form of attack that requires knowledge on many keystream elements and a huge memory. In spite of good theoretical results and estimations, the algebraic attack is not yet practically feasible.

3 A New Model of a Cryptographic Attack

The authors now propose a Known Plaintext Attack (KPA), using a regulation technique well-known in systems theory, namely a feedback type error regulation.

The controller used in the cryptanalysis can be a fuzzy controller or an unconventional controller. This technique of cryptanalysis is named *error regulation-based cryptanalysis* and it is exemplified on a simple algorithm.

The encryption function is defined as $e_{k_e}(p)=c$ and the decryption function is defined as $d_{k_d}(c)=p$.

In order to simplify the problem, it is considered a symmetric cryptosystem and one assumes that $k_e = k_d = k$.

Let us consider K_i the keys space with t bits, $K_i = (k_i^1, k_i^2, \dots, k_i^t)$, where k_i^j is 0 or 1.

The set of pairs of plaintexts and ciphertexts is noted with $S = \{(p_i, c_i), c_i = e_k(p_i)\}$ and $Card(S) = n$.

The objective of the error regulation-based cryptanalysis system is to determine the key k.

An important concept in the cryptanalysis terminology is the uniqueness distance. Shannon [1] defined the uniqueness distance as the length of an original ciphertext needed to break the cipher by reducing the number of possible spurious keys to zero in a brute force attack. That is, after trying every possible key, there should be just one decipherment that makes sense, namely the expected amount of cipher text needed to completely determine the key, assuming the underlying message has redundancy.

In the same respect, the Hamming distance between two Boolean vectors $\bar{x}, \bar{y}$ is equal with the number of positions in which they differ and it is noted with $d(\bar{x}, \bar{y})$ [14].

We have to determine the key k, therefore $e_k(p_i) = c_i, \forall (p_i, c_i) \in S$.

The schema of the error regulation-based cryptanalysis system is represented in Fig.4.

The cryptanalysis technique consists in performing the following operations:

1. a random key is selected and the c' cipher of a given p plaintext is calculated using this key;
2. the error ε as the Hamming distance between c and c' is calculated;

3. the controller block contains a certain method for the key determination, based on an analysis of the error value;
4. the key used for the plaintext encryption is generated;
5. the above steps repeat until the error is minimized, using pairs of plaintexts-ciphertexts from the known information set.

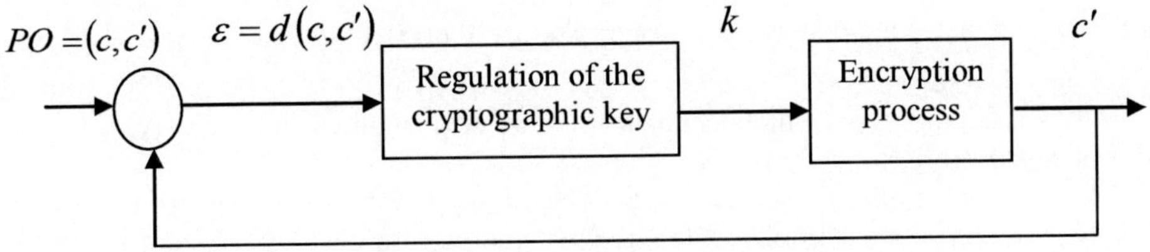

Fig. 4. Schema of the error regulation-based cryptanalysis system

PO represent the performance objectives. These are defined using the set of pairs known plaintexts and their correspondent ciphertexts:

$S=\{(p_i,c_i), c_i=e_k(p_i)\}$ with $p_i=(p_i^1,p_i^2,\ldots,p_i^s)$, $c_i=(c_i^1,c_i^2,\ldots,c_i^s)$,

where i takes values from 1 to n, where n is greater than the uniqueness distance.

ε represents the error and it is defined as the Hamming distance between two vectors.

The block of regulation of the cryptographic key contains various cryptographic attacks. The innovation consists in implementing the cryptographic attacks technique using the intermediate keys, on the basis of a feedback-type controller that performs the regulation of the cryptographic key.

The output c' is the cipher obtained using the key generated by the regulation block.

Possible scenarios that may be implemented are:

- if the obtained error is too big (that is, it has a bigger value than half of the maximum dimension of S), then the intermediate keys will be significantly changed (none of the bits of the previously found key will be preserved);
- if the obtained error is small, there will be selected a set of possible keys for which some of the bits will be changed;
- if the obtained error is around the value $n/2$, it can be started with a differential cryptanalysis. This type of attack generates a set of possible keys. These keys will be used in a linear cryptanalysis.

For example, let us consider the pair $p=(0,0)$ and $c=(1,1)$

The key is $k=(k_1,k_2)$.

The encryption function is $p_1 \oplus k_1$, $p_2 \oplus k_2$.

For example, it is chosen the intermediate key $k_i = (0,0)$.

Applying the given encryption function, it is obtained the cipher $c_i = (0,0)$ that determines a big error (the number of bits that differ is maximum, equal to the length of the cipher).

Consequently, none of the bits of the intermediate key k_i are preserved, and a new key, having extreme values, is chosen. So, it is chosen the key $k_f = (1,1)$ that generates the 0 error.

A possible controller, which can be used in an error regulation-based cryptanalysis, is a fuzzy controller.

The fuzzy controller is based on rules. The strategy of command generation used in this type of controller is implemented by means of an inference mechanism and uses a more or less natural language. A fuzzy controller may have as an associate an equivalent controller that uses conventional techniques. The inputs and the outputs of a fuzzy controller are discrete or fuzzy.

An architectural model of a fuzzy controller for processes control comprises the following components [15]:

- crisp-fuzzy conversion module ;
- knowledge base;
- decision making module based on fuzzy-inference motor reasoning;
- fuzzy-crisp conversion module.

A fuzzy controller diagram for process control is presented in Fig. 5.

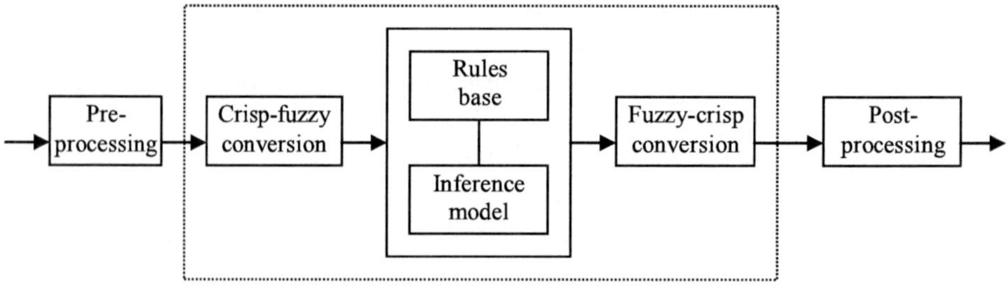

Fig. 5. A fuzzy controller diagram

The pre-processing block transforms the measured values from the measurement equipments before introducing them into the crisp-fuzzy conversion module.

The functions that can be performed by the pre-processing block are:

- normalizing or scaling the input domain to a standard values domain by using a bijective function, defined from the measured data domain to the universe domain;
- errors reduction or disposal;
- combining many measurements in order to obtain key pointers;
- sampling of the universe domain into a number of segments. The scaling function can be linear, nonlinear or mixed;

- performing approximation operations;
- determining development tendencies.

The crisp-fuzzy conversion block transforms the crisp values into fuzzy ones. The aim of this module is to allow the construction of a rules base, a fuzzy segmenting of the input spaces, output spaces respectively, and the determination of the linguistic variables used in formulation of the rules from the knowledge base [15]. The linguistic variable from the hypothesis describes an input fuzzy space, and the linguistic variable from the consequence describes an output fuzzy space.

There are seven linguistic terms used in most of the fuzzy control applications, namely:

NB-negative big, NM-negative medium, NS-negative small, ZE-zero, PS-positive small, PM-positive medium, PB-positive big.

The most used membership functions have triangular or trapezium shapes.

The triangular model of the membership function of m center and d shifting is defined according to formula 7.

$$\varphi_{m,d}(x)=\begin{cases}1-\left|\frac{m-x}{d}\right|, m-d\le x\le m+d \\ 0, otherwise\end{cases}, m\in R,\ d>0 \tag{7}$$

The trapezium model of the membership function is defined as

$$\varphi_{a,b,c,d}(x)=\begin{cases}\frac{x-a}{b-a}, a\le x<b \\ 1, b\le x\le c \\ \frac{x-d}{c-d}, c<x\le d \\ 0, x<a\ or\ x>d\end{cases}, \text{ where } a<b<c<d. \tag{8}$$

The rules base block contains a set of rules. The linguistic controller contains rules of an *if-then* format.

A fuzzy rule is a construction of an *if-then* type performed using the fuzzy implication [15].

An example of a fuzzy rule is

If x_1 is A_1 and x_2 is A_2, then y is B.

In order to define a fuzzy regulation in an error regulation-based cryptanalysis system, the concepts presented below are required.

The measurement of nearness between two code words c and c' is defined as

$$nearness(c,c')=d(c,c')/n \tag{9}$$

and it is obvious that $0\le nearness(c,c')\le 1$.

The fuzzy membership function for a codeword c to be equal to a given c' is defined as

$$\varphi(c') = \begin{cases} 0 \; if \; nearness(c, c') = z \le z_0 < 1 \\ z \qquad\qquad otherwise \end{cases} \tag{10}$$

The fuzzyfication is performed by computing the membership functions and the defuzzyfication is performed by using the method of the weight center.

The linguistic variables and the linguistic associated terms are presented in Table 3.

Table 3. Linguistic variables and linguistic associated terms

Linguistic variable	Variable type	Linguistic terms
Error (ε)	Input	ZE PS PM PB
k	Output	R C F VF

If ε is ZE (zero), then k is R (right).
If ε is PS (positive small), then k is C (close).
If ε is PM (positive medium), then k is F (far).
If ε is PB (positive big), then k is VF (very far).
The universe for the k variable is given by the keys space with t bits.

The universe for the error is given by the rational numbers from the interval $[0,1]$.

The proposed model makes possible to determine the decryption key by approximating it using intermediate keys. In the same time, it provides the opportunity to use fuzzy cryptanalysis, with a more precisely quantifying of the information theory concepts, in order to build more accurate cryptographic systems and to evaluate their strength or weakness.

4 Experimental Results

The experimental results presented in this section were obtained considering the following pair plaintext-ciphertext: $p = (1,1,0,1,0,1)$ and $c = (0,0,1,0,0,0)$. A comparison in terms of the number of intermediate keys needed to obtain the correct one was performed considering some classic cryptographic attacks and the error regulation-based cryptanalysis technique proposed by the authors.

First, the decryption key was determined by approximating it using the intermediate keys, according to the cryptanalysis technique described in the proposed model.

1. It is chosen the start key $k_1 = (0,0,0,0,0,0)$ and it is calculated the ciphertext $c_1 = (1,1,0,1,0,1)$
2. It is calculated the error $\varepsilon_1 = 5/6$, as the Hamming distance between c and c_1
3. Based on the analysis of the key value, according to the fuzzy rules, the obtained cipher determines a big error, PB-type, and the key is VF, that imposes a change of the majority of the key bits. There are performed the following operations:
$k_2 = (1,1,1,1,0,0) \rightarrow c_2 = (0,0,1,0,0,1) \rightarrow \varepsilon_2 = 1/6$ a PS-type error, corresponding to a C key, that leads to the correct key after six more steps needed to consequently modify one bit at a time.
4. The final correct key is the 8th:
$k_8 = (1,1,1,1,0,1) \rightarrow c_8 = (0,0,1,0,0,0) \rightarrow \varepsilon_8 = 0$

The conclusion is that, in this case with favorable choices, *the encryption key is obtained using 7 intermediate keys.*

Using the brute force attack, that consists in verifying all the possible keys, starting with the same initial key $k_i = (0,0,0,0,0,0)$ and consequently modifying a single bit, then 2 bits and so forth, *the number of intermediate keys is* $1+6+5\times6+4\times5+3\times4+1=70$. For bigger lengths of the key (usually 1024), the number of intermediate keys is increasing and the response time is longer.

In terms of linear cryptanalysis, the encryption key is obtained by solving the equation (1), so that every bit of the encryption key is precisely and quickly determined, *with no intermediate keys needed.*

As for the differential cryptanalysis, this method requires at least an additional pair of plaintext-ciphertext, that is *extra information*, in order to obtain the differential characteristics and more sets of possible keys.

5 Conclusions

Understanding cryptographic attacks is important to the science of cryptography, as they represent threads for the security of a cryptographic system by finding a weakness in their structure and, thus, serves to improve cryptographic algorithms.

Considering the taxonomy of the mostly used attack techniques on ciphers in cryptographic systems, the paper proposes a new approach of the cryptographic attacks by means of an error regulation-based cryptanalysis. By implementing the algorithm defining the proposed model, on the basis of a feedback fuzzy controller that ensures the regulation of the key, advantages in terms of accuracy, efficiency, and improved operating time can be emphasized. The authors consider that the proposed technique may be classified between the linear and the differential cryptanalysis techniques and it has better performances than the brute force attack.

As future direction, one may consider software implementation of the proposed model on more complex algorithms, in order to simulate and validate it.

References

1. Shannon, C.E.: Communication Theory of Secrecy Systems. Bell System Technical Journal 28(4), 656–715 (1949)
2. Kerckhoff, A.: La cryptographie militaire. Journal des sciences militaires IX, 5–38 (1883), `http://petitcolas.net/fabien/kerckhoffs/`
3. Keliher, L.: Linear Cryptanalysis of Substitution-Permutation Networks (2003), `http://mathcs.mta.ca/faculty/lkeliher/publications.html`
4. Matsui, M.: The First Experimental Cryptanalysis of the Data Encryption Standard. In: Desmedt, Y.G. (ed.) CRYPTO 1994. LNCS, vol. 839, pp. 1–11. Springer, Heidelberg (1994)
5. Langford, S.K., Hellman, M.E.: Differential-linear cryptanalysis. In: Desmedt, Y.G. (ed.) CRYPTO 1994. LNCS, vol. 839, pp. 17–25. Springer, Heidelberg (1994)
6. Kaliski Jr., B.S., Robshaw, M.J.B.: Linear cryptanalysis using multiple approximations. In: Desmedt, Y.G. (ed.) CRYPTO 1994. LNCS, vol. 839, pp. 26–39. Springer, Heidelberg (1994)
7. Nyberg, K.: Linear approximation of block ciphers. In: De Santis, A. (ed.) EUROCRYPT 1994. LNCS, vol. 950, pp. 439–444. Springer, Heidelberg (1995)
8. Knudsen, L.R.: A key-schedule weakness in SAFER K-64. In: Coppersmith, D. (ed.) CRYPTO 1995. LNCS, vol. 963, pp. 274–286. Springer, Heidelberg (1995)
9. Matsui, M.: Linear cryptanalysis method for DES cipher. In: Helleseth, T. (ed.) EUROCRYPT 1993. LNCS, vol. 765, pp. 386–397. Springer, Heidelberg (1994)
10. Biham, E., Shamir, A.: Differential cryptanalysis of DES-like cryptosystems. In: Menezes, A., Vanstone, S.A. (eds.) CRYPTO 1990. LNCS, vol. 537, pp. 2–21. Springer, Heidelberg (1991)
11. Difference Distribution Tables of DES, `http://www.cs.technion.ac.il/~cs236506/ddt/DES.html`
12. Courtois, N.T., Meier, W.: Algebraic Attacks on Stream Ciphers with Linear Feedback. In: Biham, E. (ed.) EUROCRYPT 2003. LNCS, vol. 2656, pp. 345–359. Springer, Heidelberg (2003)
13. Courtois, N.T., Bard, G.V.: Algebraic cryptanalysis of the data encryption standard. In: Galbraith, S.D. (ed.) Cryptography and Coding 2007. LNCS, vol. 4887, pp. 152–169. Springer, Heidelberg (2007)
14. Pless, V.: Introduction to Theory of Error Correcting Codes. Wiley & Sons, New York (1982)
15. Vaduva, I., Albeanu, G.: Introduction in Fuzzy Modeling. University of Bucharest Publishing House (2004)

A Designated Verifier Proxy Signature Scheme with Fast Revocation without Random Oracles

M. Beheshti-Atashgah[1], M. Gardeshi[2], and M. Bayat[3]

[1] Research Center of Intelligent Signal Processing, Tehran, Iran
m.beheshti.a@gmail.com
[2] Department of Communication & Information Technology,
Imam Hossein University, Tehran, Iran
mgardeshi@ihu.ac.ir
[3] Department of Mathematics & Computer Sciences,
Tarbiat Moallem University, Tehran, Iran
bayat@tmu.ac.ir

Abstract. In a designated verifier proxy signature scheme, proxy signature is issued for a designated receiver and only he/she can validate the signature. The fast revocation of delegated rights is an essential issue of the proxy signature schemes. In this paper, we present a designated verifier proxy signature scheme with fast revocation that has provable security in the standard model. In the our proposed scheme, we use of an on-line partially trusted server named SEM and the SEM should check whether a proxy signer signs according to the warrant or he/she exists in the revocation list. Additionally, the proxy signer must cooperate with the SEM to produce a valid proxy signature. We also propose the provable security of our scheme is based on the Gap Bilinear Diffie-Hellman ($GBDH$) intractability assumption and we will show that the proposed scheme satisfies all the security requirements for a proxy signature.

Keywords: Proxy signature scheme, Fast revocation of delegated rights, Security mediator, Provable security, Standard model.

1 Introduction

The concept of proxy signature scheme was first introduced by Mambo et al.'s in 1996 [1]. In a proxy signature scheme, an original signer can delegate his/her signing capability to a proxy signer and therefore the proxy signer can sign messages on behalf of the original signer. According to the Mambo et al.'s work [2], we can classify proxy signature schemes based on delegation types into three sets: full delegation, partial delegation and delegation by warrant. In the full delegation, the original signer gives his/her private key to the proxy signer and then the proxy signer uses it to sign messages. In the partial delegation, the original signer generates a proxy key from his/her private key and gives it to the proxy signer. The proxy signer uses the proxy key to sign messages. In the delegation by warrant, the original signer gives the proxy signer a warrant which is produced by the original signer and includes

H. Cherifi, J.M. Zain, and E. El-Qawasmeh (Eds.): DICTAP 2011, Part I, CCIS 166, pp. 535–550, 2011.

information such as the identity of the original signer, the identity of the proxy signer, a time period of the proxy validation and other information. The proxy signer uses the warrant and the corresponding private key to generate a signature. A number of proxy signature schemes have been proposed for each of three delegation types, such as [3], [4].

However, most existing proxy signature schemes have essential weaknesses [5]: First, the declaration of a valid delegation period in the warrant is useless because the proxy signer can still create a proxy signature and claim that his/her signature was done during the delegation period even if the delegation period has expired. Second, when the original signer wants to revoke the delegation earlier than his/her plan, he/she can do nothing. Therefore, the fast revocation of delegated rights is an essential issue of the proxy signature schemes.

Until now, schemes have been proposed to solve these weaknesses. For example, Sun [6] showed a time-stamped proxy signature scheme and claim that the fast revocation can be solved by using a time-stamp. Sun's scheme suffers from security weakness and cannot solve the second problem. Moreover, in using of the time-stamp technique, synchronization is a serious problem in practice. But Seo et al. [5] showed a mediated proxy signature scheme to solve the proxy revocation problem by using a special entity, named SEM, who is an on-line partially trusted server. But their proposed scheme has not provable security neither in the random oracle model described by Bellare&Rogaway [7] and in the standard model described by Waters [8] and therefore Seo et al.'s scheme did not attract many interests.

On the other hands, a designated verifier proxy signature scheme is a proxy signature scheme that the signature is issued only to a designated receiver and therefore only the designated verifier can validate the signature. Such these schemes are widely used in situations where the receiver's privacy should be protected. In 1996, Jakobsson et al. [9] first introduced a new primitive named designated verifier proofs in the digital signature schemes. After that in 2003, Dai et al. [10] proposed a designated verifier proxy signature scheme and in the last years, schemes such as [11], [12] have been proposed which have provable security in the random oracle model [7]. Yu et al. [13] also showed a designated verifier that has provable security in the standard model. Their scheme is based on the idea described by Waters [8].

In this paper, we will propose the first designated verifier proxy signature scheme with fast revocation which has provable security in the standard model and based on $GBDH$ intractability assumption. Our proposed scheme is based on Yu et al.'s scheme and we used from the proxy fast revocation technique of the Seo.

The rest of this paper is organized as follows: some preliminary works are given in Section 2. In Section 3, we present our formal models. In Section 4, our designated verifier proxy signature scheme with fast revocation is presented. In Section 5, we analyze the proposed scheme and finally conclusions will be given in Section 6.

2 Preliminaries

In this section, we review fundamental backgrounds including bilinear pairings and complexity assumptions used in this paper.

2.1 Bilinear Pairings

Let G, G_T be two cyclic multiplicative groups of prime order p and g be a generator of G. The map $e: G \times G \rightarrow G_T$ is said to be an admissible bilinear pairing if the following conditions hold true:

(1) $bilinearity$: $For\ all\ a, b \in \mathbb{Z}_p, e(g^a, g^b) = e(g, g)^{ab}$
(2) $non-degeneracy$: $e(P, P) \neq 1_{G_T}$
(3) $computability$: $There\ is\ an\ efficient\ algorithm\ to\ compute\ e(g, h) for\ all\ g, h \in G.$

2.2 Complexity Assumption

Definition 1 ($CBDH$ problem). Given $(g, g^a, g^b, g^c \in G)$ for some unknown $a, b, c \in \mathbb{Z}_p$, compute $e(g, g)^{abc}$.

Definition 2 ($DBDH$ problem). Given $(g, g^a, g^b, g^c \in G)$ for some unknown $a, b, c \in \mathbb{Z}_p$ and $w \in G_T$, decide whether $w = e(g, g)^{abc}$.

Definition 3 ($GBDH$ problem). Given $(g, g^a, g^b, g^c \in G)$ for some unknown $a, b, c \in \mathbb{Z}_p$, compute $w = e(g, g)^{abc}$ with the help of $DBDH$ oracle $\mathcal{O}_{DBDH}$.

The probability that an adversary $\mathcal{A}$ can solve the $GBDH$ problem is defined as:

$$Succ_{\mathcal{A}}^{GBDH} = \Pr[e(g, g)^{abc} \leftarrow \mathcal{A}(G, G_T, g, g^a, g^b, g^c, \mathcal{O}_{DBDH})].$$

3 Formal Models of DVPSS[1] with Fast Revocation

3.1 Outline of DVPSS

Suppose that Alice be the original signer, Bob be the proxy signer, Cindy be the designated verifier and SEM be the security mediator. A DVPSS with fast revocation consists of the following algorithms.

- **Setup:** Given a security parameter l^k, this algorithm outputs the system parameters π.
- **KeyGen:** This algorithm takes as input the system parameters π and outputs the secret/public key pair (sk_i, pk_i) for $i \in \{a, b, c\}$ denotes Alice, Bob and Cindy.
- **DelegationGen:** This algorithm takes as input the system parameters π, the warrant ω and the original signer's private key sk_a, then outputs two partial proxy keys σ_B, σ_S and a revocation identifier R_A. Alice sends (ω, R_A, σ_B) to Bob and sends (ω, R_A, σ_S) to the SEM.
- **DelegationVerify:** After receiving (ω, R_A, σ_S) and (ω, R_A, σ_B), the SEM and Bob confirm their validity.

---

[1] Designated Verifier Proxy Signature Scheme.

- **ProxyValid:** Bob wants to sign a message M. The SEM should ascertain whether the period of proxy delegation specified in the warrant ω should be valid. If Bob not be in the public revocation list; then SEM issues a partial proxy signature (Token) on the message M.
- **ProxySignGen:** This algorithm takes as input π, ω, two partial proxy keys σ_B, σ_S, the proxy signer's private key sk_b, the designated verifier's public key pk_c and a message M to produce a proxy signature σ_P.
- **ProxySignVerify:** This algorithm takes as input π, ω, public keys pk_a, pk_b, a signed message M, the proxy signature σ_P, the designated verifier's private key x_c and returns $\top$ if the signature is valid, otherwise returns $\bot$ indicating the proxy signature is invalid.
- **Transcript simulation:** This algorithm takes as input a message M, the warrant ω and the designated verifier's private key sk_{cx} to generate an identically distributed transcript σ_P^* that is indistinguishable from the original DVPS σ_P.
- **ProxyRevocation:** If Alice wants to revoke the delegation of Bob before the specific delegation period, she then asks the SEM to put (ω, R_A) in a public revocation list. In this case, the SEM does not issue any token for Bob.

3.2 Security Notions

There are three types adversary in the system as follows.

Type I: Adversary $\mathcal{A}_{\text{I}}$ only has the public keys of Alice and Bob.

Type II: Adversary $\mathcal{A}_{\text{II}}$ has the public keys of Alice and Bob, he/she additionally has the secret key of the original signer Alice.

Type III: Adversary $\mathcal{A}_{\text{III}}$ has the public keys of Alice and Bob, he/she additionally has the secret key of the proxy signer Bob.

Note that if DVPSS is unforgeable against type II and III adversary, it is also unforgeable against type I adversary.

Unforgeability against $\mathcal{A}_{II}$

The existential unforgeability of a DVPS under $\mathcal{A}_{\text{II}}$ adversary requires that it is difficult for the original signer to generate a valid proxy signature of a message M^* under the warrant ω^* that has not been signed by the proxy signer Bob. It is defined using the following game between the challenger $\mathcal{C}$ and $\mathcal{A}_{\text{II}}$ adversary:

- **Setup:** The challenger $\mathcal{C}$ runs the Setup algorithm to obtain system parameters π, and runs **KeyGen** algorithm to obtain the secret/public key pairs (sk_a, pk_a), (sk_b, pk_b) , (sk_c, pk_c) of the original signer Alice, proxy signer Bob and the designated verifier Cindy. Then $\mathcal{C}$ sends sk_a, pk_a, pk_b, pk_c to the adversary $\mathcal{A}_{\text{II}}$.
- **SEM-Sign queries:** The adversary $\mathcal{A}_{\text{II}}$ can request a partial proxy signature of SEM on the message M. $\mathcal{C}$ runs the ProxySign algorithm to obtain the partial proxy signature σ_{ps} and then sends it to $\mathcal{A}_{\text{II}}$.
- **User-Sign queries:** The adversary $\mathcal{A}_{\text{II}}$ can request a proxy signature on the message M under the warrant ω. $\mathcal{C}$ runs the ProxySign algorithm to obtain the proxy signature σ_P and then sends it to $\mathcal{A}_{\text{II}}$.

- **Verify queries:** The adversary $\mathcal{A}_{\text{II}}$ can request a proxy signature verification on a (M, ω, σ_P). If σ_P is a valid DVPS, $\mathcal{C}$ outputs $\top$ and $\bot$ otherwise.
- **Output:** Finally, $\mathcal{A}_{\text{II}}$ outputs a new DVPS σ_P^* on the message M^* under the warrant ω^*, such that
  (a) (M^*, ω^*) has never been queried during the ProxySign queries.
  (b) σ_P^* is a valid DVPS of message M^* under warrant ω^*.

The advantage of $\mathcal{A}_{\text{II}}$ in the above game is defined as $\text{Adv}_{\mathcal{A}_{\text{II}}} = \Pr[\mathcal{A}_{\text{II}} \text{ succeeds}]$.

Definition 4. An adversary $\mathcal{A}_{\text{II}}$ is said to be an $(\epsilon, t, q_{PS}, q_v)$ −forger of a DVPS if $\mathcal{A}_{\text{II}}$ in the above game: has advantage of at least ϵ, runs in time at most t, makes at most q_{PS} User-Sign queries and q_v Verify queries.

Unforgeability against $\mathcal{A}_{III}$
Similar to the last game, the following game is defined between the challenger $\mathcal{C}$ and $\mathcal{A}_{\text{III}}$ adversary:

- **Setup:** The challenger $\mathcal{C}$ runs the Setup algorithm to obtain system parameters π, and runs **KeyGen** algorithm to obtain the secret/public key pairs(sk_a, pk_a), (sk_b, pk_b), (sk_c, pk_c) of the original signer Alice, proxy signer Bob and the designated verifier Cindy. Then $\mathcal{C}$ sends sk_b, pk_a, pk_b, pk_c to the adversary $\mathcal{A}_{\text{III}}$.
- **SEM-Delegation queries:** $\mathcal{A}_{\text{III}}$ can request a partial proxy key σ_S of the SEM. $\mathcal{C}$ runs the DelegationGen algorithm to obtain two partial proxy key σ_B, σ_S and a revocation identifier R_A and then returns (ω, R_A, σ_S) to $\mathcal{A}_{\text{III}}$.
- **User-Delegation queries:** $\mathcal{A}_{\text{III}}$ can request a partial proxy key $\sigma_B$of Bob. $\mathcal{C}$ runs the DelegationGen algorithm to obtain two partial proxy key σ_B, σ_S and a revocation identifier R_A and then returns (ω, R_A, σ_B) to $\mathcal{A}_{\text{III}}$.
- **SEM-Sign queries:** The adversary $\mathcal{A}_{\text{III}}$ can request a partial proxy signature of the SEM on the message M under the warrant ω. $\mathcal{C}$ runs the ProxySign algorithm to obtain the partial proxy signature σ_{ps} and then sends it to $\mathcal{A}_{\text{III}}$.
- **User-Sign queries:** The adversary $\mathcal{A}_{\text{III}}$ can request a final proxy signature on the message M under the warrant ω. $\mathcal{C}$ runs the ProxySign algorithm to obtain the proxy signature σ_P and then sends it to $\mathcal{A}_{\text{III}}$.
- **Verify queries:** The adversary $\mathcal{A}_{\text{III}}$ can request a proxy signature verification on a (M, ω, σ_P). If σ_P is a valid DVPS, $\mathcal{C}$ outputs $\top$ and $\bot$ otherwise.
- **Output:** Finally, $\mathcal{A}_{\text{III}}$ outputs a new DVPS σ_P^* on the message M^* under the warrant ω^*, such that
  (a) ω^* has never been queried during the Delegation queries.
  (b) (M^*, ω^*) has never been queried during the ProxySign queries.
  (c) σ_P^* is a valid DVPS of message M^* under warrant ω^*.

The advantage of $\mathcal{A}_{\text{III}}$ in the above game is defined as $\text{Adv}_{\mathcal{A}_{\text{III}}} = \Pr[\mathcal{A}_{\text{III}} \text{ succeeds}]$.

Definition 5. An adversary $\mathcal{A}_{\text{III}}$ is said to be an $(\epsilon, t, q_{\omega}, q_{PS}, q_v)$ – forger of a DVTPS if $\mathcal{A}_{\text{III}}$ in the above game: has advantage of at least ϵ, runs in time at most t, makes at most q_ω SEM-Delegation and user-Delegation queries, q_{PS} SEM-Sign and User-Sign queries and q_v Verify queries.

3.3 Security Requirements

Verifiability: The designated verifier should be convinced of the original signer's agreement on the signed message.

Identifiability: Anyone should determine the identity of the corresponding proxy signer from a proxy signature.

Undeniability: The proxy signer should not be able to create the signature against anyone. This is also called "non-repudiation".

Prevention of misuse: A proxy signing key should not be used for purpose other than generating valid proxy signature. In case of misuse, the responsibility of the proxy signature should be determined explicitly.

4 Proposed DVPSS in the Standard Model

In this section, we describe our proposed DVPSS with fast revocation. In the following, all the messages to be signed will be showed as bit string of length n.

It is possible to be quest that if the bit length of input messages is more than n, what we can do? Thus for more flexibility of the scheme, we can use a collision-resistant hash function $H: \{0,1\}^* \rightarrow \{0,1\}^n$ in the first and last of the proposed scheme.

Our scheme includes the following algorithms:

- **Setup:** Let (G, G_T) be bilinear groups from prime order p. e denotes an admissible pairing and $g \in G$ is the generator of G. $u', m' \in G$ are two random integers and $u = (u_i), m = (m_i)$ are vectors of length n that is chosen at random from group G. The system parameters are $\pi = (G, G_T, p, e, g, u', m', u, m)$.
- **KeyGen:** Alice sets her secret key $sk_a = (x_a, y_a) \in \mathbb{Z}_p^2$ and computes her corresponding public key $pk_a = (g^{x_a}, g^{y_a})$. Similarly, proxy signer Bob sets his secret-public keys $sk_b = (x_b, y_b) \in \mathbb{Z}_p^2$, $pk_b = (g^{x_b}, g^{y_b})$. The secret-public keys of the designated verifier Cindy are $sk_c = (x_c, y_c) \in \mathbb{Z}_p^2$, $pk_c = (g^{x_c}, g^{y_c})$.
- **DelegationGen:** Let ω_i be the i-th bit of ω that ω is the warrant issued by the original signer and $\mathcal{W} \subseteq \{1,2,\cdots,n\}$ be the set of all i for which $\omega_i = 1$. Suppose that M is the message of length n-bit and M_j be the j-th bit of M which $M_j = 1$. The original signer Alice randomly chooses $x_{a_1}, x_{a_2}, r_{a_1}, r_{a_2} \in \mathbb{Z}_p$ such that $x_{a_1} + x_{a_2} = x_a$, $r_{a_1} + r_{a_2} = r_a$. Alice also published the value R_A.

$$\sigma_B = \left(g^{x_{a_1} y_a} \left(u' \prod_{i \in W} u_i \right)^{r_{a_1}}, g^{r_{a_1}} \right)$$

$$\sigma_S = \left(g^{x_{a_2} y_a} \left(u' \prod_{i \in W} u_i \right)^{r_{a_2}}, g^{r_{a_2}} \right) \quad (1)$$

$$R_A = g^{r_a}$$

Then Alice sends (ω, R_A, σ_B) to Bob and sends (ω, R_A, σ_S) to the SEM.

- **DelegationVerify:** To validate the correctness of (ω, R_A, σ_B), Bob computes $R_B = e(\sigma_{B_1}, g)$ and sends (ω, R_B) to the SEM. After receiving $R_S = e(\sigma_{S_1}, g)$ from the SEM, Bob checks whether the following equation is satisfy?

$$\begin{aligned} R_B R_S &= e(\sigma_{B_1}, g) e(\sigma_{S_1}, g) \\ &= e\left(g^{x_{a_1} y_a} \left(u' \prod_{i \in W} u_i \right)^{r_{a_1}}, g \right) e\left(g^{x_{a_2} y_a} \left(u' \prod_{i \in W} u_i \right)^{r_{a_2}}, g \right) \\ &= e(pk_{ax}, pk_{ay}) e(u' \prod_{i \in W} u_i, R_A) \end{aligned} \quad (2)$$

Similarly, the SEM verifies the equation by R_B.

- **Proxy-Valid:** To produce a proxy signature on a message M, Bob must cooperate with the SEM. Bob sends his identity and (ω, M, R_A, R_B) to the SEM. The SEM confirms that (ω, M, R_A, R_B) was received in the DelegationGen and DelegationVerify steps. Then before generating a partial proxy signature, the SEM must ascertain the following conditions.
  1. The time period of proxy delegation specified in the warrant ω should be valid.
  2. (ω, R_A) should not be in the public revocation list. If these two conditions hold, then the SEM performs the proxy signature generation step.
- **ProxySignGen:**
  1. The SEM randomly chooses $r_S, r_m \in \mathbb{Z}_p$ and sends the following partial proxy signature σ_{ps} to Bob.

$$\sigma_{ps} = \left(\sigma_{ps_1} \left(u' \prod_{i \in W} u_i \right)^{r_S} \left(m' \prod_{j \in M} m_j \right)^{r_m}, g^{r_S}, g^{r_m} \right) =$$

$$\left(g^{x_{a_2} y_a} \left(u' \prod_{i \in W} u_i \right)^{r_{a_2} + r_S} \left(m' \prod_{j \in M} m_j \right)^{r_m}, g^{r_S}, g^{r_m} \right) \quad (3)$$

2. Bob checks whether the following equation holds.

$$e\left(\sigma_{ps_1}, g\right) R_B = e(pk_{ax}, pk_{ay}) \cdot e\left(u' \prod_{i \in \mathcal{W}} u_i, \sigma_{ps_2} R_A\right) . e\left(m' \prod_{j \in \mathcal{M}} m_j, \sigma_{ps_3}\right) \quad (4)$$

If the above equation holds, he chooses two random integers $r_B, r'_m \in \mathbb{Z}_p$ and then computes the proxy signature as follows.

$$\sigma_{P_1} = e\left(\sigma_{ps_1}\sigma_{B_1}\left(u' \prod_{i \in \mathcal{W}} u_i\right)^{r_B} g^{x_b y_b}\left(m' \prod_{j \in \mathcal{M}} m_j\right)^{r'_m}, pk_{cx}\right)$$

$$= \left(g^{x_a y_a} g^{x_b y_b}\left(u' \prod_{i \in \mathcal{W}} u_i\right)^{\tilde{r}}\left(m' \prod_{j \in \mathcal{M}} m_j\right)^{\tilde{r}_m}, g^{x_c}\right), \quad (5)$$

$$\sigma_{P_2} = \sigma_{ps_2} R_A g^{r_B}, \sigma_{P_3} = g^{\tilde{r}_m}$$

where $\tilde{r} = r_{a_1} + r_{a_2} + r_S + r_B$ and $\tilde{r}_m = r_m + r'_m$. The proxy signature on the message M will be $(\omega, M, R_A, \sigma_P)$.

- **ProxySignVerify:** The designated verifier validates the proxy signature $\sigma_P = (\sigma_{P_1}, \sigma_{P_2}, \sigma_{P_3})$ by checking the follow equality:

$$\sigma_{P_1} = e(g^{x_a y_a}, g^{x_c}) e(g^{x_b y_b}, g^{x_c}) \cdot e\left(\left(u' \prod_{i \in \mathcal{W}} u_i\right)^{\tilde{r}}, g^{x_c}\right) e\left(\left(m' \prod_{j \in \mathcal{M}} m_j\right)^{\tilde{r}_m}, g^{x_c}\right) \quad (6)$$

$$\sigma_{P_1} = e(pk_{ax}, pk_{ay})^{x_c} e(pk_{bx}, pk_{by})^{x_c} . e\left(u' \prod_{i \in \mathcal{W}} u_i, \sigma_{P_2}\right)^{x_c} e\left(m' \prod_{j \in \mathcal{M}} m_j, \sigma_{P_3}\right)^{x_c}$$

- **ProxyRevocation:** To revoke the delegation rights, it is enough that the original signer (Alice) gives (ω, R_A) to the SEM and asks the SEM to put the (ω, R_A) in a public revocation list.

5 Analysis of the Scheme

5.1 Unforgeability

Unforgeability against adversary $\mathcal{A}_{\text{II}}$

Theorem 1. If there exists an adversary $\mathcal{A}_{\text{II}}$ who can $(\epsilon, t, q_{PS}, q_v)$ breaks our scheme, then there exists another algorithm $\mathcal{B}$ who can use $\mathcal{A}_{\text{II}}$ to solve an instance of the $GBDH$ problem with probability

$$Succ_{\mathcal{B}}^{GBDH} \geq \frac{\epsilon}{8(n+1)q_{PS}} \tag{7}$$

In time

$$t' \leq ((2n+6)q_{PS} + nq_v + 2)t_1 + (5q_v)t_2 + (3n + 12q_{PS} + q_v + 5)T_1 + (3q_v)T_2 + (q_{PS} + 4q_v)t_e$$

where t_1, t_2 are the time for a multiplication in G and G_T respectively, T_1, T_2 are the time of an exponentiation in G and G_T respectively, and t_e is the time for a pairing computation in (G, G_T).

Proof. Assume that $\mathcal{B}$ receives a $GBDH$ problem instance (g, g^a, g^b, g^c) of a bilinear group (G, G_T) whose orders are both a prime number p. His/Her goal is to output $e(g,g)^{abc}$ with the help of the $DBDH$ oracle O_{DBDH}. $\mathcal{B}$ runs $\mathcal{A}_{\text{II}}$ as a subroutine and act as $\mathcal{A}_{\text{II}}$'s challenger. $\mathcal{B}$ will answer $\mathcal{A}_{\text{II}}$'s queries as follows:

Setup: $\mathcal{B}$ chooses a random integer $l = 4q_{PS}$ and other random integer k uniformly between 0 and n. Then, $\mathcal{B}$ picks values $(x_a, y_a, r_0, r_1, \cdots, r_n) \in \mathbb{Z}_p$ at random. $\mathcal{B}$ also picks a random value x' and a random n-vector $\vec{x} = (x_i)$ where $x', x_i \in \mathbb{Z}_l$. Additionally, $\mathcal{B}$ chooses a value y' at random and a random n-vector $\vec{y} = (y_i)$ where $y', y_i \in \mathbb{Z}_l$. All of these values are kept secret by $\mathcal{B}$.

For a message M and a warrant ω, we let $\mathcal{M} \subset \{1,2,\cdots,n\}$ and $\mathcal{W} \subset \{1,2,\cdots,n\}$ be the set of all i for which $M_i = 1$ and $\omega_i = 1$. For simplicity of analysis, we defines functions $F(M)$, $J(M)$ and $K(M)$ as in [3].

(1) $F(M) = (p - lk) + x' + \sum_{i \in \mathcal{M}} x_i$

(2) $J(M) = y' + \sum_{i \in \mathcal{M}} y_i$

(3) $K(M) = \begin{cases} 0, & if\ x' + \sum_{i \in \mathcal{M}} x_i = 0\ (mod\ l) \\ 1, & Otherwise. \end{cases}$

In the next step, $\mathcal{B}$ generates the follow common parameters:

(1) $\mathcal{B}$ assigns $\vec{u} = (u_1, \cdots, u_n)$, $u_i = g^{r_i} (i = 1, \cdots, n)$ and $u' = g^{r_0}$.

(2) $\mathcal{B}$ chooses random integers $x_a, y_a \in Z_p^*$, and sets the original signers' public key as $(pk_{ax}, pk_{ay}) = (g^{x_a}, g^{y_a})$.

(3) $\mathcal{B}$ assigns the public keys of the proxy signer and the designated verifier $(pk_{bx}, pk_{by}) = (g^a, g^b)$, $pk_{cx} = g^c$, respectively. The parameters g^a, g^b, g^c are the input of the $GBDH$ problem.

(4) $\mathcal{B}$ assigns $m' = pk_{by}^{p-lk+x'} g^{y'}$, $m_i = pk_{by}^{x_i} g^{y_i}$ and $\vec{m} = (m_1, m_2, \cdots, m_n)$.
Note that, we have

$$m' \prod_{i \in \mathcal{M}} m_i = pk_{by}^{F(M)} g^{J(M)}$$

Finally, $\mathcal{B}$ returns $(G, G_T, e, p, g, u', \vec{u}, m', \vec{m})$ and $(pk_{ax}, pk_{ay}, pk_{bx}, pk_{by}, pk_{cx}, x_a, y_a)$ to adversary $\mathcal{A}_{\mathrm{II}}$.

Delegation queries: Includes the following stages.

(1) If $K_a(\omega) = 0$, $\mathcal{B}$ terminates the simulation and report failure.

(2) If $K_a(\omega) \neq 0$, this implies $F(M) \neq 0 \ (mod\ p)$ [3]. In this case, $\mathcal{B}$ chooses $x_{a_1}, x_{a_2}, r_{a_1}, r_{a_2} \in \mathbb{Z}_p^*$ randomly such that $x_{a_1} + x_{a_2} = x_a$ and $r_{a_1} + r_{a_2} = r_a$. Then $\mathcal{B}$ computes

$$\sigma_B = \left(g^{x_{a_1} y_a} \left(u' \prod_{i \in \mathcal{W}} u_i \right)^{r_{a_1}}, g^{r_{a_1}} \right)$$

$$\sigma_S = \left(g^{x_{a_2} y_a} \left(u' \prod_{i \in \mathcal{W}} u_i \right)^{r_{a_2}}, g^{r_{a_2}} \right) \tag{8}$$

$$R_A = g^{r_a}$$

ProxySign queries: SEM randomly chooses $r_S, r_m \in \mathbb{Z}_p$ and then computes the partial proxy signature σ_{PS} as follows:

$$\sigma_{PS} = \left(g^{x_{a_2} y_a} \left(u' \prod_{i \in \mathcal{W}} u_i \right)^{r_{a_2} + r_S} \left(m' \prod_{j \in M} m_j \right)^{r_m}, g^{r_S}, g^{r_m} \right) \tag{9}$$

During this stage, $\mathcal{A}_{\mathrm{II}}$

(1) If $K(M) = 0$, $\mathcal{B}$ terminates the simulation and report failure.

(2) If $K(M) \neq 0$, $\mathcal{B}$ picks the random integers $r_B, r_m' \in \mathbb{Z}_p$ and then computes the proxy signature $(\sigma_{P_1}, \sigma_{P_2}, \sigma_{P_3})$ as follows

$$\sigma_{P_1} = e\left(pk_{bx}^{-\frac{J(M)}{F(M)}} \left(m' \prod_{j \in M} m_j \right)^{\tilde{r}_m} \left(u' \prod_{i \in \mathcal{W}} u_i \right)^{\tilde{r}} g^{x_a y_a}, pk_{cx} \right),$$

$$\sigma_{P_2} = g^{\tilde{r}}, \sigma_{P_3} = g^{-\frac{a}{F(M)}} g^{\tilde{r}_m} \tag{10}$$

Where $\tilde{r} = r_{a_1} + r_{a_2} + r_S + r_B$ and $\tilde{r}_m = r_m + r'_m$.

Note that, in the above equations $\sigma_{P_3} = g^{-\frac{a}{F(M)}} g^{\tilde{r}_m} = \sigma_{P_3} = g^{\tilde{r}_m - \frac{a}{F(M)}} = g^{\hat{r}}$.

Correctness

$$\sigma_{P_1} = e\left(pk_{bx}^{-\frac{J(M)}{F(M)}} \left(m' \prod_{j\in M} m_j \right)^{\tilde{r}_m} \left(u' \prod_{i\in W} u_i \right)^{\tilde{r}} g^{x_a y_a}, pk_{cx} \right)$$

$$= e\left(g^{ab} \cdot g^{-ab} \cdot g^{-\frac{aJ(M)}{F(M)}} \left(pk_{by}^{F(M)} g^{J(M)} \right)^{\tilde{r}_m} \left(u' \prod_{i\in W} u_i \right)^{\tilde{r}} g^{x_a y_a}, pk_{cx} \right)$$

$$= e\left(g^{ab} \cdot \left(g^{bF(M)} g^{J(M)} \right)^{-\frac{a}{F(M)}} \left(pk_{by}^{F(M)} g^{J(M)} \right)^{\tilde{r}_m} \left(u' \prod_{i\in W} u_i \right)^{\tilde{r}} g^{x_a y_a}, pk_{cx} \right)$$

$$= e\left(g^{ab} \cdot \left(pk_{by}^{F(M)} g^{J(M)} \right)^{\tilde{r}_m - \frac{a}{F(M)}} \left(u' \prod_{i\in W} u_i \right)^{\tilde{r}} g^{x_a y_a}, pk_{cx} \right)$$

$$= e\left(g^{ab} \cdot \left(m' \prod_{j\in M} m_j \right)^{\hat{r}} \left(u' \prod_{i\in W} u_i \right)^{\tilde{r}} g^{x_a y_a}, pk_{cx} \right)$$

ProxySign Verify queries: Assume that $\mathcal{A}_{\text{II}}$ issues a verify query for the message/signature pair $(M, \omega, \sigma_{P_1}, \sigma_{P_2}, \sigma_{P_3})$.

(1) If $F(M) = 0$, $\mathcal{B}$ submits

$$\left(g, g^a, g^b, g^c, \frac{\sigma_1}{e(g^c, g^{y_a})^{x_a} e(g^c, \sigma_2)^{r_0 + \sum_{i\in W} r_i} e(g^c, \sigma_3)^{J(M)}} \right) \quad (11)$$

Correctness

σ_{P_1}

$$= e(pk_{ax}, pk_{ay})^{x_c} e(pk_{bx}, pk_{by})^{x_c} . e\left(u' \prod_{i\in W} u_i, \sigma_{P_2} \right)^{x_c} e\left(m' \prod_{j\in M} m_j, \sigma_{P_3} \right)^{x_c}$$

$$= e(g^{x_a}, g^{y_a})^c e(g^a, g^b)^c . e\left(g^{r_0 + \sum_{i\in W} r_i}, \sigma_{P_2} \right)^c e\left(g^{J(M)}, \sigma_{P_3} \right)^c$$

$$= e(g, g)^{abc} e(g^c, g^{y_a})^{x_a} . e\left(g^c, \sigma_{P_2} \right)^{r_0 + \sum_{i\in W} r_i} e\left(g^c, \sigma_{P_3} \right)^{J(M)}$$

Which indicates

$$\left(g, g^a, g^b, g^c, \frac{\sigma_{P_1}}{e(g^c, g^{y_a})^{x_a} e(g^c, \sigma_2)^{r_0+\sum_{i\in W} r_i} e(g^c, \sigma_3)^{J(M)}}\right)$$

Is a valid BDH tuple.

(2) If $F(M) \neq 0$, $\mathcal{B}$ can compute a valid proxy signature just as he responses to proxy signature queries. Assume that $(M, \omega, \sigma'_{P_1}, \sigma'_{P_2}, \sigma'_{P_3})$ be the signature computed by $\mathcal{B}$. Then $\mathcal{B}$ submits

$$\left(g, m' \prod_{j\in M} m_j, \frac{\sigma_{P_3}}{\sigma'_{P_3}}, g^c, \frac{\sigma_{P_1}}{\sigma'_{P_1}} e\left(g^c, \frac{\sigma'_{P_2}}{\sigma_{P_2}}\right)^{r_0+\sum_{i\in W} r_i}\right) \quad (12)$$

to the $DBDH$ oracle $\mathcal{O}_{DBDH}$. If $\mathcal{O}_{DBDH}$ returns 1, $\mathcal{B}$ outputs "valid" and otherwise, $\mathcal{B}$ outputs "invalid".

Correctness

If $(M, \omega, \sigma_{P_1}, \sigma_{P_2}, \sigma_{P_3})$ is a valid designated verifier proxy signature computed by $\mathcal{B}$, then we have

$$\sigma_{P_1} = e(pk_{ax}, pk_{ay})^{x_c} e(pk_{bx}, pk_{by})^{x_c}. e\left(u' \prod_{i\in W} u_i, \sigma_{P_2}\right)^{x_c} e\left(m' \prod_{j\in M} m_j, \sigma_{P_3}\right)^{x_c}$$

Similarly, since $(M, \omega, \sigma'_{P_1}, \sigma'_{P_2}, \sigma'_{P_3})$ is another valid designated verifier proxy signature computed by $\mathcal{B}$, then

$$\sigma'_{P_1} = e(pk_{ax}, pk_{ay})^{x_c} e(pk_{bx}, pk_{by})^{x_c}. e\left(u' \prod_{i\in W} u_i, \sigma'_{P_2}\right)^{x_c} e\left(m' \prod_{j\in M} m_j, \sigma'_{P_3}\right)^{x_c}$$

We can obtain

$$\frac{\sigma_{P_1}}{\sigma'_{P_1}} = \left(\frac{e(u' \prod_{i\in W} u_i, \sigma_{P_2})}{e(u' \prod_{i\in W} u_i, \sigma'_{P_2})}\right)^{x_c} \left(\frac{e(m' \prod_{j\in M} m_j, \sigma_{P_3})}{e(m' \prod_{j\in M} m_j, \sigma'_{P_3})}\right)^{x_c}$$

$$= e\left(g^{r_0+\sum_{i\in W} r_i}, \frac{\sigma'_{P_2}}{\sigma_{P_2}}\right)^{x_c} e\left(m' \prod_{j\in M} m_j, \frac{\sigma_{P_3}}{\sigma'_{P_3}}\right)^{x_c}$$

$$= e\left(g^c, \frac{\sigma'_{P_2}}{\sigma_{P_2}}\right)^{r_0+\sum_{i\in W} r_i} e\left(m' \prod_{j\in M} m_j, \frac{\sigma_{P_3}}{\sigma'_{P_3}}\right)^{c}$$

Therefore,

$$\frac{\sigma_{P_1}}{\sigma'_{P_1}} e\left(g^c, \frac{\sigma'_{P_2}}{\sigma_{P_2}}\right)^{r_0+\sum_{i\in w} r_i} = e\left(m' \prod_{j\in M} m_j, \frac{\sigma_{P_3}}{\sigma'_{P_3}}\right)^c$$

Which indicates that

$$\left(g, m' \prod_{j\in M} m_j, \frac{\sigma_{P_3}}{\sigma'_{P_3}}, g^c, \frac{\sigma_{P_1}}{\sigma'_{P_1}} e\left(g^c, \frac{\sigma'_{P_2}}{\sigma_{P_2}}\right)^{r_0+\sum_{i\in w} r_i}\right)$$

is a valid BDH tuple.

If $\mathcal{B}$ does not abort during the simulation, the adversary $\mathcal{A}_{\mathrm{II}}$ will output a valid DVPS $\sigma_P^* = \left(\sigma_{P_1}^*, \sigma_{P_2}^*, \sigma_{P_3}^*\right)$ on the message M^* under the warrant ω^* with success probability ϵ.

(1) If $(M^*) \neq 0$; $\mathcal{B}$ will abort.

(2) Otherwise, $F(M^*) = 0$ and $\mathcal{B}$ computes

$$\frac{\sigma_{P_1}^*}{e(g^c, g^{y_a})^{x_a} e\left(g^c, \sigma_{P_2}^*\right)^{r_0+\sum_{i\in w} r_i} e\left(g^c, \sigma_{P_3}^*\right)^{J(M)}}$$

and outputs it as the value of $e(g,g)^{abc}$.

This completes the description of the simulation. Now we have to compute $\mathcal{B}$'s probability of success. $\mathcal{B}$ will not abort if the following conditions hold.

A: $\mathcal{B}$ does not abort during the ProxySign queries.

B: $F(M^*) = 0 \ (mod\ p)$.

Finally, the success probability is $Succ_{\mathcal{B}}^{GBDH} = \Pr[A \wedge B]\epsilon$. Now, we compute this probability using Waters' technique [3].

$$\Pr[A \wedge B] = \Pr[A]\Pr[B|A] = \Pr\left[\bigcap_{i=1}^{q_{ps}} K(M_i) \neq 0\right] \Pr\left[x' + \sum_{i\in \mathcal{M}^*} x_i = lk|A\right]$$

$$= \left(1 - \Pr\left[\bigcup_{i=1}^{q_{ps}} K(M_i) = 0\right]\right) \Pr\left[x' + \sum_{i\in \mathcal{M}^*} x_i = lk|A\right]$$

$$\geq \left(1 - \frac{q_{ps}}{l}\right) \Pr\left[x' + \sum_{i\in \mathcal{M}^*} x_i = lk|A\right]$$

$$= \frac{1}{n+1}\left(1 - \frac{q_{ps}}{l}\right) \Pr[K(M^*) = 0|A]$$

$$= \frac{1}{n+1}\left(1-\frac{q_{ps}}{l}\right)\frac{\Pr[K(M^*)=0A]}{\Pr[A]}\Pr[A|K(M^*)=0]$$

$$= \frac{1}{n+1}\left(1-\frac{q_{ps}}{l}\right)\frac{1}{l-q_{ps}}\Pr[A|K(M^*)=0]$$

$$\geq \frac{1}{(n+1)l}\left(1-\frac{q_{ps}}{l}\right)\Pr[A|K(M^*)=0]$$

$$\geq \frac{1}{(n+1)l}\left(1-\frac{q_{ps}}{l}\right)\Pr\left(1-\Pr\left[\bigcup_{i=1}^{q_{ps}} K(M_i)=0\,|K(M^*)=0\right]\right)$$

$$= \frac{1}{n+1}\left(1-\frac{q_{ps}}{l}\right)^2 \geq \frac{1}{n+1}\left(1-\frac{2q_{ps}}{l}\right)$$

Therefore $Succ_{\mathcal{B}}^{GBDH} \geq \frac{1}{(n+1)l}\left(1-\frac{2q_{ps}}{l}\right)\epsilon$. We can get a simplified result by setting $l = 4q_{ps}$. Then

$$Succ_{\mathcal{B}}^{GBDH} \geq \frac{\epsilon}{8(n+1)q_{ps}}\,. \qquad \blacksquare$$

Unforgeability against adversary $\mathcal{A}_{\text{III}}$

Theorem 2. If there exists an adversary $\mathcal{A}_{\text{III}}$ who can $(\epsilon, t, q_\omega, q_{PS}, q_v)$ breaks our scheme, then there exists another algorithm $\mathcal{B}$ who can use $\mathcal{A}_{\text{III}}$ to solve an instance of the $GBDH$ problem with probability

$$Succ_{\mathcal{B}}^{GBDH} \geq \frac{\varepsilon}{3(n+1)^3\left(3(q_\omega+q_{PS})\right)^{q_v+2}} \tag{13}$$

In time

$$t' \leq \left((2n+6)q_{PS} + (n+4)q_v + (n+4)q_\omega\right)t_1 + (3q_v)t_2 + (8q_\omega + 12q_{PS} + 4q_v)T_1 + (4q_v)T_2 + (q_{PS} + 6q_v)t_e$$

where t_1, t_2 are the time for a multiplication in G and G_T respectively, T_1, T_2 are the time of an exponentiation in G and G_T respectively, and t_e is the time for a pairing computation in (G, G_T).

Proof. We are forced to omit the proof of theorem 2 due to page limitation, but it is similar to the proof of Theorem 1. ■

5.2 Security Requirements

1. Verifiability. In our scheme, since the original signer's public key is indeed to verify the proxy signature, the designated verifier can be convinced of the original signer's agreement on the signed message.

2. Undeniability. Anyone cannot find the proxy signer's private key due to the difficulty of discrete logarithm problem (DLP) and thus only proxy signer know his private key. Therefore, when the proxy signer create a valid proxy signature, he cannot repudiate it because the signature is created by using his private key (x_b, y_b).
3. Identifiability. In the proposed scheme, identity information of proxy signer is included explicitly in a valid proxy signature and ω as a form of public key. So, anyone can determine the identity of the proxy signer from the signature created by him and confirm the identity of the proxy signer from the ω.
4. Prevention of misuse. Only the proxy signer can issue a valid signature because only he know his private key (x_b, y_b). So, if the proxy signer uses the proxy key for other purposes, it is his responsibility because only he can generate it.

Moreover, the original signer's misuse is also prevented because she can not compute the valid proxy signature.

6 Conclusions

The proxy fast revocation of delegated rights is an essential issue of the proxy signature schemes. In this article, we proposed designated verifier proxy signature scheme with fast revocation capability which used from security mediator technique of Seo et al. Our proposed scheme has also provable security in the standard model based on the $GBDH$ assumption.

References

1. Mambo, M., Usuda, K., Okamoto, E.: Proxy signature: delegation of the power to sign messages. IEICE Transactions on Fundamentals 79A(9), 1338–1353 (1996)
2. Mambo, M., Usuda, K., Okamoto, E.: Proxy signature for delegating signing operation. In: Proceedings of the 3rd ACM Conference on Computer and Communications Security, March 14 -16, pp. 48–56. ACM, NewYork (1996)
3. Boldyreva, A., Palacio, A., Warinschi, B.: Secure proxy signature scheme for delegation of signing rights (May 20, 2005), http://eprint.iacr.org/096/2003
4. Yu, Y., Sun, Y., Yang, B., et al.: Multi-proxy signature without random oracles. Chinese Journal of Electronics 17(3), 475–480 (2008)
5. Seo, S.-H., Shim, K.-A., Lee, S.-H.: A mediated proxy signature scheme with fast revocation for electronic transactions. In: Katsikas, S.K., López, J., Pernul, G. (eds.) TrustBus 2005. LNCS, vol. 3592, pp. 216–225. Springer, Heidelberg (2005)
6. Sun, H.-M.: Design of time-stamped proxy signatures with traceable receivers. IEE Proceedings: Computers and Digital Techniques 147(6), 462–466 (2000)
7. Bellare, M., Rogaway, P.: The exact security of digital signatures - how to sign with RSA and rabin. In: Maurer, U.M. (ed.) EUROCRYPT 1996. LNCS, vol. 1070, pp. 399–416. Springer, Heidelberg (1996)
8. Waters, B.: Efficient identity-based encryption without random oracles. In: Cramer, R. (ed.) EUROCRYPT 2005. LNCS, vol. 3494, pp. 114–127. Springer, Heidelberg (2005)

9. Jakobsson, M., Sako, K., Impagliazzo, R.: Designated verifier proofs and their applications. In: Maurer, U.M. (ed.) EUROCRYPT 1996. LNCS, vol. 1070, pp. 143–154. Springer, Heidelberg (1996)
10. Dai, J.Z., Yang, X.H., Dong, J.X.: Designated-receiver proxy signature scheme for electronic commerce. In: Proc. of IEEE International Conference on Systems, Man and Cybernetics, vol. 1, pp. 384–389. IEEE Press, Los Alamitos (2003)
11. Huang, X., Mu, Y., Susilo, W., Zhang, F.T.: Short designated verifier proxy signature from pairings. In: Enokido, T., Yan, L., Xiao, B., Kim, D.Y., Dai, Y.-S., Yang, L.T. (eds.) EUC-WS 2005. LNCS, vol. 3823, pp. 835–844. Springer, Heidelberg (2005)
12. Lu, R.X., Cao, Z.F., Dong, X.L.: Designated verifier proxy signature scheme from bilinear pairings. In: Proc of the First International Multi-Symposiums on Computer and Computational Sciences 2006, pp. 40–47. IEEE Press, Los Alamitos (2006)
13. Yu, Y., Xu, C., Zhang, X., Liao, Y.: Designated verifier proxy signature scheme without random oracles. Computers and Mathematics with Applications 57, 1352–1364 (2009)

Presentation of an Efficient and Secure Architecture for e-Health Services

Mohamad Nejadeh[1] and Shahriar Mohamadi[2]

[1] Information of Technology Department of International Pardis Branch of Guilan University, Rasht, Iran
[2] Faculty Member Of Khajeh Nasir Toosi University,Assistant Prof,Tehran, Iran
{m_nejadeh,smohamadi40}@yahoo.com

Abstract. Nowadays a great number of activities are performed via internet. With increment in such activities, two groups of services are required for providing a secure platform: 1- Access control services, 2- communication security services. In this article we propose a secure and efficient system for establishment of secure communication in e-health. This architecture focuses on five security indicators of authorization, authentication, integrity, non-repudiation and confidentiality. This architecture uses an efficient encryption scheme, which is a combination of the public key and the symmetric key encryption systems, all of which are combined with a log strategy In this article we have used a new role-based control model to provide the security requirement of authorization for user's access to data. Data sensitivity is measured based on the labels given to the roles; and then these data are encrypted with proper cryptography algorithms. In a comparison of these architectures, you will see that this architecture enjoys an efficient mechanism, which is very suitable and practical for communication and interchange of data.

Keywords: access control; cryptography; digital signature; Log strategy.

1 Introduction

The sudden growth in use of internet in the recent years has had a significant effect on communication of people with each other, partnership in references and information and commercial models. Medical sector was not an exception and internet had a significant effect on that. E-health includes different types of health services presented via internet. In this relation the services are provided in different domains of training, information and various health and treatment services. E-health increases access of health services promotes presented services quality and efficiency. Therefore appearance of a secure ground in this domain is necessary, which is considered as one of the most challengeable problems in e-health domain.

Security in information systems means protection of systems against unauthorized changes and access of information. The most important aims of security systems include protection of confidentiality, integrity, availability and data guarantee. Confidentiality must be maintained to protect the patient's privacy: the patient's data,

H. Cherifi, J.M. Zain, and E. El-Qawasmeh (Eds.): DICTAP 2011, Part I, CCIS 166, pp. 551–562, 2011.

such as medical records, would affect the doctor's diagnosis and treatment decisions of a patient. Integrity must be conserved to ensure that the patient's data have not been altered and is up to date. The availability of the e-Health system is also of great importance; a person's life could be dependent upon the e-Health system [2].

On the other hand with exertion of access control on the basis of the rules, the rights for access of factors to objects are determined. Access control on systems mentions which people are authorized to access to which resources under which conditions and which actions they are authorized to perform on the resources. One of the access control models is role-based access control (RBAC) that has attracted much attention due to publicity. This model in the first presentations proved that it has a simpler security management as compared with the other models due to application of the concept of role and decreased management costs.

This paper presents an efficient and secure architecture for security of e-health services. In section 2 we discuss a proposed solution for creation of a secure communication. In the next sections, we propose the results of the former section in construction of a secure architecture for e-health services and present our proposed model that is presented as follows: section 3 considers access control model. Section 4 presents an efficient and secure cryptography scheme. In section 5 we mentioned digital signature. You can study Log strategy in section 6 and our proposed architecture has been presented in section 7 and finally in section 8 our paper is ended with a conclusion.

2 The Proposed Solution

E-Health security studies are still in an early stage. As far as the authors are aware, there have been only several approaches on e-Health Service Authentication and e-Health Data Transmission for example in [8], an authentication protocol is developed. The protocol uses "Timestamp" to describe and verify the security properties related to the expiration of keys and the freshness of the message. The protocol heavily relies on clock synchronization of both parties, thus, the issue of trusting each other's clock becomes a problem.

In [9], a Workflow Access Control Framework is proposed to provide more flexibility in handling e-Health dynamic behavior. The idea is to model each work task in the system as state-machines. At each state, the data access permission is granted based on the resources required to move on to the next state. For any entities involved, the information of all states statuses are stored in a lookup table to improve processing speed. However, this approach consumes a large amount of memory space since an entity must store a copy of the status of all states in the system.

To design a secured applied system and establish a secure communication and message interchange, five security needs should be satisfied:

- Integrity: prevents data change. Of course any change on information, creates some changes on the text.
- Authentication: Authentication ensures the parties with right accessing to a system.

- Authorization: Determines access control on the basis of the authorized rules, which determine that factor's rights of access to objects.
- Non-repudiation: The user must not deny the performed transaction and must provide proof in case that this situation occurs.
- Confidentiality: The confidential information must be secured from an unauthorized party.

We proposed a new style of secure architecture for e-health communications. Table 1 summarizes the requirements resulting from the security concerns, and technologies recommended. The third column of Table 1 shows the existing solutions for exertion of any of the technologies mentioned in the table.

Table 1. Security requirements along with the technologies recommended for these requirements and solutions to address them

Security	Technology	Solution
Authorization	Access control	Role model- interaction-organization
Authentication	Using a pair of keys	Biometric and Smart card
	Digital Signature	ECDSA
Integrity	Digital Signature	
Non-repudiation	Digital Signature	
	Log	Transaction Log
Confidentiality	Encryto/ Decrypto	ECC & AES

3 Access Control Model

With using model [1] we propose a new security scheme for e-health system that is examined with different algorithms for communication in e-health and the original results are presented. With using model [1], we execute our authorization control on our system. Of course it is necessary to mention that this access control model is studied for static system and does not include a dynamic and distributed system. In this frame three main elements of interaction, role and organization have been created. This model presents them in the forms of role models, interaction models and organization models:

3.1 Role Model

The role in this system assumes a peer-to-peer model. It is both a server and a client, capable of both receiving request from other roles as well as initiating requests to other roles in the system. In this scheme, an abstract role model to classify roles is presented. The detailed responsibilities of each role are not specified at this abstract level. A role can only become functional when it is instantiated with assigned position, specific set of duties, and interactions within a specific organization. The abstract model of a role is described in Fig. 1.

In this model the roles are supposed to act as initiator and reactor at the same time. If a role is able to initiate a request to other roles, then it's an initiator. If a role receives requests from other roles, then it's a reactor.

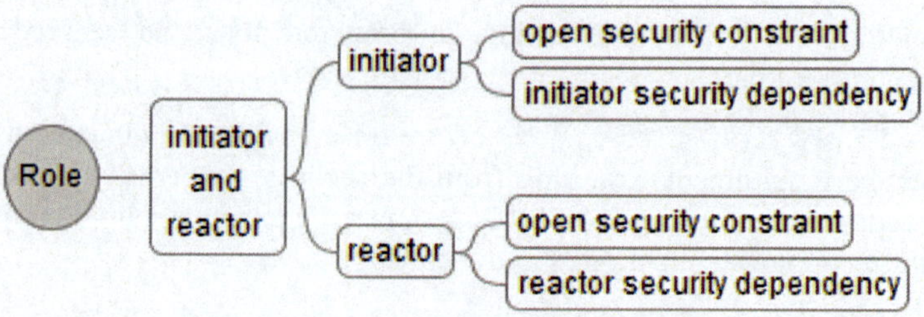

Fig. 1. The Abstract Role Model [1]

Each role in this system is associated with a set of security properties called security dependency. The security dependency describes the security constraint(s), which creates impediments and limitations for some special interactions. Therefore such limitations may be exerted to roles as a set of conditions and impediments and the roles should act in such a way not to violate from the conditions and impediments. In this system four types of security dependencies have presented: 1- Open security dependency, 2- initiator security dependency, 3- reactor security dependency, 4-initiator and reactor security dependency (Fig.2).

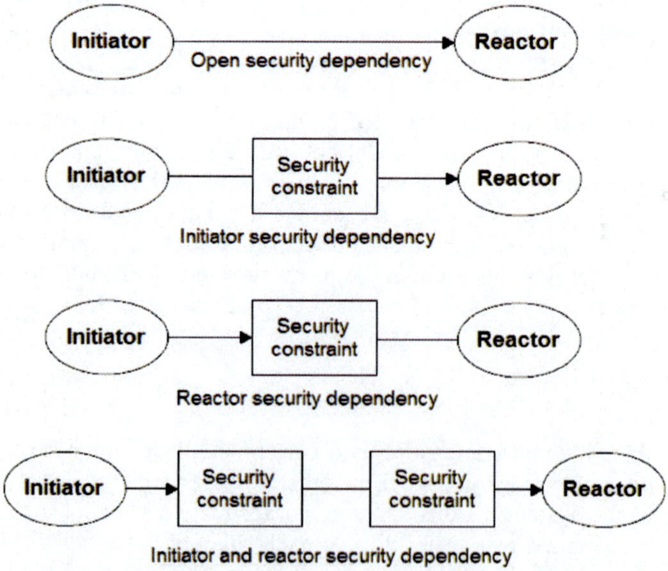

Fig. 2. Different Types of Security Dependencies [1]

3.2 Interaction Model

In this system, the interaction model is divided into two categories.

- Closed interaction: The number of participants of a particular interaction is fixed and cannot be changed for that type of interaction.
- Open interaction: The number of participants can be changed over the progress of the interaction.

Regardless whether an interaction is open or closed, four types of communication methods exist, namely, one to one, one to many, many to one and many too many.

3.3 Organization Model

Most of organizations have different structures that determine different roles for classified situations. In this model each organization model contains three important properties: 1- organization structure, 2- organization positions, and 3- organization rules.

Organizational rules dictate policies and limitation on the method of information current in and out of the organization. These rules are independent to any especial definition of drawings by organizational structures. Therefore these rules are practical for different organizations: 3 basic rules are considered for each organization: 1- The requirement to play positions, 2- the interaction direction and 3- the interaction range. For the requirement to play positions defines the restriction of what a position can do, such as: a given organization position must be played by only one role during the organization's lifetime or two positions can never be played by the same role. Interaction direction defines the information flow direction within the system. The direction can be divided into three categories, up, peers and down. The interaction range defines how far an interaction can be reached. The value can be adopted from 1 to n.

Depending on the topology of the organization, we can further divide the organizations into centralized structure, multilevel hierarchy, peers to peers and complex composite structure. When the organizational structure was selected the organization model is produced. [1]

3.4 Exertion of Role- Interaction- Organization Models on an Experimental Sample

In this section we show an original sample of e-health system, on which role-interaction- organization model has been exerted on it, in this case we have five roles, namely, a patient, a receptionist, a nurse, a general practitioner (GP) and a specialist named as role 1, role 2, role 3, role 4 and role 5. We supposed that role 1 is an initiator, role 2, 3 and 4 are initiators and reactor and role 5 is a reactor. In this model we only considered the closed and one-to- one Interaction. The transactions of each role according to the presented model in [1] are presented in the form of a label. For example I_C_S_23 means as follows: I means interaction, C means that the interaction is closed, S means that the interaction is one-to –one and 23 shows that the interaction starts from role 2 and ends with role 3 depends on the roles involved in the interaction, the numbers changed proportionally. In this stage, the roles in the current system have no clear responsibilities. For example, at this stage, there is an interaction checked in the system, I_O_S_53, which O means open interaction. As we described above, this interaction is not legitimate. We can examine the interaction from two ways. From the role model way, role 5 is a reactor role; it only receives the requests from other roles. From the interaction model way, we defined only closed interactions are allowed to be performed among roles, however, this interaction is belonged to open interaction category. Therefore, this interaction can be examined as an illegal interaction to arise.

As it was shown in Fig. 3 and with a view to the real system in the real world, our original sample performs five vital activities of patients, treatment procedure, help and general medical care and high level medical care. In our original sample, we have five positions in the organization including patient, receptionist, nurse, general practitioner (GP) and specialist. That the patient is able to explain and interchange the information. The receptionist performs the activities of explanation, interchange of information, reception and helping. The nurse is able to perform the activities of explanation, interchange of information and helping. The general practitioner performs the activities of explanation, interchange of information and helping and finally the specialist performs the activities of explanation, interchange of information and helping.

As you can see in Fig. 3, the interaction between the patient and the receptionist has open security dependency and no security constraint has been presented. The patient sets an appointment time with the doctor through the receptionist. The patient also has a domain of communication with the nurse, the general practitioner and the specialist. But whereas he cannot meet the requirements of the related security constraint, this interaction is not created directly. Therefore the receptionist follows the information related to the patient to meet the requirements of the security constraints related to the nurse and the general practitioner and hereby the interaction between the patient and the nurse or the doctor is established. For Example, the patient may not set an appointment time with the physician directly therefore the receptionist follows up the patient's information to provide a helping interaction and an interaction with the general practitioner. After performance and completion of such an interaction, places the data in a security constraint for establishment of an interaction between the patient and the physician to be able to understand what time the constraint is considered. Then the receptionist can establish an interaction with the patient and inform the patient of the appointment with the general practitioner. Therefore the appointment between the patient and the doctor is performed at the determined date and after completion of such an interaction, the determined security relations for such an interaction, which have been added to the security constraints, are deleted and the work is completed successfully.

Sometimes it is possible the nurse encounters problems while establishment of the interaction of helping to the patient and an interaction of helping with the general practitioner is required. Therefore the nurse for establishment of such an interaction first should meet the requirements of the security constraints related to the doctor, on the other hand with a view to setting of the communication domain and the organization structure the nurse needs to present a security constraint, which indicates the role, which will communicate, therefore the interaction between the nurse and the general practitioner is established and the nurse will be able to receive the procedure of the instructions required for patient's treatment.

If the general practitioner is unable to solve the patient's problem he should start a helping interaction for communication with the specialist and provide an appointment time with the specialist for the patient. In this type of interaction with a view to communication scope and organizational structure the general practitioner needs a security constraint, which indicates the role, which will communicate and on the other hand should meet the requirements of security constraints of the specialist and similar to appointment with the general practitioner, the patient needs to perform the interaction security constraint in appointment with the specialist.

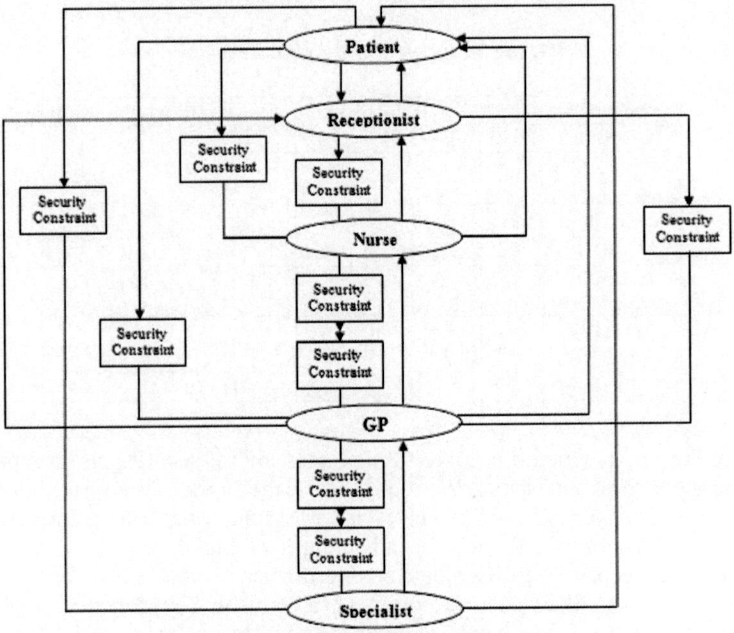

Fig. 3. The Simple Case of E-health System

4 Efficient and Secure Cryptography Scheme

With cryptography, data can be protected from others and only the authorized users will be able to read the data with decryption. Applications of cryptography include hash function, exchange of key, digital signature and certificate. Hash function emphasizes on function integrity and investigates if the document has been altered. Some examples of hash function include MD4, MD5 and Secure Hash Algorithm/ Standard (SHA/SHS). Key exchange is used in symmetrical cryptography. Symmetrical cryptographies use identical key for encryption and decryption of a message. In this section with consideration of different cryptography algorithms, the lightest and securest algorithm is selected for the architecture.

In this section, we explain the grounds required for the proposed solution on cryptography algorithms. An algorithm is considered to be a secure algorithm if and only if a) brute force is the only effective attack against it and b) the number of possible keys is large enough to make brute force attack infeasible. There are two main types of encryption algorithms: asymmetric and symmetric key algorithms. For symmetrical encryption, there are different encryption algorithms that may be used in commerce. Symmetrical algorithms such as DES, 3DES, AES and Blowfish are often compared and used in [4] and [5]. These algorithms have different specifications that have been studied by specialists and proved. But we have used different specifications of algorithms for security of different types of information. According to comparisons in [3] that has compared algorithms with a view to key size, block size, algorithm structure, rounds number and feasibility of being cracked, AES has obtained the most scores and DES the least scores with a view to security (Table 2).

Table 2. Encryption algorithms ranking

Algorithm	DES	3DES	AES	Blowfish	DEA	RC4
Key Size	7	13	17	20	10	17
Block Size	17	17	20	17	17	13
Algorithm structure	13	13	17	13	17	20
Rounds	17	20	17	17	13	10
feasibility of being cracked	4	7	7	7	7	4
TOTAL SCORE	58	70	78	74	64	64
Ranking	#6	#3	#1	#2	#4	#4

As we know, asymmetric algorithm creates more security as compared with symmetric algorithms but symmetric algorithms have higher speed, therefore we paid attention to empowering AES, which is a symmetrical algorithm, with ECC asymmetric algorithm to combine the advantages of higher speed in the symmetric algorithm with security of asymmetric algorithms. In this state for Secrete Key transfer, which was the most important problem in key transfer in symmetric algorithms, we used ECC asymmetric algorithm, which has more speed than the other asymmetric algorithms so that besides increase of speed we can guarantee more security. In this state we have only used ECC cryptography for AES key transfer.

A relative point has been given to the criteria listed in Table 2 supposing that the algorithms are secure. The domain of this relative point is between 1 and 20 that the 20 is the higher point. After presentation of the comparisons, now it's turn to select proper cryptography algorithms for data encryption.

There are different types of information in e-health with different sensitiveness. Some of them are sensitive date such as patient's medical history, medical diagnosis and results of examinations, which should not be released to the others except the patient, doctors and the related nurses. Also some data are less sensitive or not sensitive including patient's personal data, appointment times, etc. In this research the users presented in health system include: patient, receptionist, nurse, general practitioner and specialist that their working relation was presented in section 3. As it was mentioned before the interactions between the roles are presented as a label. Certainly during such interactions and communications, different types of data are sent and received. In these transactions some data may be very sensitive and therefore needing more protection or some data less sensitive and needing less protection. We separated sensitiveness of the data on the basis of the presentable labels in communications and on that basis select the related cryptography algorithm. Table 3 presents different types of communications and also the type of the selected cryptography label and algorithm.

Table 3. Relations in e-health, presented label and the selected cryptography algorithm

Relations	Label	Cryptography algorithm type
Patient, Nurse, General Practitioner, Specialist	I_C_S_13 I_C_S_15 I_C_S_45	AES (256-Bit), ECC
Patient, Nurse, General Practitioner	I_C_S_14 I_C_S_34 I_C_S_43	AES (192-Bit), ECC
Patient, Receptionist, Nurse, General Practitioner	I_C_S_12 I_C_S_23 I_C_S_24 I_C_S_32 I_C_S_42	AES (128-Bit), ECC

5 Digital Signature

A digital signature is used for one message and in brief a digital signature is an electronic signature, which may not be forged. A digital signature includes a unique mathematical fingerprint from the current message, which is also called One-Way-hash. The receiving computer receives the message and executes the same algorithm on the message, decrypts the signature and compares the results. If the fingerprints are similar, the receiver can be sure of the sender's identity and correctness of the message. This method guarantees that the message has not been altered during transfer process. In this architecture we have used a Hash algorithm for creation of a message summary and use ECDSA (Elliptical Curve Digital Signature Algorithm) [6] to guarantee Authentication. Key size in this algorithm is 192 bits including a security level equivalent to DSA (Digital Signature Algorithm) with key size of 1024. [7] The summarization algorithm used in our proposed architecture is SHA-1, which has the three following specifications:

- Message length is fixed, i.e. with each length of message its summary is the same. This length for SHA-1 is 160 bits.
- Each entrance bit is effective on exit. It means that two messages, which are only different in a bit, have different summaries.
- They are unilateral: it means that with having the message summary we cannot build the original message.

It is of special importance that with use of the mentioned method in our architecture, the security requirements of authentication, non-repudiation, integrity and confidentiality are met.

When the sender creates the message summary with use of SHA-1 function and adds it to the end of his message as digital signature and sends it to the receiver on the other part, the receiver, separated the message summary from the original message and decrypts the message summary with the sender's public key. Then he compares the summary with the original massage produced by himself and their conformity means that the sender is the person claiming so, because only he has the private key corresponding to his public key (Authentication).

Also the message data integrity has been protected, it means that the message has not been altered, because otherwise the results would not be conforming (Integrity). On the other hand, the sender cannot deny sending of message, because no other one has his private key (non-repudiation).

6 Log Strategy (Events Registration)

Along with the digital signature a log strategy is used to ensure non-repudiation. The log server is a security mechanism to protect a physician from a false repudiation. If a physician refuses to accept false diagnosis and treatment for a patient, the log server can provide the transaction records as proof. In fact Log strategy acts as a third party like a witness for performance of the service rendering and the service receiving performance method.

7 The Proposed Architecture

Fig. 3 has presented the proposed model for security of communications in e-health. In this model there are three main areas including operator's position, security communication layer and server's position. The secure communication layer provides a proper amount of security for communication.

For entrance to the system an authentication process (biometric and smart card) is required for all roles to recognize the authorized users. After authentication process was performed successfully and authentication was guaranteed, a user can execute applied processes. Whereas the main aim is to make the communications between the two sections secure, therefore before start of interchange of any type of massage, a proper security protocol should be executed so that communication is performed according to the layer. When a user enters the system through smart card and biometric for the first time, the system creates the public key for the user. The private key is protected by the user and the public key is used as the parameters, which are issued by a certificate and signed by the server. A copy of the certificate is kept in the server.

After user's authentication and his recognition as authorized, interactions between the users are performed. As it was mentioned before, the interactions of each role are presented with a label.

In Fig. 4 the sender can connect to the receiver and they can distinguish each other's validity with use of the certificates. They may request the server to investigate their certificates to make sure that the certificates are valid. If a user (sender) wishes to send a message to the receiver, the sender sends a message (message opening, saving, edition and deletion) in Message Module to the receiver.

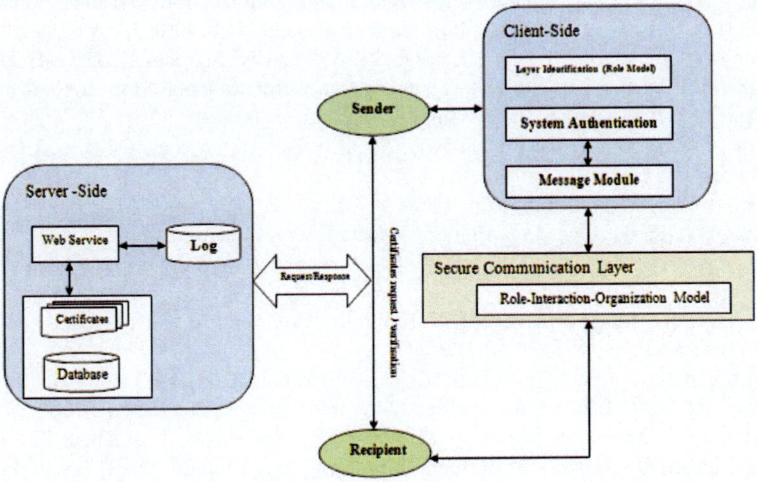

Fig. 4. The proposed model for secure interchange

8 Conclusion and Future Work

This paper has presented a modern architecture for e-health services that was examined with different algorithms for communications in e-health and the original results were presented. In our proposed architecture with composition to two cryptography algorithms of ECC and AES we could present data cryptography in a more secure method. As compared with the existing architectures, which used RSA or AES algorithms (singly), our system has been appeared more efficient. Whereas in this article we have used AES for more efficient and AES besides ECC for more security and at the same time with digital signature with use of ECDSA we could increase confidentiality, integrity, security, confidentiality and non-repudiation (of both parties) and make the non-repudiation ability more definite, also with use of a new model of role- based access control we could label the interactions between the roles and determine the level of the data sensitiveness on the basis of labels and use a cryptography algorithm proportionate to data sensitiveness, so that we can execute the proposed security frame and the related mechanisms on an e-health system and examine our architecture in future. In the future project we are trying to use a more suitable access control model so that we can apply our architecture in a dynamic and distributed environment.

References

1. Li, W., Honag, D.: A New Security Scheme for E-health System.: iNEXT – UTS Research Centre for Innovative in IT Services and Applications University of Technology, Sydney, Broadway NSW, Australia (2007)
2. Smith, E., Eloff, J.: Security in Health-care Information Systems-current Trends. International Journal of Medical Informatics 54(1), 39–54 (1999)
3. Boonyarattaphan, A., Bai, Y., Chung, S.: A Security Framework for e-Health Service Authentication and e-Health Data Transmission. Computing and Software Systems Institute of Technology University of Washington, Tacoma (2009)
4. Dhawan, P.: Performance Comparison: Security Design Choices.: Microsoft Development Network (2007), http://msdn2.microsoft.com/en-us/library/ms978415.aspx
5. Tamimi, A.-K.: Performance Analysis of Data Encryption Algorithms (2007), http://www.cse.wustl.edu/~jain/cse56706/ftp/encryption_perf/index.html
6. Vanstone, S.: Responses to NISTs Proposal. Communications of the ACM 35, 50–52 (1992)
7. Lenstra, A.K., Verheul, E.R.: Selecting cryptographic key sizes. In: Imai, H., Zheng, Y. (eds.) PKC 2000. LNCS, vol. 1751, pp. 446–465. Springer, Heidelberg (2000)
8. Elmufti, K., Weerasinghe, D., Rajarajan, M., Rakocevic, V., Khan, S.: Timestamp Authentication Protocol for Remote Monitoring in eHealth. In: The 2nd International Conference on Pervasive Computing Technologies for Healthcare, Tampere, Finland, pp. 73–76 (2008)
9. Russello, G., Dong, C., Dulay, N.: A Workflow-based Access Control Framework for e-Health Applications. In: Proc. of the 22nd International Conference on Advanced Information Networking and Applications - Workshops, pp. 111–120 (2008)

Risk Assessment of Information Technology Projects Using Fuzzy Expert System

Sanaz Pourdarab[1], Hamid Eslami Nosratabadi[2,*], and Ahmad Nadali[1]

[1] Department of Information Technology Management,
Science and Research Branch, Islamic Azad University
[2] Young Researchers Club, Science and Research Branch,
Islamic Azad University
hamideslami.na@gmail.com

Abstract. Information Technology (IT) projects are accompanied by various risks and high rate of failure in such projects. The purpose of this research is Risk assessment of IT projects by an intelligent system. Here, a Fuzzy Expert System has been designed with considering main effective variables on risk assessment as Inputs variables and level of project risk as output. Then, the system rules have been extracted from the IT experts and the system has been developed with the use of FIS tool of MATLAB software. Finally, the presented steps have been run in an Iranian Bank as empirical study.

Keywords: Risk Assessment, Information Technology Projects, Fuzzy Expert System.

1 Introduction

The rapid growth of information technology (IT) investments has imposed pressure on management to take into account the risks and payoffs in their investment decision-making. At the same time, they have been confronted with conflicting information regarding the outcome of IT investments. In today's business environment, information technology (IT) is considered to be a key source of competitive advantage. With its growing strategic importance, organizational spending on IT applications is rising rapidly, and has become a dominant part of the capital budgets in many organizations. However, to be ready for upcoming events, an organization must create an effective risk management plan, which starts with accurate and appropriate risk identification. Additional models and methods have been introduced by a variety of risk management researchers. For example, a model has been presented for risk management that is composed of nine phases [1]. The nine steps that compose the risk management process are as follows: define, focus, identify, structure, ownership, estimate, evaluate, plan, and manage. There is another paper which investigated information technology projects [2]. They identified four levels for this type of project, including process, application, organization, and inter-organization. Corresponding to

* Corresponding author.

H. Cherifi, J.M. Zain, and E. El-Qawasmeh (Eds.): DICTAP 2011, Part I, CCIS 166, pp. 563–576, 2011.

these four levels were suggested four major components of risk management, namely, identification, analysis, reducing measures, and monitoring. Barki, et al. developed a methodology and a decision support tool to assess risks of software development projects [3]. Wallace, et al. determined six dimensions of risk in IT projects and proposed a reliable and valid framework to assess them [4]. Tuysuz and Kahraman evaluated risks of IT projects using fuzzy analytical hierarchy process [5]. In software project risk management literature, there is another study which defined the software project risk assessment process independently [6]. In 2001, IEEE Standard produced the software risk management process in the life cycle (IEEE Standard, 2001). This standard suggested that risk analysis and assessment process included risk identification, risk estimation and risk evaluation. An intelligent early alarming system has been designed in a paper, to assess and trace risk to improve software quality [7]. Risk and uncertainly management use the following three-step approach: 1) Risk identification: the first step of risk management process is risk identification. It includes the recognition of potential sources of risk and uncertainty event conditions in the project and the clarification of risk and uncertainty responsibilities. 2) Risk assessment: risk and uncertainty rating identifies the importance of the sources of risk and uncertainty to the goals of the project. Risk assessment is accomplished by estimating the probability of occurrence and severity of risk impact.3) Risk mitigation: mitigation establishes a plan, which reduces or eliminates sources of risk and uncertainty impact to the project's deployment or minimize the effect of risk and uncertainty? Options available for mitigation are: control, avoidance, or transfer [8]. This article mainly focuses on the evaluation phase of the project risk management process, which is a certain common element in all approaches. The aim of this study is to construct an Expert System which evaluating the Risk level of Information Technology projects as Output based on major factors as Input variables. The factors consist of six main factors with 28 sub-factors. Some managers and IT consultants as the research Experts identify the Project Risk level according to linguistic variables based on different situations of these six main factors. Since the experts' judgment is explained with linguistic variables, using fuzzy functions and Fuzzy deduction system can be advantageous to build a basic knowledge system for evaluating IT projects. The following part of the paper is a review of Literature which includes two section .The first part explains IT project Risk and the second part describes the Fuzzy Expert system. Then Fuzzy Expert System Design Methodology will be explained. Finally the proposed system has been described.

2 Literature Review

2.1 Information Technology Projects Risk

Unsuccessful management of IT risks can lead to a variety of problems, such as cost and schedule overruns, unmet user requirements, and failure to deliver business value of IT investment. Risks of IT investments are abundant in terms of variety too.

As a definition of Risk, Chapman and Cooper define risk as "exposure to the possibility of economic or financial loss or gains, physical damage or injury or delay as a consequence of the uncertainly associated with pursuing a course of action" [9]. The American National Standard Institution defines project risk as "An uncertain event or condition that, if it occurs, has a positive or a negative effect on that least one project objective, such as time, cost, scope, or quality, which implies an uncertainly about identified events and conditions" [8].There have already been several lists of risk factors published in IS literature. There exist two streams of IS research which consider IT investment risks in different perspectives. The first stream is mainly concerned about risks in software development [10]. In this regard, Boehm [6] identified a ''Top-10'' list of major software development risks that threaten the success of projects. Barki et al. [3] identified 35 risk variables in software projects and categorized them into five factors. Building upon this, Wallace [11] conducted a survey with 507 software project managers and this resulted in six categories or dimensions of risk: team, organizational environment, requirements, planning and control, user, and project complexity. These risks can be generally treated as private risks, which are specific to projects. The second stream of research views IT investment risks from a broader perspective. It is not limited to software development process, but is extended to external factors. The risk areas that threaten the success of IT Investments can be categorized in: Private Risks and Public Risks. Private Risks can be divided in: Organizational Risks included User Risk, Requirement Risk, Structural Risk, Team Risk and Complexity Risk. Public Risks can be divided in Competition Risk and Market Environment Risk [10]. The assessment of risk during the justification process can enable management to plan for any occurrences that may arise. In doing so, managers put in place mechanisms to manage and mitigate their risks. In other words, Risk management is defined as the systematic process of identifying, analyzing, and responding to project risks [10]. Once the possible risks and their characteristics that may affect the project are identified, they must be evaluated. Risk evaluation is the process of assessing the impact and likelihood of identified risks. The aim of risk evaluation is determining the importance of risks and prioritizing them according to their effects on project objectives for further attention and action. Evaluation techniques can be mainly classified into two groups; these are qualitative methods and quantitative methods. Qualitative methods describe the characteristics of each risk in sufficient detail to allow them to be understood. Quantitative methods use mathematical models to simulate the effect of risks on project outcomes. The most commonly used qualitative methods are the probability–impact risk rating matrix, which is constructed to assign risk ratings to risks or conditions based on combining probability and impact scales, and the use of a risk breakdown structure (RBS) to group risks by source. Quantitative methods include Monte Carlo simulation, decision trees, and sensitivity analysis. These two kinds of methods, qualitative and quantitative, can be used separately or together [12]. The risk evaluation methodology focused on in another paper, consists of identification of risk factors related to IT projects and ranking them in order to make suitable decisions .The risk factors being used are: Development process, Funding, Scope, Relationship management, Scheduling, Sponsorship/Ownership, External dependencies, Project Management, Corporate environment, Requirements, Personnel and Technology. In the mentioned study, fuzzy analytical hierarchy process (FAHP) is exploited as a means of risk evaluation methodology to prioritize and organize risk factors faced in IT projects [8]. In artificial intelligence area, uncertain problems received great attention. Bayesian Belief Network (BBN) has been used in some studies to calculate software project risk impact weights and build a model to guide project manager and also to assess software project risks [13][14][15]. Fuzzy set is a qualitative method by introducing subjection functions for fuzzy problems. Artificial Neural Network (ANN) is used to assess IT project risk because of its powerful self-learning ability. A network model has been constructed to assess IT project risk [16]. Expert systems received more and more attention in risk management research because risk manager can extract knowledge from knowledge warehouse. In addition, there are some other simple methods to assess risk such as Sensitivity Analysis (SA), reason-result analysis, SRAM model, one-minute risk assessment tool and risk assessment method based on absorptive capacity [17].

2.2 Fuzzy Expert System

Fuzzy expert systems use fuzzy data, fuzzy rules and fuzzy inference, in addition to the standard ones implemented in the ordinary expert systems. The fuzzy Inference Systems (FIS) are very good tools as they hold the nonlinear universal approximation [18]. Fuzzy inference systems can express human expert knowledge and experience by using fuzzy inference rules represented in “if-then” statements. Following the fuzzy inference mechanism, the output can be a fuzzy set or a precise set of certain features [19].

Fuzzy Inference System (FIS) incorporates fuzzy inference and rule-based expert systems. There are different types of fuzzy systems are introduced. Mamdani fuzzy systems and TSK fuzzy systems are two types of fuzzy systems commonly used in literature that has different ways of knowledge representation.TSK (Takagi-Sugeno-Kang) fuzzy system was proposed in an effort to develop a systematic approach to generate fuzzy rules from a given input–output data set.

A basic Takagi–Sugeno fuzzy inference system is an inference scheme in which the conclusion of a fuzzy rule is constituted by a weighted linear combination of the crisp inputs rather than a fuzzy set and the rules have the following Structure:

$$\text{If x is A1 and y is B1, then } z1 = p1x + q1y + r1 . \qquad (1)$$

Where p1, q1, and r1 are linear parameters.TSK Takagi–Sugeno Kang fuzzy controller usually needs a smaller number of rules, because their output is already a linear function of the inputs rather than a constant fuzzy set.

Mamdani fuzzy system was proposed as the first attempt to control a steam engine and boiler combination by a set of linguistic control rules obtained from experienced human operators. Rules in Mamdani fuzzy systems are like these:

$$\text{If x1 is A1 AND/OR x2 is A2 Then y is B1} . \qquad (2)$$

Where A1, A2 and B1 are fuzzy sets. The fuzzy set acquired from aggregation of rules' results will be defuzzified using defuzzification methods like centroid (center of gravity), max membership, mean-max, and weighted average. The centroid method is very popular, in which the ''center of mass'' of the result provides the crisp value. In this method, the defuzzified value of fuzzy set A, d (A), is calculated by the formula (3).

$$d(A) = \int_A x.\mu_A(X)dx \Big/ \int_A \mu_A(X)dx \quad (3)$$

where is the membership function of fuzzy set A .Regarding our problem in which various possible conditions of parameters are stated in form of fuzzy sets, the Mamdani fuzzy systems will be utilized due to the fact that the fuzzy rules representing the expert knowledge in Mamdani fuzzy systems, take advantage of fuzzy sets in their consequences, while in TSK fuzzy systems, the consequences are expressed in form of a crisp function [20].

3 Methodology to Design Fuzzy Expert System

The general process of constructing such a fuzzy expert system from initial model design to system evaluation is shown in Fig.1. This illustrates the typical process flow as distinct stages for clarity but in reality the process is not usually composed of such separate discrete steps and many of the stages, although present, are blurred into each other.

Once the problem has been clearly specified, the process of constructing the fuzzy expert system can begin. Invariably some degree of data preparation and preprocessing is required. The first major choice the designer has to face is whether to use the Mamdani inference method or the Takagi-Sugeno-Kang (TSK) method. The choice of inference methodology is linked to the choice of defuzzification method. Once the inference methodology and defuzzification method have been chosen, the process of enumerating the linguistic variables necessary can commence. The next stage of deciding the necessary terms with their defining membership functions and determining the rules to be used is far from trivial however. After a set of fuzzy membership functions and rules has been established, the system may be evaluated, usually by comparison of the obtained output against some *desired* or *known* output using some form of error or distance function. However, it is very rare that the first system constructed will perform at an acceptable level. Usually some form of optimization or performance tuning of the system will need to be undertaken. A primary distinction illustrated in Fig. 1 is the use of either *parameter optimization* in which (usually) only aspects of the model such as the shape and location of membership functions and the number and form of rules are altered, or *structure optimization* in which all aspects of the system including items such as the inference methodology, defuzzification method, or number of linguistic variables may be altered. In general, though, there is no clear distinction. Some authors consider rule modification to be structure optimization, while others parameterize the rules [21].

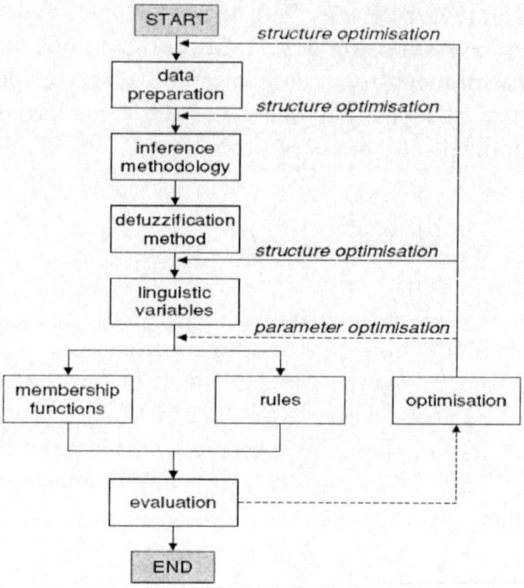

Fig. 1. Typical process flow in constructing a fuzzy expert system [21]

In this research, these steps briefly have been followed:

Step1. Clarifying the objective
Step2. Selecting the Input and output variables with the use of previous studies. Besides, the meaningful linguistic states along with appropriate fuzzy sets for each variable ought to be selected.
Step3. Determining the membership functions for the variables
Step4. Specifying the rules for making the relations clear between Inputs and outputs.
Step5. Developing the Fuzzy Expert System via FIS Tool in MATLAB Software.
Step6. Implementing the designed system in the case of Saman Iranian Bank based on the situation of the bank to identify the risk assessment of an E-banking project.
In next section the proposed system has been presented.

4 The Proposed Fuzzy Expert System

The Risk factors considered in the model as the most effective factors on IT project risks, have been selected according to the previous research. The factors have been divided into six different risk groups consisting of 28 sub-risk factors and have been categorized as follows [3] [12] [17]:

- Environment and ownership (EO): Business or corporate environment instability, Lack of Top Management commitment and support, Failure to get project plan approval from all parties, Lack of sharing responsibility.
- Relationship Management (RM): Failure to manage End-user Expectations, Lack of adequate user involvement, managing multiple relationships with stakeholders, Failure to meet stakeholders' expectations.
- Project Management (PM):Lack of effective management skills, Lack of effective project management methodology, not managing change properly, Extent of changes in the project,Unclear project scope and objectives.

- Resources and planning(RP): Resource shortage, No planning or inadequate planning, Misunderstanding the requirements, Unrealistic deadlines, Underfunding the development.
- Personnel and staffing(PS): Project team expertise, Dependence on a few key people, Poor team relationship, Lack of available skilled personnel, Project manager's experience.
- Technology(T): Technical complexity, Newness of technology, Need for new hardware and software , Project size.

The aim is assessing the Risk of an IT project in E-banking[1] field which has been implemented in Saman bank according to the main six factors status. Since the obtained opinions from the experts, managers and IT consultants, about the relation between the IT projects risk level and the Risk factors, are ambiguous and not precise, Evaluation has been done via linguistic variables. To this purpose, a Mamdani's Fuzzy Expert system has been designed. In this system, six main Risk factors have been considered as Inputs and IT risk as output. The Inputs and Output of designed fuzzy expert system have been presented in Tables 1 & 2.

Table 1. The inputs of fuzzy expert system

Sign	**Inputs**	**Interval**	**Type of membership function**	**Linguistic terms**
EO	Environment and Ownership	[0 1]	Gbell	Low(L) Medium(M) High(H)
RM	Relationship Management	[0 1]	Gaussian	Low(L) Medium(M) High(H)
PM	Project Management	[0 1]	Gbell	VeryLow(VL), Low(L), Medium(M), High(H), VeryHigh(VH)
RP	Resources and Planning	[0 1]	Gaussian2	Low(L), Medium(M), High(H)
PS	Personnel and Staffing	[0 1]	Gaussian	Low(L) Medium(M) High(H)
T	Technology	[0 1]	Gaussian	VeryLow(VL), Low(L), Medium(M), High(H) , VeryHigh(VH)

Table 2. The output of fuzzy expert system

Sign	***Output***	***Interval***	***Type of membership function***	***Linguistic terms***
ITRisk	IT Project Risk	[0 1]	Gaussian2	VeryLow(VL),Low(L), Medium(M) High(H), VeryHigh(VH)

[1] Since the information of considered bank are confidential, The Authors have not been authorized to present more details.

The system according to the obtained rules from IT experts about the relation between Input variables and Output has been designed via MATLAB software. The obtained rules can be viewed in Table 3.

Table 3. The obtained rules from the experts for designing Fuzzy expert system

	EO	*RM*	*PM*	*RP*	*PS*	*T*	*ITRisk*
1	H	M	H	H	H	VH	VL
2	M	H	M	M	H	M	M
3	L	M	VL	L	M	L	VH
4	H	L	M	H	L	L	H
5	M	H	H	M	M	M	L
6	L	M	L	L	L	VL	VH
7	M	L	VL	M	M	M	H
8	M	M	H	H	M	M	M
9	L	L	H	M	L	H	M
10	M	L	VH	H	M	M	L

After specifying Input and Output variables, Membership functions by the experts have been defined for the variables shown in Figure 2 through Figure 8.

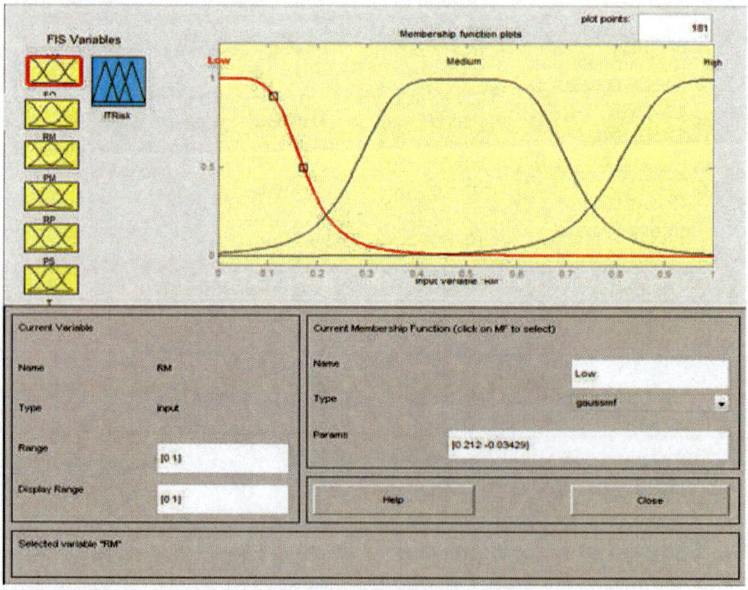

Fig. 2. Three Gbell Membership function for Environment and Ownership

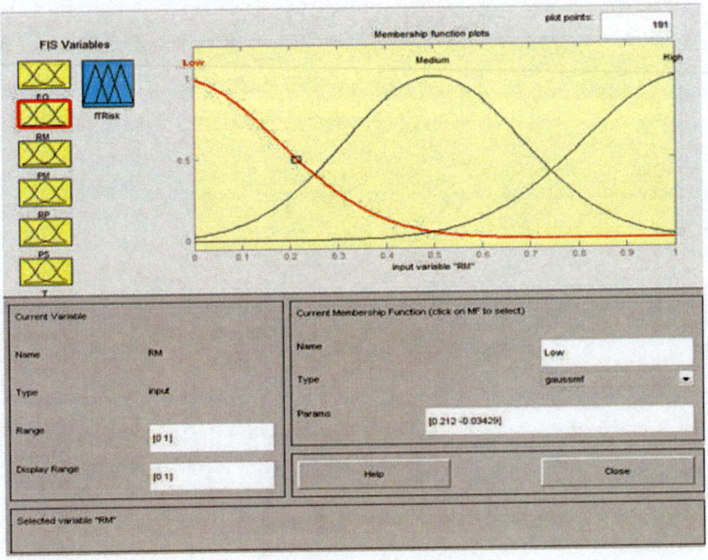

Fig. 3. Three Gaussian Membership function for Relationship Management

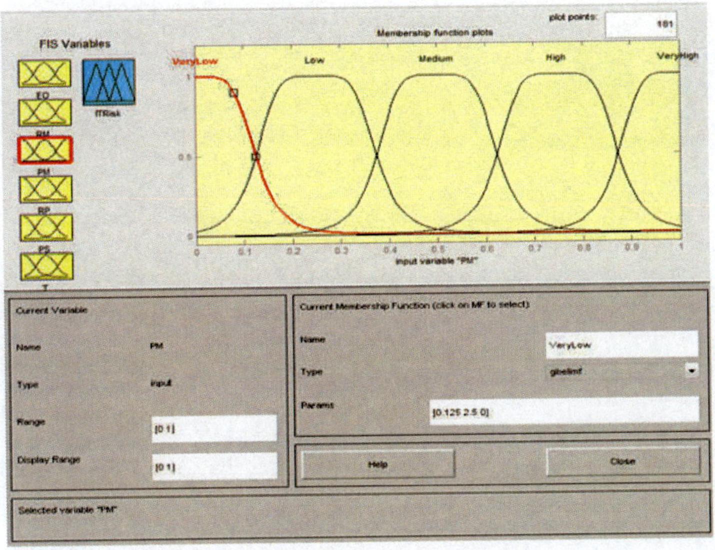

Fig. 4. Five Gbell Membership function for Project Management

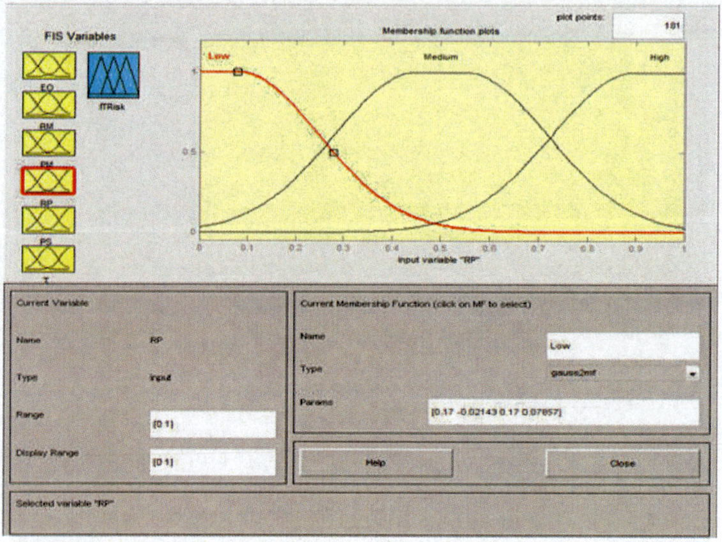

Fig. 5. Three Gaussian2 Membership function for Resources and Planning

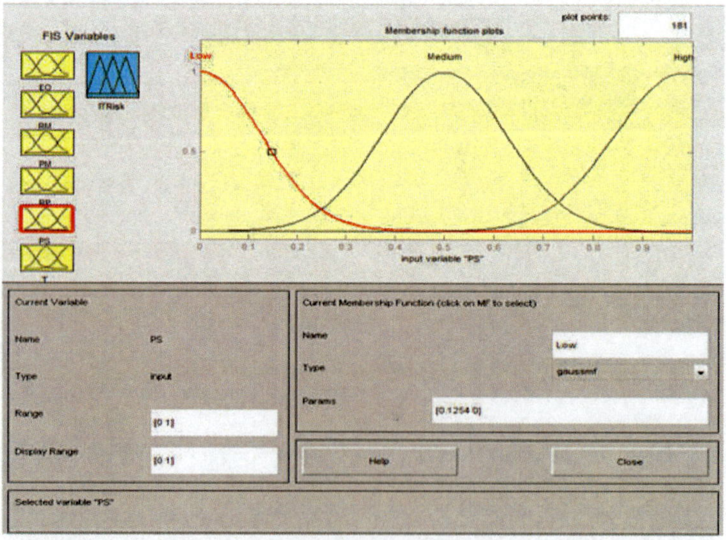

Fig. 6. Three Gaussian Membership function for Personnel and Staffing

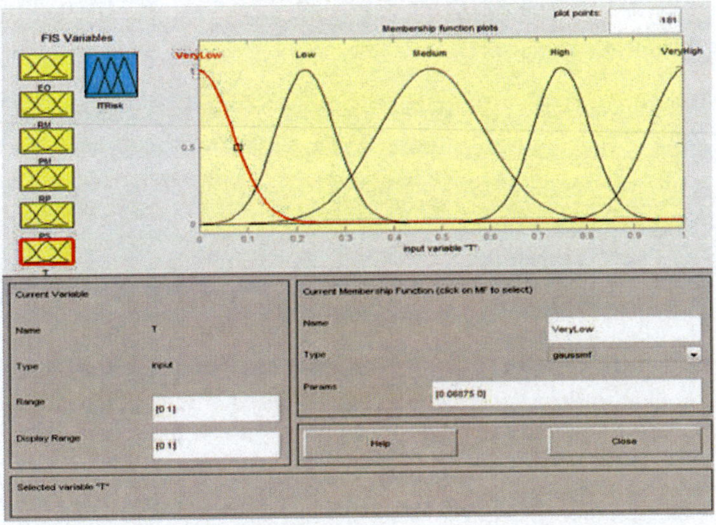

Fig. 7. Three Gaussian Membership function for Technology

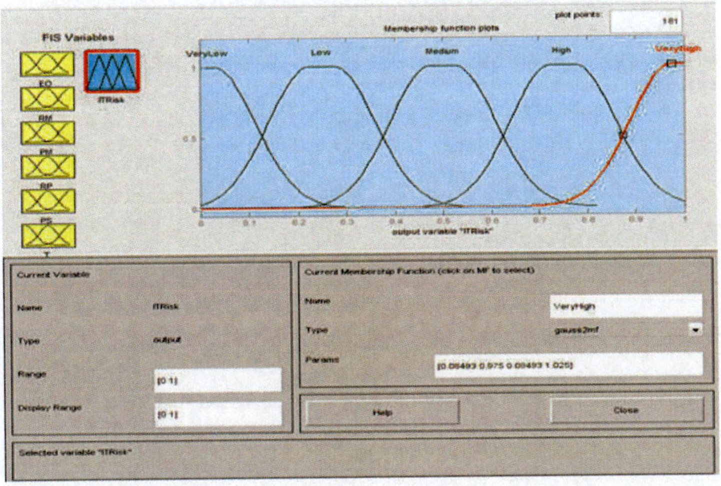

Fig. 8. Five Gaussian2 Membership function for IT project Risk

Here, Fuzzy Inference System (FIS) in MATLAB software has been used and some useful MATLAB commands to work with the designed FIS have been presented. To create an FIS, MATLAB fuzzy logic toolbox provides a user friendly interface in which they can choose the intended specification from drop-down menus.

```
>>fis = readfis ('RiskAssesment')
fis =
name: 'RiskAssesment'
type: 'mamdani'
andMethod: 'min'
orMethod: 'max'
defuzzsMethod: 'centroid'
impMethod: 'min'
aggMethod:'max'
input: [1*6 struct]
output: [1*1 struct]
rule: [1*10struct]
```

The system is able to determine the project risk based on the effective factors on IT projects risk. Regarding the proposed fuzzy expert system, the considered project has been evaluated, as shown in Figure 9.

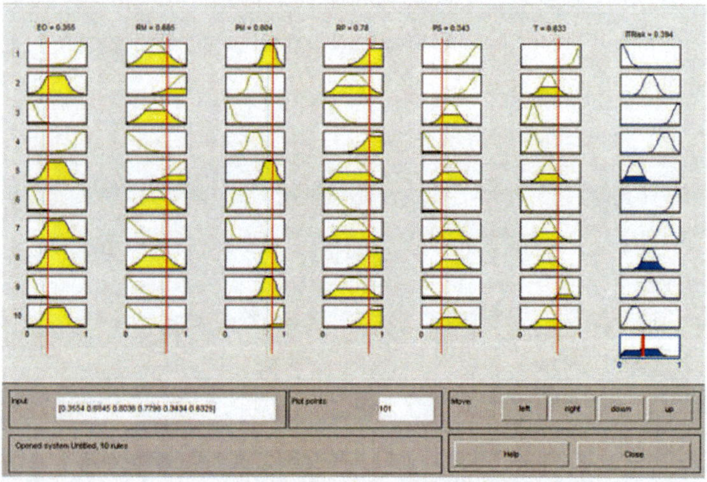

Fig. 9. Assessed Risk of E-banking project by designed fuzzy expert system

According to the experts' opinions as the inputs, the following results have been identified:

<u>Environment and ownership</u> (EO): 035	<u>Resources and planning</u>(RP): 0.78
<u>Relationship Management</u> (RM): 0.68	<u>Personnel and staffing</u>(PS): 0.34
<u>Project Management</u> (PM): 0.8	<u>Technology</u>(T): 0.63

According to the Inputs, the considered project risk has been 0.394 out of 1. The system output is shown that the considered project risk is low based on the linguistic terms. Eventually, the resulted information of the designed system has been given to the final decision makers to decide what to do about the considered project.

Designed system provides a simple yet powerful means of analysis as it gives decision makers an opportunity to consider a range of issues pertinent to existent risk in IT investment decisions before embarking upon detailed, time-consuming financial analysis of IT projects. One of the significant features for the designed system is the possibility of sensitivity analysis. The system enables user to study the parameters change effect on IT projects risk. IT managers should carefully consider factors that may push the status of an IT project from the low risk to high risk end. However, the system has been empirically tested and it is an important tool that would aid the IT experts to make a decision to launch an IT project depends on the level of its risk.

5 Conclusions

Evaluating the IT projects risk based on effective factors, was major fundamental in this paper. To reach this goal, a Mamdani's Fuzzy expert system has been designed with considering the situation of six main effective factors on projects risk as the Inputs and the Risk level as the output and Membership functions have been defined for the variables. Then, according to the rules which have been obtained from consultants and IT managers as the experts, the fuzzy expert system has been designed. This system is able to determine the IT projects risk based on effective factors as an evaluator system. The most important advantage for this Fuzzy Expert system is predicting the risk level related to IT projects and its impact on changing the effective factors status and project Risk. Finally, one of the IT projects has been evaluated.

Acknowledgement. Here, we appreciate from the IT Experts of Saman Iranian bank which has given their knowledge to use them to us as the researchers.

References

1. Chapman, C.B., Ward, S.C.: Project risk management: processes, techniques, and insights, 2nd edn., vol. 65. Wiley, Chrichester (2004)
2. Bandyopadhyay, K., Mykytyn, P.P., Mykytyn, K.: A framework for integrated risk management in information technology. Management Decision 37(5), 437–444 (1999)
3. Barki, H., Rivard, S., Talbot, J.: Toward an assessment of software development risk. Journal of Management Information Systems 10(2), 203–225 (1993)
4. Wallace, L., Keil, M., Rai, A.: How software project risk affects project performance: an investigation of the dimensions of risk and an exploratory model. Decision Sciences 35(2), 289–321 (2004)
5. Tuysuz, F., Kahraman, C.: Project risk evaluation using a fuzzy analytic hierarchy process: an application to information technology projects. International Journal of Intelligent Systems 21(6), 559–584 (2006)
6. Boehm, B.W.: Software risk management: principles and practices. IEEE Software 8(1), 32–41 (1991)

7. Liu, X.Q., Kane, G., Bambroo, M.: An intelligent early warning system for software quality improvement and project management. Journal of Systems and Software 79(11), 1552–1564 (2006)
8. Iranmanesh, H., Nazari Shirkouhi, S., Skandari, M.R.: Risk evaluation of information technology projects based on fuzzy analytic hierarchal process. International Journal of Computer and Information Science and Engineering 2(1), 38–44 (2008)
9. Chapman, C.B., Cooper, D.F.: Risk analysis: testing some prejudices. European Journal of Operational research 14(1), 238–247 (1983)
10. Chen, T., Zhang, J., Lai, K.K.: An integrated real options evaluating model for information technology projects under multiple risks. International Journal of Project Management 27(8), 776–786 (2009)
11. Wallace, L., Keil, M., Rai, M.: Understanding software project risk: a cluster analysis. Information & Management 42(1), 115–125 (2004)
12. Tüysüz, F., Kahraman, C.: Project risk evaluation using a fuzzy analytic hierarchy process: an application to information technology projects. International Journal of Intelligent Systems 21(6), 559–584 (2006)
13. Hui, A.K.T., Liu, D.B.: A bayesian belief network model and tool to evaluate risk and impact in software development projects. In: Reliability and Maintainability Annual Symposium, pp. 297–301 (2004), doi:10.1109/RAMS.2004.1285464
14. Guo, B., Han, Y.: Project risk assessment based on bayes network. Science Management Research 22(5), 73–75 (2004)
15. Feng, N., Li, M., Kou, J.: Software project risk analysis based on BBN. Computer Engineering and Application 18, 16–18 (2006)
16. Feng, N., Li, M., Kou, J.: IT project risk evaluation model based on ANN. Computer Engineering and Applications 6, 24–26 (2006)
17. Liu, S., Zhang, J.: IT project risk assessment methods: a literature review. Int. J. Services, Economics and Management 2(1), 46–58 (2010)
18. Iyatomi, H., Hagiwara, M.: Adaptive fuzzy inference neural network. Pattern Recognition 37(10), 2049–2057 (2004)
19. Juang, Y.S., Lin, S.S., Kao, H.P.: Design and implementation of a fuzzy inference system for supporting customer requirements. Expert Systems with Applications 32(3), 868–878 (2007)
20. Haji, A., Assadi, M.: Fuzzy expert systems and challenge of new product pricing. Computers & Industrial Engineering 56(2), 616–630 (2009)
21. Garibaldi, J.M.: Fuzzy Expert Systems. Stud Fuzz 173, 105–132 (2005), doi:10.1007/3-540-32374-0_6

Automatic Transmission Period Setting for Intermittent Periodic Transmission in Wireless Backhaul

Guangri Jin, Li Gong, and Hiroshi Furukawa

Graduate School of Information Science and Electrical Engineering, Kyushu University
744 Motooka, Nishi-ku, Fukuoka, 819-0395 Japan
jingr@mobcom.ait.kyushu-u.ac.jp,
kyoriki@mobcom.ait.kyushu-u.ac.jp,
furuhiro@ait.kyushu-u.ac.jp

Abstract. Intermittent Periodic Transmission (IPT forwarding) has been proposed as an efficient packet relay method for wireless backhaul. In the IPT forwarding, a source node sends packets to a destination node with a certain time interval (IPT duration) so that signal interference between relay nodes that send packets simultaneously are reduced and frequency reuse is realized which brings about the improvement of system throughput. However, optimum IPT duration setting for each node is a difficult problem which is not solved adequately yet. In this paper, we propose a new IPT duration setting protocol which employs some training packets to search the optimum IPT duration for each node. Simulation and experimental results show that the proposed method is not only very effective but also practical for wireless backhaul.

Keyword: Multi-Hop, Wireless Backhaul, IPT Forwarding, Training Packet.

1 Introduction

The high-speed data transmission with an order of 100Mbps envisioned for the next generation wireless communication systems will enforce the range of cell coverage less than 100m (a class of pico-cell), which increases the number of cells to cover the service area. Deployment of many base nodes considerably raises infrastructure costs, thus cost reduction must be key success factor for future broadband systems.

In recent years, wireless backhaul systems have drawn a great interest as one of the key technologies to reduce infrastructure costs for next generation broadband systems [1]~[2]. In wireless backhaul base nodes have capability of relaying packets by wireless, and a few of them called core nodes, serve as gateways to connect the wireless backhaul with outside backbone network (i.e. Internet) by cables. Upward packets originated from the mobile terminals (e.g. cell phone) which are associated to one of the base nodes and directed to the outside network are relayed by the intermediate relay nodes (slave nodes) until they reach the core nodes. Downward packets originated from the outside network and directed to a mobile terminal in the wireless backhaul are sent by the core nodes and relayed by slave nodes until they reach the final node to which the mobile terminal is associated (Fig. 1). With connecting base nodes by wireless, flexibility of the base nodes deployment is realized and total infrastructure costs are reduced due to few cable constructions [2].

H. Cherifi, J.M. Zain, and E. El-Qawasmeh (Eds.): DICTAP 2011, Part I, CCIS 166, pp. 577–592, 2011.

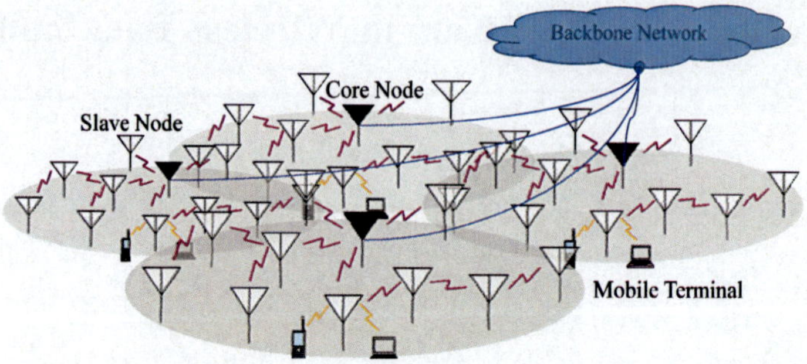

Fig. 1. Wireless backhaul system

Wireless backhaul systems traditionally have been studied in the context of Spatial TDMA (STDMA) and Ad Hoc network. STDMA can achieve collision free multihop channel access by a well-designed time slot assignment for each cell [3]~[5]. However, such a planning is not feasible in real systems because of the irregular cell forms in real environment. Additionally, frame synchronization must be managed carefully in STDMA, which induces rather difficult optimization issues [9]. As far as Ad Hoc network is concerned, many studies have contributed to improve its performance. In [6], Li et al. have indicated that an application of IEEE802.11 to wireless multihop network fails to achieve optimal packet forwarding due to severe packet loss. In [7], Zhai et al. have proposed a new packet scheduling algorithm called Optimum Packet scheduling for Each Traffic flow (OPET) which can achieve an optimum scheduling of packets by assigning high priority of channel access to the current receiver. However, overhead due to complicated hand-shakes decreases frequency reuse efficiency. In [8], Bansal et al. have indicated that the throughput of wireless multihop network decreases with the increase of hop counts.

On the other hand, we have proposed Intermittent Periodic Transmission (IPT forwarding, [9]) as an efficient packet relay method with which the system throughput can achieve a constant value. With IPT forwarding, source node intermittently sends packets with a certain time interval (IPT duration), and each intermediate relay node forwards the relay packet immediately after the reception of it. The frequency reuse space attained by the method is proportional to the given IPT duration. In [10], a series of experiments have been carried out to confirm the effectiveness of the method with real testbed. The IPT forwarding is further enhanced with the combinations of MIMO transmission [11] and directional antenna [12].

IPT duration is the most important parameter for applying the IPT forwarding method. In [13], a collision free IPT duration setting method was proposed and evaluated with computer simulations. However, the method is not feasible since it introduced some new MAC packets, which makes it difficult to be implemented with general WLAN modules. Additionally, the system throughput is not guaranteed to be maximized by the IPT durations attained by the method.

In this paper, we propose a new IPT duration setting protocol which employs training packets to search the IPT durations for each slave node. With these IPT durations, end to end throughputs for each slave node are maximized. A new metric for the training process is also presented and the proposed protocol is evaluated with both computer simulations and experiments by real testbeds.

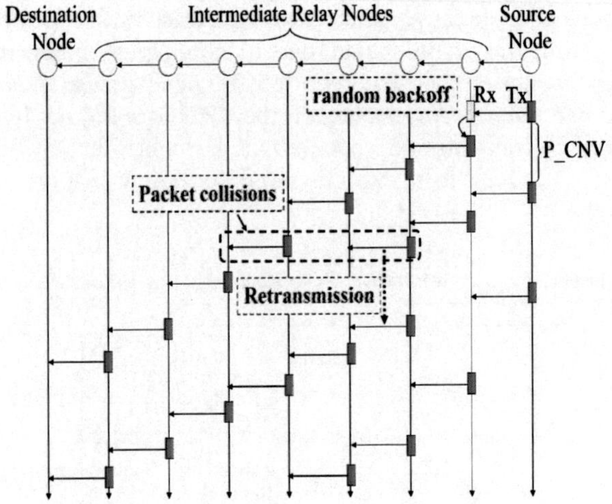

Fig. 2. Packet relay mechanism in conventional method

The rest of this paper is organized as follows. Section 2 explains the principle of the IPT forwarding and the IPT duration setting method proposed by [13]. Section 3 explains the proposed protocol in detail. In section 4, the new protocol is evaluated with both simulations and experiments. Section 5 concludes this paper.

2 Intermittent Periodic Transmission

In this section, we explain the principle of the IPT forwarding along with the conventional packet relay method. The IPT duration setting method proposed by [13] is also introduced.

2.1 Principle of IPT Forwarding

In order to clearly explain the principle of IPT forwarding, we illustrated the packet relay mechanism of the conventional CSMA/CA based method and the IPT forwarding in Fig. 2 and Fig. 3, respectively.

In the two figures, 9 nodes are linearly placed and instantaneous packet relays on the route are shown in accordance with time. All the packets to be sent are re-formatted in advance to have the same time length.

In the case of the conventional CSMA/CA based method, the source node sends packets with a random transmission period of P_CNV and each intermediate relay node forwards received packets from its preceding node with a random backoff period. In the case of the IPT forwarding, the source node transmits packets intermittently with a certain transmission period of P_IPT and each intermediate relay node immediately forwards the received packets from the preceding node without any waiting period. No synchronization is required for both the conventional method and the IPT forwarding method.

In the conventional method co-transmission space, which is defined as the distance between relay nodes that transmit packets at the same time, is not fixed. In such situations, packet collisions could occur due to co-channel interference if the co-transmission space is shorter than the required frequency reuse space, as shown in Fig. 2. On the other hand, in the case of the IPT forwarding it can be readily understood that the co-transmission space could be controlled by the transmission period of P_IPT that is given to the source node, as shown in Fig. 3 in which reuse space is assume to be 3.

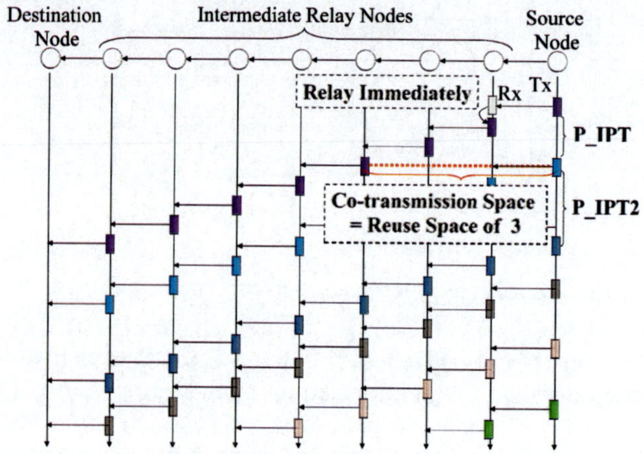

Fig. 3. Packet relay mechanism in IPT forwarding

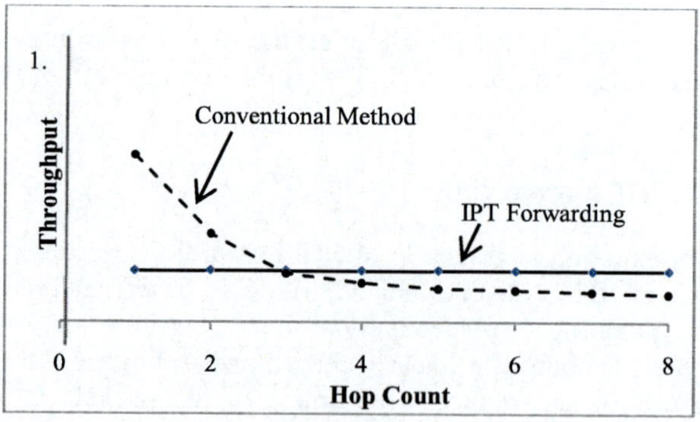

Fig. 4. Performance comparison of the conventional method and the IPT forwarding

Reduction of the packet collisions will help to reduce retransmissions and will consequently help to improve the system performance. If an adequate IPT duration is set in the core node, it is possible to remove interference between co-channel relay nodes that send packets simultaneously. If the IPT duration is equal to the threshold, the resultant throughput observed at the destination node can be maximized.

Fig. 4 schematically shows the normalized throughput versus hop count feature of the conventional method and IPT forwarding for the systems in Fig. 2 and 3. In Fig. 4, constant IPT duration is applied for all slave nodes and thus the resultant throughputs are all the same [9].

2.2 Collision-Free IPT Duration Setting

As discussed earlier, in order to achieve optimal performance the core node should set an adequate IPT duration for each slave node. However, the optimum IPT duration for each slave node depends on many environmental factors such as channel characteristics, node placements, antenna directions and so on. To make the IPT forwarding method practical, an automatic IPT duration setting method is required. To this problem, [13] has proposed a collision-free algorithm to automatically find IPT durations for each node.

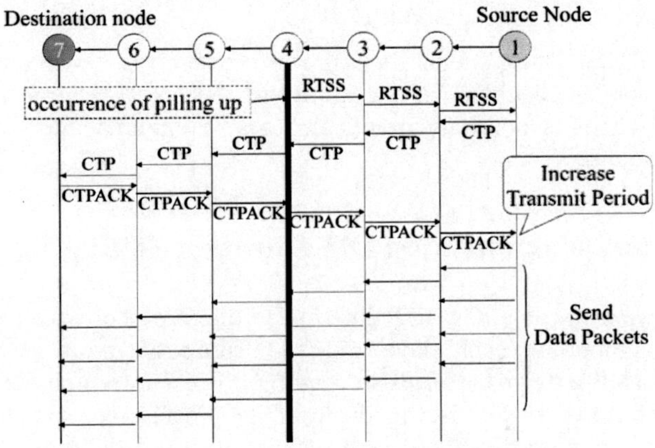

Fig. 5. Collision-Free IPT duration setting

In this subsection, we will first introduce the collision-free method and then indicate its drawbacks.

1) Summary of Collision-free method

Three new MAC layer packets, RTSS (Request to Stop Sending) packet and CTP (Clear to Pilling UP) packet and CTPACK (CTP ACKnowledgement) packet, are defined in [13] and a hand shaking algorithm is employed to find the IPT duration for each node.

As shown in Fig. 5, when the IPT duration setting started the source node (node 1) continuously sends data packets to the destination node (node 7) with certain IPT duration. If a data packet transmission fails in an intermediate node (e.g. node 4 in Fig. 5) due to interference, the node sends a RTSS packet to the source node to stop sending data packets. The source node suspends the sending of data packets immediately after reception of the RTSS packet and sends a CTP packet to the destination node. The CTP packet is relayed in the same way as that for data packet and therefore the destination node can know that all the relaying data packets are cleared out from the system by reception of the CTP packet. The destination node immediately sends a CTPACK packet to the source node on reception of the CTP packet. After receiving the CTPACK packet, the source node increases the IPT duration by one step and resumes the sending of data packets. This process repeats until no data packet forwarding failure occurs in the relaying route.

2) Drawbacks of Collision-free Method

Although the collision-free method can obtain certain IPT durations for wireless backhaul, it has some severe drawbacks as described below.

1) Since new MAC layer packets are introduced, it is difficult to be implemented by general wireless interface modules.
2) The packet transmission state is confirmed by checking the MAC state of each node. However, existing MAC drivers (e.g. MAD WiFi Driver) do not provide such functions.
3) System throughput is not guaranteed to be maximized by applying the IPT durations attained by the method.

Any modification to existing standards will cause extra costs. Since one of the major advantages for wireless backhaul is the ability to reduce costs, a new IPT duration setting method which is not only practical but also exploits the optimum system performance is required.

3 Throughput Maximization IPT Duration Setting

In this section, we propose a new IPT duration setting protocol which maximizes the end to end throughput for each slave node. The proposed protocol employs some training packets and performs a series of training process to search the optimum IPT duration for each slave node. During the training process, core node continuously sends a number of training packets to each slave with an IPT duration which increases gradually until the end to end throughput from the core node to the slave node reaches the maximum value.

Throughout this paper we assume that the route of wireless backhaul is already decided before the IPT duration setting starts and will not change during the process of the protocol.

3.1 Variables and Parameters

We defined the following variables and parameters in the new protocol.

1) Training packet
2) Number of training packets: N
3) Training time for each node: T
4) Training metric for each node: TM
5) IPT duration for each node: D (micro second)
6) Training Step in the process: Δ (micro second)

In these variables, the training packet is defined as OSI link layer's data packet with the length of 1450 Byte and identified by sequence number. The parameters *TM* and *D* are initialized whenever new training begins for a new slave node. The training metric *TM*, which is described latter in detail, is used as the criterion for the training process.

3.2 Details of the Protocol

As shown in Fig. 1, wireless backhaul can be considered as the union of a few sub systems each of which is consisted of a core node and several slave nodes belonging to it (i.e. each slave node is connected to the outside network via the other slave nodes intermediately and finally through the core node by wireless multihop fashion). We call the sub systems mesh clusters (Fig. 6) throughout this paper and the IPT duration setting is performed for each mesh cluster respectively in the same way.

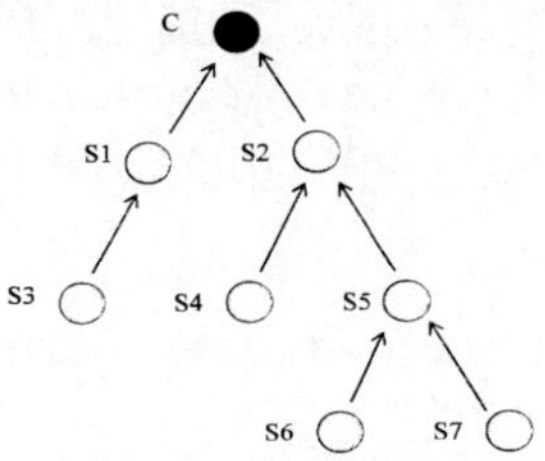

Fig. 6. Mesh cluster

Now consider a mesh cluster with a core node *C* and a set of slave nodes $\{S_1, S_2, ..., S_n\}$. For each slave node $S \in \{S_1, S_2, ..., S_n\}$, the following process is executed .

Step1: The core node *C* initializes the training metric *TM* as -1.0 and initialize *D* as D_0 for the slave node *S*, in which D_0 is a relatively small non-negative value.

Step2: The core node *C* sends *N* training packets which have the sequence number of 1, 2, ..., *N* to the slave node *S* continuously with the IPT duration of *D*.

Step3: Whenever the slave node *S* receives a training packet which is destined to it, *S* records the sequence number and the packet reception time.

Step4: If the reception of training packets destined to itself is finished, the slave node *S* sends a report packet to the core node *C* which contains the sequence number and reception time (Seq1, T_1) of the first training packet it received and the sequence number and reception time (Seq2, T_2) of the last training packet it received. The number of training packets received without duplication, *Num*, is also included in the report packet.

Step5: When the core node *C* receives report packet from the slave node *S*, it estimates actual training time spent for *S* as below.

$$\begin{aligned} \sigma &\stackrel{\text{def}}{=} (T_2 - T_1) / (Seq2 - Seq1) \\ T_{start} &= T_1 - \delta * (Seq1 - 1) \\ T_{end} &= T_2 + \delta * (N - Seq2) \\ T &= T_{end} - T_{start} \end{aligned} \quad (1)$$

According to the estimated training time *T*, a new training metric is calculated as below.

$$New\_TM = \frac{Num}{T}$$

After the computation of new training metric, the training process branches into two cases based on the value of *New_TM*.

a) If $New\_TM \leq TM$, the core node *C* finishes the training for *S* and set the IPT duration of *S* as $(D - \Delta)$ and move to the training of next slave node.
b) If $New\_TM > TM$, the core node *C* increases the IPT duration *D* by Δ, replace the training metric *TM* with *New_TM* and repeats the above ***Step2~Step5***.

Step6: The core node *C* repeats the above Step2~Step5 until the training for all the slave nodes is finished.

3.3 Features of the Protocol

We make some explanations on the new proposed protocol in this subsection.

1) Throughout the training process, we assume that the system does not provide packet relay service so that only training related packets exist in the system.
2) During the training process, if some packet loss occur, the first and last packet received by the slave node *S* could be different with the ones sent by the core node *C*. For this reason, the actual training time *T* must be re-estimated as in Step5. In formula (1), δ is the average training packet transmission time and the training start time and end time are complemented by δ, which consequently complements *T*.
3) The protocol repeats the same training process by gradually increasing the IPT duration for each slave node until its training metric reaches the maximum value. Since for each slave node the training finishes at the moment when *TM* begins to decrease, we set the IPT duration as the value of one preceding step as shown in a) of Step5.
4) It can also be easily realized that training metric *TM* is closely connected to the end to end throughput from the core node *C* to the slave node *S*. Since the protocol searches the IPT duration for each slave node which maximizes its training metric, the end to end throughput of each slave node is also maximized by the calculated IPT durations.

4 Evaluation

In this section, we evaluate the proposed protocol with both computer simulations and experiments by real testbed under indoor environment.

4.1 Evaluation by Computer Simulation

We assume IEEE802.11a as the wireless interface of each node and deployed two simulation scenarios with string topology and tree topology respectively as shown in Fig.7 (Scenario 1) and Fig.8 (Scenario 2). The simulation sites are models of West Building of ITO Campus, Kyushu-University, Japan.

Each system in the Scenarios is consisted of only one mesh cluster. The simulation parameters are shown in Table 1 and the IPT forwarding is applied.

4.2 Simulation Scenarios

In the first, we measured the end to end throughput from core node to each slave node with different IPT durations in the two simulation scenarios using the following formula (2).

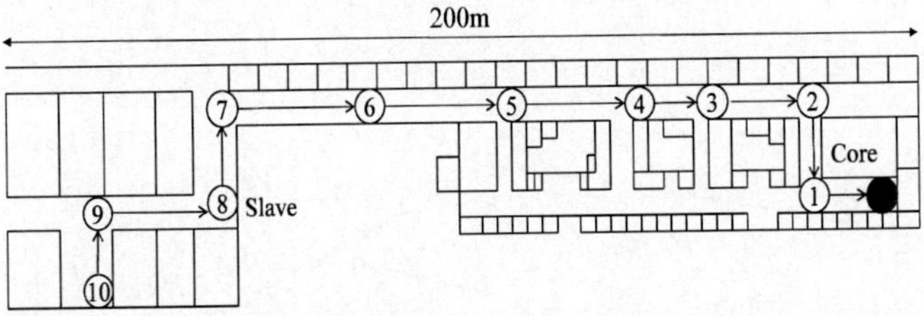

Fig. 7. Simulation site 1, string topology system

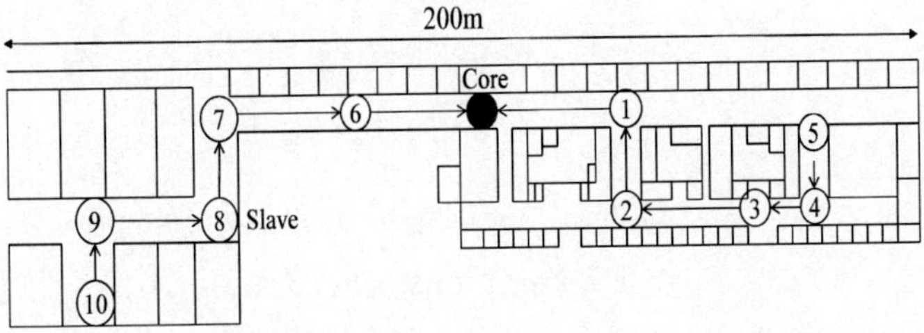

Fig. 8. Simulation site 2, tree topology system

Table 1. Simulation Parameters

MAC Model	IEEE802.11a, Basic Mode. Retry Count = 3.
PHY Model	Packet reception fails when SINR level becomes lower than 10dB.
Propagation Model	2 Ray Ground Reflection Model. No Fading Effect. 12dB Attenuation by a Wall.
Routing Method	Minimum Path Loss Routing.
Data Packet Length	1500 Byte.

$$\text{Throughput} = \frac{\text{Number of Received Packets without Duplication} * \text{Packet Length}}{\text{Transmission Time}} \quad (2)$$

In this first evaluation, IPT durations are set manually for the purpose of searching an optimum IPT duration for each slave node. Manually taken optimum IPT durations are compared with the ones to be found by the proposed protocol, afterward.

We assume that no extra traffic occurs during the measurement and the number of transmitted packets in the above formula is 2000.

After that, we performed the proposed protocol to calculate the IPT durations for each slave node with the initial value D_0 to be 0, Δ to be 100 μsec.

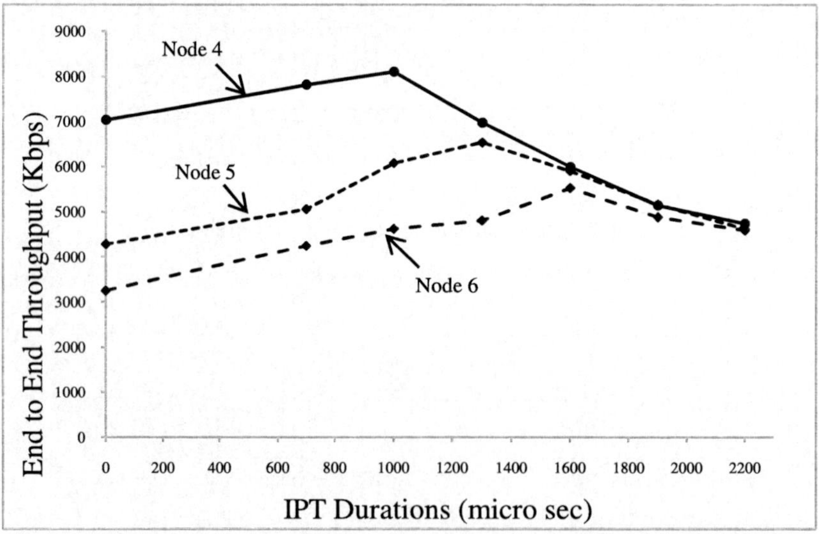

Fig. 9. IPT durations and end to end throughput for node 4, 5, 6 in simulation scenario 1

4.1.2 Simulation Results

The throughput vs. IPT duration for each slave node is shown in Fig. 9, 10 for scenario 1 and in Fig. 12 for scenario 2. The optimum IPT durations with which the end to end throughput is maximized are shown in Table 2 for scenario 1 and in Table 3 for scenario 2. The IPT durations obtained by the protocol for each slave node are shown in Fig. 11 for scenario 1 and Fig. 13 for scenario 2.

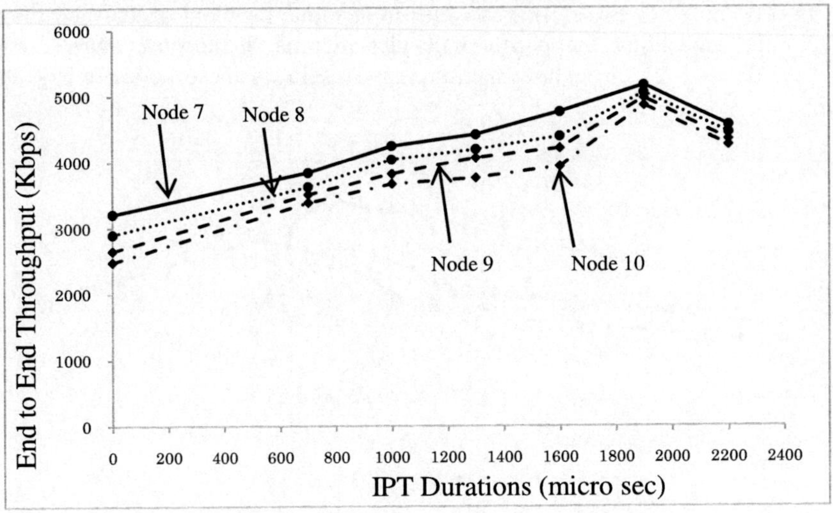

Fig. 10. IPT durations and end to end throughput for node 7, 8, 9, 10 in simulation scenario 1

Table 2. Optimum IPT durations in simulation scenario 1 (μsec)

Node 4	Node 5	Node 6	Node 7	Node 8	Node 9	Node 10
1000	1300	1600	1900	1900	1900	1900

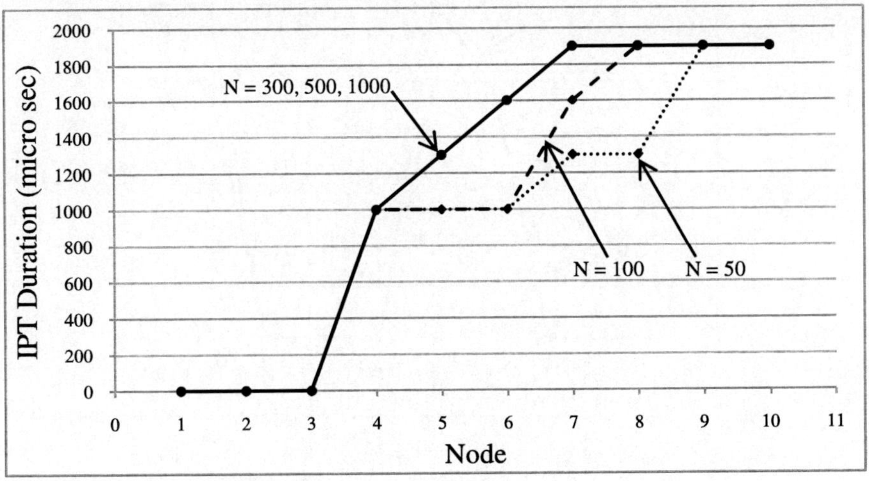

Fig. 11. Automatically calculated IPT durations in simulation scenario 1

As shown in Fig. 11 and. 13, the IPT duration calculated by the protocol is zero for node 1, 2, 3 in scenario 1 and for node 1, 2, 3, 6, 7, 8 in scenario 2. According to the feature of the IPT forwarding, it can be easily understood that the IPT durations for the slave nodes which are located within the CSMA range of the core node could be set to zero because for these nodes no hidden terminal problem occurs and thus no need to purposely adjust the packet transmission time in the core node. For this reason, we deleted the throughput measurement results of these nodes in Fig. 9, 10 and 12.

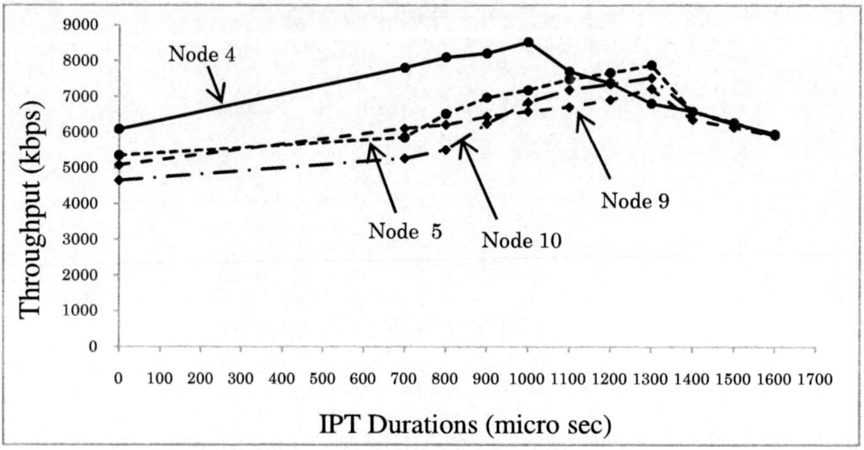

Fig. 12. IPT durations and end to end throughput for node 4, 5, 9, 10 in simulation scenario 2

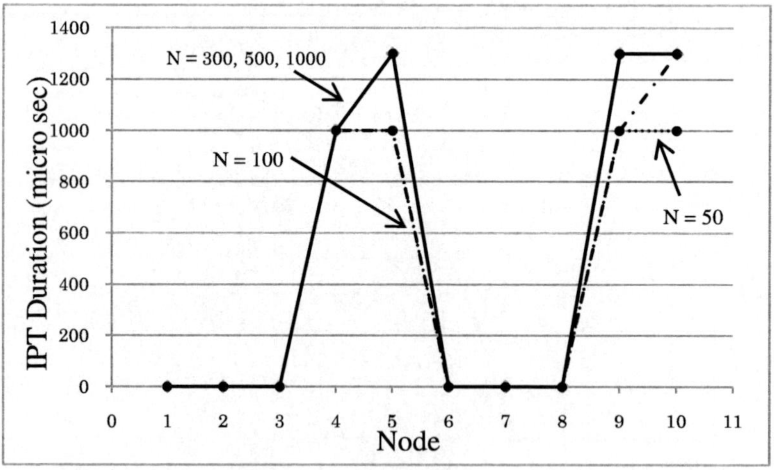

Fig. 13 Automatically calculated IPT durations in simulation scenario 2

Table 3. Optimum IPT durations in simulation scenario 2 (μsec)

Node 4	Node 5	Node 9	Node 10
1000	1300	1300	1300

In Fig. 11 and 13, the automatically calculated IPT durations match to the optimum ones in Table 2 and 3 with $N = 300, 500, 1000$. However, with relatively small values of N (50, 100 in this case), the calculated IPT durations do not match to the optimum ones. This is because with such small N, the ratio of received training packets number and N varies intensively each time and the estimation of training time is not precise enough.

Fig. 14. Picomesh LunchBox

However, with the increment of N (larger than 300 in this case), these variations are suppressed and consequently the calculated IPT durations converge to the optimum values for each slave node.

The simulation results show that with adequate parameter settings, the proposed protocol can find the optimum IPT durations for each slave node, with which the end to end throughput is maximized.

4.2 Evaluation by Experiments

In order to further confirm its performance, we implement the proposed protocol into a testbed and evaluate its performance under real indoor environment.

4.2.1 Testbed and throughput Measurement Tool

The testbed is called "Picomesh LunchBox" (LB, Fig. 14). LB is the first product of "MIMO-MESH Project" which the authors are working on [14].

LB is equipped with three IEEE802.11 modules, two of which are used for relaying packets between base nodes and the other one is used for mobile terminal access.

Each module of LB is assigned with different spectrum so that the interference between these modules could be avoided. The hardware specification of LB is shown in Table 4.

In this experiment, we use IPerf to measure the throughputs [15]. IPerf is free software which can measure the end to end throughput in various networks with a pair of server and client. Additionally, we adopt UDP mode of its two operational modes (TCP mode and UDP mode) and measure the throughput from client to server.

Table 4. Specification of LB

CPU	AMD Geode LX800
Memory	DDR 512MB
Backhall Wireless IF	IEEE802.11b/g/a ×2
Access Wireless IF	IEEE802.11b/g/a ×1
OS	Linux kernel 2.6

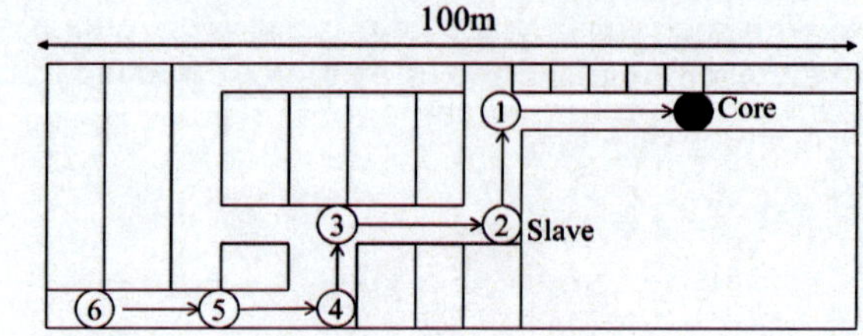

Fig. 15. Experimental site

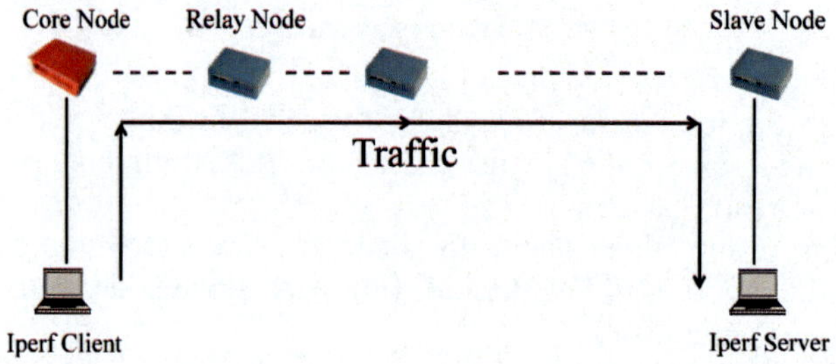

Fig. 16. Throughput measurement system

4.2.2 Experimental Scenario

We deployed a wireless backhaul system with one core node and six slave nodes in West Building of ITO Campus, Kyushu-University, Japan (Fig. 15).

At first, we measured the end to end throughput of each slave node with different IPT durations by IPerf. Specifically, we set up the IPerf client in a PC which is connected to the core node and the IPerf server in a PC which is connected to the slave node (Fig. 16). During the measurement, traffic flows from IPerf client to sever and each measuring continues 30 seconds. We also assume that no extra traffic occurs during the measurement. In this first experiment, IPT durations are set manually for the purpose of searching an optimum IPT duration for each slave node. The optimum IPT durations are compared with the ones to be found by the proposed protocol, afterward.

In the next, we performed the proposed protocol to calculate the IPT durations for each slave node with the training packet number N to be 1000 and the initial value D_0 to be 1000, Δ to be 100 μsec.

4.2.3 Result of the Experiments

The throughput vs. IPT duration for each slave node is shown in Fig. 17 and the IPT durations calculated by the proposed protocol and the protocol's run time are shown in Table 5.

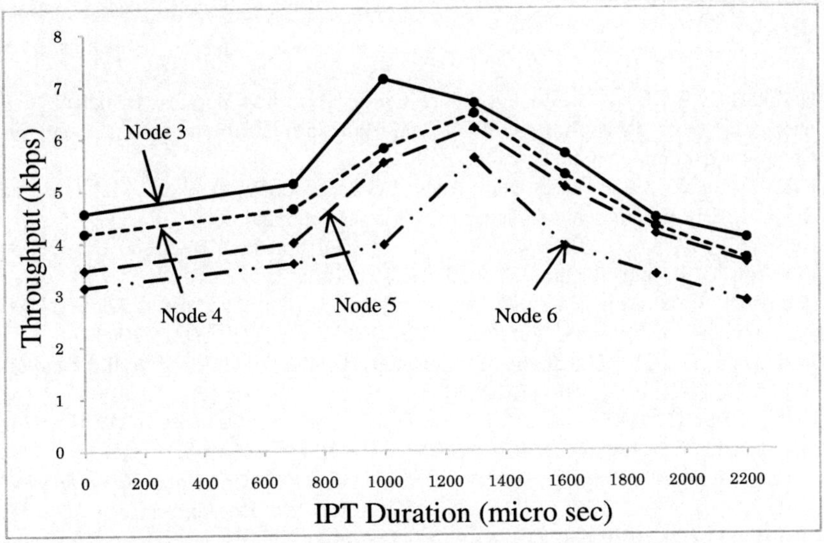

Fig. 17. IPT durations and end to end throughput for Node 3, 4, 5, 6 in experiment

Table 5. IPT durations searched by the protocol (μsec) and its run time

Node 1	Node 2	Node 3	Node 4	Node 5	Node 6	Run Time
0	0	1000	1300	1300	1300	11 (sec)

The calculated IPT durations of node 1 and 2 are zero in Table 5, which means that the two nodes are located within the CSMA range of the core node and thus we deleted the corresponding throughputs of the two nodes in Fig. 17.

As we can see from Fig. 17 and Table 5, the calculated IPT durations match to the optimum ones measured by IPerf with which the end to end throughputs reach the maximum values. With 6 slave nodes and 1000 training packets, the protocol spent 11 seconds to finish, which makes it practical enough in real applications.

5 Conclusion

In this paper we proposed a new IPT duration setting protocol which can calculate the optimum IPT duration for each slave node automatically. The proposed protocol is evaluated both with computer simulations and experiments by real testbed under indoor environment.

Evaluation results show that with the calculated IPT durations the end to end throughput of each slave node is maximized. Since the protocol does not introduce any modifications to existing standards, it could be easily implemented with general WLAN modules.

References

[1] Narlikar, G., Wilfong, G., Zhang, L.: Designing Multi-hop Wireless Backhaul Networks with Delay Guarantees. In: Proc INFOCOM 2006 25th IEEE International Conference on Computer Communications, pp. 1–12 (2006)

[2] Pabst, R., et al.: Relay-Based Deployment Concepts for Wireless and Mobile Broadband Radio. IEEE Communication Magazine, 80–89 (September 2004)

[3] Nelson, R., Kleinrock, L.: Spatial TDMA: A Collision Free Multihop Channel Access Protocol. IEEE Trans. Comm. 33(9), 934–944 (1985)

[4] Gronkvist, J., Nilsson, J., Yuan, D.: Throughput of Optimal Spatial Reuse TDMA for Wireless Ad-Hoc Networks. In: Proc. VTC 2004 Spring, 11F-3 (May 2004)

[5] Li, H., Yu, D., Gao, Y.: Spatial Synchronous TDMA in Multihop Radio Network. In: Proc. VTC 2004 Spring, 8F-1 (May 2004)

[6] Li, J., Blake, C., De Couto, D.S.J., Lee, H.I., Morris, R.: Capacity of Ad Hoc Wireless Network. In: Proc. ACM MobiCom 2001 (July 2001)

[7] Zhai, H., Wang, J., Fang, Y., Wu, D.: A Dual-channel MAC Protocol for Mobile Ad Hoc Networks. In: Proc. IEEE Workshop on Wireless Ad Hoc and Sensor Networks, in conjunction with IEEE GlobeCom, pp. 27–32 (2004)

[8] Bansal, S., Shorey, R., Misra, A.: Energy efficiency and throughput for TCP traffic in multi-hop wireless networks. In: Proc INFOCOM 2002, vol. 23-27, pp. 210–219 (2002)

[9] Furukawa, H.: Hop Count Independent Throughput Realization by A New Wireless Multihop Relay. In: Proc. VTC 2004 fall, pp. 2999–3003 (September 2004)

[10] Higa, Y., Furukawa, H.: Experimental Evaluation of Wireless Multihop Networks Associated with Intermittent Periodic Transmit. IEICE Trans. Comm. E90-B(11) (November 2007)

[11] Mohamed, E.M., Kinoshita, D., Mitsunaga, K., Higa, Y., Furukawa, H.: An Efficient Wireless Backhaul Utilizing MIMO Transmission and IPT Forwarding. International Journal of Computer Networks, IJCN 2(1), 34–46 (2010)

[12] Mitsunaga, K., Maruta, K., Higa, Y., Furukawa, H.: Application of directional antenna to wireless multihop network enabled by IPT forwarding. In: Proc. ICSCS (December 2008)

[13] Higa, Y., Furukawa, H.: Time Interval Adjustment Protocol for the New Wireless multihop Relay with Intermittent Periodic Transmit. In: IEICE, B-5-180 (September 2004)

[14] `http://mimo-mesh.com/en/`

[15] `http://iperf.sourceforge.net/`

Towards Fast and Reliable Communication in MANETs

Khaled Day, Bassel Arafeh, Abderezak Touzene, and Nasser Alzeidi

Department of Computer Science, Sultan Qaboos University, P.O. Box 36,
Al-Khod 123, Oman
{kday,arafeh,touzene,alzidi}@squ.edu.om

Abstract. A number of position-based routing protocols have been proposed for mobile ad-hoc networks (MANETs) based on a virtual two-dimensional grid partitioning of the geographical region of the MANET. Each node is assumed to know its own location in the grid based on GPS positioning. A node can also find out the location of other nodes using location services. Selected gateway nodes handle routing. Only the gateway node in a cell contributes to routing packets through that cell. This paper shows how to construct cell-disjoint paths in such a two-dimensional grid. These paths can be used for routing in parallel multiple data packets from a source node to a destination node. They provide alternative routes in cases of routing failures and allow fast transfer of large amounts of data by simultaneous transmission over disjoint paths. Performance characteristics of the constructed paths are derived showing their attractiveness for improving the reliability and speed of communication in MANETs.

Keywords: Mobile ad-hoc networks, position-based routing, 2D grid, parallel paths, reliability.

1 Introduction

Communication in a Mobile Ad-hoc Network (MANET) is a challenging problem due to node mobility and energy constraints. Many routing protocols for MANETs have been proposed which can be broadly classified in two categories: topology-based routing and position-based routing. In topology-based protocols [1], link information is used to make routing decisions. They are further divided in: proactive (table-driven) protocols, reactive (on-demand) protocols and hybrid protocols, based on when and how the routes are discovered. In proactive topology-based protocols, such as DSDV [2], each node maintains one or more tables containing routing information to other nodes in the network. When the network topology changes the nodes propagate update messages throughout the network to maintain a consistent and up-to-date view of the network. In reactive topology-based protocols, such as AODV [3], the routes are created only when needed. Hybrid protocols, such as: ZRP [4], combine both proactive and reactive approaches where the nodes proactively maintain routes to nearby nodes and establish routes to far away nodes only when needed.

The second broad category of routing protocols is the class of position-based protocols [5-8]. They make use of the nodes' geographical positions to make routing decisions. Nodes are able to obtain their own and destination's geographical position

H. Cherifi, J.M. Zain, and E. El-Qawasmeh (Eds.): DICTAP 2011, Part I, CCIS 166, pp. 593–602, 2011.

via Global Positioning System (GPS) and location services. This approach has become practical by the rapid development of hardware and software solutions for determining absolute or relative node positions in MANETs [9]. One advantage of this approach is that it requires limited or no routing path establishment/maintenance which constitutes a major overhead in topology based routing methods. Another advantage is scalability. It has been shown that topology based protocols are less scalable than position-based protocols [5]. Examples of position-based routing algorithms include: POSANT (Position Based Ant Colony Routing Algorithm) [8], BLR (Beaconless Routing Algorithm) [10], and PAGR (Power Adjusted Greedy Routing) [11].

In [12], a location aware routing protocol (called GRID) for mobile ad-hoc networks was proposed. GRID views the geographic area of the MANET as a virtual 2D grid with an elected leader node in each grid square (grid cell). Routing is performed in a cell-by-cell manner through the leader nodes. Variants of GRID have been proposed in [13] and [14] introducing some improvements to the original GRID protocol. In [13] nodes can enter a sleep mode to conserve energy and in [14] stable nodes that stay as long as possible in the same cell are selected as gateways. Several other protocols based on a similar virtual grid view have appeared in the literature such as [15] and [16].

This paper shows how to construct parallel (cell-disjoint) paths between any source cell and any destination cell in a two-dimensional grid. The constructed parallel paths can be used to provide alternative routes in case of routing path failures. They can also help speeding up the transfer of large amounts of data between a source node and a destination node. This can be achieved by dividing up the large data into pieces and sending the pieces simultaneously on multiple disjoint paths.

The remainder of the paper is organized as follows: section 2 introduces some definitions and notations; section 3 shows how to construct cell-disjoint paths in a 2D grid; section 4 derives performance characteristics of the constructed paths; and section 5 concludes the paper.

2 Preliminaries

Consider a mobile ad hoc network (MANET) composed of N mobile wireless devices (nodes) distributed in a given geographical region. The geographical area where the MANET nodes are located can be viewed as a virtual two-dimensional (2D) grid of cells as shown in figure 1. Each grid cell is a $d \times d$ square. Two grid cells are called neighbor cells if they have a common edge or a common corner. Therefore each grid cell has eight neighbor cells. A path in the 2D-grid is a sequence of neighboring grid cells. Two MANET nodes are called neighbor nodes (or neighbors) if they are located in neighbor cells. The value of d is selected depending on the minimum transmission range r such that a MANET node can communicate directly with all its neighboring nodes (located anywhere in neighbor cells). This requirement is met if d satisfies the condition: $r \geq 2d\sqrt{2}$. This can be seen by noticing that the farthest apart points in two neighboring grid cells are two diametrically opposite corners at distance $2d$ in each of the two dimensions. These two farthest apart points are at distance: $2d\sqrt{2}$.

Each grid cell is identified by a pair of grid coordinates (x, y) as illustrated in figure 1. Each MANET node has a distinctive node id (IP or MAC address). We use letters such as *A*, *B*, *S*, *D* and *G* to represent node ids. A packet sent by a MANET node can be addressed to a single node within the sender's transmission range, or it can be a local broadcast packet which is received by all nodes within the sender's transmission range.

Data packets are routed from a source node *S* to a destination node *D* over the 2D-grid structure with each routing step moving a packet from a node in a grid cell to a node in a neighboring grid cell until the destination node *D* is reached. In each grid cell one node is selected as the gateway node. Only gateway nodes participate in forwarding packets through the sequence of cells forming a routing path. A gateway node in cell (x, y) is denoted $G_{x,\ y}$. Each node can have up to eight neighboring gateway nodes (one in each of the eight neighboring cells) as shown in figure 1. Each node is able to obtain its own geographical position through a low-power GPS receiver and the location of other nodes through a location service. The location of a node is mapped to the (x, y) coordinates of the grid cell where the node is located. We show how to construct a maximum-size set of cell-disjoint paths between any two grid cells. These paths can be used for routing a set of packets simultaneously from a source node to a destination node. The packets could correspond to multiple copies of the same packet sent in duplicates for higher reliability or could be pieces of a divided up large message sent in parallel for faster delivery.

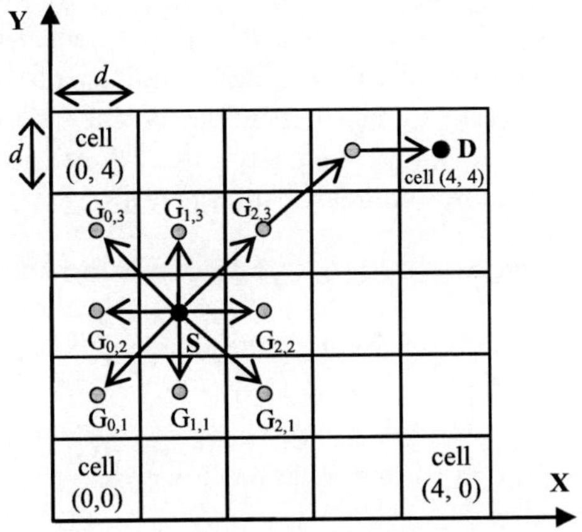

S: source node, D: destination node
$G_{x,y}$: gateway node in cell (x,y)

Fig. 1. 2D Grid View of a MANET Region

3 Cell-Disjoint (Parallel) Paths in a 2D-GRID

Let *S* be a source node located in a source cell (x_S, y_S) of a virtual 2D-grid and let *D* be a destination node (different from *S*) located in a destination cell (x_D, y_D). We show

how to construct a maximum number of cell-disjoint paths from S to D. A path from S to D is a sequence of cells starting with the source cell (x_S, y_S) and ending with the destination cell (x_D, y_D) such that any two consecutive cells in the sequence are neighbor grid cells. Two paths from S to D are called cell-disjoint (or parallel) if they do not have any common cells other than the source cell (x_S, y_S) and the destination cell (x_D, y_D). A path from S to D can be specified by the sequence of cell-to-cell moves that lead from S to D. Such sequences can be used as routing vectors to guide the forwarding of packets from source to destination.

There are eight possible moves from any cell to a neighbor cell. These eight moves are denoted: <+x>, <-x>, <+y>, <-y>, <+x, +y>, <+x, -y>, <-x, +y> and <-x, -y>. The moves <+x> and <-x> correspond to the right and left horizontal moves in the grid, the moves <+y> and <-y> correspond to the up and down vertical moves and the moves <+x, +y>, <+x, -y>, <-x, +y> and <-x, -y> correspond to the four diagonal moves. In a path description we use a superscript integer value i after a move to represent i successive repetitions of that move. For example <+x, +y>^{3} represents 3 successive <+x, +y> moves.

There are at most eight cell-disjoint paths from S to D corresponding to the eight possible starting moves: <+x>, <-x>, <+y>, <-y>, <+x, +y>, <+x, -y>, <-x, +y>, and <-x, -y>. We assume without loss of generality that $x_D \geq x_S$ and $y_D \geq y_S$ (i.e. D is north east of S). The paths for the other cases can be derived from the paths of the case $x_D \geq x_S$ and $y_D \geq y_S$ as follows: (a) if $x_D \geq x_S$ and $y_D < y_S$ then replace $+y$ by $-y$ and vice versa in all paths, (b) if $x_D < x_S$ and $y_D \geq y_S$ then replace $+x$ by $-x$ and vice versa in all paths, and (c) if $x_D < x_S$ and $y_D < y_S$ then do both replacements in all paths. We distinguish four cases in the construction of cell-disjoint paths from the source cell (x_S, y_S) to the destination cell (x_D, y_D) depending on the relationship between the distances $\delta_x = x_D - x_S$ and $\delta_y = y_D - y_S$ along the x and y dimensions (i.e. depending on the relative positions of the source and destination nodes).

Case 1: If $\delta_x > \delta_y \geq 1$ (the case $\delta_y > \delta_x \geq 1$ is symmetric and can be obtained by swapping x and y)

Table 1 lists eight cell-disjoint paths from the source cell (x_S, y_S) to the destination cell (x_D, y_D) for the case $\delta_x > \delta_y \geq 1$.

Table 1. Cell-Disjoint Paths for the case $\delta_x > \delta_y \geq 1$

Path	Source Exit Moves	Diagonal Moves	Horizontal Moves	Destination Entry Moves
π_{11}	<+x, +y>	<+x, +y>$^{\delta_y-1}$	<+x>$^{\delta_x-\delta_y-1}$	<+x>
π_{12}	<+x>	<+x, +y>$^{\delta_y-1}$	<+x>$^{\delta_x-\delta_y-1}$	<+x, +y>
π_{13}	<+y> <+x, +y>	<+x, +y>$^{\delta_y-1}$	<+x>$^{\delta_x-\delta_y-1}$	<+x, -y>
π_{14}	<+x, -y>	<+x, +y>$^{\delta_y-1}$	<+x>$^{\delta_x-\delta_y-1}$	<+x, +y> <+y>
π_{15}	<-x, +y> <+x, +y>^{2}	<+x, +y>$^{\delta_y-1}$	<+x>$^{\delta_x-\delta_y-1}$	<+x, -y><-y>
π_{16}	<-y> <+x, -y>	<+x, +y>$^{\delta_y-1}$	<+x>$^{\delta_x-\delta_y-1}$	<+x, +y>^{2} <-x, +y>
π_{17}	<-x> <-x, +y> <+x, +y>^{3}	<+x, +y>$^{\delta_y-1}$	<+x>$^{\delta_x-\delta_y-1}$	<+x, -y>^{2} <-x, -y>
π_{18}	<-x, -y> <+x, -y>^{2}	<+x, +y>$^{\delta_y-1}$	<+x>$^{\delta_x-\delta_y-1}$	<+x, +y>^{3} <-x, +y> <-x>

Each path starts with a sequence of *source exit moves* which include a move to one of the 8 neighbor cells of the source cell followed by up to four moves to reach the common exit column (the next column following the column containing the source node in the direction of the destination node). Notice that in the symmetric case $\delta_y > \delta_x \geq 1$, the term *column* should be replaced by the term *row*. Once the paths reach the exit column they all follow the same two sequences of moves namely a sequence of δ_y-1 diagonal moves of the type <+x, +y> followed by a sequence of δ_x-δ_y-1 horizontal moves of the type <+x>. Notice that in the symmetric case $\delta_y > \delta_x \geq 1$ the term *horizontal* should be replaced by the term *vertical*. These two sequences make the eight paths reach the destination entry column which is the column immediately preceding the column containing the destination cell. Once the entry column is reached the paths follow a sequence of up to five *destination entry moves* to maintain the cell-disjoint property. Figure 2 illustrates the construction with an example where $\delta_x = 5$ and $\delta_y = 2$.

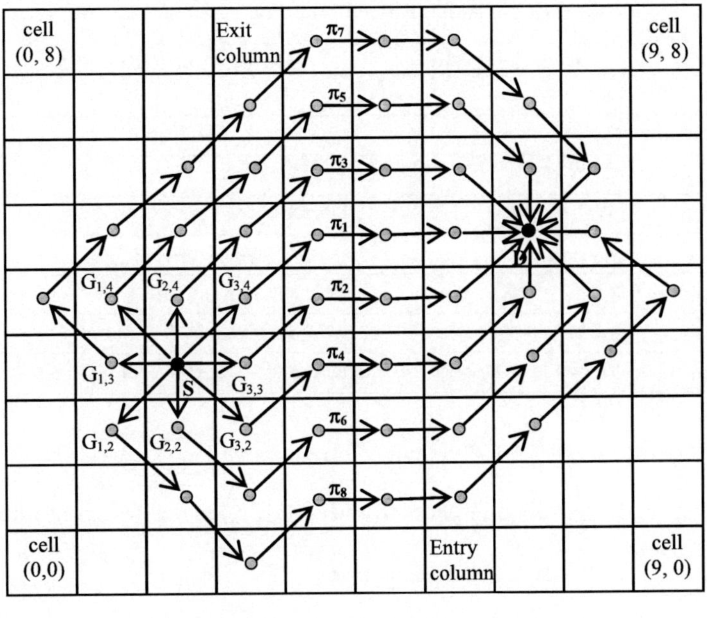

Fig. 2. Cell-Disjoint (Parallel) Paths in a 2D Grid

Case 2: $\delta_x \geq 2$ & $\delta_y = 0$ (the case $\delta_y \geq 2$ & $\delta_x = 0$ is symmetric and can be obtained by swapping *x* and *y*)

Table 2 lists eight cell-disjoint paths from source cell (x_S, y_S) to destination cell (x_D, y_D) for this case.

Table 2. Cell-Disjoint Paths for the case $\delta_x \geq 2$ and $\delta_y = 0$

Path	Source Exit Moves	Horizontal Moves	Destination Entry Moves
π_{21}	<+x>	<+x>$^{\delta x -2}$	<+x>
π_{22}	<+x, +y>	<+x>$^{\delta x -2}$	<+x, -y>
π_{23}	<+x, -y>	<+x>$^{\delta x -2}$	<+x, +y>
π_{24}	<+y> <+x, +y>	<+x>$^{\delta x -2}$	<+x, -y> <-y>
π_{25}	<-y> <+x, -y>	<+x>$^{\delta x -2}$	<+x, +y> <+y>
π_{26}	<-x, +y> <+x, +y>^{2}	<+x>$^{\delta x -2}$	<+x, -y>^{2} <-x, -y>
π_{27}	<-x, -y> <+x, -y>^{2}	<+x>$^{\delta x -2}$	<+x, +y>^{2} <-x, +y>
π_{28}	<-x> <-x, +y> <+x, +y>^{3}	<+x>$^{\delta x -2}$	<+x, -y>^{3} <-x, -y> <-x>

Case 3: $\delta_x = 1$ and $\delta_y = 0$ (the case $\delta_y = 1$ and $\delta_x = 0$ is symmetric) - Table 3 lists eight cell-disjoint paths from cell (x_S, y_S) to cell (x_D, y_D) for this case.

Table 3. Cell-Disjoint Paths for the case $\delta_x = 1$ and $\delta_y = 0$

Path	Source Exit Moves	Destination Entry Moves
π_{31}	<+x>	
π_{32}	<+x, +y>	<-y>
π_{33}	<+x, -y>	<+y>
π_{34}	<+y>	<+x, -y>
π_{35}	<-y>	<+x, +y>
π_{36}	<-x, +y> <+x, +y>	<+x> <+x, -y> <-x, -y>
π_{37}	<-x, -y> <+x, -y>	<+x> <+x, +y> <-x, +y>
π_{38}	<-x> <-x, +y> <+x, +y>^{2}	<+x> <+x, -y>^{2} <-x, -y> <-x>

Case 4: $\delta_x = \delta_y$ (in this case we must have $\delta_x = \delta_y \geq 1$)

Table 4 lists eight cell-disjoint paths from cell (x_S, y_S) to cell (x_D, y_D) for this case.

Table 4. Cell-Disjoint Paths for the case $\delta_x = \delta_y$

Path	Source Exit Moves	Common Diagonal Moves	Destination Entry Moves
π_{41}	<+x, +y>	<+x, +y>$^{\delta y-1}$	
π_{42}	<+x>	<+x, +y>$^{\delta y-1}$	<+y>
π_{43}	<+y>	<+x, +y>$^{\delta y-1}$	<+x>
π_{44}	<+x, -y>	<+x, +y>$^{\delta y-1}$	<+x, +y> <-x, +y>
π_{45}	<-x, +y> <+x, +y>	<+x, +y>$^{\delta y-1}$	<+x, -y>
π_{46}	<-y> <+x, -y>	<+x, +y>$^{\delta y-1}$	<+x, +y>^{2} <-x, +y> <-x>
π_{47}	<-x> <-x, +y> <+x, +y>^{2}	<+x, +y>$^{\delta y-1}$	<+x, -y> <-y>
π_{48}	<-x, -y> <+x, -y>^{2}	<+x, +y>$^{\delta y-1}$	<+x, +y>^{3} <-x, +y>^{2} <-x,-y>

4 Properties of the Constructed Paths

We obtain the lengths of the constructed cell-disjoint paths. These lengths are readily obtained from the tables 1, 2, 3 and 4.

Result 1: The lengths of the constructed 8 paths for each of the 4 cases are listed in Table 5.

Table 5. Lengths of the Constructed Cell-Disjoint Paths

Case	Length of Path 1	Length of Path 2	Length of Path 3	Length of Path 4	Length of Path 5	Length of Path 6	Length of Path 7	Length of Path 8
1	$\lvert\pi_{11}\rvert = \delta_x$ (optimal)	$\lvert\pi_{12}\rvert = \delta_x$ (optimal)	$\lvert\pi_{13}\rvert = \delta_x + 1$	$\lvert\pi_{14}\rvert = \delta_x + 1$	$\lvert\pi_{15}\rvert = \delta_x + 3$	$\lvert\pi_{16}\rvert = \delta_x + 3$	$\lvert\pi_{17}\rvert = \delta_x + 6$	$\lvert\pi_{18}\rvert = \delta_x + 6$
2	$\lvert\pi_{21}\rvert = \delta_x$ (optimal)	$\lvert\pi_{22}\rvert = \delta_x$ (optimal)	$\lvert\pi_{23}\rvert = \delta_x$	$\lvert\pi_{24}\rvert = \delta_x + 2$	$\lvert\pi_{25}\rvert = \delta_x + 2$	$\lvert\pi_{26}\rvert = \delta_x + 4$	$\lvert\pi_{27}\rvert = \delta_x + 4$	$\lvert\pi_{28}\rvert = \delta_x + 8$
3	$\lvert\pi_{31}\rvert = \delta_x$ (optimal)	$\lvert\pi_{32}\rvert = \delta_x + 1$	$\lvert\pi_{33}\rvert = \delta_x + 1$	$\lvert\pi_{34}\rvert = \delta_x + 1$	$\lvert\pi_{35}\rvert = \delta_x + 1$	$\lvert\pi_{36}\rvert = \delta_x + 4$	$\lvert\pi_{37}\rvert = \delta_x + 4$	$\lvert\pi_{38}\rvert = \delta_x + 8$
4	$\lvert\pi_{41}\rvert = \delta_y$ (optimal)	$\lvert\pi_{42}\rvert = \delta_y + 1$	$\lvert\pi_{43}\rvert = \delta_y + 1$	$\lvert\pi_{44}\rvert = \delta_y + 2$	$\lvert\pi_{45}\rvert = \delta_y + 2$	$\lvert\pi_{46}\rvert = \delta_y + 4$	$\lvert\pi_{47}\rvert = \delta_y + 4$	$\lvert\pi_{48}\rvert = \delta_y + 8$

We make use of the above path lengths results to derive an upper bound for the average packet delivery probability assuming parallel routing of multiple copies of a packet over the eight disjoint paths.

Result 2: In a MANET of N nodes located in a kxk two-dimensional grid, the average packet delivery probability $P_{delivery}$ using parallel routing on the cell-disjoint paths constructed in tables 1-4 satisfies:

$$P_{delivery} \geq 1\text{-}[1\text{-}(1\text{-}(1 - 1/k^2)^N)^{k+3}]^8 . \tag{1}$$

Proof: A packet will be delivered if at least one of the eight paths is not broken. For a path to be non broken we need to have for each of the grid cells along that path at least one MANET node located in that cell. If in total there are N nodes and if we assume node mobility is such that a node is equally likely to be located in any of the k^2 cells at any given time, then the probability that a given node is located in a given grid cell is: $1/k^2$. Hence the probability that a given grid cell does not host any of the N nodes is $P_{empty} = (1 - 1/k^2)^N$. The probability that a given grid cell hosts at least one node is therefore: $P_{non\ empty} = 1\text{-}(1 - 1/k^2)^N$. The probability that each of the l cells along a path π of length l hosts at least one gateway node is therefore $P_{delivery\ on\ \pi} = (1\text{-}(1 - 1/k^2)^N)^l$. This probability decreases as the path length l increases. Let us therefore find an upper bound on the average path length. Based on Table 5, the average increase over the minimum length in the eight routing paths is less than 3 in each of the four cases. It is equal to 2.5 in cases 1, 2 and 3 and it is equal to 2.75 in case 4. The maximum distance between any source cell and any destination cell is k hops (k diagonal moves). Hence the average probability of delivery on a single path satisfies: $P_{delivery\ on\ a\ single\ path} \geq (1\text{-}(1 - 1/k^2)^N)^{k+3}$. Therefore the probability of delivery on at least one of the 8 paths satisfies: $P_{delivery} \geq 1\text{-}[1\text{-}(1\text{-}(1 - 1/k^2)^N)^{k+3}]^8$. QED

The expression of $P_{delivery}$ is plotted in figure 3 as a function of the network density $\delta = N/k^2$ which is the average number of MANET nodes per grid cell. The delivery probability approaches 1 when the network density reaches 3 nodes per grid cell.

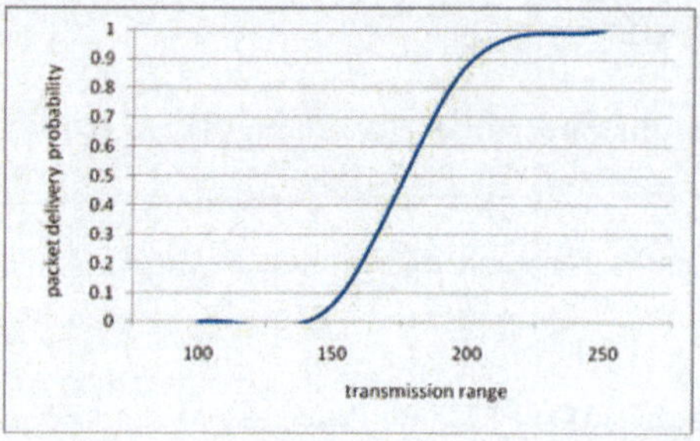

Fig. 3. Packet Delivery Probability vs Network Density

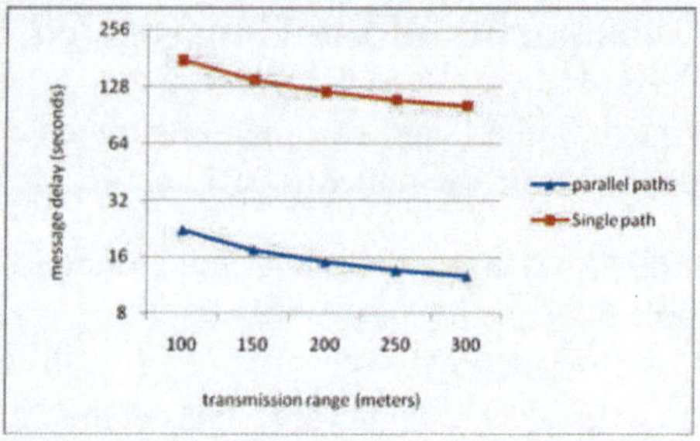

Fig. 4. Packet Delivery Probability vs Transmission Range

Notice that the value of k depends on the size of the physical area and on the transmission range. If for example we assume a square shaped physical area of size Δ meters by Δ meters ($\Delta \times \Delta$ m^2), a transmission range of r meters and if we set the grid cell size d to its maximum value $d = r/(2\sqrt{2})$, then the value of k would be: $k = \Delta/d = 2\sqrt{2}\Delta/r$. Substituting k by $2\sqrt{2}\Delta/r$ in expression (1) and plotting the packet delivery probability as a function of r for a fixed number of nodes $N = 100$ and a fixed square shaped physical area of 500 meters by 500 meters results in the plot shown in figure 4. Here we observe the impact of increasing the transmission range which results in reducing the value of k and hence the number of cells in the grid (dividing the same physical area in less but bigger cells). Less cells with the same number of nodes implies more nodes per cell in average and hence higher chance of having gateway nodes in the cells through which packets are routed.

Our last result is an estimation of the total delay to route a large amount of data of size M bytes from a source node to a destination node assuming the M bytes data is divided into packets of size p bytes each and that these packets are sent in parallel over the cell-disjoint paths. Let us assume a packet of size p bytes each requiring τ seconds delay to be sent over one hop (from a node to a neighboring node).

Result 3: The delay T for sending a message of size M bytes fragmented in packets of size p bytes each over the cell-disjoint paths described in tables 1-4 satisfies:

$$T \leq M.\tau.\,(k+8)/8p\,, \qquad (2)$$

where τ is the one-hop packet transmission delay.

Proof: The total number of packets after fragmenting the message of B bytes is: $n = B/p$. Each of the eight cell-disjoint paths between the source and the destination will route $n/8$ of these n packets. The total delay on any of the eight parallel paths is at most $(n/8)\,\tau.l_{max}$, where $l_{max} = k+8$ is the maximum path length as shown in Table 5.

QED

Figure 5 plots the maximum message delay T as a function of the transmission range. Higher transmission ranges imply less hops (shorter paths) and hence shorter delays. In this figure we have used the following settings: M = 1 megabytes, p = 1 kilobytes and τ = 8 milliseconds. The figure illustrates the amount of reduction in the communication delay resulting from sending data in parallel on the constructed disjoint paths as compared to sending the data on a single path.

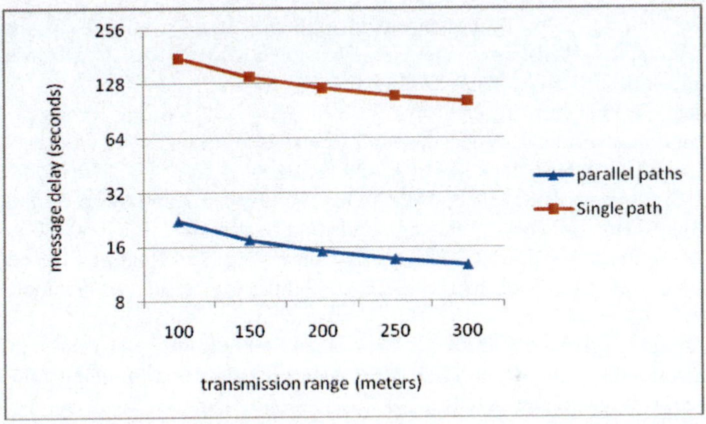

Fig. 5. Message Delay vs Transmission Range with Single and Multiple Parallel Paths

5 Conclusion

This paper has proposed a construction of cell-disjoint paths in a 2D grid structure which can be used in position-based MANET routing protocols for providing alternative routes in cases of routing path failures and for speeding up the transfer of large amounts of data between nodes. Packet delivery probability and communication delay results have been derived illustrating the attractiveness of using the constructed paths for improving the reliability and speed of communication in MANETs.

References

1. Abolhasan, M., Wysocki, T., Dutkiewicz, E.: A Review of Routing Protocols for Mobile Ad Hoc Networks. Ad-Hoc Networks 2, 1–22 (2004)
2. Perkins, C.E., Bhagwat, P.: Highly Dynamic Destination-Sequenced Distance-Vector Routing (DSDV) for Mobile Computers. In: Proc. SIGCOMM Symposium on Comm, pp. 212–225 (1994)
3. Perkins, C., Belding-Royer, E., Das, S.: Ad hoc On-Demand Distance Vector (AODV) Routing, RFC 3561 (2003)
4. Hass, Z.H., Pearlman, R.: Zone Routing Protocol for Ad-Hoc Networks, IETF, draft-ietf-manet-zrp-02.txt (1999)
5. Stojmenovic, I.: Position-Based Routing in Ad Hoc Networks. IEEE Communications, 128–134 (July 2002)

6. Giordano, S., Stojmenovic, I., Blazevic, L.: Position based routing algorithms for ad hoc networks: A taxonomy. Ad Hoc Wireless Networking. Kluwer, Dordrecht (2003)
7. Mauve, M., Widmer, J., Hartenstein, H.: A Survey on Position-Based Routing in Mobile Ad-Hoc Networks. IEEE Network Magazine 15(6), 30–39 (2001)
8. Kamali, S., Opatrny, J.: POSANT: A Position Based Ant Colony Routing Algorithm for Mobile Ad Hoc Networks. Journal of Networks 3(4), 31–41 (2008)
9. Hightower, J., Borriello, G.: Location Systems for Ubiquitous Computing. Computer 34(8), 57–66 (2001)
10. Chen, G., Itoh, K., Sato, T.: Enhancement of Beaconless Location-Based Routing with Signal Strength Assistance for Ad-Hoc Networks. IEICE Transactions on Communications E91.B(7), 2265–2271 (2010)
11. Abdallaha, A.E., Fevensa, T., Opatrnya, J., Stojmenovic, I.: Power-aware semi-beaconless 3D georouting algorithms using adjustable transmission ranges for wireless ad hoc and sensor networks. Ad Hoc Networks 8, 15–29 (2010)
12. Liao, W.-H., Tseng, Y.-C., Sheu, J.-P.: Grid: A Fully Location-Aware Routing Protocol for Mobile Ad Hoc Networks. Telecommunication Systems 18(1), 37–60 (2001)
13. Chao, C.-M., Sheu, J.-P., Hu, C.-T.: Energy-Conserving Grid Routing Protocol in Mobile Ad Hoc Networks. In: Proc. of the IEEE 2003 Int'l Conference on Parallel Processing, ICCP 2003 (2003)
14. Wu, Z., Song, H., Jiang, S., Xu, X.: A Grid-based Stable Routing Algorithm in Mobile Ad Hoc Networks. In: Proc. of the First IEEE Asia Int'l Conf. on Modeling and Simulation (AMS 2007), Thailand, pp. 181–186 (2007)
15. Wang, Z., Zhang, J.: Grid based two transmission range strategy for MANETs. In: Proceedings 14th International Conference on Computer Communications and Networks, ICCCN 2005, pp. 235–240 (2005)
16. Wu, Z., Song, H., Jiang, S., Xu, X.: A Grid-based Stable Backup Routing Algorithm in MANETs. In: International Conference on Multimedia and Ubiquitous Engineering, MUE 2007 (2007)

Proactive Defense-Based Secure Localization Scheme in Wireless Sensor Networks

Nabila Labraoui[1], Mourad Gueroui[2], and Makhlouf Aliouat[3]

[1] STIC, University of Tlemcen, Algeria
[2] PRISM, University of Versailles, France
[3] University of Setif, Algeria
labraouinabila@yahoo.fr

Abstract. Sensors' localizations play a critical role in many sensor network applications. A number of techniques have been proposed recently to discover the locations of regular sensors. However, almost all previously proposed techniques can be trivially abused by a malicious adversary involving false position. The wormhole attack is a particularly challenging one since the external adversary which acts in passive mode, does not need to compromise any nodes or have access to any cryptographic keys. In this paper, wormhole attack in DV-hop is discussed, and a Wormhole-free DV-hop Localization scheme (WFDV) is proposed to defend wormhole attack in proactive countermeasure. Using analysis and simulation, we show that our solution is effective in detecting and defending against wormhole attacks with a high detection rate.

Keywords: Range-free localization, secure localization, WSN.

1 Introduction

Recently, the wireless sensor networks (WSNs) has emerged an exciting new development in the field of signal processing and wireless communications for many innovative applications [1]. When a sensor detects an emergency event-driven, its location information should be quickly and accurately determined; sensing data without knowing the sensor's location is meaningless [2]. A straightforward solution is to equip each sensor with a GPS receiver that can accurately provide the sensors with their exact location. Unfortunately, the high costs of GPS technology are at odds with the desire to minimize the cost of individual nodes. Thus it is only feasible to fit a small portion of all sensor nodes with GPS receivers. These GPS-enabled nodes called *anchor* or *beacon nodes* provide position information, in the form of beacon message, for the benefit of *non-beacon* or *blind nodes* (i.e nodes without GPS capabilities). Blind nodes can utilize the location information finished from multiple nearby beacon nodes to estimate their own positions, thus amortizing the high cost of GPS technology across many nodes [3].

Localization in WSNs has drawn growing attention from the researchers and many range-based and range-free approaches [4, 5] have been proposed. However, almost all previously proposed localization can be trivially abused by a malicious adversary. Since location information is an integral part of most wireless sensor networks

H. Cherifi, J.M. Zain, and E. El-Qawasmeh (Eds.): DICTAP 2011, Part I, CCIS 166, pp. 603–618, 2011.

services such as geographical routing and applications such a target tracking and monitoring, it is of paramount importance to design localization to be resilient to location poisoning. However, security solutions require high computation, memory, storage and energy resources, which create an additional challenge when working with tiny sensor nodes [6,7]. A trade-off between security level and performance must be carefully balanced [6].

Motivated by the above observation, our intention in this work is not to provide any brand-new localization technique for WSNs, but to analyze and enhance the security of DV-Hop algorithm, a typical range-free approach built upon hop-count. In this paper, we propose a Wormhole-free DV-hop Localization scheme (WFDV), to thwart wormhole attacks in DV-Hop algorithm. We choose the wormhole attack as our defending target, since it is a particularly challenging attack which can be successfully launched without compromising any nodes or having access to any cryptographic keys. Hence, a solution that depends only on cryptographic techniques is clearly not effective enough to defend against wormhole attacks. The main idea of our approach is to plug-in proactive Countermeasure to the basic DV-Hop scheme named: *Infection prevention* that consists of two phases to detect wormhole attacks. The first phase applies two inexpensive techniques and utilizes local information that is available during the normal operation of sensor nodes. Advanced technique in the second phase is applied only when a wormhole attack is suspected to remove the packets delivery through the wormhole link. Thus, in case there are no wormholes in the network, the sensors do not need to waste computation and communication resources. We present simulations to demonstrate the effectiveness of our proposed scheme.

The paper is organized as follows. Section 2 describes the problem statements. Section 3 describes the system model. In section 4, we describe our proposed Wormhole-Free DV-Hop based localization in details. In Section 5, we present the security analysis. In section 6, we present the simulation results. Section 6 reviews the related work on the secure localization. Finally, Section 7 concludes this paper.

2 Problem Statements

In this section, we describe the DV-hop localization scheme, its vulnerability against the wormhole and the impact of this attack on the location accuracy.

2.1 The Basic DV-Hop Localization Scheme

Niculescu and Nath [8] have proposed the range-free DV-Hop, which is a distributed, hop by hop localization algorithm. It is easy to implement and has less demanding on the hardware conditions [9]. The algorithm implementation evolves in three steps:

In the first step, each beacon node broadcasts a beacon message to be flooded throughout the network containing the beacons location with a hop-count value initialized to zero. Each receiving node maintains the minimum hop-count value per beacon of all beacons messages it receives. Beacons are flooded outward with hop-count values incremented at every intermediate hop.

In the second step, once a beacon gets hop-count value to other beacon, it estimates an average size for one hop, which is then flooded to the entire network. The average hop-size is estimated by beacon i using the following formula:

$$HopSize_i = \frac{\sum_{j \neq i} \sqrt{(x_i - x_j)^2 + (y_i - y_j)^2}}{\sum_{j \neq i} h_{ij}} \tag{1}$$

where (x_i, y_i), (x_j, y_j) are coordinates of beacon i and beacon j, h_{ij} is the hops between beacon i and beacon j. Blind nodes receive *hop-size* information, and save the first one. At the same time, they transmit the *hop-size* to their neighbor nodes. In the end of this step, blind nodes compute the distance to the beacon nodes based hop-length and hops to the beacon nodes.

$$d_i = hopcount_i \times HopSize_i \tag{2}$$

In the third step, after the blind node obtains three or more estimated values from anchor nodes, it can compute its physical location in the network by using methods such as triangulation [10].

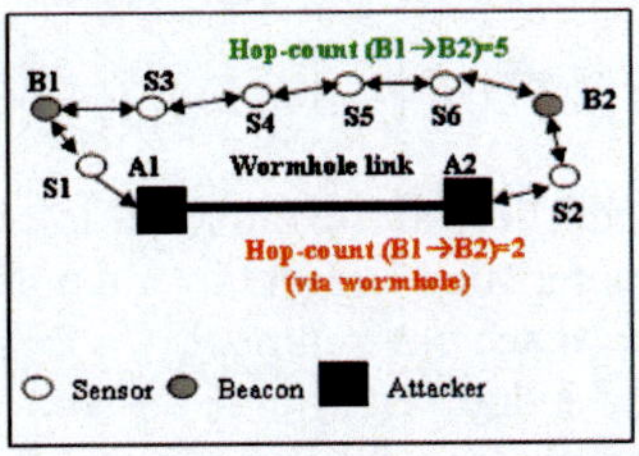

Fig. 1. Impact of wormhole attack on DV-hop localization

2.2 Impact of the Wormhole Attack on DV-Hop

The *wormhole attacks* [11, 12] are relatively easy to mount, while being difficult to detect and prevent. In a typical wormhole attack, when one attacker receives (captures) packets at one point of the network, it tunnels them through the wormhole link to the other attacker, which retransmits them at the other point of the network. Since in the wormhole attack the adversary replays recorded messages, it can be launched without compromising any network node, or the integrity and authenticity of the communication.

Launching wormhole attack in DV-hop can cause two impacts:

A. causing position error: The wormhole attack can greatly deteriorate the DV-Hop localization procedure. In can affect the first step by making the hop count abnormal; consequently, the second step is also affected and the entire localization scheme is ruined. As seen from Fig.1, a wormhole link between malicious node A1 and A2 exists. A1 receives the beacon message from B1 with a hop-count equal to 1 and tunnels it to A2. A2 replays the beacon message and transmits it to S2. Normally, beacon node B1 and B2 are 5 hops away, but in existence of a wormhole link, the hop-count between them changes to 2, which lead B2 to make a false estimation on the average hop size. In the same way, sensor nodes near B2 will assume a smaller hop counts to B1 and triangulation will provide a highly inaccurate position estimate.

B. Energy depletion: The nodes have to transmit more replayed messages under attack, and thus consume more energy than in a benign environment. It is fatal for the network with limited resource.

3 System Model

This section illustrates our system model including communication, network, and adversary models.

3.1 Simplified Path-Loss Model

In this subsection we study how to characterize the variation in received signal power over distance due to the path loss inspired from [13], [14]. Path loss is the term used to quantify the difference (in dB) between the transmitted signal power, *Pt*, and received signal power *Pr*(*d*) at distance *d* . The simple path-loss model predicts that the mean path loss, $\overline{PL}(d)$, measured in dB, at a transmitter-receiver separation distance (*d*) will be:

$$\overline{PL}(d) = \overline{PL}(d_0) + 10\gamma log_{10}\left(\frac{d}{d_0}\right) \quad (3)$$

where, $\overline{PL}(d_0)$ is the mean path loss in dB at close-in reference distance d_0, which depends on the antenna characteristics and the average channel attenuation, and γ is the path-loss exponent. In free space environment, γ = 2. The reference distance, d_0 is chosen to be 1-10 meters for indoor environments and 10-100 meters for outdoor environments. When the simplified model is used, the value of $\overline{PL}(d_0)$ is set to the free-space path gain at distance d_0 assuming omni-directional antennas:

$$\overline{PL}(d_0) = 20log_{10}\left(\frac{4\pi d_0}{\lambda}\right) \quad (4)$$

where, $\lambda = {}^{c}/_{f}$ is the wavelength of the transmitted signal (*c* is the speed of light, $3\text{x}10^8$ m/s, and *f* is the frequency of the transmitted signal in Hz). The path losses at different geographical locations at the same distance *d* (for $d > d_0$) from a fixed transmitter, exhibit a natural variability due to the environment that results in *log-normal shadowing*. It is usually found to follow a Gaussian distribution with standard deviation σ dB about the distance-dependent mean path-loss $\overline{PL}(d)$. Finally, the received signal power at a separation distance *d* based on the transmitted signal in dB is:

$$P_r(d) = P_t - \overline{PL}(d_0) - 10\gamma log_{10}\left(\frac{d}{d_0}\right) + \sigma \quad (5)$$

The IEEE 802.15.4 standard [15] addresses a simple, low-cost and low-rate communication network that allows a wireless connectivity between devices with a limited power. Recently, most of sensor platforms equip the specific RF chip which can provide the IEEE 802.15.4 physical characteristics. CC2420 RF chip is one of these RF transceivers that can be utilized for a number of sensor hardware platforms. The CC2420 RF modules can measure the received signal power as RSSI (Received Signal Strength Indicator). Based on this value, having the transmission power level, the receiver can estimate the transmitter-receiver separation distance.

3.2 Network Model

Here, we assume a static wireless sensor network composed of a number of tiny motes uniformly distributed in a field. All the nodes in the network are the same and equipped with two radios: the regular radio RF and a radio with frequency hopping (FH) capability. We assume that the network consists of a set of blind sensor nodes S of unknown location and a set of beacon nodes B which already know their absolute locations via GPS or manual configuration. We assume the communication range R of each node in the WSN is the same. We further assume that any pair of nodes in the network shares two cryptographic keys K_1 and K_2 after they discover their neighborhood. We assume all beacon nodes are uniquely identified. We also assume that the contention-based medium-access protocol is used in the networks and there is at least one RTS/CTS/Data/Ack period of time that a pair of nodes can communicate. We assume that during one execution of RTS-CTS-Data-ACK the environment is stable, thus loss of packets due to noise spike can be ignored. Hence, if the sender has successfully sent the RTS to the receiver, all of its neighbors would have received the RTS and would not contend for the channel. Therefore, the CTS will be received correctly at the sender.

3.3 Adversary Model

We assume a wormhole link is bidirectional with two endpoints (wormhole ends). The length of the wormhole link is assumed to be larger than R to avoid the endless packet transmission loops caused by the both attackers. However, we treat the wormhole attackers as external attackers which act in passive mode.

To describe our proposed solution clearly, we provide the following definitions:

Definition 1. *Local neighbor*: local neighbors of a node are all single-hop neighbor that lie in the communication range of the node.

Definition 2. *Fake neighbor*: a node is a fake neighbor if it can be communicated with via the wormhole link.

In the remaining sections of the paper, we use the following notations in Table 1:

Table 1. Notation

Notation	*Description*
$RTT_{(S1,S2)}$	RTT between node *S1* and node *S2*
$RTT_{wormhole}$	RTT of a link under wormhole attack
$AvgRTT_{S1}$	average RTT of all links from *S1* to its neighbors
w	time to tunnel a packet between two wormhole ends
n	Number of neighbors of a node
N_i	A nonce
P	Propagation delay of a legitimate link
Pt	transmitted signal power
Pr	Received signal power
E(K,M)	Encryption of message M with secret key K
HMAC(K,M)	Message digest of M using hash function with key K

4 WFDV: Wormhole-Free DV-Hop Based Localization

In this section, we describe our proposed wormhole attack resistant localization scheme, called WFDV: Wormhole-Free DV-Hop based localization. The WFDV enables sensors to determine their location and defend against the wormhole attack at the same time. Since DV-hop is well known, we focus attention mainly on the improvement upon robustness against wormhole threats. The success of wormhole attack in the first step of DV-Hop can lead to infect its second step and thus to distort the location estimate accuracy.

The Wormhole-Free DV-Hop based localization includes two phases, infection prevention and DV-Hop-based secure localization. Firstly, a proactive countermeasure named *infection prevention* is performed to prevent wormhole contamination via wormhole links. After eliminating the illegal connections, the DV-Hop localization procedure can be successfully conducted.

4.1 Infection Prevention

The infection prevention is performed before the first step of DV-Hop scheme in order to eliminate the fake connections produced by wormhole, which infect the localization procedure, by relaying and reporting a false hop-count. The aim of attacker is to perform distance reduction between two far neighbors by replaying a message from beacon nodes or from blind nodes in the first step of DV-Hop scheme. It is very difficult for nodes to distinguish the local neighbor from fake neighbor because the attacker replays a *genuine* message. In our approach, each node builds the neighbor list and tries to detect links suspected to be part of a wormhole. This prevention is very useful, because the node can detect the replayed messages and drops them immediately; avoiding transmitting replayed messages. By consequence, sensors preserve more energy and bandwidth and avoid infecting other nodes. Following are two phases of infection prevention:

– **Phase I – Neighbor List Construction (NLC):** In this step, a node S_1 simply discovers its one-hop neighbors by does one-hop broadcast of the neighbor request (NREQ) message and saves the time of NREQ sending: T_{REQ}. The NREQ receiving node responds to S_1 with the neighbor reply (NREP) message, in which it piggybacks the transmitted signal power *Pt*. The requesting node S_1 saves the time of each NREP receiving: T_{REP}.

In the NLC phase, we use two simple triggers to find out if a link should be suspected and challenged. The *first trigger* is based on the RSSI which is an inexpensive technique that assists the infection prevention to remove fake links. Taking advantage of the communication capability of the WSN, the RSSI ranging technique has the low-power, low-cost characteristics. So the WFDV only cites RSSI to assist building neighbor list, to detect fake links and remove them. The *second trigger* is based on RTT technique.

***Technique 1 :Signal Attenuation Property Check*:** Based on the path loss model presented in subsection 3.1, the received signal strength anywhere farther than the reference distance must be less than the received power at the reference distance ($\forall d > d0$: $Pr(d) < Pr(d0)$). We name this *signal attenuation property*. Therefore, if we assume the distance between every two nodes is more than the reference distance, no node can receive a message with a power more than $Pr(d0)$.

While reply messages are received, *Signal Attenuation property* is checked by node S_1. If a connection does not follow *Signal Attenuation property*, the node S_1 removes this connection and blacklists it.

```
Algorithm1. Neighbor list Construction
LocalNs=∅;  SuspectNs=∅;  TotalRTT=0;  n=0;
1. S1→*: NREQ: IDS1,N1;
2. Si→S: NREP: IDSi,N1,Pt;
3. for each reply from node Si Do
     if (Pt-Pr) < PL(d0)   {Signal attenuation property}
        then Si is a fake neighbor {Si is blacklisted}
        else
              SuspectNS1=SuspectNS1 ∪ Si
              TotalRTT=TotalRTT+ RTT(S1,Si)
              n=n+1
        endif
   End do
4.  If SuspectNS1 ≠ ∅      {RTT detection}
      then      AvgRTTS1=Total RTT/n
        For each node Si ∈ SuspectNS1  Do
          if  RTT(S1,Si)≥ k * AvgRTTS1
           then  Confirm the link (S1,Si) is suspicious
                 Execute Neighbor list repair.
           else LocalNs1= LocalNs1  ∪ Si
          end if
        End Do
     end if
```

Technique 2: RTT-Based Detection: if we assume that the attacker is smart enough to fake a RSSI value and reply the message with adjusted power that does not violate the signal attenuation property, the *Signal Attenuation Property check* becomes inefficient. In this case, a *second trigger* is used, based on the round trip delay of a link (RTT) namely *RTT-based Detection.* RTT is a measure of the time it takes for a packet to travel from a node, across a wireless network to another node and back. The RTT can be calculated as $RTT=T_{REP}-T_{REQ}$.

Let a node S_1 communicate with a neighbor node S_2. During peace time, the RTT between S_1 and S_2 is $2p$. If the direct link (S_1,S_2) is formed as a result of a wormhole attack, then the round trip time would be $RTT_{wormhole}=2(p+w+p)=2(2p+w)$. Where w is time to tunnel a packet between two wormhole ends. Thus we believe the RTT of the wormhole link should be at least two times the RTT of a normal link, even though w can be smaller than p. In Section 6 we conduct simulations to confirm this fact.

For each NREP, S_1 measures the RTT with all of the presume neighbors. If it finds one node S_i that $RTT(S_1,S_i)$ is at least k times the average RTT between S_1 and all its neighboring nodes, then the link (S_1,S_i) may be a wormhole. The value of k is the system parameter which depends on n and w. In Section 5.1 we explain how the value of k is determined. The RTT detection is similar to the scheme proposed in [16]. However, the difference is that we define deterministic threshold value while the scheme in [16] decides the threshold value based on simulations. The pseudo-code of NLC phase is presented in Algorithm 1.

– Phases II – Neighbor List Repair: Having suspected a possible wormhole link in the network, WFDV launches a series of challenges to make sure that the wormhole is correctly identified. In this phase we use frequency hopping for confirming the existence of a wormhole. The pseudo-code is presented in Algorithm 2.

```
Algorithm2. Frequency Hopping Challenge(S1,S2)
1: S1 →S2: RTS, Enc(K1,N1); (frequency f1)
2: S2 →S1: CTS,Enc(K1,f2,N1,N2),HMAC(K1,f2,N1,N2); (f1)
3: S2 switches its receiver to f2 and waits for 2*RTT(S1,S2)
   time;
4: After receiving the CTS,
   S1 →S2: RTS,Enc(K1,N2),HMAC(K2,N2);(f2)
5: if S1 receives ACK from S2 in frequency f2 within duration of
   2*RTT(S1,Si) time
       then  LocalNS1=LocalNS1 U S2
       else  S2  is fake neighbor  {S2 is blacklisted};
   end if
```

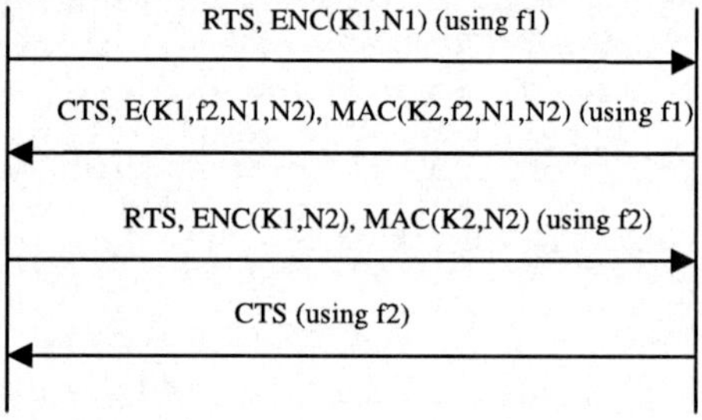

Fig. 2. Frequency Hopping Challenge

We illustrate in Fig. 2, the implementation of Algorithm2 using RTS/CTS mechanism of the contention-based medium-access (MAC) protocols in WSNs like S-MAC, T-MAC or B-MAC. In the first message, S_1 sends RTS and a nonce N_1 to S_2 using a frequency $f1$ being used for communication between them. Upon receiving this message from S_1, S_2 replies in frequency f_1 with a CTS message that contains the frequency f_2 (picked from the set of common frequencies shared by S_1 and S_2), the nonce N_1 received previously and a new nonce N_2, also encrypted with K_1. To protect the integrity of the packet, S_2 can optionally compute a message digest using HMAC function with key K_2. After replying to S_1 with CTS packet, S_2 switches its receiver to frequency f_2 and starts waiting for a packet from S_1. Here we assume the CTS always gets through if the environment conditions are stable. Later in the analysis section we discuss this assumption in depth. Immediately after receiving CTS, S_1 switches its transmitter to frequency f_2 and sends a new RTS message to S_2 that contains N_2 for the sake of authentication.

Finally, S_2 replies with a CTS packet to finish the challenge. If S_1 and S_2 are far away and become direct neighbors due to the wormhole, then by switching to the new frequency they will not be able to receive messages from each other. This is because the attacker does not know the new frequency and thus cannot forward the messages between S_1 and S_2. The use of nonces N_1 and N_2 is to avoid the replay attacks. Without the nonces, the attacker can launch the attack as follows. Suppose that the attacker has captured a CTS packet which contains an encrypted frequency f_2 that he does not know. He can store the message and try to scan all the frequencies to find out the one in which S_1 and S_2 are communicating. On correctly identifying the frequency, he can replay the same message for any new challenge between the same pair S_1 and S_2, thus effectively breaking the solution. This attack is not possible if we use nonces because they can help detect replayed messages. We can further improve the security for these messages by including the expiry time for each message.

4.2 DV-Hop Based Secure Localization

After the infection prevention step is performed, each node S_i in the network maintains a list of local neighbors $LocalN_{Si}$. Thus, while each node eliminates the fake links from its neighbor list, the DV-Hop localization procedure will be conducted. In both of first and second phase of the DV-Hop localization, every node will not forward the message received from the node out of its local neighbors list. With this strategy, the impacts of the wormhole attack on the localization will be avoided. Thus, our proposed scheme can obtain the secure localization against the wormhole attack.

5 Security Analysis

In this section we provide the security analysis of our secure localization scheme. We show the wormhole's impact on sensor node location determination is prevented proactively and DV-hop localization procedure can be successfully conducted.

5.1 Analysis of Neighbor List Construction Phase

A. Violating "Signal Attenuation Property"

Considering a simple scenario, as illustrated in Fig.3, in which adversary wants to make four fake links, S_1-D_1, S_1-D_2, S_2-D_1 and S_2-D_2. We define *victim topology* as two sets of nodes corresponding to two sides of the attack. Each node is a member of one set and its path loss to the adversary is its representative. In our scenario we assume the victim topology which is : {{45,70},{50,80}}that means there are 2 nodes in the left (right) side of attack with these path loss value. We also assume that the maximum power level of nodes is 0bBm, and the path loss at reference distance is 40dBm. M1 and M2 are relay points of the attacker and S_i and D_i nodes are victims. The adversary must change the signal strength before relaying them. Considering the power level of the adversary uses to relay a message is ΔP plus the received power, the end-to-end path loss between two close nodes should fulfill the "Signal Attenuation" property. i.e the end-to end path loss should be more than 40dBm. To maximize the chance of creation fake link, the adversary has to minimize the ΔP. however the minimum ΔP the attacker can use to make all 4 fake links is 60dBm. Therefore, when it relaying the messages of closer nodes it can be detected by the closer node in the other side because the end-to-end path loss between two close nodes is less than 40dBm which is impossible based on the Signal Attenuation property.

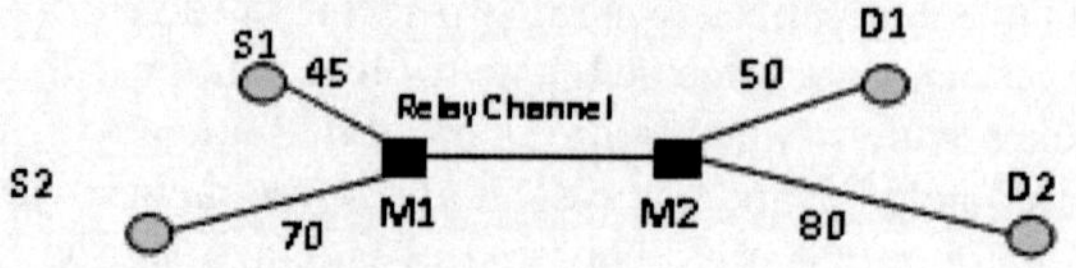

Fig. 3. A simple replay channel

B. Attacking RTT-Based Detection

In Algorithm 1 we require that $RTT_{(S1,S2)}$ be at least *k* times $AvgRTT_{S1}$ so that S_1 can start suspecting the link (S_1,S_2) to be a wormhole. Now we show how each node can determine the value of *k*. Let *n* be the number of neighbors a node has and assume that among *n* neighbors there exists at most *m* ($m< n$) wormhole link. We have:

$$RTT_{S1,S2} = 2(2p + w)$$

$$AvgRTT_{S1} = \frac{(n-m)2p + 2(2p+w)m}{n} \tag{6}$$

$$Test = \frac{RTT_{(S1,S2)}}{AvgRTT_{S1}} = \frac{2(2p+w)n}{(n-m)2p + 2(2p+w)m} \geq k \tag{7}$$

Observe that *Test* increases when *w* increases. Thus, to avoid detection, the attacker should try to decrease the value of *Test* by decreasing *w*. However, *w* is always greater than 0. Thus, if we set the threshold value *k* for $w = 0$ then the attacker will very likely be detected. In that case, $k = \frac{2n}{n+m}$ and can easily be computed by each wireless node. For example, if $n= 6$ and $m = 1$, then the threshold value *k* will be 12/7 = 1.7.

This is a deterministic value, contradicting with the one in [16], where the threshold value varies in different networks.

5.2 Analysis of Neighbor List Repair Phase

The attacker has two options to respond to the challenge: either to drop the RTS packet or to allow the packet to pass through to S_i. We now show that using any of these options is not helpful to the wormhole attack and it will eventually be discovered.

A. Dropping the RTS Packet

In our solution if S_1 does not get the CTS reply in a finite amount of time it will timeout and resend the RTS. In IEEE 802.15.4 standard each node retries *r* times (typically *r*=3) before declaring a transmission failure [16]. If a transmission failure occurs our solution considers that to be a missed challenge. If a link has *M* such continuous missed challenges, our solution declares that link to be malicious.

If node S_l is sending an RTS frame then the probability that collisions occurs is given by:

$$P[collision] = 1 - (1 - \tau)^{n-1} \quad (8)$$

Where τ is the probability of transmission at a moment t of each node and n is the number of neighbors of a node. If S_l does not get the CTS reply within a finite amount of time, it times out and resends the RTS frame. If all these r RTS frames were to collide with transmissions from other node then the probability of that happening is:

$$P[Losing\ r\ RTS] = [1 - (1 - \tau)^{n-1}]^r \quad (9)$$

The probability of failing M challenges due to wireless issues rather than wormhole is:

$$P[Failing\ M\ challenges] = [1 - (1 - \tau)^{n-1}]^{rM} \quad (10)$$

Using $M = 6$, $r = 3$, $n = 10$ and $\tau = 0.1$ we get

$$P[Failing\ M\ challenges] = 1.4 \times 10^{-4} \quad (11)$$

This probability of failing M challenges without the existence of wormhole is thus negligible. Hence the strategy of dropping RTS packets is not in the interest of the wormhole.

B. Allowing the RTS Packet Through

The other option for the wormhole is to allow the RTS to go through. We assume that (1) it is too expensive for the attacker to listen on all the available channels and (2) it is computationally infeasible for the attacker to break the encryption to obtain f_2 in a short duration. Therefore, by allowing the RTS get through the attacker has to guess the frequency f_2, because the content of the message is encrypted and integrity protected.

The probability of correctly guessing the right frequency is $1/N$, where N is the number of channels. If we further force each node to pass the challenge for δ times this probability of guessing the correct frequency every time is reduced to $1/N\delta$. Using appropriate values of δ and N this probability can be made very small. For example if N= 27 (802.15.4 network) and δ = 2 the probability is less than 1%. The wormhole thus is unlikely to pass the neighbor list repair phase.

6 Simulation

In order to investigate the effect of the wormhole attack and the ability of WFDV to detect attacks, we conduct simulation using the ns-2 simulator. First, we define the parameters used in our scenario, and then we present our simulation results.

6.1 Simulation Setup

The simulation is performed by using ns-2 version 2.29 with 802.15.4 MAC layer [17] and CMU wireless extensions [18]. Table 2 resumes the configuration that was used for ns-2.

Table 2. Simulation configuration

Number of nodes	2, 4, 100
RF range	20 m
Propagation	TwoRayGround
Antenna	Omni Antenna
Mac Layer	802.15.4
Simulation time	4 minutes

The wormhole was implemented as a wired connection with much less latency than the wireless connections. The location of the wormhole was completely randomized within the network.

6.2 Simulation Results

In order to evaluate the performance of our scheme, two parameters were tested: *"impact of wormhole attack on the RTT values"* and *"effectiveness of RTT-based detection"*.

1. Impact of Wormhole Attack on the RTT Values

We conduct simulation to study the impact of wormhole links on the RTT values. In the first scenario of simulation, we set up a simple sensor network consisting of two sensor nodes. We measure the average RTT when sending a ping packet from one mote to another and receive an acknowledgment back for the same packet.
In the second scenario of simulations, we set up a sensor network consisting of four sensor nodes including two legitimate nodes and 2 compromised nodes. We mimic a wormhole attack where a packet sent from one mote is captured at the first attacker, tunneled to the second attacker, and replayed at the second mote. The wormhole link was implemented as a wired connection. In this scenario, we verify if the RTT of a wormhole link is twice as much as that of a normal link.

We conduct both simulations for five minutes continuously and take the average of the results. Fig. 4 shows that the round trip time when the wormhole existed is much higher than that in normal case. The average RTT of sending a packet through wormhole link and a legitimate link was observed to be 15.22 ms and 7.37 ms, respectively. Thus the node can use the delay as an indicator to suspect any link.

2. Effectiveness of RTT-Based Detection

We implement the RTT-based detection in Neighbor List Construction phase, to study the effectiveness of the threshold value. We create a network topology with 100 nodes deployed randomly in a 1000meters×1000 meters field. The radio range is set to 20 meters. There is no movement of nodes and the background traffic is generated randomly by a random generator provided by ns2. The CBR connection with 4 packets per second are created and the size of the packet is 512 bytes.

In the simulation, we randomly pick a node S_1. We then create a wormhole link between S_1 and a distant node S_2. Repeating the experiment many times we can select

S_I with varying degree of neighbors. We then measure the RTT between the neighbors of S_I and calculate k (threshold) as described in sub-section 5.1. We conduct simulation for five minutes

Comparison of the simulated values to the analytical value is shown in Fig. 5. We observe that the ratio of the wormhole RTT to average RTT is always above the calculated threshold and hence we conclude that the threshold value we suggested is effective.

We can conclude that WFDV can defend the network efficiently against the wormhole attack.

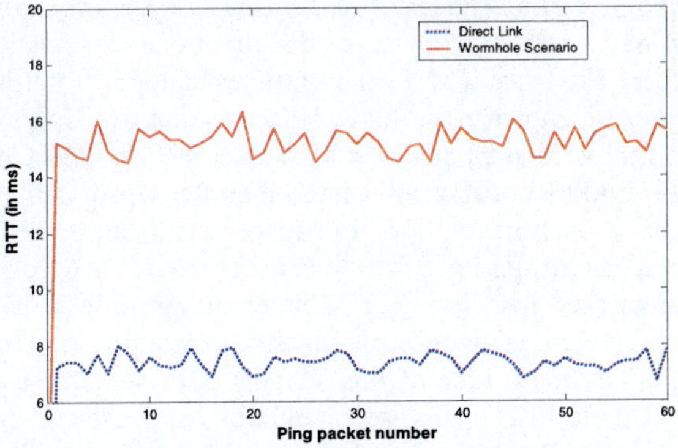

Fig. 4. Round trip time (Wormhole link and normal link)

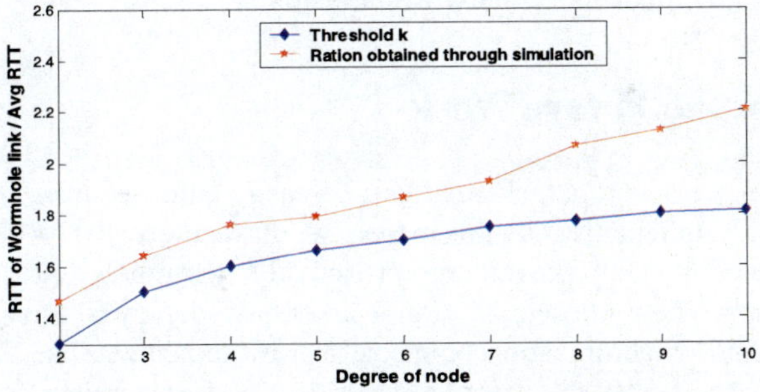

Fig. 5. Round trip time: Theoretical vs Simulation

7 Related Work

Lazos et al. proposed a robust positioning system called ROPE [19] that provides a location verification mechanism to verify the location claims of the sensors before data collection. However, the requirement of the counter with nanoseconds precision makes it unsuitable in low cost sensor networks. DRBTS [20] is a distributed reputation-based beacon trust security protocol aimed at providing secure localization in WSNs. Based on a quorum voting approach, DRBTS drives beacons to monitor each other and then enables them to decide which should be trusted. However it requires extra memory to store the neighbor reputation tables and trusted beacon neighbor tables. To provide secure location services, [21] introduces a method to detect malicious beacon signals, techniques to detect replayed beacon signals, identification of malicious beacons, avoidance of false detection and the revoking of malicious beacons. By clustering of benign location reference beacons, Wang et al. [22] proposes a resilient localization scheme that is computational efficiency. In [23], robust statistical methods are proposed, including triangulation and RF-based fingerprinting, to make localization attack-tolerant.

To achieve secure localization in a WSN suffered from wormhole attacks, SeRLoc [24] first detects the wormhole attack based on the *sector uniqueness* property and *communication range violation* property using directional antennas, then filters out the attacked locators. HiRLoc [25] further utilizes antenna rotations and multiple transmit power levels to improve the localization resolution. However, SeRLoc and HiRLoc need extra hardware such as directional antennae. In [26], Chen et al. propose to make each locator build a conflicting-set and then the sensor can use all conflicting sets of its neighboring locators to filter out incorrect distance measurements of its neighboring locators. The limitation of the scheme is that it only works properly when the system has no packet loss. In [27], Zhu et al. propose a label-based secure localization scheme which is wormhole attack resistant based on the DV-Hop localization process. The main idea of this scheme is to generate a pseudo neighbor list for each beacon node, use all pseudo neighbor lists received from neighboring beacon nodes to classify all attacked nodes into different groups, and then label all neighboring nodes (including beacons and sensors). According to the labels of neighboring nodes, each node prohibits the communications with its pseudo neighbors, which are attacked by the wormhole attack.

8 Conclusion and Future Work

Wormhole attacks are severe attacks that can be easily launched even in networks with confidentiality and authenticity. In this paper, we have presented WFDV an effective method for detecting and preventing proactively wormhole attacks in DV-hop localization scheme. The proposed solution is an easy-to-deploy solution because it does not require any time synchronization or special hardware neither. The WFDV only uses simple techniques to identify the wormhole and then performs proper actions to confirm the existence of the attack. Through simulation, we make a compelling argument showing the ability of WFDV to detect the wormhole attack. Our analysis further confirms the effectiveness of our framework. In our future work, we will implement the frequency hopping in order to analyze the energy efficiency of our proposal.

References

1. Chong, C.Y., Kumar, S.P.: Sensor networks: evolution, opportunities, and challenges. IEEE 91(8), 1247–1256 (2003)
2. Rabaey, M.J., Ammer, J.L., da Silva, J.R., Patel, D., Roundy, S.: PicoRadio supports ad hoc ultra-low power wireless networking. Computer 33(7), 42–48 (2002)

3. Pirreti, M., Vijaykrishnan, N., McDaniel, P., Madan, B.: SLAT: Secure Localization with Attack Tolerance. Technical report: NAS-TR-0024-2005, Network and Security Research Center, Dept. of Computer Science and Eng., Pennsylvania State Univ (2005)
4. Zhao, M., Servetto, S.D.: An Analysis of the Maximum Likelihood Estimator for Localization Problems. In: IEEE ICBN (2005)
5. Bahl, P., Padmanabhan, V.N.: RADAR:An In-building RF-based User Location and Tracking System. In: IEEE INFOCOM (2000)
6. Labraoui, N., Gueroui, M., Aliouat, M., Zia, T.: Data Aggregation Security Challenge in Wireless Sensor Networks: A Survey. Ad hoc & Sensor Networks. International Journal 12 (2011) (in Press)
7. Zia, T., Zomaya, A.Y.: A security framework for wireless sensor networks. In: IEEE Sensor Applications Symposium, Texas (2006)
8. Niculescu, D., Nath, B.: Ad Hoc Positioning System (APS). In: IEEE GLOBECOM 2001, San Antonio, pp. 2926–2931 (2001)
9. Wenfeng, L.: Wireless sensor networks and mobile robot control, pp. 54–60. Science Press (2009)
10. Parkinson, B., Spilker, J.: Global positioning system: theory and application. American Institute of Aeronautics and Astronautics, Washington, D.C (1996)
11. Hu, Y., Perrig, A., Johnson, D.: Packet Leashes: A Defense Against Wormhole Attacks in Wireless Ad Hoc Networks. In: INFOCOM, vol. 2, pp. 1976–1986 (2003)
12. Papadimitratos, P., Haas, Z.J.: Secure Routing for Mobile Ad Hoc Networks. In: CNDS 2002 (2002)
13. Goldsmith, A.: Wireless Communications. Cambridge University Press, New York (2005)
14. Rappaport, T.: Wireless Communications: Principles and Practice. Prentice Hall PTR, Englewood Cliffs (2001)
15. Shon, T., Choi, H.: Towards the implementation of reliable data transmission for 802.15.4-based wireless sensor networks. In: Sandnes, F.E., Zhang, Y., Rong, C., Yang, L.T., Ma, J. (eds.) UIC 2008. LNCS, vol. 5061, pp. 363–372. Springer, Heidelberg (2008)
16. Tran, P.V., Hung, L.X., Lee, Y.K., Lee, S., Lee, H.: TTM: An Efficient Mechanism to Detect Wormhole Attacks in Wireless Ad-hoc Networks. In: 4th IEEE Consumer Communications and Networking Conference (2007)
17. Zheng J.: Low rate wireless personal area networks: ns-2 simulator for 802.15.4 (release v1.1) (2007), http://ees2cy.engr.ccny.cuny.edu/zheng/pub
18. The Rice Monarch Project: Wireless and mobility extensions to ns-2 (2007), http://www.monarch.cs.cmu.edu/cmu-ns.html
19. Lazos, L., Poovendran, R., Capkun, S.: ROPE: Robust Position Estimation in Wireless Sensor Networks. In: IEEE IPSN, pp. 324–331 (2005)
20. Srinivasan, A., Teitelbaum, J., Wu, J.: DRBTS: Distributed Reputation-based Beacon Trust System. In: 2nd IEEE Int'l Symposium on Dependable, Autonomic and Secure Computing, pp. 277–283 (2006)
21. Liu, D., Ning, P., Du, W.: Detecting Malicious Beacon Nodes for Secure Localization Discovery in Wireless Sensor Networks. In: IEEE ICDCS, pp. 609–619 (2005)
22. Wang, C., Liu, A., Ning, P.: Cluster-Based Minimun Mean Square Estimation for Secure and Resilient Localization in Wireless Sensor Networks. In: the Int'l Conf. on Wireless Algorithms, Systems and Applications, pp. 29–37 (2007)
23. Li, Z., Trappe, W., Zhang, Y., Nath, B.: Robust Statistical Methods for Securing Wireless Localization in Sensor Networks. In: IEEE IPSN, pp. 91–98 (2005)

24. Lazos, L., Poovendran, R.: SeRLoc: robust localization for wireless sensor networks. ACM Transactions on Sensor Networks 1(1), 73–100 (2005)
25. Lazos, L., Poovendran, R.: HiRLoc: high-resolution robust localization for wireless sensor networks. IEEE Journal on Selected Areas in Communications 24(2), 233–246 (2006)
26. Chen, H., Lou, W., Wang, Z.: Conflicting-set-based wormhole attack resistant localization in wireless sensor networks. In: Zhang, D., Portmann, M., Tan, A.-H., Indulska, J. (eds.) UIC 2009. LNCS, vol. 5585, pp. 296–309. Springer, Heidelberg (2009)
27. Wu, J., Chen, H., Lou, W., Wang, Z.: Label-Based DV-Hop Localization AgainstWormhole Attacks in Wireless Sensor Networks. In: 5th IEEE International Conference on Networking, Architecture, and Storage (NAS 2010), Macau SAR, China (2010)

Decision Directed Channel Tracking for MIMO-Constant Envelope Modulation

Ehab Mahmoud Mohamed[1,2], Osamu Muta[3], and Hiroshi Furukawa[1]

[1] Graduate School of Information Science and Electrical Engineering,
Kyushu University, Motooka 744, Nishi-ku, Fukuoka 819-0395, Japan
[2] Permanent: Electrical Engineering Department, Faculty of Engineering,
South Valley University, Egypt
[3] Center for Japan-Egypt Cooperation in Science and Technology, Kyushu University,
Motooka 744, Nishi-ku, Fukuoka 819-0395, Japan
`ehab@mobcom.ait.kyushu-u.ac.jp`,
`{muta,furukawa}@ait.kyushu-u.ac.jp`

Abstract. The authors have proposed Multi-Input Multi-Output (MIMO)-Constant Envelope Modulation, MIMO-CEM, as power and complexity efficient alternative to MIMO-OFDM, suitable for wireless backhaul networks. Because MIMO-CEM receiver employs 1-bit ADC, MIMO-CEM channel estimation is one of the major challenges toward its real application. The authors have proposed adaptive channel estimator in static and quasi-static channel conditions. Although wireless backhaul channel conditions are theoretically considered as static and quasi-static, it suffers from some channel fluctuations in real applications. Hence, the objective of this paper is to present a decision directed channel estimation (DDCE) to track channel fluctuation in high Doppler frequency condition, and clarify the effectiveness of our method under dynamic channel. For the purpose of comparison, the performance of DDCE is compared with that of a pilot assisted linear interpolation channel tracking for MIMO-CEM. Different Doppler frequencies are assumed to prove the effectiveness of the scheme even in high channel variations.

Keywords: MIMO, Constant envelope modulation, Decision directed channel tracking, adaptive channel estimation, Low resolution ADC.

1 Introduction

Multi-Input Multi-Output Constant Envelope Modulation, MIMO-CEM, has been introduced as an alternative candidate to the currently used MIMO- Orthogonal Frequency Division Multiplexing (OFDM) used in the IEEE 802.11n standard especially for wireless backhaul network applications [1]. One of the major disadvantages of the OFDM is that the transmit signal exhibits noise like statistics, which requires high power consumption analog devices especially for RF power amplifier (PA) and analog-to-digital converter (ADC). Due to the stringent linearity requirements on handling OFDM signal, nonlinear power efficient PA like class C cannot be used for OFDM transmission. Instead, linear power inefficient PA should

H. Cherifi, J.M. Zain, and E. El-Qawasmeh (Eds.): DICTAP 2011, Part I, CCIS 166, pp. 619–633, 2011.

be used like class A and class A/B, which get OFDM a power consuming modulation scheme. In consequence, many efforts have been made so far to solve this vital problem in OFDM systems for the recent years [2]. All these drawbacks prevent OFDM from scalable design when it is extended to MIMO due to Hardware complexity; this is the reason why the IEEE802.11n standard specifies only 4×4 MIMO as a maximum MIMO-OFDM structure [3].

To cope with this issue, the authors suggested that Constant Envelope Modulation (CEM) can be used as an alternative candidate to OFDM transmission [1] [4] [5]. In this system, constant envelope Phase Modulation (PM) is used at the transmitter. Since PM signal can be viewed as differential coded frequency modulated (FM) signal, information is carried over frequency domain rather than over amplitude domain. Therefore, it is allowed to use nonlinear PA at transmitter subject to reducing spurious emission. Until now, most of the studies on PA have been investigated for linear modulation, i.e., PA has to be designed to achieve good trade-off between the requirement of linearity and the improvement of power efficiency. On the other hand, CEM systems alleviate the requirement of linearity at PA and therefore drastic improvement of power efficiency is highly expected as compared with linear modulations [6]. In [6], it is shown that the DSP circuits of 3 sector macro base station consumes only 300 watt of the 1800 watt totally consumed by the base station; about 16.667%. On the other hand, the linear PA consumes 1200 watt; about 66.7 % from the totally consumed power. The target in our further studies is to develop a nonlinear power amplifier which significantly improves power efficiency as compared with linear modulation while suppressing the out-of-band spectrum emission below the required value.

On the receiver side, intermediate frequency (IF) or radio frequency (RF) sampling results in allowing us to use low resolution ADC subject to shorter sampling interval than that required for baseband sampling. The authors suggested that 1-bit ADC is used as CEM default operation and 2 or 3 bits for CEM are optional ones [1]. Using only 1-bit ADC, there is no need for the complex analog Automatic Gain Control (AGC) circuit which greatly reduces CEM power consumption and complexity, especially when it is extended to MIMO. In addition, this low resolution ADC with IF sampling removes most analog stages (analog mixer, analog LPF and anti aliasing filter), which reduces receiver complexity. In contrast, it is a high power consuming to design ADC for OFDM systems at the IF band because of its high resolution, which gives us another superiority of CEM over OFDM regarding power consumption and complexity [7].

On the other hand, OFDM (linear modulation) has higher spectral efficiency than CEM (nonlinear modulation). This drawback of CEM is diminished by introducing MIMO; CEM should be subjected to higher MIMO branches than OFDM. Although, such a MIMO basis design of the proposed CEM transceiver necessitates high computational power required for signal processing, we can view the concern with optimistic foresight because cost for signal process is being reduced every year thanks to rapid progress on digital circuit evolution. A little improvement in power efficiency of major analog devices such as PA has been observed for the last few decades. In contrast, we have seen drastic improvements of digital devices in their power consumption and size for the same decades [8].

The proposed MIMO-CEM receiver is based upon modified Maximum Likelihood Sequence Estimation (MLSE) equalizer proposed by the authors [1], which takes into account the high quantization noise due to the low resolution ADC. The modified MLSE equalizer needs accurate multipath channel states information to replicate the received signal correctly [1], which is hard task in presence of large quantization noise attributable to low resolution ADC; where all signal amplitude information is completely destroyed in the default 1-bit resolution. Therefore, MIMO-CEM channel estimation is a big challenge to the real application; how we can accurately estimate channel information in presence of large quantization noise in addition to the AWGN noise. In [5], the authors have proposed the channel estimation method for MIMO-CEM systems, where channel parameters are estimated iteratively by an adaptive filter which minimizes the error between the replicated preamble signal and actually received one affected by a real channel and a low resolution ADC. In this method, the received preamble signal can be replicated by estimating MIMO channels whose approximates actual channels characteristics so as to mimic their effect upon the received MIMO signal when low-bit ADC is applied at the receiver. MSK and GMSK based CEM systems with the above channel estimator achieves excellent performance for different multipath Quasi-static channel scenarios in presence of severe quantization noise.

Because Wireless Backhaul suffers from channel fluctuations (dynamic channels) in real applications, the objective of this paper is to present a decision directed channel estimation (DDCE) technique for MIMO-CEM systems in frequency selective time varying channels. In which, the channel estimator in [5] is combined with a block based DDCE technique [9]-[11] in order to track channel variation. In SISO-CEM systems with DDCE, the channel estimate during current data block is estimated by using the decided value in the previous data block. Dynamic channel estimation is more challengeable issue than Quasi-static one because dynamic channel estimation and tracking has to be achieved during highly quantized received data, where all amplitude information is severely affected by a low resolution ADC and completely removed in the 1-bit case. For the purpose of comparison, we evaluate a linear interpolated pilot assisted channel tracking for SISO-CEM (SISO-CEM PAS), where two preambles are allocated at the beginning and the end of the frame and channel estimates at these two positions are used to estimate channel variation between these preambles by using a linear interpolation.

The rest of the paper is organized as follows. Section 2 gives details construction and explanations of the MIMO-CEM transceiver system. The MIMO-CEM adaptive channel estimator for quasi-static channel is given in Sec. 3. Section 4 gives the proposed SISO-CEM DDCE and the linear interpolated pilot assisted channel tracking (PAS). BER performance for MSK and GSMK based SISO-CEM systems under different f_dT_s values are evaluated in Sections 5 and 6. Section 7 gives the extension of the proposed SISO-CEM DDCE to MIMO-CEM followed by the conclusion in Section 8.

2 MIMO-CEM Transceiver System

Figures 1, 2 and 3 show the system block diagram of the SISO-CEM, 2x2 MIMO-CEM transceivers and 2x2 MIMO-CEM modified MLSE equalizer, respectively. MIMO-CEM system is mainly designed and optimized for 1-bit ADC (default operation) in order to develop a small size and power-efficient MIMO wireless backhaul relay station. When ADC resolution is only 1bit, a limiter can be used as ADC and thus complicated AGC circuit to adjust the input signal level is not needed. This fact will have a great impact on the system complexity, power consumption and cost when it is extended to MIMO, where each MIMO branch needs its own AGC-ADC circuit. On the other hand, 1-bit ADC means high nonlinear limiting function that can be expressed as:

$$f(\Theta)=\begin{cases}1 & if\ \Theta\geq 0\\ -1 & if\ \Theta<0\end{cases} \tag{1}$$

This high nonlinear function needs advanced and modified equalization and MIMO channel estimation techniques to equalize the received MIMO signal. On possible solution to the equalization problem was given by the authors through the CEM modified MLSE equalizer [1], as in Fig. 2. This modified MLSE equalizer estimates the non-linear effect (quantization noise) of the low bit ADC upon the received signal when it equalizes the channel distortion. So, it has an ability to equalize the received signal, with an acceptable BER performance [1] even if it is affected by hard limiter (1-bit ADC) under the constraints of highly estimated channel conditions H_{est}. Beside the default 1-bit ADC operation, the authors examined the 2 and 3-bit ADC cases as optional ones. Also, the authors extended SISO-CEM to MIMO-CEM and proved its effectiveness using the CEM MLSE equalizer in terms of BER performance [1].

In SISO-CEM, Fig.1, the input binary data *Inp* is convolutional-encoded (Enc) and interleaved (Π) in order to enhance BER performance especially in the default 1-bit ADC operation. The convolutionally encoded and interleaved data is constant envelope PM modulated using differential encoder followed by MSK or GMSK frequency modulation, signal *X*. The received signal is affected by multipath time varying channel *H* and additive white Gaussian noise (AWGN). On the receiver side, analog BPF filter is used to improve Signal to Noise power Ratio (SNR) of the received signal corrupted by AWGN noise. After that, the signal is converted into digital one using low resolution ADC sampled at IF band and digitally converted into baseband (IF-BB) and low pass filtered (LPF), signal *Y*. The LPF signal *Y* is equalized by the modified MLSE equalizer [1] using estimated channel characteristics $H_{est.}$ Depending upon the tradeoff between performance accuracy and computational complexity, the CEM MLSE may out Hard or Soft decisions. In Soft decision, Log Likelihood Ratio (LLR) is used as bits reliable output information. Although Soft decisions have better BER performance than Hard decisions, it requires more computational complexity. The MLSE equalizer output is then de-interleaved (Π^{-1}) and decoded using Viterbi decoder (Vit Dec) to produce the estimated input binary data $\hat{Inp}$.

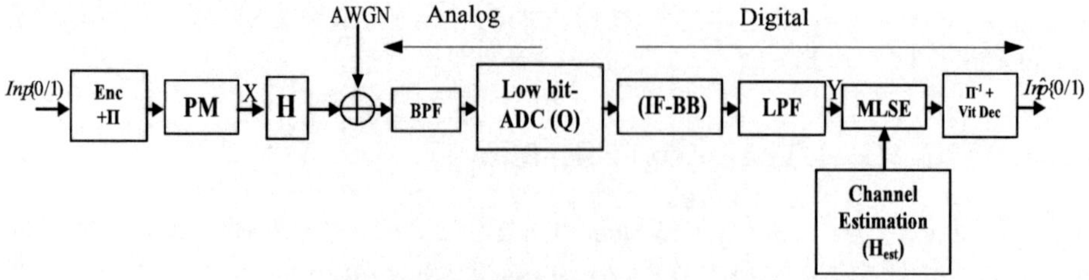

Fig. 1. The SISO-CEM transceiver

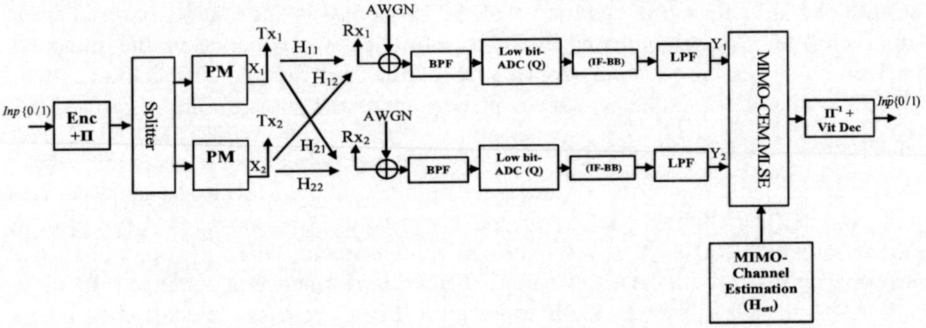

Fig. 2. The 2x2 MIMO-CEM transceiver

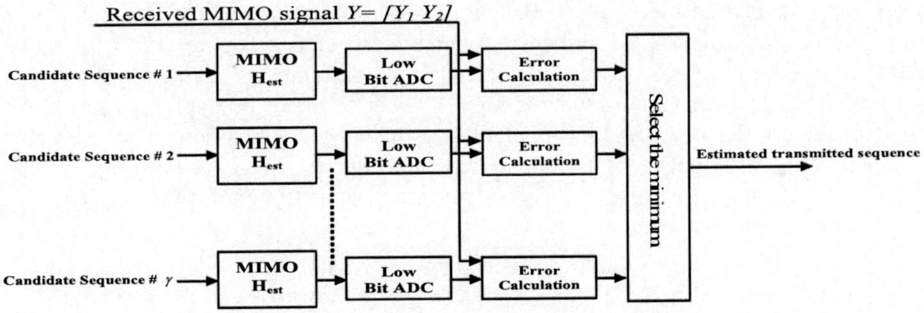

Fig. 3. The 2x2 MIMO-CEM MLSE equalizer

3 Channel Estimation for MIMO-CEM Systems

The authors have proposed an adaptive channel estimation method for SISO-CEM system and extended it to MIMO-CEM case [5], where a hard limiter as in Eq.1, is used to cut out the amplitude information of the received signal. For 1-bit CEM, although the received signal amplitude is completely lost, channel information still exists in phase fluctuation of the received signal. So for 1-bit SISO-CEM, the channel estimator (assuming no AWGN) is required to solve this non-linear equation:

$$HrdLmt\ (X * H_{est}) = HrdLmt\ (X * H),\ and\ H_{est}\ maynot\ equal\ H \qquad (2)$$

where *HrdLmt* denotes the 1-bit ADC function Eq.1, and * means linear convolution. Hence, there are infinite numbers of H_{est} which can satisfy Eq.2. This fact suggests that conventional linear channel estimation techniques like Least Squares (LS), Minimum Mean Square Error (MMSE) and correlator are not practical solutions for CEM channel estimation problem as the authors pointed out [5], because these methods deal with linear systems and have no function to deal with highly non-linear systems. Therefore, the authors proposed channel estimation strategy to find out an estimated channel whose characteristics do not necessary match the actual channel, but exactly mimic its effect upon the transmitted signal when 1-bit ADC is applied at the receiver. In other words, the target of their proposal is not to directly observe the actual channel through known preambles. Instead, they replicated the preamble received signal at the receiver in presence of the hard limiter attributable to 1-bit ADC, and channels parameters are adaptively estimated so as to minimize the MSE between the actual received signal and its replicated version $\overline{\|Y - Y_{est}\|^2}$, see Fig 4. Therefore, the authors suggested iteratively minimizing the MSE using adaptive filter processing [2]. Utilizing the estimated channel by the modified CEM MLSE equalizer, which takes the 1-bit effect into account, Fig. 3, optimum BER performance that exactly matches actual channel performance is obtained. For 2 and 3-bit ADC, the CEM system tends to be more linear. Hence, the channel estimator problem becomes more relaxed and the channel estimator approximates the actual channel characteristics.

Figure 4 shows the block diagram of the SISO-CEM adaptive filter channel estimator, where constant envelope PM modulated PN sequence X is transmitted as a known training sequence for adaptive channel estimator. The received preamble signal after frequency-down conversion and low-pass filtering in digital domain is denoted as Y. The replicated received signal Y_{est} is obtained by applying the known preamble X to the estimated channel and a given ADC function. The estimator calculates the error between the actual received signal Y and its replica Y_{est}. The adaptive filter channel parameters H_{est} is determined so as to minimize the error.

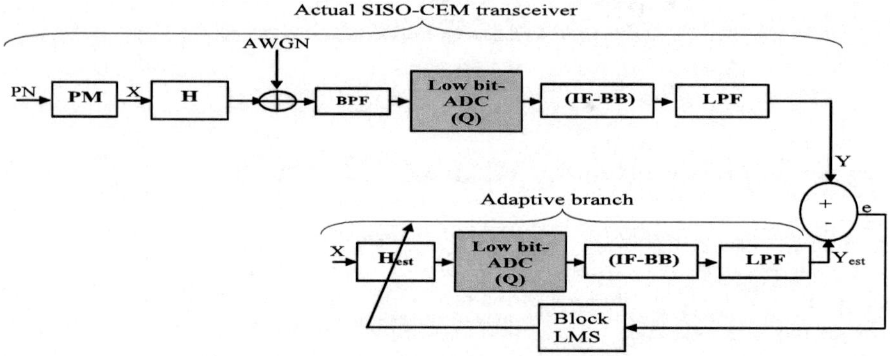

Fig. 4. The SISO-CEM adaptive channel estimator

The block least mean square (BLMS) algorithm used in adaptive process is given as:

$$H_{est}(n+1) = H_{est}(n) + \frac{u(n)}{\zeta} \sum_{i=0}^{\zeta-1} X_b^*(n\zeta+i)e(n\zeta+i) \tag{3}$$

$$e(n\zeta+i) = Y(n\zeta+i) - Y_{est}(n\zeta+i) \tag{4}$$

where $H_{est}(n)=[h_{est0}(n)\ h_{est1}(n).....h_{est(M-1)}(n)]^T$ is the estimated channel vector of length M at iteration step n, $u(n)$ is step size of recursive calculation in adaptive filter at iteration step n, and ζ is the length of the complex baseband training transmitted PM signal X_b. The suffixes ^{T} and * denote transpose and complex conjugate, respectively. X_b^* is given as:

$X_b^*(n\zeta+i)=[x_b^*(n\zeta+i)\ x_b^*(n\zeta+i-1).......x_b^*(n\zeta+i-M+1)]^T$, where M denotes channel length.

The channel estimator calculates error e given by Eq.(4) of the entire received training signal block stored at the receiver. After that, channel parameters H_{est} are updated once by the recursive calculation in Eqs.(3) and (4), where block length of BLMS is the same as preamble length. The authors also used adaptive step size $u(n)$ in order to speed up the convergence rate of the algorithm with no additional complexity result from using the BRLS algorithm. This calculation is continued until MSE becomes low enough to obtain sufficient MLSE equalization performance or the number of adaptive iterations comes to a given number N_{train}. Consequently, CEM MLSE can perform well by utilizing the estimated channel states for further symbol equalizations. In order to reduce the complexity of the adaptive processing, correlator estimator can be used to provide roughly estimated channel information as initial channel states for adaptive calculation in Eqs.(3) and (4) [5].

Utilizing the property that MIMO channels are uncorrelated, the authors extended their SISO-CEM adaptive estimator into the adaptive bank MIMO-CEM channels estimator; shown in Fig. 5 for 2x2 MIMO-CEM. In this scheme, each channel (H_{est11} and H_{est12}) are adaptively updated simultaneously and separately using the block (B-) LMS algorithm. Also, the nonlinear effect of the 1-bit ADC on the combined received MIMO signal can be taken into account by using this structure. Also, the initial values MIMO-CEM correlators are based upon sending two phase shifted PN sequences preambles from TX_1 and TX_2 simultaneously. This phase shift is used to maintain some orthogonality between the transmitted PN preambles. The phase shift must be greater than the expected channel length (M). So, they can estimate the initial values of H_{est11}, H_{est12}, H_{est21} and H_{est22} simultaneously and separately using four correlator estimators one for each channel. This adaptive bank MIMO-CEM estimator can be easily extended to more MIMO-CEM branches.

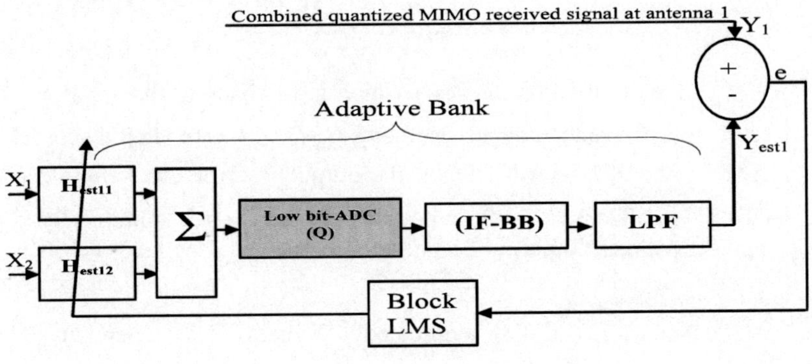

Fig. 5. 2×2 MIMO-CEM Adaptive Bank Channel Estimator for antenna 1

4 Decision-Directed Channel Tracking for SISO-CEM Systems in Time Varying Frequency Selective Channels

In this section, we propose a block based DDCE for SISO-CEM systems and compare it with the conventional linear interpolation based dynamic channel estimation technique.

4.1 Block Based Decision Directed Dynamic Channel Estimation in SISO-CEM Systems

DDCE is an effective technique to track channel fluctuation during data transmission in high Doppler frequency systems. In this section, we present a block based DDCE for dynamic channel tracking in SISO-CEM system. Figure 6 shows the SISO-CEM frame structure and its corresponding received one, where the LPF received signal Y is divided into two parts; the preamble part $Y_{(P)}$ which results from receiving the transmitted preamble PN sequence $X_{(P)}$, and the received data blocks part $Y_{(K)}$, $1 \le K \le NoOfBlocks$, which results from receiving the transmitted data blocks $X_{(K)}$ as shown in Fig. 6.

Figure 7 shows the proposed SISO-CEM (Hard/Soft) DDCE construction, including the SISO-CEM Adaptive channel estimator shown in Fig. 4, in more details. The proposed (Hard / Soft) SISO-CEM DDCE is described as follows:

1. First the channel is initially estimated $H_{est}(0)$ using the received PN preamble sequence $Y_{(P)}$ and the transmitted PN preamble sequence $X_{(P)}$. This initial estimation is done using correlator and adaptive channel estimator described in Sec. 3.
2. This initially estimated channel $H_{est}(0)$ is used to equalize the received data block $Y_{(1)}$ using the modified CEM MLSE equalizer to obtain $In\hat{p}_{Enc(1)}$ which is de-interleaved (Π^{-1}) and Viterbi decoded (Vit Dec) to find the estimated input data block $In\hat{p}_{(1)}$.
3. Two types of DDCE methods are considered in this paper, i.e., hard and soft DDCEs. In hard DDCE, the output signal of the CEM MLSE equalizer is hard decided as $In\hat{p}_{Enc(1)}$. Then, $In\hat{p}_{Enc(1)}$ is PM modulated to obtain $\hat{X}_{(1)}^{Hard}$ (the dashed line in Fig.7) which is fed back to the adaptive channel estimator. Current channel estimate $H_{est}(1)$ is estimated using H_{est} (0), $\hat{X}_{(1)}^{Hard}$, and $Y_{(1)}$. In soft DDCE, the output of error correction decoder for DDCE is utilized, i.e., soft output information, Log Likelihood Ratio (LLR) of the equalizer output, is de-interleaved (Π^{-1}) and applied to soft decision Viterbi decoder (Vit Dec) to obtain $In\hat{p}_{(1)}$ which is encoded (Enc), interleaved (Π), and PM modulated to obtain $\hat{X}_{(1)}^{Soft}$ .Then, $\hat{X}_{(1)}^{Soft}$ is fed back to the adaptive channel estimator. Similarly to hard DDCE, current channel estimate $H_{est}(1)$ is estimated using $H_{est}(0)$, $\hat{X}_{(1)}^{Soft}$, and $Y_{(1)}$.
4. Repeat steps 2,3 until $Y_{(K)} = Y_{(NoOfBlock)}$.

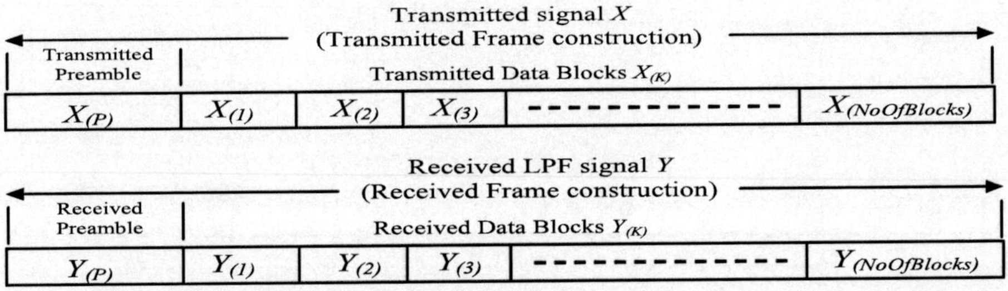

Fig. 6. The Transmitted and Received Frame structure of the proposed SISO-CEM DDCE

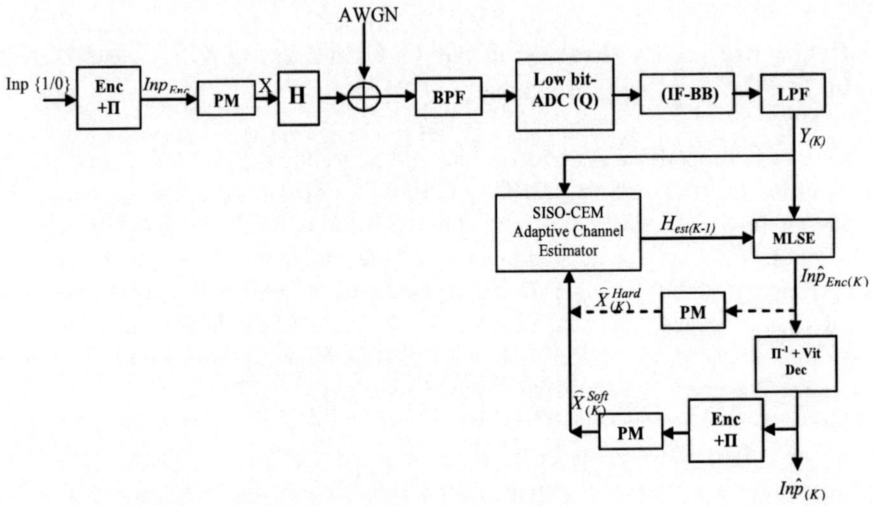

Fig. 7. The SISO-CEM (Hard/ Soft) DDCE construction, the dashed line shows DDCE Hard Decision path and the solid line shows the Soft Decision One

4.2 Pilot Assisted Linear Interpolation Channel Estimation

As a conventional pilot assisted time-varying channel estimation method, we also consider a linear interpolation based technique, where channel characteristic is estimated by taking linear interpolation between two channel estimates provided by preambles at the beginning and end of the transmission frame. Linear interpolation is used to linearly estimate the channel between these two known values. For more estimation accuracy, many pilots are shuffled with the data and then higher order interpolation can be used. Although shuffling many pilots enhances the estimation accuracy, it increases the computational complexity and reduces the spectral efficiency. In SISO-CEM PAS, we use only two PN pilot preambles blocks to track channel variation by linear interpolation as shown in Fig.8. At each pilot position $(X_{(P1)}, Y_{(P1)})$ and $(X_{(P2)}, Y_{(P2)})$ the channel is estimated using SISO-CEM correlator and adaptive channel estimator, then linear interpolation is used to estimate the channel during data part.

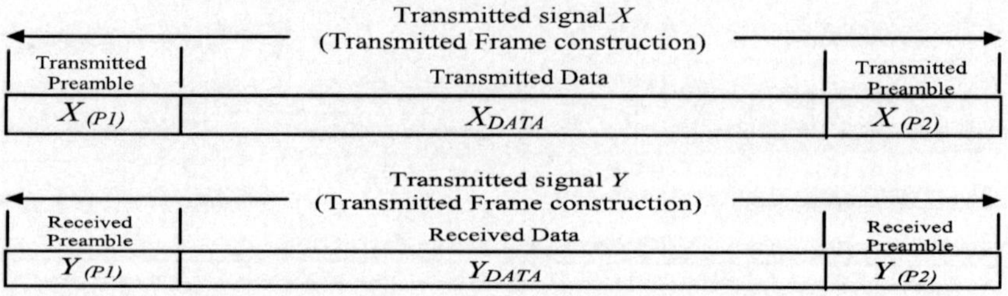

Fig. 8. The Transmitted and Received Frame structure of the proposed SISO-CEM PAS channel estimation

5 Performance Evaluation of SISO-CEM Using MSK and DDCE in Time-Varying Channels

In this section, we evaluate the performance of the proposed SISO-CEM time varying channel estimators ((Hard/Soft) DDCE, and PAS) for different f_dT_s values using MSK modulation. In SISO-CEM PAS, Soft output MLSE is used. We use the modified Jack's model (Young's model) presented in [12] to simulate the multipath time varying Rayleigh fading channel. In our evaluations, we will only concern about the 1-bit ADC case because it is considered as the MIMO-CEM default operation and the strictest non-linear case. Table 1 shows the simulation parameters used in these evaluations. The normalized preamble size is given as $\left(\frac{preamble\ size}{Total\ frame\ size}=0.14\right)$.

Figures 9-11 show BER performance of SISO-CEM systems with PAS, Hard DDCE, and Soft DDCE, respectively. In these figures, perfect means BER performance is evaluated using actual channel information, and estimated means BER performance is evaluated using estimated channel. From these figures, we can notice the superior BER performance of the SISO-CEM Soft DDCE over the other two schemes. SISO-CEM Soft DDCE can track the channel variation even in the very high Doppler frequency of f_dT_s = 0.001 with BER error floor of 0.001. On the other hand, the SISO-CEM Soft DDCE has the highest computational complexity as explained in Sec. 4. Also, the SISO-CEM Soft PAS channel estimation has a near SISO-CEM Soft DDCE performance in slow dynamic channels of f_dT_s = 0.0001. The SISO-CEM Hard DDCE has nearly the same BER performance as SISO-CEM Soft PAS channel estimator in the very high Doppler frequency of f_dT_s=0.001, but SISO-CEM Soft PAS channel estimator overcomes SISO-CEM Hard DDCE performance in slow and moderate dynamic channel conditions of f_dT_s = 0.0001, 0.0002 and 0.0005. But of course, Hard SISO-CEM DDCE BER performance overcomes the performance of Hard SISO-CEM PAS in moderate and high Doppler frequencies as it happens in Soft DDCE and Soft PAS. These figures prove the effectiveness of SISO-CEM (CEM modified MLSE equalizer and channel estimator) and in general MIMO-CEM systems (explained later) for time varying channel applications.

Table 1. Simulation parameters for performance evaluation in the MSK based SISO-CEM channel estimator

Parameter	value
f_dT_s	0.0001, 0.0002, 0.0005, and 0.001
Preamble PN sequence length.	1- For DDCE 63 chips for $f_dT_s = 0.0001$ and 0.0002, and 31 chips for $f_dT_s = 0.0005$ and 0.001 2- For PAS 62 chips (divided into parts) for $f_dT_s = 0.0001$ and 0.0002 and 30 chips for $f_dT_s = 0.0005$ and 0.001
Data Block length for DDCE	16 Symbols for $f_dT_s = 0.0001$ and 0.0002, and 12 symbols for $f_dT_s = 0.0005$ and 0.001.
B = (Preamble length) / (Total Frame length)	0.14 (For Both Techniques)
Actual Channel model H	Multipath time varying Rayleigh fading, equal gain, 4 paths, $\tau_{rms} = 1.12T_s$ (RMS delay spread), T_s is the symbol duration.
Estimated Channel Model H_{est}	4 paths separated by T_s.
ADC quantization bits	1-bit
Sampling rate at ADC	16 fs
BPF	6 order Butterworth, BW = 0.6
FEC Encoder	Conventional encoder with Constraint length = 7, Rate = ½, $g_0 = 133_8$ and $g_1 = 171_8$.
FEC Decoder	Hard / Soft Decision Viterbi Decoder for Hard/ Soft MLSE outputs respectively.

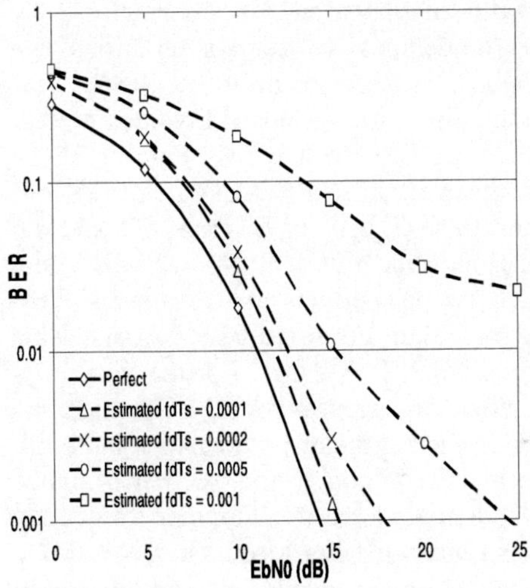

Fig. 9. BER performance using Soft Decision SISO-CEM PAS channel estimation

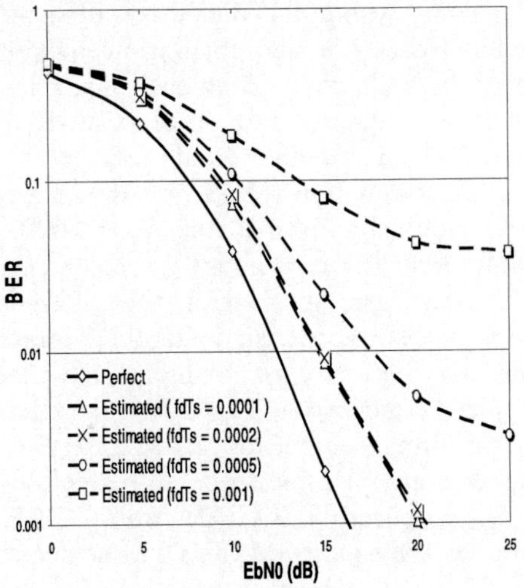

Fig. 10. BER performance using Hard Decision SISO-CEM DDCE

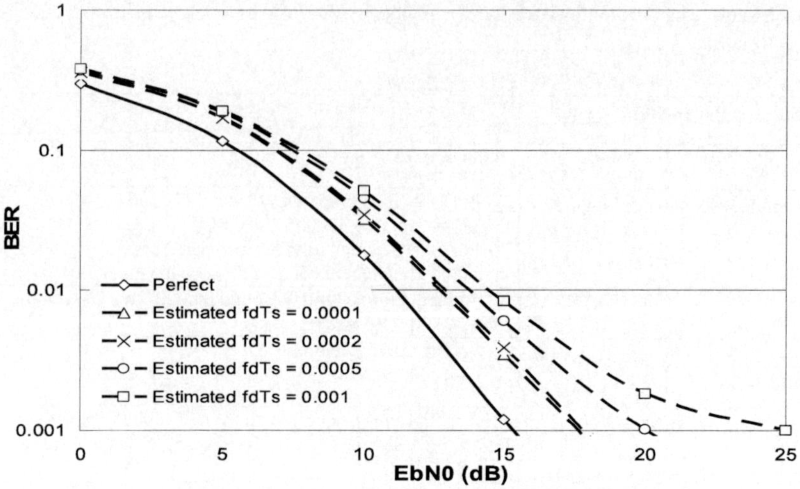

Fig. 11. BER performance using Soft Decision SISO-CEM DDCE

6 The Performance of SISO-CEM Using GMSK and Soft DDCE

GMSK modulation is applied to MIMO-CEM system in [4] to increase its spectral efficiency. Although higher spectrum efficiency than MSK is achieved using GMSK, it suffers from Inter Symbol Interference (ISI) caused by Gaussian filtering (GF) the transmitted baseband signal, i.e. there is a tradeoff between spectral efficiency improvement and BER degradation using GMSK.

In this section, we test our proposed SISO-CEM Soft DDCE for various GMSK BT values, where BT denotes 3 dB-bandwidth of Gaussian filter normalized by symbol frequency, and for various Doppler frequencies. In these simulations, we utilize the simulation parameters given in Table 1, except we only test SISO-CEM Soft DDCE scheme, and we use GMSK modulation with various BT values of 0.3, 0.5, 0.7 and 1. Another GF is used as the receiver LPF with BT=1. Figures 12-14 show the simulation results. As shown from these figures, SISO-CEM Soft DDCE works well using GMSK for f_dT_s = 0.0002 and 0.0005, and for BT = 1, 0.7 and 0.5 with no error floor. Although there is no error floor appear until EbN0 = 25 dB in the BT = 0.3 case, there is a big difference between perfect and estimated BER performances, more than 5 dB EbN0 increase to obtain the same BER of 0.01. This value may be increased for higher BER target like BER = 0.001. For the very high Doppler frequency of f_dT_s = 0.001, there is an error floor appear for all BT values, the best performance appear at BT = 1. At BT = 0.3, the estimator performance is highly degraded and far away from the perfect performance. In conclusion, the performance of the proposed SISO-CEM Soft DDCE is degraded as the Doppler frequency increases and as the GMSK BT value decreases. The worst case occurs at f_dT_s = 0.001 and BT =0.3, which means that the channel estimator needs to track a highly fluctuated channel using a strictly quantized high ISI received signal. For slow and moderate channel variations of f_dT_s = 0.0002 and 0.0005, it is recommended to use

GMSK constant envelope modulation with BT = 0.5. And, for very high channel fluctuation of $f_dT_s = 0.001$, it is recommended to use BT = 0.7 or 0.5 depending upon the system requirements, i.e., the required performance against spectral efficiency improvements.

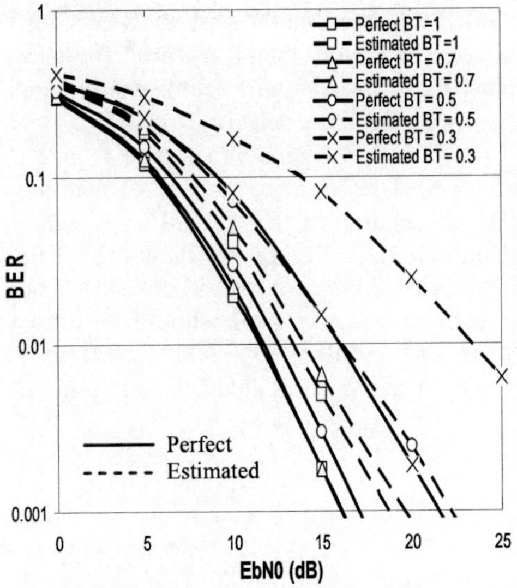

Fig. 12. BER performance using SISO-CEM sosft DDCE with $f_dT_s = 0.0002$

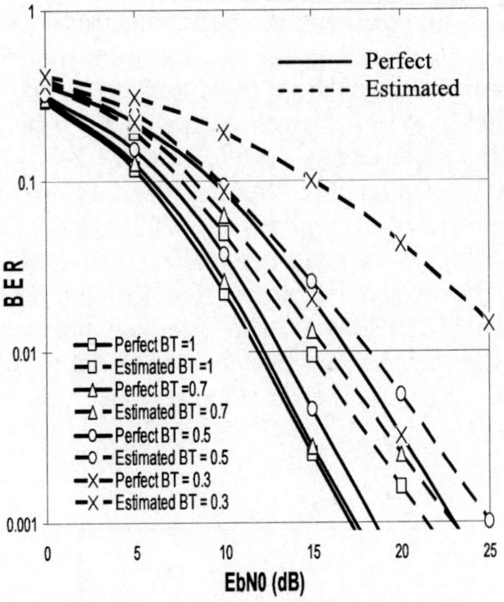

Fig. 13. BER performance using SISO-CEM sosft DDCE with $f_dT_s = 0.0005$

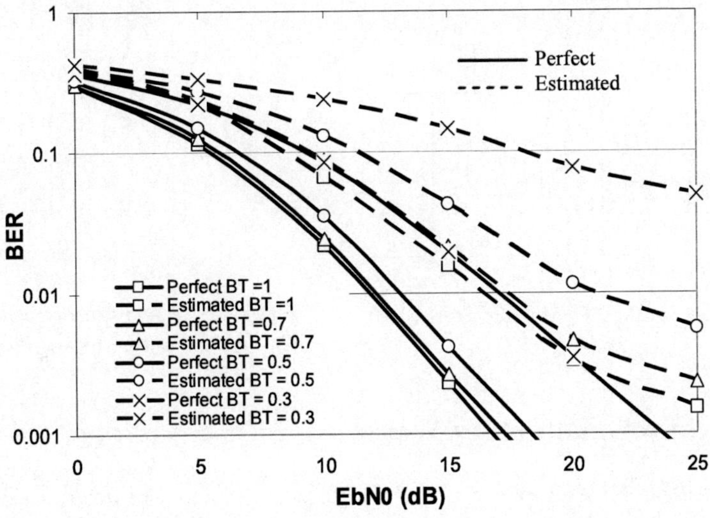

Fig. 14. BER performance using SISO-CEM sosft DDCE with $f_dT_s = 0.001$

7 Application of DDCE to MIMO-CEM Systems

Utilizing the MIMO channel estimator in Fig.5 and the proposed block DDCE scheme descried in Sec.4 for CEM systems, a direct extension of the proposed scheme into 2x2 MIMO is shown in Fig. 15. Again, the dashed line shows the DDCE Hard Decision path and the Solid line shows the Soft Decision One. We use the same steps described in Sec.4 except we use 2 transmit signals X_1 and X_2 and the corresponding received signals are Y_1 and Y_2. And, the adaptive estimator will estimate a channel matrix $\boldsymbol{H}_{est\ (K-1)}$ which consists of 4 different multipath channels $H_{est11(K-1)}$, $H_{est12(K-1)}$, $H_{est21(K-1)}$ and $H_{est22(K-1)}$. This MIMO-CEM DDCE can be extended to more than 2x2 MIMO branches. We test the 2x2 MIMO-CEM DDCE using table 1 simulation parameters except we use 2x2 MIMO-CEM configuration, Fig.2, with soft output MIMO-CEM MLSE equalizer using MSK modulation. Figure 16 shows the BER performance comparison for different f_dT_S values of 0.0002, 0.0005 and 0.001. Like the SISO-CEM DDCE case, our proposed estimator works well without any error floor for the slow and moderate dynamic channel conditions of 0.0002 and 0.0005, but there is an error floor appear on the too fast time varying channel conditions of 0.001.

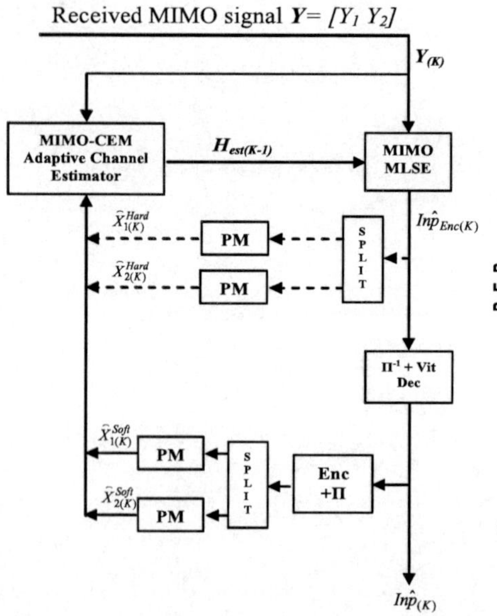

Fig. 15. The 2x2 MIMO-CEM (Hard/Soft) DDCE construction

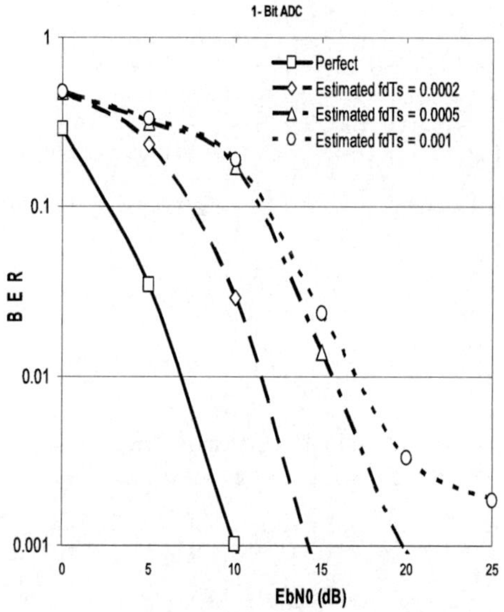

Fig. 16. BER performance using Soft Decision 2x2 MIMO-CEM DDCE

8 Conclusion and Future Works

In this paper, we have proposed a decision directed channel estimation (DDCE) for MIMO-CEM systems in time varying channel conditions with high Doppler frequencies. We proved that the proposed (Soft/Hard) DDCE works well in slow time varying conditions and soft DDCE outperforms hard one at the expense of the increased computational complexity. Also, we clarified that linear interpolation PAS and DDCE achieve good channel tracking performance for slow and moderate/high time-varying channels, respectively. Also, we evaluated SISO-CEM Soft DDCE using GMSK CEM in presence of large quantization noise attributable to 1-bit ADC on the receiver side. We recommended that BT=0.5 for moderate dynamic channels and BT =0.7 or 0.5 for fast one are suitable parameters. At the end of the paper, we presented how the proposed SISO-CEM time varying channel estimators is extended to MIMO-CEM case. Further our study items are to reduce the computational complexities of the proposed DDCE scheme in MIMO-CEM systems.

References

1. Muta, O., Furukawa, H.: Study on MIMO Wireless Transmission with Constant Envelope Modulation and a Low-Resolution ADC. IEICE Technical Report, RCS2010-44, pp.157-162 (2010) (in Japanese)
2. Hou, J., Ge, J., Zahi, D., Li, J.: Peak-to-Average Power Ratio Reduction of OFDM Signals with Nonlinear Companding Scheme. IEEE Transaction of Broadcasting 56(2), 258–262 (2010)
3. Mujtaba, S.A.: TGn sync proposal technical specification. doc: IEEE 802.11-04/0889r7, Draft proposal (2005)
4. Kotera, K., Muta, O., Furukawa, H.: Performance Evaluation of Gaussian Filtered Constant Envelope Modulation Systems with a Low-Resolution ADC. IEICE Technical Report of RCS(2010) (in Japanese)
5. Mohamed, E.M., Muta, O., Furukawa, H.: Channel Estimation Technique for MIMO-Constant Envelope Modulation Transceiver System. In: Proc. of RCS 2010, vol. 98, pp. 117–122 (2010)
6. Correia, L.M., Zeller, D., Blume, O., Ferling, D., Jading, Y., Gódor, I., Auer, G., Van Der Perre, L.: Challenges and Enabling Technologies for Energy Aware Mobile Radio Networks. IEEE Communications Magazine 48(11), 66–72 (2010)
7. Wepman, J.A.: Analog-to-Digital Converters and Their Applications in Radio Receivers. IEEE Communications Magazine 33(5), 39–45 (1995)
8. Horowitz, M., Stark, D., Alon, E.: Digital Circuit Design Trends. IEEE Journal of Solid-State Circuits 43(4), 757–761 (2008)
9. Arslan, H., Bottomley, G.E.: Channel Estimation in Narrowband Wireless Communication Systems. Journal of Wireless Communications and Mobile Computing 1(2), 201–219 (2001)
10. Ozdemir, M.K., Arslan, H.: Channel estimation for Wireless OFDM Systems. IEEE Communications Surveys 9(2), 18–48 (2007)
11. Akhtman, J., Hanzo, L.: Decision Directed Channel Estimation Aided OFDM Employing Sample-Spaced and Fractionally-Spaced CIR Estimators. IEEE Transactions on Wireless Communications 6(4), 1171–1175 (2007)
12. Young, D.J., Beaulieu, C.: The Generation of Correlated Rayleigh Random Variates by Inverse Discrete Fourier Transform. IEEE Transactions on Communications 48(7), 1114–1127 (2000)
13. Oyerinde, O.O., Mneney, S.H.: Iterative Decision Directed Channel Estimation for BICM-based MIMO-OFDM Systems. In: ICC 2010, pp. 1–5 (2010)

A New Backoff Algorithm of MAC Protocol to Improve TCP Protocol Performance in MANET

Sofiane Hamrioui[1] and Mustapha Lalam[2]

[1] Department of Computer Science, University of Sciences and Technologies Houari Boumedienne, Algiers, Algeria
[2] Department of Computer Science, University of Mouloud Mammeri, Tizi Ouzou, Algeria
s.hamrioui@gmail.com, lalamustapha@yahoo.fr

Abstract. In this paper, we propose an improvement to the Medium Access Control (MAC) protocol for better performance in the MANET (Mobile Ad Hoc Network). We are especially interested in the TCP (Transmission Control Protocol) performance parameters like the throughput and end-to-end delay. This improvement is IB-MAC (Improvement of Backoff algorithm of MAC protocol) which proposes a new backoff algorithm based on a dynamic adaptation of its maximal limit according to the number of nodes and their mobility. The evaluation of our IB-MAC solution and the study of its incidences on TCP performance are done with some of reactive (AODV, DSR) and proactive (DSDV) routing protocols, two versions of TCP protocols (Vegas and New Reno) and varying network conditions such as load and mobility.

Keywords: MANET, Performance, Protocols, MAC, IB-MAC, Transport, TCP.

1 Introduction

Mobile Ad Hoc Networks (MANET) [1] are complex distributed systems that consist of wireless mobile nodes. In such network, the MAC protocol [2], [3], [4] must provide access to the wireless medium efficiently and reduce interference. Important examples of these protocols include CSMA with collision avoidance that uses a random back-off even after the carrier is sensed idle [5]; and a virtual carrier sensing mechanism using request-to-send/clear-to-send (RTS/CTS) control packets [6]. Both techniques are used in IEEE 802.11 MAC protocol [5] which is a current standard for wireless networks.

Many applications in MANET depend on the reliability of the transport protocol. Transmission Control Protocol (TCP) [7], [8] is the transport protocol used in the most IP networks [9] and recently in ad hoc networks like MANET [10]. It is important to understand the TCP behavior when coupled with IEEE 802.11 MAC protocol in an ad hoc network. When the interactions between the MAC and TCP protocols are not taken into account, this may degrades MANET performance notably TCP performance parameters (throughput and the end-to-end delay) [11], [12], [13].

H. Cherifi, J.M. Zain, and E. El-Qawasmeh (Eds.): DICTAP 2011, Part I, CCIS 166, pp. 634–648, 2011.

In [15], we presented a study of interactions between the MAC and TCP protocols. We have shown that the TCP parameters performance (notably throughput) degrades while the nodes number increase in a MANET using IEEE 802.11 MAC as access control protocol. In [16], we have proposed solutions to the problem posed in [15], but we have just limited to a chain topology and also to the influence of the nodes number on the TCP performance.

Our contribution in this paper is the following of those done in [15] and [16]. Different topologies have been studied and another parameter which is nodes mobility has been considered. After a short presentation of the studied problem, we present our improvement IB-MAC (Improvement of Backoff of the MAC protocol) which proposes a dynamic adaptation of the maximal limit of the MAC backoff algorithm. This adaptation is as function of the nodes number in the network and their mobility. To finish, we study the incidences of this improvement on the MANET performance notably on the TCP performance.

2 Interaction between MAC and TCP Protocols

2.1 MAC IEEE 802.11 and TCP Protocols in the MANET

IEEE 802.11 MAC protocol defines two different access methods; a distributed coordination function (DCF) and polling based point coordination function (PCF). In MANET, the DCF feature is used. The DCF access is basically a carrier sense multiple access with collision avoidance (CSMA/CA) mechanism. In order to avoid collision due to the hidden terminal problem [17], [18] the node first transmits a Request To Send (RTS) control frame. The destination node responds with a Clear To Send (CTS) control frame. Once a successful RTS-CTS frame exchange takes place, the data frame (DATA) is transmitted. The receiving node checks the received data frame, and upon correct receipt, sends an acknowledgement (ACK) frame. Although the introduction of RTS-CTS-DATA-ACK frame format makes the transmission more reliable, there is still the possibility of transmission failure.

It has been shown that TCP does not work well in a wireless network [7], [19]. TCP associates the packet loss to the congestion, and then it starts its congestion control mechanism. Therefore, transmission failures at the MAC layer lead to the congestion control activation by TCP protocol then the number of packets is reduced. Several mechanisms have been proposed to address this problem [20], [21], [22], but most of them focus on the cellular architecture. The problem is more complex in MANET where there is no base station and each node can act as a router [23], [24].

The TCP Performance parameters (like the throughput and the end-to-end delay) have been the subject of several evaluations. It has been shown that these parameters degrade when the interactions between MAC and TCP are not taken into account [7], [17]. In our previous work [15], we confirmed these results by studying the effect of the MAC layer when the number of nodes increases. The major source of these effects is the problem of hidden and exposed nodes [17], [18]. The most important solution which has been proposed to the hidden node problem is the use of RTS and CTS frames [25], [26]. Although the use of RTS/CTS frames is considered as a solution to the hidden node problem, it was shown in [15] [17] [27] that it also leads to further degrade the TCP flow by creating more collisions and introduce an additional overhead. Then these two constraints decrease the TCP performance.

2.2 Related Work

In [28] [29] [30] [31] [32], many analyses of TCP protocol performance are done and several solutions on how to improve this performance are proposed. In this paper we present the most important of these solutions.

Yuki and al. [33] have proposed a technique that combines data and ACK packets, and have shown through simulation that this technique can make radio channel utilization more efficient. Altman and Jimenez [34], proposed an improvement for TCP performance by delaying 3-4 ACK packets. Kherani and Shorey [35], suggest significant improvement in TCP performance as the delayed acknowledgement parameter d increases to the TCP window size W. Allman [36], conducted an extensive evaluation on Delayed Acknowledgment (DA) strategies, and they presented a variety of mechanisms to improve TCP performance in presence of side-effect of delayed ACKs. Chandran [37] proposed TCP-feedback, with this solution, when an intermediate node detects the disruption of a route; it explicitly sends a Route Failure Notification (RFN) to the TCP sender. Holland and Vaidya [38] proposed a similar approach based on ELFN (Explicit Link Failure Notification), when the TCP sender is informed of a link failure, it freezes its state. Liu and Singh [39] proposed the ATCP protocol; it tries to deal with the problem of high Bit Error Rate (BER) and route failures. Fu et al. [40] investigated TCP improvements by using multiple end-to-end metrics instead of a single metric. They claim that a single metric may not provide accurate results in all conditions. Biaz and Vaidya [41] evaluated three schemes for predicting the reason for packet losses inside wireless networks. They applied simple statistics on observed Round-trip Time (RTT) and/or observed throughput of a TCP connection for deciding whether to increase or decrease the TCP congestion window. Liu et al. [42] proposed an end-to-end technique for distinguishing between packet loss due to congestion from packet loss by a wireless medium. They designed a Hidden Markov Model (HMM) algorithm to perform the mentioned discrimination taking RTT measurements over the end-to-end channel. Kim and al. [43] [44] proposed the TCP-BuS (TCP Buffering capability and Sequence information), like previous proposals, uses the network feedback in order to detect route failure events and to take convenient reaction to this event. Oliveira and Braun [45] propose a dynamic adaptive strategy for minimizing the number of ACK packets in transit and mitigating spurious retransmissions. Hamadani and Rakocevic [46] propose a cross layer algorithm called TCP Contention Control that it adjusts the amount of outstanding data in the network based on the level of contention experienced by packets as well as the throughput achieved by connections. Zhai and al. [47] propose a systematic solution named Wireless Congestion Control Protocol (WCCP) which uses channel busyness ratio to allocate the shared resource and accordingly adjusts the sender's rate so that the channel capacity can be fully utilized and fairness is improved. Lohier and al. [48] proposes to adapt one of the MAC parameters, the *Retry Limit* (*RL*), to reduce the drop in performance due to the inappropriate triggering of TCP congestion control mechanisms. Starting from this, a MAC-layer LDA (Loss Differentiation Algorithm) is proposed.

The approaches just presented suggest improvements to TCP performance based on MAC and TCP protocols. In our work, we propose to study the interactions between these two protocols and improve them. In what follows, we examine the interactions between MAC and TCP before proceeding to the presentation of our solutions.

3 IB-MAC (Improvement of Backoff of the MAC Protocol)

The MAC protocol is based on the backoff algorithm that allows it to determine which will access to the wireless medium in order to avoid collisions. The time backoff is calculated as follows:

$$BackoffTime = BackoffCounter * aSlotTime \quad (1)$$

In (1), aSlotTime is a time constant and BackoffCounter is an integer from uniform distribution in the interval [0, CW] and CW is the contention window who's minimum and maximum limits are (CW_{min}, CW_{max}) and are defined in advance.

The CW value is increased in the case of non availability of the channel using the following formula:

$$\begin{gathered} m \leftarrow m+1 \\ CW(m) = (CW_{min}+1)*2^{m}-1 \\ CW_{min} <= CW(m) <= CW_{max} \end{gathered} \quad (2)$$

m: the number of retransmissions.

As we have seen through the simulations presented in the [15] and [16], when the number of nodes in the network increases, the performance of TCP deteriorates. The cause of this degradation is the frequent occurrence of collisions between nodes. These collisions become more frequent with a small bachoff interval because the probability to have two or more nodes choose the same value in a small interval is greater than the probability that these nodes choose the same value in a larger interval.

Note by I this interval, SI its size, and Pr(i,x) is the probability that the node i chooses the x value in the I interval. The problem then is how to ensure that for any two nodes i and j in the network with i != j, we will have:

$$\begin{gathered} | Pr(i,x) - Pr(j,x) | = y \\ y \mathrel{!}= 0 \end{gathered} \quad (3)$$

For an important number of nodes in the network, and for a high probability that the formula **(3)** will be verified, we must have a larger S_I. To do this we wanted to make the size of S_I adaptable to the number of nodes in the network, then we intervene on one of the limits of this interval, we then propose the limit CW_{max}.

Note by n the number of nodes in the network.

Then the first part of the expression of CW_{max} will be:

$$F(n) = \log(n) \quad (4)$$

Log () is used here because we found in [15] and [16] that the effects of the large values of the nodes number on the TCP performance are almost the same.

Another factor in the deteriorating of the TCP performance is the mobility of nodes. In fact, node mobility often leads to the breakdown of connectivity between nodes, resulting in loss of TCP packets and then the degradation of the TCP performance. At the MAC protocol, when the packets losses are detected, they are associated to the collisions problem, which is not the case here. Then, more the mobility increases, more the backoff interval increases, something that should not happen because these packets are lose due to the rupture of the connectivity and no to the collisions. Therefore, we will try to find a compromise between the effect of mobility and the size of the backoff interval.

Mobility is generally characterized by its speed and angle of movement, two factors that determine the degree of the impact of mobility on packets loss. Consider a node i, in communication with another node j, then we note by:

α: the angle between the line (i, j) and the movement direction of node i,
W: the speed of mobile node i.

To consider the impact of mobility on the loss of packets is is necessary to study the effects of mobility parameters (W and α). For the effect of speed W, as in the case of number of nodes, we use a logarithmic function because for large values of speed mobility the results converge. So this is expressed as follows:

$$H(W) = \begin{cases} 1 & \text{if } W=0 \text{ (Without mobility)} \\ Log(W) & \text{else} \end{cases} \quad (5)$$

Also, the direction of the node movement determines the degree of the influence of mobility on packets loss, it is given by M_0:

$$M_0 = \begin{cases} 1 & \text{if } W=0 \text{ (without mobility)} \\ 1 & \text{if } -\Pi/4 <= \alpha <= \Pi/4 \\ \frac{1}{\sqrt{W}} & \text{else} \end{cases} \quad (6)$$

We know that when the W and M_0 increase, the packets loss increase too, it increases more when the node is moving in the opposite direction of communication. This increasing of packets loss has a negative impact on backoff interval because they can be associated to the collisions, but is not the case here (as explained above). To make this impact positive, we must use the inverse, as like follows:

$$1 / (M_0 * \log(W)) = M(W, \alpha) \quad (7)$$

$M(W,\alpha)$ decreases with the increasing of W and M_0, it decreases more when the node is moving in the opposite direction of communication.

We give now the new expression of CW_{max} as follows:

$$CW_{max}(n, W, \alpha) = CW_{max0} + F(n) * M(W,\alpha) \quad (8)$$

From (4), (5) and (7), we will have:

$$CW_{max}(n, W, \alpha) = CW_{max0} + Log(n) * (1 / (M_0 * \log(W))) \quad (9)$$

CW_{max0}: initial value of CW_{max} defined by the MAC protocol (with the 802.11 version, it is equal to 1024); M_0: see the expression (6).

In (9), the value of n is variable; it is updated always when there is a new arrived node to the network or a leaved node from the network. So, our solution also contains an agent let updating the value of n as follows:

```
Begin
……
Variable N ← 0;
……
Node_i ← NEW (Node_Class);
Add (Node_i)
N ← N+1
……
Free (Node_j)
N ← N-1;
……
End;
```

After having made the values of CW_{max} adaptive to the number of nodes used and their mobility, the IB-MAC (improved version of that given by the formula (2)) becomes:

$$\begin{aligned} m &\leftarrow m + 1 \\ CW(m) &= (CW_{min}(n) + 1)*2^m - 1 \\ CW_{min} &<= CW(m) <= CW_{max}(n, W, \alpha) \\ CW_{max}(n, W, \alpha) &= CW_{max0} + (1 / (M_0 * \log (W)))*\log(n) \end{aligned} \tag{10}$$

m: the number of retransmissions, n: the number of the nodes used.

α: the angle between the line formed by the mobile node and its corresponding node and the movement direction of this mobile node.

W: the speed of mobile node.

M_0: see the expression (6),

CW_{max0}: initial value of CW_{max}.

4 Incidences of IB-MAC on TCP Performance

4.1 Simulation Environment

The evaluation is performed through the simulation environment NS-2 (version 2.34) [49] [50]. MAC level use the 802.11b with DCF (Distributed Coordination Function), keeping the default values of model parameters. For our simulations, the effective transmission range is of 250 meters and an interference range of 550 meters. Each node has a queue buffer link layer of 50 packets managed with a mode drop-tail [51]. The scheduling packet transmissions technique is the First in First out (FIFO) type. The propagation model used is two-ray ground model [52].

Our simulations are done with some of the IETF standardised routing protocols (AODV [53], DSR [54], and DSDV [55]). DSDV is a proactive protocol, while

AODV and DSR are two reactive protocols; each one has a mechanism of its own and is totally different from each other.

The values, such as the duration of simulation, the speed of the nodes, and the number of connections have been established in order to obtain interpretable results compared to those published in the literature. The simulations are performed for 1000 seconds, this choice in order to analyze the full spectrum of TCP throughput.

We considered two cases: without and with mobility. In the first case, three topologies are studied: chain, ring and plus topologies in which always the node 1 send for the node n (see Fig. 1). The distance between two neighbouring nodes is 200 meters and each node can communicate only with its nearest neighbour. The interference range of a node is about two times higher than its transmission range.

In the mobility case, we study a random topology with two cases: weak and strong mobility. In both cases, it is only the node 1 that sends for the node n. The mobility model uses the random waypoint model [56], we justify our choice by the fact that the network is not designed for mobility and that this particular model is widely used in the literature. In this model the node mobility is typically random and all nodes are uniformly distributed in space simulation. The nodes move in 2200m*600m area, each one starts its movement from a random location to a random destination.

We used TCP NewReno [57] and TCP Vegas [58]. New Reno is a reactive variant, derived and widely deployed, and whose performances were evaluated under conditions similar to those conducted here. TCP Vegas transport protocol with proactive features and also its specific mechanism completely different from that of New Reno TCP. TCP traffic was used as the main traffic network.

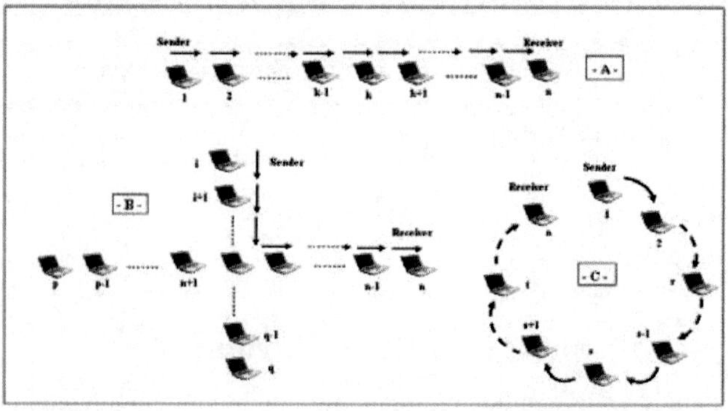

Fig. 1. Topology used in the simulations (without mobility)

4.2 Parameters Evaluation

We have simulated several scenarios with different numbers of nodes n, topologies, routing and TCP protocols, and mobility. We are interested in each scenario into two parameters. The first is the throughput which is given by the ratio of the received data on all data sent. The second parameter is the end-to-end delay which is given by time for receipt of data - the data transmission time/number of data packets received.

4.3 Simulations en Results

Scenario 1: chain topology in which node 1 sends for node n (Fig. 1. -A-).

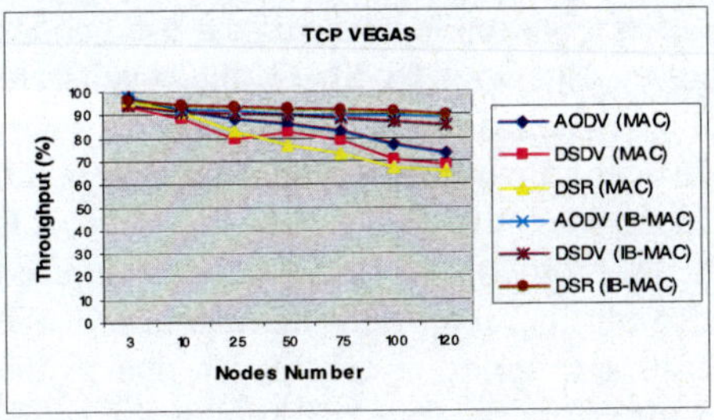

Fig. 2. Throughput with TCP Vegas and chain topology

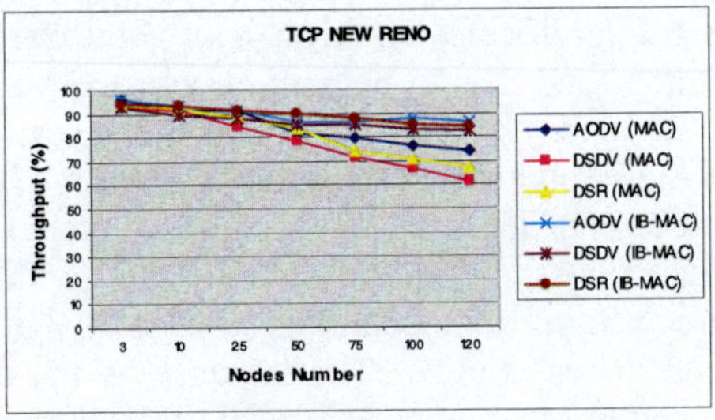

Fig. 3. Throughput with TCP New Reno and chain topology

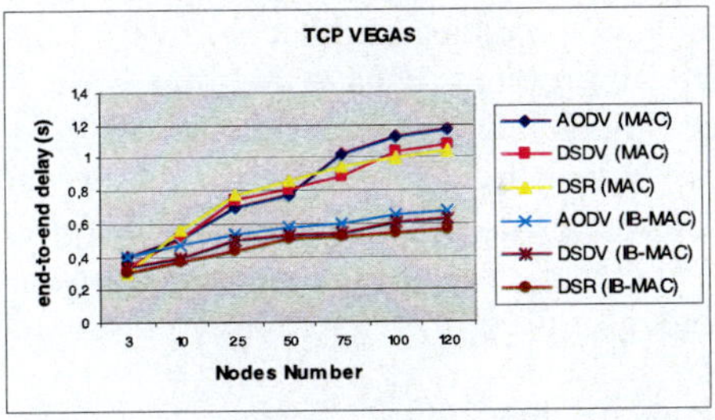

Fig. 4. End-To-End Delay with TCP Vegas and chain topology

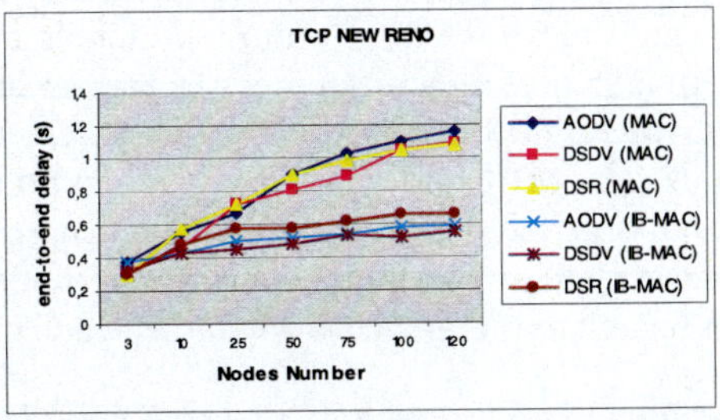

Fig. 5. End-To-End Delay with TCP New Reno and chain topology

We see, through Fig. 2, with MAC protocol, when we use TCP Vegas as transport protocol, that more the nodes number participating in the chain increases, more the throughput decreases. This result remains true with the three routing protocols used (AODV, DSDV and DSR) although there is a difference between them. We are interested in because our aim in using these protocols is just to show if the throughput parameter is independent from the used routing protocol. This degradation at a given time (from n=100 nodes) begins to take stability for the three protocols.

This degradation is due to TCP packet loss occurred, and that becomes more important with increasing size of the network. With the analysis of trace files for these graphs, we found that the frames handled at the MAC level mainly RTS and CTS are sensitive to network size, to the extent they become to large losses as the number of nodes is increased. It has been shown previously that such packet losses in such conditions of simulations are mainly due to the consequences of hidden nodes and exposed, a result that has already been achieved in our past work [15] [17] [18].

But when the IB-MAC is used as MAC protocol we see, in the same Fig. 2, that with the three routing protocols, the throughput is better. There is an important improvement of this parameter, even if there is a slight decrease when the number of nodes increases but this decrease is much smaller compared to the first case when the

MAC protocol is used. This improvement is due to the use of the adaptive nature of our solution IB-MAC to the nodes number in the network.

We have the same observations by analyzing the graphs in figure 3 where the New Reno version of TCP protocol is used. With MAC protocol, and with the three used routing protocols, the throughput values decreases with the increase of the used nodes number and star to be stable from n=100 nodes. But with IB-MAC, the results are better in terms of throughput, as in the case of TCP Vegas.

Fig. 4 and Fig. 5 show the evolution of the second parameter studied which is the end-to-end delay when the nodes number increases. With both transport protocols (TCP Vegas and TCP New Reno) and with MAC protocol, we find that with the used three routing protocols, this parameter significantly increaser with the increase of the used nodes number. The increase of the end-to-end delay is essentially due to the detection of frequent loss of TCP packets in the network more the number of nodes increased. These losses will be the cause for the frequent start of the congestion avoidance mechanism by the TCP protocol, so that will result in delaying the transmission of TCP packets and the increase in delay. This increase in delay begins to stabilize for the three routing protocols from n = 110 nodes and that below t = 1.2 s. Although the slight differences in performance, all protocols behave the same way.

Always for the end-to-end delay parameter (Fig. 4. and Fig. 5.), when the IB-MAC is used as MAC protocol we see that with the three routing protocols, the end-to-end delay is better. There is an important improvement of this parameter, even if there is a slight increase when the number of nodes increases but this decrease is smaller compared to the first case when the MAC protocol is used.

Scenario 2: plus topology in which node 1 sends for node n (Fig. 1. -B-).

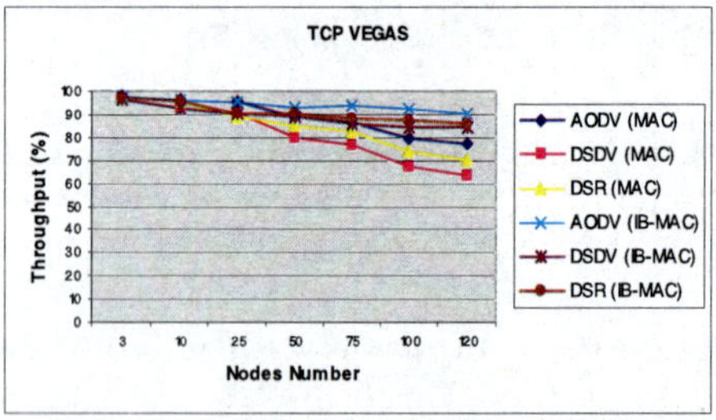

Fig. 6. Throughput with TCP Vegas and plus topology

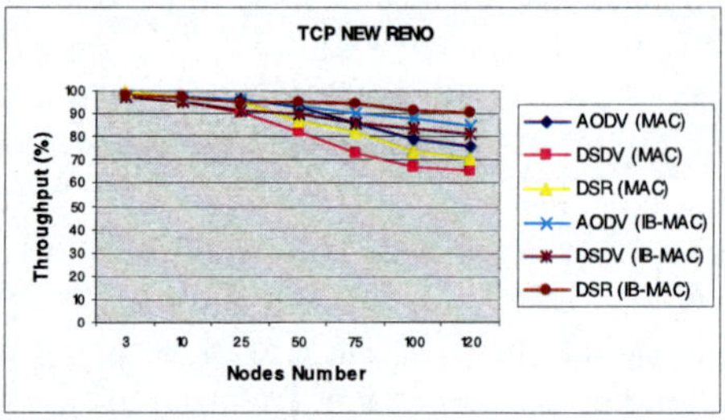

Fig. 7. Throughput with TCP New Reno and plus topology

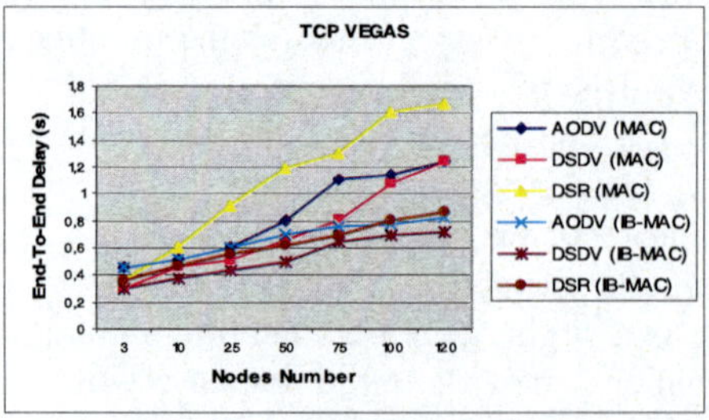

Fig. 8. End-To-End Delay with TCP Vegas and plus topology

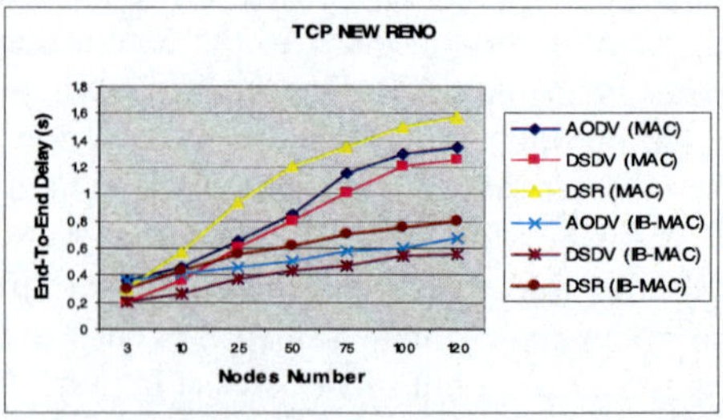

Fig. 9. End-To-End Delay with TCP New Reno and plus topology

Scenario 3: ring topology in which node 1 sends for node n (see Fig. 1. -C-).

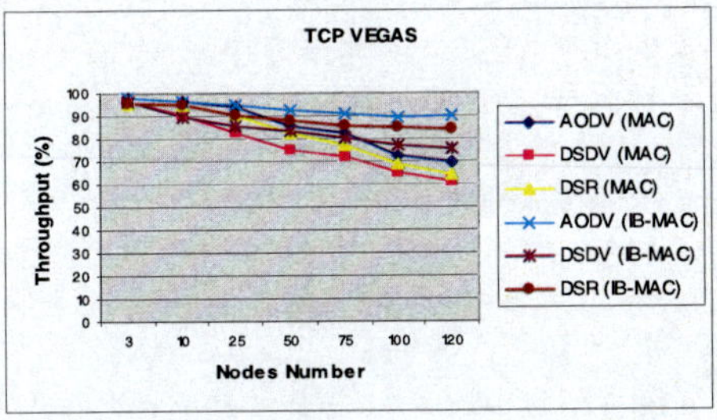

Fig. 10. Throughput with TCP Vegas and ring topology

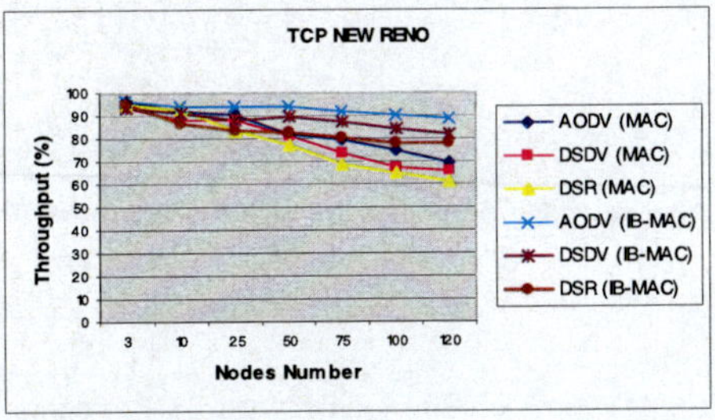

Fig. 11. Throughput with TCP New Reno and ring topology

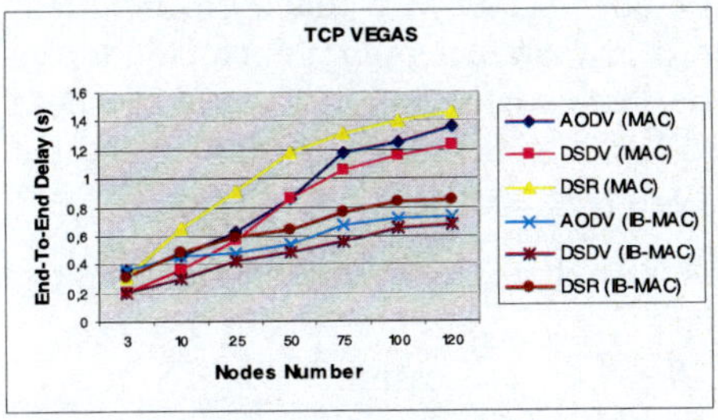

Fig. 12. End-To-End Delay with TCP Vegas and plus topology.

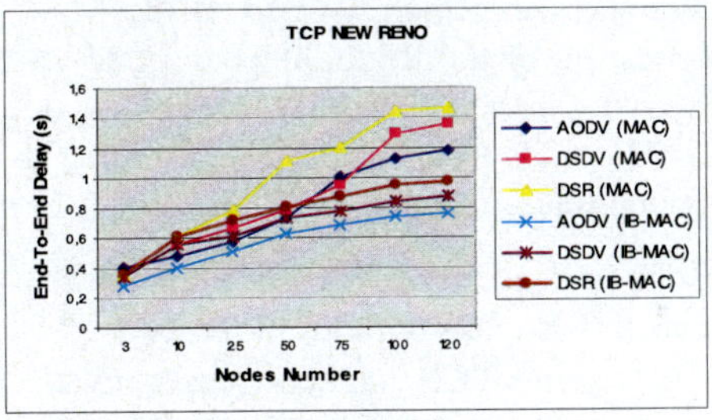

Fig. 13. End-To-End Delay with TCP New Reno and ring topology.

Through scenarios 2 and 3, we found that the results of the variation of the throughput and the end-to-end delay parameters are almost similar with those of scenario 1. So we can say that in the case where the nodes are static (no mobility), the degradation of these two parameters is presents with the different routing protocols, topology and TCP protocols. . But with IB-MAC solution, the throughput and end -to-end delay are better.

Scenario 4: random topology with weak mobility (speed W = 5 m/s).

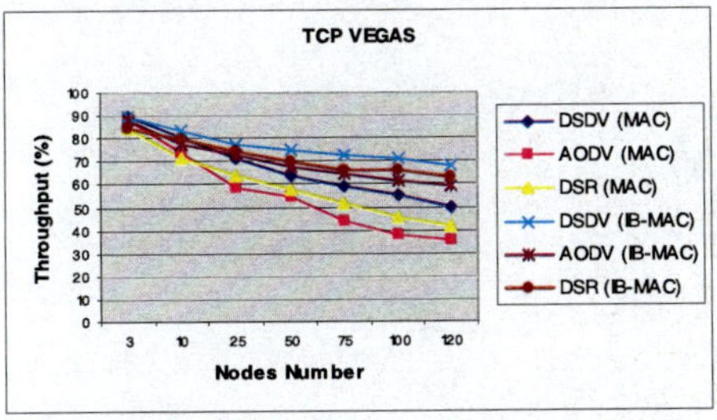

Fig. 14. Throughput with TCP Vegas with weak mobility (speed W = 5 m/s)

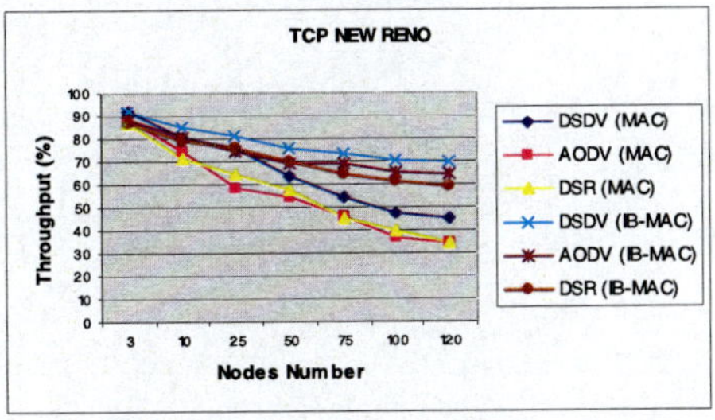

Fig. 15. Throughput with TCP New Reno with weak mobility (speed W = 5 m/s)

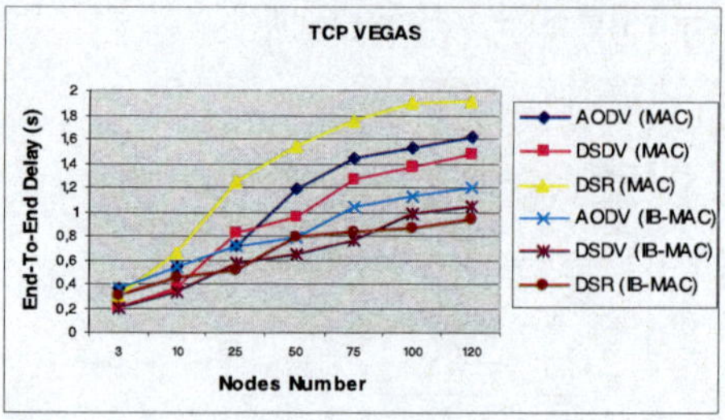

Fig. 16. End-To-End Delay with TCP Vegas and weak mobility (speed W = 5 m/s)

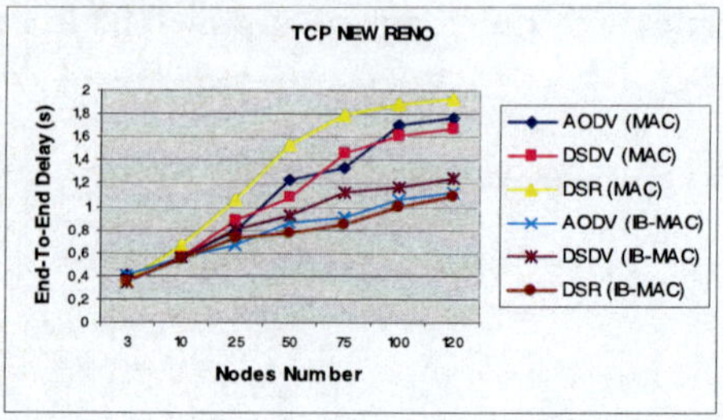

Fig. 17. End-To-End Delay with TCP New Reno and weak mobility (speed W = 5 m/s)

For the weak mobility, when the MAC protocol is used, we found an important degradation of the throughput and end-to-end delay parameters in comparison to the first case (without mobility) and that with the three routing protocols and the both TCP protocols (Vegas and New Reno). To explain this degradation, we analyzed the obtained trace files and we found:

i) The increase of RTS/CTS frames losses with the increase of nodes number in the network (first case without mobility);
ii) There are TCP packets losses even if there are successful RTS/CTS frames transmissions. In this case, these losses are caused by the unavailability route due the nodes mobility (the used route is outdated, denoted by "NRTE" in the trace file).

We deduce through i) and ii) that the mobility of nodes, although it is weak (here speed W = 5 m/s), participate to the degradation of the throughput and end-to-end delay parameters.

With our solution IB-MAC, always with weak mobility, we found an important improvement of the throughput and end-to-end delay parameters in comparison to the first case when the MAC protocol is used. This improvement is available with all the routing and transport protocols used.

Scenario 5: random topology with strong mobility (speed W = 25 m/s).

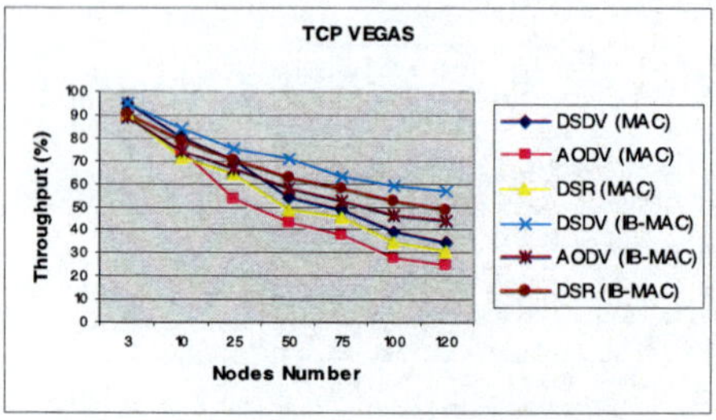

Fig. 18. Throughput with TCP Vegas with strong mobility (speed W = 25 m/s)

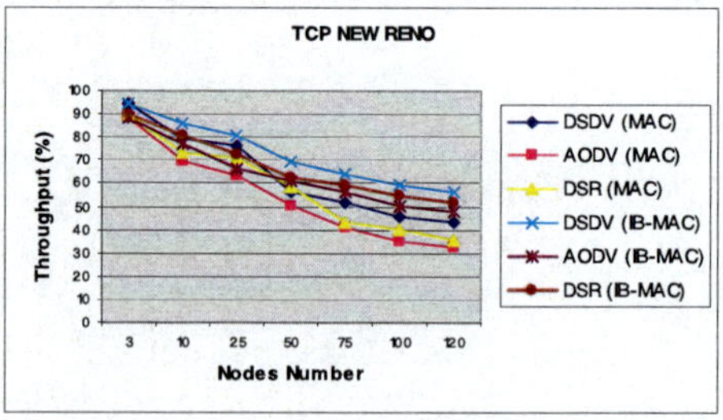

Fig. 19. Throughput with TCP NewReno and strong mobility (speed W=25 m/s)

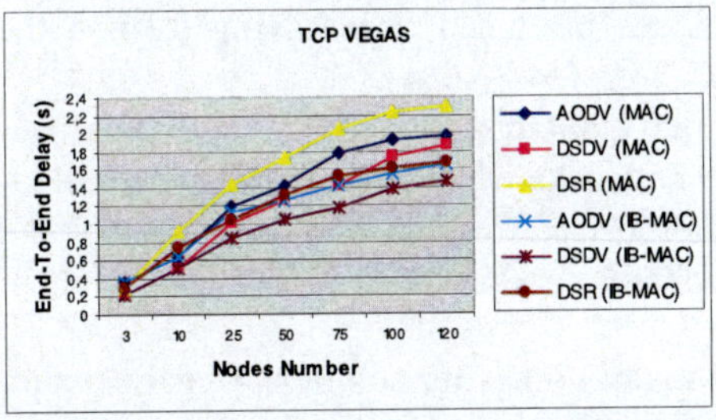

Fig. 20. End-To-End Delay with TCP Vegas and strong mobility (speed W = 25)

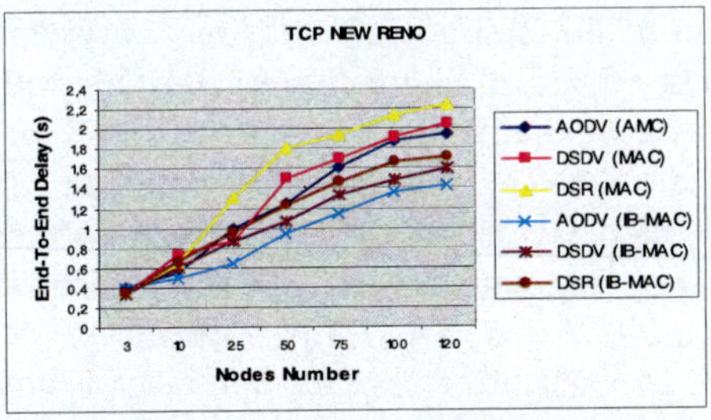

Fig. 21. End-To-End Delay with TCP New Reno and strong mobility (speed W = 25 m/s)

For strong mobility, we find that there is also a degradation of the throughput and end-to-end parameters when the MAC protocol is used, more important than the case with weak mobility because here the breaks connectivity increases then the links stability becomes more important. This degradation is observed with the three used routing protocols and the both TCP version. We have done the same analysis as above to know the reasons of this degradation; we found that the causes of this degradation are also related to those discussed in i) and ii) in weak mobility case.

In this case too (strong mobility), with our solution IB-MAC, we found an important improvement of the throughput and end-to-end delay parameters in comparison to the first case when the MAC protocol is used. This improvement is available with the routing and transport protocols used.

In fact, when the network has a weak mobility (nodes with low speeds), it presents a rather high stability; then links failure are less frequent than the case of a high mobility. Consequently, the fraction of data loss is smaller when for the case where nodes move at low speeds (strong mobility), and grows with the increase in their mobility. In the two case (weak and strong mobility), with the three routing protocols used (AODV, DSDV and DSR) and with the tow TCP versions (Vegas and New Reno), we note that with IB-MAC the network offers better results with the two TCP parameters (throughput and end-to-end delay) than those with MAC standard. This improved performance provided by IB-MAC is due to the fact that there is an adaptation of the maximal limit of the backoff algorithm, according to the nodes number and their mobility.

From these results, we can say that even in the case of a random topology where nodes are mobile (a feature specific to MANET networks) the IB-MAC solution improves the performance of TCP.

5 Conclusion

In this paper, we proposed an improvement of MAC protocol for better TCP protocol performance (throughput and end-to-end delay) in MANET. Our solution is IB-MAC which is a new Backoff algorithm making dynamic the CW_{max} terminal in depending on the number of nodes used in the network and their mobility. This adaptation is to reduce the number of collisions between nodes produced after having learned the same values of the interval Backoff algorithm.

We studied the effects of IB-MAC on the QoS in a MANET. We limited our studies on very important parameters in such networks which are throughput and end-to-end delay because they have great effects on the performance of TCP protocol and that of the total network. The results are satisfactory and show a marked improvement in the TCP and MANET performances.

As perspectives, we have to test for how many nodes our solutions remains valid, and also compare our solution to those proposed in the literature.

References

1. Basagni, S., Conti, M., Giordano, S., Stojmenovic, I.: Mobile Ad hoc Networking. Wiley-IEEE Press (2004) ;ISBN: 0-471-37313-3
2. Karn, P.: MACA - A New Channel Access Method for Packet Radio. In: Proc. 9th ARRL/CRRL Amateur Radio Computer, Networking Conference (1990)
3. Bhargavan, V., Demers, A., Shenker, S., Zhang, L.: MACAW, A Media Access Protocol for Wireless LANs. In: Proc. ACM SIGCOMM (1994)
4. Parsa, C., Garcia-Luna-Aceves, J.: TULIP - A Link-Level Protocol for Improving TCP over Wireless Links. In: Proc. IEEE WCNC (1999)
5. IEEE Std. 802.11. Wireless LAN Media Access Control (MAC) and Physical Layer (PHY) Specifications (1999)
6. Mjeku, M., Gomes, N.J.: Analysis of the Request to Send/Clear to Send Exchange in WLAN Over Fiber Networks. Journal of lightware technology 26(13-16), 2531–2539 (2008); ISSN: 0733-8724
7. Holland, G., Vaidya, N.: Analysis of TCP performance not over mobile ad hoc networks. In: Proc. ACM Mobicom (1999)
8. Hanbali, A., Altman, E., Nain, P.: A Survey of TCP over Ad Hoc Networks. IEEE Communications Surveys & Tutorials 7(3), 22–36 (2005)
9. Kurose, J., Ross, K.: Computer Networking: A top-down approach featuring the Internet. Addison-Wesley, Reading (2005)
10. Kawadia, V., Kumar, P.: Experimental investigations into TCP performance over wireless multihop networks. In: SIGCOMM Workshop on Experimental Approaches to Wireless Network Design and Analysis, E-WIND (2005)
11. Jiang, R., Gupta, V., Ravishankar, C.: Interactions Between TCP and the IEEE 802.11 MAC Protocol. In: DARPA Information Survivability Conference and Exposition (2003)
12. Nahm, K., Helmy, A., Kuo, C.-C.J.: On Interactions Between MAC and Transport Layers in 802.11 Ad-hoc Networks. In: SPIE ITCOM 2004, Philadelphia (2004)
13. Papanastasiou, S., Mackenzie, L., Ould-Khaoua, M., Charissis, V.: On the interaction of TCP and Routing Protocols in MANETs. In: Proc. of AICT/ICIW (2006)
14. Li, J.: Quality of Service (QoS) Provisioning in Multihop Ad Hoc Networks. Doctorate of Philosophy. Computer Science in the Office of Graduate Studies, California (2006)
15. Hamrioui, S., Bouamra, S., Lalam, M.: Interactions entre le Protocole MAC et le Protocole de Transport TCP pour l'Optimisation des MANET. In: Proc. of the 1st International Workshop on Mobile Computing & Applications (NOTERE 2007), Morocco (2007)
16. Hamrioui, S., Lalam, M.: Incidence of the Improvement of the Transport – MAC Protocols Interactions on MANET Performance. In: 8th Annual International Conference on New Technologies of Distributed Systems (NOTERE 2008), Lyon, France (2008)

17. Jayasuriya, A., Perreau, S., Dadej, A., Gordon, S.: Hidden vs. Exposed Terminal Problem in Ad hoc Networks. In: Proc. of the Australian Telecommunication Networks and Applications Conference, Sydney, Australia (2004)
18. Altman, E., Jimenez, T.: Novel Delayed ACK Techniques for Improving TCP Performance in Multihop Wireless Networks. In: Conti, M., Giordano, S., Gregori, E., Olariu, S. (eds.) PWC 2003. LNCS, vol. 2775, pp. 237–250. Springer, Heidelberg (2003)
19. Kuang, T., Xiao, F., Williamson, C.: Diagnosing wireless TCP performance problems: A case study. In: Proc. of SPECTS (2003)
20. Bakre, B., Badrinath, R.: I-TCP: Indirect TCP for mobile hosts. In: Proc. 15th Int. Conf. Distributed Computing Systems (1995)
21. Brown, K., Singh, S.: M-TCP: TCP for mobile cellular networks. ACM Compueer Communication Review 27(5) (1997)
22. Bensaou, B., Wang, Y., Ko, C.C.: Fair Media Access in 802.11 Based Wireless Ad-hoc Networks. In: Proc. Mobihoc (2000)
23. Gerla, M., Tang, K., Bagrodia, R.: TCP Performance in Wireless Multihop Networks. In: IEEE WMCSA (1999)
24. Gupta, A., Wormsbecker, C.: Experimental evaluation of TCP performance in multi-hop wireless ad hoc networks. In: Proc. of MASCOTS (2004)
25. Jain, A., Dubey, K., Upadhyay, R., Charhate, S.V.: Performance Evaluation of Wireless Network in Presence of Hidden Node: A Queuing Theory Approach. In: Second Asia International Conference on Modelling and Simulation (2008)
26. Marina, M.K., Das, S.R.: Impact of caching and MAC overheads on routing performance in ad hoc networks. Computer Communications (2004)
27. Ng, P.C., Liew, S.C., Sha, K.C., To, W.T.: Experimental Study of Hidden-node Problem in IEEE802.11 Wireless Networks. In: ACM SIGCOMM 2005, USA (2005)
28. Bakre, A., Badrinath, B.: I-tcp: Indirect tcp for mobile hosts. In: IEEE ICDCS 1995, Vancouver, Canada, pp. 136–143 (1995)
29. Balakrishnan, H., Seshan, S., Amir, E., Katz, R.: Improving tcp/ip performance over wireless networks. In: 1st ACM Mobicom, Vancouver, Canada (1995)
30. Brown, K., Singh, S.: M-tcp: Tcp for mobile cellular networks. ACM Computer Communications Review 27, 19–43 (1997)
31. Tsaoussidis, V., Badr, H.: Tcp-probing: Towards an error control schema with energy and throughput performance gains. In: 8th IEEE Conference on Network Protocols, Japan (2000)
32. Zhang, C., Tsaoussidis, V.: Tcp-probing: Towards an error control schema with energy and throughput performance gains. In: 11th IEEE/ACM NOSSDAV, New York (June 2001)
33. Yuki, T., Yamamoto, T., Sugano, M., Murata, M., Miyahara, H., Hatauchi, T.: Performance improvement of tcp over an ad hoc network by combining of data and ack packets. IEICE Transactions on Communications (2004)
34. Altman, E., Jiménez, T.: Novel delayed ACK techniques for improving TCP performance in multihop wireless networks. In: Conti, M., Giordano, S., Gregori, E., Olariu, S. (eds.) PWC 2003. LNCS, vol. 2775, pp. 237–250. Springer, Heidelberg (2003)
35. Kherani, A., Shorey, R.: Throughput analysis of tcp in multi-hop wireless networks with ieee 802.11 mac. In: IEEE WCNC 2004, Atlanta, USA (2004)
36. Allman, M.: On the generation and use of tcp acknowledgements. ACM Computer Communication Review 28, 1114–1118 (1998)

37. Chandran, K.: A feedback based scheme for improving TCP performance in ad-hoc wireless networks. In: Proc. of International Conference on Distributed Computing Systems (1998)
38. Holland, G., Vaidya, N.H.: Analysis of tcp performance over mobile ad hoc networks. In: Mobicom 1999, Seattle (1999)
39. Liu, J., Singh, S.: ATCP: TCP for mobile ad hoc networks. IEEE JSAC 19(7), 1300–1315 (2001)
40. Fu, Z., Greenstein, B., Meng, X., Lu, S.: Design and implementation of a tcp-friendly transport protocol for ad hoc wireless networks. In: 10th IEEE International Conference on Network Protocosls, ICNP 2002 (2002)
41. Biaz, S., Vaidya, N.H.: Distinguishing congestion losses from wireless transmission losses:a negative result. In: IEEE 7th Int. Conf. on Computer Communications and Networks, New Orleans, USA (1998)
42. Liu, J., Matta, I., Crovella, M.: End-to-end inference of loss nature in a hybrid wired/wireless environment. In: WiOpt 2003, INRIA Sophia-Antipolis, France (2003)
43. Kim, D., Toh, C., Choi, Y.: TCP-BuS: Improving TCP performance in wireless ad hoc networks. Journal of Communications and Networks 3(2), 175–186 (2001)
44. Toh, C.-K.: A Novel Distributed Routing Protocol to support Ad-Hoc Mobile Computing. In: Proc. of IEEE 15th Annual Int'l Phoenix Conf. Comp. and Commun. (1996)
45. Oliveira, R., Braun, T.: A Dynamic Adaptive Acknowledgment Strategy for TCP over Multihop Wireless Networks. In: Proc. of IEEE INFOCOM (2005)
46. Hamadani, E., Rakocevic.: A Cross Layer Solution to Address TCP Intra-flow Performance Degradation in Multihop Ad hoc Networks. Journal of Internet Engineering 2(1) (2008)
47. Zhai, H., Chen, X., Fang, Y.: Improving Transport Layer Performance in Multihop Ad Hoc Networks by Exploiting MAC Layer Information. IEEE Transactions on Wireless Communications 6(5) (2007)
48. Lohier, S., Doudane, Y.G., Pujolle, G.: MAC-layer Adaptation to Improve TCP Flow Performance in 802.11 Wireless Networks. In: WiMob 2006. IEEE Xplore, Canada (2006)
49. NS2. Network simulator, `http://www.isi.edu/nsnam`
50. Fall, K., Varadhan, K.: Notes and documentation. LBNL (1998), `http://www.mash.cs.berkeley.edu/ns`
51. Floyd, S., Jacobson, V.: Random Early Detection Gateways for Congestion Avoidance. IEEE/ACM Transactions on Networking 1, 397–413 (1993)
52. Bullington, K.: Radio Propagation Fundamentals. The Bell System Technical Journal 36(3) (1957)
53. Perkins, C.E., Royer, E.M., Das, S.R.: Ad Hoc On-Demand Distance-Vector (AODV) Routing. IETF Internet draft (draft-ietf-manet-aodv-o6.txt)
54. Johnson, D., Hu, Y., Maltz, D.: The Dynamic Source Routing Protocol (DSR) for Mobile Ad Hoc Networks for IPv4. RFC 4728, IETF (2007)
55. Perkins, C., Bhagwat, P.: Highly dynamic destination-sequenceddistance-vector routing (DSDV) for mobile computers. In: Proc. of ACM SIGCOMM Conference on Communications Architectures, Protocols and Applications, pp. 234–244 (1994)
56. Hyytiä, E., Virtamo, J.: Randomwaypoint model in n-dimensional space. Operations Research Letters 33 (2005)
57. Floyd, S., Henderson, T.: New Reno Modification to TCP's Fast Recovery. RFC 2582 (1999)
58. Xu, S., Saadawi, T., Lee, M.: Comparison of TCP Reno and Vegas in wireless mobile ad hoc networks. In: IEEE LCN (2000)

A Link-Disjoint Interference-Aware Multi-Path Routing Protocol for Mobile Ad Hoc Network

Phu Hung Le and Guy Pujolle

LIP6, University of Pierre and Marie Curie
4 place Jussieu 75005 Paris, France
{Phu-Hung.Le,Guy.Pujolle}@lip6.fr

Abstract. A mobile ad hoc network (MANET) is the network without any pre-existing communication infrastructure. Wireless mobile nodes can freely and dynamically self-organize into arbitrary and temporary network topologies. In MANET, the influence of interference is very significant for the network performance such as data loss, conflict, retransmission and so on. Therefore, interference is one of the factors that has the greatest impact to network performance. Reducing interference on the paths is a critical problem in order to increase performance of the network. In this paper, we propose a formula of interference and a novel Link-disjoint Interference-Aware Multi-Path routing protocol (LIA-MPOLSR) that was based on the Optimized Link State Routing protocol (OLSR) for MANET to increase the stability and reliability of the network. The more difference between LIA-MPOLSR and the other multi-path routing protocols is that LIA-MPOLSR calculates interference by taking into account of the geographic distance between nodes instead of hop-by-hop. We also use a mechanism to check the status of the received node before the data is transmitted through this node to increase transmission effects. From our simulation results, we show that the LIA-MPOLSR outperforms IA-OLSR, the original OLSR and OLSR-Feedback, measured by comparing packet delivery fraction, routing overhead and normalized routing load.

Keywords: Mobile Ad Hoc Networks; Multi-path; Routing Protocol; OLSR; Interference.

1 Introduction

In recent years, MANET has been widely studied because of its various applications in disaster recovery situations, defence (army, navy, air force), healthcare, academic institutions, corporate conventions/meetings, to name a few.

Currently, many multi-path routing protocols have been proposed such as on-demand protocol AOMDV [1] or proactive protocol SR-MPOLSR [2], and MPOLSR [3] etc. However, only a few multi-path routing protocols address the reduction of interference of the paths from a source to a destination.

In MANET, when a node transmits data to the others, this can cause interference to neighbor nodes. Interference reduces significantly the network performance such as

H. Cherifi, J.M. Zain, and E. El-Qawasmeh (Eds.): DICTAP 2011, Part I, CCIS 166, pp. 649–661, 2011.

data loss, conflict, retransmission and so on. To improve the network performance, we propose a formula of interference of a node, a link, a path and build a novel Link-disjoint Interference-Aware Multi-Path routing protocol (LIA-MPOLSR) that minimizes the influence of interference. The advantage of link-disjoint multi-path is that it can realise well in a quite sparse and dense network.

This paper is organized as follows. Following the first Section of introduction, Section 2 introduces the detail structure of LIA-MPOLSR protocol. Then Section 3, we compare the LIA-MPOLSR protocol with the Interference-Aware routing protocol (IA-OLSR), the original OLSR [4], OLSR-Feedback (OLSR-FB) [5]. Finally, we will summarize in Section 4.

2 The Link-Disjoint Interference-Aware Multi-Path Routing Protocol

2.1 Topology Information

In OLSR protocol, the link sensing and neighbor detection are performed by "HELLO" message. Each node periodically broadcasts "HELLO" message containing information about neighbor node and the current link status of the node.

Each node in the network broadcasts the "Topology Control" (TC) about the network topology. The information of network topology is recorded by every node. OLSR minimizes the overhead from flooding of control traffic by using only selected nodes, called Multipoint Relays (MPRs), to retransmit control messages.

Our protocol, LIA-MPOLSR, inherits all above characteristics. Moreover, LIA-MPOLSR also updates the position of all nodes, the interference level of all nodes and links.

2.2 Interference

In MANET, each node has two radio ranges, one is the transmission range (Rt) and the other is carrier sensing range (Rcs). Transmission range is the range that a node can transmit a packet successfully to other nodes without interference. The carrier sensing range is the range that a node can receive signals but cannot correctly decode the signal.

When a node transmits data, all nodes within the carrier sensing range are interfered. The level of the interference of a node depends on the distance from the transmitting node to received node.

The closer between two nodes in the network is, the higher interference impact is and vice versa.

The total interference on one node in the network is the sum of the received interference signals on that node. If the total interference signals are small enough, one can expect higher successful transmission.

In contrary, if the interference signals exceed a certain threshold, the data cannot be correctly decoded or even not detected, so interference is one of the most important factor affecting network performance. Therefore, interference reduction has been considered to increase network quality and performance.

In [6], the interference of a node is defined as the total useless signals that is transmitted by other nodes within its interference range. The interference of link and path are total useless signals transmitted by other nodes within their interference ranges.

On the other hand, the interference of a node is the total of the node within its interference range. Link interference of network is the average of the total interference of each node forming the link. Interference of a path is the total interference of the every links forming the path.

2.3 Measurement of Interference

As we know, interference of a node depends on the distance from the node to other nodes in the interference range of it. To exactly calculate the interference of a node, a link and a path we divide whole interference region of a node into smaller interference regions. The interference calculation will be more precise as we divide the interference area of a node into more smaller areas. However, it increases the calculation complexity.

In this paper, we divide the interference region into four regions. This choice is a compromise between the precision and the calculation complexity. The interference regions are following.

The whole interference of a node can be considered as a circle with a radius of Rcs (carrier sensing range), with the centre is the considered node. The four zones are determined by R_1, R_2, R_3 and R_4 as follows (Figure 1).

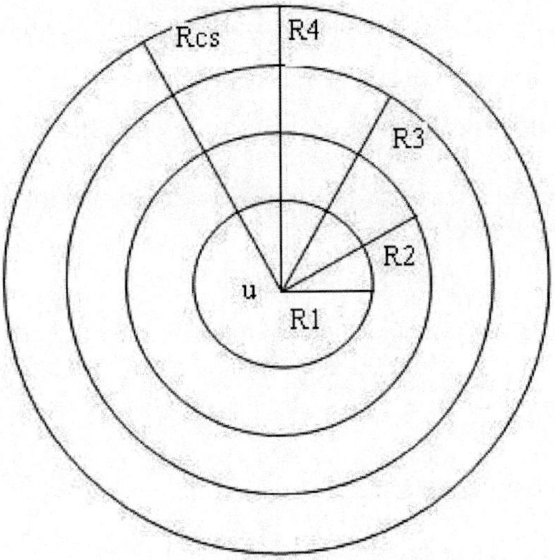

Fig. 1. Illustration of radii of interference

zone1: $0<d<=R_1$, $R_1=1/4Rcs$
zone2: $R_1<d<=R_2$, $R_2=2/4Rcs$
zone3: $R_2<d<=R_3$, $R_3=3/4Rcs$
zone4: $R_3<d<=R_4$, $R_4=Rcs$
where d is the transmitter- receiver distance.

For each zone, we assign an interference weight which represents the interference level that a node present in this zone causes to the considered node in the center.

If the weight of interference of zone1 is 1, the weight of interference of zone2, zone3 and zone4 are α, β and γ respectively ($\gamma < \beta < \alpha < 1$). We can calculate the interference of a node u in MANET as follows:

$$I(u)=n1+\alpha.n2+\beta.n3+\gamma.n4. \quad (1)$$

where n1, n2, n3 and n4 are the number of nodes in zone1, zone2, zone3 and zone4 respectively. Parameters α, β and γ are determined as follows. According to [7], in Two-Ray Ground path loss model, the receiving power (P_r) of a signal from a sender d meters away can be modeled as Eq.(2).

$$P_r = P_t\, G_t\, G_r\, h_t^2\, h_r^2/d^k \quad (2)$$

In Eq. (2), G_t and G_r are antenna gains of transmitter and receiver, respectively. P_t is the transmitting power of a sender node. h_t and h_r are the height of both antennas respectively. Here, we assume that MANET is homogeneous, that is all the radio parameters are identical at each node.

$$\alpha = (P_t\, G_t\, G_r\, h_t\, h_r/R_2^k)/(P_t\, G_t\, G_r\, h_t\, h_r/R_1^k)=R_1^k/R_2^k=0.5^k$$
$$\beta = (P_t\, G_t\, G_r\, h_t\, h_r/R_3^k)/(P_t\, G_t\, G_r\, h_t\, h_r/R_1^k)=R_1^k/R_3^k=0.33^k$$
$$\gamma = (P_t\, G_t\, G_r\, h_t\, h_r/R_4^k)/(P_t\, G_t\, G_r\, h_t\, h_r/R_1^k)=R_1^k/R_4^k=0.25^k$$

We assume that common path loss model used in wireless networks is the open space path loss which has k as 2. Therefore, $\alpha=0.25$, $\beta=0.11$, $\gamma=0.06$ and

$$I(u) = n1+0.25n2+0.11n3+0.06n4 \quad (3)$$

Based on the formula of interference of a node we can calculate the interference of the links as below:

A Link interconnecting two nodes u and v, e=(u,v); I(u) and I(v) are the interference of u, v respectively.

$$I(e)=(I(u)+I(v))/2 \quad (4)$$

Based on the formula (4), we can calculate interference of a path P that consists of links e_1 e_2 ,...,e_n

$$I(P)=I(e_1)+I(e_2)+\ldots+I(e_n)$$

2.4 LIA-MPOLSR Protocol Design

2.4.1 The Building of IA-OLSR

The Interference-Aware routing protocol (IA-OLSR) is a single path routing protocol with minimum interference from a source to a destination. We build IA-OLSR as follows.

a) Specifying n1, n2, n3, n4

According to the formula (3), the interference of a node u in MANET is
$I(u) = n1+0.25n2+0.11n3+0.06n4$

Each node of MANET has a co-ordinate (x,y). The co-ordinate of a node in MANET can be defined by writing a program in NS-2. If the co-ordinate of u, v is (x1,y1), (x2,y2), respectively then distance between u and v is

$$\sqrt{(x1-x2)^2+(y1-y2)^2} \tag{5}$$

The formula (5) is used to calculate the distances between u and all other nodes in MANET. After comparing those distances to R_1, R_2, R_3, and R_4 we will have the number of nodes in zone1, zone2, zone3, and zone4 of node u.

In IA-OLSR, topology information of MANET is maintained and updated by each node. When any node changes its status, its information and position are updated. The distances between it and other nodes are recomputed. Therefore, interference of nodes and links is recomputed too.

b) Modelling MANET as a Weighted Graph

MANET can be considered as a weighted graph (Figure 2) where nodes of MANET are vertices of the graph and the edges of the graph are any two neighbor nodes. The weight of each edge is the interference level of the corresponding link.

This graph is dynamic. The edges and the weight of them are changed when any node changes its status.

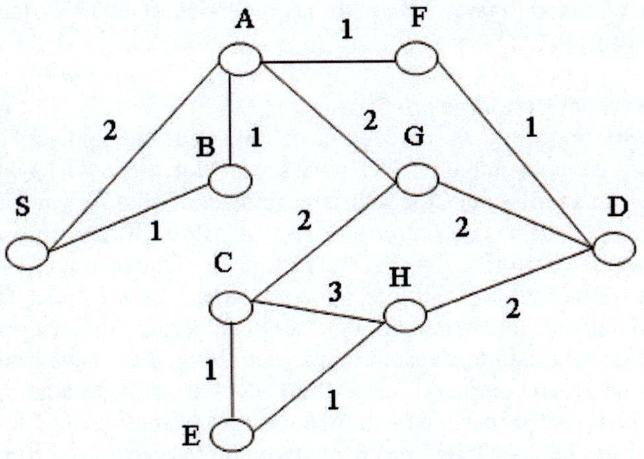

Fig. 2. Illustration of a weighted graph

c) Using Dijsktra's Algorithm

Applying Dijsktra's algorithm to the weighted graph above we will have the minimum interference path from the source to the destination.

2.4.2 Algorithm of Link-Disjoint Multi-Path

In MANET, multi-path can be divided into three categories as follows:

- Node-disjoint multi-path: the paths have only common source and destination.
- Link-disjoint multi-path: the paths can share a few common nodes but not links.
- Hybrid: Multi-path where the paths may be some common links and nodes.

To build the algorithm of link-disjoint multi-path, we perform as following steps :

- Step 1: Find the single path with minimum interference based on the IA-OLSR algorithm.

- Step 2: Dijkstra's algorithm is used one more time while avoiding any link between the source and the destination along the path found in the step 1. We then get the second minimum interference path from the source to the destination.

- Step 3: Dijkstra's algorithm is repeated for a number of times k (k=3,...,n) and while avoiding any link between the source and the destination along the paths found in the previous steps to find k-minimum interference path.

In the Figure 2, we illustrate an example for MANET that is considered as a weighted graph. The weight of each edge is set on the edge.

When applying Dijsktra's algorithm at the first time for this weighted graph with the source S and the destination D, we get the minimum interference path S-A-F-D that has the value of 4.

The second minimum interference path S-B-A-G-D is found by employing Dijsktra's algorithm once again. This path has the value of 6. This graph has not the third link-disjoint path.

2.4.3 Route Recovery and Forwarding

In LIA-MPOLSR, topology of network is maintained and updated by each node through "HELLO" message and "TC" message. Moreover, LIA-MPOLSR also updates the position of all nodes, the interference level of all nodes and links.

The mechanism of the packet forwarding in LIA-MPOLSR performs as follows.

When a node wants to forward packets to next node in the path that found, one more check has been conducted by sent node to confirm the received node. The packet will be transmitted without any problem on the path. Otherwise, the node will use immediately a different path to transmit the packet. When there have been no available paths, the paths will be recomputed. LIA-MPOLSR is also able to detect the failed link as in [5]. When the first packet is dropped it stops transmitting the packets and recalculate the routing table. These mechanisms could help to enhance the stability and reliability of the network.

3 Performance Evaluation

3.1 Simulation Environment

The protocol is implemented in NS2 with 10 Mbps channel. Traffic source is CBR. The distributed coordination function (DCF) of IEEE 802.11 for wireless LANs is used as the

MAC layer. The Two-Ray Ground and the Random Waypoint models have been used. Each node has a transmission range of 160 meters and a carrier sensing range of 400 meters. The simulation is performed on the network of 30 and 50 nodes. These nodes can move randomly within the area of 700m x 800m and the pause time is set to 0s.

3.2 Simulation Results

With the network of 50 nodes and 30 nodes, we compare four protocols LIA-MPOLSR, IA-OLSR, the original OLSR and OLSR-Feedback(OLSR-FB) for:

1-Packet delivery fraction (PDF)
2-Routing overhead
3-Normalized routing load(NRL)

a) The network of 50 nodes

In the first simulation, the nodes move randomly within the area of 700m x800m, the speed of the nodes is from 4 m/s to 10 m/s, the packet size of 512 bytes and Constant Bit Rate (CBR) changes from 320 Kbps to 1024 Kbps.

As shown in Figure 3, the PDF of LIA-MPOLSR can be approximately 13% higher than that of IA-OLSR, 39% than that of the original OLSR and 34% than that of OLSR-FB. The PDF of LIA-MPOLSR is higher than IA-OLSR, the original OLSR and OLSR-FB because LIA-MPOLSR has the backup paths and its paths were only influenced by lower interference.

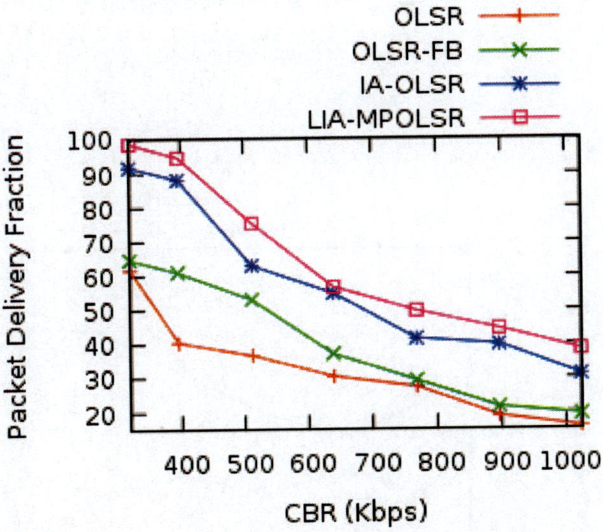

Fig. 3. Packet delivery fraction

Routing overhead of LIA-MPOLSR is possibly 6% lower than that of IA-OLSR, 11% than that of the original OLSR and OLSR-FB as shown in Figure 4. For the reason that IA-OLSR, the original OLSR and OLSR-FB have only one path. They must discover a new path when their path is broken while LIA-MPOLSR only looks for new paths when all its paths are broken, therefore, LIA-MPOLSR can reduce the quantity of the path discoveries. Moreover, the number of packet retransmissions of LIA-MPOLSR is less than IA-OLSR, the original OLSR, and OLSR-FB because its lost packets are lower.

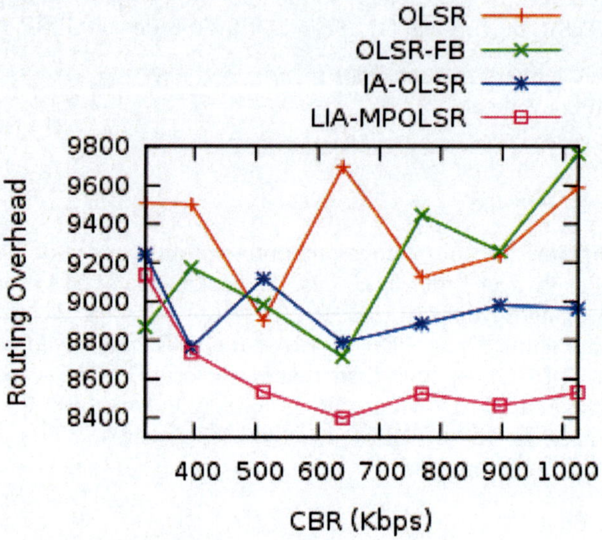

Fig. 4. Routing overhead

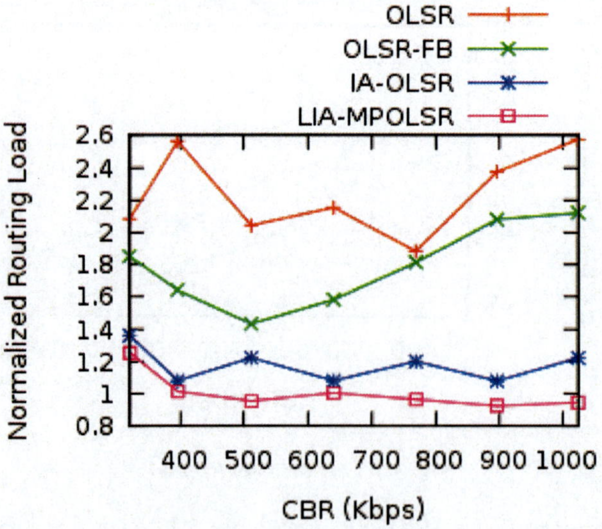

Fig. 5. Normalized routing load

Figure 5 shows that the NRL of LIA-MPOLSR decreases possibly 23% compared to that of IA-OLSR, 60% to that of the original OLSR and 50% to that of OLSR-FB. That is because the number of the lost packets and routing overhead of LIA-MPOLSR are less than IA-OLSR, the original OLSR and also OLSR-FB.

In the second simulation, the nodes move with the same speed from 1 m/s to 10 m/s, the packet size is 512 bytes and CBR value of 396 Kbps.

As shown in Figure 6, when the nodes move with the speed from 5 m/s to 10 m/s, the packets of IA-OLSR, the original OLSR and OLSR-FB were lost significantly, therefore, the PDF of LIA-MPOLSR can exceed that of IA-OLSR, the original OLSR and OLSR-FB by 17%, 48% and 40%, respectively.

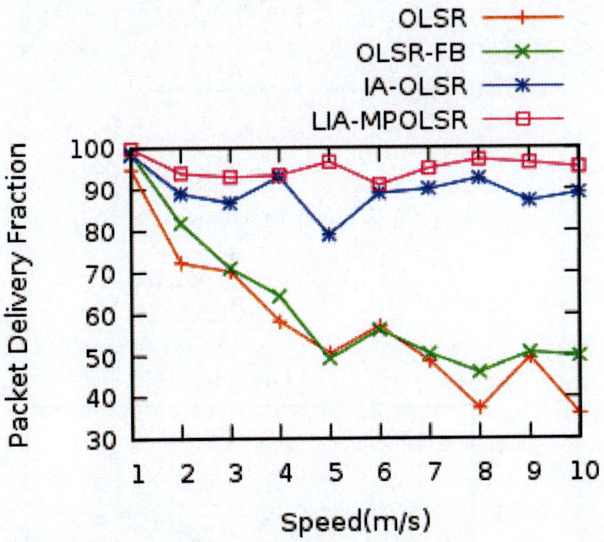

Fig. 6. Packet delivery fraction

Routing overhead of LIA-MPOLSR is about 8% less than that of IA-OLSR, 20% than that of the original OLSR and 14% than that of OLSR-FB as shown in Figure 7. Due to the fact that when the nodes move rapidly, the break of the unique path of IA-OLSR, the original OLSR and OLSR-FB always happens, thus they must look for a new path. On the contrary, LIA-MPOLSR has backup paths. Furthermore, the lost packets of IA-OLSR, the original OLSR, and OLSR-FB are more than LIA-MPOLSR, thus the number of packet retransmissions of IA-OLSR, the original OLSR and OLSR-FB increases.

For the reason that the lost packets and routing overhead of LIA-MPOLSR are lower than IA-OLSR, the original OLSR and OLSR-FB, hence the NRL of LIA-MPOLSR has the ability to reduce approximately 17% compared to that of IA-OLSR, 67 % to that of the original OLSR and 57 % to that of OLSR-FB as shown in Figure 8.

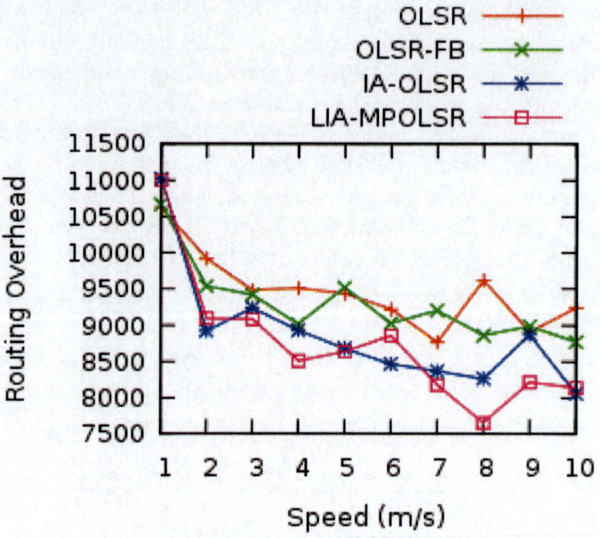

Fig. 7. Routing overhead

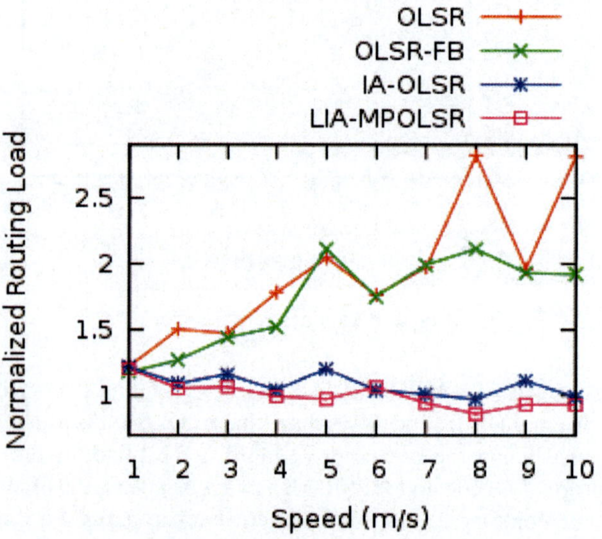

Fig. 8. Normalized routing load

b) The network of 30 nodes

The nodes move randomly within the area of 700m x800m, the speed of the nodes is from 4 m/s to 10 m/s, the packet size of 512 bytes and Constant Bit Rate (CBR) varies from 320 Kbps to 1024 Kbps.

As shown in Figure 9, the PDF of LIA-MPOLSR can only be approximately 8% higher than that of IA-OLSR, 30% than that of the original OLSR and 25% than that of OLSR-FB. It is because in a sparse network, the interference impact reduces.

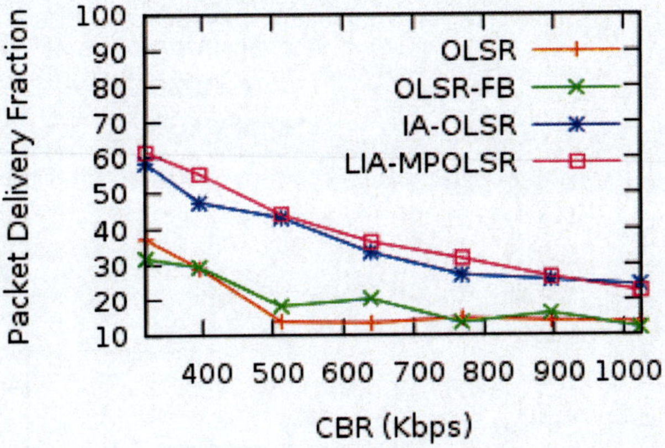

Fig. 9. Packet delivery fraction

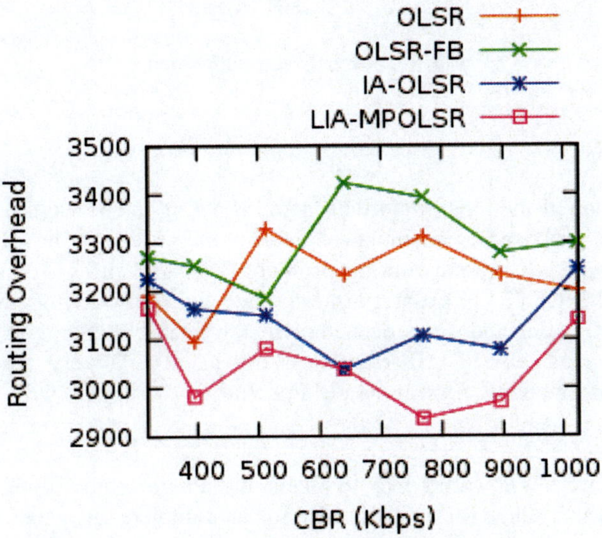

Fig. 10. Routing overhead

Routing overhead of LIA-MPOLSR is possibly 7% lower than that of IA-OLSR, 12% than that of the original OLSR and 13% than that of OLSR-FB as shown in Figure 10.

For the reason that the lost packets and routing overhead of LIA-MPOLSR are less than that of IA-OLSR, the original OLSR and OLSR-FB, therefore, the NRL of LIA-MPOLSR has the ability to reduce by 18% compared to that of IA-OLSR, 69 % to that of the original OLSR and 59 % to that of OLSR-FB as shown in Figure 11.

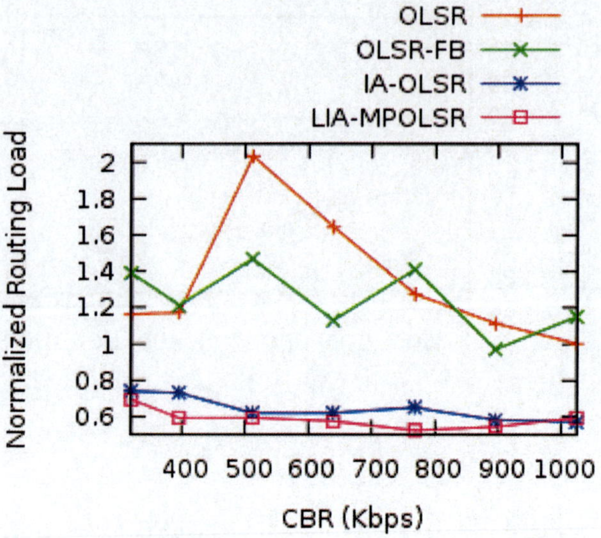

Fig. 11. Normalized routing load

4 Conclusion

Interference is one of the most important factor affecting the network performance. In this paper, we proposed a formula of interference and a novel Link-disjoint Interference-Aware Multi-Path routing protocol (LIA-MPOLSR) for mobile ad hoc network. LIA-MPOLSR calculates interference by considering the geographic distance between nodes and it has been shown significantly better than IA-OLSR, the original OLSR and also OLSR-Feedback for packet delivery fraction, routing overhead and normalized routing load. For future work, we will improve our protocol.

Acknowledgments. We would like to thank the Phare team, Lip6, University of Pierre Marie Curie, France for valuable help to can complete this paper.

References

1. Marina, M.K., Das, S.R.: On-demand Multipath Distance Vector Routing for Ad Hoc Networks. In: Proc. of 9th IEEE Int. Conf. On Network Protocols, pp. 14–23 (2001)
2. Zhou, X., Lu, Y., Xi, B.: A novel routing protocol for ad hoc sensor networks using multiple disjoint paths. In: 2nd International Conference on Broadband Networks, Boston, MA, USA (2005)
3. Jiazi, Y., Eddy, C., Salima, H., Benoît, P., Pascal, L.: Implementation of Multipath and Multiple Description Coding in OLSR. In: 4th Introp/Workshop, Ottawa, Canada
4. Clausen, T., Jacquet, P.: IETF Request for Comments: 3626, Optimized Link State Routing Protocol OLSR (October 2003)

5. UM-OLSR, http://masimum.dif.um.es/?Software:UM-OLSR
6. Xinming, Z., Qiong, L., Dong, S., Yongzhen, L., Xiang, Y.: An Average Link Interference-aware Routing Protocol for Mobile Ad hoc Networks. In: Conference on Wireless and Mobile Communications, ICWMC 2007 (2007)
7. Xu, K., Gerla, M., Bae, S.: Effectiveness of RTS/CTS handshake in IEEE 802.11 based ad hoc networks. Journal of Ad Hoc Networks 1(1), 107–123 (2003)
8. Perkins, C.E., Royer, E.M.: Ad-Hoc on demand distance vector routing. In: IEEE Work-Shop on Mobile Computing Systems and Applications (WMCSA) New Orleans, pp. 90–100 (1999)
9. Perkins, C.E., Royer, E.M.: Ad Hoc On Demand Distance Vector (AODV) Routing. Draft-ietf-manet- aodv-02.txt (November 1998) (work in progress)
10. David, B.J., David, A.M., Josh, B.: DSR: The Dynamic Source Routing Protocol for Multi-Hop Wireless Ad Hoc Networks. In: Ad Hoc Networking, pp. 139–172. Addison-Wesley, Reading (2001)
11. Olsrd, an adhoc wireless mesh routing daemon, http://www.olsr.org/
12. Perkins, C.E., Bhagwat, P.: Highly dynamic destination-sequenced distance-vector routing (DSDV) for mobile computers. In: Proceedings of ACM Sigcomm (1994)
13. Burkhart, M., Rickenbach, P., Wattenhofer, R., Zollinger, A.: Does topology control reduce interference? In: Proc. of ACM MobiHoc (2004)
14. Johansson, T., Carr-Motyckova, L.: Reducing interference in ad hoc networks through topology control. In: Proc. of the ACM/SIGMOBILE Workshop on Foundations of Mobile Computing (2005)
15. Haas, Pearlman: Zone Routing Protocol (1997)
16. Moaveni-Nejad, K., Li, X.: Low-interference topology control for wireless ad hoc networks. Ad Hoc& Sensor Wireless Networks: an International Journal (2004)
17. Lee, S.J., Gerla, M.: Split Multi-Path Routing with Maximally Disjoint Paths in Ad Hoc Networks. In: IEEE ICC 2001, pp. 3201–3205 (2001)
18. Park, V.D., Corson, M.S.: A highly adaptive distributed routing algorithm for mobile wireless networks. In: Proceedings of IEEE Infocom (1997)

Strategies to Carry and Forward Packets in VANET

Gianni Fenu and Marco Nitti

Department of Computer Science, University of Cagliari,
Via Ospedale 72, 09124 Cagliari, Italy
{fenu,marconitti}@unica.it

Abstract. The aim of this paper is to find the best strategies to carry and forward packets within VANETs that follows a Delay Tolerant Network. In this environment nodes are affected by intermittent connectivity and topology constantly changes. When no route is available and the link failure percentage is high, the data must be physically transported by vehicles to destination. Results show how, using vehicles cooperation and several carry and forward mechanisms with different deliver priorities, is possible to improve performance for free in terms of data delivery.

Keywords: VANET; Delay Tolerant Network; Carry and Forward mechanism; Idle Periods; mobility modeling.

1 Introduction

Vehicular Ad-hoc Networks or VANETs are particular type of mobile networks where nodes are vehicles and no fixed infrastructure is needed to manage connection and routing among them. Vehicles, in a pure VANET, are self-organized and self-configured thanks to "ad hoc" routing protocols that manage message exchange. These characteristics make this technology a good solution to create applications for safety purposes or simply to avoid traffic congestion. Vehicle's inside devices are also designed to access internet when a gateway is encountered. Road Side Unit (RSU) or Access Point (AP) could be used as gateways in a hybrid VANET to work as intermediates between vehicles and other networks. Often cars move at high speeds and this behavior reduces transmission capacity, creating issues like:

1. Rapid change of network topology. The state of connectivity between nodes is constantly evolving.
2. Frequent disconnections. When traffic density is low, distance between vehicles can reach several kilometers beyond the range of the wireless link and this involve link failure that can last several minutes.
3. High nodes congestion in heavy traffic conditions can affect the protocol performance.
4. High level of packet losses. Measurements of UDP and TCP transmissions of vehicles in a highway passing in front of an AP moving at different speeds, report losses on the order of 50-60% depending on the nominal sending rate and vehicle speed.

H. Cherifi, J.M. Zain, and E. El-Qawasmeh (Eds.): DICTAP 2011, Part I, CCIS 166, pp. 662–674, 2011.

5. Addressing. Every node must be addressed unambiguously.
6. Environment obstacles like tunnels, traffic jams, lakes etc. could interfere with the transmission signal.
7. Interoperability with other networks has to be achieved. Nodes must be able to exchange data with other types of networks, especially those based on fixed IP addresses.

For these reasons all standard routing protocols result inadequate to ensure good connection and achieve high performance. In order to obtain suitable routing protocols we have to exploit the characteristics of VANET. An interesting property of vehicles is that they move along roads unchanged for years and this allow recognizing specific mobility patterns. So knowing vehicles speed, direction and position we can predict their future geographic locations and plan some strategies to deliver the packets exploiting vehicles cooperation. This paper is based on a scenario already used in [1] by Fiore and Barcelos, with the difference that we measure how traffic data varies using different deliver priorities. We have introduced in our code a parameter called alpha in order to manage cooperators behavior during delivery. Alpha, in fact, can influence the choice of possible receivers for each cooperator and change, in this way, the overall amount of data delivered or the number of files completely downloaded. In this framework nodes can download information from fixed infrastructure scattered in the topology or from other vehicles. Infrastructures can be placed in highway or in urban centre. In addition AP, using vehicle information, can detect and warn the next AP on the path, which can prepare in advance the data to send or anticipate vehicles meeting. These techniques can be used to implement a carry and forward mechanism to exploit time used by vehicles to cross dark areas between different AP coverage and deliver data to nodes that travel in opposite direction. The main contribution of this paper is:

1. Definition of a Vehicular Ad Hoc Network scenario that opportunistically allows downloading packets when vehicles cross AP.
2. Definition of AP idle period and research of how traffic density influence its duration. Results are obtained with simulations executed on data taken from the multi-agent traffic simulator developed at ETH Zurich where the traffic approximates a $M/GI/\infty$ queue system.
3. Proposal of several scheduling mechanisms that exploit AP idle periods to organize distribution of packets to specific vehicles called cooperators whose task is to physically carry data toward the final destination. Giving different deliver priorities we discover how to help vehicles to finish their translation faster in order to allow them to help in future cooperation.

The paper is organized as follows: section 2 discuss related work. Section 3 describes the vehicular scenario showing the amount of AP idle periods obtained from simulations. Section 4 proposes scheduling algorithms (and related results) in order to benefit from the carry and forward concept. Section 5 offers some conclusions.

2 Related Work

In this years have been proposed several protocols to route data in VANET and we can group them in two main categories:

1. Topology-based routing that can be:
   - *Proactive* in which topology is constantly updated due to periodical collection of traffic conditions.
   - *Reactive* where the topology overview is update only when requested.
   - *Hybrid* that is a combination of the previous (proactive for near destinations and reactive for far destinations).
2. Position-based routing or geographic routing in which we need:
   - *Location service* to find the destination. This unit is important because geographic routing protocols don't use IP to address nodes that can be identified only using coordinates and unique ID.
   - *Forwarding Strategies* to send the packet to the destination reliably and as quick as possible.

Actually all the protocols studied can be situated in one of this two categories. The correct strategy must be taken, considering the feature of the network in which we're working. In our scenario, where there isn't total coverage and transmissions are affected by long delays, the best choice is the geographic routing protocol category. In particular we focus on opportunistic forwarding strategies, in which nodes schedule the forwarding of packets according to opportunities; [2], [3] e [4]. The opportunity may be based on: historical path likelihoods, [2], packet replication, [3], or on the expected packet forwarding delay, [4]. These scheduling mechanisms are based on epidemic [5] and probabilistic routing [6] and their objective is to optimize contact opportunities between vehicle and AP to forward packets in intermittent scenarios. However, these protocols don't consider how to exploit the vehicle-vehicle contacts. If we know meetings in advance, we can involve some unaware passersby in communication and let them physically carry data to destination. SPAWN, [7], is a good example of cooperative strategy for content delivery. It works using peer-peer swarming protocol (like bit torrent) including a gossip mechanism that leverages the inherent broadcast nature of the wireless medium, and a piece-selection strategy that uses proximity to exchange pieces quicker. We assume that our scenario use similar SPAWN based mechanism that works at a high abstraction level (above data-link layer) to improve the distribution of popular files among vehicles. Imagine, for example, a VANET where a group of nodes try to download the first page of the local newspaper sharing chunks of information when they meet. Unique difference between two scenarios is that SPAWN considers unidirectional traffic over highways while we consider a more complex urban environment.

3 AP Idle Time and Suitable Conditions

In this section we describe the simulation scenario and how we calculate AP idle periods using different traffic densities. Then we show results obtained and explain which are best conditions to perform Carry and Forward (C&F) mechanism in order to obtain good performance.

In our scenario vehicles download information from fixed infrastructure or AP located along roads. AP are connected via backbone and scattered among the topology without cover the whole path followed by vehicles, (intermittent connectivity). When a vehicle reaches the AP coverage for the first time obtains identification (Node-ID) and then starts to periodically broadcast its direction, speed and ID. These beacons of information converge to a common server that gets a constantly updated overview of the topology. Actually we only know status of vehicles under coverage but it's possible to predict for each of them the instant when they leave AP and start travel in dark areas due to historical paths. TCP / IP stack protocols don't provide an high data transfer to vehicles due to the harsh physical conditions in which they have to communicate, so AP are provided of storing and computing capabilities as happens in Delay Tolerant Network (DTN), [8]. If some packets are lost, AP doesn't perform retransmission immediately but waits until it finishes the block of data that was transmitting in order to optimize band. The server uses vehicles status (speed, direction, id) to choose how to manage data distribution among AP. When an AP receives data from server, starts to exchange information with its neighbors about vehicles traveling under its coverage in order to schedule packets between cooperators, hoping that they can meet the real destination while travel in dark areas. Packets are transferred from server to AP (custodians in DTN terminology) using TCP/IP stack protocols. In highway scenarios in which vehicles follow the same direction for long periods, the server predicts without doubts which will be the next AP on the path. From now on we will use specific terminology to refer to actors in the network:

- *Consumer* is a vehicle that downloads whenever has the opportunity.
- *Receiver* is a consumer that is designed to receive data from cooperators. It is discover by the C&F mechanism. Consumer usually becomes receiver if has high probability to meet cooperators during its trip.
- *Cooperator* is a common vehicle that can be used by AP to carry packets to receivers.
- *Idle period* is the time's slot in which the AP has no consumers under coverage. AP isn't really idle because it's busy to manage cooperation between cooperators but for simplicity we continue to use this term.
- *Dark area* represent the stretch of road between two coverage.

As we can see in Fig. 1, consumers can only receive data when are under AP coverage and when they leave it, have to wait to reach the next AP to resume their download. We desire to exploit this dead time using the idle periods of AP to schedule the data among cooperators. With a correct study of topology and an optimized packets distribution, cooperators will be able to meet consumers during their trip in dark areas and deliver to them the information that they are carrying.

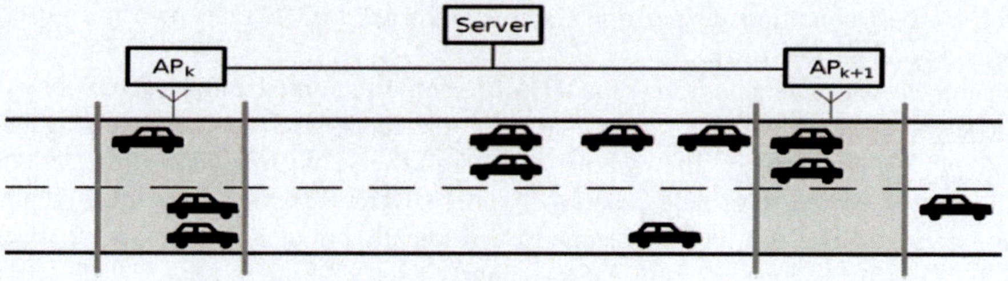

Fig. 1. Network scenario

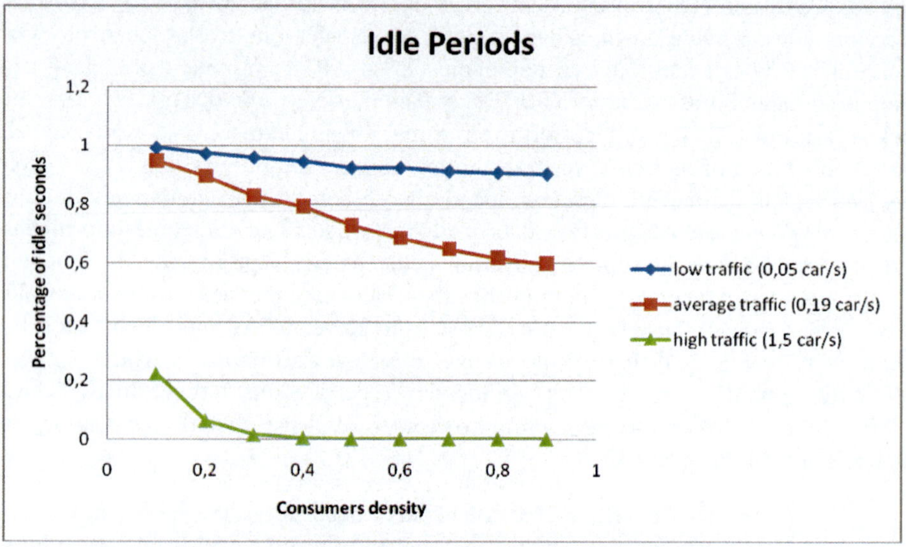

Fig. 2. Idle periods calculated with different traffic density

Our simulations use selected real-world road topologies from the area of Zurich, Switzerland, due to the availability of large-scale microscopic-level traces of the vehicular mobility, [9]. The traces reflect both macro-mobility patterns of thousands of vehicles and micro-mobility vehicle behaviors of individual drivers using a queue-based model. In particular, without loss of generality, we focus on the canton of Schlieren as summarized characteristics of low, medium and high traffic. We didn't use traditional network simulator, such as ns-2, due to the elevate number of vehicles reported in our trace. Instead, we use Matlab to manage properly this huge amount of data thanks to optimized operations between tables. In each experiment, before calculate idle periods, we have to set three parameters: (i) AP position (the choice can be made based on traffic density or environment conditions), (ii) δ or consumers density and (iii) the range of AP coverage. With these three parameters we can create, with the same traces, several frameworks in order to see the behavior of AP under different conditions. In particular the most important one is δ because allow us to set the percentage of vehicles that try to download from AP. In traces, each vehicle is identified by unique ID, so we simply performed a random decisions based on δ to establish if a node is a consumer or not.

Then, for each second of simulation, we check if there are consumers under coverage and if AP is busy. Finally we increment coverage range up a maximum of 300 mt. to see how it influences results. Fig. 2 shows simulations results; in x-axis we can see the consumers density while in y-axis the percentage of idle period (from 0 to 1).

As we can see, with low traffic density (0.05 car/s), the AP is almost always idle and also with a transmission range of 300 mt. remains free for about 88% of the simulation. In areas with average traffic density (0.19 car/s) results show a considerable amount of time usable by scheduler to manage cooperation among vehicles. A steady stream of cars instead (1.5 car/s), involves intense activity of the AP, which, even with low consumer density, remains busy to transmit data to consumers. Note that, in this last case, the time available for the scheduler becomes zero quickly and apply C&F algorithm becomes impossible. However, results obtained in this way only represent the amount of time in which AP doesn't have consumers under coverage but we don't know if, at the same time, cooperators are available for cooperation. For this reason we must introduce the concept of usable idle periods.

A second of usable idle periods occurs only when:

1. There isn't consumer under the coverage (generic idle period).
2. There is at least a cooperator under the coverage.
3. There is at least a receiver that is traveling in a dark area and is moving in the opposite direction of a cooperator (only in this case they can meet halfway). Like said before, we don't know the position of vehicles that aren't under coverage, but we assume that AP communicate among them to predict these information (in highway is pretty easy).

The scheduler works only during usable idle periods, but sometimes the necessary conditions to obtain it, rarely occur. For example, if our AP has a little transmission range (50 mt.) and we place it in a low traffic road where vehicles move at high speeds, we have very low probabilities to obtain usable idle periods. Similarly one-way streets or dead ends are not suitable for this mechanism so we have to place the infrastructure carefully. Performing experiments we notice that, in zones with a medium/high traffic flow, appropriate values of consumers density ($0.3<\delta<0.5$) and average speeds (about 20-30 km/h) the chances to apply the mechanism are relatively high.

4 Schedule Strategies and Results

In this section have been tested several mechanisms for scheduling packets in opportunistic C&F protocol in order to optimize network performance. Mainly three techniques have been proposed:

1. Distribute the available data equally among consumers.
2. Give greater priority to vehicles which have almost finished downloading their file.
3. Designate as receivers of the packets only vehicles that have more probabilities to meet cooperators.

The algorithm that implement these techniques examine the traffic second after second. Every moment consumers and cooperators state is updated by using two data structures and all AP are checked to find out which ones are free and which ones are busy. Only consumers that travel in dark areas are labeled as receivers during a particular second. For each of them, data structures are update with following information: AP target that is the AP where the consumer is directed (or where we estimate it is directed), x and y coordinates, direction and finally the file status that represent how many bits have been downloaded so far by the vehicle. Obviously file status can be filled every time consumers travel under an AP, or when they meet cooperators in dark areas. Similarly cooperators have a data structure that is updated every second with this information: AP source that is the AP where cooperator is coming from, x and y coordinate, direction, a list of possible receivers, another complementary list to the previous one with the amount of data to deliver to each receiver (transaction list) and finally a TTL (time to live) counter used to measure the lifetime of data carried. Once updated the two structures, each cooperator is able to check its receivers list to see if someone is close enough to establish a connection. If this occurs data are transferred in the amount indicated by the transaction list.

Like said in the previous section this mechanism works at an high abstraction level, above data-link layer of the TCP/IP stack because we are only interested in understand if the global scenario performance could be improved. For this reason we assume that all transmissions occur instantly without any problems related to packet losses or environmental interferences in signal. Regarding physical and data-link protocols we can suppose to use the well-know 802.11p standard. Amount of data transferred during each encounter is fixed and is based on the average link durations (around six seconds). If a vehicle finishes to download its files, it is automatically deleted from the list of consumers, and can be candidate to become a cooperator. A cooperator can carry only a predetermined amount of data, so it's better to decide in advance how to divide the packets among receivers. The division strategy, managed by scheduler, depends on the value of a parameter that we call α: if α is equal to 0 means that all data must be delivered only to the receiver which have the most advanced file status (maximum priority) while if it is equal to 1 means that data must be divided equally among all receivers (equal priority). Thus, by simply changing the α value we can determine the percentage of consumers to which give higher priority (if $\alpha = 0.2$ means that only 20% of the receivers with bigger file status will receive data). This parameter allows us to simultaneously implement the firsts two strategies for packets delivery (α=0 for maximum priority and α=1 for equal priority). For the third strategy instead we have to calculate the probability that two vehicles meet themselves during their trip, so is necessary to know, for each pair of AP, the percentage of vehicles traveling form the first to the second one and vice versa. For example with a microscopic simulator we can calculate this percentage as the ratio between the number of vehicles that generally move from AP1 to AP2 and the total number of vehicles passing through AP1. If we perform this operation for all possible pairs of AP and for both directions we can obtain an idea of traffic streams. This isn't a novel method to calculate meetings but we decide to use this for simplicity. In future study, other solutions can be proposed. For example, could be very interesting to use navigator GPS information to know vehicles destination and hypothesize which roads will be drive, using Dijkstra algorithm or studying traffic congestion. Another method consists in perform a census to know generic drivers' behaviors for each day and hour of the week in order to calculate vehicles streams.

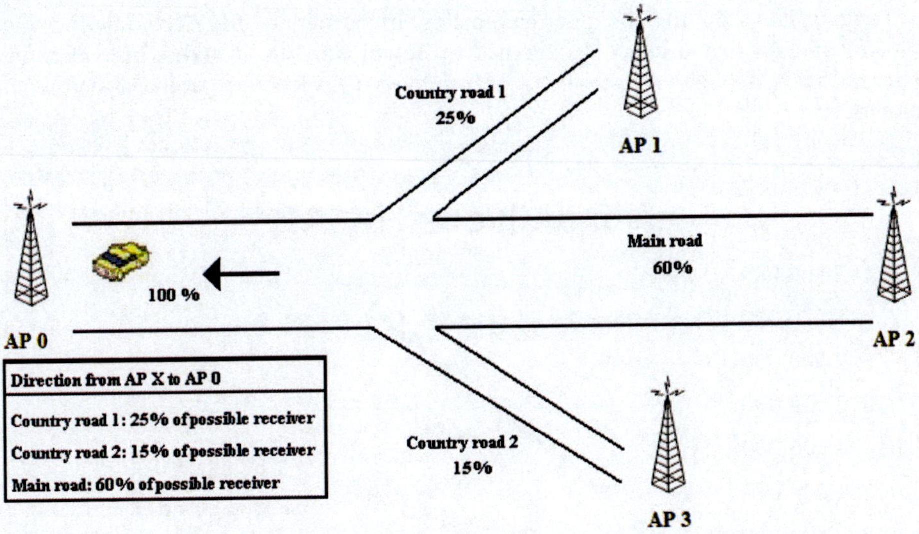

Fig. 3. in this example we assume that AP0 use traffic stream percentage to decide how to schedule data. 60% of available packets were prepared for receivers coming from AP2, 25% for receivers from AP1 and other 15% for receivers from AP3. Then data were divided properly among cooperators.

At this point, we only have to decide if our target is to optimize data transfer or ensure equity during packets distribution. If we try to optimize performance, the scheduler have to divide packets only among cooperators headed to road with high vehicles stream. All consumers that travel in low traffic zones will remain isolated. To avoid this situation, we use traffic streams to randomly decide how to schedule packets between cooperators, in order to give a connection chance to all consumers. Fig. 3 show how we make the decision.

All mechanisms discussed so far, have been tested by performing two big experiments:

1. A simulation using four AP placed in an ideal position. Between each pair of AP there aren't crossroads or bifurcations but only straight road and this situation give us the security to know in advance all possible meetings between vehicles. This experiment aims to verify the proper functioning of the strategies.
2. A simulation using three AP placed casually on the map. This is a more realistic scenario that allows us to see if protocol works in harsh conditions too.

Table 1. Simulation input parameters

Nr. AP	AP bit/s	File size	Car tran. range	AP tran. range	TTL
4	10 Mb	40 MB	200 mt.	200 mt.	60
3	10 Mb	10 MB	200 mt.	200 mt.	300

Table 1 shows simulations input parameters. In particular, "file size" describes the amount of data that each consumer has to download. Fig. 4 and 5 instead show experiments results given in terms of MB delivered respectively from AP and from cooperators.

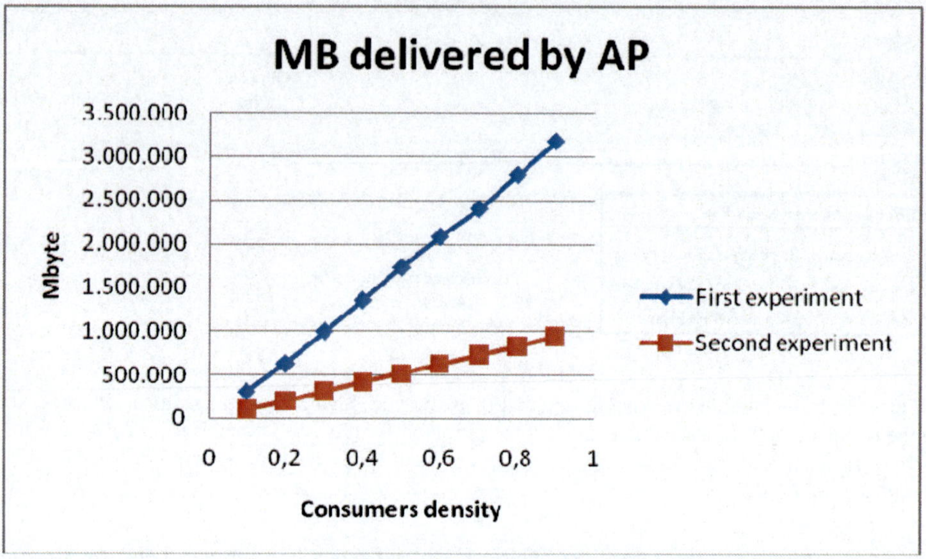

Fig. 4. Data delivered by AP

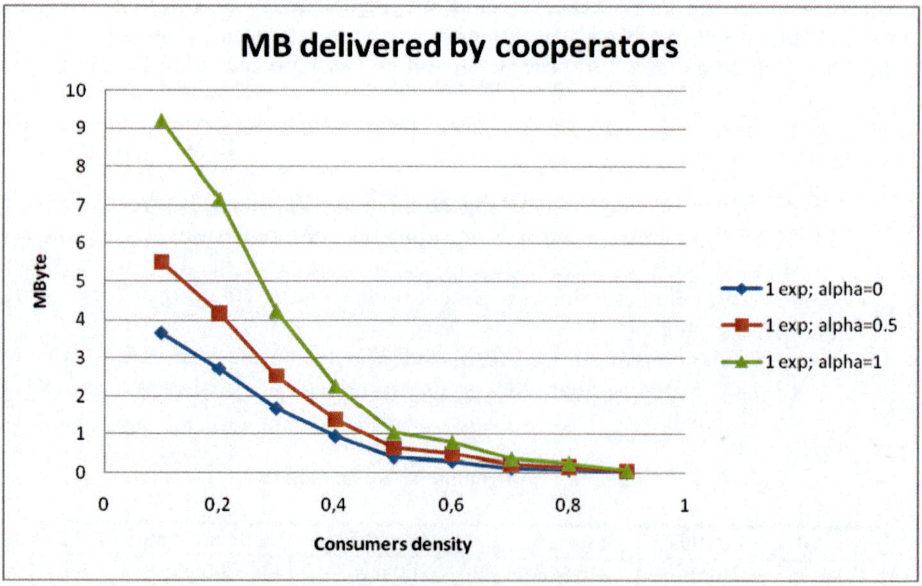

Fig. 5. Data delivered by cooperators

Analyzing results, you may notice that high percentage of packets is handed over by AP and only a small amount due C&F protocol. However, this small amount helps vehicles to finish their downloads faster improving, indirectly, network performance and effectiveness of cooperation. Since AP manages most of the packets, it's obvious that increasing the consumers' density, the amount of data distributed globally in the system increases too. In first experiment with α=0 the system delivers from a minimum of 306 GB to a maximum of 3 TB and 177 GB (in three hours of simulation from 4 AP). Instead, packets distributed by cooperators decreases with increasing value of δ. This behavior was predictable because:

- The scheduler is busier with consumer under coverage and has less time (usable idle periods) to organize cooperation between cooperators and receivers.
- More consumers mean fewer cooperators because vehicle's number is fixed.
- Every second AP must divide its amount of data (10 Mb) equally among the consumers. So more consumers means more time to complete downloads and then fewer vehicles are able to candidate as cooperators.
- More consumers also mean that the cooperators have a higher number of suitable receivers to serve and consequently there is a further slowdown in finishing downloads.

Moreover, in fig. 5 we can note how increasing α for smaller values of δ, the number of packets delivered increases. This means that an equal distribution of data among receivers produces, in terms of performance, more acceptable results. However, if our intent is to increase number of files completely downloaded then it's preferable to set a lower value of α (so we maximize priority). First simulations show that files completely downloaded rise proportionally to priority.

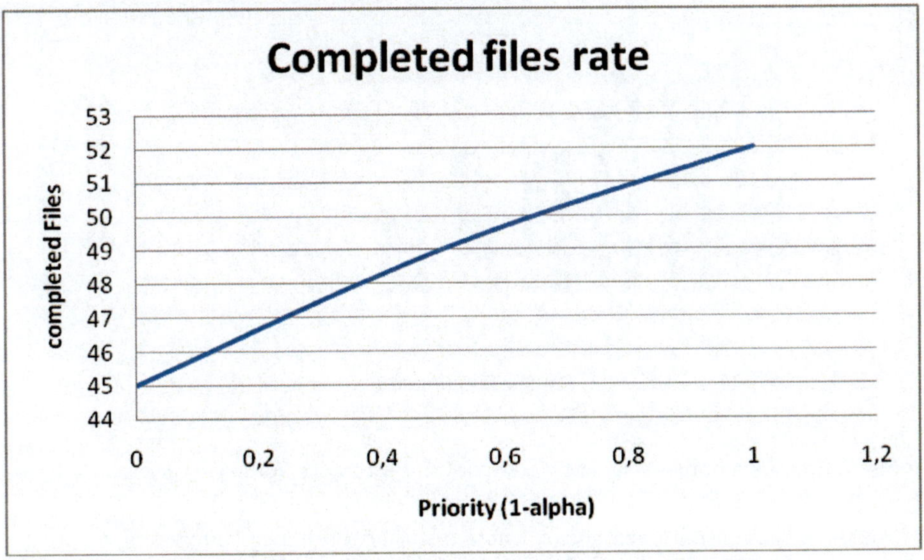

Fig. 6. Files completed rise proportionally to priority

However the more realistic scenario of second simulation give some different results. Without knowing in advance the route taken by vehicles, we must assume, through a probabilistic calculation, which will be the target AP for each consumer. Based on these assumptions (which could be wrong) we calculate for each cooperator the receivers list. For this reason in this second experiment, performances are worst respect the previous one but the protocol behavior is quite similar. The unique difference is that, in this case, the number of file completed doesn't raise proportional to priority. This happens because the algorithm only attempts to predict possible encounters that sometimes may not occur. All missed meetings result in lost opportunities to increase the overall efficiency of the network. Moreover, since AP are far apart, this forced us to set a TTL high enough to ensure that all vehicles have opportunity to meet. So, when the meeting doesn't happen, the cooperator may remain several seconds wandering on the map, before being used again for other receivers (provided along the trip encounters another free AP). This strategy issue happens when the topology has a too homogeneous traffic distribution. If, for example, road from AP1 to AP2 manage a traffic density equal to road from AP1 to AP3 means that the scheduler in AP1 has only 50% chance to properly predict meeting because it's unable to discover which road will be taken by cooperators. For this reason is better to place the AP always at principal city crossroads, especially in main streets (this allows us to predict more efficiently the meetings) or in highway (where only two directions exist). Finally fig. 7 shows the amount of file completed using different priority value.

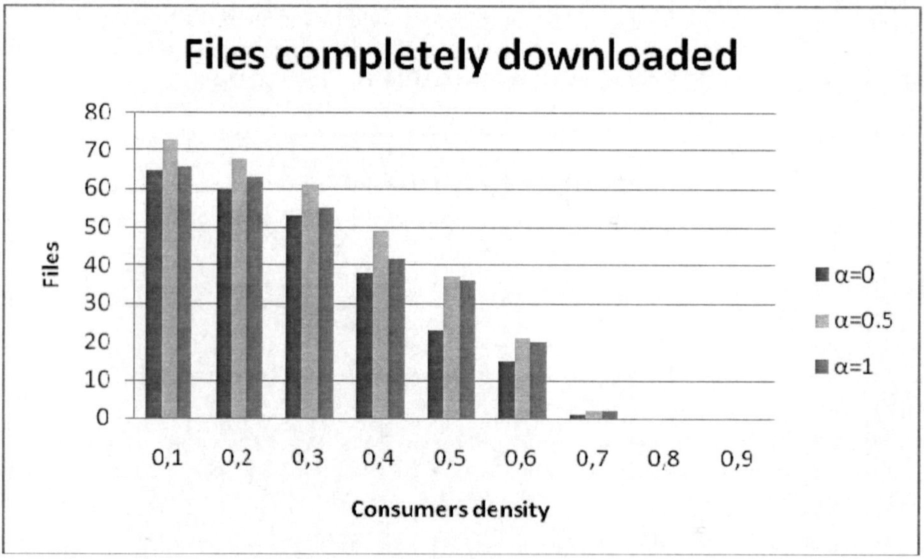

Fig. 7. Histogram of files completely downloaded. Best choice, for low δ values, is α=0.5.

For the same reason given above, random scenario produces interesting behaviors in files downloaded, especially for lower values of δ. In fact, as we can see, using average value of α (0.5) instead of high value (0) we can complete more files hoping, in this way, to increase future cooperation. It's important to remark that this approach enhances cooperative content sharing in VANETs without introducing additional overhead since we only use AP idle period to manage the scheduling process. Our intent is to improve this mechanism and conduct further experiments, increasing simulation duration and AP number in order to find out if cooperation's level increases in longer simulation, influencing positively VANET performance. We are also interested in adopting a more advanced simulation platform like one described in [10] in order to facilitates the dynamic interaction between vehicles and AP.

5 Conclusions

In this paper has been proposed a vehicular framework that opportunistically allows downloading packets when vehicles cross AP. The scenario adopts some feature from the Delay Tolerant Network, giving to AP storing and computing capabilities to manage delays, and benefits of a Carry and Forward mechanism. Using this protocol is possible to increase the global throughput of a real scenario due to the exploitation of AP idle periods. If traffic conditions, vehicles speeds, vehicles distribution and consumers density are balanced the increment of performance can be relevant. Then we explain why big idle periods don't always mean time usable by scheduler. In fact if a AP is idle but no cooperators are available for receive data to carry or no receiver is detected, this time results wasted. With this assumption we propose different strategies to schedule packets and change the protocol operation, producing different results. If our application requires the urgent delivery of some packets to a particular vehicle, we should use a high priority delivery strategy, while if the goal is to maximize the number of data sent it's better to use an equal priority delivery strategy. These behaviors were tested in two different simulations. Results have shown that in an ideal scenario, where we can predict with certainty vehicles meeting, it's possible to choose the strategy based on preferences (maximize data transfer or number of files completed) while in a random scenario we must avoid to use high priority. With high priority strategy, in fact, we places too much trust in meetings that may not occur while with a moderate priority (α=0.5) is possible to completely deliver more files.

References

1. Fiore, M., Barcelo-Ordinas, J.M.: Cooperative download in urban vehicular networks. In: IEEE 6th International Conference on Mobile Adhoc and Sensor Systems, Mass 2009, pp. 20–29 (2009)
2. Burgess, J., Gallagher, B., Jensen, D., Levine, B.N.: MaxProp: Routing for Vehicle-based Disruption Tolerant Networks. In: 25th Conference on Computer Communications, INFOCOM, pp. 1–11 (2006)
3. Balasubramanian, A., Levine, B.N., Venkataramani, A.: DTN Routing as a Resource Allocation Problem. In: Proceedings of the 2007 Conference on Applications, Technologies, Architectures, and Protocols for Computer Communications, ACM SIGCOMM 2007, New York, vol. 37(4), pp. 373–384 (2007)
4. Zhao, J., Cao, G.: VADD: Vehicle-assisted data delivery in vehicular ad hoc networks. In: 25th IEEE International Conference on Computer Communications, IEEE INFOCOM, Spain, pp. 1–12 (2006)

5. Vahdat, A., Becker, D.: Epidemic routing for partially connected ad hoc networks. Technical report, Duke University (2000)
6. Doria, A., Lindgren, A., Schelén, O.: Probabilistic routing in intermittently connected networks. SIGMOBILE Mobile Computing and Communication 7(3), 19–20 (2004)
7. Das, S., Nandan, A., Gerla, M., Pau, G., Sanadidi, M.Y.: Cooperative downloading in vehicular ad-hoc wireless networks. In: Second Annual Conference on Wireless On-demand Network Systems and Services, WONS, pp. 32–41 (2005)
8. Fall, K.: A delay-tolerant network architecture for challenged internets. In: Proceedings of the 2003 Conference on Applications, Technologies, Architectures, and Protocols for Computer Communications, SIGCOMM 2003, pp. 27–34. ACM, New York (2003)
9. Burri, A., Cetin, N., Nagel, K.: A large-scale agent-based traffic microsimulation based on queue model. In: Proceedings of Swiss transport research conference (STRC), Switzerland, pp. 3–4272 (2003)
10. Yang, Y., Bagrodia, R.: Evaluation of VANET-based advanced intelligent transportation systems. In: Proceeding of the Sixth ACM International Workshop on VehiculAr InterNETworking, VANET 2009, Beijing, China, pp. 3–12 (2009)

Three Phase Technique for Intrusion Detection in Mobile Ad Hoc Network

K.V. Arya, Prerna Vashistha, and Vaibhav Gupta

ABV-Indian Institute of Information Technology & Management Gwalior, India
{kvarya.iiitm.ac.in}
{sharma.prerna17,guptavaibhav.05086}@gmail.com

Abstract MANET is an infrastructure less network where Routing Protocols play a vital role. Most of the routing protocols assume that all the nodes in the network are fair and ready to co-operate with each other. In a network some nodes can be selfish and malicious which leads to security concerns. Therefore, Intrusion Detection System (IDS) is required for MANETs. In MANETs, most of the Intrusion Detection Systems (IDSs) are based on watchdog technique. These watchdog techniques also called overhearing techniques and suffer from some problems. In this paper an effort has been made to overcome the problems of overhearing technique by introducing an additional phase of authentication in between the route establishment and the packet transmission. Here, DSR has been modified so that discovered route will not have nodes with less remaining power. Nodes with sufficient transmission power will be taken into consideration for packet transmission at the time of route discovery.

Keywords: MANET, DSR, Watchdog, IDSs, Promiscuous.

1 Introduction

Over the next decade of the wireless communication systems, there is a tremendous need for the rapid deployment of independent mobile users. Significant examples include emergency search/rescue missions, disaster relief efforts, battlefield military operations etc. A network of such users is referred to as Mobile Ad hoc Network (MANET). These Networks are autonomous and decentralized wireless systems consisting of mobile nodes that are free to move into the network or leave the network at any point of time. This aspect of MANET makes it very unpredictable.

These nodes are the systems or devices i.e. mobile phone, laptop and personal computer that are mobile. MANETs can be host/router or both. All the activities in the network, such as delivering data packets, are being executed by the nodes, either individually or collectively. Depending on its application, the structure of a MANET varies. The MANET may operate in a standalone fashion, or may be connected to the larger Internet.

As the cost of the wireless access is decreasing, wireless could replace wired in many settings. Wireless is advantageous over wired as nodes can transmit the data while being mobile. But the distance between nodes is limited by their transmission

H. Cherifi, J.M. Zain, and E. El-Qawasmeh (Eds.): DICTAP 2011, Part I, CCIS 166, pp. 675–684, 2011.

range. But ad hoc network allows nodes to transmit their data through the intermediate nodes.

Various Routing Protocols have been proposed for MANETs [5]. Working group (WG) of Internet Engineering Task Force (IETF) is devoted for developing IP routing protocols [10]. Security in MANET is a very important issue for the basic functionality of the network. The nature of mobile ad hoc network poses a range of challenges to the security designs. MANET suffers from various attacks because of its open medium, dynamic topology, and lack of central monitoring and management. A node may misbehave by agreeing to forward the packet but fail to do so, because it is overloaded, selfish, malicious, or broken. A selfish node wants to save its battery. A node may be intended to perform something malicious and launches denial of service attack by dropping the packets. The ad hoc networks can be reached very easily by users, as well as by malicious attackers. If a malicious attacker reaches the network, the attacker can easily exploit or possibly even disable the mobile ad hoc network.

The rest of the paper is organized as follows: Section 2 presents the review of the related work. The proposed three phase technique with algorithm is explained in Section 3. In Section 4 simulation studies have been carried out to compare the performance of the proposed technique. Conclusions are given in Section 5.

2 Related Work

Security has become the primary concern in MANET. To provide security many Intrusion detection system have been proposed in literature. Marti et al. [1] proposed a technique Watchdog and Pathrater built on Dynamic Source Routing Protocol (DSR) [11] that has become the basis for many researches. Now most of the IDSs are based on this technique. Watchdog identifies the misbehaving node in the path while the Pathrater rates the path based on the watchdog results. Watchdog does this by listening to its neighboring node in promiscuous mode. If the next node does not forward the packet then it may be a malicious node. Counting of the transmit failure activities is done. If the counter exceeds a threshold the node is declared malicious and avoided by the Pathrater. Watchdog is a good technique that comes with few weaknesses that are being discussed in Marti's work. This technique performs well but it fails in case there is ambiguous collision, receiver collision, limited transmission power, false misbehavior reporting, collusion and partial dropping.

Buchegger and Boudec [9] proposed another reputation mechanism that is called Confident. Confident has four main components, namely a monitor, a reputation system, a path manager, and a trust manager. Confident remains dependent on the Watchdog mechanism, and therefore inherits many of its problems.

Core, a Collaborative Reputation mechanism proposed by Michiardi et al. [8], also uses a Watchdog mechanism. The reputation table is used which keeps track of reputation values of other nodes in the network. Since a misbehaving node can accuse a good node, only positive rating factors can be distributed in Core.

Patcha and Mishra [7] proposed an extension to the Watchdog technique by tackling the problem of collusion attack, where more than one node collaborates to do a malicious behavior. This technique is efficient only when there is little or no movement of node.

Twoack [2] solution, proposed by Balakrishnan et al., replaces Watchdog and solves the problems of the receiver collision and limited transmission power. Some specified set of actions are being performed by every set of three consecutive nodes. In Twoack all the forwarded packets are being acknowledged which leads to congestion in the network.

In [6], Hasswa et al. proposed an intrusion detection and response system called Routeguard. This technique uses the two techniques that were proposed by Marti et al., Watchdog and Pathrater, are combined to classify each neighbor node as: fresh, member, unstable, suspect, or malicious. However, when the malicious nodes are misbehaving for 50% to 60% of the time there is a slight drop in Routeguard's performance.

Enough work has been put to overcome these deficiencies. Nasser and Chen [3] proposed an Enhanced Intrusion Detection system for discovering malicious nodes in the network called Exwatchdog. Exwatchdog extends the Watchdog proposed by Marti et al [1]. They focus on one of the weaknesses of the Watchdog technique, namely the false misbehaving problem where a malicious node falsely reports other nodes as misbehaving while in fact it is the real intruder. However, there may exist a true misbehaving node is in the all available paths from source to destination then it is impossible to confirm and check the number of packets with the destination.

Roubaiey and T. Sheltami [4] proposed a mechanism, named: Adaptive Acknowledgment (AACK) that was an attempt to remove two significant problems: the limited transmission power and receiver collision. The AACK mechanism may not work well on long paths that will take a significant time for the end to end acknowledgments. This limitation will give the misbehaving nodes more time for dropping more packets. Also AACK still suffers from the partial dropping attacks (gray hole attacks).

All the previous solutions used Watchdog as the base for their techniques. Whereas, the Three phase solution, proposed by us, replaces Watchdog and solves all the problems of it.

3 Three Phase Technique

In this section we have proposed Three Phase Technique for intrusion detection in MANET which mainly consists of the route discovery through modified DSR, authentication through certification, and packet transmission after authentication is successful.

3.1 Discovery of Route Using Modified DSR

To discover the route from the source node to the destination node, a route request (RREQ) is broadcasted to all the nodes in the neighborhood. Each node upon receiving the Route Request, retransmits the request appending its address, its current power and its queue length (buffered packets that are needed to be processed) only if it has not already forwarded a copy of the RREQ. Queue length will be taken so that source node can decide whether this node will be having sufficient battery to participate in the packet transmission. The destination node returns a reply for each route request it received. Nodes with the sufficient power will be considered by the source node. The energy contained in any node is estimated as follows:

$$Power = E_c\text{-}(Q_i{*}Energy) \quad (1)$$

Where E_c represents the current energy and no. of packets in the buffer of node under consideration are represented by Q_i. In this paper we have considered decay in energy with time is very less and can be ignored. For successful transmission of the packet from source through the selected node, the estimated power should follow the relationship given in (2).

$$Power>(Num_p){*}Energy \quad (2)$$

Where Num_p is the number of packets the source wants to send to the destination.

If an intermediate node is unable to deliver the packet to the next hop, then node returns a ROUTE ERROR to source, stating that the link is currently broken. Source Node then removes this broken link from its cache. For sending such a retransmission or other packets to this same destination, if source node has another route to destination in its route cache, it can send the packet using the new route immediately after the authentication. Otherwise, it has to perform a new route discovery for this destination.

Any malicious node may reply to the request from the source by claiming to have the shortest path to the destination. To overcome this problem, source node does not initiate the data transfer process immediately after the routes are established. Instead it waits for the authenticated reply from the destination.

3.2 Authentication through Certification

Since there is no fixed infrastructure for ad hoc networks, nodes carry out all required tasks for security including routing and authentication in a self organized manner.

Each node N generates its keys (public and private) by itself using RSA algorithm [12] which stands for Rivest, Shamir and Adleman who first publicly described it. One more key is generated through the use of the hashed IP address which is unique in the network. This unique key will be then encrypted by it using its private key. Then a request is made to sign the encrypted hashed value to its neighbors. Since these nodes are in a one-hop distance from each other, they can sense their neighbor node for a while to assure that whether it should sign this encrypted hashed value of that node or not.

Thus each node in its radio range issues neighbor node a certificate that bind public key with the unique IP address of the neighbor node with issuer's private key and stores one copy of this certificate in its repository while sending another copy of certificate to the corresponding node. Each certificate issued will be valid for a defined time. When the route is established between the source and the destination, source node sends the route (list of the nodes in the path in sequence) and asks for its certificate.

Now this neighbor sends this request to its next hop node in the route. This process will continue till this request reaches the destination. The process is shown in the Fig. 1. Then the target node will add its certificate issued by the previous node in the route and forwards it to that node. As shown in the Fig. 2. The node will check its repository for the correctness of the certificate. If it is correct then it will append its certificate to that reply coming from the destination and forward it to the next hop node in the route. As shown in the Fig. 3.

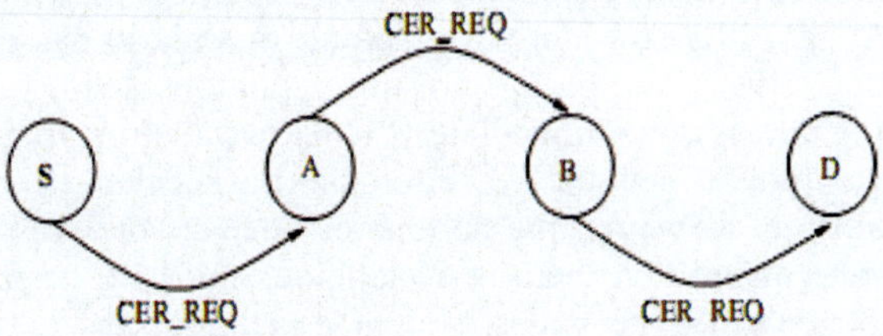

Fig. 1. Certificate request reaches to Destination D through the intermediate node A and B

Fig. 2. D transmits the certificate to B which was earlier issued by B itself

This process continues until the source node receives these certificates. After receiving certificates, source node checks the certificate appended in its repository to see that whether it is the same certificate issued by it and checks that all the certificates are received in the order of the path from the destination node to the sender as shown in the Fig. 4. Thus after authentication is done packet transmission takes place.

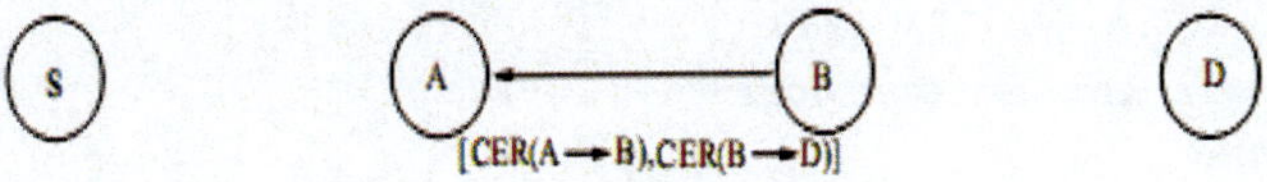

Fig. 3. B verifies the certificate correctness coming from D and appends its certificate which is issued by A with it and forward it to A

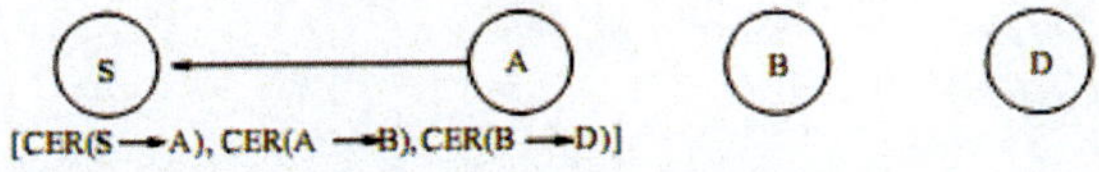

Fig. 4. S receives all the certificates of the nodes that fall in the route and verifies the sequence of the certificate

3.3 Packet Transmission after Successful Authentication

After authentication packet transmission takes place. Source node forwards the packet to its neighbor and overhears it. For each node there will be a timer that will be used when an alarm is being raised. The value of the timer will be estimated as (3):

$$Timer = T_{packet} + T_{ack} \tag{3}$$

Where T_{packet} represents the transmission time of the packet and T_{ack} is the time required for the acknowledgement to reach that node. Thus the packet drop information will not be activated before the expiry of the corresponding timer. In the proposed methodology, it is considered by default that alarm has been raised due to any collision in the network not because of any malicious activity. Therefore, at the packet drop nothing new is done immediately. Only it waits for timer expiry.

If before timer expires it gets the ACK for that packet then it is confirmed that it was actually a collision. However, the node does not gets the ACK before the timer expire then it is determined that there is a malicious node in the path. Based on the replies through the intermediate nodes, source node finds the actual culprit. If the collision occurs at the receiver, the request to forward that packet is made again and if the node tries to save its energy by not sending the packet then it will be considered as malicious node not the selfish one. In the next section, proposed algorithm is described which overcomes the problems related with the conventional overhearing technique.

4 Proposed Algorithm

In the proposed algorithm we use the modified DSR routing mechanism as described in section 3. The detailed steps of the methodology are given in the following algorithm.

1. Discover the route through modified DSR then the source node will select the nodes in the route using (4.1) and (4.2).
2. Destination node sends route reply with certificate that it has received from next hope node in the path.

```
node=SOURCE;
while(node!=DEST)
{
          Forward CER-REQ;
          node=next hope node;
endwhile
}
```

3. All intermediate node append their certificates and forward route reply. Route reply reaches to the Source node.

```
N=DEST;
S=Destination's Certificate;
while(node!=SOURCE)
      {
      forward to next hope node it's certificate appending with S.
      If any node finds the key duplicate than it is thought that it is a
      malicious node.
      }
end while
```

The performance of the proposed method is computed in terms of assessment for overhearing problem. In the next section we compare it with the conventional overhearing technique.

5 Comparison with the Overhearing Techniques

This section compares the various weaknesses of the watchdog technique along with the improvements suggested in the proposed method: Overhearing techniques such as watchdog has been bases for many researches. Now in this section we will discuss that how some add-on can really improve it. So this section is dedicated to the comparison between these two techniques.

Ambiguous collision: Ambiguous collisions may occur at node A When node B forwards the data packet towards C, and A cannot overhear the transmission due to another concurrent transmission in A's neighborhood. This problem has been solved by introducing the concept of the timer.

Receiver collision: Receiver collisions take place in the overhearing techniques when a node A overhears the data packet being forwarded by B, but C fails to receive the packet due to collisions. So in the proposed method C requests B for the retransmission of the packet.

False misbehavior: It is not possible because by the time node will be reporting that a node is malicious till that time nodes have received the ACK .So it cannot raise the false alarm. If it tries to drop the ACK packet previous node will be knowing that this is the malicious node and action will be taken against it.

Less transmission power: The problem regarding the less transmission power will be taken care at the time of the route discovery as nodes with the sufficient energy will be considered by the source node for the packet transmission.

Collusion: It is also not possible for two nodes to collude to perform some malicious activities as authentication is done. If two nodes $M1$ and $M2$ collude with each other to perform some malicious activities then the node $M0$ will not be issuing the certificate to $M1$. So path will not be set through these nodes. As shown in the Fig. 5.

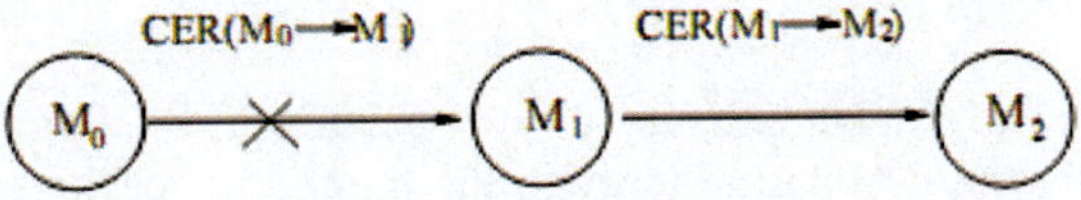

Fig. 5. Node M_1 and M_2 collude with each other and M1 authenticate M_2 even though it is malicious. So node M_0 caches that node M_1 is also malicious and does not issue certificate to M_1.

Partial Dropping: Concept of threshold has been removed completely so there is no scope for partial dropping because all the nodes are authenticated and once a packet is dropped then next packet will not be send if malicious node is there. New route will be used for further transmission.

6 Simulation Result

The performance of the Three phase technique is evaluated by simulating it on Qualnet (version-5.2). This simulation is carried out on a personal computer with an Intel processor Core 2 Due 3.4 GHz processor, 1 GHz of memory running on Microsoft windows 7 Operating system. We modified DSR module in Qualnet such that each node appends its current power and its queue length with its address. Our simulations were carried out with 80 mobile nodes moving in a 700×700 m2 flat area. Each nodes transmission range is 250 m by default. The IEEE 802.11 MAC layer was used. A random waypoint mobility model was taken with maximum speed of 15 m/sec and pause time of 3 second. All nodes are set on Promiscuous mode. We implement CBR transfers between pairs of nodes. Source and destination for each CBR link are selected randomly. The Three phase scheme is analyzed under varying traffic conditions by running simulations for networks with 8 (low traffic), 16, and 24 (high traffic) CBR pairs. Each CBR source generates packets of size 512 Bytes, and transmits 4 packets per second. Simulation time is set to 1000 seconds.

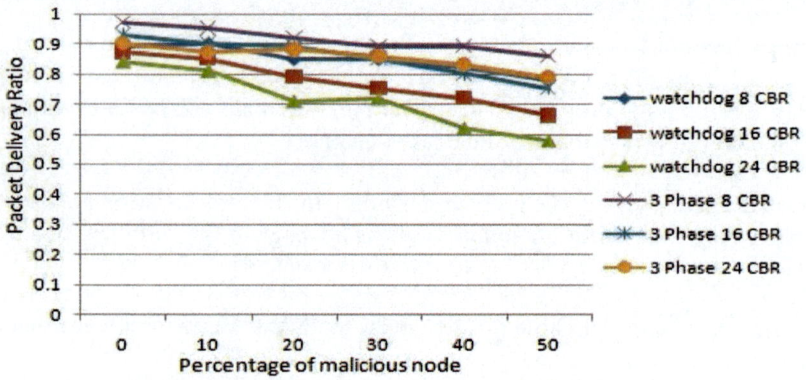

Fig. 6. Comparision of watchdog and Three phase technique in terms of packet delivery ratio

6.1 Performance Matrices

Packet delivery ratio: Packet delivery ratio is calculated by dividing the number of packets received by the destination through the number of packets originated by the source (i.e. CBR source).

Routing Overhead: The routing overhead describes how many routing packets for route discovery and route maintenance needed to be sent in order to propagate the CBR packets.

6.2 Discussion on Simulation Results

In Fig. 6 comparison of packet delivery ratio between the Three phase technique and watchdog is shown with the increasing number of misbehaving nodes. Performance is evaluated on various traffic conditions with increasing number of malicious nodes from 0 (no node is misbehaving) to 50%. When there is no malicious node, packet delivery ratio is same for both technique even in the various traffic loads. But with the increasing CBR links, performance of watchdog degrades poorly. While performance of Three Phase Technique degrades slightly. Thus comparing with the Watchdog scheme, our Three Phase scheme maintains a relatively high packet delivery ratio. Fig. 7 compares overhead in both the schemes. Overhead increase in three phase technique is due to the authentication phase. Three phase technique prevents against the malicious activity at the time of the transmission, it increases overhead up to 30% to 40%. But it is visible that the overhead increases slightly in case of three phase technique than the watchdog technique with the increase in the CBR links and number of malicious node. Thus for the larger network with the large number of CBR links this overhead increase would be up to 25% to 30%. This overhead increases with the increase of malicious node in the network and the increase in the CBR links in the network.

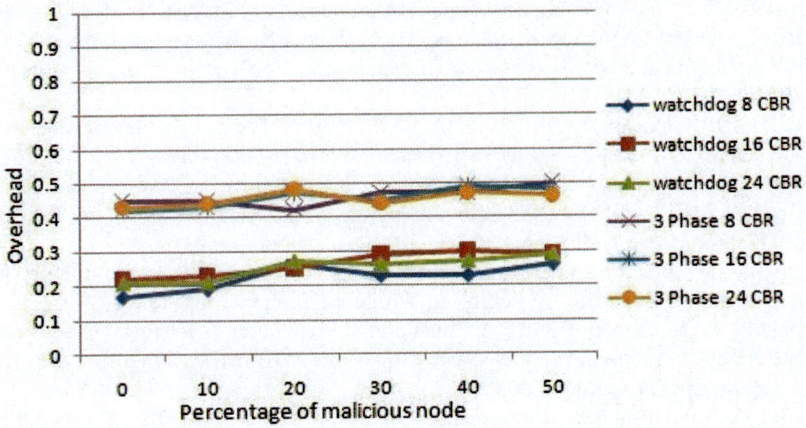

Fig. 7. Comparison of Watchdog and Three Phase Technique in terms of Overhead

7 Conclusion and Future work

This research is devoted to detect malicious and selfish nodes and mitigate their impact by avoiding them in later transmissions. In this research we improve the existing IDSs over MANETs. In specific, we solve the problems of Watchdog technique, which considered to be the base technique that is used by many of the recently IDSs. This paper proposes Three phase technique which can be added to the source routing protocol. It detects malicious nodes and handles all the collisions very efficiently with the use of the timer. It works better where collisions are highly frequent. It removes the concept of threshold which allows a malicious node to drop a certain number of packets. This technique introduces a novel phase i.e. authentication phase to provide secure and authenticated path which also lead to increased overhead.

In the future we will continue this research for more reliable and efficient technique with less overhead and authentication not only in forward but also in backward direction of the discovered route for packet transmission. At the time of authentication node has to take the certificates from its entire neighbor which is very difficult in the case when there is number of nodes are very high. This assumption may not be practical in every case that the nodes get certified from all the neighbors.

References

1. Marti, S., Giuli, T., Lai, K., Baker, M.: Mitigating Routing Misbehavior in Mobile Ad Hoc Networks. In: Sixth Annual International Conference on Mobile Computing and Networking (2000)
2. Deng, J., Balakrishnan, K., Varshney, P.K.: TWOACK: Preventing Selfishness in Mobile Ad Hoc Networks. In: IEEE Wireless Comm. and Networking Conf. (2005)
3. Chen, N., Nasser.: Enhanced Intrusion Detection System for Discovering Malicious Nodes in Mobile Ad-hoc Networks. In: IEEE International Conference on Communication (2007)
4. Roubaiey, A.l., Shakshuki, E., Sheltami, T., Mahmoud, A., Mouftah, H.: AACK: Adaptive Acknowledgment Intrusion Detection for MANET with Node Detection Enhancement. In: IEEE International Conference on Advanced Information Networking and Applications (2010)
5. Abusalah, L., Guizani, M., Khokhar, A.: A Survey of Secure Mobile Ad Hoc Routing Protocols. IEEE Communications Surveys and Tutorials 10(4) (2008)
6. Hasswa, A., Hassanein, H., Zulker, M.: Routeguard: An Intrusion Detection and Response System for Mobile Ad Hoc Networks. In: Wireless And Mobile Computing, Networking And Communication, vol. 3, pp. 336–343 (2005)
7. Patcha, A., Mishra, A.: Collaborative security architecture for black hole attack prevention in mobile ad-hoc networks. In: Radio and Wireless Conference, pp. 75–78 (2003)
8. Michiardi, P., Molva, R.: CORE: A Collaborative Reputation Mechanism to enforce node cooperation in Mobile Ad hoc Networks. In: Proc. IEEE/ACM Symp. Mobile Ad Hoc Networking and Computing (2002)
9. Buchegger, S., Boudec.: Performance Analysis of the CONFI- DANT Protocol Cooperation Of Nodes-Fairness in Dynamic Ad-hoc Networks. In: Proc. IEEE/ACM Symp. Mobile Ad Hoc Networking and Computing (2002)
10. Internet Engineering Task Force, `http://www.ietf.org/rfc.html`
11. Dyanamic Source Routing Protocol, `http://en.wikipedia.org/wiki/DynamicSourceRouting`
12. RSA, `http://en.wikipedia.org/wiki/RSA`

DFDM: Decentralized Fault Detection Mechanism to Improving Fault Management in Wireless Sensor Networks

Shahram Babaie, Ali Ranjideh Rezaie, and Saeed Rasouli Heikalabad

Department of Computer Engineering, Tabriz Branch, Islamic Azad University, Tabriz, Iran
{Hw.Tab.Au,A.Ran.Rezaie,S.Rasouli.H}@Gmail.com

Abstract. Wireless Sensor networks (WSN) are inherently fault-prone due to the shared wireless communication medium and harsh environments in which they are deployed. Energy is one of the most constraining factors and node failures due to crash and energy exhaustion are commonplace. In order to avoid degradation of service due to faults, it is necessary for the WSN to be able to detect faults early and initiate recovery actions. In this paper we propose a decentralized cluster based method for fault detection and recovery which is energy efficient namely DFDM. Simulation Results show that the performance of proposed algorithm is more efficient than previous ones.

Keywords: Wireless sensor network, Cluster-based, Fault management, Energy efficiency.

1 Introduction

In the recent years, the rapid advances in micro-electro-mechanical systems, low power and highly integrated digital electronics, small scale energy supplies, tiny microprocessors, and low power radio technologies have created low power, low cost and multifunctional wireless sensor devices, which can observe and react to changes in physical phenomena of their environments. These sensor devices are equipped with a small battery, a tiny microprocessor, a radio transceiver, and a set of transducers that used to gathering information that report the changes in the environment of the sensor node. The emergence of these low cost and small size wireless sensor devices has motivated intensive research in the last decade addressing the potential of collaboration among sensors in data gathering and processing, which led to the creation of Wireless Sensor Networks (WSNs).

A typical WSN consists of a number of sensor devices that collaborate with each other to accomplish a common task (e.g. environment monitoring, target tracking, etc) and report the collected data through wireless interface to a base station or sink node. The areas of applications of WSNs vary from civil, healthcare and environmental to military. Examples of applications include target tracking in battlefields [1], habitat monitoring [2], civil structure monitoring [3], forest fire detection [4], and factory maintenance [5].

H. Cherifi, J.M. Zain, and E. El-Qawasmeh (Eds.): DICTAP 2011, Part I, CCIS 166, pp. 685–692, 2011.

Due to the deployment of a large number of sensor nodes in uncontrolled or even harsh or hostile environments, it is not uncommon for the sensor nodes to become faulty and unreliable. Fault is an incorrect state of hardware or a program as a consequence of a failure of a component [6]. Some of the faults result from systems or communication hardware failure and the fault state is continuous in time. For example, a node may die due to battery depletion. In this paper we consider only permanent faults, faults occurring due to battery depletion in particular, which when left unnoticed would cause loss in connectivity and coverage.

Faults occurring due to energy depletion are continuous and as the time progresses these faults may increase, resulting in a non-uniform network topology. This often results in scenarios where a certain segment of the network becomes energy constrained before the remaining network. The problems that can occur due to sensor node failure are loss in connectivity, delay due to the loss in connection and partitioning of the network due to the gap created by the failed sensors.

Therefore, to overcome sensor node failure and to guarantee system reliability, faulty nodes should be detected and appropriate measures to recover connectivity must be taken to accommodate for the faulty node. Also, the power supply on each sensor node is limited, and frequent replacement of the batteries is often not practical due to the large number of the nodes in the network. In this paper, we propose a cluster based fault management scheme which detects and rectifies the problems that arise out of energy depletion in nodes. When a sensor node fails, the connectivity is still maintained by reorganization of the cluster. Clustering algorithms such as LEACH [7] and HEED [8] saves energy and reduces network contention by enabling locality of communication.

The localized fault detection method has been found to be energy-efficient in comparison with another algorithm proposed in [9]. Crash faults identification (CFI) [9] performs fault detection for the sensor network. It does not propose any method for fault recovery.

In this paper we propose a centralized cluster based method called DFDM for fault detection and recovery which is energy efficient.

The rest of the paper organized as follows: in section 2, we explain the related works. Section 3 describes the proposed algorithm with detailed. Section 4 explore the simulation parameters and result analysis. Final section is containing of conclusion and future works.

2 Related Works

In this section, we briefly review the related work in the area of fault detection and recovery in wireless sensor networks. Many techniques have been proposed for fault detection, fault tolerance and repair in sensor networks [9, 10, 11, 12]. Cluster based approach for fault detection and repair has also been dealt by researchers in [12]. Hybrid sensor networks make use of mobile sensor nodes to detect and recover from faults [13, 14, 15].

In [16], a failure detection scheme using management architecture for WSNs called MANNA, is proposed and evaluated. It has the global vision of the network and can perform complex tasks that would not be possible inside the network. However, this approach requires an external manager to perform the centralized diagnosis and the communication between nodes and the manager is too expensive for WSNs. Several localized threshold based decision schemes were proposed by Iyengar [11] to detect both faulty sensors and event regions. In [10], a faulty sensor identification algorithm is developed and analyzed. The algorithm is purely localized and requires low computational overhead; it can be easily scaled to large sensor networks. It deals with faulty sensor readings that the sensors report.

In [17], a distributed fault-tolerant mechanism called CMATO for sensor-nets is proposed. It views the cluster as an individual whole and utilizes the monitoring of each other within the cluster to detect and recover from the faults in a quick and energy-efficient way. In fault recovery scheme of this algorithm the nodes within the cluster which its cluster head is faulty join to the neighbor cluster heads which is closest to them.

There have been several research efforts on fault repair in sensor networks. In [18], the authors proposed sensor deployment protocol which moves sensor to provide an initial coverage. In [19], the authors proposed an algorithm called Coverage Fidelity maintenance algorithm (Co-Fi), which uses mobility of sensor nodes to repair the coverage loss. To repair a faulty sensor, the work in [14] proposes an algorithm to locate the closest redundant sensor, and use the cascaded movement to relocate the redundant sensor. In [15], the authors proposed a policy-based framework for fault repair in sensor network, and proposed a centralized algorithm for faulty sensor replacement. These techniques outline the ways by which mobile robots/sensors move to replace the faulty nodes. However, movement of the sensor nodes is by itself energy consuming and also to move to an exact place to replace the faulty node and establish connectivity is tedious and energy consuming.

3 Proposed Protocol

Due to the large impact of the permanent faults in the cluster head side, in this paper we explore the fault-tolerant mechanism for it.

In this section, we explain the components which considered in proposed algorithm with details.

3.1 Network Model

Let us consider a sensor network which consists of N nodes uniformly deployed over a square area with high densely. There is a sink node located in the field, and the cluster heads use multi-hop routing to send data to it. Also the nodes in each cluster use tree topology to send data to cluster head. We assume all nodes, including the cluster heads and the normal nodes, are homogeneous and have the same capabilities, and they use power control to vary the amount of transmission power which depends on the distance to the receiver.

This paper deals with the fault detection at the cluster head and recovery the other nodes after the stage of cluster formation.

As can be seen in Fig. 1, this algorithm selects a node as a manager node in each cluster so that firstly it is in radio range of cluster head and secondly it has maximum remained energy and third it has maximum number of ordinary nodes in its neighborhood. For this reason, this algorithm uses (1) to select cluster manager.

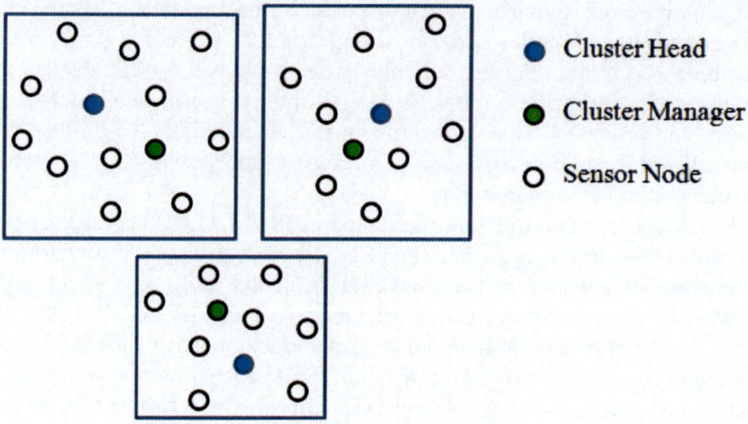

Fig. 1. Network model in DFDM

$$C\_V_{Manager} = \alpha(\frac{E_r}{E_i}) + \beta(\frac{N_{non}}{N_{aon}}) + \lambda(\frac{\Sigma E_{r\_non}}{\Sigma E_{i\_non}}) \quad (1)$$

Here, E_r is the remaining energy of the node and E_m is the amount of its initial energy. N_{non} of a node is the number of neighboring ordinary nodes which is in its transmission radio range and N_{aon} is the number of all ordinary nodes in cluster. $E_{r\text{-}non}$ is remaining energy of neighboring ordinary node and $E_{i\text{-}non}$ is its initial energy. Parameters α, β, λ determine the weight of each ratio so that sum of them is 1.

3.2 Energy Consumption Model

In DFDM, energy model is obtained from [7] that use both of the open space (energy dissipation d^2) and multi path (energy dissipation d^4) channels by taking amount the distance between the transmitter and receiver. So energy consumption for transmitting a packet of l bits in distance d is given by (2).

$$E_{Tx}(l,d) = \begin{cases} lE_{elec} + l\varepsilon_{fs} d^2 & , d \le d_0 \\ lE_{elec} + l\varepsilon_{mp} d^4 & , d > d_0 \end{cases} \quad (2)$$

Here d_0 is the distance threshold value which is obtained by (3), E_{elec} is required energy for activating the electronic circuits. ε_{fs} and ε_{mp} are required energy for amplification of transmitted signals to transmit a one bit in open space and multi path models, respectively.

$$d_0 = \sqrt{\frac{\varepsilon_{fs}}{\varepsilon_{mp}}}. \quad (3)$$

Energy consumption to receive a packet of l bits is calculated by (4).

$$E_{Rx}(l) = lE_{elec}\,. \tag{4}$$

3.3 Fault Detection

In this section, we discuss method to detect the faults in the cluster heads and report to the members of the clusters. This detection is essential for the cluster members as they have to invoke mechanism for the repair and recovery of those faults so as to keep the cluster connected.

In proposed algorithm, cluster manager is responsible to detecting the fault at the cluster head in each cluster. For this propose, cluster manager send an AWAKE message to cluster head periodically. If it does not receive any response from cluster head, it recognizes that cluster head of its cluster is fault.

3.4 Fault Recovery

In this section, we discuss the mechanism to fault recovery. The fault recovery refers to the connectivity recovery after the cluster head has failed. The cluster head faults discussed here are confined to failure due to energy exhaustion. The fault recovery mechanism is performed locally by each cluster.

If cluster head is declared failed, all the cluster members would be notified through the broadcasted CH-fail message from cluster manager.

In this time, cluster manager selects a new cluster head for this cluster among all neighboring nodes which are in its radio range according to (5).

$$C\_V_{New\_CH} = \frac{E_r}{(D_{nch\_och})^2} \tag{5}$$

Here, E_r is the remaining energy of the node and $D_{nch\text{-}och}$ is the distance between the node that wants to new cluster head and old cluster head which is faulty node.

The node is selected as a new cluster head that is closer to old cluster head and also has maximum remaining energy.

4 Simulation Results

In this section, we present and discuss the simulation results for the performance study of DFDM protocol. We used GCC to implement and simulate DFDM and compare it with the CMATO protocol.

The network is clustered using the LEACH and HEED clustering algorithms, the cluster heads then organize into a spanning tree for routing. We implement DFDM in both LEACH and HEED protocol. The transmission ranges were varied from 20 m to 120 m. Simulation parameters are presented in Table 1 and obtained results are shown below.

Table 1. Simulation parameters

Parameters	Value
Network area	200 meters × 200 meters
Base station location	(0, 0)m
Number of sensors	100
Initial energy	3J
E_{elec}	50 nJ/bit
ε_{fs}	10 pJ/bit/m2
ε_{mp}	0.0013 pJ/bit/m4
d_0	87 m
E_{DA}	5 nJ/bit/signal
Data packet size	4800 bytes
Beacon packet size	30 bytes

Fig. 2 shows the average energy loss for fault detection in DFDM and CMATO. In this evaluation, we change the transmission range at the all nodes, and measure the energy loss for fault detection.

As it can be seen, proposed protocol has performance better than CMATO in average energy loss for fault detection.

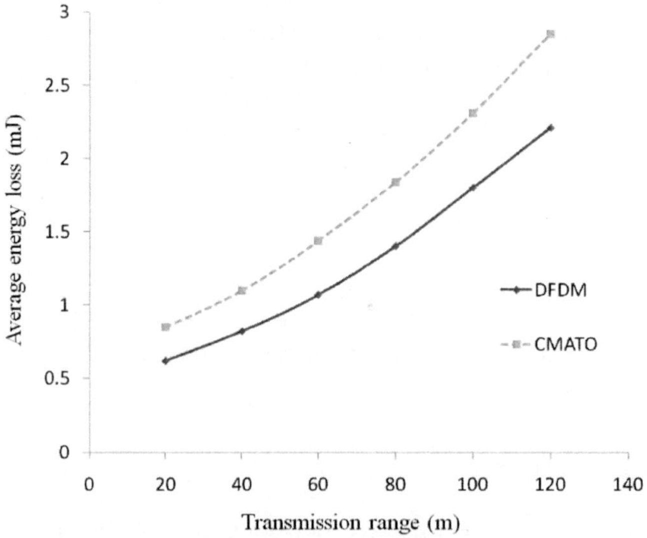

Fig. 2. Average energy loss for fault detection

4 Conclusion

In this paper we propose a decentralized cluster based method namely DFDM for fault detection and recovery which is energy efficient. Simulation Results show that the DFDM consumes less energy for fault detection and uses the new energy efficient method to fault recovery that prolongs the network lifetime.

References

1. Bokareva, T., Hu, W., Kanhere, S., Ristic, B., Gordon, N., Bessell, T., Rutten, M., Jha, S.: Wireless Sensor Networks for Battlefield Surveillance. In: roceedings of The Land Warfare Conference (LWC 2006), Brisbane, Australia, October 24 – 27 (2006)
2. Mainwaring, A., Polastre, J., Szewczyk, R., Culler, D., Anderson, J.: Wireless Sensor Networks for Habitat Monitoring. In: The Proceedings of the 1st ACM International Workshop on Wireless Sensor Networks and Applications (ACM-WSNA), Atlanta, Georgia, USA, September 28 - 28, pp. 88–97 (2002)
3. Xu, N., Rangwala, S., Chintalapudi, K., Ganesan, D., Broad, A., Govindan, R., Estrin, D.: A Wireless Sensor Network for structural Monitoring. In: Proc. ACM SenSys Conf. (November 2004)
4. Hefeeda, M., Bagheri, M.: Wireless Sensor Networks for Early Detection of Forest Fires. In: The proceedings of IEEE Internatonal Conference on Mobile Adhoc and Sensor Systems, Pisa, Italy, October 8-11, pp. 1–6. Pisa, Italy (2007)
5. Srinivasan, K., Ndoh, M., Nie, H., Xia, C(H.), Kaluri, K., Ingraham, D.: Wireless technologies for condition-based maintenance (CBM) in petroleum plants. In: Prasanna, V.K., Iyengar, S.S., Spirakis, P.G., Welsh, M. (eds.) DCOSS 2005. LNCS, vol. 3560, pp. 389–390. Springer, Heidelberg (2005)
6. Koushanfar, F., Potkonjak, M., Sangiovanni-Vincentelli, A.: Fault tolerance in wireless ad hoc sensor networks. IEEE Sensors 2, 1491–1496 (2002)
7. Heinzelman, W.B., Chandrakasan, A.P., Balakrishnan, H.: Energy-Efficient Communication Protocol for Wireless Microsensor Networks. In: Proceedings of the Hawaii International Conference on System Sciences (2000)
8. Younis, O., Fahmy, S.: HEED: A Hybrid, Energy-Efficient, Distributed Clustering Approach for Ad Hoc Sensor Networks. IEEE Transactions on Mobile Computing 3(4), 366–379 (2004)
9. Chessa, S., Santi, P.: Crash Faults Identification in Wireless Sensor Networks. Computer Comm. 25(14), 1273–1282 (2002)
10. Ding, M., Chen, D., Xing, K., Cheng, X.: Localized fault-tolerant event boundary detection in sensor networks. In: IEEE Infocom (March 2005)
11. Krishnamachari, B., Iyengar, S.: Distributed Bayesian Algorithms for Fault-tolerant Event Region Detection in Wireless Sensor Network. IEEE Transactions on Computers 53(3), 241–250 (2004)
12. Gupta, G., Younis, M.: Fault-tolerant clustering of wireless sensor networks. In: Wireless Communications and Networking, WCNC 2003, March 16-20, vol. 3, pp. 1579–1584 (2003)
13. Mei, Y., Xian, C., Das, S., Hu, Y.C., Lu, Y.H.: Repairing Sensor Networks Using Mobile Robots. In: Proceedings of the ICDCS International Workshop on Wireless Ad Hoc and Sensor Networks (IEEE WWASN 2006), Lisboa, Portugal, July 4-7 (2006)
14. Wang, G., Cao, G., Porta, T., Zhang, W.: Sensor relocation in mobile sensor networks. In: The 24th Conference of the IEEE Communications Society, INFOCOM (March 2005)
15. Le, T., Ahmed, N., Parameswaran, N., Jha, S.: Fault repair framework for mobile sensor networks. In: IEEE COMSWARE (2006)
16. Ruiz, L.B., Siqueira, I.G., Oliveira, L.B., Wong, H.C., Nogueira, J.M.S., Loureiro, A.A.F.: Fault management in event-driven wireless sensor networks. In: MSWiM 2004: Proceedings of the 7th ACM International Symposium on Modeling, Analysis and Simulation of Wireless and Mobile Systems, New York, pp. 149–156 (2004)

17. Lai, Y., Chen, H.: Energy-Efficient Fault-Tolerant Mechanism for Clustered Wireless Sensor Networks. In: Proceedings of 16th International Conference on Computer Communications and Networks, pp. 272–277 (2007)
18. Wang, G., Cao, G., Porta, T.L.: A bidding protocol for deploying mobile sensors. In: 11th IEEE International Conference on Network Protocol ICNP 2003, pp. 315–324 (November 2003)
19. Ganeriwal, S., Kansal, A., Srivastava, M.B.: Self aware actuation for fault repair in sensor networks. In: IEEE International Conference on Robotics and Automation (ICRA) (May 2004)

RLMP: Reliable and Location Based Multi-Path Routing Algorithm for Wireless Sensor Networks

Saeed Rasouli Heikalabad[1], Naeim Rahmani[2], Farhad Nematy[2], and Hosein Rasouli[1]

[1] Department of Technical and Engineering, Tabriz Branch, Islamic Azad University, Tabriz, Iran
{S.Rasouli.H,Hosein.Heikalabad}@Gmail.com

[2] Department of Technical and Engineering, Tabriz Branch, Islamic Azad University, Tabriz, Iran
{Naeim.Rahmani,Farhad_Nematy}@yahoo.com

Abstract. Considering the necessity of reliability providing and lifetime prolonging in wireless sensor networks as Quality of Service requirements, it is necessary to present a new routing algorithm that can best provide these requirements in network layer. For this purpose, we propose a new multi path routing algorithm namely RLMP which guarantees achieve to required QoS of wireless sensor networks and balances the energy consumption in all nodes. Simulation Results show that the performance of proposed algorithm in providing quality of service requirements of different applications is more efficient than previous algorithms.

Keywords: Wireless sensor network; Multi-path routing; Reliable; Energy balancing.

1 Introduction

In the recent years, the rapid advances in micro-electro-mechanical systems, low power and highly integrated digital electronics, small scale energy supplies, tiny microprocessors, and low power radio technologies have created low power, low cost and multifunctional wireless sensor devices, which can observe and react to changes in physical phenomena of their environments. These sensor devices are equipped with a small battery, a tiny microprocessor, a radio transceiver, and a set of transducers that used to gathering information that report the changes in the environment of the sensor node. The emergence of these low cost and small size wireless sensor devices has motivated intensive research in the last decade addressing the potential of collaboration among sensors in data gathering and processing, which led to the creation of Wireless Sensor Networks (WSNs).

A typical WSN consists of a number of sensor devices that collaborate with each other to accomplish a common task (e.g. environment monitoring, target tracking, etc) and report the collected data through wireless interface to a base station or sink node. The areas of applications of WSNs vary from civil, healthcare and environmental to military. Examples of applications include target tracking in battlefields [1], habitat

H. Cherifi, J.M. Zain, and E. El-Qawasmeh (Eds.): DICTAP 2011, Part I, CCIS 166, pp. 693–703, 2011.

monitoring [2], civil structure monitoring [3], forest fire detection [4], and factory maintenance [5].

However, with the specific consideration of the unique properties of sensor networks such limited power, stringent bandwidth, dynamic topology (due to nodes failures or even physical mobility), high network density and large scale deployments have caused many challenges in the design and management of sensor networks. These challenges have demanded energy awareness and robust protocol designs at all layers of the networking protocol stack [6].

Efficient utilization of sensor's energy resources and maximizing the network lifetime were and still are the main design considerations for the most proposed protocols and algorithms for sensor networks and have dominated most of the research in this area. The concepts of latency, throughput and packet loss have not yet gained a great focus from the research community. However, depending on the type of application, the generated sensory data normally have different attributes, where it may contain delay sensitive and reliability demanding data. For example, the data generated by a sensor network that monitors the temperature in a normal weather monitoring station are not required to be received by the sink node within certain time limits. On the other hand, for a sensor network that used for fire detection in a forest, any sensed data that carries an indication of a fire should be reported to the processing center within certain time limits. Furthermore, the introduction of multimedia sensor networks along with the increasing interest in real time applications have made strict constraints on both throughput and delay in order to report the time-critical data to the sink within certain time limits and bandwidth requirements without any loss. These performance metrics (i.e. delay, energy consumption and bandwidth) are usually referred to as Quality of Service (QoS) requirements [7]. Therefore, enabling many applications in sensor networks requires energy and QoS awareness in different layers of the protocol stack in order to have efficient utilization of the network resources and effective access to sensors readings. Thus QoS routing is an important topic in sensor networks research, and it has been under the focus of the research community of WSNs. Refer to [7] and [8] for surveys on QoS based routing protocol in WSNs.

Many routing mechanisms specifically designed for WSNs have been proposed [9][10]. In these works, the unique properties of the WSNs have been taken into account. These routing techniques can be classified according to the protocol operation into negotiation based, query based, QoS based, and multi-path based. The negotiation based protocols have the objective to eliminate the redundant data by include high level data descriptors in the message exchange. In query based protocols, the sink node initiates the communication by broadcasting a query for data over the network. The QoS based protocols allow sensor nodes to make a tradeoff between the energy consumption and some QoS metrics before delivering the data to the sink node [11]. Finally, multi-path routing protocols use multiple paths rather than a single path in order to improve the network performance in terms of reliability and robustness. Multi-path routing establishes multiple paths between the source-destination pair. Multi-path routing protocols have been discussed in the literature for several years now [12]. Mutli-path routing has focused on the use of multiple paths primarily for load balancing, fault tolerance, bandwidth aggregation, and reduced delay. We focus to guarantee the required quality of service through multi-path routing.

The rest of the paper organized as follows: in section 2, we explain the related works. Section 3 describes the proposed algorithm with detailed. Section 4 explore the simulation parameters and result analysis. Final section is containing of conclusion and future works.

2 Related Works

QoS-based routing in sensor networks is a challenging problem because of the scarce resources of the sensor node. Thus, this problem has received a significant attention from the research community, where many works are being made. Some QoS oriented routing works are surveyed in [7] and [8]. In this section we do not give a comprehensive summary of the related work, instead we present and discuss some works related to proposed protocol.

One of the early proposed routing protocols that provide some QoS is the Sequential Assignment Routing (SAR) protocol [13]. SAR protocol is a multi-path routing protocol that makes routing decisions based on three factors: energy resources, QoS on each path, and packet's priority level. Multiple paths are created by building a tree rooted at the source to the destination. During construction of paths those nodes which have low QoS and low residual energy are avoided. Upon the construction of the tree, most of the nodes will belong to multiple paths. To transmit data to sink, SAR computes a weighted QoS metric as a product of the additive QoS metric and a weighted coefficient associated with the priority level of the packet to select a path. Employing multiple paths increases fault tolerance, but SAR protocol suffers from the overhead of maintaining routing tables and QoS metrics at each sensor node.

K. Akkaya and M. Younis in [14] proposed a cluster based QoS aware routing protocol that employs a queuing model to handle both real-time and non real time traffic. The protocol only considers the end-to-end delay. The protocol associates a cost function with each link and uses the K-least-cost path algorithm to find a set of the best candidate routes. Each of the routes is checked against the end-to-end constraints and the route that satisfies the constraints is chosen to send the data to the sink. All nodes initially are assigned the same bandwidth ratio which makes constraints on other nodes which require higher bandwidth ratio. Furthermore, the transmission delay is not considered in the estimation of the end-to-end delay, which sometimes results in selecting routes that do not meet the required end-to-end delay. However, the problem of bandwidth assignment is solved in [15] by assigning a different bandwidth ratio for each type of traffic for each node.

SPEED [16] is another QoS based routing protocol that provides soft real-time end-to-end guarantees. Each sensor node maintains information about its neighbors and exploits geographic forwarding to find the paths. To ensure packet delivery within the required time limits, SPEED enables the application to compute the end-to-end delay by dividing the distance to the sink by the speed of packet delivery before making any admission decision. Furthermore, SPEED can provide congestion avoidance when the network is congested.

However, while SPEED has been compared with other protocols and it has showed less energy consumption than other protocols, this does not mean that SPEED is energy efficient, because the protocols used in the comparison are not energy aware.

SPEED does not consider any energy metric in its routing protocol, which makes a question about its energy efficiency. Therefore to better study the energy efficiency of the SPEED protocol; it should be compared with energy aware routing protocols.

Felemban et al. [17] propose Multi-path and Multi-Speed Routing Protocol (MMSPEED) for probabilistic QoS guarantee in WSNs. Multiple QoS levels are provided in the timeliness domain by using different delivery speeds, while various requirements are supported by probabilistic multipath forwarding in the reliability domain.

Recently, X. Huang and Y. Fang have proposed multi constrained QoS multi-path routing (MCMP) protocol [18] that uses braided routes to deliver packets to the sink node according to certain QoS requirements expressed in terms of reliability and delay. The problem of the end-to-end delay is formulated as an optimization problem, and then an algorithm based on linear integer programming is applied to solve the problem. The protocol objective is to utilize the multiple paths to augment network performance with moderate energy cost. However, the protocol always routes the information over the path that includes minimum number of hops to satisfy the required QoS, which leads in some cases to more energy consumption. Authors in [19], have proposed the Energy constrained multi-path routing (ECMP) that extends the MCMP protocol by formulating the QoS routing problem as an energy optimization problem constrained by reliability, playback delay, and geo-spatial path selection constraints. The ECMP protocol trades between minimum number of hops and minimum energy by selecting the path that satisfies the QoS requirements and minimizes energy consumption.

Meeting QoS requirements in WSNs introduces certain overhead into routing protocols in terms of energy consumption, intensive computations, and significantly large storage. This overhead is unavoidable for those applications that need certain delay and bandwidth requirements. In our work, we combine different ideas from the previous protocols in order to optimally tackle the problem of QoS in sensor networks. In our proposal we try to satisfy the QoS requirements for real time applications with the minimum energy. Our RLMP routing protocol performs paths discovery using multiple criteria such as energy remaining, probability of packet sending, average probability of packet receiving and interference.

3 Proposed Protocol

In this section, we explain the assumptions and energy consumption model used in RLMP and describe the various constituent parts of the proposed protocol.

3.1 Assumptions

We assume that all nodes are randomly distributed in desired environment and each of them is assigned a unique ID. At start, the initial energy of nodes is considered equal. All nodes in the network are aware of their location (by positioning schemes such as [24]) and also are able to control their energy consumption. Because of this assumption has been that the nodes can communicate with other nodes outside their radio range in the absence of node in their radio transmission range.

Let us assume that nodes are aware of their remaining energy and also remaining energy of other nodes in their transmission radio range (via received beacon from them). We consider that each node can calculate its probabilities of packet sending and packet receiving with regard to link quality. Predications and decisions about path stability may be made by examining recent link quality information.

3.2 Energy Consumption Model

In RLMP, energy model is obtained from [20] that use both of the open space (energy dissipation d^2) and multi path (energy dissipation d^4) channels by taking amount the distance between the transmitter and receiver. So energy consumption for transmitting a packet of l bits in distance d is given by (1).

$$E_{Tx}(l,d)=\begin{cases} lE_{elec}+l\varepsilon_{fs}d^2 & ,d\le d_0 \\ lE_{elec}+l\varepsilon_{mp}d^4 & ,d>d_0 \end{cases} \tag{1}$$

In here d_0 is the distance threshold value which is obtained by (2), E_{elec} is required energy for activating the electronic circuits. ε_{fs} and ε_{mp} are required energy for amplification of transmitted signals to transmit a one bit in open space and multi path models, respectively.

$$d_0=\sqrt{\frac{\varepsilon_{fs}}{\varepsilon_{mp}}}. \tag{2}$$

Energy consumption to receive a packet of l bits is calculated according to (3).

$$E_{Rx}(l)=lE_{elec}. \tag{3}$$

3.3 Link Suitability

The link suitability is used by the node to select the node at the next hop as a forwarder during the path discovery phase. Let N_A be a set of neighbors of node A. Then our suitability function includes the *PPS* (Probability of Packet Sending), *APPR* (Average Probability of Packet Receiving) and I_B (Interference of link A and B) and is obtained by (4).

$$l_{AB}=\max_{B\in N_A}\{PPS_B+APPR_{N_B}+1/I_B+\frac{E_A+E_B}{(D_{A\_B}+D_{B\_S})^2}\}. \tag{4}$$

In here, B is the node at the next hop. PPS_B is the probability of packet sending of node B. Each node calculates the value of this parameter by (5). $APPR_{NB}$ is the average probability of packet receiving of all neighbors of node B that obtained by (6). I_B is interference of link between A and B. In this paper, I_B is same signal to noise ratio (SNR) for the link between A and B. The relationship used in final section of (4) is used for balancing the energy consumption which introduced in [21]. E_A and E_B are remaining energies of node A and node B, respectively. $D_{A\text{-}B}$ is distance between node A and node B and $D_{B\text{-}S}$ is distance between node B and base station.

$$PPS = \frac{Number-of-Successful-Sending-Packets}{Total-Number-of-Sending-Packets}. \tag{5}$$

$$APPR_{N_B} = \left(\sum_{j=C, C \in N_B}^{for\ all\ C\ in\ N_B} PPR_j \right) / n(N_B). \tag{6}$$

In here, PPR_j is probability of packet receiving of node j which is the neighbor node of node *B*. purpose of $n(N_B)$ is the number of neighbor nodes of node *B*.

The total merit (TM) for a path *p* consists of a set of *K* nodes is the sum of the individual link merit $l_{(AB)}$ along the path. Then the total merit is calculated by (7).

$$TM_p = \sum_{i=1}^{K-1} l_{(AB)_i} \tag{7}$$

3.4 Paths Discovery Mechanism in RLMP

In multi-path routing, node-disjoint paths (i.e. have no common nodes except the source and the destination) are usually preferred because they utilize the most available network resources, and hence are the most fault-tolerant. If an intermediate node in a set of node-disjoint paths fails, only the path containing it node is affected, so there is a minimum impact to the diversity of the routes [22].

In first phase of path discovery procedure, each node collects the needed information about its neighbors by beacon exchange between them and then updates its neighboring table.

After this phase, each sensor node has enough information to compute the link suitability for its neighboring nodes.

For faster execution of multi-path discovery, this mechanism is done in parallel. For this purpose, in first, the source node broadcasts the RREQ message to all its neighbors that are closer than itself to the base station. Fig. 1 shows the RREQ message structure.

Source ID	Path ID	TM_p

Fig. 1. RREQ message structure

Then the nodes at the next hop locally computes its preferred next hop node using the link suitability function, and sends out a RREQ message to its most preferred next hop. This operation continues until sink. The TM_p parameter is updated at each hop.

To avoid having paths with shared node and to create disjoint paths, we limit each node to accept only one RREQ message with the same source ID. Those nodes that have joined to a path as a forwarder at next hop, if receive the RREQ message with same source ID from other nodes, immediately broadcast an BUSY message to it node to announce that it have been part of a path. Fig. 2 depicts this operation.

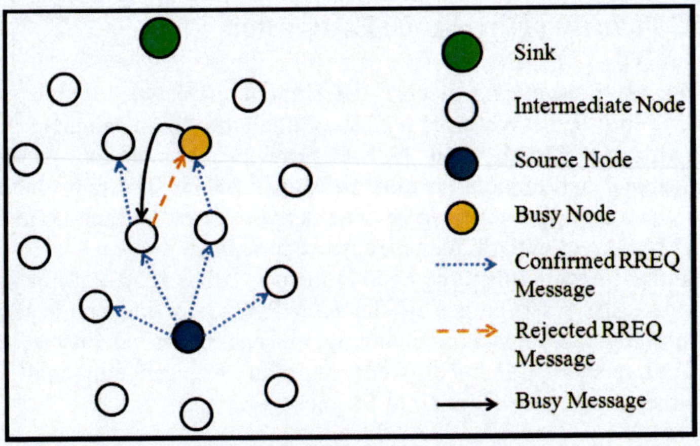

Fig. 2. RREQ and BUSY messages transmission

3.5 Path Maintenance

In order to energy saving, we reduce the overhead traffic through reducing control messages. Therefore, instead of periodically flooding a KEEP-ALIVE message to keep multiple paths alive and update merit function metrics, we append the metrics on the data message by attaching the residual energy and link quality to the data message.

3.6 Paths Selection

After the execution of paths discovery phase and the paths have been constructed, we need to select a set of paths from the N available paths to transfer the traffic from the source to the destination with a desired bound of data delivery given by α. To find the number of required paths, we assume that each path is associated with some rate *pi* (i=1, 2 … N) that corresponds to the probability of successfully delivering a message to the destination which is calculated by (8). Following the work done in [23], the number of required paths is calculated by (9).

$$P_i = 1 - \prod(1 - PSDT_j). \quad (8)$$

In here, $PSDT_j$ is the estimated packet reception rate to the node j, which is one of the nodes in the desired path.

$$k = x_a \sqrt{\sum_{i=1}^{N} p_i (1 - p_i)} + \sum_{i=1}^{N} p_i . \quad (9)$$

In here, x_a is the corresponding bound from the standard normal distribution for different levels of α. Table 1 lists some values for x_a.

Table 1. Some values for the different bounds [23]

α	95%	90%	85%	80%	50%
x_a	-1.65	-1.28	-1.03	-0.85	0

4 Simulation and Performance Evaluation

In this section, we present and discuss the simulation results for the performance study of RLMP protocol. We used GCC to implement and simulate RLMP and compare it with the MCMP and ECMP protocols. Simulation parameters are presented in Table 2 and obtained results are shown below. The radio model used in the simulation was a duplex transceiver. The network stack of each node consists of IEEE 802.11 MAC layer with 50 meter transmission range.

We assume that location of source node in the network is (250, 250) meters.

We investigate the performance of the RLMP protocol in a multi-hop network topology. We study the impact of changing the packet arrival rate on end-to-end delay, packet delivery ratio, and energy consumption. We change the real-time packet arrival rate at the source node from 10 to 55 packets/sec.

Table 2. Simulation parameters

Parameters	Value
Network area	400 meters × 400 meters
Base station location	(0, 0)m
Number of sensors	100
Initial energy	2J
E_{elec}	50 nJ/bit
ε_{fs}	10 pJ/bit/m2
ε_{mp}	0.0013 pJ/bit/m4
d_0	87 m
E_{DA}	5 nJ/bit/signal
Data packet size	512 bytes
Beacon packet size	50 bytes

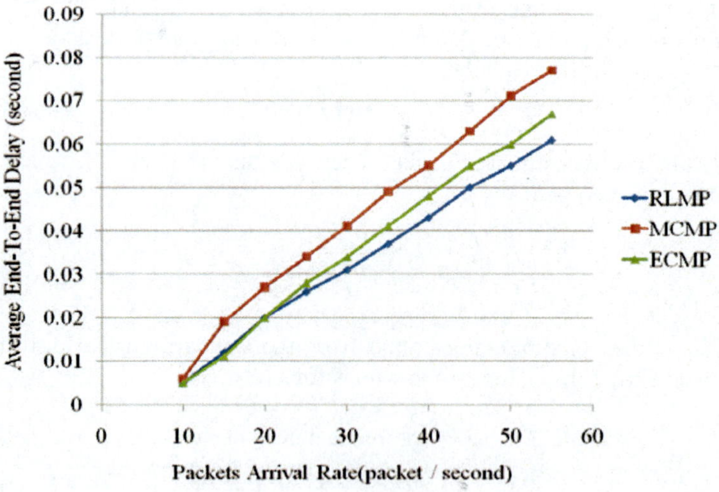

Fig. 3. Average end to end delay

4.1 Average End-to-End Delay

The average end-to-end delay is the time required to transfer data successfully from source node to the destination node.

Fig. 3 shows the average end to end delay for RLMP, MCMP and ECMP. In this evaluation, we change the packet arrival rate at the source node, and measure the delay.

As it can be seen, proposed protocol has performance better than MCMP and ECMP in average end to end delay.

4.2 Average Energy Consumption

The average energy consumption is the average of the energy consumed by the nodes participating in message transfer from source node to the destination node.

Fig. 4 shows the results for energy consumption in RLMP, MCMP and ECMP protocols. As it can be seen, in our protocol, energy consumption for packet sending is some deal optimize in comparison to the MCMP and ECMP.

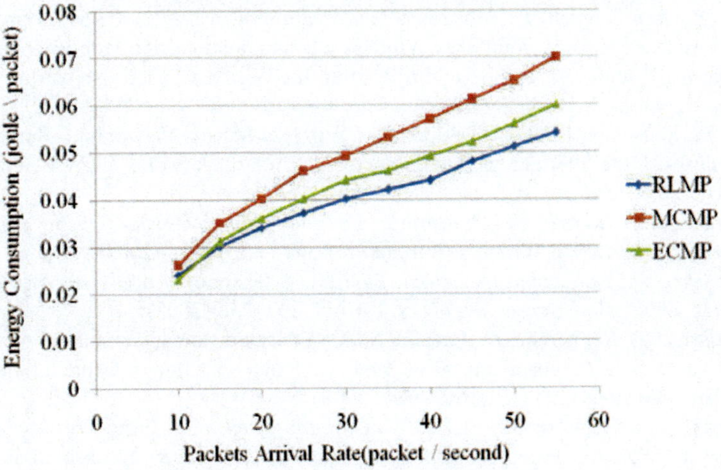

Fig. 4. Average energy consumption

5 Conclusion

In this paper, we propose the new multi path routing algorithm for real time applications in wireless sensor network namely RLMP which is QoS aware and can increase the network lifetime. Our protocol uses four main metrics of QoS with special relation in path discovery mechanism. Simulation Result shows that the performance of RLMP in end to end delay is optimized compared to the MCMP and ECMP protocols.

References

1. Bokareva, T., Hu, W., Kanhere, S., Ristic, B., Gordon, N., Bessell, T., Rutten, M., Jha, S.: Wireless Sensor Networks for Battlefield Surveillance. In: Proceedings of The Land Warfare Conference (LWC)– Brisbane, Australia, October 24-27 (2006)
2. Mainwaring, A., Polastre, J., Szewczyk, R., Culler, D., Anderson, J.: Wireless Sensor Networks for Habitat Monitoring. In: the Proceedings of the 1st ACM International Workshop on Wireless Sensor Networks and Applications (ACM-WSNA), Atlanta, Georgia, USA, September 28, pp. 88–97 (2002)
3. Xu, N., Rangwala, S., Chintalapudi, K., Ganesan, D., Broad, A., Govindan, R., Estrin, D.: A Wireless Sensor Network for structural Monitoring. In: Proc. ACM SenSys Conf. (November 2004)
4. Hefeeda, M., Bagheri, M.: Wireless Sensor Networks for Early Detection of Forest Fires. In: The Proceedings of IEEE Internatonal Conference on Mobile Adhoc and Sensor Systems, Pisa, Italy, pp. 1–6 (2007)
5. Srinivasan, K., Ndoh, M., Nie, H., Xia, C(H.), Kaluri, K., Ingraham, D.: Wireless technologies for condition-based maintenance (CBM) in petroleum plants. In: Prasanna, V.K., Iyengar, S.S., Spirakis, P.G., Welsh, M. (eds.) DCOSS 2005. LNCS, vol. 3560, pp. 389–390. Springer, Heidelberg (2005)
6. Yahya, B., Ben-Othman, J.: Towards a classification of energy aware MAC protocols for wireless sensor networks. Journal of Wireless Communications and Mobile Computing
7. Akkaya, K., Younis, M.: A Survey on Routing for Wireless Sensor Networks. Journal of Ad Hoc Networks 3, 325–349 (2005)
8. Chen, D., Varshney, P.K.: QoS Support in Wireless Sensor Networks: a Survey. In: the Proceedings of the International Conference on Wireless Networks (ICWN), pp. 227–233 (2004)
9. Al-Karaki, J.N., Kamal, A.E.: Routing Techniques in Wireless Sensor Networks: A Survey. IEEE Journal of Wireless Communications 11(6), 6–28 (2004)
10. Martirosyan, A., Boukerche, A., Pazzi, R.W.N.: A Taxonomy of Cluster-Based Routing Protocols for Wireless Sensor Networks. ISPAN, 247–253 (2008)
11. Martirosyan, A., Boukerche, A., Pazzi, R.W.N.: Energy-aware and quality of service-based routing in wireless sensor networks and vehicular ad hoc networks. Annales des Telecommunications 63(11-12), 669–681 (2008)
12. Tsai, J., Moors, T.: A Review of Multipath Routing Protocols: From Wireless Ad Hoc to Mesh Networks. In: Proc. ACoRN Early Career Researcher Workshop on Wireless Multihop Networking, July 17-18 (2006)
13. Sohrabi, K., Pottie, J.: Protocols for self-organization of a wirless sensor network. IEEE Personal Communications 7(5), 16–27 (2000)
14. Akkaya, K., Younis, M.: An energy aware QoS routing protocol for wireless sensor networks. In: The Proceedings of the MWN, Providence, pp. 710–715 (2003)
15. Younis, M., Youssef, M., Arisha, K.: Energy aware routing in cluster based sensor networks. In: The Proceedings of the 10th IEEE International Syposium on Modleing, Analysis, and Simulation of Computer and Telecommunication Systems (MASCOTS 2002), Fort Worth, October 11-16 (2002)
16. He, T., et al.: SPEED: A stateless protocol for real-time communication in sensor networks. In: The Proceedings of the Internation Conference on Distributed Computing Systems, Providence, RI (May 2003)

17. Felemban, E., Lee, C., Ekici, E.: MMSPEED: multipath multispeed protocol for QoS guarantee of reliability and timeliness in wireless sensor networks. IEEE Trans. on Mobile Computing 5(6), 738–754 (2006)
18. Huang, X., Fang, Y.: Multiconstrained QoS Mutlipath Routing in Wireless Sensor Networks. Wireless Networks 14, 465–478 (2008)
19. Bagula, A.B., Mazandu, K.G.: Energy Constrained Multipath Routing in Wireless Sensor Networks. In: Sandnes, F.E., Zhang, Y., Rong, C., Yang, L.T., Ma, J. (eds.) UIC 2008. LNCS, vol. 5061, pp. 453–467. Springer, Heidelberg (2008)
20. Heinzelman, W.B., Chandrakasan, A.P., Balakrishnan, H.: Energy-Efficient Communication Protocol for Wireless Microsensor Networks. In: Proceedings of the Hawaii International Conference on System Sciences (2000)
21. Rasouli Heikalabad, S., Habibizad Navin, A., Mirnia, M.K., Ebadi, S., Golesorkhtabar, M.: EBDHR: Energy Balancing and Dynamic Hierarchical Routing algorithm for wireless sensor networks. IEICE Electron. Express 7(15), 1112–1118 (2010)
22. Ganesan, D., Govindan, R., Shenker, S., Estrin, D.: Highly-resilient, energy-efficient multipath routing in wireless sensor networks. ACM SIGMOBILE Mobile Computing and CommunicationsReview 5(4), 11–25 (2001)
23. Dulman, S., Nieberg, T., Wu, J., Havinga, P.: Trade-off between Traffic Overhead and Reliability in Multipath Routing for Wireless Sensor Networks. In: The Proceeding of IEEE WCNC-2003, vol. 3, pp. 1918–1922 (March 2003)
24. Shi, Q., Huo, H., Fang, T., Li, D.: A 3D Node Localization Scheme for Wireless Sensor Networks. IEICE Electron. Express 6(3), 167–172 (2009)

Contention Window Optimization for Distributed Coordination Function (DCF) to Improve Quality of Service at MAC Layer

Maamar Sedrati[1], Azeddine Bilami[1], Ramdane Maamri[2], and Mohamed Benmohammed[2]

[1] Computer Science Departement, Faculté des Sciences, UHL, Université de Batna
[2] Computer Science Departement, Faculté des Sciences, UMC, Université de Constantine Algeria
msedrati@gmail.com, msedrati@univ-batna.dz

Abstract. With emergence of new multimedia and real-time applications demanding high throughput and reduced delay, the existing wireless local networks (WLANs) characterized by mobile stations with a low bandwidth and high rate error are not able to provide these QoS (Quality of Service) requirements.

After collisions during competitive access to the channel, packets must be retransmitted. These retransmissions consume enough bandwidth and increase the end-to-end delay for these packets. To address this, our solution tries to propose a new incrementing way for contention window (CW) with more realistic values in DCF (Distributed Coordination Function) at MAC layer. In order, to provide an opportunity for each station which needs to use a given channel, a way to access it after a small number of attempts called "Ret" (i.e. avoid the problem of starvation), we proposed to use "Ret" value in a new way to calculate CW values.

To show the performance of the proposed solution, simulations were conducted under Network Simulator (NS2) to measure the traffic control and packet loss ratio under various constraints (mobility, density, etc…).

Keywords: Quality of service, wireless local area networks, WLAN, DCF, MAC, CW, Network Simulator NS2.

1 Introduction

In Recent years, IEEE 802.11 [1] standard has emerged as the dominating technology for Wireless local area network (WLAN). Low cost, ease of deployment and mobility support has resulted in the vast popularity of IEEE 802.11 WLANs. They can be easily deployed in various locations. With emergence of new multimedia and real-time applications demanding high throughput and reduced delay, people want to use these applications through WLAN connections. The standard WLAN use the traditional best effort service able to support data applications. So, multimedia and real time applications require quality of service (QoS) support such as guaranteed bandwidth and low delay.

H. Cherifi, J.M. Zain, and E. El-Qawasmeh (Eds.): DICTAP 2011, Part I, CCIS 166, pp. 704–713, 2011.

The Quality of service (QoS) is the most important factor which gives which gives great satisfaction to the customer and great benefice to the providers.

Several studies has been done to improve quality of service (QoS) in network domain and particularly in ad hoc WLAN. QoS has to be guaranteed in reality at different levels of protocol architecture i.e. in different network layers (physical, network, etc.).

The medium access control (MAC) layer of 802.11 [1] are also designed to get the best effort data transmissions; the original 802.11 standard does not take QoS into account. Hence to provide QoS support IEEE 802.11 standard group has specified a new IEEE 802.11e standard [2]. which supports QoS by providing differentiated classes of service in the medium access control(MAC) layer [3], it also enhances the physical layer so that it can delivery time sensitive multimedia traffic, in addition to traditional data packets. A lot of researches are underway to ensure acceptable QoS over wireless mediums [4].

The remainder of this article is organized as follows: Section 2 describes the 802.11 legacy DCF and its limitations [5]. In section 3 we present a detailed description of the proposed solution. Section 4 evaluates the performances of our solution by comparing them to basic DCF. Finally section 5 concludes and outlines open research directions.

2 Distributed Coordination Function (DCF)

DCF is the fundamental MAC method used in IEEE 802.11 [1] and based on a CSMA/CA (Carrier Sense Multiple Access with Collision Avoidance) mechanism. The CSMA/CA (Carrier Sense Multiple Access with Collision Avoidance) constitutes a distributed MAC based on a local assessment of the channel status, i.e. whether the channel is busy or idle. If the channel is busy, the MAC waits until the medium becomes idle, and after a specified period of time called the DCF Interframe Space (DIFS). If the channel stays idle during the DIFS deference, the MAC then starts the backoff process by selecting a random backoff counter. For each slot time interval, during which the medium stays idle, the random backoff counter is decremented. If a certain station does not get access to the medium in the first cycle, it stops its backoff counter, waits for the channel to be idle again for DIFS and starts the counter again. As soon as the counter expires (becomes zero), the station accesses the medium. Hence the deferred stations don't choose a randomized backoff counter again, but continue to count down. Stations waiting for long time will have the advantage over the others which are just entered, in that they only have to wait for the remainder of their backoff counter from the previous cycle(s).

Each station maintains a contention window (CW), which is used to select the random backoff counter. The backoff counter is determined as a random integer drawn from a uniform distribution over the interval [0, CW].The larger the contention window is the greater is the resolution power of the randomized scheme. It is less likely to choose the same random backoff counter using a large CW .However, under a light load; a small CW ensures shorter access delays .The timing of DCF channel access is illustrated in Fig. 1.

An acknowledgement (ACK) frame is sent by the receiver to the sender for every successful reception of a frame. The ACK frame is transmitted after a short IFS (SIFS), which is shorter than the DIFS. As the SIFS is shorter than DIFS, the transmission of ACK frame is protected from other station's contention. The CW size is initially assigned CWmin and if a frame is lost i.e. no ACK frame is received for it, the CW size is doubled, with an upper bound of CWmax and another attempt with backoff is performed. After each successful transmission, the CW value is reset to CWmin.

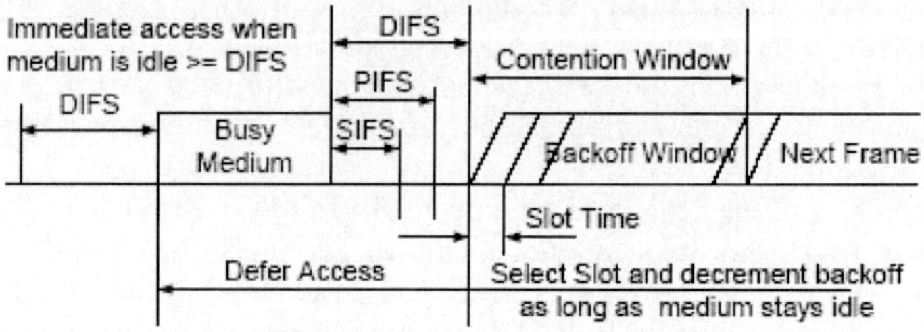

Fig. 1. The timing relationship for DCF or basic access method

An additional RTS/CTS (Request To Send / Clear To Send) mechanism is defined to solve a hidden terminal problem inherent in Wireless LAN. The successful exchange of RTS/CTS ensures that channel has been reserved for the transmission from the particular sender to the particular receiver. This is made possible by requiring all other mobile stations set their Network Allocation Vector (NAV) properly after hearing RTS/CTS and data frame. So they will refrain from transmitting when the other mobile station is in transmission. Use of RTS/CTS is much helpful when the actual data size is large compared to size of RTS/CTS. When the data size is comparable to size of RTS/CTS, the overhead caused by the RTS/CTS would compromise the overall performance [4] [5]. All of the MAC parameters including SIFS, DIFS, SlotTime, CWmin, and CWmax are dependent on the underlying physical layer (PHY).

3 The Quality of Service (QoS)

3.1 Quality of Service (QoS) and QoS Model

The quality of service (QoS) is a set of mechanisms capable to distribute the network resources on different applications in order to maximize the degree of satisfaction of each one [6]. It is characterized by a number of parameters (flow, latency, jitter and loss). From the user point of view, the QoS can be defined as the degree of its satisfaction.

A QoS model defines an architecture which provides the best possible service. This model must take into consideration all the challenges imposed by ad hoc networks, such as change of topology and constraints of energy and reliability. It describes a set of services that enable customers to select a number of warranties on some properties such as time, reliability, etc... Several QoS models are proposed in the literature: The conventional models Intserv [7] and DiffServ [8] used in wired networks are not suitable for WLAN. Many others solutions are proposed such as IEEE 802.11 DCF and Black Burst Contention Scheme (BB) extension [9], IEEE 802.11e [2], MACA (Multihop access collision avoidance) [10], MACAW (Media Access Protocol for Wireless LANs) [11], MACA/PR (Multiple Access Collision Avoidance with Piggyback Reservation) [12], etc...

Each of these solutions attempts to improve one or more parameters of the QoS.

4 Proposed Modifications

4.1 Motivations

The modification of DCF procedure is based on mechanisms that generated packets loss and inutile bandwidth consumption. Packets loss may be happen when collisions take place in channel contention mechanism. After these collisions, retransmissions are reinitiated, so they consume bandwidth and increase latency packets between communicating pairs.

4.2 Proposed Solution

Our proposal solution is made by changing CW (Contention Windows) increment function in medium access procedure DCF that use RTS and CTS at MAC layer to improve some QoS parameters such as: loss, delay and throughput.

In DCF procedure, backoff mechanism reduces the risk of collision but it does not remove this phenomenon completely. If collisions still occur, a new backoff will be generated randomly. At each collision, window size increase in order to reduce the probability of such collisions to happen again. CW values permitted by the standard will change between CWMin and CWMax values. The window lower bound is reset to CWMin when packet has been correctly transmitted [11]. We propose two functions to increment the CW value by two new calculation types (i.e. left shift) that we noted: function 1 and 2.

Backoff time for basic DCF is βi * (SlotTime) where βi is given by the following mathematical formula: $\beta i = 2^{i+k} - 1$ where i (initially equal to 1) is the transmission attempt number and k depends on the PHY layer type and SlotTime is function of physical layer parameters. There is a higher limit for “i,” above which the random range (CWmax) remains the same. When a packet is successfully transmitted, the CW is reset to CWmin.

In 802.11 standard, the chosen value are CWmin = 31, CWmax = 1023 and for k we take the value 4, so βi becomes $(\beta i = 2^{i+4} - 1)$ and i takes values from 1 to 6 (i = {1, 2, 3, 4, 5, 6}). In this case βi is the result of adding 1 to the one bit left shift of the variable CW. So after each collision, possible CW values are: {31, 63, 127, 255, 511, 1023} (see fig.2.a).

The function 1 is based on adding 3 to two bits left shift of the variable CW, where the number 3 is used to replace the two bits equal to zero after shift operation and βi becomes $(\beta i = 2^{2i+3} - 1)$. The number of retransmissions attempts after calculation is (04) (i= {1, 2, 3, 4}), if i is greater than 3 we set CW = 1023. So after each collision, possible CW values are: {31, 127, 511, 1023} (see fig.2.b).

The function 2 is based on adding 7 to three bits left shift of the variable CW, where the number 7 is used to replace the three bits equal to zero after shift operation and βi becomes$(\beta i = 2^{3i+5} - 1)$. The number of retransmissions attempts after calculation is (03) (i= {0, 1, 2}), if i is greater than 1 we set CW = 1023. So after each collision, possible CW values are: {31, 255, 1023} (see fig.2.c).

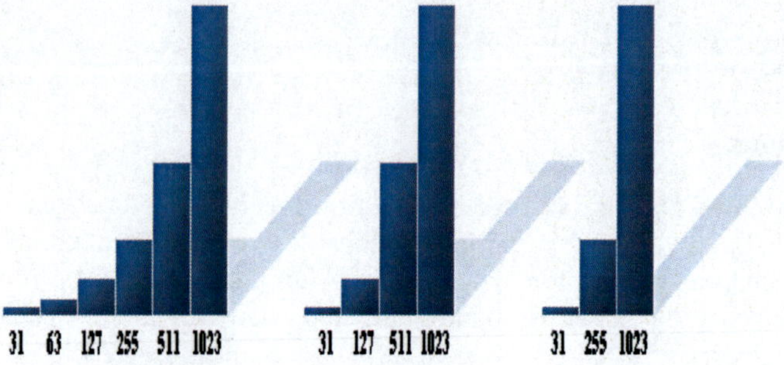

Fig. 2.a **Fig. 2.b** **Fig. 2.c**

Fig. 2. Possible CW values for (basic DCF, function 1and function 2)

5 Simulation and Evaluation

In this section, we present the result of simulation to evaluate the performance of the proposed functions under certain metrics and constraints

5.1 Constraints

In WLAN, nodes are mobile, so routes which they are parties become invalid, so we are in case to discover again new paths those generating an additional control load which consuming bandwidth. Nodes have limited energy, so it is imperative to best manage it as long as possible. Energy consumption is proportional to the number of packets processed and the type of treatment (Tx / Rx). Density (The average number of neighbors per node) they all impact on the performance of mobile wireless networks (WLAN).

5.2 Metrics

Evaluate network performances is to find if it is able to minimize packets loss, i.e. ensure if possible a transfer loss near to zero (quality criterion). Control load is required for network management but it consumes some bandwidth, over this rate is high, performance network degrades but conversely they are better (efficacy endpoint). Taking into account physical links characteristics (capacity) and current flow sharing them, when throughput (quantity of information per unit time) is higher, bandwidth is used efficiently. For some applications, it is not enough to transmit large data quantity (high speed) without loss, but it is imperative to transmit it if possible faster, i.e. short (reduced) delay in real-time applications.

To study and analyze our proposed solution based on Distributed Coordination Function (DCF) at MAC layer, we used Network Simulator (Ns2) [13] version 2.31 installed on Debian Lenny GNU / Linux.

The table below (Table 1) shows parameters used in simulation model. They represent values used in NS-2 for layer IEEE 802.11b.

Table 1. Simulation parameters

Parameter	Value
Simulation time	100s
Access medium	Mac/802_11
Routing protocol	AODV
Buffer size	50
Simulation grid	1200×1200 m
SlotTime	20 μs
SIFS	10 μs
CWMin	31
CWMax	1023
Flow	11Mb

5.3 Curves and Discussions

The desired parameters to be evaluated by simulation under different contexts (mobility and density) are: average throughput in kbps that indicates data transfer rate. Having a network system with high flow is coveted. Packets lost ratio is the rapport among successfully received and sent packets. This ration proves network reliability.

To compare these three functions, we have considered six different scenarios (Table 2) depending on the constraint of mobility and number of nodes (mobile station) with low value (10 nodes), medium value (20 nodes) and high value (50 nodes). For each scenario, we have analyzed the found results of the two functions with the basic DCF.

The packets lost and sent number, packet loss ratio and data throughput (bps) are attributes that we are going to measure.

Table 2. Different scenarios of simulation

Mobility / Nodes	low	high
10	Scenario 1	Scenario 2
20	Scenario 3	Scenario 4
50	Scenario 5	Scenario 6

Packets Sent

We have obtained the following (Table 3) by measuring the total number of packets sent in the different scenarios for the tree functions.

Table 3. Packets sent

Scenarios	1	2	3	4	5	6
Basic DCF	6433	5491	3668	3353	1626	2118
Function 1	7346	5395	3147	3966	2608	2671
Function 2	7374	5224	2778	3779	2668	2321

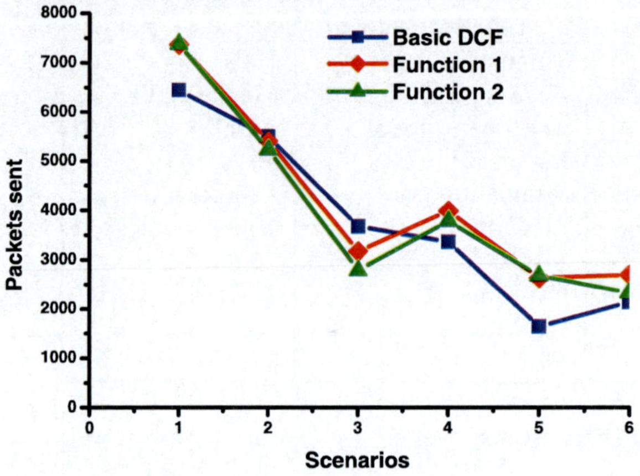

Fig. 3. Packets sent

We have noted that the three functions have the same performance, in the case of transmitted packets, except for a high number of nodes and high mobility, where the basic DCF is different from the two proposed functions

Packets Lost

Table 4 shows the total number of packets lost in the different scenarios for the tree functions (basic DSF, function 1, and function 2).

Table 4. Packets lost

Scenarios	1	2	3	4	5	6
Basic DCF	68	222	249	232	239	260
Function 1	29	103	146	181	238	146
Function 2	11	117	115	160	201	165

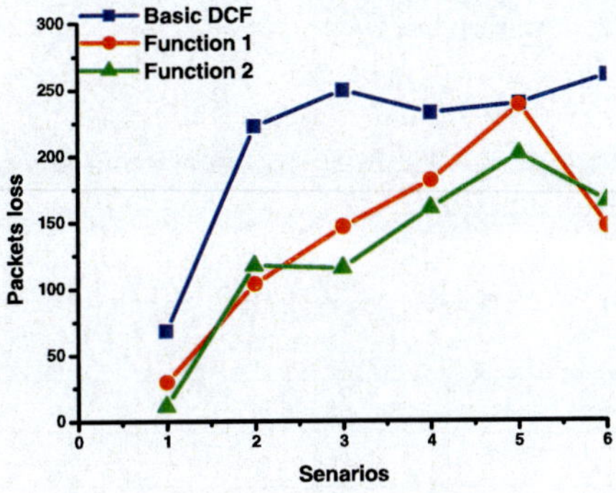

Fig. 4. Packets lost

We can see that the proposed functions give better results in all scenarios then basic DCF.

Packet Loss Ratio

The table 5 shows the packet lost ratio in the different scenarios for the tree functions. The Packet Loss ratio is defined as: (received packet number / sent packet number) * 100.

Table 5. Packet Loss ratio (%)

Scenarios	1	2	3	4	5	6
Basic DCF	1,06	4,04	6,79	6,92	14,70	12,28
Function 1	0,39	1,91	4,64	4,56	9,13	5,47
Function 2	0,15	2,24	4,14	4,23	7,53	7,11

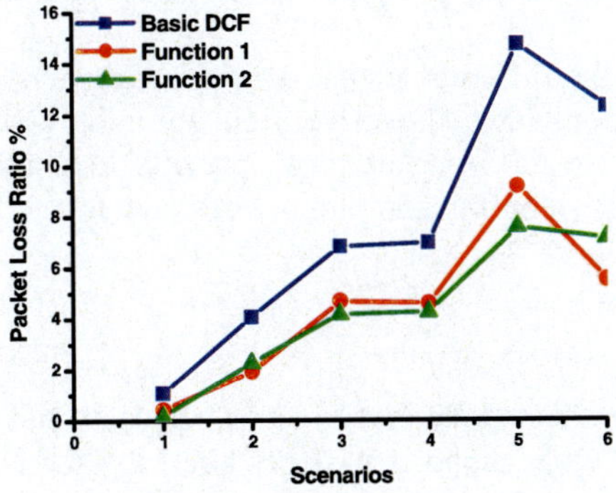

Fig. 5. Packet Loss ratio

In the packet loss ratio case, we have noted that the proposed two functions reduce significantly the packet loss parameter.

Average Throughput
We have obtained the following (Table 6) by measuring average throughput (kbps) for all scenarios for the tree functions.

Table 6. Average throughput

Scenarios	1	2	3	4	5	6
Basic DCF	6796	5703	3608	33	155	204
Function 1	7768	5654	3171	40	258	272
Function 2	7470	5465	2841	38	267	23

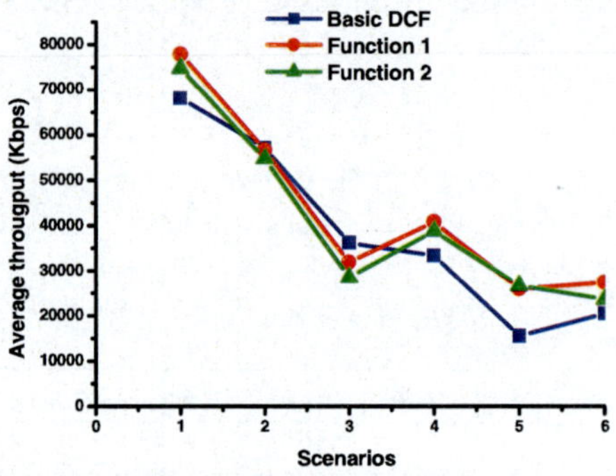

Fig. 6. Average throughput

In the case of average throughput, our functions give better results in almost all scenarios.

Based on results of the different scenarios and parameters, we can conclude that the proposed two functions have shown very encouraging results compared to basic DCF for measured parameters (packets sent, packets loss and average throughput) under the two constraints (mobility and number of nodes).

6 Conclusion

In this paper, we have evaluated the performance of our proposed solution (function 1 and 2) mechanism for QoS support in IEEE 802.11 WLAN. We have shown by simulations that the proposed solution improves QoS requirements (rate packet loss and throughput) in two constraints (mobility and density).

We plan in future work to compare the proposed solutions to others mechanisms used in WLAN such as EDFC of 802.11.e.

References

1. Cali, F., Conti, M., Gregori, E.: Dynamic Tuning of the IEEE 802.11 Protocol to Achieve a Theoretical Throughtput Limit. IEEE/ACM Trans. Networking 8(6), 785–799 (2000)
2. IEEE 802.11e draft/D4.1, Part 11: Wireless Medium Access Control (MAC) and physical layer (PHY) specifications: Medium Access Control (MAC) Enhancements for Quality of Service, QoS (2003)
3. Wu, H., Peng, K., Long, K., Cheng, S., Ma, J.: Performance of Reliable Transport Protocol over IEEE 802.11 Wireless LAN: Analysis and Enhancement. In: Proceedings of IEEE INFOCOM 2002, New York, NY (2002)
4. Anastasi, G., Lenzini, L.: QoS provided by the IEEE 802.11 wireless LAN to advanced data applications: a simulation analysis. ACM/Baltzer Journal on Wireless Networks, 99–108 (2000)
5. Chen, Z., Khokhar, A.: Improved MAC protocols for DCF and PCF modes over Fading Channels in Wireless LANs. In: Wireless Communications and Network Conference, WCNC (2003)
6. Kay, J., Frolik, J.: Quality of Service Analysis and Control for Wireless Sensor Networks. In: The 1st IEEE International Conference on Mobile Adhoc and Sensor Systems (MASS 2004), Ft. Lauderdale, FL, October 25-27 (2004)
7. Braden, R., Zhang, L., et al.: Integrated Services in the Internet Architecture: an Overview. RFC 1633 (1994)
8. Blake, S., Black, D., Carlson, M., Davies, E., Wang, Z., Weiss, W.: An Architecture for Differentiated Services. RFC 2475 (1998)
9. Veres, A., et al.: Supporting Service Differentiation in Wireless Packet Networks Using Distributed Control. In: IEEE JSAC (2001)
10. Karn, P.: MACA: a New Channel Access Method for Packet Radio. In: ARRL/CRRL Amateur Radio 9th Comp. Net, Conf. pp. 134–140 (1990)
11. Bharghavan, V., et al.: MACAW: A Media Access Protocol for Wireless LANs. In: Proc. ACM SIGCOMM (1994)
12. Lin, C.R., Gerla, M.: Asynchronous Multimedia Multihop Wireless Networks. In: IEEE INFOCOM (1997)
13. Fall, K., Varadhan, K.: The NS Manual. Vint Project, UC Berkeley, LBL, DARPA, USC/ISI, and Xerox PARC (2002)

A Novel "Credit Union" Model of Cloud Computing

Dunren Che and Wen-Chi Hou

Department of Computer Science
Southern Illinois University Carbondale,
Illinois 62901, USA
{dche,hou}@cs.siu.edu

Abstract. Cloud Computing is drawing people's attention from all walks of the IT world. It promises significant reduction of cost among many other advantages as it proclaims, including increased availability, fast provision, on-demand, and pay-per-use, etc. This paper presents a novel model of Cloud Computing, named "Credit Union" model (referred to as the CU model or CUM for short). This model is motivated by the cooperative business model of the many credit unions that have been widely practiced as a type of financial institutions world-wide. The CU model aims at utilizing the vast, underutilized computing resources in homes and offices, and transforming them into a self-provisioned community cloud that mimics the business model of a credit union, i.e., membership and credits are obtained by contributing spare computing resources. Clouds built based on the CU model, referred to as CU clouds, bear the following advantageous characteristics comparing to the general clouds: complete vendor independence, improved availability (due to reduced internet-dependence), better security, and superb sustainability (green computing). This paper expounds the principles and motivations of the CU model, addresses its implementation architecture and related issues, and outlooks prospect applications.

Keywords: Cloud Computing, Cloud Computing Model, Cloud Architecture, Green Computing, Sustainability, Community Cloud, Community Cloud Computing.

1 Introduction

Cloud Computing was the most discussed topic in the IT industry and academia in 2010, and it will likely remain to be the hottest IT topic this year and for the years to come. Cloud Computing proclaims many virtues or advantages over prior computing paradigms and models. Among them, cost reduction is probably the most attractive, at least to the CFOs (Executive Financial Officers). What are really tempting to the CFOs are the saved capital expenses that can then be turned into operational expenses. Additional cost-reduction may be obtained via improved hardware utilization, guaranteed availability (accompanied by the saved cost of failures and recovery), and the utility payment feature (i.e., the so-called pay-as-you-go model) of Cloud Computing. And for cloud service providers/vendors, cost reduction is often

H. Cherifi, J.M. Zain, and E. El-Qawasmeh (Eds.): DICTAP 2011, Part I, CCIS 166, pp. 714–727, 2011.

realized through economy of scale. Improved hardware utilization straightforwardly implies less hardware needed, less power consumed, and less electric garbage to be processed. Therefore Cloud Computing is considered an enabling technology for green computing. While the current Cloud Computing technologies already promote environmental sustainability, we believe we can go a lot farther along the line of sustainability and practice green computing more thoroughly through a new model of Cloud Computing – the "Credit Union" Model – that forms the theme of this paper.

We see unused (and often wasted) computing resources everywhere and everyday -- whether it is a power PC in office or a notebook at home, it constantly has idle CPU cycles and spare memory and disk spaces. After office hours, especially the period from mid-night to early morning, most computers are completely idle or turned off. However, on the other side of our planet, a new day is dawning, filled with complex activities that can only be perfectly and promptly accomplished with more CPU cycles and more memory spaces. Current Cloud Computing and the accordingly developed solutions cannot simply fit in here because they were not designed to utilize the vast amount, underutilized computing resources possessed by individuals and organizations for the good of the individuals and the communities.

Excessive computing resources are important assets to individuals and to the global village as a whole. To the resource owners, individuals or organizations, these assets are just like one's spare money. Spare money, if not invested, of course, will not yield any interests, but it does not flow away (let's intentionally turn a blind eye to the inflation that seems existent in every economy of this world). However, the matter is far worse when it comes to unused spare computing resources – these resources either completely vanish (like CPU cycles) or fast evaporate (depreciating their values in exponential speed) – which at the end causes a sheer waste of what might have started as a precious portion of one's capital spending.

Being practiced widely and successfully, credit unions are a type of cooperative financial institutions that are owned and controlled by their members and operated for the purpose of promoting thrift, providing credit at reasonable rates and other financial services to their members. Many credit unions exist to further community development or sustainable international development on a local level.

Our comparison between spare computing resources and spare money inspires creation of a special credit union so that both individuals and organizations can contribute their spare computing recourses and transform into community benefits or individuals' credits or even monetary interests. In other words, we can construct a computing infrastructure that is community-based, relying on members' contribution of their excessive computing recourses, such as CPU cycles, memory and disk spaces. Such a community computing infrastructure cannot be readily provisioned by current cloud vendors using existing technologies. CU clouds can only be made a reality via integration of multiple existing computing paradigms and technologies, including the fast fledging Cloud Computing, Grid Computing, and Peer-to-Peer (P2P) computing.

In this paper we present a novel, "Credit Union" model of Cloud Computing that is a specialized Cloud Computing model to serve the particular needs of a community and its members who possess spare computing resources and allow them to invest that their spare resources (just like their spare moneys) for the common good of the community and/or extra individual benefits (earned in the form of credits). Such developed community clouds (or CU clouds) may be made open to the general public to gain profits from outside; and the community members who hold sufficient credits may also choose to exchange for monetary benefits. Construction of CU clouds requires integration and utilization of several other related computing technologies that are reviewed in the next section.

The remainder of this paper is organized as follows: Section 2 reviews related technologies and related work. Section 3 defines our "credit union" model of Cloud Computing and discusses its relationships with other relevant computing models. Section 4 analyzes the scenarios of CU cloud applications and derives important characteristics that have influence on the architectural design of CU clouds. Section 5 presents illustrative architecture of CU clouds. Section 6 summarizes our discussion and points out future directions.

2 Related Technologies and Work

Our "credit union" model of Cloud Computing is not built from scratch, but on a series of underling, enabling technologies. This section, as a preliminary for the subsequent discussion, reviews the key supporting technologies and related work, with the hope of setting up a meaningful discussion context and clearing up possible confusions.

2.1 Cloud Computing

Although being widely discussed as a buzzword, *Cloud Computing* to different people still leads to rather different interpretations. We adopt the definition given by the National Institute of Standards and Technology (NIST) in 2009 [8], which we believe represents the most accepted definition for Cloud Computing [1]:

Cloud Computing is a **model** *for enabling convenient, on-demand network access to a shared pool of configurable computing resources (e.g., networks, servers, storage, applications and services) that can be rapidly provisioned and released with minimal management effort or service provider interaction.*

Obviously, the term Cloud Computing refers to a general computing model or paradigm, being companied by a rich set of enabling/supporting technologies and products and services.

It is interesting to point out the key characteristics, delivery models, and deployment modes of Cloud Computing [2]:

The **key characteristics** of Cloud Computing include *on-demand self-service*, *ubiquitous network access*, *location independent* resource pooling, *rapid elasticity*, and *pay-per-use* (or pay-as-you-go). There are three primary **delivery models**, *cloud software as s service (SaaS)*, *cloud platform as a service (PaaS)*, and *cloud infrastructure as a service (IaaS)*, and four distinct **deployment models**, *private* cloud, *community* cloud, *public* cloud, and *hybrid* cloud.

There are several other computing models that are often regarded as the supporting technologies or closely related technologies to the Cloud Computing paradigm, from time to time causing confusions. We next briefly review these supporting or related technologies and highlight their characteristics.

2.2 Other Related Computing Models

A *Distributed System* consists of multiple autonomous computers that communicate through a computer network, and interact with each other in order to achieve a common goal. *Distributed Computing* generally refers to the use of a distributed system to solve a computational problem that is divided into many tasks, each of which is solved by one computer of the distributed system.

Generally speaking, *Grid Computing* is a form of distributed computing and parallel computing, whereby a 'super and virtual computer' is (formed) composed of a cluster of networked, loosely coupled computers acting in concert to perform very large tasks. The goal of Grid Computing is to provide a consolidated high-performance computing system based on loosely coupled storage, networking and parallel processing functions linked by high bandwidth interconnects.

Obviously, distributed computing denotes a rather general concept (or model) of computing. Both Cloud Computing and Grid Computing can be regarded as a particular kind of distributed computing; and both aim at delivering abstracted computing resources. But the two shall not be confused though their distinction is fairly subtle.

The comparison between the two models made by Frischbier and Petrov [1] are interesting. We quote and adapt their comparisons below:

The two paradigms (Cloud Computing and Grid Computing) differ in their particular approaches and subjects:

(i) Cloud Computing aims at serving multiple users at the same time and elastically via resource *pooling* while Grid Computing is intended to deliver functionality at a scale and quality equivalent to a *supercomputer* via a *queuing* system;

(ii) Grids consist of resources owned and operated by different organizations while clouds are usually under a single organization's control;

(iii) Cloud services can be obtained by using a standardized interface over a network, while grids typically require running the grid fabric software locally (the fabric software was designed for unifying the interconnected grid nodes).

Here we want to point out that our "credit union" Cloud Computing model implicates a notion that is quite on the opposite of item (ii). This is just one of the several aspects that make our "credit union" model different from the general Cloud Computing model that most people have on their minds.

Two other computing notions are often referred to when Cloud Computing is discussed -- *utility computing* and *service-oriented computing* (typically manifested *as Software-as-a-Service* or *SaaS* for short). These two notions are rather generic terms, primarily referring to two aspects (or characteristics) of Cloud Computing. To help clearing up possible confusions, we provide following the definitions:

Utility computing — the packaging of computing resources, such as computation and storage, as a *metered service* similar to a traditional public utility, such as electricity.

Service-oriented computing – Cloud computing provides services related to computing and, in a reciprocal manner, *service-oriented computing* consists of the computing techniques that operate on software-as-a-service (SaaS).

It shall be clear that utility computing emphasizes the "metered" feature while service-oriented computing highlights on the "service-oriented" feature, which are both manifested by Cloud Computing.

2.3 Related Work

There is "tons" of reported work related to Cloud Computing. The leading Cloud Computing providers include Amazon [11, 12], Google [9], Microsoft [10], Salesforce [13], and more. The Linux website http://linux.sys-con.com/node/1386896 even listed The Top 250 Players in the Cloud Computing in Year 2010, yet at the same time almost everyone agrees that Cloud Computing is still in its infancy. There are also numerous well-written surveys introducing and discussing Cloud Computing and related technologies [1, 2, 3, 4, 7, 8, 14]. So in this section, we are not going to review Cloud Computing in a general way. Instead, in the following we particularly look at SETI@home [5] and Seattle [6], two important projects that might be considered as overlapping somehow with our CU model and our CU cloud project that is currently being initiated. The overlapping is actually minimal as explained below.

SETI@home: SETI@home ("Search for Extra-Terrestrial Intelligence at home") is an internet-based public volunteer computing project employing the BOINC software platform, hosted by the Space Sciences Laboratory, at the University of California, Berkeley, in the United States. Its purpose is to analyze radio signals, searching for signs of extra-terrestrial intelligence, and is one of many activities undertaken as part of SETI. Technically, SETI@home is a large Internet-based distributed system (project) for scientific computing; being an aspect of the P2P paradigm, involving shifting resource-intensive functions from central servers to workstations and home PCs. It uses millions of voluntary computers in homes and offices around the world to accomplish its computing tasks. Although it has not found signs of extraterrestrial life, the project has contributed to the IT industry and academia with the so-called "public-resource computing" model. In SETI@home, the client program repeatedly gets a work unit from the data/result server, analyzes it, then returns the results (candidate signals) to the server. The client can be configured to compute only when its host is idle or to run constantly at a low priority and as a background process. SETI@home does not contain any of the major ingredients of Cloud Computing but it is related to our work in that both use voluntary computers in office and homes with excessive computing capacities. SETI exercises *public-resource computing* for scientific discovery while our CU model aims at utilizing excessive computing resources owned be individuals and/or organizations for the common good of a community and/or the benefits of the participating individuals in the community.

Seattle: Seattle is a free, education research platform, implemented as a common denominator of Cloud Computing, Grid Computing, P2P network, distributed systems and networking on diverse platform types. As a project, Seattle reflects a *community-driven* effort that depends on resources donated by users of the software (and as such is free to use). A user (typically an educator) can install Seattle onto their personal computer to enable Seattle programs to run using a portion of the computer's resources. As an educational platform, Seattle provides many pedagogical contexts ranging from courses in Cloud Computing, Networking, and Distributed Systems, to Parallel Programming, Grid Computing, and P2P Computing. Seattle itself is not generally regarded as pursuing Cloud Computing. Seattle exposes locality and primarily provides a distributed system environment as an educational platform. Seattle uses configurable *sandboxes* to securely execute user code and monitors the overall use of key resources. Seattle is interesting to us because it relies also on public resources (resources are donated to Seattle and counted as credit for using Seattle after an instructor installs and runs the installer software on a local machine); in addition, Seattle has a preexisting base of installed computers to start with, that we might need as well for effective implementation of our CU clouds.

3 Defining the "Credit Union" Model of Cloud Computing

Much of the popularity of Cloud Computing attributes to its promise for cost reduction (from both the providers' side and the consumers' side). The reduction of cost directly contributes to environment-friendliness and thus Cloud Computing is said to be "green computing". Even though, we observe that huge amount of CPU cycles and memory and disk spaces are underutilized and/or wasted in offices and at homes, day and night (especially after midnight). It would make greater contribution to the environmental sustainability that Cloud Computing has already promised if we can recycle and reuse the large amount of unused extra computing resources. The current Cloud Computing model and techniques were not particularly designed for increasing the resource utilization of the vast amount of client computers. We are thus motivated to develop a specialized Cloud Computing mode and the accompanying techniques to carry the sustainability feature of Cloud Computing a big step forward.

Credit unions as a type of financial institutions have been practiced very successfully for the good of a community and the benefits of its members by attracting and reinvesting the spare money owned by its members. The principles and basic ideas practiced by credit unions can be extended to and incorporated by Cloud Computing. This consideration leads to a new, specialized Cloud Computing model, which we refer to as the "credit union" model (CUM). The goal of this model is to consolidate and utilize the unused excessive computing resources possessed by individuals and/or organizations in a community. This novel Cloud Computing model is defined with more details as follows.

Definition of the "Credit Union" Model of Cloud Computing (CUM): The "credit union" model of Cloud Computing is a specialized model of the general Cloud Computing paradigm. It relies on the excessive computing resources owned by the individuals and/or organizations in a community. In the setting of the CU model, computing resources are contributed by individuals and/or organization either free or for credits. Clouds built according to the CU model are referred to as CU clouds. CU clouds stick to the general principles of Cloud Computing but require specialized architecture and implementation considerations for realizing its goal.

CU clouds aim at utilizing the elapsing CPU cycles and other excessive computing resources such as memory and disk spaces owned by the individuals and/or organizations in a community; the community is not necessarily limited by the geographical boundaries. The developed CU clouds are typically deployed as a consolidated computing facility to be consumed by the community for the common good of the community, or the members (accordingly to the respective amounts of credits earned); alternatively, CU clouds as services can also open to the general public for gaining profits from the outside world – in other words, the community can independently function as a cloud service provider or simply sell its consolidated cloud infrastructures and facilities to a larger, enterprise cloud service provider.

The community oriented feature of a CU cloud makes it easy to get confused with the notion of community clouds in the general sense, but they are different. For a community cloud, in the general sense, the community and its members act only as the consumers of the cloud services that are typically provided by an enterprise cloud service provider; however, for a CU cloud, the community and its members not only are the consumers but also the service provider and owner -- they collectively own everything of their cloud, from its infrastructures, facilities, hardware and software, to full control and full management of everything of the cloud. The members of a CU cloud are voluntary participants – they are mainly attracted by the opportunity of earning credits that may be traded for monetary benefits or free use of the cloud facilities. Credits are earned through "depositing" (contributing) their excessive computing resources to the community, and, of course, the earned credits can also be donated to the community for the common good of the community.

We generally assume the opinion of Foster, *et al.* that Cloud Computing not only overlaps with Grid Computing, it shall be evolved out of Grid Computing and rely on Grid Computing as its backbone and infrastructure support [4]. Nevertheless, the two paradigms are far from being identical. Imagine that we can pull Grid Computing to one side and pull Cloud Computing to the other side, then our CU cloud model shall sit in the middle of the two paradigms, slightly shifted back from the cloud side to the grid side as shown in Figure 1, which is adopted from [4] but modified for illustrating the relationships between the new notion of CU cloud and other related computing models. In Figure 1, Web 2.0 covers almost the whole spectrum of service-oriented applications, where Cloud Computing lies at the large-scale side. Supercomputing and Cluster Computing have been more focused on traditional non-service applications. Grid Computing overlaps with all these fields and is generally considered of lesser scale than supercomputers and clouds. CU clouds sit at the low scale end of clouds but overlaps more with grid computing; in other words, CU clouds are clouds, but of less scale, and appears to have more in common with grids compared to the general cloud computing.

More specifically, what is the little extra common ground that CU clouds now find with grids? This question is answered by review the difference between clouds and grids [4]:

Clouds mostly comprise dedicated data centers belonging to the same organization, and within each data center, hardware and software configurations and supporting platforms are in general more *homogeneous* as compared with those in grid environments. In contrast, grids however build on the assumption that the resources are *heterogeneous* and *dynamic*, and each grid site may have its own administration domain and operation autonomy. However, in the context of CU clouds, we face even a more significantly heterogeneous environment of computing resources that are possessed by individuals/organizations with exclusive privilege for use. From this point of view, CU clouds shall be relocated more toward the territory of grids. This characteristic of CU clouds raises a great implementation challenge – distributing coordination and load balancing within a highly dynamic and heterogeneous system.

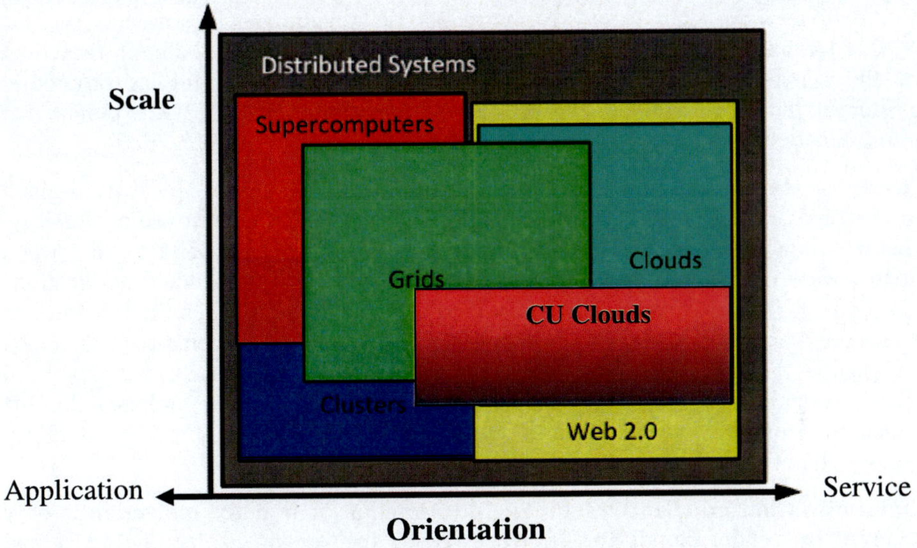

Fig. 1. Relationships between CU clouds and other related computing domains (adapted and modified from [4])

4 Prospect Applications and Implication on Implementation

The CU model has opened a brighter and broader horizon for future applications of Cloud Computing. It is more promising than the vender-provision model of today's Cloud Computing because CU clouds have the potential to diminish the concerns and flaws associated with today's Cloud Computing.

As today's cloud services are exclusively provided by enterprise venders such as Google, Amazon, and Microsoft, *vendor cloud* and *vendor Cloud Computing* are equivalent terms to today's Cloud Computing, which straightforwardly reflect the *vender provision* nature of today's clouds. Cloud Computing is generally accredited of the feature of "green computing" owing to virtualization that has been successfully used to maximize resource utilization. However, with today's Cloud Computing, such effort (on maximizing resource utilization) has only been pursued on venders' side where cloud resources are centralized and owned by the venders; resource utilization on client machines has never been a concern of today's Cloud Computing.

Our CU model will help diminish the following aspects of concerns regarding today's Cloud Computing:

Security and Privacy: While the security concern of cloud consumers is not necessarily endemic only to Cloud Computing (noticing that vendors have been taking every means to protect consumer data and applications on their clouds), privacy concern seems an issue that can never be solved by the vender-provision model of today's Cloud Computing. No matter what advance is made, users would never be without concerns when they run their mission-critical applications and/or store their sensitive data on clouds. We doubt US government departments such as DOD, CIA, and FBI will ever completely trust any vender clouds, though they long for the convenience and benefits promised by Cloud Computing as any other consumers. These government branches would more willingly accept CU clouds that will situate on their own premises under their full control.

Cascading failure: Being centrally managed and maintained by best trained professionals, vendor clouds generally enjoy the good fame of improved availability. That does not mean that the clouds are absolutely isolated from failures, and when cloud failure indeed occurs, it causes *cascading effect* to all dependent applications and services. However, users want to get their things done even when the Internet and clouds are down or the network communication is slow. In such scenarios, CU clouds demonstrate great competency and advantage over vendor clouds. Moreover, in extreme situations (e.g., at war times) a community may want to completely shut off connection from the global domain of Internet, only CU clouds may give this security option without affect ongoing applications.

Underutilization on client resources: Maximization of resource utilization is only achieved by vendor clouds for the resources on the vender's side. The CU cloud Computing can perfectly unify vendor resources and client resources, realize utilization maximization on all resources, and exercise the sustainability of green computing to the fullest.

By and large, CU clouds overcome several innate flaws (more accurately, most of the flaws are resulted from the *vendor-provision model* of today's Cloud Computing) and demonstrate undisputable advantages over the current Cloud Computing model, yet still retain all the advantage and benefits promised by Cloud Computing. CU clouds have a far better potential than vendor clouds for wide acceptance with regard to all walks of applications, from private sectors to the vast amount of communities and organizations at all levels, including government departments and those having extremely high demand for confidentiality and privacy.

As for application of CU clouds in public institutions in the United States, state laws typically disallow public assets (allocated to public universities, for example) from being used for other than the original purposes. Nevertheless, public institutions can use services delivered by their own CU clouds to enhance their original missions (education and/or research). Otherwise, the cloud services they need must be purchased from external, enterprise providers, which certainly means extra budges must be allocated. Public institutions may choose to use their self-provisioned CU clouds to promote non-profit collaborations with other local institutions at all levels, including primary and secondary schools, and community colleges. Relatively large local communities such as community colleges may deploy their CU clouds, and multiple community CU clouds may further form a cloud federation at a larger scale to better serve the varied needs of all potential consumers (individuals and organizations, local and distant) at all levels.

Next we derive two aspects of expectations from the scenarios of CU cloud applications that have implication to the architecture and implementation of CU clouds.

First, a community with CU clouds is not an enterprise cloud service provider (but this does not eliminate the possibility that the community evolves into an enterprise cloud service provider in the future just as Amazon.com, which though might be considered as an exceptional example). The primary computing resources available to community CU clouds are extracted and consolidated from autonomous machines owned by various individuals and/or organizations and are geographically distributed. This important feature of CU clouds requires every participating computer to install and run specially designed software (we can vividly call as *membership software* or a *virtual box*) that collects and virtualizes excessive resources from each participating computer. A good metaphor for such membership software might be a boy scout who participates in a food drive program, comes to your house and collects the (spare) food items you are willing to contribute.

Second, a community typically does not have a dedicated cluster of commodity computers to support their community CU clouds. Once a community decides to build a CU cloud, for the sake of overall performance (regarding system monitoring, distributing coordination, and load balancing, etc.), procurement of a few dedicated machines might be necessary or at least recommended. They will be used to represent the community clouds in the cyberspace, serving as an access portal for internal consumers and also for potential outside customers. Overall, cloud resource consolidation and management are best carried out at such dedicated machines (which may alternatively be delegated to a few relatively powerful machines contributed to the community cloud especially in case of failure or experiencing severe performance degradation). The heterogeneous and highly dynamic nature of CU clouds (hosted by varied machines, which each runs a different pack of software and yet needs to support a range of fast changing and privileged local applications first) raises a greater technological challenge that the current cloud vendors have not been confronted with.

5 Architecture and Implementation Issues

The resource environment (including hardware, software, and applications) that a CU cloud is built on are highly heterogeneous and dynamic. The unused extra computing resources at each participating computer must be extracted and consolidated through virtualization and abstraction carefully carried out locally. Because each machine must be configured in a way not to affect its local users' daily work (we refer to these users as "native users" in the context of a CU cloud), at the hardware level, the hosted architecture [7] for virtualization becomes the only rational choice, which provides partitioning on top of a standard operation system, leaving the entire working environment of the native users completely intact. In contrast, the other popular virtualization architecture, bare-metal (Hypervisor) architecture [7], though often claims more efficiency, cannot fit into to the particular scenario of CU clouds as the hypervisors need to completely take over the original host operating system that, however, is still required by the native users and their applications.

Figure 2 illustrates the architecture for implementing a *core element* in a CU cloud (a core element is a node in a CU cloud denoting the abstracted and encapsulated resources from a participating machine via virtualization). The host operating system and all local applications as well as their running environments remain intact. The virtualization module (and added layer) above each participating machine provides the ability to emulate (multiple) guest operating systems that are open to cloud applications. As the host machine is dedicated to the CU clouds, the number of virtual machine instances (VMI), at one core element is usually limited to just a few; when the host machine is found having insufficient spare resources (e.g., CPU cycles), the number of virtual instances spawned from that machine shall be accordingly reduced (even to zero in case of severe resource completion). The virtual machine management (VMM) module provides a local management console, giving the owner or native users the means to interfere the resource completion between native applications and alien applications (i.e., cloud applications). Proper implementation of the virtualization layer shall not make the native users feel obvious performance degradation due to completion between native applications and alien applications. The virtualization layer (also called Hypervisor as in [7]) gracefully mult-plexes and encapsulates the computing resources (when their utilization rate is stably below a certain threshold). As an option, device emulation may be incorporated into the Hypervisor or VM.

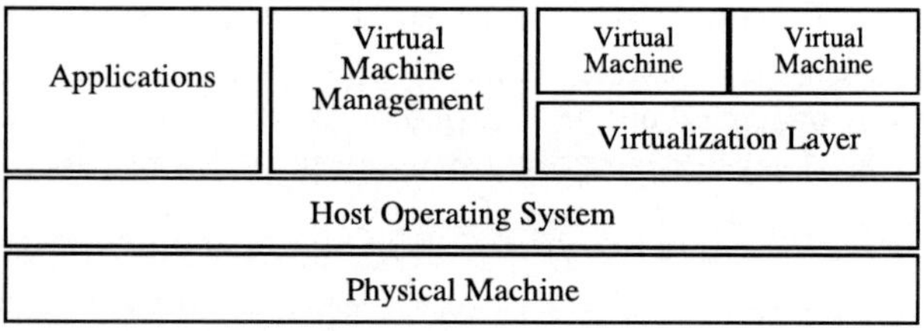

Fig. 2. Illustrative structure of a core element in a CU cloud

We take a similar way to consolidate the core elements as in [15]: taking the core element node of Figure 2 and multiply it on a physical network (typically the Internet), orchestrating the management over the entire infrastructure, and providing front-end coordination and load balancing for incoming connections with caching and filtering; this results in a whole range of consolidated virtual machine instances, which altogether are referred to as the *virtual infrastructure* hosting our CU clouds. The overall architecture that our CU clouds are situated on is depicted in Figure 3. Due to the fact that a CU cloud is physically hosted by a group of networked autonomous machines possessed by individuals or organizations, in the architecture of CU cloud (Figure 3), native users are granted (by the locally installed membership software) privileged accesses to respective host machines, as denoted by the module named "Desktop" on the upper right side of the structure (see Figure 3). As pointed out earlier, in the setting of CU clouds, we best have a few dedicated commodity machines installed to serve community-with, virtual infrastructure management. The left column in the architecture (see Figure 3) explicitly indicates the infrastructure management module.

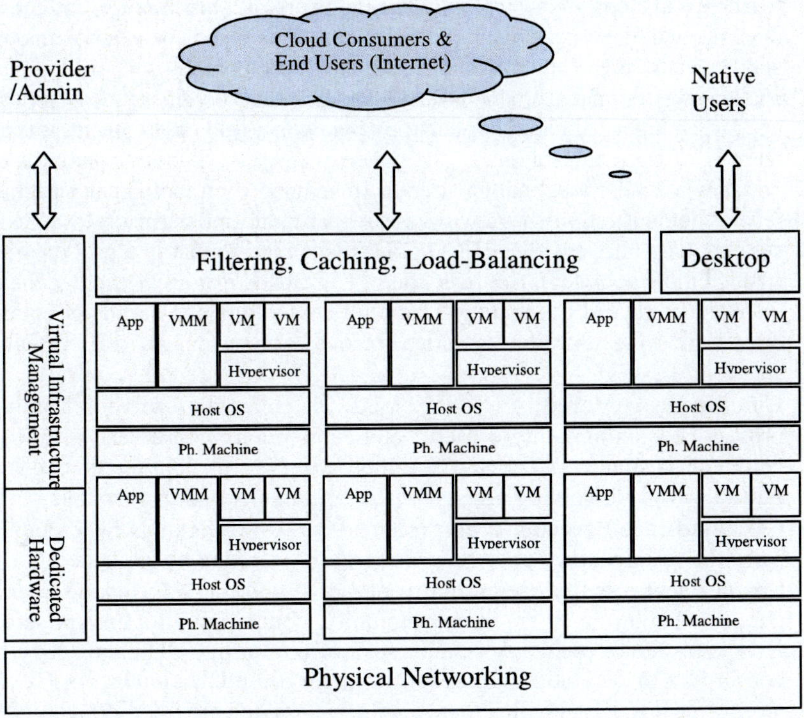

Fig. 3. Illustrative architecture of CU clouds

One prominent feature in the construction of CU clouds is resource-sharing between native users and alien applications, which happens at each core element node. While the idea of provisioning such a community-backed cloud infrastructure is exciting, the highly dynamic and heteronomous nature in a CU cloud environment implies new challenges. Virtualization must consider how to harmoniously reconcile the conflicts (resources competition) between native applications and alien applications. The inherent characteristics of a CU cloud determine that the resource management policy must first guarantee smooth running of all local applications. Furthermore, the virtualization module must be designed with the capability to automatically adjust the resources extracted at each core element node as cloud consumable resources. For example, each Hypervisor shall be able to switch to the full potential of each core element when the resource request from local applications drops to the minimum, which typically happens at the end of each work day for office computers and at the beginning of each work day for home computers.

The dynamic feature of the CU cloud infrastructure more resembles that in a grid environment. The relatively mature technologies developed by the grid community can be adapted for the construction of future CU clouds.

Before we end this section, let's summarize the key features of CU clouds as compared to vender clouds:

- **Different assumption:** CU clouds build on the assumption that computing resources are separately owned by the members of a community, and are highly dynamic and heterogeneous; typically each resource node is an autonomous node and has its own administration domain, comparable to grids, but more challenging for management because we have to coordinate local applications and large number of cloud applications (while in a grid environment, it is a small number of large applications). The governance in a CU cloud context is carried out at two levels: local administration (managing each individual machine) and federal administration (if viewing the whole cloud infrastructure as a federated system). The infrastructure of CU clouds is similar to that in a grid environment (though more complex). Construction of CU clouds may well leverage the results obtained from Grid Computing, which reflect more than a decade of community efforts in standardization, security, resource management, and virtualization support [4].
- **Community-centered:** A CU cloud is community-driven, community-provisioned, community-owned, and community-consumed – altogether, community-centered. Yet, a CU cloud reserves the option to open to the outside world for gaining profits for the community and its members.
- **CU clouds are "greener":** as explained earlier, CU clouds have potential to carry the sustainability of "Green Computing" forward by a big step.
- **Smaller scale:** as the computing resources supporting a CU cloud come from the contributing members in a community, comparing with enterprise clouds, CU clouds are of relatively smaller scale. But multiple CU clouds may form a consortium or federation and result in larger-scale CU clouds. So, CU clouds are not necessarily smaller than enterprise vender provided clouds when the envisioned technologies mature.
- **Natural digital ecosystems:** A CU cloud possesses most features of a digital ecosystem such as self-provision, self-organization, self-control, scalability, sustainability, and thus can naturally serve as an ideal platform for digital ecosystem development.
- **Ideal platform for education:** A CU cloud deployed for an educational institution can serve as a readily available and ideal platform for further the development of community education clouds.
- **Ideal platform for government:** due to the less security and privacy concern that inherently comes with the CU model.
- **Ideal platform for every community and organization**.

6 Summary

In this paper, we presented a novel Cloud Computing Model (CUM) which is based on and motivated by the widely practiced credit unions as a type of cooperative financial institutions world-wide. We discussed the architecture for CU cloud implementation and other related issues. CU clouds have important advantages over the current Cloud Computing model (which is basically a vendor-provision model). CU clouds do not come without new challenges, but that are not insurmountable. The new challenges are outlined below and form our future work to be investigated with the project that we are currently initiating:

- CU cloud specific virtualization technologies (of which a key point is how to gracefully balance cloud requirements with native applications)
- New host operating systems with built-in virtualization capability utilizing special hardware level support.
- Decentralized cloud facility management (including distributing coordination and load balancing, etc.)

PS: Just before we were to submit this paper, we notice Marinos and Briscoe's paper [16] that addresses on a highly relevant issue – Community Cloud Computing. Recognizing the potential overlaps, we highlight on a few points that differentiate our work from their: (1) CUM is based on the credit union business model; (2) CU clouds are open; (3) CUM draws upon voluntary computing [5, 6].

References

1. Frischbier, S., Petrov, I.: Aspects of Data-Intensive Cloud Computing. In: From Active Data Management to Event-Based Systems and More, pp. 57–77 (2010)
2. Tek-Tips: Defining Cloud Computing (2009), http://tek-tips.nethawk.net/blog/defining-cloud-computings-key-characteristics-deployment-and-delivery-types
3. Kossmann, D., Kraska, T.: Data Management in the Cloud: Promises, State-of-the-art, and Open Questions. Datenbank-Spektrum 10(3), 121–129 (2010)
4. Foster, I., Zhao, Y., et al.: Cloud Computing and Grid Computing 360-Degree Compared. In: Grid Computing Environments Workshop, pp. 1–10 (2009)
5. Anderson, D., Cobb, J., et al.: SETI@home: an experiment in public-resource computing. Commun. ACM 45(11), 56–61 (2002)
6. Cappos, J., Beschastnikh, I., et al.: Seattle: A Platform for Educational Cloud Computing. In: SIGCSE, pp. 111–115 (2009)
7. VMWare (White Paper): Virtulization Overview (2006), http://www.vmware.com/pdf/virtualization.pdf
8. Mell, P., Grance, T.: The NIST Definition of Cloud Computing. National Institute of Standards and Technology. Information Technology Laboratory (July 2009)
9. Google: What is Google App Engine (2010), http://code.google.com/intl/en/appengine/docs/whatisgoogleappengine.html
10. Microsoft: Windows Azure (2010), http://www.microsoft.com/windowsazure/windowsazure/
11. Amazon Elastic Compute Cloud (Amazon EC2) (2011), http://aws.amazon.com/ec2/
12. Varia, J.: Cloud Architectures (Amazon White Paper, June 2008), http://jineshvaria.s3.mazonaws.com/public/cloudarchitectures-varia.pdf
13. Salesforce (2011), http://www.salesforce.com/
14. Armbrust, M., Fox, A., et al.: A Berkeley View of Cloud Computing. Technical Report No. UCB/EECS-2009-28, http://www.eecs.berkeley.edu/Pubs/TechRpts/2009/EECS-2009-28.html
15. Jones, M. T.: Anatomy of an Open Source Cloud (2010), http://www.ibm.com/developerworks/opensource/library/os-cloud-anatomy/
16. Marinos, A., Briscoe, G.: Community Cloud Computing. In: CloudCom, pp. 472–484 (2009)

A Trial Design of e-Healthcare Management Scheme with IC-Based Student ID Card, Automatic Health Examination System and Campus Information Network

Yoshiro Imai[1], Yukio Hori[1], Hiroshi Kamano[2], Tomomi Mori[2], Eiichi Miyazaki[3], and Tadayoshi Takai[3]

[1] Graduate School of Engineering, Kagawa University
Hayashi-cho 2217-20, Takamatsu, Japan
imai@eng.kagawa-u.ac.jp
[2] Health Center, Kagawa University
2-1 Saiwai-cho, Takamatsu, Japan
[3] Faculty of Education, Kagawa University
1-1 Saiwai-cho, Takamatsu, Japan

Abstract. A Health Education Support System has been being developed for Students and university staffs of Kagawa University. The system includes an IC card reader(writer), several types of physical measuring devices (height meter, weight meter, blood pressure monitor, etc. for health examination), a special-purpose PC, distributed information servers and campus network environment. We have designed our prototype of a Health Education Support System as follows; Students and/or university staffs can utilize the above system for their health education and/or healthcare whenever they want anywhere in university. They can use IC-based ID cards for user authentication, operate the physical measuring devices very much simply, and maintain their physical data periodically. Measured data can be obtained at any point of university by means of measuring devices connected with the system on-line, transferred through campus network environment, and finally cumulated into a specific database of secured information servers. We have carried out some experiments to design our system and checked behaviour of each subsystem in order to evaluate whether such a system satisfy our requirements to build facilities to support health education described above. In this paper, we will introduce our design concepts of a Health Education Support System, illustrate some experimental results and discuss perspective problems as our summaries.

Keywords: Health Education, Cloud Computing Service, IC-based ID card, Automatic Health Examination System, e-Healthcare.

1 Introduction

Nowadays, people of the world become aware of significance about daily health problems more an more. So there have been growing interests in healthcare and

H. Cherifi, J.M. Zain, and E. El-Qawasmeh (Eds.): DICTAP 2011, Part I, CCIS 166, pp. 728–740, 2011.

its technological (i.e. industrial) approaches in individual as well as corporation. Some people, for example L. Barrett of Internet News, said, "It's a time of big changes for the health care industry as it transitions from paper-based antiquated record-keeping to digital storage of patient's records as well as administrative and other medical-related information." As he said, some of the biggest names in technology have introduced and been continuing to develop solutions designed to make medical records more accessible to patient's during their hospital visits and more portable as they change providers.

Some companies have led to participate in development and management of mobile and Cloud computing solutions by means of Internet and wireless network. For example, famous ones such as Google[1] and Microsoft[2] have introduced personal healthcare portals for patients to manage their records and/or medical histories online.

Not only industrial but also academic approaches also have been growing and spreading more widely and steadily as mentioned in the later section. Application of mobile healthcare should be considered and developed in the scope of a comprehensive architecture, as was predicted by T. Broens, M. van Sinderen [1] and so on. Cloud computing approach is one of the most efficient strategies to provide ICT-based smart applications to users (patients as well as doctors/nurse) and realize mobile healthcare environment.

On the other hand, health education is one of the most important subjects which must be achieved efficiently in all the schools and universities of the world. In order to perform suitable health education, it is necessary for doctors and nurses in university to investigate students' medical records and give their diagnosis to the according students individually. So almost all the universities, even in Japan, must provide an effective environment for health education and/or efficient support to obtain and manage students' medical records.

This paper will describe our Cloud Computing Service for a Health Education Support System, which has been designed and now under developing/tuning stages as an example of e-Healthcare Management Scheme with IC-based Student ID card, Automatic Health Screening Modules(sub-system) and Distributed Campus Information Network. The next section mentions related works/researches about e-healthcare as application of Cloud computing for healthcare support. The third section introduces design concept and explains configuration of our Health Education Support System. The fourth section reports a current status of a trial prototype of our support system with IC-based Student ID card, Automatic Health Examination System and Distributed Campus Information Network. And finally, the last section concludes our summaries and future problems.

---

1 (e.g.) Google Health
`http://www.google.com/intl/en-US/health/about/index.html`

2 (e.g.) Microsoft HealthVault
`http://www.healthvault.com/industry/index.html`

2 Related Works

This section explains precedent researches, mainly in academic approaches. And key ideas of the above related works are discussed to find and choose suitable approach and strategy for our Health Education Support System

E.-H. Kim et al. of Washington University have developed and implemented a "Web-Based Personal-Centered Electronic Health Record" system named the Personal Health Information Management System [3]. They have reported its evaluation by low-income families and elderly or disabled populations. This trial had been done for the sake of confirmation of its functionalities which are "patient-centered" and regulate inequality (i.e., "digital divide"). Usability of their system was satisfied by both patients and providers during such a trial.

W. Omar and A. Taleb-Bendiab of Liverpool John Moores University have discussed how to use some service-oriented architecture (SOA) to build an e-health monitoring system (EHMS). They specify a model for deploying discovering, integrating, implementing, managing, and invoking e-health services. They also mentioned that the above model could help the healthcare industry to develop cost efficient and dependable healthcare services [4].

M. Subramanian et al. of Cardiff University(UK) have reported their research project implementing a prototype to 'push' or 'pull' data via mobile devices and/or dedicated home-based network servers to one or more, data analysis engines [5]. This data has been practically used to evaluate diabetes risk assessment for a particular individual, and also undertake trends analysis across data from multiple individuals. Their project has been named "Healthcare@Home" and one of Research Models for Patient-Centred Healthcare Services. It employs use of the service-oriented architecture (SOA) approach. They also have shown the need for such a personalized(i.e., "patient/user-centered") health management system. In this paper, so-called patient's medical records are efficiently obtained by means of network and utilized for evaluation of diabetes risk assessment at doctor's viewpoint.

Syed Sibte Raza Abidi of Dalhousie University(Canada) has characterized "Healthcare Knowledge Management[6]," from various perspectives–such as epistemological, organizational learning, knowledge-theoretic and functional. Frontiers of healthcare knowledge management utilize a Semantic Web based healthcare knowledge management framework ,in particular, for patient management through decision support and care planning, from a knowledge-theoretic perspective. A suite of healthcare knowledge management services are aimed to assist healthcare stakeholders from a functional perspective.

E. D'Mello and J. Rozenblit of University of Arizona have pointed, in [7], "patients' medical information is dispersed on several providers' medical information systems making personal medical information management a difficult task for patients. Given this situation, there is a need for patients to be able to easily access their patient data from the different providers' systems so as to promote effective management of their medical information." And they have proposed a design for a system that will alleviate the personal health information management process for patients by providing them a single point of access to their medical information from disparate healthcare providers' systems over the Internet. Their system has been based on Extensible Markup Language (XML) web services. An evaluation of their prototype has shown that the design allows patients an easy means of managing their health information and the design is also scalable, extensible, secure and interoperable with disparate healthcare providers' information systems.

W.D. Yu and M. Chan of San Jose State University have introduced an application of electronic health record (EHR) systems [9]. They explained a service engineering modeling of the integration of a parking guidance system services with EHR system. Their integrated system has provided services for patients as well as healthcare providers. The authors have pointed that such an integrated system must be available on mobile devices in order to provide efficient and convenient e-healthcare services. And they mentioned that an according server has been implemented as a Web service server, and a mobile Web service client, along with its desktop counterpart, is a part of the integrated system. Finally they have made a point of showing that such an integrated system addresses various security issues in privacy, integrity and confidentiality of the patient's medical record data.

We will put the above researches and their results into good account in order to design and utilize our new system. In the next section, a new health management system in our university will be discussed based on some related works described above. It has been designed and then partly implemented first as our prototype which is reflected the above preceding works.

This section introduces a design concept of our Health Education Support System based on previous problems to be resolved. Our university has had some requirements to archive students' Health environment efficiently and provide Health (-keeping) education during students' school days. And then the section also explains details of the system for the sake of prototype implementation and new problems for future system management.

2.1 System Design Concept

It has been necessary for the Health Center of our university to perform regular health screening for all the students at the beginning of every first semester. Physical measuring devices must be used in decade intervals and now they can be replaced to be more intelligent and digitally precise Some kinds of such devices are not on-line and not suitable to be connected directly to the network. Operators must perform paper-based recording of students' medical data for such devices. Health screenings are always time-consuming every year. So not only students but staffs of our university have been hoping that such health screenings will be carried out more efficiently and in the relatively shorter period.

We have start discussing to realize a new Health Education Support System in order to improve our previous problems described above. Design concepts of our system are as follows:

1. System realizes acquiring data automatically from physical measuring devices at the regular health screenings.
2. System applies IC cards for Students Identification of our university to not only user authentication but also short-time recording (or temporary storage) of measured data.
3. System provides information retrieval for students' healthcare records through convenient and secure accessibility to distributed information servers in university campus network.
4. System supports health education that doctors and nurses of our university provide on-demand health consultation for questions and answers about student's health efficiently.
5. System helps students (as well as staffs of our university) to perform self-managing and maintaining for their good health.

We are implementing such a support system designed by collaboration team including members from Health Center, Faculty of Education, and Information Technology Center.

The first mission of our Health Education Support System is to reduce man power cost for regular health screenings so that system must realize automatic data acquisition from measuring device to PC and/or smart storage media. IC cards are used to authenticate students and staffs of information environment in our university and this time they will be utilized to obtain convenient and secure accessibility to our system as well as smart media to keep users' healthcare records during regular health screenings at least for their paperless operations. The system will be implemented in our distributed campus network environment using some information servers such as database, world-wide web, mail, and so on.

Such an approach will lead our system to provide Cloud computing services to its users. Namely, students and staffs who are the users of our system can easily obtain convenient accessibility and refer their healthcare records by users themselves as well as their consulting doctors and/or nurses n our university. Figure1 shows the Conceptual Configuration of our Health Education Support System. It can support ubiquitous healthcare management by means of PC manipulation with IC card authentication and using mobile phone which look like as Cloud computing services.

3 Health Education Support System

3.1 Detail of Prototype System

A prototype of our system includes following three facilities: (1) automatic acquisition of data from physical measuring devices to PC and/or IC card under user authentication, (2) data management of students' healthcare records in distributed information servers which can transfer data from/to PCs with IC cards, and (3) using mobile phones with wireless LAN-based connectivity to refer students' healthcare records within university.

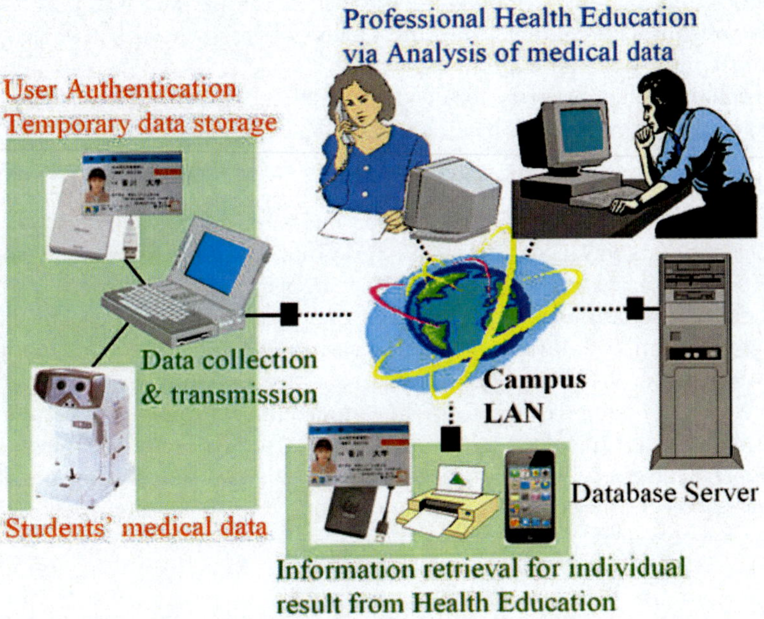

Fig. 1. Conceptual Configuration of a Health Education Support System

First of all, we start to explain (1) facility below. We have tested to perform reading operations and writing ones against IC cards for Students Identification. These operations can be carried out on Windows PC with IC card reader/writer named PaSoRi and special software library called felicalib. Hori, a member of our system development team, has recorded his experience and results to create original software for the above test in his Blogs which are frequently referred by some users in Japan who want to know usage of IC cards. (We are very sorry because his blogs [3] are written in Japanese).

Miyazaki, another member of our team, has developed software to control physical measuring devices and acquire their data for users and currently store them. And he has prepared GUI to integrate IC card-based user authentication and data transfer from measuring device to IC card. He has also reported a state of our research at an international symposium[12]. Now we can not only use IC card for Student Identification for user authentication, but also apply IC card itself into temporary storage for student medical data as a smart media. These efforts described above can let us utilize IC cards more effectively and efficiently as follows;

[3] Report of reading IC card: Yukio Hori [felica] extraction of ID and name string from FCF format by PaSoRi
`http://yasuke.org/horiyuki/blog/diary.cgi?Date=20090707`
report of writing IC card: Yukio Hori [felica] using felicalib on Cygwin software
`http://yasuke.org/horiyuki/blog/diary.cgi?Search=[felica]`

- paperless operation to memorize measured health data temporarily even under off-line environment (i.e. measuring operations with the PCs which cannot connect to the campus network)
- high reliable data integrity for students medical data in PCs and in their IC cards during regular health screenings,

Secondarily, we mention (2) facility of our prototype system. We have a lot of experiences to design and implement some kinds of information servers such as an application gateway (i.e. special-purpose information server) for some Web services to mobile systems [2]. Software of information servers are written in Java programming language because of our experiences to develop such software. The reasons to employ Java as system description language are as follows; (1) flexible absorption of differences between software developing environment and software execution one, (2) thread-based concurrent execution for several kinds of information server application, and (3) accumulation of decade-years experiences to develop server application for elated works. Distributed information servers have been easily developed for the sake of client PCs which can read and write data between IC cards.

3.2 Functions of Program Modules and Processing Flow of System

This subsection explains the detail of processing flow of our health education support system. The first half of this part shows functions and relation of program modules and its second half describes detail of data handling between IC card and Information Server as an example of processing flow of our system.

Functions and Relation of Program Modules. Program modules for the system mainly consist of ones for client PC, ones for Information Server, and one for Smart phones. Figure 2 shows functions and relation of program modules.

For example, program modules for client PC control to acquire physical measured data and to read/write data from/to IC cards. Ones for Information Server work together Web-DB system, which has been built by means of Apache and SQL server. In cooperation, both of them can play an important role to receive and/or send users' physical measured data between client PC and Information server.

A program module for mobile phones can be selected, because two types of modules for such phones have been provided. One is Java program for high-performance cellular phones, and another is Javascript for a lot of browsers (ex. Safari) of smart phones and PDAs. The former is already developed and used for another project[8], which can be customized for some types for J2ME[4]-based microCPU with CLDC[5] specification. The later has been developed with Dr. Keiichi Shiraishi of Kagawa National College of Technology, Japan as one of our research colleagues.

---

[4] Java2 Platform of MicroEdition.

[5] Connected Limited Device Configuration.

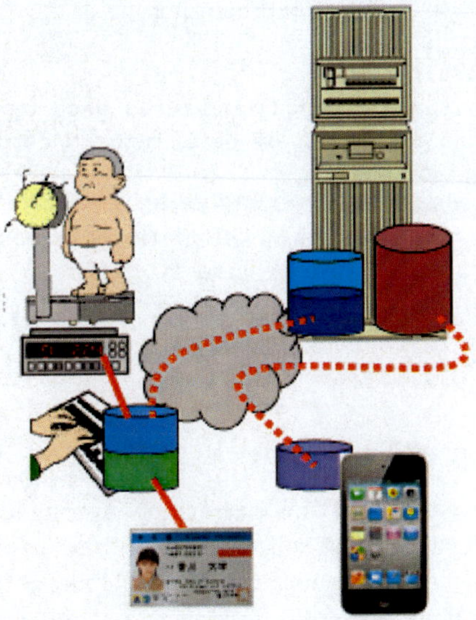

Fig. 2. Functions and Relation of Program Modules

Each module can be downloaded from Information Server to the target mobile phone according to user's request and executed on the phone in order to transfer information between them. Such a module plays a role to provide an interface of users (students of our university) and our Health Education Support System.

Detail of Processing Flow for IC card and Information Server. For the sake of giving more exact image for system, as one of examples, we will focus relation between client PC and Information Server, explain behaviour of program modules, and describe detail of processing flow. Such a flow can be expressed by means of steps from 1 to 4 as follows;

1. `Reading User ID form IC card` (getting UserInfo)
2. `Combining it with measured data from physical measuring device`
3. `Confirming combined dataset on PC` – neglectable
4. *select (a)Server-client style or (b)Standalone one*
   (a) for *Server-client style* ··· On-line processing
   - data-input mode: (client PC → Information Server (IS))
     i. `open session by UserInfo`
        (NB) executing in the Thread mode for multiple access
     ii. `transfer DateInfo, SubjectToBeMeasured to IS`
     iii. `transfer a series of PhysicalMeasuredData continuously`
     iv. `close session`
   - data-refer mode: (client PC ← IS)
     i. `open session by UserInfo`
     ii. `retrieve by means of specified condition`
     iii. `receive the appropriate record (a set of data)`
     iv. `close session`

(b) for *Standalone style* ··· Off-line processing
   - data-writing mode:
      i. `read specific area of IC card`
      ii. `modify it with a newly measured data on PC`
      iii. `write the new block of data into IC card`
   - data-reading mode:
      i. `read specific area of IC card`
      ii. `display it on PC` (this is an affirming process)
      iii. `save it with UserInfo into PC file`

Communication between client PC and Information server is secured and carried out through the university campus network.

3.3 Trial Evaluation of Prototype

In this part, trial evaluation will be performed among our prototype system and currently presented researches, whose systems and/or approaches have some analogy to ours in the relevant papers introduced below.

H.Chang and his colleagues point out that patient-centric healthcare and evidence-based medicine require health-related information to be shared among a community in order to deliver better and more affordable healthcare in their paper[10]. They also claim that it is highly valuable to develop IT technologies that can foster sustainable healthcare ecosystems for collaborative, coordinated healthcare delivery. Their assertion is that an emerging cloud computing appears well-suited to meet the demand of a broad set of health service scenarios.

Our approach is one of the same sides of their assertions and our strategy to realize Health Education Support has been achieved through our university campus network as well as IC card for student authentication. So it will be effective for users (not only students but doctors/nurses of our university) to utilize our system through distributed network environment.

L.Liao and his research team propose that the patient oriented Web-enabled healthcare service application has brought a new trend to delivery patient-centric healthcare, and it can provide an easy implementation and interoperability for complicated electronic medical records (EMR) systems in their paper[11].

Our prototype system has also provided its interface of Web-based service for clients, especially major part of users(students) with mobile phones and portable PCs. But other users(doctors/nurses) can deal with information about students' healthcare through special interface suitable to modify as well as Web-browser only for references. The reason to employ such two types of interfaces for doctors/nurse is both of security and operability. If only Web-based interface is provided, an easy implementation is fulfilled but security suitable to modify and refer information about students' healthcare is not easy to achieve.

There has been published an interesting paper[14] about the Health 2.0 and review of German Healthcare Web portals by R.Görlitz and his members of FZI (Forschungszentrum Informatik). They have searched for the German health-related web portals incorporates by means of major search engines using German key words such as "Health", "Care support", "Disease", "Nursing service" and classified the relevant links on the retrieved websites in order to compare their characteristics as well as cluster similar portals together, As one of their conclusions, they report "One striking aspect distilled from the conducted review of German health care web portals is that most of the found portals are predominantly *WEB 1.0*, for which the operator provides and controls all the information that is published."

Our system also employs basic system architecture and structure such as Web-DB cooperation, Web-based user interface, simple TCP-based communication between client PCs and Information servers, which are ones of so-called *WEB 1.0* styles. Therefore, it cannot provide up-to-date technologies for users. But our system can give users a sense of assurance through its interface, service and functionality.

4 Current State and Perspective Problems

This section describes a current state of our Health Education Support System for this year's development. Additionally, it mentions some perspective problems to manage our system in practical situation and advance the system into the next stage by stepwise refinement.

4.1 Prototype System as Cloud Service

Our project has started to provide some effective solutions to reduce time-consuming mount of services for regular health screenings and to achieve smart user authentication with IC card during Health Education (including such screenings). Members of our project belongs to Health Center(doctor/nurse), Faculty of Education, Information Technology Center, and Graduate School of Engineering. So we can distribute our tasks and/or determination of the whole system design and then assign them for specialists of each field.

Members of Faculty of Education have designed handling of physical measuring devices and IC card with help from Information Technology Center, they have also designed transferring of measured records between client PCs and Information servers, members of Information Technology Center have designed Web-DB cooperation scheme and Web-interface for Health Education Support System, and finally members of Health Center can provide health education with measured healthcare records from regular health screenings.

Users of our system have regular health screenings through user authentication by means of IC card. They can receive information about their healthcare records after IC card-based authentication and consult doctor's opinions based on their healthcare records. Users can look upon such a series of procedures as a kind of cloud computing services about healthcare.

I.K.Kim and his university's research members report that identity management has been an issue to hinder in adoption of e-Healthcare applications, and propose a methodology of Single-Sign-On for Cloud applications by utilizing Peer-to-Peer concepts to distribute processing load among computing nodes in their paper[13].

We have employed user authentication with IC card-based student identification for simple/quick procedure and moreover we have tried to utilize such an IC card as a temporary storage at the same time, especially during regular health screenings. Our approach may be effective not only for smart authentication but also for man power reduction of time-consuming regular health screenings.

4.2 Perspective Problems

Our Health Education Support System will have some perspective problems until it will have been developed and utilized in practical situation. Such problems are summarized as follows;

- System must provide several kinds of security measures to support user's accessibility for his/her medical database in the information server. Because of treatment of individual medical information, our Information Technology Center should pay its severe attention to need for security measures. It is necessary to discuss to keep high-level security measures for Health Center's operations which manage students' healthcare records and allow users to access them.
- System must allow some privileged users to access students' healthcare records in order to perform health check. Doctors and nurses of university are registered as privileged users in our system, who want to utilize statistical problem-solving libraries for data mining and analysis. Therefore, system must equip such libraries and usage services so that that privileged user can manipulate them easily for his/her efficient health check. This service is really necessary to realize Health Education Support with our system.
- System must help its users refer their healthcare records and browse health-checked results from their doctors and/or nurses for their self-health management. Several reports have told us that it must be necessary for users to improve self-managing capabilities for their healthcare. System must provide browsing service of user's healthcare information as one of Cloud computing services.
- System must show the privileged users some suitable methods to extract and select the very students whose healthcare records are applicable to searching conditions. And it must call the students to come to the Health Center of our university in order to consult their doctors/nurses about their health. Such a calling service will be implemented by means of mobile e-mail and voice message based on intention of doctors/nurses.

5 Conclusions

This paper describes our Health Education Support System and its practical services realized based on Cloud computing approach. Such a system has been included with IC card reader/writer for user authentication and temporary data storage, Automatic Health Examination Modules to allow several types of physical measuring devices to collect users'(i.e. patients') medical data, distributed information servers which can play following roles such as Database sever of medical records management, Web server of Healthcare service with Cloud interface, Mail/Communication server of periodical/emergent contacts for users (i.e. students of our university) and so on. A prototype of our system has been developed and evaluated over distributed campus information network.

Some related works are also explained and reviewed in the paper for the sake of efficient designing of our Health Education Support System. Ones of such works are worth while discussing, especially how to deal with medical records for users themselves as well as service providers. Their some good ideas contribute to design of our Health Education Support System practically and influence development of its Cloud computing services.

Our prototype is evaluated by means of comparison of similar related researches. Some researches have relatively similar approaches and others have difficult goals. But current trends are employed with Cloud service based approaches and will make such services very much fruitful on users' viewpoints. Many reports, some of which this paper has referred to, have supported such a cloud-based approaches and strategies.

Acknowledgments. The authors would like to express sincere thanks to Dr. Hiroshi Itoh and Dr. Shigeyuki Tajima, Trustees (Vice-Presidents) of Kagawa University, for their financial supports and heart-warming encouragements individually. They are also thankful to General chair Professor H. Cherifi and Reviewers for their great supervisions about our paper. This work is partly supported by the 2010 Kagawa University Special Supporting Funds.

References

1. Broens, T., Halteren, A.V., Sinderen, M.V., Wac, K.: Towards an Application Framework for Context-aware m-Health Applications. In: Proceedings of 11th Open European Summer School (EUNICE 2005), pp. 1–7 (2005)
2. Imai, Y., Sugiue, Y., Hori, Y., Iwamoto, Y., Masuda, S.: An Enhanced Application Gateway for some Web services to Personal Mobile Systems. In: Proceedings of the 5th International Conference on Intelligent Agents, Web Technology and Internet Commerce, Vienna, Austria, vol. 2, pp. 1055–1060 (2005)
3. Kim, E.-H., et al.: Web-based Personal-centered Electronic Health Record for Elderly Population. In: Proceedings of the 1st Transdisciplinary Conference on Distributed Diagnosis and Home Healthcare, pp. 144–147 (2006)
4. Omar, W.M., Taleb-Bendiab, A.: e-Health Support Services based on Service-oriented Architecture. IT Professional 8(2), 35–41 (2006)
5. Subramanian, M., et al.: Healthcare@home: Research Models for Patient-centred Healthcare Services. In: JVA 2006: Proceedings of IEEE International Symposium on Modern Computing, pp. 107–113 (2006)
6. Abid, S.S.R.: Healthcare Knowledge Management: the Art of the Possible. In: AIME 2007: Proceedings of the 2007 conference on Knowledge Management for Health Care Procedures pp. 1–20 (2007)
7. D'Mello, E., Rozenblit, J.: Design For a Patient-Centric Medical Information System Using XML Web Services. In: Proceedings of International Conference on Information Technology, pp. 562–567 (2007)

8. Imai, Y., Hori, Y., Masuda, S.: A Mobile Phone-Enhanced Remote Surveillance System with Electric Power Appliance Control and Network Camera Homing. In: Proceedings of the Third International Conference on Autonomic and Autonomous Systems, Athen, Greece, p. 6 (2007)
9. Yu, W.D., Chan, M.: A Service Engineering Approach to a Mobile Parking Guidance System in uHealthcare. In: Proceedings of IEEE International Conference on e-Business Engineering, pp. 255–261 (2008)
10. Chang, H.H., Chou, P.B., Ramakrishnan, S.: An Ecosystem Approach for Healthcare Services Cloud. In: Proceedings of IEEE International Conference on e-Business Engineering, pp. 608–612 (2009)
11. Liao, L., et al.: A Novel Web-enabled Healthcare Solution on Healthvault System. In: WICON 2010, Proceedings of The 5th Annual ICST Wireless Internet Conference (WICON), pp. 1–6 (2010)
12. Miyazaki, E., et al.: Trial of a Simple Autonomous Health Management System for e-Healthcare Campus Environment, In: Proceedings of The Third Chiang Mai University- Kagawa University Joint Symposium, CD-ROM proceedings, @Chiang Mai, Thailand (2010)
13. Kim, I.K., Pervez, Z., Khattak, A.M., Lee, S.: Chord based Identity Management for e-Healthcare Cloud Applications. In: SAINT 2010: Proceedings of 10th IEEE/IPSJ International Symposium on Applications and the Internet, pp. 391–394 (2010)
14. Görlitz, R., Seip, B., Rashid, A., Zacharias, V.: Health 2.0 in Practice: A Review of German Healthcare Web Portals. In: ICWI 2010: Proceedings of 10th IADIS International Conference WWW/Internet 2010, pp. 49–56 (2010)

Survey of Security Challenges in Grid Environment

Usman Ahmad Malik[1], Mureed Hussain[2], Mehnaz Hafeez[2], and Sajjad Asghar[1]

[1] National Centre for Physics, QAU Campus, 45320 Islamabad, Pakistan
[2] Shaheed Zulfikar Ali Bhutto Institute of Science and Technology (SZABIST), H-8/4 Islamabad, Pakistan
usman@ncp.edu.pk, hmureed@yahoo.com, mehnaz.hafeez@cern.ch, sajjad@ncp.edu.pk

Abstract. Use of grid systems has increased tremendously since their inception in 90's. With grids, users execute the jobs without knowing which resources will be used to run their jobs. An important aspect of grids is Virtual Organization (VO). VO is a group of individuals, pursuing a common goal but under different administrative domains. Grids share large computational and storage resource that are geographically distributed among a large number of users. This very nature of grids, introduces quite a few security challenges. These security challenges need to be taken care of with ever increasing demand of computation, storage and high speed network resources. In this paper we review the existing grid security challenges and grid security models. We analyze and identify the usefulness of different security models including role based access control, middleware improvements, and standardization of grid service. The paper highlights the strengths and weaknesses of the reviewed models.

Keywords: grid security, GSI, RBAC.

1 Introduction

A Grid is a collection of heterogeneous, coordinated shared resources (systems, applications and network), distributed across multiple administrative domains, for problem solving [1]. The idea of computing grids is quite similar to that of an electric grid, where a home user does not know that the electricity for his toaster is coming from which grid station. Similarly in grids, users execute arbitrary code without knowing which resources will be used to run their jobs. As the usage of grids has grown considerably, there are quite a few security challenges that need to be taken care of. There are several grid projects, which are providing hundreds and thousands of CPUs for processing and petabytes of storage. One such example is World-wide Large Hadron Collider (LHC) Computing Grid (WLCG) [2]. If a user or a grid site administrator does not have adequate knowledge of security and its implications, they can be subject to appalling compromises of security [3].

H. Cherifi, J.M. Zain, and E. El-Qawasmeh (Eds.): DICTAP 2011, Part I, CCIS 166, pp. 741–752, 2011.

Grid has an important aspect of Virtual Organization (VO). A VO is a group of individuals, institutions and resources, pursuing a common goal, but is not part of a single administrative domain and so introduces security issues in usage of grid resources [4].

Grid applications are different from traditional client-server applications because of dynamic requirement of resources, security, performance constraints, scale with respect to magnitude of the problem and amount of resources involved [8]. Unlike the client-server environment, in grids, not only users but also the applications are not trusted [6][21]. Grids have been realized for sharing resources. This sharing does not only entail simple file sharing and data exchange but also demands access facility to other computers, software and storage facilities. The conditions and parameters under which sharing should occur, must also be defined very clearly and carefully [1].

The security and integrity of these resources is of utmost importance [6][21]. This security requirement is unique. A parallel computation which needs huge computational resources, distributed across different administrative domains, demand a security infrastructure and relationships amongst these hundreds and thousands of processors distributed around the globe [8], and each of these domains have its own sets of policies and practices [7].

The set of policies and operational practices across various administrative domains are fundamentally dependant on their corresponding services, protocols, Application Programming Interfaces (APIs), and Software Development Kits (SDKs). These aspects of a domain present a major challenge in interoperability with other domains [1].

The major security challenges in grids are single sign-on, protection and delegation of credentials, mapping grid users to local users, interoperability, group communication, accessing and querying the grid information services, firewalls and Virtual Private Networks (VPN) [3][8][9]. High-speed networks connect the high performance computational grids and so network should also be protected. Most of the commercial network protocols do not provide security, confidentiality and protection against traffic analysis attacks [12]. Several research projects in the past and present have focused on providing secure technologies for the grids and several technologies have been introduced as a result of this research.

This paper is aimed at providing a literature review of existing security challenges in grid environments and the possible solutions to these problems. We would discuss different aspects of grid security models that include role based access control mechanism, standardization of grid services, use of Public Key Infrastructure (PKI), and middleware improvements. This paper will also provide a critical evaluation of various security models for grids that have been implemented so far.

The remaining part of the paper is organized as follows: section 2 covers the literature overview, critical evaluation of the security models is presented in section 3, the concluding remarks are covered in section 4.

2 Literature Review

The purpose of literature review is to emphasize the significance of security models in grid environment. A brief overview of different security challenges and their possible solutions have been reviewed. Various security models based on middleware security improvements, use of PKI, standardization of grid services, and role based access control mechanism have been discussed.

Welch et al. [4] discuss the three key functions for a grid security model. The first one is *multiple security mechanisms*. According to them the security model must be interoperable with existing security infrastructure to save investments. The second function is *dynamic creation of services*. These services must not contradict with existing set of rules and policies. The third function is *dynamic establishment of domain trusts* for frequently changing application requirements and transient users. The *Globus Toolkit* ver. 2 (GT2) security model fulfills all three functions and uses *Grid Security Infrastructure* (GSI) for implementation of security functionality. GSI security format is based on X.509 certificates and *Secure Socket Layer* (SSL). PKI is a preferred framework with respect to grid security. The *Open Grid Services Architecture* (OGSA) aligns grid technologies with web services. Globus Toolkit ver. 3 (GT3) and corresponding GSI3 provides implementation of OGSA mechanisms. A GT3 OGSA security model has been introduced, which other than fulfilling the three basic functions describes several security services like *credential processing service (CPS), authorization service (AUS), credential conversion service (CCS), identity mapping service (IMS)* and *audit service (ADS)*. This model pulls out the security from the application and places it in hosting environment. The new model has two benefits over the GT2 which are, *use of web services security protocols* and *tight least-privilege model*. The later eliminates the need of privileged network services besides making other improvements. Web Service Resource Framework (WSRF) is an alternate to OGSA for providing stateful web services. WSRF is a joint effort of Globus Team and IBM.

Moore et al. [5] have adapted Globus and Kerberos for a secure *Accelerated Strategic Computing Initiative* (ASCI) grid. The majority of the available grid technologies do not provide sufficient security, and the ones who provide use the PKI. The existing infrastructure at ASCI uses Kerberos for network authentication and a number of Kerberos/*Distributed Computing Environment* (DCE) applications are running so using PKI (GSI) is not an option. The *Generic Security Service Application Programming Interface* (GSSAPI) provides an abstraction layer for interoperability between the GSI and the Kerberos. Two major portability issues were: 1) delegation of credentials from the gatekeeper to the forked processes and 2) user-to-user communication. Both issues were resolved by modifying the Kerberos GSSAPI library source code. The GSSAPI error reporting does not always provide a meaningful error message because of its tendency to isolate higher layers. New tools and utilities have to be included to detect and report security issues. A utility for refreshing the credentials for jobs running for longer duration would also be needed. The shift to PKI in future is not totally ruled out, but in either case GSSAPI is a viable portability layer.

Butt et al. [6] have presented a two level approach; which provides a secure execution environment for shell-based applications and active runtime monitoring in grids. Traditional access control mechanism binds a user entity with a resource. This assignment is achieved through user account creation. This scheme is not feasible in grids due to large number of resources and users, non-uniform access to resources (if required), frequent changes in machine specific policies, and transient nature of jobs/projects and users. The manual work and maintenance increase the overhead manifolds. In absence of any trust relationship between the users and resources, either the malicious resources can affect the results of a user program, or a malicious user program can be dangerous for integrity of the resources. One approach is to handle security issues by putting constraints on the development environment, for assuring the safe applications, but limiting the application functionality may render it less useful. Another approach is to implement checks at compile, link and load time of the application. This can also be dodged by malicious code injection at the run time. Therefore a secure execution environment is a must requirement for security in grids. A two-level approach has been proposed by the authors. First component is a shell security module (that actively checks the user commands) has been integrated with standard command shell for enforcing the host security policy, which is managed by a configuration file. The second component is active monitoring. When a system call is invoked the kernel system-call mechanism transfers the control to the security module to check whether to allow the execution of this call or not, thus precluding malicious calls.

Azzedin et al. [7] have introduced a Trust-aware Resource Management System (TRMS). According to them quality of service and security are important for resource allocation in grids. As security is implemented as a separate sub-system [8], the *Resource Management System* (RMS) does not consider security policies and implications while allocating resources. A mechanism for computing trust and reputation has been introduced. The model divides grid systems into smaller, autonomous, single administrative entities called *grid domains* (GDs). Two virtual domains *resource domain* (RD) and *client domain* (CD) are associated with each GD. Both virtual domains, posses a set of trust attributes relevant to the TRMS and are used to compute the *Required Trust Level* (RTL) and *Offered Trust Level* (OTL). Agents having access to trust level table are associated with both CDs and RDs. If the calculated trust values are different from the existing ones, the agents update the table. A heuristic based trust-aware resource management algorithm is introduced for resource allocation based on three assumptions: 1) centralized scheduler organization, 2) non-preemptive task execution and 3) indivisible tasks.

Foster et al. [8] present a grid security policy for computational grids and a secure grid architecture based on that policy. The basic requirements of a grid security policy are: single sign-on, protection of credentials, interoperability with (site local) security infrastructures already in place, exportability, uniform certification infrastructure, and support for group communications. A grid security policy has been proposed encompassing security needs of all participating entities that includes users, applications, resources and resource owners. The security architecture presented consists of four major protocols: 1) User proxy creation protocol, 2) Resource allocation protocol, 3) Resource allocation from a process protocol and 4) Mapping registration protocol. The proposed security architecture has been implemented as part of Globus project and is called Grid Security Infrastructure (GSI). The GSI is developed on top of Generic Security Services Application Program Interface (GSSAPI) allowing for portability. The developed architecture has been deployed at Globus Ubiquitous Supercomputing Testbed Organization (GUSTO), a test-bed providing a peak performance of 2.5 teraflops.

According to [10] secure information sharing in dynamic coalitions like grids is a big security risk. Dynamic Coalition Problem (DCP) has been introduced and they have proposed a Role Based Access Control (RBAC) / Mandatory Access Control (MAC) based candidate security model, to control information sharing between entities, involved in dynamic coalitions. The focus is on federating resources. The model includes resources, services, methods, roles, signatures and time constraints and support both RBAC and MAC. A prototype of the proposed model has been implemented using Jini and Common Object Request Broker Architecture (CORBA) as middleware.

In [11] Mukhin has presented another grid security model. Grid services that span across multiple domains must be interoperable at protocol, policy and identity level. The security model emphasizes on standardization of services and federating different security mechanism. The policy must specify what it expects. The requestor of a service must know the requirements and capabilities supported by the target service so that an optimal set of security bindings can be used for mutual authentication. This information must be provided by the hosting environment for establishing a security context, for exchange of secure messages, between the requestor and the service. To achieve credential mapping proxies and gateways are used. Authorization enforcement should ensure that client's identity is understood and validated in service provider's domain. Different organizations under a VO must also establish a trust relationship to interoperate as everyone has its own security infrastructure. Secure logging is an essential service in the proposed model. The primitive security functions should be used as security services for providing authentication, authorization, identity mapping, credential conversion, audit, profile, and privacy services. The existing security technologies should be extended rather than replacing them.

Distributed Role Based Access Control (dRBAC) is best suited for controlling access to distributed resources in coalition environments [13]. dRBAC provides varying access levels and monitoring of trust relationship which other models of access control lack. Third party delegation, valued attributes, and continuous monitoring features of dRBAC achieve this functionality. The resources and principals (the ones need access to resources) both are called entities for simplification. Other constructs of dRBAC include roles, delegations, delegation, proofs and proof monitor. Two schemes of delegation include 1) self-certifying and third-party delegations and 2) assignment delegation. The valued attributes are used for defining the level of access and third parties can be assigned the right to delegate valued attributes as they can delegate roles. dRBAC also provides *delegation subscription* which provides the benefit of continuous monitoring of the trust relationship that has already been established. These are implemented using *event push* model, which minimizes the polling and also notifies the subscriber if the delegation in question has been invalidated. Wallets are used to store delegations. All newly issued delegations are stored in wallets so that they can be discovered and used by other roles.

Mao et al. [14] have introduced a partner-and-adversary threat model; which is not addressed by any of the existing grid security mechanisms. The model is based on the principal that an unknown principal becomes trustworthy if a trusted third party (e.g. a Certification Authority – CA) has introduced it into the system. A conformable policy is must for a VO, irrespective of its dynamic and ad-hoc nature. This behavior conformity is difficult to achieve in a grid environment. They introduce a *Trusted Computing* (TC) technology as a solution against the afore-mentioned threat, which is a tamper protection hardware module called *Trusted Platform Module* (TPM). The TPM works against the stronger adversary (the owner of a platform) and prevents malicious activities. Each VO member platform has a TPM with an *attestation identity key.* The *credential migration protocol* is used to move credentials from one TPM to another by a *Migration Authority* (MA). Using the TPM the chained proxy certificates are no more required. A single credential is created and stored in the TPM. This mechanism provides much stronger protection of the credentials. The members can be removed from a VO by the VO admin without letting them take away any of the VO data and without obtaining user's consent which mitigates the problem of non-conformity to the VO policy.

PERMIS [15] is a role based privilege management system. It is based on X.509 Attribute Certificates (ACs). Authentication is done using a public key certificate, whereas the attribute certificates are used for authorization. The attribute certificates bind user names with privilege attributes. The access rights are held in the privilege attributes of the AC. The PERMIS *privilege management infrastructure* (PMI) comprises of a policy, Privilege Allocator (PA), Privilege Verification Subsystem (PVS), and the PMI API. The policy defines which users have what access on which resources and what are the conditions under which the access is allowed. The policy is specified in XML. A unique identifier is assigned to each policy at the time of its creation. The PA does the signing of the policy and assignment of privileges to users. PERMIS uses RBAC to control access to resources. As the policies are signed, storing them on public LDAP repositories poses no risk of repudiation. The authentication and authorization is performed by the PVS. The authentication mechanism is application specific whereas authorization mechanism is not. PERMIS supports dynamic changes in the authorization policies.

Martinelli et al. [16] have extended the Usage Control (UCON) model in grids. Unlike traditional access control models, which rely on authorization alone, UCON relies on two more factors called obligations and conditions. Other benefits of this model include mutable attributes, which result into continuity of the policy enforcement and usage control. A policy is defined which defines which subjects have what access to which resources under what conditions. The policy also controls the order of actions performed on objects. Policy Enforcement Point (PEP) and Policy Decision Point (PDP) are two main components of the UCON architecture. The PEP is continuously monitoring for access requests to resources. As soon as a user tries to access a resource, PEP suspends it and asks PDP for decision. PDP in turn retrieves subject/object and condition parameters from the *Attribute Manager* (AM) and the *Condition Manager* (CM) respectively. If all factors are satisfied the PDP returns control to PEP with permit access, which as a result resumes the suspended action. Otherwise the access request is declined. One possibility is normal execution and completion of the process after which the access is revoked. As PDP is always active, if any of the conditions do not satisfy, even during the execution of a process, its access to the resource is revoked. The conditions are evaluated continuously by PDP.

Jung et al. [17] have presented a flexible authentication and authorization architecture for grid computing. They have presented a dynamic and flexible architecture; which provides dynamic updates to security policies and fine-grained (method-level) authorization. Currently, the security policy of a particular service should be set before its deployment. To cater any changes in the policy, the service must be stopped and re-deployed by the administrator, which is an overhead. The proposed architecture has three components: *Flexible Security* (FSecurity) *Manager*, *Security Configuration Data Controller* (SCDC), and *FSecurity Manager Cleint* (FMC). The FSecurity Manager intercepts and processes the authentication and authorization requests. It also enables the method level authorization by implementing the *fgridmap* file. The SCDC is used to manage and store the security policy information. The FMC is used to manage the service manager through a web interface. Aspect Oriented Programming (AOP) has been adopted to implement this architecture, which allows easy integration with the current system without modifying the existing architecture.

Stoker et al. [18] have presented three approaches to address the credential delegation problem in grid environment. The implementation of these three schemes (method restriction, object restriction and time-dependent restrictions) within Legion, a metacomputing software, have been discussed. The *method restriction* approach can be achieved by 1) method enumeration, which is tedious, inflexible, difficult to implement and requires a lot of changes to the code 2) compiler automation, which involves writing compilers for all of the Legion supported languages 3) method abstraction, which also requires upgrading the existing infrastructure. The *object restriction* can be achieved by 1) object classes, which would only be effective if used together with method enumeration 2) transitive trust, where remote method calls are annotated with methods being called 3) trusted equivalence classes, which has shortcomings of group definition and membership verification and implicit trust on modified objects of trusted classes objects 4) trusted application writers and developers, which allows or denies access based on credentials of the principal on behalf of whom the request is being made. The *time-dependent restrictions* require a reasonable slack time window to minimize refreshes and maximize security.

Ferrari et al. [19] have presented a flexible security system for Legion. Main components of the Legion security model are: 1) Legion Runtime Library (LRTL), which has a flexible protocol stack. The method calls are handled by an event-base model 2) the core objects. The *host objects* manage active objects and control access to processing resources. The *vault objects* manage inert objects and control storage resources. A unique Legion Object Identifier (LOID) is associated with every object and user. The user is authenticated based on his LOID and credentials. The access control is per object basis. Access Control Lists (ACLs) are used to restrict access to methods and objects. The message privacy is achieved by encryption (private mode) and integrity (protected mode). To achieve object isolation separate accounts are used to execute different user objects. The site isolation is provided by restricting messages with admin credentials within the site. The ACL mechanism has been extended to provide site-wide access control. The objects running behind a firewall have an associated proxy object running on the firewall host for providing secure access to objects. The class manager objects provide implicit set of parameters to control resource selection by the user.

An architecture for resource management model by Foster et al. [20] addresses site autonomy, heterogeneous substrate, policy extensibility, online control and co-allocation. The main components of the architecture are: Resource Specification Language (RSL), local resource manager, resource brokers, and resource co-allocator. The user specifies the job requirements in RSL, which is passed onto *Globus Resource Allocation Manager* (GRAM). The GRAM schedules the resources itself or through some other resource allocation mechanism. The GRAM *gatekeeper* performs mutual authentication and starts the job manager to perform the job. A resource broker specializes the job specifications in the RSL. It passed on the job request to an appropriate local resource manager or to a resource co-allocator for a multi-site resource request. As the number of jobs increase the failure rate at multiple sites also increases due to authorization problems, network issues, and badly configured nodes. The issue of dynamic job structure modification to minimize such failures needs to be addressed.

3 Critical Evaluation

During the literature review, three approaches of grid security models stand out. These include Role Based Access Control (RBAC), GSI, and security models based on web services. Featuring strengths of these models, the RBAC model simplifies user privilege management, it is widely accepted in the industry as a best practice. Many major software vendors offer RBAC based products. It provides efficient provisioning and efficient access control management, although in large heterogeneous environments, implementation of RBAC may become extremely complex. The GSI covers authentication and privilege delegation extensively. Addressing a wide range of security issues in grid environment is the strength of GSI.

On the other hand, one of the biggest advantages of using web services is the fact that they are not based on any specific programming language. Moreover, the web services implementation is not based on any programming data model i.e., object oriented or non-object oriented. As they are based on web technologies, which have already proven to be scalable and they pass through the firewalls fairly easily. The services normally do not require a huge framework in memory. A small application with a few lines of code could also be exposed as a Web Service. We have grouped the studied security models with respect to these three broader approaches.

Grid Security Policy and architecture [8] addresses a wide range of security challenges in grid through Grid Security Infrastructure (GSI). This model provides a base for grid security and future grid security models. Still some of the security features that are not addressed in this model include support for group context, and credential delegation. Moreover performance bottleneck is also a concern. Yet GSI establishes the base security model and is a de-facto security infrastructure for providing security in grids.

Security model for OGSA is based on GT-3 and web-services protocols [4]. The proposed security model shows improvements over previous GT-2 model. It is based on least privilege model. This model is not generalized enough and its implementation is Globus specific. On the other hand the ASCI project ports Globus system from GSI to Kerberos security [5]. GSS-API layer modifications provide interoperability between GSI & Kerberos. The solution lacks adaptability and reusability. Moreover it is against the grid philosophy of single-sign on, as Kerberos supports user authentication only and is not designed for host authentication. It is noteworthy that host authentication is an important aspect of grids.

[17] and [20] both implementations are based on Globus middleware. [17] has provided method level access with credential delegation while [20] has focused on the security aspects of resource management in Globus.

Like most of the other implementations discussed so far, [16] is also specific to Globus middleware. The UCON model has been extended to provide usage control. It provides a generic architecture, active policy decision and dynamic authorization policy.

Both [10] and [13] have attempted to map role based access techniques on grid security. [10] focuses on information sharing and security risks. It is a theoretical model that lacks implementation and validation. Whereas [13] provide credential discovery, validation, delegation and management in distributed environment. It is a strong security model in terms of valued attributes and trust monitoring credential, yet it lacks provisioning for limiting the transitive trust. Like [10] it is also a theoretical model and has no practical implementation.

[15] is yet another model that is based on RBAC like [10] and [13]. This shows the usefulness of RBAC in grids. It focuses on authorization only. Unlike [10] and [13] it has a practical implementation available with generic APIs that can be useful in other applications.

Like [4], [11] has also mapped web services security models to grid security. The proposed security model extends the existing security techniques for web services. However, it is also a theoretical model and there is no implementation and validation of the model like [10].

Secure execution environment for grid applications [6] is proposed for shell based applications. It provides more than 200% performance gain for shell-based applications only. This approach enhanced the grid by focusing on security without performance degradation. This feature makes it unique amongst other implementations reviewed in this paper as other implementations focused only on security concerns.

[14] becomes distinct from rest of the studied models as it focuses on a partner-and-adversary model. It is a hardware-based solution that provides security against strong adversary, the platform owner and dynamic VO support. Since it is a hardware-based solution, therefore it involves more cost. Moreover its dependency on an Online Certificate Revocation Authority (OCRA) is also a bottleneck.

[18] and [19] are based on Legion. [18] has focused on delegation of credentials and authorization whereas [19] has discussed the components and features for Legion security architecture. Majority of the security concerns in Legion are addressed in [19] while [18] has provided a detailed study of credential delegation using eight different approaches.

TRMS [7] is a trust model for grids and trust-aware resource management system. It has reduced security overheads and improves grid performance. Unlike other security models, it uses a heuristic based algorithm. Therefore, one cannot ensure that the current dataset represents or accounts for the future system state as well.

A complete summary of the critical evaluation along with the strengths and weaknesses is presented in Table1.

Table 1. Summary of critical evaluation of grid security models

Security Model	Area of Focus	Strengths	Weaknesses
Security model for OGSA based on GT-3 and web-services protocols [4]	Security model for OGSA using web-services security protocols (GT-3/GSI-3)	Improvements over previous GT-2 model & tight least privilege	Implementation is Globus specific
Porting Globus system from GSI to Kerberos [5]	GSS-API interoperability layer modifications	Interoperability between GSI & Kerberos using GSS-API	Lack of adaptability and reusability
Secure execution environment for grid applications [6]	Secure execution environment for grid applications	200% performance gain for shell-based applications	Useful for shell-based applications only
TRMS [7]	Trust model for grids and trust-aware resource management system	Reduced security overheads and improves grid performance	Heuristic based algorithm
Grid Security Policy and architecture [8]	Grid Security Infrastructure (GSI)	Majority of the security issues addressed, base for other security models	No group contexts and credential delegation, performance bottleneck
Information sharing & security in dynamic coalitions [10]	RBAC/MAC based security approach to address dynamic coalition problem	Uses RBAC based security	No implementation / validation of model
Grid security model based on OGSA [11]	Web services based security model for OGSA	Proposed security architecture extends the existing security technologies	No implementation / validation of the model
dRBAC for credential discovery & validation [13]	Credential discovery, delegation and management in distributed environment	Strong security model in terms of valued attributes & trust monitoring credential	No provision of limiting the transitive trust
Daonity [14]	Partner-and-adversary model, hardware based solution	Security against strong adversary, the platform owner and dynamic VO support	Hardware solution, involves more cost, dependence on OCRA
PERMIS [15]	Authorization policy and role based PMI based on RBAC	Dynamic changes in authorization policies are supported; generic APIs	Focuses only on authorization, other aspects of grid security are not addressed
Usage control in grids by extending the UCON model [16]	Usage control, authorization, conditions and obligations	Generic architecture, active policy decision, dynamic authorization policy	Implementation is Globus specific
Fine-grained and flexible security mechanism [17]	Method level authorization, credential delegation, and aspect oriented programming	Method level access, dynamic, no changes in the existing infrastructure	Implementation is Globus specific
Approaches for credential delegation in Legion [18]	Delegation of credentials and authorization in Legion framework	Eight approaches to provide detailed study of credential delegation	Legion specific, covers credential delegation only
Legion security architecture for solving metacomputing security problem [19]	Components and features in Legion security architecture	Majority of the security concerns addressed, a detailed security model	Implementation is Legion specific
Management of resources in a metacomputing environment [20]	Globus resource management architecture and components	All resource management issues have been addressed	Implementation is Globus specific

4 Conclusion

Grids are collections of coordinated shared resources, distributed across multiple administrative domains, for solving computational problems. The concept of virtual organizations in grids introduces many security challenges. As sharing of resources across different administrative domains is a challenging task with respect to security. In this paper we have reviewed the literature relating to existing grid security challenges, and different security models for grids. We have also presented the critical analysis by comparing different security models. We have observed that RBAC based systems are gaining popularity for providing grid security and services, but most of the models are theoretical and lack practical implementation. We have also observed that GSI is still an essential model for grid security. To date no single security model addresses all security concerns in grid environment. Most of the models are either middleware specific, or the problem domain they address is very small. A lot needs to be done for, generalization of the existing models, improving performance of these models, and building intelligent and self-learning security models.

References

1. Foster, I., Kesselman, C., Tuecke, S.: The Anatomy of the Grid: Enabling Scalable Virtual Organizations. International J. Supercomputer Applications 15(3) (2001)
2. World-wide LHC Computing Grid (WLCG), `http://lcg.web.cern.ch/LCG`
3. Humphrey, M., Thompson, M.: Security Implications of Typical Grid Computing Usage Scenarios. Security Working Group GRIP Forum Draft (October 2000)
4. Welch, V., Siebenlist, F., Foster, I., Bresnahan, J., Czajkowoski, K., Gawor, J., Kesselman, C., Meder, S., Pearlman, L., Tuecke, S.: Security for Grid Services. In: Proceedings of the 12th IEEE International Symposium on High Performance Distributed Computing, Seattle, Washington (June 2003)
5. Moore, P.C., Johnson, W.R., Detry, R.J.: Adapting Globus and Kerberos for a Secure ASCI Grid. In: Proceedings of ACM/IEEE Super Computing Conference, p. 54 (2001)
6. Butt, A.R., Adabala, S., Kapadia, N.H., Figueiredo, R.J., Fortes, J.A.B.: Fine-grain Access Control for Securing Shared Resources in Computational Grids. In: Proceedings of 16th International Parallel and Distributed Processing Symposium. IEEE Computer Society, FL (2002)
7. Azzedin, F., Maheswaran, M.: Towards Trust-aware Resource Management in Grid Computing Systems. In: Proceedings of 2nd IEEE/ACM International Symposium on Cluster Computing and the Grid, pp. 452–457 (2002)
8. Foster, I., Kesselman, C., Tsudik, G., Tuecke, S.: A Security Architecture for Computational Grids. In: Proceedings of ACM Conference on Computers and Security, pp. 83–91 (1998)
9. Adamski, M. et al.: Trust and Security in Grids: A State of the Art. CoreGRID White Paper (May 26, 2008), `http://www.coregrid.net/mambo/images/stories/WhitePapers/whp-0001.pdf`
10. Phillips, C.E., Ting, T.C., Demurjian, S.A.: Mobile and Cooperative Systems: Information Sharing and Security in Dynamic Coalitions. In: 7th ACM Symposium on Access Control Models and Technologies, CA, USA, pp. 87–96 (2002)

11. Mukhin, V.: The Security Mechanisms for Grid Computers. In: Proceedings 4th IEEE Workshop on Intelligent Data Acquisition and Advanced Computing Systems: Technology and Applications, pp. 584–589 (September 2007)
12. Buda, G., Choi, D., Graveman, R.F., Kubic, C.: Security Standards for the Global Information Grid. In: Military Communications Conference, Communications for Network-Centric Operations: Creating the Information Force, vol. 1, pp. 617–621. IEEE, Los Alamitos (2001)
13. Freudenthal, E., Pesin, T., Port, L., Keenan, E., Karamcheti, V.: dRBAC: Distributed Role-based Access Control for Dynamic Coalition Environments. In: Proceedings of the 22nd International Conference on Distributed Computing Systems, pp. 411–420. IEEE Computer Society Press, Los Alamitos (2002)
14. Mao, W., Yan, F., Chen, C.: Daonity: Grid Security with Behavior Conformity. In: Proceedings of 1st ACM Workshop on Scalable Trusted Computing: Applications and Compliance, Virginia, USA, pp. 43–46 (2006)
15. Chadwick, D.W., Otenko, A.: The PERMIS X.509 Role Based Privilege Management Infrastructure. In: Proceedings of 7th ACM Symposium on Access Control Models and Technologies, CA, USA, pp. 135–140 (2002)
16. Martinelli, F., Mori, P.: A Model for Usage Control in Grid Systems. In: Proceedings of International Workshop on Security, Trust and Privacy in Grid Systems, p. 520. IEEE, Los Alamitos (2007)
17. Jung, H., Han, H., Jung, H., Yeom, H.Y.: Flexible Authentication and Authorization Architecture for Grid Computing. In: Proceedings of International Conference on Parallel Processing, pp. 61–77 (2005)
18. Stoker, G., White, B.S., Stackpole, E., Highley, T.J., Humphrey, M.A.: Toward Realizable Restricted Delegation in Computational Grids. In: Hertzberger, B., Hoekstra, A.G., Williams, R. (eds.) HPCN-Europe 2001. LNCS, vol. 2110, p. 32. Springer, Heidelberg (2001)
19. Ferrari, A., Knabe, F., Humphrey, M., Chapin, S.J., Grimshaw, A.S.: A Flexible Security System for Metacomputing Environments. In: Sloot, P.M.A., Hoekstra, A.G., Bubak, M., Hertzberger, B. (eds.) HPCN-Europe 1999. LNCS, vol. 1593, pp. 370–380. Springer, Heidelberg (1999)
20. Czajkowski, K., Foster, I., Karonis, N., Kesselman, C., Martin, S., Smith, W., Tuecke, S.: A Resource Management Architecture for Metacomputing Systems. In: Feitelson, D.G., Rudolph, L. (eds.) IPPS-WS 1998, SPDP-WS 1998, and JSSPP 1998. LNCS, vol. 1459, pp. 62–82. Springer, Heidelberg (1998)
21. Adabala, S., Butt, A.R., et al.: Grid-computing Portals and Security Issues. Journal of Parallel and Distributed Computing 63(10), 1006–1014 (2003)

Hybrid Wavelet-Fractal Image Coder Applied to Radiographic Images of Weld Defects

Faiza Mekhalfa[1] and Daoud Berkani[2]

[1] Centre de Recherche en Soudage et Controle,
Signal and Image Processing Laboratory,
Route de Dely Brahim BP 64, Cheraga 16800, Algeria
f_Mekhalfa@hotmail.fr

[2] Ecole Nationale Polytechnique, Electronic Department,
10, Avenue Hassen Badi BP 182, El Harrach 16200, Algeria
dberkani@hotmail.com
http://www.csc.dz, http://www.enp.edu.dz

Abstract. Fractal image compression has the advantage in term of its ability to provide a very high compression ratio. Discrete wavelet transform (DWT) retains frequency as well as spatial information of the signal. These structural advantages of the DWT schemes can lead to better visual quality for compression at low bitrate. In order to combine the advantages of wavelet and fractal coding, many coding schemes incorporating fractal compression and wavelet transform have been developed. In this work we evaluate a hybrid wavelet-fractal coder for image compression, and we test its ability to compress radiographic images of weld defects. A comparative study between the hybrid wavelet-fractal coder and pure fractal compression technique have been made in order to investigate the compression ratio and corresponding quality of the image using peak signal to noise ratio.

Keywords: Fractal Compression, Discrete Wavelet Transform, Hybrid Wavelet-Fractal Image Coder, Radiographic Image.

1 Introduction

Image compression is a vital task for image transmission and storage. The goal of image compression techniques is to remove redundancy present in data in a way that enables acceptable image reconstruction [1]. There are numerous lossy and lossless image compression techniques and each has advantages and disadvantages [2].

Fractal coding is a lossy image compression technique. The method consists of the representation of image blocks through the contractive transformation coefficients, using the self-similarity concept. This type of compression provides a good scheme for image compression with fast decoding and high compression ratios [3], but it suffered from a large encoding time, difficulties to obtain high quality of decoded images and blocking artifacts at low bitrates. Many works

H. Cherifi, J.M. Zain, and E. El-Qawasmeh (Eds.): DICTAP 2011, Part I, CCIS 166, pp. 759–767, 2011.

combined wavelets with the fractal coding to improve a visual quality for compression at low bitrate [4] [5] [6]. Moreover, the hybrid wavelet-fractal coder can help to speedup the runtime of the pure fractal compression algorithm, with its less computational complexity [7] [8].

In the hybrid wavelet-fractal coder, wavelet transform is first applied to the image and to the resultant coefficients, fractal coding is then performed. In this paper, hybrid and pure fractal algorithms have been evaluated by applying them on standard images in first step and then tested the hybrid coder on radiographic images of weld defects. For performance analysis, we use the most popular evaluation metrics: compression ratio (CR) and peak signal to noise ratio (PSNR).

The organization of the paper is as follow. Section 2 and 3 include the fundamental principles of fractal and wavelet theories. Section 4 presents the hybrid wavelet-fractal image coder. Discussion and comparison of the results obtained with studied methods are given in section 5. Section 6 contains the conclusion.

2 Fractal Image Compression

In conventional fractal coding schemes, an image is partitioned twice into non overlapping range blocks (R) and larger domain blocks (D), which can overlap. Then each range block R_i is mapped onto one domain block $D_j(i)$ such that a transformation w_i of the domain block is a good approximation of the range block. The parameters describing the contractive affine transformation that has the minimum mean squared error (MSE) between the original range block and the coded range are saved, and we get the transforamtion $W_i = \cup w_i$, that code the image approximation [9].

The regeneration error in the fractal coding is performed by the collage theorem. This theorem guarantees that the lower the error, the closer to the attractor X_f of the image x is [10]:

$$d(x, X_f) \leq \frac{s}{1-s} d(x, X_f) \ . \tag{1}$$

where s is known as a scale factor $0 \leq s < 1$.

The decompression process is based on an iterative simple algorithm, which is started with any initial image. Then we repeatedly apply the W_i until we approximate the fixed point.

3 Discrete Wavelet Transform

Wavelets provide a multi-resolution decomposition of signal. They can give the frequency content of the signal at a particular instant of time. They can also decorrelate data, which can lead to a more compact representation than the original data. The basic idea of the wavelet transform is to represent any arbitrary signal as a superposition of a set of such wavelets or basis functions. The wavelets functions are constructed from a single mother wavelet by dilation (scaling) and translation (shifts).

The discrete wavelet transform for two dimensional signal X can be defined as follows [11]:

$$W(a_1, a_2, b_1, b_2) = \frac{1}{\sqrt{a_1 a_2}} \left(\psi(\frac{X - b_1}{a_1}, \frac{X - b_2}{a_2}) \right) . \quad (2)$$

where the indexes $W(a_1, a_2, b_1, b_2)$ represent the wavelet coefficients, a_1, a_2 are dilation, b_1, b_2 are translation and ψ is the mother wavelet. A wavelet transform combines both low pass and high pass filtering in spectral decomposition of signals [12].

The discrete wavelet transform of an image provides a set of wavelet coefficients, which represent the image at multiple scales. The decomposition into a discrete set of wavelet coefficients is performed using an orthogonal basis functions. These sets are divided into four parts such as approximation, horizontal details, vertical details and diagonal details. Another decomposition of approximation part takes place and we regenerate four new components (Fig.1.).

Fig. 1. 2 D DWT for image

4 Hybrid Wavelet-Fractal Coder

The fractal coding algorithms in the spatial domain have been extended into the wavelet domain [4] [5] [6]. The motivation for wavelet-fractal image compression stems from the existence of self similarities across subbands at the same spatial location in the wavelet domain.

Fractal image compression in the wavelet domain can be viewed as the inter-scale prediction of a set of wavelet coefficients in the higher frequency subbands from those in the lower frequency subbands. A contractive mapping associates a domain tree of wavelet coefficients with a range tree that it approximates. The approximating procedure is very similar to that in the spatial domain and it includes two steps: subsampling and determining the scaling factor. Subsampling associates the size of a domain tree with that of a range tree by truncating all coefficients in the highest subbands of the domain tree. The scale factor is the multiplied with each wavelet coefficient in the tree (Fig. 2.). Note that, an additive constant is not required in wavelet domain fractal estimation because the wavelet tree does not have a constant offset.

The detailed process of fractal coding based on wavelet domain is described below:

Let D_l denote domain tree, which has its coarsest coefficients in decomposition level l, and let R_{l-1} denote the range tree, which has its coarsest coefficients in decomposition level l-1. The contractive transformation (T) from domain tree D_l to range tree R_{l-1}, is given by [13] [14]:

$$T(D_l) = \alpha * S(D_l) . \tag{3}$$

where S denotes subsampling, and α is the scaling factor.

We consider $x = (x_1, x_2, , x_n)$ the ordered set of coefficients of a range tree and $y = (y_1, y_2, ., y_n)$ the ordered set of coefficients of a subsampled domain tree. Then the mean squared error is:

$$MSE = \sum_{i=o}^{n} (x_i - \alpha * y_i) . \tag{4}$$

We deduce that:

$$\alpha = \frac{\sum_{t=o}^{n} (x_t * y_t)}{\sum_{t=o}^{n} (y_t^2)} . \tag{5}$$

We should find the best matching domain block tree for a given range block tree. The encoded parameters are the position of the domain tree and the scaling factor. We note that the rotation and flipping have not been considered in this algorithm.

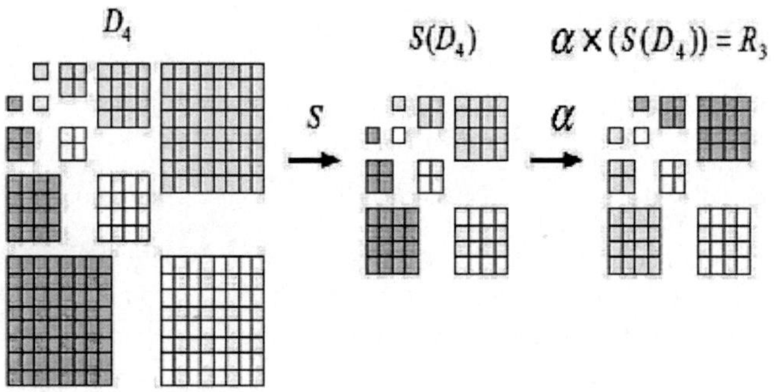

Fig. 2. Wavelet-fractal approximating

5 Experimental Results

5.1 Comparison and Discussion

The hybrid wavelet-fractal coder results have been compared with the pure traditional fractal technique [3]. The pure Jacquin's fractal coding, will be referred as FRAC, whereas the hybrid wavelet-fractal coding, referred as WFC. Simulation results were obtained by using three typical 8 bit grayscale, 256x256 images. The architecture used in experiments was a 3.4 GHZ Pentium IV Processor.

This section presents the comparison between these methods in terms of objective quality PSNR, and compression ratio CR. The fractal image compression experiments were performed by keeping range size as eight. The domain pool consists of the blocks of the partitioned image with atomic block size 16x16. By reducing the block size, the PSNR improves but with sacrificing the compression ratio. In wavelet-fractal image compression algorithm, first we decompose the image by 5-level Haar wavelet transform. Then, the block sizes of 8x8, 4x4, 2x2 and 1x1 were used from the high frequency subbands to low frequency subbands, and searched for the best pair with the same block size 8x8, 4x4, 2x2 and 1x1 within the downsampled images in the subbands with one level less. The pair matching is performed between the subbands of the 1, 2, 3, and 4 levels as domain pool and downsampled of subbands of 2, 3, 4, and 5 levels as range block, respectively. In this method for each pair matching in the horizontal, vertical, and diagonal subbands, one scale factor is stored. The calculation of scale factor is performed through equation (5).

Table 1 shows the PSNR values and the compression ratios for the two methods. The hybrid WFC coder PSNR values are better than the fractal values. The hybrid wavelet-fractal compression algorithm gives the opportunity to compress the image with high compression ratio.

Table 1. Numeric results of compression

Images	**Methods**	**PSNR (dB)**	**CR(%)**
Image 1 : Lena	FRAC	24.11	83
	WFC	25.14	86
Image 2 : Cameraman	FRAC	13.29	85
	WFC	21.35	86
Image 3 : Boats	FRAC	16.68	83
	WFC	23.83	86

Fig. 3. shows the decompressed images obtained by the studied methods. The images coded by fractal algorithm presents the blocking artifacts due to fractal block partitioned procedure. The wavelet-fractal coder presents an improvement of subjective quality compared to fractal compression algorithm. Based on the experiment results, the hybrid wavelet-fractal coder (WFC), significantly, outperforms the pure fractal algorithm (FRAC).

5.2 Application of the Hybrid Wavelet-Fractal Coder to Radiographic Images of Weld Defects

Radiographic testing is one of the most common method of non-destructive testing (NDT) used to detect defects within the internal structure of welds [15]. The radiographic films are examined by interpreters, of which the task is to detect, recognize and quantify eventual defects and to accept or reject them by referring to the non destructive testing codes and standards. This technique is used for inspecting several types of defects such as pores, crack, slag inclusion, porosity, lack of penetration, lack of fusion, etc. The detection of the defects in a radiogram is sometimes very difficult, because of the bad quality of the films, the weld thickness, and the weak sizes of defects. In recent years there has been a marked advance in the research for the development of an automatic system to detect and classify weld defects by using digital image processing and pattern recognition tools [16].

Radiographic images like any other digital data require compression in order to reduce disk space needed for storage and time needed for transmission. The lossless image compression methods can reduce the file only to a very limited degree. The application of hybrid wavelet-fractal coder allow to obtaining much higher compression ratios with a good quality of reconstructed images.

The aim of this experiment is to investigate if it is possible to apply the hybrid wavelet-fractal compression to radiographic images of weld defects. In order to test the efficiency of the hybrid coder on radiographic images, we have selected five radiographic testing images representing different weld defects: external undercut, lack of fusion, crack, lack of penetration, and porosity. Fig. 4. shows radiographic original images and the wavelet-fractal reconstructed images. We give also the PSNR values at 1.12 bpp. By examining the reconstructed images, we can deduce that this method gives acceptable results on the overall images. In case of image 1 and 4, we obtain a good subjective quality and the defects (external undercut and lack of penetration) are put in obviousness. However for the second, third and fifth one, the decompressed images have some blurred regions. In spite of this, we can distinguish the defects (lack of fusion, crack, and porosity respectively).

6 Conclusion

In this paper we have evaluated a hybrid wavelet-fractal coder. The wavelet-fractal coder has been compared to the pure fractal compression technique. Simulation results demonstrate a gain in PSNR objective measure with good compression ratio percentage. In addition to this, experiments have also been made by applying the hybrid wavelet-fractal coder on radiographic images of weld defects. The results showed that the decompressed images obtained can be used for image analysis. However, the algorithm requires some improvements to provide competitive PSNR values.

Fig. 3. Comparison of reconstructed images

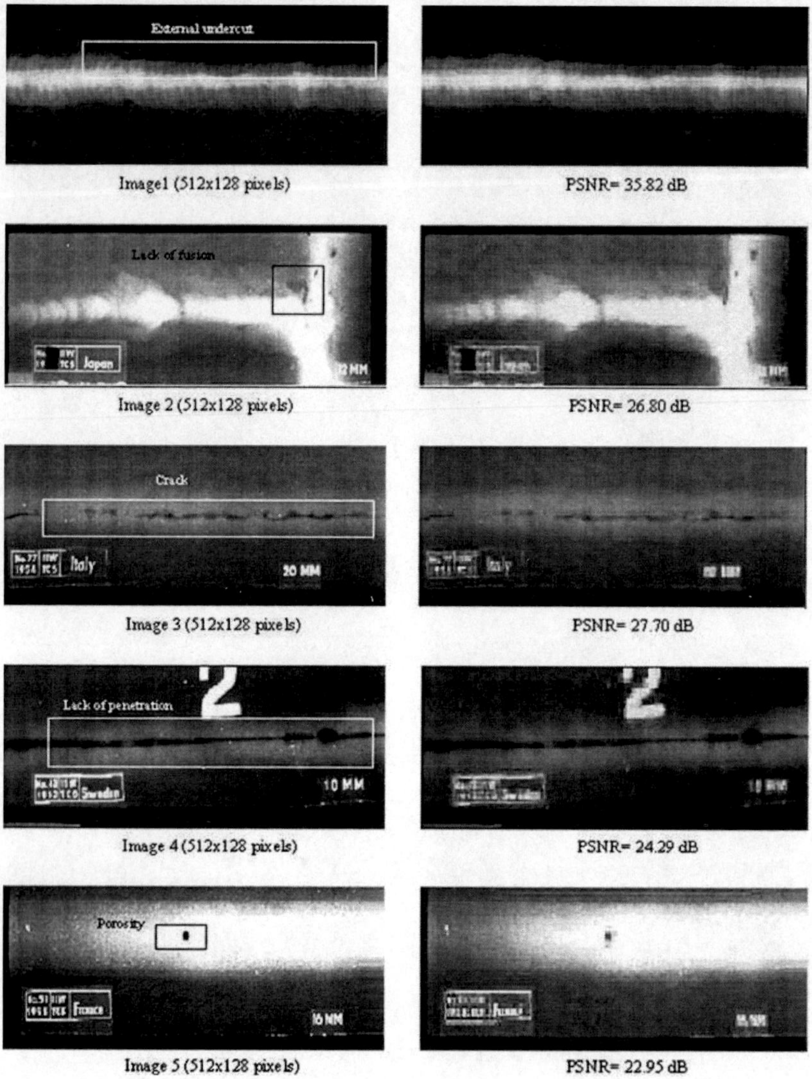

Fig. 4. Wavelet-fractal compression results (PSNR) at 1.12 bpp. Left: radiographic original images, right: reconstructed images.

References

1. Salomon, D.: Data Compression: The complete reference, 4th edn. Springer, Heidelberg (2007)
2. Bovik, A.C.: Handbook of image and Video Processing: Acedmic press, London (2000)
3. Jacquin, E.: Image Coding Based on Fractal Theory of Iterated Contractive Image Transformations. IEEE Trans. Image Process. 1(1), 18–30 (1992)
4. Rinaldo, R., Calvagnon, G.: Image Coding by Block Prediction of Multiresolution Subimages. IEEE Trans. Image Process. 4(7), 909–920 (1995)
5. Asgari, S., Nguyen, T.Q., Sethares, W.A.: Wavelet Based Fractal Transforms for Image Coding with no Search. In: IEEE International Conference on Image processing (1997)
6. Davis, G.M.: A Wavelet Based Analysis of Fractal Image Compression. IEEE Trans. Image Process. 7(2), 141–154 (1998)
7. Iano, Y., da Silva, F.S., Crus, A.L.: A Fast and Efficient Hybrid Fractal-Wavelet Image Coder. IEEE Trans. Image Process. 15(1), 98–105 (2006)
8. Duraisamy, R., Valarmathi, L., Ayyappan, J.: Iteration Free Hybrid Fractal-Wavelet Image Coder. International Journal of Computational Cognition 6(4), 34–40 (2008)
9. Koli, N.A., Ali, M.S.: A Survey on Fractal Image compression Key Issues. Inform. Technol. J. 7(8), 1085–1095 (2008)
10. Wohlberg, B., Jager, G.: A Review of the Fractal Image Coding Literature. IEEE Trans. Image Process. 8(12), 1716–1729 (1999)
11. Kharate, G.K., Ghatol, A.A., Rege, P.P.: Image Compression Using Wavelet Packet Tree. ICGST- GVIP Journal 5(7), 37–40 (2005)
12. Sadashivappa, G., AnandaBabu, K.S.: Evaluation Wavelet Filters for Image compression. Proceeding of World Academy of Science Engineering and Technology 39, 138–144 (2009)
13. Avanaki, M., Ahmadinejad, H., Ebrahimpour, R.: Evaluation of Pure Fractal and Wavelet Fractal Compression Techniques. ICGST- GVIP Journal 9(4), 41–47 (2009)
14. Kim, T., Van Dyck, R.E., Miller, D.J.: Hybrid Fractal Zerotree Wavelet Image Coding. Signal Process. Image Communication 17, 347–360 (2002)
15. Rogerson, J.H.: Defects in welds: Their prevention and their significance, 2nd edn. Applied science publishers (1985)
16. Da Silva, N., Calôla, L., Siqueira, M., Rebello, J.: Pattern Recognition of Weld Defects Detected by Radiographic Test. NDTE International 37(6), 461–470 (2004)

New Prediction Structure for Stereoscopic Video Coding Based on the H.264/AVC Standard

Sid Ahmed Fezza and Kamel Mohamed Faraoun

Department of Computer Science, Djillali Liabes University, Algeria
sidahmed.fezza@gmail.com

Abstract. The Three-dimensional video has gained significant interest recently. Many of existing 3D video systems are based on stereoscopic technology. The data of the stereoscopic video is twice of the monoscopic video at least, so the data of the stereoscopic video is very huge, efficient compression techniques are essential for realizing such applications. In this paper, stereoscopic video coding is studied, and three prediction structures for stereoscopic video coding are discussed. An improved structure is proposed after the three prediction structures were analyzed and compared. The proposed structure encodes stereoscopic video sequences effectively.

Keywords: Stereo Video Coding, Structures of Prediction, H.264/AVC.

1 Introduction

During the past decade, 3D visual communication technology has received considerable interest as it intends to provide reality of vision. Various types of 3D displays have been developed in order to produce the depth sensation. However, the accomplishment of 3D visual communication technology requires several other supporting technologies such as 3D representation, handling, and compression for ultimate commercial exploitation. Many innovative studies on 3D visual communication technology are focused on the development of efficient video compression technology.

Various choices, depending on the application, are available for representing a three-dimensional (3D) video [1]. Among these choices, there is stereoscopic video technology. Stereo video is used to stimulate 3D perception capability of human psychovisual system by acquiring two video sequences (left sequence and right sequence) of the same scene from two horizontally separated positions and then presenting the left frame to the left eye and the right frame to the right eye. The human brain can process the difference between these two images to yield 3D perception, because they provide the depth information [2]. At present, the stereoscopic video has been applied widely, such as 3D television, cinema, 3D telemedicine, medical surgery, virtual reality and so on [3]. However, the data of the stereoscopic video is twice of the monoscopic video at least, so the data of the stereoscopic video is very huge. If the stereo video is not compressed, it is difficult to store and transport the enormous amount of data, so it is necessary to compress the stereo video [4].

H. Cherifi, J.M. Zain, and E. El-Qawasmeh (Eds.): DICTAP 2011, Part I, CCIS 166, pp. 762–769, 2011.

H.264/AVC is the latest international video coding standard. It was jointly developed by the Video Coding Experts Group (VCEG) of the ITU-T and the Moving Picture Experts Group (MPEG) of ISO/IEC [5]. H.264/AVC is referred to as the part 10 of MPEG-4, or as AVC (Advanced Video coding). Compared to prior compression standards, H.264/AVC provides very high coding efficiency. For example, compared to MPEG-4 advanced simple profile, up to 50% of bit-rate reduction can be achieved [6]. Thus H.264/AVC is the best video coding standard for monoscopic video, so it is evident that the stereoscopic video coding is based on H.264/AVC.

The paper is organized as follows: The prediction structures are presented in Section 2, followed by the results of the evaluation of these structures in Section 3. In Section 4 we will describe the proposed structure. We give the experimental results in Section 5, and finally, this paper is concluded in section 6.

2 Previous Prediction Structures for Stereo Video Coding

Stereo video is the most important special case of multi-view video with N = 2 views, there are two separate video sequences: left sequence and right sequence. As we know, the data of the stereo video is twice of the monoscopic video at least, so compressing is very necessary. Compression of conventional stereo video has been studied for a long time and the corresponding standards are available.

To compress the stereo video sequences efficiently, not only redundancy of inter frames and intra frame but also the relationship between inter views should be efficiently exploited and reduced. The redundancy of inter frames in the same view can be called *temporal redundancy*, and the redundancy of the inter views at the same time can be called *disparity redundancy*. Motion compensation prediction (MCP) is used to reduce the temporal redundancy, and disparity compensation prediction (DCP) is used to reduce the disparity redundancy [7].

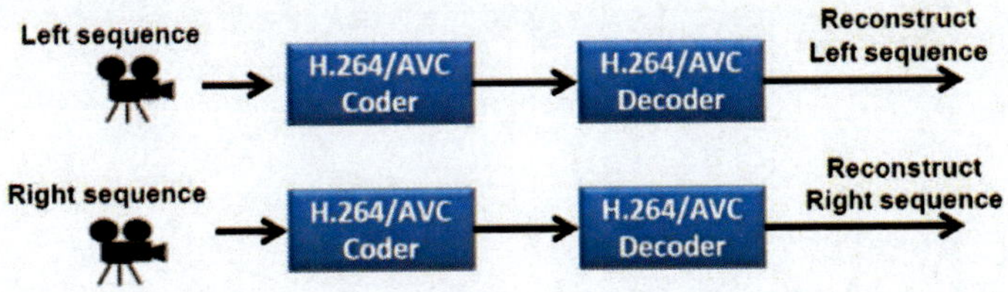

Fig. 1. Simulcast scheme

By the significant correlation considered or not, the prediction structures for stereo video coding can be classified into three types (or schemes) [8]. The three types are as follows:

- **Scheme 1:** One simple solution to stereoscopic video coding is the "simulcast" technique depicted in Figure 1. The left and right sequences are encoded independently with MCP. Figure 2 shows the prediction mode. In this structure, the temporal redundancy is used, but the relativity between the left view and right view is not exploited.

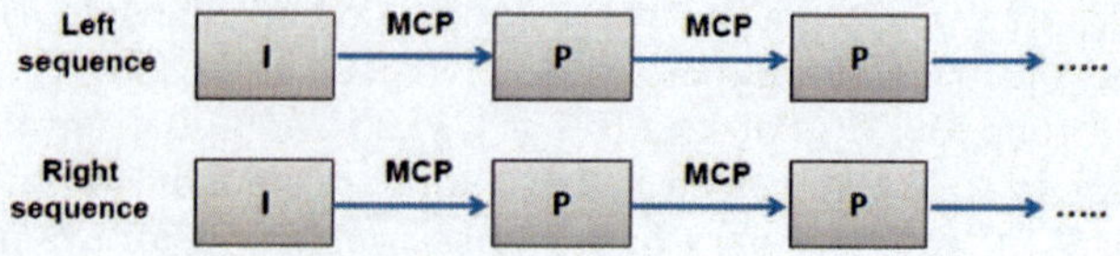

Fig. 2. The right sequence is compressed with MCP

- **Scheme 2:** The left sequence is encoded with MCP, and the right sequence is encoded with DCP. This structure is depicted in the Figure 3. In this structure, the temporal redundancy of the left sequences is used, and the relativity between the left view and right view is used. However, the temporal redundancy of the right sequence is not exploited.

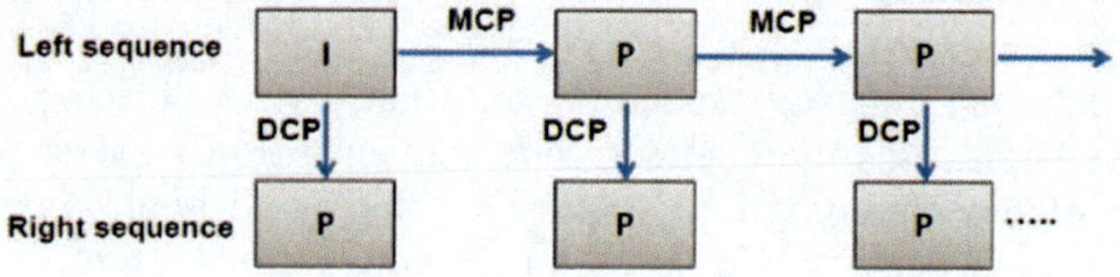

Fig. 3. The right sequence is compressed with DCP.

- **Scheme 3:** The left sequence is encoded with MCP, and the right sequence is encoded with MCP+DCP. This structure is depicted in the Figure 4. In this structure, the temporal redundancy is exploited when the left and right sequences are compressed, and the relativity between the left view and right view is exploited when the right sequence is compressed.

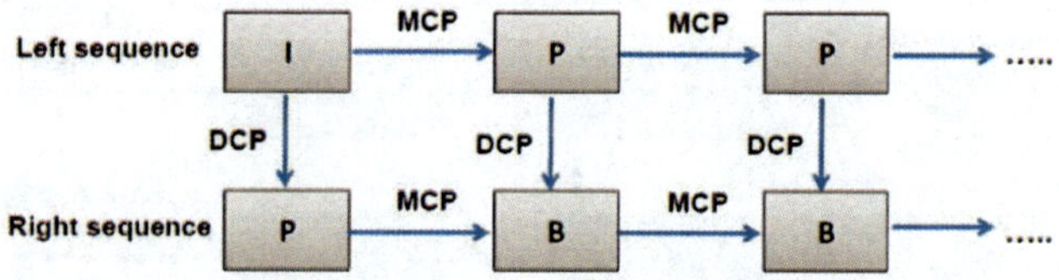

Fig. 4. The right sequence is compressed with MCP+DCP

In the three structures described above, hierarchical B pictures (see [9] for a detailed description) in temporal direction is used [10], because this hierarchical reference picture structure can achieve better performance on coding efficiency than traditional IPPP structure. Currently, the hierarchical B pictures structure is already supported by H.264/AVC. This approach based on inter-view prediction combined with hierarchical B pictures for temporal prediction was promoted by Fraunhofer HHI [10] [11], and more researches are based on a similar kind of idea. This prediction structure has coding efficiency advantages over the other configurations, at the disadvantage of being more complex [11].

3 Comparison of the Three Prediction Structures

There are two parts in our experiments. In the first one, prediction performances among the three prediction structures are analyzed. In the second, the three structures are objectively evaluated in terms of PSNR vs. bitrate. The experiments we presented are performed with JMVM 8.0 (Joint Multi-view Video Model) which is based on H.264/AVC [12]. The JMVM is the reference software for the Multiview Video Coding (MVC) project of the Joint Video Team (JVT) of the ISO/IEC Moving Pictures Experts Group (MPEG) and the ITU-T Video Coding Experts Group (VCEG) [12].

The three prediction structures are tested on the stereoscopic video sequence namely *Soccer2*. The tested stereo video sequence consist of a left and right view sequence, each with a resolution of 480×270 pixels, 0-99 encoded frame, and a frame rate of 30 fps.

The prediction performance is evaluated by the prediction error of the right view, and the rule used is SAD (Sum of Absolute Differences), with its formula as follows:

$$SAD = \frac{\sum_{y=0}^{h-1}\sum_{x=0}^{w-1} |F[x][y] - F'[x][y]|}{h \times w \times 255} \times 100\% \quad (1)$$

where $F[x][y]$ and $F'[x][y]$ denote the original data and the corresponding predicting data of the current frame, and h and w mean the height and width of the image, respectively.

Figure 5 shows the prediction performance results of three structures presented in the Section 2. Experimental results show that SAD value of the scheme 3 is lowest. Therefore, the scheme 3, combining MCP and DCP, is proved to be the best stereoscopic video coding scheme.

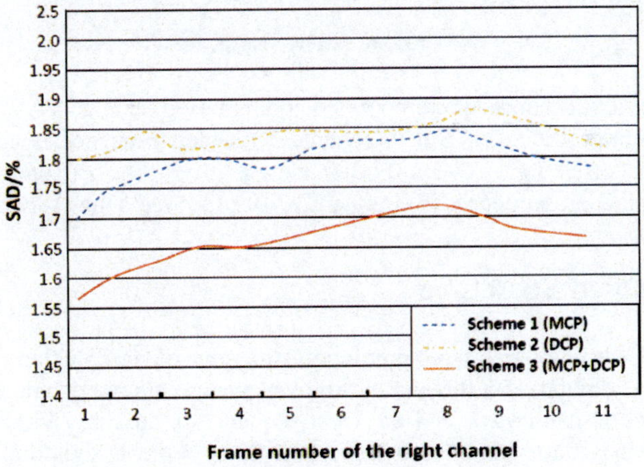

Fig. 5. Comparison of prediction errors in three schemes

For the second part of the comparison, we use the PSNR (peak-signal-to-noise-ratio) measure. Typically PSNR values are plotted over bit rate and allow then comparison of the compression efficiency of different algorithms. The PSNR measure estimates the quality of the decoded video samples compared with the original video samples, and PSNR of the luminance signal is given as:

$$PSNR_Y[db] = 10.\log_{10}\left(\frac{255^2}{MSE}\right) \tag{2}$$

MSE denotes the minimum mean squared error, which is defined as:

$$MSE = \frac{1}{N_1 N_2}\sum_{\boldsymbol{n}\in\mathbb{R}}[c(\boldsymbol{n}) - r(\boldsymbol{n}+\boldsymbol{d})]^2 \tag{3}$$

where $\mathbb{R}$ denotes a block of size $N_1 \times N_2$ and $n=(n_1, n_2)^T \in \mathbb{R}$ a pixel position within that block. c denotes the values of the pixels in the current frame, r the pixels in the reference frame.

Figure 6 shows results of performances of the three schemes. The parameters QP which means the quantization parameter is selected in schemes as follow 28, 34 and 40. The experimental results imply that the scheme 3 is better than the other schemes.

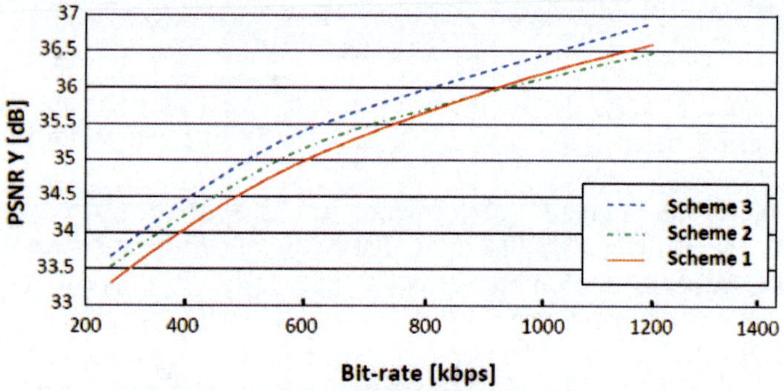

Fig. 6. PSNR results

In all the previous schemes of stereo video coding based on H.264/AVC, the scheme 3 has the best coding efficiency. But in scheme 3, the left sequence is compressed with MCP only. The correlation between the left view and right view is not exploited in the compression of the left sequence. Consequently, we proposed a new scheme.

4 The Proposed Structure

In the Section 3, we compared three prediction structures of stereo video coding based on H.264/AVC. It is obvious that the left and right sequences are not equal. It is evident that the left sequence is main view and the right sequence is auxiliary view. The auxiliary view is encoded by three kinds of schemes: In the scheme 1, temporal redundancy is exploited only; in the scheme 2, disparity redundancy is exploited only; in the scheme 3, the temporal redundancy and disparity redundancy are exploited. The main view is compressed with MCP only. In this section, we proposed a new prediction structure. In proposed structure, the left and right sequences are equal. The left and right sequences are incorporated into one sequence, and then the incorporated sequence is compressed.

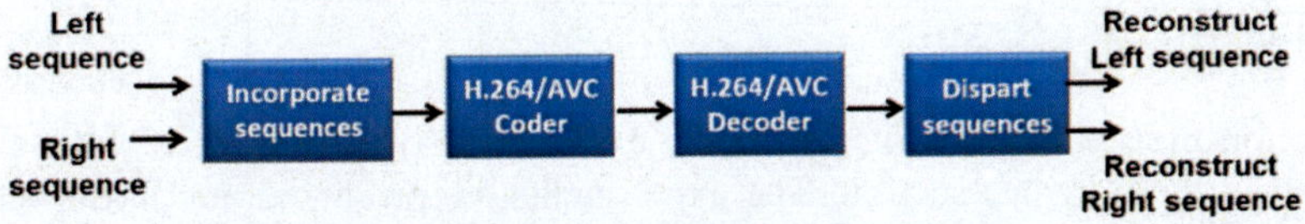

Fig. 7. The incorporated sequence

The proposed structure can be depicted by the Figure 7. The left and right sequences are incorporated firstly. Then the incorporated sequence is compressed by the coder. It exists much way for incorporate sequences. For example:

- Several left frames first, then several right frames. The several left frames can be called a group; the several right frames can be called a group too. The length of the group is not fixed. Then the incorporated sequence is encoded by H.264/AVC Coder. The relativity between the frames in the same view is exploited only.
- One left frame, and then one right frame, and so on. When the incorporated sequence is compressed, the disparity redundancy can be exploited.
- The first frame L0 (the first frame of the left sequence) is compressed independently. The second frame R0 (the first frame of the right sequence) is predicted by the first frame L0. Firstly, the frame L1 is predicted by L0, then the following R1 (the second frame of the right sequence) can be predicted by R0 or L1, or both. The results are compared, and then decides which frame is as reference frame. Next, the frame R2 is predicted by R1. After that L1 and R2 have been coded, the L2 is predicted by the L1 or R2, or both. The results are also compared, and then decides which frame is as reference frame, and so on.

We opted for this latter scheme. The prediction mode of this scheme is depicted in Figure 8. In Figure 8, the frames of both sequences (Ri and Li) are incorporated into one sequence. For clarification purpose, the incorporate sequence of figure is divided into two levels. The level 0 use only MCP (except R0), and level 1 use MCP+DCP except L0 which is coded in intra mode. So the DCP is used alternatively between the left and right sequences. The red numbers in the figure represents the coding order of the frames.

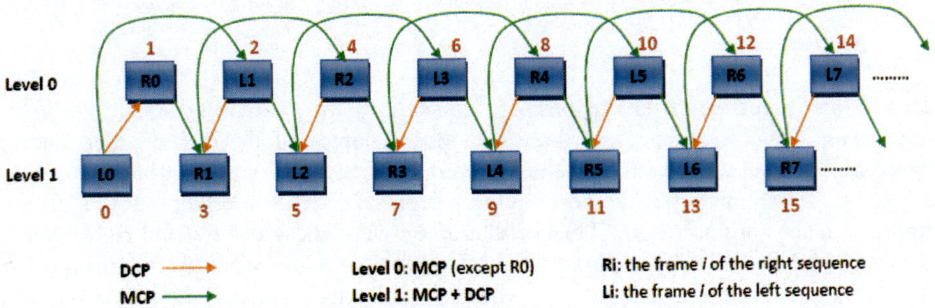

Fig. 8. The proposed structure

5 Experimental Results

This section presents the results of coding experiments with the prediction structure described in the previous section. The experiments we presented are performed with JMVM 8.0 (Joint Multi-view Video Model) which is based on H.264/AVC [12], using typical settings for MVC (see [13] for details), like variable block size, multi-reference picture, a search range of ±96, CABAC enabled and rate control using Lagrangian techniques.

We compared the performance of the proposed structure with that of three previous structures described in Section 2. The results of the experimental performed on the stereoscopic video sequence namely *Soccer2*. The tested stereo video sequence consist of a left and right view sequence, each with a resolution of 480×270 pixels, 0-99 encoded frame, and a frame rate of 30 fps. The parameters QPs used in the above schemes are 28, 34 and 40.

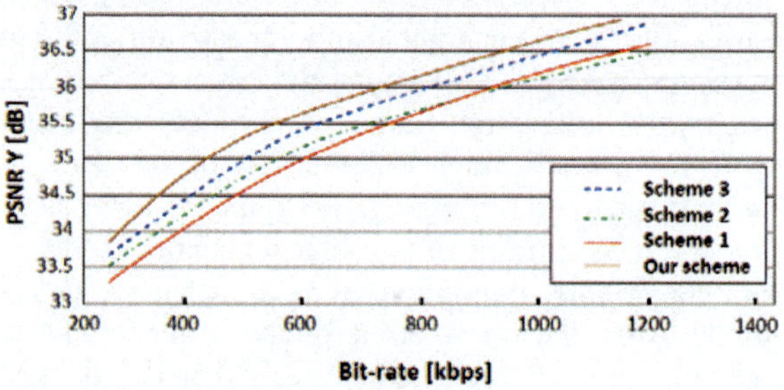

Fig. 9. Performance comparison of the proposed structure

Figure 9 shows that a significant PSNR gain with the proposed scheme compared to the three previous schemes. Furthermore it is clear that the proposed scheme can achieve up to 1.8dB gain in PSNR compared to other schemes. We tested the proposed scheme with other stereo video sequences such as *ballroom* and *puppy* and observed similar PSNR gains. Therefore, it could be concluded that the proposed scheme outperform the three previous schemes.

6 Conclusion

This paper investigates extensions of H.264/AVC for compressing stereo video sequences. Generally, there are three previous schemes of the stereo video coding based on H.264/AVC. The three schemes were analyzed and compared. In all of these schemes, the scheme 3 has the best coding performance. But in scheme 3, the left and right sequences are not equal. The correlation between the left view and right view is not exploited in the compression of the left sequence. Consequently, we proposed a new scheme. In proposed scheme, the left and right sequences are equal, the correlation between the two sequences is used by the left and right sequences alternatively. The left and right sequences are incorporated into one sequence, and then the incorporated sequence is compressed. The experimental results show that the proposed scheme is effective, and it is better in coding efficiency than the other schemes.

References

1. Onural, L., Smolic, A., Sikora, T.: An Overview of a New European Consortium: Integrated Three-Dimensional Television Capture, Transmission and Display (3DTV). In: Proc. European Workshop on the Integration of Knowledge, Semantic and Digital Media Technologies, London (2004)
2. Smolic, A., Cutchen, D.M.: 3DAV Exploration of Video-Based Rendering Technology in MPEG. IEEE Transactions on Circuits and Systems for Video Technology 14(9), 348–356 (2004); Special Issue on Immersive Communications
3. Smolic, A., Merkle, P., Müller, K., Fehn, C., Kauff, P., Wiegand, T.: Compression of Multi-View Video and Associated Data. In: Ozaktas, H.M., Onural, L. (eds.) Three-Dimensional Television: Capture, Transmission, and Display. Springer, Heidelberg (2007)
4. Park, J., Yang, K.H., Wadate, Y.I.: Efficient representation and compression of multi-view images. IEICE Transactions on Information and Systems E83-D(12), 2186–2188 (2000)
5. Draft ITU-T recommendation and final draft international standard of joint video specification (ITU-T Rec. H.264/ISO/IEC 14 496-10 AVC), in Joint Video Team (JVT) of ISO/IEC MPEG and ITU-T VCEG, JVTG050 (2003)
6. Wiegand, T., Sullivan, G.J., Bjøntegaard, G., Luthra, A.: Overview of the H.264/AVC video coding standard. IEEE Transactions on Circuits and Systems for Video Technology 13(7), 560–576 (2003)
7. Yang, W., Ngan, K., Lim, J., Sohn, K.: Joint motion and disparity fields estimation for stereoscopic video sequences. Signal Processing: Image Communication 20(3), 265–276 (2005)
8. Shiping, L., Mei, Y., Gangyi, J., Tae-Young, C., Yong-Deak, K.: Approaches to H.264-Based stereoscopic video coding. In: Proc. Third International Conference on Image and Graphics, Hong Kong, China, pp. 365–368 (2004)
9. Schwarz, H., Marpe, D., Wiegand, T.: Analysis of hierarchical B pictures and MCTF. In: IEEE International Conference on Multimedia and Expo., Toronto, Ontario, Canada (2006)
10. Merkle, P., Müller, K., Smolic, A., Wiegand, T.: Efficient Compression of Multi-View Video Exploiting Inter-View Dependencies Based on H.264/MPEG4-AVC. In: Proc. International Conference on Multimedia and Expo., Toronto, Ontario, Canada (2006)
11. Merkle, P., Smolic, A., Müller, K., Wiegand, T.: Efficient Prediction Structures for Multiview Video Coding. IEEE Transactions on Circuits and Systems for Video Technology 17(11), 1461–1473 (2007); Special Issue on Multiview Video Coding and 3DTV
12. Joint Multiview Video Model (JMVM) 8.0. JVT-AA207, Geneva, Switzerland (2008)
13. ISO/IEC JTC1/SC29/WG11: Requirements on Multiview Video Coding v.4. Doc. N7282, Poznan, Poland (2005)

Histogram Shifting as a Data Hiding Technique: An Overview of Recent Developments

Yasaman Zandi Mehran[1], Mona Nafari[2,*], Alireza Nafari[3], and Nazanin Zandi Mehran[4]

[1] Islamic Azad University, Shahre-e-Rey Branch, Tehran, Iran
zandi@srbiau.ac.ir
[2] Razi University of Kermanshah,
Department of Electrical Engineering, Kermanshah, Iran
Fax: 0098-21-88614966
m.nafari@razi.ac.ir, Mona_nafari_1362@yahoo.com
[3] Amir Kabir University of Technology,
Department of Electrical and Mechanical Engineering, Tehran, Iran
ali.heisenberg@aut.ac.ir
[4] Amir Kabir University of Technology,
Department of Biomedical Engineering, Tehran, Iran
nazaninznd@aut.ac.ir

Abstract. Histogram shifting is a data hiding technique which has been proposed since 2004. In this paper, we provide an overview of recent contributions pertaining to the Histogram shifting technique. It discusses on this method and its development in terms of payload capacity and image quality. From these discussions, we can state that which schemes are beneficial in terms of capacity-PSNR control. Overally, Histogram shifting is a valuable technique. Its practical applications are expected to grow in years to come.

Keywords: Histogram shifting, Pseudo code, predictive coding, histogram modification, difference image, block, correlation, sub-sampling.

1 Introduction

Security problems, such as interception, modification, duplication, etc on the Internet, have encountered critical situation [1]. Data hiding conceals the secret data in the cover medium (which can be a digital image) as a method that have been proposed to protect the security [2]. Reversible recovery of the cover image is preferable for some applications such as medical diagnosis, legal documents, etc [3]. Lossless restoration of the original image is required after the message is extracted. Several reversible data hiding schemes have been proposed [4][5][6]. These schemes can be divided to three category: spatial domain, frequency domain, and index domain. In the spatial domain schemes, Celik et al proposed generalized least significant bit(G-LSB) method [7]. Difference expansion data hiding was proposed by Tian in 2003 [8], in which the

* Corresponding author.

H. Cherifi, J.M. Zain, and E. El-Qawasmeh (Eds.): DICTAP 2011, Part I, CCIS 166, pp. 770–786, 2011.

redundancy of the pixels is explored. The histogram of the pixels in the image was applied by Ni et al [9] in 2006. The peak and zero pair of the histogram was explored. In the histogram-based data hiding, the number of pixels in the peak point, represents hiding capacity. Another reversible data hiding was proposed by Tsai et al[10] in 2005, in which a pair wise logical computation(PWLC) for data hiding was utilized. In the frequency domain, some reversible data hiding schemes was introduced. Fridrich et al [11] proposed LSB-based data hiding in 2001. The LSB plane of the quantized DCT coefficients was compressed. The compressed data with the secret message were embedded in the LSB bits of the coefficients. In 2002, Xuan et al. [12] explored the relationship between the bit planes of the discrete wavelet transformation (DWT) coefficients. Kamstra and Heijmans [13] proposed a data hiding scheme in 2005 that employed DWT coefficients to embed secret data. In the index domain, secret data is embedded in the vector quantized image. In 2005, a data hiding scheme was proposed by Chang and Wu [14] which was based on vector quantization (VQ).

The rest of this paper is organized as follows: In Section 2, histogram-based data hiding techniques are briefly described. In Section 3, the simulation results are illustrated. Conclusions are made in Section 4.

2 Related Works

In this paper reversible histogram based data hiding techniques and its developments since 2004 has been described, which its basic idea proposed by Ni et al in 2004 [15].

In the basic histogram shifting data hiding, first a zero point and a peak point are found. Zero point (or minimum number of pixels) corresponds to the gray scale value which no pixel in the cover image assumes. Peak point corresponds to the gray scale value with the maximum number of pixels in the cover image. The goal of finding the peak points is to increase the payload capacity as large as possible. Since the number of bits which are embedded into an image equals to the number of pixels associated with the peak points, two or more pairs of zero and peak points can be used for increasing the capacity and generally in any method which is based on image histogram (directly or indirectly), it is aimed to increase the number of peak points. Here for simplicity in illustration of the principle of the algorithm, only one pair of zero-peak values are applied.

Thus, in the next step after finding zero-peak pair, the image is scanned in a sequential order. The gray scale value of pixels between peak and zero points are incremented by 1 unit. This step is equivalent to shifting the gray scale values of pixels between peak and zero points in the histogram, to the right hand side by 1, leaving the gray scale value of peak points empty. The whole image is scanned again, once a pixel with gray scale value of peak point is encountered, if the corresponding bit to be embedded is 1, the pixel is incremented by 1, otherwise the pixel remains intact. It can be observed that the payload capacity of this algorithm equals to the number of pixels that assume the gray scale value of the peak point, when there is only one pair of zero-peak points. Clearly if the required capacity is greater than the actual capacity, more pairs of peak and zero points (maximum and minimum) is needed. The embedding algorithms which is presented below use multiple pairs of maximum and minimum points.

2.1 Pseudo Code Data Hiding Algorithm with Multiple Pairs of Peak and Zero Points

In this section for the case of three pairs of peak and zero points, a pseudo code embedding algorithm is presented which has been proposed by Ni et al in 2006 [16]. It is aimed to generate this code to reach the cases where any number of multiple pairs of peak and zero points are used. This algorithm has two phases like any other data hiding methods: Embedding process, Extraction process. These processes are described as the following.

2.1.1 Embedding Process

First for an $M \times N$ image, with gray scale value of each pixel $x \in [0,255]$:

Step.1: Generate its histogram $H(x)$.

Step.2: In the histogram $H(x)$, find three minimum point $H(b_1)$, $H(b_2)$, $H(b_3)$. Assume three minimum points satisfy the following condition:

$0 < b_1 < b_2 < b_3 < 255$

Step.3:In the intervals of $(0, b_1)$ and (b_2, b_3), find the maximum points $h(a_1)$, $h(a_3)$, respectively, and assume $a_1 \in (0, b_1)$, $a_3 \in (b_3, 255)$.

Step.4: In the intervals (b_1, b_2) and (b_2, b_3), find the maximum points in each interval. Assume they are: $h(a_{12})$, $h(a_{21})$, $b_1 < a_{12} < a_{21} < b_2$ and $h(a_{23})$, $h(a_{32})$, $b_2 < a_{23} < a_{32} < b_3$.

Step.5: Find a point having a larger histogram value in each of the following three maximum points pairs $(h(a_1), h(a_{12}))$, $(h(a_{21}), h(a_{23}))$, and $(h(a_{32}), h(a_3))$, respectively. Assume $h(a_1)$, $h(a_{23})$, $h(a_3)$ are the three selected maximum points.

Step.6: $(h(a_1), h(b_1))$, $(h(a_{23}), h(b_2))$ and $(h(a_3), h(b_3))$ are the three pairs of maximum and minimum points. For each of these three pairs, apply Steps 3-5. All of these three pairs are treated as cases of peak and zero points pairs.

2.1.2 Extraction Process

For simplicity only one pair of peak and zero points is described here, because the general cases of multiple pairs of maximum and minimum points can be decomposed as a one pair case.

Assume the grayscale value of peak and zero points are a and b, respectively. Assume $a < b$ in the marked image of size $M \times N$, where $x \in [0,255]$.

Step.1: Scan the marked image in the same sequential order as that used in the embedding procedure. If a pixel with its gray scale value $a+1$ is encountered, a bit "1" is extracted. If a pixel with its value a is encountered, a bit "0" is extracted.

Step.2: Scan the image again, for any pixel with gray scale value $x \in (a, b]$, the pixel value is subtracted by 1.

Step.3: If there is overhead information found in the extracted data, set the pixel grayscale value (whose coordinate (i, j) is saved in the overhead) as b.

2.2 Data Hiding Scheme Using Predictive Coding and Histogram Shifting

The similarity of neighboring pixels in the cover image is applied in this scheme which is proposed by Tsai et al in 2009[17]. By using the prediction technique and the residual histogram of the predicted errors of the host image, the secret data is embedded in the residual image by using a modified histogram-based approach. To increase the hiding capacity of the histogram-based scheme, the linear prediction technique is employed to process the image. Here, the pixels of the image are predicted from the residual image. Secret data are then embedded in the residual image by using a modified histogram-based approach. The proposed scheme consists of two procedures: the embedding procedure and the extraction and image restoration procedure.

2.2.1 The Embedding Procedure

According to the histogram based data hiding, the more the amplitude of a given histogram changes, the more the hiding capacity is. To apply the similarity between neighboring pixels, first the cover image is divided into 3×3, 5×5, 7×7, ... pixel blocks. One pixel in each block is selected as the basic pixel for prediction. All pixels in the block are processed by the linear prediction technique to generate the prediction errors, which is called the residual values. By calculating the difference between the basic pixel and each pixel, the prediction error is determined. Each block is sequentially processed in the same way. After processing all blocks, the residual image is generated. Next, the histogram of the residual image is generated. All values in the residual image are not employed to generate the histogram. After finding the occurrences of residual values that correspond to these non-basic pixels in the cover image, the residual histogram is generated. The residual histogram can be divided into two parts: non-negative histogram(NNH) and negative histogram (NH). After the residual histogram is generated, the secret data are embedded in the residual values of the residual image. If *sb* is the secret data to be embedded, first the pairs of peak and zero points in NNH and NH have to be searched. If there isn't enough space to embed the secret data, more pairs of peak and zero points in NNH and NH have to be searched.

Each residual value in the peak point is employed to carry 1-bit secret bit *sb*. One of two possible cases is found for such residual value. If the value of *sb* equals 1, no change is needed for the residual value. Otherwise, the residual value is shifted closer to the value of the zero point by 1. The remaining residual value ranges between the peak and zero points are shifted closer to the value of the zero point by 1. The residual values that are outside the peak and zero pairs remain unchanged. The modification for secret embedding is employed to both NNH and NH. After the secret data is embedded in the residual image, the residual stego-image is generated. By performing the reverse linear prediction on the residual stego- image, the stego-image of the proposed scheme is obtained. The residual values corresponding to the basic pixels in the cover image are not included in calculating the residual histogram. In other words, residual values are used in each block of pixels in the cover image. In addition, to provide a good image quality for the stego image, the absolute distance between the original residual value and its modified values is at most 1.Therefore, the absolute distance between one pixel in the cover image and its corresponding pixel in the stego image is at most 1.

2.2.2 The Extraction and Restoration Procedure

When the stego image and the pairs of peak and zero points are ready, the procedure can be started. First, the linear prediction technique used in the embedding procedure is applied to the stego image. Then, the residual stego-image is obtained. The pixel of the residual stego image is examined to extract the embedded secret data *sb* and to recover the original image. This procedure is similar to that of the original histogram based extraction procedure. Two different cases are considered:

1-If pixel of the residual stego image is not within the peak and zero points range, this pixel is skipped and the pixel value remains unchanged for image reconstruction.

2-Otherwise, three cases are discussed:

a) In the first case, if pixel value is in the peak point, 1-bit secret data valued at 1 is extracted and the value of pixel is unchanged.
b) In the second case, if the absolute difference between x and the peak point is 1, 1-bit secret data valued at 0 is extracted and the pixel value is replaced by the value of the peak point.
c) finally, the remaining pixels are shifted close to peak point by 1 and no secret data is extracted. After that, the embedded secret data is extracted from the stego image. The original image can be restored by performing reverse linear prediction to the reconstructed stego image.

2.3 Data Hiding Based on Histogram Modification of Difference Images

In this section, another method of histogram based data hiding technique described which has been proposed by Chia-Chen Lin et al [18] in 2008. In this scheme which is based on the difference image histogram modification, the peak point are used to hide secret messages. This method is divided into three phase: Difference histogram creating, hiding and extracting phases.

2.3.1 Creating the Histogram Phase

A difference image of an image must be generated before the hiding phase, to create a enough free space for data hiding. For a gray scale image $I(i, j)$ with $M \times N$ pixels in size, a difference image $D(i, j)$, with $M \times (N-1)$ pixels can be generated from the original image $I(i, j)$ by using following formula:

$$D(i, j) = |I(i, j) - I(i, j+1)| \quad \begin{matrix} 0 \le i \le M-1 \\ 0 \le j \le N-2 \end{matrix} \tag{1}$$

The maximum pixel values in a difference image tend to be around value 0. The peak point in the histogram of a difference image is used to create the free space for hiding messages. Therefore, by using the difference image histogram, a larger number of messages can be hided in comparison with the original image.

2.3.2 Hiding Phase

Step 1: Divide the original cover image into blocks $A \times B$ in size. Generate a difference image $D_b(i, j)$ of size $A \times B - 1$ for each block by using following formula:

$$D_b(i,j) = |I_b(i,j) - I_b(i,j+1)| \quad ,0 \le i \le A-1 \qquad (2)$$
$$0 \le j \le B-2 \quad 0 \le b \le \frac{M \times N}{A \times B} - 1$$

Step 2: Generate the histogram of the difference image $D_b(i, j)$ and record the peak point p_b for each block.

Step 3: If the pixel value $D_b(i, j)$ of block b is larger than the peak point p_b of block b, change the pixel value $D_b(i, j)$ of block b to $D_b(i, j)+1$. Otherwise, the pixel value $D_b(i, j)$ remains unchanged. The modification principle is defined as

$$D'_b(i,j) = \begin{cases} D_b(i,j)+1 & \text{if} \quad D_b(i,j) > p_b \\ D_b(i,j) & o.w. \end{cases} \qquad (3)$$

For $0 \le i \le A-1$, $0 \le j \le B-2$, $0 \le b \le \frac{M \times N}{A \times B} - 1$, where p_b is the peak point of block b.

Step 4: For the modified difference image D'_b, the pixels having grayscale values the same as peak point p_b, can be modified as follows to hide embedded message bit m:

$$D''_b(i,j) = \begin{cases} D'_b(i,j)+m & \text{if} \quad D'_b(i,j) = p_b \\ D'_b(i,j) & o.w. \end{cases} \qquad (4)$$

where p_b is the peak point of block b, and $m \in \{1,0\}$.

Step 5: Use the original image and its hidden difference image to construct the marked image by performing the inverse transformation T^{-1}. For the first two pixels in each row, the inverse operation is as follows:

$$S_b(i,0) = \begin{cases} I_b(i,0)+m & \text{if} \quad I_b(i,0) > I_b(i,1) \\ I_b(i,1) + D''_b(i,0) & o.w. \end{cases} \qquad (5)$$

$$S_b(i,1) = \begin{cases} I_b(i,0) + D''_b(i,0) & \text{if} \quad I_b(i,0) < I_b(i,1) \\ I_b(i,1) & o.w. \end{cases} \qquad (6)$$

For $0 \le i \le A-1 \quad 0 \le b \le \frac{M \times N}{A \times B} - 1$.

For any residual pixels, the inverse operation is defined as:

$$S_b(i,j) = \begin{cases} S_b(i,j-1) + D''_b(i,j-1) & \text{if} \quad I_b(i,j-1) < I_b(i,j) \\ S_b(i,j-1) - D''_b(i,j-1) & o.w. \end{cases} \qquad (7)$$

For $0 \le i \le A-1, \quad 0 \le j \le B-2, \quad 0 \le b \le \frac{M \times N}{A \times B} - 1$.

2.3.3 Extracting and Restoring Phase

The embedded message is extracted in this phase in addition to restoration of original image. The basic steps for the extraction and restoration process are as follows.

Step 1: Divide the received marked image into blocks $A \times B$ in size. Generate the difference image $SD_b(i, j)$ of block b from the received marked image by using the following formula:

$$SD_b(i, j) = |S_b(i, j) - S_b(i, j+1)| \tag{8}$$

For $0 \le i \le A-1 \quad 0 \le j \le B-2 \quad 0 \le b \le \frac{M \times N}{A \times B} - 1$.

Step 2: Perform the embedded message extracting on the difference image $SD_b(i, j)$ of block b by using the following rule:

$$m = \begin{cases} 0 & if \quad SD_b(i, j) = p_b \\ 1 & if \quad SD_b(i, j) = p_b + 1 \end{cases} \tag{9}$$

For $0 \le i \le A-1 \quad 0 \le j \le B-2 \quad 0 \le b \le \frac{M \times N}{A \times B} - 1$

Where p_b is the received peak point of block *b*. We first scan the entire difference image of block *b*. For block *b*, if the pixel with p_b is encountered, bit 0 is extracted. If the pixel with $(p_b + 1)$ is encountered, bit 1 is extracted.

Step 3: Remove the embedded message from the difference image $SD_b(i, j)$ for block b by using the following formula:

$$SD'_b(i, j) = \begin{cases} SD_b(i, j) - 1 & if \quad SD_b(i, j) = p_b + 1 \\ SD_b(i, j) & o.w. \end{cases} \tag{10}$$

Step 4: Shift some pixel values in the difference image $SD'_b(i, j)$ to obtain its reconstructed original difference image $RD_b(i, j)$ according to:

$$RD_b(i, j) = \begin{cases} SD'_b(i, j) - 1 & if \quad SD_b(i, j) > p_b + 1 \\ SD'_b(i, j) & o.w. \end{cases} \tag{11}$$

For $0 \le i \le A-1 \quad 0 \le j \le B-2 \quad 0 \le b \le \frac{M \times N}{A \times B} - 1$

Step 5: Finally, obtain the recovered original image $RH_b(i, j)$ by performing the inverse transformation T^{-1}. Similar to Step 5 in the hiding phase, for the first two pixels of each row the inverse operation is expressed as:

$$RH_b(i,0) = \begin{cases} S_b(i,0) \; if & S_b(i,0) \le S_b(i,1) \\ S_b(i,1) + RD_b(i,0) & o.w \end{cases} \tag{12}$$

$$RH_b(i,1) = \begin{cases} S_b(i,0) + RD_b(i,0) \; if & S_b(i,0) \le S_b(i,1) \\ S_b(i,1) & o.w \end{cases} \tag{13}$$

For the remaining pixels, the corresponding inverse operation is shown as

$$RH_b(i,j)=\begin{cases} RH_b(i,j-1)+RD_b(i,j-1) & \text{if} \quad S_b(i,j-1)\le S_b(i,j) \\ RH_b(i,j-1)-RD_b(i,j-1) & \text{if} \quad o.w \end{cases} \tag{14}$$

For $0\le i\le A-1 \quad 0\le j\le B-2 \quad 0\le b\le \frac{M\times N}{A\times B}-1$.

Because the hiding algorithm is based on a multilevel concept, the algorithm can be performed repeatedly to convey a large amount of embedded messages.

2.4 Data Hiding Scheme Based on Three-Pixel Block Differences

In this section a data hiding scheme has been proposed that embeds a message into an image using the two differences, between the first and the second pixels as well as between the second and the third pixels in a three-pixel block. In this method, the term "histogram" is not used necessarily, but its fundamental concepts have been indirectly applied, which are using peak points, zero points and shifting the gray scale between these two values. This scheme has been proposed by Ching-Chiuan Lin et al in 2008 [19]. In the cover image, an absolute difference between a pair of pixels is selected to embed the message. In the best case, a three-pixel block can embed two bits and only the central pixel needs to be increased or decreased by 1. First an image is divided into non-overlapping three-pixel blocks, where the maximum and minimum allowable pixel values are 255 and 0, respectively.

2.4.1 Embedding Process

Let $g(d)$ be the number of pixel pairs with absolute difference equal to d, where $0\le d\le 253$ and pixel pairs in the block which contains a pixel value equal to 0 or 255 are not considered when calculating $g(d)$. Before embedding a message, the proposed scheme selects a pair of differences M and m such that $g(M)\ge g(M')$ and $g(m)\le g(m')$ for all $0\le M',m'\le 253$. Let (b_{i0},b_{i1},b_{i2}) denote a block i with pixel values equal to b_{i0},b_{i1}, and b_{i2}, and $\max(b_{i0},b_{i1},b_{i2})$ and $\min(b_{i0},b_{i1},b_{i2})$ denote the maximum and minimum pixel values in the block, respectively. First, blocks satisfying the following two conditions are selected:

(a) $1\le b_{i0},b_{i1},b_{i2}\le 254$

(b) $\max(b_{i0},b_{i1},b_{i2})=254$ and $\min(b_{i0},b_{i1},b_{i2})=1$.

For each block i satisfying the above conditions (a) and (b), call the embedding procedure shown in Figure.1.to embed the message. The brief procedure is described in two steps. The steps are expanded in detail. After invoking the embedding procedure, if $\max(b_{i0},b_{i1},b_{i2})=255$ or $\min(b_{i0},b_{i1},b_{i2})=0$, record block i in the overhead information. For each selected block i, the sender performs the following actions:

Step1: Increase d_{i0} by 1 if $M+1\le d_{i0}\le m-1$, and increase d_{i1} by 1 if $M+1\le d_{i1}\le m-1$, where $d_{i0}=|b_{i0}-b_{i1}|$ and $d_{i1}=|b_{i1}-b_{i2}|$;

Step2: Embed a message into block i if $d_{i0}=M$ or $d_{i1}=M$;

Then, the sender scans the image again and performs the following actions for each block i with $2 \le b_{i0}, b_{i1}, b_{i2} \le 253$.

Step $1'$: Increase d_{i0} by 1 if $M+1 \le d_{i0} \le m-1$, and increase d_{i1} by 1 if $M+1 \le d_{i1} \le m-1$.

Step $2'$: Embed the overhead information and the residual message into block i if $d_{i0} = M$ or $d_{i1} = M$.

```
Procedure of embedding:
if di0 == M {
        if di1 == M
                embed 2 bits;
        else {
                if M < di1 < m
                        embed 1 bit and increase difference;
                else
                        embed 1 bit and leave unchanged;
        }
}
Else if M < di0 < m {
        if di1 == M
                increase difference and embed 1 bit;
else {
        if M < di1 < m
                increase 2 differences;
        else
                increase difference and leave unchanged;
        }
}
else {
        if di1 == M
                leave unchanged and embed 1 bit;
        else {
                if M < di1 < m
                        leave unchanged and increase difference;
                else
                        do nothing;
        }
}
```

Fig. 1. Embedding procedure

Then go to step 1 until the message is completely embedded.

2.4.2 Extraction Process

For extraction process scan the stego-image block by block in the order the message was embedded. For each block i with $1 \le b_{i0}, b_{i1}, b_{i2} \le 254$, perform the actions in accordance with the conditions listed in Figure 2. After the respective actions have been completed, save the extracted message bits in the list 1 if $\min(b_{i0}, b_{i1}, b_{i2}) = 1$ or $\max(b_{i0}, b_{i1}, b_{i2}) = 254$, and save the extracted message bits in the list 2, if $2 \le b_{i0}, b_{i1}, b_{i2} \le 253$. List-1 contains a part of the message embedded in step 1,2 and List-2 contains the message embedded in step $1'$, $2'$.

Item	Conditions	Actions
1	$di0 == M$ and $di1 == M$	Extract "00"
2	$di0 == M$ and $di1 == M + 1$ and $bi1 > bi2$	Extract "01", $bi2 = bi2 + 1$
3	$di0 == M$ and $di1 == M + 1$ and $bi1 < bi2$	Extract "01", $bi2 = bi2\text{-}1$
4	$di0 == M$ and $M + 1 < di1\ m$ and $bi1 > bi2$	Extract "0", $bi2 = bi2 + 1$
5	$di0 == M$ and $M + 1 < di1\ m$ and $bi1 < bi2$	Extract "0", $bi2 = bi2\text{-}1$
6	$di0 == M$ and ($di1 < M$ or $di1 > m$)	Extract "0"
7	$di0 == M + 1$ and $di1 == M$ and $bi0 < bi1$	Extract "10", $bi0 = bi0 + 1$
8	$di0 == M + 1$ and $di1 == M$ and $bi0 > bi1$	Extract "10", $bi0 = bi0\text{-}1$
9	$di0 == M + 1$ and $di1 == M + 1$ and $bi0 < bi1 < bi2$	Extract "11", $bi0 = bi0 + 1$, $bi2 = bi2\text{-}1$
10	$di0 == M + 1$ and $di1 == M + 1$ and $bi0 > bi1 > bi2$	Extract "11", $bi0 = bi0\text{-}1$, $bi2 = bi2 + 1$
11	$di0 == M + 1$ and $di1 == M + 1$ and $bi0 < bi1 > bi2$	Extract "11", $bi1 = bi1\text{-}1$
12	$di0 == M + 1$ and $di1 == M + 1$ and $bi0 > bi1 < bi2$	Extract "11", $bi1 = bi1 + 1$
13	$di0 == M + 1$ and $M + 1 < di1\ m$ and $bi0 > bi1 > bi2$	Extract "1", $bi0 = bi0\text{-}1$, $bi2 = bi2 + 1$
14	$di0 == M + 1$ and $M + 1 < di1\ m$ and $bi0 < bi1 < bi2$	Extract "1", $bi0 = bi0 + 1$, $bi2 = bi2\text{-}1$
15	$di0 == M + 1$ and $M + 1 < di1\ m$ and $bi0 < bi1 > bi2$	Extract "1", $bi1 = bi1 - 1$
16	$di0 == M + 1$ and $M + 1 < di1\ m$ and $bi0 > bi1 < bi2$	Extract "1", $bi1 = bi1 + 1$
17	$di0 == M + 1$ and ($di1 < M$ or $di1 > m$) and $bi0 < bi1$	Extract "1", $bi0 = bi0 + 1$
18	$di0 == M + 1$ and ($di1 < M$ or $di1 > m$) and $bi0 > bi1$	Extract "1", $bi0 = bi0\text{-}1$
19	$M + 1 < di0\ m$ and $di1 == M$ and $bi0 > bi1$	Extract "0", $bi0 = bi0\text{-}1$
20	$M + 1 < di0\ m$ and $di1 == M$ and $bi0 < bi1$	Extract "0", $bi0 = bi0 + 1$
21	$M + 1 < di0\ m$ and $di1 == M + 1$ and $bi0 > bi1 > bi2$	Extract "1", $bi0 = bi0\text{-}1$, $bi2 = bi2 + 1$
22	$M + 1 < di0\ m$ and $di1 == M + 1$ and $bi0 < bi1 < bi2$	Extract "1", $bi0 = bi0 + 1$, $bi2 = bi\text{-}1$
23	$M + 1 < di0\ m$ and $di1 == M + 1$ and $bi0 < bi1 > bi2$	Extract "1", $bi1 = bi1\text{-}1$
24	$M + 1 < di0\ m$ and $di1 == M + 1$ and $bi0 > bi1 < bi2$	Extract "1", $bi1 = bi1{+}1$
25	$M + 1 < di0\ m$ and $M + 1 < di1\ m$ and $bi0 > bi1 > bi2$	$bi0 = bi0\text{-}1$, $bi2 = bi2 + 1$
26	$M + 1 < di0\ m$ and $M + 1 < di1\ m$ and $bi0 < bi1 < bi2$	$bi0 = bi0 + 1$, $bi2 = bi2\text{-}1$
27	$M + 1 < di0\ m$ and $M + 1 < di1\ m$ and $bi0 < bi1 > bi2$	$bi1 = bi1\text{-}1$
28	$M + 1 < di0\ m$ and $M + 1 < di1\ m$ and $bi0 > bi1 < bi2$	$bi1 = bi1 + 1$
29	$M + 1 < di0\ m$ and ($di1 < M$ or $di1 > m$) and $bi0 < bi1$	$bi0 = bi0 + 1$
30	$M + 1 < di0\ m$ and ($di1 < M$ or $di1 > m$) and $bi0 > bi1$	$bi0 = bi0\text{-}1$
31	($di0 < M$ or $di0 > m$) and $di1 == M$	Extract "0"
32	($di0 < M$ or $di0 > m$) and $di1 == M + 1$ and $bi1 < bi2$	Extract "1", $bi2 = bi2\text{-}1$
33	($di0 < M$ or $di0 > m$) and $di1 == M + 1$ and $bi1 > bi2$	Extract "1", $bi2 = bi2 + 1$
34	($di0 < M$ or $di0 > m$) and $M + 1 < di1\ m$ and $bi1 < bi2$	$bi2 = bi2\text{-}1$
35	($di0 < M$ or $di0 > m$) and $M + 1 < di1\ m$ and $bi1 > bi2$	$bi2 = bi2 + 1$
36	($di0 < M$ or $di0 > m$) and ($di1 < M$ or $di1 > m$)	Do nothing

Fig. 2. Conditions and their actions for extracting process of data hiding scheme based on three-pixel block differences

2.5 Data Hiding Based on Correlation between Sub-sampled Images

In this scheme, a data hiding method is described which has been proposed by Kim[20] that modifies the difference histogram between sub-sampled images. It applies the spatial correlation in neighboring pixels to achieve higher capacity than other histogram based methods. After explanation of embedding process, extraction process have been described.

2.5.1 Embedding Process

Data embedding procedure, is composed of six steps as follows:

Step 1: Generate sub-sampled versions S_k using two sampling factors $(\Delta u, \Delta v)$ and Eq.(1) by performing sub-sampling from an original image I:

$$S_k(i, j) = I\left(i \cdot \Delta v + floor\left(\frac{k-1}{\Delta u}\right), j \cdot \Delta u + ((k-1) \bmod \Delta u)\right) \tag{15}$$

Step 2: Determine a reference sub-sampled image S_{ref} to maximize spatial correlation between the sub-sampled images. We select S_{ref} from the following Eq.(16). For example, when $\Delta u = 3, \Delta v = 3$, S_5 is determined as the reference one. It is defined as

$$S_{ref} = \left(Round\left(\frac{\Delta u}{2} - 1\right)\right) \times \Delta v + Round\left(\frac{\Delta v}{2}\right) \tag{16}$$

Step 3: Create difference images between the reference and the other destination sub-sampled images denoted by:

$$D_{ref-Des}(k_1,k_2)=S_{ref}(k_1,k_2)-D_{Des}(k_1,k_2) \tag{17}$$

where $0 \le k_1 \le M/_{\Delta v} - 1, 0 \le k_2 \le N/_{\Delta u} - 1$.

Step 4: Prepare empty bins in each histogram of the difference images according to an embedding level L, where $H = -255,...,255$. Depending on the desired degree, L affects the performance of capacity and the perceptual quality. In order to achieve this, the negative differences and then non-negative differences in the outer regions of a selected embedding range should be shifted left and right, respectively. When shifting H, only the pixels in the destination sub-sampled image are modified. The embedding procedure will use the range $[-L, L]$ in the shifted histogram. The shifted histogram H_s can be calculated as follows:

$$H_s = \begin{cases} H+L+1 & if \quad H \ge L+1 \\ H-L-1 & if \quad H \le -L-1 \end{cases} \tag{18}$$

Also, this can be obtained by:

$$D'_{ref-Des}(k_1,k_2)=S_{ref}(k_1,k_2)-S'_{Des}(k_1,k_2) \tag{19}$$

where

$$S'_{Des}(k_1,k_2)=\begin{cases} S_{Des}(k_1,k_2)-(L+1) & if \quad H \ge L+1 \\ S_{Des}(k_1,k_2)+(L+1) & if \quad H \le -L-1 \end{cases} \tag{20}$$

Step 5: Embed message $w(n)$ by modifying H_s, where $w(n)=\{1,0\}$. The modified difference image D' is scanned. Once a pixel with the difference value of $-L$ or $+L$ is encountered, the message to be embedded is checked. This process is repeated until there are no pixels with the difference value of $\pm L$. Then the embedding level decreases by 1. These scanning and embedding steps are executed until $L<0$. Likewise, only the pixels in the destination sub-sampled image are modified. The message embedding can be formulated as follows:

$$D''_{ref-Des}(k_1,k_2)=S_{ref}(k_1,k_2)-S''_{Des}(k_1,k_2) \tag{21}$$

Where

$$S'_{Des}(k_1,k_2)=\begin{cases} S'_{Des}(k_1,k_2)+(L+1) & if \quad D'=-L, w(n)=1 \\ S'_{Des}(k_1,k_2)-(L+1) & if \quad D'=L, w(n)=1 \\ S'_{Des}(k_1,k_2)+L & if \quad D'=-L, w(n)=0 \\ S'_{Des}(k_1,k_2)-L & if \quad D'=L, w(n)=0 \end{cases} \tag{22}$$

$$\text{For } L=0 \,\&\, L>0 \tag{23}$$

Step.6: Finally, obtain the marked image I_w through the inverse of the sub-sampling with the unmodified reference sub-sampled image $S_{ref}(k_1,k_2)$ and the modified destination sub-sampled images $S''_{Des}(k_1,k_2)$

2.5.2 Extraction and Restoration Algorithm

The extraction and recovery steps are as follows:

Step 1: Obtain two sampling factors $(\Delta u, \Delta v)$ and the embedding level L from the LSB of the selected pixels using the secret key.
Step 2: Generate sub-sampled versions in Eq.(1) by performing sub-sampling from the marked image I_w using the sampling factors in Step1.
Step 3: Determine a reference sub-sampled image S_{ref} by Eq.(2).
Step 4: Create difference images between the unmarked reference sub-sampled image S_{ref} and the other marked destination sub-sampled images denoted by:

$$D_{ref-W}(k_1,k_2) = S_{ref}(k_1,k_2) - S_W(k_1,k_2) \tag{24}$$

where $0 \le k_1 \le M/_{\Delta v} - 1, 0 \le k_2 \le N/_{\Delta u} - 1$ and $w = 1,\dots,\Delta u \times \Delta v$
Step 5: Extract the hidden message $w(n)$ from each difference image. The extraction process is the inverse of embedding process. After a new variable L' is set to 0, the difference image D is scanned. Once a pixel with the difference value of 1 is encountered, bit 1 is restored. If the pixel with the difference value of 0 encountered, bit 0 is restored. This process is repeated until there are no pixels with the difference value of 0 and 1. After L' is increased by 1, the difference image is scanned again, and the message is extracted using the following rule:

$$w(n) = \begin{cases} 0 & if \quad D = 2L' or - 2L' \\ 1 & if \quad D = 2L' + 1 or - (2L' + 1) \end{cases} \tag{25}$$

This scanning and extracting process is executed until $L' > L$.
Step 6: Remove the hidden message $w(n)$ from the difference images.

$$w(n) = \begin{cases} 0 & if \quad D = 2L' or - 2L' \\ 1 & if \quad D = 2L' + 1 or - (2L' + 1) \end{cases} \tag{25}$$

This scanning and extracting process is executed until $L' > L$.
Step 6: Remove the hidden message $w(n)$ from the difference images.

For $L' = 0$

$$S'_w(k_1,k_2) = \begin{cases} S_w(k_1,k_2) + L' & if \quad D(k_1,k_2) = 2L' \\ S_w(k_1,k_2) + (L'+1) & if \quad D(k_1,k_2) = 2L'+1 \\ S_w(k_1,k_2) + L' & if \quad D(k_1,k_2) = -2L' \\ S_w(k_1,k_2) - (L'+1) & if \quad D(k_1,k_2) = -2L'-1 \end{cases} \tag{28}$$

For $1 \le L' \le L$.
Step 7: Shift each histogram H_s of the difference image back to obtain its original difference histogram H as follows:

$$H = \begin{cases} H_s - L - 1 & if \quad H_s \ge 2L + 2 \\ H_s + L + 1 & if \quad H_s \le -2L - 2 \end{cases} \tag{29}$$

This can be obtained by

$$D''_{ref-W}(k_1,k_2)=S_{ref}(k_1,k_2)-S''_W(k_1,k_2) \quad (30)$$

Where

$$S''_w(k_1,k_2)=\begin{cases} S'_w(k_1,k_2)+(L+1) & if \quad H_s \geq 2L+2 \\ S'_w(k_1,k_2)-(L+1) & if \quad H_s \leq -2L-2 \end{cases} \quad (31)$$

Step 8: Finally, obtain there covered original image I through the inverse of the sub-sampling with the sub-sampled images.

In the next section, all of the described methods are simulated to illustrate a comparison in terms of quality and capacity.

3 Simulation Results

Simulation are performed to evaluate the performance of all histogram based data hiding schemes. In terms of embedding capacity and invisibility, the performance of these algorithms are measured by comparing with each other and with Ni et al's scheme. The capacity (bit per pixel) measures the amount of data that can be hidden. The peak signal to noise ratio (PSNR) is utilized to show the distortion or invisibility of the stego-image. For an $M \times N$ gray scale image, the PSNR value is defined as follows:

$$PSNR = 10 \times \log\left(\frac{255^2 \times M \times N}{\sum_{i=0}^{M-1}\sum_{j=0}^{N-1}\left(I(i,j)-I(i,j)'\right)}\right) dB \quad (32)$$

where $I(i,j)$ and $I(i,j)'$ denote the pixel values in i th row and j th column of the cover image and the stego-image, respectively. Table 1 & 2 show the maximum payload capacity, in bpp and bits respectively, that the test images can offer using all the schemes which are proposed in sections *2.1.* to *2.5.* In all simulation, three gray scale images of 512×512 pixels are tested as depicted in Figure.4. The message bits to be embedded were randomly generated using the MATLAB function.

Embedding variables of Kim's scheme[19], $(\Delta u, \Delta v)$ and $L$is adjusted to 3 and 0, respectively. Kim exploited the fact that the difference values having small magnitudes occurred frequently because of the high spatial correlation between sub-sampled images. The embedding capacity of the Kim's algorithm depends on how many the difference images are used and how many pixels having the difference values between $-L$ and L in each difference image exist. In addition, sampling factors affect embedding capacity. Pixel redundancy and spatial correlation between the determined reference sub-sampled image and the other ones are high at the selected sampling factors. From this result, the performance of capacity versus distortion depends on the characteristics of the images. In Tsai et al.'s scheme [16] the negative histogram and non-negative histogram of the residue image are employed and provided high capacity enhancement compared to original image histogram. In the simulations, these test images are first divided into blocks of 3×3 pixels and then the linear prediction is performed to generate the residual images. In other words, 8 residual values are generated for each 3×3 block. To evaluate the performance of the these methods, the hiding capacity and the stego-image quality are computed. The size of the embedded secret data is determined according to the capacity of the supported image. From this results, the performance of capacity versus distortion depends on the characteristics of the images. Tables 1 and 2 summarized comparison results of histogram-shifting based algorithms for three test images: *Lena*, *Baboon* and *Boat*. The hiding capacity of Chia Chen Lin et al's scheme[18] is equal to the sum of the number of pixels associated with the peak points of the blocks in the difference image. Based on the nature of an image, the gray scale values close to 0 in its difference image may be the maximum number of pixels. In addition, the number of pixels that correspond to the peak point in a difference image is always larger than the number in its original image. Based on this property of the difference image histogram, a large amount of embedded messages can be hidden in a marked image in comparison with its original image. The embedding performance of the Chia Chen Lin et al.'s scheme did not achieve more than 0.22 bpp for the test images, because the amount of the peak information for all blocks exceeded the whole embedding capacity. In other words, it suffered from the lack of capacity control due to the need for embedding all peaks information for blocks. Experimental results supported that Kim's algorithm achieved high embedding capacity in comparison to other reversible schemes while maintaining the distortion at a low level.

In Ni et al's scheme [14] two pairs of maximum and minimum points are utilized in data embedding and extraction process. The histogram-based Ni et al.'s scheme showed the fixed PSNR quality, 48.2dB, but the achievable capacity was a little varied for each image. In Ching-Chiuan Lin scheme [19] the peak signal to noise ratio (PSNR) is utilized to show the distortion of the stego-image. The payload capacities and PSNR values of this method are higher than Ni et al.'s in embedding process. Table 1 shows that in each level Ching Lin's scheme provides higher capacity than other schemes. Because it uses three pixel blocks and two differences in each block. The secret bits are embedded in these differences. Thus it provides high payload capacity. The second scheme that provides higher capacity is the Kim's one that uses the correlation of subsampled image, Since the secret bits are embedded in difference image of each subsampled image with the reference one. Thus it provides a large amount of space for hiding secret bits. Tsai [16] and Chia Lin have similar capacity and Ni et al scheme have almost 0.25bpp for payload capacity. For comparison of image quality and invisibility, Tsai has the highest PSNR, but the image quality of Ching Lin's scheme is satisfactory. Overall comparison between the existing reversible data hiding techniques in Terms of pure payload and the PSNR is presented in Table 1. In terms of embedding capacity(bit) and image quality(dB), the algorithms are compared with each other in 16 levels for the *Lena* as shown in Fig. 4. Ching lin scheme showed relatively high embedding capacity versus PSNR value, whereas the Tsai scheme had low embedding capacity compared to other schemes.

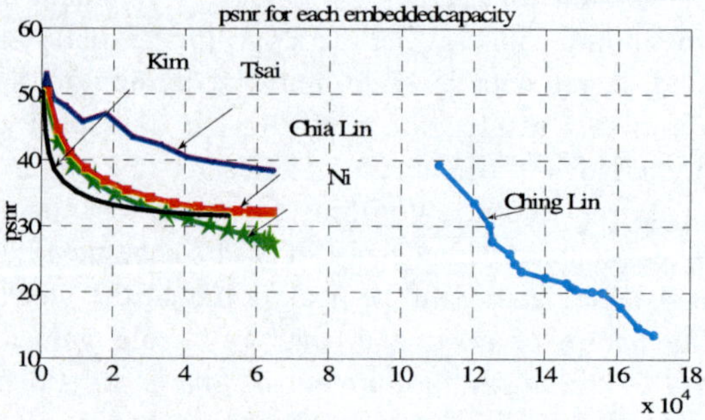

Fig. 3. Comparison of embedding capacity (bit) versus image quality (dB) of methods for test image *lena*

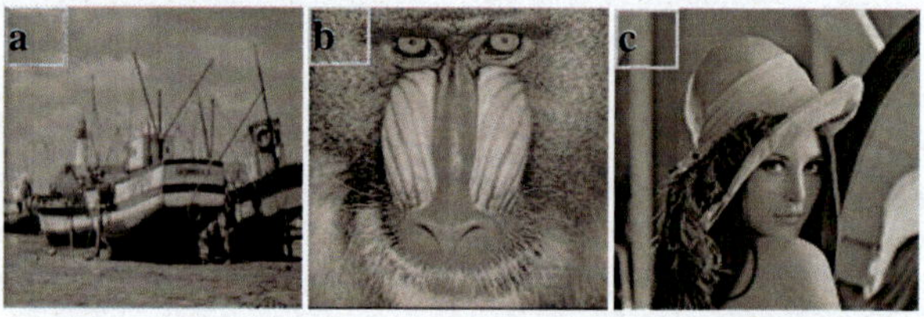

Fig. 4. Test images: (a) Boat; (b) Baboon; (c) Lena

Table 1. Comparison between histogram based data hiding algorithm in terms of the payload capacities and the PSNR values for Lena in 4 level

	Level	**1**	**2**	**3**	**4**
Kim	**PSNR(db)**	49	43.5	41.5	38.5
	Capacity (Bit/pixel)	0.07	0.225	0.34	0.44
Ni (2006)	**PSNR(db)**	48.3	48.3	48.2	48.2
	Capacity (Bit/pixel)	0.042	0.14	0.13	0.24
Tsai	**PSNR(db)**	59	55	52	50
	Capacity (Bit/pixel)	0.02	0.05	0.08	0.21
Ching Lin	**PSNR(db)**	48.67	43.02	39.64	37.21
	Capacity (Bit/pixel)	0.216	0.38	0.53	0.66
Chia Lin	**PSNR(db)**	47	43	38	37
	Capacity (Bit/pixel	0.084	0.087	0.107	0.22

Table 2. The performance of the histogram based data hiding schemes

Methods	Kim's scheme	Ni 2006's scheme	Tsai's scheme	Ching Lin's scheme	Chia Lin's scheme
PSNR(db)Lena	48.9	48.2	50.59	30.0	48.67
Capacity (Bits)	20121	5460	52322	308474	65349
PSNR(db)Baboon	48.7	48.2	51.03	30.4	48.67
Capacity (Bits)	6499	5421	18410	161118	38465
PSNR(db)Boat	68.9	48.2	47.66	30.4	48.67
Capacity (Bits)	21442	7301	53510	307193	56713

4 Conclusions

In this paper, reversible histogram-based data hiding schemes is presented which all of them have been developed in few recent years. All the schemes intend to improve the histogram-based data hiding scheme which embeds secret data in to the peak points of the image histogram. To achieve a higher hiding capacity, more peak-zero pairs are explored instead of using only one pair in each histogram. Experimental results supported that Ching Lin's scheme and Kim's algorithm achieved higher embedding capacity than other reversible schemes while maintaining the distortion at a low level and it has satisfactory PSNR for image quality. The performance of Kim's algorithm can be enhanced by deciding optimum sampling factors considering the characteristics of a given image.

Acknowledgment

The authors gratefully acknowledge the financial and support of this research, provided by the Islamic Azad University, Shahr-e-Rey Branch,Tehran, Iran.

References

1. Cheng, Q., Huang, T.S.: An Additive Approach to Transform-Domain Information Hiding and Optimum Detection Structure. IEEE Transactions on Multimedia 3(3), 273–284 (2001)
2. Artz, D.: Digital Steganography: Hiding Data Within Data. IEEE Internet Computing 5(3), 75–80 (2001)
3. Podilchuk, C.I., Delp, E.J.: Digital Watermarking: Algorithms and Applications. IEEE Signal Processing Magazine 18(4), 33–46 (2001)
4. Wang, R.Z., Lin, C.F., Lin, J.C.: Image Hiding by Optimal LSB Substitution and Genetic Algorithm. Pattern Recognition 34(3), 671–683 (2001)
5. Jo, M., Kim, H.D.: A Digital Image Watermarking Scheme Based on Vvector Quantization. IEICE Transactions on Information and Systems 9(3), 1054–1105 (2002)
6. Chang, C.C., Tai, W.L., Lin, C.C.: A Reversible Data Hiding Scheme Based on Side-Match Vector Quantization. IEEE Transactions on Circuits and Systems for Video Technology 16(10), 1301–1308 (2006)

7. Celik, M.U., Sharma, G., Tekalp, A.M.: Reversible Data Hiding. In: Proceedings of IEEE International Conference on Image Processing, Rochester, NY, vol. 158, pp. 157–160 (2002)
8. Tian, J.: Reversible Data Embedding Using a Difference Expansion. IEEE Transactions on Circuits and Systems for Video Technology 13(8), 890–899 (2003)
9. Ni, Z., Shi, Y.Q., Ansari, N., Su, W.: Reversible Data Hiding. IEEE Transactions on Circuits and Systems for Video Technology 16(3), 354–361 (2006)
10. Tai, C.L., Chiang, H.F., Fan, K.C., Chung, C.D.: Reversible Data Hiding and Lossless Reconstruction of Binary Images Using Pair-Wise Logical Computation Mechanism. Pattern Recognition 38(11), 1993–2006 (2005)
11. Fridrich, J., Goljan, M., Du, R.: Invertible Authentication. In: Proceedings of SPIE Security Watermarking Multimedia Contents, San Jose, CA, pp. 197–208 (January 2001)
12. Xuan, G., Zhu, J., Chen, J., Shi, Y.Q., Ni, Z., Su, W.: Distortionless Data Hiding Based on Integer Wavelet Transform. Electronics Letters 38(25), 1646–1648 (2002)
13. Kamstra, L., Heijmans, H.J.A.M.: Reversible Data Embedding into Images Using Wavelet Techniques and Sorting. IEEE Transactions on Image Processing 4(12), 2082–2090 (2005)
14. Chang, C.-C., Wu, W.-C.: A Reversible Information Hiding Scheme Based on Vector Quantization. In: Khosla, R., Howlett, R.J., Jain, L.C. (eds.) KES 2005. LNCS (LNAI), vol. 3683, pp. 1101–1107. Springer, Heidelberg (2005)
15. Shi, Y.Q., Ni, Z., Zou, D., Liang, C., Xuan, G.: Lossless Data Hiding: Fundamentals, Algorithms and Applications. In: Proc. IEEE Int. Symp. Circuits Syst., Vancouver, BC, Canada, vol. II, pp. 33–36 (May 2004)
16. Ni, Z., Shi, Y.-Q., Ansari, N., Su, W.: Reversible Data Hiding. IEEE Transactions on Circuit and Systems for Video Technology 16(3) (March 2006)
17. Tsai, P., Hu, Y.-C., Yeh, H.-L.: Reversible Image Hiding Scheme Using Predictive Coding and Histogram Shifting. Signal Processing 89, 1129–1143 (2009)
18. Lin, C.-C., Tai, W.-L., Chang, C.-C.: Multilevel Reversible Data Hiding Based on Histogram Modification of Difference Images. Pattern Recognition 41, 3582–3591 (2008)
19. Lin, C.-C., Hsueh, N.-L.: A Lossless Ddata Hiding Scheme Based on Three-Pixel Block Differences. Pattern Recognition 41, 1415–1425 (2008)
20. Kim, K.-S., Lee, M.-J., Lee, H.-Y., Leea, H.-K.: Reversible Data Hiding Exploiting Spatial Correlation Between Sub-sampled Images. Pattern Recognition 42, 3083–3096 (2009)

New Data Hiding Method Based on Neighboring Correlation of Blocked Image

Mona Nafari[1], Gholam Hossein Sheisi[2], and Mansour Nejati Jahromi[3]

[1] Razi University of Kermanshah, Department of Electrical Engineering, Kermanshah, Iran
m.nafari@razi.ac.ir
[2] Department of Electrical Engineering, Razi University of Kermanshah, Iran
Sheisi@razi.ac.ir
[3] Department of Electrical Engineering, Azad University South Branch
and Aeronautical College, Tehran, Iran
Nejati@aut.ac.ir

Abstract. Data hiding process hides secret data in a media and reversible image data hiding is a technique in which the cover image can be completely restored after the extraction of secret data. In this paper a simple method is proposed for reversible data hiding in image blocks, by calculation of correlation matrix before data embedding. New data hiding method in these blocks is applied, by considering the pattern of correlation matrix and correlation threshold. Experimental results show that this method is capable of providing a great embedding capacity without making noticeable distortion with high PSNR.

Keywords: Reversible data hiding, correlation matrix, thresholding, blocks, sum-block, error correlation.

1 Introduction

Data hiding techniques [1] play an important role in security of data transmission and data authentication. Image data hiding, delivers a hidden secret message by a cover image [2]. The sender hides the encrypted message in the cover image and sends it to a receiver via the Internet or other transmission media; on the other hand the receiver receives the stego-image and extracts the secret message by using the corresponding extraction and decryption processes [3]. A reversible data hiding method is the one which can extract the cover image from stego-image after the extraction of hidden data, without distortion in cover image [4][5].The proposed data hiding technique is capable of extraction of secret data and restoration of the image. In this way based on an identified standard, secret data is embedded. Chang et al in 2008 [6], proposed a data hiding method based on neighboring correlation in which they exploited the correlation of the neighboring pixels. In their scheme, any two neighboring pixels can be used to conceal one bit of secret data and a threshold T is set to control the distortion between the cover image and the stego-image. This scheme is explained in section 2.

H. Cherifi, J.M. Zain, and E. El-Qawasmeh (Eds.): DICTAP 2011, Part I, CCIS 166, pp. 787–801, 2011.

In Section 3&4, new method of data hiding and data extraction based on neighboring correlation will be introduced in detail, followed by our experimental results which will be presented in Section 5. Finally, we conclude in Section 6.

2 Related Neighboring Correlation Method

Correlation quantifies the strength of a linear relationship between two variables [7].When there is no correlation between two quantities, and then there is no tendency for the values of one quantity to increase or decrease with the values of the second quantity. Chang et al [8], measured the distance between two neighboring pixel values in order to embed secret data in the image. The hiding process of their scheme can be described as follow:

Step1: Calculate the correlation of neighboring pixels to determine whether the pixels can be used to hide information or not. In this method, the correlation is indicated by the intervals between the adjacent pixels. If the pixels are capable of hiding, then the pixels are changeable.

$$C_i = \begin{cases} 1 & if\ |I_i - I_{i+1}| \le T \ \&\ I_{i+1} + 2T \le 255 \\ 0 & o.w \end{cases} \quad (1)$$

In the equation above T is a predefined threshold which is used to control the distortion between cover image and stego-image. The bitmap C is then concatenated by the secret data to superimpose on the image.

$I_i = \{I_1, I_2 ..., I_{M\times N}\}$ is the cover image which its size is $M \times N$ pixels where $I_i \in \{0,...,255\}$. By using a bitmap $C = \{C_1, C_2, ..., C_{MxN}\}$, record whether the pixel can be used to hide the information or not.

Step2: If the pixels are changeable, the interval between the adjacent pixels for data hiding has to be increased according to the value of the secret bit.

The following extraction process is used to extract the secret data and cover image.

Step1: Determine the pixel whether it is changeable or not .

Step2: If the pixel is changeable, then the difference between the pixel and its adjacent pixel have to be figured out. If the difference is higher than the predefined threshold, then the hidden secret bit is 1, otherwise the hidden secret bit is 0.

The payload capacity of the scheme is given by Eq (2):

$$CAP_{proposed} = M \times N - \|com_c\| \quad (2)$$

Where $\|com_c\|$ is the length of the compressed bit stream of C.

The main emphasis of Chang et al method is on differences of neighboring pixels, pixel scanning, and increasing the pixel value.

3 Neighboring Blocks Correlation

The proposed method explores the neighboring pixels similarity to improve the correlation-based reversible data hiding. It is aimed to provide a higher data hiding capacity, and maintaining the quality of the image.

Correlation in an image is an illustration of the dependence and relationship between each pixel with neighboring pixels. In proposed scheme, the image is divided in to non-overlapping 2×2 blocks. In dividing process, block size plays an important role in the number of bits to be embedded. Since one bit is embedded in each block, whether it is 3×3, 5×5, 7×7 or larger, it is more advantageous to apply small sized blocks. Figure.2 gives an illustration of blocking process. Each block (central thick black block) as shown in Figure.1 (c), has 8 adjacent blocks (thin colored blocks) and each one is used in calculation of the mean correlation of the central block. If the size of an image is $M \times N$ pixels with M row and N column, then the number of blocks is calculated by Eq (3):

$$n = \frac{(M \times N - (M \times 2 + N \times 2 - 4))}{4} \tag{3}$$

Where n is the number of bits to be embedded. $2 \times M + 2 \times N - 4$ is the number of pixels at the border of an image. These pixels are used only in calculating the correlation matrix not in the procedure of data embedding; because if they are utilized in data embedding procedure, they will cause distortion at the border of the image.

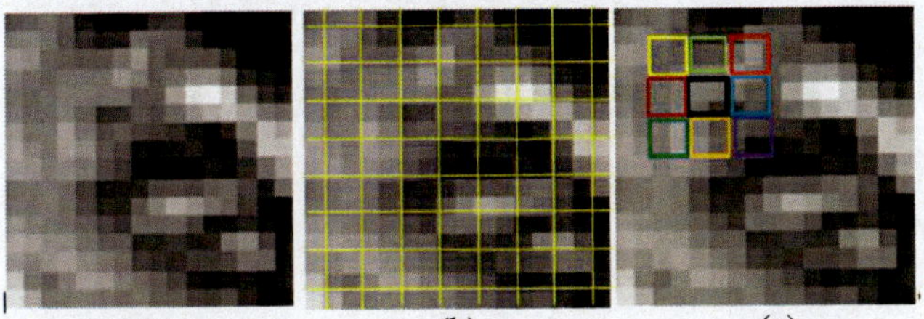

(a) (b) (c)

Fig. 1. Procedure of blocking, (a) original image (b) dividing in to 2×2 blocks (c) adjacent 8 blocks of each central block

If A and B are two matrices, the correlation of these two matrices is calculated by Eq (4):

$$c_{1:8} = \frac{\left(A - \bar{A}\right)\left(B_{1:8} - \bar{B}_{1:8}\right)}{\sqrt{\left(A - \bar{A}\right)^2 \left(B_{1:8} - \bar{B}_{1:8}\right)^2}} \tag{4}$$

A is the central block. There are n central blocks in the image. $B_{1:8}$ are the 8 adjacent blocks and $\bar{A}$ and $\bar{B}$ are the mean values of A and B respectively. In other words for each correlation calculation between block A and one of neighboring block B , Eq (5) is calculated:

$$c = \frac{(A-\bar{A})(B-\bar{B})}{\sqrt{(A-\bar{A})^2 (B-\bar{B})^2}} \tag{5}$$

Since for each block B which is at the neighboring of block A, Eq (5) is calculated, that is shown by $c_{1:8}$. For an image which has n blocks, there is $8\times n$ correlation calculation. Then, only the mean values are saved for each block; thus matrix $I_{correlation-matrix}$ is generated and it has to be normalized to the range [0 1]. Now threshold (T) is defined for each iteration of data embedding and its values is selected from the range of minimum to maximum of correlation matrix elements. Correlation in an image is an important standard for many processing procedures. For example some area in an image that has low correlation coefficients and high frequency components are not proper places for data embedding. Therefore the proposed scheme is very sensitive about the places for data embedding in the image. This threshold determines if the image block can embed a secret bit or not.

As an example, suppose an image with 8×8 pixels $I_{original-image}$, and secret data as follows:

$$I_{original-image} = \begin{bmatrix} 75 & 81 & 119 & 124 & 87 & 59 & 75 & 86 \\ 67 & 90 & 104 & 97 & 87 & 75 & 74 & 77 \\ 69 & 107 & 107 & 90 & 95 & 84 & 61 & 73 \\ 76 & 88 & 76 & 82 & 110 & 64 & 64 & 101 \\ 86 & 80 & 65 & 80 & 104 & 99 & 99 & 108 \\ 82 & 81 & 96 & 132 & 134 & 147 & 124 & 112 \\ 81 & 83 & 111 & 137 & 112 & 103 & 79 & 93 \\ 84 & 79 & 102 & 116 & 79 & 73 & 54 & 81 \end{bmatrix}$$

$$Secret - data = \{0,0,1,1,0,0,0,1,0\}$$

If the image is divided in 2×2 blocks:

$$I_{original-image} = \begin{bmatrix} 75 & 81 & 119 & 124 & 87 & 59 & 75 & 86 \\ 67 & 90 & 104 & 97 & 87 & 75 & 74 & 77 \\ 69 & 107 & 107 & 90 & 95 & 84 & 61 & 73 \\ 76 & 88 & 76 & 82 & 110 & 64 & 64 & 101 \\ 86 & 80 & 65 & 80 & 104 & 99 & 99 & 108 \\ 82 & 81 & 96 & 132 & 134 & 147 & 124 & 112 \\ 81 & 83 & 111 & 137 & 112 & 103 & 79 & 93 \\ 84 & 79 & 102 & 116 & 79 & 73 & 54 & 81 \end{bmatrix}$$

Where the blocks are:

$$\begin{bmatrix} 90 & 104 \\ 107 & 107 \end{bmatrix}, \begin{bmatrix} 97 & 87 \\ 90 & 95 \end{bmatrix}, \begin{bmatrix} 75 & 74 \\ 84 & 61 \end{bmatrix}, \begin{bmatrix} 88 & 76 \\ 80 & 65 \end{bmatrix}, \begin{bmatrix} 82 & 110 \\ 80 & 104 \end{bmatrix}, \begin{bmatrix} 64 & 64 \\ 99 & 99 \end{bmatrix}, \begin{bmatrix} 81 & 96 \\ 83 & 111 \end{bmatrix}, \begin{bmatrix} 132 & 64 \\ 137 & 112 \end{bmatrix},$$

$$\begin{bmatrix} 147 & 124 \\ 103 & 79 \end{bmatrix}.$$

The mean correlation of each identified 2×2 block with neighboring blocks is:

$$I_{correlatin-matrix} = \begin{bmatrix} 0 & 0 & 0 & 0 & 0 & 0 & 0 & 0 \\ 0 & 0.730 & 0 & 0.493 & 0 & 0.608 & 0 & 0 \\ 0 & 0 & 0 & 0 & 0 & 0 & 0 & 0 \\ 0 & 0.779 & 0 & 0.644 & 0 & 0.783 & 0 & 0 \\ 0 & 0 & 0 & 0 & 0 & 0 & 0 & 0 \\ 0 & 0.870 & 0 & 0.725 & 0 & 1.000 & 0 & 0 \\ 0 & 0 & 0 & 0 & 0 & 0 & 0 & 0 \\ 0 & 0 & 0 & 0 & 0 & 0 & 0 & 0 \end{bmatrix}$$

By normalizing the correlation matrix elements, the correlation values are in the range of 0 to 1. Neighboring blocks are the blocks which surrounded these blocks. For example for the block b_1 as follows:

$$b_1 = \begin{bmatrix} 90 & 104 \\ 107 & 107 \end{bmatrix}$$

The 8 surrounding blocks are:

$$\begin{bmatrix} 75 & 81 \\ 67 & 90 \end{bmatrix}, \begin{bmatrix} 81 & 119 \\ 90 & 104 \end{bmatrix}, \begin{bmatrix} 119 & 124 \\ 104 & 97 \end{bmatrix}, \begin{bmatrix} 67 & 90 \\ 69 & 107 \end{bmatrix}, \begin{bmatrix} 104 & 97 \\ 107 & 90 \end{bmatrix}, \begin{bmatrix} 69 & 107 \\ 76 & 88 \end{bmatrix}, \begin{bmatrix} 107 & 107 \\ 88 & 76 \end{bmatrix}, \begin{bmatrix} 107 & 90 \\ 76 & 82 \end{bmatrix}$$

Only the mean value of these 8 values has to be saved in upper left pixel of each block and the correlation block is created as : $\begin{bmatrix} 0.7305 & 0 \\ 0 & 0 \end{bmatrix}$

In fact correlation matrix in this example is a 8×8 matrix that its size is equal to the size of original image. For simplicity in addressing, a zero row and a zero column are concatenated before and after the correlation matrix. The zeros in the matrix have no effect on calculation and they are only for preserving the correlation matrix size. So they make it simpler to address the positions of secret data to be embedded.

In section 2, correlation based data hiding technique has been explained which is proposed by Chang et al, but there are some fundamental differences between this method and the method which is proposed in this paper. These differences are based on the viewpoint of the correlation term and its applications in data hiding. They are as follows:

Chang et al have used the term "correlation" in their approach but this correlation is nothing, except the difference between pixel values, but the correlation which has been used in this study, is the application of "Correlation" in its statistical concept. Furthermore, the correlation is based on image blocks.

On the other hand this difference (which has been used as correlation), is applied for determining the bit to be embedded, that it is 0 or 1. But in proposed scheme the correlation is used for determining if the blocks are embeddable or not embeddable. Thus it is aimed to have a very high quality stego-image.

4 Data Hiding Based on Correlation

In this section data hiding is implemented based on neighboring blocks correlation. If the procedure of section 3 is done for each block of an image, a correlation matrix is generated as $I_{correlation-matrix}$. In the next subsection, a data hiding method is proposed that is based on threshold and correlation of adjacent pixels.

4.1 Data Embedding

Let $M = \{m_1, m_2, ..., m_n\}$ be the secret data to be embedded. The following steps and their explanations show the procedure of data embedding.

Step1: Divide the image $I(i,j)$ in to 2x2 blocks $I_n(i,j)$, where n demonstrates nth block. Figure.2 shows a typical 2x2 block.

Step2: Use the correlation matrix $I_{correlation-matrix}$ with the size $M \times N$ pixels which is described in the last section. For having the same size as the original image, the correlation matrices have to be concatenated with zero rows and zero columns before and after the first and the last rows and columns respectively. So the correlation size is the same as the image. As it is mentioned, the value of the matrix is normalized to be in the range of 0 to 1.

Step3: Specify a threshold T to start the data embedding procedure.

Step4: Embed each bit of secret data in the block which its correlation, according to $I_{correlation-matrix}$ is higher than T or equal, as described in step 5 and 6. The embedding process starts according to the threshold that is defined. In each iteration only one bit is embedded in each block $B_n(i',j')$ where B_n demonstrates n th block which is located in i' row and j' column of all blocks:

$$i' = floor\left(\frac{i+1}{2}\right) \quad j' = floor\left(\frac{j+1}{2}\right) \tag{6}$$

In the example that is proposed in section 3, if the threshold is T=0.1, all the correlation values of correlation matrix have the desired condition to embed secret data in the image.

Step5: Sum the values of 4 pixels (figure.2) in each block that its correlation is higher or equal to the defined threshold, according to Eq (7):

n Indicates the n th block that has the embedding condition.

$$sumblock(i',j') = X(i',j') + a(i',j') + b(i',j') + c(i',j') \tag{7}$$

$x_n(i',j')$	$a_n(i',j')$
$b_n(i',j')$	$c_n(i',j')$

Fig. 2. A typical 2x2 block B_n

An additional bit has to be concatenated to each elements of correlation matrix at the upper left pixel of each block. This bit shows whether the sumblock is odd or even. If the sumblock is odd, the bit is 1. Else if the sumblock is even, the bit is 0. This bit is virtual and only works for restoring of original image from stego-image.

$$I^{*}_{correlation-matrix}=\begin{bmatrix} 0 & 0 & 0 & 0 & 0 & 0 & 0 & 0 \\ 0 & 0.730 & 0 & 1.493 & 0 & 0.608 & 0 & 0 \\ 0 & 0 & 0 & 0 & 0 & 0 & 0 & 0 \\ 0 & 1.779 & 0 & 0.644 & 0 & 0.783 & 0 & 0 \\ 0 & 0 & 0 & 0 & 0 & 0 & 0 & 0 \\ 0 & 1.870 & 0 & 1.725 & 0 & 2.000 & 0 & 0 \\ 0 & 0 & 0 & 0 & 0 & 0 & 0 & 0 \\ 0 & 0 & 0 & 0 & 0 & 0 & 0 & 0 \end{bmatrix}$$

Step6: Determine if the sumblock has an even or odd value. If the value is odd, the bit to be embedded is 0 otherwise the bit to be embedded is 1. In the example of section (3) the sumblocks are: 408,309,371,369,376,515,294,326,453

Embed the secret data by using Eq (8):

$$x_n(i',j')=x_n(i',j')+1+(sumblock_n(i',j')+m_n)\bmod 2 \tag{8}$$

$$x_1(i',j')=x_1(i',j')+1+(sumblock_1(i',j')+m_1)\bmod 2$$
$$=90+1+(408+0)\bmod 2=91$$

$$x_2(i',j')=x_2(i',j')+1+(sumblock_2(i',j')+m_2)\bmod 2$$
$$=88+1+(309+0)\bmod 2=90$$

$$x_3(i',j')=x_3(i',j')+1+(sumblock_3(i',j')+m_3)\bmod 2$$
$$=81+1+(371+1)\bmod 2=83$$

$$x_4(i',j')=x_4(i',j')+1+(sumblock_4(i',j')+m_4)\bmod 2$$
$$=97+1+(369+1)\bmod 2=99$$

$$x_5(i',j')=x_5(i',j')+1+(sumblock_5(i',j')+m_5)\bmod 2$$
$$=82+1+(376+0)\bmod 2=83$$

$$x_6(i',j')=x_6(i',j')+1+(sumblock_6(i',j')+m_6)\bmod 2$$
$$=132+1+(515+0)\bmod 2=134$$

$$x_7(i',j')=x_7(i',j')+1+(sumblock_7(i',j')+m_7)\bmod 2$$
$$=75+1+(294+0)\bmod 2=76$$

$$x_8(i',j')=x_8(i',j')+1+(sumblock_8(i',j')+m_8)\bmod 2$$
$$=64+1+(326+1)\bmod 2=65$$

$$x_9(i',j')=x_9(i',j')+1+(sumblock_9(i',j')+m_9)\bmod 2$$
$$=147+1+(453+0)\bmod 2=149$$

$$I_{stego-image} = \begin{bmatrix} 75 & 81 & 119 & 124 & 87 & 59 & 75 & 86 \\ 67 & 91 & 104 & 98 & 87 & 76 & 74 & 77 \\ 69 & 107 & 107 & 90 & 95 & 84 & 61 & 73 \\ 76 & 90 & 76 & 83 & 110 & 66 & 64 & 101 \\ 86 & 80 & 65 & 80 & 104 & 99 & 99 & 108 \\ 82 & 82 & 96 & 134 & 134 & 149 & 124 & 112 \\ 81 & 83 & 111 & 137 & 112 & 103 & 79 & 93 \\ 84 & 79 & 102 & 116 & 79 & 73 & 54 & 81 \end{bmatrix}$$

It is clear that:

If the sumblock is odd its residue in dividing by 2 is 1. If the bit to be embedded is 0, 2 is added to the pixel value x.

If the sumblock is even its residue in dividing by 2 is 0. If the bit to be embedded is 1, 2 is added to the pixel value x.

If the sumblock is odd its residue in dividing by 2 is 1. If the bit to be embedded is 1, 1 is added to the pixel value x and no bit is embedded so the block is skipped.

If the sumblock is even its residue in dividing by 2 is 0. If the bit to be embedded is 0, 1is added to the pixel value x and no bit is embedded so the block is skipped.

In other words in the case of embedding secret bit, 2 is added to the value of x; But if no bit is embedded, 1 is added to the value of x.

Step7: calculate the correlation matrix like the process mentioned in step2, $I_{correlation-matrix-after-embedding}$ and normalize it to the range [0 1].

Step8: find the mean square error (*MSE*) of correlation matrix elements before and after embedding process. This error is calculated for each elements of correlation matrix by using Eq (9):

$$MSE = \frac{\sqrt{\left(\sum_m \sum_n (I_{correlation-matrix}(m,n) - I_{correlation-matrix-after-embedding}(m,n))\right)^2}}{M \times N} \tag{9}$$

m and n are m th row and n th column of correlation matrix $I_{correlation-matrix}$ and $I_{correlation-matrix-after-embedding}$ respectively. $I_{correlation-matrix}(m,n)$ and $I_{correlation-matrix-after-embedding}(m,n)$ are the correlation values at m th row and n th column of correlation matrix $I_{correlation-matrix}$ and $I_{correlation-matrix-after-embedding}$ respectively. $M \times N$ is the number of all pixels or the number of correlation matrix elements.

Clearly, in each iteration of this algorithm, the correlation matrix before embedding is different from the correlation matrix after embedding. This difference or error which hereafter is called"MSE", is important in selection of best threshold. By decreasing this error, minimum degradation is generated in image quality; because error decreasing leads to minimum degradation in quality of the image; but the capacity has to be high enough. So this target will be met by a tradeoff between error and pay load capacity.

By executing all these process in each threshold from 0.1 to 1 with the step of 0.05, it can be judged which threshold is the best one. Because as it is mentioned, when the threshold is decreased, the payload capacity increases. On the other hand the quality of the stego-image decreases. But by extracting an error value in each threshold the pattern of decreasing of this error can be detected. This pattern is dependent on image type and payload capacity, but undoubtedly it has a descent shape.

The correlation matrix of stego-image is $I_{stego-correlation-matrix}$,as follows:

$$I_{stego-correlation-matrix} = \begin{bmatrix} 0 & 0 & 0 & 0 & 0 & 0 & 0 & 0 \\ 0 & 0.7375 & 0 & 1.4536 & 0 & 1.6651 & 0 & 0 \\ 0 & 0 & 0 & 0 & 0 & 0 & 0 & 0 \\ 0 & 0.7258 & 0 & 0.6157 & 0 & 0.759 & 0 & 0 \\ 0 & 0 & 0 & 0 & 0 & 0 & 0 & 0 \\ 0 & 1.7675 & 0 & 0.8105 & 0 & 1.0 & 0 & 0 \\ 0 & 0 & 0 & 0 & 0 & 0 & 0 & 0 \\ 0 & 0 & 0 & 0 & 0 & 0 & 0 & 0 \end{bmatrix}$$

According to Eq (8), the mean square error is 0.0078. If this process is done in thresholds 0.1 to 1 with the step of 0.1, the errors are:

0.0050, 0.0041, 0.0025, 0.0037, 0.0035, 0.0020, 0.0025, 0.0006, 0.0000, 0.0000

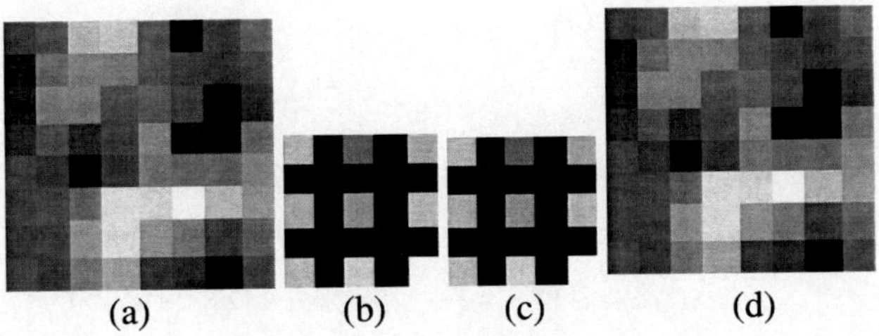

Fig. 3. (a) Original image, (b) unmarked correlation matrix, (c) marked correlation matrix and (d) marked image

As can be seen the, error is 0 at the threshold *T=1.* Because there are no elements in correlation matrix with the value of 1, thus no bit is embedded and the *MSE* is zero. Figure.3 Shows original image, unmarked correlation matrix, marked correlation matrix and marked image respectively.

4.2 Extraction Process

For extraction process, correlation matrix $I^*_{correlation-matrix}$ is needed as the overhead information. $*$ demonstrates the modified version of $I_{correlation-matrix}$

This process has some steps as follows:

Step1: Compute the sum of each block in stego-image according to the same block in $I^*_{correlation-matrix}$, that its correlation is higher or equal to the threshold defined at the beginning of embedding

Step2: Extract secret data as "*extracted(n)*" which are derived from Eq (9) to be:

$$extracted(n) = 1 - sumblock(n) \bmod 2 \tag{9}$$

The hidden data are extracted by Eq (9).

$$\begin{aligned}
extracted(1) &= 1 - sumblock(1) \bmod 2 \\
&= 1 - 409 \bmod 2 = 0 \\
extracted(2) &= 1 - sumblock(2) \bmod 2 \\
&= 1 - 311 \bmod 2 = 0 \\
extracted(3) &= 1 - sumblock(3) \bmod 2 \\
&= 1 - 372 \bmod 2 = 1 \\
extracted(4) &= 1 - sumblock(4) \bmod 2 \\
&= 1 - 370 \bmod 2 = 1 \\
extracted(5) &= 1 - sumblock(5) \bmod 2 \\
&= 1 - 377 \bmod 2 = 0 \\
extracted(6) &= 1 - sumblock(6) \bmod 2 \\
&= 1 - 517 \bmod 2 = 0 \\
extracted(7) &= 1 - sumblock(7) \bmod 2 \\
&= 1 - 295 \bmod 2 = 0 \\
extracted(8) &= 1 - sumblock(8) \bmod 2 \\
&= 1 - 327 \bmod 2 = 1
\end{aligned}$$

$$s = \{0,0,1,1,0,0,0,1,0\}$$

Step3: Restore the original image blocks as follows:

1) If $extracted(n) = 0$ and $I^*_{correlation-matrix}$ of $block(i)$ is more or equal to "1" $(I^*_{correlation-matrix}(n) \geq 1)$, subtract 2 from the upper left pixel of each block: $X=X-2$
2) If $extracted(n) = 1$ and $I^*_{correlation-matrix}$ of $block(n)$ is located between "1" and "T" $(T \leq I^*_{correlation-matrix}(n) \leq 1)$, subtract 2 from the upper left pixel of each block: $X=X-2$
3) If $extracted(n) = 1$ and $I^*_{correlation-matrix}$ of $block(n)$ is more or equal to "1" $(I^*_{correlation-matrix}(n) \geq 1)$, subtract 2 from the upper left pixel of each block: $X=X-1$
4) If $extracted(n) = 0$ and $I^*_{correlation-matrix}$ of $block(n)$ is located between "1" and "T" $(T \leq I^*_{correlation-matrix}(n) \leq 1)$, subtract 1 from the upper left pixel of each block: $X=X-1$

If the sumblock is calculated for each block of stego-image, we have:

409,311,372,370,377,517,295,327

According to step(3), the recovered image is $I_{recovered-image}$, as follows:

$$I_{restored-image} = \begin{bmatrix} 75 & 81 & 119 & 124 & 87 & 59 & 75 & 86 \\ 67 & 90 & 104 & 97 & 87 & 75 & 74 & 77 \\ 69 & 107 & 107 & 90 & 95 & 84 & 61 & 73 \\ 76 & 88 & 76 & 82 & 110 & 64 & 64 & 101 \\ 86 & 80 & 65 & 80 & 104 & 99 & 99 & 108 \\ 82 & 81 & 96 & 132 & 134 & 147 & 124 & 112 \\ 81 & 83 & 111 & 137 & 112 & 103 & 79 & 93 \\ 84 & 79 & 102 & 116 & 79 & 73 & 54 & 81 \end{bmatrix}$$

All the processing of our proposed scheme is in the spatial domain. The operation requires generating the correlation matrix of the image, determining threshold, hiding messages, and doing the inverse transformation in the spatial domain.

5 Experimental Results

To evaluate the proposed method, seven test images has been used in Figure.4 include: a) baby b) balloon c) leaves d) children e) text f) flowers g) bee, of the same size 512×512 with 256 gray scales.

All the concerned data hiding algorithms are run by the operating system *windows XP* and the program developing environment is *MATLAB 7.8*. The proposed method has been assessed by three aspects: correlation error, PSNR and pay load capacity.

The PSNR value can be computed by the following equation:

$$PSNR = 10\log_{10}\left(\frac{R^2}{MSE}\right) \tag{10}$$

R is the maximum fluctuation in the input image data type. For example, if the input image has a double-precision floating-point data type, then R is 1. If it has an 8-bit unsigned integer data type, R is 255. MSE (Mean Square Error) can be computed by equation (11) as follows:

$$MSE = \frac{\sum_{M,N}\left[I_1(m,n) - I_2(m,n)\right]^2}{M \times N} \tag{11}$$

Where M & N illustrate row and column of each image respectively. $I_1(m,n)$ & $I_2(m,n)$ are the original image and stego-image respectively. If the distortion between the cover image and the stego-image is small, the PSNR value is large. Thus, a larger PSNR value means that the quality of the stego-image is better than the smaller one. Secret data is generated by using pseudo random number generator. Based on test images, the payload capacity at threshold $T = 0.1$ (most. capacity) and PSNR at worst case are shown in Table.1. Tables.2&3 show The comparison of PSNR and payload capacity between proposed scheme and Ni et al method[9][10][11][12]. At $T=0.1$ and $T=0.85$ respectively. Table.4 shows the comparison of PSNR and payload capacity between proposed scheme and MPE method [13].

As it is seen PSNR and capacity of proposed scheme in comparison with Ni et al method (Table.2&3) is much higher. One of the most important characteristic of proposed method is that PSNR is high. PSNR and capacity in proposed method is higher than Ni et al method. Higher thresholds act more strictly than lower thresholds.

Table.4 shows the comparison of proposed scheme and MPE method in pay load capacity and PSNR. MPE shows higher capacity than the correlation threshold method. MPE embeds secret data based on modification of error prediction. So it can provide high capacity for embedding but PSNR in proposed scheme is more than twice higher than MPE method. The average PSNR in proposed method is more than 70 db, but its average is 30db and 50 db in MPE method and Ni et al method respectively.

Figure.5 shows the payload capacity in each threshold from 0.1 to 1. As it is shown in threshold 0.1, the algorithm can embed 0.25 bpp, since in this threshold almost all blocks can be used for data embedding. The capacity of seven test images decreases by increasing the threshold. At threshold $T=1$ capacity is 1500 bit or 0.02bpp. PSNR as a measurement of image quality is demonstrated in any threshold.

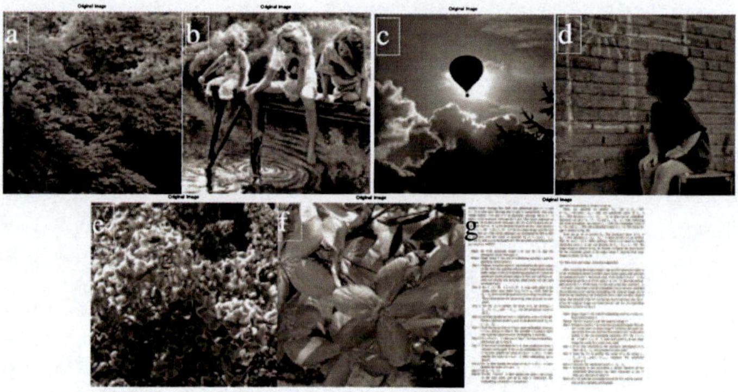

Fig. 4. a) Leaves b) children c) balloon d) baby e) Flowers f) bee g) text

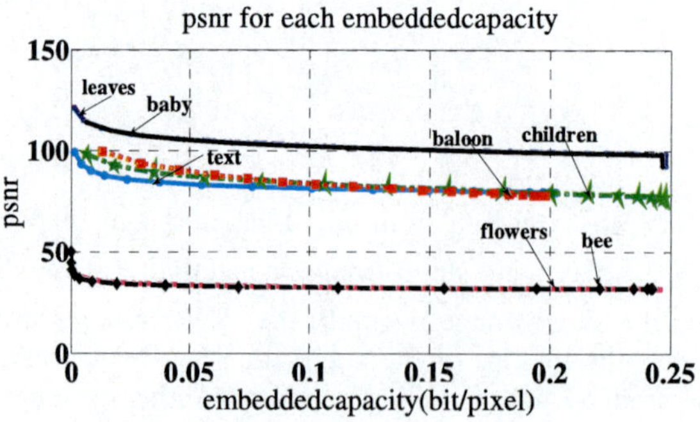

Fig. 5. PSNR vs. capacity (bit/pixel)

Table 1. Payload capacity and PSNR of proposed scheme

Test image	PSNR (db)at T=0.1(worst psnr)	Embedded capacity at T=0.1 (best case) bits
text	79.5226	52986
leaves	92.5342	64963
children	77.0790	64920
balloon	77.9409	51799
baby	92.5635	64669
flowers	31.6487	64410
Bee	31.9536	63602

Table 2. Payload capacity and PSNR of proposed scheme andcomparison with Ni method in highest capacity and lowest psnr

Test image	Proposed scheme (at T=0.1) bits	Psnr db	Ni et al.'s scheme bits	Psnr db
text	52986	79.5226	101789	60.9398
Leaves	64963	92.5342	2403	49.0190
children	64920	77.0790	1982	51.3550
balloon	51799	77.9409	27293	47.6319
baby	64669	92.5635	4315)	52.2989
flowers	64410	31.6487	2825)	49.1812
bee	63602	31.9536	3708	51.0475

Table 3. Payload capacity and PSNR of proposed scheme and comparison with Ni method in lowest capacity and highest psnr

Test image	Proposed scheme (at T=0.85) bits	PSNR(db)	Ni et al.'s scheme bits	PSNR(db)
text	2238	112.9885	101789	60.9398
Leaves	3443	111.0678	2403	49.0190
children	9313	89.1008	1982	51.3550
balloon	11934)	90.1495	27293	47.6319
baby	8009	107.4445	4315	52.2989
flowers	165	41.0177	2825	49.1812
bee	107	41.0712	3708	51.0475

Table 4. Payload capacity and PSNR of proposed scheme and comparison with MPE method in highest capacity and lowest psnr

Test image	Proposed scheme (at T=0.1) (Bits)	PSNR(db)	MPE scheme	PSNR(db)
text	52986	79.52	75933	33.41
Leaves	64963	92.53	133719	27.83
children	64920	77.07	141725	27.29
balloon	51799	77.94	90922	30.03
baby	64669	92.56	129413	28.45
flowers	64410	31.64	139466	27.38
bee	63602	31.95	120156	28.39

6 Conclusion

In this paper, we have proposed a simple and efficient reversible information hiding scheme based on neighboring correlation of gray level images. The proposed scheme intends to improve the correlation-based data hiding which embeds secret data within the upper left pixel of each block in the image and not only conceals a satisfied amount of secret information in the cover image, but also restores the cover image from the stego-image without any loss by using correlation matrix $I^{*}_{correlation-matrix}$ as the overhead information (which is one of the disadvantages of this scheme in restoration of image) to have a reversible method. The most important feature of this scheme is its high PSNR or the quality of stego-image.

References

[1] Zeng, W.: Digital Watermarking and Data Hiding: Technologies and Applications. In: Proc. Int. Conf. Inf. Syst, Anal. Synth., vol. 3, pp. 223–229 (1998)

[2] Thien, C.C., Lin, J.C.: A Simple and High-Hiding Capacity Method For Hiding Digit by Digit Data in Images Based On Modulus Function. Pattern Recognition 36(13), 2875–2881 (2003)

[3] Chan, C.K., Cheng, L.M.: Hiding Data in Images by Simple LSB Substitution. Pattern Recognition 37(3), 469–474 (2004)

[4] Wang, J., Ji, L.: A Region and Data Hiding Based Error Concealment Scheme for Images. IEEE Transformations on Consumer Electronics 47(2), 257–262 (2001)

[5] Wang, R.Z., Lin, C.F., Lin, J.C.: Image Hiding by Optimal LSB Substitution and Genetic Algorithm. Pattern Recognition 34(3), 671–683 (2001)

[6] Celik, M.U., Sharma, G., Tekal, A.M.: Lossless Watermarking for Image Authentication: A new Framework and An Implementation. IEEE Trans. Image Process. 15(4), 1042–1049 (2006)

[7] Lim, S.: Two-Dimensional Signal and Image Processing, pp. 218–237. Prentice Hall, Englewood Cliffs (1990)

[8] Chang, C.C., Lu, T.C.: Lossless Information Hiding Scheme Based on Neighboring Correlation. In: Second International Conference on Future Generation Communication and Networking Symposia (2008)

[9] Ni, Z., Shi, Y.Q., Ansari, N., Su, W., Sun, Q., Lin, X.: Robust lossless image data hiding. In: Proc. IEEE Int. Conf. Multimedia Expo., Taipei, Taiwan, R.O.C, pp. 2199–2202 (June 2004)

[10] Xuan, G., Shi, Y.Q., Ni, Z., Chai, P., Cui, X., Tong, X.: Reversible Data Hiding for JPEG Images Based on Histogram Pairs. In: Kamel, M.S., Campilho, A. (eds.) ICIAR 2007. LNCS, vol. 4633, pp. 715–727. Springer, Heidelberg (2007)

[11] Shi, Y.Q., Ni, Z., Zou, D., Liang, C., Xuan, G.: Lossless data hiding: Fundamentals, algorithms and applications. In: Proc. IEEE Int. Symp. Circuits Syst., Vancouver, BC, Canada, vol. II, pp. 33–36 (May 2004)

[12] Xuan, G., Yao, Q., Yang, C., Gao, J., Chai, P., Shi, Y.Q., Ni, Z.: Lossless Data Hiding Using Histogram Shifting Method Based on Integer Wavelets. In: Shi, Y.Q., Jeon, B. (eds.) IWDW 2006. LNCS, vol. 4283, pp. 323–332. Springer, Heidelberg (2006)

[13] Hong, W., Chen, T.S., Shiu, C.W.: Reversible Data Hiding for High Quality Images Using Modification of Prediction Errors. The Journal of Systems and Software 82, 1833–1842 (2009)

Author Index